Organizational Behavior

An Introduction to Your Life in Organizations

Rae André
Northeastern University

PEARSON

Prentice
Hall

Upper Saddle River, NJ 07458

Library of Congress Cataloging-in-Publication Data

André, Rae
    Organizational behavior: an introduction to your life in organizations / Rae André.—1e
        p. cm.
    Includes bibliographical references and index.
    ISBN 0-13-185495-X
    1. Organizational behavior.   2. Psychology, Industrial.   I. Title.
HD58.7.A478 2008
658--dc22 2007029574

Editor-in-Chief: David Parker
Product Development Manager: Ashley Santora
Assistant Editor: Keri Molinari
Marketing Manager: Anne Howard
Marketing Assistant: Susan Osterlitz
Senior Managing Editorial: Judy Leale
Associate Managing Editor: Renata Butera
Production Project Manager: Carol Samet
Permissions Project Manager: Charles Morris
AV Project Manager: Rhonda Aversa
Senior Operations Supervisor: Arnold Vila
Senior Art Director: Janet Slowik
Interior Design: Karen Quigley
Cover Design: Karen Quigley
Cover Illustration/Photo: Veer/Theo Olivieri
Illustration (Interior): ElectraGraphics, Inc.
Director, Image Resource Center: Melinda Patelli
Manager, Rights and Permissions: Zina Arabia
Manager, Visual Research: Beth Brenzel
Image Permission Coordinator: Jan Marc Quisumbing
Photo Researcher: Melinda Alexander
Composition: Preparé
Full-Service Project Management: Preparé
Printer/Binder: Quebecor/Versailles

Credits and acknowledgments borrowed from other sources and reproduced, with permission, in this textbook appear on page 556.

Pearson Prentice Hall™ is a trademark of Pearson Education, Inc.
Pearson® is a registered trademark of Pearson plc
Prentice Hall® is a registered trademark of Pearson Education, Inc.

Pearson Education LTD.
Pearson Education Singapore, Pte. Ltd
Pearson Education, Canada, Ltd
Pearson Education-Japan

Pearson Education Australia PTY, Limited
Pearson Education North Asia Ltd
Pearson Educación de Mexico, S.A. de C.V.
Pearson Education Malaysia, Pte. Ltd.

10 9 8 7 6 5

ISBN-13: 978-0-13-185495-6
ISBN-10: 0-13-185495-X

To my Dad:
dear father,
wise friend,
and consummate
businessman

Brief Contents

Appendices

Integrative Cases and Projects

Contents

Appendices

Integrative Cases and Projects

A Note for Professors

What are the unique features of *Organizational Behavior: An Introduction to Your Life in Organizations?*

Overview

1. This textbook helps readers *solve organizational problems* using OB theories.
2. The material is *personalized*.
3. The text adopts a *global* perspective on organizational challenges.
4. The chapters emphasize problem solving and active learning.
5. The end-of-chapter materials in "Apply What You Have Learned. . ." offer a variety of opportunities for practical applications, critical thinking, and explorations.
6. The problem-solving approach delivers actionable knowledge.

1. THIS TEXTBOOK HELPS READERS USE OB THEORIES TO SOLVE ORGANIZATIONAL PROBLEMS. Although most OB texts lead with theories and follow with applications, this one leads with applications and follows with theories. Using this **problem-solving approach**, students first read about the challenges that individuals face every day in organizations, and then explore the research findings that can help them to meet these challenges.

Organizational Behavior: An Introduction to Your Life in Organizations thoroughly covers the latest, most valid and practical research results. At the same time, in terms of the book's structure, problems come first and theories come next. Chapters are organized around questions oriented to managerial practice.

For example, Chapter 7: Communication and Interpersonal Relationships addresses these questions:

How can you make the communication process work for you?

What are some gender differences in communication styles?

How do you build trust in relationships?

How do you persuade others?

What communication strengths do you already have? Which skills do you need to develop?

What are some tested tactics for doing well on job interviews?

For more examples, see the Preview section that opens each chapter.

2. THE MATERIAL IS PERSONALIZED. The title suggests the personalized approach: The focus of the book is on *your life in organizations*. The text addresses students directly and informally. It asks them to actively engage with the chapter concepts by thinking about how to apply them to their own careers. It asks students to address issues as if they were managers. It also engages them by offering self-tests and short exercises throughout the chapters.

To this end, the first and last chapters of the text are organized somewhat differently than others you may have read. The first chapter opens traditionally, discussing environmental factors affecting today's organizations, but rather than cover history and methodology at this point, it discusses how these factors affect today's careers; *your career.* The last chapter invites students to keep studying OB even after this course, offering them some tools, including social science methodology and suggestions for further reading that can help them in their further explorations.

3. THE TEXT ADOPTS A GLOBAL PERSPECTIVE ON ORGANIZATIONAL CHALLENGES. This is accomplished in the following ways:

- Students learn about global issues in organizational behavior and theory throughout the book, beginning with the global context for organizational problem solving established in Chapter 1.

- The latest global research is integrated into every chapter, in every appropriate topic as space permits.

- In addition, one full chapter is devoted to understanding cross-cultural relationships.

- Many of the opening cases and end-of-chapter materials focus on international companies.

4. THE CHAPTERS EMPHASIZE PROBLEM SOLVING AND ACTIVE LEARNING. Each chapter includes:

a. *A Preview that lists the key questions and concepts the chapter will address.* This section replaces the "Questions you should be able to answer after reading this chapter" found in many of today's texts. The Previews are easy to skim, so readers get a concise overview of the chapter without having to flip through a lot of pages. The section is also a useful tool for reviewing for an exam. Finally, it is not reductionistic. I don't believe it is possible to summarize, in even a dozen questions, the contents of a complex chapter that is based on decades of interesting, high quality research.

b. *A chapter opening company case (and video supplied by Prentice-Hall).* A short case at the beginning of each chapter introduces some of the problem-solving challenges that will be addressed. Each case is based on a short (6 to 15 minute) Prentice-Hall video featuring organizational issues in a real company. The videos feature inside looks at real companies.

c. *Supporting material* within the body of the chapter enhances the book's problem focus. It includes such features as second-person questions ("What would you do if. . .?"), cases that illustrate the theory (including some more extensive cases that continue through an entire section), and many examples of what actual companies and individuals are doing to solve organizational problems.

d. *Self-assessments* are integrated within the chapter. Because of this placement, they are more likely to be completed in context and more likely to help students remember the related theory.

e. *Overviews* summarize, clarify, and, in many cases, apply material from the text at strategic points in the chapters. These are primarily study aids. They do not provide additional theory, although sometimes they do provide additional examples of how theories can be applied.

**5. THE END-OF-CHAPTER MATERIALS IN "APPLY WHAT YOU HAVE LEARNED. . ."
OFFER A VARIETY OF OPPORTUNITIES FOR PRACTICAL APPLICATIONS, CRITICAL
THINKING, AND EXPLORATIONS.** In general, the end-of-chapter materials include:

- shorter cases that can be read on the spot in class to enhance discussion during the lecture, or to fill out and reinforce the material at the end of a class.

- longer cases for group work in class, and for outside assignments.

- exercises for experiential group work, debates, and role-playing in-class.

- Explorations, primarily online, that invite students to go beyond the text for homework, short and long papers, or presentations.

- enough material to create a highly experiential course.

Specifically, the materials in "Apply What You Have Learned. . ." are:

- *World Class Companies* (or *People*) features companies that take distinctive approaches to OB problems. Short enough to be read in class, this section includes questions for discussion.

- *Advice from the Pros* offers practical ideas from professionals in the field. These integrate theory with practice, and sometimes suggest new ideas that may not yet have received research attention. This section includes questions for discussion.

- *Gain Experience.* The experiential exercises simulate organizational issues in the classroom and give students the opportunity to solve problems using the chapter theory.

- *Can You Solve This Manager's (Person's, Group's, Company's) Problem?* These problem-solving cases, of various lengths and difficulty, test the students' knowledge of the theory and their ability to apply it.

- *Explorations* is a window on the world of resources beyond this book. Although suggestive rather than exhaustive, it has several uses. It can be tailored for a variety of short and longer assignments. Professors can use the section to create homework assignments, or to suggest research topics. It can enhance online courses. It can guide advanced students who want to research chapter topics more fully.

In addition, the textbook includes a section of:

- *Integrative exercises and cases* This section focuses on longer integrative cases and projects. It includes cases, experiential exercises, and recommended term projects for both groups and individuals. (see Table 1.)

6. THE PROBLEM-SOLVING APPROACH DELIVERS ACTIONABLE KNOWLEDGE. Basing a textbook on fundamental organizational applications demonstrates how the field of organizational behavior helps managers solve practical problems.[1] Using the problem-solving approach, the contributions of the field are plain. The scope and depth of research available to address particular organizational issues is clear.

Structuring material in this way may also suggest to scholars how the field can further develop its research. Scholars interested in creating "actionable knowledge,"[2] as I am, are addressing questions such as: Are we, as a field, asking the *right* questions? Are we asking the questions to which managers need answers? Are we answering the key questions as effectively as we can? Further, what is the right mix of data-based research and practitioner knowledge in a book with this approach? We are beginning to find answers to these questions.

How Is the Book Organized?

In this textbook I do not assert a particular view on the sequence in which an OB course should be taught. Some professors like to start their course with groups, others with leadership, and still others with organizational theory. Many change their approach over time as their own perspectives and interests develop. Rather than burden you with an approach that would be limiting, I have simply organized this book in a logical fashion and made the chapters reasonably independent of each other so that you can easily rearrange them to suit your needs.

Figure 1 shows this organization, which moves from the micro level to the macro level and then, at the end of the book, covers organizational factors that have dynamic effects system-wide.

While I would recommend caution in separating logically linked chapters—in particular, the two chapters on groups, and the two on leadership—I would highly recommend that you move the groups chapters, or whichever chapters you prefer, to the front of your syllabus if that is where you want them. The one chapter that is prerequisite to most others

---

[1] For more background on why such an approach may be useful to the field, see M. R. Blood, "The Role of Organization Behavior in the Business School Curriculum," in J. Greenberg, *Organizational Behavior: The State of the Science* (Hillsdale, NJ: Lawrence Erlbaum Associates, Publishers, 1994): 207–220; C. Lundberg, "Techniques for Teaching OB in the College Classroom," in J. Greenberg, *Organizational Behavior: The State of the Science* (Hillsdale, NJ: Lawrence Erlbaum Associates, Publishers, 1994): 221–244; C. Argyris, "Reflection and Beyond in Research on Organizational Learning," *Management Learning 35* (4), 2004: 507–509.

[2] L. L. Ferguson, "How Social Science Research Can Help Management," *California Management Review 8* (4), Summer 1966:3–10; M. R. Blood, "Only *You* Can Create Actionable Knowledge," *Academy of Management Learning & Education 5* (2), 2006:209–212.

FIGURE 1

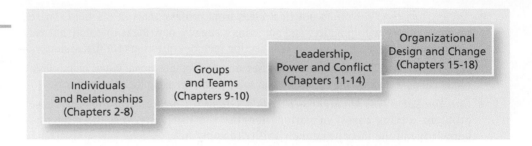

is Chapter 2: Your Personality and Style. I recommend that you cover it very early, and certainly before leadership, because personality is a factor that affects many phenomena.

What Is the Ultimate Purpose of This Book?

Studying OB can be exciting. Not just "interesting," but *exciting!* My ideal OB class is one in which students leave with the twinkle in their eye that shows an "Aha!" response, indicating that they learned something new about themselves and their future life organizations. My goal for *Organizational Behavior: An Introduction to Your Life in Organizations* is to showcase our fascinating field.

Now, not all of *us* are exciting, and even when we are, we may be just a bit less so in our 8 a.m. classes. And maybe it is just plain beyond the ken of textbook writers to make any textbook exciting. Yet, the excitement of a book about people in organizations is inherent in the field of organizational behavior—its ability to open people's eyes to new possibilities for themselves personally and for the people they will one day manage, its practical and occasionally quirky findings, and its window on a world of human adventures in a variety of organizations and cultures. In this textbook, and in your course, we are in a partnership to do our best to convey to our students that excitement!

At the same time, writing a textbook is itself either a labor of love or the manifestation of a lunatic disposition. Please help me decide which by sending me your feedback on how this text works for your classes. Contact me any time at r.andre@neu.edu.

INSTRUCTOR'S RESOURCE CENTER: Register. Redeem. Login.

www.prenhall.com/irc is where instructors can access a variety of print, media, and presentation resources available with this text in downloadable, digital format. For most texts, resources are also available for course management platforms such as Blackboard, WebCT, and Course Compass.

IT GETS BETTER. Once you register, you will not have additional forms to fill out, or multiple usernames and passwords to remember to access new titles and/or editions. As a registered faculty member, you can login directly to download resource files, and receive immediate access and instructions for installing Course Management content to your campus server.

NEED HELP? Our dedicated Technical Support team is ready to assist instructors with questions about the media supplements that accompany this text. Visit: http://247.prenhall.com/ for answers to frequently asked questions and toll-free user support phone numbers. The following supplements are available to adopting instructors.

For detailed descriptions of all of the supplements listed below, please visit: www.prenhall.com/irc

Instructor's Resource Center (IRC) on CD-ROM–ISBN: 0-13-185508-5

Printed Instructor's Manual–ISBN: 0-13-185506-9

Printed Test Item File–ISBN: 0-13-174316-3

TestGen Test Generating Software–Visit the IRC (online) for this text.

PowerPoints–Visit the IRC (both online and on CD-ROM) for this text.

NEW! Videos on DVD–ISBN: 0-13-1854968

TABLE 1 Integrative Exercises and Cases: Key Topics

■ = Primary relevance ● = Secondary relevance

Chapter	Cases			Exercises		
	Western Distribution Center, Inc.	International Rose Growers, Inc.: Managing a Small Business Start-up in the Caribbean	The Baker and Eiger Companies	The Career Self-Study Project: An Integrative Paper	The Connections Project and Paper: An Integrative Project on Leading Teams	Company Design Analysis: An Integrative Project for Teams
1 Why Mastering OB Is Essential to Your Career				●		
2 Your Personality and Style				■	■	
3 Decision Making				●	●	●
4 Fundamentals of Motivation	■			●	●	
5 Motivating Individuals in Their Jobs						●
6 Health and Stress at Work		●		●		
7 Communication and Interpersonal Relationships		●		●	●	
8 Cross-Cultural Relationships		■		●	■	
9 Groups and Their Influence	■				■	
10 Improving Team Decision-Making			●		■	
11 The Challenge of Leadership		●	●	●	●	
12 Leadership Roles and Skills				●	●	
13 Power and Influence					●	
14 Conflicts Good and Bad						
15 Designing Effective Organizations			■		■	■
16 Organizational Structure as a Design Tool	●		■			■
17 Organizational Culture						●
18 Changing Organizations						
19 OB Is for Life						
For groups?	■		●		■	■
For individuals?	●	●	●		■	
For a paper?		●	●	●	■	■
For a presentation?					■	■

TABLE 2 Ethics Coverage

Chapter	Primary Coverage	Secondary Coverage	Exercises and Cases: Primary Coverage	Exercises and Cases: Secondary Coverage
1 Why Mastering OB Is Essential to Your Career	Increased attention to organizational ethics (today)	The need for OB skills in ethics: • Personal ethics and integrity • Choosing a company to work for	Career anchors and values Explorations: • Ethics	Netflix Which OB skills are most important in which industries?: law
2 Your Personality and Style		Test use Ethical business values		Amy's Ice Creams
3 Decision Making	What is the social context of the decision?: • Make a fair decision. • Monitor biases in yourself and others. • Foster individual and organizational ethics.	Procedural justice	What can Citigroup teach Hewlett-Packard about ethical decision making?	
4 Fundamentals of Motivation	Goals may induce unethical behavior			
5 Motivating Individuals in Their Jobs				Volvo: The Uddevalla Plant
6 Health and Stress at Work				
7 Communication and Interpersonal Relationships		How do you create a trusting relationship?		*Ethical Communication* (supplementary video)
8 Cross-Cultural Relationships	Corruption: International Corruption Perceptions Index			*Global Business and Ethics* (supplementary video)
9 Groups and Their Influence	Develop an ethical group process	Deindividuation Poor decision making, such as groupthink—illusion of inherent morality		
10 Improving Team Decision Making		High-performance teams concern themselves with ethical decision making		
11 The Challenge of Leadership	How do leaders practice ethical leadership?	Leadership values: Differences in		
12 Leadership Roles and Skills	Establish a climate of respect (to deter deviant behavior)	What is the nature of negotiation: Understanding one's own ethics Firing: Account for ethical responsibilities Examining capitalism as a core value; Ethical grounds of	Advice from the Pros: How to interview executives for integrity Authentic leadership: John Tu, Kingston Technology (with supplementary video)	
13 Power and Influence	Obedience and resistance: Value of holding ethical beliefs as deterrent Does power corrupt?	Apply power tactics: But are all ethical? Should you play politics: Is it ethical? Toxic leaders: Raising ethical objections to them		Should You Play Politics?

TABLE 2 continued

Chapter	Primary Coverage	Secondary Coverage	Exercises and Cases: Primary Coverage	Exercises and Cases: Secondary Coverage
14 Conflicts Good and Bad		Whistleblowing: Need for codes of ethics		
15 Designing Effective Organizations				
16 Organizational Structure as a Design Tool				
17 Organizational Culture	How does culture promote ethical behavior? • Reconciling professional and personal values systems • Designing organizational cultures to encourage moral expression • Designing cultures to value diversity	A Once World Class Company: Arthur Andersen		
18 Changing Organizations	What are some key ethical dilemmas during organizational change?			
19 OB is for Life	What are some key ethical issues in social science research?	Who should organizations serve?: Critical theory What should OB teachers teach?		

TABLE 3 Diversity Coverage

(This list covers primarily the material on U.S. diversity. Because international coverage is so extensive in the book, it is not cited in this table, with the exception of some material on cross-cultural teams.)

Chapter	Primary Coverage	Secondary Coverage	Exercises and Cases: Primary Coverage	Exercises and Cases: Secondary Coverage
1 Why OB Is Essential to Your Career	The complex workforce: Age, gender, race	Organizational adaptations: Developing cultures that hire a diverse set of employees	IQ Solutions: Opening case	Career anchors: Discuss: How will today's workforce affect people who have your career anchor? For example, how might a diverse workforce affect your career?
2 Your Personality and Style			Can You Solve This Manager's Problem?: Different personalities— different treatment?	
3 Decision Making	Monitor biases in yourself and others			
4 Fundamentals of Motivation				
5 Motivating Individuals in Their Jobs				Psychological contracts affected by demographic differences Supplementary Prentice Hall video: Dupont
6 Health and Stress at Work		The need to address the work-life concerns of women and minorities		
7 Communication and Interpersonal Relationships	Categorizing: Social categories, stereotypes, prejudice, illusory correlation Gender styles	Trust and distrust in relationships		
8 Cross-Cultural Relationships			Cultural Awareness Exercise	
9 Groups and Their Influence	What issues arise in multicultural teams? In virtual multicultural teams? (U.S. and international)		How to Build a Cross-cultural Team (international)	
10 Improving Team Decision Making				
11 The Challenge of Leadership	How will your minority status affect your leadership opportunities?	Exploration: Ethnic minorities and leadership		
12 Leadership Role and Skills				

TABLE 3 continued

(This list covers primarily the material on U.S. diversity. Because international coverage is so extensive in the book, it is not cited in this table, with the exception of some material on cross-cultural teams.)

Chapter	Primary Coverage	Secondary Coverage	Exercises and Cases: Primary Coverage	Exercises and Cases: Secondary Coverage
13 Power and Influence				Recommended feature film: *Prisoner of Honor*
14 Conflicts Good and Bad		Team diversity interacts with team conflict to affect performance Social category diversity and relational conflict		
15 Designing Effective Organizations				
16 Organizational Structure as a Design Tool		Failure to integrate departments charged with managing diversity		
17 Organizational Culture	Culture motivates ethical behavior: Designing cultures to value diversity Will you face a glass ceiling?	Subcultures and counter-cultures are an important source of diversity		
18 Changing Organizations	Culture, changing to cultures that value diversity		Exploration: The business of diversity training Exploration: Minorities in business	
19 OB Is for Life				Supplementary video: *Channeling Human Resources: Showtime*

For Students: How to Use This Textbook

Organizational Behavior: An Introduction to Your Life in Organizations poses practical, managerial questions, and then shows you how organizational behavior theory can help you to develop answers. The book's *problem-solving approach* helps you to address crucial questions such as: How do I manage a work team? How do companies really motivate their employees? And, what can companies do to improve corporate ethics? It helps you to frame challenges you will face in organizational life using the latest and best-researched ideas.

Participate to Learn

When you actively work with an idea, you frame your experience of it in ways that will help you to remember it and apply it in the future. To really make an idea your own, something you can use effectively in the future, you have to formulate it in our own words, critically compare your own ideas with what you read, and imagine how the idea can be applied. This process of engaging with a concept is called *active learning*.

The principles of active learning suggest that you are more likely to really learn an idea if you:

- can place it in a real-life context, including the context of your own experience.
- see how it fits logically with other concepts.
- ask questions about it.
- actually use it to solve problems.
- think critically about it.
- share it.

This textbook challenges you to interact with the material in many different ways. You will be asked to apply the concepts to your own life and the lives of others. You will be encouraged to both *actively study* and *practically apply* the text material. In each chapter there is a set of learning tools—questions, self-assessments, case examples, explorations, chapter summary—that encourage your interaction with the material. These tools are primarily *organizers* and *motivators*. It is up to you to provide the critical and creative thinking about the material that, in the end, leads to your taking away some useful information from this class.

During class time, your professor will also challenge you to actively engage with the text ideas through discussions, case analyses, and exercises. You may be asked to work with other individuals and in groups. Please *volunteer* for exercises, *speak up*, *ask* questions, *criticize* theories, *praise* theories, and in any other way you can think of *get involved* in class with the material. Once you get out into the workplace it will be much more difficult than it is in class to ask challenging questions about how organizations really work. In fact, in many organizations there are taboos about asking such questions because they may imply a criticism of current management practices, even where no such criticism is intended.

So, participate now. Ask your questions now. You won't regret it.

How to Use the Study Aids in This Textbook

Each chapter of *Organizational Behavior: An Introduction to Your Life in Organizations* includes the following study aids that help you understand, enjoy, and learn the material.

1. PREVIEWS Each chapter begins with a Preview section, which lists the key questions you should be able to answer after mastering the chapter. You can use the Preview section in these three ways:

1. *Before you read the chapter, read the Preview to get a feel for the kinds of problem-solving problems the chapter will cover.*
   Why should you bother to do this? Reading and study skills experts routinely advise students to skim chapters before actually reading them. Skimming creates for you a context that enhances your subsequent ability to remember the material. In the Preview we have done the work of skimming and flipping for you.

2. *After you read the chapter use the Preview as a study aid.*
   Go back to Preview and remind yourself what the chapter said about each key question. Can you answer the question thoroughly? Do you know all the main concepts and terms that are used to answer the question?

3. *Think about how you might use the material in the future.*
   How does what you have learned enhance your knowledge of life in organizations? How might it affect your career? What skill sets does it suggest you may need? Imagine how can you "keep" this material for future use. Memorize it? Physically store it? Learn where to find it again if you ever need it?

2. SELF-ASSESSMENTS AND SHORT EXERCISES WITHIN THE CHAPTERS Each chapter in *Organizational Behavior: An Introduction to Your Life in Organizations* includes many self-evaluation instruments and some short exercises that help you to understand yourself and others while absorbing basic concepts. It is worth repeating that there is no better way to understand and remember a concept than to actively apply it to your own situation. Completing the exercises in the chapters as you come to them will help you learn the material.

3. OVERVIEWS Most chapters have one or more overviews, which are convenient summaries of some important chapter contents. These study aids have been specially designed to help you organize some of the more complex material.

4. EXPLORATIONS Going beyond your textbook by doing one or more of the recommended "explorations" will enrich your understanding of the concepts and help you to remember them. This is a good way to prepare for essay questions, papers, case analyses, and projects, because you will discover additional concepts, contexts, and examples that you can include in your write-up.

5. CHAPTER SUMMARIES Use the summaries at the end of the chapter to review key concepts and terms. In these summaries you will find two study aids for each key question asked in the chapter. First is a paragraph or two outlining basic answers to the key question. After reading the chapter, you should understand the logic behind the answers to each key question. One caution: The chapter summaries are only that—summaries. They do not cover all chapter content.

The second study aid is a list of key terms for each chapter section. After each paragraph is a list of all the terms that have been highlighted in that section of the chapter.

6. GLOSSARY ORGANIZED BY CHAPTER To help you study the full list of key terms for each chapter, check out the glossary at the end of the book. Unlike traditional glossaries, this one is organized by chapter, so that for each chapter you can find all the key terms and their definitions in one place.

Student Resources

COMPANION WEBSITE: www.prenhall.com/andre contains free access to a student version of the PowerPoint package.

VANGONOTES.COM Study on the go with VangoNotes—chapter reviews from your text in downloadable mp3 format. Now wherever you are—whatever you're doing—you can study by listening to the following for each chapter of your textbook:

- Big Ideas: Your "need to know" for each chapter
- Key Terms: audio "flashcards" to help you review key concepts and terms
- Rapid Review: A quick drill session–use it right before your test

VangoNotes are **flexible**; download all the material directly to your player, or only the chapters you need. And they're **efficient**. Use them in your car, at the gym, walking to class, wherever. So get yours today. And get studying.

SAFARIX ETEXTBOOKS ONLINE The Largest eTextbook Store on the Internet!

Developed for students looking to save money on required or recommended textbooks, SafariX eTextbooks Online saves students up to 50% off the suggested list price of the print text. Students simply select their eText by title or author and purchase immediate access to the content for the duration of the course using any major credit card. With a SafariX eText, students can search for specific keywords or page numbers, make notes online, print out reading assignments that incorporate lecture notes, and bookmark important passages for later review. For more information, or to purchase a SafariX eTextbook, visit <http://www.safarix.com>.

FEEDBACK

The author and product team would appreciate hearing from you! Let us know what you think about this textbook by writing to college_marketing@prenhall.com Please include "Feedback about Andre 1e" in the subject line.

If you have questions related to this product, please contact our customer service department online at www.247.prenhall.com.

Author Biography

Rae André received her Ph.D. in Organizational Psychology from The University of Michigan, the M.A. in Film Studies from The University of California at Los Angeles, and the B.A. (Cum Laude) in English from Cornell University. She has held professional positions at MCA, Inc., IBM, and General Motors Corporation.

Dr. André is the author or co-author of six books. These include, co-edited with Peter J. Frost, *Researchers Hooked on Teaching: Noted Scholars Discuss the Synergy Between Teaching and Research* (Sage Publications, 1996), *Positive Solitude* (HarperCollins, 1991), and, co-authored with Peter D. Ward, *The 59-Second Employee: How to Stay One Second Ahead of Your One-Minute Manager* (Houghton Mifflin Company, 1984). In addition, she has published more than 40 cases, articles, and classroom exercises in such journals as *Across the Board, The Boston Globe, Economic Development Quarterly,* the *Journal of General Management,* the *Journal of Small Business Management,* the *Journal of Management Education,* and *The New York Times.* Her work has often been described in the press, including *The Chicago Tribune, The Dallas Times Herald, Prevention Magazine, The Washington Post,* and *The Wall Street Journal.*

Currently Professor in the College of Business Administration at Northeastern University, Dr. André has taught Organizational Behavior and Theory, Introduction to Business, Business Strategy, Managing People in International Settings, and International Negotiation. Throughout her career, she has advocated the integration of rigorous classroom learning with real world experience, and, typically, her research is interdisciplinary and applied. She often studies unusual organizational forms such as business consortia, hybrid organizations, and quangos.

Dr. André has served on the Editorial Review Board of *The Journal of Management Education* and the Board of Directors of the Organizational Behavior Teaching Society. She is a member of the Academy of Management and the Authors Guild. She has been a visiting professor at the University of Pittsburgh's Semester at Sea voyage (1996), L'École Supériere du Commerce, Reims, France; the University of Waikato, New Zealand; and the Ulster University in Belfast, Northern Ireland.

Acknowledgments

The dozens of people who have created this book have performed as a real team, a virtual team, and a high performance team (see Chapter 9). For me as an author, it has been a pleasure and a fine adventure to work with them.

The highly professional Prentice Hall group that brings it all together so capably includes: Mike Ablassmeir, Senior Acquisitions Editor; Renata Butera, Associate Managing Editor; Steve Deitmer, Director of Development; Claudia Fernandez, Project Manager; Leah Johnson, Publisher's Representative; Keri Molinari, Assistant Editor; Charles Morris, Permissions Editor; Amy Ray, Freelance Editor; Carol Samet, Production Project Manager; Jeff Shelstad, Editorial Director; Janet Slowik, Senior Art Director; Denise Vaughn, Assistant Editor; and numerous other individuals who have performed well in crucial supportive roles.

The reviewers who commented with such care on early drafts (thank you so very much!) are:

Bradley Alge,	*Purdue University*
Lizabeth A. Barclay,	*Oakland University*
Eleanor H. Buttner,	*University of North Carolina–Greensboro*
Susan Eisner,	*Ramapo College*
Janice Gates,	*Western Illinois University*
Jackie Gilbert,	*Middle Tennessee State University*
Selina A. Griswold,	*The University of Toledo*
Ken Harris,	*Florida State University*
Chad Higgins,	*University of Washington*
Tai G. Kim,	*University of Delaware*
Randolph New,	*University of Richmond*
K. Praveen Parabotccah,	*University of Wisconsin–Whitewater*
Marian C. Schultz,	*University of West Florida*
Randy Sleeth,	*Virginia Commonwealth University*
Christie Kennedy Struckman,	*San Jose State University*
Sean Valentine,	*University of Wyoming*

Thanks also to the additional anonymous reviewers who gave of their time and expertise to help develop this project.

Thanks also to Lenore Kalarness, Freelance Editor, for her able support.

Special thanks go to my colleagues at the Organizational Behavior Teaching Society, including founder David L. Bradford of the Stanford Graduate School of Business, without whose inspiration and guidance over many years this book would never have been written. I have benefitted greatly from the work on organizational design by Patrick Connor. Finally, thanks to Megan André for her help and support throughout this project.

1

Why Mastering Organizational Behavior Is Essential to Your Career

Preview

What is organizational behavior, and what kinds of business challenges does it address?
What is organizational behavior (OB)?
What challenges do managers face at different organizational levels?
Why is it useful to visualize an organization as a system?

What economic and social issues challenge today's organizational leaders?
Globalization
The changing nature of work
The complex workforce

What organizational processes help companies compete in the modern economy?
Relying on teams
Innovations in attracting and keeping employees
Adaptations in organizational design
Increased attention to organizational ethics

What will your career be like in modern organizations?
The need for OB skills
Career paths and patterns
Career stages and career anchors
Career roles

How will mastering organizational behavior help you in your career?

Nidek Corporation and IQ Solutions, Inc.

Imagine that you are the head of a Japanese company that has a major division in the United States because the 160 million Americans who have vision problems are an important market for your product. How do you bridge the Japanese–American cultural gap to effectively manage both your Japanese and your American workforces?

Managing a multicultural workforce is one of the key challenges faced by business leaders today. It is the sort of challenge faced by the managers of **Nidek Corporation**, a leading innovator of ophthalmology and health care equipment. The managers at Nidek realize that U.S. and Japanese corporate cultures differ on everything from how employees greet each other to how they expect to be rewarded. To enhance company cohesion, Nidek has developed a unique hybrid of management styles from both cultures. For example, in Japan, Nidek's salespeople have a strong sense of belonging to the company, whereas in the United States loyalty tends to be low. So Nidek management uses a variety of motivation techniques to reduce turnover among its American salespeople. For instance, it encourages them to take pride in their work by developing an appreciation of the high quality of the products they sell and it helps them to make more money by allowing them to represent more than one product.

Now consider the case of **IQ Solutions**, a $30 million U.S. company that produces communications and advertising campaigns for such agencies as the U.S. Department of Agriculture (see illustration for a sample product) and the National Cancer Agency. The company's nearly 200 employees speak 18 different languages and come from diverse cultural

GREATNESS COMES FROM

DIVERSITY

USDA

backgrounds. The company believes its employee diversity adds value to the service it offers to its clients, and also enhances the quality of its employees' work life. A company spokesperson says, "We enjoy [diversity]. We embrace it. We let our people ethnically share through e-mails, through brown bag lunches, [and] through celebrations of various holidays."

What do Nidek and IQ Solutions have in common? Both companies are facing head on, and successfully, the major challenges of managing a modern workforce that is increasingly global and diverse. They also exemplify what this book is about—managing people, jobs, and organizations in a fast-paced international economy. Imagine that you are a manager in one of these companies, responsible for perhaps a dozen people. Better yet, imagine you are leading such a corporation. What would you need to know about managing the people in your organization? The answer is . . .*a lot*. And much of what you need to know is in the book you are about to read.

Organizations come in many varieties: small, medium, and large; moderately-paced and fast-paced; local and global. You should learn as much as you can about organizations, because, in all probability, you will be employed in them for the rest of your working life. Further, as a manager or an entrepreneur, you will spend most of your time working alongside the people of your company. To be successful, you must know a great deal about how to interact with them, organize them, and lead them.

What Is Organizational Behavior, and What Kinds of Business Challenges Does It Address?

What Is Organizational Behavior (OB)?

organization
A coordinated set of individuals working together on a relatively continuous basis toward common goals.

organizational behavior (OB)
The study of how people behave in organizations.

An **organization** is a coordinated set of individuals working together on a relatively continuous basis toward common goals. **Organizational behavior** (OB), is, put simply, the study of how people behave in organizations. This book focuses on behavior in business (for-profit) organizations. However, you can adapt most of its ideas for public sector (not-for-profit) organizations and government agencies as well.

Organizational behavior is a social science. This means that, by definition, its findings are based on data obtained through systematic study. People who study and apply OB hope to enhance worker well-being and organizational effectiveness by applying psychological and human systems knowledge. In addition to its own research, OB uses concepts and research from a variety of social sciences, including psychology, sociology, anthropology, economics, communication, and political science.

The field of OB offers tested principles that have a high probability of being useful to you in organizational life. Still, because human behaviors and systems are so complex, and because factors change from moment to moment, it is difficult to predict exactly what will happen next in any human relationship. Furthermore, there are often several reasonable ways to approach any given problem. Each of the chapters in this book offers you a variety of approaches that will help you diagnose and address organizational problems. In addition, the last chapter provides more details about the science of human behavior, and the history of OB research in particular, so that throughout your career you can continue to be an educated consumer of applied OB research.

Of course, OB is also about how real managers manage, and about how actual organizations function, and not all of this reality can be captured through social science alone. So throughout this text you will find many examples and cases that illustrate the complexities of organizational life.

What Challenges Do Managers Face at Different Organizational Levels?

OB covers fundamental issues that face *all* managers in an organization: how to motivate yourself and others, how to work and stay healthy, how power and politics shape careers and organizations, how leaders lead, and how managers design their companies to meet worldwide competition. Keep in mind that organizational behavior is not the same thing as **human resources management** (HRM), which is the particular organizational function responsible for selecting employees, establishing compensation systems, managing benefits, implementing training programs, and coordinating labor relations. Unlike HRM, OB is not a function; it is a set of organization-wide processes.

In this book you will learn about both **micro level** and **macro level** OB. Micro level OB covers individual, interpersonal, and group behaviors. Macro level OB covers how human systems are organized, structured, and controlled. Some experts prefer to reserve the term *organization behavior* strictly for micro level concepts and the term **organizational theory** (OT) for macro level concepts. However, in this book "organization behavior" refers to the subject as a whole, including both micro and macro dimensions.

Understanding OB helps managers solve people problems at all organizational levels. Whenever you are considering a problem at one level, you should keep in mind that all levels of an organization actively influence each other. So, for instance, a problem in your team is influenced by the characteristics of the individuals on the team as well as the culture of the organization.

See Table 1.1 for examples of the managerial challenges you will study in each chapter and at each level of analysis.

human resources management (HRM)
The particular organizational function responsible for such activities as selecting employees, and establishing compensation systems.

micro level OB
OB theory covering individual, interpersonal, and group behaviors.

macro level OB
OB theory covering how human systems are organized, structured, and controlled.

organizational theory (OT)
Term reserved for macro level concepts.

TABLE 1.1 OB Helps Managers Solve Practical Problems

At the individual level of analysis. . .	Chapters that address these problems. . .
How are you different from others and what does your uniqueness imply for your job and career choices? How can you work effectively with individuals who are different from you? How can you personally motivate others? How do you design motivating jobs? How do managers make effective decisions?	2. Your Personality and Style 3. Decision Making 4. Fundamentals of Motivation 5. Motivating Individuals in Their Jobs 6. Health and Stress at Work 7. Communication and Interpersonal Relationships 8. Cross-Cultural Relationships
At the group level of analysis. . .	
What are the kinds of workgroups you will encounter in business today? How can you be an effective group member and leader? How do you design and coach a team? a multinational team?	9. Groups and Their Influence 10. Improving Team Decision Making
With leadership across all levels. . .	
How should you approach the challenge of leadership? What are some leadership roles that you should one day be able to fill? What is the role of power in organizational life? How should you deal with conflict?	11. The Challenge of Leadership 12. Leadership Roles and Skills 13. Power and Influence 14. Conflicts Good and Bad
At the organizational systems level of analysis. . .	
How do you design an organization to meet its unique challenges? How are employees coordinated through different organizational structures? How do companies use organizational culture to promote organizational effectiveness? How do you get an entire organization to change its ways?	15. Designing Effective Organizations 16. Organizational Structure as a Design Tool 17. Organizational Culture 18. Changing Organizations

FIGURE 1.1

An Organization Is a System

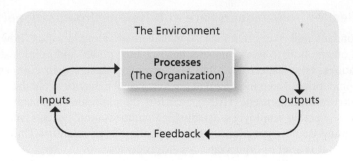

Why Is It Useful to Visualize an Organization as a System?

Before we go deeper into the study of OB and managerial challenges, let's pause to consider in depth the question, "What is an organization?" When you picture an organization in your mind, what do you see? Perhaps an organizational chart, with a company's levels and divisions? Maybe a photograph of several groups of people? Although these are both valid representations, in your role as a business decision maker, you should try to visualize an organization as a **system**. A system is a set of elements that combine to form a complex whole.[1]

According to **systems theory**, organizations are entities that transform inputs into outputs and operate within constraints imposed on them by their environments.[2] To visualize an organization as a system, see Figure 1.1.

Visualizing an organization as a system is useful because it helps you to see its basic elements quite clearly. The elements of the system are its inputs, processes, outputs, and feedback. Inputs to a company include materials, ideas, and employees. Processes are what the organization itself does to the inputs to transform them into outputs; outputs are primarily a company's products; feedback includes any sort of information that describes the outputs, such as information about how the outputs have been perceived by customers, competitors, or regulators.

For example, a manufacturing company collects inputs in the form of raw materials and processes them into an output called a product. Its customers buy the product and comment on its utility and quality, and thus give the organization's managers important feedback about how to improve the product. In a similar way, innovative companies take in information and raw materials, transform them via creative processes, and produce new technologies. Also, universities take in students and turn out educated citizens.

If you do not visualize your organization as a system, you may fail to recognize some key element. For example, suppose you are a manager under pressure to cut costs immediately. You grab the chance to buy a cheap raw material (an input), but, because you were rushed, you failed to consider that the material is hard for workers to handle (the process) and that its low quality may affect customer satisfaction (feedback). When solving an organizational problem, remembering to weigh all the essential elements ensures that you do not ignore one of them.

Beyond identifying fundamental organizational factors and introducing some key vocabulary, systems theory also illustrates that organizations exist in environments to which they must constantly adapt. Organizations that easily absorb inputs from their environments are called **open systems**. They have **permeable boundaries** that permit the free flow of information both into and out of the organization. An example of an open system is a company that does everything it can to make sure its employees understand customer needs, encouraging workers at all levels to visit with and learn from their customers. **Closed systems** are organizations that do not absorb inputs so easily because they have **impermeable boundaries** that restrict information flow. An example of a closed system is a company that only allows salespeople, rather than employees from a variety of functions, to meet customers.

Because, in a sense, open systems can learn, they are more likely than closed systems to adapt to environmental changes. Most modern organizations strive to be open systems. Only the occasional company, usually a monopoly, is so powerful that it can afford to be a closed system that ignores its environment. The key question for most modern organizations is how can the organization become more open?

---

system
A set of elements that combine to form a complex whole.

systems theory
The theory that organizations are entities that transform inputs into outputs and operate within constraints imposed on them by their environments.

open systems
Systems that easily absorb inputs from their environments.

permeable boundaries
Boundaries that permit the free flow of information both into and out of the organization.

closed systems
Systems that do not easily absorb inputs from their environments.

impermeable boundaries
Boundaries that restrict information flow

We will have more to say about organizational systems and design later in the book. For now, whenever you want to think critically about an organization, picture it as a system.

What Economic and Social Issues Challenge Today's Organizational Leaders?

Among the important environmental factors that shape today's organizations and careers are three economic and social issues: 1) globalization, 2) the changing nature of work, and 3) the complex workforce. Leaders must adapt their organizations' processes to these factors; you will probably adapt your career to them as well.

Globalization

Globalization is the modern phenomenon of the increased internationalization of business—the movement of trade, resources, and personnel across borders and regions. Many people have hoped that globalization would benefit both advanced industrial countries and the developing world. Some argue cogently that it has.[3] But others raise concerns. Nobel Prize-winning economist Joseph Stiglitz writes, "Globalization seems to have unified so much of the world against it, perhaps because there appear to be so many losers and so few winners.. . . Young French workers ask how globalization is going to make them better off—if, as they are told, they must accept the resulting lower wages and weakened job protection."[4] Similarly, Ben Bernanke, Chairman of the Board of Governors of the U.S. Federal Reserve, has argued that globalization may create an unsustainable growth in inequality among peoples.[5]

Although the United States is still the world's most powerful business engine,[6] today its companies and jobs are influenced by globalization as never before. Some observers estimate that fully 70 percent of American industry now faces foreign competition within the U.S. market.[7] Many companies no longer identify themselves with the United States, but consider themselves to be international. And although many U.S. workers will continue to have good jobs, others, mostly the unskilled, will have to compete against other unskilled workers internationally both to obtain work and to earn a living wage.

Global competition affects the nature of the work companies offer. For example, it affects whether vehicles are both designed *and* manufactured in the United States. It also affects where jobs will be located. For example, a pharmaceutical company is likely to do its genetic research in Boston, but produce its drugs in Guadalajara. Finally, globalization affects how companies manage people, including how they design their organizational structures and cultures and how they manage and motivate their employees. The Nidek case at the beginning of this chapter illustrates this well.

Certainly your career will be affected by the global economy in ways that we cannot even predict today. In response to global competitive pressures, your company may downsize, and your job may be outsourced or exported. Whether you are an employee or an entrepreneur, you may find that your best business opportunities lie on another continent. Even if you never set foot outside the United States, there is a high probability that you will have to work cross-culturally. You may have to manage a variety of cross-cultural interactions with peers, suppliers, and customers. If you make it to the top, you are increasingly likely to be part of an international management team. In a global company such as General Electric Corporation, for instance, fully one-third of the top leadership team comes from countries other than the United States.[8]

Welcome to the *world* in which you will live and work!

The Changing Nature of Work

For the purposes of this book, **work** is an activity an individual engages in to earn money. Often the term is used synonymously with **employment**, which implies that the person works for someone. A **job** is a specified task or set of tasks.

What will be the work of tomorrow, and what jobs will be available? Although no one can predict the future, by examining current statistics and trends we can make some educated guesses. There is some good news and some bad news.

globalization
The increased internationalization of business based on the movement of trade, resources, and personnel across borders and regions.

work
An activity an individual engages in to earn money.

employment
Working for someone.

job
A specified task or set of tasks an individual does as part of an occupation.

JOB GROWTH The good news is that in the U.S. economy today there are more than 145.6 million jobs, and the U.S. Department of Labor predicts that by 2014 there will be 18.9 million additional new jobs.[9] In addition to the new jobs, many existing positions will open up as companies replace retiring workers. In fact, replacement needs will create more job openings than will employment growth.[10]

Where will jobs be available? Many of the newly created jobs will be in smaller companies. It is primarily small and new companies, rather than large, existing businesses, that create jobs.[11] In fact, most recent job growth has come from companies less than two years old.[12] In total there are about 5.6 million companies in the United States. However, the number of companies with fewer than 100 employees far outstrips the number of larger companies, and only about 3,600 companies have 2,500 or more employees.[13]

Most people will work for others rather than for themselves. In 2004, wage and salary workers held about 91 percent of all jobs, and the self-employed about 9 percent. (Less than 1 percent were unpaid family workers.)[14] Even if you plan on starting your own company, chances are you will spend some time working for others. Research suggests that most company founders got their business ideas in their prior jobs,[15] where they also developed crucial contacts with customers, suppliers, and potential employees.

What industries will have the most jobs? Through 2014, the fastest growing industry sectors will be services for education and health.[16] These will include educational services at all educational levels, along with private hospitals, nursing and residential care, and individual and family services. In fact, about 3 in every 10 jobs in the country will be either in health care and social assistance or private educational services.

Which types of occupations will grow the most? The fastest growing occupational group will be professional and related occupations. About three-fourths of the growth in professional jobs will come from only three groups of professions: computer and mathematical occupations; health care practitioner and related technical occupations; and education, training, and library occupations.[17] Other fast-growing occupations will be services (such as food preparation and health care support); management, business, and financial occupations; and construction and mining.

ENTRY LEVEL HIRING For today's students there is even more good news about jobs. In recent years, the hiring of entry level workers has been surging by double digits. Data from the U.S. Bureau of the Census suggest that now and for years to come, new college graduates will be in fairly high demand.[18] This is because two members of the baby boom generation will retire for every one new college graduate who enters the job market.

As a result, today's graduates are already finding that their job opportunities are not limited to just one industry. One applicant may apply to companies as diverse as J. P. Morgan, Microsoft, and Teach for America, for example. Also, liberal arts graduates are finding that companies are willing to provide them with the on-the-job training they need to bump up their business skills.

JOB DISRUPTION So that's the good news. The bad news is that, in recent decades, the average pay of workers in rich countries, including the United States, has stagnated or even fallen.[19] On top of this, Americans work long hours, about 300 hours more per year than Europeans.[20] In addition, some U.S. workers have faced major job disruptions, leaving others to worry whether they will be next.

In the face of competitive pressures, it is fairly common for companies to go out of business. For instance, half of the 100 biggest industrial firms existing in the United States in 1974 had gone out of business by 2000.[21] Some companies choose to **downsize**, or **rightsize**—both of which mean to grow smaller by cutting employees.

downsize, rightsize
To grow smaller by cutting employees.

One source reports that in the 1990s about half of U.S. companies downsized to some extent.[22] During that period, companies often cut out a layer of middle management, and permanently laid off many workers. Remaining workers had to put in longer hours, and they became increasingly anxious about losing their jobs. At the height of the 1981 recession some 12 percent of workers were afraid of losing their jobs, whereas by the late 1990s that figure had risen to 37 percent.[23] In 2006 the number of households afraid of job loss or other income interruption in the upcoming year was 35 percent.[24]

Other challenges facing U.S. workers include having their jobs **outsourced**, or sent either to other companies or other countries. The term **offshoring** describes the particular case of outsourcing in which jobs are sent abroad. For example, in one seven-year period one multinational eliminated 59,000 jobs in Western Europe and North America while creating 56,000 new jobs primarily in east Asia and Eastern Europe.[25]

Companies have many reasons for downsizing. One reason is locating cheaper labor abroad. Formerly, companies offshored mainly blue-collar labor; however, now cheap white-collar labor is also available outside the United States, especially in countries such as India, where English is widely spoken. Another reason companies downsize American operations is that global companies increasingly find their markets are abroad, and they want to be closer to them. A third reason is that companies are likely to decide to drop functions that are not essential to their core work and business strategy. For example, just as universities hire catering companies to run their food services operations, so companies outsource peripheral functions. Fourth, failure to anticipate changes in technology has driven some companies to cut workers. For example, in 2003, Kodak predicted that the film industry would decline by about 10 percent a year in the United States; instead, it declined by closer to 30 percent. As a result, the company's bond rating was reduced to junk status, and by 2007 the company had to lay off 26,000 workers.[26] Finally, productivity increases here in the United States have also reduced the need for workers. Based in large part on information technology innovation, advances in manufacturing have been especially strong.[27] For a graphic view of the relationship between productivity and employment, see Figure 1.2.

Unfortunately, the worldwide growth of new employment opportunities is insufficient to productively employ both those who have lost their jobs and the new entrants to the labor force. At the end of 2000, unemployment worldwide stood at about 160 million workers, and most of these individuals were first-time jobseekers. Fifty million of these jobseekers were from the industrialized countries.[28]

CONTINGENT JOBS Some U.S. workers face a future of one unstable job after another. In 2001 about 4 percent of the total U.S. workforce (5.4 million workers) held **contingent jobs**, jobs that are temporary and not expected to last. In addition, 6.4 percent were independent contractors (8.6 million workers), 1.6 percent were on-call workers (2.1 million workers), 0.9 were temporary help agency workers (1.2 million workers), and 0.5 percent were contract company workers (633,000 workers).[29]

outsource
To send jobs to other companies or other countries.

offshore
To outsource jobs to other countries.

contingent jobs
Jobs that are temporary and not expected to last.

FIGURE 1.2

Fewer Workers, More Productivity 1978–2003

Source: Industrial Production Index, Federal Reserve Bank of St. Louis: Economic Research, http://research.stlouisfed,org/fred2/series/INPRO. Accessed September 17, 2006; L.J. Bivens, "Economic snapshot," Economic Policy Institute, November 30, 2005, http://www.epinet.org/content.cfm/webfeatures_snapshot_20051130. Accessed September 17, 2006. Based on data from the Bureau of Labor Statistics.

In sum, about 13 percent of the total U.S. workforce lives with unstable employment, many suffering the personal and family consequences of being laid off and out of work. Yet, while having an unstable job is bad for some workers, others view flexible work arrangements as a benefit. Workers who want to test their employability, learn new skills, and transition into permanent jobs actually benefit from temporary work opportunities. Also, employers find that having a large pool of temporary workers provides flexible opportunities for expansion.

Who are today's workers and jobseekers? In the next section we will explore the complex U.S. workforce and the challenges it presents to managers.

The Complex Workforce

The U.S. workforce is becoming more diverse with every year. In addition to the major categories of age, gender, and race, the workforce is made up of people who differ in national origin, physical ability, sexual orientation, class, and religion.

Each of these groups faces its own unique challenges, including developing a group identity and at times facing prejudice. Of course, organizations themselves face the challenge of working with their diverse workforces. American corporations spend millions of dollars annually on training programs that help individuals work and manage in organizational cultures that are diversified—in short, that help employees work with individuals who differ from themselves. In addition, age, gender, and race are **protected classes**, which means it is illegal to discriminate against an employee because of these factors. Companies and their employees must know what constitutes illegal discrimination and how to avoid it.

In addition to demographic diversity, the workforce varies widely in terms of literacy, employability, and unionization.

Next we examine how each of these factors affects organizations today.

protected classes
Groups of people defined by factors such as age, gender and race, on the basis of which it is illegal to discriminate.

AGE The U.S. workforce is aging (See Figure 1.3). By 2014 the group of American workers aged 16 to 24 will find its share of the labor force decreasing to 13.7 percent.[30] The group aged 25 to 54 will find its share shrinking to 65.2 percent. Meanwhile, workers 55 and older will find their share of the workforce growing from 15.6 percent in 2004 to 21.2 percent in 2014.

Although the U.S. workforce is aging, on the whole, it is still growing. In contrast, other developed countries are experiencing not only aging populations and workers, but population reduction and workforce shrinkage.[31] For instance, Japan's population peaked in 2005 at around 125 million people, and the country's more pessimistic forecasts predict it may shrink to about 95 million people by the year 2050. In Germany, the world's third-largest economy, the total population may shrink from 82 million to 70 to 73 million by 2030. Similar predictions are being made for most other developed countries and even for such emerging ones as China. All of these countries are struggling with how to maintain economic growth in the face of their shrinking populations.

As for young people, globally, by 2010 there will be 460 million new, young jobseekers. Two-thirds of these will be in Asia, whereas only 3 percent will be in Europe and North America.[32]

THE MILLENNIAL GENERATION In the United States, between 2000 and 2015, the number of workers aged 35 to 44 will decline by 15 percent, leading forward-thinking companies to worry about replacing their older workers and retaining their younger ones.[33] Companies will be competing to hire individuals from the Millennial generation, the 70 to 80 million individuals born in the 1980s and 1990s.

Although it may be too soon to tell how the Millennial generation will behave in the workplace, they are said to share the following characteristics:[34]

- Computer fluency
- Eagerness for feedback, evaluation, and mentoring
- Impatience to make an impact on their new organizations
- Teamwork orientation
- Desire for responsibility

FIGURE 1.3

Percent of Labor Force by Age Group, 2004 and Projected 2014

Source: U.S. Department of Labor, Bureau of Labor Statistics, Occupational Outlook Handbook, 2006–2007 Edition, http://www.bis.gov/oco/print/oco2003.htm. Accessed October 22, 2006.

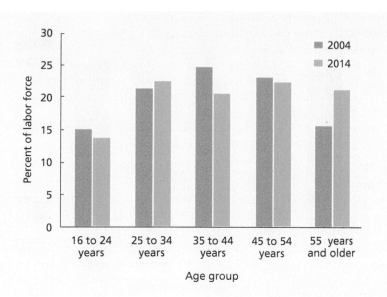

- Desire for on-the-job training to develop their skills and future careers
- Dislike for working long hours
- Weak work ethic
- Desire to balance personal and professional life
- Idealism and desire to give back to society
- Need for direction from their managers

Although some of these characteristics might be attributed to young people from any generation, young people today are receiving more attention than recent generations because they are a relatively small cohort. Their employers are working hard to understand and work with their unique set of values. It may be, too, that companies will be making a variety of cultural changes to accommodate the particular needs and values of younger workers.

GENDER In 2002, 74 percent of men and 60 percent of women aged 16 and older were in the workforce.[35] In 2002, 29 percent of men and 34 percent of women worked in a managerial or professional specialty.[36] This represented an improvement for women, who only held 22 percent of such jobs in 1993.[37] However, within this broad category women held a much larger share of the relatively lower-paying occupations. They were only 11 percent of the engineers and 19 percent of the dentists, but 98 percent of the preschool and kindergarten teachers and 93 percent of the registered nurses.[38]

Between 1979 and 2002, men's real earnings (adjusted for inflation) increased by only 1 percent, whereas women's real earnings increased by 27 percent. According to the U.S. Department of Labor, the improvement for women can be attributed mainly to their pursuit of higher education.

Between 1970 and 2001, the percentage of women aged 25 to 64 who had completed four or more years of college nearly tripled, from 11 percent to 32 percent, whereas the percentage of men with a college degree only doubled, from 16 percent to 32 percent.[39] Partly as a result, in 2001, among families in which both wives and husbands worked, 24 percent of the wives earned more money than their husbands.[40]

About 60 percent of the world's 2.8 billion workers are men and 40 percent are women.[41] In every occupation, women face higher unemployment rates and earn less money than men. They represent 60 percent of the world's 550 million working poor. Women hold 20 to 40 percent of all managerial jobs worldwide, but their representation seems to have plateaued. Countries in North America, South America, and Eastern Europe have a higher share of women in management jobs than countries in East Asia, South Asia, and the Middle East.[42]

FIGURE 1.4

Percent of Labor Force by Race and Ethnic Origin, 2004 and Projected 2014

Source: U.S. Department of Labor, Bureau of Labor Statistics, *Occupational Outlook Handbook*, 2006–2007 ed., www.bls.gov.oco/print/oco2003htm. Accessed July 20, 2006.

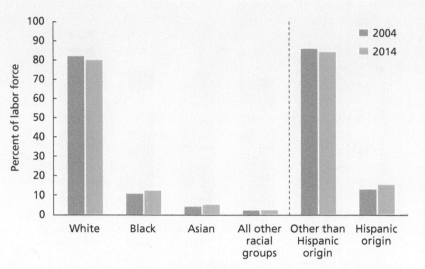

Note: The four race groups add to the total labor force. The two ethnic origin groups also add to the total labor force. Hispanics may be of any race.

RACE Although the U.S. workforce is mainly white, Hispanics, blacks, and Asian and other ethnic groups account for an increasing share. Their percentage of the national labor force will grow from 30 percent in 2004 to 34.4 percent in 2014.[43] Hispanics are projected to be the fastest growing of these four groups.

You can see these trends in Figure 1.4. In this illustration, the labor force is portrayed in two ways, as four race groups, and as Hispanics (who can be any race) and non-Hispanics.

In the future, the U.S. workforce will become even more racially diverse. By 2050 about half of all Americans will be white and half will be of a variety of other races.[44]

In addition to the diversity of the workforce, U.S. managers must concern themselves with literacy, employability, and labor unions, which we will consider next.

LITERACY Only about half of the U.S. adult population can read well enough to achieve the minimum standard considered necessary for success in a global economy.[45] The 50 percent below this standard are not illiterate in the traditional sense of not being able to read simple passages or write their name; however, they do not possess the more sophisticated skills necessary to succeed in a technologically advanced economy. On literacy tests, they perform below the average score for adults who graduated from high school. Many would have trouble reading a simple instruction manual, let alone dealing with complicated technologies.

In a 2002 study of 20 high-income countries, U.S. literacy was only average, despite the fact that the United States ranks near the top in education spending and sends significantly more of its population on to higher education. Older generations of Americans are more literate than younger generations, suggesting that in the future American literacy will drop to below average among top nations.

employability skills
Social and behavioral skills necessary for fitting into the workplace.

EMPLOYABILITY **Employability skills** are those social and behavioral skills necessary for fitting into the workplace. They include having a good work ethic and knowing how to dress, be prompt, greet coworkers, and manage one's time. In a study by the National Association of Manufacturers reporting data from U.S. employers in 20 industries, 59.1 percent listed poor basic employability skills (including attendance and having a good work ethic) as the most serious deficiency among their hourly production employees.[46] The second most serious deficiency was poor reading and writing skills, cited by 32.4 percent of the employers. The third was inadequate math skills, cited by 26.2 percent of employers.

Given these data, it is not surprising that a study by the American Management Association found that companies ranked developing and improving workforce skills eighth out of 25 issues of current corporate concern, even above such important matters as developing technological solutions to business problems (ranked number 12) and getting access to investment capital (ranked number 18).[47]

UNION REPRESENTATION Today, fewer than 13 percent of all American workers belong to unions, down from 34 percent in 1955.[48] In the private (business) sector, 8.2 percent of workers are unionized, whereas in the public (government) sector the figure is 37.2 percent. In all, today's union membership is close to 16 million people.

In 2001, union members earned 25 percent more than nonunion members in comparable jobs. This increment is referred to as the **wage differential**. Union members made a median salary of $760 per week, compared to the $599 per week of nonunion workers.

Among occupational groups the most heavily unionized are workers in education, training, and library occupations (36.1 percent), whereas the least unionized are workers in sales and office occupations (8.2 percent). Although the percentage of unionized manufacturing workers has been declining for two decades, the percentage of unionized service workers has been increasing. Rates of union membership are highest among workers 45 to 54 years old, and full-time workers are more than twice as likely as part-time workers to be union members. The largest numbers of union workers live in California, New York, and Illinois.

Workforces outside the United States typically have far higher percentages of unionized workers.[49] In Canada, Australia, and Germany, trade union membership runs more than 30 percent, whereas in Sweden it is about 80 percent. In Australia, France, and Germany, many more employees who are not themselves union members are nevertheless covered by the collective bargaining agreements that unions negotiate with management. The result is that although fewer than 10 percent of workers might belong to unions, 90 percent may be covered by union agreements, as is the case in France.

IMPLICATIONS OF THESE TRENDS Globalization, the changing nature of work and the complex workforce will all affect your life in organizations. Although a minority of workers and business owners will be able to avoid being significantly affected by today's global business environment, during your career you will probably have to contend with it. So although the focus of this book is on the United States and its practices, here you will also learn about the many cross-cultural factors in modern organizational life, and about how to develop cross-cultural knowledge and adaptability throughout your career.

You may also have to contend with the effects of job growth and disruption as they affect U.S. workers and, indeed, workers in all developed countries. Certainly you will see organizations change and evolve culturally and structurally, as they respond to global competition.

As a member of the Millennial generation, you will have excellent opportunities to find a good job in a good company, provided that you have a sound education and are willing to relocate to wherever the jobs are. You can expect companies to work hard to keep you, too. As many as a third of new employees leave within three years, and it costs a company nearly $10,000 per person to train replacements.[50]

Finally, as a result of its ethnic, cultural, and other diversity, the U.S. workforce tends to be dynamic and creative but also, at times, challenging. You may find that managing members of the diverse workforce and being a member of the diverse workforce yourself are, and will continue to be for the foreseeable future, significant issues.

wage differential
The increment of the median salary of union members compared to nonunion workers.

What Organizational Processes Help Companies Compete in the Modern Economy?

To deal with fast-paced international competition, companies work hard to foster innovation and high-quality decision making. To do this, many are relying extensively on teams. Also, many are changing the way they attract and keep trained workers. Finally, companies are making important adaptations in their organizational designs.

Relying on Teams

Today companies make extensive use of teams. This adaptation certainly makes common sense. For one thing, today's work is more complicated than ever before. It is often **knowledge work**—work that requires high levels of analysis and is performed by well-educated individuals. In contrast with manufacturing work, knowledge work usually requires the integration of the ideas of a variety of specialists. For example, designing the computer program used by the tax advisors in a tax preparation company might require the knowledge of programmers, tax lawyers, and behavioral specialists. No one individual alone has enough knowledge and ability to get the job done, so effective teamwork is absolutely necessary.

Companies also use teams because effective teams can replace expensive managers. Also, they provide highly motivating, interesting situations in which to work. Finally, members of the Millennial generation are said to be comfortable working in teams.

Innovations in Attracting and Keeping Employees

Companies that hope to attract and keep their employees cater to their preferences. For example, they may offer their employees opportunities for increasing their training, enhancing their work–life balance, and even advancing social causes.

To illustrate, Millennials (along with other generations, it must be said), want to balance their work and family lives. In a 2006 survey of 37,000 undergraduates, this was their number-one career goal.[51] As a result, some companies now offer flexible work schedules. At the systems engineering firm Lockheed Martin, some employees work nine-hour days and get every other Friday off. Pharmaceutical giant Merck & Company is considering enhancing vacation time in order to stay competitive with other companies in the same industry: Eli Lilly & Company offers new employees 17 vacation days, for instance. Companies also want to retain their talented young women after they become mothers. The consulting firm Booz Allen Hamilton strives to achieve this by creating meaningful internal jobs for its young female consultants who want to reduce their travel time.[52]

Members of the Millennial generation also want on-the-job training, and according to the 2006 *BusinessWeek* ranking of Top 50 Employers, most of the top companies now provide extensive training programs.[53] Student internships are popular, too. Students learn a lot from them, and, increasingly, companies are relying on them to recruit permanent employees.

Millennials are also highly interested in companies that show social responsibility.[54] To meet this interest, at investment firm Goldman Sachs & Company the standard company match of $2000 for charitable contributions has been raised to $10,000. Recruits at cigarette maker Philip Morris USA are also wooed on the social responsibility theme: They are offered the opportunity to work on technologies that make cigarettes less harmful.

Adaptations in Organizational Design

So far we have focused on how companies are adapting their micro level processes to the changing times. But how are they adapting their macro level processes?

To begin with, companies today strive to be lean. They want to operate with as few employees as possible, and with the least costly payroll, and so, as we have seen, they rightsize and outsource.

Companies also want to be less bureaucratic and defensive and more innovative and enterprising. Although they may hold onto some departments that emphasize bureaucratic procedures and plans—departments such as accounting and manufacturing—large companies, like IBM and General Electric, now emphasize flexibility for their companies as a whole. For example, a company may try to become a **boundaryless organization**, in which the internal barriers to communication and information are removed among the organization's functions (such as engineering, marketing, and manufacturing) and between domestic and foreign operations.[55] The concept of the boundaryless organization was popularized by General Electric's iconic former head Jack Welch. The boundaryless approach is based on the assumptions that good ideas come from all parts of the organization and that all parts of the organization should be thinking about customers. A related approach is

knowledge work
Work that requires high levels of analysis and is performed by well-educated individuals.

boundaryless organization
Organization in which the internal barriers to communication and information are removed among the organization's functions and operations.

employee empowerment. Using this technique, companies allow employees to make decisions that traditionally were made by managers alone.

Some companies make system-wide process improvements. For example, they might focus on enhancing quality in their **core competencies**, which are the operations in which a company excels, and outsource peripheral functions to other companies that can do them better because they specialize in them. Or, since many foreign manufacturers compete so effectively on quantity, U.S. companies often focus on quality. To do this they are likely to adopt systems for **total quality management** (TQM)—organization-wide processes that emphasize excellence in outcomes such as product reliability and durability. They might also adopt full-scale changes like **re-engineering**, the redesign of business processes to improve performance on such outcomes as cost, quality, service, and speed.[56] Re-engineering is usually applied simultaneously to many different organizational processes. For example, it might involve changing a company's work units from functional departments to process teams, and changing people's jobs from simple tasks to multi-dimensional tasks.

Today companies also want to keep and protect any process that gives them a competitive advantage. For this reason, they emphasize **organizational learning**, the process by which knowledge acquired by individuals is embedded in organizational memory.[57] For example, when a manager figures out a new way to achieve efficiency, his or her company must somehow hold on to this knowledge so the company can continue to use it. Organizational learning is also important because loyalty between companies and their employees is often low. Employees who move on to other opportunities may take critical information with them.

Organizations are also interested in developing cultures that are flexible and adaptable. One way to achieve this is to hire a diverse set of employees. Not only do companies that value diversity hire workers from a variety of backgrounds, they make sure that talented people from all backgrounds are given the experience and contacts they need to move up in the corporation. Having an innovative culture is also highly valued today. Companies compete for top talent, and design human systems that will develop their ideas.

Finally, some organizations have developed new forms. Partnerships are popular. Rather than continually shop for the best price among all suppliers, for example, a company may choose to structure an ongoing relationship with only one or two. When a company wants to enter a foreign market, it may even partner with its former foreign competitors. Another adaptive form is the **networked organization**, which is comprised of loosely joined companies that may have quite different designs, each adapted to a separate environment, but which are organized through one core holding company. Richard Branson's Virgin group of companies is an example of a highly successful networked organization that includes an airline, a mobile phone company, and a personal electronics company, among others, all benefiting from the Virgin brand, financing, and management style.

employee empo
Allowing employees
decisions that traditi
made by managers a

core competencies
The operations in which a
company excels.

total quality management (TQM)
Organization-wide processes that emphasize excellence in outcomes such as product reliability and durability.

re-engineering
The redesign of business processes to improve performance on such outcomes as cost, quality, service, and speed.

organizational learning
The process by which knowledge acquired by individuals is embedded in organizational memory.

networked organization
An organization comprised of loosely joined companies that may have quite different designs, each adapted to a separate environment, but that are organized through one core holding company.

TABLE 1.2 Overview: How Companies Adapt Their Organization-Wide Processes and Designs to the Global Business Environment

How do organizations adapt?	Examples
Organizations become leaner.	They emphasize rightsizing and they practice outsourcing.
Organizations become less bureaucratic and more innovative.	They emphasize their core competencies and break down barriers between functions and between divisions.
Organizations implement process improvements.	They improve quality in a variety of ways through total-organization programs such as total quality management and re-engineering.
Organizations hold on to and develop their best practices.	They facilitate organizational learning through leadership and participation.
Organizations develop flexible and innovative cultures.	They hire for diversity and excellence, then design systems that motivate these kinds of employees.
Organizations adopt new forms.	They enter into partnerships with suppliers and competitors, and form or join networks that provide mutual advantages.

Increased Attention to Organizational Ethics

In the wake of numerous corporate scandals, from the demise of Enron to corruption at Fannie Mae, managers are also paying increased attention to organizational ethics. One reason for their interest is that companies that make a commitment to organizational ethics perform better financially than those that do not.[58] In addition, organizations want to avoid the corporate deaths caused by unethical behavior at companies like Arthur Andersen, and, in fact, to avoid any scandal at all that may tarnish their reputations.

transparency

Visibility into organizational decision making to assess its truthfulness.

A further factor is that stakeholders, including stockholders and governments, are demanding **transparency**—visibility into organizational decision making to assess its truthfulness—especially in functions like accounting that have been at the center of a series of major corporate scandals. Finally, many organizational leaders and members are themselves concerned individuals who want to manage ethically. It may be that at least some of the individuals who commit white-collar crimes just do not see themselves as criminals. Why is that, and what can be done about it?

As a result of such concerns, many U.S. companies today recognize the need to establish dedicated processes for incorporating ethical standards into business decisions. The processes they establish go far beyond merely publishing a code of ethics. An additional issue is that internationally, there is a wide range of business-government-societal systems that have an equally wide range of views, laws, and ethical standards. It is incumbent on U.S. companies and businesspeople doing business in another country to learn that country's way of doing things, and, at the same time, to realize that U.S. laws govern their business behavior abroad.

Throughout this book we will have much more to say about how companies can improve organizational ethics.

What Will Your Career Be Like in Modern Organizations?

All of the issues described in this chapter will affect your career. Because the business world is now so complex and fast-paced, to enhance your job opportunities you must be aware of major trends like the ones we have just discussed, and you must be adaptable.

The Need for OB Skills

In today's competitive environment, one strategy for success is to optimize your OB skills along with your professional specialty. When the business of your company changes, the need for interpersonal, group, and leadership skills endures. Whatever your professional training, it is useful to develop a reputation as a person who knows how to get results through people. *Become known not only as an excellent technician but also as a person who is savvy about management and leading.*

How do company recruiters view OB skills? In a recent study of recruiters at 85 business schools, recruiters ranked the following skills most highly[59] (the percent of recruiters who ranked the skill as "very important" is also noted): 1) communication and interpersonal skills (89 percent); 2) the ability to work well within a team (87 percent); 3) personal ethics and integrity (86 percent); 4) analytical and problem-solving skills (84 percent); 5) work ethic (83 percent); and 6) fit with the corporate culture (75 percent).

The kinds of OB skills needed in modern business organizations are detailed in Table 1.3.

The Special Case for Ethics. As you examine this list, you may be wondering why being ethical is considered a skill. Isn't being a good person what ethics is all about? Unfortunately, in today's complicated world, being a good person only goes so far. Just as companies today are re-envisioning and refocusing their commitments to ethics, so must individuals. For example, soon you will make an important decision that reflects modern ethical complexities: When you graduate, you will choose a company to work for.[60] Are you willing to work for just any company? Of course not. For each company you consider, you want to know what its goals are, what values its culture stands for, and whether, based on your values, you personally want to work there. Would becoming an employee of this company be consistent with your own values and help you continue to develop into the kind of person you want to be? The answers to these questions are neither simple nor easily determined.

TABLE 1.3 Meet Today's Organizational Challenges with OB Skills

These modern environmental factors. . .	. . .Influence organizations to adapt by becoming more. . .	. . .And influence individuals to obtain particular OB skills, such as being. . .
Globalization	Flexible	Effective group members
The nature of jobs	Fast-paced	Team leaders
The diverse, changing, and internationally competitive workforce	Knowledgeable	Ethical
	Ethical	Culturally adaptable
	Innovative	Interpersonally competent
		Networkers
		Leaders of organizational change
		Emotionally well-grounded
		Continual learners
		Creative (especially in teams)
		Physically healthy and adaptable in the face of stress

However, knowing how to approach the problem specifically and thoroughly is an ethics skill that you can further develop.

Career Paths and Patterns

Faced with the uncertainties of the future, you are no doubt wondering what path your career will follow. Given that you are already succeeding as an undergraduate or graduate college student, you are well on your way to finding a job in the desirable **primary labor market** that includes professional, managerial, and other white-collar jobs. These jobs generally provide high incomes, relative security, and good benefits. No doubt you hope to avoid jobs in the **secondary labor market**, dead-end positions with few benefits and little security.

Then, too, you may already have set your career expectations to deal with future changes. For one thing, you may have already anticipated that career patterns, described next, change with the times.[61] Most likely your career will follow one of the following four basic patterns.

A **steady state career** is characterized by a lifetime of employment in one job, changing employers infrequently. You might be a stockbroker your entire life, for instance, in one or two companies. In the mid-twentieth century this pattern was common.

A **spiral career** is one in which you follow a variety of interests based on your skills. Over the course of their lives, people in spiral careers develop various interests around one core interest. You could be a stockbroker for a while, then a financial analyst, and later an independent financial planner.

A third kind of career is the **transitory career** in which an individual moves among many different unrelated positions. For example, you might be a stockbroker for a few years, then an entrepreneur in a catering business, and still later take up aqua farming.

Finally, a **linear career** is one in which a person stays within the same profession, but changes jobs and companies fairly frequently, moving up the ladder. You might be a stockbroker for some years in a couple of different companies, then advance in a series of financial services companies to manager, vice-president, and president. This is the kind of pattern that is most common today.

Linear careers are often referred to as **boundaryless**, which means that they are characterized by increased movement between organizations.[62] In 1983 the median period for which men aged 55 to 64 had been with their current employers was 15.3 years, but by 2000 it had declined to 10.2 years.[63] Since large corporations cannot provide stable, lifetime careers, individuals who work for them today are likely to move from one company to another, to identify with the market for their skills rather than with their present employer, and to obtain career support from extra-organizational networks and information.[64] Today about 40 percent of mid-level managers are in frequent contact with professional recruiters.[65]

primary labor market
The market that includes professional, managerial, and other white-collar jobs.

secondary labor market
The market of jobs with few benefits and little security.

steady state career
A career in which one remains in one job long-term, changing employers infrequently.

spiral career
A career in which one follows a variety of interests based on one's skills.

transitory career
A career in which one moves among many different unrelated positions.

linear career
A career in which one stays within the same profession, but changes jobs and companies fairly frequently, moving up the ladder.

boundaryless career
A linear career characterized by increased movement between organizations.

You are probably keenly aware that in today's turbulent job market you need to keep your skills, reputation, and network polished at all times. Indeed, some companies openly recognize today's business uncertainties and will actively encourage you to look out for yourself by keeping your skills and networks up-to-date. One way of dealing with career uncertainty is to start your own company. If this is your choice you are not alone: In the United States the number of one-person businesses, for example, is growing by 4 to 5 percent per year.[66]

Career Stages and Career Anchors

Whatever your career pattern, your career is likely to unfold in a set of logical *stages* in which your goals and activities will change and evolve.[67] Research suggests that careers advance through five stages.

Stage 1: *Preparation.* In the first stage you prepare for the work world. You study career options, set goals, and study to acquire the knowledge and skills you need to meet your goals.

career anchor

An occupational self-concept based on one's self-perceived talents, abilities, values, needs, and motives.

During this stage, you begin to develop a set of beliefs called **career anchors**. A career anchor is "a person's occupational self-concept, based on his or her self-perceived talents, abilities, values, needs, and motives."[68] It develops based on a person's assessment of his or her talents, skills, and areas of competence, along with his or her main motives, needs, goals, and values.[69] As you develop your career anchor or anchors, you will naturally take into account the various contextual factors described earlier in this chapter.

The five most common career anchors are:[70]

1. Technical or functional competence. (For instance, you are an engineer and a darned good one.)
2. Managerial competence. (You enjoy managing people, budgets, and projects.)
3. Security and stability in your job. (You want security first and foremost; you would be attracted to a military or governmental job.)
4. Creativity and entrepreneurship. (You love to start businesses but after they are up and running you sell them and move on.)
5. Autonomy and independence. (You like to work creatively and on your own, with minimal or no supervision.) See the section "Gain Experience" at the end of this chapter to complete an assessment of your career anchors.

Stage 2: *Organizational Entry.* During this period, you explore different jobs and get a feel for different types of companies. Some students enter this stage while still at university by taking relevant summer jobs or attending schools that offer internships and cooperative education. In recent years, top MBA (Master of Business Administration) programs have required their applicants to be well into this stage, with four or five years of experience under their belts before applying. Today programs are more flexible because they want to attract women before they have children, and because they need to compete with other professions, such as law, that do not have this requirement. For example, at Stanford in 2006, the average number of years of work experience for the incoming MBA class was 3.8, compared with an average of 5 years in 2001.[71]

Stage 3: *Early Career.* You establish yourself in a specific job, in a specific company, and work hard to be successful.

career plateau

Stage at which one is seen as a solid company citizen, but not in line for advancement.

Stage 4: *Middle Career.* During this stage you continue to work. Perhaps you reach the top of the company. Or perhaps you come to a **career plateau** in which you are seen as a solid company citizen, but are not in line for advancement.

Stage 5: *Late Career.* Finally, you wind down your commitment to the company and to your career, and you plan the details of your retirement.

Career Roles

role

The behavior expected of someone who holds a particular status.

At some point in your career you are likely to face an important choice about the type of **role** you want to fulfill in organizational life. A role is the behavior expected of someone who holds a particular status.[72] In professional careers especially, you may one day have to choose between the roles of **independent contributor** and **manager**. Not everyone wants to become a manager, and companies today, especially those involved in knowledge work, recognize that there are many other ways to be a strong organizational contributor.

Let's say you become a successful marketing researcher: You develop into a highly knowledgeable professional, a practical problem solver, and an excellent team player. You have become a successful independent contributor—someone who works without subordinates to do an important organizational job. Clearly, your job is different from that of a manager—someone who works through people to accomplish the work of an organization. One day, having watched you perform in this role successfully over a number of years, your division manager offers you a promotion to the role of manager. In this position, you will definitely make more money. However, you have always loved doing consumer research, and you enjoy the professional recognition you continue to earn as a top researcher. You have a tough decision to make. Should you drop your role as an independent contributor in favor of this new role of manager? Which role will make you happier in the long run?

To help you make this decision, you should be clear about what a manager does. Among other things, managers motivate subordinates, make decisions, set goals, run teams, and monitor processes. Hour by hour, their work is characterized by brevity, variety, and fragmentation.[73] Some of their days are "normal," bringing a heavy load of meetings and communications.[] Other days are devoted to managing crises or catching up. In Table 1.4 you can see a comprehensive list of the roles that managers perform.

So do you want to be a manager? Although "management" is the label most often used to describe satisfying careers in organizations, in reality it is not the only route you can

independent contributor
Someone who works without subordinates to do an important organizational job.

manager
Someone who works through people to accomplish the work of an organization.

TABLE 1.4 The Ten Basic Managerial Roles

Interpersonal Roles	Activities	Example
1. Figurehead	Represents the organization on formal occasions	A division leader addresses the stockholders at the annual stockholder meeting.
2. Liaison	Interacts with peers and others outside the organization in order to gain favors and information, including serving on corporate boards	The CEO serves on the boards of two other corporations.
3. Leader	Selects and motivates employees	A manager has to select 20 percent of her employees to fire during a downsizing, and has to keep the remaining employees motivated.
Informational Roles		
4. Monitor	Receives and collects internal information in order to develop a thorough understanding of his organization	Sam Walton, founder of Wal-Mart, held daily meetings to review key organizational statistics, which had to be summarized on just one page.
5. Disseminator	Brings information from the environment into the organization	The manager of an engineering group attends a conference on sustainable production processes, and briefs other managers on what she learned.
6. Spokesperson	Sends information from the organization into its environment, including managing public relations	The CEO writes an editorial on improving U.S. productivity for a major newspaper.
Decision-Making Roles		
7. Entrepreneur	Directs meetings to develop strategies and initiate change	A manager observes but does not get involved in an important meeting so group members will feel comfortable voicing creative ideas.
8. Disturbance Handler	Mobilizes the organization to quickly react when it is threatened	The manager of a storage facility mobilizes his company to deal with a major fire.
9. Resource Allocator	Decides where the organization will direct its efforts, including budgeting and scheduling	The director of research and development (R&D) funds one project but not others.
10. Negotiator	Enters into negotiations on behalf of the organization	The head of purchasing negotiates a major contract with a supplier.

Source: Based on H. Mintzberg, *The Nature of Managerial Work*, New York: Harper & Row, 1973.

TABLE 1.5 Overview: Careers

Career Patterns	Steady state—lifetime employment in one job
	Spiral—one skill set leads to a variety of jobs
	Transitory—jobs have no particular pattern
	Linear—a lifetime in one profession, but in different jobs and companies
Career Stages	Preparation for working—You develop career anchors and skills.
	Organizational entry—You try out a variety of jobs and organizations.
	Early career—You set career goals in a company.
	Middle career—You either move up in the company or plateau.
	Late career—You reduce your commitment and make plans to retire.
Career Roles	Independent contributor—You work in a key job without subordinates.
	Manager—You manage others to meet organizational goals.

take. Being aware of different organizational roles and your preferences about them is an important factor in planning a satisfying and successful career.

Table 1.5 summarizes the various career patterns, stages, and roles that you may experience during your career.

How Will Mastering Organizational Behavior Help You in Your Career?

In this chapter you have read about the context and issues that shape today's organizations and careers. How can this textbook help you to meet these challenges and have a successful career?

Imagine you are standing in the end zone of a football field and have just received the opening kickoff. You realize this is not your typical game when you observe that the field is not filled with your team and 11 opponents, but with thousands of people. There is no possible way you can run around or through all these people. Sometimes you cannot even tell which ones are on your side and which ones are your opponents.

These are the people you will meet in the game of business. They are your bosses, subordinates, and co-workers. They are the individuals who will make up your professional network, the people you will admire, and the characters you will try to work around. It is only with and through these people that you will achieve your goals.

Mastering the essentials of organizational behavior will help you play the game of life in organizations by improving your judgment about these individuals, and the groups and companies they populate.

In particular, studying OB will help you to:

- Understand yourself so you can figure out where and how to fit in, and so you can create teams and organizations that will help others to do the same.
- Become familiar with a variety of well-researched techniques for solving behaviorally based organizational problems.
- See organizations in all their fascinating and challenging complexity, perhaps with an eye to leading one.
- Obtain the vocabulary and fundamental understandings that will allow you to continue to learn about organizational life well beyond this book and this course.

How can you maximize the probability of reaching your career goals? Start by learning all you can about organizational behavior, then run out onto the playing field, and start shaking hands.

Apply What You Have Learned. . .

World Class Company: Netflix

In 2005 Netflix exemplifies the kind of company that is scrambling to make it in today's fast-paced global economy.[74] Chief executive Reed Hastings founded the company because he had already started up and sold a successful software company and then saw a new opportunity. Spurred by advances in technology and the annoyance of a $40 late payment from a video store, Hastings founded Netflix and quickly made it America's leading online DVD-rental company.

Currently, the business straddles the offline and online worlds, offering DVDs in the mail for a flat fee each month, and downloaded rentals from a collection of 50,000 titles. (A typical neighborhood video store has about 3,000 titles.) On average, Netflix mails out 1 million DVDs a day.

So far Netflix has faced down, and also become partners with, Wal-Mart. It now faces competition from Blockbuster. Meanwhile, the technology, marketing, and legalities of downloading DVDs are still developing. Hastings has thought about going international, and his company has imitators from France to Australia, but he has chosen to fight his U.S. battles first. Hastings concentrates on service, and Netflix has been ranked by a leading market research firm as the top Internet retailer for customer satisfaction.

As of this writing, Netflix is a small company employing about 1,000 people at corporate headquarters and shipping centers. Netflix's Web site touts the company's ethics. (Hastings is himself a Peace Corps veteran.) Everywhere in their market Netflix sees opportunities to vastly improve service. "Fun" is defined as meeting interesting challenges with great colleagues, and being part of a demanding but rewarding high-performance team. Employees' performance appraisals are based on a 360-degree (from peers, subordinates, and superiors) anonymous review twice a year. The company is "anti-bureaucratic and anti-hierarchical. . . [You will be encouraged to] propose alternative business strategies, independent of your formal position, or laugh with the CEO. Just be insightful."[75]

Discuss

1. What characteristics of modern organizations does Netflix exemplify? Describe what type of an organization it is, what type of jobs its workers perform, and the probable characteristics of its workers.
2. What would be the advantages of working for Netflix? the disadvantages?
3. Do you think Netflix will be around a decade from now?

Advice from the Pros

Which OB Skills Are Most Important in Which Industries?

If your goal is to one day make it into a top management position, here's some expert advice for you. Experts in different industries emphasize different skills and tactics. However, they all suggest acquiring OB skills and knowledge.

An IT (Information Technology) expert[76] advises. . . Develop people skills, leadership ability, and a systems perspective.

Technical skills, people skills, and leadership skills must *all* be excellent. Be ambitious, not necessarily to climb the ladder, but to discover innovations that are possible to achieve through your work. In your job, avoid too much internal focus. Always strive to stay in touch with the big picture for your company

—*According to R. Lampman,*
Senior Vice President of Research, Hewlett-Packard

An expert in the health industry[77] advises. . . Understand the importance of mentors, networking, and power.

In the first five years, get a job in a health-care organization, find a mentor, and work on a project that has an important impact on the bottom-line. Then find a position in which you can begin to make contacts among leaders in the health care industry. Plan to take on more people and bigger budgets as you move up

—*According to D. J. Hilferty,*
President and CEO,
AmeriHealth Mercy/Keystone Mercy Health Plan

An expert in the entertainment industry[78] advises. . . Don't expect high level rewards in your first jobs.

Take any job to get your foot in the door. Don't think about making more money, think about acquiring more experience in whatever your passion is. Don't worry about credentials because people from business, law, and film schools can all make it in this industry. Have a long-term plan. Get into a visionary company, find a mentor, and network widely.

—According to N. Tellem,
President of CBS Entertainment

An expert in the investment-banking industry[79] advises. . . Become an effective one-to-one communicator.

Get an undergraduate degree in finance or economics and an MBA. Learn, and love learning about, how investments are structured to drive companies. Be able to communicate your knowledge. Since an analyst's view is narrow, eventually try to find a job in which you get a broad exposure to the business.

—According to E. Billings,
Co-CEO and Co-chairman of Friedman,
Billings, Ramsey Group

An expert in law firms[80] advises. . . Cultivate ethical approaches to business problems.

You need the legal skills of reasoning, writing, and speaking. You need integrity. Develop the types of skills appropriate for your specialty. Litigators and finance lawyers need different oral presentation skills, for example. To succeed, you will need intelligence, stamina, and the kind of sound judgment your clients can rely on.

—According to D. de Hoyos,
Managing Partner of Mayer,
Brown, Rowe & Maw

Experts in international business say. . . develop cross-cultural skills and a supportive family.

You need to be a hard-working, well-credentialed, career-committed professional to succeed in international business.[81] Increasingly important are acquiring a graduate degree, developing an explicit international focus, having personal experience living outside the United States, and mastering foreign language skills. International assignments are risky, posing business, personal, and family challenges.[82] However, if you succeed, they are highly fulfilling, offering a rich experience of life and constant opportunities for learning. Of course, having international work does not necessarily mean living abroad, and managers who are repatriated still enjoy the international aspects of their jobs.

Moving up the ladder in an international company can be tricky. For example, high-flyers from one country may not be accepted as leaders in another country because of cultural biases.[83] Also, only 22 percent of a sample of human resources executives in *Fortune* 500 companies believe that expatriates' international assignments are rewarded with career advancement.[84]

Discussion

Break into groups based on which of the preceding experts most closely relates to your career interest.

1. Discuss whether you agree or disagree with the expert's advice, especially as it refers to the OB skills that are important in this profession.
2. What additional OB skills do you think might be important in this profession? List five or six additional skills and be prepared to tell why you chose them.

Gain Experience

I. Career Anchors and Values

You are your own career manager, a significant responsibility. Understanding what motivates you in your career and how today's business environment may affect you can be very useful over the long term. In this exercise, you will have the opportunity to think about your career in the context of your career anchors and the business environment as discussed in this chapter.

Part I What is your career anchor?

For each numbered item below, prioritize choices *a* through *e* according to their importance to you, with

5 = the activity you enjoy or want the most, and

1 = the activity you enjoy or want the least.

(For example, you might set rank *a* as number 2, *b* as number 4, and so on.

1. In general, I really enjoy
   ___ a. working on challenging problems.
   ___ b. organizing and leading people.
   ___ c. routine and stability.
   ___ d. lots of opportunity to be creative.
   ___ e. my independence.

2. When I am working, I have the most fun when:
   ___ a. I am absorbed in a hands-on project.
   ___ b. I am working in a team.
   ___ c. I can be pretty certain about how things will turn out.
   ___ d. I am thinking up business ideas.
   ___ e. I am doing my own thing apart from others.

3. The most important thing to me in a job is:
   ___ a. having the opportunity to work on interesting problems.
   ___ b. the opportunity to lead and manage.
   ___ c. knowing my paycheck is secure.
   ___ d. figuring out how to sell a product.
   ___ e. being left alone to do my work.

Now add up your points for each letter, and write the totals below. Your highest point total is your strongest career anchor.

Career Anchor	Total Points
a. Technical and analytical competence. (You are an engineer, writer, scientist, accountant—and a darned good one.)	
b. Managerial competence. (You are good at managing people, budgets, and projects.)	
c. Security and stability in your job. (You want security first and foremost; you would enjoy a military or government job.)	
d. Creativity and entrepreneurship. (You love to start businesses, and you often sell them and move on after they are up and running.)	
e. Autonomy and independence in your work. (You work creatively and on your own, with minimal or no supervision.)	

The maximum score for an anchor is 15. If you have two high scores, realize that both are important to you. This exercise is only a very simple way of helping you to systematize your thinking about career anchors. You might want to spend more time outside of class thinking in more depth about what motivates you in your choice of career.

Part II   Discussion

Your professor will assign you to a group based on your preferred career anchor. (For more popular anchors, more than one group will be necessary.) In your group, introduce yourself and briefly describe why this anchor is important to you. Then discuss and be prepared to report to the class on the following questions:

1. How will today's global business environment affect people who have your career anchor? For example, how is having to compete globally likely to affect you?
2. How will today's work affect people who have your career anchor? For example, how will job growth or job disruption affect you?
3. How will today's workforce affect people who have your career anchor? For example, how might your career be affected by a diverse workforce? by literacy and employability issues? by unionization?

Part III   And what about your values?[85]

Your professor will hand you an index card. In the upper right-hand corner note down your first career choice. On the rest of the card, write your *fantasy obituary.* You are totally free to write down whatever you want in your obituary, which will most likely reflect your aspirations, achievements, and desired lifestyle. Turn these cards in to your professor, who will redistribute them randomly to the class for discussion.

II. Is Geography Destiny?

Are you willing to devote a few minutes to a task that will teach you something not only about a crucial organizational context but also about yourself? Read further and follow the directions.

1. Take out an $8\frac{1}{2}$ by 11 inch sheet of paper and a pen or pencil. Here's your assignment: Draw a picture of the entire world, including the outlines and names of as many countries as you can. You have five minutes.
2. Next, jot down the answers to the following questions:
   a. What geographical feature or country did you put at the center of your world?
   b. What regions of the world do you know well? Why do you know them so well?
   c. What regions of the world do you know less well? Why?
   d. If you had unlimited time to finish out your world, what else would you add?
3. Don't put away your map yet; further challenges await!
   a. Label on your map the countries that are the United States' top trading partners. Try for the top five, labeling the country with which the United States trades the most "#1" and proceeding down your list.
   b. Next, indicate the five American states that have the most international trade, assigning an A to the state with the most trade, and so on.
4. Share your map with a partner and have him or her count the number of countries you correctly placed and identified.

Discussion

1. What can this task teach you?
2. What did you put at the center of the map?
3. How did you do?
   Some years ago, a poll conducted for the National Geographic Society showed that the average adult American could only name four European countries from their outlines on a map, and fewer than six of the 50 United States. One in four could not find the Pacific Ocean. The worst-performing group was those ages 18 to 24.[86]
4. Consult Appendix 1 at the back of this book, where you will find a map of the world that gives you answers to some of the questions above.

Can You Solve This Manager's Problem?

The Young President's Vision

You have taken over the presidency of your father's successful software engineering firm, a 50-employee business that designs and installs computer networks for moderate-sized businesses in the northwestern United States. Your engineering staff numbers 35 individuals, with an average age of 38. The rest of your employees are support staff, including salespeople, accountants, secretaries, and maintenance workers.

Having worked as the company's vice president for new product development for several years, you realize the company has great potential for growth, especially in Japan. However, you are also aware of some crucial personnel problems. Of your ten top managers, five key ones are in their fifties and you suspect some of them may retire early. Even though your company has a pleasant family feel about it, you have difficulty competing for software engineers against the larger businesses in the region because of the higher salaries they offer. There is a significant lack of international experience among your employees: For one thing, only one engineer and one secretary speak Japanese fluently (and you yourself get by with a limited vocabulary), and only three of your younger engineers have lived abroad for an extended period.

Based on the growth you anticipate both domestically (80% of the total) and internationally (20% of the total), you envision that your company will double its engineering staff within three years. To do this effectively, you believe your company must become known as the kind of company people really want to work for.

You have scheduled for tomorrow a meeting of your three vice-presidents and the director of human resources management. They are eager to hear in much greater detail about your three-year vision. Tonight you have to sit down and decide exactly what to tell them.

Assignment

Divide into small groups. Your job, as a team, is to lay out the details of the young president's vision. To create your vision, use what you have read in the chapter about:

1. the challenges that face today's organizational leaders, including globalization, the changing nature of work, and the complex workforce.
2. the modern organizational processes that help companies compete.

Each group should list the key elements (8 to 10) of its vision and be ready to present its vision to the class.

Chapter Summary and Key Terms

What is organizational behavior, and what kinds of business challenges does it address?

OB is, put simply, the study of how people behave in organizations. It helps managers solve problems by applying the findings of social science. It is not the same thing as HRM, which is a particular organizational function. From the micro level to the macro level in an organization, OB helps managers solve a variety of practical problems.

An organization is a system with inputs, processes, and outputs. It utilizes feedback to constantly evolve. When you visualize organizations as systems, you are better able to recognize fundamental business factors, keep context in mind, and stress the importance of adapting to the environment.

organization   4
organizational behavior (OB)   4
human resources management (HRM)   5
micro level OB   5
macro level OB   5
organizational theory (OT)   5
system   6
systems theory   6
open systems   6
permeable boundaries   6

closed systems   6
impermeable boundaries   6

What economic and social issues challenge today's organizational leaders?

Today's organizational leaders must understand the force of globalization, the changing nature of work, and the complexities of the workforce. Some of the key issues related to the changing nature of work are job growth, job disruption, and contingent jobs. Some that are related to the complex workforce are age, gender, race, literacy, employability, and union representation.

globalization   7
work   7
employment   7
job   7
downsize, rightsize   8
outsource   9
offshore   9
contingent jobs   9
protected classes   10
employability skills   12
wage differential   13

What organizational processes help companies compete in the modern economy?

Today's companies try to foster innovation and high quality decision making. They rely extensively on teams, and they are improving the way they attract and keep trained workers. They are emphasizing ethics. Companies also adapt their organizational processes. They attempt to become boundaryless, empower employees, emphasize core competencies, re-engineer processes, and develop organizational learning.

knowledge work   14
boundaryless organization   14
employee empowerment   15
core competencies   15
total quality management (TQM)   15
re-engineering   15
organizational learning   15
networked organization   15
transparency   16

What will your career be like in modern organizations?

Although no one can predict how job opportunities will change, careers are typified by patterns, stages, and role choices. These days, both workers and companies expect that individuals will work for many different companies during their lifetimes. It is a good idea to be aware of your career anchors, which influence your career choices.

primary labor market   17
secondary labor market   17
steady state career   17
spiral career   17
transitory career   17
linear career   17
boundaryless career   17
career anchor   18
career plateau   18
role   18
independent contributor   19
manager   19

How will mastering organizational behavior help you in your career?

OB is an integrative discipline that provides practical information and insights for your life in organizations. Enhancing your OB skills along with your professional specialty is one way to improve your career prospects.

Explorations

1. Careers

  A. To learn more about the growth of various careers and industries, read the most current Career Guide to Industries, published by the U.S. Department of Labor, Bureau of Labor Statistics, at www. bls.gov.

  B. Check out http://www.acinet.org/acinet to find out things like how much money you can earn in the same type of job in different parts of the country (you can ask precise questions, such as "What do accountants and auditors get paid in Fresno, CA?"), and what the fastest growing occupations are for college grads.

  C. If you are trying to decide which career is for you, one classic self-help manual is Richard Bolles' *What Color Is My Parachute?*

  D. Try this exercise: Imagine you are 90 years old, and you are thinking back on your life. What did you do during your life that mattered to you? Which of your accomplishments do you value the most? What are your regrets? How did your career choices influence your life?

2. How much will you make?

For comparisons of wages, earnings, and benefits of workers by race, age, sex, and union membership see www.bls.gov: "Overview of BLS Statistics on Wages, Earnings, and Benefits."

3. To keep up on international business

Consult publications such as *The Economist* and *The Financial Times*, along with the international journals in your field of interest. International journals with specific OB content include *Journal of International Business Studies* and the *International Journal of Management*. However, you are also likely to find international content in any OB journal.

4. Ethics

To learn about business ethics, Web search for "business ethics" for a variety of private and public resources. This will help you discover the ethics issues that are most important in business today. Also, check out the *Journal of Business Ethics* in your library's online database. For a comprehensive view, read Joel Makower's *Beyond the Bottom Line: Putting Social Responsibility to Work for Your Business and The World.*

References

[1] *Webster's Encyclopedic Unabridged Dictionary of the English Language,* (New York: Portland House, 1989).

[2] See D. Katz and R. L. Kahn, *The Social Psychology of Organizations* (New York: Wiley, 1966).

[3] J. Bhagwati, *In Defence of Globalisation* (New York: Oxford University Press, 2004).

[4] J. Stiglitz, "We Have Become Rich Countries of Poor People," *The Financial Times* September 7, 2006, www.ft.com. Accessed September 16, 2006.

[5] S. Stern, "Managers Will Miss the Voice of the Proletariat," *The Financial Times*, September 4, 2006, www.ft.com. Accessed September 16, 2006.

[6] "Playing leapfrog," *The Economist*, September 14, 2006, http://www.economist.com/surveys/displaystory.cfm?story_id=E1_SRSRTPN. Accessed September 16, 2006.

[7] M. Javidan and R. J. House, "Cultural Acumen for the Global Manager: Lessons from Project Globe," *Organizational Dynamics 29* (4), Spring 2001:289–305.

[8] *Growing in an Uncertain World: General Electric 2003 Annual Report* (Fairfield, CT: General Electric Company, 2004):7.

[9] U.S. Department of Labor, Bureau of Labor Statistics, *Occupational Outlook Handbook,* 2006–2007 ed., www.bls.gov/oco/print/oco2003.htm. Accessed July 20, 2006.

[10] U.S. Department of Labor, Bureau of Labor Statistics, "The 2006–07 Career Guide to Industries," Bulletin 2601, http://www.bls.gov/oco/cg/print/indchar.htm. Accessed July 23, 2006.

[11] R. Abrams, "All Hat, No Cattle" (New York: Inc.com., 2004), http://www.inc.com/articles/2004/03/allhatnocattle.html. Accessed April 29, 2007.

[12] R. Abrams, "All Hat, No Cattle" (New York: Inc.com., 2004), http://www.inc.com/articles/2004/03/allhatnocattle.html. Accessed April 29, 2007.

[13] U.S. Census Bureau, "Employment Size of Employer Firms, 2001," in Statistics about Business Size (including Small Business), http://www.census.gov/epcd/www/smallbus.html. Accessed September 21, 2005.

[14] U.S. Department of Labor, Bureau of Labor Statistics, *Occupational Outlook Handbook,* 2006-2007 ed., www.bls.gov/oco/print/oco2003.htm. Accessed July 20, 2006.

[15] P. G. Audia and C. I . Rider, "A Garage and an Idea: What More Does an Entrepreneur Need?" *California Management Review 48* (1), Fall 2005:6–28.

[16] U.S. Department of Labor, Bureau of Labor Statistics, *Occupational Outlook Handbook,* 2006–2007 ed., www.bls.gov/oco/print/oco2003.htm. Accessed July 20, 2006.

[17] U.S. Department of Labor, Bureau of Labor Statistics, *Occupational Outlook Handbook,* 2006–2007 ed., www.bls.gov/oco/print/oco2003.htm. Accessed July 20, 2006.

[18] U.S. Census Bureau, "U.S. Interim Projections by Age, Sex, Rce, and Hispanic Origin," 2004. Internet Release Date: March 19, 2004, http://www.census.gov/ipc/www/usinterimproj/. Accessed September 16, 2006.

[19] "Economics Focus: On the Hiking Trail: Globalisation is Generating Huge Economic Gains. That is No Reason to Ignore Its Costs," *The Economist* 380 (8493): September 2, 2006: 66.

[20] "America's Economy," *The Economist* August 29, 2006, http://www.economist.com/research/Backgrounders/display Backgrounder.cfm?bg=937843. Accessed September 17, 2006.

[21] "Masters of the Universe," *The Economist 381* (8498), October 7, 2006:18–20.

[22] D. McGinn and K. Naughton, "How Safe is Your Job?" *Newsweek*, February 5, 2001:36–43.

[23] A. Greenspan, quoted in W. Greider, *The Soul of Capitalism* (New York: Simon and Schuster, 2003):13.

[24] Leo J. Shapiro and Associates, "Consumers Calm Down," September 11, 2006, http://www.ljs.com/NATSEP06ns.htm. Accessed October 10, 2006.

[25] D. E. Westney, "ABB—Through the Strategic Design Lens," in D. Ancona, T. Kochan, M. Scully, J. Van Maanen, and D. E. Westney, *Organizational Behavior & Processes* (Cincinnati, Ohio: South-Western College Publishing, 1999): Module 2, 27–39.

[26] "Another Kodak Moment," *The Economist* May 12, 2005, www.economist.com/research/articles. Accessed October 15, 2005.

[27] "American Manufacturing: Lean and Unseen," *The Economist,* July 1, 2006:55–56.

[28] International Labour Organization, "World Employment Report 2001: Life at Work in the Information Economy," www.ilo.org/public/english/support/publ/wer/overview.htm: 1. Accessed March 30, 2004.

[29] "Labor Month in Review," *Monthly Labor Review Online 124* (6), June 2001:2.

[30] U.S. Department of Labor, Bureau of Labor Statistics, *Occupational Outlook Handbook,* 2006–2007 ed., www.bls.gov/oco/print/oco2003.htm. Accessed July 20, 2006.

[31] "Survey: The Near Future: The New Demographics," *The Economist*, November 1, 2001.

[32] International Labour Organization, *World Employment Report 2001: Life at Work in the Information Economy,* World Employment Report 2001: Life at Work in the Information Economy, www.ilo.org/public/english/support/publ/wer/overview.htm: 2. Accessed March 30, 2004.

[33] S. M. Jacoby, *Employing Bureaucracy: Managers, Unions, and the Transformation of Work in the 20th Century (Revised Edition)* (Mahwah, New Jersey, Lawrence Erlbaum Associates Publishers, 2004):222.

[34] L. Gerdes, "The Best Places to Launch a Career: The Top 50 Employers for New College Grads," *BusinessWeek Online,* September 18, 2006, www.businessweek.com. Accessed September 15, 2006.

[35] R. Spraggins, "Women and Men in the United States: March 2002," *Current Population Reports,* U.S. Department of Commerce, U.S. Census Bureau, March 2003:3.

[36] U.S. Department of Labor, Bureau of Labor Statistics, *Women in the Labor Force: A Databook* (February 2004):25–26.

[37] U.S. Department of Labor, Bureau of Labor Statistics, *Women in the Labor Force: A Databook* (February 2004):8–10.

[38] U.S. Department of Labor, Bureau of Labor Statistics, *Women in the Labor Force: A Databook* (February 2004):1.

[39] U.S. Department of Labor, Bureau of Labor Statistics, *Women in the Labor Force: A Databook* (February 2004):8–10.

[40] U.S. Department of Labor, Bureau of Labor Statistics, *Women in the Labor Force: A Databook* (February 2004):58.

[41] "More Women Join World's Workforce: Obstacles Persist; U.S. Women Managers Advance," International Labor Office, Washington Office, May 20, 2004, http://www.us.ilo.org/ studies/workingwomen_04.cfm. Accessed May 20, 2004. Cites a study of 353 Fortune 500 companies by the Catalyst organization.

[42] L. Wirth, *Breaking Through the Glass Ceiling: Women in Management—Update 2004* (Geneva, Switzerland: International Labor Office, 2004).

[43] U.S. Department of Labor, Bureau of Labor Statistics, *Occupational Outlook Handbook,* 2006-2007 ed., www.bls.gov/oco/print/oco2003.htm. Accessed July 20, 2006.

[44] U.S. Census Bureau, "U.S. Interim Projections by Age, Sex, Race, and Hispanic Origin,"http://www.census.gov/ipc/www/usinterimproj/. Accessed September 16, 2006.

[45] A. Sum, I. Kirsch, and R. Taggart, *The Twin Challenges of Mediocrity and Inequality: Literacy in the U.S. from an International Perspective* (Princeton, NJ: Educational Testing Service, 2002); National Institute for Literacy, Facts & Statistics, Workforce Education, http://www.nifl.gov/nifl/facts/workforce.html. Accessed September 12, 2006.

[46] National Association of Manufacturers, Anderson Center for Workforce Success, *The Skills Gap 2001: Manufacturers Confront Persistent Skills Shortages in an Uncertain Economy* (Washington, DC: National Association of Manufacturers, 2002).

[47] American Management Association, *American Management Association Research Survey: Corporate Concerns* (New York, NY: American Management Association, 2001).

[48] U.S. Department of Labor, "Union Members in 2003," news release, January 21, 2004, http://www.bls.gov/cps/.

[49] International Labour Organization, "Labor Statistical Database," www.ilo.org.

[50] L. Gerdes, "The Best Places to Launch a Career: The Top 50 Employers for New College Grads," *BusinessWeek Online,* September 18, 2006, www.businessweek.com. Accessed September 15, 2006.

[51] Survey by Universum Communications, reported in L. Gerdes, "The Best Places to Launch a Career: The Top 50 Employers for New College Grads," *BusinessWeek Online,* September 18, 2006, www.businessweek.com. Accessed September 15, 2006.

[52] S. Shellenbarger, "The Mommy Drain: Employers Beef Up Perks to Lure New Mothers Back to Work," *The Wall Street Journal,* September 28, 2006:D1.

[53] L. Gerdes, "The Best Places to Launch a Career: The Top 50 Employers for New College Grads," *BusinessWeek Online,* September 18, 2006, www.businessweek.com. Accessed September 15, 2006.

[54] L. Gerdes, "The Best Places to Launch a Career: The Top 50 Employers for New College Grads," *BusinessWeek Online,* September 18, 2006, www.businessweek.com. Accessed September 15, 2006.

[55] J. Welch with J. A. Byrne, *Jack: Straight from the Gut* (New York: Warner Business Books, 2003):186.

[56] M. Hammer and J. Champy, *Re-Engineering the Corporation: A Manifesto for Business Revolution* (New York: HarperBusiness, 2001):35.

[57] C. Argyris and D. Schön, *Organizational Learning: A Theory of Action Perspective* (Reading, MA: Addison-Wesley Publishing Company, 1978).

[58] C. C. Verschoor, "A Study of the Link between a Corporation's Financial Performance and Its Commitment to Ethics," *Journal of Business Ethics 17* (1998):1509–1516. See also L. L. Embley, *Doing Well While Doing Good* (Englewood Cliffs, NJ: Prentice Hall, 1993).

[59] R. Alsop, "The Top Business Schools: Recruiters' M.B.A. Picks," *The Wall Street Journal Online,* September 20, 2006, http://online.wsj.com/article/SB115860376846766495.html?mod=2_1245_1. Accessed September 20, 2006.

[60] E. M. Hartman, "Can We Teach Character? An Aristotelian Answer," *Academy of Management Learning & Education 5* (1), 2006:68–81; R. Klimoski, "Introduction. Aristotle as a Business Ethics Professor," *Academy of Management Learning & Education 5* (1), 2006:66–67.

[61] M. J. Driver, "Careers: A Review of Personal and Organizational Research," in C. L. Cooper and I. T. Robertson, eds., *Key Reviews in Managerial Psychology: Concepts and Research for Practice* (New York: John Wiley & Sons, 1994):237–269.

[62] P. M. Valcour and P. S. Tolbert, "Gender, Family and Career in the Era of Boundarylessness: Determinants and Effects of Intra- and Inter-organizational Mobility," *International Journal of Human Resource Management 14* (5), August 2003:768–787.

[63] "Masters of the Universe," *The Economist 381* (8498), October 7, 2006:18–20.

[64] M. B. Arthur, "The Boundaryless Career: A New Perspective for Organizational Enquiry," *Journal of Organizational Behavior 15,* 1994:295–306; S. Svenja and M. B. Arthur, "The Boundaryless Career," in J. Greenhaus and G. Callanan, eds., *The Encyclopedia of Career Development* (Thousand Oaks, CA: Sage, forthcoming 2006): forthcoming.

[65] "Masters of the Universe," *The Economist 381* (8498), October 7, 2006:18–20.

[66] "Masters of the Universe," *The Economist 381* (8498), October 7, 2006:18–20.

[67] J. H. Greenhaus, *Career Management* (New York: Dryden, 1987).

[68] B. Lawrence, "Career Anchor," in N. Nicholson, ed., *The Blackwell Encyclopedic Dictionary of Organizational Behavior* (Cambridge, MA: Blackwell, 1995):44–45.

[69] E. H. Schein, *Career Anchors: Discovering Your Real Values* (San Francisco: Pfeiffer: An Imprint of Jossey-Bass Inc., Publishers, 1993).

[70] B. Lawrence, "Career Anchor," in N. Nicholson, ed., *The Blackwell Encyclopedic Dictionary of Organizational Behavior* (Cambridge, MA: Blackwell, 1995):44–45. Schein includes three additional categories: Service/Dedication to a Cause, Pure Challenge, and Lifestyle. See E. H. Schein, *Career Anchors: Discovering Your Real Values* (San Francisco: Pfeiffer: An Imprint of Jossey-Bass Inc., Publishers, 1993).

[71] R. Knight, "Top Schools Recruiting Younger MBAs," *The Financial Times,* September 13, 2006, http://www.ft.com. Accessed September 25, 2006.

[72] J. C. Macionis, *Sociology* , 10th ed. (Upper Saddle River, NJ: Pearson/Prentice Hall, 2005):141.

[73] H. Mintzberg, *The Nature of Managerial Work* (New York: Harper and Row Publishers, 1973):31.

[74] "Movies to Go: Can Netflix's Reed Hastings Succeed in the Battle to Deliver Movies Online?" *The Economist* July 7, 2005, www.economist.com. Accessed October 15, 2005; http://www.netflix.com. Accessed October 15, 2005.

[75] "Top Ten Reasons to Join Netflix," http://www.netflix.com/Jobs?id=5245. Accessed October 15, 2005.

[76] Views of R. Lampman, director of Hewlett-Packard Labs and senior vice president of research, in E. Weinstein, "Advice From the Top: Climbing the Ladder in the IT Industry," *The Wall Street Journal Online,* April 7, 2004.

[77] Views of D. J. Hilferty, president and CEO of AmeriHealth Mercy/Keystone Mercy Health Plan, in M. Ballinger, "Advice From the Top: Climbing the Ladder in the Health Industry," *The Wall Street Journal Online,* March 31, 2004.

[78] Views of N. Tellem, president of CBS Entertainment, in J. Murphy, "Advice from the Top: Climbing the Ladder in TV Entertainment," *The Wall Street Journal Online,* March 29, 2004.

[79] Views of E. Billings, a founder, co-CEO and cochairman of Friedman, Billings, Ramsey Group in Arlington, Va., in E. Schulte, "Advice from the Top: Climbing the Ladder in the Banking Industry," *The Wall Street Journal Online,* March 31, 2004.

[80] Views of D. de Hoyos, managing partner of Mayer, Brown, Rowe & Maw, in N. S. Malik, "Advice from the Top: Climbing the Ladder in U.S. Law Firms," *The Wall Street Journal Online*, April 15, 2004.

[81] M. L. Egan, M. Bendick Jr., and J. J. Miller, "U.S. Firms' Evaluation of Employee Credentials in International Business," *International Journal of Human Resource Management 13* (1), February 2002:76–88.

[82] Twenty-four Finnish managers interviewed for V. Suutari, "Global Managers: Career Orientation, Career Tracks, Lifestyle Implications and Career Commitment," *Journal of Managerial Psychology 18* (3), 2003:185–207.

[83] "National Divisions Bar European Leaders from International Careers," *Financial Management (UK) (CIMA)*, November 2000:5.

[84] J. Hauser, "Managing Expatriates' Careers," *HR Focus 76* (2), February 1999:11.

[85] As suggested by P. Prasad, "Restoring Connections in the OB Classroom," in R. André and P. Frost, Eds., *Researchers Hooked on Teaching: Noted Scholars Discuss the Synergies of Teaching and Research,"* (Thousand Oaks, CA: Sage, 1997:213–223.)

[86] W. A. McDougall, "Why Geography Matters," *American Educator*, Spring 2001, www.aft.org/american_educator/spring2001/geography.html (poll conducted in 1989). Accessed May 29, 2004.

2 Your Personality and Style

Preview

What is your personality?
Where does personality originate?
How do psychologists determine an individual's personality?
How can you know whether a psychological test is a good one?
What is a personality profile? What is the Big Five personality profile?
What is your personality profile, as assessed with the Big Five?

How is the study of personality traits applied in organizations?
What does the Big Five profile of personality predict in organizations?
How does the Myers-Briggs Type Indicator assess personality?
What do the Big Five and the MBTI have in common?
What are some personality variables that are especially important in organizations?
What is a psychological disorder?

What is your emotional style and why is it important in organizational life?
Genetic determinants of emotions
Environmental determinants of emotions
Task determinants of emotions
What suggests emotional competence on the job?

What cognitive abilities contribute to your personal style?
Analytic ability
Creative ability
Practical intelligence

What values and attitudes contribute to your personal style?
Values
Attitudes
Can values and attitudes change?

Amy's Ice Creams

"I started Amy's Ice Creams when I was 24 and I am now 29. . . ." How's that? Build a 100,000-gallon-per-year business in just five years? Amy Miller continues, "I am now 29 . . . and holding, because you never grow old at the ice cream store."[1]

Today Amy Miller is the happy owner of the Texas ice cream stores that bear her name. In 2005 the chain of more than a dozen stores celebrated its twentieth anniversary by giving out free ice cream at every store.

Amy Miller, once a pre-med major at Tufts University, spent from 1979 through 1984 working for Steve's Ice Cream, a national chain of ice cream shops. She opened stores for Steve's in both Manhattan and Coconut Grove, Florida. She was a manager in the very first Bertucci's, now a chain of Italian restaurants. She also earned her MBA from the University of Texas at Austin.

Are Amy Miller's personality and style reflected in her company? You bet. Consider the following:

When Steve's Ice Cream was sold to a large corporation, Amy decided she did not want to work in a bureaucratic culture and chose to open her own shop instead. She and her business partner, Scott Shaw, chose college town Austin, Texas, as their site.

The mission statement of Amy's company is to make people's day. "What we know is that people come into the ice cream store here not 'cause they're hungry. They're here 'cause they're with their family and they want to experience something together or some special moment. Or they're sad; they just had an exam and they want to treat themselves so they feel better."[2]

Also, Amy's "makes it a rule to spend money participating in events with local charities rather than on advertising."[3]

Finally, Amy Miller's goal is to have Amy's last for 100 years, even though she won't be here to see it.

Like Amy Miller, you are a unique individual who brings a particular style to your work and life. Your individuality depends in part on such biographical characteristics as your gender, age, physical appearance, race, nationality, and sexual preference. It also depends on the psychological characteristics that we will focus on in this chapter—namely, your personality, cognitive abilities, attitudes, and values. By better understanding yourself you can better understand others and become a more effective and satisfied manager.

What Is Your Personality?

personality
The unique pattern of enduring thoughts, feelings, and actions that characterize an individual.

Personality is the unique pattern of enduring thoughts, feelings, and actions that characterize an individual.[4] It is the expression of the sum total of who you are biologically, psychologically, and behaviorally. To describe it you must factor in everything about you, from your inherited biological characteristics to the habits, emotional expressions, and social skills you have acquired during your lifetime.

Understanding your style and personality helps you face organizational life with confidence. Knowing your strengths allows you to play to them, and knowing your weaknesses allows you to manage them. Also, when you know who you are, you can figure out where you best fit in. For example, would you perform well in a work group filled with extraverts? Should you work in a bureaucratic company, or would you thrive in a company with an entrepreneurial spirit? Finally, understanding how you differ from others helps you appreciate and work with the human differences you will experience every day on the job.

Where Does Personality Originate?

heredity
Genetic factors.

environment
Non-genetic factors.

Some researchers believe that genetic factors (**heredity**) and non-genetic factors (**environment**) appear to have approximately equal effects in shaping one's personality.[5] Others suggest that genetic factors are somewhat less influential than environmental factors.[6] Certainly, it is safe to say that both your genetic makeup and your life experiences can influence your personality in important ways.

GENETIC FACTORS Studies comparing identical and non-identical twins raised both apart and together confirm the hypothesis that genes contribute significantly to personality. Among other things, identical twins raised apart show relatively greater similarity than non-identical twins raised apart in their general activity level, emotionality, anxiety, and sociability.[7]

What are some of the more important influences of our genes?

Intelligence is a complex trait that is influenced by many genes, along with environmental factors.[8] In childhood, genes account for about 40 percent of individual differences in IQ scores, whereas in adolescence and young adulthood they account for 60 percent of such individual differences, and in later life 80 percent.[9]

subjective well-being
Happiness.

Also, happiness, known to psychologists as **subjective well-being**, is to a great extent inherited. A study based on a sample of 2,310 middle-aged twins compared their genetic predisposition to happiness with such environmental factors as income, socioeconomic status, marital status, educational attainment, and religious commitment. It found that the situational factors hardly predict happiness at all, whereas almost half of the variation in subjective well-being is genetic.[10] A retest on a smaller portion of this sample after intervals of 4.5 years and 10 years suggested that the influence of a person's genetic inheritance is even stronger than the first study described. There is even some evidence that a person's temperament is significantly determined by their genetic inheritance. Analysis of data on an international sample of 5,085 men and women aged 14 and over found that, although it is modified by culture, a person's childhood personality endures into adulthood.[11] Also, research on children reared in the same family suggests that it is primarily shared genetics, rather than shared experiences, that make the children resemble one another.[12]

ENVIRONMENTAL FACTORS Family life is a major influence on personality. A famous stage manager, for instance, attributes her success in part to her large family. Growing up among 10 children taught her how to remain calm amid chaos, an essential skill when managing a theatric production, in which so much can go wrong.[13]

Peer group influences also play a role in personality development. Peer groups are an important context that influences young adolescents' achievement, beliefs, and behaviors.[14] For example, the nature of a young student's peer group influences not only whether he or she likes and enjoys school, but also his or her level of achievement throughout the school year.

Finally, the society in which you are raised influences your personality.[15] For example, some cultures are individualist and some are collectivist. Americans are raised to be individualistic. One study found that 70 percent of a sample of American students believed they were superior to their peers, and 60 percent believed they were in the top 10 percent on a variety of personal qualities.[16] Chinese, in contrast, are taught collectivist values that subjugate their individual selves for the greater good of the family, the company, and society.[17]

SITUATIONAL FACTORS The immediate situation in which you find yourself also affects which aspects of your personality are displayed. Stressful situations, such as an employment interview, are likely to constrain your behavior. Thus, you are likely to act more conservatively in a job interview than you would in a leisure activity like a picnic in a park.[18]

Also, although personality is relatively stable over time, it is occasionally altered by life events, such as moving from one culture to another, or by physiological changes caused by illness or trauma.[19] For instance, individuals who are raised in a poor country until their teen years are likely to lack a belief in their personal self-efficacy. However, after living in the United States for some years, their confidence in themselves may increase, simply because their new life circumstances allow them to achieve more.

How Do Psychologists Determine an Individual's Personality?

Although psychologists sometimes study personality by directly observing individuals, the most popular way to study personality is by administering personality tests. These tests are convenient and inexpensive to administer, and they have been shown to be useful in many walks of life. Personality tests measure **personality traits**, which are characteristics that individuals display over time and across situations.[20]

In a moment you will be invited to take a personality test that should be of interest to you. The results of the test are used to predict, among other things, how different individuals are likely to react when they succeed or fail at a task. How should you approach this test?

Often psychologists give their clients a general idea about the goals of an upcoming test but decline to discuss the test in great detail. In this way, they hope to maximize the usefulness of the results by minimizing their client's natural tendency to over-interpret or even, at times, to "game" the test. This will be our approach here, too.

When you take the psychological tests and personal profiles in this book you should try to answer each question honestly. Avoid looking for patterns among the questions or trying to manipulate your score. Being honest with yourself will allow you to learn the most about your personality. If you want to learn why the test was written the way it was, you can do so after you've taken the test. This way, you will not spoil the test's validity for you.

Now go to Table 2.1 and follow the instructions.

Then go to Table 2.2 to record and score your answers by circling the answers you chose in Table 2.1.

a. For each time you chose the answer preceded by the *highlighted* statement, give yourself 3 points if you circled "slightly closer" and 4 points if you circled "much closer."

b. For each time you chose the answer preceded by the *unhighlighted* statement, give yourself 2 points if you circled "slightly closer" and 1 point if you circled "much closer."

Now add up your score, which is the total number of points you earned for the 11 questions. The possible range of scores is from 11 (a high internal LOC) to 44 (a high

---

peer group influences
The influences of people of approximately the same age, social status, and interests.

personality traits
Characteristics that individuals display over time and across situations.

TABLE 2.1 Internal–External Locus of Control Test

For each question, circle the letter next to the statement that is closer to your own opinion. Then circle whether you feel the response is "slightly closer" or "much closer" to your opinion than the other response is.

1. a. Many of the unhappy things in people's lives are partly due to bad luck.

    b. People's misfortunes result from the mistakes they make.

    Slightly closer   Much closer

2. a. In the long run, people get the respect they deserve in this world.

    b. Unfortunately, an individual's worth often passes unrecognized no matter how hard he tries.

    Slightly closer   Much closer

3. a. The idea that teachers are unfair to students is nonsense.

    b. Most students don't realize the extent to which their grades are influenced by accidental happenings.

    Slightly closer   Much closer

4. a. Becoming a success is a matter of hard work; luck has little or nothing to do with it.

    b. Getting a good job depends mainly on being in the right place at the right time.

    Slightly closer   Much closer

5. a. What happens to me is my own doing.

    b. Sometimes I feel that I don't have enough control over the direction my life is taking.

    Slightly closer   Much closer

6. a. The average citizen can have an influence in government decisions.

    b. This world is run by the few people in power, and there is not much the little guy can do about it.

    Slightly closer   Much closer

7. a. In my case, getting what I want has little or nothing to do with luck.

    b. Many times we might just as well decide what to do by flipping a coin.

    Slightly closer   Much closer

8. a. Who gets to be boss often depends on who was lucky enough to be in the right place first.

    b. Getting people to do the right thing depends upon ability; luck has little or nothing to do with it.

    Slightly closer   Much closer

9. a. Most people don't realize the extent to which their lives are controlled by accidental happenings.

    b. There is really no such thing as "luck."

    Slightly closer   Much closer

10. a. In the long run, the bad things that happen to us are balanced by the good ones.

    b. Most misfortunes are the result of lack of ability, ignorance, laziness, or all three.

    Slightly closer   Much closer

11. a. Many times I feel that I have little influence over the things that happen to me.

    b. It is impossible for me to believe that chance or luck plays an important role in my life.

    Slightly closer   Much closer

Source: Adapted from G. K. Valecha and T. M. Ostrom, "An Abbreviated Measure of Internal–External Locus of Control," *Journal of Personality Assessment 38,* 1974: 369–376. Based on research by J. B. Rotter, "Generalized Expectancies for Internal Versus External Control of Reinforcement," *Psychological Monographs 80* (1), 1966: Whole No. 609.

TABLE 2.2 Scoring Key for the Internal–External Locus of Control Test

		Points	
1.	a. Many of the unhappy things in people's lives are partly due to bad luck.	Slightly closer = 3	Much closer = 4
	b. People's misfortunes result from the mistakes they make.	Slightly closer = 2	Much closer = 1
2.	a. In the long run, people get the respect they deserve in this world.	Slightly closer = 2	Much closer = 1
	b. Unfortunately, an individual's worth often passes unrecognized no matter how hard he tries.	Slightly closer = 3	Much closer = 4
3.	a. The idea that teachers are unfair to students is nonsense.	Slightly closer = 2	Much closer = 1
	b. Most students don't realize the extent to which their grades are influenced by accidental happenings.	Slightly closer = 3	Much closer = 4
4.	a. Becoming a success is a matter of hard work; luck has little or nothing to do with it.	Slightly closer = 2	Much closer = 1
	b. Getting a good job depends mainly on being in the right place at the right time.	Slightly closer = 3	Much closer = 4
5.	a. What happens to me is my own doing.	Slightly closer = 2	Much closer = 1
	b. Sometimes I feel that I don't have enough control over the direction my life is taking.	Slightly closer = 3	Much closer = 4
6.	a. The average citizen can have an influence in government decisions.	Slightly closer = 2	Much closer = 1
	b. This world is run by the few people in power, and there is not much the little guy can do about it.	Slightly closer = 3	Much closer = 4
7.	a. In my case, getting what I want has little or nothing to do with luck.	Slightly closer = 2	Much closer = 1
	b. Many times we might just as well decide what to do by flipping a coin.	Slightly closer = 3	Much closer = 4
8.	a. Who gets to be boss often depends on who was lucky enough to be in the right place first.	Slightly closer = 3	Much closer = 4
	b. Getting people to do the right thing depends upon ability; luck has little or nothing to do with it.	Slightly closer = 2	Much closer = 1
9.	a. Most people don't realize the extent to which their lives are controlled by accidental happenings.	Slightly closer = 3	Much closer = 4
	b. There is really no such thing as "luck."	Slightly closer = 2	Much closer = 1
10.	a. In the long run, the bad things that happen to us are balanced by the good ones.	Slightly closer = 3	Much closer = 4
	b. Most misfortunes are the result of lack of ability, ignorance, laziness, or all three.	Slightly closer = 2	Much closer = 1
11.	a. Many times I feel that I have little influence over the things that happen to me.	Slightly closer = 3	Much closer = 4
	b. It is impossible for me to believe that chance or luck plays an important role in my life.	Slightly closer = 2	Much closer = 1

external LOC). When given to a large sample of white males, the median score of an almost identical test was 22.1.[21]

How should you interpret your results? **Locus of control** (LOC) refers to the extent to which individuals believe that they can control events that affect them. Individuals with a high **internal locus of control** believe that events result primarily from their own behavior and actions. Those with a high **external locus of control** believe that powerful others, fate, or chance primarily determine events. In the test, the answers with highlighted letters and the higher scores are the more "external" answers. So what was your result on the test and what do you make of it? Before you read on, you might want to take a moment to reflect on what you think your score suggests about your attitudes and behavior in organizations.

People differ in their sense that there is a connection between their personal characteristics and actions and the outcomes they experience. Individuals with a high internal LOC believe that any reinforcement they receive is contingent on their own behavior,

locus of control (LOC)
The extent to which individuals believe that they can control events that affect them.

internal locus of control
The tendency to believe that events result primarily from one's own behavior and actions.

external locus of control
The tendency to believe that powerful others, fate, or chance primarily determine events.

whereas individuals with high external LOC believe any reinforcement they receive comes from outside of themselves and is a result of luck, chance, or the intervention of powerful others.[22] Typically, individuals with a high internal LOC have better control of their behavior than individuals with a high external LOC. They are more likely than externals to become politically involved, and are more likely to attempt to influence other people. They are more active in seeking information and knowledge concerning their situation than externals are. They are also more likely to assume that their efforts will be successful.

Being an internal brings some advantages in an organization. When applying for a job, internals interview better initially and are more likely to get that coveted second interview.[23] On the job, individuals with internal LOC have more positive work attitudes and act more positively than individuals with external LOC.[24] Internals are also more likely to have stronger self-esteem and to develop healthier lifestyles, resulting in less absenteeism.[25] Externals tend to be more anxious.[26]

Salespeople with an internal LOC believe any rewards they receive (such as extra compensation) or punishments that come their way (such as failure to be promoted) are due to their own sales-related performance.[27] In contrast, salespeople with an external LOC do not perceive much relationship between their sales behavior and their sales outcomes. Externals generally believe that their rewards and punishments are subject to fickle and unstable forces, such as the whims of others. Executives who are more internal tend to pursue more innovative strategies and adopt longer time horizons.[28]

International studies find similar results. For example, in a study done in 24 nations and territories, primarily among managers from entry level to the top of corporate hierarchies, people with internal LOC had higher job satisfaction and absence of physiological strain.[29] People with higher internal LOC tend to have a stronger sense of psychological well-being, a finding that holds true in a wide variety of cultures, including both those that are more individualistic, such as the United States, the United Kingdom, and South Africa, and those that are more group-oriented, such as Japan and China.[30]

You will not be surprised to learn that similar patterns are found among students. Students high in external LOC believe they have little control over their final grades. They are less likely than internals to assume personal responsibility for their course performance and are more prone than internals to blaming their professors for their grades. The result is they tend to rank their instructors lower on course evaluations.[31]

How Can You Know Whether a Psychological Test Is a Good One?

Does the locus of control test really tell you something true and useful about yourself? Hopefully, yes. Psychologists work hard to create personality tests (which are also called personality "instruments") that are valid and reliable. A **valid test** is one that measures what it says it measures, and a **reliable test** is one that when repeated will give similar results.

The Internal–External Locus of Control Test is a well-researched test that successfully meets both of these criteria. It is valid because it has been shown—not just once, but many times—to measure the extent to which people believe that they themselves, rather than fate and situational factors, control the events and outcomes in their lives. The test does actually tell you how your beliefs compare with those of a large, well-differentiated group of people who have also taken the test. Also, the test is reliable because researchers have demonstrated that if you take the test again at some future time, say, six months from now, you will in all probability get the same results.

Finally, as we have seen, the test is useful. It has been shown to predict important differences in behavior on the job as well as in other aspects of life.

Not all tests are created equal, of course. Fill out a typical *Cosmo* quiz and you are not likely to be using an instrument that is particularly valid or reliable. Such "tests" can help you to order your thoughts or compare your ideas with those of others, but they do not meet psychologists' rigorous standards for accurately mirroring personal reality over time.

If you find a random test on the Internet and you want to tell whether it is a good one, you should examine its origins carefully. Has the test been researched extensively, and has this research been published in reliable scholarly outlets? Scholarly journals have rigorous

valid test
A test that measures what it says it measures.

reliable test
A test that will give similar results if it is repeated.

requirements regarding how research is conducted, and articles accepted for publication have been read carefully and judged according to professionally accepted standards.

Of course, asking whether a test is a good one also suggests we should examine how the test is used. Test-use and test-manipulation are two important ethical issues. Because of privacy concerns, whether or not companies should use personality tests at all is debatable, and in some places the law attempts to control their use. For example, a company might be permitted to use only a test that has been shown in the research to be correlated with effectiveness in a certain job, and not other tests. An additional issue concerns individual gaming of the tests. Is it ethical to misrepresent yourself on a personality test? What do you think?

What Is a Personality Profile? What Is the Big Five Personality Profile?

During the second half of the twentieth century, research psychologists were busy creating and testing a large number of discrete personality traits. After many years of focusing on the discovery of personality traits, they began to summarize and organize all of the personality traits that had been identified up to that time. Their goal was to develop a **personality profile**, a test that describes an individual's whole personality, rather than just the separate traits that make up that personality.

Today, using sophisticated statistical techniques to summarize the most valid and reliable psychological traits, researchers have identified five fundamental dimensions that define an individual's personality.[32] These five dimensions have been known by various names, including the "Norman Five," after early researcher W. T. Norman,[33] and "five factor theory." We will refer to them here by what has become the customary term: the "Big Five."

The Big Five model clusters different personality traits into enduring dimensions of personality that together describe the whole person. Each of the five factors represents a **continuum** on which an individual's score may fall anywhere to the left, the right, or somewhere in the middle. The ends of the continuum are its poles, such as (extreme) extraversion and (extreme) introversion.

As you work with the Big Five, keep in mind that in the science of psychology, language is always a limitation. Much as psychologists would prefer to use nonjudgmental, neutral terminology when they name the poles of a personality continuum, sometimes there is simply no accurate way to describe the opposite of a given trait. Our language, far from being a scientifically objective measure of the world, is really a reflection of our own human biases. For example, what is the opposite of "agreeableness"? Is it really "disagreeableness," an idea with so many negative connotations? Might it not be something less judgmental, such as "self-absorbed"? Although they are not intended to be, some terms you will read in the Big Five classifications may seem critical. Thus, when you work with the Big Five, try to view all of its terms dispassionately, factoring in the reality that a word can suggest—but is not—an individual's, or your own, behavioral reality.

The Big Five personality factors are:

1. Extraversion and energy (sometimes referred to as "sociability," or "surgency") versus introversion and passivity.

   People who are extraverts are sociable, fun-loving, affectionate, friendly, and talkative. They exhibit warmth, gregariousness, assertiveness (some say dominance), activity, excitement-seeking, and positive emotions. Interest in enjoying others' company and the ability to be assertive are important components of extraversion. This pole of the variable is not all positive and lighthearted, however. According to one research team, "What is essential to recall. . . is that liking people does not necessarily make one likable. Salesmen, those prototypic extraverts, are generally happier to see you than you are to see them."[34]

   The opposite pole on this continuum is introversion and passivity. People high on introversion are retiring, sober, reserved, submissive, aloof, inhibited, quiet, unengaged emotionally, solitudinous, and task oriented.

2. Adventurous versus traditional (also referred to as "openness versus closedness").

   Open individuals are defined by their preference for variety, independence, and liberal beliefs. They care more for acquiring rich and varied experiences than for developing

personality profile
A test that describes an individual's whole personality, rather than just the separate traits that make up that personality.

continuum
A continuous series.

their cognitive (thinking) ability. People who exhibit openness are likely to be original, imaginative, and daring. They typically have a broad range of interests, including fantasy, aesthetics, feelings, actions, ideas, and values.

Often they are seen by themselves and others as somewhat more intelligent than most. Although intelligence itself is not one of the Big Five factors, intelligence predisposes a person to openness, and it can be developed by openness.

The opposite pole of this continuum represents being relatively closed to experience. The person who is closed to experience is conventional, down-to-earth, and conforming. He or she likes routine and does not have a lot of curiosity.

3.   Agreeableness versus tough-mindedness.

The person who is agreeable exhibits trust, sympathy, generosity, forgiveness, open-mindedness, flexibility, gullibility, and cheerfulness. Persons may be what we might call too agreeable, in which case they are dependent, overly cooperative, and self-effacing.

The opposite end of this continuum is tough-mindedness. Especially self-centered, these people are likely to set themselves against others. They tend to be critical, skeptical, antagonistic, unsympathetic, uncooperative, stubborn, and blunt. Some would argue that their sense of attachment is defective; others would argue that they are highly independent. Because they are often working against people, the tough-minded are seen as narcissistic, perfectionist, arrogant, and self-righteous. Certainly they have a drive for mastery. Some are overtly aggressive; others may be polished manipulators. They may exhibit overt or inhibited hostility.

4.   Conscientiousness versus undirectedness.

Exhibiting the trait of conscientiousness means being careful and thorough, preferring to live one's life deliberately. It is associated with reliability, hard work, self discipline, neatness, and ambition. It is somewhat related to being moralistic. Conscientiousness is related to having a need for achievement.

Its opposite pole, undirectedness, suggests a person who is disorganized, lax, sloppy, thoughtless, aimless, unstable, and unambitious.

5.   Emotionality (also called neuroticism) versus stability.

Being high in emotionality suggests anxiety, hostility, depression, self-consciousness, impulsiveness, and vulnerability. Because they must deal more often with disruptive emotions, individuals high in emotionality may use inappropriate coping responses, such as hostile reactions and wishful thinking. They are more likely than the average person to adopt irrational beliefs, such as self-blame.

The opposite pole to emotionality is stability—being even-tempered, comfortable, hardy, unemotional, relaxed, calm, and self-satisfied.

What Is Your Personality Profile, as Assessed with the Big Five?

You have learned that the best way to profile your personality using the Big Five is to take a personality test designed to measure it. Although the following short adjective checklist is less valid than a longer, question-based test, it does give you a workable idea of your personality profile. To profile your personality based on the Big Five, read the lists of adjective pairs in Table 2.3 and choose the word in each pair that best describes you.[35] For each pair, select the word that most accurately describes you most of the time. Then simply add up the columns. The column with the higher number suggests the pole of the continuum that best describes your personality.

A couple of cautions. First, each list has 10 pairs. If your numbers for a dimension are very close (5 and 5, or 4 and 6) you fall in the middle range on that dimension and should take particular care in how strongly you interpret it. Also, these lists are what psychologists call **transparent**, meaning that the profile is easy to manipulate according to how you might like to be rather than how you are. Therefore, to get a more valid result, it would be useful to have a few friends, relatives, or colleagues who know you well complete the checklists and share them with you.

transparent
Easy to manipulate to attain desired results.

TABLE 2.3 Profile Your Personality Using the Big Five

Big Five Factor 1: Introversion and Passivity versus Extraversion and Energy

retiring.. sociable
sober... fun-loving
reserved.. affectionate
aloof... friendly
inhibited.. spontaneous
quiet... talkative
passive.. active
loner... joiner
task-oriented.................................... person-oriented
follower... leader

Introverted and passive	Extraverted and high energy

Big Five Factor 2: Traditional versus Adventurous (Sometimes referred to as Closed versus Open)

conventional.................................... original
down-to-earth.................................. imaginative
uncreative....................................... creative
narrow interests................................ broad interests
not curious...................................... curious
unadventurous.................................. daring
conforming...................................... independent
prefer routine................................... prefer variety
traditional....................................... untraditional
inartistic... artistic

Traditionalist (closed)	Adventurer (open)

Big Five Factor 3: Tough-minded versus Agreeable

critical.. lenient
serious.. cheerful
competitive...................................... cooperative
skeptical... trusting
argumentative.................................. agreeable
stubborn... flexible
egocentric....................................... selfless
cynical.. gullible
manipulative.................................... straightforward
proud... humble

Tough-minded (self-centered)	Agreeable (other-centered)

Big Five Factor 4: Conscientious versus Undirected

well organized.................................. disorganized
careful.. careless
reliable... undependable
punctual.. late
self-reliant...................................... dependent
businesslike..................................... playful
persevering...................................... quitting
hardworking..................................... lazy
practical.. impractical
conscientious................................... negligent

Conscientious	Undirected

Big Five Factor 5: Stable versus Emotional

calm... worrying
relaxed... high-strung
even-tempered.................................. temperamental
secure.. insecure
patient.. impatient
not envious...................................... envious, jealous
adaptable.. vulnerable
objective... subjective
comfortable...................................... self-conscious
self-satisfied.................................... self-pitying

Stable	Emotional

Source: Adapted from R. R. McCrae and P. T. Costa, Jr. "Validation of the Five-Factor Model of Personality Across Instruments and Observers." *Journal of Personality and Social Psychology 52* (1), 1987: 81–90. These lists are intended to provide a quick assessment to be used only for teaching purposes.

Now summarize your profile here by circling the appropriate poles in Table 2.4.

TABLE 2.4 Your Big Five Profile Summarized

I am...	Or...	This finding is strong (one pole was checked at seven or more times) or borderline (poles were checked about evenly):	
Introverted and passive	Extraverted and high energy	Strong	Borderline
A traditionalist (closed)	An adventurer (open)	Strong	Borderline
Tough-minded (self-centered)	Agreeable (other-centered)	Strong	Borderline
Conscientious	Undirected	Strong	Borderline
Stable	Emotional	Strong	Borderline

How Is the Study of Personality Traits Applied in Organizations?

Companies use Big Five profiles, as well as individual personality traits, for a variety of purposes in organizational life. Applying these tools, they attempt to predict both individual success and individual failure.

What Does the Big Five Profile of Personality Predict in Organizations?

The Big Five personality profile is widely used today in such on-the-job processes as employee selection, performance appraisal, motivation, and team building.[36] Among the many well-documented findings (see Table 2.5) are that a higher score on conscientiousness predicts that a person will be motivated to perform well in a job, whereas a higher score on neuroticism predicts the opposite.[37] Also, personality types are related to individual thinking styles. Extraverts and open-minded individuals have complex thinking styles and are especially creative in generating ideas, whereas neurotics favor simplistic thinking and conventional styles.[38] Interestingly, the research suggests that personality is unrelated to cognitive ability.[39]

GETTING ALONG VERSUS GETTING AHEAD In organizational life, most people want to both get along and get ahead.[40] However, to get along individuals must seem cooperative, compliant, friendly, and positive, and they must be seen by others as good team players and organizational citizens. For example, helping a coworker who is late on a project is getting along. People who get along demonstrate interpersonal skill, work well with others, show positive attitudes, and share credit. On the other hand, to get ahead, individuals must take the initiative, seek responsibility, compete, and try to be recognized, and they must be seen by others to be getting results and providing leadership. People who get ahead work with energy, show effort, value productivity, and show concern for quality. Coming to work early and staying late are examples of behaviors aimed at getting ahead.

Sometimes successful job performance requires getting along, and other times it requires getting ahead. Recent research suggests that in real life getting along and getting

TABLE 2.5 How the Big Five Personality Factors Predict Personal Behaviors

Factor	Strongly correlates with:	Moderately correlates with:
Extraversion and energy	Alcohol consumption, popularity, parties attended (number per month), attractiveness, dating variety (number dated during a year), routinely exercises	Fraternity interest, participation in sports
Adventurousness	Intelligence, plays musical instruments	Liberal arts
Agreeableness	Gender Honesty (–) Tobacco consumption	Religiosity (–) Dating variety (–) Dieting behavior (–) Driving fast
Conscientiousness	Gender, intelligence, honesty, gradepoint average (–) Alcohol consumption	(–) Traffic violations
Emotionality	Gender (–) Intelligence	(–) Attractiveness (–) Routinely exercises

Caution: Some of these are self-perception measures, and are thereby best taken with a grain of salt, especially the factors attractiveness, intelligence, popularity, femininity, religiosity, and honesty. The sign (–) means the correlation is negative. For example, the more agreeable you are, the less likely you are to consume tobacco or alcohol.

Source: Adapted from S. V. Paunonen, "Big Five Factors of Personality and Replicated Predictions of Behavior," *Journal of Personality and Social Psychology 84* (2), 2003: pp. 411–424. Reprinted by permission of S.V. Paunonen, Ph. D and the American Psychological Association.

ahead are both associated with low neuroticism; that is, good emotional adjustment.[41] However, getting along correlates with the Big Five personality dimensions of agreeableness and conscientiousness, whereas getting ahead correlates with the personality dimensions of extraversion (in particular, its component factor of ambition, but not its component factor of sociability) and openness. Thus the person who is most likely to both get along and get ahead will be extraverted, open, agreeable, conscientious, and, of course, well adjusted.

CROSS-CULTURAL AND OTHER APPLICABILITY It has been learned, too, that the Big Five personality profile is quite likely to be applicable to people from many countries.[42] A study of highly diverse cultures (American, German, Portuguese, Hebrew, Chinese, Korean, and Japanese) with languages from five distinct language families strongly suggests that the Big Five personality trait profile is universal.

However, predictive as the Big Five is, it is not without its critics.[43] Researchers contend that some personality traits are not captured by the five variables. Also, complex behaviors, such as donating blood or working toward self-improvement, have many causes, only some of which are personality variables, and only some of which variables are included in the Big Five. Caution in using the Big Five for such applications is recommended.

How Does the Myers-Briggs Type Indicator Assess Personality?

The Myers-Briggs Type Indicator (MBTI) is a famous personality profile that has been taken by millions of people in business and education.[44] It is used primarily to help individuals find a fit between their personality and a job, and to help companies develop strategies for using personality type to improve selection, retention, performance, and interpersonal relations.

Developed by Katherine Briggs and Isabel Briggs Myers, the MBTI is based on the work of Karl Jung, a psychological pioneer who, like Sigmund Freud, worked in the pre-scientific era in which psychologists based their theories on observation. Based on his clinical practice and other personal observations, Jung came to believe that differences among people fall into four categories. Myers and Briggs label these categories as follows: 1) introversion versus extraversion, 2) sensing versus intuition, 3) thinking versus feeling, and 4) judging versus perceiving.[45] The MBTI measures individual personalities along these four continuums to create 16 (4 × 4) personality types.

Research that has checked out the validity of the MBTI, along with the widespread use of the MBTI and similar instruments, suggests that understanding your personality using Jungian theory can help you to recognize the types of jobs that you will enjoy and be good at.[46] For example, if you have the profile ISTJ (introverted, sensing, thinking, and judging) you would probably like work that is technical in nature, performed in a stable and traditional organization in which results are tangible and measurable. Depending on your interests, you would probably enjoy being in a job similar to that of an auditor, a supply-chain manager, or a mechanical or electrical engineer.

Some researchers have urged caution in applying the MBTI too broadly, suggesting, for example, that as a tool for leadership development it is limited.[47] Its authors also caution that feedback from the test should always be given interactively by a trained professional, and that all types must be presented as valuable.[48] Today the test continues to be used widely in organizations as a diagnostic tool.

What Do the Big Five and the MBTI Have in Common?

Interestingly, the similarities between the observation-based MBTI and the research-based Big Five personality profile are substantial. Research that directly compares the two has shown that the four MBTI types rather closely resemble four of the five dimensions of the Big Five personality profile.[49] (The remaining Big Five factor, stability versus emotionality, does not figure into the MBTI at all because it measures a dimension more closely related to emotion than to the cognitions and attitudes that are the focus of the MBTI[50]). See Table 2.6 for a comparison of the Big Five and the MBTI.

TABLE 2.6 Overview: A Comparison of the Big Five and MBTI Personality Factors

MBTI Factor #1 Big Five Factor #1	Extraversion (E) Extraversion and Energy	Introversion (I) Introversion and Passivity	Strong relationship
MBTI Factor #2 Big Five Factor #2	Sensing (S) Traditionalist (closed)	Intuition (N) Adventurer (open)	Strong relationship
MBTI Factor #3 Big Five Factor #3	Thinking (T) Tough-minded (self-centered)	Feeling (F) Agreeable (other-centered)	Moderate relationship
MBTI Factor #4 Big Five Factor #4	Judging (J) Conscientious	Perceiving (P) Undirected	Moderate relationship

Among the four core factors common to both personality profiles, two relationships are strong and two are moderate. The MBTI factor extraversion–introversion is strongly associated with the Big Five factor extraversion–introversion, and the MBTI sensation–intuition factor is strongly associated with the Big Five factor traditionalist–adventurer (closed versus openness) factor. The MBTI thinking–feeling factor is moderately associated with the Big Five tough-minded–agreeableness factor, and the MBTI judging–perceiving factor is moderately associated with the Big Five conscientiousness–undirected factor.[51] Thus, if you were to take both tests, it is *very* likely that you will have the same answers on dimensions one and two, and *somewhat* likely you will have the same answers on dimensions three and four.

Why is this comparison useful? Understanding the similarities and differences between the Big Five personality profile and the MBTI is important because both are widely used today. If you analyze your personality profile using the Big Five model as you did earlier, it is useful to be able to translate that profile into an MBTI profile, because in organizational life you will almost certainly need that profile. (Knowing your MBTI profile is also useful, we hear, in the online dating scene.)

What Are Some Personality Variables That Are Especially Important in Organizations?

As you read further in this text, you will find discussions of many additional personality traits and related concepts. These include self-monitoring, the belief in self-efficacy, the need for achievement, the need for affiliation, dysfunctional personality traits, and Machiavellianism. Before we leave our basic discussion of personality, however, several personality traits warrant special mention here because of their particular relevance to business and organizations.

SELF-ESTEEM Self-esteem is the evaluation you make of yourself in terms of your worth as a human being.[52] Conceptually it is closely related to locus of control, emotional stability, and self-efficacy (a person's expectation that he or she can perform).[53] Self-esteem has a strong influence on a person's sense of well-being.[54] The sense of well-being is also strongly influenced by the traits of extraversion and neuroticism, and by one's life circumstances.

Interestingly, people generally develop attitudes and behave in ways that maintain their current level of self-esteem.[55] In organizations, employees with high self-esteem are likely to develop positive work attitudes, such as job satisfaction, and they are likely to perform at a high level. In contrast, but consistent with their self-image as incompetent, employees with low self-esteem are likely to develop both negative work attitudes and unproductive work behaviors.

RISK-TAKING Risk-taking is the tendency to take the chance of a loss in order to make a larger gain. It is a personality trait that is one of the components of the Big Five factor of extraversion.[56] Although risk-taking is an important concept in business, as a personality trait and personal predisposition it has not been widely studied. One reason it has been relatively ignored may be that it is hard to study. Risk-taking is a complex, multifaceted concept that involves attitudes toward taking risks, choices in risky situations, personal and business risks, and risky threats as well as risky opportunities. Highly sophisticated research methods are required to measure it accurately. Nevertheless, one study of 500 top-level Canadian executives was able to combine the many facets of risk into a set of practical tests, with interesting results.[57] It found that the most successful executives— those who were wealthier, had higher incomes, higher positions, and more authority— were the biggest risk-takers. The most mature executives—that is, those who were older, had longer seniority with their company, and had fewer dependents—were the most risk averse. Not surprisingly, executives from large banks showed significantly less risk-taking than executives from other types of businesses.

COMPETITIVENESS People who like to win even if the activity is not very important are competitive. Like risk-taking, competitiveness contributes to the Big Five factor of extraversion.[58] Typical questionnaire items that measure competitiveness are, "I enjoy working in situations involving competition with others," and "I feel that winning is important in both work and games."[59]

Competitiveness in organizational life is closely linked with goal setting.[60] For example, when they believe themselves to be working in a competitive organizational culture, salespeople who are highly competitive set higher goals and perform better. Salespeople who are not particularly competitive set low goals for themselves whether or not they believe themselves to be working in a competitive culture. They also perform less well.

Competitiveness is linked to how people see themselves in relation to others. For one thing, competitive people see relationships in terms of power. They believe that non-cooperation is strong and intelligent, whereas cooperation is weak and unintelligent.[61] On the other hand, compared with cooperative people, when their group is in a competition with another group, competitive people are especially cooperative with their own group members, and they become especially flexible in their thinking.[62] It seems that whether as an individual or as a group member, competition motivates them to perform.

Finally, competitiveness is closely linked with a person's motive to achieve, and both of these personality traits together predict a person's pace of life.[63] The higher their competitiveness and achievement motivation, the more likely it is that people's life is fast-paced. Indeed, a study of 31 countries confirms that competitive cultures are fast-paced cultures. Examples of fast-paced nations and cultures are Japan, Hong Kong, and many of the European nations. Slow-paced nations include the People's Republic of China (surprisingly enough), Greece, Brazil, and Mexico.

What Is a Psychological Disorder?

Individuals who have a **psychological disorder** suffer significant pain and stress, and also maladaptive functioning, due to biological factors, learned habits, or mental processes, rather than situational influences.[64] Sometimes individuals with psychological disorders cannot work. Other times they do work, but they exhibit such abnormal behavior that they stress the people they work with. The worst case, perhaps, is when managers with psychological disorders misuse their power over others.

Sometimes psychological disorders originate in a physically unhealthy mind and can be treated with drugs. Other times they originate in "deep-seated personal conflicts, bad habits, negative life experiences, daily stress, faulty processing of information, and sociocultural factors."[65] The American Psychiatric Association today identifies several hundred psychological disorders.

Two of the psychological disorders you would be likely to find in a business context are **narcissistic personality disorder** and **antisocial personality disorder**. Individuals who have a narcissistic personality disorder appear arrogant and self-important. They have an exaggerated sense of their own achievements and talk about them incessantly. They "feel entitled to special treatment *by* others but are markedly lacking in empathy *for* others."[66] Often these individuals move up rapidly through their organizations, until

psychological disorder
A psychological condition which causes significant pain, stress and maladaptive functioning, due to biological factors, learned habits, or mental processes, rather than situational influences.

narcissistic personality disorder
A disorder characterized by arrogance, self-importance, a feeling of entitlement to special treatment by others, and a marked lack of empathy for others.

antisocial personality disorder
A disorder characterized by the lack of anxiety, remorse of guilt; psychopathy, sociopathy.

someone discovers that they cannot really manage people effectively, and that they actually harm those under them because they take credit for their work and hinder their growth.

Individuals with an antisocial personality disorder (formerly called "psychopaths" or "sociopaths") lack anxiety, remorse, or guilt.[67] In the United States, it is estimated that about 3 percent of men and 1 percent of women have this disorder.[68] They will do anything to get what they want, and they may actually be charming and intelligent as they fleece their customers and business associates.

What Is Your Emotional Style and Why Is It Important in Organizational Life?

emotion

A momentary, elementary feeling of pleasure or displeasure, and of activation or deactivation.

mood

An ongoing cycle of feelings that are *not* intense enough to interrupt one's ongoing thought processes.

affect

The manner in which one expresses one's emotions.

An **emotion** is a momentary, elementary feeling of pleasure or displeasure, and of activation or deactivation.[69] It is a temporary positive or negative experience that you feel as happening to you yourself, is generated in part by your cognitive appraisal of the particular situation, and is accompanied by both your learned and your automatic physical responses.[70] Many researchers today distinguish between emotion and **mood**. You experience an emotion as beginning and ending, and it is intense enough to disrupt your thinking processes. In contrast, a mood is an ongoing cycle of feelings that are *not* intense enough to interrupt your ongoing thought processes.[71]

Your emotional style is the way you express your emotions, and it is closely related to your personality. When you express your emotions, you are said to be demonstrating **affect**.[72] Affect is one component in the Big Five factor of emotionality, and it can be either negative or positive. In the Big Five test, for example, a pattern of negative affect is suggested if you agree with statements such as "I am easily displeased with things at work."[73] In contrast to individuals who have a pattern of negative affect, individuals with positive affect are more optimistic about themselves and their surroundings. They also perceive their world as less stressful.[74]

felt emotions

Emotions which are experienced; may or may not be appropriate to express to others.

displayed emotions

The emotions which one expresses to others.

Managing emotions on the job can be challenging. Whenever you feel an emotion at work, you must decide whether it is appropriate to display it in the circumstance in which you find yourself. Sometimes you'll decide that your **felt emotions** should not become **displayed emotions**. For instance, you might feel frustrated over a setback but decide that expressing frustration in front of your boss shows weakness, or you might feel elated over a business success, but suppress your happiness because you do not want to make your coworkers jealous.

Genetic Determinants of Emotions

To some extent your emotional style is innately determined. As evidence, consider two facts. First, certain emotions are common to all human beings. The six universal emotions are anger, fear, sadness, happiness, disgust, and surprise.[75] Second, when presented with stimuli that elicit basic emotions, all humans react with similar facial responses.[76] Thus, you can be pretty sure that if you sense that your colleague from another country seems to be happy, sad, or angry, he or she really is.

Further, your predisposition to a certain intensity of emotion is probably inherited. We have already pointed out that people's level of subjective well-being, or happiness, is stable over the course of their lives.[77] Studies of twins suggest that their genetic make-up predicts their happiness more than having either money or popularity. Also, over time, people who win the lottery are not happier than those who do not.[78]

In addition, your emotions are closely integrated with your physical make-up. Interestingly, people who are asked to make the facial expressions commonly associated with certain emotions report actually *feeling* the emotions.[79] Making posed facial expressions can even affect your judgment. When participants in a research study were asked to smile, they tended to form more positive impressions of others than those who were not asked to smile.[80] (No wonder bosses like their employees to smile at them!) Furthermore, people who are happier or more optimistic have stronger immunity against disease. They are also less likely to die of chronic disease, and are likely to live longer. People who are frequently distressed and angry get sick, or feel sick, more often. They also have more dental problems and heal more slowly after surgery.[81]

Environmental Determinants of Emotions

Some of your emotional responses are habits that you have learned from others.

For instance, your family life has taught you how to express your emotions, and it has also influenced you in ways that make you want to emote. When individuals repeatedly exhibit highly charged emotions in the office, there is some likelihood that they have failed to resolve emotional family issues. Their emotional outbursts are likely to continue until they recognize the true source of their problem. Today, family systems therapy helps managers avoid emotional inefficiency in the office by showing them how the dynamics of their family lives, now and in the past, affect their behavior with their work teams.[82]

Different societies have different **emotion cultures**, which are characteristic emotional styles, [83] and these emotion cultures also influence individual emotional style. For example, women generally smile more than men do, but the extent to which this is true varies by nationality, ethnicity, and age.[84] For example, women and men from the United States and Canada show larger differences in their amount of smiling (with women smiling significantly more) than do participants from the United Kingdom.

Sometimes the emotion culture a society thinks it has is not the emotion culture it actually has. For instance, in the United States many people believe that women are more emotional and more emotionally expressive than men. We tend to believe that women feel and express sadness more than men do, and that men feel and express anger more than women do. These beliefs instruct both women and men as to what their appropriate emotional roles are, and when their feelings and expressions deviate from the cultural norm, individuals try to change them. However, a recent large scale U.S. research study suggests that, contrary to our cultural beliefs, women do not report more frequent emotional experiences than men.[85] Also, the study found no differences between men and women in how often they feel angry. Although the research found that women do report more negative feelings than men do, it determined that women's more frequent negative emotions are best explained by their lower household incomes.

Task Determinants of Emotions

Certain tasks elicit emotional arousal in large numbers of people. Speaking in front of a group is one such task. Forty percent of Americans rank public speaking as a major fear inducer, right up there with snakes, spiders, and heights.[86]

Another task that leads to emotional arousal is test taking. Individuals tend to perform best on tests when their emotional arousal is moderate rather than high or low. High emotional arousal tends to impair their ability to perform, in which case they are said to be suffering from **test anxiety**.[87]

Recent research has identified a phenomenon called **stereotype threat** that explains some of the excessive emotional arousal and reduced performance that occurs when members of minority groups take a test.[88] Studies focusing on gender and race have shown that when members of minority groups are reminded about the negative stereotypes of their groups' cognitive abilities just before a test, their performance on the test is impaired.[89] In one study, women and men about to take a difficult math test heard the stereotype that men usually outscore women on such tests. In comparison with control groups, the women who heard this stereotype had significantly lower scores, whereas the men's scores were unaffected.

What Suggests Emotional Competence on the Job?

Since emotions influence both human relations and cognitive performance, **emotional competence** is a quality that is highly valued by today's employers. Emotional competence, also referred to as "emotional intelligence" and "EQ," is a multi-faceted personal characteristic that includes self-awareness, psychological self-management, social awareness and empathy, and relationship management.[90]

Emotional competence is related to many work-related outcomes. To begin with, it is one of the factors that predicts how well a job candidate succeeds in a job interview.[91] The candidates most likely to be hired are those that make interviewers like them, demonstrate self-control, and project confidence. Once on the job, emotionally

emotion cultures
The characteristic emotional styles of different societies.

test anxiety
The impairment of one's ability to perform on a test due to high emotional arousal.

stereotype threat
A phenomenon in which individuals have impaired performance on a test after being reminded about the negative stereotypes of their groups' cognitive abilities.

emotional competence
Emotional intelligence or "EQ"; a multifaceted personal characteristic that includes self-awareness, psychological self-management, social awareness and empathy, and relationship management.

competent individuals demonstrate positive work attitudes, altruistic behavior, and successful task performance.[92] In a study of senior managers in non-profit organizations, emotional competency also helped individuals manage the work–family conflicts that were affecting their career commitment. Finally, **emotional incompetence**, including being habitually angry and having low self-control, contributes to workplace aggression.[93]

Different companies have different cultural norms about **emotional display**—the manner and extent of emotional expression. Many companies follow norms of impersonality, in which intense positive or negative emotional displays are unwelcome.[94] In these organizations, display of emotions is considered to be detrimental to performance. Other companies, however, favor an approach called **bounded emotionality**, in which certain constrained emotional expressions are encouraged at work in order to encourage community building and personal well-being.[95] In these organizations, such emotional expressions as shedding tears would be acceptable on some occasions. One company that employs the philosophy of bounded emotionality is The Body Shop International, a publicly owned multinational firm in the cosmetics industry that has an unusually high number of women in its managerial ranks.

Some jobs require the expression of particular emotions. This aspect of work is referred to as **emotional labor**, which is the effort, planning, and control needed to express certain specific emotions while performing a job.[96] Call center workers, teachers, tour guides, bank tellers, and airline flight attendants all face frequent situations in which they feel emotions but do not dare to express them. As employees who are performing emotional labor, they are bound by organizational **display rules**, guidelines about how they must interact with others, usually customers. At Walt Disney World, the display rule is that Mickey never, never gets angry; at McDonald's the staff is always helpful and enthusiastic.[97]

One problem with emotional labor is the frequent occurrence of **emotional dissonance**, the inconsistency we experience between a felt emotion (such as being angry at a customer) and our emotional expression (forcing ourselves to be pleasant toward that customer). Emotional dissonance is a significant factor in job stress:[98] It is not easy for Mickey to stay cool when he has been kicked in the shins for the tenth time. Many companies today recognize the special challenges of emotional labor. They make a point of creating a strong service culture in which the norms and values for treating customers are clear, and as part of this culture they encourage employees to find meaning and value in treating customers well.[99] They also are clear about rewarding employees for displaying the mandated emotions, and they try to hire employees who are most likely to be comfortable displaying the job-appropriate emotions.

We will have more to say about emotions at appropriate places throughout this book, including how emotions affect decision making, how emotions motivate, and how individuals monitor emotions during conflict and negotiation.

What Cognitive Abilities Contribute to Your Personal Style?

Cognitive abilities are another important component of your personal style. In recent years they have typically been described using the **triarchic theory of intelligence**, a model that includes analytic, creative, and practical components.[100] Analytic ability helps you calculate a company's investment return; creative ability allows you to imagine new products and markets; practical ability lets you figure out what to do if you are stranded at the airport and have to get a crucial report to your boss.

Analytic Ability

Among the characteristics of effective managers and leaders are superior reasoning and problem-solving skills. People who make good decisions enhance the probability that their companies will succeed, whereas people who make bad decisions enhance the probability of failure. In the early 1980s Roger Smith, Chairman of General Motors Corporation,

---

emotional incompetence
Lack of emotional intelligence.

emotional display
The manner and extent of emotional expression.

bounded emotionality
An approach in which certain constrained emotional expressions are encouraged at work in order to encourage community building and personal well-being.

emotional labor
The effort, planning, and control needed to express certain specific emotions while performing a job.

display rules
Guidelines about how employees must interact with others, usually customers.

emotional dissonance
The inconsistency experienced between one's felt emotion(s) and one's emotional expression.

triarchic theory of intelligence
A model of cognitive abilities which includes analytic, creative, and practical components.

analytic ability
Reasoning and problem-solving skills.

decided that, in the future, robots would produce cars, and he invested $45 billion in this idea.[101] By the late 1980s, after a major transfer to automation, GM had lost even more market share, and plant productivity was falling every year. Among other errors, Smith had failed to account for unintended consequences: Automation severely limits flexibility, and requires expensive high-level technicians. For the amount of money Smith had spent, GM could have bought both Toyota and Nissan.

Intelligence quotient, or IQ, is the most widely used measure of analytic ability. Today an **IQ test** is any test used to measure analytic intelligence on an objective, standardized scale.[102] IQ tests are made up of sub-scales (sub-tests). For example, the widely used Stanford-Binet test measures verbal reasoning (including comparing and contrasting concepts), quantitative reasoning (doing math problems), abstract-visual reasoning (describing why you should do something), and working memory (when you hear a string of numbers, how many can you remember, and how many can you repeat in reverse order?).

IQ scores correlate reasonably well with high school grades,[103] and with the ability to learn on the job.[104] In a classic 60-year-long study, children with high IQ scores were well above average in terms of academic and financial success as adults.[105]

IQ tests are designed to differentiate among individuals so that their scores are distributed on a bell-shaped curve called a **normal distribution**, also called a "normal curve." Researchers generally strive to create psychological tests that give results approximating the normal curve because such results tell us something about the majority members of a population but also about the unusual members of that population. For example, the average IQ is 100. Of the total population, around 68 percent falls within +/– 1 σ (σ is the symbol for standard deviation) of the mean IQ, or between 85 and 115. Individuals with scores below 85 and above 115 are unusual.

Given that you are reading this text, your IQ is almost certainly in the 50 percent of the population that is above average, and you are probably at the high end. As a manager, it is often important to keep in mind that 50 percent of the population is also below average.

Creative Ability

Creativity is the ability to produce innovative, high-quality ideas and products.[106] Creative people are characterized by 1) expertise in their field, based on their own significant learning experiences; 2) creative skills that include the capacity to generate many solutions to a problem, the ability to drop outmoded problem-solving habits, persistence at problem solving, willingness to take risks, and willingness to work hard; and 3) the motivation to produce creatively for intrinsic, personal reasons rather than for extrinsic rewards.[107]

Guy Laliberté has all the hallmarks of a creative individual in business. He started out as a fire-breathing street performer. In 1984, he founded, and today continues to manage, Cirque du Soleil, a 3500-member global entertainment company that has transformed going to the circus into an upscale experience. He prefers to refer to himself as a "guide" rather than a boss, and while he plans new shows, chooses the directors, and furnishes the funding, he delegates the routine work to others. His company gives 1 percent of its gross revenue to social projects like Cirque du Monde, circus workshops for street children in 18 countries. Laliberté's press director, who cannot always count on getting in contact with him, says, "What can I say, he's an artist."[108]

Practical Intelligence

Practical intelligence, also called "situational judgment," is essentially common sense.[109] Fundamental to practical intelligence is **tacit knowledge**, the action-oriented knowledge one acquires and that allows an individual to achieve goals he or she personally values.[110]

Tacit knowledge is measured by giving individuals written descriptions of workplace scenarios involving problems with coworkers, with the work itself, and with supervisors, and asking them to identify how they would behave. Critics of the theory of practical intelligence argue that it is really only job knowledge, and that traditional measures of intelligence are more valid.[111]

---

intelligence quotient (IQ)
The most widely used measure of analytic ability.

IQ test
Any test used to measure analytic intelligence on an objective, standardized scale.

normal distribution
A distribution of scores with a bell-shaped curve or "normal curve."

practical intelligence
Common sense, also called "situational judgment."

tacit knowledge
The action-oriented knowledge one acquires that allows one to achieve goals one personally values.

Yet, consider this example. Art Fry was a new-product development researcher at 3M, a diversified technology company, when he was introduced to a strange adhesive.[112] Always a practical guy—as a kid in Iowa he would turn spare lumber into toboggans—he did not at first know what to do with the stuff. But then his scrap paper bookmarks kept falling out of his church choir hymnal, and in a moment he had the idea for Post-it® notes. There was more to do, however. It took Fry years to convince the company to manufacture the product. Yet one year after its introduction, Post-it® notes were named the company's outstanding new product.

While performance on intelligence tests begins to decline in middle adulthood, performance on measures of practical intelligence continue to improve until old age.[113] In business management and sales, for example, practical intelligence increases with age and experience.[114]

What Values and Attitudes Contribute to Your Personal Style?

cognitions
Ways of knowing.

belief
The conviction that a particular matter is true or false.

value
A broad principle underlying one's beliefs; an abstract standard of goodness that is often defined by the culture one lives in.

attitude
The combination of one's beliefs about something (one's cognitions) with one's feelings (affect) and actions (behavior) toward it.

Beliefs, attitudes, and values are characteristic aspects of our **cognitions**—our ways of knowing. A **belief** is a particular matter that one considers to be true or false.[115] An example is, "I believe workers are treated fairly in most companies."

A **value** is a broad principle that underlies one's beliefs. Values are abstract standards of goodness that are often defined by the culture we live in.[116] They are more stable and more difficult to change than either beliefs or attitudes. "All companies should provide health benefits to their employees" is a value statement.

An **attitude** to a given object combines our beliefs about that object (our cognitions) with our feelings (affect) and actions (behavior) toward it.[117] The statement "Because my company doesn't treat its employees well, I dislike it and I am thinking of quitting," describes an employee's attitude towards his or her company.

Values

Individuals' values are interrelated with their personalities.[118] For instance, introverts are likely to value solitude, and conscientious types are likely to value—you guessed it—conscientiousness.

Like personality traits, values can be summarized in sets. One well known set is the Schwartz "values circumplex," a description of international values based on research in 40 countries.[119] S. H. Schwartz and his colleagues believe that all values are best understood in terms of two dimensions. The first dimension is "self-transcendence versus self-enhancement," which is the degree to which a person is self-centered versus other-centered. The other dimension is "openness to change versus conservation," the degree to which a person enjoys innovation versus preserving the status quo. You may have noticed that these dimensions are similar to the Big Five personality dimensions "tough-minded versus agreeable" and "adventurous versus traditional."

Figure 2.1 illustrates the most important values held by individuals in the nations Schwartz and his colleagues studied. For example, some societies hold more benevolent values, whereas others hold more hedonistic values. Along the same lines, some companies value tradition, whereas others value stimulation and excitement.

job involvement
The belief that there is a relationship between an individual's performance in a job and his or her own self-worth.

work centrality
The general importance of work in an individual's life compared with other activities, such as leisure, spending time with friends, or family events.

WORK VALUES Among the work values that are particularly important in organizations today are job involvement, work centrality, and business ethics.

Job involvement is the belief that there is a relationship between an individual's performance in a job and his or her own self-worth.[120] Companies prefer to see their employees psychologically involved with their jobs because such involvement is related to lower absenteeism and less quitting.[121] On the other hand, being highly involved with one's job can exacerbate an individual's reaction to any types of stressors that threaten his or her performance, increasing the probability of illness and heavy alcohol use.[122]

A related value in organizations is **work centrality**, the general importance of work in an individual's life compared with other activities, such as leisure, spending time with

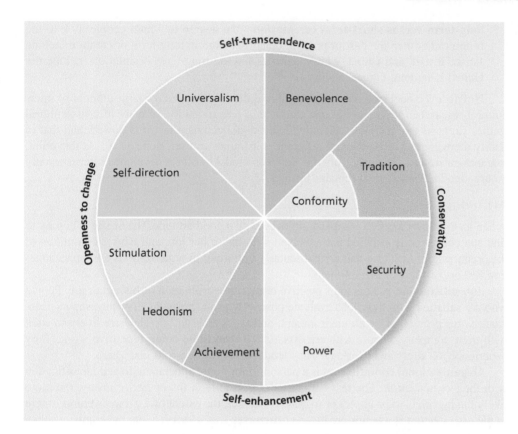

FIGURE 2.1

The Schwartz Values Circumplex

Source: S. H. Schwartz, G. Melech, A. Lehmann, S. Burgess, M. Harris and V. Owens, "Extending the Cross-Cultural Validity of the Theory of Basic Human Values with a Different Method of Measurement," *Journal of Cross-Cultural Psychology 32*, September 2001: 519–542. Copyright ©2001 by Sage Publications. Reprinted by permission of Sage Publications, Inc.

friends, or family events.[123] This value today tends to spark some controversy. Some employers want to hire only workers who put work first in their lives. Others encourage their employees to have a reasonable **work–life balance**, to proportion their time and commitment between work life and personal life. Some social critics question the benefits of working long, hard hours, and wonder how paid work has become so central in people's lives.[124]

Finally, holding **ethical business values** is a topic that is widely discussed in today's organizations. Some companies are now interviewing job candidates for ethical values by asking them multiple questions about how they have handled ethical situations in the past, and then evaluating and cross-checking their responses.[125]

VALUES IN GLOBAL CONTEXT In the last two decades of the twentieth century, the study of values in different cultures was strongly influenced by the work of researcher Geert Hofstede, who used data on 116,000 IBM personnel worldwide to develop a five-factor scale that differentiated among the work-related values of 40 nationalities.[126] Hofstede's five sets of work-related values are:

1. **power distance**—the extent to which people accept an unequal distribution of power in their society. Countries with high power distance include Brazil, India, and Mexico; countries with low power distance include Austria, Israel, and Denmark.[127]

2. **uncertainty avoidance**—the extent to which people feel threatened by uncertainty and ambiguity. Countries high on uncertainty avoidance include Greece, Japan, and France; countries low on uncertainty avoidance include Denmark, Sweden, and Great Britain.

3. **individualism versus collectivism**—the degree to which people prefer to act individually or in groups. Individualistic countries include the United States, Australia, and the Netherlands; collectivist countries include Venezuela, Taiwan, and Greece.

4. **tough versus nurturing orientation**—taking a competitive view of the world versus a relationship-oriented view. Countries scoring high for toughness include Japan, Austria, and Venezuela; countries scoring low include Sweden, Denmark, and Thailand.

work life balance
A proportioning of time and commitment between work life and personal life.

ethical business values
Principles/standards governing the handling of ethical situations in the workplace.

5. long-term versus short-term orientation—the degree to which people look to the future rather than the past or present. Countries high in long-term orientation include Japan, Brazil, and China, while countries low on long-term orientation include the United Kingdom, France, and Israel.[128]

Hofstede's model, and debates about its validity, have spurred a large amount of inter-cultural research.[129] To cite but one example, a reexamination of a set of cross-cultural studies suggests that the Hofstede individualism–collectivism factor is flawed, and that in reality there are few cross-cultural differences in values and self-concept.[130] At this point, researchers are moving away from the Hofstede model to others developed internationally on broader data bases, yet it remains influential.

Attitudes

When an employer says, "I want an employee with a good attitude," he or she is hoping to find someone who is satisfied and involved with his or her job, and who is committed to the organization. Attitudes that are particularly important to organizations are job satisfaction and organizational commitment.

job satisfaction
A person's positive or negative evaluation of his or her job.

Job satisfaction is a person's positive or negative evaluation of his or her job. People who are satisfied with their jobs evaluate positively such factors as their pay, supervision, chances for promotion, work environment, and tasks they do.[131] They are likely to stick with their company. People who are dissatisfied tend to be doing repetitive work. They experience job stress and overload. They tend to look for new jobs elsewhere.

organizational commitment
A person's emotional attachment to and identification with his or her organization.

Organizational commitment is a person's emotional attachment to and identification with their organization. The less committed a person is to his or her company, the more likely the person is to be absent or to quit.[132] In fact, the extent of a person's commitment to the organization is a better predictor of **turnover** (his or her leaving the company) than job satisfaction is.[133]

turnover
When an individual leaves a company.

Can Values and Attitudes Change?

Companies hire and promote workers based on their attitudes, but they also measure and shape their employees' attitudes once they are on the job. Employers often measure employee attitudes using **attitude surveys**, which are written questionnaires that tap job satisfaction, organizational commitment, and company-specific attitudes, such as employees' views about their bosses and workgroups. Then they set out to shape attitudes that favor the company.

attitude surveys
Written questionnaires that tap job satisfaction, organizational commitment, and company-specific attitudes.

For example, most companies want their employees to agree with company policies and conform to the corporate culture. How can they influence their employees' attitudes in these matters?

One way to change people's attitudes is to get them to change their behaviors. That's right, their *behaviors*. Interestingly, experiments have shown repeatedly that when individuals publicly behave in ways that are inconsistent with their privately held attitudes, they are likely to change their attitudes to be consistent with their behavior.[134] To illustrate, a manager of a less-than-committed worker, such as a new employee, might put that worker in charge of a public relations campaign that praises the company. By doing this, the manager can reasonably expect that the employee will develop a more favorable attitude toward the company.

Why is this tactic likely to work? Individuals are likely to change their attitudes when they begin to experience some discomfort about them. When individuals believe that their attitudes are inconsistent with each other, or that their attitudes and behaviors are inconsistent, they experience **cognitive dissonance**.[135] Experiencing cognitive dissonance is actually physiologically arousing and somewhat uncomfortable,[136] so an individual will try to reduce the discomfort. Thus, when the new, somewhat skeptical employee finds herself promoting the company, her attitude toward the company improves because changing her mind makes her feel more comfortable.

cognitive dissonance
Anxiety that results from simultaneously holding contradictory attitudes, or from behaving in ways that contradict one's beliefs.

The phenomenon of cognitive dissonance applies primarily to attitudes that are strong and clearly defined.[137] In contrast, when attitudes are weak and vague, a person's self-perception may actually play a larger role in determining his or her behavior. **Self-perception theory** suggests that under some circumstances people do not feel uncomfortable when their attitudes and behaviors differ. What they do instead is observe their own behavior and then deduce what their attitude must be from what they see.[138] For example, students who smile at their professor may deduce that they like the professor. Or, in the example in the previous paragraph, the employee who positively promotes her company deduces that she herself must like the company. This theory is most predictive when people have not developed a strong attitude toward something.

Do these relationships between attitudes and behaviors hold in all cultures? Probably not. For example, discrepancies between attitudes and behaviors may be more stressful for people in individualist cultures than people in collectivist cultures.[139] In individualist cultures, attitudes are seen as "who I am" and are carefully protected. In collectivist cultures, however, behaving in ways that are at odds with your own individual values probably feels less threatening because the individual values are seen as relatively less important to begin with.

self-perception theory
A theory which suggests that under some circumstances people do not experience cognitive dissonance when their attitudes and behaviors differ, but rather observe their own behavior and deduce what their attitude must be from what they see.

In Conclusion

In this chapter we have asked the question "What is your personality and style?" and answered it by discussing personality, cognitive abilities, values, and attitudes. Although we do not have the space here to provide a test for each personality trait or each cognitive skill, we have given you the opportunity to take an important psychological test, the Locus of Control, and to sketch your psychological self-portrait using the widely applied Big Five personality profile. You will have more opportunities to take more tests throughout this text. Also, check out the "Explorations" section at the end of this chapter for suggestions that will help you to explore your personality beyond the pages of this book.

How important is this kind of knowledge in business today? Jerry Jurgensen, chief executive officer of Nationwide, one of the largest diversified insurance and financial services companies in the world, puts it this way: "Managers need to understand the different ways people are wired—the differences in their interpersonal styles. In our work at Nationwide, much of our cultural transformation is grounded in our ability to better understand our individual styles. This is very real and very important for people to understand. It is critical to preparing students to be leaders and managers to teach them to recognize and appreciate the differences in the ways that people are wired; the sooner they recognize this, the more effective they can be."[140]

Apply What You Have Learned. . .

World Class Personality

The Rebel Billionaire

What do you make of a guy who believes business should be fun, who is dyslexic, a reluctant public speaker, and who cries in public? The man in question is the kind of person who, in the midst of a hostage crisis, would notice the irony of "the Virgin cabin crew with their red miniskirts and red stiletto shoes walking past the group of Iraqi soldiers in the vast empty airport."[141] The kind of man who, while facing death and vowing he will never again put himself in that position, at the same moment realizes he will most certainly take on the same kind of challenge again.

Meet Richard Branson, the "rebel billionaire" (after his television show of the same name). Having moved from his first venture *Student* magazine into Virgin Records, Branson went on to create an empire of, at last count, some 50 companies. Branson is known more for developing companies than for running them; although he typically maintains a financial stake, his laissez-faire style of management gives leaders of his companies full decision making powers.

Branson is one of the outstanding business personalities of our times. He himself points out that he is independent, stubborn, cunning, a team player, affectionate, irreverent towards authority, and competitive. When he left his English preparatory school at age 17, his headmaster's parting words to him were, "Congratulations, Branson. I predict that you will either go to prison or become a millionaire."[142]

On the opening page of his autobiography, we meet Branson as he is writing a posthumous letter for his two children. About to embark on a dangerous balloon adventure, he knows he may not survive. "Dear Holly and Sam," he writes, "Life can seem rather unreal at times. Alive and well and loving one day. No longer there the next.

"As you both know I always had an urge to live life to its full. That meant I was lucky enough to live the life of many people during my 46 years. I loved every minute of it and I especially loved every second of my time with both of you and Mum."[143]

Characteristically, Branson sees his business and personal life as one seamless event. Just before the balloon launch, one of his flying partners has to pull out because of illness. "Rory and I met and hugged each other. We both cried. As well as becoming a close friend as our third pilot on the balloon flight, Rory had been joining forces with me recently on a number of business deals. Just before we had come to Morocco, he had bought a share in our new record label, V2, and had invested in Virgin clothes and Virgin Vie, our new cosmetics company."[144]

Branson says he became an entrepreneur "almost by default" and that if someone would have called him that in the early days, he would have asked his partner what it meant. "I certainly didn't regard myself as a businessman. Businessmen were middle-aged men in the city who wore pin-striped suits, had wives and two to four children in the suburbs, and were obsessed with making money. Of course, we wanted to make money on *Student*, too; we needed money to survive. But we saw it as much more a creative enterprise than a moneymaking one. Later it became apparent to me that business could be a creative enterprise in itself. . . . Above all, you want to create something you are proud of."[145]

Branson suggests that one way he compensated for his dyslexia was by becoming more intuitive with people. Here is a classic story: Mike Oldfield, the shy genius behind Virgin's early album *Tubular Bells*, walked into Branson's houseboat on the afternoon of his first major concert and announced he could not go on stage that night. Branson, appalled but recognizing Mike to be as stubborn as he was himself, suggested they go for a drive in his vintage Bentley. "I knew that Mike had always admired this battleship gray car with its faded red leather seats. I hoped that a soothing drive past the [music hall] would put Mike in a different frame of mind. We drove off with Mike sitting bolt upright."[146] Passing the concert hall, where fans were beginning to gather, Oldfield reaffirmed that he could not go on stage. Branson merely asked him if he would like to drive, and he agreed. After a while, Branson said, "Mike, would you like to have this car? As a present?" "A present?" said Mike. "Come off it! It was your wedding present!" "No, all you have to do is then drive it around to the [concert hall] and go up onstage tonight. It's yours." After a few moments, Mike agreed. "It's a deal," he said.[147] Oldfield performed, and although he never learned to like the limelight, *Tubular Bells* went on to be wildly successful.

Branson never let his dyslexia, which made him a "dunce" at math and spelling, interfere with his ventures. He offers this advice:

> I found that it was only when I was using real numbers to solve real problems that math made any sense to me. If I was calculating how much a Christmas tree would grow or how many budgies would breed, the numbers became real and I enjoyed using them. . . . I worry about all the people who have been classified as stupid by. . . IQ tests. Little do these people know that often these IQ tests have been dreamed up by academics who are absolutely useless at dealing with the practicalities of the outside world. I loved doing real business plans.

For his television reality show, Branson established the rule that he would never ask his contestants to do things that he would not do. In one segment, each contestant was asked to jump into the arms of another contestant who was strung out on a wire over a deep gorge. If the contestant fell, he or she was bungeed (belayed on a flexible rope), but also fell hundreds of feet. After the competition, fifty-something Branson, while asserting he has a certain fear of heights, also attempted the jump. He fell, flipping over and over and twisting in the rope, to return bloodied but obviously satisfied.

In another segment, a contestant who had to take a penalty was put into a sleek capsule along with Branson and swung out over the river above 360-foot Victoria Falls. Branson told the guy they were going to make the world's first attempt to go over the falls in a capsule, so was he ready? Three times Branson asked him, and three times the answer was yes. Then Richard (as the contestants referred to him) told the unfortunate contestant that he had just failed a test. The contestant had not even looked at the falls and had merely accepted the challenge on Richard's authority. Had they actually gone over the falls they most certainly would have died. Richard made his point that, in life as in business, all risks should be calculated ones. The guy was eliminated from the competition.

Branson says that the two questions he is asked most often are why he risks his neck ballooning and where is the Virgin Group going? He says:

> [Ballooning] is one of the few great challenges left. . . . As soon as I've banished the terrors of each actual flight, I once again feel confident that we can learn from our mistakes and achieve the next one safely.

> The wider question of where the Virgin Group will end up is impossible to answer. . . . Some people say that my vision for Virgin breaks all the rules and is too wildly kaleidoscopic; others say that Virgin is set to become one of the leading brand names of the next century. . . . As for me, I just pick up the phone and get on with it.[148]

Discuss

1. Describe Richard Branson's personality using the Big Five profile and other personality tests.
2. Why is Branson successful in business?
3. Many of Branson's companies are in entertainment, transportation, and aligned industries. Would he be a successful entrepreneur in other industries?

Source: Based on R. Branson, *Losing My Virginity: How I've Survived, Had Fun, and Made a Fortune Doing Business My Way.* Times Business, Random House, 1998.

 ## Advice from the Pros

How Executive Coaches Analyze Personality–Role Fit

Executive coaches are private consultants, such as psychologists or communication experts, who help executives improve and adapt their personal styles. Imagine that you are a high-level executive who has been asked to take on a new role. Perhaps you are a chief operations officer who has been asked to move abroad to take over the same function in a country in which you do not speak the language. Or perhaps you are a career engineer who has been asked to take on the job of marketing a new product aimed at engineers like yourself.

Should you accept or not? Your executive coach would counsel you to think about whether the stretch between your personal style, including your personality, and the style demanded by the role is big or small, and good or bad. Your choices boil down to those on the Personality-Role Fit Grid (see Table 2.7 on page 54).

Discussion

1. Thinking ahead to your own career, describe a job in each quadrant; that is, one in which you would be comfortable, one that would be a challenge, one that would incite your resistance, and one that would create stress. Share these with the class.
2. Defend your position:

   In your career, you should take on primarily those tasks that allow you to play to your natural personality and style.

   OR

   In your career, you should take on many different kinds of tasks, adapting your style to whatever challenges come your way.

TABLE 2.7 **The Personality–Role Fit Grid**

	A Small Stretch (Taking on a role that is close to your personal style and personality)	**A Big Stretch (Taking on a role that is very different from your personal style and personality)**
A Good Stretch (The role feels good and seems to be an opportunity.)	**I. Comfort** Being in this role is likely to give you feelings of fulfillment, contentment, and enthusiasm, and a sense that "I am in the right job." You are willing to adapt temporarily to others' differing personal styles. Example: You accept a promotion from stockbroker to manager of a team of brokers. Both jobs suit your extraverted, tough-minded, conscientious self.	**II. Challenge** Being in this role gives you a sense of meeting a personal challenge and enhancing your personal development. You are increasingly comfortable with others' personal styles. You make sure you get your personal needs met outside of this role. Example: You are a chief operations officer who takes over the same function in a country in which you do not speak the language. However, you are adventurous and learn languages easily. Your family adapts well in other cultures.
A Bad Stretch (The role feels bad and seems like it might be a career threat.)	**III. Resistance** In this role you experience boredom, stagnation, lack of challenge, and lack of flexibility. You are unwilling to adapt to others' styles Example: You are a career engineer who accepts the job of marketing a new product aimed at engineers like yourself. However, you are an introvert, and strongly prefer analytic jobs and working on your own to interacting with a team and with customers.	**IV. High stress** In this role you feel demotivated and stressed and have a hard time coping. You feel like "I can't go on with this" and begin to look for other jobs and opportunities. You may feel depressed. Example: After college, where you studied literature and enjoyed a small group of close friends, your father asks you to join the dynamic sales force of his small insurance company.

Source: Adapted from "Executive Coaching: How to Manage Role Stretch," http://www.teamtechnology.co.uk/executivecoaching.htm. Accessed July 11, 2005.

Gain Experience

The Personality Interview

1. Each student finds a partner. The partners should not know each other well.
2. Adopt the following roles:
   a. *Interviewer*—The job of the interviewer is to determine the Big Five personality profile of the interviewee (excluding the neuroticism dimension) by asking the interviewee questions about herself or himself. The interviewer may not ask direct questions about what the interviewee's profile is. For example, he or she may not ask, "Are you an introvert?" or "Are you energetic?"
   b. *Interviewee*—The role of the interviewee is to answer the interviewer's questions truthfully. The interviewee should not answer any direct questions about his or her profile or characteristics.
3. The interviewer interviews the interviewee for four minutes, looking for clues to the following four dimensions:

   a. Extraversion versus introversion.
   Extraverts are sociable, energetic, fun-loving, affectionate, friendly, and talkative; exhibit warmth, gregariousness, assertiveness (some say dominance), activity, excitement seeking, and positive emotions. Introverts are retiring, sober, passive, reserved, submissive, aloof, inhibited, quiet, unengaged emotionally, solitudinous, and task oriented.
   b. Adventurous versus traditional.
   Adventurous individuals are defined by their preference for variety, independence, and liberal beliefs; enjoy acquiring rich and varied experiences rather than developing their cognitive (thinking) ability; are likely to be original, imaginative, daring, and intelligente; have a broad range of interests, including fantasy, aesthetics, feelings, actions, ideas, and values. Traditional individuals are relatively closed to experience, conventional, down-to-earth and conforming; like routine and do not have a lot of curiosity.

c. Agreeable versus tough-minded.

Agreeable individuals exhibit trust, sympathy, generosity, forgiveness, open-mindedness, flexibility, gullibility, and cheerfulness; if too agreeable, may be dependent, fawning, and self-effacing.

Tough-minded individuals are especially self-centered, likely to set themselves against others, critical, skeptical, antagonistic, unsympathetic, uncooperative, stubborn, rude, narcissistic, perfectionist, arrogant, self-righteous, independent, have a drive for mastery; overtly aggressive or polished manipulators; may exhibit overt or inhibited hostility.

d. Conscientious versus undirected.

Conscientious individuals like being careful and thorough; prefer to live their life deliberately; are reliable, hard working, self disciplined, neat, ambitious, moralistic; have a high need for achievement.

Undirected individuals are disorganized, lax, sloppy, thoughtless, aimless, unstable, unambitious, and weak-willed.

4. The interviewer writes down the personality profile of the interviewee, but does not show it to the interviewee yet.

5. Switch roles and repeat the process.

6. Share the personality profiles and discuss their accuracy. (5 minutes)

7. Discussion

a. Which personality dimensions were easiest to determine? Which were hardest?

b. If you were interviewing a candidate for a job, how would you apply your knowledge of the Big Five personality profile?

 ## Can You Solve This Manager's Problem?

Different Personalities—Different Treatment?

George, the associate director of marketing and advertising, was walking along a long corridor with his boss, Sam. The two were on their way to a meeting in the department's plush conference room. As they passed Joe's office, George impulsively stuck his head through the open door. Joe was in charge of developing marketing plans for a couple of the company's moderately important products.

"Hey, Joe, how's it going?" said George.

Joe was on the phone but put his party on hold. "Going great. I'm on top of the Winco project and should have a report out later today. I can't wait to make the presentation."

"Terrific. Looking forward it. Up for a game of tennis later this week?"

"Sure thing."

"I'll phone you," said George. As Joe went back to his call, George and Sam continued down the hall. "Hold on, Sam. I need to check in here with Carol." George knocked politely on Carol's door, which was only slightly ajar.

"Come in."

George opened the door and stood in front of Carol's desk. Carol was his ace marketing researcher, a Ph. D. in psychology with great statistical analysis talent. She looked up from her computer as he said, "Carol, how are you doing today?"

"Well, thanks. Busy. There's a lot of good data coming in on the Dalton project."

"I just stopped by to see when the report will be up."

"Let's see here. I have scheduled it to be completed for Thursday morning."

"Great. I definitely want to see that product move. Could you e-mail the report to me as soon as you finish it please?"

"Sure thing."

George turned and continued his walk with Sam.

After a moment Sam said, "You know George, I have been meaning to touch base with you about that corporate mandate to do a better job of managing diversity, especially in light of our weak record of keeping our top performing women. Just now I couldn't help but notice how you treated Joe and Carol quite differently, and I wonder if you could explain why you did that?"

Discussion

1. In what ways does George treat Joe and Carol differently?

2. *Why* does he treat them differently?

3. If you were in George's shoes, what would you say to Sam?

Defend your position

Select one of the following positions and be ready to defend it.

Managers should treat all employees alike despite their personality differences.	*Managers should treat all employees differently according to their unique personalities.*
Some points to consider:	Some points to consider:
Treating employees differently can lead to accusations of favoritism and bias.	People with different personalities are motivated differently.
Treating employees differently may lead to legal complaints of discrimination.	One-size-fits all interpersonal interactions might leave Joe bored (if they are too formal) or Carol stressed (if they are too informal).
A basic principle of bureaucracy is that when bosses adopt an impartial demeanor, all, not just some, of their employees feel appreciated.	Organizational cultures are made stronger by recognizing and valuing employee diversity.
Adopting professional standards creates an organizational culture that values merit rather than politics.	If employees understand the rationale for treating people differently, they will accept it. Training group members to understand the different types of personalities in their group can promote not only mutual acceptance but also group creativity. It just makes common sense to interact with others based on your personality and theirs.

Chapter Summary and Key Terms

What is your personality?

You are a unique individual, different from others psychologically in terms of your special combination of personality, cognitive abilities, attitudes, and values.

Extensive research suggests that personality is both genetically and environmentally determined. Psychologists often measure personality using well-researched paper and pencil questionnaires that measure traits. A test's academic research credentials are your best guide to whether it is valid, that is, to whether it actually measures what it claims to measure.

Some personality tests measure traits. Other tests, including the well-researched Big Five personality test, profile your personality overall by summarizing a variety of traits into general factors.

personality   32
heredity   32
enviroment   32
subjective well-being   32
peer group influences   33
personality traits   33
locus of control (LOC) 35
internal locus of control   35
external locus of control   35
valid test   36
reliable test   36
personality profile   37
continuum   37
transparent   38

How is the study of personality traits applied in organizations?

The Big Five profile and the MBTI have much in common and are both widely used for such activities as performance appraisals and team building. In addition, personality continuum traits that are particularly important in organizations are locus of control, self-esteem, risk-taking, and competitiveness.

psychological disorder   43
narcissistic personality disorder   43
antisocial personality disorder   43

What is your emotional style and why is it important in organizational life?

Your emotional style is determined in part by your genetic make-up and in part by what you have learned about emotional expression. On the job, emotional competence is a valued skill.

Since you have completed the Big Five mini-version in this chapter, you already have a short sketch of your emotional style. See your results for Factor Five, "Stable versus Emotional." Different organizations have different norms concerning what emotions are appropriate to display on the job.

emotion   44
mood   44
affect   44
felt emotions   44
displayed emotions   44
emotion cultures   45
test anxiety   45
stereotype threat   45
emotional competence   45
emotional incompetence   46
emotional display   46
bounded emotionality   46

What cognitive abilities contribute to your personal style?

Cognitive abilities include analytic, creative, and practical abilities. Companies are interested in how well you can perform in each of these areas.

What values and attitudes contribute to your personal style?

Individuals bring sets of beliefs, values, and attitudes to the workplace. Important work values today include job involvement and work centrality. When you are interpreting the behavior of people from other countries, consider how their values may differ from your own, using the guidelines established by researchers Schwartz and Hofstede. Attitudes that employers often measure are job satisfaction and organizational commitment.

Explorations

1. Take the Big Five personality test.

Of all the explorations in this book, this is one of the best and most useful! To take a complete version of the Big Five and get detailed feedback on your personality, do a Web search for IPIP-NEO and Personality Test Center.

2. Explore your personality further.

Make a list of the personality traits you think you have inherited and the ones you think you have learned. Which ones would you like to change if you could?

3. Learn about happiness.

Martin Seligman has written extensively on happiness and related subjects. His Web site, www.authentichappiness.org, hosts a variety of personality tests.

4. Learn about unhappiness.

To learn more about how your personal life might be interfering with your work life, explore the practice and ideas behind family therapy. A book that includes practical suggestions for related self-exploration is Dan Neuharth's *If You Had Controlling Parents* (New York: Quill, 1999).

References

[1] http://www.amysiccrcram.com/dearamy/index.asp. Accessed September 25, 2005.

[2] "Amy's Ice Cream," Out on the Porch Video, News 36, October 11, 2005. http://www.kxan.com/Global/story.asp?S=2510107. Accessed September 25, 2005.

[3] http://www.amysicecream.com/charities/index.asp. Accessed September 25, 2005.

[4] D. A. Bernstein, L. A. Penner, A. Clarke-Stewart, and E. J. Roy, *Psychology* (Boston and New York: Houghton Mifflin Company, 2003):518.

[5] J. C. Loehlin and J. Nicholls, *Heredity, Environment and Personality* (Austin: University of Texas, 1976):92. See also R. Plomin, K. Asbury, and J. F. Dunn, "Why Are Children in the Same Family So Different? Nonshared Environment a Decade Later," *Canadian Journal of Psychiatry 46*, April 2001:225–233.

[6] D. A. Bernstein, L. A. Penner, A. Clarke-Stewart, and E. J. Roy, *Psychology* (Boston and New York: Houghton Mifflin Company, 2003):A–5.

[7] A. D. Pickering and J. A. Gray, "The Neuroscience of Personality," in L. Pervin and O. John, eds., *Handbook of Personality: Theory and Research*, 2nd ed. (New York: Guilford, 1999):277–299. See also D. C. Rowe, "Genetics, Temperament, and Personality," in R. Hogan, J. Johnson and S. Briggs, eds., *Handbook of Personality Psychology* (San Diego: Academic Press, 1997):367–386.

[8] R. Plomin, M. J. Owen, and P. McGuffin, "The Genetic Basis of Complex Human Behaviors," *Science 264*, June 17, 1994:1733–1739.

[9] M. McGue, T. J. Bouchard Jr., W. G. Iacono, and D. T. Lykken, "Behavioral Genetics of Cognitive Ability: A Life-Span Perspective," in R. Plomin and G. E. McClearn, eds., *Nature, Nurture and Psychology* (Washington, DC: American Psychological Association, 1993):59–76. See also R. Plomin, *Development, Genetics and Psychology* (Hillsdale, NJ: Erlbaum, 1986).

[10] D. Lykken and A. Tellegen, "Happiness is a Stochastic Phenomenon," *Psychological Science 7* (3), May 1996:186–189.

[11] R. R. McCrae, P. T. Costa, F. Ostendorf, A. Angleitner, M. Hrebickova, M. D. Avia, J. Sanz, M. L. Sanchez-Bernardos, M. E. Kusdil, R. Woodfield, P. R. Saunders, and P. B. Smith, "Nature over Nurture: Temperament, Personality, and Life Span Development," *Journal of Personality and Social Psychology 78* (1), January 2000:173–186.

[12] R. Plomin, K. Asbury, and J. F. Dunn, "Why Are Children in the Same Family So Different? Nonshared Environment a Decade Later," *Canadian Journal of Psychiatry 46,* April 2001:225–233.

[13] R. J. Hughes, "Behind the Scenes: Andrea 'Spook' Testani, Stage Manager," *The Wall Street Journal,* October 14, 2005:W9.

[14] A. M. Ryan, "The Peer Group as a Context for the Development of Young Adolescent Motivation and Achievement," *Child Development 72* (4), July/August 2001:1135–1150.

[15] H. C. Triandis and E. M. Suh, "Cultural Influences on Personality," *Annual Review of Psychology 53* (1), 2002:133–160.

[16] H. R. Markus and S. Kitayama, "Culture and the Self: Implications for Cognition, Emotion, and Motivation," in L. A. Peplau and S. Taylor, eds., *Sociocultural Perspectives in Social Psychology* (Upper Saddle River, NJ: Prentice Hall, 1997):157–216.

[17] D. Y. Ho and C. Chiu, "Component Ideas of Individualism, Collectivism, and Social Organization: An Application in the Study of Chinese Culture," in U. Kim, H. C. Triandis, C. Kagitcibasi, S. Choi and G. Yoon, eds., *Individualism and Collectivism: Theory, Method and Applications* (Thousand Oaks, CA: Sage, 1994): 137–156.

[18] W. Mischel, "The Interaction of Person and Situation," in D. Magnusson and N. Endler, eds., *Personality at the Crossroads: Current Issues in Interactional Psychology* (Hillsdale, NJ: Erlbaum, 1977):166–207.

[19] D. C. Funder, "Personality," *Annual Review of Psychology 52* (1), 2001:197–221.

[20] D. A. Bernstein, L. A. Penner, A. Clarke-Stewart, and E. J. Roy, *Psychology* (Boston and New York: Houghton Mifflin Company, 2003):SIG-30.

[21] "Abbreviated 11-Item Rotter IE Scale," in J. P. Robinson and P. R. Shaver, "Measures of Social Psychological Attitudes," (Ann Arbor, Michigan: Institute for Social Research, 1973): 235–236.

[22] H. M. Lefcourt, "Internal versus External Control of Reinforcement: A Review," *Psychological Bulletin 65,* 1966:206-220. See also J. B. Rotter, "Generalized Expectancies for Internal versus External Control of Reinforcement," *Psychological Monographs 80* (1, whole no. 609), 1966. For a research overview, see H. M. Lefcourt and K. Davidson-Katz, "Locus of Control and Health," in C. R. Snyder and D. R. Forsyth, eds., *Handbook of Social and Clinical Psychology* (New York: Pergamon Press, 1991):246–266.

[23] K. W. Cook and C. A. Vance, "The Relation of Candidate Personality with Selection-Interview Outcomes," *Journal of Applied Social Psychology 30* (4), April 2000:867–885.

[24] Y. Y. Chung and C. G. Ding, "Development of the Sales Locus of Control Scale," *Journal of Occupational & Organizational Psychology 75* (2), June 2002:233–245.

[25] R. T. Keller, "Predicting Absenteeism from Prior Absenteeism, Attitudinal Factors, and Nonattitudinal Factors," *Journal of Applied Psychology 68* (3), August 1983:536–540.

[26] P. E. Spector, "Behavior in Organizations as a Function of Employee's Locus of Control," *Psychological Bulletin 91,* May 1982:482–497.

[27] Y. Y. Chung and C. G. Ding, "Development of the Sales Locus of Control Scale," *Journal of Occupational & Organizational Psychology 75* (2), June 2002:233–245.

[28] D. Miller, M. F. R. Kets de Vries, and J. Toulouse, "Top Executive Locus of Control and Its Relationship to Strategy-Making, Structure, and Environment," *Academy of Management Journal 25,* 1982:237–253.

[29] P. E. Spector, C. L. Cooper, J. I. Sanchez, M. O'Driscoll, K. Sparks, P. Bernin, A. Büssing, P. Dewe, P. Hart, L. Luo, K. Miller, L. F. R. De Moraes, G. M. Ostrognay, M. Pagon, H. Pitariu, S. Poelmans, P. Radhakrishnan, V. Russinova, and V. Salamatov, "Do National Levels of Individualism and Internal Locus of Control Relate to Well-Being: An Ecological Level International Study," *Journal of Organizational Behavior 22* (8), December 2001:815–832.

[30] P. E. Spector, C. L. Cooper, J. I. Sanchez, M. O'Driscoll, K. Sparks, P. Bernin, A. Bossing, P. Dewe, P. Hart, L. Lu, K. Miller, L. R. De Moraes, G. M. Ostrognay, M. Pagon, H. D.Pitariu, S. A. Y. Poelmans, P. Radhakrishnan, V. Russinova, V. Salamatov, J. F. Salgado, "Locus of Control and Well-Being at Work: How Generalizable ar Western Findings?" Academy of Management Journal 45, Issue 2 April 2002:453–466.

[31] P. W. Grimes, M. J. Millea, and T. W. Woodruff, "Grades—Who's to Blame? Student Evaluation of Teaching and Locus of Control," *Journal of Economic Education 35* (2), Spring 2004:129–147.

[32] P. T. Costa Jr., R. R. McCrae, and J. L. Holland, "Personality and Vocational Interests in an Adult Sample," *Journal of Applied Psychology 69* (3), 1984:390–400; R. R. McCrae and P. T. Costa Jr., "Validation of the Five-Factor Model of Personality across Instruments and Observers," *Journal of Personality & Social Psychology 52* (1), 1987:81–90; R. T. Hogan, "Personality and Personality Measurement," in M. D. Dunnette and L. M. Hough, eds., *Handbook of Industrial and Organizational Psychology*, 2nd ed. (Palo Alto, CA: Consulting Psychologists Press, 1991):878–879.

[33] See N. G. Waller and Y. S. Ben-Porath, "Is It Time for Clinical Psychology to Embrace the Five-Factor Model of Personality?" *American Psychologist,* September 1987:887–889.

[34] R. R. McCrae and P. T. Costa Jr., "Validation of the Five-Factor Model of Personality across Instruments and Observers," *Journal of Personality & Social Psychology 52* (1), (1987):81–90.

[35] Adapted from R. R. McCrae and P. T. Costa Jr., "Validation of the Five-Factor Model of Personality across Instruments and Observers," *Journal of Personality & Social Psychology 52* (1), 1987:81–90.

[36] R. P. Tett and D. D. Burnett, "A Personality Trait-Based Interactionist Model of Job Performance," *Journal of Applied Psychology 88* (3), June 2003:500–517.

[37] T. A. Judge and R. Ilies, "Relationship of Personality to Performance Motivation: A Mega-Analytic Review," *Journal of Applied Psychology 87* (4), August 2002:797–807.

[38] L. Zhang and A. J. Huang, "Thinking Styles and the Five-Factor Model of Personality," *European Journal of Personality 25* (6), November/December 2001:465–476.

[39] J. G. Rosse, H. E. Miller, and L. K. Barnes, "Combining Personality and Cognitive Ability Predictors for Hiring Service-oriented Employees," *Journal of Business and Psychology 5* (1991):431–445.

[40] J. Hogan and B. Holland, "Using Theory to Evaluate Personality and Job-Performance Relations: A Socioanalytic Perspective," *Journal of Applied Psychology 88* (1), 2003:100–112.

41 J. Hogan and B. Holland, "Using Theory to Evaluate Personality and Job-Performance Relations: A Socioanalytic Perspective," *Journal of Applied Psychology 88* (1), 2003:100–112.

42 R. R. McCrae and P. T. Costa, "Personality Trait Structure as a Human Universal," *American Psychologist 52* (5), May 1997:509–516. See also A. A. J. Hendriks, M. Perugini, A. Angleitner, F. Ostendorf, J. A. Johnson, F. De Fruyt, M. Hřebíčková, S. Kreitler, T. Murakami, D. Bratko, M. Conner, J. Nagy, A. Rodríguez-Fornells, and I. Ruisel, "The Five-Factor Personality Inventory: Cross-Cultural Generalizability across 13 Countries," *European Journal of Personality 17* (5), September/October 2003:347–373.

43 S. V. Paunonen, G. Haddock, F. Forsterling, and M. Keinonen, "Broad versus Narrow Personality Measures and the Prediction of Behavior across Cultures," *European Journal of Personality 17* (6), November/December 2003:413–433.

44 I. B. Myers, M. H. McCaulley, N. L. Quenk, and A. L. Hammer, *MBTI Manual: A Guide to the Development and Use of the Myers-Briggs Type Indicator*, 3rd ed. (Palo Alto, CA: Consulting Psychologists Press, Inc., 1998).

45 C. G. Jung, *Psychological Types* (Princeton: Princeton University Press, 1971). Originally published as C. G. Jung, *Psychologische Typen* (Zurich, Switzerland: Rascher Verlag, 1921).

46 P. D. Tieger and B. Barron-Tieger, Do What You Are: Discover the Perfect Career for You Through the Secrets of Personality Type, 2nd ed. (Boston: Little, Brown and Company, 1995).

47 J. Michael, "Using the Myers-Briggs Type Indicator as a Tool for Leadership Development? Apply with Caution," *Journal of Leadership & Organizational Studies 10* (1), Summer 2003:68–81. See also W. L. Gardner and M. J. Martinko, "Using the Myers-Briggs Type Indicator to Study Managers: A Literature Review and Research Agenda," *Journal of Management 22* (1), 1996:45–83.

40 The Myers & Briggs Foundation. http://www.myersbriggs.org/my%5Fmbti%5Fpersonality%5Ftype/take%5Fthe%5Fmbti%5Finstrument/. Accessed September 18, 2005.

49 R. R. McCrae and P. T. Costa Jr., "Reinterpreting the Myers-Briggs Type Indicator from the Perspective of the Five-Factor Model of Personality," *Journal of Personality 57* (1), March 1989:17–40.

50 R. R. McCrae and P. T. Costa Jr., "More Reasons to Adopt the Five-Factor Model," *American Psychologist*, February 1989:451–452.

51 R. R. McCrae and P. T. Costa Jr., "More Reasons to Adopt the Five-Factor Model," *American Psychologist*, February 1989:451–452.

52 D. A. Bernstein, L. A. Penner, A. Clarke-Stewart, and E. J. Roy, *Psychology* (Boston and New York: Houghton Mifflin Company, 2003):647.

53 J. E. Bono and T. A. Judge, "Core Self-Evaluations: A Review of the Trait and Its Role in Job Satisfaction and Job Performance," *European Journal of Personality 17*, 2003:S5–S18.

54 E. Diener, S. Oishi, and R. Lucas, "Personality, Culture and Subjective Well-Being: Emotional and Cognitive Evaluations of Life," *Annual Review of Psychology 54* (1), 2003:403–425.

55 J. L. Pierce, D. G. Gardner, L. L. Cummings and R. B. Dunham, "Organization-Based Self-Esteem: Construct Definition, Measurement, and Validation," *Academy of Management Journal 32* (3), September 1989:622–648, 622, 623.

56 M. J. Schmit, J. A. Kihm, and C. Robie, "Development of a Global Measure of Personality," *Personnel Psychology 53* (1), Spring 2000:153–194.

57 K. R. MacCrimmon and D. A. Wehrung, "Characteristics of Risk Taking Executives," *Management Science 36* (4), April 1990:422–435.

58 M. J. Schmit, J. A. Kihm, and C. Robie, "Development of a Global Measure of Personality," *Personnel Psychology 53* (1), Spring 2000:153–194.

59 R. Lynn, *The Secret of the Miracle Economy: Different National Attitudes to Competitiveness and Money* (London: The Social Affairs Unit, 1991). See also B. Kirkcaldy, A. Furnham and R. Levine, "Attitudinal and Personality Correlates of a Nation's Pace of Life," *Journal of Managerial Psychology 16* (1), 2001:20–35.

60 S. P. Brown, W. L. Cron, and J. W. Slocum, "Effects of Trait Competitiveness and Perceived Intraorganizational Competition on Salesperson Goal Setting and Performance," *Journal of Marketing 62* (4), October 1998:88–98.

61 W. G. B. Liebrand, R. Jansen, V. M. Rijken, and C. Suhre, "Might Over Morality: The Interaction Between Social Values and the Interpretation of Decision Making in Experimental Games," *Journal of Experimental Social Psychology 22*, 1986:203–215; C. G. McClintock and W. B. G. Liebrand, "Role of Interdependence, Individual Orientation, and Another's Strategy in Social Decision Making: A Transformational Analysis," *Journal of Personality and Social Psychology 55*, 1988:396–409.

62 P. J. Carnevale and T. M. Probst, "Good News About Competitive People," in C. De Dreu and E. Van de Vliert, eds., *Using Conflict in Organizations* (Thousand Oaks, CA: Sage, 1997):129–146.

63 B. Kirkcaldy, A. Furnham and R. Levine, "Attitudinal and Personality Correlates of a Nation's Pace of Life," *Journal of Managerial Psychology 16* (1), 2001:20–35.

64 Based on a more detailed definition in American Psychiatric Association, *Diagnostic and Statistical Manual of Mental Disorders*, 4th ed., (Washington, D.C.: American Psychiatric Association, 1994.)

65 S. Kassin, *Psychology*, 4th ed., (Upper Saddle River, NJ: Prentice Hall, 2004):624.

66 D. A. Bernstein, L. A. Penner, A. Clarke-Stewart, and E. J. Roy, *Psychology* (Boston and New York: Houghton Mifflin Company, 2003):589.

67 D. A. Bernstein, L. A. Penner, A. Clarke-Stewart, and E. J. Roy, *Psychology* (Boston and New York: Houghton Mifflin Company, 2003):590.

68 American Psychiatric Association, *Diagnostic and Statistical Manual of Mental Disorders*, 4th ed. rev., (Washington, D.C.: American Psychiatric Association, 1994, 2000); author, as cited in D. A. Bernstein, L. A. Penner, A. Clarke-Stewart, and E. J. Roy, *Psychology* (Boston and New York: Houghton Mifflin Company, 2003):590.

69 M. Seo, L. F. Barrett, and J. M. Bartunek, "The Role of Affective Experience in Work Motivation," *Academy of Management Review 29* (3), 2004:423–439. Much of this section on emotion is based on the research analyzed in this article.

70 D. A. Bernstein, L. A. Penner, A. Clarke-Stewart, and E. J. Roy, *Psychology* (Boston and New York: Houghton Mifflin Company, 2003):413.

71 M.S. Clark and A. M. Isen, "Toward Understanding the Relationship Between Feeling States and Social Behavior," in A. Hastorf and A.M. Isen, (eds.) *Cognitive social Psychology* (New York: Elsevier, 1982):73–108; R. B. Zajonc, "Emotions," in D. Gilbert, S. T. Fiske, and G. Lindzey, eds., *Handbook of Social Psychology 1*, 4th ed. (Boston: McGraw-Hill, 1998):591–634; A. P. Brief and H. M. Weiss, "Organizational Behavior: Affect

in the Workplace," *Annual Review of Psychology 53*, 2002:279–307.

[72] D. Watson, "The Vicissitudes of Mood Measurement: Effects of Varying Descriptors, Time Frame, and Response Formats on Measures of Positive and Negative Affect," *Journal of Personality and Social Psychology 55* (1), 1988:128–141.

[73] M. J. Schmit, J. A. Kihm, and C. Robie, "Development of a Global Measure of Personality," *Personnel Psychology 53* (1), Spring 2000:153–194:Appendix B.

[74] D. Watson, "The Vicissitudes of Mood Measurement: Effects of Varying Descriptors, Time Frame, and Response Formats on Measures of Positive and Negative Affect," *Journal of Personality and Social Psychology 55* (1), 1988:128–141.

[75] H. M. Weiss and R. Cropanzano, "Affective Events Theory: A Theoretical Discussion of the Structure, Causes and Consequences of Affective Experiences at Work," in B. M. Staw and L. L. Cummings, eds., *Research in Organizational Behavior 18* (Greenwich, CT: JAI Press, 1996):17–19.

[76] R. B. Zajonc, "Emotions," in D. Gilbert, S. T. Fiske, and G. Lindzey, eds., *Handbook of Social Psychology 1*, 4th ed. (Boston: McGraw-Hill, 1998):591–634.

[77] D. T. Lykken, *Happiness: What Studies on Twins Show Us About Nature, Nurture, and the Happiness Set Point* (New York: Golden Books, 1999).

[78] "Happier and Healthier?" *Consumer Reports on Health 16* (3), Consumers Union, March 2004:1–4.

[79] P. Ekman, R. W. Levenson, and W. V. Friesen, "Autonomic Nervous System Activity Distinguishes Among Emotions," *Science 221*, 1983:1208–1210.

[80] H. Ohira and K. Kurono, "Facial Feedback Effects on Impression Formation," *Perceptual and Motor Skills 77* (3, Pt. 2), 1993:1251–1258.

[81] "Happier and Healthier?" *Consumer Reports on Health 16* (3), March 2004:1–4.

[82] M. Conlin, "I'm a Bad Boss? Blame My Dad," *Business Week*, May 10, 2004:60–61.

[83] S. A. Shields, *From the Heart: Gender and the Social Meaning of Emotion* (New York: Cambridge University Press, 2002).

[84] M. LaFrance, M. A. Hecht, and E. L. Paluck, "The Contingent Smile: A Meta-Analysis of Sex Differences in Smiling," *Psychological Bulletin 129* (2), March 2003:305–334.

[85] R. W. Simon and L. E. Nath, "Gender and Emotion in the United States: Do Men and Women Differ in Self-Reports of Feelings and Expressive Behavior?" *American Journal of Sociology 109* (5), March 2004:1137–1176.

[86] Gallup poll results reported in M. Dolliver, "These Are a Few of Our Least-Favorite Things," *Adweek 42* (13), March 26, 2001:14.

[87] B. G. Turner, D. C. Beidel, S. Hughes, and M. W. Turner, "Test Anxiety in African-American School Children," *School Psychology Quarterly 8*, 1993:140–152.

[88] C. M. Steele, "A Threat in the Air: How Stereotypes Shape Intellectual Identity and Performance," *American Psychologist 52*, 1997:613–629.

[89] S. Spencer, C. M. Steele, and D. Quinn, "Under Suspicion on Inability: Stereotype Threats and Women's Math Performance," unpublished manuscript, 1997.

[90] D. Goleman, *Working with Emotional Intelligence* (New York: Bantam, 1999). For a critique of the emotional intelligence concept, see M. Davies, L. Stankov, and R. D. Roberts, "Emotional Intelligence: In Search of an Elusive Construct," *Journal of Personality & Social Psychology 75* (4), October 1998:989–1015.

[91] S. Fox and P. E. Spector, "Relations of Emotional Intelligence, Practical Intelligence, General Intelligence, and Trait Affectivity with Interview Outcomes: It's Not All Just 'G'", *Journal of Organizational Behavior 21*, 2000:203–220.

[92] A. Carmeli, "The Relationship between Emotional Intelligence and Work Attitudes, Behavior and Outcomes: An Examination among Senior Managers," *Journal of Managerial Psychology 18* (8), 2003:788–813.

[93] S. C. Douglas and M. J. Martinko, "Exploring the Role of Individual Differences in the Prediction of Workplace Aggression," *Journal of Applied Psychology 86* (4), August 2001:547–559.

[94] B. E. Ashforth and R. H. Humphrey, "Emotion in the Workplace: A Reappraisal," *Human Relations 48* (2), February 1995:97–125.

[95] J. Martin, K. Knopoff, and C. Beckman, "An Alternative to Bureaucratic Impersonality and Emotional Labor: Bounded Rationality at the Body Shop," *Administrative Science Quarterly 43* (2), June 1998:429–469.

[96] J. A. Morris and D. C. Feldman, "The Dimensions, Antecedents, and Consequences of Emotional Labor," *Academy of Management Review 21*, 1996:986–1010.

[97] A. Bryman, "McDonald's as a Disneyized Institution," *American Behavioral Scientist 47* (2), October 2003:154–167.

[98] C. Maslach, W. B. Schaufeli, and M. P. Leiter, "Job Burnout," *Annual Review of Psychology 52*, 2001:397–422.

[99] S. W. Brown, "The Employee Experience," *Marketing Management 12* (2), March/April 2003:12–13.

[100] R. J. Sternberg, *The Triarchic Mind* (New York: Cambridge University Press, 1988).

[101] J. Menkes, *Executive Intelligence: What All Great Leaders Have* (New York: HarperCollins, 2005.)

[102] D. A. Bernstein, L. A. Penner, A. Clarke-Stewart, and E. J. Roy, *Psychology* (Boston and New York: Houghton Mifflin Company, 2003):346.

[103] N. Brody and H. Ehrlichman, *Personality Psychology: The Science of Individuality* (Upper Saddle River, NJ: Prentice Hall, 1998).

[104] N. Brody, "Intelligence, Schooling, and Society," *American Psychologist 52* (10), October 1997:1046–1050.

[105] M. H. Oden, "The Fulfillment of Promise: 40-Year Follow-up of the Terman Gifted Group," *Genetic Psychology Monographs 17*, 1968:3–93.

[106] D. K. Simonton, "Creativity and Genius," in L. Pervin and O. John, eds., *Handbook of Personality Research*, 2nd ed. (New York: Guilford, 1999):629–652.

[107] T. M. Amabile, B. A. Hennessey, and B. S. Grossman, "Social Influences on Creativity: The Effects of Contracted-For Reward," *Journal of Personality & Social Psychology 50* (1), January 1986:14–23.

[108] "Lord of the Rings," *The Economist,* February 3, 2005, www.economnist.com/research/articles. Accessed October 15, 2005.

[109] R. J. Sternberg, R. K. Wagner, W. M. Williams, and J. A. Horvath, "Testing Common Sense," *American Psychologist 50*, 1995:912–927. See also R. J. Steinberg and R. K. Wagner, eds., *Practical Intelligence: Nature and Origins of Competence in the Everyday World* (New York: Cambridge University Press, 1986).

[110] R. J. Sternberg, "Managerial Intelligence: Why IQ Isn't Enough," *Journal of Management 23* (3), 1997:475–493.

[111] F. L. Schmidt, and J. E. Hunter, Tacit knowledge, practical intelligence, general mental ability and job knowledge, *Current Directions in Psychological Science*, 2(1), 1993: 8–9.

112 "Art Fry and the Invention of Post-it Notes," http://www.3m.com/about3M/pioneers/fry.jhtml. Accessed October 4, 2006.

113 S. W. Cornelius and A. Caspi, "Everyday Problem Solving in Adulthood and Old Age," *Psychology and Aging 2,* 1997:144–153.

114 R. J. Sternberg, R. K. Wagner, and L. Okagaki, "Practical Intelligence: The Nature and Role of Tacit Knowledge in Work and at School," in H. Reese and J. Puckett, eds., *Advances in Lifespan Development* (Hillsdale, NJ: Erlbaum, 1993):205–227.

115 J. J. Macionis, *Sociology* 10th edition (Upper Saddle River, NJ: Prentice Hall), 2005:65.

116 D. A. Bernstein, L.A. Penner, A. Clarke-Stewart, and E. J. Roy, *Psychology* (Boston and New York: Houghton Mifflin Company, 2003): 65.

117 D. A. Bernstein, L.A. Penner, A. Clarke-Stewart, and E. J. Roy, *Psychology* (Boston and New York: Houghton Mifflin Company, 2003): 660.

118 S. Roccas, L. Sagiv, S. H. Schwartz, and A. Knafo, "The Big Five Personality Factors and Personal Values," *Personality and Social Psychology Bulletin 28* (6), June 2002:789–801.

119 S. H. Schwartz, G. Melech, A. Lehmann, S. Burgess, M. Harris and V. Owens, "Extending the Cross-Cultural Validity of the Theory of Basic Human Values with a Different Method of Measurement," *Journal of Cross-Cultural Psychology 32,* September 2001:519–542.

120 M. R. Frone and M. Russell, "Job Stressors, Job Involvement and Employee Health: A Test of Identity Theory," *Journal of Occupational & Organizational Psychology 68* (1), March 1995:1–11.

121 G. J. Blau, "Job Involvement and Organizational Commitment as Interactive Predictors of Tardiness and Absenteeism," *Journal of Management,* Winter 1986:577–584.

122 M. R. Frone and M. Russell, "Job Stressors, Job Involvement and Employee Health: A Test of Identity Theory," *Journal of Occupational & Organizational Psychology 68* (1), March 1995:1–10.

123 K. P. Parboteeah and J. B. Cullen, "Social Institutions and Work Centrality: Explorations Beyond National Culture," *Organization Science 14* (2), March/April 2003:137–148.

124 S. Beder, *Selling the Work Ethic: From Puritan Pulpit to Corporate PR* (London: Zed Books, 2000).

125 K. Williams, "Interviewing for Integrity," *Strategic Finance 85* (11), May 2004:21.

126 G. Hofstede, *Culture's Consequences: International Differences in Work Related Values* (Beverly Hills, CA: Sage, 1980); G. Hofstede, "Cultural Constraints in Management Theories," *Academy of Management Executive 7,* 1993:81–94.

127 E. F. Jackofsy, J. W. Slocum Jr., and S. J. McQuaid, "Cultural Values and the CEO: Alluring Companions?" *Academy of Management Executive 2* (1), February 1988:39–49.

128 P. E. Spector, "An International Study of the Psychometric Properties of the Hofstede Values Survey Module 1994: A Comparison of Individual and Country/Province Level Results," *Applied Psychology: An International Review 50* (2), April 2001:269–281.

129 B. McSweeney, "Hofstede's Model of National Cultural Differences and Their Consequences: A Triumph of Faith—a Failure of Analysis," *Human Relations 55* (1), January 2002:89–118; P. E. Spector, "An International Study of the Psychometric Properties of the Hofstede Values Survey Module 1994: A Comparison of Individual and Country/Province

Level Results," *Applied Psychology: An International Review 50* (2), April 2001:269–281.

130 D. Oyserman, H. M. Coon, and M. Kemmelmeier, "Rethinking Individualism and Collectivism: Evaluation of Theoretical Assumptions and Meta-Analyses," *Psychological Bulletin 128* (1), January 2002:3–72.

131 T. R. Mitchell, B. C. Holtom, and T. W. Lee, "How to Keep Your Best Employees: Developing an Effective Retention Policy," *Academy of Management Executive 15* (4), November 2001:96–108.

132 J. L. Pierce and R. B. Dunham, "Organizational Commitment: Pre-Employment Propensity and Initial Work Experiences," *Journal of Management,* Spring 1987:163–178.

133 R. T. Mowday, L. W. Porter, and R. M. Steers, *Employee Organizational Linkages: The Psychology of Commitment, Absenteeism, and Turnover* (New York: Academic Press, 1982).

134 J. Stone and J. Cooper, "A Self-Standards Model of Cognitive Dissonance," *Journal of Experimental Social Psychology 37,* 2001:228–243.

135 L. Festinger, *A Theory of Cognitive Dissonance* (Stanford, CA: Stanford University Press, 1957).

136 A. J. Elliott and P. G. Devine, "On the Motivational Nature of Cognitive Dissonance: Dissonance as Psychological Discomfort," *Journal of Personality & Social Psychology 67,* 1994:382–394.

137 D. Dunning, "On the Motives Underlying Social Cognition," in A. Tesser and N. Schwarz, eds., *Blackwell Handbook of Social Psychology: Intraindividual Processes* (Oxford, England: Blackwell, 2001):348–374.

138 D. J. Bem, "Self-Perception: An Alternative Interpretation of Cognitive Dissonance Phenomena," *Psychological Review 74* (3), May 1967:183–200.

139 S. J. Heine and D. R. Lehman, "Culture, Dissonance, and Self-Affirmation," *Personality and Social Psychology Bulletin 23,* 1997:389–400.

140 R. L. Lewicki, "Jerry Jurgensen, Chief Executive Officer of Nationwide, on Mintzberg's *Managers Not MBAs,*" *Academy of Management Learning & Education 4* (2), 2005:240–243, 242.

141 R. Branson, *Losing My Virginity: How I've Survived, Had Fun, and Made a Fortune Doing Business My Way* (Times Business, Random House,1998):228.

142 R. Branson, *Losing My Virginity: How I've Survived, Had Fun, and Made a Fortune Doing Business My Way* (Times Business, Random House,1998):37

143 R. Branson, *Losing My Virginity: How I've Survived, Had Fun, and Made a Fortune Doing Business My Way* (Times Business, Random House,1998):3.

144 R. Branson, *Losing My Virginity: How I've Survived, Had Fun, and Made a Fortune Doing Business My Way* (Times Business, Random House,1998):4.

145 R. Branson, *Losing My Virginity: How I've Survived, Had Fun, and Made a Fortune Doing Business My Way* (Times Business, Random House,1998):43.

146 R. Branson, *Losing My Virginity: How I've Survived, Had Fun, and Made a Fortune Doing Business My Way* (Times Business, Random House,1998):93.

147 R. Branson, *Losing My Virginity: How I've Survived, Had Fun, and Made a Fortune Doing Business My Way* (Times Business, Random House,1998):93–94.

148 R. Branson, *Losing My Virginity: How I've Survived, Had Fun, and Made a Fortune Doing Business My Way* (Times Business, Random House,1998):11.

3 Decision Making

Preview

When considering how to make a decision, what principles should guide your thinking?
Organizational decision making is both rational and psychological
Rational problem solving is more complicated than it looks

When you are designing a decision-making process, what three major factors should you weigh?
What type of problem are you solving?
What are the attributes, strengths, and weaknesses of the individuals who will make the decision?
What is the social context of the decision?

How can you use experts effectively?

How can you use technology to improve decision making?

How can you implement decisions successfully?

Victorinox and the Swiss Army Knife

Imagine losing 10 percent of your business literally overnight. This is what happened to Victorinox, a Swiss company with 1,000 employees, after the World Trade Center tragedy of September 11, 2001. Victorinox is the company that makes the Swiss Army Knife, the versatile tool selected for display at the New York Museum of Modern Art and used by millions of customers worldwide.[1] The knife even goes into space as part of the official equipment of space shuttle crews. It is clearly a great product. Yet, suddenly, after 9/11, passengers were no longer allowed to carry knives onboard airplanes. Sales dipped drastically. What should the company have done?

Making decisions under pressure is just one of the many decision-making skills you must acquire as a manager. Some decisions require analytic ability; others require creative ability; some require both. All decisions require selecting the right process for the type of decision to be made. In this case, imagine the CEO of Victorinox convening a meeting of his executive team. He would know that under pressure, teams are not likely to make the kind of creative decisions the situation required. He would have to design the decision process carefully. For example, he would resist the temptation to make a quick decision and try instead to give his people the time they needed to develop creative solutions. He might even send his team home for the day, knowing full well that his committed employees would think about the problem and come back to the table with fresh ideas.

Ultimately, Victorinox decided to diversify the company's product line, creating a variety of new gadgets, such as Swiss Cards with pens, magnifying glasses, and LEDs. Today the company markets 100 different models of the original knife as well as 38,000 other pocket tools.

Decision making is a core organizational activity. In organizational life you will be heavily involved in making decisions, and, of course, you want to be an effective decision maker. This chapter describes the decision-making process and helps you develop sound strategies for making effective decisions.

When Considering How to Make a Decision, What Principles Should Guide Your Thinking?

Human decision making is a logical process that develops alternatives and selects the best among them. However, it is not as straightforward as it looks. Researchers continue to discover pitfalls in the rational decision-making process—pitfalls that savvy business decision makers anticipate and manage. To help you make better decisions in your company, consider that decision making is both rational and psychological, and that it may be a lot more complicated than it seems.

Organizational Decision Making Is Both Rational and Psychological

In business and economics a widespread assumption is that individuals, households, and organizations always make rational (reasonable and logical) choices based on their economic self-interest, and that because of this practice, free competition optimizes prices, wages, and markets. This **rational–economic model** of behavior is rooted in the eighteenth-century work of economist Adam Smith. It assumes that a person making a decision has complete and perfect information and is able to process this information accurately and without bias.[2]

Today the rational–economic model is taught to approximately 1.4 million undergraduates every year in their introductory economics courses. At the same time, it is so controversial that it has split the academic discipline of economics.[3] Its critics argue that basing our understanding of human economic behavior solely on self-interest ignores other factors that influence decision making, such as people's values and emotions, and the social context in which the decision is made.

In fact, research has shown that decisions are often made to satisfy criteria other than self-interest. For example, sometimes individuals merely want a quick resolution to a problem. At other times they may want their decisions to reflect a moral principle.[4] The Open Source software movement, in which people create free software and offer it over the Internet, is one example of altruism that does not perfectly fit the rational–economic model.

Nobel Prize winner Herbert Simon was an early critic of the rational–economic model. Simon argued for a model of human decision making based on what he termed **bounded rationality**.[5] His idea is that rationality is constrained, or "bounded," by numerous individual and environmental factors, including the limitations of the human mind, the complexity and uncertainty of problems, and time pressures. As an alternative, Simon proposed the **administrative model** of decision making, which emphasizes that decision makers 1) process only limited, manageable amounts of information rather than identifying all alternatives, 2) use shortcuts and rules of thumb when processing information, and 3) choose solutions that seem adequate but are actually less than optimal, a process known as **satisficing**, which we will discuss below.

In 2002, psychologist Daniel Kahneman won the Nobel Prize in Economic Sciences for research he conducted with his late colleague Amos Tversky on non-rational influences on people's choices, specifically on how judgments and decisions are made under conditions of uncertainty.[6] Kahneman and Tversky's research showed that when solving a problem, people often apply "rules of thumb" rather than rational analysis. In addition, individuals often base their decisions on factors that traditional economists tend to ignore, like the need for fairness or the influence of past events.

Today Kahneman and Tversky's work is part of the popular field of **behavioral economics**, which studies a variety of psychological and situational influences on decision making. Behavioral economists argue that relying solely on the rational–economic model distorts reality. They apply a broader, more psychological approach to understanding such business decisions as how people value securities, how consumers make choices, and how contracts are negotiated.

---

rational–economic model
A model of behavior which assumes that a person making a decision has complete and perfect information and is able to process this information accurately and without bias.

bounded rationality
The idea that rationality is constrained, or "bounded," by numerous individual and environmental factors.

administrative model
A model of decision-making which emphasizes that decision makers 1) process only limited, manageable amounts of information 2) use shortcuts and rules of thumb, and 3) choose solutions that seem adequate but are actually less than optimal.

satisficing
Choosing solutions that seem adequate but are actually less than optimal.

behavioral economics
The study of a variety of psychological and situational influences on decision.

In organizations, managers use a variety of both cognitive and social processes to make decisions.[7] In this chapter we will first examine the rational basis of decision making, then follow up with a look at some important non-rational influences.

Rational Problem Solving Is More Complicated than It Looks

Rational problem solving is a series of stages through which an individual or group moves.[8] See Table 3.1 for a set of problem-solving stages that is widely considered to be logical and rational.

Rather than a blueprint for action, this list of eight stages for problem solving is simply a guideline. If you were to use it to make a decision, you would be well within the norms for business; however, for any number of practical reasons, managers often choose to deviate from it.

COMPLICATIONS TO THE RATIONAL PROCESS There are numerous complications to the rational problem-solving process. For one thing, the stages of rational problem solving may happen simultaneously or in different sequences, and sometimes managers skip a stage entirely.[9] In addition, each stage in the process can be quite complex. For instance, there is much more to the earliest stages of problem solving than simply identifying a problem and setting out to investigate it.[10] There is some probability that the problem will not be identified correctly at the start, and some backtracking may be necessary to clarify it. Also, early in the process managers need to consider who should be invited to participate in the decision making.[11] Finally, in the process of formulating the problem, individual decision makers have to make judgments about whether there is enough information to make the decision, and how much urgency seems to be required.[12] All of these issues complicate and lengthen the problem-solving process—and this is only at the early stages!

Implementing a decision can also be problematic. For example, sometimes bad decisions are covered up. Often this happens because of **escalation of commitment**, the tendency to continue on a course of action once money has been spent or effort has been invested, despite signals that a project is failing. Escalation of commitment might occur

rational problem solving
A series of decision making stages through which an individual or group moves.

escalation of commitment
The tendency to continue on a course of action once money has been spent or effort has been invested, despite signals that a project is failing.

TABLE 3.1 Stages of Rational Problem Solving

Decision-Making Stage	Key Issues and Actions
1. Identify the problem or opportunity.	What business problem will be solved? What market opportunity presents itself? Be sure to identify the problem or opportunity accurately.
2. Formulate your objective(s).	Faced with this problem or opportunity, what is the company's goal? What are the criteria that must be met before decision makers conclude that a good decision has been made?
3. Familiarize yourself with the problem.	Learn all that you can about the problem, including its causes and effects.
4. Generate alternative solutions.	What are the possible solutions to this problem? Collect data about the appropriateness of each alternative, including its potential outcomes and whether it can realistically be achieved.
5. Evaluate the alternatives.	Which solutions meet the criteria established for an effective decision? How do these solutions compare in terms of costs and benefits?
6. Choose the best alternative.	Which alternative best meets the company's goal?
7. Implement the alternative.	Take action. Commit organizational resources.
8. Follow up with evaluation of the results.	Did the action solve the problem or seize the opportunity? Compare the results obtained with the goals and criteria originally established.

Source: Adapted from W. C. Wedley and R. H. G. Field, "A Predecision Support System," *Academy of Management Review 11,* 1984:407–466.

because the individuals responsible for the bad decision need to save face with their colleagues, or simply because they want to hide their mistakes.[13] The phenomenon is also called the "sunk cost effect" and the "Concorde fallacy."[14] British Airways provides an example: In the 1970s, the company launched its fleet of fast and expensive Concorde airplanes despite projections that the project would never be profitable. It was such a risky venture that as the prototype for the jet approached its completion, even the British minister for aerospace dismissed its prospects as "hopeless."[15] Sure enough, in 2003, the fleet was finally decommissioned. Today escalation of commitment is a problem well known to major organizations. To prevent it they use a variety of means, including internal audits and oversight by their boards of directors.[16] Certainly managers should closely question anyone who justifies future costs by pointing to past ones.

HOW EXECUTIVES USE THE RATIONAL PROBLEM-SOLVING PROCESS Executives spend much of their time involved in the rational problem-solving process.[17] They spend time surveying their company's economic, technical, political, and social environment for threats and opportunities, and even more time thinking about and discussing with others how to invent, design, and develop alternative sources of action. Actually choosing a course of action from the available possibilities takes somewhat less time, because the problem and its likely consequences have already been identified. Executives typically spend the *least* amount of time implementing decisions because it is usually their subordinates who are responsible for this task.

When You Are Designing a Decision-Making Process, What Three Major Factors Should You Weigh?

No single decision-making process fits all decisions. You cannot expect that proceeding through the stages in the rational problem-solving process will work every time, nor can you assume that logically choosing among alternatives is the only kind of decision making you will be using in business. For instance, sometimes making a good decision requires applying creativity or intuition.

In this section we will examine the major factors to consider when you are designing a decision-making process—that is, when you are "deciding how to decide." The three factors are: 1) the type of problem to be solved, 2) the nature of the individuals who will make the decision, and 3) the potential impact of the social context of the decision.

What Type of Problem Are You Solving?

When deciding how to decide, you need to assess: 1) whether your organization's decision makers will be primarily choosing between alternatives, or primarily creating new ideas; 2) whether the decision is programmed or non-programmed; and 3) whether the decision will be made under conditions of uncertainty.

DOES THE PROBLEM REQUIRE CONVERGENT THINKING OR DIVERGENT THINKING?
Convergent thinking is "the ability to apply logic and knowledge to narrow down the number of possible solutions to a problem."[18] Convergent thinking helps companies develop a clear direction that focuses the organization. As an employee, you would be using convergent thinking if you were deciding which supplier to choose or which advertising campaign would do well with your target market. A person's ability to use convergent thinking is measured by standard intelligence tests.

An example of a problem emphasizing convergent thinking is deciding which of several individuals to promote. This problem requires choosing between options and determining a course of action. You would apply reason and logic to solve it, applying a logical process such as that illustrated in Table 3.1.

In contrast, figuring out which business trends might affect your company's strategy over the next decade is a problem that demands **divergent thinking**, "the ability to think along many paths to generate many solutions to a problem."[19] Divergent thinking helps companies be flexible and responsive in the face of market, technological, and other changes. As an employee, you would be using divergent thinking if you were trying to

convergent thinking
The ability to apply logic and knowledge to narrow down the number of possible solutions to a problem.

divergent thinking
The ability to think along many paths to generate many solutions to a problem.

imagine all the different tactics your competitors might use to defeat you in the market. Divergent thinking ability is measured by tests of creativity.

An example of a problem involving divergent thinking is creating a new product. To approach this problem, you would rely on creative problem-solving tools, such as intuition, inspiration, and brainstorming. You would encourage innovative thinking to help your team discover new ideas and novel approaches that challenge the status quo.

Of course, business problems are often complex, requiring both kinds of thinking. Here is an example:

> As president of a multinational, you are worried about slumping profits in Sweden, a problem that was first identified by the quarterly financial analysis of all your Scandinavian subsidiaries (a convergent process). So, you direct your people to search broadly in your Swedish subsidiary and the Swedish market for an explanation (a divergent process). In meetings with key company managers, you settle on one or two key factors that need to be improved (a convergent process), and you, yourself, vow to avoid these problems in the future by being in better touch with trends in the Swedish subsidiary and its markets (a divergent process). To help you do this, you hire a Scandinavian consultant (a convergent process).

Researchers advise us that, unfortunately, relatively few individuals are experts at both convergent thinking (as measured by an IQ test) and divergent thinking (as measured by tests of creativity). Although creativity does require a certain level of intelligence,[20] the correlation between individuals' scores on intelligence tests and tests of creativity is rather low.[21] The ability to combine both intelligence and creativity in making decisions is one definition of wisdom.[22] However, because wisdom is in short supply, managers often try to improve organizational problem solving by creating teams of people that have a mix of convergent and divergent decision-making strengths.

DOES A READY-MADE (PROGRAMMED) SOLUTION FOR THE PROBLEM ALREADY EXIST? Another way of characterizing decisions is that some are **programmed** and routine, while others are **nonprogrammed** and nonroutine.[23] When individuals make programmed decisions, they follow explicit decision rules.[24] Often the decision rules are written down, and anyone who can understand and follow the established procedure can make the decision. Programmed decisions are common in organizational life. For example, managing inventories, estimating costs, and setting production schedules generally involve making programmed decisions. In companies, lower level employees typically make more of the programmed decisions.[25]

Nonprogrammed decisions have no identifiable rules for developing solutions. The criteria ultimately used to make such decisions may not have been known at the beginning of the decision-making process. The solution ultimately selected may not have been envisioned at the outset. Making nonprogrammed decisions requires judgment. In companies, upper level managers typically make more of the nonprogrammed decisions.

When a problem is structured, even though it is also complicated it can be solved using a whole menu of programming techniques developed by a company's operations research experts.[26] When a problem is not structured, it is sometimes delegated to a group, because a group can use a variety of interactional methods to explore it further. (Chapters 9 and 10 on groups and teams will explore team decision making in greater detail.)

WILL THE DECISION BE MADE UNDER CONDITIONS OF UNCERTAINTY? As the poet Robert Burns once said, "The best-laid plans of mice and men often go awry."[27] In other words, even decisions made thoughtfully and thoroughly sometimes lead to undesirable outcomes. Such decisions are said to be made under conditions of uncertainty and are therefore termed **risky decisions**. For example, despite extensive marketing research, a company can never be certain that its new product will sell.

When making decisions under conditions of uncertainty, decision makers are often forced to make choices among complex alternatives.[28] For example, where should the

programmed decisions
Decisions that are made by following explicit (often written) rules.

nonprogrammed decisions
Decisions that are made by using judgment, rather than by following explicit rules.

risky decisions
Decisions made under conditions of uncertainty.

company invest its limited resources? in entering a new market? paying down its debt? developing new products? Unfortunately, under circumstances in which the choices have many attributes, people tend to focus on the one attribute that is important to them.[29] As human beings, our short-term memory is simply not large enough to keep a large number of issues in mind at the same time long enough to evaluate them.[30] One way companies cope with this human weakness is by creating written reports to ensure that the many attributes of various problem–solution scenarios are kept in front of their decision makers.

Under conditions of uncertainty, decision makers are also forced to estimate the probabilities and risks of outcomes, and to anticipate that some outcomes simply cannot be known. Under these circumstances, individual decision makers are, again, prone to a variety of human weaknesses. One is the tendency toward **loss aversion**; that is, when faced with an equal probability of gaining or losing, a person will often choose not losing as the preferred outcome.[31] Another is the **gambler's fallacy**, people's tendency to believe that random events will correct themselves. For example, after losing on one flip of the coin, an individual will believe that he or she has a higher probability of winning on the next flip.[32] Based on the gambler's fallacy, a person might reason, "The stock market has been depressed for a long time, so it has to go up." A third weakness is that, when estimating the probabilities of extremely likely or extremely unlikely events, people tend to overestimate the likelihood of the unlikely events occurring and underestimate the likelihood of the likely events occurring.[33] For example, you are unlikely to win the lottery, and you are likely to lose your money by playing it, but you play it anyway. Or, given the low success rate of small businesses, you know that your small business is likely to fail, but you start it anyhow.

Organizations attempt to overcome these individual decision-making weaknesses by training people to be aware of them, having savvy leaders, and using well-trained teams to make decisions.

What Are the Attributes, Strengths, and Weaknesses of the Individuals Who Will Make the Decision?

To design an effective decision-making process, also consider the personalities, problem-solving styles, and other attributes of your decision makers.

RECOGNIZE INDIVIDUAL PERSONALITIES Understanding the personalities of the decision makers is an important factor in making an effective decision.[34] For example, the Big Five personality variables of conscientiousness and openness are clearly related to decision making and fact-finding abilities.[35] Based on your knowledge of the Big Five (see Chapter 2), can you imagine what the relationship might be? The answer is that people who are characterized as having a high degree of conscientiousness and openness display fast and clear thinking, provide sound insights, and are, of course, well-organized. People who have a lower degree of conscientiousness and openness to new ideas are slower, less insightful, and less well organized.

Risk propensity, the tendency to take risks, is another personality trait to weigh. For instance, there is an ongoing debate as to whether entrepreneurs have a higher tendency to take risks than managers do. It has long been thought that entrepreneurs are risk takers, and some research suggests that entrepreneurs whose goal it is to grow their companies (as opposed to just wanting a family income) are the highest risk takers of all.[36] However, other research contradicts this view, showing, for instance, that many small ventures are started while the owner holds onto another job and is making only a small capital investment in the company.[37] Most likely, a person's tendency to take a risk when making a decision is a complicated matter involving both personality and circumstances.[38]

RECOGNIZE INDIVIDUAL PROBLEM-SOLVING STYLES Individuals also have preferred decision-making styles, suggesting that they are better able to solve some problems than others. These styles are related to their personalities. What is your preferred decision-making style? The Decision Style Inventory in Table 3.2 will help you to find out. It differentiates people based on the degree to which they need structure (based on the personality trait "intolerance for ambiguity") and the degree to which they are interested in human and social concerns versus task and technical concerns.[39] The Decision Style Inventory is a

---

loss aversion
The tendency to choose not losing as the preferred outcome, when faced with an equal probability of gaining or losing.

gambler's fallacy
The tendency to believe that random events will correct themselves.

risk propensity
The tendency to take risks.

TABLE 3.2 The Decision Style Inventory

Instructions: Rank the four alternatives as either 1, 2, 4, or 8, with the highest number indicating your highest degree of preference. Each response in any set of four must be ranked differently; that is, you cannot use a number more than once for each question. At the end, total your scores in each column. Your highest score indicates your preferred decision-making style.

	2 Directive Style	**4** Analytical Style	**3** Conceptual Style	**1** Behavioral Style
1. My prime objective is to:	1 have a position with status.	1 be the best in my field.	4 achieve recognition for my work.	2 feel secure in my job.
2. I enjoy jobs that:	1 are technical and well defined.	2 have considerable variety.	4 allow independent action.	8 involve people.
3. I expect people working for me to be:	2 productive and fast.	8 highly capable.	4 committed and responsive.	1 receptive to suggestions.
4. In my job, I look for:	1 practical results.	4 the best solutions.	2 new approaches or ideas.	8 a good working environment.
5. I communicate best with others:	8 on a direct one-to-one basis.	2 in writing.	4 by having a group discussion.	1 in a formal meeting.
6. In my planning I emphasize:	8 current problems.	4 meeting objectives.	1 future goals.	2 developing people's careers.
7. When faced with solving a problem, I:	1 rely on proven approaches.	2 apply careful analysis.	4 look for creative approaches.	8 rely on my feelings.
8. When using information, I prefer:	1 specific facts.	4 accurate and complete data.	2 broad coverage of many options.	8 limited data that are easily understood.
9. When I am not sure about what to do, I:	8 rely on intuition.	1 search for facts.	2 look for a possible compromise.	4 wait before making a decision.
10. Whenever possible, I avoid:	4 long debates.	8 incomplete work.	1 using numbers or formulas.	2 conflict with others.
11. I am especially good at:	1 remembering dates and facts.	4 solving difficult problems.	2 seeing many possibilities.	8 interacting with others.
12. When time is important, I:	8 decide and act quickly.	4 follow plans and priorities.	1 refuse to be pressured.	2 seek guidance or support.
13. In social settings, I generally:	2 speak with others.	1 think about what is being said.	8 observe what is going on.	4 listen to the conversation.
14. I am good at remembering:	2 people's names.	1 places where I met others.	4 people's faces.	8 people's personalities.
15. The work I do provides me:	8 the power to influence others.	1 challenging assignments.	4 achieving my personal goals.	2 acceptance by the group.
16. I work well with those who are:	8 energetic and ambitious.	1 self-confident.	2 open-minded.	4 polite and trusting.
17. When under stress, I:	2 become anxious.	1 concentrate on the problem.	8 become frustrated.	4 am forgetful.
18. Others consider me:	4 aggressive.	1 disciplined.	2 imaginative.	8 supportive.
19. My decisions typically are:	8 realistic and direct.	2 systematic or abstract.	1 broad and flexible.	4 sensitive to the needs of others.
20. I dislike:	1 losing control.	4 boring work.	2 following rules.	8 being rejected.
Total points:	79	57	62	9b

Source: A. J. Rowe and R. O. Mason, *Managing with Style: A Guide to Understanding, Assessing, and Improving Decision Making* (San Francisco: Jossey-Bass, 1987):40–41. Reprinted by permission of Alan J. Rowe.

TABLE 3.3 Preferred Decision-Making Styles Based on Preferences for Structure, and Human versus Task Orientation.

	High Tolerance for Ambiguity (Low Need for Structure)	Low Tolerance for Ambiguity (High Need for Structure)
Oriented to Task and Technical Concerns	Analytical *Solves problems by analysis, planning, and forecasting*	Directive *Solves problems by applying operational objectives in a systematic and efficient way*
Oriented to Human and Social Concerns	Conceptual *Solves problems by exploring new options, forming new strategies, being creative, and taking risks*	Behavioral *Solves problems through people*

forced-choice test

A test which requires one to make subtle choices about one's preferences.

forced-choice test—one that requires you to make sometimes subtle choices about your preferences.

Your highest score indicates your preferred decision-making style.

Now take a look at Table 3.3, which compares the four decision-making styles identified by the Decision Style Inventory. The designers of this test report that typical scores are directive, 75; analytical, 90; conceptual, 80; and behavioral, 55.[40] How do you compare with these norms? Do your scores make sense to you in terms of the kinds of decision-making roles you have enjoyed in the past? Would you be able to get along with a boss or subordinate whose decision-making style is the opposite of yours?

If the contents of this test are familiar to you, it may be because it correlates well with the MBTI (Jungian) personality inventory and is also related to the Big Five personality inventory. Analytical and conceptual decision makers tend to be extraverts and intuitives, whereas directive and behavioral decision makers tend to be sensors and thinkers.[41] The analytic and conceptual decision makers would prefer, and might be better at, solving problems that require seeing possibilities, applying creativity or analysis, and dealing with complexity and ambiguity. In contrast, the directive and behavioral decision makers would prefer, and might do better at, solving problems that require keeping track of details, remembering things from the past (including people's names), providing a realistic context to the problems, carrying out orders, and being supportive of others.[42]

ASSESS CREATIVE PROBLEM-SOLVING ABILITIES Creativity is another way in which individual decision-making styles differ. Individual creativity requires three characteristics: expertise, creative-thinking skill, and a sense that a task is something one enjoys doing.[43] The characteristics of expertise and enjoyment are self-explanatory, but what is creative-thinking skill? It includes two basic capabilities: divergent-thinking ability and insight.[44]

To illustrate, to create a painting that is a masterpiece, you must have the ability to draw and paint, the insight to imagine your subject in a new light, the self-confidence to show your unconventional treatment to the world, and the ability to enjoy the work so that you will persevere when others would have given up. In the same way, to design a marketable new toothbrush, you (or your team) must know a great deal about how people use toothbrushes and how manufacturers make them, be able to imagine a new design and the market for it, and be confident enough to sell your project to corporate higher-ups.

Mike Lazaridis invented the Blackberry late one night in 1997, while sitting in his basement.[45] He suddenly had the insight that a tiny keyboard could be more efficient than a large one, *if* people use their thumbs. Before this, people had ridiculed the idea of such a tiny keyboard. But Lazaridis was an expert. He had been an inventor and scientist since childhood, and he had in mind that combining computers with wireless technology should be useful. Also, he had a way to persevere: He had already founded a company called Research in Motion to develop new ideas.

Creative problem solving helps companies produce useful and novel ideas ranging from new products to innovative business strategies. Keep in mind that in business, creativity emerges from groups as well as individuals. As a manager, you can enhance creativity in teams by hiring creative individuals for decisions that require creativity, by assigning people to tasks they are interested in, by training your team to make more effective decisions, and by creating a culture that supports innovation. You will reduce creativity if you: 1) closely supervise the decision-making process, 2) set constraints on how the work will be done, 3) foster competition among the creators, 4) focus on how the product will be evaluated, and 5) emphasize extrinsic rewards.[46]

To get some idea about how creative you are personally, take the short self-test in Table 3.4.

TABLE 3.4 Are You Down-to-Earth, or Not?

In each pair, circle the description that fits you best:

1. **a.** I prefer to approach routine tasks in short bursts.
   b. I am known for being able to pursue routine tasks over long periods of time.

2. **a.** I enjoy doing tasks that require a high level of accuracy.
   b. If a task requires a high level of accuracy, I prefer to delegate it to someone else.

3. **a.** I am quite sensitive to people.
   b. I am not particularly sensitive to people.

4. a. People who know me well see me as undisciplined.
   b. People who know me well see me as methodical.

5. a. I often challenge rules.
   b. I seldom challenge rules.

6. **a.** I approach tasks from unsuspected angles.
   b. I approach tasks methodically.

7. a. I am interested in careers such as accounting, electrical engineering, logistics management, police work, pharmacy, and dentistry.
   b. I am interested in careers such as sales, journalism, public relations, human resources management, and advertising account management.

8. **a.** I get passionately involved in tasks that interest me.
   b. I seldom get passionately involved in tasks.

9. a. When working in groups, I am seen as a nonconformist.
   b. When working in groups, I am seen as a team player.

10. a. When solving problems, I doubt myself a lot.
    b. When solving problems, I seldom doubt myself.

11. **a.** I am a traditional person.
    b. I am an untraditional person.

12. **a.** I enjoy doing many different activities during the day.
    b. I enjoy working on one activity for a significant part of the day.

13. a. I enjoy working under time pressure.
    b. I do not enjoy working under time pressure.

14. **a.** I enjoy collaborating with others on projects.
    b. I enjoy working by myself on projects.

Scoring:

Indicators of creativity are:

1-a, 2-b, 3-b, 4-a, 5-a, 6-a, 7-b, 8-a, 9-a,10-b,11-b, 12-b, 13-b, 14-b.

For each of these answers, give yourself one point. Add up the points. The higher your score, the more likely you are to use creativity in decision making. An average score is 6.1 (based on a sample of 53 undergraduate business students enrolled in organizational behavior classes).

Although no one can look inside your brain to see just how creative you really are, you can make some educated guesses based on your habits and preferences and the feedback you get from others. This self-test gives you a sense of whether you enjoy using creative-thinking skills; whether, like the proverbial starving artist, you sometimes get passionate about your work; and whether your style includes a lot of divergent thinking and insight. The test is based upon a variety of sources that describe creative people.[47]

You also might want to take a look at your score for the Big Five Factor "traditional versus adventurous" in Chapter 2. Most likely, if you are a traditionalist, you are probably not highly creative, while if you are an adventurer, you probably are creative.

UNDERSTAND THE VALUE AND LIMITATIONS OF INTUITION Amazingly enough, even when executives are familiar with traditional, logical decision-making tools, they use them infrequently. And even when they do use them, they seldom accept the results if the results contradict their intuitions.[48] **Intuition** is a decision-making tool that integrates experience, goals, and values without using direct reasoning. It is either unconscious or relatively automatic.

intuition
An unconscious or relatively automatic decision-making process that integrates experience, goals, and values without using direct reasoning.

Researchers are beginning to understand how intuition works. For one thing, it involves matching patterns, a process in which a person matches elements they perceive in their environment with some unconscious category, pattern, or feature.[49] For example, an engineer with experience building bridges will easily recognize the problems inherent in a new bridge site. Intuition also involves reasoning by association, a process by which a person links different elements of information to each other. The engineer knows that the design must take into account how the speed of the water affects the size of the bridge pylons. Finally, intuitive decision makers develop mental models that are based on their experiences of the world.[50] The engineer has in mind a design process that has worked in the past and is suitable for designing most bridges.

image theory
A theory which says that how a decision-maker manages and coordinates images is the essence of the intuitive decision-making process.

According to **image theory**, how a decision maker manages and coordinates images is the essence of the intuitive decision-making process. In business, what matters are the decision-maker's images of the organization's governing principles, goals, plans for attaining these goals, and likely results of implementing these plans. For example, over time a CEO develops a set of images about his or her company, including what motivates his or her management team, which employees are truly motivated to improve productivity, and what the company's culture really is. He or she draws on these images as a basis for devising and implementing change.[51]

The higher up the corporate ladder, the more prevalent is the use of intuition. Forty-five percent of corporate executives report that they rely heavily on intuition rather than facts in running their businesses.[52] A study of thousands of public and private sector managers confirmed that higher-level managers make more use of intuition than middle and lower-level managers.[53] It also found that managers in general administrative and policy positions use intuition more than managers in financial management, and that women use intuition more than men.

One reason top managers rely on intuition is because they must constantly make choices in turbulent environments where problems do not lend themselves to the techniques of cost–benefit analysis or reasoning based on probabilities.[54] Also, executives dislike using data-based analysis because it is backward looking rather than future-oriented and is therefore seen as providing little guidance.[55] In other words, executive decision makers prefer to rely on their own vision of the future.

Executives themselves report that they use intuition the most when[56]:

- There is a high level of uncertainty.
- There is little precedent.
- Variables are not scientifically predictable.
- There are few available facts.
- The facts do not clearly point the way to go.
- Time is limited and there is pressure to be right.
- There are several plausible alternative solutions, with good arguments for each.

Today powerful new technological support tools can help executives quickly sort through huge databases and vast numbers of alternatives to improve their decision-making capabilities. Using these technologies avoids the human tendency to see patterns where patterns do not exist. It also prevents decision makers from categorizing problems based on their past experience, a practice that prevents them from recognizing totally new phenomena.

To find how intuitive you are, take the third and last self-test of the chapter, in Table 3.5.

TABLE 3.5 Test Your Intuitive Powers

For each item, circle the answer that best describes you.

1. When working on resolving a problem, do you prefer to:
   a. be told what the problem is, but be left free to decide how to solve it?
   b. get very clear instructions about how to go about solving the problem before you start?

2. When working on a project, do you prefer to work with colleagues who are:
   a. realistic?
   b. imaginative?

3. Do you admire people most who are:
   a. creative?
   b. careful?

4. Do the friends you choose tend to be:
   a. serious and hard working?
   b. exciting and often emotional?

5. When you ask a colleague for advice on a problem you have, do you:
   a. seldom or never get upset if he/she questions your basic assumptions?
   b. often get upset if he/she questions your basic assumptions?

6. When you start your day, do you:
   a. seldom make or follow a specific plan?
   b. usually make a plan to follow?

7. When working with numbers, do you find that you:
   a. seldom or never make factual errors?
   b. often make factual errors?

8. Do you find that you:
   a. seldom daydream during the day and really don't enjoy doing so?
   b. frequently daydream during the day and enjoy doing so?

9. When working on a problem do you:
   a. prefer to follow the instructions or rules when they are given to you?
   b. often enjoy circumventing the instructions or rules when they are given to you?

10. When you are trying to put something together, do you prefer to have:
    a. step-by-step written instructions on how to assemble the item?
    b. a picture of how the item is supposed to look once assembled?

11. Do you find that the person who irritates you *the most* is the one who appears to be:
    a. disorganized?
    b. organized?

12. When an unexpected crisis comes up that you have to deal with, do you:
    a. feel anxious about the situation?
    b. feel excited by the challenge of the situation?

Scoring the Survey

To score the survey, complete the following steps.

1. Total the number of "a" responses you have circled for questions 1, 3, 5, 6, and 11. Enter that total in the space provided in the scoring chart in Table 3.6.   2. Total the number of "b" responses circled for questions 2, 4, 7, 8, 9, 10, and 12. Enter that total in the space provided in the scoring chart.   3. Add the "a" and "b" totals. This represents your Intuitive Score. Enter that score in the space provided in the scoring chart.   4. Because there is a total of 12 questions in this part of the survey, take the number 12 and subtract your Intuitive Score. The result equals your Thinking Score. Enter this score below.

TABLE 3.6 Scoring Chart for "Test Your Intuitive Powers"

Total "a" responses = _____ 4

Total "b" responses = _____ 4

Intuitive Score (a + b) = 8   _____ 8

Thinking score 12 minus _____ 8 _____ = 4

Interpreting the Survey

If your higher score is *Intuitive*, you have the ability to base your decisions on unknowns or possibilities. You have the potential ability to apply ingenuity to problems, to see how best to prepare for the future and to tackle difficulties with zest. You are more likely to prefer management situations that are unstructured, fluid, and spontaneous. With a high score for intuition, you have the potential ability to function best in occupations that are characterized by crisis or rapid change and environments in which you are asked to chart new, emerging trends from data including many unknowns. You also prefer to solve new and different problems versus the same or similar problems time after time.

On the other hand, if your higher score is *Thinking*, you have the ability to apply experience to problems, to bring up pertinent facts, to keep track of essential details, and to face difficulties with realism. You have the potential to function best in occupations that demand the ability to work logically; in environments in which attention to detail, procedures, and precision are valued highly; and in environments in which you are asked to implement existing policies usually made elsewhere.

If your Intuitive and Thinking scores are tied, you have the potential to rely on both feeling cues and factual cues to guide your decisions. However, there is the danger that you will have a difficult time making up your mind about which set of cues you should listen to. Therefore, it is quite possible that you will be either slow in making critical decisions or will have difficulty making a decision at all, without experiencing considerable stress.

Source: Adapted from W. H. Agor, "Test Your Intuitive Powers: AIM Survey," in W. H. Agor (ed.) *Intuition in Organizations* (Newbury Park, CA: Sage Publications, 1989): 133–144. AIM Survey copyright © by ENFP Enterprises, El Paso TX 1989.

BE AWARE OF COMMON CONSTRAINTS ON HUMAN REASONING Human reasoning is imperfect. The pitfalls to look out for include relying too heavily on your intuition (as we just discussed), reasoning illogically, and allowing your emotions to influence your decision. In this section we will examine why humans often fail to reason logically.

The limits of formal reasoning. **Formal reasoning**, also known as deductive reasoning, uses rules of logic to make a decision.[57] Any problem that can be solved using an algorithm (a formula) utilizes this kind of reasoning. Unfortunately, individuals don't always use logic effectively. For example, consider this reasoning: All CEOs are conservative. Richard Branson is a CEO. Therefore Richard Branson is conservative. Of course, this is illogical because our premise is incorrect. It is not true that all CEOs are conservative. Our conclusion is also not true: Branson, the founder of Britain's Virgin Group, has an unusually wide range of business ventures and is still hoping to make it around the world in a balloon. He is clearly not conservative, and the starting premise is clearly wrong. Yet individuals may not think to challenge the incorrect premise of a decision, and so will adopt the illogical conclusion.

Certainly you can imagine many circumstances in which the premises of a decision are incorrect, especially in the uncertain world of business. Furthermore, it turns out that when decision makers know in advance that the premises for a decision are uncertain, they are mainly interested in determining how believable, rather than how logical, the decision's outcomes are. For example, cutting production costs may not actually improve a company's bottom line, given that it might reduce product quality, but it is still an idea that most managers can get behind.

The limits of informal reasoning. When a conclusion, though supported by a premise, does not necessarily follow from the premise, we have an instance of **informal reasoning**, or inductive reasoning. Informal reasoning, although guided to some extent by the

formal reasoning
Deductive reasoning, which uses rules of logic to make a decision.

informal reasoning
Inductive reasoning, which is guided to some extent by rules of formal reasoning, but has no deterministic methods (i.e., its methods are debatable).

rules of formal reasoning, has no deterministic methods. In other words, its methods are debatable. For example, how many teenagers would you have to survey before you conclude that most teenagers need skin care products? You cannot possibly survey "most teenagers," so you survey some number of teenagers that you perceive to be enough. But how many really is enough? Reasonable individuals might reasonably disagree on this point.

The influence of heuristics. Sometimes, rather than follow the principles of formal reasoning, decision makers use heuristics. A **heuristic** is a mental decision-making shortcut.[58] Although heuristics do help us to simplify decisions, our tendency to use these "rules of thumb" can also inhibit decision-making effectiveness.[59] Researchers have had a lot of fun pointing out just how bad our human heuristics really are.[60]

heuristic
A mental decision-making shortcut.

For example, decision makers often select the first alternative they think of that meets their minimum requirements, instead of taking the time to weigh and choose the best alternative among a large array of options. This is called the **satisficing heuristic**.[61] (As we will see in Chapter 9, on group decision making, groups have the same tendency.) For example, a college student may register for a class because it fills a block in her or his schedule, only to discover later that the class is uninteresting, way over her or his head, and likely to pull down her or his grade-point average. In this case, the student has fallen prey to a person's tendency to stop searching for better options once an acceptable option has been found. Because she or he is satisficing, the student is not **optimizing**, or maximizing, her or his decision-making effectiveness.

satisficing heuristic
Selecting the first alternative one thinks of that meets one's minimum requirements, instead of taking the time to weigh and choose the best alternative among a large array of options.

optimizing
Maximizing one's decision-making effectiveness.

Another common weakness is that decision makers look for familiar patterns without assessing why certain patterns exist or whether they are likely to continue. This is called the **representativeness heuristic**. For example, when investors see that stocks are moving in a certain direction, they gradually begin to assume that the trend is a representation of other trends they have perceived in the economic data, while in reality it is not likely to be. Relying on the representativeness heuristic suggests one reason why investors can be overconfident in predicting when a stock market move will take place.[62]

representativeness heuristic
Looking for familiar patterns without assessing why certain patterns exist or whether they are likely to continue.

Yet another problematic rule of thumb is the **availability heuristic**, by which people make judgments based on the information that is mentally "available" to them at any given moment rather than conducting a thorough, realistic appraisal. What makes an event mentally available? Variables that can affect an event's mental availability and your judgment include how recent or emotionally charged the event is. For example, a television story of a train wreck is likely to turn you off to train travel even though train travel is much safer than driving.[63]

availability heuristic
Making judgments based on the information that is mentally "available" at any given moment rather than conducting a thorough, realistic appraisal.

Confirmation bias is the tendency to seek out and favor evidence that supports one's beliefs. This common bias prevents individuals from discovering evidence that disconfirms their beliefs, and leads them to make decision errors.[64] Suppose an auditor examining a company's finances develops a particular hypothesis about an irregularity that is discovered. Thereafter, the auditor will more readily perceive information that confirms the hypothesis and less readily perceive information that disconfirms the hypothesis.[65] Corporate boards often find it hard to exit from underperforming businesses because they fail to seek data that would refute their belief that the business will eventually pull out of its slump.[66]

confirmation bias
The tendency to seek out and favor evidence that supports one's beliefs.

Decision making is also subject to **unconscious bias**. Individuals suffer from the illusion that they are objective observers and actors, although they are not.[67] To illustrate, it turns out that examining a fingerprint for the purposes of a criminal investigation is not the rational science many suppose it to be. Why? Because examiners themselves are subject to unconscious bias. They look at a variety of data points to assess a match, and although their judgment tends to be good, it is not infallible. In one telling case, a suspected assailant left his fingerprint on a glass, but an examiner failed to find a match between the print and other fingerprints in the police database, a database that also happened to include the prints of a man not involved in the crime.[68] Later, when the innocent man was named as a suspect, a fingerprint examiner who knew the print he was examining came from this suspect examined the glass again. This time he "discovered" a match between the print on the glass and the innocent man's print in the

unconscious bias
The illusion that one is an objective observer and actor; reliance on preconceived opinions about someone or something.

database. The innocent man served six years in jail before being exonerated by DNA evidence.

overconfidence

Over-reliance on one's ability to make accurate predictions.

Decisions are also vulnerable to the effects of **overconfidence**. Research shows that people's confidence in their predictions routinely outstrips their accuracy.[69] One reason may be that at the moment when they evaluate the soundness of their conclusions, people forget how many elements of their reasoning could be wrong.[70] Overconfidence is in part culturally determined. For example, Chinese students are more likely than American students to show this bias. It has been hypothesized that because students in China are not encouraged to challenge their teachers, they do not challenge what they tell themselves either. Thus, they appear more confident than self-challenging Americans.[71]

implicit egotism

The tendency to prefer things which are connected with one's positive associations about oneself.

Pushing the analysis of human decision-making foibles yet further, several researchers have identified a phenomenon called **implicit egotism**.[72] Because most people possess positive associations about themselves, they prefer things that are connected with those positive associations. These preferences extend even to simple things, such as the letters in a person's name. To illustrate, ten studies assessed the role of implicit egotism as it relates to two familiar decisions: where people choose to live and what people choose to do for a living. The results indicated that people are disproportionately likely to live in places whose names resemble their own first or last names (people named Louis are disproportionately likely to live in St. Louis). People also disproportionately choose careers whose labels resemble their names (for instance, people named Dennis or Denise are overrepresented among dentists). The authors conclude that implicit egotism may influence even our major life decisions.

TABLE 3.7 **Overview: Pitfalls and Remedies in Human Reasoning**

Problem	Example	Remedy
Satisficing heuristic—selecting the first alternative rather than the best alternative	A student takes a class because it fits his schedule, only to discover that he hates the subject.	Take the time to weigh and choose among a variety of carefully considered alternatives.
Representativeness heuristic—basing decisions on familiar patterns	A student chooses to study medicine because her parents are both doctors, discovering later that she would have been much happier in business.	Assess why the patterns exist and whether they are likely to continue.
Availability heuristic—making judgments based on easily available information	When deciding what classes to take, a student bases his decisions on dorm gossip.	Do a thorough search for information before deciding.
Confirmation bias—selectively paying attention to information that supports your beliefs	A sophomore surfing the Web to learn more about recreational drugs fails to absorb information about their dangers.	Seek opinions from people with opposing points of view and opinions.
Unconscious bias—relying on preconceived opinions about someone or something.	Students asked to play the roles of the buyer and the seller of a fictitious company are asked to estimate the company's worth, and are rewarded if their estimates come close to those of impartial experts. Despite the incentive, the sellers still value the company more than the buyers.[73]	Understand what one's own biases are likely to be in any given decision.
Overconfidence—overreliance on one's ability to make accurate predictions	Rob predicts that he and Amber will win the race, failing to take into account the likely sabotage by all of the other participants.	Test predictions and judgments on other people, especially skeptics.
Implicit egotism—a preference for things connected with oneself	Harry is attracted to Sally in part because their names are rather similar.	Be aware of the phenomenon, and ask others to point it out if they suspect it in your behavior.

ANTICIPATE EMOTIONAL INFLUENCES Thinking is both an intellectual process and an emotional experience. An anxious decision maker is likely to focus on the threatening aspects of a decision.[74] A sad decision maker is likely to recall negative information.[75] A happy decision maker is likely to look for positive information.[76] Depending on their own emotional patterns, managers' judgment may be biased toward more pessimistic or more optimistic evaluations of a situation.[77]

People in positive-feeling states are likely to follow more superficial, unsystematic, and stereotype-based decision-making processes, whereas people experiencing negative-feeling states are likely to carefully and systematically execute a structured decision process.[78] In addition, people experiencing positive-feeling states are more likely to engage in divergent thinking: They categorize things in a broader, more inclusive, and flexible fashion that leads to creativity and enhanced performance on complex tasks.[79] People experiencing negative-feeling states exert more effort and are more systematic in their information processing; they are also likely to make more accurate and unbiased judgments.[80] These findings may explain why successful artists tend to be amusing whereas successful accountants tend to be serious.

When individuals postpone or avoid making choices, emotional influences may be at work.[81] According to the "old sergeant syndrome," soldiers who spend long periods fighting on the front lines—those who witness death and have no hope for transfer—tend to avoid making the very decisions that might protect them under fire.[82] They might, for example, fail to wear protective gear. In short, humans sometimes delay and avoid decisions for rational reasons, but they may also do so because of fear or regret.

A related phenomenon is that, under stress, individuals sometimes regress to more paranoid and infantile modes of thinking. In this condition they are much less able to handle subtle differences and complexities and are more likely to think in terms of all or nothing, black or white, good or bad, or superior or inferior.[83]

What Is the Social Context of the Decision?

Understanding the social context in which a decision is made is also important. Consider such factors as a person's need to feel accepted, their belief in the group's superior judgment, and the impact of participation. Also, consider how issues of fairness, bias, ethics, and culture affect decision making.

ACKNOWLEDGE SOCIAL INFLUENCES A 1952 experiment performed by Solomon Asch demonstrated that under some circumstances individuals will literally deny their own perceptions in order to agree with the other members of their group, even when the group consists of strangers.[84] Asch placed his individual subjects in seven- to nine-person groups. In each of the groups, all of the other members were Asch's confederates. Then Asch asked each group member to describe the length of a particular line segment. The lengths were all obvious. (See Figure 3.1.) But in 7 of 12 trials, the confederates deliberately lied about what they thought the length of the segment was, saying comparison line C matched the standard line A. Interestingly, more than 70 percent of the time the subjects agreed with them.

Certainly this research shows that people's decisions are influenced by others. Yet what is the explanation for the subjects' behavior?

Asch himself suggested that social pressure put on the individuals led them to conform. People went along with the others to avoid being social outcasts. While this is in part true, subsequent research showed that additional explanations are also needed. In a variation on Asch's experiment, subjects were placed anonymously into groups of people that they would not meet face-to-face and whose answers they could only observe indirectly through an electrical signal.[85] Unobserved by and unconnected to the others, the subjects pushed a button to give their answers. Interestingly, they gave nearly as many wrong responses as Asch's original subjects did. The explanation? The subjects thought that all the other people *could not be wrong*. A large group of people had reached a decision different from their own, and, based on their own experience with the validity of unanimous decisions, figured the group must be right.

FIGURE 3.1

Asch's Line Judgment

Under what circumstances would you assert that the match to Standard Line A is Comparison Line C?

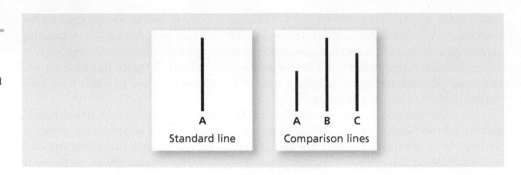

A
Standard line

A   B   C
Comparison lines

In yet another variation on Asch's experiment, one of the experimenters' confederates gave the right answer, agreeing with the subject. This social support drastically reduced the probability that the subject would give the wrong answer. In this situation, only 10 percent conformed to the majority view.[86]

Today it may be that people are somewhat less conforming than they were in Asch's time, and we know that culture also affects how likely people are to conform.[87] Nevertheless, social pressures continue to be an important factor in decision making.

DECIDE WHO SHOULD BE INVOLVED IN THE DECISION As the leader of a work team, you must decide whether to involve your subordinates in a decision or make it yourself.[88] Although encouraging participation is often useful, it is no panacea. There is no single approach to decision making, whether autocratic, consultative, or totally participative, that can be used effectively for all types of decisions.[89] When it comes to deciding whether to involve your employees in a decision, time-tested research by Victor Vroom and Phillip Yetton suggests you have a choice among these basic methods:[90]

Autocratic Alternatives
1. You solve the problem or make the decision yourself using information available to you at the present time.
2. You obtain the necessary information from your subordinates and then decide on a solution to the problem yourself. You may or may not tell your subordinates what the problem is, but you do not expect them to help you to generate or evaluate alternative solutions.

Consultative Solutions
3. You share the problem with the appropriate subordinates individually, eliciting their ideas and suggestions about how to solve the problem without bringing them together as a group, but *you* make the decision.
4. You share the problem with your subordinates in a group meeting, eliciting their collective ideas about how to solve the problem, but *you* make the decision.

Group Alternatives
5. You share the problem with your subordinates as a group. Together you generate and evaluate alternatives and try to reach a consensus about what to do. Your role is to coordinate the discussion and make sure that the critical issues are discussed. You do not try to get the group to accept your preferred solution, and you accept any solution that has the support of the entire group.

How do you decide which of these five alternatives to select? Here are some issues to consider[91]:

1. Does the problem require a high-quality decision?
2. Do you have enough information to make a high-quality decision?
3. Is the problem structured?
4. Is acceptance of the decision by your subordinates important for effective implementation?
5. If you were to make the decision by yourself, is it reasonably certain that it would be accepted by your subordinates?
6. Do your subordinates share the organizational goals to be attained in solving this problem?
7. Is conflict over the preferred solutions likely to occur among your subordinates?

MAKE A FAIR DECISION Everyone wants to believe that the decisions that involve them are just.[92] They expect **procedural justice** (also called *procedural fairness*),[93] which is using formal decision-making procedures that are fair.[94] For example, people want procedures to be trustworthy, which means that they are consistently applied over time. They also want procedures to be free of personal bias, accurate, correctable, participative, and ethical.

Why do fair procedures matter so much? One key explanation is that procedural justice communicates two important messages about a person's membership in his or her work group. The first message is whether the person is respected by members of the group, and the second is whether the person should feel pride in the group as a whole.[95]

In the United States, procedurally fair treatment results in increased job satisfaction, organizational commitment, and organizational citizenship behaviors, whereas unfair treatment results in a variety of retaliatory behaviors.[96] However, judgments of procedural justice vary by culture. People in individualistic cultures, such as the United States, prefer more formal procedures, whereas those in collectivist cultures, such as China, show no preference between formal and informal procedures.[97]

Organizational scientists generally study people's *perceptions* of justice—their subjective evaluations of the appropriateness of a given outcome or process.[98] However, one problem with relying on perceptions is that the process that is perceived to be fair may not be the process that is actually fair. For example, some tools that human resources departments use for personnel selection are perceived by job candidates as unfair, even though the tools are more valid than other tools commonly used.[99] Consider, for instance, how pre-employment interviews are structured: Job applicants believe that unstructured interviews, in which they have an open-ended, flexible talk with the interviewer, are fairer than structured interviews, in which the interview is based primarily on predetermined questions. Research tells us the opposite: that structured interviews are more accurate in assessing candidates.[100] Another misperception is created by a person's success: People evaluate a selection process somewhat more favorably when it leads to a positive outcome for them than when it leads to a negative outcome for them.[101]

In addition to procedural justice, people want **interactional justice**,[102] which is being treated respectfully when formal organizational procedures are carried out.[103] Interactional justice is morally appropriate conduct that suggests that managers have other people's well-being in mind.[104] Employees want to be treated with honesty, consideration, and courtesy. They also want decision-making processes to be explained to them.[105] For example, if you need to lay people off, you should tell them the truth and listen to their responses respectfully, and you should explain to them how management made the decision.

MONITOR BIASES IN YOURSELF AND OTHERS When we are making a decision, it sometimes takes a conscious effort to overcome our unconscious biases that unfavorably stereotype others but favor ourselves, our group, and those that can benefit us. Here are some conscious strategies to help you eliminate your own biases.[106]

1. Collect data that reveal your own and others' prejudice. One way to do this is to examine decisions systematically. For example, ask people to analyze the contributions of *all* group members before accepting the assertion that one group member has made the biggest contribution.

2. Ask yourself whether your environment is reinforcing harmful stereotypes. For example, does your company value a particular group of high achievers, all of whom are cast in the same mold? Are they perhaps from the same demographic group? Cues in your environment shape your own implicit attitudes. Be aware of these influences on your own perceptions and self-image. If you are in the minority in your company, and you discover that you have been negatively stereotyped, move on to a company in which people like you lead. Or, if this is impractical, go out of your way to observe companies in which people like you do actually lead.

procedural justice
Using formal decision-making procedures that are fair; also called "procedural fairness."

interactional justice
Treating people respectfully when formal organizational procedures are carried out.

3. Before relying on your intuition to make a decision, try to put yourself into the shoes of the people who will be affected. What do *they* believe about the problem? How will each of them be affected? What will be their reactions to proposed decisions? Putting yourself in their shoes may help you to double-check your own biases.

4. When choosing people to consider for any special opportunity or benefit, start with a list of names of all employees who have relevant qualifications. Then, after you make a preliminary choice, think about the people who did *not* make it to your short list. Are they different from you in some way? Do they fail to meet prevailing stereotypes of the "best" person for the opportunity? Consider carefully what would happen if you gave them the proposed opportunity or benefit.

FOSTER INDIVIDUAL AND ORGANIZATIONAL ETHICS It is clear that, faced with making business decisions totally on their own, individuals are likely to act reasonably according to their own values and beliefs. However, when making that same decision in an organizational setting, surrounded by others, individuals are subjected to a variety of social pressures that are likely to cloud their judgment. In an organization it is relatively easy to pass the buck because you think, "This decision should be made by my boss." And it becomes relatively easy to rationalize a harmful behavior because others are doing the same thing, taking the view that "that's business." Today it is widely accepted that such moral blindness characterizes many business decisions,[107] and companies realize they must establish not just ethics codes and ethics offices, but also organization-wide cultures that foster ethical decision making.

ethical dilemma
Any situation or decision that requires moral judgment.

Companies that want to establish an ethical decision-making process first teach their employees to recognize **ethical dilemmas** as they arise.[108] An ethical dilemma is any situation or decision that requires moral judgment. Sometimes the moral choice is between right and wrong behaviors; other times it is between two seemingly right behaviors. In addition, companies empower individuals to communicate their issues to others without fear of reprisal, and they set up specific processes to deal with those issues.

To make sure that the importance of ethical decision making is highlighted throughout their organizations, some businesses also employ corporate ethics officers. These individuals act as counselors with whom employees can talk confidentially about ethical dilemmas. They may also conduct training programs on how to improve ethical aspects of business decision making.[109]

The perceived importance of ethics and social responsibility to the success of a company is influenced by the individual's own ethical perspective as well as by the culture of the organization. (Organizational culture will be covered in greater detail in Chapter 17.) Furthermore, a study of the decision-making processes of managers in Spain, Turkey, Great Britain, and the United States suggests that both individual ethics and the organizational culture are important regardless of one's country.[110]

In the end, both individual and sociocultural processes influence whether a decision will be ethical. Each individual in an organization is accountable to both him- or herself and others. The Bentley College Center for Business Ethics suggests that in organizational life, each individual should become a "practical philosopher"—an ethical decision maker—by asking himself or herself the following questions when facing a decision requiring moral judgment:[111]

1. Is it right?
2. Is it fair?
3. How does it "smell"? (What is your instinctive reaction to it?)
4. Who gets hurt?
5. Would you be comfortable if the details of your decision were reported on the front page of your local newspaper?
6. What would you tell your child to do?

ACCOUNT FOR CULTURAL INFLUENCES Much of the research on individual and group decision making has been conducted with American and other English-speaking groups. As more cross-cultural studies are conducted, differences in decision-making styles and influences will undoubtedly be discovered. For instance, it has been suggested that how employees view participative decision making depends on forces outside of the decision-making process, including sociopolitical, legal, historical, and sociocultural factors.[112] The impact of culture on decision making is likely to be related to whether a culture is individualistic or more group oriented, and whether it has a high or low emphasis on hierarchical relationships.

How Can You Use Experts Effectively?

Naturalistic decision making is decision making that occurs in real-world settings, often under time pressure.[113] Under these conditions, it is common for managers to turn to experts (individuals with in-depth knowledge and experience) to help them make a decision. Exactly how do experts make decisions in complex, naturalistic environments under time and resource limitations? And how good are their decisions? Can you always rely on your experts?

Researchers believe that experts seldom use the methods that traditional models of decision making would predict.[114] In fact, they ignore conventional methods such as deductive logical thinking, analysis of probabilities, and statistical methods in favor of intuition, mental simulation, metaphor, and storytelling. Using intuition allows experts to size up a situation quickly. Using mental simulation lets them imagine how a course of action might be carried out; using metaphors allows them to draw on their experiences by suggesting parallels between the current situations and other situations; and using storytelling helps them consolidate their experiences to make them available in the future to themselves or others.

In field settings a typical decision maker will not make comparisons among alternatives but will instead consider only a single option. In only about 5 percent of decisions do people really make comparisons among options.[115] Experts recognize immediately that a particular course of action is the best because they have already seen it in practice. They let their intuition—in this case, their experience incorporated at an unconscious or threshold level of consciousness—be their guide.

Basing a decision on intuition grounded in experience is sometimes a reasonable choice. "Experts see the world differently," points out researcher Gary Klein. "They see things the rest of us cannot. Often experts do not realize that the rest of us are unable to detect what seems obvious to them."[116] For example, experts see patterns that novices do not notice and anomalies, such as events that did not happen and other violations of expectations. They see the big picture, differences too small for novices to detect, and their own limitations.

Relying on experts can be either a decision-making strength or a decision-making weakness. On the plus side, experts have knowledge based on experiences that, in comparison with beginners, allows them to readily find analogies between the current problem and past problems.[117] Over time they have developed a set of underlying principles, and they go ahead and apply these principles to the current decision while beginners are still focused on surface features. Sometimes, the unique cognitive approaches taken by experts can be captured through in-depth interviews and transferred to others.[118]

On the minus side, when confronted with a truly novel situation, experts are sometimes bound by their experience. Their very expertise can be their downfall because they may see what they expect to see, and they may fail to recognize when a proposed solution is incorrect.[119] In truly novel situations, experts actually become nonexperts and should make decisions just like everyone else—collecting information, generating alternatives, and making a choice.

So use your experts, by all means. But understand that the validity of the advice they offer depends on the nature of the problem to be solved.

How Can You Use Technology to Improve Decision Making?

The type of technology used to improve decision making varies depending on the employees involved in the decision and the technological devices available to them.[120] Typically, at lower levels of the organization, technological application is limited to the use of

naturalistic decision making Decision making that occurs in real-world settings, often under time pressure.

programmed decision-making processes. For example, a service technician making a house call might have a pager that tells him or her where to travel to next, but a program may have selected the destination. At middle levels, professionals and managers may have an enterprise portal that provides personalized access to corporate information and applications used for nonprogrammed decisions. Similarly, senior managers may have digital dashboards—programs that show them in real time how their business is doing overall.

The case of the Spanish clothing retailer Inditex, known for its 550 Zara stores worldwide, suggests how information technology (IT) and human decision-making processes can be integrated effectively.[121] About one-fourth the size of Gap, Inditex is more profitable than Gap, H&M, or Benetton. Yet the company spends only 0.5 percent of its revenues on IT, in contrast to the U.S. retail industry average of 2 percent. Inditex uses an inside-outside approach to its IT development. This means that it focuses on company needs and then develops IT to serve those needs, rather than searching outside the company for the latest technological enhancements. It also uses simple technology rather than complex technology wherever possible. Fundamentally, the company keeps human decision making as the driver and core process for the organization, while utilizing technology to facilitate information gathering and sharing. Thus, store managers can decide what fashions to order, and specialists can make production and volume decisions for each garment, using IT to help them to communicate and to organize large amounts of constantly changing data. Employees feel empowered not only because they make many important decisions but because the IT they understand is the IT they use.

expert systems
Computer programs that mirror some aspects of human decision-making processes.

Another application of technology to decision making is the use of **expert systems**, computer programs that mirror some aspects of human decision-making processes. Such systems usually maintain a knowledge base containing facts and known relationships in a particular problem area, along with rules of thumb or other ways of making judgments based on that knowledge.[122] For instance, a pharmaceutical distributor might use an expert system to handle the daily problem of balancing the workload of the company and improving the efficiency of its drivers making deliveries. To date, expert systems have been most useful when applied to decisions that are relatively programmed.

How Can You Implement Decisions Successfully?

implementation
Putting a solution into effect using a definite plan or procedure.

Ultimately, decision making must be followed by **implementation**, which is putting a solution into effect using a definite plan or procedure.[123] Thinking about problems and developing solutions are only first steps. To avoid falling victim to "analysis paralysis," you must subsequently turn ideas into action.

When executive search firms hunt for top executives, they look for excellence in all aspects of decision making *and* implementation. Among the key characteristics they seek in an executive are a reputation for achieving results (which is based largely on sound convergent thinking leading to effective decisions) and the ability to think strategically (which is based on divergent thinking leading to taking a broad view). Implementation abilities they look for include interpersonal skills, such as avoiding hubris and arrogance; the ability to fit into a company's culture; and communication skills, including the ability to convey complex ideas clearly and succinctly.[124]

In Conclusion

Clearly, whether your personal goals include climbing the ladder to the executive suite, or simply succeeding in organizational life, you must 1) appreciate both the rational and the nonrational sides of decision making, 2) enhance your—or your team's—abilities for convergent and divergent thinking, and 3) develop your implementation skills.

Consider this advice on decision implementation from the late management expert Peter Drucker.[125] Always practical, Drucker pointed out that you have not really made a decision until people know:

- the name of the person accountable for carrying it out;
- the deadline that needs to be met;

- the names of the people who will be affected by the decision and who therefore must know about, understand, and approve the decision—or at least not be strongly opposed to it;

- the names of the people who have to be informed of the decision, even if they are not directly affected by it.

Also, to effectively implement decisions, managers must focus on opportunities rather than problems, know how to run effective meetings, and take responsibility for communicating their action plans and information needs to their subordinates.

We will discuss the numerous challenges of implementation throughout the rest of this book, especially in the chapters on motivation, one-to-one relationships, group decision making, leadership, and change. Also note that we continue the discussion of decision making in Chapters 9 and 10, on the effective use of groups and teams.

Apply What You Have Learned . . .

World Class Company: Google, Inc.

Google is one of the most successful Internet search engine companies, indexing billions of Web pages in more than 30 languages.[126] Yet it is still a relatively small company. Over a period of two years beginning in 2001, the staff of Google quintupled to a number only slightly more than 1,000.[127] In 2005, Google had about 4,000 employees worldwide,[128] while in 2006 this number had grown to 8,000. Many of these employees are engineers.

The company's culture has always been informal. A company motto is "You can be serious without a suit."[129] Google is well known for hiring based on ability rather than experience, and people are likely to be multitalented. One chief operations engineer, for example, was also a licensed neurosurgeon. The company also likes to hire managers who are strong-willed individuals out to change the world.

Company headquarters is the Googleplex, where most people eat in the Google café and mix there with other departments. Hierarchy is minimized: Skating over a corporate officer during roller hockey is not a problem. But perhaps the signature characteristic of the company's culture is that engineers have one day a week to work solely on their own pet projects.

How does Google make decisions? Consider how its top management team operates. As Google has grown, the decision-making process of its top management team has evolved. Google was founded in 1998 by Stanford computer science graduate students Larry Page and Sergey Brin, who after three years hired an experienced Silicon Valley manager, Eric Schmidt, as Chairman and CEO. Schmidt says that when he arrived at Google, he found that, "There was a staff meeting on Wednesday for two hours, which was fascinating because it would wander from interesting topic to interesting topic. But somehow out of that, decisions were made."[130]

Schmidt undoubtedly systematized the top-level business decision making at Google. Nevertheless, at least when it employed fewer than 4,000 people, the company's decision-making style continued to be unusual. Schmidt says that whenever high-level decisions were made, two people would have to agree. This typically meant two of the top three—Page, Brin, and Schmidt himself. Much of the time, the three ran the company as a triumvirate, collaborating on both product and business decisions. "The way it really works is that if it's really important [one of us] drives the three of us to agree. . . . We, in fact, drive to consensus. Now, if two people agree, then the third person is yelled at for a while and vice-versa. And by the way, it rotates around," says Schmidt.[131]

In general, the people at Google like to make decisions as much in the open as possible. Schmidt says, "We don't like people to go off and make a decision. We try to make decisions in as large a group as possible by as few people as possible."[132] Teams make decisions by consensus, leaving room for individuals to bring their unique insights.

In an interview, Marissa Mayer, Google's 31-year-old vice-president in charge of product launches, describes how the company maintains creativity among its product managers. "We bring together a team of people who are really passionate about [a] subject. . . . We still don't do very high-definition product specs. If you write a 70-page document that says this is the product you're supposed to build, you actually push the creativity out with process. [We don't want to discourage] the engineer who says, you know what, there's a feature here that you forgot that I would really like to add. You don't want to push that creativity out of the product."[133]

Discuss

1. Describe decision making at Google.
2. In general, how does decision making in small companies differ from decision making in large companies?

Advice from the Pros

How Hollywood Producers Decide Which Writer Is Creative

After two years in Los Angeles, parking cars by night and writing TV scripts by day, you are eager to sell your creative ideas to a producer. Your goal is to join the writing team on *Desperate Nannies*. At last, you get the big call. You are invited to come down to the studio . . . to take a pencil and paper test of your creativity? to show samples of your creative writing? No. You have been invited to make a 20-minute pitch to a producer.

How do people who hire creative talent assess creativity? Many professionals, including those in marketing, film production, product design, and venture capital funding, rely on the face-to-face interview, or "pitch." A recent study of pitching in Hollywood provides some interesting views of how producers use their experience and intuition to evaluate a writer's creativity.

Producers listening to a pitch use a two-part mental process to evaluate a candidate's creativity.

Part 1. Producers Categorize the Person

First, the producer intuitively categorizes the writer in terms of a) cues that suggest the level of his or her creativity, and b) cues that suggest the level of his or her *lack* of creativity. Here are some of the resulting categories, along with the behavioral cues that producers use to make their judgments and related comments by the producer-interviewers themselves:

The Artist: High Creative Potential

Cues: quirky, unconventional, unpredictable, passionate, extreme, obscure, unpolished/anxious

Producer's comment: "There's this one guy, a real artist. But he's one of those . . . guys whose social graces are not so intact. . . . He's a bit of a nonconformist, certainly, and his hair might be wild, . . . He's incredibly shy. . . ."

The Journeyman: Moderate Creative Potential

Cues: Writerly, uses drama, natural, writes to a formula

Producer's comment: "A journeyman who's creative, can take what is a formulaic story . . . but it still works because, within that formula, he spun it so uniquely."

The Nonwriter: Low Creative Potential

Cues: Slick, writes to a formula, jaded, desperate

Producer's comment: "You know, you don't want to come off as a used car salesman; you don't want it to be a laundry list. . . ."

Interestingly, while assessing creativity, the producer is also assessing lack of creativity. The cues for noncreativity include being too slick, appearing desperate, having a memorized pitch, and presenting a long list of ideas. Says one producer, "You should never pitch more than one, maybe two projects at a time. Never, never, never. There's not a buyer in the world that you can convince that you have the same passion for five different projects. What you're selling is your passion. You're rarely selling the idea. You are selling you. You are selling your commitment, your point of view."

Part 2. Producers Categorize the Relationship

During the pitch the producers also categorize the relationship between themselves and the interviewee. This categorization has only two outcomes: Either they perceive a

likely creative collaboration, or they perceive they might be pairing an expert with an incompetent.

A collaboration is likely if the relationship between the producer and the interviewee during the interview is characterized by enthusiasm, competition, "we" language, asking questions, "a-ha" experiences, and sharing of ideas. As one Oscar-winning writer put it, "I think that magic is perhaps the most important part of the pitch. And in a sense . . . it's a seduction, a promise of what lies ahead. At a certain point the writer needs to pull back and let the producer project himself as the creator of the story. And let him project what he needs onto your idea that makes the story whole for him."[134]

A negative pairing is likely if the exchange includes lecturing, tuning out, arguing, and making bureaucratic requests ("Why don't you send me copies of your previous submissions?"). Says one producer "In an unsuccessful pitch, the person just doesn't yield or doesn't listen well. My time is valuable and if I start to tell someone my concerns and they aren't listening, I start to get tuned out to them and then my mind starts to drift. And when I realize I am not really listening to them anymore and thinking about other projects, then I know they are in trouble. . . . I don't like to hurt people's feelings, but I don't have a lot of time to waste, and I start thinking about other things."[135]

Do the producers make good decisions?

Not according to the theory of creativity in decision making. For example, producers view anxiety as a motivator for creativity, even though the research suggests that anxiety actually constrains creativity.[136] Also, they view inexperience as likely to enhance creativity, whereas research suggests that creativity is more likely to be enhanced by extensive, diverse experience.

So what should you do if your pitch is rejected? Remember, that's just show business.

Source: Based on K. D. Elsbach and R. M. Kramer, "Assessing Creativity in Hollywood Pitch Meetings: Evidence for a Dual-Process Model of Creativity Judgments," *Academy of Management Journal 46* (3), June 2003:283–301.

Discuss

1. How effective is the producers' method for choosing creative writers?
2. To what extent does the producers' method for choosing writers illustrate the theory presented in this chapter on how intuitive decisions are made? on how naturalistic decisions are made?
3. Suggest some additional decision-making methods for choosing writers.

Gain Experience

I. Fit the Process to the Decision

Do decision-making processes differ depending on the type of decision being made? In this exercise, you will find out. In groups of 4 or 5, solve the first problem below in Table 3.8. Before going on to the next problem, report to the class on the following:

1) your decision; 2) how much time it took; 3) who was involved in the decision, and how they decided; 4) how satisfied your group members are with the process they used to make the decision; and 5) how satisfied your group members are with the quality of your decision.

At the end of the exercise, consult Table 3.9 on page 87 for a description of the process that is typical of each type of decision.

Source: This exercise is based in part on theory presented in J. D. Thompson and A. Tuden, "Strategies, Structure, and Processes of Organizational Decisions," in J. D. Thompson, P. B. Hammond, R. W. Hawkes, B. H. Junker, and A. Tuden, *Comparative Studies in Administration* (Pittsburgh: University of Pittsburgh Press, 1959). The source of the evil moneylender problem is unknown.

II. Make the President's Decision

The president of your university is thinking of [choose a current controversy, such as changing the calendar of the university from semesters to quarters; adding a cooperative education component to the curriculum, thus adding one year to a students' college education (or removing such a component); requiring a semester abroad (or dropping such a requirement)].. . . How should the president go about making this decision?

In groups of 4 or 5, design a decision-making process for the president.

TABLE 3.8   Fit the Process to the Decision: Solve these problems

1. The curve

A professor grades on a curve and realizes only one of the following four students can receive an "A." Which one should it be? When your group has made its decision, raise a hand to let your professor know you are ready for the discussion.

	1st Test	2nd Test	3rd Test	Participation
John	80	90	95	Average
Carol	80	85	90	Excellent
Tom	95	90	90	Average
Bob	90	95	80	Poor

2. The player

A university (not yours) has admitted illiterate football players. Bo, a senior, is one of these. Injured, Bo can no longer play. Should Bo be allowed to graduate with his B.S. in business, which is his major subject? When you have arrived at a solution, raise a hand to let the professor know you are ready for the discussion.

3. The evil moneylender

An old moneylender offers to cancel a merchant's debt in order to keep him from going to prison if the merchant will give the moneylender his lovely daughter. Horrified yet desperate, the merchant and his daughter agree to let Fate decide. The moneylender said he would put a black pebble and a white pebble in a bag, and the girl will draw one pebble. The white pebble will cancel the debt and set the girl free; the black one will cancel the debt but make the girl the moneylender's. If she refuses to pick, her father will go to prison. From the pebble-strewn path they are standing on, the moneylender picks two pebbles and quickly puts them in the bag, but the girl sees he has picked up two black pebbles. What would you do if you were the girl? When your group has answered this question, have a member whisper it to your professor to find out if it is correct.

TABLE 3.9 Under Which Circumstances Should You Use Each Decision-Making Method?

	What is the best size of the decision-making unit?	Will making the decision involve weighing conflicting personal values?	What decision-making skills are needed?
1. A programmed decision based on computation Ex. Grading	The smallest possible decision unit	Few conflicts. In fact, the problem appears to be "common sense"	Math; computer programming
2. An unprogrammed decision based on weighing different values Ex. Pass or fail Bo?	An intermediate-sized decision unit	Some conflicts	Group process
3. A creative decision based on inspiration Ex. Moneylender problem	The context of the group is useful, but the individual usually "decides"	No	Creativity; intuition

Can You Solve This Manager's Problem?

I. What Can Citigroup Teach Hewlett-Packard about Ethical Decision Making?

Put yourself in the shoes of Mark V. Hurd, Hewlett-Packard's chairman and chief executive during the company's 2006 public and internal crisis over "pretexting." It seems that HP's board wanted to discover which of its members were providing information to reporters, and set out to investigate the leaks. To do this, the board contracted much of the detective work to outside companies, such as Security Outsourcing Solutions. This company had worked for HP for more than eight years, and was dependent on HP for about half its revenue.

One of the tactics Security Outsourcing Solutions used was pretexting. Fundamentally, pretexting is obtaining information on a false pretext, such as pretending to be someone you are not in order to gain your victim's confidence. In the HP case, one board member quit because he believed the company had obtained his personal phone records as part of the leak investigation.[137] The California attorney general accused the company of hiring people to tail some HP directors, and of attempting a sting on a reporter in order to get her to reveal her source. The company also thought about sending spies into newsrooms disguised as janitors. Allegedly the company also used tracer software, which when attached to an e-mailed document allows the sender to determine the Internet addresses where the document is opened. In its defense, the company argued that its lawyers had concluded that pretexting was legal.

So imagine you are Mark Hurd, and, for the sake of our discussion, let's assume you had no idea that any of this was going on. (In fact, Hurd testified before Congress that he failed to read an internal report on the investigation, and that he did send a booby-trapped e-mail to a reporter in an attempt to trace the leaks.[138]) Let's also assume that the chairwoman of the board of directors in charge of the investigation has resigned, and she and four others face felony charges.

One day things will get back to normal in your company, you hope, but in the meantime you want to make sure that HP does everything it can to regain its previously stellar reputation. A crucial aspect of your investigation is answering the question "How did the HP board make the series of bad decisions that got them into this mess?"

You pick up an article by *The Financial Times* that begins, "Of the world's top financial institutions none has done more than Citigroup under Chuck Prince's leadership to address ethical problems and attempt to instill an ethical culture. Citigroup has nonetheless been plagued by high-profile ethical lapses, underlining how difficult it can be to embed sound values in a diverse and complex international organization."[139] Here, you think, you might learn something useful. Citigroup had been a prominent provider of financial services to such corporate trouble-makers as Enron, WorldCom, and Parmalat, and had since made a major effort to make sure its employees followed ethical standards. Its new goals for its people include being a company with the highest standards of ethical conduct, an organization people can trust, and a company dedicated to community service.

However, the article points out that since Citigroup's new emphasis on ethics, its London operations had become embroiled in a scandal in which bond traders exploited a weakness in a particular bond market, and by making a mass order, had stung each of their competitors for millions of dollars. As stated in the article, "From an ethical point of view, some outside Citigroup as well as within argued that this was a market for professional traders who knew how to look after themselves. In this view, exploiting a structural weakness in the [bond] market was fair game. Others felt Citigroup had cynically breached a gentleman's agreement central to the workings of the market. Either way, Citigroup's traders were undoubtedly flouting the bank's stated ethical values which declared that 'we treat our customers, suppliers, and competitors fairly.'"[140] The article goes on to note that one company leader had admitted, in a leaked e-mail, that the company had made a bad decision in this instance, having failed to fully consider the transaction's impact on its clients and competitors. Chuck Prince called the trade "knuckleheaded." The traders were suspended, but later were allowed to return to work.

As you ponder the Citigroup dilemma, you wonder what you should do next at HP.

Discuss

1. In what ways did the HP decision-making process go wrong?
2. What is the difference between legal decisions and ethical decisions?
3. In both the Citigroup case and the HP case, key values conflicted. What were those values?
4. How can Mark Hurd make sure that in the future, HP decisions will be both legal and ethical?

II. Improving Customer Service in a Telecommunications Company

You are the new vice-president of human resources management for a telecommunications company that employs 45,000 workers. You have just returned from your first annual conference with the other senior executives of the company. At the event, you volunteered to chair a taskforce to look into improving customer service across the company. Ninety percent of the company's customer service is delivered by hourly employees. Yet the most recent annual employee opinion survey suggests that the majority of hourly employees are dissatisfied with their workloads and with how they are treated in the company. Seventy percent of the hourly workers are unionized.

In a few hours you will chair a meeting with the company's four other vice-presidents on your task force. Because they attended the annual conference, you know each of them to some extent. They are all line managers, accountable for the profits and losses of their respective divisions.

■ The *VP for Business Lines* has held her position for one year, having been promoted to the job after 10 years in the company's finance branch. Her reputation for conscientiousness is widespread.

■ The *VP for Private Lines* is a marketing professional who has held his job for four years. He has a well-deserved reputation for discovering and developing business opportunities.

■ The *VP for Online Services* holds an executive MBA and has experience in a broad range of line positions in your company. Her division has recently undergone a series of layoffs that have left employees at all levels of her division nervous.

■ The *VP for Long Distance Services* is an exceptionally busy, hands-on manager who has come up through the company ranks and enjoys focusing on day-to-day operations. He has flown in for the afternoon meeting and will depart immediately afterward.

■ The *VP for Human Resource Management*. You, yourself, are an expert on organizational change and a positive, energetic person. You recently attended an inspiring two-day seminar on total quality management, a program that trains employees company-wide in statistical, managerial, and behavioral skills for improving quality. Adding this up-to-date knowledge to your 15 years of experience in human resource management, you feel especially well qualified to take on the work of the task force.

You see your immediate task as having two parts.

First, you wonder how best to design the decision-making process that will solve the customer service problem. Second, you wonder how to approach the upcoming meeting.

Discussion Questions

1. What are the likely strengths and weaknesses of each of the participants in this decision? What heuristics are they most likely to use?
2. What type of problem is being solved?
3. What aspects of the social context should be considered?
4. How should you approach the upcoming meeting?

Chapter Summary and Key Terms

When considering how to make a decision, what principles should guide your thinking?

Keep in mind that organizational decision making is both rational and psychological. Rational problem solving is more complicated than it looks. Problems occur both during the decision-making process and during the implementation of a decision. A common problem is escalation of commitment, the tendency to continue on a course of action because so many resources have already been expended.

rational–economic model   64
bounded rationality   64
administrative model   64
satisficing   64
behavioral economics   64
rational problem solving   65
escalation of commitment   65

When you are designing a decision-making process, what three major factors should you weigh?

Recognize that different types of problems generally require different types of decision making. When deciding "how to decide," consider 1) the type of problem you are solving, 2) the attributes, strengths, and weaknesses of the individuals who will make the decision, and 3) the social context of the decision.

How can you use experts effectively?

Recognize experts' strengths and weaknesses. Compared with beginners, they are good at solving problems that require knowledge based on experience; however, in truly novel situations, they may see what they have learned to see, or they may approach the problem just as anyone else would.

How can you use technology to improve decision making?

You are likely to find different organizational levels using different technologies. Senior managers may have digital dashboards that show them in real time how their business is doing, while employees at lower levels might have pagers that direct them as to what to do next. Information technology and expert systems are both useful aids to human decision making.

How can you implement decisions successfully?

After making the decision, be sure responsibilities for implementing the decision are assigned and that those to whom they are assigned know they will be held accountable. Implementation will be covered in greater detail throughout the rest of this book, especially in the chapters on communication, group decision making, leadership, change, and motivation.

Explorations

1. Tools for improving logical decision making

At www.mindtools.com[141] you will find a section on decision making that offers a variety of tools for organizing decisions, including pareto analysis (logical steps to take in choosing what to change), force field analysis (analyzing the pressures for and against a choice), and grid analysis (making a choice by taking into account a large number of factors).

2. Creativity in business decision making

Do a Web search for "business creativity." How often is creativity required in business, do you think?

3. Explore your own unconscious biases

To examine your own unconscious attitudes, visit implicit.harvard.edu or www.tolerance.org/hidden%5fbias. Here you will find Implicit Association Tests that reveal unconscious beliefs by asking you to make split-second associations to different types of people. Your results may surprise you!

4. Explore with the professionals

Visit the Web site for the Society for Judgment and Decision Making at www.sjdm.org. SJDM is a professional group of psychologists, economists, decision analysts, and others dedicated to the study of decision making. Their Web site includes course syllabi with useful references on decision making in negotiations, government, medicine, and business.

5. How human factors in decision making affect the stock market

Read Robert J. Shiller's *Irrational Exuberance* (Princeton, NJ: Princeton University Press, 2000), which describes how psychological, cultural, and other factors affect stock market prices.

References

1 Based in part on Victorinox: International Media Service. http://www.victorinox.com/newsite/downloads/medien_e.pdf. Accessed September 25, 2005.

2 H. A. Simon, "Rational Decision Making in Organizations," *American Economic Review 69*, 1979:493–513.

3 P. Monaghan, "Taking On 'Rational Man': Dissident Economists Fight for a Niche in the Discipline," *The Chronicle of Higher Education 49* (20), January 24, 2003:A12.

4 C. E. Zsambok and G. Klein, eds., *Naturalistic Decision Making* (Mahwah, NJ: Erlbaum, 1997). See also H. R. Arkes and P. Ayton, "The Sunk Cost and Concorde Effects: Are Humans Less Rational Than Lower Animals?" *Psychological Bulletin 125* (5), September 1999:591–600.

5 H. A. Simon, *Administrative Behavior* (New York: Free Press, 1957). See also J. G. March and H. A. Simon, *Organizations* (New York: Wiley, 1958).

6 The Nobel Prize is not awarded posthumously.

7 V. H. Vroom and P. W. Yetton, *Leadership and Decision-Making* (Pittsburgh, PA: University of Pittsburgh Press, 1973).

8 H. Simon, *The New Science of Management Decision* (Englewood Cliffs, NJ: Prentice Hall, 1977); B. Bass, *Organizational Decision Making* (Homewood, IL: Irwin, 1983).

9 D. A. Cowan, "Developing a Process Model of Problem Recognition," *Academy of Management Review 11* (4), 1986:763–776.

10 D. Kahneman and A. Tversky, "Choices, Values, and Frames," *American Psychologist 39*, 1984:341–350.

11 W. C. Wedley and R. H. G. Field, "A Predecision Support System," *Academy of Management Review 11*, 1984:407–466.

12 D. A. Cowan, "Developing a Process Model of Problem Recognition," *Academy of Management Review 11* (4), 1996:763–776.

13 B. M. Staw and J. Ross, "Behavior in Escalation Situations: Antecedents, Prototypes, and Solutions," *Research in Organizational Behavior 9*, 1987: 39–78.

14 H. R. Arkes and P. Ayton, "The Sunk Cost and Concorde Effects: Are Humans Less Rational Than Lower Animals?" *Psychological Bulletin 125*(5), September 1999:591–600.

15 Grant Thornton, "Britain Feared Concorde Would Fail," DeHavilland Information Services, plc. www.grant-thornton.co. Accessed March 9, 2005.

16 A. Zardkoohi, "Do Real Options Lead to Escalation of Commitment?" *Academy of Management Review* 29 (1), January 2004:111–119.

17 H. A. Simon, *The New Science of Management* (Englewood Cliffs, New Jersey: Prentice-Hall, Inc., 1960).

18 D. A. Bernstein, L. A. Penner, A. Clarke-Stewart, and E. J. Roy, *Psychology* (Boston and New York: Houghton Mifflin Company, 2003):374.

19 D. A. Bernstein, L. A. Penner, A. Clarke-Stewart, and E. J. Roy, *Psychology* (Boston and New York: Houghton Mifflin Company, 2003):373. See also J. P. Guilford and R. Hoepfner, *The Analysis of Intelligence* (New York: McGraw-Hill, 1971).

20 D. K. Simonton, *Genius, Creativity and Leadership* (Cambridge: Harvard University Press, 1984). See also R. J. Sternberg, "What Is the Common Thread of Creativity: Its Dialectical Relation to Intelligence and Wisdom," *American Psychologist 56*, 2001:360–362.

21 F. Barron and D. M. Harrington, "Creativity, Intelligence, and Personality," *Annual Review of Psychology 52*, 1981:439–476. See also D. K. Simonton, "Creativity and Genius," in L. Pervin and O. John, eds., *Handbook of Personality Research*, 2nd ed. (New York: Guilford, 1999):629–652.

22 R. J. Sternberg, "What Is the Common Thread of Creativity: Its Dialectical Relation to Intelligence and Wisdom," *American Psychologist 56*, 2001:360–362.

23 P. C. Nutt, *Why Decisions Fail: Avoiding the Blunders and Traps That Lead to Debacles* (San Francisco: Berrett-Koehler, 2002). See also P. C. Nutt, "The Formulation Process and Tactics Used in Organizational Decision Making," *Organization Science 4,* 1993:226–251.

24 P. Soelberg, "Unprogrammed Decision Making," *Academy of Management Proceedings*, 1966:3–16.

25 P. C. Nutt, *Why Decisions Fail: Avoiding the Blunders and Traps That Lead to Debacles* (San Francisco: Berrett-Kohler, 2002). See also P. C. Nutt, "The Formulation Process and Tactics Used in Organizational Decision Making," *Organization Science 4,* 1993:226–251.

26 W. C. Wedley and R. H. G. Field, "A Predecision Support System," *Academy of Management Review 11*, 1984:407–466.

27 R. Burns, "To a Mouse on Turning Her Nest with the Plough, November, 1795," originally published in *Robert Burns, Poems, Chiefly in the Scottish Dialect* (Kilmarnock, 1786). http://eir.library.utoronto.ca/rpo/display/poem337.html (online text copyright I. Lancashire, Department of English, University of Toronto, 2003).

28 G. Edwards, "The Alcohol Dependence Syndrome: A Concept as Stimulus to Enquiry," *British Journal of Addiction 81*, 1987:171–183.

29 A. Tversky, "Elimination by Aspects: A Theory of Choice," *Psychological Review 79*, 1972:281–299; F. R. Kardes, "Psychology Applied to Consumer Behavior," in A. M. Stec and D. A. Bernstein, eds., *Psychology: Fields of Application* (Boston: Houghton Mifflin, 1999).

30 J. R. Bettman, E. J. Johnson, and J. Payne, "A Componential Analysis of Cognitive Effort in Choice," *Organizational Behavior and Human Decision Processes 45*, 1990:111–139.

31 A. Tversky and D. Kahneman, "Loss Aversion in Riskless Choice: A Reference Dependent Model," *Quarterly Journal of Economics 106* (4), November 1991:1039-1061; R. Dawes, "Behavioral Judgment and Decision Making," in D. Gilbert, S. T. Fiske, and G. Lindzey, eds., *Handbook of Social Psychology 1*, 4th ed. (Boston: McGraw-Hill,1998):497–549.

32 A. Tversky and K. Kahneman, "Judgment under Uncertainty: Heuristics and Biases," *Science,* September 1974: 1124–1131.

33 D. Kahneman and A. Tversky, "Choices, Values and Frames," *American Psychologist 39*, 1984:341–350.

34 A. J. Rowe and R. O. Mason, *Managing with Style: A Guide to Understanding, Assessing and Improving Decision Making* (San Francisco: Jossey-Bass, 1987).

35 K. H. Craik, A. P. Ware, B. Staw, S. Zedeck, J. Kamp, and C. O'Reilly III, "Explorations of Construct Validity in a Combined Managerial and Personality Assessment Programme," *Journal of Occupational & Organizational Psychology 75* (2), June 2002:171–193.

[36] W. H. Stewart and P. L. Roth, "Risk Propensity Differences Between Entrepreneurs and Managers: A Meta-analytic Review, *Journal of Applied Psychology 86*, 2001:145–153.

[37] J. B. Miner and N.S. Raju, "Risk Propensity Differences Between Managers and Entrepreneurs and Between Low- and High-Growth Entrepreneurs: A Reply in a More Conservative Vein," *Journal of Applied Psychology 89* (1), February 2004:3–13.

[38] H. T. Keh, M. D. Foo, and B. C. Lim, "Opportunity Evaluation under Risky Conditions: The Cognitive Processes of Entrepreneurs, " *Entrepreneurship: Theory & Practice 27* (2), Winter 2002:125–148.

[39] A. J. Rowe and R. O. Mason, *Managing with Style: A Guide to Understanding, Assessing, and Improving Decision Making* (San Francisco: Jossey-Bass, 1987).

[40] A. J. Rowe and R. O. Mason, *Managing with Style: A Guide to Understanding, Assessing, and Improving Decision Making* (San Francisco: Jossey-Bass, 1987):39.

[41] A. J. Rowe and R. O. Mason, *Managing with Style: A Guide to Understanding, Assessing, and Improving Decision Making* (San Francisco: Jossey-Bass, 1987):197.

[42] A. J. Rowe and R. O. Mason, *Managing with Style: A Guide to Understanding, Assessing, and Improving Decision Making* (San Francisco: Jossey-Bass, 1987):85–86.

[43] T. M. Amabile, "Motivating Creativity in Organizations," *California Management Review,* Fall 1997:42–52.

[44] R. J. Sternberg and J. E. Davidson, eds., *The Nature of Insight* (Cambridge, MA: MIT Press, 1995).

[45] "Mr. BlackBerry Sends a Message," *The Economist Technology Quarterly*, September 23, 2006:36–38.

[46] T. M. Amabile, *KEYS: Assessing the Climate for Creativity* (Greensboro, NC: Center for Creative Leadership, 1995); T. M. Amabile, "Stimulate Creativity by Fueling Passion," *Blackwell Handbook of Principles of Organizational Behavior* (Oxford: Blackwell Publishing, 2000):331–341.

[47] Based on M.J. Kirton, "Adaptors and Innovators: A Description and Measure," *Journal of Applied Psychology*, 61 (5) 1976: 622–629; R. J. Sternberg and J. E. Davidson, eds., *The Nature of Insight* (Cambridge, MA: MIT Press, 1995); P.D. Tieger and B. Barron-Tieger, *Do What You Are* (Boston: Little, Brown and Company, 1995); T. M. Amabile, "Motivating Creativity in Organizations," *California Management Review,* Fall 1997:42–52; T. Amabile, C. N. Hadley, and S. J. Kramer, "Creativity Under the Gun," *Harvard Business Review 80* (8), August 2002:52–60.

[48] D. J. Isenberg, "How Senior Managers Think," *Harvard Business Review*, November/December 1984:81–90.

[49] E. Dane and M. G. Pratt, "Exploring Intuition and Its Role in Managerial Decision-Making," Paper provisionally accepted in the *Academy of Management Review.*

[50] "Understanding & Supporting Decision Making: An Interview with Gary Klein," *Information Knowledge Systems Management 2* (4), 2001:291–296.

[51] L. R. Beach and T. R. Mitchell, "Image Theory: A Behavioral Theory of Image Making in Organizations," in B. Staw and L. L. Cummings, eds., *Research in Organizational Behavior 12* (Greenwich, CT: JAI Press, 1990):1–41.

[52] E. Bonabeau, "Don't Trust Your Gut," *Harvard Business Review 81* (5), May 2003:116–123.

[53] W. A. Agor, "The Intuitive Ability of Executives: Findings from Field Research," in W. H. Agor, ed., *Intuition in Organizations: Leading and Managing Productively* (Newbury Park, CA: Sage Publications, 1989):145–156.

[54] D. A. Schon, *The Reflective Practitioner—How Professionals Think in Action* (New York: Basic Books, 1983).

[55] L. D. Phillips, "Systems for Solutions," *Datamation*, April 1985:26–29.

[56] W. A. Agor, "The Intuitive Ability of Executives: Findings from Field Research," in W. H. Agor, ed., *Intuition in Organizations: Leading and Managing Productively* (Newbury Park, CA: Sage Publications, 1989):145–156.

[57] L. J. Rips, *The Psychology of Proof: Deductive Reasoning in Human Thinking* (Cambridge, MA: MIT Press, 1994).

[58] G. Gigerenzer, P. M. Todd, and ABC Research Group, *Simple Heuristics That Make Us Smart* (New York: Oxford University Press, 2000).

[59] R. Matthews, "Business Life Science & Technology: Handy Rules for Effective Decision Making," *The Financial Times* April 29, 2005, http://search.ft.com/searchArticle?query Text=handy+rules+for+effective&y=0&javascriptEnabled= true&id=050429001302&x=0. Accessed October 5, 2006.

[60] Beginning with A. Tversky and K. Kahneman, "Judgment Under Uncertainty: Heuristics and Biases," *Science,* September 1974:1124–1131.

[61] H. A. Simon, *Models of Man: Social and Rational* (New York: Wiley, 1957).

[62] R. J. Shiller, *Irrational Exuberance* (Princeton, NJ: Princeton University Press, 2000):144–145.

[63] P. Slovic, "Facts versus Fears: Understanding Perceived Risk," paper presented at science and public policy seminar sponsored by the Federation of Behavioral and Psychological and Cognitive Sciences, Washington, DC, 1984.

[64] R. S. Nickerson, "Confirmation Bias: A Ubiquitous Phenomenon in Many Guises," *Review of General Psychology 2,* 1998:175–220.

[65] J. J. McMillan and R. A. White, "Auditors' Belief Revisions and Evidence Search: The Effect of Hypothesis Frame, Confirmation Bias, and Professional Skepticism," *Accounting Review 68* (3), July 1993:443–465.

[66] "Lex COLUMN: Failing Businesses," *The Financial Times*, July 12, 2004, www.ft.com. Accessed September 25, 2006.

[67] M. R. Banaji, M. H. Bazerman, and D. Chugh, "How (Un)Ethical Are You?" *Harvard Business Review 81* (12), December 2003:56–64.

[68] S. Begley, "Despite Its Reputation, Fingerprint Evidence Isn't Really Infallible," *Wall Street Journal*, June 4, 2004:B1.

[69] B. Fischoff and D. MacGregor, "Subjective Confidence in Forecasts," *Journal of Forecasting 1*, 1982:155–172.

[70] G. W. Pitz, "Subjective Probability Distributions for Imperfectly Known Quantities," in Lee W. Gregg, ed., *Knowledge and Cognition* (Potomac, MD: Lawrence Erlbaum Associates, 1975):29–41.

[71] G. N. Wright and L. D. Phillips, "Cultural Variation in Probabilistic Thinking: Alternative Ways of Dealing with Uncertainty," *International Journal of Psychology 15,* 1980:239–257; J. F. Yates, Y. Zhu, D. L. Ronis, D. F. Wang, H. Shinotsuka, and T. Masanao, "Probability Judgment Accuracy: China, Japan, and the United States," *Organizational Behavior and Human Decision Processes 43,* 1989:145–171.

[72] B. W. Pelham, M. C. Mirenberg, and J. T. Jones, "Why Susie Sells Seashells by the Seashore: Implicit Egotism and Major Life Decisions," *Journal of Personality & Social Psychology 82* (4), April 2002:469–487.

[73] As discussed in M. H. Bazerman, G. Loewenstein, and D. A. Moore, "Why Good Accountants Do Bad Audits," *Harvard Business Review* 80 (11), November 2002:96–102.

[74] T. Dalgleish and F. N. Watts, "Biases of Attention and Memory in Disorders of Anxiety and Depression," *Clinical Psychology Review 10*, 1990:589–604.

[75] S. Hartlage, L. B. Alloy, C. Vazquez, and B. Dykman, "Automatic and Effortful Processing in Depression," *Psychological Bulletin 113*, 1993:247–278.

[76] A. M. Isen, "Positive Affect and Decision Making," in M. Lewis and J. M. Haviland-Jones, eds., *Handbook of Emotion,* 2nd ed. (New York: Guilford, 2000):417–435.

[77] K. Daniels, "Asking a Straightforward Question: Managers' Perceptions and Managers' Emotions," *British Journal of Management 14* (1), March 2003:19–22.

[78] H. Bless, G. Bohner, N. Schwarz, and F. Strack, "Mood and Persuasion: A Cognitive Response Analysis," *Personality and Social Psychology Bulletin 16*, 1990:331–345.

[79] N. Murray, H. Sujan, E. R. Hirt, and M. Sujan, "The Influence of Mood on Categorization: A Cognitive Flexibility Interpretation," *Journal of Personality & Social Psychology 59*, 1990:411–425.

[80] R. C. Sinclair, "Mood, Categorization Breadth, and Performance Appraisal: The Effects of Order of Information Acquisition and Affective State on Halo, Accuracy, Information Retrieval, and Evaluations," *Organizational Behavior and Human Decision Processes 42*, 1988:22–46.

[81] C. J. Anderson, "The Psychology of Doing Nothing: Forms of Decision Avoidance Result from Reason and Emotion," *Psychological Bulletin 129* (1), January 1, 2003:139–167.

[82] I. Janis and L. Mann, "Emergency Decision Making: A Theoretical Analysis of Responses to Disaster Warnings," *Journal of Human Stress 3*, 1977b:35–48.

[83] D. Ho, "Ways of Understanding: How Our 'States of Mind' Affect Our Thinking and Creativity in Networking," *Mental Health Practice 6* (7), April 2003:30–33.

[84] S. E. Asch, "Opinions and Social Pressure," *Scientific American 193*, 1955:31–35.

[85] M. Deutsch and H. B. Gerard, "A Study of Normative and Informational Social Influences upon Individual Judgment," *Journal of Abnormal and Social Psychology 51*, 1955:629–636.

[86] S. E. Asch, "Effects of Group Pressure upon the Modification and Distortion of Judgments," in H. Guetzkow, ed., *Groups, Leadership, and Men* (Pittsburgh: Carnegie Press, 1951):177–190.

[87] R. Bond and P. B. Smith, "Culture and Conformity: A Meta-Analysis of Studies Using Asch's (1952, 1956) Line Judgment Task," *Psychological Bulletin,* January 1996:111–137.

[88] V. H. Vroom and P. W. Yetton, *Leadership and Decision Making* (Pittsburgh, PA: University of Pittsburgh Press, 1973). See also V. H. Vroom and A. G. Jago, *The New Leadership: Managing Participation in Organizations* (Englewood Cliffs, NJ: Prentice Hall, 1988).

[89] D. M. Schweiger and C. R. Leana, "Participation in Decision Making," in E. Locke, ed., *Generalizing from the Laboratory to Field Settings: Findings from Research in Industrial Organizational Psychology, Organizational Behavior and Human Resource Management* (Lexington, MA: Lexington Books, 1986).

[90] Based on V. H. Vroom and P. W. Yetton, *Leadership and Decision Making* (Pittsburgh, PA: University of Pittsburgh Press, 1973). See also J. T. Ettling and A. G. Jago, "Participation under Conditions of Conflict: More on the Validity of the Vroom-Yetton Model," *Journal of Management Studies,* January 1988:73–83; R. H. G. Field and R. J. House, "A Test of the Vroom-Yetton Model Using Manager and Subordinate Reports," *Journal of Applied Psychology,* June 1990:362–366.

[91] V. H. Vroom and A. G. Jago, *The New Leadership: Managing Participation in Organizations* (Englewood Cliffs, NJ: Prentice Hall, 1988).

[92] J. Thibaut and L. Walker, *Procedural Justice: A Psychological Analysis* (Hillsdale, NJ: Erlbaum, 1975); M. A. Korsgaard, L. Roberson, and R. D. Rymph, "What Motivates Fairness? The Role of Subordinate Assertive Behavior on Manager's Interactional Fairness," *Journal of Applied Psychology,* October 1998:731; M. A. Konovsky, "Understanding Procedural Justice and Its Impact on Business Organizations," *Journal of Management*, 2000:489–511; J. A. Colquitt and J. Greenberg, "Organizational Justice: A Fair Assessment of the State of the Literature," in J. Greenberg, ed., *Organizational Behavior: The State of the Science*, 2nd ed. (Mahwah, NJ: Lawrence Erlbaum Associates, 2003).

[93] For a discussion of terminology appropriate to this research, see G. S. Leventhal, "What Should Be Done with Equity Theory? New Approaches to the Study of Fairness in Social Relationships," in K. Gergen, M. Greenberg, and R. Willis, eds., *Social Exchange: Advances in Theory and Research* (New York: Plenum Press, 1980):27–55.

[94] G. S. Leventhal, "What Should Be Done with Equity Theory? New Approaches to the Study of Fairness in Social Relationships," in K. Gergen, M. Greenberg, and R. Willis, eds., *Social Exchange: Advances in Theory and Research* (New York: Plenum Press, 1980):27–55. See also R. Cropanzano and J. Greenberg, "Progress in Organizational Justice: Tunneling through the Maze," in C. L. Cooper and I. T. Robertson, eds., *International Review of Industrial and Organizational Psychology 2* (New York: John Wiley, 1997):317–372.

[95] T. Tyler, P. Degoey, and H. Smith, "Understanding Why the Justice of Group Procedures Matters: A Test of the Psychological Dynamics of the Group-Value Model," *Journal of Personality & Social Psychology 70* (5), May 1996:913–930.

[96] D. P. Skarlicki and R. Folger, "Retaliation in the Workplace: The Roles of Distributive, Procedural, and Interactional Justice," *Journal of Applied Psychology 82*, 1997:434–443.

[97] K. Leung and E. A. Lind, "Procedural Justice and Culture: Effects of Culture, Gender, and Investigator Status on Procedural Preferences," *Journal of Personality & Social Psychology 50*, 1986:1134–1140.

[98] R. Cropanzano and J. Greenberg, "Progress in Organizational Justice: Tunneling through the Maze," in C. L. Cooper and I. T. Robertson, eds., *International Review of Industrial and Organizational Psychology 2* (New York: John Wiley, 1997):317–372.

[99] M. A. Konovsky, "Understanding Procedural Justice and Its Impact on Business Organizations," *Journal of Management 26* (3), 2000:489–512.

[100] G. P. Latham and B. J. Finnegan, "Perceived Practicality of Unstructured, Patterned and Situational Interviews," in H. Schuler, J. L. Farr, and M. Smith, eds., *Personnel Selection and Assessment: Individual and Organizational Perspectives* (Hillsdale, NJ: Erlbaum, 1993):41–55.

[101] D. E. Conlon and W. H. Ross, "The Effects of Partisan Third Parties on Negotiator Behavior and Outcome Perception,"

Journal of Applied Psychology 78, 1993:280–290; R. H. Lowe and S. H. Vodanovich, "A Field Study of Distributive and Procedural Justice as Predictors of Satisfaction and Organizational Commitment," *Journal of Business and Psychology 10,* 1995:99–114.

[102] J. Brockner and B. M. Wiesenfeld, "An Integrative Framework for Explaining Reactions to Decisions: The Interactive Effects of Outcomes and Procedures," *Psychological Bulletin 120,* 1996:189–208.

[103] R. J. Bies and J. S. Moag, "Interactional Justice: Communication Criteria of Fairness," in R. Lewicki, M. Bazerman, and B. Sheppard, eds., *Research on Negotiation in Organizations 1* (Greenwich, CT: JAI Press, 1986):43–55.

[104] R. Folger and R. Cropanzano, *Organizational Justice and Human Resource Management* (Thousand Oaks, CA: Sage, 1998).

[105] R. J. Bies and J. S. Moag, "Interactional Justice: Communication Criteria of Fairness," in R. Lewicki, M. Bazerman, and B. Sheppard, eds., *Research on Negotiation in Organizations 1* (Greenwich, CT: JAI Press, 1986):43–55.

[106] M. R. Banaji, M. H. Bazerman, Max H., and D. Chugh, "How (Un)Ethical Are You?" *Harvard Business Review 81* (12), December 2003:56–64.

[107] W. M. Hoffman and E. S. Petry Jr., "Business Ethics at Bentley College," *Moral Education Forum 16,* Fall 1991:1–8.

[108] A. B. Carroll, "The Pyramid of Corporate Social Responsibility: Toward the Moral Management of Organizational Stakeholders," *Business Horizons 34* (4), 1991:39–48.

[109] G. R. Weaver, L. K. Trevino, and P. L. Cochran, "Corporate Ethics Practices in the Mid-1990s: An Empirical Study of the Fortune 1000," *Journal of Business Ethics,* February 1999:283–294.

[110] S. J. Vitell and J. G. P. Paolillo, "A Cross-Cultural Study of the Antecedents of the Perceived Role of Ethics and Social Responsibility," *Business Ethics: A European Review 13* (2–3), July 2004:185–199.

[111] W. M. Hoffman and E. S. Petry Jr., "Business Ethics at Bentley College," *Moral Education Forum 16,* Fall 1991:1–8.

[112] A. Sagie and Z. Aycan, "A Cross-Cultural Analysis of Participative Decision Making in Organizations," *Human Relations 56* (4), April 2003:453–473.

[113] G. Klein, "The Recognition-Primed Decision (RPD) Model: Looking Back, Looking Forward," in C. E. Zsambok and G. Klein, eds., *Naturalistic Decision Making* (Mahwah, NJ: Erlbaum, 1997):285–292.

[114] G. Klein, *Sources of Power: How People Make Decisions* (Cambridge, MA: MIT Press, 1998).

[115] "Understanding & Supporting Decision Making: An Interview with Gary Klein," *Information Knowledge Systems Management 2* (4), 2001:291–296.

[116] G. Klein, *Sources of Power: How People Make Decisions* (Cambridge, MA: MIT Press, 1998):147.

[117] R. E. Mayer, *Thinking, Problem Solving, and Cognition,* 2nd ed. (New York: Freeman, 1992).

[118] L. G. Militello and R. J. B. Hutton, "Applied Cognitive Task Analysis (ACTA): A Practitioner's Toolkit for Understanding Cognitive Task Demands," *Ergonomics 41* (11), November 1998:1618–41.

[119] B. Fischoff and P. Slovic, "A Little Learning . . .: Confidence in Multicue Judgment Tasks," in R. Nickerson, ed., *Attention and Performance 8* (Hillsdale, NJ: Erlbaum, 1980).

[120] "Survey: The Real-Time Economy, Timely Technology," *The Economist,* January 31, 2002. Accessed May 2004.

[121] A. McAfee, "Do You Have Too Much IT?" *MIT Sloan Management Review 45* (3), Spring 2004:18–21.

[122] J. B. Barsanti, "Expert systems: Critical success factors for their implementation," *Information Executive 3* (1):30–34.

[123] *Webster's Encyclopedic Unabridged Dictionary of the English Language* (New York: Portland House, 1989).

[124] J. Rau, *Secrets from the Search Firm Files* (New York: McGraw Hill Trade, 1997).

[125] P. F. Drucker, "What Makes an Effective Executive," *Harvard Business Review 82* (6), June 2004:58–63.

[126] M. Castelluccio, "Google—An Index for the World," *Strategic Finance 84* (11), May 2003:51–52.

[127] "Managers to Watch,"(cover story) *Business Week,* Issue 3865, January 12, 2004: 65.

[128] B. Elgin, "Managing Google's Idea Factory," *BusinessWeek* Issue 3953, October 3, 2005:88–90.

[129] "The Google Culture," http:// www.google.com/corporate/culture.html. Accessed October 5, 2006.

[130] M. Mangalindan, "The Grown-Up at Google," *Wall Street Journal–Eastern Edition, 243* (61) March 29, 2004:B1, B5 :B1.

[131] M. Mangalindan, "The Grown-Up at Google," *Wall Street Journal–Eastern Edition, 243* (61) March 29, 2004:B1, B5 :B5.

[132] M. Mangalindan, "The Grown-Up at Google," *Wall Street Journal–Eastern Edition, 243* (61) March 29, 2004:B1, B5 :B1.

[133] "Inside Google's New-Product Process," *BusinessWeek Online,* June 30, 2006, http://www.businessweek.com. Accessed September 16, 2006.

[134] K. D. Elsbach and R. M. Kramer, "Assessing Creativity in Hollywood Pitch Meetings: Evidence for a Dual-Process Model of Creativity Judgments," *Academy of Management Journal 46* (3), June 2003:283–301:296.

[135] K. D. Elsbach and R. M. Kramer, "Assessing Creativity in Hollywood Pitch Meetings: Evidence for a Dual-Process Model of Creativity Judgments," *Academy of Management Journal 46* (3), June 2003:283–301:296.

[136] C. Ford, "A Theory of Individual Creative Action in Multiple Social Domains," *Academy of Management Review 21,* 1996:1112–1142.

[137] P. Waldman and D. Clark, "California Charges Dunn, 4 Others in HP Scandal," *The Wall Street Journal Online* October 5, 2006:A1. http://online.wsj.com/article/SB115997015390082371-search.html?KEYWORDS=mark+hurd&COLLECTION=wsjie/6month. Accessed October 5, 2006.

[138] P. Lattman, "Have You Hurd? Apple & HP's CEOs Have Kept Their Jobs," *The Wall Street Journal Online* October 5, 2006. http://blogs.wsj.com/law/2006/10/05/hurd-and-jobs-keep-their-jobs/. Accessed October 5, 2006.

[139] J. Plender and A. Persaud, "The Day Dr. Evil Wounded a Financial Giant," *The Financial Times,* August 22, 2006, http://search.ft.com/searchArticle?queryText=the+day+dr+evil&y=0&javascriptEnabled=true&id=060822007792&x=0. Accessed October 5, 2006.

[140] J. Plender and A. Persaud, "The Day Dr. Evil Wounded a Financial Giant," *The Financial Times,* August 22, 2006, http://search.ft.com/searchArticle?queryText=the+day+dr+evil&y=0&javascriptEnabled=true&id=060822007792&x=0. Accessed October 5, 2006.

[141] C. Chao and S. Horng. "Development and Cost-Effective Application of an Expert System for Improving Productivity: A Real-World Case Study, " *International Journal of Management 20* (3), September 2003:360–376.

4 Fundamentals of Motivation

Advanced Software Systems, Inc. (Assyst)

Sunil Kuman is the President of Advanced Software Systems, Inc., a company that provides integration services to both commercial and government enterprises. In the late 1990s, as other high technology companies were going bust, Mr. Kumar (see photograph) made two decisions that paid off. One was to focus on government as a customer. The other was to keep the company private and to grow the business by involving employees in an ESOP—an employee stock ownership plan. The ESOP, established by Assyst in 2000, gives employees ownership of the company, and provides both the company and its owners considerable tax deductions. Retained earnings are plowed back into the business. Although ESOPs vary in their design, and some designs are controversial, this one seems to be working.

One challenge of the plan is to reach out to employees and help them really understand that it is something for the long term. The ESOP is not a stock option plan. You cannot sell stocks in an ESOP until you leave the company or retire. At the same time, all employees in the company are shareholders. A trust owns the stock for them, and their valuation is the amount of stock they have times the price of the stock.

Another challenge is the paperwork. At the beginning of every year the company has to provide details of its profit and loss and a forecast for the next three to five years. Since stock is an important component of the wage, management has to learn to estimate future earnings consistently so that the forecasted earnings and actual earnings are as close as possible. However, the plan appears to be highly motivating. As one employee puts it, you watch out for what other employees are doing. If another employee is abusing something, they are kind of abusing you, too." There is also greater openness and a general family atmosphere in which everyone shares both successes and pressures.

Management expects that over the years employees will learn to think out of their normal realm of control and figure out how to bring the company even more business. Already clients see the company in a favorable light because an employee-owned company is seen as relatively stable. Also, there is more job security, and turnover is only 6 percent. The company believes its future looks extremely optimistic. Employee ownership encourages entrepreneurship among all organizational members, and they are always enthusiastic to adopt new services and technology that will help the company to grow . . . perhaps phenomenally.

motivation

An individual's direction, intensity, and persistence of effort in attaining a goal.

intrinsic motivators

Inner influences that cause a person to act.

extrinsic motivators

External influences that cause a person to act, including both rewards and punishments.

To succeed in your job, you must be able to motivate yourself. To implement organizational decisions, you must be able to motivate others. When you are trying to improve someone's motivation, including your own, should you count on "will power"? rewards? social pressures? In this chapter you will explore the principles of motivation that are most likely to be useful guides as you address this complicated puzzle.

Motivation is an individual's direction, intensity, and persistence of effort in attaining a goal.[1] To motivate, you must be able to influence 1) what behaviors people choose, 2) how much effort they exert, and 3) how long they maintain their efforts toward attaining organizational goals.

What Makes People Work Harder, Smarter, and More Positively?

Motivators fall into two categories.[2] **Intrinsic motivators** are inner influences that cause a person to act. They include personality, emotion, needs, motives, goals, and expectations. **Extrinsic motivators** are external influences that cause a person to act, including both rewards and punishments. Of course, as marketing and other motivation experts know, intrinsic and extrinsic motivators interact all the time. Show a customer an innovative product (extrinsic) and suddenly they "need" it (intrinsic). Conversely, a person's expectations can be so high (intrinsic) that no product or reward (extrinsic) will satisfy them. Thus motivation is really an interactive process between individuals and their environment, between the internal and the external.

Motivation Is a Complex Process

To see some of the many variables that affect a person's motivation, take a look at the model by Edwin A. Locke and Gary P. Latham shown in Figure 4.1.

Overall, Locke's and Latham's model reflects what we have just said, that who you are and the goals you set interact with numerous factors in your organizational environment to influence personal and organizational outcomes. Note, for instance, the large variety of influences that lead up to performance and outcomes.

Yet even such a comprehensive picture of the motivation process fails to make explicit some motivational factors that researchers have targeted in recent years, including instinct, energy, and emotion. It is primarily a cognitively based model that focuses on "cold" thinking processes to the exclusion of the "hot" emotional processes that today are considered to be important as well.[3]

Money—the Universal Reinforcer

To illustrate just how complex the process of motivation is, let's think for a moment about a motivator we all understand: money. Assume for the sake of argument that you are a young person seeking your first real paycheck and that you are thinking "I will do *anything* for money!" Really? Anything?

Your boss directs you to constantly criticize your employees in order to "motivate" them. Will you comply "for the money"? Your boss humiliates you every day. Will you stick around "for the money"? You might answer, "Well, it all depends. . . . How much criticism? How much humiliation?" And, of course, "How much money?" On the other hand, you might assert categorically, based on your personal values, simply no, and that no amount of money will motivate you to say anything different.

Consider the issue of money in terms of Abraham Maslow's classic theory of motivation.[4] Maslow proposed (too simplistically, as it turned out) that people prioritize their needs in this order: 1) physiological needs, 2) safety needs, 3) social needs, 4) esteem needs, and 5) self-actualization needs. In other words, people take care of 1) their hunger and shelter and sexual needs before they worry about 2) making themselves safe from physical and mental harm, and after these two needs are fulfilled they go on to worry about what are known as "higher order needs," which are 3) feeling loved and accepted, 4) achieving self-respect, achievement, and autonomy and 5) achieving their full personal potential (called

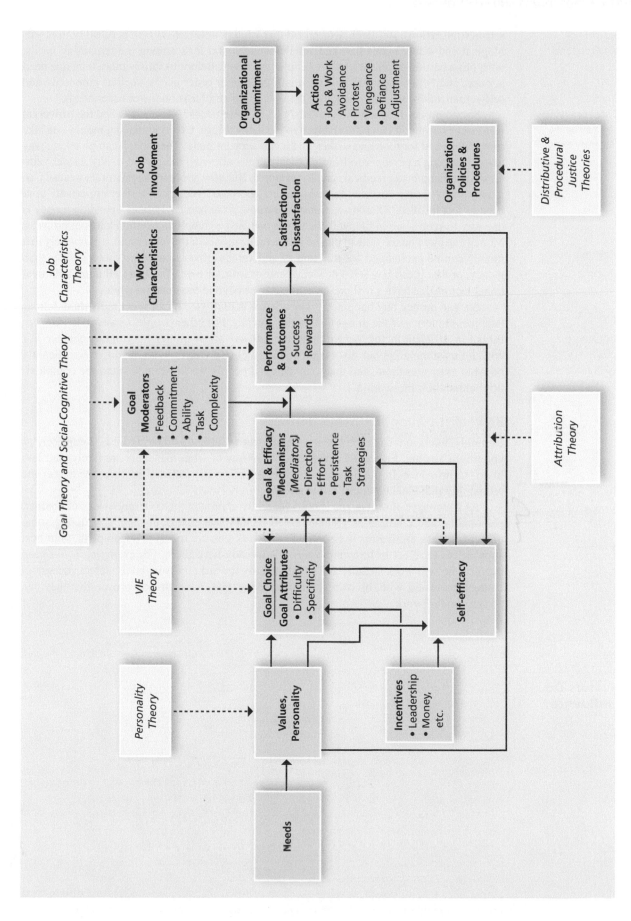

FIGURE 4.1   An Integrated Model of Work Motivation

Source: E. A. Locke and G. P. Latham, "What Should We Do About Motivation Theory? Six Recommendations for the 21st Century," *Academy of Management Review* 29(1), July 2004:388–403, 390. See also E. Locke, "The Motivation to Work: What We Know," in M. Maehr and Pintrich, eds. *Advances in Motivation and Achievement*, Vol. 10 (Greenwich, CT: JAI Press, 1997): 375–412. Academy of Management Review by E. A. Locke & G. P. Latham. Copyright 2001 by Academy of Management (NY). Reproduced with permission of The Academy of Management (NY).

self-actualization
Achieving one's full personal potential.

universal reinforcer
Money, because it can be exchanged for so many things.

self-actualization). Research determined that what people *actually* do is fulfill both physiological and safety needs first and simultaneously, and that, among the remaining needs, none has a particular priority.[5] Also, people will often attempt to satisfy more than one need at once, and, when their attempts to satisfy the higher order needs, such as autonomy and self-actualization, are frustrated, they then put more emphasis on lower order needs.[6]

So can money help a person to satisfy all of these needs? Money is called the **universal reinforcer** because it can be exchanged for so many things. Certainly having money can take care of the need for food and shelter, and it can attract a mate. Then too, it can go a long way toward keeping a person safe from physical harm—allowing the person to buy a safer vehicle or command better medical care, for example. But how about the higher order needs? Can money really meet your need to be loved and accepted? your need to feel important? your need to feel fulfilled? Of course, money can throw great parties. Further, spending money is one way to keep score in life, with the things one buys symbolizing certain kinds of prowess. Money can buy you the time to pursue self-actualization. On the other hand, it is unlikely that money can be exchanged for the kind of self-esteem that is based on factors other than money, or that it can buy self-knowledge and growth, or love. These are all human motivational factors that have a real presence in our lives beyond the material world.

So, can money buy happiness? The answer is that, yes, it can, *if* an individual defines happiness in terms of the things that money can buy. For other people, however, it is a helpful but insufficient factor. We will have more to say about money later in this chapter. For now, let us summarize our discussion so far by noting that individuals differ significantly on what motivates them, and that to understand people we must understand the complexities behind their motivation.

Be Realistic About Motivating Others

Certainly, managers can motivate their employees, but not as directly or as completely as you might assume. Figure 4.2 presents an overview of what managers are likely, and less likely, to influence. In the figure, the farther the motivator is from the core, the higher the probability that a manager can influence it.

As a manager of others you should generally approach the core motivators of instinct, personality, and emotion as predetermined factors you cannot change. If utilizing some aspects of these motivators is essential to the work you are trying to accomplish, your best approach is to select or hire employees that already have them. For example, if you need people who will work steadily and evenhandedly toward company goals, select successful college graduates, who, by completing their education, have already proven that they can do this kind of work.

FIGURE 4.2

What Motivators Do Managers Influence?

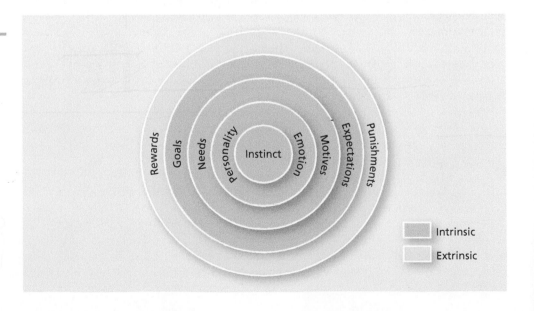

Once employees are on the job, you will be able to influence some needs and motives, but not others. However, you can certainly influence people's goals and expectations in the organization, and you also control many organizational rewards and punishments.

How Can a Manager Tap an Employee's Intrinsic Motivation?

The main intrinsic factors that motivate us are our personality, emotions, needs and motives, goals, and beliefs. Although researchers separate and identify these concepts in order to study them, they certainly interact with one other. Personality and emotion are both grounded in our physiology, for example, and our emotional states affect our goals. Managers can tap some aspects of intrinsic motivation more easily than others. For example, they are likely to select for personality, because it is relatively unchangeable. On the other hand, they are likely to try to influence an individual's goals, beliefs, and expectations.

Personality

It is reasonable to assume that individuals are motivated in some way by each of the Big Five personality factors. For example, a tendency to extraversion and energy suggests that a person is motivated to pursue social and also exciting behaviors. A tendency to tough-mindedness increases the probability that when pushed, an individual will become stubborn and not exert much effort. A tendency to conscientiousness suggests a person will persevere in a task.

However, the research identifying the Big Five is recent enough that researchers are only beginning to explore the relationship of the five composite factors to existing theories of motivation. Meanwhile, they have already examined extensively a number of separate personality traits to discover their effects on motivation. Among the most relevant in organizational life are locus of control, core self-evaluations, and independent and interdependent self-concepts.

INTERNAL–EXTERNAL LOCUS OF CONTROL Having studied personality, you know that locus of control (LOC) is the extent to which you believe that your actions influence whether rewards, reinforcements, and other outcomes in life will come your way.[7] Whether individuals have a tendency to attribute outcomes to their own actions (internal locus of control) or to circumstances they do not control (external locus of control) is clearly related to their motivation.

For one thing, it affects individuals' expectations for future performance. When people with a high external LOC succeed or fail at a task, they do not change their expectations for their performance on subsequent tasks. Why? Because they believe they succeeded or failed not because of their own effort but because of chance or fate. Externals tend to have more absenteeism and to be less satisfied with and involved with their jobs.[8] Because externals are neither reinforced by success nor punished by failure, managers are often puzzled as to how to motivate them.[9]

In comparison, people with internal LOC are more motivated on the job, and they also earn more money.[10] They perceive that they have more autonomy and control in their work, are more satisfied with their jobs, and stay in their jobs longer.[11] Internals also tend to see their supervisors more positively.[12]

Should a manager hire internals rather than externals? Not necessarily. In terms of performance, internals do better than externals in work that requires initiative and independent action, complex information processing and learning, or high motivation with rewards contingent on greater effort.[13] However, externals perform better in work that requires compliance and conformity. If the work does not require high motivation and does not give rewards contingent on greater effort—in a situation in which the employee's hourly pay is determined by a collective bargaining agreement, for example—externals perform at least as well as internals. Also, externals are more

TABLE 4.1 Core Self-Evaluation

Instructions: Below are several statements about you with which you may agree or disagree. Using the following response scale, indicate your agreement or disagreement with each item by placing the appropriate number on the line preceding that item.

1. Strongly disagree
2. Disagree
3. Neutral
4. Agree
5. Strongly agree

1. ___2___ I am confident I get the success I deserve in life.
2. ___5___ Sometimes I feel depressed.
3. ___5___ When I try, I generally succeed.
4. ___5___ Sometimes when I fail I feel worthless.
5. ___5___ I complete tasks successfully.
6. ___1___ Sometimes, I do not feel in control of my work.
7. ___3___ Overall, I am satisfied with myself.
8. ___1___ I am filled with doubts about my competence.
9. ___3___ I determine what will happen in my life.
10. ___2___ I do not feel in control of my success in my career.
11. ___5___ I am capable of coping with most of my problems.
12. ___5___ There are times when things look pretty bleak and hopeless to me.

To get your score:

a. Add up your score for all of the odd numbered questions (Questions 1, 3, 5, 7, 9, 11) and put it here: ___23___

b. For all even-numbered questions (Questions 2, 4, 6, 8, 10, 12), which are reverse-scored, subtract your answer from 6, and then add up the total. Put your answer here: ___13___

c. Add a and b. Put your answer here: ___36___

d. Divide c by 12. This is your score: _____

e. An average score is 3.88, with a standard deviation of .54 (based on four different samples).

Source: T. A. Judge, A. Erez, J. E. Bono, and C. J. Thoresen, "The Core Self-Evaluations Scale: Development of a Measure," *Personnel Psychology 56* (2), Summer 2003:303–331. This measure is nonproprietary (free) and may be used without permission.

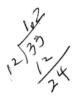

even-mannered because whether they succeed or fail on a task, their expectations for success or failure on subsequent tasks do not change.

CORE SELF-EVALUATIONS Before reading on, complete the short self-evaluation in Table 4.1. Then read the following theory behind the test.

Self-efficacy is a person's generalized belief in his or her ability to execute a course of action in any given situation.[14] Self-efficacy is related to individuals' willingness to put forth effort and perform, to persist, to be resilient in the face of failure, to solve problems effectively, and to maintain self-control.[15] Having a high sense of self-efficacy results in greater success in new endeavors, and this success, in turn, reinforces one's initial assessment of self-efficacy.[16] In short, having a high sense of self-efficacy is highly motivating.

The test you have just taken is the Core Self-Evaluations Scale, which measures self-efficacy in combination with internal locus of control, emotional stability, and self-esteem.[17] Individuals with a higher positive self-evaluation are more productive at

self-efficacy

A person's generalized belief in his or her ability to execute a course of action in any given situation.

work,[18] and they have more job satisfaction and life satisfaction as well.[19] It remains to be seen how individuals can improve their own self-concept and whether managers can influence a person's positive self-concept by showing them they can be effective on the job.

INDEPENDENT AND INTERDEPENDENT SELF-CONCEPTS People who have an image of themselves as autonomous individuals are known as **independents**. They believe that their rights and feelings outweigh those of the groups to which they belong. In contrast, **interdependents** think of themselves as linked with others through their status and social roles. They focus on the stability and harmonious functioning of their group.[20]

Independents generally live in cultures that value **individualism**, which is the emphasis on the importance of individual freedoms and rights often found in developed Western countries such as the United States. Interdependents are likely to live in countries that value **collectivism**, an emphasis on social harmony and stability that is often found in Asia and the Southern Hemisphere.[21]

In general, independents are motivated to help themselves, whereas interdependents are motivated to help their groups. The implication for managers is that they need to take these differences into account when they move between the two types of cultures and attempt to motivate individuals with these different self-concepts. For example, managers might emphasize individually based rewards in one culture and group-based rewards in another.

independents
People who think of themselves as autonomous individuals.

interdependents
People who think of themselves as linked with others through their status and social roles.

individualism
An emphasis on the importance of individual freedoms and rights.

collectivism
An emphasis on social harmony and stability.

Emotion

You are already familiar with the idea that emotions are temporary feelings of pleasure and displeasure, and of activation and deactivation.[22] Based on this way of thinking, Figure 4.3 depicts our core emotions on a two-dimensional scale based on a) how pleasant they are and b) how activated, or energized, we feel when experiencing them.

Emotions are primitive and universal, based on a constant stream of physical changes that we experience both consciously and unconsciously.[23] At every moment, one is experiencing some sort of emotional state which can be neutral, as indicated by the center point of Figure 4.3, or a blend of the two dimensions.

How do our core emotions influence motivation? For one thing, it seems that we humans automatically and continually evaluate our ongoing experiences relative to our goals,[24] and our emotions act as a sort of barometer of how well we "feel" we are doing. For example, our emotions suggest to us whether the current situation is safe or not.[25] Emotions are also a primary driver of where we focus our conscious attention, affecting how we set goals and make decisions.[26] They can even motivate in and of themselves because they may create a state of disequilibrium that we find uncomfortable.[27]

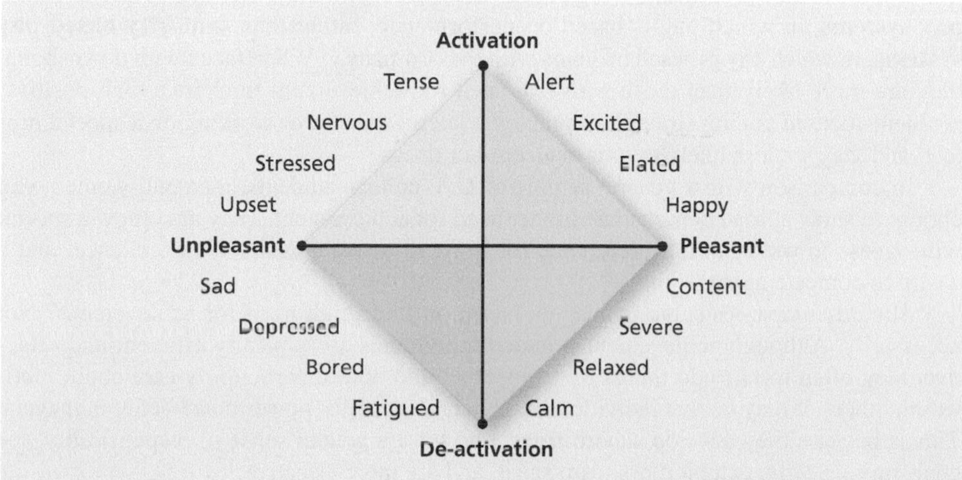

FIGURE 4.3

The Two-Dimensional Structure of Core Emotions

Source: M. Seo, L. F. Barrett, and J. M. Bartunek, "The Role of Affective Experience in Work Motivation," *Academy of Management Review* 29 (3), July 2004:423–439, 426. Copyright 2004 by Academy of Management (NY). Reproduced with permission of The Academy of Management (NY).

Having studied decision making in Chapter 3, you know that whether you are experiencing positive or negative core emotions also affects how you make decisions. People feeling positive emotions tend to have a higher expectation that their chosen course of action will lead to a successful outcome, suggesting they are more likely than people in negative-feeling states to persevere in a course of action.[28]

Finally, emotions can be activated outside of our conscious awareness, leaving us vulnerable to a variety of environmental influences. Even an exposure to an emotion-evoking stimulus that is as short as 1/250 of a second, so fast as to be outside of our awareness, can affect our attitudes and motivation.[29]

In conclusion, it is clear that emotions motivate people as they work, and that, depending on the situation, they have both productive and counterproductive influences. So-called negative emotions such as anxiety and stress, when not extreme, actually motivate people to do better in situations where precision and thoroughness are important. Although the so-called positive emotions enhance creativity and flexibility, they can also foster overconfidence and perseverance in situations where such behaviors are unwarranted.

Needs and Motives

needs
Unconscious patterns, some developed early in life and some perhaps instinctive, that lead to emotional and behavioral preferences.

Needs are unconscious patterns, some developed early in life and some perhaps instinctive, that lead to emotional and behavioral preferences.[30] David McClelland identified three needs that are especially important in organizational life: the need for power, the need for achievement, and the need for affiliation. Humanistic psychologists suggest there are six universal human needs: autonomy, personal growth, positive relations with others, purpose in life, environmental mastery, and self-acceptance.[31] Evolutionary psychologists have identified still more needs, arguing that humans instinctively need to reproduce and preserve life.[32]

need for achievement
The desire to succeed by setting and reaching goals.

need for power
The desire for dominance and social control.

need for affiliation
The desire to establish and deepen social relationships.

MCCLELLAND'S NEEDS THEORY The **need for achievement** is the desire to succeed by setting and reaching goals. Managers who have a high need for achievement focus on their accomplishments. The **need for power** is the desire for dominance and social control. Managers with a high need for power focus on building power through influencing others. The **need for affiliation** is the desire to establish and deepen social relationships. Managers with a high need for affiliation focus on improving their personal popularity.

The need for achievement has received a great deal of research attention. People with a high need for achievement are motivated most strongly by tasks that are neither too easy nor too hard.[33] This happens because, although they appreciate a challenge, they also do not want to fail. In contrast, those with a low need for achievement prefer the really easy or the really hard tasks. If they succeed, they maintain a positive self-image, whereas if they fail, they can rationalize that the task was so difficult the failure did not reflect on them personally.

merit-based pay systems
Pay systems in which pay is based on performance.

seniority-based pay systems
Pay systems in which pay is based on years with the company.

It follows that people with a high need for achievement are motivated by **merit-based pay systems**, in which pay is based on performance, rather than **seniority-based pay systems**, in which pay is based on years with the company.[34] When faced with downsizing, they are more likely than those with low need for achievement to choose such positive, problem-focused coping strategies as taking a lateral transfer or working on a special project, and they are less likely to turn to alcohol or drugs.[35]

In comparison with a general sample of U.S. college students, men and women who choose to study abroad demonstrate higher need for achievement. They also show a special willingness to work hard, a preference for difficult tasks, a desire for excellence, and a desire to compete against others.[36]

Should companies select managers based on their high need for achievement? Not necessarily. Although achievement-oriented individuals are typically efficient and effective, they often want to do things by themselves and do not particularly care about motivating others. It may be that individuals with a high need for power make better managers. This is because they develop subordinates who have a greater sense of responsibility, see goals more clearly, exhibit more team spirit, and are more effective.[37]

HUMANISTIC NEEDS Humanistic writers argue that, if today's companies hope to motivate their knowledge workers, as well as workers who face continual job uncertainty, managers should pay attention to meeting individual needs such as personal growth and purpose in life.[38] Companies that can make work meaningful to their employees can motivate and retain them, they assert. Giving individuals autonomy in decision making, providing opportunities for personal growth through challenging assignments and training, encouraging positive interpersonal relationships and social support on the job, relating the work the company does to the individual's overall purpose in life, and encouraging self-acceptance can all enhance meaning.

Aligned with this way of thinking is the notion of **humanistic capitalism**, based in companies that foster humane behavior and the appreciation and preservation of human achievements.[39] Quality of work life programs aimed at making work a more creative experience, redesigning organizations to reduce bureaucratic-style management, and the growth of corporate philanthropy are all seen as positive signs in a trend toward work that is "fulfilling, fun, and part of an integrated plan to accomplish a personal mission."[40]

> **humanistic capitalism**
> The idea that companies should foster humane behavior and the appreciation and preservation of human achievements.

THE NEEDS TO REPRODUCE AND PRESERVE LIFE Researchers in the field of **sociobiology** suggest that the most fundamental, instinctual, human needs are to reproduce and preserve life.[41] They assert that these genetically predetermined needs can be met in part through organizations, in which personality predicts success. For example, extraverts are likely to identify the social hierarchies in their organizations, figure out who has power and who can be trusted, and use these hierarchies to become personally successful. Further, being agreeable, emotionally stable, conscientious and open may result in a greater likelihood of being promoted to a higher paying position. This greater economic success results in a higher likelihood of 1) finding a partner with whom to have children and 2) of living in a safe environment that preserves the family.

Unlike most of the theories presented in this book, the theories of sociobiology remain untested, in part because testing them is difficult. At this point they are as much belief as fact, and because of their complexity, critics suggest that testing them will be a long-term challenge.[42]

> **sociobiology**
> A field that studies how natural selection, previously used only to explain the evolution of physical characteristics, shapes behavior in animals and humans.

EXPLICIT MOTIVES **Explicit motives** are the reasons people give for their actions.[43] For example, a person might explain their many friendships by asserting, "I am a people person." Unlike implicit motives (which are also called "needs"), explicit motives are conscious. They can be categorized according to themes, such as the set of reasons you give for your achievements or the set of reasons you give for wanting power.[44]

People differ as to whether they have primarily **extrinsic** or primarily **intrinsic aspirations**.[45] People with extrinsic aspirations have explicit motives such as enhancing their wealth, image, and popularity. People with intrinsic aspirations have explicit motives such as enhancing their self-acceptance, personal affiliations, and community contribution.

A classic set of explicit managerial motives is summarized by the Theory X versus Theory Y model proposed by Douglas McGregor.[46] On the one hand, **Theory X managers**:

> **explicit motives**
> The reasons people give for their actions; conscious motives.
>
> **extrinsic aspirations**
> Explicit motives that are materialistic and social.
>
> **intrinsic aspirations**
> Explicit motives that are psychological and interpersonal.

- tell their people what to do,
- judge their performance,
- and reward and punish them.

> **Theory X managers**
> Managers who tell their people what to do, judge their performance, and reward and punish them.

Their explicit motives for these actions are their beliefs that a manager's job is primarily to assess productivity; that the average person seeks security above all, prefers to be directed, and has relatively little ambition; and that the human dislike of work is so strong that generally no reward is strong enough to overcome it.

In contrast, **Theory Y managers**:

- emphasize relationships
- encourage self-control
- encourage active and responsible participation of individuals in decisions affecting their careers.

> **Theory Y managers**
> Managers who emphasize relationships, encourage self-control, and encourage active and responsible participation of individuals in decisions affecting their careers.

Their explicit motives are their beliefs that they should create a climate conducive to individual employees' growth; that the capacity for imagination, ingenuity, and creativity in problem-solving is widely distributed in the population; and that companies should move decisions downward in the organization to maximize individual responsibility and encourage learning.

Goals

Goals are major motivators in both organizational and private life, and the process of setting goals has been researched extensively. When motivating yourself or others it is a good idea to follow several well-established principles for goal setting.

SET SPECIFIC GOALS A review of nearly 400 goal setting studies indicates that, for a variety of both mental and physical tasks, setting specific goals is more motivating than establishing vague directions.[47] It is better to say "I will try to study 3 hours a day" than "I will study harder, " or "I will cold call 100 customers today" rather than "I will do my best." It is even better to say "I will study from 9 until 12" and "I will make 20 calls per hour." However, this principle is subject to the limitations described next.

SET TOUGH BUT ACHIEVABLE GOALS What do you imagine motivates people the most: telling them to do their best, setting a moderately difficult goal for them to achieve, or setting a difficult goal? According to the research, individuals put forth more effort and work more persistently to attain difficult goals.[48] This holds true whether people set the goals themselves, set the goals in consultation with others, or the goals are assigned to them.[49] People tend to believe that trying for hard goals will develop their skills, prove their competence, and give them a sense of achievement. They also believe that, in contrast with pursuing easier goals, pursuing harder goals will lead to more pride and self-respect.[50]

ESTABLISH FEEDBACK FOR GOAL ACHIEVEMENT Individuals pursuing a task are likely to set their goals for improvement based on the performance feedback provided to them by the job itself, and also by their bosses, subordinates, and coworkers. This feedback is an important part of the goal-performance equation. Goal seekers who also seek feedback are more likely to be successful.

For example, in a study of employees who were requested to continuously improve their work in quantity and quality, the individuals who actively sought feedback produced more work and work of higher quality.[51] The active seekers did things like read performance reports and ask supervisors and coworkers their perceptions of their performance in order to get the feedback they needed to improve their performance.

KEEP IN MIND THAT LEARNING GOALS MOTIVATE DIFFERENTLY THAN PERFORMANCE GOALS **Learning goals** are concerned with developing competence in an activity, while **performance goals** are concerned with demonstrating competence one has already acquired. In achievement-related situations, some people have a tendency to pursue learning goals whereas others prefer to pursue performance goals.[52] For example, some salespeople enjoy the process of learning how to sell effectively, while others only care about the positive evaluations that they receive from their managers and colleagues.

Research on salespeople suggests that improving their productivity depends considerably on developing a learning orientation rather than a performance orientation. Adopting a learning approach motivates individuals to plan, to alter sales approaches depending on the situation, and to develop the confidence to use a wide variety of sales approaches.[53] People who set performance goals are likely to avoid a new challenge if they don't think they can be successful at it. Also, when they fail, they are likely to quit.[54]

ACCOUNT FOR THE LIMITATIONS OF GOAL SETTING **Goals may restrict judgment.** In some circumstances setting goals can destroy the very behaviors management hopes to increase. This is true, for example, when employees' on-the-spot judgments are an essential factor in productivity. In this circumstance, establishing specific goals restricts employee creativity and effectiveness. For example, at Nordstrom, a company famous for

learning goals
Goals concerned with developing competence in an activity.

performance goals
Goals concerned with demonstrating competence one has already acquired.

its customer support, employees are told to use their judgment in all situations when dealing with customers. Similarly, at Southwest Airlines, employees are encouraged to "do what it takes to make the customer happy."[55] These companies have learned that setting specific goals about how to behave restricts employees' ability to react creatively and effectively to their customers' varied needs.

Goals may induce unethical behavior. Another concern is revealed in a recent study of ethics and goal setting. This interesting study showed that in a laboratory setting that protected anonymity, people who had established specific goals but had not met them were more likely to lie about having achieved them than were people who had told themselves they were just "doing their best."[56] The lying occurred whether or not the individuals expected to receive a monetary reward for achieving their goals. The lying was most likely to occur when people fell just short of achieving their goals. The researchers concluded that, in general, managers need to be aware that goal setting can have unfortunate side effects, and that they should be particularly vigilant about unethical behavior when employees are close to a goal or deadline.

Beliefs and Expectations

Theories that describe how beliefs and expectations affect motivation include expectancy theory and equity theory.

EXPECTANCY THEORY Do you *believe* that if you try hard you will be able to perform well? Do you *expect* that if you perform well your performance will be rewarded? Do you *believe* that the rewards you will receive will be valuable to you?

The **expectancy theory** of motivation proposes that an individual's effort is determined primarily by his or her beliefs in three key areas.[57]

First is the belief, known as **expectancy**, that one's effort will lead to an acceptable level of performance. Although in general effort does improve performance, you can imagine circumstances in which it might not. Hard-working individuals might find that their work is sabotaged by jealous coworkers, for example. So individuals weigh whether or not they expect their performance to pay off.

Second is **instrumentality**, the belief that the performance level one achieves will result in specific positive and/or negative outcomes. This belief depends on one's previous experience with similar tasks.

Third is **valence**, the belief that the outcome attained will be personally valued. When individuals are uncertain about what might happen after their performance improves, their motivation is reduced.

Expectancy theory asserts that a person's motivation can be measured by assigning weights to each of these beliefs and then multiplying them together. The implication is that if any one of the beliefs is very low, then a person's motivation will be very low.

The validity of expectancy theory has been widely debated.[58] The theory has received some support, but it has also been criticized on the grounds that its three key variables are too vague and the theory overall is too complex to measure and apply. Nevertheless, the theory has been useful to managers because it poses important questions, encouraging them to pay attention to 1) whether employees perceive that their effort will actually lead to improved performance, 2) whether individuals perceive that their behaviors will lead to particular outcomes, and 3) understanding what outcomes an employee prefers. Managers can motivate their employees by making sure that all of these conditions are met. Suppose a manager adds a high-performing individual to a weak team in hopes that the individual will boost the team's performance. Somehow, the manager must convince that individual that his or her effort will actually improve the team's performance, and that he or she will be rewarded for the effort. The manager should also determine, in advance, whether this is the kind of challenge the employee enjoys.

EQUITY THEORY When you receive a reward, do you accept it happily and get on with your life, or do you compare it with what others have received to see how well off you "really" are? **Equity theory** predicts that you will weigh the ratio of your effort (and other

---

expectancy theory
A theory of motivation which proposes that one's effort is determined primarily by one's beliefs in three key areas: expectancy, instrumentality, and valence.

expectancy
The belief that one's effort will lead to an acceptable level of performance.

instrumentality
The belief that the performance level one achieves will result in specific positive and/or negative outcomes.

valence
The belief that the attained outcome will be personally valued.

equity theory
A theory which predicts that one will weigh the ratio of one's effort (and other job inputs such as one's experience and ability) to one's rewards against that of others.

job inputs, such as your experience and ability) to your rewards against that of others.[59] If you discover an inequity, there will be negative consequences for you and your organization.

For example, if you worked hard and achieved a bonus, but your colleague worked little and achieved the same bonus, you perceive an inequity. Because you feel you have been treated unfairly, you may become dissatisfied with your job and less committed to your company, and you are likely to be absent more often and might even quit.[60] On the other hand, if you believe you have been treated fairly, and if your job demands are reasonable rather than extreme, you are likely to perform better and feel more satisfied.[61]

One interesting question is "What is your standard for comparison?" You might compare yourself with others you know within your company—for instance, those who have similar abilities and training or others in your job category—as well as others you know outside of your company—for instance, others in your profession.[62] Most likely you develop a mental set of a variety of people that you use simultaneously for the sake of comparison. Alternatively, you may simply weigh your own investment of skills and energy against the outcomes you personally achieve.[63]

distributive justice
The perceived fairness of outcomes in terms of how rewards and resources are allocated in an organization

To deal with perceived inequities and their negative outcomes for an organization, managers attempt to achieve **distributive justice**, the perceived fairness of outcomes in terms of how rewards and resources are allocated in an organization.[64] Although recent research suggests that measuring distributive justice can be problematic for researchers,[65] the importance of the process for managers remains undisputed. Managers typically have to decide, for example, whether distributing rewards and resources based on an employee's contribution is better than distributing them based on need.

When trying to be fair, managers must take into account existing organizational and social norms. The most prominent norms affecting how rewards are allocated are equality, merit, need, and efficiency.[66] Individuals generally weigh all or most of these principles simultaneously when making judgments about fairness. Thus, being perceived as fair remains a complicated problem for managers.

How Do Managers Motivate Using Rewards and Punishments?

Behavior modification theory suggests that our behavior is controlled by extrinsic factors—namely, the reinforcements and punishments that come our way from our environment.[67] When used in the workplace, behavior modification is often referred to as **OB mod** (organizational behavior modification).[68]

OB Mod
Organization behavior modification: An approach that focuses on changing behavior using reward and punishment.

Classic behavior modification as taught by psychologist B. F. Skinner and applied in organizations focuses on changing observable behaviors.[69] For example, managers would use OB mod to motivate people to wear their safety goggles, but they would probably not use it to enhance employee commitment. Although theorists after Skinner suggested that the reinforcement–punishment technique could also be used for understanding and influencing cognitive behavior,[70] in recent years this approach has received little attention by either scholars or managers.

So, in organizations, as elsewhere, the goal of an OB mod program is to change observable behaviors. Because the behaviors are observable, they are also quantifiable. Of course, for a program to be useful to a company, the behaviors identified should also be performance-related.

Imagine that a manager wants to achieve a production quota, which is not itself an observable *behavior*. An experienced manager will identify the actual behaviors that are most likely to lead to achieving the production quota. These might include unloading supplies rapidly and stocking supplies in the right place. Having identified the key behaviors, the manager will reinforce them, and perhaps punish counter-productive activities, such as being late or mis-stocking. Of course, organizational processes include thousands of behaviors. The manager's skill lies in identifying key behaviors that will affect the production quota. Also, because changing any behavior involves a fairly elaborate program and managers have limited resources, the manager must choose wisely.

The Five-Step OB Mod Approach

Behavior modification is a straightforward program of five steps.[71] Here's how it works.

STEP 1. IDENTIFY THE TARGET BEHAVIOR You choose a key performance-related behavior that is observable and quantifiable, as in the following self-management situation.

> For example, you believe you could be more productive in your job if you spent less time surfing the Web for fun, so you decide that the behavior to target is the number of minutes you spend surfing while on the job. (By the way, you are not alone: In a poll of 10,000 people, 44.7 percent said Web surfing for personal use is their number-one distraction at work.)[72]

STEP 2. ESTABLISH A BASELINE FOR THE TARGET BEHAVIOR You count the number of times the target behavior occurs naturally—that is, before you start to reinforce it. Managers establish baselines by asking individuals who perform the behavior to record it, or by employing trained observers. Each approach has its advantages. Using trained observers may be more accurate, but it is also likely to be more costly and may not be accepted by the workers observed. Asking workers to take the baseline themselves involves them, thus encouraging their acceptance and enhancing their understanding of the program. However, when individuals are involved in taking their own baseline data, it is important that everyone involved be aware that, because of their additional attention, the workers' performance is likely to improve irrespective of whether a reinforcement is being offered at that time.

> For a full week you keep a log of when, where, and how much time you spend surfing the Web while in the office. You also write notes on any other factors that seem relevant, such as what you surf for and whether others around you encourage or discourage your surfing.

STEP 3. ANALYZE THE ANTECEDENTS AND THE CONSEQUENCES OF THE BEHAVIOR This antecedents–behaviors–consequences analysis is often referred to as the **A-B-C's of behavior modification**. What are the antecedents and consequences of the target behavior? That is, what situational factors precede the behavior and give the individual some cue to initiate it? And then, what happens after the behavior is exhibited?

A-B-C's of behavior modification
Study of the interaction of the antecedents to a behavior, a behavior, and the consequences of that behavior.

> You analyze the circumstances, or antecedents, of the surfing. For example, based on your diary you observe that you tend to surf first thing in the morning when you want to read the news, and mid-afternoon when you want to plan your evening.
>
> Second, you analyze the consequences of surfing, and discover these include reduced concentration and lower productivity. For example, you figure out that once your concentration is broken by surfing, it takes half an hour for you to develop that concentration again. And that sometimes after your mid-afternoon surfing session you just throw in the towel and quit working for the rest of the day. This may be because you needed to spend time thinking about personal issues that came up in the surfing. You also analyze the existing punishment and rewards for your behavior, including such immediate factors as negative feedback from coworkers who know you are surfing, and such longer-term factors such as how surfing may affect your possibilities for a raise or promotion.

reinforcement
Any event that increases the probability of a behavior.

STEP 4. INTERVENE WITH A PROGRAM THAT EMPHASIZES REINFORCEMENT The goal in this step is to reinforce the desired behavior and extinguish any behaviors that interfere with the desired behavior. How is this done exactly? By following a logical plan to reinforce the target behavior and punish behaviors that interfere with it.

Reinforcement is any event that increases the probability of a particular behavior. You can reinforce in two ways: 1) by giving a person something he or she wants, or 2) by removing something he or she dislikes. These behavioral consequences are called, respectively, **positive reinforcement** (also called "reinforcement by application") and **negative reinforcement** (also called "reinforcement by removal"). In business, the three main reinforcements are money, feedback on performance, and recognition.[73]

positive reinforcement
Giving a person something he or she wants, to increase the probability that he or she will behave in a particular way.

negative reinforcement
Removing something a person dislikes, to increase the probability that he or she will behave in a particular way.

contingent

Given on the condition that a particular behavior is performed.

reward

A desired consequence which is typically given for general performance, rather than being contingent on specific behaviors.

punishment

Any event that decreases the probability of a behavior.

punishment by application

Doing something to a person that he or she dislikes.

punishment by removal

Taking away from a person something that he or she wants.

extinction

Stopping all rewards.

Note that negative reinforcement is not the same thing as punishment! In OB mod "negative reinforcement" is a technical term that actually means to increase the likelihood that a behavior will occur rather than to decrease that likelihood. For example, your employees have a tendency to be late. You tell them that if the behavior of being on time improves, and continues at a certain level, you will remove the detested time clock. In short, you reinforce productive behavior by removing something noxious in the employees' environment—namely, the time clock.

Note, too, that the reinforcer must be given **contingent** on the performance of the target behavior. This means that, the person only gets the reinforcer if he or she performs the behavior. If a desired consequence is not made contingently, it is often called a **reward**. Rewards are given for general performance rather than specific behaviors.

Punishment is any event that decreases the probability of a behavior. You can punish people by doing something to them that they dislike or by taking away from them something they want. These two approaches are called **punishment by application** (and sometimes "positive punishment") and **punishment by removal**. A related technique is simply stopping all rewards, which is called **extinction**.

See Figure 4.4 for a graphic overview of these concepts. The figure illustrates the four choices, in addition to extinction, that management has in intervening to change behavior, and that you have when you manage yourself. Which choice is best? The evidence is overwhelming that, whenever possible, managers, and you, should emphasize reinforcement. One reason to emphasize the positive is that a company generally hopes to create a positive culture. In addition, individuals who are punished often react with anger, avoidance, and/or aggression.

Use punishment only in the most extreme circumstances. For example, you might use punishment when an unwanted behavior is creating an unsafe situation. In some cases, extinction can be used to decrease an unwanted behavior. If punishment or extinction must be used, however, it should be accompanied by positive reinforcement of any new behaviors that are in the desired direction.[74]

Whatever consequence you choose, you should deliver it as close in time as possible to the occurrence of the target behavior. Also, rather than holding back your reinforcers until the target behavior is fully achieved, reinforce small improvements made

FIGURE 4.4

The Universe of Managerial Choices Using Reinforcement and Punishment

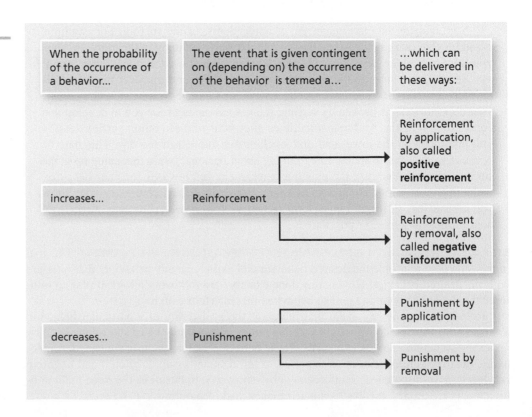

along the way. This practice is called **shaping**. Behavior change does not happen all at once. New behaviors are typically learned little by little, and reinforcing along the way enhances performance. Homework and quizzes shape behavior before a big exam, for example. Without them, the exam itself could wind up as a shock—and a punishing experience.

Throughout the process, collect data on the progress that is made. Graph the data and display it. Typical OB mod progress graphs show how performance has changed over time.

In summary, during this step of the program, you should give feedback that is:

- contingent on the occurrence of the target behavior, or some part of it,
- positive,
- specific,
- immediate, and
- graphic.

Based on your analysis, you determine that you need to cut your personal Web surfing to 10 minutes per day. However, because you are currently surfing for nearly two hours each day, stopping "cold turkey" seems impossible. Deciding that you will work gradually toward your goal, you set up a calendar with targets for each day and each week, and you establish rewards and punishments that are contingent on your meeting those targets. Use your imagination here. For example, as a reward for meeting your daily goal, each evening you could put a set amount of money into a pot, to be spent for something special at the end of the week. Or you might reward yourself with a favorite food, a call to a friend, or a particular TV show. (If you don't meet your goals, by the way, you don't get these.) You might use punishment, too: Have a friend call you at random times when you are supposed to be working rather than surfing, and if the friend catches you online, your punishment may be to pay him or her 10 bucks, or perhaps to not go out on Friday night. Sound costly? Only you can decide what it is worth to you to change your behavior.

STEP 5: EVALUATE THE INTERVENTION TO SEE IF IT CHANGED THE DESIRED BEHAVIOR At the end of the intervention, evaluate your progress using the data you have collected. Answer the question "Did the intervention lead to performance improvement in observable and quantifiable terms?" Typically, companies collect more data months or years after an intervention has ended to see if the improvement has continued.

Sometimes managers continue a reinforcement program indefinitely, but more often they **fade out** the reinforcers, reducing them systematically over a period of time. During this period they hope that workers will make the new behavior a habit, the behavior will become intrinsically motivating, and/or naturally existing reinforcers will emerge to maintain it.

After tinkering with your rewards and punishments and developing a program that really does motivate you to surf less, you meet your target of surfing only 10 minutes per workday. Presumably, you will find some satisfaction in this accomplishment. But have you also achieved better productivity? If not, you must reassess your assumption that less surfing leads to higher productivity, and you may have to design a new program around other productivity-enhancing behaviors.

Business Applications of OB Mod

OB Mod at Emery Air Freight. In a classic case, OB mod was used to improve shipping procedures in an air freight company.[75] The management of the company first did a performance audit to determine what behaviors had the most impact on profit. They determined that to reduce handling costs, employees should make better use of empty container space by consolidating small shipments. Specifically, rather than handling each small package separately, they should put small packages going to the same destination into one large package.

Next, the company measured baseline frequencies of this consolidation behavior. Whereas 90 percent of the employees believed they had been making maximum use of the

shaping
Reinforcing small improvements made along the way.

fading out
Reducing reinforcers systematically over a period of time.

empty container space, the audit team found that only 45 percent were actually doing so. Of course, as soon as the baselines were taken, performance rose.

Managers also assessed whether their employees knew how to accomplish the targeted behavior and determined they did not need further training.

Finally, managers began to reinforce the desired behavior. They had received a notebook in which 150 different types of nonmonetary rewards were suggested, including detailed praise and approving smiles. Using these simple and inexpensive techniques, they reinforced package consolidation whenever they saw it. The result of the project? Over a few years the intervention saved the company millions of dollars.

OB Mod at Stanford Group Company. In a more recent case, OB mod–based sales team training produced a large increase in revenues for a financial services company.[76] Although the company had routinely offered a variety of training programs to its sales force, it had not targeted specific behaviors that would have business results. Its training had simply been too general. It had resulted in personal development, but, as one manager put it, "Something was missing. For lack of a better word, it was accountability."[77]

After analyzing the problem, the company set two goals: to create new revenue for the firm, and to improve relationships with existing clients. Management decided it could accomplish these general goals through increasing referrals, deepening personal relationships, and expanding opportunities with existing accounts. The company then broke these goals down to a behavioral level. This level was called an "execution blueprint" and included who would do what, how they would do it, what they would say, how often it would happen, and what the potential outcomes should be.

Next, assisted by a coach, each person created a strategy for changing his or her own behavior. Each week members reported their results to their team. Interpersonal interactions with their coaches, peer pressure, and the fear of falling behind all motivated the members of the sales team. Within a few weeks they began to see results on the bottom line, which also reinforced the changed behavior.

Within six months the sales team registered a 350 percent increase in calls to initiate new sales, a 130 percent increase in referrals, a 150 percent increase in contacts with new prospects, and a 56 percent increase in revenue from new accounts.

How Do Managers Use Behavior Modification to Design Performance Appraisals and Reward Systems?

In addition to establishing the technique for organizational behavior change that you have just learned, behavior modification theory has had other significant impacts on management practices, including the design of performance appraisals and reward systems.

The Design of Performance Appraisals

The theory has influenced how performance appraisals are done. What should be the basis for a performance appraisal—a manager's judgment, performance results, or observed behaviors? One way to evaluate a person is **judgment-based evaluation**, in which a manager rates employees on traits that management has deemed to be important. For example, employees might be rated on a scale from low to high on their "willingness to take initiative" or their "honesty." Unfortunately, such evaluations are highly subject to the **halo effect**, in which a manager's overall impression of the employee, whether positive or negative, colors every item in the evaluation.[78]

Another way to evaluate employees is to use **results-based evaluation**, rating them on their performance over time. For example, managers set goals for their employees at the beginning of the year, and measure their progress by how well they have met these goals at the end of the year. This is a widely used approach that encourages setting specific goals and, often, includes employees in the goal setting process. One weakness is that it may fail to account for factors beyond the employee's control. For example, it might not adjust for the fact that a salesperson's results slump when the economy slows during the year.

judgment-based evaluation
Rating employees based on traits that management deems to be important.

halo effect
The influence of a manager's overall impression of the employee on every item of the evaluation.

results-based evaluation
Rating employees based on their performance over time.

TABLE 4.2 A Behaviorally Anchored Rating Scale Measuring Innovation

My direct supervisor. . .

1. usually objects to changes and new ideas and finds excuses why they cannot be implemented.

2. seldom experiments with new ideas or methods of doing things.

3. would be angry with me for interfering in his/her area of responsibility, so I never approach my manager with a suggested change.

4. neither encourages nor discourages new ideas from employees.

5. gives feedback to employees on their ideas and suggestions, even if they are not adopted.

6. would accompany an employee to discuss and promote the employee's idea to another manager.

7. experiments with new ideas in order to examine whether they are profitable/feasible to adopt on a large scale.

8. encourages us to discuss individual mistakes in our group, so we learn how to avoid the problem in the future.

9. sends employees to other locations in the company and elsewhere to learn about innovative processes and other ways of doing business.

10. encourages partnerships with other departments in order to implement new ideas.

In this example, a highly innovative supervisor might exhibit a behavior as high as a 10, while one who is not innovative might receive a 1.

Source: Adapted from C. A. Ramus and U. Steger, "The Roles of Supervisory Support Behaviors and Environmental Policy in Employee 'Ecoinitiatives' at Leading-Edge European Companies," *Academy of Management Journal 43* (4), August 2000:605–626.

A third way to evaluate performance is the **behaviorally based evaluation**.[79] In this OB mod approach, observable behaviors are rated on a quantifiable measure, such as their frequency, and the frequency of the behaviors is summarized in a **behaviorally anchored rating scheme** (BARS). The BARS approach rewards target behaviors and is generally perceived to be fair.

Table 4.2 is an example of a BARS evaluation question that measures a manager's innovation. It was used to assess supervisors' reactions to employees' innovative environmental ideas in European companies considered to be on the leading-edge of environmental responsibility.[80] (The study found, by the way, that even in companies with a strong environmental commitment, supervisors used less supportive behaviors when managing environmental activities, as compared with general business activities.) An employee rating the supervisor decides how supportive the supervisor is by assigning him or her a number, based on the supervisor's typical behavior, from the following list. The list begins with the least supportive behaviors and ends with the most supportive.

behaviorally based evaluation
An approach in which observable behaviors are rated on their frequency or other quantifiable measure, and these ratings are summarized in a "behaviorally anchored rating scheme" (BARS).

behaviorally anchored rating scheme (BARS)
An approach which rewards target behaviors and is generally perceived to be fair.

The Design of Reward Systems

Extensive research based on the principles of operant conditioning, which is the learning theory that is the foundation of behavior modification, tells us that the timing of reinforcers influences their impact on performance. Read through Table 4.3 to see the effect of different schedules of reinforcement on behavior.

To help you work with this chart, try taking this quiz after studying it. (You will find the answers on page 112.)

1. You want very much for your workers to improve the quality of the widgets they produce. Which schedule should you rule out?

2. You want your wait staff to use formal serving techniques at all times. Which schedule would be practical?

3. You desperately want the workers in your telephone call center to answer more calls per hour. Which schedule would be best?

4. During the week you want to put in more hours studying for this course, so you enlist a friend to "manage" you. Which schedule of reinforcement should they use?

TABLE 4.3 **Schedules of Reinforcement and Their Effects**

Schedule of Reinforcement	Definition	Example	Effect on Performance
Fixed interval	The reinforcer is given after a fixed period	Weekly paycheck	Leads to average and irregular performance
Variable interval	The reinforcer is randomly given after a variable period often determined randomly	Unannounced inspections for safety, quality, attendance); recognition visits of managers; unexpected pay raises	Leads to moderately high and stable performance: Individuals work hard so they are responding correctly when the reinforcement is offered
Fixed ratio	The reinforcer is given after a fixed number of responses	Piece work pay systems: The worker earns a fixed amount for every part produced, room cleaned, and so on	Leads quickly to very high and stable performance.
Variable ratio	The reinforcer is given after a variable number of responses, often determined randomly	A sales bonus is tied to selling a certain number of accounts, but the number varies around a mean; this is called the "slot machine effect" because the reinforcer will be received "soon"	Leads to very high performance

Answers: 1) Fixed interval: Weekly paychecks reinforce very little. 2) Variable interval: You wander randomly and unannounced through the dining room, reinforcing good behaviors with smiles, and afterwards doling out praise for good behaviors observed. 3) The "best" system would be the fixed-ratio system, in which employees' pay depends on how many calls per hour they handle and which encourages both high and stable performance. BUT prepare for a decrease in quality and an increase in customer dissatisfaction! In real life, managers have to make trade-offs between efficiency and quality. 4) Promising to take you out for a drink on Friday (fixed interval) would be a poor idea indeed: You would not be likely to increase your studying until late in the week (Friday afternoon perhaps?). Paying you a dollar every time the friend catches you studying (variable interval) would encourage you to study and to keep studying at a pretty good level. Fixed-ratio and variable-ratio schedules would not be practical unless the friend is able to count the number of hours you were studying.

The Misuse of Rewards

Managements often misuse rewards, effectively wasting them by reinforcing the wrong behaviors or no behaviors at all.[81] For example, in many companies managers hope to foster teamwork, but they continue to reward only the best team members. Or they hope for innovative thinking and risk taking, but primarily reinforce using proven methods and not making mistakes. OB mod theory encourages managers to carefully examine the relationship between the organizational behaviors they truly want and the rewards they are actually giving.

Sometimes, too, managers misuse the reward process by giving trivial awards for important contributions. For example, an employee who gives the company a cost-saving suggestion worth thousands of dollars may feel entitled to more than a coffee mug and a pat on the back.

Limitations of Behavior Modification

Behavior modification has to date been most successful when applied to simple tasks. In a manufacturing setting with well-defined, simple jobs and relatively low wages, for example, money applied as a reinforcer under the OB mod model increased performance 31.7 percent, whereas a more routine managerial intervention only increased performance 11 percent.[82] In this setting, pay had a stronger impact on performance than either social recognition or performance feedback did.

For the more complex tasks in professional and managerial work, feedback typically has the strongest effect on work performance, followed by social recognition and then money. Unfortunately, in this type of work, behavioral approaches such as BARS, while effective, are cumbersome to apply.

What Organizational Systems Do Companies Use to Motivate Their Employees?

All companies develop systems for motivating their employees. They may design their systems according to the principles of motivation we have just covered, or they may uncritically choose systems with which they have some experience. Most companies emphasize pay, but many also emphasize feedback, rewards, goals, and participation. ESOPs, described below, utilize both intrinsic and extrinsic motivation and are quite popular.

Systems That Emphasize Pay

One of the fundamental questions managers ask themselves is, "If I pay my workers more, will they perform better?" Although the research on the success of making pay contingent on general performance (called **pay for performance**) shows mixed results, in contrast, the research on using **pay** as a reinforcement for **targeted behaviors** clearly suggests that it is effective. When individuals' pay is contingent on their achieving specific targets, performance increases, on average, 33 percent in manufacturing organizations and 13 percent in service organizations.[83]

pay for performance
Making pay contingent on general performance.

pay for targeted behaviors
Making pay contingent on the achievement of specific targets.

Many organizational observers are convinced that, when designing organizational systems for motivational purposes, applying reinforcement theory is essential. As one consultant puts it, "A company is always perfectly designed to produce what it is producing. If it has quality problems, cost problems, productivity problems, then the behaviors associated with those undesirable outcomes are being reinforced. This is not conjecture. This is the hard, cold reality of human behavior."[84]

Knowing how important these principles are, some managements today are rethinking their traditional pay programs. For example, we know that it is important to make rewards contingent on performance.[85] So Home Depot pays relatively high wages, but it also expects sales associates to provide a high level of customer service. Making pay contingent on performance can occur through gain sharing (meaning that when productivity improves, so does pay), profit sharing, stock ownership, pay for skill (you are paid to improve a skill or learn new skills), and various forms of individual and team incentives.

We also know that it is important to deliver rewards close in time to the performance of the targeted behaviors.[86] Applying this principle means abandoning such traditional pay systems as weekly paychecks and end of the year bonuses. Some companies today are adopting **variable-pay programs** that blend a set salary, sometimes a relatively modest one, with pay contingent on some output measure, and they design the variable component to come close in time to the targeted behavior. For example, one company has adopted the practice that, after it has achieved its profit goal for that quarter, it makes bonus payments to workers. Another uses monthly bonuses to motivate claims processors to increase the number of calls they handle.[87] Such programs not only motivate employees, but they often also save companies money.

variable-pay programs
Programs that blend a set salary with pay contingent on some output measure.

Systems That Emphasize Feedback and Recognition

Which reward should a manager emphasize—monetary rewards, performance feedback, or recognition? An overview of all the studies that have compared these rewards suggests that it may not be cost effective for managers to spend time and financial resources on applying all three of these reinforcers simultaneously. This is because the nonfinancial reinforcers alone appear to produce the same results.[88]

In other words, if workers' pay is generally satisfactory—that is, if it seems fair and reasonable and meets their basic needs—offering modest increments in pay is not likely to change their behavior, but emphasizing feedback and recognition might. See Table 4.4, which lists some of the organizational rewards managers can use along with pay.

Systems That Emphasize Goals

Management by Objectives (MBO)
A system in which supervisors and their subordinates jointly decide the individual employee's goals for the year and pay is contingent on meeting these goals.

In a **Management by Objectives (MBO)** system supervisors and their subordinates jointly decide the individual employee's goals for the year.[89] These goals are determined in part by input from top management about the company's plan for the year, and in turn the company's plan is based on the sum of the many goals set by its employees. The employees' rewards for the year depend on how well they meet their goals. Thus the system emphasizes employee participation and goal setting along with accountability, and has the potential to tap both intrinsic and extrinsic motivators.

In 1992 MBO was widespread among *Fortune* 500 firms.[90] Today, although goal-setting programs are common, they are seldom called MBO; instead, companies are likely to use similar thinking in the management practices known as self-managed work teams or quality circles.[91] Of course, all such systems are subject to the limitations on goal setting that we have already mentioned earlier in this chapter.

Systems That Emphasize Participation

quality circles
Teams of employees who meet to discuss quality improvements.

self-managed teams
Autonomous groups that take on some of the tasks typically done by supervisors, with the theory that empowering workers will motivate them to work harder and be more committed to their organization.

Quality circles are teams of employees who meet to discuss quality improvements.[92] Adapted from Japan in the 1980s as part of organization-wide programs for Total Quality Management, the American version of quality circles lacked some of the cultural reinforcers for the practice and has recently become less popular. However, the quality circle movement increased management interest in using autonomous work groups to make decisions.

Self-managed teams are autonomous groups that take on some of the tasks typically done by supervisors.[93] The theory is that empowering workers will motivate them to work harder and be more committed to their organization. Participation in self-man-

TABLE 4.4 What Are Some Typical Organizational Rewards?

Material Rewards	Social Rewards	Task Rewards	Personal Rewards
Pay in its various forms—salary, bonuses, stock options, benefits, perks	Praise and recognition by managers and peers	Sense of accomplishment and achievement	Opportunities to learn Sense of self-worth
Job security	Promotion, both upward and laterally into desired positions	Doing something worthwhile	Career opportunities, and other longer-term chances for growth and development
Financial security		Sense of responsibility and autonomy	
	Appreciation from customers and clients		
	Respect and friendship from coworkers		

aged teams is associated with higher levels of perceived empowerment and employee satisfaction for workers, but the opposite for supervisors.[94] The use of self-managed teams has also been associated with employment reductions, leading workers to be skeptical about the practice.[95]

Systems That Maximize Intrinsic and Extrinsic Motivation

Employee stock ownership plans (ESOPs) are particular plans that allow employees to buy stock. There is a wide range of ESOPs. In some companies, employee participation is not part of the plan, and the ability to buy company stock seems to employees like just one more benefit the company offers. In other companies, such as the case of Assyst presented at the beginning of this chapter, employees feel and are treated like owners (and, indeed, in many companies they *are* owners). In these kinds of companies, the ESOPs motivate both extrinsically and intrinsically by giving employees access to financial results and business unit strategies, training them to use this information, and sharing the financial rewards with them. The employee incentive system is usually tied to the strategic priorities of the business. Instead of merely telling employees what they can gain financially if the company succeeds, managers describe the logic behind the plan and show exactly how individual rewards are tied to the business performance.

> **employee stock ownership plans (ESOPs)**
> Particular plans that allow employees to buy stock.

When ESOP programs fail to show employees the cause-and-effect relationship between work and success, between productivity and profits, they fail to motivate either intrinsically or extrinsically. According to one expert, "Too many incentive programs seem to operate behind a veil of mystery. Rewards are dangled in front of employees for faster production, higher quality, and less rework without any explanation for why speed and rework are being targeted for improvement. Simply put, the problem with many incentive programs is that they seem random and conflicting."[96]

Another problem with ESOPs is that employees are vulnerable if the value of their company stock plunges. Despite these problems, in the United States today there are about 11,000 ESOPs or similar plans covering 8.5 million employees.[97] Shareholder returns may be as much as 12 percent more than similar companies without ESOPs.[98]

When Motivating Yourself and Others, Also . . .

Weigh Recent Trends

Motivating employees is a complicated business, and most managers can learn more about how to motivate effectively.[99] In this last section, we leave you with some issues to consider as you approach motivating others and yourself.

Consider, to begin with, that with U.S. jobs becoming more information-based and complex, it will be increasingly difficult to fit workers into common molds that specify standards for individual productivity and increasingly difficult to motivate people based on such standards. In addition, the workplace has become more team-oriented, reducing opportunities for rewarding individuals. These trends suggest that companies may be wise to emphasize intrinsic motivators, like becoming the kind of company employees are proud to work for.

Second, since long-term relationships between employees and their companies are declining, the motivating value of such relationships is being lost. This raises questions about how people are energized to engage in behaviors that primarily benefit the company even though they are not particularly committed to it, and how people will sustain effort for the company in the face of organizational changes and insecure job prospects.

Finally, some theorists believe that monetary reward alone will never be a sufficient motivator because it does not reduce conflicts of interest and make people pursue common goals.[100] Perhaps the only way to build common goals for a company is to emphasize nonmaterial, human goals, such as making jobs interesting and meaningful. By this way of thinking, even profit-sharing programs are a necessary but insufficient way to motivate workers.

Take National Culture into Account

Any manager who works in a new culture must study how workers in that culture are motivated. Although the basic principles of motivation are likely to apply broadly to human beings, all learned behaviors are culture bound. For example, managerial attitudes vary across cultures. The percentage of difference in managerial job attitudes that can be attributed to nationality is estimated to be about 28 percent.[101]

Cultures differ, too, on how they value work itself. For instance, in Japan, the degree of general importance that work has in the life of the individual at any given point is high, whereas in Germany it is low.[102]

Cultures also differ in terms of the motivation systems they will accept. For example, some cultures react favorably to MBO, while others dislike these sorts of systems.[103] German managers value decentralization, two-way dialogue, a de-emphasis on hierarchy; however, they enjoy formalization—having clear goals, measuring outcomes, and making rewards contingent on behavior. So we should not be surprised that Germans favor MBO. On the other hand, because of people's ambivalent views about authority, MBO has not been favorably received in France.

Motivate Yourself to Motivate Others

Have you ever tried to improve your athletic performance, change an unhealthy habit such as smoking, or make more efficient use of your time? If you succeeded, how did you do it? If you failed, why was that?

One of the best ways to learn how to motivate others is to learn how to motivate yourself. After all, if you can't change your own behavior, how can you hope to change the behavior of others? How can you expect to be a role model? You can learn a great deal about motivation by working to change your own behaviors, with the added benefit that you will have done something to improve yourself.

Here is some parting advice about motivation from organizational consultant Nathaniel Branden[104]:

- If we are blind to our own feelings and emotions, we will be blind to the feelings and emotions of others.
- If we do not have the discipline to keep ourselves task-focused, we will not be able to inspire that focus in others.
- If we do not model self-responsibility, we cannot teach it.
- If we do not exemplify integrity, we cannot inspire it in others.
- If we cannot manage ourselves, we are unfit to manage others.

Apply What You Have Learned. . .

World Class Company: Hiscox plc

"Not many people grow up wanting to be in insurance, so we have to attract the best people by being a first-rate employer," notes the chief executive officer of Hiscox plc, the United Kingdom's leading specialist insurance group.[105] The company has evidently achieved its goal. In 2004 it was the top financial services company on the London *Sunday Times'* "100 Best Companies to Work For" list.

In the United Kingdom, Hiscox has 350 employees. More than 70 percent of them own company stock, on which the company gives them a 20 percent discount.

One of the key aspects of the Hiscox management system is commitment to employee development. Beyond its regular performance and development appraisals, the company helps employees develop a "Hiscox Career Roadmap." It also does competency appraisals that help employees determine their own development needs. It makes a significant investment in employee training.

Andrew Underwood, Head of Political Risks, is an employee who was given the opportunity to move up and try a new career direction despite not having the prerequi-site advanced degree. He says of the company, "The management are very supportive of what we are doing, and in providing guidance and making themselves available." Not surprisingly, he believes the best thing about working for Hiscox is the career opportunities it has given him. He describes his workday as rather structured, including internal meetings, discussion of client cases, client meetings, and underwriting—all in all, the best way to meet client needs. He also relates to the company's emphasis on excellence. "We are never satisfied."

Among Hiscox's employees, 82 percent believe they are able to make a difference to the success of the company, and 83 percent say they are excited at the direction in which the company is going.

Discuss

1. Identify the intrinsic motivators at Hiscox.
2. Identify the extrinsic motivators at Hiscox.
3. Why is opportunity for career growth such a powerful motivator?

Advice from the Pros

The Seven Deadly Demotivators (and What to Do About Them)

1. **Politics** Base decisions on objective, written criteria. Search out and eliminate any "unwritten rules" for granting rewards, promotions, and resources.
2. **Unclear expectations** Avoid sending too many messages. When everything is a priority, nothing is a priority.
3. **Unproductive meetings** Make sure the meeting is necessary and that the right people attend. Develop a group of skilled meeting leaders. Prepare a results-oriented agenda with one or a few key items and distribute it in advance. Expect participants to have done some preparation for the meeting. Encourage all to participate. Start and end on time, evaluate the effectiveness of the meeting, and follow up to make sure that action items are started.
4. **Hypocrisy** Monitor the consistency between words and deeds. For example, don't say "we value you" and then give no tangible display that you actually do value the person. Practice what you preach. Avoid exaggerated claims that you cannot live up to.
5. **Constant change** Employees seldom resist change when they believe it is clearly important for organizational success. Let them know what is happening and why, and keep them up to date. Respond to their concerns openly and honestly.
6. **Withholding information** When in doubt, over-communicate.
7. **Low-quality standards** Since most quality problems are due to poorly designed or mismanaged operational systems, be sure to involve employees in goal setting and process improvement. Empower a problem-solving team to investigate and solve the problem. Refuse to produce poor-quality products.

Discuss

1. Based on your experience at school, home, or work, add to this list of demotivators.
2. Relate the demotivators to the theories of motivation in the chapter: What theories explain why these practices are demotivating?

Source: D. R. Spitzer, "The Seven Deadly Demotivators," *Management Review 84* (11), November 1995:56–60. Dr. Spitzer is president of the consulting firm Dean R. Spitzer & Associates in Lakeland, Florida.

Gain Experience

I. The McClelland Consultants

As a consultant, you are used to meeting many different kinds of people. Your new client is a CEO who wants your guidance in choosing a successor. You suspect, from your preliminary communications, that this CEO has a strong need for (*insert here one of McClelland's three needs*). You want to tailor your approach to the CEO based on your knowledge of this, his most basic need. Consider how to act, how to dress, what approach to recommend in choosing the successor, what topics would be good for small talk, and anything else you can think of that might make your interaction with the CEO more effective.

You will work in groups, and each group will be assigned a CEO with one of the three needs. Brainstorm how you would approach your first meeting with this CEO, knowing that he or she has:

a. a high need for affiliation

or

b. a high need for achievement

or

c. a high need for power

Be prepared to share your ideas with your class. Is there any one style that fits all situations?

II. Reinforcement and Punishment

Two students volunteer to be employees, while the rest of the class take the role of their managers. The two step outside the classroom. One at a time they will come back in and be asked to find the professor's keys, which will be hidden somewhere in the room. Their managers are not allowed to speak or gesture to them, but they can give them other feedback.

III. Solve a Practical Problem Using Behavior Modification

Now that you have seen how behavior modification works, see if you can use it to figure out how to exercise more. Use the five-step OB mod approach to design a program in which you will exercise four times a week for 30 minutes each day.

Can You Solve This Manager's Problem?

The Wait Staff Blues

Headwaiter Stan Boss manages 20 wait staff at an upscale restaurant. In his small city, finding experienced servers is hard. When a vacancy occurs, it often takes two weeks or more to fill the position. The restaurant pays its wait staff a minimal wage, assuming rightly that they will make good to excellent money in tips. Each employee keeps 80 percent of his or her tips, giving 20 percent into a pool that goes to pay busboys and then is split overall.

Although most of his staff is efficient and effective, at the moment Stan is juggling several personnel problems.

Sally Staid is a good server who is often 30 to 45 minutes late for her 4 p.m. shift. She commutes a long distance by car and frequently complains traffic is a problem. So far, other staff have been able to compensate for her absence, but Stan can see that resentment is building.

Walt Waiter is a suave server who is popular with the customers. However, he often has childcare issues and needs to leave before his shift ends at midnight. Again, others can compensate for his absence, but resentment is building.

Andy Carver is a lazy server who earns lousy tips. However, the rest of the staff tolerate him because he is very funny, helping the evening to fly by. Stan is considering firing him because he fails to uphold the quality service ideals of the restaurant.

Discuss

1. Is Stan motivating his employees effectively?
2. What should Stan do to change the behaviors of Sally, Walt, and Andy?
3. Can you imagine any systematic approach to motivation that will solve Smith's problems once and for all?

Chapter Summary and Key Terms

What makes people work harder, smarter, and more positively?

Motivating people at work involves many factors. Managers attempt to use both intrinsic and extrinsic motivators, but must be realistic about their ability to control others' behavior. The universal reinforcer, of course, is money.

motivation   96
intrinsic motivators   96
extrinsic motivators   96
self-actualization   98
universal reinforcer   98

How can managers tap an employee's intrinsic motivation?

Managers can tap some aspects of a person's intrinsic motivation more easily than others. If a job requires a certain type of personality or emotion, for example, managers should select appropriate individuals. On the other hand, managers might reasonably attempt to influence an individual's goals, beliefs, or expectations.

self-efficacy   100
independents   101
interdependents   101
individualism   101
collectivism   101
needs   102
need for achievement   102
need for power   102
need for affiliation   102
merit based pay systems   102
seniority-based pay systems   102
humanistic capitalism   103
sociobiology   103
explicit motives   103
extrinsic aspirations   103
intrinsic aspirations   103
Theory X managers   103
Theory Y managers   103
learning goals   104
performance goals   104
expectancy theory   105
expectancy   105
instrumentality   105
valence   105
equity theory   105
distributive justice   106

How do managers motivate using rewards and punishments?

The theory that behavior can be controlled by extrinsic factors—namely, reinforcements and punishments—is called behavior modification. The goal of an organizational behavior modification, or OB Mod, program is to change observable and quantifiable behaviors, such as how many sales calls an associate makes in a day. OB Mod has sparked many business applications.

OB mod   106
A-B-C's of behavior modification   107
reinforcement   107
positive reinforcement   107
negative reinforcement   107
contingent   108
reward   108
punishment   108
punishment by application   108
punishment by removal   108
extinction   108
shaping   109
fading out   109

How do managers use behavior modification to design performance appraisals and reward systems?

Managers can choose either judgment-based, results-based, or behaviorally based performance appraisals. Those that are behaviorally based target behaviors and are generally seen as fair, but they can only be used in jobs in which the behaviors to be rewarded can be easily identified. In general, when designing reward systems, managers should be careful to reward the right behaviors, and to choose appropriate schedules of reinforcement.

judgment-based evaluation   110
halo effect   110
results-based evaluation   110
behaviorally based evaluation   111
behaviorally anchored rating scheme (BARS)   111

What organizational systems do companies use to motivate their employees?

Although all companies use a variety of motivators, some emphasize certain motivators more than others. For example, one company might emphasize pay, whereas another might emphasize feedback and recognition. A somewhat controversial system that is in wide use today is the Employee Stock Ownership Plan, or ESOP.

pay for performance   113
pay for targeted behaviors   113
variable-pay programs   113
Management by Objectives (MBO)   114
quality circles   114
self-managed teams   114
employee stock ownership plans (ESOPs)   115

When motivating yourself and others, also. . .

Weigh recent trends, take national culture into account, and motivate yourself to motivate others.

Explorations

1. Do a Web search for "motivation," and analyze what you discover.

Generally, you find a mishmash of inspirational advice and guru-speak. How does what you have read in this chapter differ from this kind of advice?

2. Do further research about ESOPs to determine whether they are the most motivating system.

For some interesting stories about managing ESOPs see two articles in the *Harvard Business Review*:

    a. Robert Frey, "Empowerment or Else," *HBR 71* (5), September/October 1993: 80–88. This is a detailed and compelling description of how Frey turned around a small, unionized manufacturing company called Cin-Made by using employee empowerment and profit sharing.

    b. Bill Gross, "The New Math of Ownership," *HBR 76* (6), November/December 1998: 68–74. His view of ESOPs? "You can't expect employees to think and act like owners unless you make them true owners."

Do a Web search for the National Center for Employee Ownership. Their site describes many of the technical details associated with establishing ESOPs.

Do a Web search for "'ESOP' and 'scandal'" to learn how some companies have used ESOPS *against* their employees.

3. Are some sources of motivation subconscious?

Edwin A. Locke, in an article entitled "What Should We Do About Motivation Theory? Six Recommendations for the Twenty-First Century," (*Academy of Management Review,* July 2004) suggests that we should try harder to understand subconscious sources of motivation and that we should use introspection more to study motivation. What do you think?

4. Want more info on behavior modification?

A classic book that shows how to use behavior modification in organizational life is F. Luthans and R. Kreitner's *Organizational Behavior Modification and Beyond* (Glenview, IL: Scott, Foresman, 1985).

References

[1] J. W. Atkinson, *Introduction to Motivation* (Princeton, NJ: Van Nostrand, 1964); J. P. Campbell and R. D. Pritchard, "Motivation Theory in Industrial and Organizational Psychology," in M. D. Dunnette, ed., *Handbook of Industrial and Organizational Psychology* (Chicago: Rand McNally, 1976):63–130; E. A. Locke and G. P. Latham, *A Theory of Goal Setting and Task Performance* (Englewood Cliffs, NJ: Prentice Hall, 1990); R. Kanfer, "Motivation Theory and Industrial and Organizational Psychology," in M. D. Dunnette and L. M. Hough, eds., *Handbook of Industrial and Organizational Psychology 1* (Palo Alto, CA: Consulting Psychologists Press, 1991):76–170. See also E. E. Lawler III, *Motivation in Work Organizations* (Monterey, CA: Brooks/Cole, 1973):2–5; C. C. Pinder, *Work Motivation in Organizational Behavior* (Upper Saddle River, NJ: Prentice Hall, 1998).

[2] S. Kassin, *Psychology,* 4th Edition (Upper Saddle River, NJ: Prentice Hall, 2004).

[3] J. P. Forgas and J. M. George, "Affective Influences on Judgments and Behavior in Organizations: An Information Processing Perspective," *Organizational Behavior and Human Decision Processes 86,* 2001:3–34.

[4] A. Maslow, *Motivation and Personality* (New York: Harper & Row, 1954).

[5] M. A. Wahba and L. G. Bridwell, "Maslow Reconsidered: A Review of Research on the Need Hierarchy Theory," *Organizational Behavior and Human Performance 15* (2), April 1976:212–240; J. Rauschenberger, N. Schmitt, and J. E. Hunter, "A Test of the Need Hierarchy Concept by a Markov Model of Change in Need Strength," *Administrative Science Quarterly 25* (4), December 1980:654–670.

[6] C. P. Alderfer, "An Empirical Test of a New Theory of Human Needs," *Organizational Behavior & Human Performance 4* (2), May 1969:142–175.

[7] P. E. Spector, "Development of the Work Locus of Control," *Journal of Occupational Psychology (61)*, 1988:335–340.

[8] P. E. Spector, "Behavior in Organizations as a Function of Employee's Locus of Control," *Psychological Bulletin 91,* May 1982:482–497.

[9] J. B. Miner, *Industrial–Organizational Psychology* (New York: McGraw-Hill, 1992).

[10] P. E. Spector, "Behavior in Organizations as a Function of Employee's Locus of Control," *Psychological Bulletin 91,* May 1982:482–497.

[11] P. E. Spector, "Behavior in Organizations as a Function of Employee's Locus of Control," *Psychological Bulletin (91)* 1982:482–497.

[12] P. E. Spector, "Behavior in Organizations as a Function of Employee's Locus of Control," *Psychological Bulletin (91)* 1982:482–497.

[13] J. B. Miner, *Industrial–Organizational Psychology* (New York: McGraw-Hill, 1992):151.

[14] A. Bandura, *Social Foundations of Thought and Action* (Englewood Cliffs, NJ: Prentice Hall, 1982):122.

[15] M. E. Gist and T. R. Mitchell, "Self-Efficacy: A Theoretical Analysis of Its Determinants and Malleability," *Academy of Management Review 17* (2), 1992:183–211; T. A. Judge, A. Erez, J. E. Bono, and C. J. Thoresen, "Are Measures of Self-

Esteem, Neuroticism, Locus of Control, and Generalized Self-Efficacy Indicators of a Common Core Construct?" *Journal of Personality & Social Psychology 83* (3), September 2002:693–710.

16 A. Bandura, *Social Foundations of Thought and Action* (Englewood Cliffs, NJ: Prentice Hall, 1986).

17 A. Erez and T. A. Judge, "Relationship of Core Self-Evaluations to Goal Setting, Motivation, and Performance," *Journal of Applied Psychology 86* (6), December 2001:1270–1279; T. A. Judge, A. Erez, J. E. Bono, and C. J. Thoresen, "Are Measures of Self-Esteem, Neuroticism, Locus of Control, and Generalized Self-Efficacy Indicators of a Common Core Construct?" *Journal of Personality & Social Psychology 83* (3), September 2002:693–710. See also D. L. Bandolas, K. Yates, and T. Thorndike-Christ, "Effects of Math Self-Concept, Perceived Self-Efficacy, and Attributions for Failure and Success on Test Anxiety," *Journal of Educational Psychology 87*, 1995:611–623; J. Carifio and L. Rhodes, "Construct Validities and the Empirical Relationships between Optimism, Hope, Self-Efficacy, and Locus of Control," *Work 19*, 2002:125–136.

18 A. Erez and T. A. Judge, "Relationship of Core Self-Evaluations to Goal Setting, Motivation, and Performance," *Journal of Applied Psychology 86* (6), December 2001:1270–1279.

19 T. A. Judge, A. Erez, J. E. Bono, and C. J. Thoresen, "The Core Self-Evaluations Scale: Development of a Measure," *Personnel Psychology 56* (2), Summer 2003:303–331.

20 H. R. Markus and S. Kitayama, "Culture and the Self: Implications for Cognition, Emotion, and Motivation," *Psychological Review 98*, 1991:224–253; Y. Kim, T. Kasser, and H. Lee, "Self-Concept, Aspirations, and Well-Being in South Korea and the United States," *Journal of Psychology 143* (2), 2003:277–290.

21 H. C. Triandis, *Individualism and Collectivism* (Boulder, CO: Westview Press, 1995).

22 M. Seo, L. F. Barrett, and J. M. Bartunek, "The Role of Affective Experience in Work Motivation," *Academy of Management Review 29* (3), 2004:423–439. Much of this section on emotion is based on the research analyzed in this article.

23 M. Seo, L. F. Barrett, and J. M. Bartunek, "The Role of Affective Experience in Work Motivation," *Academy of Management Review 29* (3), 2004:423–439. Much of this section on emotion is based on the research analyzed in this article.

24 M. Seo, L. F. Barrett, and J. M. Bartunek, "The Role of Affective Experience in Work Motivation," *Academy of Management Review 29* (3), 2004:427.

25 N. Schwarz, "Feelings as Information: Informational and Motivational Functions of Affective States," in E. T. Higgins and R. M. Sorrentino, eds., *Handbook of Motivation and Cognition: Foundations of Social Behavior 2* (New York: Guilford Press, 1990):527–561.

26 S. Kitayama, "Affective Influence in Perception: Some Implications of the Amplification Model," in G. Matthews, ed., *Cognitive Science Perspectives on Personality and Emotion* (New York: Elsevier, 1997):193–257.

27 B. L. Fredrickson, "The Role of Positive Emotions in Positive Psychology: The Broaden-and-Build Theory of Positive Emotions," *American Psychologist 56*, 2001:218–226.

28 J. D. Meyer, Y. N. Gaschke, D. L. Braverman, and T. W. Evans, "Mood-Congruent Judgment Is a General Effect," *Journal of Personality & Social Psychology 63*, 1992:119–132.

29 P. Winkielman, R. B. Zajonc, and N. Schwarz, "Subliminal Affective Priming Resists Attributional Interventions," *Cognition and Emotion 11*, 1997:433–465.

30 H. M. Kehr, "Integrating Implicit Motives, Explicit Motives, and Perceived Abilities: The Compensatory Model of Work Motivation and Volition," *Academy of Management Review 29* (3), 2004:479–499.

31 C. Ryff, "Happiness Is Everything, or Is It? Explorations on the Meaning of Psychological Well-Being," *Journal of Personality & Social Psychology 57*, 1989:1069–81.

32 D. M. Buss, "Evolutionary Personality Psychology," in M. R. Rosenzweig and L. W. Porter, eds., *Annual Review of Psychology 42*, 1991:459–491.

33 D. C. McClelland, *Human Motivation* (Glenview, IL: Scott, Foresman, 1985).

34 D. B. Turban and T. L. Keon, "Organizational Attractiveness: An Interactionist Perspective," *Journal of Applied Psychology 78*, 1993:184–193.

35 D. Rotondo, "Individual-Difference Variables and Career-Related Coping," *Journal of Social Psychology 139* (4), August 1999:458–473.

36 M. L. Schroth and W. A. McCormack, "Sensation Seeking and Need for Achievement among Study-Abroad Students," *Journal of Social Psychology 140* (4), August 2000:533–535.

37 D. C. McClelland and D. H. Burnham, "Power Is the Great Motivator," *Harvard Business Review 81* (1), January 2003:117–126.

38 See W. Greider, *The Soul of Capitalism: Opening Paths to a Moral Economy* (New York: Simon & Schuster, 2003). Also, social researcher J. Naisbitt describes a "new American work ethic." See J. Naisbitt and P. Aburdene, *Megatrends 2000* (New York: Avon, 2000, reissue edition of 1991 book).

39 R. Kristoff, "The Birth of Capitalism's Conscience," *Business & Society Review (1974) 61*, Spring 1987:27–30.

40 R. Kristoff, "The Birth of Capitalism's Conscience," *Business & Society Review (1974) 61*, Spring 1987:27–30, 29.

41 D. M. Buss, "Evolutionary Personality Psychology," *Annual Review of Psychology 42* (1), 1991:459–491.

42 L. R. Caporael, "Evolutionary Psychology: Toward a Unifying Theory and a Hybrid Science," *Annual Review of Psychology 52* (1), 2001:607–628.

43 D. C. McClelland, R. Koestner, and J. Weinberger, "How Do Self-Attributed and Implicit Motives Differ?" *Psychological Review 96*, 1989:690–702; D. C. McClelland, "Scientific Psychology as a Social Enterprise," working paper, Boston University, 1995.

44 J. C. Brunstein, O. C. Schultheiss, and R. Grässmann, "Personal Goals and Emotional Well-Being: The Moderating Role of Motive Dispositions," *Journal of Personality & Social Psychology 7*, 1998:494–508.

45 H. R. Markus and S. Kitayama, "Culture and the Self: Implications for Cognition, Emotion, and Motivation," *Psychological Review 98*, 1991:224–253; Y. Kim, T. Kasser, and H. Lee, "Self-Concept, Aspirations, and Well-Being in South Korea and the United States," *Journal of Psychology 143* (3), 2003:277–290.

46 D. McGregor, *The Human Side of Enterprise* (New York: McGraw-Hill Book Company, Inc., 1960).

47 E. A. Locke and G. P. Latham, *A Theory of Goal Setting and Task Performance* (Englewood Cliffs, NJ: Prentice Hall, 1990).

[48] E. A. Locke and G. P. Latham, *A Theory of Goal Setting and Task Performance* (Englewood Cliffs, NJ: Prentice Hall, 1990).

[49] G. P. Latham, "Motivate Employee Performance through Goal-Setting," *Blackwell Handbook of Principles of Organizational Behavior,* 2000:107–119.

[50] A. J. Mento, E. A. Locke, and H. J. Klein, "Relationship of Goal Level to Valence and Instrumentality," *Journal of Applied Psychology 77* (4), August 1992:395–405.

[51] R. W. Renn and D. B. Fedor, "Development and Field Test of a Feedback Seeking, Self-Efficacy, and Goal Setting Model of Work Performance," *Journal of Management 27* (5), 2001:563–583.

[52] D. C. Molden and C. S. Dweck, "Meaning and Motivation," in C. Sansone and J. M. Harackiewicz, eds., *Intrinsic and Extrinsic Motivation: The Search for Optimal Motivation and Performance* (San Diego: Academic Press, 2000).

[53] H. Sujan, B. A. Weitz, and N. Kumar, "Learning Orientation, Working Smart, and Effective Selling," *Journal of Marketing 58* (3), July 1994:39–53.

[54] B. Weiner, *Human Motivation* (New York: Holt, Rinehart & Winston, 1980).

[55] R. Spector and P. D. McCarthy, *The Nordstrom Way: The Inside Story of America's #1 Customer Service Company* (New York, NY: John Wiley & Sons, 1995):16; C. A. O'Reilly III and J. Pfeffer, "Southwest Airlines: Using Human Resources for Competitive Advantage (A)," Stanford University, Graduate School of Business, March 6, 1995:7; J. A. Chatman and S. E. Cha, "Leading by Leveraging Culture," *California Management Review 45* (4), Summer 2003:20–34.

[56] M. E. Schweitzer, L. Ordóñez, and B. Douma, "Goal Setting as a Motivator of Unethical Behavior," *Academy of Management Journal 47* (3), June 2004:422–432.

[57] V. H. Vroom, *Work and Motivation* (New York: Wiley, 1964); L. W. Porter and E. E. Lawler III, *Managerial Attitudes and Performance* (Homewood, IL; Irwin, 1968).

[58] R. J. House, H. J. Shapiro, and M. A. Wahba, "Expectancy Theory as a Predictor of Work Behavior and Attitudes: A Reevaluation of Empirical Evidence," *Decision Sciences 5,* 1974:481–506; T. Connolly, "Some Conceptual and Methodological Issues in Expectancy Models of Work Performance," *Academy of Management Review 1,* 1976:37–47; J. B. Miner, *Industrial–Organizational Psychology* (New York: McGraw-Hill, 1992).

[59] J. S. Adams, "Toward an Understanding of Inequity," *Journal of Abnormal and Social Psychology 67,* 1963:422–436; J. S. Adams, "Inequity in Social Exchange," In L. Berkowitz (ed.), *Advances in Experimental Social Psychology* (New York: Academic Press, 1965):267–299.

[60] T. W. Taris, R. Kalimo, and W. B. Schaufeli, "Inequity at Work: Its Measurement and Association with Worker Health," *Work & Stress 16* (4), 2002:287–301.

[61] O. Janssen, "Fairness Perceptions as a Moderator in the Curvilinear Relationships Between Job Demands, and Job Performance and Job Satisfaction," *Academy of Management Journal 44* (5) 2001:1039–1050.

[62] T. P. Summers and A. S. DeNisi, "In Search of Adams' Other: Reexamination of Referents Used in the Evaluation of Pay," *Human Relations 43* (6), 1990:497–511: R. T. Lee and J. E. Martin, "Internal and External Referents as Predictors of Pay Satisfaction Among Employees in a Two-Tier Wage Setting," *Journal of Occupational Psychology 64* (1) March 1991:57–66.

[63] T. W. Taris, R. Kalimo, and W. B. Schaufeli, "Inequity at Work: Its Measurement and Association with Worker Health," *Work & Stress 16* (4), 2002:287–301.

[64] M. L. Ambrose and R. Cropanzano, "A Longitudinal Analysis of Organizational Fairness: An Examination of Reactions to Tenure and Promotion Decisions," *Journal of Applied Psychology 88* (2), April 2003:266–275.

[65] J. M. Paterson, A. Green, and J. Cary, "The Measurement of Organizational Justice in Organizational Change Programmes: A Reliability, Validity and Context-Sensitivity Assessment," *Journal of Occupational & Organizational Psychology 75* (4), December 2002:393–408.

[66] J. T. Scott, R. E. Matland, P. A. Michelbach, and B. H. Bornstein, "Just Deserts: An Experimental Study of Distributive Justice Norms," *American Journal of Political Science 45* (4), October 2001:749–767.

[67] A. Bandura, *Principles of Behavior Modification* (New York: Holt, Rinehart and Winston, 1969).

[68] F. Luthans, *Organizational Behavior Modification* (New York: Scott Foresman, 1975).

[69] B. F. Skinner, *About Behaviorism* (New York: Vintage Books USA, 1976).

[70] D. Meichenbaum, *Cognitive-Behavior Modification: An Integrative Approach* (New York: Plenum Press, 1977).

[71] F. Luthans and A. D. Stajkovic, "Reinforce for Performance: The Need to Go Beyond Pay and Even Rewards," *Academy of Management Executive 13* (2), May 1999:49–57.

[72] D. Malachowski, "Wasted Time at Work Costing Companies Billions,"http://www.salary.com. Accessed September 16, 2006.

[73] F. Luthans and A. D. Stajkovic, "Reinforce for Performance: The Need to Go Beyond Pay and Even Rewards," *Academy of Management Executive 13* (2), May 1999:49–57.

[74] F. Luthans and A. D. Stajkovic, "Reinforce for Performance: The Need to Go Beyond Pay and Even Rewards," *Academy of Management Executive 13* (2), May 1999:49–57.

[75] "At Emery Air Freight: Positive Reinforcement Boosts Performance," *Organizational Dynamics 1* (3), Winter 1973:41–50.

[76] "Behavior-Based Sales Team Training Produces a 56% Increase in Revenues," *Managing Training and Development 04-04,* April 2004:1, 10–12.

77 "Behavior-Based Sales Team Training Produces a 56% Increase in Revenues," *Managing Training and Development 04-04,* April 2004:1, 10–12:10.

78 R. Jacobs and S. W. Kozlowski, "A Closer Look at Halo Error in Performance Ratings," *Academy of Management Journal 28* (1), 1985: 201–212.

79 P. O. Kingstrom and A. R. Bass, "A Critical Analysis of Studies Comparing Behaviorally Anchored Rating Scales (BARS) and Other Rating Formats," *Personnel Psychology 34* (2), Summer 1981:263–289; P. G. Benson , M. R. Buckley, and S. Hall, "The Impact of Rating Scale Format on Rater Accuracy: An Evaluation of the Mixed Standard Scale," *Journal of Management 14* (3), 1988:415–423.

80 C. A. Ramus and U. Steger, "The Roles of Supervisory Support Behaviors and Environmental Policy in Employee 'Ecoinitiatives' at Leading-Edge European Companies," *Academy of Management Journal 43* (4), August 2000:605–626.

81 S. Kerr, "On the Folly of Rewarding A, while Hoping for B," *Academy of Management Journal 18* (4), December 1975:769–783; S. Kerr, "On the Folly of Rewarding A, while Hoping for B," *Academy of Management Executive 9* (1), February 1995:7–14.

82 A. D. Stajkovic and F. Luthans, "Differential Effects of Incentive Motivators on Work Performance," *Academy of Management Journal 44* (3), June 2001:580–590.

83 A. D. Stajkovic and F. Luthans, "A Meta-Analysis of the Effects of Organizational Behavior Modification on Task Performance, 1975–95," *Academy of Management Journal 40* (5), October 1997:1122–1149.

84 A. C. Daniels, *Bringing Out the Best in People* (New York: McGraw-Hill, 1995):27, quoted in F. Luthans and A. D. Stajkovic, "Reinforce for Performance: The Need to Go Beyond Pay and Even Rewards," *Academy of Management Executive 13* (2), May 1999:49–57.

85 F. Luthans and A. D. Stajkovic, "Reinforce for Performance: The Need to Go Beyond Pay and Even Rewards," *Academy of Management Executive 13* (2), May 1999:49–57.

86 F. Luthans and A. D. Stajkovic, "Reinforce for Performance: The Need to Go Beyond Pay and Even Rewards," *Academy of Management Executive 13* (2), May 1999:49–57.

87 "Work Week: A Special News Report about Life on the Job—And Trends Taking Shape There," *The Wall Street Journal,* April 6, 1999:A1.

88 F. Luthans and A. D. Stajkovic, "Reinforce for Performance: The Need to Go Beyond Pay and Even Rewards," *Academy of Management Executive 13* (2), May 1999:49–57.

89 P. F. Drucker, *The Practice of Management* (New York: Harper & Row, 1954); S. J. Carroll and H. L. Tosi, *Management by Objectives: Applications and Research* (New York: Macmillan, 1973).

90 G. S. Odiorne, "MBO Means Having a Goal and a Plan Not Just a Goal," *Management 44* (1), September 1992:8–11.

91 J. W. Gibson and D. V. Tesone, "Management Fads: Emergence, Evolution, and Implications for Managers," *Academy of Management Executive 15* (4), November 2001:122–131.

92 G. R. Gray, "Quality Circles: An Update," *SAM Advanced Management Journal 58* (2), 1993:41.

93 J. W. Gibson, D. V. Tesone, and C. W. Blackwell, "Management Fads: Here Yesterday, Gone Today?" *SAM Advanced Management Journal 68* (4), Fall 2003:12–18.

94 S. E. Black, L. M. Lynch, and A. Krivelyova, "How Workers Fare When Employers Innovate," *Industrial Relations 43* (1), January 2004:44–66.

95 S. E. Black, L. M. Lynch, and A. Krivelyova, "How Workers Fare When Employers Innovate," *Industrial Relations 43* (1), January 2004:44–66.

96 D. Paul, "Incentive Plans Can Work," *Harvard Business Review 72* (2), March/April 1994:178.

97 National Center for Employee Ownership, http://www.nceo.org/library/history.html. Accessed August 15, 2006.

98 J. E. Godfrey, "Does Employee Ownership Really Make a Difference?" *CPA Journal 70* (1), January 2000:13, citing research by H. Mehran of the Northwestern University J. L. Kellogg Graduate School of Management. See also C. Rosen and M. Quarrey, "How Well Is Employee Ownership Working?" *Harvard Business Review 65* (5), September/October 1987:126–129.

99 Much of the discussion in this section is based on N. Ellemers, D. De Gilder, and S. A. Haslam, "Motivating Individuals and Groups at Work: A Social Identity Perspective on Leadership and Group Performance," *Academy of Management Review 29* (3), July 2004:459–478.

100 I. F. Sorauren, "Non-Monetary Incentives: Do People Work Only for Money?" *Business Ethics Quarterly 10* (4), October 2000:925–944.

101 M. Haire, E. E. Ghiselli, and L. W. Porter, *Managerial Thinking: An International Study* (New York: Wiley, 1966).

102 MOW International Research Team, *The Meaning of Working: An International Perspective* (London and New York: Academic Press, 1985).

103 S. S. Schneider, "National versus Corporate Culture: Implications for Human Resource Management," *Human Resource Management 27* (2), 1988:231–246.

104 N. Branden, *Self-Esteem at Work: How Confident People Make Powerful Companies* (San Francisco: Jossey-Bass Publishers, 1998):93–94.

105 http://www.hiscox.com/docs/abouthx/careers/Underwood.pdf. Accessed July 8, 2004.

5

Motivating Individuals in Their Jobs

Preview

Why do managers work hard to motivate their employees?
Reason 1. To avoid the consequences of job dissatisfaction
Reason 2. To attract and keep workers
Reason 3. To enhance task performance and organizational outcomes
Reason 4. To inspire organizational citizenship

How do managers design motivating jobs?
Job characteristics model
Creating jobs that motivate

How does an employer fit a person to a job?
Consider personality and skills
Consider individual values

What is the process of matching a person and a job?

How do companies use scheduling to motivate?
Flextime and the compressed workweek
Telecommuting
Job-sharing

How do companies use the physical environment as a motivator?

How do managers design fair and effective performance appraisals?
Meritocracy
The role of human judgment
In practice

How do companies use organizational culture to motivate their employees?
See Chapter 17: Organizational Culture

Dr. Martens

At Dr. Martens, motivating employees was a constant challenge. From its startup on April 1st, 1960, until recent times, the company had been an integral part of its local community in the British Midlands. It had employed, mostly in England, up to 3,200 people. The employees crafted the company's distinctive shoes and boots for markets worldwide. However, in 2003 Dr. Martens outsourced all of its production to Asia, eliminating 1,000 jobs in the United Kingdom.

In modern times Dr. Martens has faced a declining footwear industry and a tight labor market, and a key issue has been recruiting and retaining qualified workers. Before moving production to Asia, Dr. Martens had developed a wide range of approaches to motivating employees in their jobs. Company spokesman Howard Johnstone emphasized the following approaches, among others:

- The company hired the right people in the first place, looking for those whose values fit into the culture and who were ambitious.

- With a market focused on youthful customers, the company tried, to some extent, to reflect that youth among its employees. Yet, because the young employees seemed to be able to survive on 4 day's pay rather than 5, the company's major human resources problem was absenteeism.

- It gave employees authority, training, and resources.

- Acknowledging that all individuals have their weaknesses, management tried to bring out people's strengths, for their own benefit and that of the company.

■ The company encouraged employee input and made employees part of the decision-making process. It says it wanted them to feel part of the big picture.

■ The company wanted people to feel they were being treated equitably and fairly.

■ Dr. Martens offered modern facilities with state-of-the art equipment.

■ It offered convenient hours of work and free transportation from outlying areas.

■ It offered an employee club with facilities for parties, and through the club offered activities and trips.

■ Employees could buy the company's products at a discount.

■ Dr. Martens was involved in the community, sponsoring events ranging from football to theatre to charities.

While trying to maintain a presence in England, Dr. Martens was under competitive pressure to move production abroad. Ultimately, it succumbed to that pressure. Although its motivational practices were valid ones, in the end all such practices have to be considered in the context of the potential for offshoring jobs.

In the last chapter we examined fundamental theories of motivation and some of their applications in business. In this chapter we focus more specifically on how managers design various aspects of their organizations to motivate their employees. Generally managers design extrinsic factors in the hopes of influencing their employees' intrinsic motivation to work.

In this chapter we will examine how managers design motivating jobs, how they match employees with jobs, and how they use scheduling, the physical environment of the workplace, and performance appraisals to motivate. Later in the book we devote an entire chapter to the important motivational influences of a company's culture.

Why Do Managers Work Hard to Motivate Their Employees?

job
A specified task or set of tasks an individual does as part of an occupation.

task performance
The behaviors, both mental and physical, that individuals exhibit in pursuit of organizational goals.

organizational citizenship
Behaviors on behalf of the organization that go well beyond normal job expectations, and which may even serve a larger societal purpose.

A **job** is a task or set of tasks an individual does as part of an occupation. Some bosses do not bother to create motivating jobs. They reason, "The employees are being paid, aren't they?" or "I have jobs, and they need work, and that should be enough motivation." Do you think they are right? Can you imagine why employers make the effort to design motivating work for their employees?

Actually, there are a number of reasons why employers want their people to be motivated. For one thing, they want to avoid the consequences to the company of employees who are *dissatisfied* with their work, including such counterproductive behaviors as tardiness, theft, and loafing. Second, companies want to attract and keep the best possible workers. Third, they want to enhance their employees' **task performance**—the behaviors, both mental and physical, that individuals exhibit in pursuit of organizational goals.[1] Finally, they hope to inspire **organizational citizenship**, behaviors on behalf of the organization that go well beyond normal job expectations,[2] and which may even serve a larger societal purpose. In short, good managers always motivate for a reason, and they have plenty of reasons for caring about motivation.

Reason 1: To Avoid the Consequences of Job Dissatisfaction

Extensive research on job dissatisfaction suggests that unhappy employees tend to respond in one of four ways.[3] The first two ways are active responses, one of which is counterproductive and one of which is productive for the company. When dissatisfied employees quit an organization altogether in response to job dissatisfaction, their approach is called an **exit**. In contrast, when they choose to stay in their company and actively try to improve conditions there, or try to come up with better ways of doing things and advocate changes to make things better, their approach is called **voice**.

The second two responses are passive. Employees may respond with **loyalty**, which is accepting the status quo without raising any objections or making suggestions for improvements, or they may exhibit **neglect**, staying in the company and exhibiting passive withdrawal behaviors such as minimizing their effort. Taken as a whole, these four active and passive behaviors comprise the **EVLN** (Exit, Voice, Loyalty, Neglect) **model** of job dissatisfaction.

Employee dissatisfaction is only useful to companies if their employees respond in an active rather than a passive manner. Dissatisfied employees who cope actively and who have a commitment to continue in the organization are likely to energetically pursue new organizational options. However, the two passive responses to job dissatisfaction are particularly dysfunctional for organizations.[4] When employees ignore problems (loyalty) or withdraw from problems (neglect), not only does their dissatisfaction persist, it can spread to other employees.

Replacing an employee is expensive. A *Business Week* study in the U.S. estimates that replacement costs are over $10,000 for about half of all jobs, and are over $30,000 for 20 percent of all jobs.[5] In general, the rule of thumb is that replacement costs tend to be about 50 to 60 percent of a person's annual salary.[6] In some countries the costs are even higher: An industry analysis in the U.K. suggests that it costs a company somewhere between one and two years' pay and benefits to replace an employee.[7]

Some obvious costs of employee turnover are the cost of attracting and selecting a new employee, the premium salary that must be paid for the new hire, and the cost of processing their application. Underlying costs include time lost to management interviews, time spent training and socializing the new employee, lost productivity of the job leaver during their notice period, and finally, the lost productivity of the leaver's team.

In IT (information technology), for example, a key project team member who leaves takes along key knowledge of systems and technical experience.[8] The loss of this expertise can translate into project delays, reduction in quality, and a drop in service levels. The company faces potential costs in lost business due to unhappy customers. The turnover also creates stress because remaining employees have to pick up the slack and may experience a reduction in morale.

Employees with good job opportunities elsewhere are likely to choose the exit option. The top three reasons why IT professionals quit, for example, are: 1) they are offered a promotion at another company; 2) they receive a significant increase in a base salary; and 3) they find few career advancement and development opportunities in their current job.[9] In fact, these are the main reasons why most people leave a job.

People who are committed to their organizations are more likely to speak up rather than exit, as are those with the personality traits of high conscientiousness, high extroversion, and low neuroticism. However, employees who have spoken up unsuccessfully in the past are more likely to choose exit and neglect.[10]

Reason 2: To Attract and Keep Workers

One way employers hope to attract and keep workers is by influencing employees' attitudes towards their jobs, coworkers, and company. In another chapter, we learned that an attitude is a person's reaction toward another person, object, or idea. It can be positive, negative, mixed, or indifferent.[11] The most studied work-related attitudes are job satisfaction and organizational commitment.

exit
Dissatisfied employees quit an organization in response to job dissatisfaction.

voice
Dissatisfied employees choose to stay in their company and actively try to improve conditions there.

loyalty
Dissatisfied employees accept the status quo without raising any objections or making suggestions for improvements.

neglect
Dissatisfied employees stay in the company and exhibit passive withdrawal behaviors such as minimizing their effort.

EVLN model
A model of job dissatisfaction comprised of two active behaviors: exit and voice, and two passive behaviors: loyalty and neglect.

job satisfaction
A collection of attitudes about the various parts of the job.

JOB SATISFACTION **Job satisfaction** is a collection of attitudes about the various parts of the job.[12] It can be measured simply by asking a person, "Overall, how satisfied are you with your job?"[13]

Are Americans satisfied with their jobs? It depends on whom you ask. A report by the Conference Board and Industry Research Group notes that, in 2003, 49 percent of Americans were satisfied with their jobs.[14] However, the study also found that only 20 percent were satisfied with their employers' promotion and bonus policies, and only about a third were satisfied with their pay. (In 1995, the first time this Conference Board survey was done, 58 percent of Americans had reported that they were satisfied with their jobs.) However, among workers in the $50,000+ income group, job satisfaction fell from 67 percent in 1995 to 53 percent in 2003, and satisfaction fell the most among workers ages 35 to 54. One reason employees today are less satisfied with their jobs than they were a decade ago is the continuing efforts of employers to enhance productivity by reducing staff.

A more positive view comes from a 2003 Gallup poll finding that 44 percent of employed Americans were completely satisfied with their current jobs, with another 41 percent somewhat satisfied. Eleven percent were somewhat dissatisfied, and only 4 percent were completely dissatisfied with their jobs.[15] This report also suggested that the percentage of the workers completely satisfied with their jobs increased from 28 percent in 1989 to 44 percent in 2003, whereas during this time the percentage of dissatisfied workers did not really change. The poll also asked workers how satisfied they were with a number of factors that can lead to job satisfaction. The factor they said they were least likely to be satisfied with is the amount of on-the-job stress they experience.

How do these statistics compare with satisfaction figures worldwide? An international study suggests that although the majority of Americans, Western Europeans, and Latin Americans are satisfied with their jobs, Eastern Europeans and Asians are somewhat less satisfied.[16] Four out of five workers around the world describe themselves as very or somewhat satisfied with their jobs. One-third even report that they are very satisfied. Workers in Denmark are by far the happiest employees, with 61 percent describing themselves as very satisfied with their jobs. They are followed by Indians (55 percent), Norwegians (54 percent), U.S. workers (50 percent), and the Irish (49 percent). In contrast, only about 10 percent of Hungarians and Ukrainians are very satisfied in their jobs, and among Asian workers, only 11 percent of Chinese, 14 percent of South Koreans, and 16 percent of Japanese are very satisfied.

Whereas all of these figures are interesting, we do have to treat them with a grain of salt. For one thing, when a survey asks a single question, it may be that dissatisfied employees are reluctant to reveal their true feelings because they would have to admit to themselves that they have made a poor job choice.

What influences job satisfaction and dissatisfaction? Any one of the factors discussed in our chapter on motivation is a possibility. The extent to which people are treated equitably, the extent to which their needs are met, and the extent to which their personality affects their general sense of well-being are all likely to be important influences. One intriguing question that researchers have attempted to answer is whether job satisfaction is primarily a function of organizational life or of a person's personal predisposition to being contented. The latest studies suggest that job satisfaction is a result of both personal predispositions and organizational conditions.[17]

organizational commitment
Employees' involvement with, identification with, and emotional attachment to their organization.

continuance commitment
Employees' objective (non-emotional) decision that it is in their best interest to remain with the organization.

normative commitment
Feeling of obligation to remain with one's company.

ORGANIZATIONAL COMMITMENT When employees are involved with their organization, identify with their organization, and have an emotional attachment to it, they are said to exhibit **organizational commitment**.[18] Organizational commitment has an affective (which, as you recall, means "emotional") component insofar as people are emotionally involved with their company and perceive they have a relationship with it. A related but slightly different idea is the notion of **continuance commitment**, which occurs when employees decide that it is in their own best interest, objectively speaking, to remain with the organization. This kind of commitment lacks an affective, relational component. Sometimes, too, employees feel what is called **normative commitment**, which is a feeling of obligation to remain with their company.[19]

Oftentimes individuals are committed to their organizations but not committed to their jobs. They stay on in work they dislike because they want or need to stay in their company.

Others are committed to their jobs but not to their organizations. In 2001, 10 percent of American workers left their employers; of these, 6 percent took jobs with other companies, 1 percent started their own companies, and 3 percent retired.[20]

An interesting recent survey conducted in the United Kingdom suggests that employees there are reducing their commitment to their employers in favor of commitment to themselves. Almost 6 out of 10 employees intend to spend less time on the job and more time improving their personal life, with their top resolution being to exercise regularly. According to the researchers, these findings suggest that people still want to move up the career ladder but believe that to do this, they need the energy that comes from having a decent work/life balance.[21]

There is no way to establish a fixed set of criteria for "good jobs" and "bad jobs," because no such set is likely to capture what is obvious to particular employees about their own particular jobs.[22] Measures of job satisfaction and employee commitment are subjective. This is appropriate because these concepts measure important psychological aspects of the individuals' relationships with their employers.

PSYCHOLOGICAL CONTRACTS A **psychological contract** is the individual's belief about the exchange between himself or herself and his or her employer.[23] In past generations, the psychological contract between workers and their employers was often fairly clear: The worker gave good work in return for steady and often lifetime employment. Today, however, contracts are more typically based on the notion of **employability**, the idea that workers' abilities and competencies are the basis for their job security.[24] Psychological contracts are affected by a variety of management trends, including restructuring, downsizing, increased reliance on temporary workers, demographic diversity, and foreign competition. Such trends muddy psychological contracts because of the uncertainty they cause for both employees and organizations.

Despite their intellectual understanding of work-world uncertainty, some employees today feel that the terms of their psychological contracts have been broken. For example, one study found that in a sample of recent MBA graduates, 55 percent believed that during the previous two years their employers had broken some aspect of their psychological contract.[25]

Whereas in the past a psychological contract between worker and employer could be assumed, in turbulent times it is more important than ever that employees and organizations explicitly discuss their mutual obligations. When there are cultural differences between the employee and the managers responsible for establishing the psychological contract, or when an employee lacks knowledge of the norms of the company or industry, it is especially important to mutually develop clear expectations.[26]

> **psychological contract**
> The individual's belief about the exchange between himself or herself and his or her employer.
>
> **employability**
> The idea that workers' abilities and competencies are the basis for their job security.

Reason 3: To Enhance Task Performance and Organizational Outcomes

The third reason companies work hard to motivate their employees is to improve productivity and other organizational outcomes.

ENHANCE JOB PERFORMANCE AND PRODUCTIVITY For many years now there has been an academic debate about whether worker satisfaction actually leads to increased worker productivity. The research to date suggests that overall job satisfaction is moderately related to a person's job performance.[27] That is, if people are generally satisfied with their jobs, they are somewhat more likely to perform them better than if they are dissatisfied with them. However, the research now suggests that in terms of causality it is likely that productivity leads to satisfaction rather than vice versa. In other words, it is probably less true that happy workers make productive organizations than that productive organizations develop happy workers.[28]

The implications for managers are that it is safe to assume that, although the relationship is complex, there is some sort of relationship between worker satisfaction and productivity, and that certainly an unsatisfied worker is a counterproductive worker.[29] Also, managers should not assume that by trying to make their workers happy they will make them more productive. Rather, helping workers to be more productive is more likely to lead to satisfaction than the other way around. For example, giving workers better resources for doing their work is more likely to enhance productivity than is giving them a longer lunch hour. Can employers afford to ignore creating a good place in which to work? No, of course not, because we also know that employees with high affective commitment have stronger work motivation and somewhat higher job performance. In short, whatever managers can do to enhance organizational affective commitment can help—although it will not definitely determine—job performance and productivity.[30]

Some research suggests that satisfaction with one's job is most likely to lead to productivity among those employees who have complex jobs in which they are able to choose between maximizing their personal productivity and doing less.[31] It follows that among professional, supervisory, and managerial employees, the relationship between job satisfaction and job performance is particularly strong, perhaps because these individuals have strong opportunities for rewards and intrinsic satisfaction in their jobs.

REDUCE ABSENTEEISM AND TURNOVER Job satisfaction predicts both whether employees will be absent from their jobs and whether they are likely to leave them, although it predicts turnover more strongly than absenteeism.[32] Interestingly, satisfaction is actually less important in predicting the performance of a company's superior performers, probably because companies reward these people in many ways,[33] some of which are independent of the job itself.

INCREASE COMPETITIVE ADVANTAGE At the organizational level, it can reasonably be argued that a happy organization is a productive organization. Studies show that employees who share positive attitudes positively affect such factors as customer satisfaction, and such aspects of company performance as profit and controllable costs.[34]

For example, recent research by marketing experts suggests a relationship between employee satisfaction and customer satisfaction, and between employee satisfaction and profitability. These relationships are described by the **employee customer profit chain model**.[35] The model suggests that employees' satisfaction with their jobs and company leads to less turnover, more motivated staff, and consistent service. These benefits in turn lead to customer perceptions of value, customer satisfaction, and less customer turnover. All of these factors then lead to higher revenue and profits. Using a similar model, researchers at Sears studied data from 800 stores and found that employees' attitudes toward their company and their jobs did indeed lead to positive employee behaviors toward customers.[36]

Of course, managers and employees alike must deal with some fundamental realities underlying motivation and jobs. For one thing, the most efficient job is often the most boring job.[37] Finding ways to motivate people in these jobs has been and will continue to be a challenge.

Also, the nature of a person's work must be understood in terms of many factors, of which motivation is only one. Other important factors are working conditions, the physical difficulty of the work, and the ergonomic design of the work. Today researchers are beginning to use multidisciplinary models to account simultaneously for a variety of factors in determining work outcomes.[38]

Reason 4: To Inspire Organizational Citizenship

A final motivational goal that an organization may hold is to inspire organizational citizenship. Organizational citizenship behaviors improve group performance because they help people work together.[39] The five categories of citizenship behavior are: 1) conscientiousness—carrying out individual task performance well beyond the minimum required levels; 2) altruism—helping others; 3) civic virtue—participating in the political life of the organization; 4) sportsmanship— taking a positive attitude and not complaining; and 5) courtesy—treating others with respect.[40]

Organizational citizenship influences many aspects of organizational life. Not only is it correlated with job satisfaction, perceived fairness, and organizational commitment,[41] it also contributes to customer satisfaction and financial results. Conscientious employees go beyond customer expectations, and altruistic employees help both internal and external customers. Employees who exhibit civic virtue are likely to make suggestions to improve overall quality and customer satisfaction. Those who exhibit sportsmanship and courtesy create a positive climate among employees that spills over to customers.[42]

How Do Managers Design Motivating Jobs?

One creative way to motivate individuals in their jobs is to change the nature of the jobs themselves.

Consider this business scenario: You are the new owner of the Coffee Emporium. You purchased the Emporium because you have been drinking coffee there for years and

employee customer profit chain model
A model which suggests that employees' satisfaction with their jobs and company leads to less turnover, more motivated staff, and consistent service.

have observed two things. First, the coffee is fabulous. Second, none of the employees seems to have a particular job. Mainly high-school students, they waste a lot of time talking with each other and hanging out, and, all in all, having too much fun to be really productive. As the new owner, you see an opportunity to streamline the coffee-making process to make more profit.

You have read with interest the works of Frederick Winslow Taylor, the man who, early in the twentieth century, introduced the world to the principles of **scientific management**. The core principle of scientific management is that breaking work down into its smallest parts maximizes efficiency because each part is relatively simple to learn and do. A further advantage to scientific management is that, when a job is easily learned, workers can easily be replaced. You believe that the Emporium crew can brew more types of coffees faster and serve more customers more quickly if each employee has one definite job and group interaction is minimized. Thus, you will make more money if one person sorts the coffee supplies, another stocks the coffee behind the counter along with cream and sugar, another takes orders, another brews, another delivers the coffee to the customer at the counter, and finally, another rings it up. This way, each person gets to be an expert at a particular job, and because each job is well defined, he or she will stick to it better and become more efficient. Employees who don't stick to their jobs can be fired and replaced by other job-hungry students.

Luckily, you have recently come across a very long counter that will allow you to separate the workers from each other as much as possible so that their work will not be interrupted by unnecessary fooling around. Also, you have found some cheap partitions that will keep the workers who sort and stock the coffee out of sight of the other employees and the customers. As a final touch to your reorganization, you write out a thorough procedures manual, including what each individual is responsible for, how to maximize efficiency in each job, and how the work should flow from one person to the next. With procedures spelled out so clearly, you are confident that your modestly capable but low-salaried manager can do the job adequately.

Secure in the thought that you have maximized organizational efficiency, you take off on what you believe is a well-earned vacation. A week later, sunning at the beach, you take a call from your manager informing you that he has just shut down your business. A few days after he implemented your system, most of your employees quit. They then badmouthed the company to other students, ruining your reputation as an employer so that your manager couldn't hire anyone else. Worse yet, right up until the store closed, the coffee was getting worse and worse.

Job Characteristics Model

What should you do? Here's an idea. Turn straight to your OB textbook and look up the job characteristics model.[43] This model suggests that a person's intrinsic motivation in a particular job depends on three critical psychological states. These states are 1) the extent to which a person experiences the job to be meaningful, 2) the extent to which a person experiences responsibility for doing the job fully and well, and 3) the extent to which a person sees the results of her or his labor. In addition, the model suggests that five **core job characteristics** foster the development of these psychological states. These characteristics are: 1) **skill variety**—the extent to which a job involves a variety of different activities that require different skills and abilities; 2) **task identity**—the extent to which a job involves the completion of a whole identifiable piece of work; 3) **task significance**—the degree to which a job is perceived by the worker as being important and having a significant impact on others; 4) **autonomy**—the degree to which a job provides freedom and discretion in scheduling the work and in determining the procedures to be used; and 5) **feedback**—the extent to which performing a job results in the worker receiving clear information about the effectiveness of his or her performance.

The core job characteristics interact with the critical psychological states in the following ways: Skill variety, task identity, and task significance influence a person's experienced meaningfulness in their job; autonomy and feedback influence a person's experienced responsibility and their knowledge of results. See Figure 5.1.

scientific management
Principles introduced by Taylor, including the idea that breaking work down into its smallest parts maximizes efficiency because each part is relatively simple to learn and do and therefore workers can easily be replaced.

core job characteristics
Five characteristics that describe what makes a job motivating.

skill variety
The extent to which a job involves a variety of different activities that require different skills and abilities.

task identity
The extent to which a job involves the completion of a whole identifiable piece of work.

task significance
The degree to which the job is perceived by the worker as being important and having a significant impact on others.

autonomy
The degree to which the job provides freedom and discretion in scheduling the work and in determining the procedures to be used.

feedback
The extent to which performing the job results in the worker receiving clear information about the effectiveness of his or her performance.

FIGURE 5.1

Job Characteristics Model

Source: J. R. Hackman and G. R. Oldham, *Work Redesign* (Reading, MA: Addison-Wesley Publishing Company, 1980): 90. Reproduced by permission of Pearson Education Inc., Upper Saddle River, New Jersey.

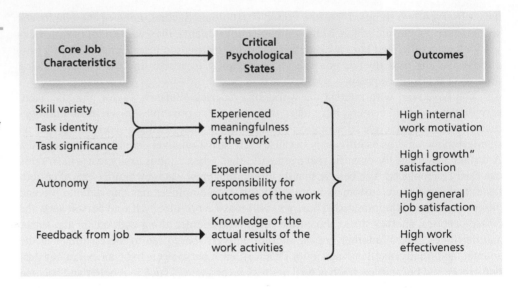

How does all this apply back at the Coffee Emporium? In the pursuit of efficiency, you, like many managers before you, have "streamlined" your employees' jobs, and in the process, you have made them less motivating. To begin with, you have reduced your workers' autonomy. You have given them strict rules and regulations and separated them so much physically that they have become, at best, mechanical instruments of your policies. No fun at all. Second, you have reduced their feedback because they are no longer saying things to each other like, "Hey, Sam, that coffee's too thin." Also, whereas all workers used to at least see the customers and sometimes interact with them, now those who are stuck behind the partition, or at the beginning of the line, get no customer feedback. Third, task identity is down because workers now don't get to see the whole process from beginning to end, and whereas they did not each perform that process individually before, they had at least felt some ownership through their interaction with their team members. Next, skill variety is down. Whereas previously workers helped each other out, now they are doing only one particular, assigned task. Dullsville, and no chance to learn new skills. Finally, task significance is also reduced, because workers don't see the connection between their own work and the goal of serving an excellent cup of coffee to a satisfied customer.

In real life, as the owner of a small company like the Emporium, you might well have intuited at least some of these potential problems. But suppose for a moment that you are in a business that has not a handful of workers, but 300 or even 1,000. Wouldn't you be tempted to maximize efficiency? To help you decide what approach would *really* work, researchers J. R. Hackman and G. R. Oldham have created a survey called the **job diagnostic survey** (JDS),[44] which assesses any job based on the five core job characteristics, as well as some related factors. From these data one can develop a **motivating potential score** (MPS) for any job. Managers can administer the survey to their employees to find out with some precision which characteristics of their jobs are motivating to them and which are not.

Here are some examples of the questions in the survey:

1. *Skill Variety* How much variety is there in your job? That is, to what extent does the job require you to do many different things at work, using a variety of your skills and talents?

2. *Task Identity* To what extent does your job involve doing a *whole and identifiable piece of work?* That is, is the job a complete piece of work that has an obvious beginning and end, or is it only a small *part* of the overall piece of work, which is finished by other people or by automatic machines?

job diagnostic survey (JDS)
A survey which assesses any job based on the five core job characteristics and some related factors.

motivating potential score (MPS)
An employee's score on the job diagnostic survey, which shows with some precision which characteristics of his or her job are motivating to him or her.

3. ***Task Significance*** In general, how *significant or important* is your job? That is, to what extent are the results of your work likely to significantly affect the lives or well being of other people?
4. ***Autonomy*** How much *autonomy* is there in your job? That is, to what extent does your job permit you to decide *on your own* how to go about doing the work?
5. ***Feedback*** To what extent does *doing the job itself* provide you with information about your work performance? That is, does the actual *work itself* provide clues about how well you are doing—aside from any "feedback" coworkers or supervisors may provide?

Also, to what extent do *managers or coworkers* let you know how well you are doing on your job?

The questions shown here are merely representative of the full survey, which asks more detailed questions about each of the motivational components. However, should you want to use these for a simple project, such as analyzing your current job in contrast with your friends' jobs, they can be answered with an "extent" scale, in which 1 = "not at all," 2 = "to a little extent," 3 = "to some extent," 4 = "to a great extent," and 5 = "to a very great extent."

In any pool of employees, some are more motivated than others. Hackman and Oldham include in their survey a measure of **growth need strength**, the degree to which an individual values complex, challenging work. In general, people with low growth need strength do respond favorably to improvements in their jobs, but they will not respond as favorably as people with high growth need strength.[45]

growth need strength
The degree to which an individual values complex, challenging work; one of the measures included in the job diagnostic survey.

To measure growth need strength, you would use a set of items like the following one: Indicate the *degree* to which you personally *would like* to have each characteristic present in your job[46]:

1. Stimulating and challenging work
2. Chances to exercise independent thought and action in my job
3. Opportunities to learn new things from my work
4. Opportunities to be creative and imaginative in my work
5. Opportunities for personal growth and development in my job
6. A sense of worthwhile accomplishment in my work

Back at the Emporium, you manage to convince your former employees to come back for two hours, paying them a bonus to do so. They agree to take the JDS. You calculate the motivating potential score for their jobs using the formula shown in Figure 5.2.

Alternatively, you could simply treat each core job characteristic as an independent variable, which is what you decide to do.[47] You also decide to measure some other employee attitudes, such as how satisfied workers are with their coworkers. The results from your survey are shown in Figure 5.3.

Creating Jobs That Motivate

Based on the data from your survey, you conclude that the jobs you have created are not particularly motivating. So your next task is to improve your workers' motivation by changing the nature of their jobs. In general, there are three approaches to making jobs more motivating. One is **job enlargement**. This practice is also referred to as "horizontal loading," because it broadens an individual's work—for example, instead of having one specialized task to do, an employee might have several. At the Emporium, for instance, the two individuals who currently sort the coffee and stock the counter might each spend half a day sorting

job enlargement
Broadening an individual's work; "horizontal loading."

$$\text{Motivating potential score (MPS)} = \left[\frac{\text{Skill variety} + \text{Task identity} + \text{Task significance}}{3}\right] \times \text{Autonomy} \times \text{Feedback from the job}$$

FIGURE 5.2
Calculating the Motivating Potential Score (MPS)

FIGURE 5.3

Employee Motivation at the Coffee Emporium Under "Efficient" New Management

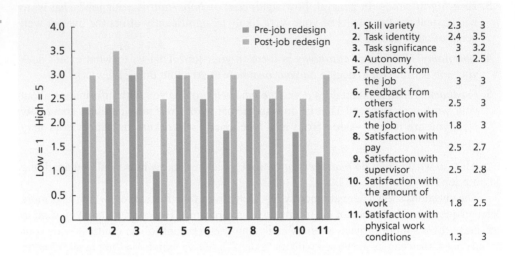

		Pre-job redesign	Post-job redesign
1.	Skill variety	2.3	3
2.	Task identity	2.4	3.5
3.	Task significance	3	3.2
4.	Autonomy	1	2.5
5.	Feedback from the job	3	3
6.	Feedback from others	2.5	3
7.	Satisfaction with the job	1.8	3
8.	Satisfaction with pay	2.5	2.7
9.	Satisfaction with supervisor	2.5	2.8
10.	Satisfaction with the amount of work	1.8	2.5
11.	Satisfaction with physical work conditions	1.3	3

job rotation
Giving workers more variety by rotating them from one kind of job to another kind of job.

job enrichment
Redesigning jobs so that workers have more autonomy, responsibility, and feedback; also called "vertical loading" because it moves decision making lower in the hierarchy.

and half a day stocking. Research suggests, however, that the motivational impact of enlarging jobs is likely to be small.[48] This is because one routine task is like another, and some workers dislike changing their habitual work patterns to take on something new.

A second approach is **job rotation**—giving workers more variety by rotating them from one kind of job to another kind of job. At the Emporium, for instance, the worker who stocks might also sometimes serve customers. Job rotation gives employees a broader view of organizational tasks and allows them to cross-train to perform those tasks. Of course, the jobs must be sufficiently different to provide meaningful cross-training.

Finally, **job enrichment** is redesigning jobs so that workers have more autonomy, responsibility, and feedback. This approach is also called "vertical loading" because it moves decision making lower in the hierarchy. For example, you might allow your workers to do a complete task and assess their own performance. Job enrichment attempts to improve upon *all* of the factors described in the job characteristics model. Here are five ways in which you might enrich an employee's job, with examples of how you might do this at the Emporium:

1. **Put two or more tasks together** to create a larger, more meaningful and more challenging piece of work. For example, at the Coffee Emporium, one person might be in charge of all aspects of the coffee sorting and stocking up until an order is taken. Others could be in charge of taking an order, making the coffee, and serving it.

2. **Create natural work units**, establishing work based on meaningful tasks. For example, making excellent coffee could be seen as a meaningful task, or interfacing with customers from the time the coffee is poured to the time that it is rung up at the cash register might be seen as a meaningful task.

3. **Establish client relationships**. Establishing a direct relationship between workers and customers increases feedback as well as autonomy and skill variety for the employee. You bought the Emporium because you saw the employees interacting with the customers. Even though their job was "just" making the coffee, they enjoyed and learned from this interaction, and customers enjoyed it as well.

4. **Expand jobs vertically**. Allow employees to take over some of the jobs that were previously assigned to management, thus providing them with increased autonomy. You might allow employees to work out their schedules together, or figure out better ways to interact with customers.

5. **Open feedback channels**. Feedback can come from the job itself, from customers, or from managers. It should come routinely, not just occasionally. For example, give employees the opportunity to call customers to see how they liked the coffee and their experience at the Emporium. Give them specific performance feedback about how much money they saved or earned for the company in a given period.

FIGURE 5.4

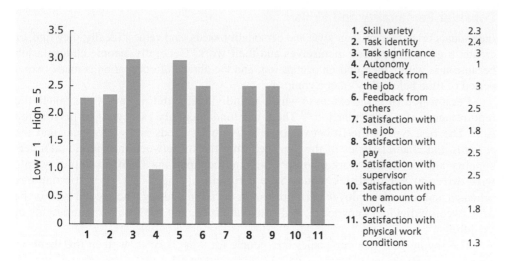

1. Skill variety	2.3
2. Task identity	2.4
3. Task significance	3
4. Autonomy	1
5. Feedback from the job	3
6. Feedback from others	2.5
7. Satisfaction with the job	1.8
8. Satisfaction with pay	2.5
9. Satisfaction with supervisor	2.5
10. Satisfaction with the amount of work	1.8
11. Satisfaction with physical work conditions	1.3

Motivation at the Coffee Emporium after Company Crisis and Intervention

IMPROVING WORK AT THE COFFEE EMPORIUM Now the partitions have come down. The long counter has been replaced by a short one. Two employees are assigned to sort, stock, and make the coffee; the others serve individual customers beginning with taking their order, then pouring their coffee, then ringing up their order, and then, sometimes, following up to find out how they like their drink. Your people now work in teams, and the teams have some discretion for determining their work hours and daily tasks. Both production and customer teams are encouraged to get feedback directly from the customers. A few months after redesigning their jobs, you repeat the JDS. The results of this survey are shown in Figure 5.4.

The average score for how motivated your employees are in their jobs (items 1 to 6) has increased from 2.2 to 2.9, a figure that you judge is not too bad for jobs in a coffee shop. Pay satisfaction and task significance have gone up the least, and only slightly, suggesting that, although employees feel generally more positive about their work, the pay is still coffee shop pay and the importance of the task has not really changed. The scores that *have* gone up significantly are autonomy (a cherished value among the students), satisfaction with physical work conditions (an essential aspect of any workplace), and task identity (the sense of contributing to a whole piece of work). You are pretty sure that the resulting increase in overall job satisfaction will help you rebuild your reputation as an employer, although this will take time. Best of all, your coffee is at least as good as before and the customers are once more flocking to your door.

Some caveats: When applying the job diagnostic survey in real life, it is important to keep in mind its limitations. For one thing, responses to the job diagnostic survey can easily be faked.[49] Also, results can be distorted by employees' desire to be consistent. For example, if they hate their jobs, they are also likely to say they are dissatisfied overall even though that might not actually be true. The results should always be checked against other data, such as your own and others' observations. When you are interpreting the JDS, it is also important to keep in mind that the job characteristics are not independent of each other, and therefore, if a job scores high on one characteristic, it is likely to score high on others.

Of course, to motivate your employees in their jobs, you do not need a survey. Understanding the fundamental psychological principles on which it is based will help you to design jobs well in the first place.

How Does an Employer Fit a Person to a Job?

Employers fit employees to jobs by taking into consideration their personalities, skills, and values, and by analyzing jobs themselves to develop clear profiles of what kind of person would be best for a particular position.

Consider Personality and Skills

Individuals bring to a job their style and personality, skills, and values. Ideally, they find, or create, a good fit between themselves and their work. Generally, people choose a job because it is within their chosen occupation, and the choice of occupation is made over a period of time before they enter a company.

person–job fit

The extent to which an individual's abilities and traits match the requirements of a particular job.

Person–job fit is the extent to which an individual's abilities and traits match the requirements of a particular job.[50] There are fundamentally two types of person–job fit.[51] The first type is the fit between the individual's needs and preferences and the rewards and characteristics of the job, including the fit between the individual's personality and particular work environments and occupations.[52] For example, people with different personalities would have different attitudes toward particular pay schemes and toward employee participation in decision making. The second type is the fit between individual knowledge, skills, and abilities, and the ability requirements of the job.

The saying goes that companies hire people for what they know, then fire them for who they are. But savvy companies work hard to avoid such hiring failures. Companies are interested in person–job fit because they realize that matching individuals' abilities and aptitudes with the ability requirements of a job positively affects job performance, and that matching an individual's needs with the particular need-fulfilling characteristics of a job affects job satisfaction.[53]

A popular, widely researched theory of person–job fit is J. L. Holland's model of vocational choice. Holland suggests that there are six fundamental personality types, and that for each of these types there are certain occupations that are "congruent," or, a good fit. See Table 5.1.

Although fitting a category of person with a type of job is predictive and somewhat useful, we should keep in mind that people also adapt in their jobs.[54] People adapt to jobs,

TABLE 5.1 Personality Type and Occupational Type According to Holland

This personality type. . .	Prefers activities such as. . .	Dislikes activities that. . .	Typical Occupations
Realistic	Systematic and specific manipulation of objects such as tools, machines, or even animals	Involve educational or therapeutic goals	Surveyor, mechanic
Investigative	Observational, symbolic, systemic, and creative investigation of physical, biological and cultural phenomena in order to understand and control them	Require persuasion, repetition, or social interaction	Chemist, physicist
Artistic	Ambiguous, free, unsystematized work that requires manipulating physical and human characteristics to create art forms or products	Require being explicit and systematic	Artist, writer
Social	Manipulation of others to train, cure, or enlighten them	Require being explicit and systematic, especially when required to *work with* materials, tools, or machines	Education, social science, teacher, counselor
Enterprising	Manipulation of others to attain organizational goals or economic gain	Require making observations, and acting in systematic ways or symbolical capacities	Business administration, marketing, sales, executive
Conventional	Explicit and systematic manipulation of data to attain organizational goals or economic gain	Require sensitivity to ambiguity, autonomy, exploration, or anything unsystematized	Accounting, business education, clerk

Source: Based on J. L. Holland, *Making Vocational Choices: A Theory of Vocational Personalities and Work Environments* (Odessa, FL: Psychological Assessment Resources, 1997).

and even change them, soon after they start them. They personalize various aspects of their jobs, from ignoring both constraints and precedents to negotiating special privileges.[55] Also, with rapid changes in technology, jobs themselves evolve over time and jobholders must continue to adapt to them. So although fitting a person to a job is useful, it is important to keep in mind that the target is always moving.

Today Holland's theory is being challenged by researchers because his six personality factors have received less validation than the factors identified by the Big Five theory of personality.[56] Also, Holland's model does not include the Big Five factor of stability (low neuroticism), which has been shown to be a powerful predictor of vocational career success.[57] At the same time, since no aspect of the Big Five correlates well with Holland's realistic type, it has been suggested that the two models might profitably be used together.

Consider Individual Values

Today many employees hope to express and develop themselves at work, to the point of bringing their personal value systems to bear on organizational decisions.[58] This trend can be attributed to a variety of social factors.[59] For one thing, people today are spending significantly more time on the job than did previous generations, so the workplace itself is where many social developments are likely to occur. For another thing, people are finding their identities less in relationship to a single company and more in relationship to their personal self-direction,[60] so their personal values may be relatively conscious and important to them. Finally, Baby Boomers who matured in the iconoclastic 1960s and 1970s are trying to maintain their idealistic identities and are bringing these values to work.[61]

For example, some workers seek to increase their experience of meaning, or spirituality, in life by merging their personal and professional values in their jobs. When they experience organizational values systems congruent with their own, such employees are more willing to commit to organizational goals and responsibilities.[62] They also experience greater satisfaction, stay with their company longer, and perform better.[63]

Of course, values systems are sometimes incongruent. For example, although about half of Americans label themselves as environmentalists,[64] management theory is often based on anti-environment assumptions. These include the belief in the necessity of increasing economic growth and the belief in the supremacy of technological development for controlling natural systems.[65] Such values incongruence can be reduced in companies when both employees and managers try to find common ground. On the one hand, top management can learn to reframe environmental issues in the language of the workplace culture. For example, they may seek to "improve operational efficiency" by reducing the input of total or hazardous materials, or by minimizing the output of wastes. Or they may "reduce risk management costs" by limiting damaging environmental exposures for employees. For their part, employees can learn to be "multilingual," adopting the language of their organization while also introducing the language of environmentalism.[66] They can reconcile their spiritual selves with their organizational selves by working to make the organization consistent with their beliefs.[67]

What Is the Process of Matching a Person and a Job?

The actual process of fitting a person to a job begins with a **job analysis**, in which a company determines what work needs to be done and what skills and abilities are necessary to perform the work. Often job analysis is done by a company's human resources department.

Companies use a variety of techniques to perform job analyses, including directly observing jobs and asking job incumbents to describe their jobs. Generally, it is believed that a variety of informants should be asked their opinions about what is needed in a given job. The list of informants might include job incumbents, supervisors, people from different parts of the organization, people from different demographic backgrounds, and anyone who depends on the work product of the job, for example, internal and external customers.[68] Doing a sound job analysis is critical because all later decisions in the

job analysis
The first step in the process of fitting a person to a job: determining what work needs to be done and what skills and abilities are necessary to perform the work.

job description

The second step in the process of fitting a person to a job: the details of what the work will be.

job specifications

The third step in the process of fitting a person to a job: the details of what skills, education and experience are required to perform the work.

procedural process

How the selection process is performed.

social process

The process of enhancing the social and emotional aspects of selection for a job.

employment process—including personnel selection, training, performance appraisal, and compensation—depend on it.[69]

The job analysis is followed by a written **job description** and **job specifications** which detail, respectively, what the work will be, and what skills, education, and experience are required to perform it. Two important aspects of what the work will be are the degree to which an employee works alone rather than with other people, and the amount of time working on projects versus processes.[70]

The next step is to attract job candidates and select from among them. Managers must first be concerned with **procedural process**—how the selection process is performed. For example, they must decide which procedure obtains the best candidates—doing interviews? administering performance-based tests? contacting references? Today managers are also interested in creating an effective **social process** during selection. This includes enhancing the social and emotional aspects of selection, including how much participation and control of the process the candidate has, how the candidate receives feedback during the process, and how candidate privacy is respected.[71]

How Do Companies Use Scheduling to Motivate?

Today many companies offer a variety of flexible scheduling arrangements for their employees. Research suggests that flextime and commuting, for example, are positively related to job satisfaction, retention, and productivity.[72]

Flextime and the Compressed Workweek

job description

Flextime is allowing employees to choose their own hours, and today more than a quarter of all full-time wage and salary workers do this either formally or informally.[73] Generally, flextime employees choose their hours around a common core, such as 9 a.m. to 3 p.m., during which they are required to be in the office. This arrangement is called a **gliding schedule**. Other forms of flextime include the **compressed workweek** and even variable-week schedules, which require working a certain number of hours during a certain number of days or weeks.

flextime

Allowing employees to choose their own hours.

gliding schedule

A form of flextime in which employees are allowed to choose their own hours around a common core of time during which they are required to be in the office.

compressed workweek

A form of flextime in which employees are allowed to work a certain number of hours during a certain number of days or weeks.

Early research suggested that the availability of flextime arrangements in a company is related to improvements in job satisfaction and performance, and reductions in absenteeism and turnover.[74] It is certainly a popular option. It is used by 99 percent of top-rated IT companies, for example,[75] and 59 percent of all organizations, as reported by human resources professionals.[76]

For example, at the Milwaukee-based financial-services firm Robert W. Baird & Company, flexible work arrangements are credited with significantly helping the bottom line. Since the company implemented such programs as compressed workweeks, flexible schedules and hours, and job-sharing, its revenues have tripled and it has grown from a regional brokerage firm into a national and international investment-banking and investment-management firm. During this time, employee ownership of the company has also grown, from 20 percent to 93 percent. More than 40 percent of the company's workforce has some sort of flexible arrangement.

Recent studies indicate that flextime attracts primarily workers who face pressures from family or school responsibilities, and it does not increase a company's attraction for those who do not have this sort of conflict.[77] One particularly interesting field experiment occurred in a large public utility company that implemented gliding-schedule flextime.[78] This company and its labor union agreed to test flextime for a year in one large sub-unit, while, for purposes of comparison, not implementing flextime in a second large sub-unit. The flextime unit experienced large reductions in absences, although no reduction in employee turnover, and when management subsequently discontinued the flextime, absences returned to former levels.

However, the experiment also demonstrated how hard it is to implement such a program in a complex working environment. The main reason the company terminated the experiment was that it could not extend flexible scheduling to all employees. One problem was that some divisions required work coverage 24 hours a day, seven days a week. Also, some field service jobs did not lend themselves to flexible scheduling because customers would not appreciate very early or very late service calls. Further, the company feared that unequal access to flexible scheduling would lead to an unmanageable number of transfers into flextime jobs, and it was not able to flexibly schedule first-level supervisors in such a way as to cover all non-supervisory personnel who were on flextime. Other problems included how to calculate overtime, schedule group meetings, and assign shift work fairly. In the end, both union and management felt the program was not viable.

Telecommuting

Telecommuting is any work arrangement that allows employees to do some of their work at home, often via a **virtual relationship** that is primarily conducted through technology.[79] A study of U.S. human resources professionals suggests that more than 37 percent of their companies offer telecommuting options.[80] Telecommuting is also used in other countries. The Spanish bank Banesto allows some workers, often women, to work at home.[81] Doing credit risk analysis, for example, can be done using a portable computer, and the company is happy to evaluate staff on their performance rather than on their hours in the office.

Contrary to what you might expect, telecommuting is actually less attractive to people with high pressures from family or school than it is to those with low pressures.[82] It seems that people with high work-family pressures prefer to clearly separate their roles rather than constantly deal with role conflicts. One interpretation is that some parents prefer to get out of the house rather than deal with the kids!

Consider that telecommuting may be bad for your career. A study of telecommuting management accountants found that participating in a particular type of alternative scheduling causes the telecommuters to be rated lower in productivity even when their productivity did not warrant this judgment.[83] In fact, participation in any form of alternative scheduling affected management's perception of the employee's long-term career potential. Telecommuters were perceived as less likely to be selected for special projects, and more likely to have substandard performance in the future. They were assigned to less challenging tasks, and their promotions were delayed.

telecommuting
Any work arrangement that allows employees to do some of their work at home.

virtual relationship
Telecommuting that is primarily conducted through technology.

Job-Sharing

Job-sharing allows two or more persons to share one job, each working part time. The workers share both the responsibilities and the benefits of one position. For example, one manager might work Mondays, Wednesdays, and Fridays, while his or her co-manager works Tuesdays and Thursdays. Or each person might work three days, with one day of overlap. The team communicates daily, using phones, faxes, and e-mail, and at work the team members share a desk and work on each others' projects.

The arrangement has been used successfully with nurse managers, improving their job satisfaction and general well-being,[84] and with bank managers.[85] It allows companies to keep experienced workers that they might otherwise lose. One version has been used successfully in Nordic countries to convert workers approaching the age of retirement to partial pensions and semi-retirement, thus creating job openings for younger unemployed workers.[86]

job sharing
Allowing two or more persons to share the responsibilities and the benefits of one job position, each working part time.

How Do Companies Use the Physical Environment as a Motivator?

Next to salaries, offices are usually a company's largest expense.[87]

There is some evidence that the design of the physical workplace affects both commitment and job satisfaction, as well as whether an individual is inclined to accept a position at a company.[88] In one poll of 200 senior managers, 90 percent believed that improvements in office design can increase employee productivity.[89]

Early research on the psychological effects of the work environment was done by Abraham Maslow.[90] Maslow set up three different office spaces and invited his subjects into one of them. He then asked the subjects to study photographs of different people.

When the subjects were in the "beautiful" office, a comfortable room with warm colors, mahogany desk, Navajo rug, paintings and sculptures, the subjects tended to rate the people in the photographs as being energetic and personally effective. When the subjects were in the "ugly" office, characterized by its small size, grey paint, and clutter of boxes, tools, and junk, the participants rated the people in the photographs as fatigued and sick. Being in an "average" room, which was also grey, with two mahogany desks, metal bookcases and filing cabinets, and no art, solicited responses only slightly better than the ugly office. (The average room, by the way, was characterized as "a professor's office." No comment.) The conclusion: Décor affects attitude.

Today, evidence for the environment–productivity connection is still primarily anecdotal.[91] A redesign at Ethicon Endo-Surgery Inc., a division of Johnson & Johnson, has been credited with significantly influencing both the number of new products developed and with revenues. At Parker LePla, a brand development and public relations firm in Seattle, a new work environment featuring live trees, café type tables and chairs, and a fountain and pond, was credited with reducing employee stress. One redesign saved a company 20,000 hours in a year because the rooms, facilities, and technology were much more accessible. Many companies are also concerned about such fundamental factors as enhancing the air quality and reducing the noise pollution in their office buildings.[92]

> **open plan office**
> An office design in which traditional, individual (cellular) spaces are replaced by individual work units organized into one large room.

Today a popular design is the **open plan office, in which** traditional individual, **cellular spaces** are replaced by individual work units organized in one large room. Companies use this plan when they want high interpersonal interaction among employees. Also, this plan often saves money because each individual worker requires less space.[93]

> **cellular spaces**
> Traditional, individual work spaces.

A case in point is the redesign of offices at Monster.com. Traditional enclosed offices were abandoned in favor of a colorful, flexible, and unconventional space, leading 90 percent of the company's employees to agree that the new physical environment improved the company's attractiveness as an employer. Among the company's new employees, 68 percent said the physical environment was an important factor in their decision to accept the new position.

Although companies such as Intel and Hewlett-Packard prefer open plan offices because they express their values, companies such as Microsoft use closable individual offices because the work performed requires uninterrupted thinking.[94] Some individuals, notably introverts who recharge better in solitude than in the company of others, and people who find noise distracting, find open plan offices stressful.

In this intriguing area, more research is needed.

How Do Managers Design Fair and Effective Performance Appraisals?

> **performance appraisal**
> The formal evaluation of an employee's performance.

Performance appraisal is the formal evaluation of an employee's performance. Performance appraisals serve a variety of purposes. They give employees valuable feedback and determine their compensation, and they help companies to categorize employees for such purposes as promotion, demotion, and training.

Meritocracy

> **meritocracy**
> A system in which people are rewarded according to established standards of performance.

A **meritocracy** is a system in which people are rewarded according to established standards of performance, such as how many clients they see, how much money they bring in, or how many calls they answer in a set amount of time. In addition to performance alone, some meritocracies take into consideration factors such as effort and circumstances. Behaviorally anchored rating schemes, discussed in the previous chapter, are often perceived to be fair, as are performance-based schemes.

Students, who have spent most of their lives in organizations called schools, where merit is measured constantly (if imperfectly) and every effort is made to make appraisals (tests, papers, and so on) fair, often expect their workplace to be the same way. Yet, the notion of meritocracy is an ideal that many organizations fail to achieve.[95] Rather, in organizational life a whole range of human factors, from expectations and biases to close personal ties, affect how performance is appraised and rewarded.

You know that for some jobs, managers can quantify results and use them as a basis for a performance appraisal. For example, in a manufacturing environment, the number and quality of products made by an individual or group is measurable. In a call center, the number of calls handled per hour is easily tracked by computer. Yet in many jobs, measuring performance is so difficult that it is not even attempted. How does one quantify how well a public relations executive represents the company? or a social worker handles a client? In such situations, organizations prefer to look at results rather than performance. Indeed, the two are often equated.

Even where quantified results exist, judgment about extenuating factors often enters into the equation. Sam sold more widgets than Sally, but, in comparison to Sally, Sam was assigned a territory with a higher concentration of potential widget customers. Thus Sally had to work very hard to find clients and make her sales, whereas Sam had the luxury of calling on known customers. Who should be rewarded? On the basis of merit and hard work one would argue for Sally. But organizational realities would often give the nod to Sam, who on paper produced more and even had time left over to develop relationships with his boss and the other higher-ups who would appraise him.

The Role of Human Judgment

So although many companies try to make formal performance ratings fair, they may fail to do so. For one thing, for a variety of individual, social, and organizational reasons, individual raters may simply choose not to be fair.

For another thing, raters are not perfectly capable of accurately rating performance.[96] They are prone to a variety of errors based on such factors as taking inadequate samples of job behaviors, having preset expectations and faulty perceptions, and failing to know about or examine changes in the ratees' jobs or job environments.[97]

For example, evaluators' expectations influence their evaluations. After a supervisor has formed an impression of a person, he or she tends to discount anything that disconfirms that impression, and also tends to rate the individual's performance based on that impression as well.[98] Also, raters who feel positively toward a ratee are more likely to be lenient, whereas raters who feel negatively are more likely to be tough.[99] This problem occurs even when a **360 degree performance appraisal** (in which employees are appraised by bosses, coworkers, and subordinates) is used. The same relationship between liking and leniency holds for ratings by superiors and peers and subordinates.

360 degree performance appraisal
An appraisal of an employee by his or her bosses, coworkers, and subordinates.

Do you think it is likely that individuals who practice impression management tactics such as complimenting their bosses get better performance evaluations? If your intuition says this is the case, you are right. But why? One way to get better performance evaluations is to be similar to one's boss in terms of gender, race, or age.[100] For example, within the United States, it has been shown that both African-American and white raters consistently give higher ratings to members of their own race.[101] But, in addition, practicing impression management can increase how much a boss likes a subordinate *and* the extent to which a boss sees their subordinate as similar to themselves.

In Practice

How does one do an effective performance appraisal? Based on the research we have discussed so far in this book, here are some general guidelines.

- **Consider carefully what behaviors and outcomes you want to evaluate.** What you evaluate (and reward) is what you will get. (Based on the principles of behavior modification.)

- **Keep in mind the psychological contract between worker and employer.** Both sides should strive to fulfill their commitments in this contract and to manage losses when the existing contracts are hard to keep. (Based on the principles of the psychological contract.)

- **Keep in mind that, in addition to actual fairness, perception of fairness matters.** Do not use a biased or subjective rating scale, for example. (Based on the principles of procedural justice).

- ***When delivering a performance evaluation, separate feedback from reward.*** This allows the employee to react separately to the feedback and the rewards, and his or her possibly emotional reaction to one aspect will not overshadow discussion of the other. (Based on principles of emotion.)

- ***Consider cultural differences.*** When entering a non-U.S. culture, do your homework. A multiplicity of factors will influence how, or even whether, a performance appraisal is done. Research indicates that culture matters particularly at two stages in the process: when selecting the person or persons to do the performance appraisal, and when selecting behaviors to appraise.[102] To avoid biases in international appraisals, one strategy is to avoid selecting appraisers from a single ethnic group. An analysis of behavior preferences based on the appraiser's cultural orientation is also desirable. For example, Asians are more likely than their Caucasian counterparts to react unfavorably toward provocative, egocentric, and showing off behaviors.

- ***Know the law related to performance appraisal.*** Information from the appraisal may be used in litigation by an employee claiming to have been a victim of discriminatory practices or by an employer defending his or her position. Be aware of the protected classes (discussed in Chapter 1).

How Do Companies Use Organizational Culture to Motivate Their Employees?

Later in this text, we devote a full chapter to organizational culture, including how it can be used to motivate people in their jobs. Culture is indeed an important motivator! Don't overlook it.

Apply What You Have Learned. . .

World Class Company: Volvo—The Uddevalla Plant

Part A. How Were Jobs Redesigned?

In 1989 Volvo opened a new assembly plant in Uddevalla on the west coast of Sweden. Rather than running cars down one long line, the plant utilized small teams to build complete cars. The conventional assembly line uses a conveyer belt to pass one car at a time in front of the worker, who puts together the same parts on each car. In contrast, under the Volvo team approach, work groups assemble sections of cars, and they work on several cars at a time.

Major components of the cars are subassembled by one set of teams. These employees rotate jobs and are responsible for managing quality control, selecting new team members, and assigning jobs. Then the final assembly teams work on four cars at a time to complete them. They plan their own schedules and work pace. They tend to prefer jobs that take several hours to complete, rather than jobs that take just a few minutes.

All teams receive extensive training so they can understand how to assemble the cars and, also, how to work together.

When defects are discovered after production, the corrections are returned to the team.

Discuss

Using Hackman's model of job design, contrast the motivating potential of the Uddevalla Plant job designs with that of conventional assembly lines.

Part B. Was the Experiment a Success?

The Volvo experiment has been both praised and derided. On the one hand, it has been called noble and humanistic. As one observer put it, "The plant's almost unreal lack of noise and movement combined with its clean and bright interior contribute to a low-stress work environment that is reflected in the team members and how they work together."[103] Typical automobile plants are noisy, dirty, and physically and mentally stressful. Volvo initiated the new plant with its innovative job design during an industrial labor crisis when Swedish manufacturers were having a hard time recruiting workers. At the time, it succeeded in retaining workers at a much higher rate than average for Swedish industry.

On the other hand, the experiment has been criticized as inefficient. Often the team approach requires significantly more time to build a car. There are high costs for selecting and training workers.

Despite the drawbacks, one researcher suggests the subsequent closing of the Uddevalla plant in 1992 was primarily due to a lack of new product development on the part of the company.[104] Christian Berggren points out that, based on customer evaluations, the plant had a clear edge in quality and the workers found smart technical solutions that reduced equipment costs and tools by one-half compared with conventional line assembly. Also, the job design and equipment at the plant created large improvements in how the work was done ergonomically and psychologically. Long-term projections suggested that the plant would have low turnover and low costs for repetitive strain injuries and workers compensation.

Discuss

1. Would you want to work at the Uddevalla Plant? Why or why not?
2. What social and economic conditions must exist before such plants are viable in your state? worldwide?

Advice from the Pros

Ten Dumb Things Managers Do to People in Their Jobs

Have any of the demotivators on the following list happened to you?

- Your manager fails to give you a clear idea of what you are supposed to do, and then wonders why you fail to perform.
- Management creates policies for every imaginable contingency, and so cannot meet your needs when a truly new problem arises.
- Conversely, management creates so *few* policies that the job seems totally political, with rewards given out on the basis of favoritism rather than merit.
- Your bosses teach you that your ideas are easily vetoed, and then wonder why you never make suggestions.
- Conversely, your bosses ask you often for your ideas, but never use them. Nor do they tell you whether or not your idea has been seriously considered.

- Your manager goes ahead and makes a decision and only later asks you for your input.
- Your company identifies a few people breaking rules and company policies and then chides the whole workforce about these infractions.
- Because a few employees can't be trusted, your company watches everyone closely and punishes every small mistake.
- Your company publishes expectations and policies, but does nothing when employees ignore them.
- Your manager asks you to change the way you are doing something but doesn't give you any guidelines about how to do so. He or she labels you or your coworkers who ask questions "resisters."

Source: Adapted from "Twenty Dumb Things Organizations Do to Mess Up Their Relationship with People" by management consultant Susan H. Heathfield, a specialist in human resource related systems. For the other 10 see:

http://humanresources.about.com/b/a/077132.htm

Discuss

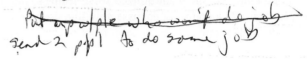

1. List three really dumb things that organizations have done to you that do not appear in the list above. These should be things that have demotivated you when it came to meeting organizational goals.
2. Share these with the class. What do these dumb things have in common?

Gain Experience

I. Good Jobs, Bad Jobs

1. In groups of three to five members, each student describes the worst job he or she has had.
2. The group selects one of these jobs and rates the job on Hackman and Oldham's (1980) core job characteristics using the scale low, medium, and high. One member of the group describes the job and their analysis to the class.

3. Repeat for the best job the students have ever had.
4. Select one of the worst jobs and, as a class, redesign it.

II. Defend Your Position: Do Stock Options Motivate Executives To Do More For Their Company's Shareholders?

See Table 5.2 for some points to consider. . .[105]

TABLE 5.2

Yes, stock options do motivate executives to do more for shareholders.	No, stock options do not motivate executives to do more for shareholders.
Executives who run their company effectively should be highly rewarded, and money is the best reward.	Executives who pay too much attention to their options and the price of the company stock may neglect the running of the company.
If the stock goes up, the executive gains right along with the shareholders.	Executives should be motivated by salaries and bonuses that are given at the discretion of the board of directors, not by their speculations in the stock market.
Options for executives are like ESOPs for employees: They motivate them both intrinsically and extrinsically.	Executives merely manipulate the stock prices so they themselves can buy low and sell high.
Executives want autonomy; they do not want their compensation to be determined solely, or even primarily, by their board of directors.	The Sarbanes-Oxley Act required managers to disclose the granting of stock options more quickly, but not quickly enough.
Using stock options rewards excellence and punishes weakness.	Unless all granting, exercise, buying, and selling of stock options is made public in advance, executives will always manipulate them for their personal advantage despite what effect this has on stockholders.
Without stock options, executives pay more attention to building their power base than increasing the stock value.	
Top executives require top rewards. If one company offers an executive some stock options, to be competitive other companies must offer them, too.	Executives should be motivated by their interesting jobs and their stockholders, not by extrinsic rewards.

Can You Solve this Manager's Problem?

Motivating Innovation at Samsung

Walk now in the shoes of Jong-Yong Yun, CEO of the Korean electronic products company Samsung. Samsung ranks number 1 in the world in eight product categories, including computer monitors, big LCD screens, and flash memory chips. In 2005, your goal is to double the number of number 1 rankings in three years and triple them in five years.

To achieve these ambitious goals, you invest heavily in research and development (R&D). In fact, you have 17 research centers and 27,000 researchers worldwide, in a total workforce of 113,600.

A compelling question is, when you bring together teams of your top engineers, designers, and researchers to develop and perfect particular products, how do you motivate them to do their best?

Consider that you are setting up a research center in South Korea. Specifically,

1. How would you convince your people that their task is significant?
2. How would you create a physical place that gives priority to creativity?
3. How would you schedule the workday for this place?

At this point, your professor will share with you what Samsung actually did.

4. What is the company's psychological contract with these high-power workers? Consider their commitment to the company, their autonomy, and their work–family balance.
5. Compare employee motivation at Samsung with motivation in typical U.S. companies.

Chapter Summary and Key Terms

Why do managers work hard to motivate their employees?

Managers want to avoid the consequences of job dissatisfaction, attract and keep workers, enhance task performance and organizational outcomes, and perhaps even inspire organizational citizenship.

job   126
task performance   126
organizational citizenship   126
exit   127
voice   127
loyalty   127
neglect   127
EVLN model   127
job satisfaction   128
organizational commitment   128
continuance commitment   128
normative commitment   128
psychological contract   129
employability   129
employee customer profit chain model   130

How do managers design motivating jobs?

They use the job characteristics model to diagnose and improve intrinsic job motivation. This model is based on improving five job characteristics: feedback, autonomy, task significant, task identity, and skill variety. They create jobs that motivate using job enlargement, job rotation, and job enrichment.

scientific management   131
core job characteristics   131
skill variety   131
task identity   131
task significance   131

autonomy   131
feedback   131
job diagnostic survey (JDS)   132
motivating potential score (MPS)   132
growth need strength   133
job enlargement   133
job rotation   134
job enrichment   134

How does an employer fit a person to a job?

Employers assess individuals in terms of their personalities, skills, and values. They also perform a job analysis to determine what tasks need to be done and what skills and abilities are needed to accomplish them. They write up a job description that describes what type of individual should perform which tasks.

person–job fit   136

What is the process of matching a person and a job?

The process of matching a person and a job is a multi-phased process that begins with a job analysis.

job analysis   137
job description   138
job specifications   138
procedural process   138
social process   138

How do companies use scheduling to motivate?

They use flextime, compressed workweeks, telecommuting, and job-sharing. Flexible work schedules are typically set around a common core of hours, an arrangement that is called a gliding schedule. Telecommuting is typically handled through a virtual relationship. Job sharing allows two people to share one job, each working part time.

How do companies use the physical environment as a motivator?

Next to salaries, offices are a company's greatest expense. To motivate their employees, managers need to consider whether to use cellular or open plan offices, and whether to bother with creating spaces that are attractive.

How do managers design fair and effective performance appraisals?

Although managers attempt to assess people on their merits, they also know that this is sometimes impossible. Effective managers do all they can to be aware of the role of human judgment in performance appraisals, including the existence of bias and the role of human errors in decision making. They also educate themselves about the importance of such factors as psychological contracts, procedural justice, cultural differences, and the law.

How do companies use organizational culture to motivate their employees?

See Chapter 17: Organizational Culture.

Explorations

1. Telework

Check out http://www.telework.gov for advice on everything from how to determine good candidates for telework (telecommuting) to how to supervise teleworkers.

2. Flextime

Web search for flextime and job-sharing applications.

3. Motivating new employees

For a hands-on approach to motivating new employees see Diane Arthur's *Recruiting, Interviewing, Selecting, & Orienting New Employees* (American Management Association, 1998).

4. Giving an effective performance appraisal

See Dick Grote, *The Performance Appraisal Question and Answer Book: A Survival Guide for Managers* (New York: AMACOM, 2002).

References

[1] Adapted from J. P. Campbell, "The Definition and Measurement of Performance in the New Age," in D. R. Ilgen and E. D. Pulakos, eds., *The Changing Nature of Performance: Implications for Staffing, Motivation, and Development* (San Francisco: Jossey-Bass, 1999):399–429.

[2] D. W. Organ, "Organizational Citizenship Behavior: It's Construct Clean-Up Time," *Human Performance 10*, 1997:85–97.

[3] D. Farrell, "Exit, Voice, Loyalty and Neglect as Responses to Job Dissatisfaction: A Multidimensional Scaling Study," *Academy of Management Journal, 26*, 1983:596–607; M. J. Withey and W. H. Cooper, "Predicting Exit, Voice, Loyalty and Neglect," *Administrative Science Quarterly 34*:521–539.

[4] J. Zhou and J. M. George, "When Job Dissatisfaction Leads to Creativity: Encouraging the Expression of Voice," *Academy of Management Journal 44* (4), August 2001:682–696.

[5] *BusinessWeek*, April 20, 1998, cited in T. R. Mitchell, B. C. Holtom, and T. W. Lee, "How to Keep Your Best Employees: Developing an Effective Retention Policy," *Academy of Management Executive 15* (4), November 2001:96–108.

[6] B. Wysocki, "Retaining Employees Turns into a Hot Topic," *Wall Street Journal*, September 8, 1997: *B1*.

[7] G. Ramsay-Smith, "Employee Turnover: The Real Cost," *Strategic HR Review 3* (4), May/June 2004:7.

[8] C. A. Hacker, "Turnover: A Silent Profit Killer," *Information Systems Management 20* (2), Spring 2003:14–18.

[9] C. A. Hacker, "Turnover: A Silent Profit Killer," *Information Systems Management 20* (2), Spring 2003:14–18.

[10] M. J. Withey and I. R. Gallatly, "Exit, Voice, Loyalty and Neglect: Assessing the Influence of Prior Effectiveness and Personality," *Proceedings of the Administrative Sciences Association of Canada, Organizational Behavior Division 20*, 1999:110–119; M. J. Withey and I. R. Gallatly, "Situational Determinants of Exit, Voice, Loyalty and Neglect," *Proceedings of the Administrative Sciences Association of Canada*, Saskatoon, Saskatchewan, June 1998.

[11] S. Kassin, *Psychology* (Upper Saddle River, NJ: Prentice Hall, 2004):521.

[12] E. A. Locke, "The Nature and Causes of Job Satisfaction," in M. Dunnette, ed., *Handbook of Industrial and Organizational Psychology* (Chicago: Rand McNally, 1976).

13 M. S. Nagy, "Using a Single-Item Approach to Measure Facet Job Satisfaction," *Journal of Occupational & Organizational Psycholog, 75* (1), March 3002:77–86; V. Scarpello and J. P. Campbell, "Job Satisfaction: Are All the Parts There?" *Personnel Psychology 36,* 1983:577–600.

14 G. Koretz, "Hate Your Job? Join the Club," *BusinessWeek,* October 6, 2003:40.

15 C. McMurray, "U.S. Workers: More Productive, but Less Secure," *Gallup Poll Tuesday Briefing,* September 16, 2003:1–4.

16 "The World at Work: Majority of Americans, Western Europeans, Latin Americans Are Satisfied with Jobs; Eastern Europeans and Asians Give Less Glowing Endorsement of Their Job Life," www.ipsos-na.com/news/pressrelease. cfm?id=1134, January 8, 2001. Accessed July 8, 2004.

17 T. A. Judge and J. E. Bono, "Relationship of Core Self-Evaluations Traits—Self-Esteem, Generalized Self-Efficacy, Locus of Control, and Emotional Stability—With Job Satisfaction and Job Performance: A Meta-Analysis," *Journal of Applied Psychology 86* (1), February 2001:80–92; R. P. Steel and J. R. Rentsch, "The Dispositional Model of Job Attitudes Revisited: Findings of a 10-Year Study," *Journal of Applied Psychology 82* (6), December 1997:873–879.

18 R. T. Mowday, L. W. Porter, and R. M. Steers, *Employee Organizational Linkages: The Psychology of Commitment, Absenteeism, and Turnover* (New York: Academic Press, 1982).

19 J. P. Meyer, "Organizational Commitment," *International Review of Industrial and Organizational Psychology 12,* 1997:175–228.

20 "Job-Hopping: The Big Picture," *BusinessWeek,* September 10, 2001:16.

21 "Managers Resolve to Spend Less Time at Work," *Management Services 48* (3), March 2004:7.

22 J. A. Ritter and R. Anker, "Good Jobs, Bad Jobs: Workers' Evaluations in Five Countries," *International Labour Review 141* (4), 2002:331–358.

23 E. H. Schein, *Organizational Psychology* (Englewood Cliffs, NJ: Prentice Hall, 1965); D. M. Rousseau and J. M. Parks, "The Contracts of Individuals and Organizations," in L. L. Cummings and B. M. Stowe, eds., *Research in Organizational Behavior 15* (Greenwich, CT: JAI Press, 1993):1–47.

24 P. R. Sparrow, "Transitions in the Psychological Contract: Some Evidence from the Banking Sector," *Human Resource Management Journal 6,* 1996:75–92.

25 S. L. Robinson and D. M. Rousseau, "Violating the Psychological Contract: Not the Exception but the Norm," *Journal of Organizational Behavior 15,* 1994:245–259.

26 E. W. Morrison and S. L. Robinson, "When Employees Feel Betrayed: A Model of How Psychological Contract Violation Develops," *Academy of Management Review, 22* (1), 1997:226–256.

27 T. A. Judge, C. J. Thoresen, J. E. Bono, and G. K. Patton, "The Job Satisfaction—Job Performance Relationship: A Qualitative and Quantitative Review," *Psychological Bulletin 127* (3), 2001:376–407; M. M. Petty, G. W. McGee, and J. W. Cavender, "A Meta-Analysis of the Relationships Between Individual Job Satisfaction and Individual Performance," *Academy of Management Review 9* (4), October 1984:712–721.

28 C. Ostroff, "The Relationship between Satisfaction, Attitudes, and Performance: An Organizational Level Analysis," *Journal of Applied Psychology 77* (6), 1992:963–974; B. Schneider, P. J. Hanges, D. B. Smith, A. N. Salvaggio, "Which Comes First, Employee Attitudes or Organizational Financial and Market Performance?" *Journal of Applied Psychology 88* (5), October 2003:836–850.

29 T. A. Judge, C. J. Thoresen, J. E. Bono, and G. K. Patton, "The Job Satisfaction–Job Performance Relationship: A Qualitative and Quantitative Review," *Psychological Bulletin 127* (3), 2001:376–407; W. H. Turnley and D. C. Feldman, "The Impact of Psychological Contract Violations on Exit, Voice, Loyalty and Neglect," *Human Relations 52* (7), 1999:895–922.

30 D. W. Organ and K. Ryan, "A Meta-Analytic Review of Attitudinal and Dispositional Predictors of Organizational Citizenship Behavior," *Personnel Psychology,* Winter 1995: 775–802,791; J. A. LePine, A. Erez, and D. E. Johnson, "The Nature and Dimensionality of Organizational Citizenship Behavior: A Critical Review and Meta-Analysis," *Journal of Applied Psychology 87* (1) 2002:52–56.

31 M. M. Petty, G. W. McGee, and J. W. Cavender, "A Meta-Analysis of the Relationships between Individual Job Satisfaction and Individual Performance," *Academy of Management Review 9* (4), October 1984:712–721.

32 K. D. Scott and G. S. Taylor, "An Examination of Conflicting Findings on the Relationship between Job Satisfaction and Absenteeism: A Meta-Analysis," *Academy of Management Journal,* September 1985:599–612; R. W. Griffeth, P. W. Hom, and S. Gaertner, "A Meta-Analysis of Antecedents and Correlates of Employee Turnover: Update, Moderator Tests, and Research Implications for the Next Millennium," *Journal of Management 26* (3), 2000:463–488, 479

33 D. G. Spencer and R. M. Steers, "Performance as a Moderator of the Job Satisfaction–Turnover Relationship," *Journal of Applied Psychology 66* (4) August 1981:511–514.

34 A. M Ryan, M. J. Schmit, and R. Johnson, "Attitudes and Effectiveness: Examining Relations at an Organizational Level," *Personnel Psychology 49* (4):853–882.

35 J. I. Heskett, W. E. Sasser, and L. A. Schlesinger, *The Service Profit Chain* (New York: Free Press, 1997); D. J. Koys, "The Effects of Employee Satisfaction, Organizational Citizenship Behavior, and Turnover on Organizational Effectiveness: A Unit-Level, Longitudinal Study," *Personnel Psychology, 54*(1):101–114.

36 A. J. Rucci, S. P. Kirn, and R. T. Quinn, "The Employee–Customer–Profit Chain at Sears," *Harvard Business Review 76,* January/February 1998:82–87.

37 J. R. Edwards, J. A. Scully and M. D. Brtek, "The Nature and Outcomes of Work: A Replication and Extension of Interdisciplinary Work-Design Research," *Journal of Applied Psychology 85* (6):860–68.

38 M. A. Campion, "Interdisciplinary Approaches to Job Design: A Constructive Replication with Extensions," *Journal of Applied Psychology 73* (3), 1988:467–481.

39 D. W. Organ and K. Ryan, "A Meta-Analytic Review of Attitudinal and Dispositional Predictors of Organizational Citizenship Behavior," *Personnel Psychology 48* (4), 1995:775–802.

40 D. W. Organ, *Organizational Citizenship Behavior* (Lexington, MA: Lexington Books, 1998).

41 D. W. Organ and K. Ryan, "A Meta-Analytic Review of Attitudinal and Dispositional Predictors of Organizational Citizenship Behavior," *Personnel Psychology 48* (4), 1995:775–802.

42 D. J. Koys, "The Effects of Employee Satisfaction, Organizational Citizenship Behavior, and Turnover on Organizational Effectiveness: A Unit-Level, Longitudinal Study," *Personnel*

Psychology 54 (1), Spring 2001:101–114; S. M. Walz and B. P. Niehoff, "Organizational Citizenship Behaviors and Their Effect on Organizational Effectiveness in Limited-Menu Restaurants," *Academy of Management Best Paper Proceedings*, 1996:307–311.

[43] J. R. Hackman, "Work Design," in J. R. Hackman and J. L. Suttle, eds., *Improving Life at Work* (Santa Monica, CA: Goodyear, 1977):115–120; J. R. Edwards, J. A. Scully, and M. D. Brtek, "The Nature and Outcomes of Work: A Replication and Extension of Interdisciplinary Work-Design Research," *Journal of Applied Psychology 85* (6), December 2000:860–868.

[44] J. R. Hackman and G. R. Oldham, "Motivation through the Design of Work: Test of a Theory," *Organizational Behavior and Human Performance*, August 1976:250–79.

[45] For a discussion of factors influencing growth need strength, see P. C. Bottger and I. K.-H. Chew, "The Job Characteristics Model and Growth Satisfaction: Main Effects of Assimilation of Work Experience and Context Satisfaction," *Human Relations 39* (6), June 1986:575–94.

[46] Adapted from J. R. Hackman and G. R. Oldham, *Work Redesign* (Reading, MA: Addison-Wesley Publishing Company, 1980). See this book for a more complete set of questions.

[47] M. G. Evans and D. A. Ondrack, "The Motivational Potential of Jobs: Is a Multiplicative Model Really Necessary?" in S. L. McShane, ed., *Organizational Behavior, ASAC Conference Proceedings 9* (5), Halifax, Nova Scotia, 1988:31–39.

[48] M. A. Campion and C. L. McClelland, "Follow-Up and Extension of the Interdisciplinary Costs and Benefits of Enlarged Jobs," *Journal of Applied Psychology 78* (3), June 1993:339–351.

[49] J. R. Hackman and G. R. Oldham, *Work Redesign* (Reading, MA: Addison-Wesley Publishing Company, 1980).

[50] D. F. Caldwell and C. A. O'Reilly, III, "Measuring Person–Job Fit with a Profile-Comparison Process," *Journal of Applied Psychology 75* (6), 1990:648–657.

[51] P. D. Converse, F. L. Oswald, M. A. Gillespie, K. A. Field, and E. B. Bizot, "Matching Individuals to Occupations Using Abilities and the O*Net," *Personnel Psychology 57* (2), Summer 2004:451–487.

[52] J. L. Holland, *Making Vocational Choices: A Theory of Vocational Personalities and Work Environments* (Odessa, FL: Psychological Assessment Resources, 1997); S. H. Osipow, "Convergence in Theories of Career Choice and Development: Review and Prospect," *Journal of Vocational Behavior 36*, 1990:122–131; I. B. Myers, M. H. McCaulley, N. L. Quenk, and A. L. Hammer, *MBTI Manual: A Guide to the Development and Use of the Myers-Briggs Type Indicator*, 3rd ed. (Palo Alto, California: Consulting Psychologists Press, Inc., 1998).

[53] An early work is R. V. Dawis and L. H. Lofquist, *A Psychological Theory of Work Adjustment* (Minneapolis, MN: University of Minnesota Press, 1984).

[54] A. Furnham, "Vocational Preference and P-O Fit: Reflections on Holland's Theory of Vocational Choice," *Applied Psychology: An International Review 50* (1), January 2001:5–29.

[55] M. Argyle, A. Furnham, and J. Graham, *Social Situations* (Cambridge: Cambridge University Press, 1981).

[56] A. Furnham, "Vocational Preference and P-O Fit: Reflections on Holland's Theory of Vocational Choice," *Applied Psychology: An International Review 50* (1), January 2001:5–29.

[57] J. Salgado, "The *Five* Factor Model of Personality and Job Performance in the European Community," *Journal of Applied Psychology, 82* (1):30–43.

[58] I. Mitroff and E. Denton, "A Study of Spirituality in the Workplace," *Sloan Management Review 40*, Summer 1999:83–92.

[59] A. J. Hoffman, "Reconciling Professional and Personal Value Systems: The Spiritually Motivated Manager as Organizational Entrepreneur," in R. A. Giacalone and C. L. Jurkiewicz, *Handbook of Workplace Spirituality and Organizational Performance* (Armonk, New York: M. E. Sharpe, 2003):193–208.

[60] D. T. Hall and P. Mirvis, "The New Protean Career: Psychological Success and the Path with a Heart," in D. T. Hall, ed., *The Career Is Dead, Long Live the Career: A Relational Approach to Careers* (San Francisco: Jossey-Bass, 1996):15–45.

[61] K. C. Cash, "A Framework for Accommodating Religion and Spirituality in the Workplace," *Academy of Management Executive 14* (3), 2000:124–34.

[62] B. Posner and W. Schmidt, "Values and the American Manager: An Update Updated," *California Management Review 34*, 1992:80–94.

[63] J. Chatman, "Matching People and Organizations: Selection and Socialization in Public Accounting Firms," *Administrative Science Quarterly 36* (3), September 1991: 459–484.

[64] Statistics on this point vary, and change. For example, the annual Gallup/Earth Day Poll found that in 2002, 47 percent of Americans held a negative view of the environment's condition; however, a declining percentage of voters favored protection of the environment over economic growth. (Source: G. Gugliotta and M. Allen, "Environmental Community Takes a Swing at Bush," *Washington Post* April 23, 2003, accessed October 12, 2004). In the mid-1990s, about three-quarters of Americans labelled themselves as environmentalists, including 21 percent who labeled themselves "active environmentalists." (Source: *Times Mirror Magazines*, reported in "The Environmental Two-Step," *Environmental Health Perspectives 104* (4), April 1996.)

[65] A. J. Hoffman, "Reconciling Professional and Personal Value Systems: The Spiritually Motivated Manager as Organizational Entrepreneur," in R. A. Giacalone and C. L. Jurkiewicz, *Handbook of Workplace Spirituality and Organizational Performance* (Armonk, New York: M. E. Sharpe, 2003):193–208; H. Daly and J. Cobb, *For the Common Good* (Boston: Beacon Press, 1994); T. Gladwin, J. Kennelly, and T. Krause, "Shifting Paradigms for Sustainable Development: Implications for Management Theory and Research," *Academy of Management Review 20*, 1995:874–907.

[66] D. Meyerson and M. Scully, "Tempered Radicalism and the Politics of Ambivalence and Change," *Organizational Science 6*, 1995:585–600.

[67] A. J. Hoffman, "Reconciling Professional and Personal Value Systems: The Spiritually Motivated Manager as Organizational Entrepreneur," in R. A. Giacalone and C. L. Jurkiewicz, *Handbook of Workplace Spirituality and Organizational Performance* (Armonk, New York: M. E. Sharpe, 2003):201; Aspen Institute, *Uncovering Value: Integrating Environmental and Financial Performance* (Washington, DC: Aspen Institute, 1998).

[68] D. M. Truxillo, M. E. Paronto, M. Collins, and J. L. Sulzer, "Effects of Subject Matter Expert Viewpoint on Job Analysis Results," *Public Personnel Management 33* (1), Spring

2004:33–46; see also R. D. Gatewood, H. S. Feild, G. T. Milkovich, and J. W. Boudreau, *Human Resource Management* (Homewood, IL: Irwin, 1991).

[69] W. F. Casio, *Applied Psychology in Personnel Management*, 3rd ed. (Englewood Cliffs, NJ: Prentice Hall, 1987):42.

[70] K. McManus, "Spend Your Time Wisely," *Industrial Engineer 36* (1), January 2004:18.

[71] E. Derous and K. De Witte, "Looking at Selection from a Social Process Perspective: Towards a Social Process Model on Personnel Selection," *European Journal of Work & Organizational Psychology 10* (3), September 2001:319–342.

[72] B. B. Baltes, T. E. Briggs, J. W. Huff, J. A. Wright, and G. A. Neuman, "Flexible and Compressed Workweek Schedules: A Meta-Analysis of Their Effects on Work-Related Criteria," *Journal of Applied Psychology 84* (4), 1999:496–513; E. J. Hill, B. C. Miller, S. P. Weiner, and J. Colihan, "Influences of the Virtual Office on Aspects of Work and Work/Life Balance," *Personnel Psychology 51*, 1998:667–683; L. T. Thomas and D. C. Ganster, "Impact of Family-Supportive Work Variables on Work-Family Conflict and Strain: A Control Perspective," *Journal of Applied Psychology 80* (1), 1995:6–15; J. T. Trent, A. L. Smith, and D. L. Wood, "Telecommuting: Stress and Social Support," *Psychological Reports 74*, 1994:1312–134.

[73] T. M. Beers, "Flexible Schedules and Shift Work: Replacing the '9-to-5' Workday?" *Monthly Labor Review 123* (6), June 2000:33–40.

[74] A. R. Cohen and H. Gadon, *Alternative Work Schedules* (Reading, MA: Addison-Wesley, 1980).

[75] M. Keefe and E. Fanning, "Computerworld 100 Best Places to Work in IT 2004," *Computerworld 38* (24), June 14, 2004:34–41.

[76] *SHRM 2001 Benefits Survey* (Society for Human Resource Management Foundation, 2001).

[77] B. L. Rau and M. M. Hyland, "Role Conflict and Flexible Work Arrangements: The Effects on Applicant Attraction," *Personnel Psychology 55* (1), Spring 2002:111–136.

[78] D. R. Dalton and D. J. Mesch, "The Impact of Flexible Scheduling on Employee Attendance and Turnover," *Administrative Science Quarterly 35* (2), June 1990:370–387.

[79] B. L. Kirkman, B. Rosen, C. B. Gibson, P. E. Tesluk, and S. O. McPherson, "Five Challenges to Virtual Team Success: Lessons from Sabre, Inc.," *Academy of Management Executive 16* (3), August 2002:67–79.

[80] *SHRM 2001 Benefits Survey* (Society for Human Resource Management Foundation, 2001).

[81] L. Crawford, "More Than a Name," *The Financial Times,* October 15, 2005. FT.com. Accessed October 15, 2005.

[82] B. L. Rau and M. M. Hyland, "Role Conflict and Flexible Work Arrangements: The Effects on Applicant Attraction," *Personnel Psychology 55* (1), Spring 2002:111–136.

[83] K. E. Frank and D. J. Lowe, "An Examination of Alternative Work Arrangements in Private Accounting Practice," *Accounting Horizons 17* (2), June 2003:139–151.

[84] S. Acorn and J. Williams, "Job Sharing at the Managerial Level," *Nursing Management 28* (5), May 1997:46–47.

[85] P. Lunt, "Want to Share a Job? Some People Do," *ABA Banking Journal 86* (3), March 1994:88.

[86] T. Miyakoshi, "The Efficacy of Job-Sharing Policy," *Applied Economics Letters 8* (7), July 2001:437–439.

[87] "Re-Engineering Offices," *Economist 337* (7942), November 25, 1995:91.

[88] H. A. Earle, "Building a Workplace of Choice: Using the Work Environment to Attract and Retain Top Talent," *Journal of Facilities Management 2* (3), December 2003:244–257.

[89] L. Wah, "The Power Office," *Management Review 87* (5), May 1998:10–14.

[90] A. H. Maslow and N. L. Mintz, "Effects of Esthetic Surroundings: Initial Effects of Three Esthetic Conditions upon Perceiving 'Energy' and 'Well-Being' in Faces," *Journal of Psychology 41,* 1956:247–254.

[91] L. Wah, "The Power Office," *Management Review 87* (5), May 1998:10–14.

[92] "Workplace Changes That Improve Performance," *Maintenance Management* (Issue 2610) October 2000: 9–10; M. A. Hofmann, "Employers Tuning in to the Dangers of Noise," *Business Insurance 39* (31) August 1, 2005:11–15.

[93] "Re-Engineering Offices," *Economist 337* (7942), November 25, 1995:91.

[94] T. E. Deal and A. A. Kennedy, *The New Corporate Cultures: Revitalizing the Workplace After Downsizing, Mergers and Reengineering* (Reading, Massachusetts: Perseus Books, 1999).

[95] See for example J. L. Pearce, *Organization and Management in the Embrace of Government* (Mahwah, NJ: Lawrence Erlbaum, 2001).

[96] C. G. Banks and K. R. Murphy, "Toward Narrowing the Research–Practice Gap in Performance Appraisal," *Personnel Psychology 38,* 1985:335–345; A. S. Tsui and B. Barry, "Interpersonal Affect and Rating Errors," *Academy of Management Journal 29,* 1986:586–599.

[97] See J. P. Campbell, M. D. Dunnette, E. E. Lawler, III, and K. E. Weick, *Managerial Behavior, Performance, and Effectiveness* (New York: McGraw-Hill, 1970).

[98] E. A. Hogan, "Effects of Prior Expectations on Performance Ratings: A Longitudinal Study," *Academy of Management Journal 38* (2), 1995:232–260.

[99] A. S. Tsui and B. Barry, "Interpersonal Affect and Rating Errors," *Academy of Management Journal 29* (3), September 1986:586–599.

[100] S. J. Wayne and R. C. Liden, "Effects of Impression Management on Performance Ratings: A Longitudinal Study," *Academy of Management Journal 38* (1), February 1995:232–260.

[101] K. Kraiger and J. K. Ford, "A Meta-Analysis of Ratee Race Effects in Performance Ratings," *Journal of Applied Psychology 70* (1), 1985:56–65.

[102] J. Li and L. Karakowsky, "Do We See Eye-to-Eye? Implications of Cultural Differences for Cross-Cultural Management Research and Practice," *Journal of Psychology 135* (5), September 2001:501–17.

[103] R. R. Rehder, "Sayonara, Uddevalla?" *Business Horizons* November-December, 1992:8–18,13.

[104] C. Berggren, "Volvo Uddevalla: A Dead Horse or a Car Dealer's Dream? An Evaluation of the Economic Performance of Volvo's Unique Assembly Plant 1989–1992." Stockholm, Royal Institute of Technology, Department of Work Science, 1993.

[105] Based on information in "Executive Pay: Taking Stock of Options," *The Economist,* July 22, 2006:13.

6

Health and Stress at Work

Preview

What is your image of a healthy work environment?

Do you really need to be concerned about stress at work?

How does stress affect on-the-job performance?

What are some common stressors at work?
Job stressors
Physical factors
Work–personal life issues

How might stress affect your health?
Fight or flight; tend and befriend
The stress response
Physiological effects

Do you have a predisposition to stress?
Personality traits
Workaholism
Type A–Type B Personality Pattern
Hardiness

How can you cope with stress at work?
Recognize the symptoms of stress
Recognize burnout
Identify the stressors in your life
Develop a general coping strategy
Manage
. . .ideas and emotions
. . .physical and behavioral factors
. . .your environment
. . .your time

What do companies do about employee stress?
Analyze the costs of stress
Set goals for becoming a healthy organization
Establish company programs: The case of work–life balance
Coach managers to recognize issues of health and productivity

Waterford Crystal

Waterford Crystal is the Irish company that makes high-quality crystal objects, including customary gifts for heads of state, prestigious trophies such as the one for the Super Bowl, and unique objects such as the crystal ball that fell in Times Square at the millennium celebration. In recent years Waterford has undergone significant change, losing many of its skilled employees to downsizing and layoffs. As the company's head of human resources puts it, change is relatively easy when a company is under duress, but it is more difficult when a company is successful. Though Waterford had been successful, management felt that the company was relying too much on outdated manual labor techniques and too little on new technologies, and that it had to take cost out of the system. Thus the layoffs.

To help its people through the downsizing process, the company invested heavily in training and communication. For example, about 6 percent of its payroll was invested in training. The company also invited employees to talk with counselors at its expense.

Today the company makes a point of hiring people who have the ability to innovate and think out of the box. It finds individuals who are adaptable to change, then gives them the necessary tools to succeed. It also works to build a level of trust by informing its employees extensively about the business. An informal company motto is "Explain, explain, explain, and then train, train, train." It strives to build a work culture that is pleasant and stress free. The job itself is often stressful enough; for instance, if a piece an employee is working on breaks, it has to be started all over again, no matter how expensive it may have been.

In a company that plans to double its business every four to five years, it is clear that business pressures on the employees are considerable.

What Is Your Image of a Healthy Work Environment?

For individuals, healthy work environments are those that promote healthy behavior patterns, leading to a sound body and mind and the prevention of disease and sickness.[1] Because of individual differences and preferences, however, one person's healthy workplace may be another person's toxic environment. From management's perspective, a healthy work environment balances two factors: workers' health and satisfaction, and the performance of the organization.[2] A healthy work organization is one that maximizes the integration of employees' goals for well-being with company objectives for profitability and productivity.[3]

Each of us has a private model for a healthy work life. Your own model is implicit in your search for the "right" job, career, and company. In choosing among options, you factor in whether you would be mentally and physically capable of doing the work and whether you would be able to accommodate to the pace, uncertainty level, and status of the job. You consider many other factors as well, including whether you believe you will enjoy and, in turn, be accepted by, the people who work in the company.

Renowned career counselor Richard Bolles suggests that, to clarify your goals for health and satisfaction at work, you should consider four questions in depth.[4]

The first question is simply *What's happening around here?* To feel comfortable in a work setting you must have a coherent idea about what its characteristics are and what you are supposed to do there. As author Bolles so colorfully puts it, to feel comfortable in any setting you have to be able to answer the most basic questions about it, such as, "Where am I? How did I get here? What on earth is happening? Is this truly a jungle? What kind of a jungle is it? Are there dangerous beasts or people here? What kind of food and drink is available?"[5]

Second, you want to know *How do I survive?* in the work setting. In assessing the prospects for health in a job, you want to know whether you can survive physically, asking questions such as: Can I take the hours (long hours, perhaps, or a night shift, or hours that conflict with outside responsibilities)? Can I take the travel? Can I really sit at that computer all day without harming my body? You also want to know whether you can survive emotionally: Can I deal with the tyrannical CEO? Can I cope with being different? Finally, you want to know whether you can survive spiritually: "Will this setting challenge my beliefs and maybe even change them in ways I would find intolerable? Will it help me advance my beliefs in the world?"

Bolles's third question is *What is my meaning or mission?* Along with having a good idea about what is happening and whether you are going to survive in a job, you also want to know whether doing the work will fulfill your sense of filling your time in a worthwhile way.

Finally, you want to ask *How can I be effective?* You want to know that you are doing your work in the most effective, efficient, and competent way. Finding jobs in which you can be effective motivates you to improve the way you are working toward your goals.

Knowing your own personal goals for healthy work alerts you to potential stressors that could disrupt your health. In the remainder of this chapter we will examine stress in organizational life with an eye to helping you identify it and deal with it.

Do You Really Need to Be Concerned About Stress at Work?

stress
A state of tension experienced when one's usual modes of coping are insufficient.

Stress is a state of tension you experience when your usual modes of coping are insufficient. Some of the common stressors at work are the stress of the job itself, physical factors such as repetitive stress injuries, and conflicts between your work and your personal life. In international jobs you may face the stress of culture shock, which we will cover in Chapter 8: Cross-Cultural Relationships.

stressor
Any event that causes a person to feel stress.

A **stressor** is any event that causes you to feel stress. In the workplace you are likely to face stress when you experience extraordinary demands, annoying constraints, or diffi-

TABLE 6.1 A Healthy Work Environment For *(Your Name Here)*

Here is a set of open-ended questions to help you develop your own personal description of a healthy work environment. Defining a healthy work environment will help you to set concrete goals to aid your search for the right job and company. Open-ended questions allow you to be individualistic, creative, and thorough in your answers. Jot down your responses to the following:

1. On the job I want to be treated. . . *with respect, given the tools to do the job and allowed to do it,*
2. In my company I want to be included whenever. . . *decisions are made that affect how I do my job*
3. The company should reward me. . . *by recognizing what I do, possibly giving me a raise/year, listen, also making sure I get the help I need*
4. My biggest rewards from my life in organizations will come when. . . *they really put the consumer first*
5. I want to be a member of an organization that has these goals. . . *job rotation*
6. I want to work for an organization that has structures and procedures and a culture that. . .
7. On the job I will be happiest when my time is spent. . .
8. I plan to divide the time between my work life and personal life. . .
9. I want to work with colleagues who. . .
10. The physical setting in which I work. . .
11. My bosses will be. . .
12. My company will help give meaning to my life because. . .

cult interpersonal relationships.[6] Sometimes you see stress in a positive light, as when you are enjoying solving a problem. When stress is experienced as positive it is called **eustress**. On the job, this is the kind of tension you experience when you face a challenging but feasible opportunity.[7] For instance, nurses in intensive care units must focus on what are clearly important tasks. Experiencing some stress allows them to actively and positively engage in their demanding work.[8]

Job stress is the harmful physical and emotional responses that occur when the requirements of the job do not match a worker's capabilities, resources, or needs.[9] How likely are you to experience job stress? The National Institute of Occupational Safety and Health (NIOSH) is the division of the U.S. Department of Health and Human Services responsible for conducting research and making recommendations for the prevention of work-related illness and injury. According to NIOSH, job stress has become a common and costly problem in the American workplace, leaving few workers untouched. Also, a study by a major insurance company reports that one-fourth of employees view their jobs as the number one stressor in their lives.[10] Problems at work are more likely to result in health complaints than either financial or family problems.[11] Three-fourths of employees believe that workers have more on-the-job stress than 20 years ago.[12] Job-related stress is an important measure of employees' well-being.[13]

Job stress costs organizations billions of dollars in employee disability claims, employee absenteeism, and lost productivity.[14] It is estimated that $700 million a year is spent by companies that need to replace the 200,000 men aged 45 to 65 who die of or are incapacitated by coronary artery disease alone.[15]

eustress
A state of stress which is experienced as positive.

job stress
The harmful physical and emotional responses that occur when the requirements of the job do not match a worker's capabilities, resources, or needs.

How Does Stress Affect On-the-Job Performance?

Challenge is an important aspect of healthy and productive work because it energizes you psychologically and physically and motivates you to learn new skills. When you meet a challenge, you feel satisfied and relaxed. But at what point does a challenge become a stressor?

Stress affects job performance in the following ways: When employees are put under low stress their performance is likely to be low; under moderate stress their performance is likely to be high; yet when they are put under extreme stress, their performance suffers.[16] See Figure 6.1.

FIGURE 6.1

The Relationship Between Stress and Job Performance

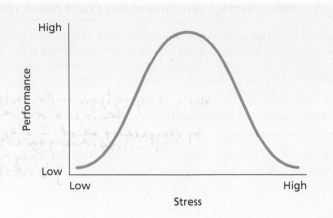

Why can't employees cope under conditions of extreme stress? It seems that during moderate stress they can manage to continue to do their job, attempting to use whatever resources are at their disposal to be productive, but once the stress is high, their emotions interfere, causing withdrawal, hostility, and aggression.

Managers aware of this relationship between stress and performance strive to motivate their employees just enough to keep their performance high without pushing them over the edge of the curve. Newer research suggests that although the u-shaped curve is intuitively appealing, previous research may have been inadequate, and it now seems likely that even moderate stress can be detrimental to performance.[17]

What Are Some Common Stressors at Work?

Organizational stressors have various origins, including the nature of the job, physical factors, and work–personal life conflicts. We will examine each of these in turn. Of course, managing interpersonal relationships, including working with difficult people, can also be stressful. This topic is covered in various places in this book, but see in particular "Leader as Disciplinarian" in Chapter 12: Leadership Roles and Skills, "Characteristics That Derail Leadership" and "Nonrational Influences in Leadership" in Chapter 11: The Challenge of Leadership, and all of Chapter 7: Communication and Interpersonal Relationships.

Job Stressors

As noted above, job stressors originate in the nature of the job itself,[18] and have a psychological impact on the worker. They include role conflict, role ambiguity, cognitive demands, and overload.

role
The behavior expected of someone who holds a particular job.

role conflict
The existence of two or more sets of role expectations for an individual's work which are incompatible with each other.

role ambiguity
Situation in which people do not know clearly what has to be done in their jobs.

insufficient authority
Situation in which someone needs to complete a job but doesn't have enough authority to make important decisions.

ROLE CONFLICT A **role** is behavior expected of someone who holds a particular job. When two or more sets of role expectations exist for an individual's work, and the compliance with one set of expectations results in the person's inability to comply with the other, we say that the individual is experiencing **role conflict**.[19] Role conflict occurs, for instance, when an employee receives incompatible requests from two or more people, or works under incompatible policies and guidelines, or receives assignments without adequate resources and materials for doing them.

ROLE AMBIGUITY Similarly, **role ambiguity** occurs when people do not know clearly what has to be done in their jobs. For example, an engineer might read in an employee manual that it is necessary to conform to all environmental regulations, yet his or her boss might say not to bother. A related concept is **insufficient authority**, which occurs when an employee needs to complete a job but doesn't have enough authority to make important decisions.[20]

COGNITIVE DEMANDS Sometimes your responsibilities for a job are beyond your ability to make decisions effectively, given the nature of the work or the time frame in which the decisions are required.[21] For example, a worker might frequently be required to solve problems with no obvious correct answer.

The cognitive demands imposed by technological change strain workers to keep up and strain relationships when bosses are not conversant with the same technologies as their subordinates. For instance, managers in developing countries experience stress because, when implementing new technologies, they may be forced to deal with inadequately trained workforces along with the imposition of deadlines.[22]

OVERLOAD Psychologists typically define work **overload** as the situation in which the amount of work in a person's job is beyond his or her ability to do alone.[23] Having too much work and too little time routinely leads to negative behavioral, psychological, and physiological outcomes.[24]

Working long hours is a related type of overload. For example, researchers have found high levels of a stress hormone in women who work large amounts of overtime.[25] Today companies such as Alcan, Eli Lilly, and Texas Instruments are actually taking steps to reduce workloads.[26] They are encouraging executives to be better role models by managing their own workloads, and encouraging employees to push back and say, "Enough." Boston Consulting Group keeps track of consultants' total hours in a weekly "Red Zone Report," and counsels employees who fall into the red zone, which suggests they are working too many hours.

overload
Situation in which the amount of work in a person's job is beyond his or her ability to do alone.

Physical Factors

Workers face a variety of potential physical stressors on the job, including the stress caused by commuting, repetitive work, noise, biogenic triggers, safety concerns, travel, and shift work.

COMMUTING An interesting finding related to people who have distinct preferences for daytime or night time activities (often referred to as "morning types" and "evening types") is that although commuting to work by car is stressful for both, morning types find the evening commute more stressful than the morning commute, while evening types find the morning commute more stressful.[27] People who are neither morning nor evening types but fall somewhere in between find the morning and evening commutes about equally stressful, and find neither commute to be as stressful as the stress reported by the morning and evening types.

REPETITIVE STRESS INJURIES About 600,000 workers miss work each year because of **repetitive stress injuries**, including wrist pain from typing or back injuries from awkward lifting. About 16 percent of all workplaces have adopted formal ergonomics programs to train workers to avoid and manage these effects.[28]

repetitive stress injuries
Injuries caused by repetitive motions while working.

NOISE **Noise** is unwanted sound. Exposure to noise can increase stress levels and reduce productivity. Office noise has been shown to result in employee discomfort and stress,[29] and background noise interferes with complex cognitive tasks.[30]

Workers in open-office environments with low intensity noise are more stressed than workers in quiet work environments. They show signs of both physiological stress and psychological stress.[31]

noise
Unwanted sound.

BIOGENIC TRIGGERS **Biogenic triggers** are foods that create a stress response all by themselves irrespective of other conditions.[32] They include coffee, tea, soda with caffeine, and amphetamines. They can cause stress symptoms such as rapid heartbeat and loss of sleep. The caffeine in two cups of coffee can add 16 beats a minute to your heart rate and make you more irritable and anxious.[33]

biogenic triggers
Foods that create a stress response all by themselves irrespective of other conditions.

SAFETY ISSUES Most responsible employers attempt to ensure the safety of their workers; nevertheless, there exists a continuum of jobs from relatively less hazardous to relatively more hazardous, with increased stress related to the more hazardous jobs. As technologies have improved and the workplace in general has become more safe, researchers have increasingly looked to company culture to explain differences in how safe companies are. For example, companies with lower commitment and involvement by higher levels of management tend to have more safety accidents.[34]

The process of managing safety can itself create stress. For example, after an accident, a company is likely to focus on and correct safety problems, but as time goes by management interest may seem to wane and employees may consider the company's safety interest to be just window-dressing. To reduce such reactions, managers must develop a safety culture that clarifies as often as necessary that the company is interested in both production and safety.[35] By establishing this dual focus, a company sends the message to workers that it does not want them to burn out or feel overwhelmed, and that the company will not cancel or ignore safety improvements

TRAVEL STRESS Business travel can also be stressful, including such pre-trip stressors as planning the trip, completing key tasks before the trip, and taking care of home and family issues. During the trip, potential stressors include the quality of hotel accommodations and communications; health concerns such as sleep, exercise, diet, and travelers' illnesses; and smoking and alcohol consumption.[36] An industry study of 600 individuals who travel by air at least once a month found that two out of every five suffer headaches, back pain, neck pain, or sleeplessness while traveling, and almost three out of five experience significant fatigue.[37] Fifty percent of unmarried and 75 percent of married business travelers find it difficult to be away from home for extended periods.[38]

Travelers are less productive on the road, and half say they need up to two days to catch up on work responsibilities they left behind.[39] On the other hand, business trips can also provide a welcome respite from one's daily work: One study discovered that even after hardworking business trips, employees tend to experience a reduction in job stress and burnout upon returning home.

SHIFT WORK Doing shift work—working full 8-hour shifts outside of normal daytime working hours—is related to health problems, possibly because working at night is more likely to lead to poorer health habits such as increased smoking and being overweight.[40] Shift workers who move back to day work often cite health reasons for their move.[41]

People who have distinct preferences for daytime or nighttime activity may have trouble adjusting to work hours that run counter to their preferences, whereas some people may not show a distinct preference.[42] **Circadian rhythms** are patterns in our bodies that are kept in cycle by environmental cues, of which the most important is light.[43] These patterns include body temperature, heart rate, and hormone production,[44] and they affect our alertness and activity level.[45] Among shift workers, continual disruption of the circadian rhythm is a source of chronic (ongoing) stress.[46]

circadian rhythms
Patterns in our bodies that are kept in cycle by environmental cues, especially light.

Work–Personal Life Issues

Work–life conflict—the inability to balance work and personal life demands—contributes significantly to stress at work, affecting turnover, productivity, job satisfaction, commitment, and costs.[47] In the United States, in particular, failure to achieve a healthy work–life balance has been a recent concern.[48] High job demands and rising household financial needs have created well-documented personal and societal problems, including lower life satisfaction, higher rates of family strife and divorce, and a rising incidence of substance abuse.

Companies today need to address such employee work–life concerns as inflexible work hours; the effect of differential compensation and advancement on men, women, and minorities; inadequate long-term saving plans; and limited resources for day care, elder care, and adoptions.[49]

TABLE 6.2 Overview: Stressors at Work

Job Stressors	Description
Role conflict	When complying with one set of expectations prevents you from complying with a second set of expectations in your job—for example, when you get requests from two bosses, or when you are asked to do two things at once
Role ambiguity	When what you are supposed to do is unclear
Cognitive demands	When your job responsibilities are beyond your cognitive capabilities
Overload	When the amount of work you are assigned is too much for you to do by yourself
Physical Factors	
Commuting	Traveling to your job is long, arduous, and at the wrong time of day for you.
Repetitive stress injuries	Performing the same tasks over and over to the point that your body is injured.
Noise	Unwanted sound increases stress.
Biogenic triggers	What you ingest affects your well being—for example, caffeine raises your heart rate.
Safety issues	Hazardous jobs and environments are stressful.
Travel stress	Traveling one or more times per month can become annoying (although at times it is relaxing).
Shift work	Working 8-hour shifts outside of normal working hours disrupts your circadian rhythm.
Work–Personal Life Issues	
Work-life conflict	The inability to take charge of both your home and your work life is stressful.

How Might Stress Affect Your Health?

How you react to the stress in your life is related to your health in both the short term and the long term.

Fight or Flight; Tend and Befriend

People's response to stress has long been described as **flight or flight**, a set of survival responses that have been passed down to modern human beings from their ancestors. In response to stressors, it has been hypothesized that humankind either flees or fights back, and that our bodily response to stress equips us for these strategies. Increased adrenalin lets us run faster, for example.

Describing the stress response in this way reminds us that stress is a part of our biological inheritance, while suggesting that it may be out of line with our needs in a quite different modern era. While your body is preparing to take on a mastodon attack, the stressor you actually face is an irate customer.

Moreover, the stress response is really fairly complicated. For one thing, recent research suggests that women may differ from men in their response to stress.[50] While both sexes share the capacity for fight or flight, women tend to use this approach less. In the face of stress, they are more likely to seek the nurturing and support of familiar people.

fight or flight
A set of survival responses in which humankind either flees or fights back in response to stressors.

tend and befriend
Responding to stressors by seeking the nurturing and support of familiar people.

This **tend and befriend** response may have conferred an evolutionary benefit by promoting survival and reducing risk for women and their children. While men's aggression has been shown to be related to higher testosterone levels, women's behavior appears to be related to the hormones estrogen and oxytocin. People with high oxytocin levels are calmer, more relaxed, less anxious, and more social. The hormonal difference between men and women also explains, in part, why women are less vulnerable than men to stress-related illnesses such as hypertension and alcohol and drug abuse.

For another thing, medical research has developed a considerable body of knowledge about the complexities of stress reactions, as we shall see next.

The Stress Response

stress response
The body's reaction to a stressor.

The **stress response** is your body's reaction to a stressor. When you become stressed, your brain activates three response systems.[51]

First, the motor cortex sends signals directly to the musculoskeletal system. Your muscles, especially in the jaw, shoulders, and back, tighten to face the threat.

Second, the cerebral cortex signals the hypothalamus, which in turn stimulates the sympathetic and parasympathetic nervous systems. As the sympathetic nervous system readies the heart to speed up, adrenaline is released and blood pressure, heart rate, and the volume of blood being pumped all increase. Meanwhile, the parasympathetic nervous system is slowing down other parts of the body by releasing other hormones. While the blood flow is sent to the brain and muscles it is reduced in the skin and digestive organs. As a result of all these hormones, you sweat (the better to cool yourself should you have to run away), your heart beats faster, and your breathing becomes quick and shallow (the better to run). Unfortunately, this same hormonal bath increases the cholesterol, triglycerides, and glucose in your blood, enhancing the blood profile that increases the risk of cardiovascular disease.

Third, via the pituitary gland three additional hormones—cortisol, corticosterone, and aldosterone—are released. In moderation, these help boost your immune system, but when their release is sustained over time, they wear out the immune system. People under continuous stress chronically stress their immune systems, and are prone to many illnesses.

Physiological Effects

The chemical changes in a person's body during stress have numerous long-term, detrimental effects on health. A review of the health effects of stress, anxiety, and anger suggests the following[52]:

STRESS AND ANGER BOTH INCREASE YOUR SUSCEPTIBILITY TO PHYSICAL ILLNESS Stress is clearly associated with an increase in upper respiratory infections, and perhaps even with cancer. Anger and hostility are also related to various physical illnesses. Angry and hostile people get sick more, stay sick longer, and are more likely to die from cardiovascular disease.

Stress is hazardous to your health because it impairs your immune system, an effect that has been demonstrated even at the level of the cells in the body. For example, a study of medical students before and during course examinations showed physiological changes to their immune systems because of the stress they were under.[53] Later, half of the students were assigned to take relaxation training. The more the students practiced relaxation techniques, the stronger their immune system remained during an examination period.

When a person's immune system is impaired because of stress, the result is an increased vulnerability to illness. For instance, chronic life stress is clearly associated with vulnerability to developing colds. Stress also predicts a slower rate of recovery from illness. A study of dental students who received voluntary wounds showed that their rate of healing was about 11 days for healing during a high-stress examination period versus about 8 days during a more relaxing vacation period; that is, healing was about 40 percent slower during the high-stress period.[54]

STRESS INFLUENCES PAIN PERCEPTION, WITH HIGH ANXIETY BEING RELATED TO LOW PAIN TOLERANCE Anxiety is related to the threshold at which we feel pain. The more anxious we feel, the more likely we are to feel pain. It is also related to the intensity of the pain: More stress equates to more intensity.

STRESS IS RELATED TO CORONARY HEART DISEASE A review of 50 research studies concluded that high levels of life stress predict coronary heart disease.[55] The connection between stress and disease is often measured in high cholesterol levels. Working with nonhuman primates, researchers found that dominant monkeys living under conditions of stress and eating a diet typical of North Americans had more than twice as much atherosclerosis ("hardening of the arteries") as dominant monkeys living under nonstressed conditions.

Do You Have a Predisposition to Stress?

Today it is well known that your personality contributes to how you experience the stressors in your life.

Personality Traits

Certain personality traits influence your experience of stress. For instance, people with high internal locus of control perceive their jobs as less stressful than do people with high external locus of control.[56] And people whose self-efficacy is high react less strongly to work overload and the strain of having to work long hours.[57] People who *believe* they are highly effective in coping with stress also have better-functioning immune systems.[58]

Workaholism

Researchers have worked to identify constellations of personality traits that relate to stress. For example, **workaholics**, people who rank high on the traits of work involvement and a drive to work,[59] report higher levels of stress, exhibit higher levels of perfectionism, and report more health-related problems than nonworkaholic workers.[60] More research must be done, however, because it has also been learned that it is important to differentiate between enthusiastic and nonenthusiastic workaholics—those who report high enjoyment of their work and those who report low enjoyment of their work. While both types of workaholics scored higher on perfectionism and job stress than other workers, as you can imagine, nonenthusiastic workaholics report more work–life conflict, less overall life satisfaction, and less purpose in life than do enthusiastic workaholics.[61]

workaholism
Excessively high ranking on the traits of work involvement and a drive to work.

Type A–Type B Personality Pattern

Another constellation of personality traits that is related to stress is the **Type A–Type B personality** pattern. Answer the questions in Table 6.3 to rate yourself, then read the analysis that follows here.

The generally accepted description of the Type A behavior pattern includes the following: 1) Physical characteristics include a loud voice, quick speech, psychomotor activity, and facial muscle tension. 2) Related attitudes and emotions are hostility, impatience, anger, and aggressiveness. 3) In terms of motivation, the Type A is high on achievement motivation, competitiveness, and ambition. 4) Behaviorally, Type As appear alert and hyperactive and have high work involvement. 5) Cognitively, they want control of their environment.[62]

The Type B behavior pattern is just the opposite. Type B men, for example, are not hostile.[63] Because they have high self-esteem, they don't feel the need to take control of their total environment, but rather have developed the art of overlooking imperfections. For one thing, they accept others' faults. If a bad driver gets in their way, they become more cautious but are unlikely to become angry.[64] Type Bs rarely feel tense or bring tension into their families.

Persons who exhibit the Type A behavior pattern have long been believed to experience more stress and to be more prone to cardiovascular disease than those who exhibit the Type B pattern.[65] However, in recent years the relationship of the Type A behavior pattern to stress and cardiovascular disease has been challenged because earlier research only examined the relationships predicted by the Type A–B pattern overall, rather than by its distinctive components. More recent research examining the components separately indicates that it is actually only the emotional components of Type A behavior that predict stress and cardiovascular disease. Some research suggests that it is the emotions anger,

Type A–Type B personality
A constellation of personality traits that predict one's reaction to stressors.

TABLE 6.3 Type A Behavior Patterns

Indicate the extent to which you agree with the following statements using this scale:

1 = I don't agree at all.	2 = I agree to a little extent.	3 = I agree to some extent.	4 = I agree to a great extent.	5 = I agree to a very great extent.

1. _____ I am seldom in a rush.

2. _____ I hate having to wait.

3. _____ I am quick-tempered.

4. _____ I talk more loudly than most people.

5. _____ I drive hard to get things done.

6. _____ I am hot-headed.

7. _____ I speak more quickly than most people.

8. _____ I have a strong need to excel.

9. _____ I get annoyed when someone ignores me.

10. _____ I seldom interrupt others.

11. _____ I get furious when criticized.

12. _____ I think about work all the time.

13. _____ When I get frustrated, I want to hit someone.

14. _____ I am more restless and fidgety than most people.

15. _____ I prefer to linger over a meal and enjoy it.

Your response to this set of statements can give you an indication of two aspects of your self: whether 1) you are Type A or Type B, and 2) you have a tendency to be angry compared with others. The questions are suggestive rather than definitive: If you suspect you are at risk and want to do something about this, you should consult a licensed psychologist.

To assess your Type A–Type B pattern:

Step 1: Add up your scores for items 2, 4, 5, 7, 8, 12, and 14. Put your score here. _____ This is your total for Step 1.

Step 2: For each of questions 1, 9, and 15, subtract your score from 6.

In other words,

a. Question 1: 6 – (your score) = _____

b. Question 9: 6 – (your score) = _____

c. Question 15: 6 – (your score) = _____

        Add up the totals for a, b, and c: _____. This is your total score for Step 2.

Step 3: Add your scores for Steps 1 and 2 and put the total here. _____

Interpretation: You are probably a Type A if your score is 40 or more, Type B if your score is 20 or less.

To assess your tendency to be angry:

Add up your score for items 3, 6, 9, 11, and 13 and put the total here. _____

Interpretation: You have a strong tendency to anger if your score is 20 or more.

Source: Based on information in R. H. Rosenman, "The Interview Method of Assessment of the Coronary-Prone Behavior Pattern," in T. Dembroski, S. Weiss, J. Shields, S. Haynes, and M. Fienlieb, eds., *Coronary-prone Behavior* (New York: Springer-Verlag, 1978):55–70; D. C. Ganster, J. Schaubroeck, W. E. Sime, and B. T. Mayes, "The Nomological Validity of the Type A Personality Among Employed Adults," *Journal of Applied Psychology 76* (1), 1991:143–168; E. D. Eaker, L. M. Sullivan, M. Kelly-Hayes, R. B. D'Agostino, Sr., and E. J. Benjamin, "Tension and Anxiety and the Prediction of the 10-Year Incidence of Coronary Heart Disease, Atrial Fibrillation, and Total Mortality: The Framingham Offspring Study," *Psychosomatic Medicine 67* (5), September 1, 2005:692–696.

hostility, and aggressiveness (the **AHA! Syndrome**) that are the major predictors of car-diovascular disorders.[66] The 10-year Framingham Offspring Study published in 2004 found that male participants high in anger are more likely to develop an irregular heart rhythm, and, also, to have died from any cause during the study. However, for women, there was no significant association between anger, hostility, or Type A behavior and the risk of developing heart disease or dying of any cause.[67]

AHA! Syndrome
Tendency to experience anger, hostility and aggressiveness.

Hardiness

Finally, it has been hypothesized that individuals can be rated on their **hardiness**, attitudes that buffer them from the negative effects of stress.[68] You are hardy if you exhibit a combination of three attitudes. The first is commitment, which is defined as the tendency to involve yourself in, rather than being alienated from, whatever you are doing or encounter. Second is control, which is the tendency to feel and act as if you are influential rather than helpless in life. Third is chal-lenge, the belief that change is normal and interesting rather than a threat to your security. While psychological attitudes no doubt affect your experience of stress, the research on hardiness per se is mixed. Most recently a study has shown that hardiness as currently defined is only mod-estly predictive of stress and health, and that it is predictive for men but not women.[69]

hardiness
Holding attitudes which buffer you from the negative effects of stress.

How Can You Cope with Stress at Work?

Recognize the Symptoms of Stress

Learn to recognize some basic warning signals of stress.[70] Work through the checklist in Table 6.4 to learn the most common ones.

TABLE 6.4 The Basic Warning Signs of Stress

Using the scale below, work through this checklist indicating how often you are troubled by each of the following:

0 = Never or rarely   1 = Occasionally   2 = Frequently   3 = Always or nearly always

Physical symptoms

Lack of appetite _____

Headaches _____

Craving for food when under pressure _____

Indigestion _____

Constipation or diarrhea _____

Sweating for no good reason _____

Difficulty sleeping _____

Cramps and muscle spasm _____

Restlessness _____

Constant tiredness _____

Tight neck or shoulders _____

Impotency or frigidity _____

Eczema _____

Waking up in the morning and feeling tired after an early night _____

Behavioral symptoms

Excessive smoking _____

Excessive use of alcohol _____

Teeth grinding _____

Bossiness _____

Compulsive eating _____

Inability to get things done _____

Emotional symptoms

Constant irritability _____

Crying at small problems _____

Anger _____

Loneliness _____

Boredom—inability to find meaning in anything _____

Feeling unable to cope _____

Nervousness _____

Feeling the target of other people's animosity _____

Feeling powerless to change things _____

Lack of interest in doing things after returning home from work _____

Cognitive symptoms

Difficulty making decisions _____

Loss of sense of humor _____

Lack of creativity _____

Trouble thinking clearly _____

Inability to finish one task before rushing into another _____

Scoring: How many symptoms of stress did you rate a 2 or 3? Any one symptom suggests a concern; having several symptoms suggests a pattern. This is just a checklist, rather than a well-designed psychological test. Use your judgment to decide if your stress is excessive.

Recognize Burnout

Job burnout is a mismatch between a person and his or her job, or between a person and his or her workplace, that is frequently associated with stress.[71] Mismatches may occur in the areas of workload, individual control over one's work, rewards, one's sense of community at work, fairness, and values.

Symptoms of job burnout are:

1. Exhaustion: feeling drained and lacking the mental or physical energy to perform.
2. Cynicism: evaluating and reacting negatively to your job, your work, and the people with whom you work. You think negatively about your workplace and your coworkers, and you perform at just a minimum level.
3. Negative self-evaluation: a declining sense of effectiveness in your job. You are self-critical, and in general have a negative sense of yourself and your work.

Burnout may lead to depression, not only about one's job, but about one's self and life.

Identify the Stressors in Your Life

We just looked at symptoms of stress. Now let's take a look at potential causes of stress in your life. How stressful is your life right now? Complete Table 6.5 to find out.

Develop a General Coping Strategy

Once you have identified a stressful situation, or a set of them, you need to take action. In general, there are five ways you might approach a stressful situation.[72] These are:

1. Active coping: You make a plan of action and follow it.
2. Distancing: You try to keep away from the situation for a while.
3. Seeking social support: You ask people who have had similar experiences for advice.
4. Resignation: You decide there is nothing you can do to change the situation.
5. Restraint: You try to avoid expressing your feelings.

While no one approach can be recommended in all cases, research indicates that, on the job, active coping is likely to be your best strategy. It has been shown to effectively decrease psychological stress for all of the typical job stressors. Nonactive coping techniques (distancing, seeking social support, resignation, and restraint) may be useful in responding to major life events and to traumatic or short-term stressors, but they appear not to be effective in responding to ongoing daily and routine stressors. This is probably because they do not directly alter the source of the problems. A person may want to use active coping in conjunction with other methods. For example, using distancing for a while can give people an opportunity to rest and refocus, while seeking social support can give them an opportunity to obtain the emotional and practical support that will enable them to confront challenges more effectively.

Some suggested steps for active coping are[73]:

1. Identify the stressors and their effects.
2. Decide which stressors can and cannot be changed.
3. List specific steps you can take to cope with the stress. (These may involve managing your cognitions, emotions, behaviors, physical reactions, environment, or time, all of which will be discussed below.)
4. Implement your coping plan.
5. Observe changes in the stressors and your responses to them.
6. Reevaluate your coping methods to improve results if you need to.

Manage Ideas and Emotions

Cognitive restructuring is substituting for emotionally charged ideas about a stressor ideas that are more solution-oriented.[74] For example, when facing a deadline, you might have a tendency to say to yourself things like, "I'll never get this done on time," and "If I

TABLE 6.5 How Stressful Is Your Life Right Now? Rank-Ordered Life Events

If you have experienced any of these life events in the last 12 months, circle the point value "earned," then add up your total number of points.

Life Event	Point Value
1. Death of spouse/mate	87
2. Death of close family member	79
3. Major injury/illness to self	78
4. Detention in jail or other institution	76
5. Major injury/illness to close family member	72
6. Foreclosure on loan/mortgage	71
7. Divorce	71
8. Being a victim of a crime	70
9. Being the victim of police brutality	69
10. Infidelity	69
11. Experiencing domestic violence/sexual abuse	69
12. Separation or reconciliation with spouse/mate	66
13. Being fired/laid-off/unemployed	64
14. Experiencing financial problems/difficulties	62
15. Death of a close friend	61
16. Surviving a disaster	59
17. Becoming a single parent	59
18. Assuming responsibility for sick or elderly loved one	56
19. Loss of or major reduction in health insurance/benefits	56
20. Self/close family member being arrested for violating the law	56
21. Major disagreement over child support/custody/visitation	53
22. Experiencing/involved in auto accident	53
23. Being disciplined at work/demoted	53
24. Dealing with unwanted pregnancy	51
25. Adult child moving in with parent/parent moving in with adult child	50
26. Child develops behavior or learning problem	49
27. Experiencing employment discrimination/sexual harassment	48
28. Attempting to modify addictive behavior of self	47

Life Event	Point Value
29. Discovering/attempting to modify addictive behavior of close family member	46
30. Employer reorganization/downsizing	45
31. Dealing with infertility/miscarriage	44
32. Getting married/remarried	43
33. Changing employers/careers	43
34. Failure to obtain/qualify for a mortgage	42
35. Pregnancy of self/spouse/mate	41
36. Experiencing discrimination/harassment outside the workplace	39
37. Release from jail	39
38. Spouse/mate begins/ceases work outside the home	38
39. Major disagreement with boss/coworker	37
40. Change in residence	35
41. Finding appropriate child care/day care	34
42. Experiencing a large unexpected monetary gain	33
43. Changing positions (transfer, promotion)	33
44. Gaining a new family member	33
45. Changing work responsibilities	32
46. Child leaving home	30
47. Obtaining a home mortgage	30
48. Obtaining a major loan other than home mortgage	30
49. Retirement	28
50. Beginning/ceasing formal education	26
51. Receiving a ticket for violating the law	22

Scoring:

If you have more than 300 points, you have about a 75 percent chance of experiencing health problems because of your stress.

If you have 151 to 299 points, you have about a 50 percent chance of experiencing health problems because of your stress.

If you have up to 150 points, you will probably not experience health problems because of your stress.

Source: C. J. Hobson, J. Kamen, J. Szostek, C. M. Nethercut, J. W. Tiedmann, and S. Wojnarowicz, "Stressful Life Events: A Revision and Update of the Social Readjustment Rating Scale," *International Journal of Stress Management,* 5(11), 1998:1–23. The Hobson et al scale furthers original research by T. H. Holmes and R. H. Rahe, "The Social Readjustment Rating Scale," *Journal of Psychosomatic Research, 11* (Pergamom Press Ltd., 1967):213–18. Copyright © 2004, Springer Netherlands. Reproduced with permission.

fail. . .[substitute here your own version of "my parents will disown me and my friends will draw and quarter me"]." But it is far better to coach yourself than to worry. Say to yourself, "Take this one step at a time," and "Even if I fail to meet the deadline, I will have tried my best." Such cognitive coping does not eliminate stressors, of course, but it does help you to put them into perspective and thus make them less emotionally disruptive.[75]

During stressful times our beliefs also come into play. Authors Aggie Casey and Herbert Benson of the Harvard Medical School point out that a common myth about stress is that "I must feel stressed in order to succeed."[76] Other myths, which are part of the traditional core work ethic in the United States, include the idea that work is noble, and that the harder the work, the more noble it is. This core work ethic is sometimes extended to include the beliefs that the more discomfort is involved, the more noble the work is, and that leisure is an inferior and perhaps virtueless activity.[77] Under these myths, being stressed out becomes a good thing.

Do you like others to know how hard you work? believe that people who work longer hours are better workers? feel awkward in the presence of your boss (suggesting you quite seriously want to please him)? find it difficult to relax on weekends? If your answer is "yes" to these questions, you are committed—and perhaps overly committed—to the work ethic.

You might want to consider the advice of Australian stress expert Paul Wilson, who writes, "Slavish commitment to vague or abstract masters (such as corporations) and ideals is not necessarily in your best interest, especially if you have a tendency to worry about work and to take it too seriously. It is far better to challenge what you believe in and what you believe you want from your work, *then* to make your commitments. When you are working toward goals that *you* define and believe in, you will be more calm about your work."[78]

Wilson suggests this exercise that you can do right now. Imagine that you are 65 years old. Think back over your life: What did success really mean to you? What did you really accomplish? Doing this simple exploration can help you to clarify you personal goals and to strike what is for you the right balance between them and your life in organizations.

Manage Physical and Behavioral Factors

To manage stress effectively, you must concern yourself with your body as well as your mind.

GET ENOUGH SLEEP AND EXERCISE Although the amount of sleep needed by healthy people varies, most need seven to eight hours a night.[79] Getting enough sleep is a recommended stress reducer for employees and executives alike.[80] Being under stress may affect your sleep patterns. In a study of healthy undergraduates, those who were told that upon awakening they would have to give a 15-minute speech on a topic that would be chosen for them had changes in their heart rate patterns similar to those of insomniacs.[81]

According to the U.S. Surgeon General, most people should exercise 30 minutes a day most days of the week.[82] Yet fewer than one in four Americans exercise enough to obtain any significant health benefits. The exercise does not have to be vigorous—yoga, swimming, and walking all qualify. The health benefits of even moderate exercise include improving your mood and strengthening your immune system.

Some businesspeople take their exercise to extremes and advocate doing so.[83] Even training for marathons and triathlons has gained popularity. The CEO of a real estate company in Portland, Maine, spends 20 hours a week on a bicycle, and asserts that when he is on the bike he can think up new business ideas without interruption. The COO of a Connecticut asset management firm does Ironman contests to ward off insomnia. The CEO of a Philadelphia insurance company reimburses his 1,100 employees for gym memberships and gives them a longer lunch hour if they work out. And the ex-CEO of online travel service Expedia.com suggests that patiently building one's physical capacities can lead to more patience in building one's business.

LEARN TO RELAX When you relax, your metabolism, heart rate, blood pressure, breathing rate, and muscle tension all decrease.[84] These responses are exactly the opposite of what happens during the fight or flight response. Not only does relaxation let you feel calm in the moment, when practiced regularly it may buffer your long-term sensitivity to stress. For instance, research suggests that people who regularly elicit what is popularly called **the relaxation response** experience the same stress hormones that others do, but they do not react as strongly to them.[85]

the relaxation response
The elicitation of a relaxed state, in which the body slows down.

There are many paths to relaxation.[86] Practicing deep breathing is one way. Simply sit or lie in a comfortable place and breathe long and slowly through your nose. Try to make your diaphragm work for you. Experiment by placing one hand flat against your chest and one hand flat against your abdomen. Which hand moves the most when you breathe? Try to make it the one on your abdomen.

Another method is meditation. Sit in a quiet, comfortable place. Relax your body by taking some long, deep breaths. Concentrate on . . . something. Some people like to concentrate on one word. Others like a phrase or phrases. Others like to concentrate on the sensation of their breath leaving their nostrils. As your thoughts intrude upon this concentration, try not to avoid the internal monologue but don't encourage it either, just let it be there and, gently, refocus. Do this for 10 to 20 minutes.

Some people like to relax using a guided meditation. Get a tape, or make a tape, that guides you through a physical relaxation routine and then guides your thoughts gently and beautifully through a landscape or into a piece of music. Or guide your meditation by relaxing your body a bit at a time, part by part, beginning with your toes and moving on up to your head.

Still others like to combine more intense physical exercise along with their cognitive relaxation. They practice gentle yoga—stretching and breathing in various postures while concentrating on your body and its reaction. Or they practice aerobic exercise like swimming, biking, or walking while focusing on the cadence of their movements.

See "Gain Experience: Progressive Relaxation" at the back of this chapter for an exercise you can use to relax sitting at your desk or lying comfortably in a quiet place. The exercise is based on the idea that tensing your muscles before relaxing them is a particularly effective way to relax. Try it now. You deserve it!

PRACTICE EFFECTIVE ERGONOMICS When sitting at a desk, sit up straight when working at your keyboard. Don't slouch or hunch over.[87] Don't use your chin to hold the receiver against your shoulder when you talk on the telephone. Doing this builds up strain in your neck muscles. Every 10 minutes, take a 30-second break from tasks that require repetitive movements. Change your position, straighten your posture, stand up, and flex your neck and fingers.

Take a five-minute break every hour or two and walk around the room. Research suggests that taking regular rest breaks can be an effective means of maintaining performance, managing fatigue, and controlling the accumulation of risk during prolonged tasks.[88]

Manage Your Environment

Not all, but some, stressors in your environment can be managed. Here are some interesting ideas that will help you identify them and cope. Why not try a:

TECHNOLOGY FAST:

Unplug *all* communication devices at least once a week for several hours.

PEOPLE FAST:

Set aside a block of hours each week during which you speak to no one.

"NOISE" FAST:

Devote at least 20 minutes a day to doing absolutely nothing. Just sit and be. Focus on something to help you escape your stream of consciousness.

WEEKEND FAST:

Make a list of the tedious chores you often do on weekends and post it on the refrigerator. Then do not do *any* of those things until Monday! (This is your author's personal favorite.)

NEWS FAST:

For three days do not read, watch, or listen to the news.

FIGURE 6.2

Pie Charts of Your Average Day and Your Preferred Day

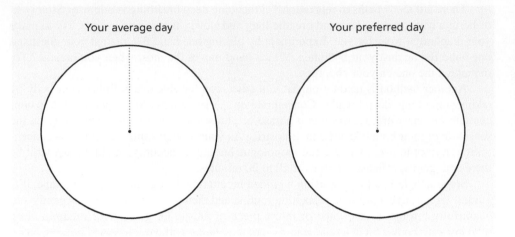

Manage Your Time

Time management is an essential skill that can help you reduce stress in both your personal and professional life.

In the space provided in Figure 6.2, complete a pie chart of how you spend your average day, then draw a second pie chart that shows how you would prefer to spend your time. What differences do you discover?

Want a more accurate portrait? If you are so motivated, keep a time log for a week. Write down everything you do, when the activity begins and ends, and how much time it took. At the end of the week, review your data. Critically examine your activities. Did you spend enough time doing the important things? Did you spend too much time on unimportant things? Did you manage your time, or did time manage you?

If deadlines stress you out, or you feel you waste time on the job, you may need to study basic principles of time management. First, you need to find out how you waste time by doing the exercises we just mentioned.

Then set goals for yourself. There is a direct relationship between goals and time. According to Dr. Walter Pauk, the Cornell University learning and study skills expert, "When you have a goal firmly in mind, you will think of objectives rather than activities. You will make better decisions, speak and write more forcefully, and treat time as a precious commodity."[89] Pauk goes on to point out that when you set goals, you avoid falling victim to the four great "robbers of time":

1. Laziness—"I don't feel like doing it right now."
2. Sidetracks—"I'll get the news on the Web and then I'll start working."
3. Procrastination—"I'll do it later."
4. Daydreaming—"Some day I'll amaze them."

Finally, you need to plan your time, and of course stick to the plan. Whether you use a paper and pencil or an electronic planner, plan the days in the month and the hours in the days. Be sure you can see a whole month at a time so that future events are not "forgotten." Discover your prime time for working: Are you a morning or a night person, or someone with no preference? Do your priority tasks then.

By learning to manage time, you will avoid the stressors of being a time-waster: failure to do your job on time, failure to be competitive, and failure to live up to your ability.

What Do Companies Do About Employee Stress?

Concerned companies understand that stress can negatively affect both their employees and the bottom line. They set goals for becoming a healthy organization, set up programs for their employees, and coach their managers to be aware of the stress factor.

Analyze the Costs of Stress

About half of the 2 million people who die every year in the United States die of preventable causes. In fact, in 1990 the leading causes of death in the United States were tobacco usage (400,000 people), diet and activity patterns (300,000 people), and alcohol consumption (100,000 people).[90] It is not surprising, then, that today more than 80 percent of U.S. businesses with 50 or more employees have some form of wellness program, the most popular of which are exercise programs, stop-smoking clinics, back-care programs, and stress management.[91]

Why do companies invest in these programs? Because they find that stress and its related diseases can be costly to them in terms of both productivity and profits. For example, a study of 46,000 workers undertaken by six major companies confirmed that stress is a major contributing factor to the companies' higher medical costs. Employees with high stress and stress-related factors along with physical risk factors for heart disease had medical bills three times higher than other employees.[92]

Relating stress to quality and costs, an insurance industry study on the effects of stress prevention programs in hospital settings found that the frequency of medication errors by hospital staff in a 700-bed hospital declined by 50 percent after stress prevention activities were implemented.[93] In a second study, there was a 70 percent reduction in malpractice claims in 22 hospitals that implemented stress prevention activities. In a matched group of 22 hospitals that did not implement stress prevention activities, there was no reduction in claims. In these studies program activities included 1) employee and management education on job stress, 2) changes in hospital policies and procedures to reduce organizational sources of stress, and 3) establishment of employee assistance programs.

Set Goals for Becoming a Healthy Organization

A healthy organization, according to the National Institute for Occupational Safety and Health (NIOSH), is one that has:

- low rates of illness,
- low rates of injury,
- low rates of disability, and
- is competitive in the marketplace.[94]

One way that companies reduce stress and achieve these goals is by paying attention to their own cultures and processes. Characteristics of a healthy organization include recognition of employees for good work performance, opportunities for career development, an organizational culture that values the individual worker, and management actions that are consistent with organizational values.[95]

Companies also undertake direct stress interventions. These can be categorized according to a medical model, in which the earlier interventions are the more desirable.[96] In this model, 1) primary stress interventions are those that are preventive in nature because they try to avoid a health problem by illuminating the root causes, including appropriate selection, placement, and training[97]; 2) secondary stress interventions mitigate potential health problems, by offering relaxation training, for example; and 3) tertiary interventions treat the problem after it has been manifest; an example is an employee assistance program that provides counseling. Unfortunately, companies do not always focus on the most practical type of intervention. A study of British employers found that whereas only 12 percent provide information about childcare and 2 percent offer services such as childcare or financial help with child care, 56 percent spend money on counseling for stress.[98]

Establish Company Programs: The Case of Work–Life Balance

The culture of the software industry is such that the boundary between work and life is often blurred, and workers seldom attach to one organization. Even so, in this industry a company that takes an accommodating approach to its employees' nonwork commitments can create greater organizational commitment.[99] Furthermore, the commitment can be created among a company's most desirable employees. An IBM survey of its workforce demonstrated that the company's highest performers are the ones most likely to consider their ability to balance work and personal responsibilities when making a decision to stay with the company. Employees overall rated work–life balance issues as 6th of 16 factors that keep them with the company. However, IBM's top performers, as identified by performance review ratings, ranked balance issues 2nd of those 16 factors.[100]

Company programs that help employees to balance their home and work life often provide counseling, research, and referrals on issues such as child care and eldercare. Their advocates argue that companies that use them benefit in terms of employee time saved, increased motivation and productivity, employee retention, decreased health care costs, and reduced absenteeism.[101] A high-level corporate officer at DuPont commented on his own company's policy, "Managers like me who have had the comfort of relying on our spouses to handle most family issues often fail to understand how critical such programs are to our employees [whose spouses work] and, therefore, to our business success. We now have empirical data that confirms employees who take advantage of DuPont's work/life programs are more committed than the average employee."[102]

Of course, companies institute a wide range of programs for managing stress at work, including but not limited to improving physical conditions; offering opportunities during the workday to exercise and eat well; and providing training in ergonomics, worker safety, and relaxation.

In particular, addressing employee vacation time has become an important issue. In the private sector about 25 percent of workers get no paid vacation time, and an additional 33 percent only take a seven-day vacation.[103] Many employees are afraid to leave for the two weeks that are due to them, fearing they might miss crucial developments in the office. To encourage its people to relax, the accounting firm PricewaterhouseCoopers now shuts down its entire national organization twice a year, for about 5 days around the Fourth of July and 10 days around the Christmas holidays. This ensures that people can walk away and not worry about what is happening in the office. The company also tracks vacation days spent and reminds employees to use theirs up.

Coach Managers to Recognize Issues of Health and Productivity

Some practical approaches that managers can take to alleviate employee stress include[104]:

- improving physical working conditions, including reducing employees' exposure to noise, toxins, and chemicals;
- redesigning jobs to reduce the incidence of repetitive-strain injuries;
- maintaining job demands at healthy levels;
- providing healthy work schedules that include rotating shifts, using flextime, and reducing forced overtime;
- offering stress management training; and
- encouraging social support from coworkers and supervisors.

In the end. . .

"Manage yourself to manage others" is an axiom of organizational life. It is never more true than when applied to managing your stress. When it comes to coping on the job, not only are you your own best manager, you are a role model to those you manage.

Apply What You Have Learned. . .

World Class Companies: Companies with Award-Winning Wellness Programs

The United States

The Wellness Councils of America give annual awards to companies that exemplify best practices for workplace wellness.[106] Their top award is the Platinum Award. Among the recent award winners are Syngenta of North Carolina and International Truck and Engine Corporation of Illinois.

Syngenta is a global agribusiness that is the U.S. sales leader in crop protection products, including herbicides and pesticides, and related products. Although its North American base is in Greensboro, North Carolina, it has half a dozen offices and also numerous field employees across the United States. Its application for the Platinum Award covered about 2,200 employees. Syngenta does not contract out its health services to an HMO (health management organization); rather, it insures its employees itself. Initiated in 1998, its Reaping Rewards Wellness Program has an employee participation rate of 74 percent (2005), up from 56 percent in 1998. In addition to its U.S. initiative, the company hopes to take wellness global by aiming for a global minimum standard of health and wellness for all its employees.

In recent years, Syngenta employees have been asked to establish personal wellness goals. Then the company's Health Services Staff coaches them on how to meet those goals. The company offers many wellness initiatives, including a pedometer competition to encourage exercise, on-site Weight Watchers classes, and stress management classes. The company's objective is to create a healthier employee population which, in turn, will be more productive and have less absenteeism. It monitors its return on investment in wellness programs by keeping track of such things as health-insurance claims, pharmacy claims, and health risk results, and it selects topics for its wellness programs based on these results. For example, between 2002 and 2005 total cholesterol among employees went down 4 percent, and the number of employees considered at risk based on their cholesterol was reduced from 45 percent to 34 percent.

International Truck and Engine Corporation manufactures trucks, engines, school buses, and parts, and also offers financing. It uses a wellness initiative called "Vital Lives" to endorse wellness, prevention, and safe behaviors as preferred lifestyle choices for employees *and* their families. The company has about 14,500 active employees at 26 sites, but the total number of people its program covers, including retirees, is about 79,000. According to the company, the initiative has enhanced productivity, reduced absenteeism and turnover, and avoided unnecessary health care costs. The company spends about $412K annually for the program, but, while national health care costs have outpaced inflation, its own costs have been relatively controlled. A key aspect of the program is that it is decentralized; 26 local Vital Lives teams made up of volunteer union and non-union employees implement the programs. Annually, there is a two-day wellness summit to provide learning and networking opportunities for the employees. Also, employees are given incentives for healthy behaviors: Active employees who do not smoke receive a $50 monthly reduction in their health care premium. And the company offers a variety of wellness programs, such as a nutrition-based "Spring Tune-Up" challenge, a fitness-based "Trucking Across North America" challenge, and either a health club subsidy or a subsidized onsite fitness center.

Canada

In western Canada, a similar award goes to companies that create workplaces that foster psychological well-being among employees.[107] Two companies that have won the British Columbia Psychological Association's Award Psychologically Healthy Workplace Award are Vancouver City Savings Credit Union and Petro-Canada Burrard Products Terminal.

Vancouver City Savings Credit Union is Canada's largest credit union. Among its initiatives are: 1) An "open door" policy with respect to mental health. This policy encourages employees to give management feedback about what they need, and it empowers employee teams to implement the feedback results. 2) An Employee Advisory Committee, which addresses ideas and concerns about benefits, salaries, training, policies, and staff programs. 3) A "living well" council, which helps employees take responsibility for their health. 4) Recognition programs, whereby employees are encouraged and supported to share recognition with their colleagues.

Petro-Canada Burrard Products Terminal processes oil for gasoline, distillates, and jet fuel. Its key health intervention is based on employee involvement. Sixty percent of the company's workers are union members. Since 1995 the company has worked hard to develop a culture of mutual respect, and it attributes its safety record (only one injury in the last nine years), its operating expense reduction and reduced absenteeism rate to that culture.

Discussion

1. List the programs these companies have put in place.
2. What do these programs have in common?

Advice from the Pros

What's in a Nap?

Winston Churchill, Albert Einstein, and John F. Kennedy did it. Companies such as the petrochemical firm Nova Chemicals Corporation and the financial software company Intuit Canada encourage it. What is this unusual activity?

It's napping, or, in business speak, *power napping*.

Sleep specialists suggest that a 20- to 60-minute nap significantly boosts performance, and that a short rest before a night shift increases alertness by approximately 30 percent. Napping reduces stress. And psychology researcher Carlyle Smith points out that napping also helps people remember things they have just learned.

So some companies are going with the idea. In some facilities, Inuit Canada furnishes resting rooms with beds, fresh linens, and extra blankets. Gould Evans, a Missouri design firm, offers a "spent tent"—a tent and sleeping bag, with eyeshades and soft music—set up in their offices. At London public relations firm Firefly Communications, employees work in often-hectic open offices, but their recharge room offers relaxation for up to 30 minutes in a comfortable chair with soothing music and low lighting.

A person's circadian rhythm, the internal pattern of sleep and wakefulness, takes a dip between 2 and 4 P.M. (also between 2 and 4 A.M.). During that time critical thinking, creativity, and motor coordination all dip.

So, perhaps you should consider Winston Churchill's advice: "Don't think you will be doing less work because you sleep during the day. That's a foolish notion held by people who have no imagination." Mr. Churchill should know. He continued his daily napping right through World War II.

Discuss

1. How many students in the class like to nap? Those who nap, why do you nap? Those who do not nap, why not? Do you think napping helps you perform better?
2. Have you ever worked in an organization that encouraged napping? How about one that looked the other way if someone fell asleep at his or her desk?
3. What guidelines for power-napping programs would you suggest for any business?

Sources: J. Traves, "You Snooze, You Win," *Canadian Business 78* (17), August 29, 2005:52–53; "Sleeping on the Job?" *Employee Benefits,* June 2004:32.

Gain Experience

I. Progressive Relaxation

In general, what you will do here is alternately tense and relax your muscles, deepening your full body relaxation as you include more and more muscle groups. Tense each muscle group for several seconds (7 to 10 is usually about right), then relax for another 10 seconds or so. If anything recommended here is uncomfortable for you, adapt the exercise to your own needs.

Lie on the floor in a place that is warm, comfortable, dim, and quiet. Lie on your back with your hands at your sides, your legs uncrossed, your shoes off. Just lie there for several minutes, taking deep breaths and exhaling slowly. (Chair option: This exercise can be adapted for an office or classroom in which lying on the floor is not a good option.)

Beginning with your right hand, make a tight fist . . . and relax. Repeat.

Press your right arm down to the ground (or to the back of your chair) . . . and relax. Repeat.

Moving to your left hand, make a tight fist . . . and relax. Repeat.

Press your left arm down to the ground (or to the back of your chair) . . . and relax. Repeat.

For your facial muscles . . . first . . .

Pull back the sides of your mouth in an exaggerated smile . . . and relax. Repeat.

Pucker up your face around your nose . . . and relax. Repeat.

Raise your eyebrows as high as you can . . . and relax. Repeat.

For your upper back and neck . . .

Slide your chin down your chest, without touching it, stretching as far as you can . . . and relax. Repeat.

For your chest. . .

Pull your shoulder blades together under your back . . . and relax. Repeat.

For your abdomen. . .

Make all the muscles hard . . . and relax. Repeat.

Moving to your feet . . .

Curl your right foot into a ball, as though trying to make a fist . . . and relax. Repeat.

Point your toe to your head (stretching the calf) . . . and relax. Repeat.

Press your entire leg down to the floor (or down on your chair) . . . and relax. Repeat.

Curl your left foot into a ball, as though trying to make a fist . . . and relax. Repeat.

Point your toe to your head (stretching the calf) . . . and relax. Repeat.

Press your entire leg down to the floor (or down on your chair) . . . and relax. Repeat.

Now, just lie there for a few moments, enjoying this state of relaxation. Breathe deeply. Recognize muscles in your body that the exercise did not include, and which may be important to you to focus on in the future. Recognize which muscles were included but which need still more relaxation.

II. Visualization

Your professor will guide you in a visualization. Visualizations are useful for:

1. further, deeper relaxation. Listening to a visualization is particularly useful for those people who find they get distracted by their thoughts when trying to relax or meditate, and for those who simply enjoy the interesting trips they take when imaging/imagining.
2. problem solving in a nonlinear fashion, through visualization. When you think about a problem while in a state of deep relaxation, you are probably thinking about it in a divergent, or holistic, rather than a convergent, or focused, way. Also, some athletes, such as platform divers, swear by visualization as a technique that helps them integrate what they have learned.

III. Do You Spend Your Time, Or Waste It?

1. List from memory everything you did yesterday, from the time you got up until the time you went to bed. Estimate the time spent on each item.
2. When your list is complete, critically examine your activities. Did you spend enough time doing important things? Did you spend too much time on unimportant things? Did you manage your time, or did outside influences have significant impacts?

Chapter Summary and Key Terms

What is your image of a healthy work environment?

Write out your answers to the following four questions raised earlier in this chapter: What's happening around here? How do I survive? What is my meaning or mission? How can I be effective?

Do you really need to be concerned about stress at work?

Stress is a state of tension people feel when their usual modes of coping do not work. Whether you are a manager or not, whether you are personally stressed or not, stress will be a factor in your work team and company. Job stress has become a common and costly problem in the American workplace.

stress   152
stressor   152
eustress   153
job stress   153

How does stress affect on-the-job performance?

Under low stress performance is likely to be low. Under moderate stress performance is likely to be high. However, under extreme stress, performance suffers.

What are some common stressors at work?

Common stressors are the job itself, physical factors, and work-personal life issues.

role   154
role conflict   154
role ambiguity   154
insufficient authority   154
overload   155
repetitive stress injuries   155
noise   155
biogenic triggers   155
circadian rhythms   156

How might stress affect your health?

Physiologically and psychologically, men and women react to stress somewhat differently. However, being constantly under stress without developing the ability to cope with it endangers the health of both. Stress may impair your immune system and enhance your perception of pain. It is related to the development of coronary heart disease.

fight or flight   157
tend and befriend   158
stress response   158

Do you have a predisposition to stress?

How do you know whether you are a Type A workaholic who is likely to have a heart attack before you are fifty? The self-test in this chapter may send you exploring beyond this book.

workaholism   159
Type A–Type B personality   159
AHA! Syndrome   161
hardiness   161

How can you cope with stress at work?

Learn to recognize the symptoms of stress, including burnout. Identify the stressors in your life. Create a plan for active coping, and put your plan for self-management into action. Get support from others.

job burnout   162
cognitive restructuring   162
the relaxation response   164

What do companies do about employee stress?

Many companies today educate themselves about the costs of stress and set goals for becoming a healthy organization. They establish programs for their employees and coach their managers to recognize the links between employee health and productivity.

Explorations

1. Company stress management programs
Web search these key words to find out more about organizational programs for stress management: stress+programs+companies. Use your academic data bases to search for more details.

2. Health management in Britain and Canada
For an international perspective, Web search: British+government+workplace+health or Canada+government+workplace+health.

3. NIOSH
Check out the National Institute for Occupational Safety and Health at http://www.cdc.gov/niosh/homepage.html

4. Wellness Councils of America
The Wellness Councils of America is an organization dedicated to "helping organizations of all kinds build and sustain results-oriented wellness programs." Find out more about the council at www.welcoa.org.

5. Relaxation
Learn more about the "relaxation response" on the Web.

6. If you believe you have a problem with stress. . .
Here are some excellent books:

Meyer Friedman, M.D., and Diane Ulmer, R.N, M.S., *Treating Type A Behavior and Your Heart* (New York: Alfred A. Knopf, 1984). Despite the fact that this is an older book, it treats the anger–hostility component of Type A behavior extensively and intelligently. (Feel free to ignore the authors' recommendation to read, as therapy, Proust's seven-volume novel *Remembrance of Things Past*. They themselves admit this may be a stretch.)

Read and do the exercises in Richard N. Bolles's *The Three Boxes of Life and How to Get Out of Them: An Introduction to Life/Work Planning* (Berkeley, CA: Ten Speed Press, 1978). Bolles is the author of the classic career guide *What Color Is Your Parachute?* mentioned in Chapter 1's "Explorations."

Paul Wilson, *Calm at Work* (Penguin Books Australia Ltd.: 1997) has dozens of good introspections and helpful hints. Available most readily in England and Australia, and on the Web.

Check out your university counseling centers, which is likely to have stress management resources especially designed for students

There are many commercial Web sites that provide a variety of testing and counseling services. Look for Stress Busters, Mind Tools, and Stress Free Net, among others.

7. For recent perspectives on students, stress, and lifestyle read:
M.S. Cole, H. S. Field, and S. G. Harris, "Student Learning Motivation and Psychological Hardiness: Interactive Effects on Students' Reactions to a Management Class," *Academy of Management Learning & Education (3)* 1, March 2004:64–85.

L. Spencer, "Results of a Heart Disease Risk-Factor Screening Among Traditional College Students," *Journal of American College Health 50* (6), May 2002: 291–296.

References

[1] Adapted from S. E. Taylor, *Health Psychology*, 4th ed. (New York: McGraw-Hill, 1998).

[2] D. Jaffe, "The Healthy Company: Research Paradigms for Personal and Organizational Health," in S. Sauter and L. Murphy, eds., *Organizational Risk Factors for Job Stress* (Washington DC: American Psychological Association, 1995):13–40.

[3] S. Sauter, S. Lim, and L. Murphy, "Organizational Health: A New Paradigm for Occupational Stress Research at NIOSH," *Japanese Journal of Occupational Mental Health 4*, 1996:248–254.

[4] R. N. Bolles, *The Three Boxes of Life and How to Get Out of Them: An Introduction to Life/Work Planning* (Berkeley, CA: Ten Speed Press, 1978).

[5] R. N. Bolles, *The Three Boxes of Life and How to Get Out of Them: An Introduction to Life/Work Planning* (Berkeley, CA: Ten Speed Press, 1978).

[6] A. P. Brief, R. S. Schuler, and M. Van Sell, *Managing Job Stress* (Boston: Little, Brown, 1981).

[7] Hans Selye, *The Stress of Life* (New York: McGraw-Hill, 1978).

[8] B. L. Simmons and D. L. Nelson, "Eustress at Work: The Relationship between Hope and Health in Hospital Nurses," *Health Care Management Review 26* (4), Fall 2001:7–18.

[9] S. Sauter, L. Murphy, M. Colligan, N. Swanson, J. Hurrell, Jr., F. Scharf, Jr., R. Sinclair, P. Grubb, L. Goldenhar, T. Alterman, J. Johnston, A. Hamilton, and J. Tisdale, *Stress at Work,* Department of Health and Human Services Publication no. 99–101 (Cincinnati OH: National Institute for Occupational Safety and Health, January 7, 1999).

[10] Northwestern National Life data, reported in S. Sauter et al., *Stress at Work,* Department of Health and Human Services Publication no. 99–101 (Cincinnati OH: National Institute for Occupational Safety and Health, January 7, 1999). Accessed May 26, 2004.

[11] St. Paul Fire and Marine Insurance Company study, reported in S. Sauter et al., *Stress at Work,* Department of Health and Human Services Publication no. 99–101 (Cincinnati OH: National Institute for Occupational Safety and Health, January 7, 1999). Accessed May 26, 2004.

[12] Princeton Survey Research Associates study, reported in S. Sauter et al., *Stress at Work,* Department of Health and Human Services Publication no. 99–101 (Cincinnati OH: National Institute for Occupational Safety and Health, January 7, 1999). Accessed May 26, 2004.

[13] J. H. Browne, "Benchmarking HRM Practices in Healthy Work Organizations," *American Business Review 18* (2), June 2000:54–61.

[14] J. L. Xie and J. Schaubroeck, "Bridging Approaches and Findings Across Diverse Disciplines to Improve Job Stress Research," in P. L. Perrewé and D. C. Ganster, eds., *Research in Occupational Stress and Well-Being 1,* 2001:1–53.

[15] S. Cartwright and C. L. Cooper, *Managing Workplace Stress* (Thousand Oaks, CA: Sage, 1997).

[16] C. R. Anderson, "Stress, Performance, and Coping: A Test of the Inverted-U Theme," *Academy of Management Proceedings,* 1975:152–154.

[17] L. A. Muse, S. G. Harris, and H. S. Field, "Has the Inverted-U Theory of Stress and Job Performance Had a Fair Test?" *Human Performance 16* (4), 2003:349–364.

[18] A. Shimazu and S. Kosugi, "Job Stressors, Coping, and Psychological Distress among Japanese Employees: Interplay between Active and Non-Active Coping," *Work & Stress 17* (1), January 2003:38–51.

[19] P. L. Perrewé, K. L. Zellars, G. R. Ferris, A. M. Rossi, C. J. Kacmar, and D. A. Ralston, "Neutralizing Job Stressors: Political Skill as an Antidote to the Dysfunctional Consequences of Role Conflict," *Academy of Management Journal 47* (1), February 2004:141–152.

[20] A. Shimazu and S. Kosugi, "Job Stressors, Coping, and Psychological Distress among Japanese Employees: Interplay between Active and Non-Active Coping," *Work & Stress 17* (1), January 2003:38–51.

[21] T. D. Wall, P. R. Jackson, and S. Mullarkey, "Further Evidence on Some New Measures of Job Control, Cognitive Demand and Production Responsibility," *Journal of Organizational Behavior 16* (5), September 1995:431–455; A. Shimazu and S. Kosugi, "Job Stressors, Coping, and Psychological Distress among Japanese Employees: Interplay between Active and Non-Active Coping," *Work & Stress 17* (1), January 2003:38–51.

[22] S. Cartwright and C. L. Cooper, *Managing Workplace Stress* (Thousand Oaks, CA: Sage, 1997).

[23] C. Cammann, M. Fichman, G. D. Jenkins, and J. Klesh, "Michigan Organizational Assessment Questionnaire," in S. E. Seashore, E. E. Lawler, P. H. Mirvis, and C. Cammann, eds., *Assessing Organizational Change: A Guide to Methods, Measures, and Practices* (New York: Wiley-Interscience, 1983):71–138.

[24] P. W. Spector, D. J. Dwyer, and S. M. Jex, "The Relationship of Job Stressors to Affective Health, and Performance Outcomes: A Comparison of Multiple Data Sources," *Journal of Applied Psychology 73* (1), 1988:11–19; S. M. Jex and T. A. Beehr, "Emerging Theoretical and Methodological Issues in the Study of Work-Related Stress," in K. M. Rowland and G. R. Ferris, eds., *Research in Personnel and Human Resources Management 9* (Greenwich, CT: JAI Press, 1991):311–365.

[25] U. Lundberg and B. Hellström, "Workload and Morning Salivary Cortisol in Women," *Work & Stress 16* (4), October 2002:356–63.

[26] S. Shellenbarger, "Taking Back the Weekend: Companies Help Employees Cut Back on Overwork," *The Wall Street Journal,* May 18, 2006:D1.

[27] C. Langford and A. I. Glendon, "Effects of Neuroticism, Extraversion, Circadian Type and Age on Reported Driver Stress," *Work & Stress 16* (4), 2002:316–334.

[28] K. Clark, "Pain in the Bottom Line," *U.S. News & World Report 129* (21), November 27, 2000:58.

[29] L. J. Loewen and P. Suedfeld, "Cognitive and Arousal Effects of Masking Office Noise," *Environment and Behaviour, 24,* 1992:381–395; E. Sundstrom, J. P Town, and R. W. Rice, "Office Noise, Satisfaction, and Performance," *Environment and Behaviour, 26,* 1994: 195–222.

[30] S. Banbury and D. C. Berry, "Disruption of Office-Related Tasks by Speech and Office Noise," *British Journal of Psychology 89* (3), August 1998:499–517.

[31] G. Evans and D. Johnson, "Stress and Open-Office Noise," *Journal of Applied Psychology 85* (5), October 2000:779–783.

[32] A. Casey and H. Benson, *Mind Your Heart: A Mind/Body Approach to Stress Management, Exercise, and Nutrition for Heart Health* (New York: Free Press, 2004):96.

[33] S. Cohen, "De-stress for Success," *Training & Development 51* (11), November 1997:76–80.

[34] M. J. Smith, H. H. Cohen, and A. Cohen, "Characteristics of a Successful Safety Program," *Journal of Safety Research 10,* 1978:5–15.

[35] R. A. Carrillo, "Safety Leadership: Managing the Paradox," *Professional Safety,* July 2005: 31–34.

[36] R. S. DeFrank, R. Konopaske, and J. M. Ivancevich, "Executive Travel Stress: Perils of the Road Warrior," *Academy of Management Executive 14* (2), May 2000:58–71.

[37] Citing a study by Kensington Technology Group, "Road Weary and Inefficient: Business Travelers Aren't Productive," *Industrial Engineer 36* (2), February 2004:66.

[38] C. Fisher, "Business on the Road," *American Demographics 20,* 1998:44–47.

[39] M. Westman and D. Etzion, "The Impact of Short Overseas Business Trips on Job Stress and Burnout," *Applied Psychology: An International Review 51* (4), October 2002:582–592.

[40] M. Kivimäki, P. Kuisma, M. Virtanen, and M. Elovainio, "Does Shift Work Lead to Poorer Health Habits? A Comparison Between Women Who Had Always Done Shift Work with Those Who Had Never Done Shift Work," *Work & Stress 15* (1), January 2001:3–13.

[41] M. Härmä, "Individual Differences in Tolerance to Shift Work: A Review," *Ergonomics 36,* 1993:101–109.

[42] J. A. Horne and O. Ostberg, "A Self-Assessment Questionnaire to Determine Morningeveningness in Human Circadian Rhythms," *International Journal of Chronobiology 4,* 1976:97–110; C. Langford and A. I. Glendon, "Effects of Neuroticism, Extraversion, Circadian Type and Age on Reported Driver Stress," *Work & Stress 16* (4), 2002:316–34.

[43] R. S. DeFrank, R. Konopaske, and J. M. Ivancevich, "Executive Travel Stress: Perils of the Road Warrior," *Academy of Management Executive 14* (2), May 2000:58–71.

[44] R. S. DeFrank, R. Konopaske, and J. M. Ivancevich, "Executive Travel Stress: Perils of the Road Warrior," *Academy of Management Executive 14* (2), May 2000:58–71.

[45] K. Wright, "Times of Our Lives," *Scientific American 14* (3), June 2004:42–49.

[46] K. Steenland, "Shift Work, Long Hours, and CVD: A Review," in P. L. Schnall, K. Belkic, P. Landsbergis, and D. Baker, eds., *The Workplace and Cardiovascular Disease: Occupational Medicine State of Art Reviews 15* (1) (Philadelphia, PA: Hanley & Belfus, 2000):7–17.

[47] C. J. Hobson, L. Delunas, and D. Kesic, "Compelling Evidence of the Need for Corporate Work/Life Balance Initiatives: Results from a National Survey of Stressful Life-Events," *Journal of Employment Counseling 38* (1), March 2001:38–44.

[48] C. J. Hobson, L. Delunas, and D. Kesic, "Compelling Evidence of the Need for Corporate Work/Life Balance Initiatives: Results from a National Survey of Stressful Life-Events," *Journal of Employment Counseling 38* (1), March 2001:38–44.

[49] J. Polach, "HRD's Role in Work-Life Integration Issues: Moving the Workforce to a Change in Mindset," *Human Resource Development International 6* (1), March 2003:57–68.

[50] E. Goode, "Response to Stress Found That's Particularly Female," *The New York Times,* May 19, 2000:A22; S. E. Taylor, *The Tending Instinct: Women, Men, and the Biology of Nurturing* (New York: Times Books, 2002).

[51] A. Casey and H. Benson, *Mind Your Heart: A Mind/Body Approach to Stress Management, Exercise, and Nutrition for Heart Health* (New York: Free Press, 2004):54.

[52] R. M. Suinn, "The Terrible Twos—Anger and Anxiety: Hazardous to Your Health," *American Psychologist 56* (1), January 2001:29–36.

[53] J. Kiecolt-Glaser, R. Glaser, E. Strain, J. Stout, K. Tarr, J. Holliday, and C. Speicher, "Modulation of Cellular Immunity in Medical Students," *Journal of Behavioral Medicine 9*, 1986:5–21.

[54] P. Marucha, J. Kiecolt-Glaser, and M. Favagehi, "Mucosal Wound Healing Is Impaired by Examination Stress," *Psychosomatic Medicine 60*, 1998:362–365.

[55] S. Manuck, J. Kaplan, and K. Matthews, "Behavioral Antecedents of Coronary Heart Disease and Atherosclerosis," *Arteriosclerosis 6*, 1986:2–14.

[56] L. R. Murphy, "A Review of Organizational Stress Management Research," *Journal of Organizational Behavior Management*, Fall/Winter 1986:215–227.

[57] S. M. Jex and P. D. Bliese, "Efficacy Beliefs as a Moderator of the Impact of Work-Related Stressors: A Multilevel Study," *Journal of Applied Psychology 84* (3), June 1999:349–361.

[58] S. A. Wiedenfeld, A. O'Leary, A. Bandura, S. Brown, S. Levine, and K. Raska, "Impact of Perceived Self-Efficacy in Coping with Stressors on Coping with the Immune System," *Journal of Personality and Social Psychology 59*, 1990:1082–1094.

[59] C. A. Bonebright, D. L. Clay, and R. D. Ankenmann, "The Relationship of Workaholism with Work-Life Conflict, Life Satisfaction, and Purpose in Life," *Journal of Counseling Psychology 47* (4), October 2000:469–476.

[60] J. T. Spence and A. S. Robbins, "Workaholism: Definition, Measurement, and Preliminary Results," *Journal of Personality Assessment 58*, 1992:160–178; A. Kanai, M. Wakabayashi, and S. Fling, "Workaholism among Employees in Japanese Corporations: An Examination Based on the Japanese Version of the Workaholism Scales," *Japanese Psychological Research 38*, 1996:192–203.

[61] C. A. Bonebright, D. L. Clay, and R. D. Ankenmann, "The Relationship of Workaholism with Work-Life Conflict, Life Satisfaction, and Purpose in Life," *Journal of Counseling Psychology 47* (4), October 2000:469–476.

[62] M. Friedman and R. Rosenman, *Type A Behavior and Your Heart* (New York: Alfred A. Knopf, 1974).

[63] M. Friedman and D. Ulmer, *Treating Type A Behavior And Your Heart* (New York: Alfred A. Knopf, 1984).

[64] M. Friedman and D. Ulmer, *Treating Type A Behavior And Your Heart* (New York: Alfred A. Knopf, 1984):76.

[65] M. Friedman and R. Rosenman, *Type A Behavior and Your Heart* (New York: Alfred A. Knopf, 1974).

[66] F. Palmero, J. L. Diez, and A. B. Asensio, "Type A Behavior Pattern Today: Relevance of the JAS-S Factor to Predict Heart Rate Reactivity-Jenkin's Activity Scale," *Behavioral Medicine*, Spring 2001:28–36.

[67] E. D. Eaker, L. M. Sullivan, M. Kelly-Hayes, R. B. D'Agostino, Sr., and E. J. Benjamin, "Tension and Anxiety and the Prediction of the 10-Year Incidence of Coronary Heart Disease, Atrial Fibrillation, and Total Mortality: The Framingham Offspring Study," *Psychosomatic Medicine 67* (5), September 1, 2005:692–696.

[68] S. C. Kobasa, "Stressful Life Events, Personality and Health: An Inquiry into Hardiness," *Journal of Personality and Social Psychology (37)*, 1979: 1–11; S. C. Kobasa, S. R. Maddi, and S. Kahn, "Hardiness and Health: A Prospective Study," *Journal of Personality and Social Psychology (42)*, 1982: 168–177.

[69] S. Klag and G. Bradley, "The Role of Hardiness in Stress and Illness: An Exploration of the Effect of Negative Affectivity and Gender," *British Journal of Health Psychology 9 (Part 2)*, 2004:137–161.

[70] S. Cartwright and C. L. Cooper, *Managing Workplace Stress* (Thousand Oaks, CA: Sage, 1997); A. Casey and H. Benson, *Mind Your Heart: A Mind/Body Approach to Stress Management, Exercise, and Nutrition for Heart Health* (New York: Free Press, 2004).

[71] J. Nelson, "Christina Maslach," *New Zealand Management 52* (3) April 2005:43–45.

[72] A. Shimazu and S. Kosugi, "Job Stressors, Coping, and Psychological Distress among Japanese Employees: Interplay between Active and Non-Active Coping," *Work & Stress 17* (1), January 2003:38–51.

[73] S. E. Taylor, *Health Psychology*, 4th ed. (New York: McGraw-Hill, 1998).

[74] A. A. Lazarus, *Behavior Therapy and Beyond* (New York: McGraw-Hill, 1971).

75 M. H. Antoni, D. G. Cruess, S. Cruess, S. Lutgendorf, M. Kumar, G. Ironson, N. Klimas, M. A. Fletcher, and N. Schneiderman, "Cognitive-Behavioral Stress Management Intervention Effects on Anxiety, 24-Hour Urinary Norepinephrine Output, and T-Cytoxic/Suppressor Cells Over Time Among Symptomatic HIV-infected Gay Men," *Journal of Consulting and Clinical Psychology 68 (1)*, 2000:31–45.

76 A. Casey and H. Benson, *Mind Your Heart: A Mind/Body Approach to Stress Management, Exercise, and Nutrition for Heart Health* (New York: Free Press, 2004).

77 P. Wilson, *Calm at Work* (Ringwood, Victoria, Australia: Penguin Books, 1997):37.

78 P. Wilson, *Calm at Work* (Ringwood, Victoria, Australia: Penguin Books, 1997):39.

79 J. F. Coates, "Sleeping on the Job: Some Considerations for HR," *Employee Relations Today 30* (4):11–21.

80 W. Atkinson, "Stress," *Risk Management 51* (6), June 2004:20–24.

81 Study by M. Hall, "Acute Stress Affects Heart Rate Variability During Sleep," *Psychosomatic Medicine 66* (1):56–62, reported in "Study Shows How Stress May Affect Sleep Patterns," *Biotech Week,* March 3, 2004:609.

82 A. Casey and H. Benson, *Mind Your Heart: A Mind/Body Approach to Stress Management, Exercise, and Nutrition for Heart Health* (New York: Free Press, 2004):214.

83 S. Max, "And Now, The Chief Endurance Officer," *BusinessWeek/online* October 17, 2005. http:// www.businessweek.com/print/magazine/content. Accessed October 15, 2005.

84 A. Casey and H. Benson, *Mind Your Heart: A Mind/Body Approach to Stress Management, Exercise, and Nutrition for Heart Health* (New York: Free Press, 2004):57.

85 A. Casey and H. Benson, *Mind Your Heart: A Mind/Body Approach to Stress Management, Exercise, and Nutrition for Heart Health* (New York: Free Press, 2004):57.

86 A. Casey and H. Benson, *Mind Your Heart: A Mind/Body Approach to Stress Management, Exercise, and Nutrition for Heart Health* (New York: Free Press, 2004):66ff.

87 Based on information provided by C. Grant, research associate at the University of Michigan Center for Ergonomics, in S. Cohen, "De-Stress for Success," *Training & Development 51* (11), November 1997:76–80.

88 P. Tucker, "The Impact of Rest Breaks Upon Accident Risk, Fatigue and Performance: A Review," *Work & Stress 17* (2), April 2003:123–137.

89 W. Pauk and J. P. Fiore, *Succeed in College!* (Boston: Houghton Mifflin Company, 2000):23.

90 J. M. McGinnis and W. H. Foege, "Actual Causes of Death in the United States," *JAMA: The Journal of the American Medican Association 270* (18), November 10, 1993:2207–2212.

91 According to the Wellness Councils of America. http://www.welcoa.org/wellworkplace/index.php?cat=1&page=1. Accessed September 22, 2005.

92 R. Goetzel, D. Anderson, R. Whitmer, R. Ozminkowski, R. Dunn, and J. Wasserman, "The Relationship between Modifiable Health Risks and Health Care Expenditures: An Analysis of the Multi-Employer HERO Health Risk and Cost Database," *Journal of Occupational and Environmental Medicine 40*, 1998:843–54.

93 J. W. Jones, B. N. Barge, B. D. Steffy, L. M. Fay, L. K. Kuntz, and L. J. Wuebker, "Stress and Medical Malpractice: Organizational Risk Assessment and Intervention," *Journal of Applied Psychology 73*(4), 1988:727–735.

94 S. Sauter et al., *Stress at Work,* Department of Health and Human Services Publication no. 99–101 (Cincinnati OH: National Institute for Occupational Safety and Health, January 7, 1999). Accessed May 26, 2004.

95 J. Landauer, "Bottom-Line Benefits of Work/Life Programs," *HR Focus 74* (7), July 1997:3–4.

96 S. Cartwright, C. Cooper, and L. Murphy, "Diagnosing a Healthy Organization: A Proactive Approach to Stress in the Workplace," in S. Sauter and L. Murphy, eds., *Organizational Risk Factors for Job Stress* (Washington DC: American Psychological Association, 1995):217–33.

97 J. M. Ivancevich and M. T. Matteson, "Promoting the Individual's Health and Well-Being," in C. L. Cooper and R. Payne, eds., *Causes, Coping and Consequences of Stress at Work* (New York: Wiley, 1988).

98 "Work-Life Stress Costs Billions," *Financial Management*, June 2001:46.

99 D. Scholarios and A. Marks, "Work-Life Balance and the Software Worker," *Human Resource Management Journal 14* (2), 2004:54–64.

100 J. Landauer, "Bottom-Line Benefits of Work/Life Programs," *HR Focus 74* (7), July 1997:3–4.

101 J. Landauer, "Bottom-Line Benefits of Work/Life Programs," *HR Focus 74* (7), July 1997:3–4.

102 J. Landauer, "Bottom-Line Benefits of Work/Life Programs," *HR Focus 74* (7), July 1997:3–4.

103 T. Egan, "The Rise of Shrinking-Vacation Syndrome," *The New York Times* August 20, 2006:18.

104 J. Cahill, P. Landsbergis, and P. Schnall, "Reducing Occupational Stress: An Introductory Guide for Managers, Supervisors, and Union Members," Presentation at the Work Stress and Health '95 Conference, Washington D. C., September 1995, cited in *Training & Development 51* (11), November 1997:76–80.

105 See www.welcoa.org for workplace award executive summaries for these and other companies.

106 "Winners Named in Psychologically Healthy Workplace Award," 2004, http://www.psychologists.bc.ca/ Workplace Award.html. Accessed July 11, 2005.

7

Communication and Interpersonal Relationships

Preview

How can you make the communication process work for you?
A model of communication
Receiving the message
Decoding the message and forming a response
Encoding the response
Transmitting the response

How can you use nonverbal behaviors to communicate more effectively?

How can understanding gender styles improve your ability to communicate on the job?

How do you build trust in relationships?
What is trust?
How do you create trusting relationships?
Trust and lying

How do you persuade others?
The communicator
The message
The audience

What communication strengths do you already have? Which skills do you need to develop?
Communication competencies
Self-monitoring
Personal orientation to others
Active listening

What are some tested tactics for doing well on job interviews?
Make a good first impression
Present yourself favorably
Be aware of company responsibilities and tactics for interviews

Communicating in the Global Marketplace

Corporate communication goofs. You hear about them all the time. "Come alive with the Pepsi generation!" was translated for the Chinese market and became "Pepsi brings your ancestors back from the grave!" Gerber tried to sell baby food in Africa using its traditional packaging—a cute baby on the label, along with the name of the food. Only trouble was, in Africa, where literacy is low, the picture on a jar always shows what the product is. . . .Now you, of course, would never make such communication gaffes, would you?

Well, there's a lot more to global communication than meets the eye. For example, it is common today for people to chat across time zones and even days. You are working in Boston, and need to contact your counterpart in New Zealand. Let's see, what time is it there? For that matter, what day is it? A Bostonian's rule of thumb is that New Zealand is 10 hours ahead and one day behind. (But is that with or without daylight savings time?) Go figure.

Communicating globally involves understanding a whole host of issues involving differences in language, culture, and time. The person who becomes really good at it will first master being a good communicator at home. . . .

communication
The exchange of thoughts, opinions, or information by speaking, writing, or other means

In this chapter we explore interpersonal **communication**, the exchange of thoughts, opinions or information by speaking, writing, or other means.[1] Understanding communication will help you turn the communication process into a practical business tool. In this chapter, for instance, you will learn how to evaluate male and female communication styles, build trust in relationships, persuade others, evaluate your personal communication style, recognize some of your current communication strengths and weaknesses, and use your knowledge of communication to approach a job interview.

How important is it to be a good communicator? Consider that today executive coaching in the United States is a billion-dollar business that revolves around helping people build better relationships through *communication*.[2]

How Can You Make the Communication Process Work for You?

conduit metaphor
The idea that language transfers thoughts and feelings from person to person rather like a pipe transfers water from place to place.

English speakers typically describe the communication process using the **conduit metaphor**, which assumes that language transfers thoughts and feelings from person to person rather like a pipe transfers water from place to place. This metaphor suggests that speakers and writers transfer their thoughts and feelings into words, that words contain the thoughts and feelings, and that listeners or readers somehow extract the thoughts and feelings from the words.[3] To understand how influential the conduit metaphor is, consider that English speakers often say that they "transfer ideas from person to person," or that they "exchange ideas through words."

Although this metaphor for communication has its uses, and, in fact, we are going to use it to organize the discussion here, it has an unfortunate side effect, too. The problem is that it suggests that communication is a straightforward, free-flowing process that requires little effort, which is far from the truth.[4] This belief may lead organizational leaders to devote limited resources to programs that help their employees become better communicators when, in reality, many employees would benefit from such programs.

In particular, we should all be sensitive to the fact that people themselves individually determine the meanings of words, and that meanings are not "transferred."[5] Words do not mean, *people* mean. The result is that communicators inevitably communicate unintended meanings, and receivers create meanings and act on the basis of their own meanings. The receiver's meaning may approximate the communicator's intended meaning, or it may not.

unintentionality
The communication of unintended meanings.

noise
Any disturbance that disrupts the communication process.

Therefore, there is a certain amount of **unintentionality** in the communication process. Unintentionality is one aspect of **noise**, which is defined as any disturbance that disrupts the communication process. The object of improving communication is to reduce noise and increase understanding of what is actually meant.

Imagine you have a "communication problem." The first step in solving it is to answer the question, What exactly do you mean when you say you have a communication problem? As you will see next, the answer can be fairly complex.

A Model of Communication

See Figure 7.1 for a model that suggests how the communication process works.

Various aspects of communication can be understood using this model. Most commonly the model refers to how we use language. When someone speaks to us, we hear them, figure out what they really mean, think about what we want to say, figure out how to say it, and then speak our response—sometimes all in an instant. However, events other than speech also communicate. A scent communicates, for example. When you receive the message that your nose has perceived a scent, you might decode that scent as "Cheap perfume," form the response "Better avoid this person who has such bad taste in perfume," encode the response "Be polite but escape," and transmit your response by smiling politely and sidling away.

Here is an example of how the verbal communication process works in practice. The situation is that an employee has just complimented the boss on his new suit.

THE BOSS

Receives the message: That employee has just complimented me on my new suit.

Decodes the message: I'm being buttered up.

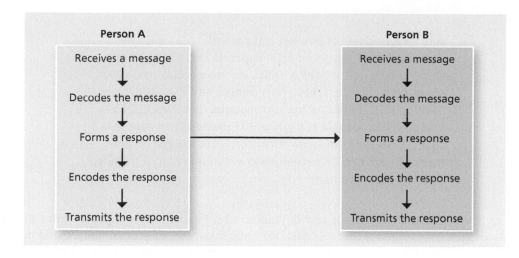

FIGURE 7.1

A Model of Communication

Forms a response: Be polite, but don't let him think he can butter me up so easily.

Encodes the response: Say "thank you" but don't encourage more behaviors such as this one.

Transmits the response: The boss politely says, "Thank you," but does not stop to talk.

THE EMPLOYEE

Receives the message: My boss gave me a friendly smile but left abruptly.

Decodes the message: Is the boss just being polite?

Forms a response: I should be careful not to overdo it. I'll turn the compliment into a joke.

Encodes the response: "I have one exactly like it!"

Transmits the response: (calling lamely after the boss as he recedes down the hall) "I have one too!" (The boss wonders what exactly this strange employee is trying to tell him).

As you can deduce from the complexities and subtleties in this example, there are many places in which communication can go wrong. Even what seem to be simple exchanges of information are often misinterpreted. To help you become a better communicator, let's examine some of the common issues that arise at each phase in the communication process.

Receiving the Message

To begin with, you must pay attention to how you receive a message. Many communication problems can be traced back to this crucial process.

UNDERSTANDING THE MESSAGE The first issue is clarity: Did you hear and understand the message the way the sender intended? Not only are messages complex, but human abilities to receive them are imperfect, subject to factors such as perceptual errors and overload (see below) that create noise.

So when you receive an important communication, it is often a good idea to check it out with the sender in this way: "I heard you say x. Can I please take a moment to check out with you whether what I heard, and how I interpreted it, are what you intended to communicate? Okay? Here's what I heard. . ."

SELECTIVE ATTENTION Another factor in the communication process is the problem of **selective attention**. At any given moment we humans can focus on only *some* of the stimuli that come our way, while other stimuli are disregarded. If we were not designed to perceive the world in this way, our brains would soon be overwhelmed with stimuli. To illustrate this, take a look at the passage in Figure 7.2, which contains two messages. Read aloud, as quickly as possible, the message in *red*.

Now close your eyes and answer this: How many of the words in blue can you remember? Probably not many, even though you "saw" the blue words, and many of them appear more than once.

selective attention
Focusing only on some stimuli while disregarding others.

FIGURE 7.2

Read Aloud the Message in Red

Any time students of intellect and potential DOG are CAR involved HAT in GRASS an BLUE experiment ONE like FIELD this PEN one, HOT it TAPE is TABLE incumbent CLOUD on PINK those TREE who WELL have FISH created KEY the CREAM task VIEW to DOG make CAR the HAT material GRASS as BLUE silly ONE as FIELD possible PEN while HOT making TAPE sure TABLE that CLOUD the PINK subjects TREE in WELL the FISH experiment KEY are CREAM treated VIEW without rancor or ridicule.

This exercise demonstrates how difficult it is for human beings to pay attention to more than one thing at a time.[6] In fact, the more conscious effort that you expend in paying attention to a message, the less likely it is that you can successfully divide your attention with another task. Think about the implications of this principle for using a cell phone while driving,[7] or talking to your boss on the phone while simultaneously reading your e-mail.

Some individuals pride themselves on their ability to multitask—that is, to do more than one thing at once. However, according to Linda Stone, a researcher and former Microsoft and Apple executive, in reality such individuals are primarily paying "continuous partial attention" to a variety of inputs.[8] Thus, various media, from text messages to face-to-face conversations, are constantly vying for a person's undivided attention. Based on this reality, researchers are working to develop media that know when to interrupt you . . . and when not to. Such media are called **augmented cognition systems**. The Pentagon, for example, is working on a CogPit, a smart cockpit for fighter aircraft that will read the changes in a pilot's brainwaves and how he is interacting with the controls to determine if the pilot's task is too delicate to be interrupted.[9] Microsoft Research is working on Busy-Body, a system that gauges how busy the user is and whether a new input is important enough to interrupt her or him.

Meanwhile, as a busy individual, knowing about the phenomenon of selective attention is prerequisite to dealing with it. Realize that at times you may miss important inputs, and actively solicit information only when you are truly prepared to concentrate on it. And, it bears repeating in this context, talk with the sender to be sure that your interpretation of his or her message is the same as the intended message: Maybe you were not concentrating as well as you should have been when you first heard it.

augmented cognition systems
Media that know when to interrupt you, and when not to.

OVERLOAD Given human cognitive limitations, it is easy to understand how our message-rich, responsibility-rich jobs and lives can overload us. A study by Pitney Bowes found that the typical white-collar worker at a *Fortune* 1,000 firm sends and receives an average of 190 messages a day in electronic and paper formats.[10] One market research firm predicts that soon, by e-mail alone, there will be more than 60 billion messages sent each year.[11] A British psychologist has even identified a new mental disorder caused by too much information—the Information Fatigue Syndrome.[12]

Of course, there is a big difference between miscellaneous information and useful knowledge. Because some jobs are overloaded with information, a critical skill to develop is **information filtering**. Employees may have to remind themselves (or be reminded by their bosses) that their job is to do something for their company, not to process data.

information filtering
Focusing only on useful knowledge rather than miscellaneous information.

A related problem is that, when a person is overloaded, messages that are actually important are likely to be lost or distorted. For example, while killing all your junk mail, you might accidentally delete a subordinate's e-mail, or you might fail to read carefully the one dozen e-mails that all come in on the same subject.

When managers perceive a communication overload, they can do a number of things to alleviate it. Skills that come into play include the ability to reduce input, to organize it, and to reduce your own contribution of relatively useless messages. Sometimes managers establish gatekeepers, such as personal assistants, to screen their inputs.

The other side of the coin is that, when you are sending a message to others who are overloaded, confirm that your message is heard and understood. To accomplish this, managers sometimes practice redundancy—for example, sending a message through more than one channel. They might also follow up on their communication to verify whether it was received and understood.

Decoding the Message and Forming a Response

When you decode a message, you interpret its meaning both cognitively *and* socially. That is, you try to figure out what exactly the communicator was trying to tell you, but also what he or she was implying. After you decode the message, you form a response by deciding what reply to send. As so often happens, we human beings manage to find less than perfect ways of doing these things.

ATTRIBUTING CAUSES *Why* is your boss behaving in a particular way? When you answer this question, you are making an **attribution**. Attribution is the process of explaining the causes of people's behavior, including your own. When making attributions, we sometimes make mistakes.

For example, the **fundamental attribution error** occurs when, in assigning causality to another person's behavior ("why did that person do that?"), we are more likely to believe that the action was caused by the *actor* than to believe it was caused by the situation. Meanwhile, if we were to ask the actor to tell us what caused the action, the actor is more likely to say his or her behavior was caused by the *situation*.[13]

Here is an example of a situation leading to some fundamental attribution errors:

Behavior: A student gets many questions wrong on a test.

Likely attribution by the professor: He or she gives little weight to the difficulty of the questions, and decides the student did not study enough.

Likely attribution by the student: He or she gives little weight to partying late the night before the test, and decides the test questions were unreasonable.

When making attributions, people weigh whether the behavior they are interpreting is unique to the particular situation (distinctiveness), whether it is consistent from situation to situation (consistency), and whether other individuals faced with the same situation would respond in the same way (consensus). If the behavior is highly unique (the individual does it only once, for instance) and other people would probably respond in the same way, a person is more likely to say the behavior was caused by the situation. If the behavior is highly consistent from situation to situation, a person is more likely to say it was caused by the individual.[14]

A related error is **self-serving bias**. This is the tendency to attribute one's successes to one's personal attributes while attributing one's failures to—you guessed it!—external causes. Why did the student get a good grade on the test? "I succeeded in that test because I am so intelligent, not because it was so easy."

Interestingly enough, the fundamental attribution error is a phenomenon typical of Western, individualistic cultures. In cultures that focus more on individuals as they exist within the contexts of their family and society, people are more likely to err by attributing causality to situations.[15]

CATEGORIZING Because society is a complex place, individuals use mental shortcuts to make sense of it.[16] For one thing, we put people into social categories, groups of individuals that we perceive to have similar characteristics: old and young, rich and poor, men and women, Republicans and Democrats. This process obviously has some utility. For instance, it helps us make a best guess as to how to communicate with a member of a group, and it allows us to simplify how we remember people.[17]

At the same time, creating social categories, or **stereotypes**, invites **prejudice**, which is a preconceived opinion, either favorable or unfavorable, of others. It is useful to think of prejudice as literally "pre-judging" an individual according to your beliefs about the attributes of the group or groups to which that person belongs. All of us need to routinely

attribution
The process of explaining the causes of people's behavior, including your own.

fundamental attribution error
Mistakenly believing that an action was caused by the actor rather than the situation.

self-serving bias
The tendency to attribute one's successes to one's personal attributes while attributing one's failures to external causes.

stereotypes
Social categories.

prejudice
A preconceived opinion, either favorable or unfavorable, of others.

illusory correlation
The process by which we categorize an entire group based on the behavior of a handful of people in that group.

monitor our prejudgments. For example, a problem occurs when a belief is based on an **illusory correlation**, the process by which we categorize an entire group based on the behavior of a handful of people in that group.[18]

Prejudice in a one-to-one relationship is typically overcome by recognizing it and then making an effort to get to know the other person well. The better you know a person, the less likely you are to rely on stereotypes to understand him or her. However, experiencing prejudice in a one-to-one relationship differs from experiencing it as a member of a group, in which a variety of social pressures make prejudice more difficult to overcome.[19]

SUPPORTING PSYCHOLOGICAL IDENTITY Developing a psychological identity is known to be a critical task of adolescence.[20] "Who am I?" is the question young people ask themselves as they search for groups in which they feel they belong. Yet, in fact, we continue to mold our psychological identities throughout our lives. They are an important way in which we locate ourselves within our social environment, and a way in which we present ourselves to others.

possible selves
Concrete ideas about what our psychological identity is or may become.

As we develop ideas about our psychological identity, we imagine **possible selves**, concrete ideas about what our psychological identity is or may become.[21] Possible selves represent individuals' "sense of what they might become, what they would like to become, and what they are afraid of becoming."[22] Individuals' possible selves change over the course of their lives as their opportunities and constraints change.

In general, people prefer individuals and activities that confirm their own identities, and they will interpret events in such a way as to protect their identities. One reason people try to manage the impression they make on others, a process called **impression management**, is to protect this self-concept.[23] Individuals' choices about how to act, including what to say, are based not only on their own needs and goals but on their interpretation of the social world and how they believe it will receive any messages they send.[24] Thus, by attempting impression management, individuals are not necessarily being superficial or deceptive.

impression management
The attempt to manage the impression one makes on others.

self-presentation strategy
A type of impression management which seeks to make the actor more appealing through both verbal and nonverbal cues.

There are two main types of impression management. The first type is the **self-presentation strategy**, which seeks to make the actor more appealing through both verbal and nonverbal cues, including smiling, eye contact, and touching. The second type is the **other-enhancement strategy**, which demonstrates that the actor favorably evaluates or agrees with the other, including flattery, favor-doing, and opinion conformity.[25]

other-enhancement strategy
Favorably evaluating or agreeing with another person, including flattery, favor-doing and opinion conformity.

Putting in face time, time devoted to being seen in the office whether or not one is working, is an example of impression management. If standard work hours are 9 to 5, yet most people routinely stay in the office until 7 pretending to work, an individual may have to decide whether it is work output or presence, or perhaps both, that is required to impress management.[26] Of course, if an individual's self-concept is based on goal achievement rather than pretense, he or she will find this sort of impression management very difficult to do without feeling resentment.

Practicing impression management on the job can be useful. Several studies have shown that impression management by subordinates does improve their performance ratings.[27] However, attempts to make a favorable impression on one's boss are most likely to be effective if the boss himself or herself perceives that the employee is similar to him or her in terms of demographics such as gender, race, and age.[28]

The processes of attribution, categorizing, and protecting one's psychological identity are all factors that affect how you decode and respond to a message. Once you have decided what you want to reply, the next step is to figure out how to get your response across to others.

Encoding the Response

When encoding the response, you translate your idea into a form that others can recognize, typically into written or spoken language. You choose the words and symbols that you believe will best communicate your ideas.

During encoding, your most important goal is to be as clear as possible in both your writing and speaking. However, achieving clarity is sometimes a problem. Effective writing and speaking are skills that must be nurtured. For example, you have to monitor your use of **jargon**, which is language comprehensible only to certain groups.

jargon
Language which is comprehensible only to certain groups.

For example, do you know what "eat your own dog food" means in corporate life? At Microsoft, the phrase describes the company's use of its own software, a mandated, company-wide practice.[29]

Transmitting the Response

Your next challenge is to decide which **medium**, or communication channel, is the best one for delivering your message.[30] Firing someone via e-mail is quite different from firing him or her in person. In short, choose your medium carefully.

Two important factors to consider when choosing a medium for your message are whether the medium is rich or lean, and whether it is formal or informal.

IS THE MEDIUM RICH OR LEAN? Media are considered rich or lean depending on the amount and type of information they can portray and the amount of feedback they allow. A rich medium can portray complicated information, both factual and personal, and allows for a great deal of feedback. A lean medium is best used for simple, straightforward information without a lot of interpersonal context or the need for feedback.

Here are some common media. Which do you think is the richest medium? the leanest?

- Face-to-face conversation
- Video-mediated communication
- Telephone conversation
- Postal mail
- E-mail

In fact, these media are ordered top to bottom from richest to leanest. For example, if the nature of your message is concrete and precise (simple and straightforward), you should consider e-mail (a lean medium). Distributing information is an appropriate use of a lean medium. However, take into account that not all e-mail is equally lean: Text messaging among friends can be highly creative and personal, for example.

In contrast, if your message is rather vague, involving nuance and emotion (complicated), you should choose a video-mediated or a face-to-face conversation (rich mediums). Evaluating a job candidate for a professional role would best be done through a rich medium.

If the nature of your message is emotional, you should probably use a rich medium. (Avoid the temptation to discuss a sensitive personnel problem in a memo, for instance.) You would also choose a rich medium, such as a face-to-face conversation, if you want more feedback or faster feedback.

IS THE MEDIUM FORMAL OR INFORMAL? Formal channels of communication are those that are sanctioned by your organization. One formal channel is communication via the organizational hierarchy, in which a person communicates upward, downward, or laterally. Not all formal channels of communication are based in the existing hierarchy, however. In fact, some are set up explicitly to avoid the hierarchy. For example, an **open door policy** encourages employees to go "around" their bosses, when necessary, to take their message to someone higher up in the organization. Anonymous employee suggestion boxes and personnel surveys are similar channels that companies use to get around the communications problems in status and inequality that are inherent in hierarchical communication.

Informal channels of communication are all those that are outside of formal channels. They tend to be based on informal networks in the organization and may cut across hierarchies. Sometimes called "the grapevine," informal channels are an important aspect of organizational information sharing because they communicate information that would not otherwise be known.[31] The grapevine often operates through informal leaders in the organization. Of course, the quality of information in the grapevine varies. Sometimes it is incomplete and inaccurate; other times it is the only way to get the truth.

See Table 7.1 for an overview of effective communication.

medium
Communication channel, such as face to face conversation or a text message.

open door policy
A policy that encourages employees to take their message to someone higher up in the organization than their boss.

How Can You Use Nonverbal Behaviors to Communicate More Effectively?

So far, we have been considering primarily verbal (oral and written) communications. How important is the nonverbal aspect of communication—behaviors such as our actions, body movements, facial expressions, gestures, dress, or where we choose to deliver a message? The answer is: *enormously important.*

For example, body language communicates two primary things: liking and openness towards an individual, and the relative status of two individuals.[32] Facial expressions are probably the most powerful component of body language. Smiling can convey such emotions as joy, embarrassment, self-satisfaction, or approval. Eye contact is generally used to invite social interaction, and lack of eye contact to discourage social interaction. Men sometimes use staring, which, when aimed at women, sometimes suggests claiming dominance and defining women as sexual objects.[33] Women, on the other hand, seldom use this tactic.

Gestures can convey many things, from insults to invitations. Touching can convey intimacy and caring, but also, in male–female relationships, a claim to dominance.

How you move and position your body can convey status. For example, adopting a relaxed posture in another's presence is often an indication of higher status. When two people are talking, the person who is sprawling back in his or her chair, arms crossed casually behind his or her head, is not likely to be the subordinate!

In general, powerful people act more freely and spontaneously and subordinates act more formally and self-consciously. Bosses can put their feet up on the desk, or

TABLE 7.1 Overview: Checklist for Effective Communication

When receiving the message. . .	Check with the sender to be sure you understand the message. Pay attention and avoid distractions. Design your work to prevent overload.
When decoding the message and forming your response. . .	Audit your thinking for attribution errors including: ■ the fundamental attribution error. ■ self-serving bias. Monitor your tendency to categorize. Ask yourself how your proposed response will influence your self-concept. Consider how your attempts at impression management may influence your self-concept.
When encoding your response. . .	Strive for clarity. Avoid jargon.
When transmitting your response. . .	Choose the appropriate medium; that is: ■ a rich medium such as face-to-face conversation for emotional and subtle messages, and messages that require more and faster extensive feedback. ■ a lean medium such as e-mail if you want concrete and precise feedback. Choose the appropriate channel; that is: ■ a formal channel for organizationally sanctioned communication. ■ an informal channel for all other information. Use non-verbal forms of communication appropriately: actions, body language, facial expressions, gestures, dress, and where you are when you deliver your message.

swear, or interrupt others, whereas subordinates sit formally, speak politely, and display deference through silence.[34]

The more powerful also use more **personal space**, the area around a person that they claim to maintain privacy. Men typically command more personal space than women, and they are more likely to intrude on women's space than vice versa.[35]

Finally, *where* you deliver your message is also a factor. Just as the marriage proposal offered on a lovely beach is more likely to be accepted, so the meeting held in appropriate business surroundings is more likely to be effective.

personal space
The area around a person that he or she claims in order to maintain privacy.

How Can Understanding Gender Styles Improve Your Ability to Communicate on the Job?

Men and women communicate differently. These differences are less obvious in written communication, but more obvious when the communication is verbal and nonverbal.[36] Linguist Deborah Tannen has researched men's and women's conversational rituals in the workplace and discovered a variety of differences, including these:

■ Men are more likely than women to view an interpersonal interaction as a negotiation of relative status and power. In a conversation, they are more likely to assert their power by giving advice, using combative language, interrupting, and talking more than the person they are with.[37]

■ Women who ask questions are more focused on getting information, whereas men refrain from asking questions because they are focused on the impression their asking will make on others. Men will not ask for help because it puts them in a one-down position.38

■ When making a decision, women are more likely to downplay their certainty, whereas men are more likely to downplay their doubts.[39]

■ Conversational rituals that men often use include banter, joking, teasing, and playful put-downs, and expending effort to avoid the one-down position in the interaction. Women often try to maintain an appearance of equality. They try to take into account the effect of the exchange on the other person, and to downplay the speakers' authority so they can get the job done without being obvious about wielding power.[40]

■ Men usually employ **report talk**, in which information is exchanged. Women also use report talk, but they are more likely than men to engage in **rapport talk**, aimed at relationship building.[41]

report talk
Conversation in which information is exchanged.

rapport talk
Conversation that is aimed at relationship building.

■ Girls learn that to get the best results as leaders they should phrase their ideas as suggestions rather than orders, and they should phrase their reasons for the suggestions as the good of the group. Women tend to be overly modest and play down their authority, a style that is easily misinterpreted as weak and indecisive. Boys, on the other hand, experience many more hierarchical groups growing up. They don't criticize the leader as "bossy," because they expect the high-status boys to give orders and push low-status boys around.[42]

■ Men are more likely than women to use **agonism**, a warlike, oppositional format, to accomplish a range of interactional goals that have nothing literally to do with fighting. Men will heatedly argue and then be as friendly as ever, whereas women are likely to take the fighting for real and to be amazed that the men can still be friends.43

agonism
A warlike, oppositional style of interaction used to accomplish a range of interactional goals that have nothing literally to do with fighting

Individuals who are in the minority in a company and/or are not in powerful positions, may be seen by others as different and inferior. Typically, it is women who play a minority role, and because of their status, in meetings they may literally not be listened to. Tannen found that even if a man and a woman talk for exactly the same amount of time in a meeting, people tend to think the woman talked too much. Many women she interviewed reported they often suggest ideas in meetings, only to have them ignored. However, when a man makes the same suggestion, people tend to listen attentively.

double-bind

The fact that a woman who acts the passively feminine role that society has traditionally dictated for women may be perceived as weak, while a woman who acts assertively may be perceived as bossy.

In general, a woman who acts the passively feminine role that society has traditionally dictated for women may look weak, while a woman who acts assertively may be criticized as bossy. This is called the **double-bind**.[44] It is likely to be other women, rather than men, who have negative perceptions about assertive communication that comes from women.[45] Some women react to the problem of the double-bind by using strategies such as modulating how often they speak so as to not appear too dominating. Others decide that being seen as aggressive is a price worth paying for being listened to.[46]

How Do You Build Trust in Relationships?

In this section we examine the nature of trust. We discuss how to build trusting relationships and why lying should be seen as a relational skill.

What Is Trust?

Trust is a foundation of effective communication. Both a psychological and a sociological concept, trust characterizes individuals and can also be understood in the context of one-to-one relationships, groups, and organizations.[47]

On the one hand, individuals are said to be trusting. Indeed, the ability to trust is studied as a personality trait,[48] and, as you may recall, it is a component of the Big Five factor of agreeableness. On the other hand, in situations involving two or more persons, trust is a kind of mutual faithfulness on which all social relationships ultimately depend.[49]

calculus-based trust

Trust based on the belief that another person may be deterred from acting against our interests.

identification-based trust

Trust based on the belief that another person identifies (empathizes) with our interests and values, and is likely to look out for them.

Why is trust so important? Trust is a foundation for interpersonal relationships and the basis for stability in social institutions and markets.[50] In predicting future events that depend on relationships, trust is one way of reducing complexity: Instead of analyzing a situation from all angles and at a great cost in time, we simply trust.[51] Trust is also a way of increasing personal initiative, because, without it, individuals would spend a great deal of time figuring out the social complexities that surround them.

There are two fundamental types of trust. One kind is **calculus-based trust**, which is based on our belief that another person may be deterred from acting against our interests.[52] This is the kind of trust we typically find in professional relationships. We trust that our boss will be polite to us because if he is not, he faces being ostracized by other managers.

The second kind of trust is **identification-based trust**, which is based on our belief that another person identifies with—that is, empathizes with—our interests and values, and is likely to look out for them. This is the kind of trust found in "relational" interpersonal contracts.

TABLE 7.2 Trust and Distrust in Relationships

High Trust Characterized by hope, faith, confidence, assurance, and initiative	*Engaged* Example: A close family or team, or a highly cohesive organization	*Oppositionally Engaged* Example: Trading alliances between business partners from different countries and different cultures
Low Trust Characterized by no hope, no faith, no confidence, passivity, and hesitance	*Unengaged* Example: Casual acquaintances	*Negatively Engaged* Example: Enemies
	Low Distrust Characterized by no fear, absence of skepticism, absence of cynicism, low monitoring, and no vigilance	*High Distrust* Characterized by fear, skepticism, cynicism, wariness and watchfulness, and vigilance

Source: Adapted with permission from R. J. Lewicki, D. J. McAllister, and R. J. Bies, "Trust and Distrust: New Relationships and Realities," *Academy of Management Review, 23* (3), July 1998:438–58. Copyright 1998 by ACADEMY OF MANAGEMENT (NY). Reproduced with permission of THE ACADEMY OF MANAGEMENT (NY).

Although more research needs to be done in this area, it now seems that trust and distrust are not simply the extremes of a one-dimensional continuum that runs from more trusting to less trusting/distrust. Rather, people judge a relationship on the extent to which they trust it and, *separately*, on the extent to which they distrust it.[53] See Table 7.2.

For example, the global economy runs on both trust and distrust. We trust our company, and our trading partners, to work with us, but we also know that we have some distrust in these relationships because they are dependent on the vagaries of downsizing, mergers, imperfect agreements, and other business factors. By this way of thinking, **trust** is defined as one party's optimistic expectation of the behavior of another, when the other must make a decision about how to act, and **distrust** is defined as the expectation that others will not act in one's best interests and may deliberately seek to cause harm.[54]

To the extent that organizations focus on rational decision making and expediency, it is difficult for them to create trust. In a fully rational world, organizations only trust their employees to the extent that employees align their abilities, knowledge, and goals with those of the organization. Likewise, employees only trust their employers when their employers' goals are aligned with their own. In areas outside of these alignments, particularly areas in which beliefs and values matter, employees are, essentially, distrusted by their organizations, and organizations are distrusted by their employees. So although we may be interested in building trust in order to enhance efficiency and effectiveness in business relationships, we also create extensive contracts and written agreements to manage the possible downside consequences of distrust.

trust
One party's optimistic expectation of the behavior of the other, when the other must make a decision about how to act.

distrust
The expectation that another will not act in one's best interests and may deliberately seek to cause harm.

How Do You Create Trusting Relationships?

Trust is not a commodity or a belief. Rather, it is one characteristic of effective interpersonal processes. Thus, trust can be created, and it can be restored. Developing trust between individuals requires that both of them take responsibility for developing a variety of effective interpersonal practices, including relational and emotional skills.[55]

CREATING TRUST IS A RELATIONAL SKILL Trust is created by using promises, commitments, offers, demands, expectations, and explicit and tacit understandings.[56] It is established through dialogue and conversation, by making and keeping promises, and by setting and meeting expectations.

Trust also depends on respect for one's fellow human beings, an intent that is conveyed to others by such communication and interpersonal behaviors as being on time for meetings, respecting individuals' personal space, and answering e-mails. Being seen as high in credibility and trustworthiness is essential for effective leaders. At one major bank, officers who are caught in even the smallest infraction are fired, not necessarily because of the infraction itself, but because their behavior erodes trust.[57]

CREATING TRUST IS ALSO AN EMOTIONAL SKILL Trust is also an emotion that is essential to our well being. Without it we are alienated and paranoid, and through it we define our relationships to the world. It has been suggested that trust is a kind of optimism, whereas distrust is a kind of pessimism.[58]

The ability to trust is at least partly learned. In a survey, 1,245 randomly selected college professors were asked how much they give to charity each year.[59] About 9 percent of the economics professors, whose professional training teaches that people act only in their own self interest, gave nothing. In contrast, even though their incomes were lower than the economists', the proportion of professors in other disciplines giving nothing ranged only between 1.1 and 4.2 percent. Also, the economists gave less to big charities such as the United Way and viewer-supported public television. Further research showed that it was their training in economics, rather than their personal predispositions, that reduced the economists' altruism.

Probably narrowly self-interested behavior is ultimately self-defeating, because in the long run, people who trust and cooperate do better than untrusting isolates. So we each need to examine and understand our ability to trust. Whether to trust poses an existential dilemma, as it may be that *believing* in the viability of human commitments is a necessary first step to making ourselves trustworthy, and to trusting.[60]

Trust and Lying

Even lying is, in part, a relational skill.[61] Consider that to do something like extend an invitation or make a request commits the speaker to defining aspects of himself or herself, the other person, and the relationship between the two. The act of inviting someone to do something, for example, presupposes a relationship between you and that person. If the person rejects your invitation directly, the rejection causes you to lose face and may jeopardize the relationship.

So a person who doesn't want to accept an invitation may lie to protect the face of the person issuing the invitation. "Actually, my calendar is totally full next week. I'm so sorry." Such a lie may actually reinforce the person's own identity as a considerate, cooperative person. This occurs despite the fact that his or her lie goes against standard moral injunctions to avoid lying. By this way of thinking, lying is important not so much because it "interferes with trust" (although it can do that, too), but because people want to maintain relationships, avoid conflicts, and prevent the loss of face.

How Do You Persuade Others?

Persuasive communication is aimed at changing **attitudes**, which are tendencies to think, feel, or act either positively or negatively toward stimuli in our environment.[62] To persuade effectively, you must control the characteristics of the communicator, the message, and the audience.[63]

You should also weigh which of two routes to persuasion is better.[64] The **central route** focuses on the argument you are making. When you use this route, you persuade others by basing your argument on carefully processed information and elaborating upon an argument logically. In contrast, the **peripheral route** focuses on the communicator. Using this approach, you pay little attention to carefully processing information and you only somewhat elaborate an argument, but you persuade through personal cues such as confidence and attractiveness.

What characteristics of the communicator, the message, and the audience are important?

The Communicator

First, is the communicator **credible**?[65] There are two aspects of credibility—competency, the extent to which an individual is perceived to be knowledgeable in their field, and trustworthiness, the extent to which a person is believed to be telling the truth without compromising it for political or personal gain.

Second, is the communicator **likable**? As we have already seen, those who are physically attractive or like us demographically are more likely to influence us than those who are unattractive and unlike us.

The Message

The message should be matched to the audience. Here are some ways to do this:

AVOID EXTREME POSITIONS Research suggests that communicators are more persuasive if their position is not too far removed from that of their audience. People spend more time scrutinizing what they consider to be extreme material and are more likely to discount it than if the material is closer to their own view.[66] Also, the more personally important the issue is to them, the more stubborn the audience is.[67]

CONTENT RICH OR CONTENT POOR? Should you entertain or inform? use few data points or many? The answer is that if your audience is not highly involved in the subject, you can be more superficial, relying on slogans, one-liners, and slick graphics to make your case. However, if your audience is highly involved with the subject, if you use these slick tactics at all, they must be grounded in lots of fact-based content.[68]

---

attitudes
Tendencies to think, feel, or act either positively or negatively toward stimuli in our environment.

central route
A persuasion strategy which focuses on the argument that one is trying to make.

peripheral route
A persuasion strategy which focuses on the communicator, using personal cues such as confidence and attractiveness.

credible communicator
A communicator with sufficient competency (knowledge in one's field) and trustworthiness (the extent to which one is believed to be telling the truth).

likable communicator
A communicator with personal traits (often including personal attractiveness and demographic similarity) that endear him/her to the receiver.

FRAME YOUR MESSAGE EFFECTIVELY You are invited to invest in a venture that has a 30 percent chance of failure. Would you part with your hard-earned cash under these odds? Now consider this alternative: You are invited to invest in a venture that has a 70 percent chance of success. So what do you think? It all depends how you "see" the issue, doesn't it? **Framing** a message is describing it in a way that is most likely to lead to the outcome you want.[69] Framing is an effective strategy because people's patterns of decision making are somewhat predictable.

framing
Describing a message in a way that is most likely to lead to the outcome you want.

Keep in mind these principles when framing a decision:

Frame the Consequences Negatively. Framing a decision in terms of its negative consequences is more persuasive than framing it in terms of its positive consequences.[70] Imagine you want to downsize your company, and you hope your team of managers will support the reduction in the workforce. Question: Are you more likely to elicit your managers' cooperation if you frame the problem in terms of the costs to the company of not downsizing (such as loss of pricing advantage and market share) or if you frame it in terms of the merits of being the right size of company to match the competition and be profitable? Answer: Frame the problem in terms of the costs to the company of not downsizing.

Fear Tactics Must Include Instructions for Coping. Messages with high fear content work better than messages with low fear content as long as they tell the audience how to deal with the problem.[71] Safety training films work better when they show mangled bodies rather than accident statistics, and also demonstrate safe techniques, for example.

Frame the Risks in Terms of Losses. When you want someone to take a risk, it is better to frame a decision in terms of the probability of suffering losses rather than the probability of making a gain. Research on the **risky choice framing effect** suggests that when you emphasize the gains to be made, people suddenly become risk averse, whereas if you emphasize the ills to be escaped, they become interested in taking the risk.[72] As your company's marketing chief, you hope to convince top management to invest heavily in a certain new product. Would you frame the choice in terms of the benefits to the company, such as revenue enhancement, or in terms of what competitors will do to the company if they go to market first with a similar product? Go to the head of the class if your answer is to stir up worry about the competition.

risky choice framing effect
People's tendency to become risk averse when possible gains to be made are emphasized, but to become more interested in taking the risk when possible ills to be escaped are emphasized.

Frame the Attributes Positively. The **attribute framing effect** suggests that when you want people to think positively about a characteristic, you should describe it in positive terms. This straightforward concept is used widely in marketing: It is more inviting to describe meat as 75 percent lean than it is to describe it as 25 percent fat.[73] You can apply the concept to decision making as well. Present your program as having made 90 percent of its target and you are more likely to see it continued than if you present it as having failed to meet 10 percent of its target.[74]

attribute framing effect
People's tendency to think positively about a characteristic when it is described in positive terms.

The Audience

Communicating effectively also depends on understanding who your audience is and why they might be likely to change their minds.

UNDERSTAND YOUR AUDIENCE'S NEEDS People vary in terms of their ability to think critically about the contents of a message, and they also vary in their motivation to listen to it. Take these factors into account as follows: If your audience has the ability and motivation to listen to your message, focus on the strength and quality of your arguments. If they lack these characteristics, concentrate on factors other than the argument itself, such as your appearance and your ability to evoke emotion.[75]

WHY PEOPLE CHANGE THEIR ATTITUDES There are competing theories about why people change their attitudes. One approach is **cognitive dissonance theory**, which suggests that individuals want their attitudes and beliefs to be consistent with each other and also with their behavior.[76] Thus, people who smile at those they dislike experience some discomfort because their behavior does not match their attitude. Literally hundreds of studies have shown that when people publicly engage in behaviors that run counter to their attitudes, they are likely to change their attitudes.[77] It follows that, if you can induce people to engage in behaviors that

cognitive dissonance theory
A theory about why attitudes change which suggests that individuals want their attitudes and beliefs to be consistent with each other and also with their behavior.

run counter to their attitudes, you may change their attitudes. One way this principle has been applied is to attempt to reduce racial prejudice by bringing people of different races together in positive situations. If different races interact positively, it is believed, their attitudes toward each other will improve. Research has shown, however, that people change their attitudes primarily to reestablish a positive view of themselves, and that if they can achieve this positive view of self in some way other than changing their attitudes, they will.[78] For example, an individual might be likely to donate to a charity that assists a racial minority rather than change his or her attitude about that minority.

self-perception theory

A theory about why attitudes change which suggests that when people are not sure of their attitudes, they simply infer them from their behavior.

A different explanation for why attitudes change is offered by **self-perception theory**, which suggests that when people are not sure of their attitudes, they simply infer them from their behavior. This process also makes attitudes consistent with behavior.

Probably both theories are correct. Cognitive dissonance theory applies to situations in which our attitudes are clear and strong and any inconsistency among them has an important impact on one's self-concept, whereas self-perception theory applies to situations when attitudes are less clear.[79]

Let us not forget, either, that people may be induced to change their attitudes by any number of motivational tactics, including observation of various stimuli and models, and the use of rewards and punishments.

PUT THE AUDIENCE IN A GOOD MOOD Research shows that people who are in a positive emotional state are more readily persuaded.[80] It seems that when in a good mood people become mentally lazy and more uncritically accept your point of view.[81] So tell a joke, offer food and drink, go on retreat in a great place . . . use your imagination!

What Communication Strengths Do You Already Have? Which Skills Do You Need to Develop?

Learning the cognitive and analytical skills taught in academic courses is only part of making a successful career. It is also important to excel in a variety of social and interpersonal skills, which is why gaining experience in social settings outside of the classroom is a big plus.

Communication Competencies

No list of skills can be comprehensive, but the list provided in Table 7.3 is one you should find useful. After looking at the list, next consider the extent to which you utilize the important interpersonal approaches of self monitoring, personal orientation to others, and active listening.

Self-Monitoring

self-monitoring

An individual's tendency to actively construct his or her public image to achieve social goals.

The personality trait of **self-monitoring** is an individual's tendency to actively construct his or her public image to achieve social goals.[82] Before we discuss why self-monitoring is useful, get a sense of what your self-monitoring profile is by taking the quiz in Table 7.4.

Individuals differ in their ability and willingness to monitor their self-expressions in social situations. The higher your score on the Self-Monitoring Quiz, the more likely you are to monitor your self-expression. High self-monitors ask themselves, "Who does this situation want me to be and how can I be that person?" whereas low self-monitors ask, "Who am I and how can I be me in this situation?"[83] The former willingly adapts to the situation, whereas the latter thinks, "What you see is what you get."

High self-monitors are more likely than low self-monitors to occupy central positions in an organization's social networks.[84] They are also more likely to emerge as leaders in groups.[85] It may not surprise you to hear that a study of undergraduate seniors found marketing students to be significantly more likely than MIS or accounting majors to be self-monitors. Thus, marketing majors are more likely to attempt to control the impressions they make on others, portray a deliberate image, adjust their behavior to any situation, read others' emotions, have good intuition, and tell whether others consider a joke to be in poor taste. They are also more likely to be able to identify others who are lying to make an impression.[86]

What are the implications of your self-monitoring style for life in organizations? As one set of researchers put it, even if you cannot change your self-monitoring orientation,

TABLE 7.3 Communication Competencies

Rate the extent to which you are competent on each of the skills listed below using the following scale. (For verification of your view, you may also want to ask someone who knows you well to do the same task.)

1 = to a very little extent or not at all, 2 = to a little extent, 3 = to some extent, 4 = to a great extent, 5 = to a very great extent

Self-awareness

_____ I read my own emotions well.

_____ I recognize the impact of my emotions on others.

_____ I sometimes use my "gut" sense to guide decision making.

_____ I know my strengths and limitations.

_____ I have a sense of my own self-worth.

Self-management

_____ I control my potentially disruptive emotions.

_____ I am trustworthy.

_____ I adapt to changing situations.

_____ I overcome obstacles.

_____ I manage message overload.

_____ I am ready to seize opportunities.

_____ I see the upside in events.

Social awareness

_____ I take an active interest in others' concerns.

_____ I recognize customer needs.

_____ I recognize the needs of my bosses.

_____ I recognize the needs of my subordinates.

Relationship management

_____ I have a range of tactics to use in persuasion.

_____ I make a good first impression.

_____ I present myself favorably.

_____ I am assertive.

Now rank your competencies to develop a sense of where your strengths and weaknesses lie. Based on what you learn, you can develop a plan for enhancing your skills.

you can change your behavior to some extent to reduce any negative impacts.[87] For instance, low self-monitors like to belong to cliques in which individuals have similar attitudes. They choose their friends on the basis of liking and they like to be with the same set of friends no matter what the activity. Meanwhile, high self-monitors invest little emotion in relationships, choosing their friends based on how closely their skills match the activity at hand. If you are a low self-monitor you can consciously resolve to overcome your inclination to retreat into stable friendship cliques by deliberately widening your friendship network. High self-monitors are susceptible to pressure from others, causing them to have more workload because of the larger number of connections in their interpersonal network. Their personal challenge is to avoid accepting too many different work responsibilities while still maintaining friendships.

Personal Orientation to Others

Next, how much are you really interested in others? People differ in whether they are more proself or prosocial.[88]

Research suggests that people with prosocial orientations are especially concerned about how they present themselves to others. This concern translates into behaviors, too: Prosocials actually do make more positive impressions on others.[89]

personal orientation to others
The extent to which an individual is interested in other people.

TABLE 7.4 Self-Monitoring Quiz

Instructions: How well does each statement below describe you? Use the following scale.

Inaccurate to a very great extent = 1	Inaccurate to a great extent = 2	Somewhat accurate = 3	Accurate to a great extent = 4	Accurate to a very great extent = 5

1._____ I would make a good actor.

2._____ I hate being the center of attention.

3._____ I put on a show to impress people.

4._____ I am likely to show off if I get the chance.

5._____ I am the life of the party.

6._____ I am good at making impromptu speeches.

7._____ I would not make a good comedian.

8._____ I like to attract attention.

9._____ I use flattery to get ahead.

10._____ I don't like to draw attention to myself.

Scoring:

Step 1: For each of questions 2, 7, and 10, subtract your answer from 6. For example, if you answered "2" to question 2, your score for that question is 6 − 2 = 4. Sum these three answers and put the total here: _____

Step 2: For the remaining questions, total your score and put it here: _____.

Step 3: Sum Steps 1 and 2 to get your total score: _____.

Comparison: An average score for undergraduates who are primarily business students is about 25 points (n = 111).

Source: International Personality Item Pool. (A Scientific Collaboratory for the Development of Advanced Measures of Personality Traits and Other Individual Differences, http://ipip.ori.org/, 2001. Accessed November 3, 2005).

If you are more proself you are likely to be:

- Individualistic
- Competitive

If you are more prosocial you are more like to be:

- Cooperative
- Altruistic
- Egalitarian
- Maximin (This term refers to a person's desire to maximize the outcomes for the individual who receives the lowest outcomes. Essentially, if you exhibit this tendency, you like rooting for the underdog.)

Active Listening

As one pundit puts it, "You hear with your ears, but you listen with your ears and your mind." However, hearing comes naturally, while listening does not. **Active listening** is a strategy of paying attention in order to assess the emotional and informational content of a message and establish rapport with the speaker.

Whether you are a manager or a salesperson, a secretary or an accountant, being a good listener is an essential business skill. Merely marginal listening occurs when you hear the words but are easily distracted and allow your mind to wander.[90] Evaluative listening occurs when you concentrate on what is being said but do not pick up nonverbal cues or subtle verbal cues. Truly active listening only occurs when you receive a message, process it, and respond so as to encourage further communication.

A rule of thumb for interviewers is that they should talk only about 30 percent of the time and listen about 70 percent of the time.[91] Many interviewers, upon being videotaped, are chagrined to learn that they are talking far too much. Listening is especially important

active listening
A strategy of paying attention in order to assess the emotional and informational content of a message and establish rapport with the speaker.

in sales. Managers of insurance agents believe that for agents selling insurance, listening is actually more essential than either speaking or writing.[92]

How good are you at listening? See Table 7.5 to find out what you *should* be doing.[93]

One important aspect of active listening is the ability to ask good questions.[95] You probably already know the difference between **closed questions** and **open questions**. The former can be answered with a yes or no, whereas the latter encourage elaborate responses. When you ask a closed question you tend to pause or even end a dialogue. In contrast, when you ask an open-ended question you tend to move a dialogue along. In addition, a dialogue may be cut off because one person simply avoids asking any questions at all. This

closed questions
Questions which can be answered with a yes or no.

open questions
Questions which encourage elaborate responses.

TABLE 7.5 Characteristics of Effective Listening

Effective sensing is receiving all cues from the speaker. Verbal skills: ■ Hearing what is said ■ Noting the inflection with which it is said ■ Attending to the message ■ Sensing the tone of the message. Nonverbal skills: ■ Picking up on body language, facial expressions, and personal space. ■ Using all your senses, not just hearing.	Example: An effective insurance agent pays attention to what the client has to say, and conveys this attention by not being easily distracted.[94]
Effective processing is thinking about the material you have received. ■ Understanding: ascribing accurate meaning to the words and to the emotions, thoughts, and feelings behind the words ■ Interpreting: assessing the implications of the message ■ Evaluating: assessing the importance of the message ■ Remembering: committing new material to memory	Example: An effective insurance agent asks questions to clarify what the client is saying and identifies the client's key points. The agent restates the points to confirm that he or she has understood them. The agent separates facts from opinions and is open to ideas and suggestions.
Effective responding is assuring the speaker that listening has occurred, encouraging communication to continue, and monitoring your own responses carefully. Verbal skills: ■ Acknowledging what is said ■ Agreeing with some of it, paraphrasing it, and asking questions ■ Using an appropriate tone of voice and familiar words Nonverbal skills: ■ Maintaining appropriate eye contact, facial expressions, head nods, and body language	Example: To indicate listening, an agent nods and maintains good posture. The agent has good listening manners: He or she does not interrupt and does not behave in distracting ways, such as playing with hair or jewelry.

may happen because one party may be uninterested in what the other party has to say or may be reluctant to seem too intrusive, or because one party may feel uncertain about his or her ability to follow up on the other party's answer.

What Are Some Tested Tactics for Doing Well on Job Interviews?

A job interview is a meeting of two strangers. Typically it is the first one-to-one relationship you will have in your organization. How can theory about communications and relationships help you to establish rapport and get the job? In practice, what do you need to know about job interviews?

Make a Good First Impression

To begin with, not only is it important to make a good first impression, it is *very* important to make a good first impression. Consider this interesting research. Two Harvard university psychologists showed 10-second clips of teachers to raters, who then judged the teachers on a 15-item list of qualities.[96] Then the researchers repeated the experiment with 5-second clips of the same teachers using different raters. Allowing for statistical error, the results for the 10-second and 5-second clips were identical. Intrigued, the researchers then repeated the experiment using 2-second clips, and again got results that were essentially the same! Finally, the researchers compared the 2-second ratings by complete strangers with student ratings of the same teachers after a full semester of classes, and, again, the ratings were in close agreement. But, you might be saying, this experiment was done with students, and who knows what criteria they used to rate their teachers? What really happens in job interviews?

To investigate a business application of their experiment, the researchers have obliged us with one last iteration. Interviewers trained for six weeks in employment-interviewing techniques interviewed 98 volunteers for 15 to 20 minutes and then rated them. Later, 15-second clips of each interview, including the applicant entering the room, shaking hands with the interviewer, and sitting down, were shown to independent raters. The opinions of the raters who saw the candidates for 15 seconds correlated strongly with those of the trained interviewers who saw the candidates for 15 to 20 minutes. This is but the latest in a series of research studies indicating that first impressions matter.[97]

Now that you get the picture, what can you do about this phenomenon? Physically attractive people are perceived as having more positive traits than are less attractive people,[98] so pay attention to grooming, adopt good posture, and smile. A study of college students seeking jobs found that if you are conventionally attractive, dressing well can increase your chances of being hired. In the study the attractive people who dressed appropriately increased their chances of being hired from 82 percent to 100 percent. For subjects who were unattractive, however, dressing well only increased their chances for being hired from 68 percent to 76 percent. The study also demonstrated how life can be unfair: Poorly dressed, attractive candidates were hired more often than well-dressed, unattractive candidates.

Once a first impression is established, raters are actually more highly influenced by it than by a candidate's later performance. This phenomenon is called **first impression bias**. Interviewers show relatively high positive regard to attractive applicants, selling the company to them and giving them job information while gathering less information from them.[99] According to this phenomenon, even when someone who is initially rated highly suffers a downturn in performance on the job, it is likely they will continue to be rated highly.[100]

first impression bias
The phenomenon in which raters are more highly influenced by a candidate's first impression once it is established than by that candidate's later performance.

Present Yourself Favorably

You can present yourself most favorably by using impression management techniques as well as by finding companies that are looking for people specifically like you.

IMPRESSION MANAGEMENT TECHNIQUES Can impression management help you in an interview? Although little research has been done in this area, some results are suggestive. Politicians, for example, can learn to control their nonverbal behavior to convey an impression of being powerful.[101] A weak applicant might be able to do the same thing. At the same time, a strong applicant who has poor self-presentation skills has to be concerned about creating a false negative impression.

An exploratory study of interviewers and applicants in a campus placement office suggests that applicants do indeed use a wide range of impression management tactics, and that these have a potentially large effect on how well they are evaluated and whether they receive a job offer.[102] Self-promotion was the most frequently used tactic, and both self-promotion and demonstrating a fit with the company influenced the interviewer's ratings of the interviewee. Here is a list of the most popular self-promotion strategies used by job applicants in the study (in no particular order):

The applicants told stories about:

- How they chose their careers or became interested in the company
- Past job duties and work history
- Scholastic activities and achievements
- Leisure or travel activities
- Extracurricular activities

They also made statements about themselves as:

- Successful and competent
- Goal- or results-oriented
- Highly motivated, organized or energetic
- Someone with strong interpersonal and communication skills
- An effective leader
- Flexible and open to growth

Most applicants tried to construct positive self-images in two or more categories.

A caveat is in order here. The research on self-promotion has focused on the job application process in the United States, a highly individualized culture. In collectivist cultures, and in international companies, other tactics will undoubtedly be necessary. More research needs to be done in this important area.

WHAT TYPE OF PERSONALITY IS THE COMPANY LOOKING FOR? (DOES IT KNOW?) Why do companies do job interviews at all? Why not simply look at a candidate's credentials and recommendations, give him or her a test for skills, and call it a day? In fact, the cumulative research suggests that, beyond cognitive tests, the typical employment interview does not add substantially to predictions of job performance or productivity.[103] Still, most companies want to *see* the person they are considering hiring.

Chief among the characteristics employers are looking for is a certain type of personality. In saying this, a company may simply mean they are looking in general for a good fit between the candidate and themselves, and they may judge this fit based on their own common sense. Of course, we know that such an approach will be subject to many kinds of problems, from the company's inadequate decision-making processes to various types of communication bias. For instance, "a good fit" is likely to translate into "someone like me." Despite these limitations, the inferences of applicant personality traits made in the initial interview influences the number of follow-up interviews and job offers.[104]

Ideally, companies research the specific personality traits that predict job performance and then interview for candidates with these traits. How successful are they, in the interview, in identifying the personality traits they seek? One study has explored how well interviewers can identify the Big Five personality traits in a 30-minute, introductory interview.[105] The results suggest that interviewers can get to know job candidates almost as well as their friends know them, but that they can assess some traits more readily than others. An interviewer can most easily assess extraversion, agreeableness, and adventurousness/openness to experience, but is somewhat less effective in assessing what are actually the two most job-relevant traits—conscientiousness and emotional stability. This may be because interviewees can successfully use impression management to look good on these two traits in the interview (though they can't fool their friends).

Be Aware of Company Responsibilities and Tactics for Interviews

How good is a particular company in managing its people? If you are going on a job interview, you are about to find out. Good interviewing practices used by savvy companies include structured interviewing, awareness of the dynamics of social exchange, and professional standards of etiquette. Debatable practices include the currently popular "interview inquisition."

STRUCTURED INTERVIEWS Because of communication distortions like impression management, judgmental errors, and perceptual limitations, informally conducted interviews typically fail to predict an applicant's performance on the job. However, structuring job interviews makes them almost as valid as mental ability tests.[106]

Interviews can be structured in several different ways.[107] To begin with, panel interviewing, in which candidates meet with a panel of three to five people all at once, improves decision-making by reducing the effects of individual bias.[108] It also increases the information the interviewers gather. With one person focusing on interacting effectively with the candidate, the others on the panel can focus on observing the candidate.[109] Such highly structured processes are sometimes performed in **assessment centers**, training and development facilities staffed by professional interviewers and assessors, and designed with such useful amenities as rooms with one-way mirrors.

Another sort of structure is provided by having clear job descriptions, which outline the activities to be performed in the job and their rationale, and using these job descriptions to help avoid sidetracks during the interview. Job descriptions are often based on a formal job analysis, a company's detailed description of the job, its relation to other jobs, and the knowledge and skills needed to do the job.[110] This kind of information is used most effectively when summarized in a rating form tailored to the specific job being filled. For example, a rating form for a particular clerical position would include, among other things, 1) proofreading reports, 2) organizing the work of others, 3) telephone communications, and 4) handling of confidential information.[111] Asking a potential employee about each of these in turn would be more effective than asking general questions about organizational or telephone ability.

Finally, additional structure can be achieved by anchoring questions to behavior. Prior to the interview, the company develops examples of what constitutes poor, marginal, and good behavior in key aspects of the job. These are assigned points accordingly. For example, candidates for the position of stock analyst might be asked how they would organize their research on a particular industry, and their answers would be rated in comparison to what the company considers to be weak, average, and excellent approaches. Each candidate is asked identical valid and job-related questions, and after the interview the panel members rate and compare their responses.

THE EFFECTS OF SOCIAL EXCHANGE Implicit in any job interview are the interviewee's expectations for **social exchange**, which is the ongoing give-and-take between the employee and the organization. In particular, employees hope for care and concern in return for their commitment. If new employees feel cared for by an organization, they are likely to feel obliged to it.[112]

Social exchange is implicit in a **realistic job preview**, a recruitment procedure in which, rather than relying on a rosy picture, organizations give both favorable and unfavorable work information to candidates.[113] Being realistic lowers overly inflated pre-entry expectations, and inoculates employees against problems they face on the job because they are expecting them. It signals that the company cares enough about the new employee to tell him or her the truth. Widely researched, realistic job previews have been shown to contribute to organizational commitment and improved workplace performance.[114] One rea-

assessment centers
Training and development facilities staffed by professional interviewers and assessors, and designed with amenities such as rooms with one-way mirrors.

social exchange
The ongoing give-and-take between the employee and the organization.

realistic job preview
A recruitment procedure in which organizations give both favorable and unfavorable work information to candidates.

son realistic job previews are effective is that they convey concern for the individual, which in turn creates greater commitment.

ETIQUETTE TO EXPECT FROM COMPANIES   An interviewer has to hold up his or her side of the communication process or risk alienating the interviewee. Also, poor professional interviewing can harm the reputation of a company.[116]

As a candidate you should expect your interviewer to: 1) Be honest. 2) Turn off the phone and eliminate interruptions. 3) Avoid making negative comments about your qualifications. 4) Be on time, courteous, and professional. 5) Spend the majority of the time (about 70 percent) listening. 6) Set aside a specific amount of time for the interview and then not exceed it, out of respect for your time. 7) Thank you for taking the time to come in, and clarify how any financial matters are to be settled before you leave the building. 8) Follow up on whatever actions were committed to during the interview.

THE "INTERVIEW INQUISITION"   Today stress- and puzzle-intensive interviews are fairly popular.[116] Interviewers pose one or more puzzles of logic, some of which are insolvable, to interviewees and ask them to solve them on the spot. Examples include, "Why do mirrors reverse right and left instead of up and down?" and "If you could remove any one of the 50 states, which would it be?"[117]

The mainstream interest in the technique is generally attributed to its use by Microsoft. ("How would you design Bill Gates's bathroom?" is one fabled question.) The company, which receives about 12,000 résumés a month, asserts that the puzzles are an egalitarian way to structure an interview, cutting through formal credentials, such as the school a candidate attended, and presentation cues, such as how the candidate dresses, to get the candidate to actually demonstrate his or her logic, imagination, and problem-solving ability.

Critics argue that it is not clear what the brainteasers measure and that they do not measure whether a candidate will be a valuable employee. Whether a test of problem-solving ability should be delivered in the stressful medium of a job interview is a related issue.

In Conclusion

This chapter covers a lot of ground, from what the communication process is to how you can make it work for you. Most people need to learn even more about building effective one-to-one relationships through communication. Whatever your interpersonal specialty, be it sales, negotiation, or managing subordinates, there are many books and courses available to help you continue to improve your skills.

Apply What You Have Learned...

World Class Company: The Mayo Clinic

Some organizations take communication very seriously. The Mayo Clinic is one such place.[118] One of the best known academic medical centers in the world, with sites in Minnesota, Florida, and Arizona, every year Mayo Clinic serves more than half a million patients from 150 countries. As part of numerous efforts designed to ensure these patients have a positive experience, the organization employs a full time communications ("comm") team. As spokesperson Amy Davis puts it, "Mayo Clinic employees create our brand every day in every interaction they have with every patient. It's not only the physicians, nurses, and therapists, but also the housekeepers, parking attendants, and every other Mayo employee who interacts with patients or supports those that do."[119]

A primary principle of the comm team is to get "the right information to the right people the right way."[120]

What exactly does the comm team do? Here are some examples.

- Every year it reviews in depth three sets of data about its more than 38,000 U.S. employees—the employee satisfaction survey, survey results from the *Fortune* 100's Best Places to Work survey (it often makes the list), and employee demographic data. It does this in order to fully understand its employees and face down stereotypes about them.
- It networks with employees to find out about their concerns. Each member of the comm team picks 10 employees whom they know informally and sends them e-mails once or twice a month, which they can respond to if they feel they are not too busy. The e-mails ask such questions as "What one question

would you like to ask our CEO?" and "What do you think of May's participation in healthcare reform?"

- It creates personal communication plans for Mayo's top managers. These plans include key messages and tactics. A writer is assigned to each CEO or CAO (chief administrative officer) and works with them regularly to collaborate on creating messages for employees.
- The comm team hired a storytelling consultant to help top managers develop and use their own stories in their communications.
- The comm team develops its own processes as a team, constantly challenging its members to bring problems and challenges rather than updates and reports to group meetings. It also works hard to help members utilize their unique strengths. "That means making sure your best crisis communicator isn't overwhelmed with deadline-driven projects and that your creative 'think outside the box' communicator isn't drooping from constant operational writing projects. It means making sure you are giving people the kinds of projects that motivate them to do their best."[121]

Discuss

1. Which particular one-to-one relationships does Mayo focus on?
2. What communication principles does the motto "get the right information to the right people the right way" suggest?
3. What else do you think a communication team might do for a company?

Advice from the Pros

Etiquette for Electronic Communication

Respect the Receiver

When you call or e-mail someone, identify yourself clearly. "Hi, this is Ralph Oliva from Great University. I am trying to reach Ms. Johnson." Sign your e-mails and PowerPoint presentations with the source of the communication and how to get back to that source.

Match the Medium to the Message

When conveying good news, it may be OK to use an impersonal medium. But when conveying bad news use voice-to-voice or face-to-face communication.

When you need a lengthy, complex, detailed answer, send your message several ways, such as with an e-mail, a PowerPoint attachment, and a phone call.

Avoid Angry E-mail

Respect the dignity of the person you are angry with and deliver the message personally, especially if this will improve your business relationship. Remember that an angry e-mail lives on in cyberspace forever, and may be a problem when it is discovered later.

Avoid Spam-Nation

Deliver value in every communication. If you are selling something, package it in a communication that conveys real value.

Avoid Phone Annoyances

Make your outgoing voicemail message brief. Don't say "Your call is very important to me" or include long explanations about how your answering system works. Answer your phone messages.

Don't use your cell phone in public places. You'll avoid creating noise pollution as well as inadvertently sharing business secrets with strangers.

Source: Based on "Respecting Your Receiver," by R. A. Oliva, executive director of the Institute for the Study of Business Markets (ISBM), *Marketing Management 13* (3), May/June 2004:40–42.

Discuss

1. What electronic communication problems have you experienced?
2. Do you agree with this advice? What further advice would you give?
3. This chapter lists media in terms of how rich they are as a medium of communication. E-mail is considered the leanest medium. What enriches an e-mail? What are its limitations?

More Advice from the Pros

How to Impress at Job Interviews

1. Prepare thoroughly by researching the company (its annual report, Web site, and other literature) and be ready for stock questions such as "What interests you about this company?" and "What are your strengths and weaknesses?"
2. Arrive on time. Consider making the trip once ahead of time to discover potential bottlenecks.
3. Make a good first impression. Always wear a suit even if you know the company has a relaxed dress code.
4. Be polite to receptionists and all employees. The impression you make on them may count.
5. Sell yourself. Even if it is on your résumé, describe the progress you have made through school, or, later, through your career, and mention any special expertise you have.
6. Ask relevant questions, such as why the position is available and what the future of the company is

likely to be. Avoid salary and benefits talk at the first interview.
7. Find out what the next stage of the hiring process and what the timeframe for the next step are. Thank the interviewer for his or her time. If you are excited about the company, say so.
8. If you receive a rejection letter, do not be afraid to write the interviewer to ask why this happened and whether there is anything you could do differently in future interviews.

Source: Based on M. Ingram, "How to: Impress at Job Interviews," *Financial Management* (CIMA), March 2002:41. Mark Ingram is European managing director of the financial recruitment firm David Charley International.

Discuss

1. Do you agree with this advice? Why or why not?
2. What other advice would you add to these tips?

 ## Gain Experience

I. Effective Listening

A. **Pair up** for these challenging assignments. Your professor will tell you when to start and end your conversations.

Exercise 1. Have a conversation with your partner, but do not use the word "I."

Exercise 2. One person starts the conversation with a sentence, and the other begins his or her response with the last word or phrase of the first person's sentence.

Exercise 3: Describe something, and then at the end of your description add "and that's all."

B. **Form a large group.**

Exercise 4: Speak a letter of resignation, with each person in the group adding only one word.

Source: Second City Communication—Prentice Hall video, 2005.

II. Job Interview Improv

In this exercise three job candidates interview for a sales position. The effectiveness of the job interview will be evaluated by a consulting team.

Step 1. Ten volunteers take the following roles:
   Job candidates (3)
   Interviewers (2)
   Consulting teams
   Consultants to the job candidates (3)
   Consultants to the interviewers (2)

Step 2. The whole class: read the following description of ABC Company and the job it is seeking to fill. Address any questions of fact.

ABC Company is a medium-sized pharmaceutical company that sells a line of 20 specialized heart medicines directly to doctors in their offices. It employs a sales staff of 300 individuals nationwide, organized into 8 regions. In its current interview process, the company is looking for a sales rep to cover just the territory that is your state. The job will entail 80 percent travel, 10 percent office time, and 10 percent home-based work. The rep will be compensated based on a modest salary plus a significant commission. Successful sales reps can expect their territory to be enlarged in the future.

Step 3.

A. The (3) candidates

Leave the room. Discuss together how as candidates in the interview you can demonstrate the behaviors on the "Checklist for candidates." Decide the order in which people will interview. When ready, all three candidates return to the classroom.

Checklist for Candidates

1. The candidate made a good first impression.
2. The candidate promoted himself or herself by telling stories about how he or she chose a particular career, became interested in the company, or has performed in past jobs.
3. The candidate made self-image statements about himself or herself as successful and confident.
4. The candidate made self-image statements about his or her goal- and results-orientation.
5. The candidate made self-image statements about himself or herself as highly motivated, organized, or energetic.
6. The candidate appeared to be friendly and active (extroverted).
7. The candidate appeared to be cooperative and flexible (agreeable).
8. The candidate thanked the interviewer for his or her time and clarified what the next stage of the interview process will be.

B. The (2) interviewers

Meet and discuss together how you as a team can meet the following criteria for good interviewing. Decide on questions to ask the candidates.

Checklist for Interviewers

1. The team was courteous.
2. The team was professional.
3. The team established trust with the candidate.
4. The team spent most of its time listening (70 percent or more).
5. The team did not exceed the time allotted to the interview.
6. The team practiced active listening, receiving messages and responding in such a way as to encourage further communication.
7. The team elicited enough information to make a good decision.

8. The team gave the candidate a positive impression of the company.

C. The (3) consultants to the candidates

Study the Table 7.6 checklist of desirable candidate behaviors. Meet as a group to discuss and clarify what behaviors could exemplify each item. Decide on a set of questions to the candidates. Be prepared to time the interviews (5 minutes each).

D. The (2) consultants to the interviewers.

Study the Table 7.7 checklist of desirable interviewer behaviors. Meet as a group to discuss and clarify what behaviors could exemplify each item.

Step. 4. The interview team conducts 5-minute job interviews with each of the three candidates. The consultants to the candidates numerically rate each candidate after their interview. The consultants to the interview team take notes and numerically rate the team at the end of the three interviews.

Step. 5. Consultants finalize their ratings and then give feedback to the candidates and interviewers. Emphasize what the candidates and interviewers actually did, as well as what they might have done that would have enhanced their performance. Class members provide additional feedback.

III. Job Interview Preparation Questions

Divide into groups of four or five. Each group will be assigned one or more questions to answer.[123] In your group, each person should spend a few minutes writing down the answers to the question assigned. Then share your responses with each other and be ready to share the best ones with the class.

1. Give an example of a time when you successfully took charge of a group and helped guide it to get the job done.
2. Describe a time when you had to make a tough strategic decision. Why was the decision tough and what did you do?
3. What strategies have you used in the past to make sure that your department got what it needed?
4. Think about a time when you made a decision you knew would not be popular. How did you convey the decision to subordinates and senior leaders?
5. Describe a time when you successfully persuaded a group to your point of view. How did you go about it?
6. What was the most successful project that you ever worked on? Why was it successful and what was your specific role?
7. What was the most difficult budgeting challenge you have ever faced and how did you handle it?

Table 7.6 Desirable Candidate Behaviors

To what extent did a candidate exhibit the following behaviors? (1 = not at all, 2 = to a little extent, 3 = to some extent, 4 = to a great extent, 5 = to a very great extent)

	Candidate #1	Candidate #2	Candidate #3
1. The candidate made a good first impression.			
2. The candidate promoted himself or herself by telling stories about how he or she chose a particular career, became interested in the company, or has performed in past jobs.			
3. The candidate made self-image statements about himself or herself as successful and confident.			
4. The candidate made self-image statements about his or her goal- and results-orientation.			
5. The candidate made self-image statements about himself or herself as highly motivated, organized, or energetic.			
6. The candidate appeared to be friendly and active (extroverted).			
7. The candidate appeared to be cooperative and flexible (agreeable).			
8. The candidate thanked the interviewer for his or her time and clarified what the next stage of the interview process will be.			

Table 7.7 Checklist: Desirable Interviewer Behaviors

To what extent did the interview *team* exhibit the following behaviors? (1 = not at all, 2 = to a little extent, 3 = to some extent, 4 = to a great extent, 5 = to a very great extent)

Desirable interviewer behaviors	What is the extent to which the interview team exemplified these behaviors?
1. The team was courteous.	
2. The team was professional.	
3. The team established trust with the candidate.	
4. The team spent most of its time listening (70 percent or more).	
5. The team did not exceed the time allotted to the interview.	
6. The team practiced active listening, receiving messages and responding in such a way as to encourage further communication.	
7. The team elicited enough information to make a good decision.	
8. The team gave the candidate a positive impression of the company.	

Chapter Summary and Key Terms

How can you make the communication process work for you?

A one-to-one communication is often, and inadequately, conceptualized as a series of steps. Pitfalls in communicating include selective attention, overload, categorizing, erroneous attributions, and the desire to support one's own psychological identity. When responding to a communication, it is important to choose the appropriate medium, based on whether it is rich or lean, formal or informal.

communication   178
conduit metaphor   178
unintentionality   178
noise   178
selective attention   179
augmented cognition systems   180
information filtering   180
attribution   181
fundamental attribution error   181
self-serving bias   181
stereotypes   181
prejudice   181
illusory correlation   182
possible selves   182
impression management   182
self-presentation strategy   182
other-enhancement strategy   182
jargon   182
medium   183
open door policy   183

How can you use nonverbal behaviors to communicate more effectively?

Keep in mind that nonverbal communication is powerful: Pay attention to such behaviors as facial expressions, gestures, and entering an individual's personal space.

personal space   185

How can understanding gender styles improve your ability to communicate on the job?

Men are more likely to use report talk and agonism, whereas women are more likely to use rapport talk and to misunderstand agonism. Women and other minorities may find themselves in a double-bind when it comes to meeting both their traditional roles and their business roles.

report talk   185
rapport talk   185
agonism   185
double-bind   186

How do you build trust in relationships?

Trust is either calculus-based or identification-based. Trust is both an emotional skill and a relational skill. It may be also a personality trait. Lying affects relationships because people want to maintain relationships, avoid conflict, and avoid loss of face.

calculus-based trust   186
identification-based trust   186
trust   187
distrust   187

How do you persuade others?

Key issues relate to the communicator, the message, and the audience. Is the communicator credible and likable? Is the message extreme? content-rich? effectively framed? What are the needs and mood of the audience? Can you change people's minds by applying the theory of cognitive dissonance?

attitudes   188
central route   188
peripheral route   188
credible communicator   188
likable communicator   188
framing   189
risky choice framing effect   189
attribute framing effect   189
cognitive dissonance theory   189
self-perception theory   190

What communication strengths do you already have? Which skills do you need to develop?

Assess your strengths and weaknesses. Learn what your personal orientation to others is, and whether you are a self-monitor. Practice active listening.

self-monitoring   190
personel orientation to others   191
active listening   192
closed questions   193
open questions   193

What are some tested tactics for doing well on job interviews?

Understand the importance of making a good first impression and adopt an impression management strategy for the interview. Know what the company is looking for in terms of personality. Understand that a company also has a role in designing a good interview.

first impression bias   194
assessment centers   196
social exchange   196
realistic job preview   196

Explorations

1. Look for opportunities to practice effective communication.

Reading about communication is not enough. . . You have to practice. Your university probably offers a variety of courses in communication, including public speaking and persuasion. Look for those that emphasize hands-on practice. Consider, as well, experiential courses in negotiation and leadership.

2. Join Toastmasters International . . .

Which is an organization whose mission is to "make effective communication a worldwide reality." Check out the group's Web site to find experiential training programs near you, at a reasonable cost.

3. For reading at your leisure . . .

- An excellent book on assertiveness training is Robert E. Alberti and Michael L. Emmons' book *Your Perfect Right: Assertiveness and Equality in Your Life and Relationships.* Attend an interactive workshop if possible.
- The classic book on persuasion is Dale Carnegie's *How to Win Friends and Influence People* (New York: Pocket, 1990), first published in 1937 and still, amazingly, a bestseller. (At this writing, it is number 107 at Amazon.com.)

4. On the Web. . .

Research "communication training" to learn about the large number of companies involved in selling this service. What types of training are particularly popular today?

References

1 *Webster's Encyclopedic Unabridged Dictionary of the English Language* (New York: Portland House, 1989).

2 P. Dvorak, "Construction Firm Rebuilds Managers to Make Them Softer," *The Wall Street Journal* May 16, 2006:A1.

3 M. Reddy, "The Conduit Metaphor: A Case of Frame Conflict in Our Language about Language," in A. Ortony, ed., *Metaphor and Thought* (Cambridge, England: Cambridge University Press, 1979):284–324.

4 S. R. Axley, "Managerial and Organizational Communication in Terms of the Conduit Metaphor," *Academy of Management Review 9* (3), July 1984:428–437.

5 S. R. Axley, "Managerial and Organizational Communication in Terms of the Conduit Metaphor," *Academy of Management Review 9* (3), July 1984:428–437.

6 N. Moray, "Attention in Dichotic Listening: Affective Cues and the Influence of Instructions," *Quarterly Journal of Experimental Psychology 11,* 1959:56–60.

7 See D. L. Strayer, F. A. Drews, and W. A. Johnston, "Cell Phone–Induced Failure of Visual Attention During Simulated Driving," *Journal of Experimental Psychology: Applied 9* (1) 2003:23–32

8 "Computers that Read Your Mind," *The Economist Technology Quarterly* September 23, 2006:24–25.

9 "Computers that Read Your Mind," *The Economist Technology Quarterly* September 23, 2006:24–25.

10 J. McCafferty, "Coping with Infoglut," *CFO 14* (9), September 1998:101–103.

11 The prediction is for 2006. T. Peterson, "Coping with Infoglut," *Computerworld, 37*(25), June 23, 2003:40.

12 J. McCafferty, "Coping with Infoglut," *CFO 14* (9), September 1998:101–103.

13 L. Ross, "The Intuitive Psychologist and His Shortcomings: Distortions in the Attribution Process," in L. Berkowitz, ed., *Advances in Experimental Social Psychology 10* (New York: Academic Press, 1977):174–221.

14 H. H. Kelley, "The Processes of Causal Attribution," *American Psychologist 28,* 1973:107–128.

15 J. G. Miller, "Culture and the Development of Everyday Social Explanation," *Journal of Personality and Social Psychology 46,* 1984:961–978.

16 S. T. Fiske, "Stereotyping, Prejudice, and Discrimination," in D. Gilbert, S. T. Fiske, and G. Lindzey, eds., *Handbook of Social Psychology 2,* 4th ed. (Boston: McGraw-Hill, 1998):357–414.

17 J. F. Dovidio, K. Kawakami, and S. L. Gaertner, "Reducing Contemporary Prejudice: Combating Explicit and Implicit Bias at the Individual and Intergroup Level," in S. Oskamp, ed., *Reducing Prejudice and Discrimination* (Hillsdale, NJ: Erlbaum, 2000):137–163.

18 D. L. Hamilton and J. Sherman, "Social Stereotypes," in R. S. Wyer and T. K. Srull, eds., *Handbook of Social Cognition,* 2nd ed. (Hillsdale, NJ: Erlbaum, 1994).

19 S. Brickson, "The Impact of Identity Orientation on Individual and Organizational Outcomes in Demographically Diverse Settings," *Academy of Management Review 25* (1), 2000:82–101; F. J. Flynn, "Identity Orientations and Forms of Social Exchange in Organizations," *Academy of Management Review 30* (4), 2005:737–750.

20 H. Erickson, *Identity: Youth and Crisis* (New York: Norton, 1968).

21 H. Markus and P. Nurius, "Possible Selves," *American Psychologist 41,* 1986:954–969.

22 H. Markus and P. Nurius, "Possible Selves," *American Psychologist 41,* 1986:954–969,954.

23 B. R. Schlenker and M. F. Weigold, "Self-Identification and Accountability," in R. A. Giacalone and P. Rosenfeld, eds., *Impression Management in the Organization* (Hillsdale, NJ: Erlbaum, 1989):21–43.

24 S. Zirkel, "Social Intelligence: The Development and Maintenance of Purposive Behavior," in R. Bar-On and J. D. A. Parker, eds., *The Handbook of Emotional Intelligence: Theory, Development, Assessment and Application at Home, School and in the Workplace* (San Francisco: Jossey-Bass, 2000):3–27.

25 E. E. Jones, *Ingratiation* (New York: Appleton-Century-Crofts, 1964); J. T. Tedeschi and V. Melburg, "Impression Management and Influence in the Organization," in S. B. Bacharach and E. J. Lawler, eds., *Research in the Sociology of Organizations 3* (Greenwich, CT: JAI Press, 1984):31–58; S. J. Wayne and R. C. Liden, "Effects of Impression Management on Performance

Ratings: A Longitudinal Study," *Academy of Management Journal 38* (1), February 1995:232–260.

26 B. Munck, "Changing a Culture of Face Time," *Harvard Business Review 79* (10), November 2001:125–130.

27 D. Kipnis and S. M. Schmidt, "Upward Influence Styles: Relationship with Performance Evaluations, Salary, and Stress," *Administrative Science Quarterly 33*, 1988:528–542; S. J. Wayne and M. K. Kacmar, "The Effects of Impression Management on the Performance Appraisal Process," *Organizational Behavior and Human Decision Processes 48*, 1991:70–88; G. R. Ferris, T. A. Judge, K. M. Rowland, and D. E. Fitzgibbons, "Subordinate Influence and the Performance Evaluation Process: Test of a Model," *Organizational Behavior and Human Decision Processes 58*, 1994:101–135;S. Zivnuska, K. Kacmar, L. A. Witt, D. S. Carlson, and V. K. Bratton, "Interactive Effects of Impression Management and Organizational Politics on Job Performance," *Journal of Organizational Behavior 25* (5), 2004:627–640.

28 S. J. Wayne and R. C. Liden, "Effects of Impression Management on Performance Ratings: A Longitudinal Study," *Academy of Management Journal 38* (1), February 1995:232–60.

29 F. Warner, "Microsoft Eats the Dog Food," *Fast Company 62*, August 2002:46. http://www.fastcompany.com/magazine/62/microsoft.html. Accessed February 26, 2007.

30 M. McLuhan, *Understanding Media: The Extensions of Man* (New York: McGraw Hill, 1964).

31 P. V. Lewis, *Organizational Communication: The Essence of Effective Management*, 3rd ed. (New York: Wiley, 1987).

32 A. Mehrabian, *Nonverbal Communication* (Chicago: Aldine-Atherton, 1972).

33 N. Henley, M. Hamilton and B. Thorne, "Womanspeak and Manspeak: Sex Differences in Communication, Verbal and Nonverbal," in J. J. Macionis and N. V. Benokraitis, eds., *Seeing Ourselves: Classic, Contemporary and Cross-Cultural Readings in Sociology*, 2nd ed. (Englewood Cliffs, NJ: Prentice Hall, 1992):10–15.

34 L. Smith-Lovin and C. Brody, "Interruptions in Group Discussions: The Effects of Gender and Group Composition," *American Journal of Sociology 54* (3), June 1989:424–35; C. Johnson, "Gender, Legitimate Authority, and Leader-Subordinate Conversations," *American Sociological Review 59* (1), February 1994:122–35.

35 N. Henley, M. Hamilton and B. Thorne, "Womanspeak and Manspeak: Sex Differences in Communication, Verbal and Nonverbal," in J. J. Macionis and N. V. Benokraitis, eds., *Seeing Ourselves: Classic, Contemporary and Cross-Cultural Readings in Sociology*, 2nd ed (Englewood Cliffs, NJ: Prentice Hall, 1992):10–15.

36 L. R. Smeltzer and J. D. Werbel, "Gender Differences in Managerial Communication: Fact or Folk-Linguistics?" *Journal of Business Communication 23* (2), Spring 1986:41–50.

37 D. Tannen, *You Just Don't Understand: Men and Women in Conversation* (New York: Ballantine Books, 1990); M. Crawford, *Talking Difference: On Gender and Language* (Thousand Oaks, CA: Sage, 1995).

38 D. Tannen, *Talking from 9 to 5: How Women's and Men's Conversational Styles Affect Who Gets Heard, Who Gets Credit, and What Gets Done at Work* (New York: William Morrow and Company, Inc., 1994):24, 28.

39 D. Tannen, *Talking from 9 to 5: How Women's and Men's Conversational Styles Affect Who Gets Heard, Who Gets Credit, and What Gets Done at Work* (New York: William Morrow and Company, Inc., 1994):35–36.

40 D. Tannen, *Talking from 9 to 5: How Women's and Men's Conversational Styles Affect Who Gets Heard, Who Gets Credit, and What Gets Done at Work* (New York: William Morrow and Company, Inc., 1994):23.

41 D. Tannen, *You Just Don't Understand: Men and Women in Conversation* (New York: Ballantine Books, 1990).

42 N. Maltz and R. A. Borker, "A Cultural Approach to Male–Female Miscommunication," in J. J. Gumperz, ed., *Language and Social Identity* (Cambridge: Cambridge University Press, 1982):196–216; D. Tannen, *Talking from 9 to 5: How Women's and Men's Conversational Styles Affect Who Gets Heard, Who Gets Credit, and What Gets Done at Work* (New York: William Morrow and Company, Inc., 1994):39–40.

43 D. Tannen, *Talking from 9 to 5: How Women's and Men's Conversational Styles Affect Who Gets Heard, Who Gets Credit, and What Gets Done at Work* (New York: William Morrow and Company, Inc., 1994):57,58; D. Tannen, *The Argument Culture: Moving from Debate to Dialogue* (New York: Random House, 1998).

44 K. H. Jamieson, *Beyond the Double Bind: Women and Leadership* (New York: Oxford University Press, 1997).

45 D. L. Mathison, "Sex Differences in the Perception of Assertiveness Among Female Managers," *Journal of Social Psychology 126* (5), October 1986:599–606.

46 D. Tannen, *Talking from 9 to 5: How Women's and Men's Conversational Styles Affect Who Gets Heard, Who Gets Credit, and What Gets Done at Work* (New York: William Morrow and Company, Inc., 1994):289.

47 J. D. Lewis and A. Weigert, "Trust as a Social Reality," *Social Forces 63* (4), June 1985:967–985.

48 P. R. Shaver and C. Hazan, "Attachment," in A. L. Weber and J. H. Harvey, eds., *Perspectives on Close Relationships* (Boston: Allyn and Bacon, 1994):110–130.

49 G. Simmel (1900), translated by Tom Bottomore and David Frisby, *The Philosophy of Money* (London: Routledge & Kegan Paul, 1978).

50 R. J. Lewicki, D. J. McAllister, and R. J. Bies, "Trust and Distrust: New Relationships and Realities," *Academy of Management Review 23* (3), July 1998:438–458.

51 N. Luhmann, *Trust and Power* (Chichester, England: Wiley, 1979).

52 R. J. Lewicki and C. Wiethoff, "Trust, Trust Development, and Trust Repair," in M. Deutsch and P. T. Coleman, eds., *The Handbook of Conflict Resolution* (San Francisco: Jossey-Bass, 2000):86–107.

53 R. J. Lewicki, D. J. McAllister, and R. J. Bies, "Trust and Distrust: New Relationships and Realities," *Academy of Management Review 23* (3), July 1998:438–458.

54 T. Govier, "Is It a Jungle Out There? Trust, Distrust, and the Construction of Social Reality," *Dialogue 33*, 1994:237–252.

55 F. Flores and R. C. Solomon, "Creating Trust," *Business Ethics Quarterly 8* (2), April 1998:205–232.

56 F. Flores and R. C. Solomon, "Creating Trust," *Business Ethics Quarterly 8* (2), April 1998:205–232.

57 F. Flores and R. C. Solomon, "Creating Trust," *Business Ethics Quarterly 8* (2), April 1998:205–232.

58 K. Jones, R. Hardin and L. C. Becker, "A Symposium on Trust," *Ethics 107* (1), 1996:4–61.

59 R. Frank, T. Gilovich and D. Regan, "Does Studying Economics Inhibit Cooperation?" *Journal of Economic Perspectives 7* (2), 1993:159–171.

60 F. Flores and R. C. Solomon, "Creating Trust," *Business Ethics Quarterly 8* (2), April 1998:205–232.

61 N. Rodriguez and A. L. Ryave, "The Structural Organization and Micropolitics of Everyday Secret Telling Interactions," *Qualitative Sociology 15* (3), Fall 1992:297–318.

62 I. Ajzen, "Nature and Operation of Attitudes," *Annual Review of Psychology 52*, 2001:27–58; A. H. Eagly and S. Chaiken, *The Psychology of Attitudes* (Fort Worth, TX: Harcourt Brace Jovanovich, 1993).

63 G. Bohner and N. Schwarz, "Attitudes, Persuasion and Behavior," in A. Tesser and N. Schwarz, eds., *Blackwell Handbook of Social Psychology: Intraindividual Processes,* 2001:413–435.

64 J. T. Cacioppo, R. E. Petty, and S. L. Crites, "Attitude Change," in V. S. Ramachandran, ed., *Encyclopedia of Human Behavior* (San Diego: Academic Press, 1993).

65 S. Chaiken and D. Maheswaran, "Heuristic Processing Can Bias Systematic Processing: Effects of Source Credibility, Argument Ambiguity, and Task Importance on Attitude Judgment," *Journal of Personality and Social Psychology 66,* 1994:460–473.

66 K. Edwards and E. E. Smith, "A Discomfirmation Bias in the Evaluation of Arguments," *Journal of Personality and Social Psychology 71*, 1996:5–24.

67 J. R. Zuwerink and P. G. Devine, "Attitude Importance and Resistance to Persuasion: It's Not Just the Thought That Counts," *Journal of Personality and Social Psychology 70,* 1996:931–944.

68 R. E. Petty and D. T. Wegener, "The Elaboration Likelihood Model: Current Status and Controversies," in S. Chaiken and Y. Trope, eds., *Dual Process Theories in Social Psychology* (New York: Guilford, 1999):41–72.

69 I. P. Levin, S. L. Schneider, and G. J. Gaeth, "All Frames Are Not Created Equal: A Typology and Critical Analysis of Framing Effects," *Organizational Behavior and Human Decision Processes 76*, 1998:141–188.

70 B. E. Meyerowitz and S. Chaiken, "The Effects of Message Framing on Breast Self-Examination Attitudes, Intentions and Behavior," *Journal of Personality & Social Psychology 52*, 1987:500–510.

71 F. Gleicher and R. E. Petty, "Expectations of Reassurance Influence the Nature of Fear-Stimulated Attitude Change," *Journal of Experimental Social Psychology 28,* 1992:86–100.

72 S. Highhouse and P. Yüce, "Perspectives, Perceptions, and Risk-Taking Behavior," *Organizational Behavior and Human Decision Processes 65* (2), February 1996:151–167.

73 I. P. Leven and G. J. Gaeth, "Framing of Attribute Information Before and After Consuming the Product," *Journal of Consumer Research 15*, 1988:374–378.

74 I. P. Levin, "Associative Effects of Information Framing," *Bulletin of the Psychonomic Society 25,* 1987:85–86.

75 R. E. Petty and D. T. Wegener, "The Elaboration Likelihood Model: Current Status and Controversies," in S. Chaiken and Y. Trope, eds., *Dual Process Theories in Social Psychology* (New York: Guilford, 1999):41–72.

76 L. Festinger, *A Theory of Cognitive Dissonance* (Evanston, IL: Row, Petersen, 1957).

77 J. Stone and J. Cooper, "A Self-Standards Model of Cognitive Dissonance," *Journal of Experimental Social Psychology 37,* 2001:228–243.

78 C. M. Steele, S. J. Spencer and M. Lynch, "Self-Image Resilience and Dissonance: The Role of Affirmational Resources," *Journal of Personality and Social Psychology 64,* 1993:885–896.

79 D. Dunning, "On the Motives Underlying Social Cognition," in A. Tesser and N. Schwarz, eds., *Blackwell Handbook of Social Psychology: Intraindividual Processes* (Oxford, England: Blackwell, 2001):348–374.

80 N. Schwarz, H. Bless, and G. Bohner, "Mood and Persuasion: Affective States Influence the Processing of Persuasive Communications," *Advances in Experimental Social Psychology 24,* 1991:161–199.

81 A. M. Isen, "Positive Affect, Cognitive Processes, and Social Behavior," in L. Berkowitz (ed.), *Advances in Experimental Social Psychology 20* (New York: Academic Press, 1987):203–253.

82 M. Snyder, "Self-Monitoring of Expressive Behavior," *Journal of Personality and Social Psychology 30*, 1974:526–537; S. Gangestad and M. Snyder, "To Carve Nature at Its Joints: On the Existence of Discrete Classes in Personality," *Psychological Review 92,* 1985:317–349; S. W. Gangestad and M. Snyder, "Self-Monitoring: Appraisal and Reappraisal," *Psychological Bulletin, 126*, 2000:530–555; A. Mehra, M. Kilduff, and D. J. Brass, "The Social Networks of High and Low Self-Monitors: Implications for Workplace Performance," *Administrative Science Quarterly, 46*(1), March 2001:121–45.

83 A. Mehra, M. Kilduff, and D. J. Brass, "The Social Networks of High and Low Self-Monitors: Implications for Workplace Performance," *Administrative Science Quarterly, 46* (1), March 2001:121–145, 124.

84 A. Mehra, M. Kilduff, and D. J. Brass, "The Social Networks of High and Low Self-Monitors: Implications for Workplace Performance," *Administrative Science Quarterly 46* (1), March 2001:121–145, 124.

85 S. J. Zaccaro, R. J. Foti, and D. A. Kenny, "Self-Monitoring and Trait-Based Variance in Leadership: An Investigation of Leader Flexibility across Multiple Group Situations," *Journal of Applied Psychology 76*, 1991:308–315.

86 N. M. Noel, C. Michael, and M. G. Levas, "The Relationship of Personality Traits and Self-Monitoring Behavior to Choice of Business Major," *Journal of Education for Business 78* (3), January/February 2003:153–157.

87 A. Mehra, M. Kilduff, and D. J. Brass, "The Social Networks of High and Low Self-Monitors: Implications for Workplace Performance," *Administrative Science Quarterly 46* (1), March 2001:121–145.

88 D. M. Messick and C.G. McClintock, "Motivational Basis of Choice in Experimental Games," *Journal of Experimental Social Psychology 4*, 1968:1–25; D. M. Kuhlman and A. F. J. Marshello, "Individual Differences in Game Motivation as Moderators of Preprogrammed Strategy Effects in Prisoner's Dilemma," *Journal of Personality and Social Psychology 32*, 1975: 922–931; G. P. Knight, A. G. Dubro, and C. Chao, "Information Processing and the Development of Cooperative, Competitive and Individualistic Social Values," *Developmental Psychology 21*, 1985:37–45.

89 J. Iedema and M. Poppe, "The Effect of Self-presentation on Social Value Orientation," *Journal of Social Psychology 134* (6), December 1994:771–782.

90 S. B. Castleberry and C. D. Shepherd, "Effective Interpersonal Listening and Personal Selling," *Journal of Personal Selling and Sales Management XIII*, Winter 1993:35–49.

91 P. Lewis, "Learning to Ask Good Questions," *Journal of European Industrial Training 13* (9), 1989:4–8.

92 V. P. Goby and J. H. Lewis, "The Key Role of Listening in Business: A Study of the Singapore Insurance Industry," *Business Communication Quarterly 63* (2), June 2000:41–51.

93 Adapted from L. B. Corner and T. Drollinger, "Active Empathetic Listening and Selling Success: A Conceptual Framework," *Journal of Personal Selling & Sales Management 19* (1), Winter 1999:15–29.

94 V. P. Goby and J. H. Lewis, "The Key Role of Listening in Business: A Study of the Singapore Insurance Industry," *Business Communication Quarterly 63* (2), June 2000:41–51.

95 P. Lewis, "Learning to Ask Good Questions," *Journal of European Industrial Training 13* (9), 1989:4–8.

96 Research by N. Ambady and R. Rosenthal, cited in W. Poundstone, "Impossible Questions: Do Applicants Who Answer Them Correctly Make Better Hires?" *Across the Board*, September/October 2003:44–48. See N. Ambady, and R. Rosenthal "Half a Minute: Predicting Teacher Evaluations from Thin Slices of Nonverbal Behavior and Physical Attractiveness," *Journal of Personality and Social Psychology 64*, 1993: 431–41.

97 N. R. Bardack and F. T. McAndrew, "The Influence of Physical Attractiveness and Manner of Dress on Success in a Simulated Personnel Decision," *Journal of Social Psychology 125(6)*, 1985:777–78; R. Bull and N. Runsey, *The Social Psychology of Facial Appearance* (London: Springer-Verlag,

1988); E. Smith and D. Mackie, *Social Psychology*, 2nd ed (Philadelphia: Taylor & Francis, 2000).

98 K. K. Dion, E. Berscheid, and E. Walster, "What Is Beautiful Is Good," *Journal of Personality and Social Psychology 24,* 1972:285–290; M. Snyder, E. D. Tanke, and E. Berscheid, "Social Perception and Interpersonal Behavior: On the Self-Fulfilling Nature of Social Stereotypes," *Journal of Personality and Social Psychology, 35*, 1977:656–666.

99 T. W. Dougherty, D. B. Turban, and J. C. Callender, "Confirming First Impressions in the Employment Interview: A Field Study of Interviewer Behavior," *Journal of Applied Psychology 79* (5), October 1994:659–665.

100 J. L. Schrag, "First Impressions Matter: A Model of Confirmatory Bias," *Quarterly Journal of Economics 114* (1), February 1999:37–82; S. E. Asch, "Forming Impressions of Personality," *Journal of Abnormal Social Psychology 41*, 1946:1230–1240.

101 B. R. Schlenker, Impression Management: The Self-Concept, Social Identity, and Interpersonal Relations (Monterey, CA: Brooks/Cole, 1980).

102 A. L. Kristof and C. K. Stevens, "Applicant Impression Management Tactics: Effects on Interviewer Evaluations and Interview Outcomes," *Academy of Management Proceedings*, 1994:127–131.

103 M. A. Campion, E. D. Pursell, and B. K. Brown, "Structured Interviewing: Raising the Psychometric Properties of the Employment Interview," *Personnel Psychology 41*, 1988:25–42; L. C. Walters, M. R. Miller, and M. J. Ree, "Structured Interviews for Pilot Selection: No Incremental Validity," *International Journal of Aviation Psychology 3*, 1993:25–38; F. L. Schmidt and J. E. Hunter, "The Validity and Utility of Selection Methods in Personnel Psychology: Practical and Theoretical Implications of 85 Years of Research Findings," *Psychological Bulletin 124*, 1998:262–274.

[104]D. F. Caldwell and J. M. Burger, "Personality Characteristics of Job Applicants and Success in Screening Interviews," *Personnel Psychology 51*, 1998:119–136.

[105]M. R. Barrick, G. K. Patton, and S. N. Haugland, "Accuracy of Interviewer Judgments of Job Applicant Personality Traits," *Personnel Psychology 53* (4), Winter 2000:925–951.

[106]A. I. Huffcutt and A. W. Arthur, Jr., "Hunter and Hunter (1984) Revisited: Interview Validity for Entry-Level Jobs," *Journal of Applied Psychology 79*, 1994:184–190; W. H. Weisner and S. F. Cronshaw, "A Meta-Analytic Investigation of the Impact of Interview Format and Degree of Structure on the Validity of the Employment Interview," *Journal of Occupational Psychology 61*, 1988:275–290.

[107]C. Daniel and V. Sergio, "Structured Interviewing Simplified," *Public Personnel Management 20* (2), Summer 1991:127–134.

[108]M. Rothstein and D. N. Jackson, "Decision-Making in the Employment Interview: An Experimental Approach," *Journal of Applied Psychology 65* (3), 1980:271–283.

[109]C. R. Nordstrom, R. J. Hall, and L. K. Bartels, "First Impressions Versus Good Impressions: The Effect of Self-Regulation on Interview Evaluations," *Journal of Psychology 132* (5), September 1998:477–491.

[110]H. S. Feild and R. D. Gatewood, "Matching Talent with the Task," *Personnel Administrator 32* (4), April 1987:113–126.

[111]H. G. Osburn, C. Timmreck, and D. Bigby, "Effect of Dimensional Relevance on Accuracy of Simulated Hiring Decisions by Employment Interviewers," *Journal of Applied Psychology 66* (2), 1981:159–165.

[112]Y. Ganzach, A. Pazy, Y. Ohayun and E. Braynin, "Realistic Job Preview, Social Exchange and Organizational Commitment," *Academy of Management Proceedings*, 2000:1–6

[113]J. Weitz, "Job Expectancy and Survival," *Journal of Applied Psychology 40, 1956*:245–247; S. L. Rynes, "Recruitment, Job Choice and Post-Hire Consequences: A Call for New Research Directions," in M. D. Dunnette and L. M. Hough, eds., *Handbook of Industrial and Organizational Psychology, 2*, 2nd ed. (Palo Alto, CA: Consulting Psychologists Press, 1956):399–444.

[114]B. M. Meglino, E. C. Ravlin, and A. S. DeNisi, "A Meta-Analytic Examination of Realistic Job Preview Effectiveness: A Test of Three Counterintuitive Propositions," *Human Resource Management Review 10* (4), Winter 2000:407–434; S. L. Premack and J. P. Wanous, "A Meta-Analysis of Realistic Job Preview Experiments," *Journal of Applied Psychology 70*, 1985:706–719.

[115]J. Krug, "Interviewing Etiquette," *Journal of Management in Engineering 13* (4), July/August 1997:16.

[116]W. Poundstone, "Beware the Interview Inquisition," *Harvard Business Review 81* (5), May 2003:18–19.

[117]W. Poundstone, "Beware the Interview Inquisition," *Harvard Business Review 81* (5), May 2003:18–19, 18.

[118]A. Davis, "Taking Communication to the Next Level at Mayo Clinic," *Strategic Communication Management 10* (5), August/September 2006:14–17.

[119]A. Davis, "Taking Communication to the Next Level at Mayo Clinic," *Strategic Communication Management 10* (5), August/September 2006:14–17, 14.

[120]A. Davis, "Taking Communication to the Next Level at Mayo Clinic," *Strategic Communication Management 10* (5), August/September 2006:14–17, 17.

[121]A. Davis, "Taking Communication to the Next Level at Mayo Clinic," *Strategic Communication Management 10* (5), August/September 2006:14–17, 15.

[122]Based on A. Lazarus, "Preparation Is Key to Successful Job Interviews," *Physician Executive 30* (3), May 2004:48–50.

8 Cross-Cultural Relationships

Preview

What characterizes Americans—what characterizes *you*—culturally?

Western business customs are accepted worldwide—so why should you study other cultures?

What cultural differences interest managers?
Perceptual differences
Nonverbal differences
Differences in attitudes and values
Personality differences
Differences in psychological contracts

What do you need to know about developing business relationships with America's most important trading partners?
Canada
The People's Republic of China
Mexico
Japan
The Federal Republic of Germany

What characterizes the successful individual working overseas?

How can you develop cross-cultural skills?
Use the Big Five personality theory
Understand your tolerance for ambiguity
Evaluate differences in values
Develop cultural intelligence
Understand culture shock
Gain experience
Attend cross-cultural training

What should companies do to support their expatriates?

How should you prepare for a short-term international assignment?

Global HRM: The Case of Sam Lafayette

Samuel Lafayette sold his house, polished up his college French (at company expense), and took his family to Paris to start up a new division for his company. Working under a three-year contract, he threw himself into the work. Unfortunately, things didn't work out quite as he had hoped. He and his family hated the assignment, and they returned to the United States early.

Samuel felt that he had been let down by his company, and misinformed. As he complained to two HR directors in a tense meeting, he felt his family was left swimming. The adjustment was difficult for his young children. The list of schools that the company had provided was inadequate. It had been difficult for his wife to find friends among the French neighbors. Now he and his family are back in New York City, and they are, as he puts it, "homeless," with "nothing to show for it." To add insult to injury, upon returning home, Samuel's company would only offer him a position at a lower level, although at the same salary. Samuel's reaction? "Unacceptable!"

But there is another side to the story. Six months before his departure—in plenty of time for him to take advantage of it—Samuel had been offered an employee assistance program to help him with the pending cross-cultural experience. The program would have involved him and his entire family in learning how to cope with living in France. He declined it, perhaps believing that most of the adjustment would be his own rather than his family's. Meanwhile, the company had invested millions in the new start-up, and Samuel had broken his three-year contract. Despite the fact that Samuel was a valued employee who had been with the company nine years, the company felt it was dealing generously with him.

This scenario is not unusual. Working cross-culturally is one of the hazards of being involved in a global business. Of course, it is also one of its pleasures!

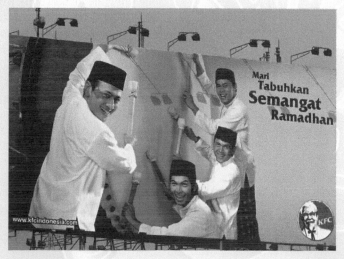

culture
A set of shared beliefs and values about what is desirable in a community, and the set of behaviors and practices that support these values.

national culture
The thoughts, emotions, and behaviors rooted in common values and societal conventions of a particular society.

Even if international business will not be a significant part of your career, there is a strong probability that in your job you will sometimes work with people of other nationalities and cultures. You might routinely talk on the telephone to customers in Brazil, for example. Or you might have the opportunity to work in Hong Kong for a time. You might work with subcultures right in your own country, too. This chapter introduces a variety of approaches that, whatever your level of involvement, will help you manage the cross-cultural relationships you will encounter.

Culture is a set of shared beliefs and values about what is desirable in a community, and the set of behaviors and practices that support these values.[1] **National culture** includes the thoughts, emotions, and behaviors rooted in common values and societal conventions of a particular society.[2] Of course, most nations also have subcultures, groups that are themselves unique. This is a factor that cross-cultural travelers must always take into account.

What Characterizes Americans—What Characterizes *You*—Culturally?

How do you answer this question? "I'm unique," you might say, "An individual. There's no one like me." Of course! However, do you also sense that, assuming you are an American, you come from an entire culture of individualists? And have you ever experienced a culture in which individuals actually describe themselves quite differently?

To understand cultural differences, the first culture you should study is your own. Table 8.1 presents an informal test of your cultural acumen with respect to Americans in business. In each category managers from two countries are compared. Your job is to choose which manager is the American.[3] Circle either "x" or "y". As you read through the categories, also try to figure out what the other country is. Hints: It is the same country for all categories, and it is in Europe.

Now check your answers in Appendix 2.

In the overview in Table 8.2, you will find a summary of the American characteristics just illustrated. You will learn still more about Americans as you read through the chapter.

Western Business Customs Are Accepted Worldwide—So Why Should You Study Other Cultures?

Trick question! The Western business customs that count the most are *not* accepted worldwide. Typically, it is only the superficial customs that have been adopted. So your counterpart in Japan may dress as you do and may enjoy going out for a few beers after work as you do, but he (rarely a she) does not think about these behaviors the same way you do. For one thing, he thinks of his Western-design business suit as Japanese, and when he goes out after work with colleagues, he is actually just extending his business day into a different mode that often lasts quite late into the evening. And there are many, many more important differences in how he views himself, his family, his company, and his country.

Obviously, these cultural differences can get in the way of effective communication. For instance, two individuals from different cultures may make incorrect attributions about each other's behavior. Consider this example. An American supervisor, accustomed to managing subordinates by encouraging their participation, is talking with a Greek subordinate, who expects to be told what to do.[4]

The American asks: How long will it take you to finish this report?

The American is *thinking*: I am asking him to participate.

The Greek is *thinking*: He is the boss. Why doesn't he just tell me when he wants it?

The Greek replies: I don't know. How long should it take?

The American is *thinking*: He is refusing to take responsibility.

The Greek is *thinking*: I asked him for an order.

The American responds: You are in the best position to figure out how long the job should take.

TABLE 8.1 Which Is the American Way of Business?

What is the culture's. . .?	Characteristics of Cultures X and Y	Who is the American?
1. Fundamental approach to business decision making	X managers prefer to rely on certitudes, such as regulations or mathematical rules. This can be an advantage because they can rally quickly and unanimously to an issue that is elucidated by a commonly accepted rule. Y managers prefer to discuss issues, and to create or to find what they think is the right way to handle an issue. This comparison is borne out in the X and Y school systems: X students listen to the "truth" as told by the teacher, whereas Y students are expected to give their opinion and to participate in the learning experience.	X or Y?
2. Preferred mode of decision making	X managers are used to working alone, and making decisions alone. They often consider group meetings to be a waste of time. Y managers take meetings a lot more seriously, seeing them as the basis of their decisions. They tend therefore to achieve more results in group meetings than X managers, who believe they will actually be more efficient when making a decision alone.	X or Y?
3. How work groups make decisions	X group meetings are usually informal, with all people present speaking, and a natural leader appearing throughout the discussion. Y meetings are more formal, with a known leader managing the discussion; typically this person will be the highest in the hierarchy, or the oldest one.	X or Y?
4. Reaction to problems	A typical X reaction to an unexpected problem will be to shift the decision to a higher level of responsibility through a memorandum, and therefore to avoid a conflict at the current level of decision making. Y managers are more likely to emphasize the potential benefits of facing conflicts; they will look for a group meeting involving all parties to solve the problem.	X or Y?
5. Workplace relationships	X managers greet easily every person they meet, even if they do not know the person. Y people are reserved, and keep some distance in order to avoid any status mistake; however, they usually go and shake hands with everybody in their department in the morning, whereas X people say a vague "hello." In X companies, doors are kept open, therefore inviting people to speak with each other; doors are only closed in case of private meetings. In Y, it is usual that all doors be closed to let people work alone in peace. Y develop deep personal relationships with a few colleagues, whereas X, perhaps because they move more frequently from company to company, place less emphasis on such relationships.	X or Y?
6. Attitudes toward time	X managers are always rushing, trying to achieve the highest efficiency during they workday. Y people want to control their own time, and want to be able to take a break if they think they need it. They focus on effectiveness rather than on efficiency. As a result, X managers hardly take the time to eat a sandwich at noon, whereas Y usually enjoy a hot meal with several courses. X tend to accomplish things earlier in the day; Y tend to get more done later in the day.	X or Y?

The American is *thinking*: He refuses to take responsibility.

The Greek is *thinking*: What nonsense. I'd better give him an answer.

In this dialogue each side is misjudging the other. The American has no clue that participation is seldom used in Greek businesses, and the Greek has no clue that participation is either possible or useful. Rather than trying to understand each other, each labels the other as a dummy. Any one of thousands of cultural differences could cause such a problem.

TABLE 8.2 Overview: Characteristics of Americans in Cultural Perspective

Assumptions about decision making	Discussing issues openly is valued. Discussion is a good way to figure out the right way to handle an issue.
Preferred mode of decision making	Meetings are taken seriously. Meetings are the basis of decisions and accomplish important tasks.
Group decision making	Meetings are informal, with all people present speaking, and a natural leader appearing during the discussion.
Conflict management	Facing conflict is seen as a positive, whether between individuals or groups.
Workplace relationships	The expectation is of friendly and open but impersonal relationships. People expect to greet and speak with each other easily.
Attitudes toward time	Hurried, Americans want to achieve the highest efficiency during their workday.

On the other side of the coin, some countries appear to be characteristically capable of integrating a variety of cultures, and can be called welcoming cultures. It has been pointed out, for example, that foreign executives are more comfortable working in Britain than in some other countries.[5] Of the 50 largest British firms in 2004, 17 were run by foreigners, compared with only 5 of the top 50 in Germany and America, and 3 in France. Middle management ranks are filled with foreigners, too. As one executive headhunter asserts, "Britain is not by any stretch of the imagination a chauvinistic nation. [In contrast,] French business is dominated by graduates of the grandes écoles, and the Americans are very monocultural."[6]

In terms of the adjustment difficulties they pose for U.S. employees, the regions of the world rank as follows, from the most to the least difficult:[7]

- Africa
- Middle East
- Far East
- South America
- Eastern Europe/Russia
- Western Europe/Scandinavia
- Australia and New Zealand

What Cultural Differences Interest Managers?

Let's next examine some of the key cultural differences that you should be aware of when you interact with foreign nationals in business. We will be using nationality as our unit of analysis, but of course we should keep in mind that this approach is imperfect. Within any country, individual behavioral patterns will span a wide range, and subcultures exist. Perhaps you are familiar with U.S. subcultures that are themselves quite different from the predominant culture, for example. Therefore, in any cross-cultural interaction, you should use cultural knowledge not to make judgments, but to form hypotheses about the behavior you observe.

Here are some examples of the important cultural differences you may encounter.

Perceptual Differences

Perceptual differences include those posed by high and low context cultures and monochronic and polychronic cultures.

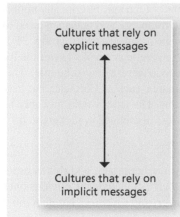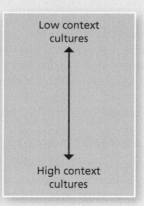

FIGURE 8.1

High Context versus Low Context Cultures

Sources: J. Demorgon, and M. Molz, "Bedingungen und Auswirkungen der Analyse von Kultur(en) und interkulturellen Interaktionen," in A. Thomas, (ed.) Psychologie interkulturellen Handelns, (Göttingen: Hofgrefe, 1996):43-105; E. Hall, *Beyond Culture,* (New York: Doubleday, 1976).

HIGH AND LOW CONTEXT CULTURES When interacting with others, people from **high context cultures** rely extensively on situational cues such as physical context, body language and status, whereas people from **low context cultures** rely extensively on explicit codes, especially the spoken and written word.[8] Which characterizes Americans, do you think? Here's a hint: People from high context cultures emphasize relationships and empathy, whereas people from low context cultures emphasize sending and receiving accurate messages.[9]

The United States is, of course, a low context culture, along with Canada, Germany, Switzerland, the Scandinavian countries, and Great Britain. High context cultures include Japan, China, Korea, Mexico, and the Arab countries. For more comparisons, see Figure 8.1.

Unless they recognize and accept their differences, individuals from low context cultures may get frustrated with those from high context cultures. Problems occur when high context types insist upon spending time building relationships, won't "get down to business," and won't "put it in writing." Because they need to establish the social context of their relationships, people from high context cultures exchange significantly more messages and offers during e-business negotiations than people from low context cultures.[10] For their part, people from high context cultures may find those from low context cultures to be pushy and impersonal, and, unless the low context individuals change their ways, they are unlikely to trust them. The failure to recognize differences in cultural context and adjust their own behaviors is a major reason why expatriate leaders, in particular, fail in their international assignments.[11]

MONOCHRONIC AND POLYCHRONIC CULTURES Cultures can also be described in terms of **polychronicity**, the preference for having multiple activities occurring at the same time, versus **monochronicity**, the preference for scheduling tasks separately and for focusing on just one task at a time.[12] These have been referred to respectively as "harmonic time vision" and "clock time vision." [13] Polychronic cultures emphasize involving people and completing transactions, whereas monochronic cultures emphasize adhering to schedules.

In the former, individuals prefer to organize activities by scheduling two or more events at one time, whereas in the latter they prefer to schedule only one event at a time. In either case, individuals believe that their preference is the best way to do things.

Both individuals and their cultures can be characterized in this way.[14] Individual North Americans are said to be monochronic relative to Latin Americans, for example. Time for North Americans is an important commodity, to be measured and valued, whereas in Latin America it is fluid and flexible. Interestingly, Japanese favor monochronicity when using technology and when dealing with non-Japanese, but favor polychronicity in almost everything else.[15]

high context cultures
Cultures in which people rely extensively on situational cues such as physical context, body language and status when interacting with others.

low context cultures
Cultures in which people rely extensively on explicit codes, especially the spoken and written word, when interacting with others.

polychronicity
The preference for having multiple activities occurring at the same time.

monochronicity
The preference for scheduling tasks separately and for focusing on just one task at a time.

As you can imagine, the awareness of different perceptions of time may be critically important for global teams, especially those that meet in virtual environments, and managers need to appreciate the different time perceptions that may exist among the members of their group.[16] For example, a typical American way to run a teleconference is to create separate blocks of time for discussion and decision making, and require participants to adhere to the schedule. This approach may work well with people from monochronic cultures, such as Germans, but may annoy those from polychronic cultures, such as Saudi Arabians. The latter would probably be uncomfortable with a tightly scheduled agenda and would be less disciplined in sticking to it.

Nonverbal Differences

In cross-cultural relationships, nonverbal behaviors are always important, and this is especially true in high context cultures. In business, nonverbal behaviors include the obvious ones such as hand gestures, posture, facial expressions, eye contact, and touching, but also more subtle ones such as interpersonal distance, walking behavior, use of cosmetics, and silence.[17] Nonverbal differences may also include contextual factors such as architecture or graphic symbols (for example, the pictures indicating the men's room and the women's room).

Each nonverbal behavior sends a message, and, in a foreign culture, the message must be interpreted with care. Each communication can mean 1) something different in the other culture than it does in yours; 2) nothing in your culture, but something in theirs; or 3) the same thing in their culture as in yours. For example, the A-Ok gesture as used in the United States means that things are great, but in Japan it signifies money, and in Brazil it is an obscenity. In Japan, scratching one's head and saying "saa" suggests embarrassment, whereas to an American this behavior signals nothing.[18]

Differences in Attitudes and Values

FUNDAMENTAL VALUES ACROSS THE WORLD Are we moving toward a uniform McWorld, in which Western cultural values dominate? Probably not. A longitudinal study of world values including 65 societies representing 75 percent of the world's population suggests that economic development is certainly associated with shifts away from rigid values toward values that are increasingly rational, tolerant, trusting, and participatory.[19] However, the study also tells us that the broad cultural heritage of a society remains. That is, whether a society has its roots in, for example, Protestantism, Roman Catholicism, Orthodoxy, Confucianism, or Communism continues to affect its culture despite modernization through economic growth.

Take a look at the World Values Survey Global Cultural Map (Figure 8.2) to see which countries are most like each other. On the map, proximity suggests similarity.

The map arrays cultures on two sets of values. The vertical axis represents traditional versus industrialized values. Traditional values include, among other things, strong religious ties, an emphasis on family, and favorable attitudes toward army rule, whereas industrialized values are the opposite. The horizontal axis represents survival values versus self-expression values. Survival values include the belief that men make better political leaders than women, dissatisfaction with household financial status, and rejection of foreigners, homosexuals, and people with AIDS. Self-expression values are the opposite.

TABLE 8.3 Out There. . .

In which culture . . .

. . .do people move their head from side to side to show they are listening and agreeing with you?

. . .would you be likely to encounter a manager sleeping during meetings?

. . .do people often say "I'll call you" but do not really mean it?

. . .would you be likely to encounter very long periods of silence after you ask someone a question?

. . .is it extremely rude to show the soles of your shoes?

Answers to Table 8.3: India, Japan, the United States, Japan, any Muslim culture

FIGURE 8.2

World Values Survey Global Cultural Map

Source: R. Inglehart and W. E. Baker, "Modernization, Cultural Change and the Persistence of Traditional Values," *American Sociological Review* 26, February 2000: 29. Reprinted by permission of Ronald Inglehart.

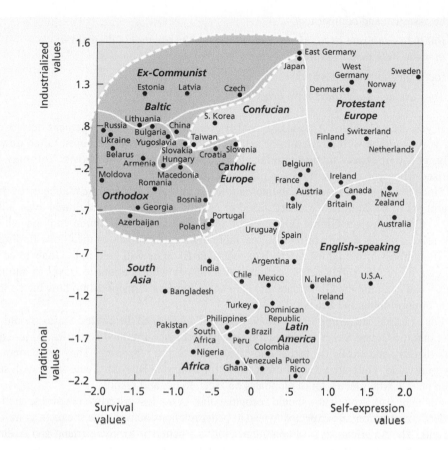

As you can see, richer countries rank relatively high on both industrialized and self-expression values. Note, however, that the United States is more traditional than many cultures in Europe.

THE VALUE OF WORK IN A PERSON'S LIFE Work is but one of life's activities. Can you count on your employees to be committed to it? When managing in another culture, it is useful to know how important work is to your employees compared with other aspects of their lives.

For example, work is much more important in the lives of Japanese than in the lives of the Germans or British.[20] As a manager you could expect to demand more of your employees' time if your company is in Japan.

VALUES IN THE WORKPLACE Understanding cultural differences in the values people use and express at work is also important. For example, understanding these differences helps companies develop strategies for moving employees between cultures, and for cultivating global leadership talent.

The first major study to examine such differences was Geert Hofstede's analysis of IBM employees from 40 countries, which we discussed in detail in Chapter 2.[21] Based on Hofstede's research,[22] it is known that, relative to managers in other countries, American managers tend to:

- place some value on equality.

  On Hofstede's power distance dimension, they rate below average.

- enjoy to some extent the challenge posed by business uncertainties.

  On the uncertainty avoidance dimension they rate below average.

- emphasize and reward individual rather than group effort.

  They rate high on individualism.

■ be assertive and competitive.

But they don't rate as highly as some others on the toughness dimension: they are only somewhat tough.

■ focus on short term paybacks.

They are definitely short-term oriented.

If you are an average American manager going on a tour of management duty overseas, you would be well advised to be self-conscious about these attributes. Often unwittingly, you will expect to find similar characteristics among your hosts. You may be surprised when you discover they see the world quite differently.

Since the Hofstede research, an international study of 18,000 middle managers by 150 researchers in 62 countries was organized to profile world business cultures even more fully.[23] Called Project Globe, this research identifies nine work dimensions on which work-related values differ worldwide. See Table 8.4 for a summary of the Globe findings.

The authors of the Globe research expect their findings will help individuals to communicate more effectively across cultures. A manager who is about to travel to another country can examine the Globe data and gain some important insights into how the people in that country think and behave.

For example, according to the Globe findings, a visitor to the United States should be aware that the United States is among the high performance-oriented countries. Americans speak directly and explicitly and employ lots of facts and reasoning. They are economically motivated. They are very different from, for example, Russians, who view with suspicion people who place a lot of emphasis on facts, logic, and results.

For their part, Americans should recognize that in the less assertive countries, such as Sweden, conversations are expected to lead to better relations between the speakers as well as to results. The American style of communication is a better fit for Switzerland and Austria, where the process of communication is highly structured and formal. In these countries, meetings are planned in advance, with a clear agenda. Messages are expected to describe explicit procedures. As compared with Sweden, there is less emphasis on relationship building.

CORRUPTION A dark side of cultural differences in business values is the prospect of discovering more corruption than you are used to, including bribery and other types of unfair business practices. To illustrate, the Transparency International Corruption Perceptions Index charts levels of corruption in 133 countries. Although the index focuses on the abuse of public office for private gain, it has clear implications for the private sector. In particular, U.S. managers have to be wary of such illegal activities as the use of payoffs to government officials. (See Table 8.5.)

Personality Differences

Some researchers are curious about the relationship between culture and personality. For example, a study of 13,118 students in 31 countries suggests that the relationship of self-esteem to life satisfaction is stronger in individualistic countries than in collectivist countries.[24] This is because in collectivist countries the self plays a less prominent role in the lives of individuals. Another study suggests that the Big Five personality trait of openness/adventurousness predicts success in cross-cultural training performance.[25] Studies like these may eventually provide the building blocks for a thorough knowledge of the relationship between personality and culture. Certainly many personality tests, including the Big Five inventory, do have cross-cultural validity,[26] and can be used for this purpose.

Even so, a concern among theorists has been that using personality inventories developed in one culture to measure behavior in a different culture is problematic. Who is to know whether the culture being measured behaves at all like the culture in which the test was created? Probably it is better to develop tests within a culture so they can be shown to measure what actually matters there. Recently researchers have developed a test of personality factors related to job performance and validated it with 2,000 individuals, primarily managers, in 13 countries.[27] The results suggest that the test, called the Global Measure of

TABLE 8.4 Work Values in Global Perspective

Dimension	Cultures low on this dimension. . .	Cultures high on this dimension. . .
Institutional emphasis on collectivism versus individualism: *To what extent does the society foster group activities rather than individual autonomy?*	Value autonomy and individual freedom and base rewards on individual performance. Value self-interest more strongly than the collective good. Examples: Argentina, Greece, Italy	Value group harmony and cooperation and use rewards to recognize the group instead of the individual. People are motivated by others' satisfaction. Examples: Japan, South Korea, Sweden
Future orientation: *To what extent does the society encourage future-oriented behaviors such as planning, investing in the future, and delaying gratification?*	Emphasize instant gratification and shorter horizons for planning. Examples: Argentina, Italy, Russia	Save for the future and emphasize longer time-frames for planning. Examples: The Netherlands, Singapore, Switzerland
Assertiveness: *To what extent does the society encourage its members to be tough, confrontational, assertive and competitive rather than modest and tender?*	Value cooperative relations, harmony and loyalty, and show sympathy for the weak. Examples: Sweden, New Zealand	Value competition and winners. Examples: Austria, U.S.
Power distance: *To what degree do members of a society expect power to be unequally shared?*	Expect less differentiation between people who have power and those who do not. Favor stronger participation in decision making. Examples: Denmark, the Netherlands	Expect obedience toward superiors and clearly distinguish between people and power with status and people without it. Examples: Russia, Spain, Thailand
Performance orientation: *To what extent does the society encourage performance improvement and excellence?*	Emphasize loyalty and belonging, are uncomfortable experiencing feedback, and pay attention to a person's family and background rather than performance. Competition is associated with defeat. Examples: Argentina, Italy, Russia	Have a "can-do" attitude and believe in taking the initiative. They prefer a direct, explicit style of communication and tend to have a sense of urgency. Examples: Hong Kong, Singapore, United States
In-group collectivism: *To what extent do members of a society take pride in membership in small groups such as their family and circle of close friends, and the organizations in which they are employed?*	Do not give family members and close friends any form of special treatment, and people do not feel an obligation to ignore rules or procedures to take care of close friends. Examples: Denmark, Sweden, New Zealand	Take pride in their families and in their employing organizations. Being a member of a family and of a close group of friends—an in-group—is very important and family members and close friends ends have strong expectations of each other. Examples: China, India, Iran
Humane orientation: *What is the degree to which the society encourages and rewards individuals for being fair, altruistic, generous, caring, and kind to others?*	Motivate using power and material possessions, and self-enhancement is important. Assertive styles of conflict resolution are preferred, and people are expected to solve their own problems. Examples: France, Singapore, West Germany	Value human relations, sympathy, and support for others—especially the weak. Individuals are expected to care for others. People are friendly, sensitive and tolerant, and value harmony. Examples: Ireland, Malaysia, the Philippines
Uncertainty avoidance: *To what extent do people seek orderliness, consistency, structure, formalized procedures, and laws in their daily lives to alleviate the unpredictability of future events?*	Have a strong tolerance of ambiguity and uncertainty, are used to less structure in their lives, and are less concerned about following rules and procedures. Examples: Greece, Russia, Venezuela	Prefer orderliness and consistency, structured lifestyles, clear social expectations, and many rules and laws. Examples: Germany, Sweden and Switzerland
Gender differentiation: *To what extent does the society maximize gender role differences?*	Offer women relatively high status and authority; men and women have similar levels of education. Examples: Denmark, Hungary, Poland	Give men higher social status. Few women have authority. Examples: China, Egypt, South Korea

Source: Based on information in M. Javidan and R. J. House, "Cultural Acumen for the Global Manager: Lessons from Project Globe," *Organizational Dynamics* 29 (4), Spring 2001:289–305.

TABLE 8.5 International Corruption Perceptions Index 2004

This table includes only the United States's top 10 trading partners and other countries of interest. A higher CPI signifies that a country is perceived as less corrupt.

Country Rank	Country	CPI 2004 score
1	Finland	9.7
5	Singapore	9.3
11	United Kingdom	8.6
12	Canada ◄	8.5
15	Germany ◄	8.2
17	Ireland	7.5
17	United States	7.5
22	France ◄	7.1
22	Spain	7.1
24	Japan ◄	6.9
26	Israel	6.4
28	Uruguay	6.2
29	United Arab Emirates ◄	6.1
35	Taiwan ◄	5.6
39	Malaysia ◄	5.0
42	Italy	4.8
44	South Africa	4.6
47	South Korea ◄	4.5
59	Brazil	3.9
62	Cuba	3.7
64	Mexico ◄	3.6
71	Saudi Arabia	3.4
71	China ◄	3.4
114	Venezuela	2.3
133	Indonesia	2.0
145	Bangladesh	1.5

◄ = A Top Ten U.S. Trading Partner, January 2004

Source: Transparency International, "Reprinted from the International Corruption Perception Index, 2004 Copyright. *Transparency International: the global coalition against corruption.* Used with permission. For more information, visit http://www.transparency.org."

Personality (GPI), is as cross-culturally transferable as the Big Five test. In the future, it will be used to assess employees for selection, development, coaching, and feedback purposes.

Differences in Psychological Contracts

The ability to understand cross-cultural differences in the psychological contracts between employees and their companies is another skill in the international manager's repertoire.[28] Because the relationship between the company and the employee is voluntary, it is important to know what exactly keeps the two together.

For example, what is the nature of the exchange between the two parties under conditions in which the employee has some degree of personal freedom? Also, how does society itself influence this exchange? Differences in societies create differences in psychological contracts and work behavior.[29] Among the main societal influences on work behavior are the laws governing the employer–employee relationship, the existence of legal protections for employees, the existence of a market economy, the power of the government relative to business, and the right to engage in collective bargaining.

One concern is that cultural differences in psychological contracts may lead to cultural conflicts within a company. Consider the problem that occurred when the American Chrysler Company merged with Germany's Daimler-Benz, creating Daimler Chrysler.[30] In the U.S. company, executives were receiving multimillion-dollar compensation packages, a normal circumstance for the American culture. But a German executive refused to accept such compensation, pointing out that in his small hometown, such a large pay gap between him and his neighbors would cause great bitterness. (What he actually said was, "In the small town where I live, if I went to the market after someone had said I made $20 million . . . they'd destroy my house."[31]) In societies like Germany and Japan, where psychological contracts between employee and employers are influenced by social norms aimed at maintaining some status equality, companies that want to reward high performers often give perks instead of money.

In another example, consider the conflict generated by the differing psychological contracts in Australia and the United States. In the United States, notions of equality, justice and fairness translate into equality of opportunity but not equality of outcomes. Individuals have equal opportunity to find their way into a social system that is then stratified into many levels. In Australia, on the other hand, equality means seeking greater equality of outcome in terms of a high minimum standard of living for *all*. Australians admire a person who overcomes adversity and remains modest more than they admire high achievers or leaders.[32] An American leader working in Australia might offend his or her coworkers by demanding a fancy office and pursuing a lavish lifestyle.

Of course, there are many other structural factors in a society that influence how people interact. Though just as important as those we have just discussed, they are beyond the scope of this book. They include the sizes and types of companies present in the culture. They also include the nature of competition, intercompany relationships, business–government relationships, and laws and legal systems. The international manager who expects to partner with other nationalities or live in another country must study all of these. For example, it is essential to understand socialism and its effects on commerce if you are going to do business in Scandinavia, and it is essential to understand how centralized governments work if you are going to do business in The People's Republic of China.

What Do You Need to Know About Developing Business Relationships with America's Most Important Trading Partners?

Among the major countries with which the United States does business are Canada, China, Mexico, Japan, and Germany. See how well you can do on the test in Table 8.6, which asks you to match one cultural characteristic of each of these countries with the proper country.

After completing the test in Table 8.6, read the brief descriptions of what you can expect in terms of cultural differences when doing business in these countries. The descriptions are included here to alert you to some possible differences you will encounter across cultures, rather than to provide an in-depth portrait of each culture. They are based on the Project Globe research as well as on what country experts say about doing business there.

When going abroad for business, you should always read up on a country. Hopefully, your company will help you learn as much as possible by providing cross-cultural training and contacts in the culture.

Canada

Canada is a multicultural society in which the two dominant subcultures are the English Canadians and the French Canadians. Other strong ethnic groups are Asian, Dutch, German, Italian, Polish, Scandinavian, and Ukrainian. In the French sector, located in Quebec province, the official language is French, whereas in the rest of Canada it is English.

Like the United States, Canada is a relatively low-context culture, in which individual achievement and individual welfare are more important than the welfare of the group or

TABLE 8.6 Do You Know as Much as the Project Globe Research Team?

Project Globe tells us which countries are high and which are low on nine dimensions. Match the country with the dimension. For each dimension there is only one correct answer.

Canada	1. One of the most assertive countries in the world.
Mexico	2. Neither high nor low on any characteristic.
China	3. One of the most future-oriented countries in the world.
Japan	4. One of the countries most likely to avoid uncertainty.
Germany	5. One of the most in-group collective countries of the world.
United States	6. One of the most performance oriented countries in the world.

Source: Based on information in M. Javidan and R. J. House, "Cultural Acumen for the Global Manager: Lessons from Project Globe," *Organizational Dynamics* 29 (4), Spring 2001:289–305.

Answers: 1. Japan, 2. Mexico, 3. Canada, 4. Germany (former West), 5. China, 6. United States.

maintaining group priorities.[33] Employees in Canada, like those in the United States, are highly individualistic, relatively short-term oriented, and about average in terms of aggressiveness and competitiveness.[34] Canadians are said to suffer from national identity anxiety because of their close proximity to the powerful United States. Certainly their fears of over-dependence on the U.S. economy are well-founded, as about 85 percent of their exports go to the United States.[35]

Canadians are friendly and conservative. They are more likely than people in the United States to practice the formalities of etiquette. French Canadians are more attentive to protocol than are English Canadians.

The People's Republic of China

China is highly export-oriented and, since the mid-1990s, has been second only to the United States in receiving foreign direct investment.[36] According to its government, thousands of companies, mostly in manufacturing, have been started either by direct investment or joint ventures. As China develops a viable legal system, investment may grow. In 2004, for example, a new law reformed the granting of licensing rights. It remains to be seen how well it will be enforced.

Chinese companies are likely to be strongly paternalistic, basing their practices in part on those of the state-owned enterprises that once monopolized the country. For example, it is not unusual for them to provide housing, cafeterias, entertainment, and basic education. At the same time, it is not unusual for companies to ignore the laws that ostensibly provide protection for workers in the private sector, such as those requiring contributions to social security programs or those requiring collective employee representation.

In the case of a toy company employing 30,000 workers in a province near Hong Kong, managers take a patronizing view of the employees, saying they do not want to work hard to better themselves. Most employees in the plants are young women. Managers speak to them as parents and use substantial amounts of punishment. Employees appear to be more compliant than committed.

When doing business with Chinese, it is important to focus not on the individual Chinese person but rather on the group. Because it is one of the most in-group collec-

CHAPTER 8 • CROSS-CULTURAL RELATIONSHIPS   **221**

tive countries, avoid self-centered "I" conversations. Chinese may also be more reserved than North Americans, both in speech and gestures. Among the more difficult aspects of the culture for Americans are the concepts of face and guanxi.[37] Face refers to the combination of dignity, self-respect, prestige, and one's social standing and position as perceived by others. It is important that Westerners use caution when hosting nationals, especially in public, to preserve and enhance face. Guanxi refers to relationships that imply the exchange of favors and gifts, and is commonly practiced in Chinese business.

Here's a cultural oddity: As recently as 2002, height requirements for jobs and even school admissions have been common in China.[38] For example, Shanghai's East China University of Politics and Law requires male students to be at least 1.70 meters (5 feet 6 inches) and females 1.60 meters (5 feet ½ inches). It is thought that height is important in jobs that carry authority and in leisure industry jobs where physical attractiveness is a bonus.

Mexico

From the 1940s to the mid-1980s Mexico protected domestic firms from international competition by severely restricting imports.[39] Wealth continued to be concentrated in a small proportion of the population, and throughout the economy, monopolies controlled important segments. These influences have led to several factors that characterize the Mexican work culture.

One factor is the existence of an invisible caste system. This is evident in commercials for all consumer products, which typically exclude brown faces. At the same time, most Latin Americans deny the prevalence of any caste system.

Another factor is that Mexican management decision making is more paternalistic, authoritarian, and hierarchical than in the United States, and encouraging participation is seen as a weakness. Mexican firms are almost always managed by an owner and a team of relatives or close friends. In choosing someone to fill a position, family loyalties are valued over management skills.

In the Mexican legal system, litigation is rare and judges are seldom bound by precedents. Business is based so highly on personal relationships that laws are enforced according to political influence. For example, it may be impossible to collect a debt. In this atmosphere, developing personal relationships is essential so that one is not cheated.

Mexicans believe it is more important to be nice than to be objective, and that it is all right to lie if people's feelings are preserved. Whereas Americans and Canadians tend to see Mexicans as emotional and undisciplined, Mexicans tend to see Americans and Canadians as emotionless, insensitive, and manipulative.

Japan

Japan is the business world's toughest culture. It ranks number one in being aggressive, competitive, and interested in acquiring money and things.[40] Like Canada and the United States it is a low power-distance culture hostile to institutions in which power is distributed in a highly unequal fashion. The salary ratio between executives and lower-level employees is relatively low.

Japan is long-term oriented, and expects both close and long-lasting relationships with service providers based on reliability, responsiveness, and empathy. Japanese strongly prefer to avoid uncertainty. They respect propriety and order. They are also relatively collectivist. Their families are closer than those in the United States , but not as close as those in China.

Japanese base interpersonal relationships on the concept of amae, a term that cannot be directly translated but which means roughly that although status should be taken into account, the person of higher status should behave in a paternal fashion toward the person of lower status. Thus, a boss is as much a father figure as a mentor, and is expected to be concerned for an employee's family. Japanese also respect seniority and age. Maintaining face is also important.

TABLE 8.7 Before You Travel to Japan. . .

If you were traveling to Japan, what aspects of the Japanese culture should you study? Here is a partial list:

Protocol around using the meishi (business card)

Nonverbal language

- Shaking hands versus bowing
- Typical Japanese gestures
- How the Japanese use silence, especially in negotiating

The importance of using shokainin (introducers)

The role of "yes" and "no" in Japanese, including ways to avoid saying "no"

How Japanese view women and other races

How Japanese use consensus decision making

The importance of "face" and preventing "loss of face"

How and why individuals separate their public posturing from their private thoughts (tatemae and honne)

Etiquette, including seating arrangements, table manners, and gift-giving

---

Japanese and Americans differ in the amount of personal disclosure they are comfortable with. To establish trust, Americans often reveal progressively more details about themselves, whereas Japanese maintain more personal privacy. As a result Americans may see Japanese as secretive and aloof, and Japanese may see Americans as stupidly blunt.

In groups and organizations, Japanese deemphasize the individual. In fact, a common Japanese saying is "The nail that sticks up gets hammered down." New recruits to Japanese companies spend many years working as equals on a team before a few are chosen to be leaders. If you were to travel to Japan to do business, you would need to learn a great deal about the culture. See Table 8.7 for a list of some key cultural characteristics.

The Federal Republic of Germany

Germany is a highly structured society.[41] Modern German business practices are influenced by a number of factors, including laws that give workers the right to codetermine many business practices, strong government involvement, issues relating to integrating the former East and West sectors financially and culturally, and regulations imposed under the EU (European Union). Business and government work closely together. The government even has control or equity participation in hundreds of firms, and there are many joint government and business enterprises.

Germany is a vast welfare state that supports its workers with five or six weeks of paid vacation, liberal pensions, bonuses, and medical and dental care. In recent years Germany has had a slow-growing economy, and interest in changing generous government social programs and protective labor laws has grown.[42] People in the eastern part of the country are significantly less satisfied with their opportunities than those in the west, suggesting immigration from east to west will continue.[43]

Germans as individuals tend to be organized, disciplined, and unspontaneous. They are also very private, emphasizing close family ties and making a strong distinction between acquaintances and friends.

When doing business, Germans are formal and conservative. They are also title conscious, placing importance on using the correct title when addressing someone. Promises made verbally or in print are legally binding, prompting some of the reticence for which Germans are known.

What Characterizes the Successful Individual Working Overseas?

In a speech to GE employees, Jack Welch, the iconic leader of General Electric, once pointed out, "The Jack Welch of the future cannot be me. I spent my entire career in the United States. The next head of General Electric will be somebody who spent time in Bombay, in Hong Kong, in Buenos Aires. We have to send our best and brightest overseas and make sure they have the training that will allow them to be the global leaders who will make GE flourish in the future."[44]

Here is a summary of the personal characteristics of the individual who is likely to be effective working overseas:[45]

- **General professional qualifications**

    Appropriate educational background and experience

    Commitment to the overseas job

    Recognition that professional and technical skills may have to be modified to fit local conditions

- **Interpersonal skills**

    Openness to the ideas, beliefs and points of view of others

    Respect for others; attentiveness and concern; and the ability to acknowledge and respond to others in ways that make them feel valued

    Good listening skills with an ability to accurately perceive the needs and feelings of others

    Relationship-building skills; an ability to maintain relationships; trusting and cooperative

    Calm in the face of interpersonal conflict or stress

    Sensitivity to and awareness of local social, political, and cultural realities

- **Individual traits**

    Assertive and quick to act or to propose a plan of action

    Self-confidence with regard to personal goals and judgment

    Frank and open in dealing with others

    Flexible and non-ethnocentric

    Extraverted—outgoing, enjoys people

- **Realistic pre-departure expectations**

    Realistically aware of the constraints and barriers to effective performance but fairly optimistic about success

    Some concerns about living overseas

    Positive expectations for a rewarding experience

- **If married, has a spouse who. . .**

    Has similar qualifications

- **Language ability**

Inability to speak the local language is perhaps the greatest cultural barrier an individual faces. Even when the importance of language is recognized and individuals work to learn the language of their host culture, language still poses a formidable barrier. One reason is that literal translation so often fails. For example, qualifying words like "terrible" and "fantastic" may or may not convey the meaning or level of intensity that they convey in your culture. Another reason is that language reflects aspects of the culture that may be unknown to you. For example, in Japan it is unacceptable to say "No," which disturbs interpersonal harmony, and if you use this word, despite being an American, you will be considered rude. In China, the language itself reflects the fact that Chinese organize objects in a more relational and less categorical way than do European Americans.[46]

How Can You Develop Cross-Cultural Skills?

How do you develop the attitudes and skills that are necessary for working cross-culturally? The possibilities range from performing self-assessments, to attending cross-cultural training, to gaining international experience.

Use the Big Five Personality Theory

To begin with, you should assess whether you would enjoy working in cross-cultural situations. Recall from an earlier chapter our discussion of the Big Five personality dimensions: 1) Extraversion versus introversion, 2) Adventurous versus traditional, 3) Agreeable versus tough-minded, 4) Conscientious versus undirected, 5) Emotionality (also called neuroticism) versus stability.

Does your score on the Big Five personality traits suggest you are adventurous and agreeable, or traditional and tough-minded? In general, an adventurous person, a person who is open to experience, is likely to enjoy working in exotic new places, whereas a traditionalist will not.[47] An agreeable person is also relatively adaptable in new cultures, and he or she is more likely to pick up on cultural differences than a tough-minded individualist.

However, what would happen if an agreeable person were plunked down into a tough-minded culture? The stress of adapting there might be high. Obviously it is a good idea to consider the fit of your predispositions to a particular culture before you pursue an assignment there.

For example, an expatriate living in Taiwan, a Confucian culture like many of those in east and southeast Asia, must adapt to its collectivistic beliefs. Such a culture directs behavior toward the good of the group, rather than to that of the individual. Its citizens tend to be relationship oriented. Inequality between people in different power positions is seen as relatively desirable (in contrast with the United States). Preserving harmony is also highly desirable. Based on these factors alone, U.S. expatriates in Taiwan would be expected to experience sharp cultural contrasts.

A study of expatriate adjustment in Taiwan examined which Big Five traits predicted a good adjustment to each of three factors: the work environment, interpersonal interactions with local Taiwanese, and general living conditions.[48] It found the following: When it comes to adjustment to the Taiwanese work environment, expatriates who are adventurous do well. When it comes to interpersonal interactions, extraversion and agreeableness predict success, probably because they help a person develop friendship ties. Finally, when it comes to general living adjustment, including adapting to the cost of living, shopping, food, and housing, extraverts and the adventurous adjust well to living in Taiwan.

Understand Your Tolerance for Ambiguity

Historically, a variety of tests have been developed to assess cross-cultural adaptability.[49] These include measures of self awareness ("self-monitoring"), self-confidence, and the predisposition to culture shock. Some of these factors are now encompassed by the Big Five. However, one classic personality test that has been used fairly often deserves special mention. The test measures a trait called **tolerance for ambiguity**.[50] It asks people the extent to which they agree with statements like:

tolerance for ambiguity
The extent to which someone enjoys complexity and novelty, and tolerates problems in which there is no clear answer.

1. A person who leads an even, regular life in which few surprises or unexpected happenings arise, really has a lot to be grateful for.
2. It is more fun to tackle a complicated problem than to solve a simple one.
3. People who fit their lives to a schedule probably miss most of the joy of living.
4. Many of our most important decisions are based upon insufficient information.
5. Teachers or supervisors who hand out vague assignments give a chance for one to show initiative and originality.

If you strongly agree with statements 2 through 5, and disagree with statement 1, you are likely to tolerate ambiguity well. You are more likely to enjoy complexity and novelty, and to tolerate problems in which there is no clear answer. On the other hand, if you disagree with these kinds of statements, you are likely to have a high intolerance for ambiguity and you are less likely than others to enjoy relating cross-culturally.

Evaluate Differences in Values

In addition, pay attention to any differences in values between yourself and the nationals of other countries. Researchers are beginning to discover that certain differences in values can be particularly problematic for expatriate adjustment. In particular, people whose identity rests on values such as equality and social justice risk harming their self-image in cultures that do not hold similar values.[51] They may find working in such cultures to be particularly disturbing on a personal level.

In like fashion, foreign nationals who must adjust to the U.S. culture must also pay attention to the different values they find here. For example, they are not likely to be familiar with U.S. laws and customs relating to sexual harassment in the workplace. A Swedish pharmaceutical firm had to pay millions of dollars in damages to more than 300 women who had been sexually harassed at the company's Illinois plant.[52] A Japanese company was sued after it recommended that a woman claiming sexual harassment confront her harasser alone in his office to work things out.

Develop Cultural Intelligence

Some researchers suggest that to adapt well to new cultures, as well as to manage multicultural teams and in multicultural environments, individuals need to develop **cultural intelligence**.[53] This is the ability to "think about thinking," and to develop and expand your behavioral repertoire, often on the spot.

cultural intelligence
The ability to think "about thinking" and to develop and expand one's behavioral repertoire.

When interacting with a person from a different culture, people with high cultural intelligence do three things. First, they observe a variety of cues to the other person's behavior and assemble them to make sense of what the other person is actually experiencing Next, they have the motivation to persist in their attempts to understand the other person, despite receiving mixed signals and being confused. Third, they choose and execute the right actions to respond appropriately.

As an overall strategy, when working with people from other cultures, learn to use the following approaches:[54]

- When communicating cross-culturally, assume that differences exist until you learn otherwise.
- Suspend judgment: Focus on describing to yourself the behaviors you observe, rather than on evaluating them.
- Do your best to empathize with the people you encounter, assessing who they are, how they became who they are, and how their culture has shaped them.
- Finally, develop hypotheses about the causes of their behavior, and keep testing those hypotheses with them and others, paying careful attention to their reaction and feedback, until your understanding of the culture deepens.

Understand Culture Shock

On some international assignments, whether to an unfamiliar region of one's own country or to another culture altogether, employees are stressed by being in a cultural environment in which business practices, organizational dynamics, and interpersonal life are new and different. In these new cultures, they may experience **culture shock** (also called "acculturative stress"), which is a sense of disorientation in interpreting the myriad unfamiliar environmental, business, and social cues they encounter.[55] For example, a U.S. businessperson in Japan may find that the consensus-oriented, nonconfrontational Japanese are an enigma. Feeling confused and stressed, she or he may not be as productive as expected. [56]

culture shock
A sense of disorientation in interpreting the myriad unfamiliar environmental, business, and social cues one encounters in a new culture; "acculturative stress."

On long-term assignments, businesspeople entering into a new culture go through a predictable set of stages of culture shock.[57] At first they see the culture from their own ethnocentric perspective, judging it by their own values and beliefs. Like tourists, in this "contact" stage they tend to be curious and euphoric.

After some period of time, however, they tire and may withdraw into their own private world. In this "disintegration" stage they experience confusion and disorientation as they recognize the significant differences between their own and the host culture. Whereas previously they saw the cultural differences as interesting, now they find them annoying. They get worn down by having to work hard to accomplish what, at home, are simple tasks.

FIGURE 8.3

**The Culture Shock
Curve**

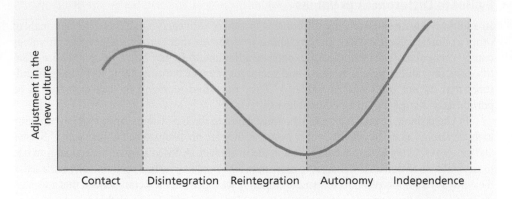

During the "reintegration" stage, people may become angry and suspicious and reject the cultural differences by stereotyping and judging the other culture. They overcompensate by asserting their own cultural values.

In the fourth stage, "autonomy" individuals begin to accept the legitimacy of the cultural differences and are less defensive and more relaxed. One symptom of their increasing comfort level is that they begin to communicate nonverbally in the style of the new culture.

Finally, people reach a stage of "independence" in the culture, in which they actually value and appreciate the cultural differences and can express trust, humor, and love in the new setting.

Business travelers who visit another culture for days or weeks typically experience only the first one or two stages of culture shock: They are curious and happy to be there, but they may also become disoriented, confused, or even depressed. However, experienced travelers may avoid culture shock altogether.

Often it is the "trailing spouse," the spouse who follows his or her partner abroad, who experiences the most serious culture shock. As suggested in our opening case for this chapter, the spouse has to deal with many of the issues of family resettlement, including dealing with housing, schools, foods, and transportation, to say nothing of finding amusement. Typically, this spouse must accomplish all this in a language that he or she doesn't know. Meanwhile, the working partner is at the office all day in a relatively busy and supportive setting. He or she enjoys routine, prestige, and interesting challenges.

In recent years, executives have been attracted to China because of its high growth. For their part, Chinese companies have welcomed managers with experience in Western companies, in order to modernize their own management methods and develop their image as global businesses. However, there have been notable failures among non-Chinese executives for such companies as the Bank of China and Jin Jiang Hotels.[58] As usual, the most common reason for failure to succeed in the People's Republic of China is family failure to adjust. Families have particular trouble in Chinese rural settings. However, executives, too, have had some difficulties both fitting into the existing company cultures and moving them from relationship-oriented to performance-oriented. Exceptions to the latter problem are Lenovo, the company that bought IBM's PC division, and CNOOC, the large oil company.

reentry shock
Culture shock that happens in reverse upon returning to one's own culture.

After living abroad for an extended period, some individuals experience **reentry shock**, culture shock that happens in reverse upon repatriation.[59] They find living in their home country to be stressful, at least for some months. Having lived abroad, they are acutely aware of their own culture, and they may not agree with it or like it. They may be bored with colleagues who now seem narrow-minded. They may have lost some prestige on their return home, as well, having enjoyed enhanced prestige in their international position. Once again they must adapt.

Gain Experience

Gaining experience in different cultures is invaluable. Travel to other countries and having international contacts count, but living there for extended periods is even better. The experience of having worked through all of the stages of the culture shock curve is one that cannot be replicated in reading or training. Of course, to gain the full benefit of living abroad, it is important to actually experience the local culture rather than to stay in an enclave of that remains overwhelmingly American.

Experienced internationals know that locating a **cultural interpreter**, a person who can explain the psychological and social basis of local behaviors and attitudes, is important. Often companies that send employees abroad will appoint one or more local employees, in addition to the boss, to fill this role. For longer assignments, too, they are likely to send employees on a preliminary visit to help them determine their fit with the culture. If an employer does not offer these kinds of contacts, it is important that an employee working abroad find them on his or her own.

cultural interpreter
A person who can explain the psychological and social basis of local behaviors and attitudes.

Attend Cross-Cultural Training

Finally, employees can participate in cross-cultural training. Companies are interested in fostering their employees' cross-cultural skills because they know that, for example, sending people on overseas assignments is expensive. One estimate is that cost of a failure—an employee returning home before his or her contract is up—is at least 2.5 times the expatriate's salary.[60] The cost of having an employee fail to do a job well after starting the assignment is also high.[61] Therefore, many companies today select their international employees based not only on their skills but also on their personality and adaptability. They are also likely to evaluate the adaptability of their spouse and family. And they offer training.

One type of training focuses on developing country-specific knowledge. In a **cultural assimilator**, an individual is presented with a scenario that takes place in the country to which he or she will travel and is asked to describe how he or she would react in such a situation. The cultural assimilator teaches about elements in the culture that are likely to be challenging.

cultural assimilator
A cross-cultural training method in which an individual is presented with a scenario that takes place in the country to which he or she will travel and is asked to describe how he or she would react in such a situation.

Other types of training develop cross-cultural skills that would be applicable in any culture.[62] A variety of role-plays, simulations, and field visits are used to increase awareness of communication differences and other cultural factors. Some of these are included at the end of the chapter.

What Should Companies Do to Support Their Expatriates?

In addition to your personal characteristics and skills, your success as an expatriate depends on your job satisfaction and integration into your new organization.[63] Expatriates who are satisfied in their jobs and better integrated into their new organizations also adjust better cross-culturally.

Thus it is crucial that multinationals put in place human relations policies and practices that will help their expatriates achieve job satisfaction. Also, they should go out of their way to encourage their expatriates to develop strong work-related interpersonal relationships and networks.

How Should You Prepare for a Short-Term International Assignment?

Consider that years-long assignments overseas may be declining, and that it is more likely that you will be asked to make one- or two-week trips to other cultures. You may not have much time to get ready for the trip. What preparation is absolutely necessary? Here are some essentials:

- Learn a dozen key phrases in the host language.
- Learn the essential *faux pas* to avoid.
- Learn the friendly gestures, such as gift-giving, that are expected.
- Learn the key business customs, especially those related to decision making, negotiation, and entertaining.

- If at all possible, identify a cultural interpreter here at home and pick his or her brain.

- In the time you have before departure, learn as much as you can about the country, from its geography to its government and arts. Also learn about the region. There are dozens of books and Web sites available to help you.

- Finally, rest up beforehand, anticipate jet lag, relax and enjoy the trip.

In Conclusion

In today's global business environment, cross-cultural adaptability is a skill that is likely to come in handy. In addition, if you anticipate an international career, or even just one international assignment, it is essential that you assess your own capabilities and get the training you need to adapt in the host culture.

Bon voyage, and

祝您好運 [†]

[†]good luck!

Apply What You Have Learned. . .

World Class Company: Lincoln Electric's Cultural Lessons from International Expansion

Lincoln Electric, one of the world's leading manufacturers of arc-welding products, is famous for its long-term success with an incentive system that ties worker productivity to worker pay.[64] Rather than being given hourly wages or a salary, U.S. factory workers at Lincoln are paid on the basis of how many units they individually produce, and, depending on how much cash the company has at the end of the year, they also earn an annual bonus. The workers are graded twice a year on four performance factors: the quality of their work, the quantity of their work, their dependability, and their cooperation.

Historically, the bonus contributes more than 50 percent of the Lincoln employees' incomes. In many years, hundreds of them have earned $70,000 to $80,000 and some have made more than $100,000. Since employees at Lincoln act much like entrepreneurs, the company can get by with a supervisor-to-worker ratio of 1 to 100. (In most U.S. factories the ratio is 1 to 25.) The company's absentee rate is between 1.5 and 2 percent, and its turnover rate is only 3.5 percent. The average workweek is between 43 and 58 hours. Up until the time it went international, the company had never failed to pay a bonus.

In the late 1980s, facing international competition, Lincoln bought eight plants in Europe and Mexico and built three green-field (new) plants in Brazil, Japan, and Venezuela. As Donald Hastings, former chief executive officer put it, "None of us had any significant international experience. No one on the board, including me, ever seriously challenged [this expansion]. We believed that because we were so successful in the United States, we could be successful anywhere."[65]

Many factors contributed to what eventually became a significant retrenchment internationally for Lincoln, including a world recession and the acquisition of significant debt. Among these factors were cross-cultural misunderstandings and miscalculations. Corporate management had little experience running a complex, international company. And because American managers did not know how to run the foreign operations, the company relied on local expertise.

When Hastings moved to Europe to manage the damage, he discovered that the Lincoln Electric culture had had little influence on the local operations. He held meetings in which each salesman was required to describe his territory and customers, and what he was planning to do to get new business, only to realize that none of them had ever before been required to commit themselves to a plan in front of other people. When he asked his managers to develop a plan for increasing market share, their reaction was that you should never take an account from a competitor because the competitor will in turn take one

away from you. When he went on an announced visit to a plant in Germany, three workers were found sleeping on the job. In addition, people in Japan would not buy Lincoln's products because the company had not taken on a business partner there.

Lincoln set out to turn the situation around. Admitting the company's inadequacies, in the fall of 1993 management scaled down operations in Europe, and closed down their plants in Germany, Brazil, Venezuela, and Japan. At the same time, in the United States they developed new products for sale through Wal-Mart and Home Depot, and they offered special promotions to long-time distributors. While many U.S. companies were downsizing, Lincoln raised its sales goals from $1.8 million to $2.1 million per day, and went from using 75 to 80 percent of its manufacturing capacity to more than 100 percent by hiring new workers.

People dug in. In manufacturing, bottleneck areas were identified and experienced people were asked to do more. Many in the bottleneck areas worked holidays and postponed vacations. Altogether about 450 people gave up 614 weeks of vacation, and some people worked seven days a week for months. Lincoln met and surpassed its sales goals, and even increased market share in countries where it had closed its operations. By the end of 1993, the company was able to increase revenues and profits enough in the United States to pay off its major loans, and the bonus was paid with borrowed money. By mid-1994 its foreign operations were also profitable.

In retrospect, Hastings says, the company should have paid more attention to the strong expressions of concern from employees who had seen some of the risks in the international expansion. Years before the expansion program, the company should have initiated a selection and training program for internationalizing the top management team. Management should have challenged their own assumption that people all over the world would be willing to work harder to enhance their incomes.

Today the company is back on track financially, and it has an internationally experienced board and management team. Its incentive management program has been successfully exported to Mexico. In its unionized plant there, in a culture that disdains piecework, Lincoln introduced the piecework system with two workers. After these two started to make more money than their coworkers, other workers wanted to join the system too. It took two years, but the entire plant finally adopted piecework. In 2004 Lincoln Electric acquired controlling interest in several welding businesses in China.

Discuss

1. List the major cultural problems Lincoln Electric faced when it went international.
2. Describe what Lincoln should have done to forestall these problems.

3. How likely is that companies today would identify and deal with such problems earlier than Lincoln did? What factors would influence this process?

Advice from the Pros

The Internationalable Employee

Lennie Copeland and Lewis Griggs are well known cross-cultural consultants in the United States, and producers of the well known film series *Going International* and *Valuing Diversity.* Here is some of their advice about cross-cultural assignments:

- Some people are not cut out for international work. There is no shame in finding out that you are really better suited to working in Chicago than in Karachi.
- Some people will be happy working in some cultures but not others.
- Curiosity is essential for the international cat. Successful expatriates study the cultural patterns, business norms, and national character of their host countries. They study everything from history and art to politics and economics.
- Successful international candidates have a geocentric (literally "world-focused") view.
- "Flexible" does not mean weak; it means, as the Japanese say, "hard like water"—flowing, bending, but powerful.

- Successful candidates are resourceful, with plenty of internal resources and a willingness to ask for help from others.
- Foreigners will accept your *faux pas* if they sense your sincere goodwill.
- Bring a lively sense of humor.

Source: This advice is drawn from Copeland and Griggs' book *Going International: How to Make Friends and Deal Effectively in the Global Marketplace* (New York: Random House and New American Library, 1985).

Discuss

1. Are you cut out for international work, or not? Explain your answer.
2. What is a geocentric view? Where do you acquire it? Who do you know who really has it?
3. Describe an amusing cross-cultural situation in which you or someone you know has been involved. Why was it funny? Did everyone involved think it was amusing, or were some people uncomfortable?

Gain Experience

I. Culture Shock in the Classroom

Stand up, find a partner and move to a place in the room where furniture does not come between you or get in your way. Talk to each other until your professor asks you to stop. When he or she asks you to stop, freeze in position.

II. Cultural Awareness Exercise

Becoming aware of your own heritage and cultural background as well as your pride in that background makes it easier to see sources of cultural pride in other cultural and ethnic backgrounds. In this exercise, participants are asked to discuss characteristics of their own cultural groups and to identify sources of pride in their own culture, and then to repeat the exercise from the point of view of a member of a different culture.

The purposes of this exercise are:

1. To explore sources of pride in one's cultural background.
2. To identify stereotypes of other cultural groups.
3. To develop appreciation for cultural diversity.

4. To develop empathy with members of disadvantaged groups.

Step 1. The class is divided into as many groups of 10 to 14 as possible, with even numbers in each group. Half of each group should form a circle, facing outwards, with the other half forming a concentric circle, facing inward, paired one-to-one with a member of the inner circle.

Members will discuss each of the following topics for about four minutes, two minutes for each of the partners. At a signal from the instructor, the outer circle shifts one position to the left, creating new pairings.

1. Describe your cultural background. You can define this as narrowly or as broadly as you would like, but try to focus on what distinguishes you culturally from others.
2. Of what aspects of your cultural background are you most proud?

3. Describe some of the customs, rituals, and/or ceremonies associated with your cultural group.
4. Describe a member of your cultural group, excluding members of your family, who is a good role model for others in that cultural group.
5. Describe a situation where you felt out of place as a result of being different from others.

Step 2. Repeat the same process but this time each group is to adopt the identity of another culture. For example, one group might be assigned to respond to the topics from the perspective that every member of the group was Hispanic. As many different cultural groups can be assigned as there are circles in the class. Reassemble the class and discuss the exercise.

Discuss

1. What did you learn about yourself here?
2. What did you learn about other cultures, in general? Specifically?
3. What made you comfortable or uncomfortable?

Source: G. Coombs and Y. Sarason, "Culture Circles: A Cultural Self-Awareness Exercise," *Journal of Management Education 22* (2) April 1998: 218–226. Copyright © 1998 by Sage Publications. Reprinted by permission of Sage Publications, Inc.

III. Intercultural Negotiation

Divide into groups of 5 to 7. The groups will be further divided into Americans and X-ians. By way of introduction to the exercise, all participants should read the following instructions for the Americans.

Briefing Sheet for Americans

You are two (or more) Americans, male and female, both well-known journalists. Both of you have M.A.'s in journalism from recognized schools and have spent several years in international travel and reporting on political, cultural, and artistic subjects in a number of countries.

Never at a loss to detect a possible story, you are pleased to encounter three people in a restaurant in Athens whom you have met once before briefly. You do not remember their names, but do remember that they are from Country X, a rather exotic and unusual place not often visited by foreigners. Country X is one of those places in the world about which there are more legends than facts. It is known, however, to be a society with highly developed arts, literature, and gardens (which are apparently some kind of art form), and with an atmosphere of being inaccessible and not too interested in getting into the world tourism business. One of the intriguing things about which speculation sometimes appears in the Sunday supplements is the X-ian Queen's Garden Festival, which apparently takes place once a year and which no outsider has ever visited or photographed. To be able to attend and photograph the festival, especially to be the first, would be a true journalistic coup.

In this exercise, you will approach the X-ians at their restaurant table and ask to join them. Talk with them about general subjects for about 15 minutes. Then find a pretext to leave the table for one or two minutes and decide together what would be the best way to approach your real subject: Can you get permission to observe the next Queen's Garden Festival and do a story with pictures?

Try not to let your conversation run on too long. After you return from conferring, make your request to the X-ians. You will get a yes or no answer. At that point, the exercise is over, and you excuse yourselves again and leave.

Source: Adapted from T. Gochenour, "The Owl," in T. Gochenour, ed., *Beyond Experience: An Experiential Approach to Cross-Cultural Education*, 2nd ed. (Yarmouth ME: Intercultural Press Inc., 1993): 128–133. Reprinted by permission of Theodore Gochenour.

 ## Can You Solve this Manager's Problem?

The People's Republic of China (PRC): A Research Project *(to be completed outside of class)*

You are a general manager in a medium-sized transportation and distribution company. You have just been informed that, beginning in four weeks, you will be spending four months on a project in the People's Republic of China. Your task is to develop a list of resources that will help you to adjust culturally in this assignment. You are working from your actual situation, in your city and state. Your project will be evaluated on the quality of your findings. For example, did you identify some really top experts on China, or not?

Do all of the following:

1. Identify five or six books that you should read about the PRC. For each book, describe in a couple of paragraphs why it is essential reading. Select your books to cover as broad a range of issues about China as possible, rather than just one or two issues. For instance, do not just select books on government; instead, choose books on government, education, culture, economics, and so on.
2. Identify two or three academic and/or well-researched articles that specifically address issues of cross-cultural adjustment in the PRC. Based on these, list the top 10 issues that you will face.
3. Find one good Web site that describes issues of cross-cultural adjustment in the PRC. Based on this, list five top issues that you will face.
4. Identify an individual who might actually serve as a cultural interpreter for you. Describe his or her qualifications, how you would contact this person, how much

time you would like to spend with him or her, and what you would like to learn from him or her.

5. Identify one place where your company could send you to gain experience in this culture before your actual assignment begins. You have a budget of $3,500 and three days available for this immersion training.

6. Identify and watch one good movie filmed in the PRC. Summarize what you learned from it in a few paragraphs.

7. Looking back on your research, what are its limitations? its strengths? How could a good HRM department have helped you in your research?

Chapter Summary and Key Terms

What characterizes Americans—what characterizes *you*—culturally?

Culture is a set of shared beliefs, values, and practices. It is important to understand the differences and similarities between how Americans and others do business.

culture   210
national culture   210

Western business customs are accepted worldwide—so why should you study other cultures?

This is a trick question: In fact, Western business customs are not accepted worldwide, and cultural differences can get in the way of effective communication. However, some countries, such as Great Britain, seem especially capable of welcoming and integrating a variety of cultures.

What cultural differences interest managers?

Be on the lookout for a variety of cultural differences that might cause misunderstandings. Among the most important are differences in perceptions, nonverbal behaviors, attitudes and values, personalities, and psychological contracts.

high context cultures   213
low context cultures   213
polychronicity   213
monochronicity   213

What do you need to know about developing business relationships with America's most important trading partners?

You should study any culture you are likely to do business with. The countries with which the United States trades the most are Canada, Mexico, China, Japan, and Germany.

What characterizes the successful individual working overseas?

Characteristics include professional credentials appropriate to the job, interpersonal skills, individual flexibility and other personality traits, realistic expectations, language capability, and, if married, a spouse with similar traits. Whatever your professional credentials, always research the host culture.

How can you develop cross-cultural skills?

Gain international experience. Identify a cultural interpreter. Understand your tolerance for ambiguity. Although some companies provide cross-cultural training, many do not. You may be lucky enough to get some in-depth coaching, but more likely you will have to read and experience on your own. Understand culture shock.

tolerance for ambiguity   224
cultural intelligence   225
culture shock   225
reentry shock   226
cultural interpreter   227
cultural assimilator   227

What should companies do to support their expatriates?

Companies should do everything they can to ensure that their expatriate employees develop job satisfaction, as well as supportive colleagues and networks.

How should you prepare for a short-term international assignment?

Most probably, your international assignments will be short ones. A checklist of things to do before you go includes learning some key phrases in the host language, knowing *faux pas* to avoid, and mastering essential business customs.

Explorations

1. ExpatExchange: A World of Friends Abroad . . . is an informative Web site that includes everything from travel warnings to the fun cultural quiz of the week. Check it out at www.expatexchange.com

2. American Citizens Abroad . . . is an advocacy organization. See www.aca.ch.

3. What is it like to work overseas?
Check out www.peacecorps.gov for cross-cultural stories told by Peace Corps volunteers. Or, for a more business-oriented view, Web search for "working overseas," and review some of services offered by the sites.

4. Gain cross-cultural experience at home. . . Take an international student to lunch.

5. Find country details
For helpful hints on visiting a country, read the "worldguide" at www.Lonelyplanet.com.

6. Do essential reading
For books providing authoritative cultural overviews check out this specialty publisher: http://www.interculturalpress.com/. A particularly interesting read is *Americans at Work: A Guide to the Can-Do People* by Craig Storti (Yarmouth, ME: Intercultural Press, 2004), a cultural guide to the U.S. workplace for non-Americans.

7. Conduct further research
To learn more about Project Globe and its findings consult the GLOBE Web site by searching for "Project Globe" and "University of Calgary." For more on the world values survey search for "World Values survey" and "Institute for Social Research." *The Economist* regularly publishes excellent "country briefings" that focus on economic and other structural attributes of nations.

8. Take that semester abroad!

References

[1] M. Javidan and R. J. House, "Cultural Acumen for the Global Manager: Lessons from Project Globe," *Organizational Dynamics* 29 (4), Spring 2001:289–305.

[2] C. Nakata and K. Sivakumar, "Instituting the Marketing Concept in a Multinational Setting: The Role of National Culture," *Journal of the Academy of Marketing Science* 29 (3) 2001:255–275.

[3] Adapted from R. André and G. Quinquis, "Socofrance, S.A.: An American and French Negotiation Simulation," *Journal of Management Education* 24 (4), August 2000:501–519.

[4] Adapted from H. C. Triandis, *Interpersonal Behavior* (Monterey, CA: Brooks/Cole, 1977):248.

[5] "Outside In," *The Economist* December 29, 2004. http://www.economist.com/research/articles. Accessed October 15, 2005.

[6] Peter Breen of Heidrick Struggles, quoted in "Outside In," *The Economist* December 29, 2004. http://www.economist.com/research/articles. Accessed October 15, 2005.

[7] J. S. Black, H. B. Gregersen, and M. E. Mendenhall, *Global Assignments: Successfully Expatriating and Repatriating Global Managers* (San Francisco: Jossey-Bass Publishers, 1992).

[8] E. T. Hall, *Beyond Culture* (Garden City, NY: Anchor Press/Doubleday, 1976).

[9] M. Munter, "Cross-Cultural Communication for Managers," *Business Horizons* 36 (3), May–June 1993:69–78.

[10] S. Koeszegi, R. Vetschera, and G. Kersten, "National Cultural Differences in the Use and Perception of Internet-based NSS: Does High or Low Context Matter?" *International Negotiation* 9 (1), 2004:79–109.

[11] M. Martinko, "Culture and Expatriate Failure: An Attributional Explication," *International Journal of Organizational Analysis* 7 (3), July 1999:265–293.

[12] M. H. Onken, "Temporal Elements of Organizational Culture and Impact on Firm Performance, *Journal of Managerial Psychology* 14 (3/4), 1999:231–244.

[13] C. Saunders, C. Van Slyke, and D. R. Vogel, "My Time or Yours? Managing Time Visions in Global Virtual Teams," *Academy of Management Executive* 18 (1) February 2004:19–31, 25

[14] D. L. Persing, "Managing in Polychronic Times," *Journal of Managerial Psychology* 14 (5), 1999:358–373; A. C. Bluedorn, T. J. Kalliath, M. J. Strube, and G. D. Martin, "Polychronicity and the Inventory of Polychronic Values: The Development of an Instrument to Measure a Fundamental Dimension of Organizational Culture," *Journal of Managerial Psychology* 14 (3/4) 1999:205–30; E. T. Hall, and M. P. Hall, *Understanding Cultural Differences*, (Yarmouth, ME: Intercultural Press, 1990).

[15] A. C. Bluedorn, C. Felker Kaufman, and P. M. Lane, "How Many Things Do You Like to Do at Once? An Introduction to Monochronic and Polychronic Time," *Academy of Management Executive* 6 (4), November 1992:17–26.

[16] C. Saunders, C. Van Slyke, and D. R. Vogel, "My Time or Yours? Managing Time Visions in Global Virtual Teams," *Academy of Management Executive* 18 (1), February 2004:19–31.

[17] J. C. Condon and F. S. Yousef, *An Introduction to Intercultural Communication* (Indianapolis: Bobbs-Merrill, 1975).

[18] P. R. Harris and R. T. Moran, *Managing Cultural Differences: Leadership Strategies for a New World of Business* 4th ed. (Houston, Texas: Gulf Publishing Company, 1996).

[19] R. Inglehart and W. E. Baker, "Modernization, Cultural Change, and the Persistence of Traditional Values," *American Sociological Review* 65, 2000:19–51.

[20] MOW International Research Team, *The Meaning of Work: An International Perspective* (London: Academic Press, 1987):83.

[21] G. Hofstede, *Culture's Consequences: International Differences in Work Related Values* (Beverly Hills, CA: Sage,

1980). Hofstede credits M. H. Bond for his contribution to developing the fifth factor, which is derived in part from Confucian values discovered in Asia. Hofstede's work is criticized in B. McSweeney, "Hofstede's Model of National Cultural Differences and Their Consequences: A Triumph of Faith—a Failure of Analysis," *Human Relations 55* (1), January 2002:89–118.

22 G. Hofstede, "Cultural Constraints in Management Theories," *Academy of Management Executive 7* (1) February 1993:81–94.

23 M. Javidan and R. J. House, "Cultural Acumen for the Global Manager: Lessons from Project Globe," *Organizational Dynamics 29* (4), Spring 2001:289–305.

24 E. Diener and M. Diner, "Cross-Cultural Correlates of Life Satisfaction and Self-Esteem," *Journal of Personality and Social Psychology 68* (4), April 1995:653–663.

25 F. Lievens, E. Van Keer, M. M. Harris, and C. Bisqueret, "Predicting Cross-Cultural Training Performance: The Validity of Personality, Cognitive Ability, and Dimensions Measured by an Assessment Center and a Behavior Description Interview," *Journal of Applied Psychology 88* (3), June 2003:476–487.

26 R. R. McCrae and P. T. Costa, Jr., "Personality Trait Structure as a Human Universal," *American Psychologist 52* (5), May 1997:509–517; V. Benet-Martinex and O.P. John, "Toward the Development of Quasi-indigenous Personality Contructs," *American Behavioral Scientist 44* (1), September 2000:141–157; M.S. Katigbak, A. T. Church, M. A. Guanzon-Lapeña, A. J. Carlota, and G. H. Del Pilar, "Are Indigenous Personality Dimensions Culture Specific? Philippine Inventories and the Five-Factor Model," *Journal of Personality & Social Psychology 82* (1), January 2002:89–101.

27 M.J. Schmit, J.A. Kihm, and C. Roble, "Development of a Global Measure of Personality," *Personnel Psychology 53* (1), 2000:153–193.

28 D. M. Rousseau and R. Schalk, *Psychological Contracts in Employment* (Thousand Oaks, CA: Sage Publications Inc., 2000):1; D. M. Rousseau and J. M. Parks, "The Contracts of Individuals and Organizations," *Research in Organizational Behavior 15* (1993):1–43.

29 P. S. Goodman, F. Olivera, and R. Ranganujam, *Linkages between Societal Culture and Organizational Practices* (Unpublished paper, Carnegie Mellon University, 1998).

30 D. M. Rousseau and R. Schalk, *Psychological Contracts in Employment* (Thousand Oaks, CA: Sage Publications Inc., 2000):287.

31 H. W. Jenkins, "Just Another German Car Company," *The Wall Street Journal,* May 26, 1999:A23, as cited in D. M. Rousseau and R. Schalk, *Psychological Contracts in Employment* (Thousand Oaks, CA: Sage Publications Inc., 2000):287.

32 G. W. Renwick, "A Fair Go For All: Australian/American Interactions," (Yarmouth, ME: Intercultural Press, 1991).

33 E. T. Hall, *Beyond Culture.* (Garden City, NY: Doubleday, 1976).

34 G. Hofstede, *Culture's Consequences: International Differences in Work Related Values* (Beverly Hills, CA: Sage, 1980).

35 K. Warn, "Economy: Can the Good Times Keep on Rolling?" *Financial Times,* October 31, 2002.

36 Information in this section is based on P. R. Harris and R. T. Moran, *Managing Cultural Differences: Leadership Strategies for a New World of Business 4th ed.* (Houston, Texas: Gulf Publishing Company, 1996); F. L. Cooke, "Foreign Firms in China: Modelling HRM in a Toy Manufacturing Corporation," *Human Resource Management Journal 14* (3), 2004:31–52; R. Yee, "Licensing Laws," *International Financial Law Review 23* (8), August 2004:52.

37 A. Sergeant and S. Frenkel, "Managing People in China: Perceptions of Expatriate Managers," *Journal of World Business 33* (1), Spring 1998:17–34.

38 "Discrimination in China: No Small Matter," *The Economist* March 2, 2002:42–43.

39 Information in this section is based on P. R. Harris and R. T. Moran, *Managing Cultural Differences: Leadership Strategies for a New World of Business* 4th ed. (Houston, Texas: Gulf Publishing Company, 1996); N. D. Kling, J. F. Alexander, R. Martinez, and D. E. McCorkle, "NAFTA Revisited: The Role of Business Educators," *Journal of Education for Business 73* (6), July/August 1998:336–343.

40 G. Hofstede, *Culture's Consequences: International Differences in Work Related Values* (Beverly Hills, CA: Sage, 1980); P. R. Harris and R. T. Moran, *Managing Cultural Differences: Leadership Strategies for a New World of Business 4th ed.* (Houston, Texas: Gulf Publishing Company, 1996); O. Furrer, B. S. Liu, and D. Sudharshan, "The Relationship Between Culture and Service Quality Perceptions," *Journal of Service Research 2* (4), 2000:355–371.

41 This section is based on P. R. Harris and R. T. Moran, *Managing Cultural Differences: Leadership Strategies for a New World of Business 4th ed.* (Houston, Texas: Gulf Publishing Company, 1996); and H. Fassbender, M. Kliger, and J. Kluge,

"What Germans Really Think," *McKinsey Quarterly 3*, 2002:145–148.

[42] H. Fassbender, M. Kliger, and J. Kluge, "What Germans Really Think," *McKinsey Quarterly 3*, 2002:145–148.

[43] H. Fassbender, M. Kliger, and J. Kluge, "What Germans Really Think," *McKinsey Quarterly 3*, 2002:145–148.

[44] M. Javidan and R. J. House, "Cultural Acumen for the Global Manager: Lessons from Project Globe," *Organizational Dynamics 29* (4), Spring 2001:289–305.

[45] F. Hawes and D. J. Kealey, *Canadians in Development: An Empirical Study of Adaptation and Effectiveness on Overseas Assignment* Technical Report. (Ottawa, Canada: Publisher Unknown, 1979); J. S. Black, M. Mendenhall, and G. Oddou, "Toward a Comprehensive Model of International Adjustment: An Integration of Multiple Theoretical Perspectives," *Academy of Management Review 16* (2), April 1991:291–317.

[46] J. Li-Jun, Z. Zhiyong, and R. E. Nisbett, "Is It Culture or Is It Language? Examination of Language Effects in Cross-Cultural Research on Categorization," *Journal of Personality & Social Psychology 87* (1), July 2004:57–65.

[47] M. B. Teagarden and G. D. Gordon, "Corporate Selection Strategies and Expatriate Manager Success," in J. Selmer, ed. *Expatriate Management: New Ideas for International Business.* (Westport, CT: Quorum Books, 1995).

[48] T. Huang, S. Chi, and J. J. Lawler, "The Relationship Between Expatriates' Personality Traits and Their Adjustment to International Assignments," *International Journal of Human Resource Management 16* (9), September 2005:1656–1670.

[49] C. H. Lee and K. J. Templer, "Cultural Intelligence Assessment and Measurement," in P. C. Earley and S. Ang, eds., *Cultural Intelligence: Individual Interactions Across Cultures,* (Stanford, CA: Stanford University Press, 2003):185–208.

[50] "Intolerance of Ambiguity," in J. P. Robinson and P. R. Shaver, *Measures of Social Psychological Attitudes* (Ann Arbor, Michigan: Institute for Social Research, The University of Michigan, 1973):401–405; S. Budner, "Intolerance of Ambiguity," *Journal of Personality 30*, 1962:29–50.

[51] A. E. M. Van Vianen, I. E. De Pater, A. L. Kristof-Brown, and E. C. Johnson, "Fitting In: Surface- and Deep-level Cultural Differences and Expatriate's Adjustment," *Academy of Management Journal 47* (5), 2004:697–709.

[52] J. S. Lublin, "Harassment Law in U.S. Is Strict, Foreigners Find," *The Wall Street Journal* Mary 15, 2006:B1.

[53] P. C. Earley and R. S. Peterson, "The Elusive Cultural Chameleon: Cultural Intelligence as a New Approach to Intercultural Training for the Global Manager," *Academy of Management Learning & Education 3* (1), March 2004:100–115.

[54] N. Adler, *International Dimensions of Organizational Behavior,* 4th ed., (Cincinnati, OH: Southwestern, 2002).

[55] K. Oberg, "Culture Shock: Adjustment to New Cultural Environments," *Practical Anthropology 7,* 1960:177–82; R. D. Hayes, "The Executive Abroad: Minimizing Behavioral Problems," *Business Horizons 15*, June 1972:87–93; J. W. Berry, M. H. Segall, and Y. H. Poortinga, eds., *Cross-Cultural Psychology: Research and Applications,* 2nd ed. (New York: Cambridge University Press, 2002).

[56] R. G. Linowes, "The Japanese Manager's Traumatic Entry into the United States: Understanding the American–Japanese Cultural Divide," *The Academy of Management Executive 7* (4), 1993:21–40.

[57] K. Oberg, "Culture Shock and the Problem of Adjustment to New Cultural Environments" (Washington D.C.: Foreign Service Institute, 1958).

[58] "Recruitment: Apply Within," *The Economist*, September 23, 2006:74–75.

[59] P. R. Harris and R. T. Moran, *Managing Cultural Differences: Leadership Strategies for a New World of Business* (Houston: Gulf Publishing Company, 1996):142.

[60] P. J. Dowling, D. E. Welch, and R. S. Schuler, *International Human Resource Management* (Cincinnati, OH: Southwestern, 1999).

[61] M. Duane, *Policies and Practices in Global Human Resource Systems.* (Westport, CT: Quorum, 2001).

[62] K. Cushner, and D. Landis, "The Intercultural Sensitizer," in D. Landis and R. S. Bhagat, eds., *Handbook of Intercultural Training,* 2nd ed., (Thousand Oaks, CA: Sage, 1996):185–201.

[63] H. Lee, and C. Lieu, "Determinants of the Adjustment of Expatriate Managers to Foreign Countries: An Empirical Study," *International Journal of Management 23* (2), June 2006: 302–311.

[64] R. M. Hodgetts, "A Conversation with Donald F. Hastings of the Lincoln Electric Company," *Organizational Dynamics 25* (3) Winter 1997:68–74; D. F. Hastings, "Lincoln Electric's Harsh Lessons from International Expansion," *Harvard Business Review 77* (3), May–June 1999:163–174; "Lincoln Electric to Acquire Welding Businesses in China," *Gases & Welding Distributor 48* (2) March/April 2004:12.

[65] D. F. Hastings, "Lincoln Electric's Harsh Lessons from International Expansion," *Harvard Business Review 77* (3), May–June 1999:163–174.

Groups and Their Influence

Preview

Why are groups so important to organizations?
Groups are a key building block of organizations
Groups represent a power structure in organizations
Groups may make *better* decisions than individuals alone
Groups may make *worse* decisions than individuals alone
Group membership influences individual identity and decision making

What key factors define a group?
The nature of groups
How groups motivate their members

What is a team?
What are teams really like in the workplace?
What are high-performance teams?

How do groups and teams evolve over time?
Stages of group development
How *short-term* groups evolve

What special issues do you face when managing a self-directed team?

What special issues do you face when managing a virtual team?

What issues arise in multicultural teams? In virtual multicultural teams?

Student Advantage

Student Advantage, the company that offers a well-known student discount card, is looking for team players. If you come through their door with your head down ready to get something done, you are probably in the wrong place. What the company really wants is employees who enjoy collaboration. For example, they expect their people to be able to get beyond titles, and to be comfortable being managed by someone 10 years their junior or their senior.

Each team at Student Advantage has a unique culture. In the New York office, for instance, the sales team is pretty formal. The Web team, on the other hand, looks and acts like it is living in a college dormitory. These differences make sense because the teams have different jobs. It is a part of their job description for the Web team to be as lively as they are and as interested as they are in student life.

Student Advantage started to focus on building teams when it reached about 70 to 100 employees. Now it faces the challenge of keeping those teams coordinated without losing either their unique characteristics or the cohesiveness of the company. Today organizations worldwide are facing similar issues regarding team management (see accompanying photo of an Asian team in a manufacturing plant).

Why Are Groups So Important to Organizations?

Figure 9.1 shows a typical organizational chart. Can you identify all the groups in this company? Before reading further, circle on the chart every group that you can find. Use your imagination. Some might not be so obvious. When you are done, turn to Appendix 3 to see all the possibilities.

How did you do? (Most people miss a few.) One of the purposes of this chapter is to encourage you to put groups on your radar screen. Sure, people know about the various departments, their own work groups, and the top management groups of their organizations. But are these all the groups that exist in a company? And are they the only groups that matter? As you read on, you will learn that organizations today have many different types of groups, and that they are enormously influential.

Much of today's business is done with and through groups, which are also referred to as teams. It is estimated that about 80 percent of *Fortune* 500 companies have about half of their employees on teams.[1] Furthermore, although teams used to be found primarily in manufacturing, today they are found widely in service industries as well.

Clearly, being aware of groups and understanding how to manage them are prerequisite to being an effective employee and manager. Groups are important because they are a key component of organizations, because they have both strengths and weaknesses as decision-making units, and because they affect the satisfaction and performance of their individual members.

Groups Are a Key Building Block of Organizations

group
Two or more people who spend time with each other, experience emotional ties, share a common frame of reference, and are behaviorally interdependent.

formal groups
A group which is officially designated by an organization to accomplish its tasks, such as a functional group or a project group.

A **group** is two or more people who spend time with each other, experience emotional ties, share a common frame of reference, and are behaviorally interdependent.[2] **Formal groups** are those officially designated by an organization to accomplish its tasks. They may be permanent or temporary, but in either case they are crucial building blocks of the organization. Here are some examples of the formal groups that you are likely to find in a company:

- *Functional groups* are those assigned particular, permanent tasks. Examples are the accounting department, the human resources management department, and the production group. As you will read below, groups are actually relatively small units. Thus, in a large firm, a department or division is, technically speaking, not a group but, rather, is made up of smaller work group*s*, units that have some common task to complete. In a small firm, on the other hand, a department might well be a group.

- *Cross-functional groups* bring together individuals from a variety of functional groups to accomplish a task. Temporary or permanent, they work on problems that require input from a variety of functions and, also, they promote the exchange of information and goodwill among the functional groups. An example is a group comprised of individuals from engineering, customer service, marketing, and production that is charged with enhancing the quality of an existing product.

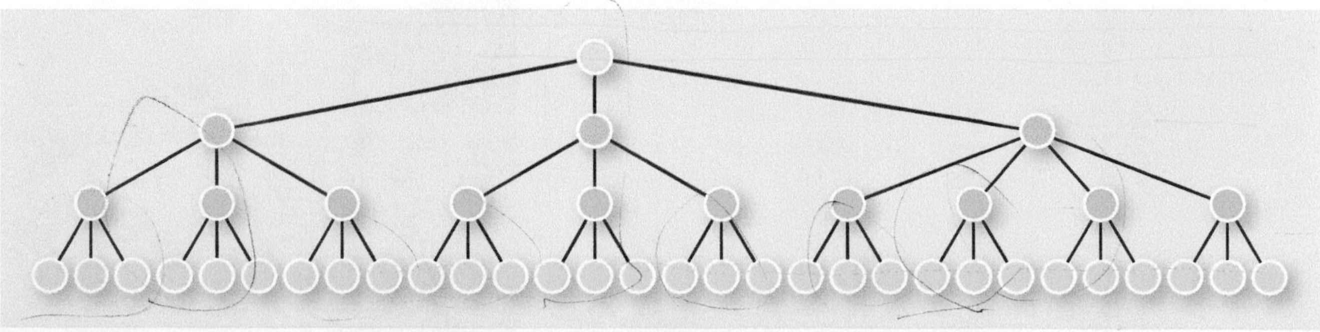

FIGURE 9.1 Can You Find the Groups in this Organization?

- *Project groups* are temporary groups that work on a time-limited task such as deciding whether to open a branch in another country. They are also called "temporary task forces." Often project groups are cross-functional.

- *Affinity groups* are associations of employees who come together because of their gender, race, ethnicity, or other traits. Among other roles, affinity groups help companies to innovate. For example, an affinity group of Hispanics at Frito-Lay, a division of PepsiCo, helped the company develop a line of guacamole-flavored potato chips that became a $100 million product.[3]

- *The executive group* includes the heads of the company and those people who routinely work with them. Typically the executive group is cross-functional and includes all of the main divisions of the company.

Informal groups are social groups that have no official designation by the organization yet have some common interests and personal ties. In an organization these might include groups based on family relationships (for example, all of the Jones relations), professional credentials (a company's engineers), demographics (the younger and older workers, or workers with and without children), and interests (the golfers).

informal groups
A social group which has no official designation by the organization, in which individuals have some common interests and personal ties.

Groups Represent a Power Structure in Organizations

Both formal and informal groups have power in the organization. Of course, formal groups are given power officially, and they are allotted resources to accomplish their sanctioned objectives. Although informal groups are not granted resources in this way, they have power because they acquire and exchange information and contacts, and because they give social support to their members.

Obviously, some groups are more powerful than others. Among formal groups, the executive group is always powerful because it controls resources. Beyond this group, typically it is the groups that are more central to the organization's mission that are the most powerful. For example, a sales division may be powerful because it is close to the customer and has important knowledge about customer needs. Powerful groups are allotted a larger portion of an organization's resources, whereas less critical groups are given fewer resources.

However, informal groups also have power. For example, even though he is only loading trucks for the summer, the CEO's nephew is a powerful person by virtue of his family group membership. Similarly, you might on occasion observe that it is an informal group of friends that actually runs a company, despite the fact that formal titles suggest otherwise. Often you can detect this phenomenon by observing who lunches with whom on a regular basis.

Because individuals gain much of their power through their group memberships, it is important to be aware of the organizational power of both formal and informal groups. If you are hoping to ascend to the top level of the company, learn which formal group is the best vehicle to the top and join it. Also, decide which informal group memberships might contribute to your career advancement. Join the jogging group, make friends with the boss's kid, or start a monthly lunch for your professional group.

Sometimes individuals decide that, alone, they do not have enough power in their organization, so they form groups whose purpose is to lobby management. When what employees seek is better salaries and working conditions, these interest groups may evolve into labor unions. For this reason, some companies squelch interest groups that work outside of sanctioned management channels. They instruct employees to work one-on-one with their managers to resolve issues, and, if this process is unsatisfactory, to work the issue up through the organization. They may explicitly forbid their employees to form other groups.

Sometimes, too, groups develop whose purpose is to subvert organizational goals. For instance, a group of employees may organize together to punch each other in and out on a time clock. Obviously it is in the company's best interest to limit the power of these kinds of groups.

Groups May Make *Better* Decisions Than Individuals Alone

You are a manager with a decision to make. Should you make the decision alone, or should you let your subordinates make it? Consider the potential advantages of group decision making over individual decision making. Here are some assets of group decision making[4]:

1. Groups bring a greater total sum of knowledge to a problem.
2. Groups bring a greater number of approaches to a problem.
3. Groups tend to take more innovative approaches to solving a problem.
4. Participation in decision making helps people understand the solution.
5. Participation in decision making helps people accept a solution.

How effective are groups in contrast to individuals? A study of 222 team learning groups found that group decision making provided an average quality improvement of 8.8 percent over a group's most knowledgeable member, with at least some improvement evident in 97 percent of the groups.[5] However, the level of conflict in a group must also be taken into account. Too much conflict reduces effectiveness.

Groups May Make *Worse* Decisions Than Individuals Alone

In deciding who should make a decision, you should also consider that under certain circumstances groups make worse decisions than individuals alone. The major liabilities of group decision making are[6]:

1. Groups may be influenced by a dominant individual.
2. Social pressure on individuals can significantly affect their judgment: Individuals may vote with their friends, authorities, or superiors rather than assert their own opinion.
3. Groups have a tendency to make risky decisions, accepting a plausible early solution rather than working to find an optimal solution. This is termed the **risky shift**.
4. It is more difficult to fix responsibility for a decision on a group than on an individual.

In addition to these liabilities, group decision making is time-consuming. When speed is essential, decision making by one individual is preferable.

Group Membership Influences Individual Identity and Decision Making

In the following sentence, fill in the blanks with the first three words that come to you. "I am a(n) _independ_, a(n) _woman_, and a(n) _friend_ ."

Did you write primarily words that describe you as an individual, or did you include words that describe you in terms of the groups to which you belong? For example, "I am a scuba diver, smart, and a junior at High-Powered University" includes two statements about your individual identity and one about your social identity.

Your **social identity** consists of your belief about the groups to which you belong.[7] Social identity is important because these beliefs are part of your self-concept,[8] and as such they influence how you act and feel. Individuals usually derive their social identities from more than one social group.[9]

We gain a lot from our established social identities. The feeling of belonging to something greater than ourselves, the comfort of fitting in, and the status accorded to us are just some of the benefits of group membership. In addition, our sense of well-being is influenced by how we see ourselves in comparison with specific reference groups.[10] For example, to boost self-esteem, minorities in business may compare their own status with that of other minorities rather than with that of the majority.

However, group membership also causes identity problems. For one thing, being a member of a highly cohesive group can cause **deindividuation**—the loss of your objective self-awareness and, as a result, a reduction in your desire to adhere to personal and societal values. When group members are highly similar to one another and mutual attraction is high, individuals tend to conform to the group's values and ignore their own. "Individuals in such groups often report unconcern about what other people [outside the group] might think of their behavior, show a lack of future orientation and

risky shift
The tendency to make risky decisions; accepting a plausible early solution rather than working to find an optimal solution.

social identity
A part of your self concept that depends on your beliefs about the groups to which you belong.

deindividuation
The loss of your objective self-awareness, reducing your desire to adhere to personal and societal values.

planning, a loss of personal identity, and drug-like altered states of awareness."[11] As a result, when making a decision, individuals may conform to the group's values and ignore their own morals and ethics.

A related concern is that having a distinctive social identity sets a person, and their group, apart from others. When you belong to an **in-group**, which is a group that commands members' esteem and loyalty, typically there is a corresponding **out-group**, a group toward which the group members feel some opposition or competition.[12] When carried to extremes, the strong social identity fostered by a cohesive group can lead to prejudice, discrimination, and intergroup conflict.

If, for instance, the research and development (R &D) engineers in a company form a highly cohesive group, they may unfavorably stereotype the company's other engineers, thus setting the stage for unproductive conflict when the two groups must work together.

Whether or not individuals tend to disparage out-groups depends upon how secure they are in their own social identities. Individuals with secure social identities and those with insecure social identities both take pride in their groups, but those with secure identities are less likely to engage in behaviors that disparage out-groups.[13]

in-group
A group that commands members' esteem and loyalty.

out-group
A group toward which the group members feel some opposition or competition.

What Key Factors Define a Group?

When joining or managing a group, it is important to be conscious of the group's goals, size, norms, cohesion, and internal roles. You should also be aware of the kind of motivational gains, or losses, you can expect from the group.

The Nature of Groups

COMMON GOALS Groups have a unity of purpose. They convene for a reason, which could be as complicated and important as developing a new business strategy, or as simple and tangential as choosing regular lunch partners.

SMALL SIZE Generally, effective work groups are small in size. As one set of researchers put it, "Virtually all effective teams we have met, read or heard about, or have been members of have ranged between 2 and 25 people. . . . A large number of people, say 50 or more, can theoretically become a team. But groups of such size are more likely to break into sub-teams rather than function as a single unit. . . . Large numbers of people have trouble interacting constructively as a group, much less doing real work together. Ten people are far more likely than 50 are to work through their individual, functional, and hierarchical differences toward a common plan and to hold themselves jointly accountable for the results."[14]

Small size fosters participation and cohesion in part because of the simple fact that as groups grow larger, each individual member has less air time for themselves and fewer opportunities to interact with the other group members. See Figure 9.2 for an illustration of how increasing group size soon leads to a large and potentially unmanageable number of relationships. By the way, if the group expands to eight members there are 28 interactions, whereas if it gets as large as 9, that number grows to 36.

Other effects of size are that, as a work group increases in numbers, its leader is more likely to attempt to direct and control it, and that subordinates are somewhat more likely to be dissatisfied overall.[15] Also, subordinates are less likely to get individual recognition. Finally, as size increases, group productivity is likely to go down.[16]

All other factors aside, the ideal size for a work group is thought to be five people, the optimum tradeoff between having enough information and different approaches to a problem while still allowing each member to have a voice. Even so, in the typical five-person group, it is likely that only two people will do nearly 70 percent of the talking.[17] A consultant on teams notes, "This is an area that is debated a lot. Research shows that group processes seem to deteriorate after 10 to 12 people. Six people, plus or minus one or two, seems to be ideal."[18] However, when a group is made up of six people, it has a tendency to subdivide into two teams of three.

FIGURE 9.2

Increasing Group Size Rapidly Increases the Number of Relationships

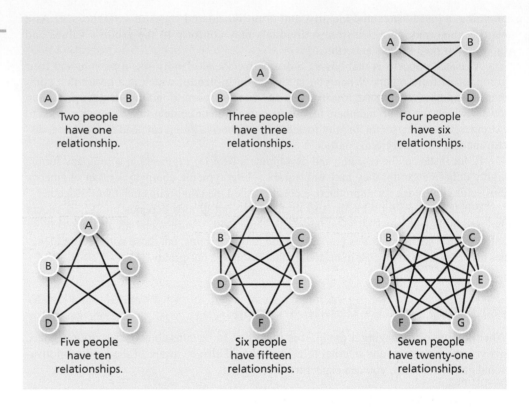

Two people have one relationship.

Three people have three relationships.

Four people have six relationships.

Five people have ten relationships.

Six people have fifteen relationships.

Seven people have twenty-one relationships.

norms

Informal rules which regulate and standardize group members' behaviors.

NORMS All groups develop **norms**, which are informal rules which regulate and standardize group members' behaviors.[19] Norms clarify the central values of a group, simplify and make predictable what behaviors are expected from group members, and help the group avoid interpersonal conflicts. Generally, groups enforce norms only for those behaviors that are viewed as important by most group members. Groups develop norms about such activities as performance standards, social arrangements and appearances, and the allocation of rewards and resources. For example, a particular group might develop the norms of working long hours, keeping to themselves, and sharing rewards equally.

Norms can sometimes be surprising. A new employee at a *Fortune* 100 company spends hours enhancing a presentation with interesting graphics, only to discover that the company norm is KISS (Keep it simple, Stupid) and that the time spent on the extras is considered company time wasted. How can you avoid a similar mistake? Norms originate in explicit statements made by group members, critical events in the group's history, habits that develop early in the group's life, and expectations brought from other groups. Because they are not written down, you need to observe your group carefully and to develop relationships with experienced colleagues who can advise you.

cohesion

The sum of all the forces acting on members to remain in a group, including the degree to which members of a group are personally attracted to each other.

COHESION When a group is perceived as a predictable source of positive feelings and emotion, its members are likely to develop stronger emotional ties to it than if it is perceived as a source of negative feelings or emotion.[20] This person–group bond reflects **cohesion**, the sum of all the forces acting on members to remain in a group,[21] including the degree to which members of a group are personally attracted to each other.[22] We are only beginning to understand whether and how cohesiveness improves group performance.[23] In smaller groups (those with three to seven members) it now seems that cohesiveness somewhat improves a group's overall performance.[24]

conformity

The tendency for people to change their behavior to match group norms.

However, cohesion can also lead to **conformity**, the tendency for people to change their behavior to match group norms. As we learned from the Asch experiments in Chapter 3, individuals in groups will often go along with the majority view, even denying their own perceptions to do so.[25] Under these conditions, the diversity of opinions and approaches that is a major strength of group decision making is lost. In further experiments, Asch investigated whether having allies in a group affects group decision making. First, he tested the power of one confederate acting as a dissenter in a group of 16 people, the rest of whom were the naïve subjects of the experiment. When the lone confederate gave an obviously wrong answer, the rest of the group laughed with amusement and disdain. However, when Asch increased the number of confederates giving the wrong answer to three, despite the fact that the confederates' answers were still obviously incorrect, the attitude of the majority turned to seriousness and increased respect. From these experiments, Asch concluded that both the withdrawal of social support and the amassing of social support should be explicitly considered when one is thinking about the formation and distortion of judgments in groups.[26]

ROLES **Roles** are "shared expectations about how a particular person in a group ought to behave."[27] Roles indicate what tasks a person should perform, and what socioemotional support a person should provide. For example, parenthood is a role, and parents are expected to maintain the household and nurture their children. Being the leader of a group is also a role, although the expectations for the role differ depending on the nature of the group. Leaders in traditional work groups are expected to direct the group and to give a modest level of personal support to group members, whereas leaders in self-managed work groups are expected to be a liaison to resources outside the group, to coach the group, and to support group members in their own roles.

Sometimes individuals lack the knowledge, ability, or motivation to perform a role well, and are said to be experiencing **role strain**. Also, individuals may find that they are trying to fill two roles that conflict, such as mentoring a junior employee and also evaluating that employee's performance. This is called **interrole conflict**.

How Groups Motivate Their Members

Sometimes group members exert greater task effort than comparable individual performers.[28] This is called a **motivation gain**. Why does it happen?

One gain in motivation is called **social compensation**, which occurs when individuals increase their own efforts to compensate for the anticipated poor performance of other members of their group.[29] In order for social compensation to occur, group success must be extremely important to the capable group member. Otherwise, the member is likely to loaf.

Another motivational gain originates in the **Köhler effect**, in which less capable members of groups actually increase their effort.[30] This phenomenon occurs when the less capable member perceives his or her contribution is crucial to the group, or when the member's evaluation within the group is crucial to him or her personally. Less capable members may also increase their effort when their group is involved in intergroup competition.[31]

What Is a Team?

You may have noticed that, aside from the opening case, so far in this chapter we have talked a lot about groups but have seldom mentioned the word "team." This is because, although in practice the terms are often used interchangeably, we can also make the case that groups and teams are not exactly the same thing. A team is always a group, but a group is not always a team. There's something special about a "team," and about "teamwork," isn't there? In this section, we will examine what makes a group into a team.

In technical terms, when group members do not have to interact very much to complete a task, they are called **working groups**.[32] An example is an accounting group in which each member individually analyzes different data, and at the end of the month the group manager assembles the data to complete a report. In such groups, individuals interact little while doing their work, and they seldom, if ever, meet to discuss their joint product. In business it is common for managers to refer to even this sort of group as a team, even though technically it is only a working group.

In contrast to working groups, **teams** engage in *collective* action to produce joint work products. They have common goals, a common approach, and mutual accountability.[33] Together, they risk conflict, loss of face, and all of the other emotional pitfalls of interpersonal interaction. An example is a group of chemical, electrical, and mechanical engineers who have been charged with developing and producing a new product.

---

roles
Shared expectations about how a particular person in a group ought to behave.

role strain
The strain someone experiences when he or she lacks the knowledge, ability, or motivation to perform a role well.

interrole conflict
The situation that arises when someone finds that he or she is trying to fill two roles that conflict.

motivation gain
Situation in which group members exert greater task effort than comparable individuals.

social compensation
A gain in motivation which occurs when individuals increase their own efforts to compensate for the anticipated poor performance of other members of their group.

Köhler effect
A gain in motivation in which a less capable member of a group actually increases his or her effort.

working group
A group whose members do not have to interact very much to complete a task.

team
A group whose members act collectively to produce joint work products.

Because of their interactive nature, teams must be well designed, as follows:

1. They must be the right size: small enough to interact effectively, large enough to integrate the necessary information and provide the necessary contacts.

2. Teams must have the right mix of skills, that is, a complementary skill set that is necessary for doing the team's task. This means teams must have:

   a. The proper technical and functional expertise. For example, the development of a new product requires both engineering and marketing expertise.

   b. The proper decision-making expertise. Teams must appropriately identify the nature of the problem they face and the decision-making expertise that is required to solve that problem.

   c. Interpersonal skills. These include a variety of group process skills, including active listening, the ability to take one's turn in leading the team, and the ability to assume a variety of process roles.[34]

What Are Teams Really Like in the Workplace?

TEAM CHARACTERISTICS Data from a survey of 515 executives in a variety of industries suggests that, in their companies, teams tend to vary in size from two to eighty members, but that the modal team size is five.[35] More than half of teams are self-managing, whereas nearly 40 percent are led by their managers. On average, teams work together for one to two years. The most common type of team is the cross-functional project group.

TEAM PROBLEMS When asked about their greatest sources of frustration and challenge, team managers say that developing and sustaining high motivation is at the top of the list.[36] Second is minimizing confusion and coordination problems. The third-largest issue is fostering creativity and innovation, and the fourth is finding adequate training for team members. These common problems suggest that the key skills needed by team managers today are the ability to:

- Motivate
- Manage conflict
- Provide leadership and direction
- Foster innovation
- Minimize confusion and coordination problems

TEAM TASKS Companies use teams for a wide variety of tasks. Microsoft uses teams to target and serve specific sets of customers.[37] Motorola Inc. has sent a team of researchers to the far reaches of China to explore customer preferences.[38]

Teams with different types of tasks face different types of risks and opportunities. For example, task forces set up to do a temporary and immediate job have the advantage of having a clear purpose and deadline, but the disadvantage that they are a new work team that needs to learn to work together. Teams that produce a product, on the other hand, have the advantage that their work is continuous over time. They can build skills around the needs of their task. But they face the risk that they may insulate themselves from the customers and become too technologically oriented.[39] See Table 9.1 for more on how different types of teams take on special risks and opportunities.

What Are High-Performance Teams?

Teams can be differentiated based on their stage of development, with high-performance teams the most highly evolved.

A **potential team** is really trying to improve its performance, but it has not yet achieved some of the goals of a real team. For example, it does not require collective accountability of the team members, it has not developed clarity about its task, and it lacks the discipline to hammer out a group process.

potential team
A team which is trying to improve its performance but has not yet achieved some of the goals of a real team.

TABLE 9.1 Examples of Risks and Opportunities for Teams Performing Different Tasks

	Risks	Opportunities
Customer service teams	The team may lose its involvement with the parent organization.	The company values the team's ability to bridge the gap between the parent organization and its customers.
Task forces	Both the team and the work are new.	Having a clear purpose and deadline may lead to both a sense of accomplishment and organizational rewards.
Human service teams	Teams are likely to be under emotional stress.	Serving people has inherent significance.
Groups that perform	Organizational support is likely to be skimpy.	Because they have a competitive spirit and/or perform before an audience, playing is encouraged.
Top management teams	The team lacks inherent controls because there is no one to push back on it. Also, it may be out of touch with the rest of the organization.	The team has lots of power to accomplish goals in and through the organization. It is also self-designing, enabling it to adapt to changing conditions.

Source: Adapted from J. R. Hackman, "Creating More Effective Work Groups in Organizations," in J. R. Hackman, ed., *Groups That Work (and Those That Don't): Creating Conditions for Effective Teamwork* (San Francisco: Jossey-Bass, 1990):489.

A **real team** is a group that is committed to a common purpose and working collectively toward their goals, while holding themselves mutually accountable for achieving them.

A **high-performance team** has all the characteristics of a real team, but in addition, its members are deeply committed to each other's personal growth and success. The high-performance team significantly outperforms other teams. However, high-performance teams of this nature are fairly rare.

Obviously, any group that has a task to perform would set for itself the goal of becoming a real team or a high-performance team. How do they achieve that goal?

For one thing, the manager of the team must set clear performance challenges.[40] In fact, these performance outcomes must be the primary reason for choosing to use a team in the first place. If individuals alone or work groups could achieve the same outcome, the team would not be necessary, and, therefore, is likely to fail.

At the same time that managers establish group performance goals, they should also consider establishing group rewards. One way to motivate and involve individuals to build a high-performance team is to reduce the level of individually based rewards, while increasing the level of group-level–based rewards.

Third, managers should try to minimize status differences. To do this, they can point out that the group may share a threat from competitive outsiders, or in other ways develop a common identity for all group members. They can encourage long-term relationships among group members.

Finally, real teams and high-performance teams include an element of trust. In teams, trust is a person's willingness to rely on others in situations where it would be possible for the other to take advantage of them.[41] Trust promotes effective teamwork by facilitating creativity, learning, and risk-taking. It takes various forms, including trusting people to be competent and perform, trusting them to approach their task with integrity, and trusting them to have concern and respect for others.[42] Trust facilitates cooperation,[43] and it reduces the need to monitor other people's behavior and to formalize procedures and contracts to control that behavior.[44]

real team
A group whose members are committed to a common purpose and working collectively toward their goals, while holding themselves mutually accountable for achieving them.

high-performance team
A rare type of real team whose members are deeply committed to each other's personal growth and success, and which significantly outperforms other teams.

How Do Groups and Teams Evolve Over Time?

You have been chosen to be part of a management group that has been asked to develop a greenfield (totally new) site to build a new brand of motorcycle using self-directed work groups. To choose the site, design a building, and set up the manufacturing process, you will work with 15 people who will meet several times a week over the course of at least a year. These people represent a wide variety of departments and functions in your company, from marketing and strategic planning to engineering and supply chain management. Different levels are also represented, from the lowest level up through the top management team. From the standpoint of the theory of group management, how should you frame your task?

For openers, keep in mind both the **process** and the **content** of the group decision making. The process is the pattern of interpersonal relationships in the group. It is *how* the group decides. A **process consultant**, by the way, is someone who helps a group interact more effectively. Content, on the other hand, is the task that the group is involved in. It is *what* the group is deciding—the problem it is trying to solve.

Stages of Group Development

Usually a new group proceeds through a set of reasonably predictable stages, each of which addresses and resolves particular aspects of the group's process. Sometimes these stages overlap. In each stage, the group risks failure if it does not manage its process well.[45] As a group's manager, your job is to help ensure that each stage progresses appropriately.

Let's take a look at each stage in turn, with an eye to suggesting what you as the group's manager might do to help your group move forward through that stage.

STAGE 1: FORMING In this stage, group members orient themselves to the task at hand. They identify and clarify their task, and they explore the manner in which the group can be used to perform the task. During this stage, group members are also getting a feel for what interpersonal behaviors are acceptable in the group, including who will lead the group, how much participation is expected, and who will form alliances with whom.

STAGE 2: STORMING As the members of the group develop an understanding of the task and their roles, they also develop an understanding of potential issues and limitations. It is only natural that some conflict will develop around what resources the group uses, how group leadership will be handled, how much commitment is required of the members, and other task and process concerns.

STAGE 3: NORMING During this stage, group members move beyond conflict to develop an in-group feeling and cohesiveness. They evolve standards, roles, and norms that give structure to group interactions. Individuals become more comfortable expressing more personal opinions, and understanding of how the group will proceed is achieved by all the group members.

STAGE 4: PERFORMING During this stage, interpersonal processes become the tool for accomplishing the group's task. The group channels its energy toward the task, and individual roles become flexible and functional.

STAGE 5: ADJOURNING[46] Termination of the group involves ending the task and allowing the members to disengage from each other in a gradual, supportive way. Some researchers have proposed that groups follow a life cycle, and that the end of the life of the group is an important stage in the group's development.[47] In groups that have been together for a long time, strong interpersonal feelings may have developed, and the group needs some time and structure for disbanding emotionally.

See Table 9.2 for an example of how a team might progress through these stages, and some appropriate interventions that the team's manager might make.

process
The pattern of interpersonal relationships in the group; *how* the group decides.

content
The task that the group is involved in; *what* the group is deciding.

process consultant
Someone who helps a group interact more effectively.

TABLE 9.2 How Managers Can Help Their Groups Through the Stages of Group Development: An Example

Stage of Group Development	What the Group Is Doing...	How the Manager Can Help...
Forming	During the first month, your new project team meets together daily to discuss the project goals. The team also meets with top management to get more information An important part of these early meetings is getting to know each other and beginning to get a feel for your team members' potential strengths and weaknesses. Individual agendas may or may not come to the fore, but are likely to emerge if they are pressing (for example, if one person is determined to lead the group).	Your role is to make sure that team members take responsibility for getting the information they need, and to make sure they have plenty of opportunities to get to know each other.
Storming	The group tries to set an agenda for the project in general and for the next six months in particular. However, some group members disagree about leadership. Some think the group should have one leader throughout the project. Others are not so sure. They think that the group has many potential leaders, and that these people all want to contribute to the group, as well as get credit for at least some of the leadership. The group decides to bring in a process consultant to help with decision making. The consultant runs the group through a three-day team-building workshop, during which the group decides to share leadership depending on the task at hand. However, one or two group members are still not totally convinced that this is the way to go...	Your main role as the group's manager is to ensure that the group does not drive conflicts underground and fail to address and resolve them.
Norming	The group tries out the idea of sharing leadership and begins to gets comfortable with it as different people take on different roles depending on their talents and preferences. For example, it decides that early in the project, the marketing expert in the group will take charge, and that when it comes time to designing the plant, the leadership will shift to an engineer. The group makes clear that some of these roles are developmental: Group members should have the opportunity, where feasible, to stretch themselves. The group members who had reservations about sharing leadership are able to conform to the group's wishes. In addition to its regular meetings, the group plans to have a luncheon meeting outside the office once a month. The group also decides that group members who are late for meetings can expect to receive a friendly phone call from the chair of the day asking them to explain why.	Your role as manager is to help the group clarify and implement appropriate roles and norms.
Performing	The group works hard for the rest of the year. Individuals contribute their particular expertise to approach tasks and problems as they arise, and most final decisions are made by the group. The group only votes when the problem is relatively trivial or when it is extremely pressed for time (which is seldom). All really important decisions are reached by consensus.	Your main job as manager is to check in with the group to make sure their process is continuing effectively. If it is not, either work with them yourself or obtain outside help from internal or external consultants.
Adjourning	Its developmental work done, the group meets for a full day to debrief its work and plan how the group members will stay involved with the project as it is implemented. Informally, group members talk about what's next for each of them. The group has a celebratory lunch on the company.	Your job as manager is to promote your group's success in the company, including the rewards that come with that success. (Also, pay the bill.)

FIGURE 9.3

The Punctuated Equilibrium Model

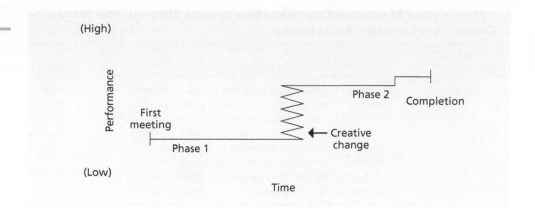

How *Short-Term* Groups Evolve

Sometimes a group's process is triggered more by the members' awareness of time factors and deadlines than by the need to complete an absolute amount of work in a specific developmental stage. When this happens, groups run only for the short term, and they follow a pattern that differs from the five-stage approach in Table 9.2.[48]

In its first meeting, the group develops a framework of assumptions and norms, including a plan, and the group sticks with these approaches throughout the first half of its life. During this first half of its deliberations, the group may show little visible progress because, although individual members are gathering information, the group as a whole is unmotivated to integrate all of their information or revise its initial plan for approaching the task.

About halfway through the allotted time, the group changes its mode. At this point, it attempts to capitalize on the learning its members have accomplished so far and it reevaluates its basic plan. Subsequently the group enters phase two, during which its revised plan is implemented. During this phase, again there is likely to be no visible progress, until, nearing the end of the assignment, there is a final push to meet group goals.

Although the midpoint is typically the point at which groups reappraise their plans, this is not always the case. The point at which a reappraisal is accomplished differs because of individual differences among the group members. For example, the individuals in the group may notice and think about deadlines differently. They may also differ in their sense of time urgency and time perspective.[49] For these reasons, the composition of the group significantly affects its time planning and its ability to meet deadlines.

The model for the behavior of short-term groups that we have just described is the **punctuated equilibrium model** (see Figure 9.3). In sum, this model suggests that time-pressured groups progress through long periods of inertia, punctuated by concentrated, creative periods of significant change.[50] Since so many business processes are time-constrained, understanding how such groups function is an important topic for today's researchers.

punctuated equilibrium model
A model which suggests that time-pressured groups progress through long periods of inertia, punctuated by concentrated, creative periods of significant change.

What Special Issues Do You Face When Managing a Self-Directed Team?

self-directed team
A group that is responsible for a whole product or service and makes its own decisions about task assignments and work methods.

A **self-directed team** is a group that is responsible for a whole product or service, and that makes its own decisions about task assignments and work methods. In some cases acting without a supervisor, the team is responsible for managing its own support services, including things such as maintenance, purchasing, and quality control. It may even perform personnel functions such as hiring and firing team members and determining pay increases. Such teams are also called autonomous work groups, self-managed work teams, and self-regulating work teams.[51]

Managers of self-directed teams must change their orientation from directing and leading to coaching and assisting. On a daily basis, their job is to back their people, get them what they need to do the job, educate them, and work with them as a member of the team.[52] For many managers, this transition from traditional management styles to participative management styles is difficult. As the CEO of Xerox put it, "It's gut wrenching. The hardest person to change is the line manager. After he's worked like a dog for five or ten years to get promoted, we have to say to him or her, 'All those reasons you wanted to be a manager? Wrong.'"[53]

There are any number of reasons why traditional team leaders do not want to change their leadership practices.[54] One key reason is that becoming a coach rather than a leader can be experienced as a demotion. Titles often change along with the role, so that someone called a "manager" might become a "facilitator."

Also, to encourage an egalitarian climate in the group, sometimes managers are asked to give up their traditional perks, such as preferred parking spaces or a spacious office. In addition, in many instances the new team leader role has not been well-defined: Often team leaders need training in how to coach, including the fundamentals of group process and decision making, but also in how to represent their group in the organization. If the organization does not define these new behaviors, the leaders may be confused about what exactly they should be doing.

Another problem may be that some managers are concerned about losing their jobs due to this transition. In truth, a substantial reduction in management positions does tend to be associated with the introduction of self-managed teams.[55] Finally, many team leaders find that although they are being asked to coach, they themselves are being directed. The hypocrisy of expecting managers to manage in a way that is different from the way they are managed themselves may not sit well with them.

On the other hand, it appears that when employees are given more power, a number of business conditions improve. Approximately half of the companies in a survey of the *Fortune* 1000 report that employee involvement improved profitability and competitiveness.[56] This is because empowerment improves employee trust in management, the quality of management decisions, a variety of organizational processes and procedures, implementation of technology, and employee safety and health.

What Special Issues Do You Face When Managing a Virtual Team?

A **virtual team** is a group of employees situated in distant locations whose members have unique skills and must collaborate using technology to accomplish their assigned tasks.[57] IBM has been using virtual teams since it went global in the 1970s,[58] and today about one-third of its employees participate at some point in such teams.

Virtual teams can be quite complex. For example, they may have members from more than one organization, and from a variety of time zones. They may have members from more than one function, or more than one national culture.[59] Also, virtual teams can interact in a variety of ways. They may meet: 1) at the same time and same place, such as in face-to-face meetings, 2) at the same time but in a different place, such as via audio- or video-conference, 3) at a different time but the same place, such as using a chat room on a network, or 4) at a different time and a different place, such as by exchanging e-mail messages.

A common type of virtual team is the **networked team**, which consists of people who collaborate to achieve a common goal across time, distance, or organizational boundaries.[60] Another type is the **parallel team**, which carries out special assignments that the regular organization does not want to do, also working across time, distance, or organizational boundaries. Other types of virtual teams include product development teams, which conduct projects for users over a long period of time, work teams that perform regular and ongoing work, service teams, and even some management teams.

The use of virtual teams is expanding exponentially in business today because 1) virtual teams can respond rapidly and flexibly to global business challenges, 2) traveling and

virtual team
A group of employees situated in distant locations whose members have unique skills and must collaborate using technology to accomplish their assigned tasks.

networked team
A virtual team which consists of people who collaborate to achieve a common goal across time, distance, or organizational boundaries.

parallel team
A virtual team which carries out special assignments that the regular organization does not want to do, and also works across time, distance, or organizational boundaries.

having continual face-to-face meetings is not particularly efficient or effective, 3) virtual teams lessen the disruption of people's lives because people don't have to travel to meet, and 4) they help people to broaden their careers and perspectives by working in a variety of cultures and organizations on a variety of tasks and projects.[61]

Theoretically, a virtual team could be a work group, a real team, or a self-directed team. However, the latest research indicates that virtual teams are so unique that they really deserve separate treatment. For example, researchers are becoming interested in the amount of time virtual teams work together as opposed to apart, as contrasted with **co-located work teams** (teams that always work together). One interesting question is how much time the team needs in face-to-face meetings in order to develop mutual understanding and cohesion.

The research on virtual teams is still relatively limited. However, we can venture some hypotheses about what processes work for them.[62] For example, we now know that empowering virtual teams—giving them more participation, knowledge, and responsibility—helps them improve their own process, including how well they seek feedback, discuss errors, and experiment with innovative ideas. Empowerment of virtual teams may also improve customer satisfaction. However, we also know that for virtual teams to be effective, team members must demonstrate a particularly high level of initiative and proactivity.

Of course, virtual teams face many communication challenges.[63] One is compensating for lack of nonverbal elements in communications, things such as smiles and voice levels. A second challenge is building personal relationships via primarily technological interaction. Finally, virtual teams are especially challenged when they need to access and leverage the unique knowledge possessed by each member.

What Issues Arise in Multicultural Teams? In Virtual Multicultural Teams?

Since most modern companies rely extensively on teamwork, and global companies are no exception, there is a strong probability that you will one day become a member of a multicultural team. For example, you might serve on a team comprised of multiple nationalities that is responsible for developing and launching a product in several countries, or you might serve on a team that is responsible for developing a product delivery strategy for Europe.

A variety of problems may emerge. For one thing, multicultural teams tend to develop tensions grounded in their diversity.[64] As noted by Percy Barnevik, the former President and CEO of the global engineering company ABB, "Multinational teams do not happen naturally. On the contrary, the human inclination is to stick to its own kind. If in selecting a manager the choice is between a compatriot with a familiar background, and a foreigner whose credentials appear strange and whose language is difficult to understand, objective criteria tend to lose out."[65] For example, IBM (based in the United States), Siemens (based in Germany), and Toshiba (based in Japan) formed a joint venture to develop a computer chip.[66] The IBMers complained that the Germans planned too much. The Germans complained that the Japanese would close their eyes and "rest" during meetings—a common Japanese practice among higher-ups who have delegated managing the meeting to their subordinates. The Japanese complained about sitting in small, individual offices and having to speak English.

For another thing, consider the influence of status and power and how these are viewed cross-culturally. A team of all Chinese managers has a common framework for interpreting the meaning of hierarchy in their organization. Their framework would include the idea that older managers have more status. But mix an American or two into their team and immediately these assumptions come into question and may, indeed, become a source of conflict. Factor in different cultural attitudes to everything from time management to gender roles, and multinational team management indeed suggests many challenges.

Finally, consider the issues that faced a certain company's human resources project team, a team that was quite stressed. The team consisted of five members, each of whom

co-located work team
A team that always works together.

represented the HR group of a different country in Latin America or South America.[67] The group was a time-limited project team in which five nationalities and one ethnicity were represented. There were four women and one man on the team, and team members ranged in age from 35 to 55. The team was not functioning well. Why? For one thing, each member had different goals and priorities, as dictated by the unique challenges and constraints they faced in their particular region. For another thing, outside of the project itself, there was little cooperation among the countries, in part because their national cultures were quite different.

To diagnose the difficulties that may arise on multicultural teams, national culture and ethnicity must be added to all of the factors already discussed in this chapter. Among other things, to better understand and guide their multinational teams, managers must understand the extent to which a team shares the same mind set, the extent of overt interpersonal conflict, and the influence of members' personal and cultural identities.

In Conclusion

In this chapter we have explored the importance and nature of groups, paying special attention to that particular type of group that is called a team. (See Table 9.3 for an overview of the main types of teams.) Whatever the nature of the group, as a manager your goal is to maximize its assets and minimize its liabilities, and to see that group members enjoy, learn, and profit from their group experience. Our next chapter is even more applied. In it, you will learn how to design and coach a team, and how to represent your team in the larger organization of which it is a part.

TABLE 9.3 Overview: Types of Teams

Potential team: a group that is really trying to improve its performance, but does not require collective accountability of the team members, has not developed clarity about its task, and lacks the discipline to hammer out a group process.

Real team: a group that is committed to a common purpose and working collectively toward its goals, while holding themselves mutually accountable for achieving them.

High-performance team: a group that has all the characteristics of a real team, but in addition, its members are deeply committed to each other's personal growth and success.

Self-directed team: a group that is responsible for a whole product or service, and that makes its own decisions about task assignments and work methods. These teams are also called autonomous work groups, self-managed work teams, and self-regulating work teams.

Virtual team: a group of employees situated in distant locations whose members have unique skills and must collaborate using technology to accomplish their assigned tasks.

Networked team: people who collaborate to achieve a common goal across time, distance, or organizational boundaries.

Parallel team: people who carry out special assignments that the regular organization does not want to do, also working across time, distance, or organizational boundaries.

Multinational team: a group comprised of two or more nationalities or ethnicities.

Apply What You Have Learned . . .

World Class Company: W. L. Gore & Associates

At W. L. Gore & Associates, the manufacturer of GoreTex Registered Trademark fabric and other materials, teams are the core building block of the organization.[68] Associates are hired not only for their technical skills but also their team, communication, and problem-solving skills. For instance, in a job interview a candidate might be asked to describe a time he or she had a conflict with a team member, or to tell how he or she solved a problem that was impeding a team project.

At Gore, project teams and business units communicate directly with each other without benefit of a hierarchy. Instead of bosses, teams have "sponsors." Natural leaders evolve during projects, and they gain followers by being very good at what they do. Employees don't have titles, either; instead, they "make commitments." The company believes this design motivates employees to take responsibility. As one engineer puts it, "One reason that I've stayed with Gore for my entire professional career is for the freedom that I have. I find that I am motivated by setting my own goals. As long as these goals are aligned with company objectives, a support structure is provided, enabling me to be successful."[69]

Compensation is determined by about 15 committees, one for each functional area. These committees include local specialists who can recognize technical excellence in that particular function, and, also, typically, a generalist who hails from elsewhere in the company. A human resources professional is also included to make sure the process is fair. The compensation teams use extensive internal feedback to rank associates from highest to lowest, based on their contribution to the success of the business. The people ranked highest are paid more than those who are ranked lowest.

Bill Gore established the company's unique team culture when he founded W. L. Gore & Associates in 1958. The company's core values are:[70]

1. Fairness to each other and everyone with whom we come in contact.
2. Freedom to encourage, help, and allow other associates to grow in knowledge, skill, and scope of responsibility.
3. The ability to make one's own commitments and keep them.
4. Consultation with other associates before undertaking actions that could impact the reputation of the company by hitting it "below the waterline."

Is Gore a laid-back place to work? *Au contraire*. As one PR professional there puts it, "People have a misconception that this is a soft corporate culture, but this is a pretty tough environment for people to be in. We put a lot of responsibility on individuals to be personally successful and to work toward business success."[71]

The people at W. L. Gore & Associates have a saying that if you are not inventing it, making it, or selling it, you are wasting your time. Today, with 6,500 associates in 45 locations around the world, Gore has been identified by *Fortune* magazine as one of the 100 best places to work in America.

Discuss

1. Identify the teams in this company.
2. How does the teamwork motivate the associates?
3. Gore rewards individuals, not teams. What do you think of their reward process? If even this forward-looking company does not reward teams, what does this say about the theory that team-based rewards create more effective teams?

Advice from the Pros

How to Build a Cross-Cultural Team

Two manufacturing companies, both with markets throughout Europe, merged.[72] One company was French, and the other was British (from the United Kingdom). Immediately after the merger, cultural differences began to interfere with decision making in the new company's work groups. Both sides saw business as inefficient, and there was a lot of griping about the incompetence of "the other side."

The president of the new company, committed to developing an open, collaborative culture company-wide,

hired consultants, who set up a two-day workshop on group process. Fourteen top people, seven French and seven British, attended. They included the president and the two levels of management just below him.

At the beginning, each participant was asked to make a short presentation about his role and department, and the others were asked to critique his style. The French found that about half of the U.K. participants were hard to understand because they spoke quickly and used a lot of jargon. They also felt the U.K. participants were too laid back and detached. For their part, the U.K. participants found the

French too enthusiastic, especially in terms of their body language. The French approach was dubbed too emotional. It was perceived to be irrational and lacking in credibility.

Next, the French and the U.K. participants each simulated a meeting that was critiqued by their counterparts in the other country. Distinct patterns were discovered. In the United Kingdom, for instance, the purpose of meetings is to agree on actions and make decisions. People expect to stick to an agenda, deviating only if new priorities emerge, and they generally agree on specific follow-up actions. They are time conscious, and, it goes without saying, they are expected to attend. In France, in contrast, it is acceptable to stray from the agenda. The purpose of meetings is not necessarily to decide but rather to give input to decisions. The key decision maker may not even be at the meeting. And French people are not time conscious—they come and go, and there may be side discussions.

Next, the participants discussed and debated which style was more useful for the company, and they decided that either style could be appropriate depending on the circumstance. A French-style meeting would be best when the decision involved general policy and marketing issues, whereas a U.K.-style meeting would be best when quick action was needed.

Finally, several simulated meetings were conducted to put new skills into practice and build cross-cultural teamwork. By the end of the workshop, the company was able to develop guidelines for how they wanted to conduct future meetings, and subsequent follow-up suggested they were able to do a better job cross-culturally. An additional training course was run for 10 other managers.

What advice do the consultants have for developing cross-cultural teams?

Consultant Mel Berger points out that cross-cultural training for teams must take into account the different learning styles of the cultures. In this instance, both cultures were comfortable learning through consensus. The role of the consultant was to design the learning events and facilitate communication, and sub-groups were comfortable voicing their opinions. However, some cultures prefer a style in which the consultant acts as the expert and people expect to be told how to behave. Still others prefer a style in which participants give personal feedback and debate with each other, and the consultant provides stimulating tasks and feedback.

Says Berger, "At the core of cross-cultural teamwork is mutual respect for different approaches, values, and deeply held attitudes to work and life . . . we must recognize the added dimension and complexity of living in a multicultural world of work. We must train managers and all boundary crossers to adapt their skills to the cultural context in which they find themselves."[73]

Discuss

1. Describe the British and French cultural groups in terms of their goals, norms, and cohesion.
2. List some of the difficulties experienced by this and other typical multinational teams.
3. How can the company ensure that the learning from this cross-cultural workshop is transferred back to actual meetings in the company?

Gain Experience

Recognizing Teams and Their Power

Individually. . .

Think about a small group (not more than eight people) you know that has (or had) power. It could be either a formal or an informal group, inside a business or not.

1. Why is this group memorable to you?
2. List the characteristics of the group in terms of its
   Size
   Goals
   Norms (informal rules)
   Cohesion
   Roles (expectations for particular individuals)
3. Was it a potential team, real team, or high-performance team? Give two reasons why you believe it fits the particular type.

In groups of three or four. . .

1. Share why the team is memorable to you.
2. Choose the most interesting team and be prepared to describe it (in terms of the details above) to the class.

Can You Solve this Manager's Problem?

Allaboutself.com

Mia Cipirano, founder of a Web site for working women called allaboutself.com, needs to cut costs by eliminating some of the expensive perks enjoyed by her staff. Talking with her process consultant, she muses about whether to create a team to help her do this, and about the leadership of the team. Is the team likely to agree with her goal? Should she choose Mike the Web-master, who is smart and spends so much time in his office working really hard, or should she choose Anita, who likes and motivates people?

Discuss

1. Is the group she creates likely to agree with Mia's goal? What will happen if they disagree?
2. Is a group likely to be effective in making this decision? Why or why not?
3. If Mia puts together a five-member team, who should lead it, Mike or Anita?
4. What would you advise Mia to say to the team as they come together for the first time?
5. What can Mia do to ensure that the team moves toward a high-performance stage of development?

Chapter Summary and Key Terms

Why are groups so important to organizations?

Groups come in many types and are used throughout organizations. They represent a key building block of organizations, and they suggest power relationships. Depending on the circumstances, they may make better or worse decisions than individuals.

group   238
formal groups   238
informal groups   239
risky shift   240
social identity   240
deindividuation   240
in-group   241
out-group   241

What key factors define a group?

Groups are characterized by unity of purpose, small size, norms, cohesion, and roles. Individuals may exert more effort working in groups than if working alone.

norms   242
cohesion   242
conformity   242
roles   243
role strain   243
interrole conflict   243
motivation gain   243
social compensation   243
Köhler effect   243

What is a team?

All teams are groups, but not all groups are teams. Types of groups include working groups, potential teams, real teams, and high-performance teams. The major difference between working groups and teams is that teams actually work on projects together. Real teams and high-performance teams have a significant element of trust among team members.

working group   243
team   243
potential team   244
real team   245
high-performance team   245

How do groups and teams evolve over time?

There are two models for group evolution. Usually groups proceed through the stages of forming, storming, norming, performing, and adjourning. Time-pressured groups may progress from long periods of inertia through concentrated periods of energy and change.

process   246
content   246
process consultant   246
punctuated equilibrium model   248

What special issues do you face when managing a self-directed team?

Teams that are responsible for a whole product or service and make many of their own decisions are widely used in business today. Managing such teams requires dropping the traditional directive style and adopting a coaching style, a transition that is not always easy for either managers or employees.

self-directed team   248

What special issues do you face when managing a virtual team?

Managing or being a member of a virtual team differs from managing or being a member of a co-located team. For example, virtual teams meet in a variety of ways. They also tend to be complex, and they face unique communication challenges.

virtual team   249
networked team   249
parallel team   249
co-located work team   250

What issues arise in multicultural teams? In virtual multicultural teams?

When working in a multicultural team, you must consider national culture and ethnicity. Team members must consider how members' cultural identities affect their interactions, and they may face more interpersonal conflict than might occur in homogeneous teams.

Explorations

1. How different social science disciplines think about groups

Web search for "groups," matched separately with "sociology," "anthropology," "communication," "psychology," and "political science." How do these different disciplines approach the topic of groups? What applications of group theory seem to interest them?

2. Groups in context

Examine the abstracts for articles in the journal *Group Dynamics: Theory, Research, and Practice.* These are available through PsychInfo, the Social Sciences Citation Index, and other databases. In what other contexts besides business are groups studied? What are the fields of the researchers who study groups?

3. Virtual groups

Web search for "virtual group." What do you learn about virtual meetings and virtual collaboration?

References

[1] C. Joinson, "Teams at Work," *HR Magazine 44* (5), May 1999:30–36.

[2] J. M. Levine and R. L. Moreland, "Group Socialization: Theory and Research," in W. Stroebe and M. Hewstone, eds., *European Review of Social Psychology 5* (Chichester, England: Wiley, 1994): 305–336; J. M. Levine and R. L. Moreland, "Small Groups," in D. T. Gilbert, S. T. Fiske, and G. Lindzey, *The Handbook of Social Psychology 2*, 4th ed. (New York: McGraw-Hill,1998):415–469.

[3] F. Johansson, "Masters of the Multicultural," *Harvard Business Review 83* (10) October 2005:18–19.

[4] N. R. F. Maier, "Assets and Liabilities in Group Problem Solving: The Need for an Integrative Function," *Psychological Review,* April 1967:239–249; P. H. Hill, "Decisions Involving the Corporate Environment," in W. C. Swap and Associates, eds., *Group Decision Making* (Beverly Hills, CA: Sage Publications, 1984): 251–279; R. A. Cooke and J. A. Kernaghan, "Estimating the Difference between Group versus Individual Performance on Problem-Solving Tasks," *Group & Organization Studies 12* (3), September 1987:319–342.

[5] L. K. Michaelsen, W. E. Watson, and R. H. Black, "A Realistic Test of Individual versus Group Consensus Decision Making," *Journal of Applied Psychology 74* (5), October 1989:834–839.

[6] N. R. F. Maier, "Assets and Liabilities in Group Problem Solving: The Need for an Integrative Function," *Psychological Review,* April 1967:239–249; P. H. Hill, "Decisions Involving the Corporate Environment," in W. C. Swap and Associates, eds., *Group Decision Making* (Beverly Hills, CA: Sage Publications, 1984):251–279.

[7] D. A. Bernstein, L. A. Penner, A. Clarke-Stewart, and E. J. Roy, *Psychology* (Boston and New York: Houghton Mifflin Company, 2003):650. Thanks to these authors, too, for suggesting a question similar to the one that opens this paragraph.

[8] L. R. Troop and S. Wright, "Ingroup Identification as the Inclusion of Ingroup in the Self," *Personality & Social Psychology Bulletin 2*, 2001:585–600.

[9] M. B. Brewer, "The Many Faces of Social Identity: Implications for Political Psychology," *Political Psychology 22* (1), 2001:115–125.

[10] R. K. Merton, "Social Structure and Anomie," *American Sociological Review 3* (6), October 1938: 672–682; J. Mirowsky and C. Ross, "Working Wives and Mental Health," Presentation to the American Association for the Advancement of Science, New York, 1984.

[11] W. C. Swap, "Destructive Effects of Groups on Individuals," in W. C. Swap and Associates, eds., *Group Decision Making* (Beverly Hills, CA: Sage Publications, 1984):73.

[12] J. C. Macionis, *Sociology* 10th ed. (Upper Saddle River, NJ: Pearson/Prentice Hall, 2005):168.

[13] J. W. Jackson and E. R. Smith, "Conceptualizing Social Identity: A New Framework and Evidence for the Impact of Different Dimensions," *Personality & Social Psychology Bulletin 25* (1), 1999:120–135.

[14] J. R. Katzenbach and D. K. Smith, "The Discipline of Teams," *Harvard Business Review 71* (2), March/April 1993:111–120.

[15] See also J. Thomas and C. F. Fink, "Effects of Group Size," in L. L. Cummings and W. E. Scott, eds., *Readings in Organizational Behavior and Human Performance* (Homewood, IL: Irwin, 1969):99–124; B. Mullen, C. Symons, L. Hu, and E. Salas, "Group Size, Leadership Behavior, and Subordinate Satisfaction," *Journal of General Psychology 116* (2), April 1989:155–70.

[16] B. Mullen and R. F. Baumeister, "Group Effects on Self-Attention and Performance: Social Loafing, Social Facilitation, and Social Impairment," in C. Hendrick, ed., *Review of Personality and Social Psychology* (Beverly Hills: Sage, 1987):189–206; B. Mullen, D. A. Johnson and S. D. Drake, "Organizational Productivity as a Function of Group Composition: A Self-Attention Perspective," *Journal of Social Psychology 127* (1987):143–150.

[17] M. E. Shaw, "Distribution of Participation as a Function of Group Size," *The Psychology of Small Group Behavior* (New York: McGraw-Hill, 1981).

[18] Doug Johnson, Associate Director of the Center for the Study of Work Teams, University of North Texas, in C. Joinson, "Teams at Work," *HR Magazine 44* (5), May 1999:30–36, 36.

[19] D. C. Feldman, "The Development and Enforcement of Group Norms," *Academy of Management Review 9* (1), January 1984:47–53.

[20] E. J. Lawler, S. R. Thye, and J. Yoon, "Emotion and Group Cohesion in Productive Exchange," *American Journal of Sociology 106* (3), November 2000:616–657.

[21] L. Festinger, "Informal Social Communication," *Psychological Review 57*, 1950:271–282.

[22] M. E. Shaw, *Group Dynamics* (New York: McGraw-Hill, 1981).

[23] R. N. Nibler and K. L. Harris, "The Effects of Culture and Cohesiveness on Intragroup Conflict and Effectiveness," *Journal of Social Psychology 143* (5), October 2003:613–631.

[24] B. Mullen and C. Copper, "The Relationship between Group Cohesiveness and Performance: An Integration," *Psychological Bulletin 115,* 1994: 210–277.

[25] S. Asch, *Social Psychology* (Englewood Cliffs, NJ: Prentice Hall, 1952).

[26] S. Asch, "Effects of Group Pressure Upon the Modification and Distortion of Judgments," in H. Guetzkow, ed., *Groups, Leadership, and Men: Research in Human Relations* (New York: Russell & Russell, 1963):177–190.

[27] J. M. Levine and R. L. Moreland, "Small Groups," in D. T. Gilbert, S. T. Fiske, and G. Lindzey, *The Handbook of Social Psychology 2,* 4th ed. (New York: McGraw-Hill, 1998): 415–469, 426.

[28] N. L. Kerr and R. S. Tindale, "Group Performance and Decision Making," in *Annual Review of Psychology 55,* 2004:623–655, 628–629.

[29] S. J. Karau, and K. D. Williams, "The Effects of Group Cohesion on Social Loafing and Social Compensation," *Group Dynamics: Theory, Research, and Practice 1,* 1997:156–168.

[30] O. Köhler, Kraftleistungen bei Einzelund Gruppenabeit [Physical Performance in Individual and Group Situations] *Ind. Psychotech. 4* 1926:209–226.

[31] N. L. Kerr and R. S. Tindale, "Group Performance and Decision Making," in *Annual Review of Psychology 55,* 2004: 623–655, 628–629.

[32] These definitions are provided in J. R. Katzenbach and D. K. Smith, *The Wisdom of Teams* (New York: HarperBusiness Essentials, 2003).

[33] J. R. Katzenbach and D. K. Smith, "The Discipline of Teams," *Harvard Business Review 71* (2), March/April 1993: 111–120.

[34] J. R. Katzenbach and D. K. Smith, "The Discipline of Teams," *Harvard Business Review 71* (2), March/April 1993:111–120.

[35] L. L. Thompson, *Making the Team: A Guide for Managers* (Upper Saddle River, NJ: Pearson/Prentice Hall, 2000).

[36] L. L. Thompson, *Making the Team: A Guide for Managers* (Upper Saddle River, NJ: Pearson/Prentice Hall, 2000).

[37] C. A. April, "Microsoft Stakes Out the Middle," *VARBusiness 21* (21), October 3, 2005:33–36.

[38] D. Roberts and D. Rocks, "China: Let a Thousand Brands Bloom," *BusinessWeek online* October 17, 2005, http://www.businessweek.com/print/magazine/content. Accessed October 15, 2005.

[39] J. R. Hackman, "Creating More Effective Work Groups in Organizations," in J. R. Hackman, ed., *Groups That Work (and Those That Don't): Creating Conditions for Effective Teamwork* (San Francisco: Jossey-Bass, 1990).

[40] J. R. Hackman, "Why Teams Don't Work," in R. S. Tindale, L. Heath, J. Edwards, E. J. Posavac, F. B. Bryant, Y. Suarez-Balcazar, E. Henderson-King, and J. Myers, *Theory and Research on Small Groups* (New York: Plenum Press, 1998).

[41] M. Williams, "In Whom We Trust: Group Membership as an Affective Context for Trust Development," *Academy of Management Review 26* (3), July 2001:377–396.

[42] D. L. Duarte and N. T. Snyder, *Mastering Virtual Teams: Strategies, Tools, and Techniques that Succeed* (San Francisco: Jossey-Bass, 1999):139.

[43] P. M. Blau, *Exchange and Power in Social Life* (New York: Wiley, 1964); L. G. Zucker, "Production of Trust: Institutional Sources of Economic Structure, 1840–1920," in B. M. Straw & L. L. Cummings, eds., *Research in Organizational Behavior 8* (Greenwich, CT: JAI Press, 1986):53–111; J. S. Coleman, "Social Capital in the Creation of Human Capital," *American Journal of Sociology 94* (supplement), 1998:95–120.

[44] W. W. Powell, "Neither Market nor Hierarchy: Network Forms of Organization," in B. M. Straw & L. L. Cummings, eds., *Research in Organizational Behavior 12* (Greenwich, CT: JAI Press, 1990):295–336.

[45] B. W. Tuckman, "Developmental Sequence in Small Groups," *Psychological Bulletin 63* (6), 1965:384–399.

[46] B. W. Tuckman and M. A. C. Jensen, "Stages of Small-Group Development Revisited," *Group & Organization Studies 2* (4), December 1977:419–427.

[47] G. Gibbard and J. Hartman, "The Oedipal Paradigm in Group Development: A Clinical and Empirical Study," *Small Group Behavior 4* (3), 1973:305–349.

[48] C. J. G. Gersick, "Time and Transition in Work Teams: Toward a New Model of Group Development," *Academy of Management Journal 31* (1), March 1988:9–41.

[49] M. J. Waller, J. M. Conte, C. B. Gibson, and M. A. Carpenter, "The Effect of Individual Perceptions of Deadlines on Team Performance," *Academy of Management Review 26* (4), October 2001:586–600.

[50] N. Eldrege and S. Gould, "Punctuated Equilibrium: An Alternative to Phyletic Gradualism," in T. J. M. Schopf, ed., *Models in Paleobiology* (San Francisco: Freeman, Cooper and Company, 1972):82–115.

[51] E. E. Lawler, III, S. A. Mohrman, and G. E. Ledford, Jr., *Employee Involvement and Total Quality Management: Practices and Results in Fortune 1000 Companies* (San Francisco: Jossey-Bass, 1992).

[52] Bill Eaton (member of the Levi Strauss executive committee) in K. Fisher, *Leading Self-Directed Work Teams: A Guide to Developing New Team Leadership Skills* (New York: McGraw-Hill, 1993).

[53] W. H. Davidow and M. S. Malone, *The Virtual Corporation: Structuring and Revitalizing the Corporation for the 21st Century* (New York: Harper Collins Publishers, 1992):177.

[54] K. Fisher, *Leading Self-Directed Work Teams: A Guide to Developing New Team Leadership Skills* (New York: McGraw-Hill, 1993).

[55] E.E. Lawler, III, S. A. Mohrman, and G. E. Ledford, Jr., *Employee Involvement and Total Quality Management: Practices and Results in Fortune 1000 Companies* (San Francisco: Jossey-Bass, 1992).

[56] E. E. Lawler, III, S. A. Mohrman, and G. E. Ledford, Jr., *Employee Involvement and Total Quality Management: Practices and Results in Fortune 1000 Companies* (San Francisco: Jossey-Bass, 1992).

[57] J. Lipnack and J. Stamps, *Virtual Teams: People Working across Boundaries with Technology,* 2nd ed. (New York: Wiley, 2000).

[58] C. Joinson, "Managing Virtual Teams," *HR Magazine 47* (6), June 2002:68–73.

[59] D. L. Duarte and N. T. Snyder, *Mastering Virtual Teams: Strategies, Tools, and Techniques That Succeed* (San Francisco: Jossey-Bass, 1999).

[60] D. L. Duarte and N. T. Snyder, *Mastering Virtual Teams: Strategies, Tools, and Techniques That Succeed* (San Francisco: Jossey-Bass, 1999).

[61] D. L. Duarte and N. T. Snyder, *Mastering Virtual Teams: Strategies, Tools, and Techniques That Succeed* (San Francisco: Jossey-Bass, 1999).

[62] D. L. Duarte and N. T. Snyder, *Mastering Virtual Teams: Strategies, Tools, and Techniques That Succeed* (San Francisco: Jossey-Bass, 1999).

[63] D. B. Roebuck, S. J. Brock, and D. R. Moodie, "Using a Simulation to Explore the Challenges of Communicating in a Virtual Team," *Business Communication Quarterly 67,* (3), September 2004:359–367.

[64] See S. C. Schneider and J. Barsoux, *Managing Across Cultures* (Harlow, England: FT Prentice Hall, 2003.)

[65] P. Barnevik, "Making Local Heroes International," *Financial Times,* January 17, 1994:8.

[66] E. S. Browning, "Side by Side. . . " *The Wall Street Journal,* May 3, 1994.

[67] P. E. Earley and C. B. Gibson, *Multinational Work Teams: A New Perspective* (Mahwah, New Jersey: Lawrence Erlbaum Associates, Publishers, 2002).

[68] Based on information in K. A. Field, "Giving Engineers the Freedom to Engineer," *Design News* 58 (15) August 5, 2002:41, D. Anfuso, "Core Values Shape W. L. Gore's Innovative Culture," *Workforce 78* (3), March 1999:48–51, *and* "Fortune 100 Best Places to Work For," http://money.cnn.com/magazines/fortune/bestcompanies/snapshots/1542.html, accessed May 29, 2007.

[69] K. A. Field, "Giving Engineers the Freedom to Engineer," *Design News* 58 (15) August 5, 2002:41

[70] D. Anfuso, "Core Values Shape W. L. Gore's Innovative Culture," *Workforce 78* (3), March 1999:48–51, 49.

[71] D. Anfuso, "Core Values Shape W. L. Gore's Innovative Culture," *Workforce 78* (3), March 1999:48–51, 53.

[72] M. Berger, "Going Global: Implications for Communication and Leadership Training," *Industrial and Commercial Training 30* (4), 1998:123–127, 126.

[73] M. Berger, "Going Global: Implications for Communication and Leadership Training," *Industrial and Commercial Training 30* (4), 1998:123–127, 127.

10

Improving Team Effectiveness

Preview

How do you design a team?

How can you set a clear and energizing direction for your team?

How do you coach the team?
Choose people with team potential
Get the group off to a good start
Develop group roles
Monitor participation
Enhance personal alignment
Utilize experts effectively
Develop an ethical group process
Delegate and empower

Be aware of the pitfalls in group decision making
Groupthink
Social loafing
Polarization
Social facilitation
Consider structuring the group decision making

How do you run an effective meeting?
Open the meeting with a clear focus
Create a culture that fosters participation
Keep the team focused on its task
End with a task focus

How do you interface for your team to obtain information, resources, and rewards?
Build relationships between the team and the broader organization
Scout for the information the team needs
Nurture both external and internal support
Implement team-based rewards
Obtain team training

How do you lead a virtual team?

How do you lead a multicultural team? A virtual multicultural team?
Special issues of multicultural virtual teams

Corporate Coaching International

Being an effective group is not just about communicating well together. It's about developing depth in both relationships and problem-solving skills. It's about the ability to confront each other in a healthy way. So says Lois Frankel, CEO of Corporate Coaching International, (see accompanying photo) a process consultation firm that helps management groups become more effective.

Frankel's specialty is taking groups off-site for developmental seminars. What do they do there? They sit on the floor. They draw pictures of boats. They climb through the trees in groups. What are they learning? How to be better group members, leaders, and managers.

For one thing, participants are learning about themselves. Frankel helps people see themselves as others see them and to decide whether or not they want to change. She helps them develop the skills they need to make the transition. For another thing, participants learn about the importance of group roles— the task roles that move the team's project forward, and the group building and maintenance roles that improve the group process. Teams also learn how to turn conflict into a positive force. And they do all these things with the other members of their actual company work group.

Does this sound like fun to you? Could you trust your group enough to allow them to help you to grow? Could you help others in your group develop their skills as team players?

You now know that groups are interesting, ubiquitous, and powerful. So how do you manage one? As the manager of a group, your goal is to maximize your team's potential for efficient decision making and collective action by encouraging constructive dissent and learning. To accomplish this goal, you must meet four conditions.[1]

First, design your team well. Second, ensure that your team has a clear, energizing direction. Third, coach instead of directing. Finally, interface between your team and the rest of your organization to make sure the team has the appropriate information and resources it needs, and, of course, the appropriate rewards. In this chapter we will describe each of these tasks in detail, providing you with a set of clear guidelines for managing an effective team. One caution: This chapter focuses on managing teams in the United States. To manage teams in other countries, including multicultural teams, you would have to take into account a host of cross-cultural differences.

How Do You Design a Team?

When you are designing a real team, the first consideration is its size. The team should be as small as possible given the nature of the work to be done. Ask yourself the question, "How small can the group be and still have the human resources needed to accomplish the assigned task?"[2] Research seldom contradicts the view that small groups are the most effective. One exception is that uncovering the individual expertise in a group may be easier to do in larger groups, a situation that we will discuss later in the chapter.[3]

The optimal size of a group is five, because this is generally thought to be small enough to be time-efficient, yet large enough to contain a diversity of viewpoints and approaches. If you need a large number of people in order to make a decision, you should consider breaking them into teams of five, and then convening the larger group to integrate their findings.

Give your team clear boundaries by being explicit about who is in the group and who is not. Given the politics inherent in organizational life, this may be more difficult than it first appears. Yet, being clear about who is a member is important when it comes to assigning responsibility for group successes and failures. Also, when there is ambiguity about who is in the group and who is not, members become frustrated by not knowing who to include in meetings and who they can count on for help. The group's effectiveness may suffer. Although in the initial stages of convening a group membership may be left unclear, at some point it is necessary for the group to be able to say "this is who we are" and move on from there.[4]

Choose the members of your team for both their task skills and their interpersonal skills. Business today often depends on knowledge specialists, and it is quite likely that some individuals will have in-depth information that other individuals do not have. However, having task expertise should be accompanied, if at all possible, by having the interpersonal skills that will bring out that expertise. As mentioned above, recent research has indicated that groups are not as good at revealing the expertise held by their individual members as we previously had thought.[5] You cannot assume that putting experts together in a room will lead to the actual use of their expertise if the group does not have process skills.

Finally, design a team that has a high probability of developing cohesion, because more cohesive groups are more productive.[6] The art is to put together groups comprised of individuals who are not too similar, but on the other hand who are not too different. Certainly they cannot be so different that they cannot work together.[7] A group's heterogeneity may originate in gender, race, nationality, profession, age, values, schools attended, skills, cognitive ability, or personal traits. Heterogeneous teams experience more conflict, and take longer to coalesce into real teams.[8] At the same time, in those situations in which complex problems require innovative solutions, they are generally more effective.[9]

Recently, researchers have begun to study personality diversity in groups. One study assessed how cognitive ability, job-specific skills, and/or personality traits predict work-team performance. It found that indeed, personality variables are an important factor in team effectiveness. In particular, the personality traits of agreeableness and conscientiousness predict greater team effectiveness. Agreeable team members tend to have the skills necessary for effective teamwork, including the ability to cooperate with others, whereas conscientious individuals focus on accomplishing team goals.[10] Related research has found that extraversion and emotional stability also enhance team effectiveness.[11]

How Can You Set a Clear and Energizing Direction for Your Team?

Begin by distinguishing between work group goals and real team goals. In work groups, it is individuals who have goals, and it is the manager who organizes the product of these individual goals into a final product that represents what the group has achieved. In a real team, in contrast, the group has responsibility for an entire project, and the members decide among themselves how they will accomplish the work.

Energize your group by making sure that the task the group has taken on requires group, rather than individual, decision making. The team should be convinced of the benefits of having a team perform the task. If the task could be done more efficiently and effectively by individuals working alone, the team will not view its time and effort as legitimate.

Set clear goals for your team. You are likely to confuse your team when, in a well-meaning but misguided spirit of participation, you assemble them, tell them in general what needs to be accomplished, and then let them work out the details.[12] Groups require structure, and part of that structure is setting clear goals. Setting a clear goal involves helping the group members to understand their mission, the resources they will have to carry out that mission, and their mutual accountability for achieving the mission. It does not mean assigning the group a specific task to do.

Encourage your group to set challenging rather than vague goals. When group members agree to take on a challenging goal such as meeting a difficult performance target, as opposed to a vague goal such as "do your best" or "try your hardest," they work harder and are more satisfied with their group experience.[13] It may be that setting challenging goals works because, in the process of goal setting, group members learn more about their task, and they experience more feelings of capability.[14]

Make clear to your group whether their task is to satisfice or optimize—that is, whether achieving a pretty good decision is okay or whether the group needs to strive hard for a high-quality decision. The group needs to know how much time and how many resources it has to solve the problem at hand. Some researchers suggest that groups are inherently more likely to be useful when performing satisficing rather than optimizing operations. Often groups do not need to perform near their upper limits, because the simple combination of their judgments produces a reasonably accurate decision.[15]

Group members should understand the nature of the group's tasks, too. In Table 10.1, you can see the different types of tasks that group members should be able to recognize.

Because different types of tasks require different decision-making processes, understanding the type of decision a group is facing is a crucial aspect of helping the group to set clear goals, and otherwise be effective.[16] Group members should be able to distinguish between performance tasks, in which the group is required to solve a problem and implement a solution, and learning tasks, in which groups are asked to learn, analyze, and plan.

TABLE 10.1 Types of Group Tasks

Performance tasks versus learning tasks:

Is the group primarily solving a problem and implementing a solution or analyzing and planning?

Tasks using convergent thinking versus tasks using divergent thinking:

Is the group selecting the best solution from a number of options or searching for a variety of solutions?

Intellective tasks versus judgment tasks:

Is the group using reasoning to make a decision, or is it making a moral judgment?

Likewise, asking groups to practice convergent thinking, in which they resolve disagreements about their preferences, is very different from asking them to practice divergent thinking, in which they search for and brainstorm a variety of solutions. Finally, asking groups to attempt to discover the true or correct answer in what is known as an "intellective" task, is different from asking them to decide on a moral value or appropriate position in what is know as a "judgment" task. Groups, like individuals, use different processes to make different types of decisions.

Sometimes, managers create teams as a deliberate sham.[17] The group may have been set up to buy time while the real decision makers behind the scenes make the actual decisions, or it may have been created to give angry people a place to blow off steam, or to provide a platform for a politically important manager to speak. Keep in mind that creating such pseudo-teams and giving them false work creates frustration and skepticism about future teams in which an individual might be invited to work.

Finally, be sure that your appraisal system reinforces team goals. Telling group members that they are a team and then treating them as individuals, giving them individual assignments and rewarding them individually, sends mixed messages.[18] "If you keep individual compensation in place, you get individuals working instead of a team. You still have to have individual compensation components, as well as team-based rewards," says one expert.[19]

Often real teams become self-directed teams, finding leadership among themselves rather than in a manager. Today, four out of five companies in the *Fortune* 1000 use self-directed teams,[20] Unisys Corporation's self-directed teams set goals based on their plant's business plan. Relying on such teams, the company's Plymouth, Michigan, operation doubled its ability to ship products without doubling its workforce. The Unisys teams also presented the company with a business plan calling for a 10-hour-a-day, four-day workweek, and as a result, the company allowed them to use one of two different work-hour plans. The plant's internal teams consultant notes, "We have fewer managers now, which means fewer people hanging over employees' necks. The plant is a pleasant place to walk into."[21] Of course, using self-directed teams instead of managers also reduces costs.

How Do You Coach the Team?

When working with traditional work groups, managers often direct, organize, and reward. When managing a real team, however, they do fewer of these things and a lot more coaching. As team expert Doug Johnson says, "Managers have to transition from command and control to coach and facilitate. Instead of focusing on day-to-day details, they can think strategically. They don't give up power, they just have different power. Early on, managers may have to jump in and help with a decision. After the team has matured, you don't jump in—you give a time factor and let the team have a chance to resolve the issue."[22]

As a team manager, where should you focus your energies? Should you worry mainly about the process of your team or about the decision the team is making? Leaders who focus their energy solely on their task are more likely to lead their group to a worse decision than those who *also* focus on the process by which the group decides.[23] More specifically, when managers assume a leadership role with respect to their group's task, they do tend to increase their group's confidence. However, when they assume a leadership role with respect to the group's process, they not only increase their group's confidence and improve the process overall, they *also* enhance the quality of the group's decision.

Teams are most likely to be open to coaching: 1) at the beginning of a project, 2) at the midpoint of a project, when about half the work has been done and/or about half of the allotted time has passed, and 3) at the end, when a piece of work has been finished.[24] Like athletic coaches, at the beginning of the project team leaders should focus on motivation, in the middle on consultation—for example, revising the team strategy—and finally, at the end, on education that builds individual and team learning for the next project.[25]

As a coach, your job is to choose a good team and then keep team members focused on being productive and successful. You need to model effective group behaviors and teach your team about effective group process. Managers also advocate for their teams. In this section, we will examine these and related processes.

Choose People with Team Potential

Being an effective group member is a skill that can be taught and learned. However, prerequisite to being an effective group member is to enjoy or at least accept working as a part of a group. A team's morale can be disrupted by group members who would prefer to be working alone.[26] This is one reason why, when building teamwork-based organizations, some companies prefer to start up entirely new units rather than train existing workers to be team players. Boeing Company's Airlift and Tanker Programs did exactly that in its greenfield Macon, Georgia, site.[27] The company formed about 60 teams in production and support functions within its 800-person workforce. General Motors' Saturn plant works on similar principles. The company both hires and trains people to be team players, and every team member goes through at least 92 hours of training in problem solving and people skills.[28]

Team members should be flexible individuals willing to step into different group roles as needed, including group leadership. They should understand the essentials of group process that we are discussing in this chapter. Finally, they should have some experience in teams.

Get the Group Off to a Good Start

The initial stages of a group are essential to its ultimate effectiveness. In addition to helping teams set and understand their goals, and designing a team well to begin with, there are several other things that managers can do to launch their teams effectively.

Fundamentally, group members must accept their task, and then define it in such a way as to make it comprehensible and applicable to everyone in the group. Sometimes they have to elaborate upon the task, and in some instances, they have to redefine it so there are no misunderstandings about it and no wasted effort. Task redefinition is a natural part of what a group does,[29] and by acknowledging this and discussing it, issues about the group's goals can be resolved.

The norms of the group and the roles of group members will develop as the group works together. As the group manager, you should be aware of any emerging group norms that may contradict those of management. In the worst case, you want to avoid the kind of problem that the Federal Aviation Administration has faced with some of its air traffic controllers.[30] In one key New York facility controllers were allowed to set their own work schedules, and the choices they made led to millions of dollars in unnecessary overtime spending. To prevent such problems, managers should give their group an indication of what norms should be valued in the group. For example, you may want to let the group know your expectations for who will participate and how long meetings will be. When the group members take responsibility for planning and monitoring their own performance, they should be encouraged to explore the implications of accepting this responsibility. Finally, both you and your group should recognize that, over time, group norms and individuals' roles will evolve. You can assist by helping your group renegotiate its processes. Although it would be inappropriate for a manager of a real team to change a group's design and processes, what you *could* do is provide occasions for explicit review and renegotiation of your group's process and goals.

Develop Group Roles

Effective groups foster constructive disagreement among group members. They welcome creative and tentative ideas. They allow for the expression of feelings as well as ideas. Leadership shifts in such groups depending on the circumstances. Expertise is recognized. Voting is minimized. To foster these and related characteristics, a team must be self-conscious and proactive about its group process, and members must be able to fulfill a variety of roles.

Team members fulfill primarily two types of roles. In **group task roles**, they facilitate and coordinate group problem-solving, and they directly improve the content of the decision. In **group-building and maintenance roles**, they build group centered attitudes and a group orientation, and they maintain and perpetuate such group-centered behavior.[31] The team manager can help by educating group members about these roles and encouraging

group task roles
Roles of team members which involve facilitating and coordinating group problem-solving and directly improving the content of the decision.

group-building and maintenance roles
Roles of team members which involve building group-centered attitudes and a group orientation, and maintaining and perpetuating such group-centered behavior.

them to be more aware of their responsibility to fulfill them. (Career hint: If you are ever invited to take part in a group at a company assessment center, displaying your ability in a variety of group roles will be a major asset.)

TASK ROLES   The following roles facilitate group problem solving. In these roles, group members improve the process by which a decision is made, and indirectly improve the decision. As you read the list, think about how often you have adopted these roles in the groups of which you have been a member.

Information-giver: offers facts, generalizations, and examples.

Information-seeker: asks others for information that clarifies suggestions made by the group, such as authoritative information or facts.

Opinion-giver: evaluates group members' suggestions.

Opinion-seeker: asks for clarification of the values and attitudes behind suggestions made by group members.

Elaborator: develops group members' suggestions with examples and further meanings, gives a rationale for them, and proposes how a particular suggestion might work out if the group adopts it.

Initiator: suggests new ideas or new approaches to the problem the group is addressing, including new procedures or new ways of organizing the group.

Summarizer: summarizes group members' ideas, or approaches, to this point in the discussion.

Orienter: defines the position of the group with respect to its goals.

Recorder: the person who records the group decisions and thus provides the group memory.

GROUP-BUILDING AND MAINTENANCE ROLES   The next roles build group cohesion and improve group process. Which of these have you used in the past?

Encourager: praises, agrees with, and accepts the contributions of other group members.

Gatekeeper: encourages the participation of others, either by encouraging it directly ("John, what do you think about this?") or by limiting the input of the more talkative members ("Let's limit each of our contributions so we all get a turn").

Harmonizer: mediates the differences between other group members, attempting to relieve tension and reconcile disagreements.

Compromiser: when in conflict with another group member, offers a compromise by yielding, admitting an error, or disciplining himself or herself to maintain group harmony.

Group Observer: observes and records group process, to enrich the group's evaluation of its own procedures.

Follower: passively accepts the ideas of others, serving as an audience for the group.

Standard-setter: expresses standards for the group to achieve.

A team can evaluate and improve its own process by using these two lists of roles as checklists for monitoring its actual behaviors. During a meeting, an assigned group member can observe these behaviors as they occur and, afterward, the group member can report on who fulfilled which roles. In general, and especially during the early stages of a project, it is a good idea for a group to take 10 minutes at the end of each meeting to debrief its own process. See Table 10.2 for a summary of the characteristics of an effective group.

Monitor Participation

An effective coach is always aware of the amount and type of participation of each group member. Here are some of the questions you might ask yourself about your team:

- Who talks most frequently? Why? To what extent is this participation useful? counterproductive?

TABLE 10.2 Overview: The Characteristics of an Effective Group

In an effective group:

- Group members often disagree.
- Criticism is constructive and not personal.
- Tentative and creative ideas are encouraged.
- Feelings as well as ideas are expressed.
- Leadership shifts depending on the task and the members' skills.
- Expertise is recognized and used.
- Group members know and practice a variety of process (task and maintenance) roles.
- Decisions are reached by consensus.
- There is little or no voting.

- Who talks least frequently? Why? What effect does this lack of participation have on the group?
- Who talks to whom?
- Who interrupts others? Who interrupts whom? Do group norms accept or reject interruptions?
- Are the members with the most to contribute participating?
- How are quiet members handled?
- How are disruptive members handled?

You can chart participation in a group by using a **sociogram**, a visual representation of who talks to whom.[32] Take a look at the sociogram in Figure 10.1. In it, directional arrows run from each team member to the others, and from each team member to the team as a whole (as indicated by the arrows that point to the middle of the group). Note how frequently each group member addresses the others by observing the marks on the appropriate arrow. Also note that any interruption is noted with an "i." Encouraging others is noted with an "e."

sociogram
A visual representation of who talks to whom.

Now assume that the people in the Figure 10.1 sociogram are sitting around a round table in the positions in which you see them on the chart. What is happening in this group, do you think?

A typical pattern emerges here. Namely, it is primarily two individuals who carry the conversation. In addition, note that these high participators, Hortense and Sam, are sitting across from each other. (Hint: When you want to talk to someone in a group, plan to sit

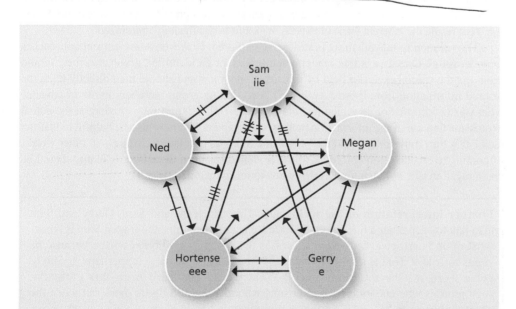

FIGURE 10.1

A Diagnostic Sociogram for a Team

across from them. When you want to avoid someone in a group, sit next to them.) What else does this sociogram tell you about this group's process? (See the box at the bottom of this page for the answer.)

Of course, who talks is important as well. Research suggests that, unfortunately, the amount of talking in a group is best predicted by an individual's dominance and confidence rather than his or her expertise.[33] At the same time, when experts do participate, they are likely to have an especially strong influence on the group.[34]

Sociograms have various structures and can serve various purposes. You can use a sociogram such as the one just illustrated to review common communication patterns with a group. Or you can create a sociogram of people's preferences. A manager might ask his or her employees, "Who in our team would you most like to work with on the new task force?" and based on the responses, he or she can map the important relationships on the team. Today some consultants use sociograms to help top management teams make sense of their own decision-making processes.

Enhance Personal Alignment

In any group, it is important to keep in mind that group members have their own individual goals, and that the group's process should take these into account whenever possible. A manager who allocates group tasks based solely on the company's needs risks alienating the employees: They may simply disengage mentally and do little but put in their time in the group.

According to experts, **alignment** is the process of promoting individual buy-in to team goals while at the same time stimulating individual learning.[35] A group's vision and core values should reflect the vision and core values of its individual members. For example, in the customer service department of a large European transportation organization, when teamwork was explicitly designed to reflect both the goals of individual team members and the department's goals, within one year the department became the highest-scoring department in the company in terms of customer satisfaction.

Utilize Experts Effectively

When a manager convenes a group of experts, he or she hopes and expects that their expertise will actually be drawn out and used by the group. Research suggests, that unfortunately, this is not generally the case. In fact, groups have a tendency to be less than optimal users of the information that is held by their group members. They tend to base their discussions on the information that is already collectively known by the group members, and fail to discover and use the in-depth information that is held by individual experts in the group.[36] Technically, this phenomenon is termed the shared versus unshared information paradigm, but we shall refer to it simply as **expert loss**.[37] What appears to happen is that group members are more comfortable discussing their mutual knowledge than they are with integrating new knowledge that comes from their individual expertise. As a result, the inherent value of experts in groups is significantly minimized.

The solution to this dilemma is still being explored. However, some current approaches may be useful. One idea is that leaders themselves, or an identified group member, should point out the special expertise held by individual members and should then directly elicit the desired information from those members.[38] Also, letting group members know in advance what sort of information is available from each individual expert may encourage the actual expression and use of the information held by such experts.[39] It may also be helpful to instruct teams that they must try to avoid the pitfall of coming to premature closure—in other words, of coming to a conclusion before all of the evidence has been discussed.[40] Teams should be encouraged to take as much time as they need to make their decisions.

alignment
The process of promoting individual buy-in to team goals while at the same time stimulating individual learning.

expert loss
The minimization of the inherent value of experts in a group because of the tendency of groups to base discussions on information that is already collectively known by the group members.

> **Further interpretation of the sociogram:** Like Hortense and Sam, Gerry and Sam also talk to each other a fair amount. Hortense is definitely an encourager. Sam is somewhat of an interrupter. Only Sam addresses the group as a whole, perhaps because he wants to lead it. Ned is a quiet member. Megan is also quiet and is, perhaps, trying to get a word in (she interrupts once). What we do not learn from this particular sociogram is who encourages or interrupts whom. We could figure these out when the observer places an "e" or "i" on the communication line in place of the tic mark.

Develop an Ethical Group Process

Ethical conduct in group decision making involves not only the outcome of the decision but the process of making the decision. Let's consider three particular process dilemmas.

To the extent that a member of a group is denied the right to participate fully in a decision-making process, that person is typically not held accountable for that group's decisions and actions. Suppose you have just joined a work group, and as a new member, you deliberately maintain a polite but non-participatory role. The group goes on to make an unethical decision. To what extent are you responsible for that decision? You had the right to speak up, but you didn't. You might have done something to derail the decision, or at least you could have protested or dissociated yourself from it, but you did not.

Here is another dilemma. Although practical reasoning is also ethical reasoning,[41] groups are typically charged with making practical decisions rather than ethical ones. It becomes a matter of group norms whether ethical aspects of the decision even enter into the process. These group norms derive, of course, from the norms of the organization of which the group is a part. But what if your organization neglects ethics, whereas you personally care about ethical reasoning?

Another issue concerning ethical decision making by groups is the fact that the more the group commands the loyalty of the individual member, the less loyal to his or her own beliefs and values that member is likely to be. Through the process of deindividuation, discussed in Chapter 9, individual ethical standards may be diluted, or radicalized. Yet, as one writer points out, the individual ethical standard is a precious commodity:

> Ethically, individuals may well be regarded as having greater worth than any of the groups to which they belong, whereas the decisions of groups may be far more important than those of all but a few individuals. . . . The human race can survive the ethically unjustifiable decisions of many individuals acting individually. . . . Whether it could survive certain ethically unjustifiable decisions of individuals acting as or on behalf of a group is doubtful. . . . It is within the power of several different groups, but no private individuals acting on their own, to perpetuate crimes on a planetary scale. If nothing else does, surely this should argue for the primary importance of the ethical aspects of group decision making.[42]

What are some ways to preserve and increase ethical group decision making? Here are seven rules of thumb:[43]

1. Make the rules of membership fair, both for those who are already members and those who would like to become members.

2. Give all members equal freedom to advocate their views.

3. Avoid assuming that your view should prevail merely because you are the chairperson or because you advocate it strongly. Expect others and yourself to support your arguments with reasoning.

4. During the decision-making process, make clear to yourself and others the ethical aspects of each of the decision alternatives under discussion.

5. Clearly distinguish between the benefits and harms for the group itself, and for those outside the group who will be affected by the decision.

6. Identify the ethical norm or norms underlying your preferred alternative. Are you applying the same norm in other situations?

7. When voting is necessary, make sure all votes are equal. Adopt fair rules for decision making.

Delegate and Empower

While taking into account the philosophy of your company, it is often important to foster the decision-making autonomy and empowerment of your work team. Some of the issues that are likely to arise when empowering a group are described by Ken Meyer, coordinator of work groups at Coldwater Machine Company, LLC in Coldwater, Ohio.[44] Meyer notes that as his company moved toward self-directed teams, some associates realized for the first time exactly what their supervisor had been doing, and were nervous about assuming those responsibilities, especially considering they would be taken on in addition to their normal workload. A related issue is that, whereas employees want more control of their work, they may not like the idea of teamwork itself. Finally, for empowerment to work, team members need to see exactly how improving their team decision making will affect the company's productivity overall.

Of course, some managers have trouble delegating. Consider the plight of the senior executive of a large Midwestern bank who desperately wanted to empower the team of high-level bank executives that reported to him—and heavily depended on him to boot. He recognized that during meetings they relied on his opinions, yet he had trouble declining to attend meetings, because when he did so he felt uninformed.[45] Research suggests that, in contrast with excellent team leaders, average leaders are more fearful about delegating, often making decisions for the team in secret.[46] Average leaders are also more likely to hesitate when their team suggests something radical, whereas superior leaders might say something like, "It's not what I think; it's what you think." It is crucial that the leader of a self-directed team avoid being too controlling.

Be Aware of the Pitfalls in Group Decision Making

Effective group coaches teach their group members about the major pitfalls in group decision making. Here are some of the primary processes that can lead a group toward unethical or ineffective decision making.

Groupthink

groupthink
The mode of thinking people adopt when the desire to agree becomes so dominant in a cohesive group that it overrides realistic appraisal of alternative courses of action.

The term **groupthink** refers to the mode of thinking that persons adopt when the desire to agree becomes so dominant in a cohesive group that it overrides realistic appraisal of alternative courses of action.[47] When a group is highly cohesive, group members may avoid criticizing their leaders' or colleagues' ideas. Because they fail to criticize, they fail to create the conflict that leads to better decision making.

What are the precursors to groupthink? One is that the greater the social cohesion of the group, the more each member wants to avoid creating disunity: When making decisions in a group, people prefer supportive to conflicting information.[48] Putting a team under time pressure and isolating it from outsiders are the other main precursors of groupthink.

When a group is experiencing groupthink, it displays a set of characteristics known as the symptoms of groupthink.[49] These are:

1. *The illusion of invulnerability* Groups are overly optimistic and willing to take extraordinary risks because members reassure each other that they are on the right course.

2. *Collective rationalization* Groups discount warnings that if taken seriously might lead them to reconsider their decisions; they rationalize them away by reemphasizing their own point of view.

3. *The illusion of inherent morality* Victims of groupthink believe unquestioningly in the inherent morality of their group, leading them to ignore the ethical and moral consequences of their decisions.

4. *Stereotyping outsiders* Group members characterize outside groups with different opinions as weak, stupid, or irrelevant. In this way the opinions of outsiders are neutralized.

5. *Direct pressure* Members of the group apply direct pressure to individuals who question the validity of the group's decisions or point out their shared illusions.

6. *Self-censorship* Individuals keep silent about their own misgivings, minimizing even to themselves the importance of their doubts.

7. *The illusion of unanimity* The group holds the illusion that all members are in agreement with its decisions and approaches. This group illusion follows from the previous symptom in which individuals censor their doubts.

8. *Self-appointed mind guards* Individuals in the group take it upon themselves to protect the group and its leader from any information that might disconfirm their beliefs in their effectiveness and morality.

In a group that is experiencing groupthink, the group process is less than optimal. Typically, the group limits its discussions to only a few alternative courses of action–often only two—without surveying all of the alternatives that might prove useful. Even when it learns of potential problems with its initial preferred decision, the group fails to reexamine that decision. Group members also fail to reexamine other alternatives that they have rejected. In addition, they make little attempt to integrate information from experts outside their group. They show interest in facts and opinions that support their preferred position, but ignore facts and opinions that do not. Finally, they spend little time trying to imagine, let alone deal with, the negative consequences of their preferred course of action.

In 1986 the space shuttle *Challenger* exploded soon after liftoff, killing seven astronauts, including Christa McAuliffe, the first teacher trained for space travel. Transcripts of the deliberations leading up to the launch suggest that groupthink characterized the faulty decision to launch when the weather was too cold. For example, the shuttle launch team was under pressure from the company and the public to launch, and individuals inside the engineering team were pressured to remain silent about their concerns that o-rings in the spacecraft would malfunction at lower temperatures. Other individuals kept silent about their own misgivings. If the groupthink had been caught in time, perhaps the Challenger disaster would never have happened.

Good coaches teach their teams how to prevent groupthink. Remedies for groupthink include:

1. The leader of the group should assign the role of critical evaluator to each member, and should encourage group members to express their objections and doubts. At the same time, the leader needs to accept criticism of his or her own judgments.

2. The leader or leaders in any group or policy-making body should initially adopt an impartial stance, instead of stating their personal preferences, which might unduly influence the group.

3. A concerned organization should set up more than one group to work on the same task, thus preventing one group from being insulated from other views.

4. The group should invite experts to each meeting and encourage them to challenge the group members' core assumptions and decisions.

5. After reaching a preliminary consensus, the group should hold a "second-chance" meeting in which every member is invited to express all of his or her residual doubts.

Cohesive groups that are put under pressure do not always fall into the groupthink pattern.[50] For one thing, having a strong, directive leader can sometimes enhance a cohesive team's performance.[51] Perhaps the main contribution of the theory of groupthink to our understanding of groups is to remind us that phenomena that are traditionally seen as positive aspects of groups, such as cohesiveness, may not always lead to improved group outcomes.[52]

Social Loafing

Social loafing is defined as a reduction in motivation and effort when individuals work in groups compared to when they work individually.[53] Most people who have worked in groups have experienced the phenomenon of social loafing. Either they have loafed themselves, or they have seen others doing it. Social loafing is a consistent phenomenon, of moderate magnitude, that occurs in a variety of groups and in many different populations.

Individuals are more likely to loaf when:[54]

social loafing
A reduction in motivation and effort when individuals work in groups compared to when they work individually.

■ They are working on tasks that are not meaningful to them, or are not personally involving.

■ Their individual work will not be compared with a group standard.

- Their individual outputs cannot be evaluated by the group.
- They are working with strangers.
- They expect the other group members to perform well.
- Their inputs to the task are redundant with those of other group members.

Men and women, individuals from a variety of cultures, and people doing different tasks all practice social loafing. However, social loafing is stronger for males than for females, and for groups from western cultures compared to eastern cultures. It is relatively strong among individualists,[55] and among those who see themselves as better than others.[56]

People who work in groups that are highly cohesive,[57] or who anticipate punishment for poor performance, are less likely to loaf.[58] Social loafing tends to be eliminated when group members are working with close friends or teammates, but it is not eliminated when one is working with coworkers who are merely acquaintances.[59]

Polarization

polarization
The tendency of groups to make more extreme decisions than individuals, in either a more adventurous direction (risky shift) or more conservative direction (cautious shift).

Groups tend to make more extreme decisions than individuals do. To illustrate, take a moment to think about the following situation:

Mr. A, an electrical engineer who is married and has one child, has been working for a large electronics corporation since graduating from college five years ago. At this company, he is assured of a lifetime job with a modest, though adequate, salary, and he will receive liberal pension benefits upon retirement. On the other hand, it is very unlikely that his salary will increase much before he retires. While attending a convention, Mr. A is offered a job with a small, newly founded company that has a highly uncertain future. The new job would pay more to start, and would offer the possibility of an ownership share, if the company survives in its competition with larger firms.

Imagine that you are advising Mr. A. What is the lowest probability of the new company proving to be financially sound that you would consider acceptable in order to advise Mr. A to take the new job? Commit your answer to paper here:_____. Now read on.

Individuals typically respond that the probability that the new company will survive would have to be nearly two-thirds before they would advise Mr. A to accept the new position.[60] In contrast, groups are likely to advise Mr. A to take the job when the company has only a slightly better than fifty/fifty chance of succeeding. The group's advice illustrates the risky shift (first defined in Chapter 9) that characterizes group decision making.

cautious shift
The phenomenon in which a group behaves more conservatively than individuals would behave.

Groups can move the other way, too, toward conservatism. This means that when individuals are cautious, groups may be even more cautious. This is referred to as the **cautious shift**.

Polarization of a group toward either the risky shift or the cautious shift is caused by at least two phenomena. The first is the need to be right. In a group, the need to be right depends in large part on what the other people in the group think, and the more people who express a particular opinion, the more valid that opinion appears to be. This is because individuals depend on the information that the others in their group provide to them, and they are not particularly critical of it. The second factor is that people want to be liked, and when they bend their attitudes toward those of the group, they are more likely to be accepted. Obviously, the need to be right and the need to be liked are related to the pressures to conform in groups that we have discussed elsewhere in this chapter and this book.

Social Facilitation

social facilitation
The enhancement of or detraction from a person's performance which results from that person being in the presence of others.

Working in the presence of others may influence people to alter their behavior. **Social facilitation** is when being in the presence of others enhances or detracts from a person's performance.[61] It is explained by the following process. In the presence of others, individuals feel some emotional arousal, such as excitement or tension. When they find themselves in this state of arousal, they tend to display the response that is most typical of their behavior in that setting. If that automatic response happens to be the most adaptive in the situation, then, great, the individual's performance will be effective. But if the response is not the most adaptive in that situation, the individual's performance will be ineffective.

Thus, if an individual is performing a task that is well learned, the presence of others facilitates that task. But if the individual is performing a task that is not well learned, the presence of others hinders the performance of the task. One explanation for this effect is that people are afraid of being evaluated by others.

Making decisions in groups can be particularly stressful because individuals may become defensive when their work is criticized. Even legitimate differences of opinion may be experienced as critical or threatening. Group members' emotional reactions can lead to polarization of the group or withdrawal of individual group members, reducing decision-making effectiveness. Furthermore, emotional patterns can affect an entire group, especially when the group shares common goals.[62] For instance, a group may share such emotions as sadness, anger, or euphoria.

Consider Structuring the Group Decision Making

Over the years, experts have developed several interesting and useful ways to structure group decision making. These include brainstorming, electronic brainstorming, nominal group technique, the Delphi method, and electronic enhancements.

BRAINSTORMING Brainstorming is a way of structuring a group's process to generate a large number of ideas. People tend to have a great deal of faith in this method of idea generation because it makes common sense that our ideas are stimulated by the ideas of others, and that others' ideas are stimulated by our own.[63]

Brainstorming is the following process:[64]

- In a meeting, group members express their ideas spontaneously.
- Group members encourage each other to say whatever ideas occur to them, even if they are crazy or similar to what has already been said.
- Criticism and evaluation of the ideas is not permitted.
- The ideas are collected.
- After the brainstorming is over, the ideas are evaluated.

Despite the fact that group brainstorming is widely believed to be useful and is widely used, brainstorming is less productive than having the same number of people working alone and then collecting and organizing their ideas. Analysis of a dozen studies of groups of three or more shows that none of the brainstorming groups produced results superior to the alternative of having individuals work initially alone and then collecting their ideas.[65] (This process is called a nominal group technique and will be described below.)

Why does brainstorming fail? For one thing, people are apprehensive about having their ideas evaluated by the group. Also, some group members take a free ride; they do not work as hard in the group as they would alone. Finally, groups are subject to the phenomenon known as **production blocking**, which is the obvious fact that only one person can speak at a time, thereby limiting the ability of the group to generate ideas.

production blocking
The fact that only one person can speak at a time, which limits the ability of the group to make ideas.

ELECTRONIC BRAINSTORMING The goal of generating a large number of ideas can also be met by using electronic brainstorming. All group members enter their ideas into a database simultaneously. One advantage of this method is that individuals are not forced to find a break in the conversation in order to express their own ideas. Another is that they can see each others' ideas and instantly react to them. This technique also reduces evaluation apprehension, especially if the contributions to the database are provided anonymously.

Electronic brainstorming is significantly more productive than traditional brainstorming.[66] However, the benefits of electronic brainstorming are lost if individuals are restricted by rules requiring them to take turns, or if there are delays in posting individuals' ideas. Whether groups that want to generate a high number of ideas should use electronic brainstorming or nominal group technique is a toss-up. This decision should be made based on the availability of the technology and assessment of which technique the users would prefer.

NOMINAL GROUP TECHNIQUE This process for generating a lot of ideas is very simple.[67] The members of the group work alone to create ideas, and then they meet to pool and organize them. There are various ways to implement nominal group technique. Members write down their ideas individually, then meet as a group and list the ideas publicly, one by one, describing each fully until all ideas are put forth. Another method is to take these steps electronically.

THE DELPHI METHOD The Delphi method structures the group communication process to help a group of individuals to handle a complex problem.[68] Delphi is unlike brainstorming in that ideas are not collected simultaneously. It builds on nominal group technique by structuring the initial input and adding a step allowing reanalysis of one's own position.

It begins with 1) individual contributions of information and knowledge, then proceeds to 2) a group judgment of these contributions, and continues with 3) an opportunity for individuals to revise their views based on feedback from the group. This procedure can be continued for several rounds. Usually, some degree of anonymity is provided for the individual responses.

The Delphi method is especially useful for forecasting because it captures individual perspectives and expertise, but also allows individuals to revise their views based on feedback. For example, it has been used to assess potential policy options in businesses, explore urban planning options in governments, and reveal social values in groups. In general the technique is most useful when the problem will be solved by a group's subjective judgments rather than by precise analytical techniques.

Here's how it works in practice. Once a problem is identified, a subgroup of people is assigned to create a questionnaire about the problem that is then sent to a larger group. (This phase can be significantly enhanced by electronic communications.) The larger group responds, and the subgroup summarizes the results. At this point, individuals are given an opportunity to change their input. The subgroup then develops a new questionnaire, and once again the larger group is invited to respond. By these means, the full group develops an understanding of key terminologies and areas of agreement and disagreement. If there is important disagreement, a third round is conducted to establish the reasons for the differences and to evaluate them. A final round is conducted after an evaluation of all the previous information is summarized and fed back to the larger group for its consideration.

Some of the virtues of the Delphi method are that individuals who respond anonymously are more likely to be frank, individual responses are considered without group-based time and social pressures, and group process variables such as the influence of bosses and the size of the group are minimized or eliminated. Its weaknesses include the possibilities for poor techniques for summarizing and presenting the group response, failure to explore disagreements, and assuming that the Delphi method should take the place of all other discussion.

ELECTRONIC ENHANCEMENTS One promising area for improving group decision making is the use of software to facilitate collaborative problem-solving, any activity in which groups of two or more people develop a plan for the design of a complex system that will solve an existing problem.[69] It is hoped that collaboration tools, often referred to as **groupware**, will improve interpersonal interaction by simplifying group processes and reducing social barriers to effective communication. Groupware also allows team members at different locations worldwide to communicate.

groupware
Collaboration software tools which are intended to improve interpersonal interaction.

Today groupware is used primarily for information sharing, document authoring, messaging systems, computer conferences, group calendars, project management, and support for team building.[70] It is hoped that in the future it will do more to incorporate the psychology of decision making into its programs. For example, we can imagine groupware that requires a group to identify and utilize its experts.

How Do You Run an Effective Meeting?

In real teams the role of leader rotates depending on the nature of the problem and the skills of the group members. Therefore, in addition to being conversant with group process and being effective team members, all group members need to know how to run an effective meeting.

Open the Meeting with a Clear Focus

When people attend a meeting they want answers to three crucial questions: "Why am I here?" "What are we going to do?" and "What's in it for me?"[71] Smart leaders make sure their meetings address these questions.

Open a meeting by telegraphing the purpose of the meeting. In some way answer the questions "Why are we here?" and "What are we trying to accomplish?"

Next, discuss the process that will be followed. In real teams the group itself usually decides this process and sets the agenda.

Third, describe the payoff of the meeting, answering the question for the participants, "What's in it for me?" Discuss how the team and its individual members will benefit from the meeting.

Create a Culture That Fosters Participation

In an ongoing real team, participation is likely to emerge naturally. However, when necessary, a variety of techniques can be used to encourage people to participate. Here is a short list of approaches to creating a team culture that encourages participation:

- Be sure people come to the meeting prepared.
- Pose open-ended questions to the group.
- Call on people directly.
- Summarize and restate ideas that come from the group.
- Maintain eye contact.
- Wait for answers; don't jump into awkward pauses.
- Describe to the group what you have observed about their process.

Of course, individuals differ in their participative styles. Some will be skilled at taking and keeping the floor, making direct requests, and making their own comments seem original, whereas others will be skilled at linking their comments to those of others and supporting others' remarks.[72] (These styles are characteristic of, respectively, men and women.) It is a good idea for managers to recognize these stylistic differences and to coach individuals and the group to recognize them as well.

Keep the Team Focused on Its Task

One of the most common problems with meetings is that they become routine. The established norms for the meetings, rather than the amount or type of work that needs to be accomplished, come to dominate the meeting's agenda and process. For example, consider an executive group that meets at a particular time each week for two hours. This is probably a bad idea. Since the work the team needs to accomplish varies week by week, so should the amount of time devoted to the meeting.

To avoid such problems, some companies have meeting rooms in which there is no furniture. Nothing shortens a meeting like making people stand. The governor of New Hampshire, former businessman Craig Benson, holds most of his meetings at a large table that is the height of a bar. Everyone stands. (Also, department heads who arrive late are locked out.) Says Benson, "Sit-down meetings tend to be more relaxed. There's no hurry to get things over . . . Figure it out. If you have a meeting that can be done in 15 minutes, and it takes 30 minutes, and there are 10 people involved, that's 150 minutes wasted. Multiply that by dozens of meetings, 52 weeks a year, and you'll see how much time we save."[73]

Here is a list of additional process recommendations for keeping your team focused:

- Reinforce on-task comments: Answer them, make eye contact with the speaker, and build on them.
- Restate the objectives of the meeting.
- When an individual goes on a tangent, summarize the discussion to that point, and then ask someone to comment on your summary.
- When someone goes off-task, ask them a yes/no question, and then ask someone else an open-ended question.

■ Use an easel to collect information, so people can stay on track with the ideas that are being expressed. If appropriate to the nature of the problem being solved, use an agenda, and stick to it.

End with a Task Focus

At the end of the meeting, but before the meeting is called to a close, be sure people have clear assignments. Answer any questions and make referrals to outside sources of information before the meeting ends. Also at the end of the meeting, take time to reinforce those members who have stayed on task, and acknowledge the group's accomplishments.

Alfred Sloan, head of General Motors from the 1920s to the 1950s, and a highly effective businessman, followed up on every meeting.[74] Immediately after a meeting, Sloan would write a short memo to one of the meeting participants summarizing the discussion, conclusion and work assignments. He would specify a deadline and who was accountable for accomplishing the assignment, then copy the memo to everyone at the meeting. As business writer Peter Drucker noted, each of Sloan's memos was a small masterpiece, and it was through them that Sloan developed into an outstandingly effective executive.

How Do You Interface for Your Team to Obtain Information, Resources, and Rewards?

As the leader of a real team you have one final, crucial job: running interference for your team with the rest of the organization. As team leader, you need to discover in the organization the rewards, information, resources, and training that your group needs. In addition, you must continually keep the group informed about developments in other work groups and the company as a whole, and with customers and suppliers.[75]

Running interference is especially important when you are coaching or leading a self-directed team. A study of 300 self-managed teams in a large manufacturing plant of a *Fortune* 500 company found that having a leader that effectively represents the team to the organization is more likely to contribute to team success than any other factor.[76] What exactly does the coach do for the team? Let's take a look.

Build Relationships Between the Team and the Broader Organization

To build relationships between the team and the broader organization, leaders must be socially and politically aware. Managing the boundary between the team and the organization is crucial.[77] This means that leaders must be aware of organizational norms about how much freedom teams should have. Violating such norms can cause trouble for the team vis-à-vis the company.

They must also build team trust, and care for their team members. Whereas average leaders see team members' personal problems as impediments to accomplishing the team's work, superior leaders defend their team members and run offense for them in the company.[78]

Scout for the Information the Team Needs

To acquire the information needed by the team, leaders must seek information from other managers, peers, and specialists, be able to "read" team members accurately to assess their practical and psychological needs, and systematically and inquisitively investigate potential problems.

For instance, leaders must keep team members up-to-date on organizational politics and policies. Also, superior leaders collect maximum amounts of input from their team members about a problem before attempting to work toward a solution.

Nurture Both External and Internal Support

Team leaders must be able to obtain external support as well as to influence their team. Average leaders seek external support less frequently and are less successful in obtaining it than are superior leaders.[79]

Also, superior leaders find ways to convince their teams about organizational necessities. One effective leader of a manufacturing team went to her accounting department to get data that would impress upon her team how the company lost money when the manufacturing line was down.

Implement Team-Based Rewards

Effective group coaches work hard to get their companies to use team-based rewards. This means not only that the team is rewarded based on their performance as a whole, but also that the organization as a whole understands the importance of this need. Better yet, the organization as a whole should have a culture that commonly rewards group behavior.

As more companies have shifted their management styles to a team-oriented approach, the need to pay careful attention to group reward systems has increased. The best programs include high levels of communication with employees about the specifics of the rewards system, a strong involvement of team members in the plan's design and implementation, and a perception by the team members that the pay system is fair.[80]

Today the norm of rewarding individual group members rather than the team as a whole remains strong in many organizational cultures. When running counter to their organization's culture, team leaders who want their team members to be committed to the group may have to resort to a variety of other approaches. See Table 10.3 for ideas about what factors motivate individuals to be committed to their team as opposed to their own self-interest.

Obtain Team Training

Often, group leaders must advocate within their organization to obtain for their teams the training that they need. One kind of training that is particularly useful is training in team building. This focuses on helping groups to better understand and manage their own group process. Possible topics for team building include principles of team design, problem solving and quality improvement, and team social skills.[81]

Some companies foster team cohesion by running off-site training programs at locales as exotic as high-ropes courses and cattle ranches.[82] The research is mixed as to whether these team-building activities are successful. One problem, of course, is that teams are constantly changing, and a one-time intervention and training can therefore only have a limited effect. Another problem is that off-site training often does not fully generalize to the workplace. On the other hand, removing teams to remote sites can help the team members to release their creativity and break down bad habits.

TABLE 10.3 How to Motivate Individuals in Teams

What motivates individuals to be committed to their team?	What motivates individuals to be committed to their own self-interest?
■ Rewards are based on the group as a whole.	■ Rewards are based on individual performance.
■ Individuals see themselves as like other members.	■ Individuals see themselves as different from other group members.
■ Individuals are confident that their opinions will be valued even if deviant.	■ Individuals fear the negative consequences of giving an unpopular opinion.
■ Status differences in the group are minimized.	■ Status differences in the group influence how decisions are made.
■ The team faces a shared threat.	■ The team faces internal competition for scarce resources.
■ The team is long-term.	■ The team is short-term.
■ Team members form friendships.	■ Team members are acquaintances rather than friends.

How Do You Lead A Virtual Team?

Table 10.4 shows some of the things that managers can do to assist virtual project teams to succeed. The behaviors are organized according the first four stages of group process.[83] As you can see, some of these recommendations would be valid for any team, whereas some are particularly tailored to the needs of the virtual team.

How Do You Lead a Multicultural Team? A Virtual Multicultural Team?

In what might be called a "rush to structure," some multicultural teams dive right into their task without addressing how their cultural differences will affect how the group does its work.[84] Such teams are likely to have serious problems, and even to fail. However, multicultural teams that take the time to develop effective working relationships by understanding their differences are even better than monocultural teams at identifying problems and generating solutions to those problems.[85]

Sometimes a manager encourages a multinational team to develop a **hybrid culture**, in which rules, expectations, and roles are understood and shared by all members.[86] Such a culture may induce members to empathize with each other, develop common goals, and improve communication. More research needs to be done on how teams that have formed hybrid cultures would change and adapt over time. However, experts recommend that teams should avoid both too much homogeneity and too much heterogeneity.[87] In other words, developing a team culture is productive, but ignoring all differences is counterproductive.

If part of getting a multicultural team off to a good start is addressing its cultural differences, what differences should a manager focus on? Among the main differences to deal with are the following:

1. Consider how the purpose of meetings is perceived. In a joint venture between British and German firms, the Germans were always well prepared for meetings because they value technical competence and expect to demonstrate it.[88] The British, on the other

hybrid culture
A culture which a manager encourages a multinational team to develop in which rules, expectations, and roles are understood and shared by all members.

TABLE 10.4 What Managers Can Do to Assist Virtual Teams

In the Forming Stage...	In the Storming Stage...	In the Norming Stage...	In the Performing Stage...
• Offer a realistic preview of what it is like to work in a virtual team. • Develop a clear team mission. • Develop a definite team identity. • Seek advice from team members who have team experience. • Obtain top management support.	• Offer at least some face-to-face team building. • Provide conflict-resolution training. • Help the team to resolve its conflicts by getting directly involved.	• Assign to the team an individual who can coach members in the skills for managing virtually. • Clearly specify the team's task requirements. • Clearly specify what individuals are accountable for, and when their work must be completed. • Establish procedures for sharing informationm. • Clarify norms for dealing with task, social, and organizational factors.	• Be sure that the departmental and company culture support the virtual team. • Establish sponsors for the team within the organization. • Support the team with resources.

Source: Adapted from S. A. Furst, M. Reeves, B. Rosen, and R. S. Blackburn, "Managing the Life Cycle of Virtual Teams," *Academy of Management Executive 18* (2), May 2004:6–20.

hand, being generalists, expected to gain information with which to develop a broader perspective on the project. They asked a lot of naïve questions that irritated the Germans. This team took nearly a year to get up to speed.

2. Think about what developing "a sense of purpose" might mean in different cultures. Although in the United States we often prefer explicit goals and objectives, in high-context cultures such as Japan this approach may be considered naïve because so much of the context of the decision will change. Also, clearly articulating a vision robs it of its subtlety and sophistication. Vision is seen as something more intuitive than tangible.

3. Weigh how, and even whether, to develop an agenda.[89] Germans depend heavily on agendas, to the point where their reluctance to deviate from an agenda troubles Americans who might like to go back and revisit a topic that has already been covered. French managers clearly dislike the one-item-at-a-time approach. They prefer to consider all issues simultaneously because they may be interrelated. They have many balls in the air at the same time.

4. Discuss how ideas about leadership differ, and which styles will be used. German group leaders gain their position because of their technical competence, whereas in France leaders are chosen because of the power and political influence they hold in their organization.[90] In the United States, we often emphasize choosing a group leader based on interpersonal competency.

5. Finally, language is a key issue. When not speaking in their native language, participants may feel uncomfortable. Not only is there an issue of understanding, there is an issue of power. Defining the language that will be used by the team is one way in which management keeps power. People who speak that language are often seen as "in" the group, whereas others are seen as "out." Some recommendations for managing language issues in multicultural teams include asking participants to speak slowly and request clarification of their points.[91] Also, when someone gets frustrated trying to make a point in a language not their own, encourage them to speak in their native language and have it translated.

Special Issues of Multicultural Virtual Teams

Because many virtual teams work globally, recognizing cultural influences is particularly important. For example, cultural views of time are based on different ethnic and national orientations, and they may affect how team members perceive deadlines and define team success.[92]

When interactive problem solving is an important role of the team, it may be important to make a deliberate effort to build team cohesion. Some companies deliberately understaff a team in order to force it to work together. Most, however, develop explicit processes for team building. For example, a transatlantic team at Wellcome, a British pharmaceutical company, planned to work together on a project for three years.[93] Within its first three months the team met together for two days on three occasions. At the first meeting the team developed a vision, whereas at the second it defined goals and assigned work. The third meeting was devoted to process issues. The team members completed questionnaires about things such as what language they preferred to work in to sort out interpersonal problems that might arise, and what strengths each individual brought to the team. Later the team conferenced regularly by telephone and met face-to-face every quarter. This start-up was considered quite successful because the team had developed mutual understandings and a recognizable working pattern.

Of course, leadership style is also an important variable in global virtual teams. One study discovered that in global teams from Europe, Mexico, and the United States, highly effective virtual team leaders acted as mentors and exhibited a high degree of empathy toward other team members, while at the same time they were able to assert their authority without being seen as inflexible or overbearing. Also, the effective leaders were found to be very good at providing regular, detailed and prompt communication with their peers, and in articulating responsibilities to the virtual team members.[94]

For a summary of ideas on how to manage a multicultural virtual team, see Table 10.5.

TABLE 10.5 **Managing Multicultural Virtual Teams**

To successfully manage a multicultural virtual team:

- Choose team members who are self-sufficient, responsible, and adaptable.
- Train them in teamwork, including cross-cultural aspects.
- Train them in the technologies they will use, and make sure the technology is reliable at all sites.
- Build the team by developing relationships among team members, preferably with face-to-face meetings, which are especially important in multicultural teams.
- Establish a communication plan that regularizes communication patterns, including how often to communicate.
- Where languages differ, emphasize written communication for the regular meetings rather than phone or conference calls. (People are usually more comfortable reading and writing, rather than speaking, a second language.)
- Pay attention to status differences, including those related to language, ensuring that individuals in the minority are heard.

Source: Based on information in S. Canney Davison and K. Ward, *Leading International Teams*. (London: McGraw-Hill, 1999):156; P. J. Caproni, *The Practical Coach* (Upper Saddle River, NJ: Prentice Hall, 2001):270–271.; S. C. Schneider and J. Barsoux, *Managing Across Cultures* (Harlow, England: FT Prentice Hall, 2003); S. Murray, "Virtual Teams: Global Harmony Is Their Dream," *The Financial Times*, May 11, 2005, http://financialtimes.com. Accessed May 18, 2006.

In Conclusion

You now know a great deal about how to coach a team. See the overview in Table 10.6 for a summary of the characteristics of high performance teams, which should now be familiar to you. If you find that you actually enjoy learning about group process, and are eager to learn more (such as attending an off-site team-building session), you are well on your way to becoming an effective manager in a team-based company.

TABLE 10.6 **Overview: High-Performance Teams**

Their design	Their process	Their outcomes
Small	Group process	Decision-making excellence
Clear boundaries	Clear and energizing goals	Implementation
Task skills	Constructive conflict	effectiveness
Interpersonal skills	Creativity	Personal growth and
Cohesion	Expression of feelings	satisfaction
	Revolving leadership	
	Empowerment	
	Ethical decision making	
	Manager as coach	
	Organizational process	
	Team rewards	
	Performance appraisal reflects group contribution and effectiveness	

Apply What You Have Learned. . .

World Class Companies: Japanese

When it comes to group decision making, Japanese companies sometimes do things very differently than U.S. companies.[95] For example, *nemewashi* is the Japanese practice of informally sounding out people's ideas about a project or a course of action *before* a formal proposal is drawn up. When practiced before a meeting, nemewashi ensures that when members meet in person, the group will exhibit consensus rather than disagreement. Exhibiting consensus at a meeting is desirable in the Japanese culture.

The way it works is that before the meeting, one or two employees interview all the invited participants to obtain their views. These employees are chosen for their neutrality on the project or action. Oftentimes it is the youngest employees who interview all the others. By circulating among the participants they not only get to know them and their views better, they also get to be known themselves.

Japanese believe that it is *outside* of the meeting that they are most likely to get people's true feelings (referred to as *honne*). By assessing views beforehand, the influence of false fronts (referred to as *tatemae),* through which people in a meeting are likely to express face-saving or socially acceptable ideas, is avoided. Also, they believe, outside the meeting people who have strong objections to the project or action, or who have new ideas, can air them without worrying about what others, especially their superiors, may think. Finally, the technique of nemewashi assures that everyone's opinion will be taken into account, and it saves face for people whose ideas are not accepted.

After their first interviews of all participants, the interviewers coordinate all of the participants' views in a written document. Then they circulate that document among the participants again and again, until all of them can agree to it and sign off on it. At the actual meeting, the "decision" is less like a discussion and more like an announcement.

The term *nemewashi* originally meant the binding up of the roots of a tree to ready it for transplanting. Today the term describes in poetic fashion how some Japanese groups coordinate their ideas and achieve consensus even before they meet.

Discuss

1. Although the practice of nemewashi is quite different from the process of group decision making used in the United States, it still helps to build teams. Why?
2. Could nemewashi be adapted to the U.S. culture? How would it improve upon traditional team decision making? What would be its drawbacks?

Advice from the Pros

When Crowds Are Better Than Groups

In his book *The Wisdom of Crowds* writer James Surowiecki tells the story of the hunt for the U.S. submarine *Scorpion,* which disappeared in 1968 on its return to Newport News after a tour of the North Atlantic. The Navy knew the sub's last reported location, and it had a vague idea of how far it might have traveled after that last contact. Still, this left it to search a circle 20 miles wide and thousands of feet deep. The task seemed hopeless.

A Naval officer came up with a novel plan for locating the ship. He made up a series of scenarios for what might have happened and assembled a team of men that included mathematicians, submarine specialists, and salvage men. However, instead of asking them to consult together to figure out the sub's whereabouts, he asked each of them to wager how likely each of the scenarios was, offering bottles of liquor as prizes. The men bet on a large variety of factors, such as why the sub ran into trouble and the steepness of its last descent. The officer assembled all the guesses, then, using a statistical technique called Baye's theorem, which calculates how new information about an event changes a person's earlier expectations of how likely the event was, calculated the group's collective estimate of the sub's location.

Of course, no one piece of information held by any one man could come close to accurately making such a prediction. How accurate do you think the summation of the team's predictions was? Author Surowiecki points out that economists have long been familiar with the phenomenon of groups being smarter than the most intelligent people in them. In 1906, British scientist Francis Galton observed some 800 people in a weight-judging competition at a local fair. Individuals guessed the weight of a fat ox, slaughtered and dressed, to try to win a prize. The crowd guessed that the ox would weigh 1,197 pounds. It came in at 1,198.

Voodoo economics, or the wisdom of crowds?

Although crowds do not always make the best decision, they typically beat all but a few individuals. Four conditions that characterize wise crowds are:

1. Diversity of opinion, with each individual having at least a touch of private information (totally unsubstantiated opinions must not be included).
2. Independent opinions, uninfluenced by other individuals.
3. Decentralized opinions, such that individuals draw on local, specialized knowledge.
4. A final aggregated opinion, using some means to turn the individual opinions into a collective decision.

Should your company develop new product X? Perhaps it should let a team of experts decide, using the process described above. Not convinced? Consider that the *Scorpion* was found 220 yards from where the group responses predicted it would be.

Discuss

1. In the chapter you learned that perhaps groups are more useful for making satisficing rather than optimizing decisions. Discuss the wisdom of crowds in light of this finding.
2. Where might the wisdom of crowds apply in business and organizational life?

Source: Based on J. Surowiecki, *The Wisdom of Crowds: Why the Many Are Smarter Than the Few and How Collective Wisdom Shapes Business, Economies, Societies, and Nations* (New York: Doubleday, 2004).

Gain Experience

I. Class Demonstration: A Group Process Fishbowl

A group of five students meets in front of the class (as in a "fishbowl," with other students looking in on them) to do the following task. Using the form below on task and maintenance roles and effective group process, the other students observe and analyze the group process.

The task:

Discuss: Some people think that professors should actively encourage quiet class members to speak up, for instance by calling on them even though they do not raise their hand. Others feel that students who want to be quiet should be allowed to, and that giving quiet students extra help is unfair. Decide where your group stands on this issue and write down a two-sentence "Open letter to professors" stating how you believe professors should act toward quiet students. Your task is finished when you give this letter to your professor.

Group Process Observation Form

On the form below, put a mark next to each behavior that you observe. Afterward answer the questions below.

Task and Maintenance Roles	Name:	Name:	Name:	Name:	Name:
1. Information-giver					
2. Opinion-giver					
3. Elaborator					
4. Summarizer					
5. Orienter					
6. Recorder					
7. Encourager					
8. Gatekeeper					
9. Compromiser					
10. Standard-setter					

Definitions

1. *Information-giver:* offers facts, generalizations, or examples.
2. *Opinion-giver:* evaluates other group members' ideas.
3. *Elaborator:* develops suggestions with examples and rationales, proposes how a suggestion might work out.
4. *Summarizer:* summarizes group ideas or approaches to this point in the discussion.
5. *Orienter:* defines the position of the group with respect to its goals.
6. *Recorder:* records the group decisions.
7. *Encourager:* praises others and agrees with them.
8. *Gatekeeper:* encourages quiet members and helps set limits on talkative members.
9. *Compromiser:* changes his or her own position or admits an error
10. *Standard-setter:* expresses standards for the group to achieve.

Additional Questions

Who talked the most?
Who talked the least?
Were tentative and creative ideas encouraged?
Were feelings as well as ideas expressed?
Was the decision reached by consensus?
How might the group process have been improved?

II. Can You Keep This Group on Point?

The class breaks up into groups of five. Each group includes one leader, one consultant, and three followers. The task of the group is to come up with a recommendation of a person to be your university commencement speaker, along with a rationale for the choice and a list of alternatives. The group will discuss for about five minutes.

Leader Role

You are the leader of a group. Can you keep the group on point? Think about how you will use the following techniques 1-5:

1. Reinforce on-task comments: Answer them, make eye contact with the speaker, and build on them.
2. Restate the objectives of the meeting.
3. When an individual goes on a tangent, summarize the discussion to that point, and then ask someone to comment on your summary.
4. When someone goes off-task, ask him or her a yes/no question, and then ask someone else an open-ended question.
5. Use a notepad to collect information, so people can stay on track with the ideas that are being expressed.

Consultant Role

Your job is to take note of how well the leader uses the techniques for keeping a group on track. You may also occasionally help the leader to do a better job, by suggesting to them how they might use a particular technique. Use this form:

Technique	How often used. . . (use hatch marks)	Examples of when the leader used this technique
Reinforces an on-task comment by answering it.		
Reinforces an on-task comment by making eye contact with the speaker.		
Reinforces an on-task comment by building on it.		
Restates the objectives of the meeting.		
When an individual goes on a tangent, summarizes the discussion to that point, and then asks someone else to comment on your summary.		
When someone goes off-task, asks them a yes/no question, and then asks someone else an open-ended question.		
Uses a notepad to collect information and keep people on track.		

Follower Roles

Follower Number 1: This follower pretty much goes along with the leader, although he or she is somewhat distractible (about 10 percent of the time).

Followers Number 2 and 3: These followers are more interested in having a good time than in making this decision, although they are still professional to their boss and are not totally against doing it (they cooperate about 60 percent of the time).

III. Brainstorming Versus Nominal Group Technique

The class is divided into an equal number of groups of four or five. Half of the groups will use brainstorming to develop their ideas, and half will use the nominal group method.

1. **Do the task**: In groups, your task is to come up with a list of six ways your university could improve student life (life beyond academics, including dorms, socializing, meals, travel, entertainment, etc.). You must use the method assigned to your group—either brainstorming or nominal group technique. (Go back to the chapter descriptions to see how to run your group.)
2. **Share and vote**: Write down your six items on the board for the entire class to see. After all lists are generated, students will vote on the one they think is has the best ideas—that is, serious ideas that could really be implemented if a reasonable amount of resources became available.

Discussion

1. Describe the process the groups actually used.
2. Which groups were more efficient?
3. Which groups produced the best ideas?

IV. Leading and Following in a Virtual Team (A project for outside of class)

The purpose of this exercise is to investigate the role of leadership in virtual teams. In this project all of your team's interactions must be through e-mail. No face-to-face or phone conversations are allowed. You will receive your team assignment from your instructor by e-mail.

V. Sociogram Demonstration

Two groups of seven students each write their names on two pieces of paper. Put the first set of seven pieces in one container, and the second set of pieces in another. Select a name from the first container (the choosers), and then one from the second container (the chosen). Throw away the first name, replace the second name in the second container, and record that the first name chose the second name.

Draw a bull's eye with the number of concentric circles matching the largest number of times anyone is chosen, plus one. In the outside circle write a zero, and the names of the people who were never chosen. In the next circle write "1" and the names of those who were chosen once, and so on until you complete all circles. Then draw arrows from every single chooser to the person they chose.

Discuss

1. What might a sociogram such as this one tell us about the relationships among these people?
2. In this demonstration, individuals were chosen by random drawing. But consider what might happen if the choosers were given some criterion on which to choose. For example, they might be asked to choose the person they would most like to work with on a group project, or they might be asked to choose the person they would most like to lead their group. How could a manager use this process? What cautions would you advise?
3. Which other student would you most like to have in your professional network? Seven students volunteer to create a sociogram using this question. After they have created the sociogram (your professor may ask them to do this outside of the classroom using pseudonyms), discuss the results and how they felt about the experience.

 ## Can You Solve this Manager's Problem?

The Virtual Work Team

T. A. Stearns is a national tax accounting firm whose main business is its popular tax preparation service for individuals. Stearns' superior reputation is based on the high quality of its advice and the excellence of its service. Key to the achievement of its reputation are the superior computer data bases and analysis tools that its agents use when counseling clients. These programs are developed by highly trained individuals, usually lawyers and tax accountants who picked up programming skills on the side.

The programs that these individuals produce are highly technical both in terms of the tax laws they cover and the code in which they were written. Perfecting them requires high levels of programming skill as well as the ability to understand the law. New laws and interpretations of existing laws have to be integrated quickly and flawlessly into the existing regulations and analysis tools.

The work is carried out in a virtual environment by four programmers in the greater Boston area. Four work sites are connected to each other and to the company by e-mail, telephone, and conferencing software. Formal meetings among all of the programmers take place only a few times a year, although the workers sometimes meet informally outside of these scheduled occasions.

The following paragraphs describe the members of the virtual work team.

Tom Andrews is a tax lawyer, a graduate of State University and a former hockey player there. At 35 years old, Tom has worked on the programs for 6 years and is the longest-standing member of the group. Along with his design responsibilities, Tom is the primary liaison with Stearns. He is also responsible for training new group members. Single, he works out of his farm in Southern New Hampshire where in his spare time he enjoys hunting and fishing.

Cy Crane, a tax accountant and computer science graduate of State University, is 32 years old, married with two children, ages 4 and 6. His wife works full time in a law firm in downtown Boston, while he commutes from his kitchen to his home office in their home in the Boston suburbs. In his spare time he enjoys biking and fishing.

Marge Dector, tax lawyer, graduate of Outstate University, is 38 years old and is married with two children, ages 8 and 10. Her husband works full time as an electrical engineer at a local defense contractor. She lives and works in her suburban Boston home, and she enjoys golf and skiing.

Megan Harris, tax accountant and graduate of Big Time University, is 26 years old and single. She recently relocated to Boston to take advantage of the wide range of opportunities in her field and to enjoy the beauty of New England. She works out of her Back Bay apartment.

In the course of their work, these four people exchange e-mail messages many times every day, and it is not unusual for one of them to step away from guests or children to log on and check in with the others. Often their e-mails are amusing as well as work-related. Sometimes they help each other with the work, as, for example, when a parent with a sick child is facing a deadline. Tom occasionally invites the others to visit with him on his farm, and once in a while Marge and Cy get their families together for dinner. About once a month the whole group gets together for lunch.

All of these workers are on salary, which, according to company custom, each has negotiated separately and secretly with management. A major factor in their commitment to the job is its flexibility. Although they are required to check in regularly during every workday, they could do the work whenever they want to. When they get together, they often joke about the managers and workers who have to be in the office during specific hours, referring to them as "face timers" and to themselves as "free agents."

When the programmers are asked to make a major program change, they often develop programming tools called macros, which help them to do their work more efficiently. These macros greatly enhance the speed at which a change can be written into the programs. Cy in particular really enjoys hacking around with macros. For example, on one recent project, he became obsessed by the prospect of creating a shortcut that could save him a huge amount of time. One week after he had turned in his code and his release notes to the company, Cy bragged to Tom that he had created a new macro that had saved him eight hours of work that week. "The stripers are running," he had said, "And I want to be on the beach." Tom was skeptical about the shortcut, but after trying it out in his own work, he found that it actually did save him many hours.

T. A. Stearns has an employee suggestion program that rewards employees for innovations that save the company money. The program gives an employee 5 percent of the savings generated by their innovation over a period of three months. The company also has a profit sharing plan. Tom and Cy feel that the small amount of money that would be generated by a company reward would not offset the free time that they gain using their new macro. They want the time either for leisure or for other consulting, and furthermore, they agree that because the money comes out of profits, the money is really coming out of the employees' pockets anyhow. There seems to be little incentive to share their innovation macro with management.

They also believe that their group could suffer if management learns about the innovation. They can now do the work so quickly that only three programmers might be needed. If management were to learn about the macro, one of them would probably lose their job, and the remaining workers would have more work thrown at them.

Cy and Tom decide that there is not enough incentive to tell the company about the macro. However, they are just entering their busy season and they know that everyone in the group would be stressed by the heavy workload. They decide to distribute the macro to the other members of their group and swear them to secrecy.

Over lunch one day, the group sets for itself a level of production that it feels would not arouse management's suspicion. Several months pass, and they use some of their extra time to push the quality of their work even higher. The rest of the time gained they use for their own personal interests.

Dave Regan, the manager of the work group, picked up on the innovation several weeks after it was first implemented. He had wondered why production time had gone down a bit, while quality had shot up, and he got his first inkling of an answer when he saw an e-mail from Marge to Cy thanking him for saving her so much time with his "brilliant mind." Not wanting to embarrass his group of employees, Dave hinted to Tom that he wanted to know what was happening, but he got nowhere. He did not tell his own manager about his suspicions, reasoning that since both quality and productivity were up he did not really need to pursue the matter further.

Then one day Dave heard that Cy had boasted about his trick to a member of another virtual work group in the company. Suddenly the situation seemed to have gotten out of hand. Dave took Cy to lunch and asked him to explain what was happening. Cy told him about the innovation, but he insisted that the group's actions had been justified to protect itself.

Dave knows that his own boss will soon hear of the situation, and that he will be looking for answers—from him.

Discuss

1. Why is this group a team?
2. What characteristics of the team predispose it to making ineffective decisions?

3. What are the characteristics of groupthink that are manifested in the work team?
4. Has Dave been an effective group leader? What should Dave do now?

Source: © 1999 by Rae André. Used with permission.

Chapter Summary and Key Terms

How do you design a team?
To design a team effectively, you should first consider its size. Then set clear boundaries about who is and who is not on the team, choose members based on their task and interpersonal skills, and choose a group that is likely to develop cohesion. It is probably a good idea to choose members who exhibit the personality characteristics of agreeableness and conscientiousness.

How can you set a clear and energizing direction for your team?
One goal of the team must be that people will work together to accomplish their task. Be sure the task actually requires group decision making. Also, consider that you only confuse the team if you treat team members as individuals, giving them individual tasks and rewarding them individually. Structuring your team's work is also important: Help them to understand their mission, resources, and mutual accountability.

How do you coach the team?
There are many facets to effective team coaching. Make sure your people have team potential, then get them off to a good start by helping them to understand their goals. Make sure they accept (and perhaps redefine) their task, and monitor how well their group roles are developing. Help the team learn and practice both group task roles and group-building roles. Encourage participation from all team members and get individuals to buy into the group. Teach the group how to use experts and how to maintain an ethical decision making process. Delegate to your team and empower them.

group task roles   263
group-building and maintenance roles   263
sociogram   265
alignment   266
expert loss   266

Be aware of the pitfalls in group decision making.
Common pitfalls include groupthink, social loafing, and polarization. Teach them to understand the effects of social

facilitation on the group's decisions. Make available to them a variety of structures for group decision making including electronic brainstorming, nominal group technique, and the Delphi method.

groupthink   268
social loafing   269
polarization   270
cautious shift   270
social facilitation   270
production blocking   271
groupware   272

How do you run an effective meeting?
Open the meeting with a clear focus, create a culture that fosters participation. Keep the team focused on its task, and also end with a task focus.

How do you interface for your team to obtain information, resources, and rewards?
Make it a point to look around in your organization for rewards, information, resources, and training that your team can use. Design reward systems that reward teamwork, not just individual work.

How do you lead a virtual team?
Helping a virtual team through the stages of group process is similar to managing any new project team. However, you should pay special attention to providing a realistic preview of how the team will interact, establishing at least some face-to-face meetings, and ensuring that the company culture supports virtual teamwork.

How do you lead a multicultural team? A virtual multicultural team?
Multicultural teams must address how cultural differences might affect their interactions. When the team is virtual, recognizing cultural differences is especially important, and it may be worthwhile to invest in team building.

hybrid culture   276

Explorations

1. Team building

Web search for "team building" and analyze what you find. For instance, what is "team building," really, as described by the consulting companies you discover? Who does it? What are some interesting ways of doing it?

2. Training groups

Check out antgrasshopper.com. What do you think about this training company's philosophy of mixing business with pleasure?

3. Sociograms

Web search for "sociogram" and describe several of the applications you find there. If you come across any exercises or software, try them out and report on what you learn.

References

[1] J. R. Hackman, "Group Influences on Individuals in Organizations," in M. D. Dunnette and L. M. Hough (eds.), *Handbook of Industrial & Organizational Psychology 3,* 2nd ed., (Palo Alto, CA: Consulting Psychologists Press, 1990):235–50. We have used Hackman's four conditions to structure this discussion, while developing it based on both his and others' research.

[2] J. R. Hackman, "The Design of Work Teams," in J. W. Lorsch, ed., *Handbook of Organizational Behavior* (Englewood Cliffs, NJ: Prentice-Hall, 1987):315–342; J.Z. Rubin, "Introduction," in W. C. Swap and Associates, eds., *Group Decision Making* (Beverly Hills, CA: Sage Publications, 1984):15–44.

[3] G. E. Littlepage and H. Silbiger, "Recognition of Expertise in Decision-Making Groups: Effects of Group Size and Participation Patterns," *Small Group Research 23* (3) 1992:344–355.

[4] R. Hackman, "The Design of Work Teams," in J. W. Lorsch, ed., *Handbook of Organizational Behavior* (Englewood Cliffs, NJ: Prentice-Hall, 1987):315–342.

[5] N. L. Kerr and R. S. Tindale, "Group Performance and Decision Making," in *Annual Review of Psychology 55,* 2004:623–655.

[6] N. L. Kerr and R. S. Tindale, "Group Performance and Decision Making," in *Annual Review of Psychology 55,* 2004:623–655.

[7] J. R. Hackman, "Group Influences on Individuals in Organizations," in M. D. Dunnette and L. M. Hough, eds., *Handbook of Industrial & Organizational Psychology 3,* 2nd ed., (Palo Alto, CA: Consulting Psychologists Press, 1990):235–50.

[8] K. Y. Williams and C. A. O'Reilly, "Demography and Diversity in Organizations: A Review of 40 Years of Research," in B.M. Staw and L.L. Cummings, eds., *Research in Organizational Behavior 20* (Greenwich, CT: JAI, 1998):77–140.

[9] L. H. Pelled, K. M. Eisenhardt, and K. R. Xin, "Exploring the Black Box: An Analysis of Work Group Diversity, Conflict, and Performance," *Administrative Science Quarterly 44,* 1999:1–28.

[10] G. A. Neuman and J. Wright, "Team Effectiveness: Beyond Skills and Cognitive Ability," *Journal of Applied Psychology 84* (3), June 1999:376–89.

[11] M. R. Barrick, G. L. Stewart, M. J. Neubert, and M. K. Mount, "Relating Member Ability and Personality to Work-Team Processes and Team Effectiveness," *Journal of Applied Psychology 83* (3), June 1998:377–394.

[12] J. R. Hackman, "Group Influences on Individuals in Organizations," in M. D. Dunnette and L. M. Hough, eds., *Handbook of Industrial & Organizational Psychology 3,* 2nd ed., (Palo Alto, CA: Consulting Psychologists Press, 1990):235–50, 498.

[13] C. C. Durham, K. Knight, and E. A. Locke, "Effects of Leader Role, Team-Set Goal Difficulty, Efficacy, and Tactics on Team Effectiveness," *Organization Behavior and Human Decision Processes 72* (2) 1997:203–231; S. R. Johnson, A. C. Ostrow, F. M. Perna, and E. F. Etzel, "The Effects of Group versus Individual Goal Setting on Bowling Performance," *Sport Psychology 11* (2) 1997:190–200.

[14] N. L. Kerr and R. S. Tindale, "Group Performance and Decision Making," in *Annual Review of Psychology 55,* 2004:623–655.

[15] N. L. Kerr and R. S. Tindale, "Group Performance and Decision Making," in *Annual Review of Psychology 55,* 2004:623–655.

[16] D. E. Hyatt and T. M. Ruddy, "An Examination of the Relationship Between Work Group Characteristics and Performance: Once More. . . ," *Personnel Psychology 50* (3), 1997:553–585.

[17] J. R. Hackman, "The Design of Work Teams," in J. W. Lorsch, ed., *Handbook of Organizational Behavior* (Englewood Cliffs, NJ : Prentice-Hall, 1987): 315–342, 335.

[18] J. R. Hackman, "Group Influences on Individuals in Organizations," in M. D. Dunnette and L. M. Hough, eds., *Handbook of Industrial & Organizational Psychology 3,* 2nd ed., (Palo Alto, CA: Consulting Psychologists Press, 1990): 235–50, 493.

[19] Doug Johnson, Associate Director of the Center for the Study of Work Teams, University of Texas at Austin, in C. Joinson, "Teams at Work," *HR Magazine 44* (5), May 1999:30–36, 35.

[20] E. E. Lawler III, *High Involvement Management* (San Francisco, CA: Jossey-Bass, 1986); G. Taninecz, T. H. Lee, A. V. Feigenbaum, B. Nagle, and P. Ward, "Best Practices and Performances: Manufacturers Tackling Leading-Edge Initiatives Generally Reap the Best Results," *Industry Week,* December 1, 1997:28–43; E. E. Lawler III, *Strategies for High Performance Organizations* (San Francisco, CA: Jossey-Bass, 1998).

[21] Molly Lamb, in C. Joinson, "Teams at Work," *HR Magazine 44* (5), May 1999:30–36, 35.

[22] C. Joinson, "Teams at Work," *HR Magazine 44* (5), May 1999:30–36.

[23] R. S. Peterson, "A Directive Leadership Style in Group Decision Making Can Be Both Virtue and Vice: Evidence From Elite and Experimental Groups," *Journal of Personality & Social Psychology, 72* (5) May 1997:1107–1121.

[24] 1 J. R. Hackman, "Why Teams Don't Work," in R. S. Tindale, L. Heath, J. Edwards, E. J. Posavac, F. B. Bryant, Y. Suarez-Balcazar, E. Henderson-King, and J. Myers, eds., Theory and Research on Small Groups (New York: Plenum Press, 1998):245–267.

[25] 1 V. U. Druskat and J. V. Wheeler, "Managing from the Boundary: The Effective Leadership of Self-Managing Work Teams," Academy of Management Journal 46 (4), August 2003:435–457;V. U. Druskat and J. V. Wheeler, "How to Lead a Self-Managing Team," *MIT Sloan Management Review 45* (4), Summer 2004:65–71.

[26] J. D. Shaw, M. K. Duffy and E. M. Stark, "Interdependence and Preference for Group Work: Main and Congruence Effects on the Satisfaction and Performance of Group Members," *Journal of Management 26* (2), 2000:259–279.

[27] C. Joinson, "Teams at Work," *HR Magazine 44* (5), May 1999:30–36,35.

[28] "Team Players," *Executive Excellence 16* (5), May 1999:18.

[29] J.R. Hackman, "Toward Understanding the Role of Tasks in Behavioral Research," *Acta Psychologica 31,* 1969:97–128.

[30] S. McCartney, "FAA Reins in Air-Traffic Controllers," *The Wall Street Journal* August 2, 2005:D1.

[31] K. F. Benne and P. Sheats, "Functional Roles of Group Members," *Journal of Social Issues, 4* (2), 1948: 41–49.

[32] Adapted from D. Ancona, T. Kochan, M. Scully, J. Van Maanen, and D. Eleanor Westney, *Managing for the Future: Organizational Behavior & Processes* (Cincinnati, OH: South-Western College Publishing, 1999).

[33] G. E. Littlepage, G. W. Schmidt, E. W. Whisler, and A. G. Frost, "An Input-Process-Output Analysis of Influence and Performance in Problem-Solving Groups," *Journal of Personality and Social Psychology 69* (5), November 1996:877–899.

[34] P. C. Bottger, "Expertise and Air Time as Basis of Actual and Perceived Influence in Problem Solving Groups," *Journal of Applied Psychology 69,* 1984:214–221.

[35] R. Angel and H. Rampersad, "Improving People Performance: The CFO's New Frontier," *Financial Executive* October 2005, 45–48.

[36] G. Stasser and W. Titus, "Pooling of Unshared Information in Group Decision Making: Biased Information Sampling During Discussion," *Journal of Personality & Social Psychology, 48,* 1985:1467–1478.

[37] N. L. Kerr and R. S. Tindale, "Group Performance and Decision Making," *Annual Review of Psychology 55,* 2004:623–655.

[38] J. R. Larson Jr., C. Christensen, T. M. Franz, and A. S. Abbott, "Diagnosing Groups: The Pooling, Management, and Impact of Shared and Unshared Case Information," *Journal of Personality & Social Psychology 75* (1), July 1998:93–108.

[39] G. Stasser, D. D. Stewart, and G. M. Wittenbaum, "Expert Roles and Information Exchange During Discussion: The Importance of Knowing Who Knows What," *Journal of Experimental Social Psychology 31,* 1995: 244–265;G. Stasser, S. I. Vaughan and D. D. Steward, "Pooled Unshared Information: The Benefits of Knowing How Access to Information Is Distributed Among Group Members," *Organizational Behavior & Human Decision Processes 82* (1), May 2000:102–116.

[40] J. R. Larson Jr., C. Christensen, T. M. Franz, and A. S. Abbott, "Diagnosing Groups: The Pooling, Management, and Impact of Shared and Unshared Case Information," *Journal of Personality & Social Psychology 75* (1), July 1998: 93–108.

[41] H. Bedau, "Ethical Aspects of Group Decision Making," in W. C. Swap and Associates, eds., *Group Decision Making* (Beverly Hills, CA: Sage Publications, 1984):115–150, 122.

[42] H. Bedau, "Ethical Aspects of Group Decision Making," in W. C. Swap and Associates, eds., *Group Decision Making* (Beverly Hills, CA: Sage Publications, 1984):115–150.

[43] H. Bedau, "Ethical Aspects of Group Decision Making," in W. C. Swap and Associates, eds., *Group Decision Making* (Beverly Hills, CA: Sage Publications, 1984):115–150.

[44] C. Joinson, "Teams at Work," *HR Magazine 44* (5), May 1999:30–36.

[45] V. U. Druskat and J. V. Wheeler, "How to Lead a Self-Managing Team," *MIT Sloan Management Review 45* (4), Summer 2004:65–71.

[46] V. U. Druskat and J. V. Wheeler, "Managing from the Boundary: The Effective Leadership of Self-Managing Work Teams," *Academy of Management Journal 46* (4), August 2003:435–457;V. U. Druskat and J. V. Wheeler, "How to Lead a Self-Managing Team," *MIT Sloan Management Review 45* (4), Summer 2004:65–71.

[47] I. L. Janis, *Victims of Groupthink: A Psychological Study of Foreign-Policy Decisions and Fiascoes* (Boston: Houghton Mifflin, 1972).

[48] S. Schulz-Hardt, D. Frey, C. Lüthgens, and S. Moscovici, "Biased Information Search in Group Decision Making," *Journal of Personality and Social Psychology 78* (4) 2000:655–669.

[49] I. L. Janis, *Victims of Groupthink: A Psychological Study of Foreign-Policy Decisions and Fiascoes* (Boston: Houghton Mifflin, 1972).

[50] B. Mullen and C. Copper, "The Relation Between Group Cohesiveness and Performance: An Integration," *Psychological Bulletin 115* (2) 1994:210–227.

[51] R. S. Peterson, P. D. Owen, P. E. Tetloc, E. T. Fan, and P. Martorana, "Group Dynamics in Top Management Teams: Groupthink, Vigilance, and Alternative Models of Organizational Failure and Success," *Organization Behavior and Human Decision Process 73,* 1998:272–305.

[52] G. Whyte, "Recasting Janis's Groupthink Model: The Key Role of Collective Efficiency in Decision Fiascoes," *Organizational Behavior and Human Decision Processes 73:* 185–209; B. Mullen and C. Copper, "The Relation Between Group Cohesiveness and Performance: An Integration," *Psychological Bulletin 115* (2) 1994:210–227.

[53] B. Latané, K. Williams and S. Harkins, "Many Hands Make Light the Work: The Causes and Consequences of Social Loafing," *Journal of Personality and Social Psychology 37* (6), 1979:822–832; S. J. Karau and K. D. Williams, "Social Loafing: A Meta-Analytic Review and Theoretical Integration," *Journal of Personality & Social Psychology, 65* (4) 1993:681–706.

[54] S. J. Karau and K. D. Williams, "Social Loafing: A Meta-Analytic Review and Theoretical Integration," *Journal of Personality & Social Psychology, 65* (4) 1993: 681–706.

[55] J. A. Wagner, III, "Studies of Individualism and Collectivism: Effects on Cooperation in Groups," *Academy of Management Journal 38* (1) 1995:152–172; M. Erez and A. Somech, "Is Group Productivity Loss the Rule or the Exception? Effects of Culture and Group-Based Motivation," *Academy of Management Journal 39(6)* 1996:1513–1537.

[56] E. Charbonnier, P. Huguet, M. Brauer, and J. M. Montiel, "Social Loafing and Self-Beliefs: People's Collective Effort Depends on the Extent to Which They Distinguish Them-

selves as Better Than Others," *Social Behavior and Personality 26* (4) 1998:329–340; P. Huguet, E. Charbonnier, and J. M. Montiel, "Productivity Loss in Performance Groups: People Who See Themselves as Average Do Not Engage in Social Loafing," *Group Dynamics 3* (2) 1999:118–131.

[57] S. Worchel, H. Rothgerber, E. A. Day, D. Hart, and J. Butemeyer, "Social Identity and Individual Productivity Within Groups," *British Journal of Social Psychology 37*, 1998:389–413.

[58] J. A. Miles and J. Greenberg, "Using Punishment Threats to Attenuate Social Loafing Effects Among Swimmers," *Organization Behavior and Human Decision Processes 56*, 1993:246–265.

[59] S. J. Karau and K. D. Williams, "Social Loafing: A Meta-Analytic Review and Theoretical Integration," *Journal of Personality & Social Psychology, 65* (4) 1993:681–706.

[60] J. A. F. Stoner, *A Comparison of Individual and Group Decisions Involving Risk,* Unpublished Masters Thesis, Massachusetts Institute of Technology, School of Industrial Management, 1961; J. A. F. Stoner, "Risky and Cautious Shifts in Group Decision: The Influence of Widely Held Values," *Journal of Experimental Social Psychology 4,* 1968:442-459.

[61] R. B. Zajonc, "Social Facilitation," *Science 149,* 1965:269–274; R. B. Zajonc, "Compresence," in P. B. Paulus, ed., *Psychology of Group Influence* (Hillsdale, NJ: Lawrence Erlbaum Associates, 1980):35–60; J. R. Aiello and E. A. Douthitt, "Social Facilitation from Triplett to Electronic Performance Monitoring," *Group Dynamics 5,* 2001:163–180.

[62] P. Totterdell, "Catching Moods and Hitting Runs: Mood Linkage and Subjective Performance in Professional Sport Teams," *Journal of Applied Psychology 85,* 2000:848–859.

[63] M. Diehl and W. Stroebe, "Productivity Loss in Brainstorming Groups: Toward the Solution of a Riddle," *Journal of Personality & Social Psychology 53,* 1987:497 509; M. Diehl and W. Stroebe, "Productivity Loss in Idea-Generating Groups: Tracking Down the Blocking Effect," *Journal of Personality and Social Psychology 61* (3), 1991:392 403; P.B. Paulus, M. T. Dzindolet, G. Poletes, and L. M. Camacho, "Perception of Performance in Group Brainstorming: The Illusion of Group Productivity," *Personality and Social Psychology Bulletin 19,* 1993:78–89.

[64] A.F. Osborn, *Applied Imagination* (2nd ed.) (New York: Scribner, 1957).

[65] R. B. Gallupe, W. H. Cooper, M. Grisé, and L. M. Bastianutti, "Blocking Electronic Brainstorms," *Journal of Applied Psychology 79* (1) 1994:77–86.

[66] R. B. Gallupe and W. H. Cooper, "Brainstorming Electronically," *Sloan Management Review 35* (1), Fall 1993:27–36.

[67] A. L. Delbecq, *Group Techniques for Program Planning: A Guide to Nominal Group and Delphi Processes* (New York: Scott, Foresman, 1975).

[68] H.A. Linstone and M. Turoff, eds., *The Delphi Method: Techniques and Applications,* (Reading, MA: Addison-Wesley Publishing Company, 1975.

[69] J. DeFranco-Tommarello and F. P. Deek, "Collaborative Problem Solving and Groupware for Software Development," *Information Systems Management,* Winter 2004:67–82.

[70] V. Zwass, *Foundations of Information Systems* (Boston, MA: Irwin McGraw-Hill, 1998).

[71] S. Buckholz S. Buckholz and T. Roth, *Creating the High-Performance Team* (New York: John Wiley & Sons, 1987).

[72] D. Tannen, *You Just Don't Understand: Men and Women in Conversation* (New York: Ballantine Books, 1990).

[73] David E. Rosenbaum, "The New Hampshire Governor: A Businessman With a Businesslike Plan," *The New York Times,* August 8, 2004:19.

[74] P. F. Drucker, "What Makes an Effective Executive," *Harvard Business Review 82* (6), June 2004:58–63.

[75] D. E. Hyatt and T. M. Ruddy, "An Examination of the Relationship between Work Group Characteristics and Performance: Once More into the Breech," *Personnel Psychology, 50* (3) Autumn 1997: 553–585.

[76] V. U. Druskat and J. V. Wheeler, "Managing from the Boundary: The Effective Leadership of Self-Managing Work Teams," *Academy of Management Journal 46* (4), August 2003:435–457; V. U. Druskat and J. V. Wheeler, "How to Lead a Self-Managing Team," *MIT Sloan Management Review 45* (4), Summer 2004:65–71.

[77] J. L. Cordery and T. D. Wall, "Work Design and Supervisory Practice: A Model," *Human Relations 38* (5), 1985:425–441; D. G. Ancona and D. F. Caldwell, "Bridging the Boundary: External Activity and Performance in Organizational Teams," *Administrative Science Quarterly 37* (4), December 1992:634–665; S. G. Cohen, L. Chang, and G. E. Ledford, "A Hierarchical Construct of Self-Management Leadership and Its Relationship to Quality of Work Life and Perceived Work Group Effectiveness," *Personnel Psychology 50* (2), Summer 1997:275–308; J. R. Hackman, *Leading Teams: Setting the Stage for Great Performances* (Boston, MA: Harvard Business School Press, 2002).

[78] V. U. Druskat and J. V. Wheeler, "Managing from the Boundary: The Effective Leadership of Self-Managing Work Teams," *Academy of Management Journal 46* (4), August 2003:435–457; V. U. Druskat and J. V. Wheeler, "How to Lead a Self-Managing Team," *MIT Sloan Management Review 45* (4), Summer 2004:65–71.

[79] V. U. Druskat and J. V. Wheeler, "Managing from the Boundary: The Effective Leadership of Self-Managing Work Teams," *Academy of Management Journal 46* (4), August 2003:435–457; V. U. Druskat and J. V. Wheeler, "How to Lead a Self-Managing Team," *MIT Sloan Management Review 45* (4), Summer 2004:65–71.

[80] L. N. McClurg, "Team Rewards: How Far Have We Come?" *Human Resource Management 40 (1),* Spring 2001: 73–86.

[81] R. Wellins, W. Byham and G. Dixon, *Inside Teams: How 20 World-Class Organizations Are Winning Through Teamwork* (San Francisco, CA: Jossey-Bass Publishers, 1994).

[82] R. W. Woodman and J. J. Sherwood, "The Role of Team Development in Organizational Effectiveness: A Critical Review," *Psychological Bulletin 88,* 1980:166–186; G. E. Huszczo, "Training for Team Building," *Training and Development Journal 44,* February 1990: 37–43; P. McGraw, "Back from the Mountain: Outdoor Management Development Programs and How to Ensure the Transfer of Skills to the Workplace," *Asia Pacific Journal of Human Resources 31,* Spring 1993: 52–61; E. Sundstrom, K. De Meuse, & D. Futrell, "Work Teams: Applications and Effectiveness," *American Psychologist, 45,* 1990:120–133.

[83] S. A. Furst, M. Reeves, B. Rosen, and R. S. Blackburn, "Managing the Life Cycle of Virtual Teams," *Academy of Management Executive 18* (2), May 2004:6–20.

[84] S. Canney Davison, C. Snow, S. Snell, and D. Hambrick, *Creating High Performing Transnational Teams: Processes, Phases and Pitfalls,* ICEDR REPORT, 1993:122.

[85] W. E. Watson, K. Kumar, and L. K. Michaelsen, "Cultural Diversity's Impact on Interaction Process and Performance: Comparing Homogeneous and Diverse Task Groups," *Academy of Management Journal 36* (3), 1993:590–602.

[86] R. A. Schweder and R. A. LeVine, *Culture Theory: Essays on Mind, Self and Emotion* (New York: Cambridge University Press, 1984); R. P. Rohner, "Culture Theory," *Journal of Cross-Cultural Psychology 18,* 1987:8–51; P. C. Earley and E. M. Mosakowski, "Creating Hybrid Team Cultures: An Empirical Test of Transnational Team Functioning," *Academy of Management Journal 43,* 2000:26–49.

[87] S. C. Schneider and J. Barsoux, *Managing Across Cultures* (Harlow, England: FT Prentice Hall, 2003):238.

[88] S. C. Schneider and J. Barsoux, *Managing Across Cultures* (Harlow, England: FT Prentice Hall, 2003):223.

[89] S. C. Schneider and J. Barsoux, *Managing Across Cultures* (Harlow, England: FT Prentice Hall, 2003):225.

90 S. Canney Davison, C. Snow, S. Snell, and D. Hambrick, *Creating High Performing Transnational Teams: Processes, Phases and Pitfalls,* ICEDR REPORT, 1993:125.

91 P. A. Orleman, "The Global Corporation: Managing Across Cultures, " Masters Thesis, University of Pennsylvania, 1992.

92 C. Saunders, C. Van Slyke, and D. R. Vogel, "My Time or Yours? Managing Time Visions in Global Virtual Teams," *Academy of Management Executive 18* (1), February 2004:19–31.

93 S. Canney Davison and K. Ward, *Leading International Teams* (London: McGraw-Hill, 1999):156.

94 T. R. Kayworth and D. E. Leidner, "Leadership Effectiveness in Global Virtual Teams," *Journal of Management Information Systems 18* (3), Winter 2001/2002:7–40.

95 Based on R. M. March, *The Japanese Negotiator: Subtlety and Strategy Beyond Western Logic* (Tokyo: Kodansha International, 1990).

11

The Challenge of Leadership

Marie Alexander, President and CEO, Quova, Inc.

As the head of Quova, Inc., a leading company in the science of geolocation (determining the geographical location of a Web surfer in order to help companies target their Web marketing), Marie Alexander (see accompanying photo) uses a "hands-under" leadership style. Her philosophy is to always be there to lift people up and help them to accomplish more, but also to catch them if they fall. She strives to help people understand what they are capable of and sets the bar higher and higher so people can achieve more both for their careers and for Quova. Alexander has a degree in music therapy and has had a varied career, including running an amusement park. Nationally she has been a leading supporter of the Family and Medical Leave Act, which allows family members up to 12 weeks a year of unpaid, job-protected leave to recover from a serious illness or to care for a new child or seriously ill family member.

Alexander believes her nurturing style works partly because she is a woman. "I think it is possible for both genders to think in these ways, but then at the same time I do think by being a woman it probably opens things up and makes it easier for me to express these things. . . . It makes it easier and more accepted for me to be nurturing in a work environment, for people to see that I would have a level of compassion because those are typically traits that are typically very acceptable in a woman, while I think that historically for a man it is very difficult for him to express those feelings and have people open up. . . . "

One thing Alexander nurtures in her company is conflict. She sees conflict as a positive thing and believes that if you are not seeing any conflict within the company the organization is not growing. Rather, what you are probably getting is passive-aggressive behavior. So she works to create a culture that rewards honesty. What this means in terms of behavior is

that if someone is thinking about an issue, he or she is encouraged to bring it out into the open and discuss it so all parties can come to a resolution.

An aspect of leadership that Alexander finds challenging is firing people. You have to balance your responsibility for one person with your responsibility for the organization as a whole, she says, and sometimes your decisions may not be popular. Although her organization can be supportive, such a decision can still be difficult. The personal emotional cost and the impact on other people's lives can be, as she puts it, "a bit weighty."

Alexander practices excellence with a heart. She believes you can never expect too much from your employees, and that a big part of what a company can accomplish together is what they all can visualize. She also believes that you can achieve wealth in more ways than just financially. "A big part of our philosophy is that regardless of the financial outcome of this, if we have not done what we are doing in a way that enriches our lives then we don't believe that we've been successful."

There are several reasons why this chapter is entitled "The *Challenge* of Leadership." To begin with, companies are challenged when they try to figure out what kind of leadership is best for their organization. They are also challenged when they try to ensure that they will always have the kind of leadership they want. Companies must be concerned with such questions as "What skills and experience should we develop in our leaders at all organizational levels?" "Can we develop interpersonal processes among our employees that might substitute for leadership? For example, might we empower employees so well that they do not really need much leadership?"

Secondly, individuals like you who are planning their careers often wonder whether they have "the right stuff" to succeed as leaders in business and corporate life. You are likely to find yourself challenged by a complicated set of questions regarding your own leadership goals: Are you a leader yourself? Do you want to become one? Where will you find leadership opportunities?

Finally, researching and understanding leadership is itself a challenge. It is not always easy to nail down leadership developments using conventional social science methodology. This is in part because leaders are typically on the move and at the forefront of change, so conventional models may simply not apply to them. Furthermore, the range of leadership behaviors is extensive, necessitating complex research approaches. Sometimes, too, the origins of leadership behaviors are psychologically subtle, requiring analyses, such as psychoanalytic ones, in which relatively few researchers are trained.

Is Marie Alexander's leadership style the best one for her company? for every company? Well, it all depends. . . . In this chapter we take on the challenge of understanding leadership in organizations. In the next chapter we will examine some of the particular roles leaders play and the core skills they need in today's organizations.

What Is Leadership, Really?

You can find examples of leadership at all different levels of an organization and in many different modes. It is fair to say that no one concept of leadership encompasses all instances of leadership in an organization. Rather, in every organization there are numerous concepts of leadership and numerous examples of leaders in a variety of places.

A Short History of Leadership Research

For centuries, management theorists, political scientists, historians, philosophers and others have pondered the nature of leadership. What is the source of their fascination?

For one thing, leaders are powerful. They may lead well or poorly, but either way the fate of everyone under their influence hangs in the balance. Leaders are potential liabilities. As executive scandals have demonstrated all too frequently, sometimes leaders consolidate power, enable corruption, and cheat their followers. On the other hand, leaders are wonderfully useful to companies and society. They motivate people to organize and accomplish all kinds of important, complicated projects that would otherwise remain undone.

Another reason leaders are interesting is that they act as role models to others. Often their followers identify with them, and they may even be inspired by them. Subordinates are likely to view their leaders as persons to emulate, and may increase their own effort and productivity as a result. Leaders are among our most influential teachers.

There are two major streams of leadership research—studies that focus primarily on individual leaders, and studies that focus on leadership as a dynamic, interactive influence process among individuals. These two approaches are as old as Plato and Aristotle. Circa 400 B.C., these philosophers presented, on the one hand, the idea that leadership is a rare blend of wisdom and truth usually possessed by only one person in a society, and on the other hand, the idea that wisdom is *never* limited to just one person.[1] In the next two sections, we will examine these two important approaches from a theoretical perspective. Later in the chapter we will examine their practical applications.

Understanding Individual Leaders

By far the more widespread approach to leadership is the one that studies individual leaders. Since the main kind of leadership people have seen through the ages has been one-person rule, the predominance of this approach is not surprising.

THE TRAIT APPROACH Before the development of a scientific approach to human behavior, theorists, who were often historians, attempted to identify "great men." They studied political leaders such as Alexander the Great and Abraham Lincoln to discover why and how they influenced others. Often researchers looked for common characteristics that these leaders shared, including social attributes like class, education, and race, and physical features like height, appearance, and age.

After social science techniques for studying personality and ability were invented in the twentieth century, researchers used their new methodology to search for personality traits that might be common among leaders. For example, they might ask themselves what traits Howard Stringer (head of Sony), Ralph Alvarez (head of McDonald's), and Steven Jobs (head of Apple Computer) have in common.

Researchers looked for ability characteristics such as intelligence, knowledge and speaking skills, and personality traits such as dominance, emotional control, and introversion-extraversion.[2] This research continues today. It is important because studying leadership traits helps companies to select leaders, and because it helps individuals plan their own career development.

THE BEHAVIORAL STYLE APPROACH Many leadership theorists are not satisfied with the idea that leadership is simply a function of a leader's innate traits. Believing that at least some leaders are made, not born, they suggest that leadership can be learned, and today they do research to determine what skills are most important. For example, leaders can learn how to delegate and how to encourage participation. Studying leadership behaviors guides companies to determine which skills are important in which jobs, and to select leaders accordingly. It also helps them to assure that their future leaders get appropriate training and experience.

THE CONTINGENCY APPROACH Other researchers study the fact that leadership is not a function of either traits or skills alone, but in part depends on the situation in which a potential leader finds herself or himself. For example, a young college graduate sent into an auto plant to manage a group of workers twice his or her age might never be fully accepted as the group leader. In contrast, a graduate of a university who enters into a management training program in a company dominated by graduates of the same school is likely to find his or her leadership initiatives welcomed. Leadership theories that take into account both the leader

contingency theory
A leadership theory that takes into account both the leader and the situation in which the leader is performing, because the leader's effectiveness is contingent upon that situation.

and the situation in which the leader is performing are called **contingency theories** because the leader's effectiveness is *contingent* upon the situation. Early contingency theorists were Frenchman Henri Fayol (1841–1925) and German Max Weber (1864–1920).[3]

Today, the contingency approach has a variety of uses. It helps companies develop different leaders for different situations, train leaders to be flexible in the face of a variety of situations, and create situations that allow for a variety of leadership styles. Understanding contingencies helps individuals find leadership opportunities in which they will shine, and to develop the flexibility to perform well in a variety of situations.

ALTERNATIVE APPROACHES Today some researchers express dissatisfaction with all of these approaches, in part because their results have been inconsistent.[4] Some have even suggested abandoning the concept of leadership altogether, replacing it with the study of reward and punishment or the use of power and influence tactics. Still others suggest that it is the perception of leadership that really matters. These debates have not been resolved.

Understanding Shared Leadership

Sometimes—and increasingly, in today's complex business organizations—leadership is shared. This means that decision making is broadly distributed among two or more individuals rather than centralized in the hands of one person.[5] By this way of thinking, leadership is an activity that is distributed among the members of a group or organization. For example, after Herb Kelleher retired as head of Southwest Airlines Co., he handed over the reins of the company to *two* successors, one of whom held the title of president and the other the title of CEO.[6] Also, at the computer company Dell, for years the Chairman and the CEO worked in adjoining offices with a glass wall between them.[7] The door in this wall was never closed. CEO Kevin Rollins pointed out, "It's a myth that one person can really run a company. Either he doesn't actually run it, or he dies trying."[8] In 2007 Michael Dell again became the single leader of his company, a move that was interpreted less as an attempt to change decision-making processes and more as an attempt to restore employee and investor confidence based on his historically visionary leadership.[9]

Mary Parker Follett (1868–1933), an early theorist in the area of shared leadership, proposed that, rather than following only the formally authorized leader, a group should follow the leadership of whichever person has the most knowledge and skill pertaining to the particular problem at hand.[10] The idea that leadership within a group could actually be shared rather than being only top-down was at that time a novel concept. Today, however, we know that shared leadership can improve organizational performance.[11] In virtual teams, for example, shared leadership is a better predictor of effectiveness than is the leadership of the appointed team leader.[12]

One common form of shared leadership is bringing in a new CEO and giving the chairmanship of the board of directors to the former CEO.[13] On the plus side of this arrangement, the new chairman is bound to be well-informed. The shared leadership can help the company by enriching the information and approaches available, and by providing more flexibility and adaptability than relying on one fallible individual. On the minus side, the new chairman may avoid letting go of power, and may attempt to defend his or her way of doing things.[14]

Creating opportunities for shared leadership suggests that a company is dedicated to developing its leadership capacity. Consultant James O'Toole writes, "In many successful companies, *leadership is treated as an institutional capacity and not solely as an individual trait....* Instead of asking 'What qualities do we need to develop in our leader?' these companies continually ask, 'What qualities do we need to develop in our organization?'"[15] O'Toole points out that the multinational communications company Motorola has a pattern of company self-renewal that extends over decades, yet the company has never had a take-charge type of leader. Instead, Motorola has been led by many different types of individuals, and it has made sure that leadership talent runs deep in the organization.

leadership
The ability of individuals to influence, motivate, and enable others to contribute to effectiveness and success of their organization.

A Practical Definition of Leadership

Given all the different ways of thinking about leadership, you may well imagine that defining **leadership** is challenging. For our purposes here, we are going to settle on a particular definition that is highly practical. In 1994, 54 researchers from 38 countries initiated Project

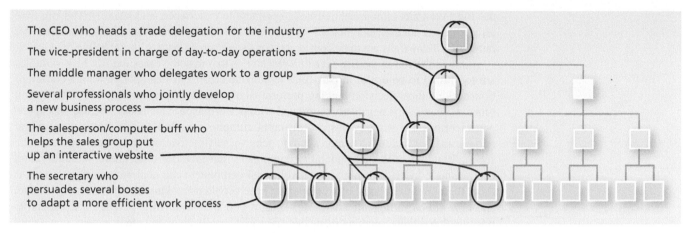

The CEO who heads a trade delegation for the industry

The vice-president in charge of day-to-day operations

The middle manager who delegates work to a group

Several professionals who jointly develop a new business process

The salesperson/computer buff who helps the sales group put up an interactive website

The secretary who persuades several bosses to adapt a more efficient work process

FIGURE 11.1   Who Is Leading in This Organization?

GLOBE to analyze leadership practices worldwide. Collectively, they defined leadership as the ability of individuals to influence, motivate, and enable others to contribute to the effectiveness and success of their organizations.[16] Like most definitions of leadership (and there are many), this one focuses on the idea that leadership is a form of social influence.[17] That is, one person influences one or more individuals who are either in a one-to-one relationship with the leader or in a group or organization run by the leader.

Where is leadership found in organizations? The answer is *everywhere*. Take a look at Figure 11.1 for some examples.

Theorists differentiate between **formal leaders**, those who have formal or legal authority to direct others in their organizations, and **emergent leaders**, those who exert significant influence over others despite having no formally allocated authority.[18] They also find it useful to distinguish among the roles of leader, **manager** and **independent (or "professional") contributor**.[19] Whereas the leader of the organization is concerned with its mission and philosophy, its managers are concerned with developing competitive advantage, and its professionals are concerned with improving the quality of products and services. The leader's main responsibility is to stimulate change; the manager's is to produce predictable results; the professional's is to produce as much as possible.

Why Are Some People Leaders While Others Are Followers?

Just as we know that personality develops through both nature and nurture, so we now know that there is no definitive answer to the question of whether leaders are born or made. Why are some people leaders while others are followers? One reason is their innate traits, and another reason is their learned behaviors. Additional factors are whether they develop leadership skills, whether they have opportunities to gain leadership experience, and whether they want to lead. In this section we will examine leadership traits, and in the following sections we will examine the other factors that also determine how some people develop into leaders.

Of course, what you might like to know right now is whether you have the abilities and skills to be a leader, and, if not, how you can get them. So let's plunge into an examination of the leadership traits that have been identified as predictive of leadership.

Traits That Predict Leadership

There are many ways to lead. None of the research results we discuss next should prevent you from assuming a leadership position if you really want it. However, in recent years researchers have identified a variety of personality traits that do correlate with leadership. These traits suggest whether you will want to lead, and whether you will be an effective leader.

According to research applying the Big Five model of personality, leaders' most consistent trait is extraversion.[20] Being an extravert predicts not only whether a person will become a leader but also whether she or he will be an effective leader. Leaders are also likely to exhibit

formal leader
A leader who has formal or legal authority to direct others in his or her organization.

emergent leaders
A leader who exerts significant influence over others despite having no formal authority.

manager
An individual who is concerned with developing competitive advantage for a company by creating predictable results.

independent contributor
Someone who is concerned with improving the quality of products and services, and whose main responsibility is to produce as much as possible; a "professional contributor."

the Big Five traits of conscientiousness, openness to experience, and stability. The Big Five research does not conclude that all, or even most, leaders will exhibit all of these traits, but rather that if any traits are to be considered consistent across leaders, these are the ones.

One limitation of the Big Five trait research is that in some cases the Big Five variables are too broad to be useful in particular circumstances.[21] For example, although conscientiousness predicts decision making performance in stable organizational contexts, during times of change it is negatively correlated with performance. This is because the concept of conscientiousness actually has two different components. One component is a volitional component that includes a person's will to achieve, self-motivation, and efficaciousness. The second component is a dependability component that includes orderliness, reliability, and cautiousness. Individuals high on the volitional component can deal with change. However those high on the dependability component have problems making decisions during change, and may not be sufficiently adaptable. Thus, if you were evaluating people for a leadership position that required making many decisions in a rapidly changing environment, you would want to look not just at their conscientiousness scores but also at their dependability scores.

The emergence of leaders can also be attributed to higher levels of intelligence,[22] dominance (including the desire to lead others),[23] and general self-efficacy (which, as you will recall, is the belief that one can successfully perform a behavior necessary to produce a desired outcome.)[24] In addition to these personality characteristics, knowledge of the business is an important factor in determining who will be an effective leader.[25]

Consider Meg Whitman, President and CEO of eBay, one of the strongest brands on the Internet.[26] Is she intelligent? Well, she studied calculus, chemistry, and physics in her first year at Princeton (but enjoyed selling advertising for a student magazine a lot more!). Does she have the desire to lead others? Whitman went on to obtain her M.B.A. at the Harvard Business School and has held a series of top jobs at such companies as Walt Disney Company; Bain & Company, a consulting firm; FTD, Inc., a floral products company; and Hasbro Inc., a toy company. Knowledge of the business? She brought the extensive experience in branding she had gained at all these companies to the presidency of eBay when it had only 30 employees. Self-efficacy? We can only suppose so: With personal holdings valued at $1.6 billion, and a family as well, today Whitman is one of the richest people in the world.

Personality characteristics that in the past were thought to be related to leadership but are now considered inessential are self-monitoring (the ability to control one's expressive behaviors)[27] and agreeableness.[28] It is now believed that high self-monitors are unlikely to adopt firm and consistent strategic visions. Over the years, agreeableness has been consistently found to be unrelated or only slightly related to organizational leadership.

Traits That Derail Leadership

Although some characteristics predict leadership, others derail it. Leadership incompetence is associated with untrustworthiness, over control, exploitation, micro-management, irritability, unwillingness to use discipline, and an inability to make good staffing and business decisions.[29]

Because the Big Five model measures primarily positive characteristics, it cannot pick up dark side characteristics—irritating tendencies that alienate subordinates and interfere with an individual's ability to lead a team.[30] However, future research on a new global measure of personality will test the extent to which the following characteristics, referred to as **derailing traits**, undermine leadership[31]:

derailing traits
Personality tendencies which undermine leadership, including egocentrism and manipulation.

1. **Egocentrism**—being self-centered and egotistical, suggested by appearing overly involved with and concerned about one's own well being and importance; an inflated evaluation of personal skills and abilities; appearing condescending to others; and an attitude of entitlement to position and rewards.

2. **Manipulation**—being self-serving and sly, suggested by a tendency to try to cover up mistakes; the ability to protect oneself by shifting blame onto others; carefully sharing information to serve one's own purpose to the detriment of others; and a willingness to take advantage of others.

3. Micro-managing—the tendency to overmanage once a person has advanced to higher levels of management, as suggested by: staying involved in too many decisions rather than passing on responsibility; doing detailed work rather than delegating it; and staying too involved with direct reports rather than building teamwork among the staff.

4. Intimidation—using power in a threatening way, as suggested by acting cold and aloof; an abrasive approach to others; a bullying style; and the use of knowledge or power to create fear in or subdue others.

5. Being passive-aggressive—avoiding confronting others, conveying acceptance or cooperation and at the same time appearing to behave in uncooperative and self-serving ways, as suggested by: communicating or implying cooperation; conveying acceptance by lack of objection; or expressing support for another person's idea; but behaving in contradictory ways that serve one's self-interest or potentially undermine the efforts of others who are possible threats.

Unfortunately, dark side characteristics are hard to detect because they are likely to coexist with high levels of self-esteem and good social skills.[32] New hires are able to hide them, and often it is only after individuals are on the job and have been evaluated by their subordinates that the problems become known.

Managers who exhibit dark side behaviors are known to be able to improve them, but to do so they need intensive training over many months rather than the several-day, standardized leadership training programs that are typically available in companies.[33]

The Choice to Lead

Some people want to lead and some people don't. Do you personally want to be a leader? When faced with this question, you should factor in several things.

To begin with, what are your goals in life? Consider, for example, how you see the ideal relationship between your work and your personal life. Research suggests that although young people highly value having a balance between home and work, the longer they stay with a company, the longer the hours they actually work and the more conflicted they feel about their work/personal life balance.[34] Young people work longer hours in part because they become more involved with their work, but also because they believe that spending more hours at work demonstrates commitment, at least in one's early career stages.[35] However, they usually hope that their situation is only for the short term. To achieve your own life goals, it is important to keep in mind what you want to accomplish long term: Is it leadership in a business organization or, is it intellectual, community, or cultural leadership? Or something else entirely?

Of course, you should also weigh your choices about leadership in light of your own career goals.[36] If your main career anchor is utilizing your managerial competence or becoming an entrepreneur, yes, you will definitely choose to become a leader and should work hard to enhance your leadership skills. However, you might choose not to become a leader if your career anchors include using your technical/functional competence, obtaining security and stability, or developing autonomy and independence.

Another consideration is financial. Typically leaders earn more than followers, although in some professions this is not the case. For example, sometimes the star surgeon or the master engineer, both independent contributors, earn more than the head of the hospital or department. Also, take into account that some companies take steps to minimize the salary differential between managers and independent contributors.

Finally, you should consider the extent to which you have the traits typically associated with leaders, keeping in mind that the traits that have been identified in the literature are primarily correlates with, not determinants of, leadership. Not having traditional leadership traits may suggest some concerns to you, but should not determine your decision about whether to lead. For example, how should you approach the question of whether to lead if you are an introvert who is also a traditionalist rather than being open to new experiences? Such a profile might mean that you won't find leading to be as natural to you as it is to an extraverted and open person, but on the other hand, you might derive great satisfaction from leading a group of people who appreciate your style. You might be very much appreciated as

TABLE 11.1 Overview: Personal Characteristics That Predict or Derail Leadership

Characteristics That Predict Leadership	Characteristics That Derail Leadership
Extraversion	Being untrustworthy
Conscientiousness	Being over controlling
Openness to experience	Exploiting
Emotional stability	Micro-managing
Intelligence	Irritability
Dominance	Being unwilling to discipline
General self-efficacy	Inability to make good staffing and/or business decisions

a leader of engineers or IT professionals, for instance, who are likely to approach problems and relationships in an analytical style that resembles yours.

Also, it is possible to adopt a personal style that is different from your preferred one. For instance, if you are an introvert, you might deliberately emphasize extraversion at work, then fall into your more natural style at home. However, extraverts, in addition to being friendly, are active people who are full of energy, and these characteristics may be hard to imitate. If you lack these characteristics, you should carefully assess whether you can compete with those who have them, because with leadership comes responsibility, and often long hours at work. For an overview of traits that predict or derail leadership, see Table 11.1.

Of course, the choice to lead is not yours alone. A group or organization must also choose you, a factor that we will discuss later in the chapter.

Can You Learn to Be a Leader?

As we have seen, some leadership characteristics are inherent in your personality. However, many, perhaps most, leadership skills can be learned. Early research at Ohio State University and the University of Michigan helped shift the focus of the field from a trait approach to a more situational, behavioral-based view.[37] The scientists reasoned that if leader behaviors could be observed, they could be taught, thus opening up opportunities for leadership to a broader range of individuals than ever before.[38]

What Is Your Leadership Style? Structured or Considerate—or Both?

According to the Ohio research, most leadership behaviors can be categorized on two dimensions. The first, **consideration**, is the degree to which a leader shows concern and respect for followers, looks out for their welfare, and expresses appreciation and support for them.[39] The second, **structure**, (also referred to as "initiating structure"), is the degree to which a leader defines and organizes his or her role and the roles of followers, is oriented toward goal attainment, and establishes clearly defined patterns and channels of communication.[40] Take the short test in Table 11.2 to determine your preferences on these two dimensions.

What does your preference mean for your life in organizations? Both consideration and structure are related to leadership effectiveness.[41] Considerate leaders are more satisfying to followers and more likely to motivate them. Showing consideration for subordinates also affects how effective a leader is overall. On the other hand, structure affects a leaders' job performance and the performance of his or her group or organization. In short, both sets of behaviors are useful skills.

Organizational applications of this model have focused on instructing leaders on how to acquire the behavioral skills that they lack. For example, if you are high on considera-

consideration
The degree to which a leader shows concern and respect for followers, looks out for their welfare, and expresses appreciation and support for them.

structure
The degree to which a leader defines and organizes his or her role and the roles of followers, is oriented toward goal attainment, and establishes clearly defined patterns and channels of communication; also called "initiating structure."

tion but low on structure, you would benefit from training on how to set and enforce clear standards for performance, including how to give negative feedback. If you are high on structure and low on consideration, you would benefit from training that enhances your interpersonal skills, such as programs in effective listening and empathy. Your ultimate goal is to score high, or skilled, on both dimensions.[42]

charismatic leader
A leader who is able to exert an unusual amount of influence on his or her followers, often through a combination of his or her personal characteristics, goals and also some extraordinary circumstances.

Do You Have the Potential to Be a Charismatic Leader?

Why is it that some leaders are able to achieve extraordinary levels of follower motivation, commitment, loyalty, and performance? **Charismatic** leaders are leaders that exert an unusual amount of influence on their followers, generally because of some combination of

TABLE 11.2 The Leadership Behavior Description Questionnaire (LBDQ)

Instructions: Read each item carefully and think about how frequently, when you are leading or managing a group, you engage in the behavior described by the item. Respond to the items using this scale:

Never = 1   Seldom = 2   Occasionally = 3   Often = 4   Always = 5

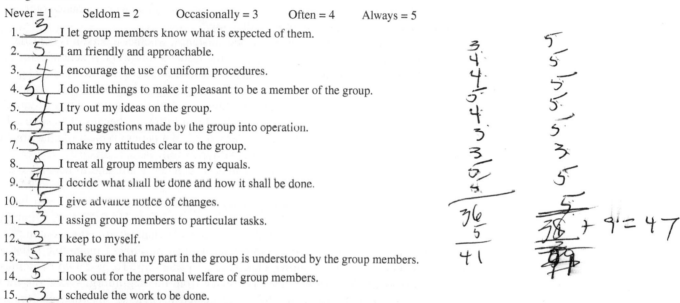

1. __3__ I let group members know what is expected of them.
2. __5__ I am friendly and approachable.
3. __4__ I encourage the use of uniform procedures.
4. __5__ I do little things to make it pleasant to be a member of the group.
5. __4__ I try out my ideas on the group.
6. __5__ I put suggestions made by the group into operation.
7. __5__ I make my attitudes clear to the group.
8. __5__ I treat all group members as my equals.
9. __4__ I decide what shall be done and how it shall be done.
10. __5__ I give advance notice of changes.
11. __3__ I assign group members to particular tasks.
12. __3__ I keep to myself.
13. __5__ I make sure that my part in the group is understood by the group members.
14. __5__ I look out for the personal welfare of group members.
15. __3__ I schedule the work to be done.
16. __5__ I am willing to make changes.
17. __5__ I maintain definite standards of performance.
18. __1__ I refuse to explain my actions.   6 - 1 = 5
19. __5__ I ask group members to follow standard rules and regulations.
20. __2__ I act without consulting the group.   6 - 2 = 4

Scoring

Structure: Ten questions measure your tendency to use structure: Add up your total score for questions 1, 3, 5, 7, 9, 11, 13, 15, 17, and 19.

Consideration: Ten questions measure your tendency to provide consideration to your group. Add up your score for questions 2, 4, 6, 8, 10, 12, 14, and 16. Then for each of questions 18 and 20, subtract your score from 6. Calculate your total score for all 10 questions.

A higher score indicates a higher tendency to apply this type of leadership.

Your structure score: _____   Your consideration score: _____

Source: Based on Staff Members, Ohio State Leadership Studies and the Bureau of Business Research, *Leader Behavior Description Questionnaire—Form XII Self* (Columbus, Ohio: Fisher College of Business, 1962); R. M. Stogdill, *Manual for the Leader Behavior Description Questionnaire—Form XII* (Columbus, Ohio: Fisher College of Business, the Ohio State University, 1963). Courtesy of Fisher College of Business, Ohio State University.

their persona, their goals, and some serendipitous extraordinary circumstances. The major characteristics of charismatic leaders are:[43]

1. Self-confidence—being confident in terms of both personal ability and judgment.

2. Vision—articulating a vision, often with an emphasis on ideology. The greater the disparity between the leader's idealized goal and the status quo, the more likely the leader will be seen as having extraordinary vision.

3. Unconventional behavior—exhibiting behaviors that are novel, unconventional, and counter to norms.

4. Environmental sensitivity—being realistic about available resources and possible constraints, about what can and cannot be accomplished.

5. Sensitivity to followers—being responsive to the needs and abilities of subordinates.

6. Role modeling—developing an image as a change agent, somebody who "makes things happen."

Additional personal traits that suggest charisma include being trustworthy, credible, morally worthy, innovative, esteemed, and powerful.[44] Personal characteristics of charismatic leaders also include a set of influence behaviors, including a charismatic communication style and visionary content in what they say.[45]

Charisma is in the eye of the beholder. For instance, whether a person is considered "trustworthy" depends on value judgments by the leader's followers. A school principal is likely to appear charismatic because of acts of kindness toward troubled kids, whereas a military leader seems charismatic because of courage in combat. Hitler was "trustworthy" insofar as many German people trusted him to pull their country out of economic depression, and he was "morally worthy" to his loyal followers because he espoused a vision for a better Germany. Tragically, Hitler exhibited a pattern typical of charismatic leaders: Because of the intense relationship with their followers, charismatic leaders are likely to believe their own ideas are better than they actually are, and to become overconfident and autocratic.

Oprah Winfrey has all the characteristics of a charismatic leader. Oprah is not only an accomplished actress and talk show host, she heads HARPO Entertainment Group, and is a partner in Oxygen Media, Inc., a cable channel aimed a women.[46] In 2003, she became the first African-American woman on *Forbes* magazine's list of billionaires. Oprah has long shown charismatic leadership. To give two examples, the content of her talk show has been visionary from the beginning. When she took on the popular *Donahue* show in 1986, she bested it because she focused less on informing her audience and more on building rapport with them. Later she also took an unconventional route when she shared her own love of reading and encouraged her viewers to read as well. Not only is Oprah innovative, she is trustworthy and caring, by all accounts with her employees as well as in public. As one communication expert puts it, "Oprah exhorts viewers to improve their lives and the world. She makes people care because she cares. That is Winfrey's genius, and will be her legacy."[47] *Time* magazine named Winfrey one of the 100 Most Influential People of the 20th Century.

See Table 11.3 for examples of how a charismatic style contrasts with the considerate style and the structured style of leadership.[48]

With training, individuals can learn to enhance several charismatic influence behaviors, including increasing their number of body gestures, telling more stories and more emotionally appealing stories, using analogies to give an emotional charge to their message, and using an animated voice tone.[49] Displaying these behaviors in presentations is somewhat more effective than normal presentation behaviors in influencing performance and attitudes of subordinates.

However, whether a charismatic leader emerges also depends on the situation.[50] Five interacting factors are essential for producing charismatic leadership. Note that several of them are situational:[51]

TABLE 11.3 Overview: Comparing Charismatic, Considerate and Structured Leadership Styles

	Charismatic Leadership	Considerate Leadership	Structured Leadership
Content of the leader's message	Articulates an overarching goal	Exhibits concern for the personal welfare of the employee	Explains the nature of the task
	Communicates high performance expectations	Engages in participative two-way conversations	Decides in detail what should be done and how it should be done
	Exhibits confidence in subordinates	Emphasizes the comfort, well-being, and satisfaction of the participant	Emphasizes the quantity of the work to be accomplished within the specified time
	Empathizes with the needs of subordinates		
		Friendly and approachable	Maintains definite standards of work performance
Style in which the message is delivered	Powerful, confident and dynamic	Warm voice tone	Neither warm nor cold; businesslike.
	Captivating, engaging voice tone	Sits on edge of desk, leans toward employee, maintains direct eye contact, relaxed posture and friendly facial expressions	Moderate level of speech intonation
	Dynamism and energy, such as pacing, sitting on the edge of the desk, direct eye contact, relaxed posture, and animated facial expressions		Sits behind the desk, maintains intermittent eye contact
			Neutral facial expression, with little smiling or head nods

Source: Based on J. M. Howell and P. J. Frost, "A laboratory study of charismatic leadership," *Organizational Behavior and Human Decision Processes 43,* 1989:242–269.

1. An extraordinarily gifted person
2. A social crisis or situation of desperation
3. A set of ideas providing a radical solution to the crisis
4. A set of followers who are attracted to the exceptional person and who come to believe that he or she is directly linked to transcendent powers
5. The validation of that person's extraordinary gifts and transcendence by repeated successes

Consider the charisma of Jack Ma, the man who, according to *The Economist,* is regarded as the godfather of the Internet in China.[52] Ma's genius is in his ability to envision Internet solutions to business problems in a country that badly needs new approaches. He came onto the scene at just the right time, when China's small businesses were eager but uninformed and unempowered, and created Alibaba, the private e-commerce firm that is today the world's largest business-to-business (B2B) marketplace. He also developed online communities and social networking. He turned e-commerce itself into a community by letting buyers and sellers message each other and post photographs and personal details on the site. Ma is an exceptional person, so well regarded in China that at a recent speech he needed six bodyguards to escape on-line traders who wanted to greet him. He prides himself on not being a geek so that he can put himself in the shoes of an ordinary customer, and he does not read business books or cases. Instead, he has the gift of vision in a time and place of extraordinary change and opportunity. He also has some powerful friends, such as Yahoo!'s Jerry Yang, and thousands of grateful customers.

In summary, modern research on charismatic leaders suggests that they are both born and created. On the one hand, the answer to the question, "Do you have the potential to be a charismatic leader?" lies in whether you exhibit certain personal characteristics, including a vision. As Robert F. Kennedy said, "Some men see things as they are and ask why? I dream things that never were and ask, why not?"[53] On the other hand, there is also some truth in the statement made by a famous military commander that "There are no great men. There are only great challenges which ordinary men are forced by circumstances to meet."[54]

Do You Have the Potential to Be a Transformational Leader?

In addition to the types of leadership we have just discussed, organizational behavior researchers also distinguish between transactional and transformational leaders.[55] **Transactional leaders** are those who manage their followers, contingently reinforcing them based on whether they meet organizational goals. For example, a transactional leader would be likely to tell an employee what to do to earn organizational rewards and would not be likely to encourage initiative. Transactional leaders are often referred to simply as "managers."[56] They use a mix of consideration and structure leadership behaviors.

In contrast, **transformational leaders** motivate their followers to move beyond their personal self-interest for the good of the group or organization.[57] Such leaders are likely to enthusiastically encourage an employee to speak up and would make an effort to find out what an employee wants and help them to get it.[58] GE has had two transformational leaders in succession. Jack Welch was a transformational leader who led the company out of bureaucracy and into a more competitive organizational form, whereas Jeffrey R. Immelt has emphasized creativity and innovation.[59] Transformational leaders emphasize the following techniques:[60]

1. Idealized influence (charisma)—they display conviction, take difficult stands, represent important values, and are admired as role models.

2. Inspirational motivation—they articulate an appealing vision for the future, challenge followers by setting high standards, talk optimistically with enthusiasm, and provide encouragement and meaning for what needs to be done.

3. Intellectual stimulation—they question assumptions, stimulate in others new perspectives and methods, and encourage ideas and reasons.

4. Individualized consideration—they treat other individuals respectfully, considering their individual needs, abilities and aspirations; they advise, teach, and coach.

Is charisma really an important component of transformational leadership? Some researchers believe that it is unnecessary and even counterproductive. They argue that transformational leaders can operate and effectively "transform" an organization using only the three other techniques: inspirational motivation, intellectual stimulation, and individualized consideration.[61] They point out that charismatic leadership focuses subordinates on connecting with and emulating the leader, whereas transformational leadership focuses subordinates on the articulated mission at hand.[62] Furthermore, while charismatic leaders foster dependency relationships with followers, relying on commitment and unquestioned obedience, transformational leaders achieve extraordinary change by directing followers' commitment and energies toward the organization and its goals while downplaying loyalty to them personally.[63]

In fact, leaders with personally charismatic traits may have to overcome the impact of their charisma in order to lead visionary companies effectively. As researcher Jerry Porras observes, "A good example is Wal-Mart founder Sam Walton. He was a very charismatic larger-than-life character. He had to overcome that in order to build a great organization, because people were inclined to rely on him or always look for him to have the right answers. Walton had to work very hard to create in his organization structures, cultures, policies, and procedures that would overcome people wanting to depend on him, and ways of operating so the company would remain great long after he was gone."[64]

---

transactional leader
A leader who manages his or her followers, contingently reinforcing them based on whether they meet organizational goals, and who is unlikely to encourage initiative.

transformational leader
A leader who motivates his or her followers to move beyond their personal self-interest for the good of the group or organization, and who is likely to encourage initiative.

In Sum...

Can leadership be learned? To the extent that transactional, charismatic, and transformational leadership are based in particular behaviors, the answer is yes. Perhaps the main issue for individuals is the question "What type of leader do I want to be?" After making that determination, the list of desirable skills you should obtain is reasonably clear.

One innovative way for today's young leaders to identify and pick up leadership skills is **peer-to-peer leadership development**.[65] Two young officers who had been friends at West Point pioneered this idea for the U.S. Army. They had learned a lot about leadership just by sitting down and sharing with each other their leadership problems and solutions, and thought why not do the same thing on a Web site? Company-Command, an internal Army Web site, was created to provide a forum where junior officers can share advice. One of its major strengths is its capability to create knowledge based on the daily challenges of frontline individuals. In fast-paced battle environments such as Iraq, traditional leadership ideas may become outdated quickly, and officers respect the opinion of peers who have recent experience. One message to take away from this approach is the importance of learning from your peers.

peer-to-peer leadership development
A model for leadership development which involves peers sitting down and sharing with each other their leadership problems and solutions, and which is able to create knowledge based on first-hand experience in fast-paced environments.

Will You Be an Effective Leader? As a Leader How Would You . . . ?

Successful leaders assess the contingencies in any situation and act accordingly. As we discussed earlier, theorists call their approach the "contingency perspective" on leadership. When using the contingency perspective, you pose to yourself questions such as "What factors in this situation seem to matter most?" and "Where and how should I focus my energy?"

In this section we will investigate a number of leadership contingencies, including how leaders guide their followers to valued goals, how they adapt their own behavior to the nature of the task, how they use their own ideas and knowledge when leading, how they interact with their followers, and how they identify factors that may actually make their leadership irrelevant. As a leader how would you. . . ?

. . . Guide Your Followers to Goals That the Company Values? (Path-Goal Theory)

Path-goal theory suggests that leaders motivate their followers to attain work-related goals by increasing the number and kinds of personal payoffs to them. They also motivate by making the paths to these payoffs easier to travel by clarifying them, reducing road blocks and pitfalls, and increasing opportunities for personal satisfaction along the way.[66]

For example, suppose the manager of an accounting department wants her employees to produce the company's quarterly reports in half the time they currently take. She could simply tell her employees the goal and let them try to accomplish it, but this approach would probably be ineffective. Path-goal theory suggests that the leader would be more effective if she would: 1) promise a group reward for achieving the goal, 2) be clear about exactly how much time she expects the group to spend, 3) make sure the employees are not distracted by other work and are not slowed down by inefficient technology, and 4) rotates some of the work so that individuals can learn new aspects of the reporting process and thus improve their skill base.

An important focus of path-goal theory is how leaders affect their followers' expectations. Research findings suggest that leaders should try to influence:

- The value to followers of their behavior and effort itself (You may recall from another chapter that this value is often referred to as a valence, a term from the expectancy theory of motivation.)
- The value to followers of attaining the goal
- The value to followers of the extrinsic outcomes
- The followers' estimate of how probable it is that their behavior and effort will actually lead to achieving the goal
- The followers' estimate of how probable it is that attaining the goal will actually lead to receiving the desired extrinsic outcomes

More recent research on path-goal theory assumes that, in addition to being rational and goal-oriented, human beings hold feelings, aesthetic values, and self-perceptions. This research suggests that people are motivated by enhancing their self-esteem and having faith in a better future.[67] By this way of thinking, leaders should somehow motivate followers to go beyond their narrow self-interest to promote the interests of the group or organization as a whole. To achieve this end, path-goal theorists today add several self-concept factors to the list that leaders should try to influence.[68] These include helping followers to maintain:

- self-consistency,
- self-esteem and self-worth, and
- hope.

Most likely it is charismatic leaders, rather than transactional leaders, who influence their followers' self-concepts. They exert their influence through such behaviors as providing explanations based on ideology ("This company stands for the American way of life") and expressing confidence in their followers ("You have met tough challenges in the past. I know you can conquer this one").

. . . Adapt Your Behavior to the Situation? (Work Unit Leadership Theory)

In order to influence the factors (such as those just discussed) that motivate subordinates, work unit leadership theory suggests that leaders should analyze factors in their work unit and act accordingly. For example, to be effective, you should assess your followers' environments and abilities and behave in ways that complement them. In addition, you should try to compensate for subordinate deficiencies, improve subordinate satisfaction, and enhance individual and group performance.[69]

To these ends, you can choose from among the set of behaviors described in Table 11.4. The list is quite comprehensive, a nearly exhaustive overview of any leader's choices for how to behave in any given situation.

A simpler model that also matches a leader's behavior with the situation is Fred Fiedler's model of leadership. Fiedler compared structure-oriented leaders with consideration-oriented leaders (he referred to them as "task-oriented leaders" and "relationship-motivated leaders," respectively) and found that structure-oriented leaders perform best in situations in which they have either very high control or relatively low control, whereas consideration-oriented leaders perform best when they have moderate control. Any shift in the amount of control affects leadership effectiveness.

Another way of saying this is that in situations that the leader does not control, such as when a hard-to-meet deadline is imposed from an external source, offering structure is

---

TABLE 11.4 **What Should a Leader Do? A Comprehensive List of Leadership Behaviors**

Path-goal clarifying behaviors—clarifying subordinate's paths to accomplishing a goal

Achievement-oriented leader behavior—stressing pride in subordinate's work and their own self-evaluation based on personal accomplishment

Work facilitation-planning, scheduling, coordinating, monitoring, coaching, reducing obstacles, and providing resources

Supportive leader behavior—providing psychological support

Interaction facilitation—facilitating collaborative and positive interaction among subordinates

Group-oriented decision process—posing problems, not solutions, to the group; searching for the mutual interests among group members with respect to solving problems; encouraging participation of all group members; generating a variety of alternatives

Representation and networking—presenting the group in a favorable manner to others in the organization, and maintaining positive relationships with influential outsiders

Value-based leader behavior—arousing subordinates' cherished values and unconscious motives by articulating a vision of a better future, displaying passion for that vision, demonstrating self-confidence, and evaluating followers and the group or organization positively

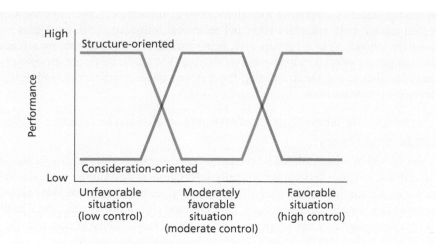

FIGURE 11.2

Fiedler's Model of Leadership Style and Effectiveness

more likely to motivate workers than offering consideration. On the other hand, when the leader has lots of control, simply telling subordinates what to do may be more effective than offering support. It is when a leader has a moderate level of control that offering consideration seems to be most effective—for example, when motivating workers to achieve day-to-day tasks under reasonable deadlines. See Fiedler's model in Figure 11.2.

How much stress employees are experiencing is also an important factor in predicting which leadership style will be effective.[70] For example, when employees are under high stress (and their leader has low control), a structure-oriented style works best. This finding has led to the approach we will examine next—cognitive resource theory.

. . . Use Your Own Ideas and Knowledge to Improve Group Performance? (Cognitive Resource Theory)

Researchers Fred Fiedler and Joe Garcia propose that the critical factor that determines which leadership style is likely to be most effective in which situation is whether the situational factors create anxiety and uncertainty for the leader. Under stress, leaders are likely to reduce their use of deliberative and analytical thinking and increase their use of previously learned knowledge and habitual reactions. In other words, too much stress nullifies leaders' ability to apply their intelligence to solving the problem, and encourages unthinking solutions. Not only are stressed leaders likely to rely on their past experience rather than on analysis of the current situation, they are more likely to rely on their basic personality characteristics, defenses, and emotions than on more rational approaches.

To deal with the stress factor, you should recognize the stress inherent in the situation, and monitor your own responses accordingly. You should seek out other individuals who can help you recognize your stress and its potential effects on your decision making.

. . . Interact with Your Followers? (Leader–Member Exchange Theory)

According to leader-member exchange (LMX) theory, the quality of the supervisor-subordinate relationship tells us whether a leader will lead successfully.[71] For example, high-quality relationships between leaders and their followers enhance employees' organizational commitment[72] and frequency of promotion.[73] However, the quality of the leader-member relationship depends on whether the subordinate has a high internal locus of control,[74] how much effort the parties put into developing the relationship, and whether they intend to develop the relationship in the future.[75]

How do you know which leader-member relationships are good ones? One way is to assess a relationship based on such factors as the mutual affection, loyalty, and professional respect the leader and follower have for each other. Also consider their mutual perception of whether or not their counterpart is making a significant work contribution.

Another way to discover differences in leader-member relationships is by comparing how well the leader treats members of an in-group versus members of an outgroup.[76]

When the leader is interacting with an in-group of subordinates, their relationships should reflect mutual trust, respect, liking, and reciprocal influence. Also, the leader is likely to favor the individuals in the group, give them valuable resources and autonomy, and respect them as people worth developing and motivating. The leader treats out-group members differently, disfavoring them, offering them fewer valuable resources, and doing little to develop or motivate them.[77]

. . . Determine When Your Leadership Is Irrelevant? (Substitutes for Leadership Theory)

Some factors in organizational life undermine and negate leaders' ability to influence their subordinates. These factors are typically referred to as substitutes for leadership.[78] For example, a leader's attempts to clarify paths and goals might be redundant because his followers have already identified them. Or followers' own professional values might negate the goal-orientation of their superiors: An engineer might refuse to rush a job to deadline because he knows that doing so will compromise quality and safety.

Although support for the idea that leadership is actually neutralized by substitutes is not overwhelming,[79] it is also true that the substitutes for leadership factors are important determinants of employee attitudes, behaviors and role perceptions. Probably the best advice to you is that, when trying to figure out what leadership approach is best for a particular situation, try to keep these factors in mind.

In Table 11.5 you can examine some typical characteristics of subordinates, the task, and the organization, and see whether they are likely to negate two kinds of leadership we have already discussed: consideration-based leadership and structure-based leadership.

As a Leader, You Also Need to Know How To . . .

In addition to the theories above, which primarily promote leadership styles to enhance organizational productivity, leaders must know how to practice ethical leadership, understand the nonrational side of leadership, and deal with cultural myths about leadership.

TABLE 11.5 How Subordinate, Task and Organizational Characteristics Neutralize Leadership

These factors. . .	Neutralize consideration-based leadership	Neutralize structure-based leadership
Individuals' ability, experience, training, and knowledge neutralize. . .		X
Individuals' indifference to organizational rewards neutralizes. . .	X	X
Tasks that are unambiguous and routine neutralize. . .		X
Tasks that are intrinsically satisfying neutralize. . .	X	
Organizational formalization, including explicit plans, goals and areas of responsibility, neutralizes. . .		X
Closely knit, cohesive work groups neutralize. . .	X	X

Source: Based on S. Kerr and J. M. Jermier, "Substitutes for Leadership: Their Meaning and Measurement," *Organizational Behavior & Human Performance 22*, 1978:375–403; P. M. Podsakoff, B. P. Niehoff, and S. B. MacKenzie and M. L. Williams, "Do Substitutes for Leadership Really Substitute for Leadership? An Empirical Examination of Kerr and Jermier's Situational Leadership Model," *Organizational Behavior and Human Decision Processes 54*, 1993:1–44.

Practice Ethical Leadership

Among the top personal leadership characteristics sought by corporate recruiters are honesty and trustworthiness.[80] However, it is not sufficient for leaders themselves to be honest and fair. They must also know how to lead others to behave ethically.[81] Having a reputation as a moral person tells followers what the leader will do, but it does not tell them what *they* are expected to do. A leader must also become a moral manager, a person who interacts with others to enhance ethical decision making.[82]

What are the factors that go into being a moral manager? A moral manager:

- Leads others on the ethical dimension
- Lets subordinates know what is expected
- Holds subordinates accountable
- Sets ethical standards
- Communicates ethics messages
- Role models ethical conduct
- Uses rewards and punishments to guide ethical behavior in the organization

Unfortunately, it is common for both moral and immoral individuals to practice ethically silent leadership, which is failing to provide leadership in the area of ethics. When their leaders remain silent, employees wonder where their leaders stand or whether they care about ethics at all. "The ethically silent leader is not perceived to be unethical but is seen as focusing intently on the bottom line without setting complementary ethical goals. There is little or no ethics message coming from the top. But silence represents an important message. . . . Employees are likely to interpret silence to mean that the top executive really doesn't care how business goals are met, only that they are met, so employees act on that message."[83]

The bottom line is that to be effective moral leaders, executives should model ethical behavior *and* hold their followers accountable for ethical conduct.

Examine the Nonrational Side of Leadership

Learning how to lead effectively goes beyond acquiring skills: It sometimes requires looking inward as well. Like all human beings, leaders are subject to cognitive and emotional distortions that can lead to irrationality and even intentional destructiveness.[84]

When leaders' unconscious fantasies and out-of-awareness behaviors affect their management practices, their organizations may be at risk.[85] At one point, when competitors were developing new products, Henry Ford's irrational dislike of producing any vehicle other than the Model-T (he once kicked to pieces a slightly modified version) nearly pushed the Ford Motor Car Company into bankruptcy.[86] Extremely self-centered CEOs tend to favor extreme strategies and lots of change, as opposed to modestly evolving strategies and stability.[87] Their companies tend to perform either extremely well, or extremely poorly, and, in general, to exhibit highly changeable performance. Unfortunately, driven personalities are unlikely to change, especially when, as CEOs, they hold so much power. Often it takes a dramatic organizational failure to unseat them.

A modern leader well-known for being self-centered and strong-willed is Larry Ellison, founder of Oracle, the maker of database software used by large companies worldwide. The joke in Silicon Valley is, "What's the difference between God and Larry Ellison?" "God doesn't believe he is Larry Ellison." After 30 years with Ellison at the helm, Oracle has no successor in line to replace him.[88] Yet, in recent years, industry insiders have determined that Ellison's investments have become risky.[89]

The more centralized an organization is and the more power the CEO has, the greater the impact of the CEO's personality on the company's culture, strategy, and structure.[90] Because of their influential positions, it is especially important that leaders understand how their unconscious agendas can drive them to irrational behavior that affects their company. In fact, you might argue that leaders have a moral *responsibility* to understand themselves so as not to victimize either themselves or the people they lead.[91] Leaders can learn more about themselves in many different ways. However, entering psychotherapy or taking on executive coaching with a trained professional are likely to be most effective.

Five unconscious fantasies of leaders, along with the type of corporate culture each fantasy is likely to create, are shown in Table 11.6.

TABLE 11.6 Some Unconscious Fantasies of Leaders and Their Impact on Company Culture

The leader's unconscious style...	...Leads to these typical behaviors...	...Which are based on these unconscious beliefs (i.e., fantasies)...	...And create these kinds of company cultures...
Paranoid	Shows a lot of suspicion, including mistrusting others, being hypersensitive and hyper-alert.	Believing that one is threatened by an external danger and must be ready to attack and resist.	People emphasize distrust, suspicion and the identification of enemies. Interpersonal relations between leaders and subordinates are hostile and persecutory. Leaders may want to attack others to defend against their own fear of persecution. The company tends to react rather than anticipate.
Obsessive-compulsive	Shows compulsiveness, insists others submit to his or her methods.	Wishing not to be at anyone's mercy and so exerting a tight control over one's surroundings.	Mistrust between leaders and subordinates is widespread. Control rests on direct supervision rather than on goodwill and shared objectives. Ritualistic, with many controls monitoring internal operations.
Dramatic	Superficially warm and charming, but in fact lacks sincerity and takes others for granted.	Needing to be at center stage in order to attract attention or impress; behaves dramatically and narcissistically (excessively self-centered)	Subordinates attracted to this type of leader are often dependent and insecure. They idealize their charismatic leaders and are therefore easy to control. Dramatic firms are often hyperactive, impulsive risk-takers.
Depressive	Acts depressed and dependent, lacks initiative	Feeling incapable, unworthy, or powerless	Negativity and inactivity are pervasive, along with lack of confidence, extreme conservatism, and insularity. Accomplishes mainly work that is programmed, routinized, and requires no special initiative.
Schizoid	Because the leader is detached, second-tier managers run the company and compete with each other for power. The company's focus is internal, emphasizing personal ambitions. Company strategy depends on shifting coalitions.	Wishing to maintain distance in relationships with others, in order to avoid pain and conflict.	Because the leader is detached, second-tier managers run the company and compete with each other for power. The company's focus is internal, emphasizing personal ambitions. Company strategy depends on shifting coalitions.

Sources: L. Lapierre, "Exploring the Dynamics of Leadership," in M. F. R. Kets de Vries and Associates, *Organizations on the Couch: Clinical Perspectives on Organizational Behavior and Change* (San Francisco: Jossey-Bass Publishers, 1991):69–93; M. F. R. Kets de Vries and D. Miller, "Leadership Styles and Organizational Cultures: The Shaping of Neurotic Organizations," in M. F. R. Kets de Vries and Associates, *Organizations on the Couch: Clinical Perspectives on Organizational Behavior and Change* (San Francisco: Jossey-Bass Publishers, 1991):243–263.

Recognize Myths About Leadership

Myths about leadership are widespread, and if you do not recognize them, they might trip you up, because myths have a way of becoming guidelines, which can be a significant problem in real life organizations.

One of today's popular myths is that tough leaders are the best leaders. "You're fired!" has become a well known slogan in the United States, suggesting that organizations require tough leaders able to make difficult choices and act decisively. Yet, according to analysts, there is little evidence that tough bosses improve business success. For example, "America's Toughest Bosses," as identified by *Fortune* magazine, do not necessarily achieve top financial results for their companies. Over one five-year period, the median return on shareholder's equity for seven "tough boss" companies ranged from 7.3 to 18.1 percent. The median for the *Fortune* 500 during the same period was 13.8 percent.[92]

A second modern myth is that leaders must be excellent technical analysts, able to think their companies to success. Many observers believe this emphasis distracts leaders from such concerns as improving motivation, commitment, and morale. As writers Jeffrey Pfeffer and John Veiga argue, "Emphasizing analytical skills over interpersonal, negotiating, political, and leadership skills inevitably leads to errors in selection, development, and emphasis on what is important to an organization."[93]

Students of leadership like yourself should take a hard look at myths about leadership. Choosing which leaders to emulate and which skills to learn is part of your own leadership challenge.

Will You Get a Chance to Lead?

Opportunities to lead are limited, especially if an "opportunity" is defined narrowly as a promotion to a higher position. Lack of leadership opportunities is one reason why some individuals leave their companies. Whether you actually will get a chance to lead in your company will depend on several factors, including what kind of leadership the company needs and values (and these may differ), and what kind of leadership training and experience you can acquire.

What Type of Leadership Does Your Company Need?

Surprisingly little research has been done that addresses this question directly, but common sense suggests that some companies, especially those operating in stable business environments in which bureaucratic decision making predominates, require transactional leaders, whereas others, especially those that need to radically change, require charismatic and transformational leaders. Certainly, whatever your leadership skills, the system in which you find yourself is going to shape your opportunities to lead.

Your opportunities will also be determined by the different needs at different organizational levels. How many charismatic lower-level supervisors are really necessary? Not many. Most likely lower levels of a company are filled with transactional leaders, only some of whom have the capability and desire to be charismatic or transformational leaders as they move up in the corporate hierarchy. An equally interesting question is whether at the top levels of a company there is room for more than a single charismatic leader. It may be that one charismatic leader drives out others.

What Type of Leadership Is Valued in Your Company?

The type of leadership a company values and the type it actually needs may differ. Consider the plight of a company that values and promotes transactional leaders but faces a competitive crisis in which transformational leadership is essential. Where will the company suddenly find its transformational leader? Conversely, imagine a company in a mature product market that is, by some accident of fate, run by a transformational leader. In all probability this leader will attempt to move the company in a new direction, or get bored with it and leave.

The type of leadership that is valued in a company depends in part on the **prototypes** (that is, the ideal models) of leadership that are held by the individuals in that company. The study of leadership prototypes is called **implicit leadership theory**, because individuals

prototype of leadership
The models of ideal leadership that are held by the individuals in a company.

implicit leadership theory
The study of leadership prototypes, which individuals hold implicitly.

hold prototypes implicitly, as unchallenged personal assumptions.[94] Personal assumptions about the traits and abilities that characterize an ideal business leader are stored in a person's memory and come into play when an individual interacts with his or her leader. These prototypes help followers make sense of what their leaders are doing.[95]

Where do individuals' prototypes come from? Individuals form their leadership prototypes based on their social experiences, interpersonal interactions, and experiences with actual leaders.[96] For example, greater height may be part of individuals' leadership prototypes. Taller individuals are more likely than shorter individuals to emerge as leaders, a finding that is true of both men and women.[97] On average, taller individuals are also more likely to make more money, a phenomenon that is especially likely to be true in occupations where persuasion and negotiation are important, such as sales and management. Compared to a person who is 5 feet 5 inches tall, a person who is 6 feet tall is likely to make almost $166,000 more over the course of a 30-year career.

In general, individuals base their prototypes of their ideal leader on six traits—four positive traits and two negative ones.[98] The four positive prototypical traits comprise what is termed the **leadership prototype**. They are sensitivity/compassion, intelligence, dedication, and dynamism/energy. The two negative traits comprise the **leadership antiprototype**. They are tyranny (being dominant, selfish, and manipulative) and masculinity (being male and masculine). With regard to the last set of traits, it is thought that although masculine attributes often predict leader emergence and advancement, such attributes are not developmental and constructive for followers, and thus are not seen by followers as desirable traits.[99]

Students of psychology will not be surprised to learn that individuals judge others to be competent leaders depending on how much they resemble themselves. In one study, goal-oriented versus people-oriented participants were asked to judge two individuals on their potential as leaders.[100] One of the individuals exhibited primarily goal-oriented behaviors; the other exhibited primarily social skills. The goal-oriented participants rated the goal-oriented individuals more favorably on leadership ability than did their socially oriented counterparts. However, the socially oriented participants perceived the socially skilled individuals as having more leadership potential. In a similar way, subordinates are somewhat more inclined to view supervisors with personality traits similar to their own as leaders.[101] Similarly, recruiters are more likely to say someone has "leadership potential" if that person has the same personality traits as the recruiter. Unfortunately, when individuals label others as effective leaders merely because they meet their own personal ideal, companies may not get the type of leadership they need.[102]

Do you meet the leadership prototype held by the influential individuals in your company, including your boss and the top managers? Implicit leadership theory suggests that the more similar your leadership style is to that of powerful decision makers, the higher the probability that you will be valued as a leader. Being different presents a dilemma to both individuals and organizations. Leadership theorists point out that, "People's self-serving notions of who is likely to succeed can influence their willingness to permit others opportunities to try. And . . . people's self-concepts and views of social categories such as leadership are intertwined, with the potential to color their judgments of who qualifies as a leader . . . with obvious consequences."[103]

Will Your Company Identify You as a Leader?

Unfortunately, companies tend to overlook individuals who fail to exhibit traditional leadership characteristics. Such individuals may not be tall or extraverted, for instance. One way to identify hidden leaders is to use sociograms and similar analyses of social networks to identify the individuals with whom people really relate.

Consider the case of soccer coach Sasho Cirovski of the University of Maryland Terapins, who brought his bottom-ranked team up to qualify for six straight NCAA tournaments, and then watched it precipitously decline.[104] He had made his two strongest players co-captains, but found they were relying too much on him and were not being proactive enough on the field. Cirovski realized that he had recruited talent, but not leaders. Stymied, he asked his brother, a human resources executive, to help him out.

His brother told him to let his team identify their own leaders by giving them a survey, asking questions such as "Whom do you rely on when the team needs motivation?" and

"Whom do you consult when you need input on making a minor personal decision?" Based on the survey results, Cirovski found that one young man was clearly the go-to guy for the team. He was a quiet sophomore who had been a promising local, but not a top recruit. Cirovski made him co-captain, and the team rallied behind him and started to win. He continued to be an effective leader until he graduated.

How Will Your Minority Status Affect Your Leadership Opportunities?

You are an X in a company run by Ys. What are your chances of being offered leadership opportunities? The research presented here focuses primarily on women in male-dominated organizations. However, other minorities have similar issues.

LEADERSHIP POTENTIAL Searching for explanations as to why there are more men than women in leadership positions, researchers have investigated gender differences in leadership styles. A recent review of 45 studies found some small differences between men and women.[105] Specifically, when they act as transactional leaders, women are somewhat more likely to systematically reward their followers, whereas men are somewhat more likely to pay attention to followers' mistakes and failures to meet standards, and to wait until problems become severe before attending to them. Men are also more likely to practice what is called laissez-faire leadership, which is being frequently absent and uninvolved during critical situations. Because all of the aspects of leadership style on which the women were stronger do predict leadership effectiveness, whereas those on which the men were stronger either have no relationship with effectiveness or predict ineffectiveness, the researchers concluded that women certainly have the inherent ability to perform well in leadership roles. However, additional research suggests that men and women's effectiveness as leaders depends on the setting in which they find themselves.[106] Women are likely to perform less well, and are perceived as performing less well, in settings in which leadership is defined in highly masculine terms. For example, they would be especially challenged in military settings. Men are likely to perform less well, and are perceived as performing less well, in settings in which leadership is defined in less masculine terms, especially in educational organizations and in governmental and social service organizations.

In short, gender should not be used as a predictor of what styles of leadership behaviors an individual will exhibit.[107] Whether for hiring and promotion or for business school admissions, people should be considered as individuals.

It is expected that people's stereotypes about the gender of leaders and managers will weaken in future. Also, to the extent that organizations learn to prefer more participative and less autocratic styles, it appears that women will fare at least as well as men in leadership roles. These analyses do not directly address how to prevent gate-keepers to leadership positions from choosing individuals who are like themselves in terms of gender or other demographic characteristics. However, they do suggest that gatekeepers might be educated to overlook gender in favor of style.

LEADERSHIP VALUES Another view of gender differences and leadership examines disparities in men's and women's values. For example, a study in the *Journal of Business Ethics* suggests that women may not relate to a business orientation that focuses on amassing wealth, on game theory, and on rationality to the exclusion of other human factors. Women want to include issues of morality, for example, in any discussion of self-interest.[108] A separate British study found that men tend to define success quantifiably, in terms of high salary, status, and material possessions such as cars, whereas women tend to define it in terms of emotional and interpersonal well-being, including being seen as experts in their field, having an intrinsically interesting job, and balancing work and personal life.[109]

It has been argued that women's participation in MBA programs internationally has plateaued at about 20 to 30 percent in part because women are turned off by programs that emphasize competition and impersonality, and in which good teaching is associated with charisma, expert power and authority, and maleness.[110] They prefer learning in programs based on helping participants with their personal issues, in cultures that are intimate and developmental, and in which good teaching involves sharing relevant experience and encouraging self-analysis.

This view of gender differences has many implications that have not yet been studied. The obvious one is that as leaders, men and women, and in fact people with any sorts of differences, may pursue somewhat different goals, and it may be important that they each find organizations that share their perspective.

What Do We Know About Leadership Cross-Culturally?

Until recently most research on leadership was done in the United States. Certainly most of the research reported in this chapter is based on studies of American leaders leading American employees. Its application to other countries remains to be tested.

Interesting questions that companies would like to know more about include what leadership traits, if any, are universally desirable, and what traits are universally undesirable.[111] Also, what is the prototype for outstanding leaders in different cultures around the world? When transporting leaders from one culture to another, what predicts whether they will be effective? One interesting research project in two Western and three Asian cultures suggests that leader supportiveness, leader charisma, and rewarding subordinates contingently show universal positive impacts.[112] But a great deal more research is needed.

A major goal of Project GLOBE is to develop a more international perspective on leadership. For example, the GLOBE researchers have discovered some national differences in attitudes toward leadership. Some cultures tend to romanticize leadership and to value both organizational and political leadership. These include the U.S., British, Eastern European, French, German, Russians, Arab, Asian, and Latin American cultures. Other countries are skeptical about leaders and are concerned that leaders tend to accumulate and abuse power. These include the Netherlands, Scandinavian countries, and the Germanic-speaking sector of Switzerland.

Implicit Theories of Leadership

The GLOBE researchers studied six implicit theories of leadership to find out what their international subjects, all middle managers, believe about them. See Table 11.7 for descriptions of the theories and how the middle managers rank them according to their importance.

Leader Attributes

Finally, as an individual, you may be wondering what attributes of leaders are valued by middle managers worldwide. Table 11.8 lists the universal positive leader attributes discovered by Project GLOBE.

In Conclusion

In this chapter we have reviewed the basic theories of leadership with an eye to helping you make some basic decisions about the role of leadership in your career. Should you decide that you definitely want to pursue leadership roles, the fundamental characteristics you need are noted here. In the next chapter, we will look at the skills leaders must have in order to excel in some of their most important roles.

TABLE 11.7 **Overview: What Middle Managers Around the World Believe About Leadership**

Leadership Category	Leadership Behaviors	Middle Managers' Views
Desirable Behaviors		
Charismatic/Value-Based Leadership	Visionary, inspirational, self-sacrificing, shows integrity, decisive, performance oriented	Considered the *most* desirable set of behaviors in most cultures
Team-Oriented Leadership	Collaborative, team integrator, diplomatic, not malevolent, administratively competent	A desirable set of behaviors in most cultures
Acceptable Behaviors		
Participative Leadership	Involves others in decision making and is not autocratic	An acceptable set of behaviors in most cultures
Autonomous Leadership	Individualistic, independent from both superiors and subordinates, autonomous, and unique	An acceptable set of behaviors in most cultures. Reported to be slightly effective in most countries of Eastern Europe and Germanic Europe except the Netherlands; ineffective in most Latin American, Middle Eastern and Anglo countries
Humane Leadership	Modest and humanely oriented	An acceptable set of behaviors in most cultures
Unacceptable Behaviors		
Self-Protective Leadership	Self-centered, status conscious, conflict inducer, face-saver, procedural (formal and ritualistic)	An unacceptable set of behaviors to be in most cultures; reported slightly effective by managers in Albania, Taiwan, Egypt, Iran, and Kuwait; in all other nations, considered an impediment to highly effective leadership.

Source: R. J. House, P. J. Hanges, M. Javidan, P. W. Dorfman, and V. Gupta, eds., *Culture, Leadership and Organizations: The GLOBE Study of 62 Societies* (Thousand Oaks, CA: Sage Publications, 2004).

TABLE 11.8 **Universal Positive Leader Attributes**

Trustworthy	Motivational
Just	Dependable
Honest	Intelligent
Has foresight	Decisive
Plans ahead	Effective bargainer
Encouraging	Win-win problem solver
Positive	Administratively skilled
Dynamic	Communicative
Motive arouser	Informed
Confidence builder	Coordinator
Team builder	
Excellence oriented	

Source: P. W. Dorfman, P. J. Hanges, and F. C. Brodbeck, "Leadership and Cultural Variation: The Identification of Culturally Endorsed Leadership Profiles," in R. J. House, P. J. Hanges, M. Javidan, P. W. Dorfman, and V. Gupta, eds., *Culture, Leadership and Organizations: The GLOBE Study of 62 Societies* (Thousand Oaks, CA: Sage Publications, 2004):669–719.

Apply What You Have Learned. . .

World Class Company: Consumer Products Inc. Hires a Consultant

Having adopted a new growth strategy, Consumer Products Inc. (CPI), an international manufacturer of foods, home care, and personal care products, set out to develop an innovative, enterprise culture.[113] (CPI is a pseudonym for an actual company.) The company decided that by changing the style of its leaders in several major business groups, it could make company-wide changes such as the following:

- Moving from endless debate to developing candid discussions and the energy to move quickly

- Moving from a lack of accountability to having people take ownership for their commitments

- Moving from slow and cautious decision making to more risk taking

- Moving from exhausting bureaucratic processes to energized and innovative action instigated from lower levels in the company

- Moving from having a lot of unnecessary work to empowering employees to refuse work that is not clearly aligned with the company's strategic priorities

The company hired the consulting firm The Forum Corporation (a real company) to train its managers in the skills associated with the types of leaders who can grow a business. These skills included different skills for different organizational levels. For example, a high-level leader might learn how to inspire and motivate, and how to obtain valid information on the competition and market. Leaders lower in the hierarchy would learn how to target and motivate innovation, how to listen, and how to receive feedback. Over a three-month period, at each management level—vice-presidents, directors, managers, and individual contributors—Forum consultants coached individuals and gave them feedback about their emerging leadership behaviors. A key aspect of the program was that the training and

learning occurred on the job and on site rather than off the job and off site. Each individual was required to set challenging business and personal leadership goals to execute in the course of day-to-day business. At the end of the program, individuals met to share stories and lessons learned.

What did the company accomplish through training its leaders to adopt new behaviors? Here are some examples:

- A supervisor dramatically changed his style and made himself more accessible to his employees. Because of this, two factory workers collaborated to make a process improvement that saved the company $125,000.

- A vice-president adopted a new cross-functional team approach to customer relations and made a significant breakthrough.

- One team leader cited his team's increased passion and risk-taking.

- A vice-president noted, "In the end it's okay to enlist the support of others, it's okay not to have all the answers, and it's okay to share that vulnerability with others. It helps bring you closer together."

Discuss

1. How have CPI's leaders adapted their approaches to the company's new strategic focus? (See work unit leadership theory in this chapter.)

2. How have CPI's leaders guided their followers to valued goals? (See path-goal theory in this chapter.)

3. How have CPI's leaders changed the supervisor-subordinate relationship? (See leader-member exchange theory in this chapter.)

4. In situations where a company is moving from a more bureaucratic to a more enterprising design, what factors in the company's culture might encourage its leaders to return to their old ways?

Advice from the Pros

Tom Peters on Talent

Management consultant Tom Peters lists the following intangible attributes that mark management talent. According to Peters, a true talent. . .

- Displays curiosity, passion, and a sense of fun
- Loves action and pressure
- Thrives on WOW—that is, he or she has things he or she *loves* to talk about, like personal accomplishments

that have defied conventional wisdom, or the job that nobody else wanted that he or she turned into a success

- Is not a clone of others
- Is intelligent, and therefore thinks at a high level
- Knows how to finish the job
- Inspires others
- Is committed to finding talent for the company

Discuss

1. Based on the descriptions of leadership in this chapter, what kind(s) of leader is Peters describing?
2. Based on what you have learned in this chapter and this book, what is different about Peter's view of leaders? Do you think he is right?

Source: Based on T. Peters, *Re-imagine!* (London: Dorling Kindersley Limited, 2003):254.

Gain Experience

"The Apprentice on Steroids"

Michael Cunningham runs an MBA class entitled "Management and Business Planning" that requires students to write a business plan, critique it, and then develop it for live businesses. The course is the capstone of an entrepreneurial program, and it the students' last course in the MBA program. Typically the course has 40 students.

In 2005, the first session of the class took place just days after Hurricane Katrina. The professor decided to put up $25,000 in seed money and charged his students with coming up with effective ways to make money to help the victims of the hurricane. What followed has been described as *"The Apprentice* on steroids." Can you imagine what

happened during the course of the class, from October through the end of December?

You are the students in Professor Cunningham's class. In teams, develop a plan for helping the victims. Write down and be prepared to present the essential points of your plan.

Discuss

1. The class and professor select the best plan. Then compare your plans with those of Dr. Cunningham's class.
2. Discuss the process that was used to develop the best plan.
3. Discuss the role of leadership in implementing the plan.

Can You Solve this Manager's Problem?

Choose Carly Fiorina's Next Job

Carly Fiorina is described as "elegant and intellectually versatile."[114] As chief executive of Hewlett-Packard (HP), in 2005 the world's second largest computer maker after Dell, she "was photogenic, mixed with celebrities and behaved like one, and seemed to do bold things–above all, her controversial merger with Compaq, another computer maker."[115] Her vision for the merger, which was announced in 2001, was to create a larger, leaner, and more powerful company from the two rivals. As of 2006 the merger was successful, although more time would be needed to ascertain its longer term impacts.[116]

Fiorina's high style upset her more conservative HP colleagues, and stockholders, too. Evidently, Fiorina resisted suggestions that she hire a chief operating officer to help her with management details.[117] She also had a harsh management style, which clashed with the normally collegial HP culture.

Under Fiorina, Hewlett-Packard lost ground to both Dell and IBM. At age 50, Fiorina was fired from Hewlett-Packard after a five year tenure and awarded a $21 million severance package. She was replaced by a man who would be likely to tend to operational issues, and who, some

argued, would execute strategy better and not be "jetting around, talking about the world economy."[118] Fiorina asserts, "My firing was not about performance. So I can only conclude it was about a set of personal agendas and dysfunction."[119]

One way to assess Fiorina's leadership style is to listen to what she says on various topics. Here are a few selections.

On Being Who You Are

Soon after she was fired from HP, Fiorina gave a commencement address that she opened with, "My fellow job seekers. . . ."[120] She asserted that she likes big challenges, and chose a challenging career path in a male-dominated industry. At the end of your life, she said, "If people ask you what your greatest accomplishment was, my guess is, it will be something that happened inside you, that no one else ever saw, something that had nothing to do with outside success, and everything to do with how you decide to live in the world."

Some interesting facts are that at the age of 23 Fiorina was a law school dropout with no clear direction in life, yet by the age of 45 she was named "The Most Powerful Woman in Business" by *Fortune.*[121]

On Managing People at HP

To quote Fiorina, "The company belongs to them—not to the Board, or the founders, or the families of the founders. The people of HP are HP. My job as CEO was to build new skills and capabilities, as well as new confidence and aspiration. . . . My job was to lead the transformation of a once-great company that now was floundering by unlocking the potential of its people and its assets.

"Over the years, I received tens of thousands of messages from employees. . . . In that entire time, only one was unsigned. The authors of all the other e-mails, both those who were supportive and those who were critical, let me know who they were as well as what they thought. I am deeply grateful for the candor and wisdom of the people of HP."[122]

On Changing a Company Strategy

Upon reading writer Alfred D. Chandler's idea that strategy should be "ennobling," Fiorina found that this made sense to her.[123] Fear is only a temporary motivator, she believes, while pursuing a worthy purpose is a motivator that lasts.

When pursuing a strategy, pursuing change too slowly can draw the criticism "too conservative," while pursing change too quickly can draw the criticism, "too radical." As CEO, Fiorina was often criticized as too radical.

On American Competitiveness

Late in 2005 Fiorina described the uproar that she had caused earlier that year when, in a reporters' roundtable in Washington, she had said, "No American has a God-given right to a job."[124] She received angry letters, she said, from people who saw her as "callous and unfeeling," and the reaction surprised her. She argues that this response may suggest that Americans are feeling too entitled, that "nothing about our future is inevitable or guaranteed: not our jobs, or our leadership, or our standard of living." Furthermore, she notes, Americans are only 4 percent of the world's population, and there are at least 300 million educated competitors outside of the United States, twice as many people as the size of our workforce, who are highly motivated to create the companies, jobs, and innovations of the future.

On Her Marriage

"I loved [my husband] because he loved that I was capable. He told me he thought I would run the company some day. I laughed and told him it was ridiculous, and although I truly thought it was, I loved him for thinking it was possible. More than that, he found it thrilling, not threatening."[125]

Discuss

1. What kind of a leader is Carly Fiorina?
2. Make a recommendation to Ms. Fiorina on what her next job should be.

Chapter Summary and Key Terms

What is leadership, really?

Leadership is a form of social influence in which one person influences one or more individuals to enhance the effectiveness of the organization. Formal leaders have legitimate authority based on their organizational position, whereas emergent leaders get things accomplished through others despite having no authority.

contingency theory   294
leadership   294
formal leader   295
emergent leaders   295
manager   295
independent contributor   295

Why are some people leaders while others are followers?

Some people are leaders because they have standard leadership traits such as extraversion, openness to experience, and intelligence. However, not all leaders exhibit the standard set of traits. It is also true that not everyone wants to lead.

derailing traits   296

Can you learn to be a leader?

Leader behaviors include two dimensions. First, leaders who exhibit consideration demonstrate concern and respect for followers and look out for their welfare. Second, leaders who initiate structure define roles and organize people to meet goals and establishing effective communications. Most managers can learn both sets of behaviors.

Charismatic leaders exert an unusual amount of influence on their followers, generally because of their self-confidence, vision, unconventional behavior, and other characteristics. Research suggests that some of these characteristics can be learned.

consideration   298
structure   298
charismatic leader   299
transactional leader   302
transformational leader   302
peer-to-peer leadership development   303

Will you be an effective leader? As a leader how would you . . . ?

Leaders have a variety of tools at their command. For example, path-goal theory describes how leaders influence their followers' perceptions of their path to a valued goal. Work unit theory shows you how to adapt your leadership style to the situation.

Other important tools are based on cognitive resources theory, leader-member exchange theory, and substitutes for leadership theory.

As a leader, you also need to know how to. . .

Practice ethical leadership, examine the nonrational side of leadership, and recognize modern myths about leadership.

Will you get a chance to lead?

Whether you will get an opportunity to lead depends on the type of leadership your company needs and values. Bureaucratic companies need primarily transactional leaders, for example. Companies that need to radically change require transformational leaders.

Implicit leadership theory tells us that individuals have in their minds prototypes of ideal leaders. The more similar your leadership style is to that of powerful decision makers, the higher the probability that you will be valued as a leader.

What do we know about leadership cross-culturally?

Project GLOBE asks questions such as "What is the prototype for outstanding leaders in different cultures around the world?" More research needs to be done in this area.

Explorations

1. Emulate your favorite leader

Divide a page into three columns. Choose a leader you admire, read up on him or her, and then list his or her leadership characteristics down the left-hand column. In the middle column, rate the extent to which you yourself have these characteristics (1 = not at all, 2 = to a little extent, 3 = to some extent, 4 = to a great extent, 5 = to a very great extent). In the final column, assuming you would like to have each characteristic, describe what you need to do to acquire it.

2. Ethnic minorities and leadership

N. R. Narayanamurthy, chairman and chief mentor at Infosys Technologies, is the first Indian to win the Ernst & Young World Entrepreneur of the Year Award. Research his background and the background of other U.S. business leaders who come from ethnic minorities (Asian, African-American, or Latino). Do ethnic minorities have the same backgrounds as other U.S. business leaders, or not?

3. Nonrational leadership

Describe two instances of leadership that you think are nonrational. These can be from your personal experience, or from information you find on the Web. What circumstances may explain these individuals and their behaviors? What have been the effects of this nonrationality?

4. What kind of leader are you?

Web search for and take at least five leadership tests/surveys. Did you find tests that you think are particularly valid and useful? What strengths and weaknesses did you discover?

5. Watching Fiorina

You can read more about Fiorina's 25 years in business in her memoir *Tough Choices*. Also Web search to find her May 23, 2005 speech "The End of Manifest Destiny" to the Detroit Economic Club and her May 7, 2005 commencement address to the North Carolina Agricultural and Technical State University.

References

[1] J. O'Toole, J. Galbraith, and E. E. Lawler III, "The Promise and Pitfalls of Shared Leadership: When Two (or More) Heads Are Better Than One," in C. L. Pearce and J. A. Conger, eds., *Shared Leadership: Reframing the Hows and Whys of Leadership* (Thousand Oaks, CA: Sage Publications, 2003):250–267.

[2] A. Bryman, *Charisma and Leadership in Organizations* (London: Sage, 1992).

[3] C. L. Pearce and J. A. Conger, "All Those Years Ago: The Historical Underpinnings of Shared Leadership," in C. L. Pearce and J. A. Conger, eds., *Shared Leadership: Reframing the Hows and Whys of Leadership* (Thousand Oaks, CA: Sage Publications, 2003):1–18.

[4] D. N. Den Hartog and P. L. Koopman, "Leadership in Organizations," in N. Anderson, D. S. Ones, H. K. Sinangil and C. Viswesvaran, eds., *Handbook of Industrial, Work and Organizational Psychology 2* (London: Sage Publications, 2001):166–187.

[5] C. L. Pearce and J. A. Conger, "All Those Years Ago: The Historical Underpinnings of Shared Leadership," in C. L. Pearce and J. A. Conger, eds., *Shared Leadership: Reframing the Hows and Whys of Leadership* (Thousand Oaks, CA: Sage Publications, 2003):1–18.

[6] J. Greene, P. Coy, J. E. Ellis, R. Berner and C. Edwards, "After the Icon Exits: How Companies from Standard Oil to Wal-Mart Have Fared Once Their Legendary Chiefs Moved On," *BusinessWeek Online* July 3, 2006, http://www.businessweek.com. Accessed September 16, 2006.

[7] T. A. Stewart and L. O'Brien, "Execution without Excuses," *Harvard Business Review,* March 2005:102–111.

[8] T. A. Stewart and L. O'Brien, "Execution without Excuses," *Harvard Business Review,* March 2005:102–111:109.

[9] J. Palmer and B. Alpert, "The Return of Michael Dell: No Quick Fix for His Company," *Barron's* February 5, 2007:35.

[10] C. L. Pearce and J. A. Conger, "All Those Years Ago: The Historical Underpinnings of Shared Leadership," in C. L. Pearce

and J. A. Conger, eds., *Shared Leadership: Reframing the Hows and Whys of Leadership* (Thousand Oaks, CA: Sage Publications, 2003):1–18.

[11] D. G. Bowers and S. E. Seashore, "Predicting Organizational Effectiveness with a Four Factor Theory of Leadership," *Administrative Science Quarterly 11,* 1966:238–263.

[12] C. L. Pearce, Y. Yoo, and M. Alavi, "Leadership, Social Work and Virtual Teams: The Relative Influence of Vertical vs. Shared Leadership in the Nonprofit Sector," in R. E. Riggio and S. Smith Orr, eds., *Improving Leadership in Nonprofit Organizations* (San Francisco, CA: Jossey-Bass, 2004):180–203.

[13] R. F. Felton, "Splitting Chairs: Should CEOs Give Up the Chairman's Role?" *McKinsey Quarterly 4,* 2004:48–57; R. F. Felton and S. C. Y. Wong, "How to Separate the Roles of Chairman and CEO," *McKinsey Quarterly 4,* 2004:58–69.

[14] "Split and Stay," *The Economist 375* (8426), May 14, 2005:68; C. M. Daily and D. R. Dalton, "CEO and Board Chair Roles Held Jointly or Separately: Much Ado about Nothing?" *Academy of Management Executive 11* (3), August 1997:11–20.

[15] J. O'Toole, "When Leadership Is an Organizational Trait," in W. Bennis, G. M. Spreitzer, and T. G. Cummings, eds., *The Future of Leadership: Today's Top Leadership Thinkers Speak to Tomorrow's Leaders* (San Francisco, CA: Jossey-Bass, 2001):158–174, 162–163.

[16] R. J. House and M. Javidan, "Overview of GLOBE," in R. J. House, P. J. Hanges, M. Javidan, P. W. Dorfman, and V. Gupta, eds., *Culture, Leadership and Organizations: The GLOBE Study of 62 Societies* (Thousand Oaks, CA: Sage Publications, 2004):9–28, 15.

[17] R. J. House and M. L. Baetz, "Leadership: Some Empirical Generalizations and New Research Directions," in B. M. Staw, ed., *Research in Organizational Behavior 1* (Greenwich, CT: JAI Press, Inc., 1979):341–423.

[18] R. J. House and M. L. Baetz, "Leadership: Some Empirical Generalizations and New Research Directions," in B. M. Staw, ed., *Research in Organizational Behavior 1* (Greenwich, CT: JAI Press, Inc., 1979):341–423, 344.

[19] R. E. Boyatzis, "Beyond Competence: The Choice to Be a Leader," *Human Resource Management Review 3* (1), 1993:1–14.

[20] R. Hogan, G. J. Curphy, and J. Hogan, "What We Know about Leadership: Effectiveness and Personality," *American Psychologist 49* (6), June 1994:493–504; T. A. Judge, R. Illies, J. E. Bono, and M. W. Gerhardt, "Personality and Leadership: A Qualitative and Quantitative Review," *Journal of Applied Psychology 87* (4), 2002:765–780.

[21] J. A. LePine, J. A. Colquitt, and A. Erez, "Adaptability to Changing Task Contexts: Effects of General Cognitive Ability, Conscientiousness, and Openness to Experience," *Personnel Psychology 53* (3), Autumn 2000:563–593.

[22] R. G. Lord, C. L. De Vader, and G. M. Alliger, "A Meta-Analysis of the Relation between Personality Traits and Leadership Perception: An Application of Validity Generalization Procedures," *Journal of Applied Psychology 71,* 1986:402–410; T. A. Judge, R. Ilies, and A. E. Colbert, "Intelligence and Leadership: A Quantitative Review and Test of Theoretical Propositions," *Journal of Applied Psychology 89* (3), 2004:542–552.

[23] L. V. Nyquist and J. T. Spence, "Effects of Dispositional Dominance and Sex Role Expectations on Leadership Behaviors," *Journal of Personality & Social Psychology 50,* 1986:87–93.

[24] J. A. Smith and R. J. Foti, "A Pattern Approach to the Study of Leader Emergence," *Leadership Quarterly 9* (2), Summer 1998:147–160. For a review of traits see R. Hogan, G. J. Curphy and J. Hogan, "What We Know about Leadership: Effectiveness and Personality," *American Psychologist 49* (6), June 1994:493–504.

[25] W. G. Bennis and B. Nanus, *Leaders: The Strategies for Taking Charge* (New York: Harper & Row, 1985).

[26] C. Fishman, "Face Time with Meg Whitman," *Fast Company 46,* April 2001:72; "The 100 Most Powerful Women," Forbes.com/lists/2005/11/5AW7.html. Accessed September 25, 2006.

[27] D. V. Day, D. J. Schleicher, A. L. Unckless, and N. J. Hiller, "Self-Monitoring Personality at Work: A Meta-Analytic Investigation of Construct Validity," *Journal of Applied Psychology 87,* 2002:390–401. These results contrast with those presented in S. J. Zaccaro, R. J. Fote, and D. A. Kenny, "Self-Monitoring and Trait-Based Variance in Leadership: An Investigation of Leader Flexibility across Multiple Group Situations," *Journal of Applied Psychology 76,* 1991:308–315. For a further discussion see J. Antonakis, "Why 'Emotional Intelligence' Does Not Predict Leadership Effectiveness: A Comment on Prati, Douglas, Ferris, Ammeter, and Buckley (2003)," *International Journal of Organizational Analysis 11* (4), 2003:355–361.

[28] T. A. Judge, J. E. Bono, R. Illies, and M. W. Gerhardt, "Personality and Leadership: A Qualitative and Quantitative Review," *Journal of Applied Psychology 87,* 2002:765–780. These results contrast with those reported in R. Hogan, G. J. Curphy, and J. Hogan, "What We Know about Leadership: Effectiveness and Personality," *American Psychologist 49* (6), June 1994:493–504. For a further discussion see J. Antonakis, "Why 'Emotional intelligence' Does Not Predict Leadership Effectiveness: A Comment on Prati, Douglas, Ferris, Ammeter, and Buckley (2003)," *International Journal of Organizational Analysis 11* (4), 2003:355–361.

[29] V. J. Bentz, "A View from the Top: A Thirty Year Perspective of Research Devoted to Discovery, Description, and Prediction of Executive Behavior," paper presented at the 93rd Annual Convention of the American Psychological Association, Los Angeles, CA, August 1985; M. M. Lombardo, M. N. Ruderman, and C. D. McCauley, "Explanations of Success and Derailment in Upper-level Management Positions," *Journal of Business and Psychology 2,* 1988:199–216; L. W. Hellervik, J. F. Hazucha, and R. J. Schneider, "Behavior Change: Models, Methods and a Review of the Evidence," in M. D. Dunnette and L. M. Hough, eds., *Handbook of Industrial and Organizational Psychology 3,* 2nd ed. (Palo Alto, CA: Consulting Psychologists Press, 1992); M. W. McCall and M. M. Lombardo, "Off the Track: Why and How Successful Executives Get Derailed," *Technical Report 21* (Greensboro, NC: Center for Creative Leadership, 1993).

[30] R. Hogan, G. J. Curphy and J. Hogan, "What We Know About Leadership: Effectiveness and Personality," *American Psychologist 49* (6), June 1994:493–504.

[31] M. J. Schmit, J. A. Kihm, and C. Roble, "Development of a Global Measure of Personality," *Personnel Psychology 53* (1), 2000:153–193.

[32] G. Harris and J. Hogan, "Perceptions and Personality Correlates of Managerial Effectiveness," paper presented at the 13th Annual Psychology in the Department of Defense Symposium, Colorado Springs, CO, April 1992.

33 D. B. Peterson and M. D. Hicks, "How to Get People to Change," workshop presented at the Eighth Annual Conference of the Society for Industrial and Organizational Psychology, San Francisco, CA, May 1993.

34 J. Sturges and D. Guest, "Working to Live or Living to Work? Work/Life Balance Early in the Career," *Human Resource Management Journal 14* (4), 2004:5–20.

35 A. Coffey, "Timing Is Everything: Graduate Accountants, Time and Organizational Commitment," *Sociology 28* (4), 1994:943–956.

36 B. Lawrence, "Career Anchor," in N. Nicholson, ed., *The Blackwell Encyclopedic Dictionary of Organizational Behavior* (Cambridge, MA: Blackwell, 1995):44–45.

37 G. W. Yunker and J. G. Hunt, "An Empirical Comparison of the Michigan Four-Factor and Ohio State LBDQ Leadership Scales," *Organizational Behavior & Human Performance 17* (1), October 1976:45–65; C. A. Schriesheim and B. J. Bird, "Contributions of the Ohio State Studies to the Field of Leadership," *Journal of Management 5* (2), Fall 1979:135–145.

38 R. T. Morris and M. Seeman, "The Problem of Leadership: An Interdisciplinary Approach," *American Journal of Sociology 56,* 1950:149–155; R. M. Stogdill, *Leadership and Structures of Personal Interaction* (Columbus, OH: Bureau of Business Research, Ohio State University, 1957): Research Monograph 84; R. M. Stogdill and A. E. Coons, *Leader Behavior: Its Description and Measurement* (Columbus, OH: Bureau of Business Research, Ohio State University, 1957):Research Monograph 84.

39 B. M. Bass, *Bass and Stogdill's Handbook of Leadership* (New York: Free Press, 1990); T. A. Judge, R. F. Piccolo, and R. Ilies, "The Forgotten Ones? The Validity of Consideration and Initiating Structure in Leadership Research," *Journal of Applied Psychology 89* (1), 2004:36–51.

40 E. A. Fleishman, "Twenty Years of Consideration and Structure," in E. A. Fleishman and J. G. Hunt, eds., *Leader Behavior: Its Description and Measurement* (Columbus OH: Bureau of Business Research, 1973):120–133; T. A. Judge, R. F. Piccolo, and R. Ilies, "The Forgotten Ones? The Validity of Consideration and Initiating Structure in Leadership Research," *Journal of Applied Psychology 89* (1), 2004:36–51.

41 D. N. Den Hartog and P. L. Koopman, "Leadership in Organizations," in N. Anderson, D. S. Ones, H. K. Sinangil and C. Viswesvaran, eds., *Handbook of Industrial, Work and Organizational Psychology 2* (London: Sage Publications, 2001):166–187; T. A. Judge, R. F. Piccolo, and R. Ilies, "The Forgotten Ones? The Validity of Consideration and Initiating Structure in Leadership Research," *Journal of Applied Psychology 89* (1), 2004:36–51.

42 R. R. Blake and J. S. Mouton, *The Managerial Grid* (Houston, TX: Gulf, 1964); R. R. Blake and J. S. Mouton, "Management by Grid Principles or Situationalism: Which?" *Group and Organization Studies 7,* 1982:207–210.

43 For a review see K. Kim, F. Dansereau, and I. Kim, "Extending the Concept of Charismatic Leadership: An Illustration Using Bass's (1990) Categories," in B. J. Avolio and F. J. Yammarino, eds., *Transformational and Charismatic Leadership 2* (Amsterdam: JAI Press, 2002):143–172.

44 W. L. Gardner and B. J. Avolio, "The Charismatic Relationship: A Dramaturgical Perspective," *Academy of Management Review 23* (1), January 1998:32–58.

45 A. J. Towler, "Effects of Charismatic Influence Training on Attitudes, Behavior, and Performance," *Personnel Psychology 56* (2), Summer 2003:363–381.

46 Details on Winfrey come from: "Biography: Academy of Achievement," http://www.achievement.org. Accessed September 25, 2006; "The *Time* 100," http://www.time.com/time/time100/artists/profile/winfrey3.html. Accessed September 25, 2006.

47 "The *Time* 100," http://www.time.com/time/time100/artists/profile/winfrey3.html. Accessed September 25, 2006.

48 J. M. Howell and P. J. Frost, "A Laboratory Study of Charismatic Leadership," *Organizational Behavior and Human Decision Processes 43,* 1989:243–269.

49 A. J. Towler, "Effects of Charismatic Influence Training on Attitudes, Behavior, and Performance," *Personnel Psychology 56* (2), Summer 2003:363–381.

50 J. G. Hunt, K. B. Boal, and G. E. Dodge, "The Effects of Visionary and Crisis-Responsive Charisma on Followers: An Experimental Examination," *Leadership Quarterly 10* (3), Fall 1999:423–448.

51 H. M. Trice and J. M. Beyer, "Charisma and Its Routinization in Two Social Movement Organizations," *Research in Organizational Behavior 8,* 1986:113–164.

52 "Face Value: China's Pied Piper," *The Economist,* September 23, 2006:78.

53 R. F. Kennedy, "Ted's Eulogy for Robert," *The New York Times,* June 9, 1968:53, as quoted in J. G. Hunt, K. B. Boal, and G. E. Dodge, "The Effects of Visionary and Crisis-Responsive Charisma on Followers: An Experimental Examination," *Leadership Quarterly 10* (3), Fall 1999:423–448.

54 W. F. "Bull" Halsey, quoted in B. Lay Jr. and F. D. Gilroy, *The Gallant Years (film)* (Hollywood, CA: United Artists, 1959), as quoted in J. G. Hunt, K. B. Boal, and G. E. Dodge, "The Effects of Visionary and Crisis-Responsive Charisma on Followers: An Experimental Examination," *Leadership Quarterly 10* (3), Fall 1999:423–448.

55 J. M. Burns, *Leadership* (New York, Harper & Row, 1978); B. Bass, *Leadership and Performance Beyond Expectations* (New York, Free Press, 1985).

56 A. Zaleznik, "Managers and Leaders: Are They Different?" in W. W. Rosenbach and R. L. Taylor, eds., *Contemporary Issues in Leadership* (Oxford: Westview Press, 1993):36–56.

57 B. M. Bass, "Does the Transactional–Transformational Leadership Paradigm Transcend Organizational and National Boundaries?" *American Psychologist 52* (2), February 1997:130–137.

58 D. Vera and M. Crossan, "Strategic Leadership and Organizational Learning," *Academy of Management Review 29* (2), April 2004:222–240.

59 B. Nussbaum, R. Berner, and D. Brady, "Get Creative!" *BusinessWeek* Issue 3945, August 1, 2005:60–68.

60 B. M. Bass and B. J. Avolio, "Developing Transformational Leadership: 1992 and Beyond," *Journal of European Industrial Training 14,* 1990:21–27; B. M. Bass, "Does the Transactional–Transformational Leadership Paradigm Transcend Organizational and National Boundaries?" *American Psychologist 52* (2), February 1997:130–137.

61 J. E. Barbuto, "Taking the Charisma Out of Transformational Leadership," *Journal of Social Behavior and Personality 12* (3), 1997:689–697.

62 B. M. Bass, *Leadership and Performance Beyond Expectations* (New York: Free Press, 1985).

63 J. E. Barbuto, "Taking the Charisma Out of Transformational Leadership," *Journal of Social Behavior and Personality 12* (3), 1997:689–697.

64 J. Nelson, "Jerry Porras—How Important Are Charismatic Leaders to Visionary Companies?" *New Zealand Management 52* (2), March 2005:40–42.

65 N.M. Dixon, "Peer-to-Peer Leadership Development," *Harvard Business Review 84* (2), February 2006: 56–57.

66 R. J. House, "A Path-Goal Theory of Leader Effectiveness," *Administrative Science Quarterly 16* (3), 1971:321–338.

67 B. Shamir, R. J. House, and M. B. Arthur, "The Motivational Effects of Charismatic Leadership: A Self-Concept Based Theory," *Organization Science 4* (4), November 1993:577–594.

68 R. J. House and B. Shamir, "Toward the Integration of Transformational, Charismatic, and Visionary Theories," in M. M. Chemers and R. Ayman, eds., *Leadership Theory and Research: Perspectives and Directions* (San Diego, CA: Academic Press, Inc., 1993):81–107.

69 R. J. House, "Path-Goal Theory of Leadership: Lessons, Legacy, and a Reformulated Theory," *Leadership Quarterly 7,* 1996:323–352.

70 F. E. Fiedler, "Personality, Motivation Systems, and Behavior of High and Low LPC Persons," *Human Relations 25,* 1972:391–412; F. E. Fiedler and J. E. Garcia, *Improving Leadership Effectiveness: Cognitive Resources and Organizational Performance* (New York: Wiley, 1987).

71 C. R. Gerstner and D. V. Day, "Meta-Analytic Review of Leader-Member Exchange Theory: Correlates and Construct Issues," *Journal of Applied Psychology 82,* 1997:827–844.

72 D. Duchon, S. G. Green, and T. D. Taber, "Vertical Dyad Linkage: A Longitudinal Assessment of Antecedents, Measures, and Consequences," *Journal of Applied Psychology 71* (1986):56–60.

73 M. Wakabayashi, G. Graen, M. Graen, and M. Graen, "Japanese Management Progress: Mobility into Middle Management," *Journal of Applied Psychology 73,* 1988:217–227.

74 R. Martin, G. Thomas, K. Charles, O. Epitropaki, and R. McNamara, "The Role of Leader-Member Exchanges in Mediating the Relationship between Locus of Control and Work Reactions," *Journal of Occupational & Organizational Psychology 78* (1), March 2005:141–147.

75 J. M. Maslyn and M. Uhl-Bien, "Leader-Member Exchange and Its Dimension: Effects of Self-Effort and Other's Effort on Relationship Quality," *Journal of Applied Psychology 86* (4), 2001:697–708.

76 F. Dansereau, J. Cashman, and G. Graen, "Instrumentality Theory and Equity Theory as Complementary Approaches in Predicting the Relationship of Leadership and Turnover amongst Managers," *Organizational Behavior & Human Performance 10,* 1973:184-200.

77 R. Martin, G. Thomas, K. Charles, O. Epitropaki, and R. McNamara, "The Role of Leader-Member Exchanges in Mediating the Relationship between Locus of Control and Work Reactions," *Journal of Occupational & Organizational Psychology 78* (1), March 2005:141–147.

78 S. Kerr and J. M. Jermier, "Substitutes for Leadership: Their Meaning and Measurement," *Organizational Behavior & Human Performance 22,* 1978:375–403.

79 P. M. Podsakoff, B. P. Niehoff, S. B. MacKenzie, and M. L. Williams, "Do Substitutes for Leadership Really Substitute for Leadership? An Empirical Examination of Kerr and Jermier's Situational Leadership Model," *Organizational Behavior and Human Decision Processes 54,* 1993: 1–44.

80 R. Alsop, "Recruiters Sound Off," *The Wall Street Journal Online,* September 20, 2006, http://online.wsj.com/article/SB115862959400467098.html?mod=JR-Business-Schools-Sept-2006. Accessed September 20, 2006.

81 L. K. Treviño and M. E. Brown, "Managing to Be Ethical: Debunking Five Business Ethics Myths," *Academy of Management Executive 18* (2), May 2004:69–81.

82 L. K. Treviño and M. E. Brown, "Managing to Be Ethical: Debunking Five Business Ethics Myths," *Academy of Management Executive 18* (2), May 2004:69–81, 75.

83 L. K. Treviño and M. E. Brown, "Managing to Be Ethical: Debunking Five Business Ethics Myths," *Academy of Management Executive 18* (2), May 2004:69–81, 77.

84 M. F. R. Kets de Vries, "Introduction: Exploding the Myth that Organizations and Executives Are Rational," in M. F. R. Kets de Vries and Associates, *Organizations on the Couch: Clinical Perspectives on Organizational Behavior and Change* (San Francisco, CA: Jossey-Bass Publishers, 1991):1–24; W. Q. Judge, *The Leader's Shadow: Exploring and Developing the Executive Character* (Thousand Oaks, CA: Sage Publications, 1999).

85 S. Finkelstein and D. Hambrick, *Strategic Leadership* (St. Paul, MN: West Educational Publishing, 1996).

86 "The Changing Nature of Leadership," *The Economist 335* (7918), June 10, 1995:57.

87 A. Chatterjee and D. C. Hambrick, "The Narcissistic CEO: An Exploratory Study of Indicators and Strategic Consequences," Paper presented at the Academy of Management Annual Meeting, Atlanta, GA, 2006.

88 V. M. Barret, "Irreplaceable?" *Forbes 178* (3), August 14, 2006:82–91.

89 V. M. Barret, "Irreplaceable?" *Forbes 178* (3), August 14, 2006:82–91

90 M. F. R. Kets de Vries and D. Miller, "Leadership Styles and Organizational Cultures: The Shaping of Neurotic Organizations," in M. F. R. Kets de Vries and Associates, *Organizations on the Couch: Clinical Perspectives on Organizational Behavior and Change* (San Francisco, CA: Jossey-Bass Publishers, 1991):243–263.

91 L. Lapierre, "Exploring the Dynamics of Leadership," in M. F. R. Kets de Vries and Associates, *Organizations on the Couch: Clinical Perspectives on Organizational Behavior and Change* (San Francisco, CA: Jossey-Bass Publishers, 1991):69–93.

92 L. Lapierre, "Exploring the Dynamics of Leadership," in M. F. R. Kets de Vries and Associates, *Organizations on the Couch: Clinical Perspectives on Organizational Behavior and Change* (San Francisco, CA: Jossey-Bass Publishers, 1991):69–93; M. F. R. Kets de Vries and D. Miller, "Leadership Styles and Organizational Cultures: The Shaping of Neurotic Organizations," in M. F. R. Kets de Vries and Associates, *Organizations on the Couch: Clinical Per-*

spectives on Organizational Behavior and Change (San Francisco, CA: Jossey-Bass Publishers, 1991):243–263.

93 J. Pfeffer and J. F. Veiga, "Putting People First for Organizational Success," *Academy of Management Executive 13,* May 1999:37–48.

94 J. Pfeffer and J. F. Veiga, "Putting People First for Organizational Success," *Academy of Management Executive 13,* May 1999:37–48.

95 R. G. Lord and G. M. Alliger, "A Comparison of Four Information Processing Models of Leadership and Social Perception," *Human Relations 38,* 1985:47–65; R. G. Lord, C. L. De Vader, and G. Alliger, "A Meta-Analysis of the Relation between Personality Traits and Leadership Perceptions: An Application of Validity Generalization Procedures," *Journal of Applied Psychology 71* (3), 1986:402–410.

96 R. A. Kenney, B. M. Schwartz-Kenney, and J. Blascovich, "Implicit Leadership: Theories Defining Leaders Described as Worthy of Influence," *Personality and Social Psychology Bulletin 22,* 1996:1128–1143.

97 O. Epitropaki and R. Martin, "Implicit Leadership Theories in Applied Settings: Factor Structure, Generalizability and Stability over Time," *Journal of Applied Psychology 89,* 2004:293–310.

98 T. A. Judge and D. M. Cable, "The Effect of Physical Height on Workplace Success and Income: Preliminary Test of a Theoretical Model," *Journal of Applied Psychology 89* (3), 2004:428–441.

99 O. Epitropaki and R. Martin, "Implicit Leadership Theories in Applied Settings: Factor Structure, Generalizability and Stability over Time," *Journal of Applied Psychology 89,* 2004:293–310.

100 S. M. Ross and L. R. Offerman, "Transformational Leaders: Measurement of Personality Attributes and Work Group Performance," *Personality and Social Psychology Bulletin 23,* 1997:1078–1086.

101 D. Dunning, M. Perle, and A. L. Story, "Self-Serving Prototypes of Social Categories," *Journal of Personality & Social Psychology 61,* 1991:957–968.

102 T. Keller, "Images of the Familiar: Individual Differences and Implicit Leadership Theories," *Leadership Quarterly 10* (4), Winter 1999:589–607.

103 T. A. Judge, R. F. Piccolo, and R. Ilies, "The Forgotten Ones? The Validity of Consideration and Initiating Structure in Leadership Research," *Journal of Applied Psychology 89* (1), 2004:36–51.

104 R. O. McElwee, D. Dunning, P. L. Tan, and S. Hollmann, "Evaluating Others: The Role of Who We Are versus What We Think Traits Mean," *Basic & Applied Social Psychology 23* (2), June 2001:123–136, 135.

105 J. McGregor, "Game Plan: First Find the Leaders," *BusinessWeek Online,* August 21, 2006, http://www.businessweek.com. Accessed September 15, 2006.

106 A. H. Eagly, M. C. Johannesen-Schmidt, and M. L. van Engen, "Transformational, Transactional, and Laissez-Faire Leadership Styles: A Meta-Analysis Comparing Women and Men," *Psychological Bulletin 129* (4), 2003:569–591.

107 A. H. Eagly, S. J. Karau, and M. G. Makhijani, "Gender and the Effectiveness of Leaders: A Meta-Analysis," *Psychological Bulletin 117* (1), January 1995:125–145.

108 J. L. Robinson and J. Lipman-Blumen, "Leadership Behavior of Male and Female Managers, 1984–2002," *Journal of Education for Business,* September/October 2003:28–33.

109 C. MacLelland and J. Dobson, "Women, Ethics, and MBAs," *Journal of Business Ethics 16,* 1997:1201–1209.

110 J. Sturges, "What It Means to Succeed: Personal Conceptions of Career Success Held by Male and Female Managers at Different Ages," *British Journal of Management 10,* 1999:239–252.

111 S. Vinnicombe and V. Singh, "Women-Only Management Training: An Essential Part of Women's Leadership Development," *Journal of Change Management 3* (4), 2003:294–306.

112 H. C. Triandis, "Foreword," in R. J. House, P. J. Hanges, M. Javidan, P. W. Dorfman, and V. Gupta, eds., *Culture, Leadership and Organizations: The GLOBE Study of 62 Societies* (Thousand Oaks, CA: Sage Publications, 2004):xv–xix.

113 P. W. Dorfman and J. P. Howell, "Leadership in Western and Asian Countries: Commonalities and Differences in Effective Leadership," *Leadership Quarterly 8* (3), Fall 1997:233–274.

114 This company's name and other details are disguised. The information for this case was collected in 2004.

115 "Exit Carly," *The Economist* February 10, 2005, http://www.economist.com/ articles. Accessed October 15, 2005.

116 "Hurd's Instinct," *The Economist,* March 31, 2005, http://www.economist.com/research/articles. Accessed October 15, 2005.

117 R. A. Burgelman and W. McKinney, "Managing the Strategic Dynamics of Acquisition Integration: Lessons from HP and Compaq," *California Management Review 48* (3), Spring 2006.

118 "Exit Carly," *The Economist* February 10, 2005, http://www.economist.com/ articles. Accessed October 15, 2005.

119 "Hurd's Instinct," *The Economist* March 31, 2005, http://www.economist.com/research/articles. Accessed October 15, 2005.

120 "Fiorina's 'Choices,'" *Newsweek CXLVIII* (16), October 6, 2006:12.

121 C. Fiorina, Commencement Address, North Carolina Agricultural and Technical State University, May 7, 2005, http://www.carlyfiorina.com/speeches. Accessed February 9, 2007.

122 C. Fiorina, *Tough Choices: A Memoir,* New York: Penguin, 2006: Front flap.

123 C. Fiorina, *Tough Choices: A Memoir,* New York: Penguin, 2006: 174.

124 C. Fiorina, *Tough Choices: A Memoir,* New York: Penguin, 2006: 83.

125 C. Fiorina, "The End of Manifest Destiny," *Speech to the Detroit Economic Club,* May 23, 2005, http://www.carlyfiorina.com/speeches. Accessed February 9, 2007.

126 C. Fiorina, *Tough Choices: A Memoir,* New York: Penguin, 2006:36.

12 Leadership Roles and Skills

Preview

What is the leader's role in special teams?
Project management
E-Leadership

What do leaders need to know about negotiation?
What is the nature of negotiation?
Internal versus external negotiation
Interpersonal skills for negotiating
Learning how to negotiate

What is unique about the leadership role of executives and CEOs?
Mid-level leaders need to develop executive skills
CEOs manage meaning for their company
CEOs' traditional and new roles

How do leaders act as disciplinarians?
Recognize abusive behaviors and bullying
Causes of employee deviance
Managing workplace deviance
Interpersonal approaches to difficult people
Organizational approaches to difficult people

When should a leader stop leading and follow instead?
When to stop leading
Managing up

As a leader, what aspects of your personal philosophy are likely to have the most influence on others?
Authenticity and integrity
Spirituality
Influence and responsibility
Examining capitalism as a core value

How do leaders act as talent scouts and mentors?
Finding and developing talent
Mentoring
Succession planning

Lawrence H. Summers
President, Harvard University

In a speech to a conference on women and science, former Harvard University President Larry Summers mused that perhaps women are not genetically capable of becoming top scientists. Attempting to explain why more women are not found in high level jobs in science and engineering, he said, "The unfortunate truth—I would far prefer to believe something else. . . is that the combination of the high-powered job hypothesis and the differing variances [in intelligence] probably explains a fair amount of this problem." Summers' remarks were repeated nationwide, as protests from faculty and outside commentators mounted. Many in the Harvard community took the opportunity to point out that Summers already had had problems in his relationship with his faculty. Some called for his resignation.

As you will learn in this chapter, leaders are not perfect. They tend to believe they are more versatile than they really are. They are likely to be overconfident, seeing their own responses, whatever they are and whoever they offend, as totally appropriate.

When leaders are executives, one of their key roles is to manage meaning for their companies, helping those below them in the organizational hierarchy to define who they are and what they are doing. As President of Harvard, Larry Summers was certainly in such a role. In fact, because of the worldwide reputation of Harvard, his influence on managing meaning could be expected to spread to educational institutions far beyond Cambridge, Massachusetts. It is also true that leaders must be good negotiators. They must speak clearly in ways that promote listening, and be assertive without damaging relationships.

Facing the uproar, Larry Summers sent a letter of apology to the members of the Harvard Community. He wrote, "I was wrong to have spoken in a way that has resulted in an unintended signal of discouragement to talented girls and women. As a university president, I consider nothing more important than helping to create an environment, at Harvard and beyond, in which every one of us can pursue our intellectual passions and realize our aspirations to the fullest possible extent."[1]

What do you think was the impact of this incident on Harvard and on Summers' ability to lead the university?

Virtually every subject in this book offers some guidance to leaders. We have covered a wide range of topics—from how managers create trust and design decisions, to how leaders motivate groups and inspire individuals to be committed to their organizations. However, leaders are so essential to company effectiveness that it is worth discussing here some of their additional, crucial roles. In this chapter you will learn about a variety of roles, from negotiator to talent scout, that, to be a successful leader, you should be able to fill.

What Is the Leader's Role in Special Teams?

This section takes an in-depth look at two important team leadership roles: leading project teams, and leading virtual teams. Although we have discussed these topics in our chapters on groups and teams, here we provide additional insight into the leadership function itself.

Project Management

project management team
A group that comes together for a finite period of time to perform a variety of tasks to meet an organizational objective.

Project management teams are groups that come together for a finite period of time to perform a variety of tasks to achieve an organizational objective.[2] Because they are finite, project management teams provide organizations with both focus and flexibility. They are particularly common in product design and manufacturing firms, management consulting, and information technology units. America Online, the communications technology company, typically has 1,000 projects running at any one time, with project lengths varying from a few weeks to a year.[3] It starts up 20 to 30 new projects every week.

Project management is so important that today it is seen as an organizational specialty in its own right, with its own journals and research.[4] The role of project manager/leader involves about 50 percent strategy and understanding of the business environment, about 40 percent management, and about 10 percent applying technical knowledge.[5] Effective project management involves focusing on results, leading well, and creating a synergistic, multi-disciplinary team that succeeds or fails as a unit.[6] It requires a leader who can move across boundaries and hierarchies, inspire confidence, and command support and action.[7] Project managers must be able to deal with such problems as the conflict that accompanies budget and scheduling constraints, the organizational politics that arise during cross-functional work, and the intellectual challenges inherent in the complexity of the project work itself.[8]

Research suggests that project leaders differ from general managers in that they tend to be more task-oriented and less people-oriented.[9] At the same time, although project leaders have lower than average levels of sociability and gregariousness, they have higher than average levels of empathy and an inner need to be liked.

The most important competencies needed by project managers are team building, leadership, and decision making.[10] When defining the project's work, timing, procedures, and control are critically important. Also, to guarantee project success, project leaders must build fast, flexible teams that can "dynamically and creatively work toward established objectives in a changing environment."[11] This requires that the project managers foster effective networking and cooperation among all of the individuals involved in the project, including people from different parts of their own organization, people from different organizations, subcontractors, vendors, and customers. It also requires that they meet the needs of their team members, who tend to want professionally stimulating and challenging work environments and opportunities for accomplishment and recognition.[12]

When their projects go wrong, it is generally because the project leaders have not achieved a balance between the dual task and people orientations characteristic of good project managers. Another issue for project managers is that they are often scattered throughout a company, and may experience isolation unless drawn together into an informal community of their own.

E-Leadership

The ability to communicate rapidly and widely using technologies like e-mail and the Internet poses many leadership challenges. When a team's work is mediated by information technology, leaders must adapt their styles.[13]

Technology enhances the capability of organizations to be boundaryless, with information flowing across both traditional functional lines and levels as well as between customers and company representatives. Not only is the amount of information enhanced, opportunities for interpersonal interaction are, too. Leaders can coach via e-mail, for example, by sending memos reinforcing targeted behaviors, sharing stories and articles of particular interest, or promoting important aspects of the organization's culture. E-leadership also changes an organization's bases of power. Leaders must be aware that more people can have more voice than ever before, a reality that both enhances and detracts from the communication process.

The following are some of the concerns leaders have about e-communication. When using technology-enhanced communication, leaders are challenged to:[14]

- understand the interpersonal characteristics of the technology in use and adapt their leadership style to it. For example, if the technology suggests cooperation, how can the leader with a directive style adapt?

- figure out how to add value to the exchange of information. If your followers are solving problems all by themselves online, what should be the leader's role?

- move from being a content leader (focused on the problem) to being a process leader (focusing on the process by which the team will solve the problem). Whether you are leading face-to-face or virtually, your team is empowered because, via technology, it has access to vast amounts of information. In fact, individual team members are likely to have expertise far beyond your own. What process enhancements can you add? Perhaps your team may even be able to lead itself, in which case your job must either evolve or be put in jeopardy.

- develop strategies for balancing face-to-face interactions with interactions that happen virtually via technology. For example, can the leadership style of consideration be shown via technology? At the same time, when using technology, how much structure is too much structure? Some leaders may overuse technology because it is convenient.

- put a plan into place for learning how to best use information technology to improve your own and others' efforts and quality of work life.

What Do Leaders Need to Know About Negotiation?

A negotiation is a situation in which two or more parties must make a decision about their interdependent goals and objectives.[15] In this situation, the parties are committed to a peaceful means for resolving their dispute or making their deal, and there is no clear, established method for making the decision. Famous modern negotiators include the Hollywood executive Michael Ovitz, who brokered an ill-fated but nevertheless remarkable deal between MCA, Inc., and Matsushita in 1990, and former U.S. Senator George Mitchell, who in the mid-1990s served as chairperson of the successful peace negotiations in Northern Ireland, and later became Chairman of the Walt Disney Company.

negotiation
A situation in which two or more parties must make a decision about their interdependent goals and objectives.

Leaders are frequently called upon to be negotiators. Whether you are negotiating a deal for your company or an agreement between two internal departments, knowing how to handle yourself and influence others are crucial skills. Negotiating is a complex human activity and learning how to negotiate effectively requires a course in itself. Here we will summarize some of the basic aspects of the negotiator role.

What Is the Nature of Negotiation?

In general, leaders must be able to diagnose any negotiation situation and select the optimal strategies and approaches, both behavioral and analytical.[16] At the same time, they must understand their own personality, ethics, and values, because these affect how they interpret the situation.

To begin with, to be successful in negotiation, leaders must examine their assumptions about the process itself. For example, if you assume the situation is one of competition and bargaining, you may actually create a win-lose solution, and, of course, the losing party may eventually try to get even. If, in contrast, you assume negotiation always involves compromise, you run the risk of relegating both sides to getting less than they really want or need. Finally, if you assume negotiation is a win-win process, both sides are most likely to get what they need. Of course, some situations are actually win-lose situations, whereas others are win-win. The trick is determining which is which.

Likewise, if you assume a negotiation situation requires the use of tactics and manipulation, you will fail to build a solid relationship for the future. Negotiations go wrong when negotiators fail to learn about the other side and their needs, make impossible demands, or poison the atmosphere with a belligerent, offensive manner.[17] Negotiations should take into consideration both parties' priorities for material and relationship outcomes. If the relationship is at all valued, negotiators should attempt to solve the other party's problems as well as their own. In most cases, tactics should be used only for self-defense.

Being an effective negotiator does not mean being glib and devious (although a few negotiators are). Rather, successful business negotiating typically involves exchanging information and resources in a way that satisfies the different and sometimes conflicting needs of the participants. Although not all differences can be solved this way, many can.

Finally, to be a successful negotiator, you must understand conflict and how you personally react to it. Many individuals are uncomfortable and even afraid of conflict. Often they would just as soon avoid it. Perhaps they are afraid they will not perform well under conflict. After all, their emotions are involved. Or they may be afraid that they will damage the relationship with the persons with whom they are negotiating. Gaining negotiation experience can go a long way toward assuaging such fears.

Internal versus External Negotiation

Negotiating inside the company differs from negotiating outside of the company in one crucial way. When a leader is negotiating inside, hierarchical relationships come into play and legitimate power (the power of the position) matters. For example, as the head of a company dealing with two warring departments, you have the power to require people to deal with their issues and you can impose a settlement if necessary.

However, when negotiating with outsiders, the clarity about power relationships that is found in a hierarchy does not exist. You must assess who has more power in the relationship and how that power is likely to influence the negotiation process and the final deal. Your own power as leader is now diminished, too, and you are likely to find yourself negotiating with the other party as an equal. If you are used to being a leader, this role may be new to you, and uncomfortable.

When Michael Ovitz brought MCA and Matsushita together, he was extraordinarily careful not to offend MCA head Lew Wasserman, who was used to being in total charge of an empire. In fact, it was Ovitz's role as broker between two powerful, egocentric men that made the negotiation possible in the first place. Working out the details of the deal itself, although not an inconsiderable task, was much less important to the final outcome.

Interpersonal Skills for Negotiating

What interpersonal skills are most likely to be helpful to you in negotiation situations? Here are six fundamental ones:[18]

1. **Expressing strong feelings appropriately.** Develop a range of expressions, from rationally talking about your feelings, to increasing the emotional content of your communication, to letting emotions take charge. Choose the expression most appropriate to the situation.

2. **Remaining rational in the face of strong feelings.** Sometimes we allow our emotions to overwhelm our rationality, particularly when someone is attacking us or when we believe that the other party is not really listening to us. Both parties must find a way to acknowledge the other party's feelings. When emotions overwhelm rationality, withdraw from the situation. State your reasons for doing so and explain that you will return.

3. **Being assertive without damaging the relationship.** Be "soft on people" by avoiding personal judgments, acknowledging the merit of the other side's position, and being considerate and polite. At the same time, stand up for your own position.

4. Improving a relationship without damage to a particular negotiation. Sometimes negotiators are afraid to be open and warm to the other party, or to acknowledge some validity in their views, for fear such approaches will prejudice the outcome. Keep in mind that good relationship building helps achieve positive outcomes. Build the relationship outside the negotiation itself. Or build it in temporally discrete time segments within the negotiation, such as before and after debating a particular point.

5. Speaking clearly in ways that promote listening. Use short, clear statements and ask the other party, politely, to repeat back what you have said. Use "I" statements, such as "I'm feeling discriminated against," instead of "you" statements, such as "You are discriminating against me."

6. Actively inquiring and listening. Separate understanding the other party's arguments from judging and responding to those arguments. Repeat back their statements in their own words. Ask about the reasoning behind their arguments.

Learning How to Negotiate

Being an effective negotiator is a complex business. It involves understanding how power works in relationships, how negotiations move through different phases, how the social context affects the process, and how to use third parties. Even more interesting, today the entire process may occur in an international context, requiring leaders to be savvy about power and negotiation styles in cultures quite different from their own. For example, Ovitz had to study the Japanese culture intensively in order to smooth the Matsushita-MCA deal.

Given the importance and complexities of the negotiation process, it is not surprising that in recent years courses on negotiation have become increasingly popular in the business community.

What Is Unique about the Leadership Role of Executives and CEOs?

Executives are individuals who have no immediate superiors, often by virtue of being owners, or who substantially control the conditions of their subordinates.[19] They are leaders at the highest level in their company, and they play a number of crucial roles. Although top leaders of a company can have a variety of titles, we will refer to them here as CEOs.

Mid-Level Leaders Need to Develop Executive Skills

The strengths that help managers to lead well at lower levels are not the same as those they need to succeed as CEO. Many mid-level leaders derail on their way to the top. It is often the case that managers who climb the hierarchy because they are excellent technicians and problem solvers later find that their careers derail because they lack people management and strategic skills.[20] Bose Corporation, realizing this problem, takes a three-tiered approach to management development, with one tier for first-line managers, a second for middle- and upper-level managers, and a third for senior executives.[21] It makes sure that as managers move up they acquire the new skills that are appropriate for their new jobs.

A related problem is that, as they move up, executives often fail to drop their task-oriented leadership styles in favor of the relationship-oriented styles needed in higher level jobs.[22] They may fail to meet business objectives, too, in part because in higher level leadership positions, personal technical excellence simply cannot substitute for the productivity that comes from excellent teamwork.

Ascending leaders also derail when they fail to adapt during transitions. For example, they may fail to adapt to a new boss with a different style. Or they may become overly dependent on one skill and fail to develop others. They may fail to adapt to the demands of a new job, new organizational culture, or changes in their market. It is therefore crucial that managers learn how to learn to deal with change and complexity.[23]

Unfortunately, executives tend to believe they are more versatile than they really are.[24] For example, they are likely to believe they can easily make the change from being a task-oriented leader to a relationship-oriented leader and, in general, to appropriately change their leadership style to fit most circumstances. Even when executives' peers, subordinates, and superiors (if any) all agree on their evaluation of an executive's style, the executives themselves often fail to be able to acknowledge their viewpoint.

In sum, leaders tend to do what they are good at and tend to view their response as the appropriate one. To change, their first order of business is not necessarily to learn a new skill but to unlearn old ones . . . to learn to place less value on their own tough-mindedness or technical competence, for example. Such a change can require deep personal evaluation, but it can be aided by giving them positive feedback about their overall competence.

CEOs Manage Meaning for Their Company

Leadership researcher James March writes, "Leadership is a combination of poetry and plumbing. The leaders that I admire keep the toilets working and also express themselves and, even more, *lead other people to know who they are and what to do*"(italics added).[25] Executive leaders not only plan, organize, and control, but also manage meaning.

The process of making meaning and sense for their company begins when CEOs reflect on their own life stories, their personal theories of leadership, and their connection to their organizations.[26] CEOs develop a personal theory of leadership and a philosophy for their company, then choose language, symbols, and signals that convey these meanings to organizational members.[27]

One thing CEOs accomplish as they manage meaning is absorb uncertainty for the company. In the face of uncertainty and risk, the top leader acknowledges the reality, but makes the case for, and encourages, the company to forge ahead.[28] Successful executives turn fear of failure into hope for success.

For some three decades, Warren Buffett has published an annual letter to the stockholders of Berkshire Hathaway in which he writes candidly about his company. His business wisdom is so well appreciated that the letter is eagerly awaited and read widely in the business community. In a recent letter he focused on uncertainty:

> Our gain in net worth during 2005 was $5.6 billion, which increased the per-share book value of both our Class A and Class B stock by 6.4 percent. Over the last 41 years (that is, since present management took over) book value has grown from $19 to $59,377, a rate of 21.5 percent compounded annually.
>
> We had a decent year in 2005. . .
>
> My goal in writing this report is to give you the information you need to estimate Berkshire's intrinsic value. I say "estimate" because calculations of intrinsic value, though all-important, are necessarily imprecise and seriously wrong. The more uncertain the future of a business, the more possibility there is that the calculation will be wildly off-base. . . .[29]

Buffett goes on to explain with characteristic wit how Berkshire is positioned—in particular how *well* Berkshire is positioned—in this uncertain world. He praises his managers extravagantly (one is a "remarkable entrepreneur") and tells folksy stories. In short, his personal style and analysis are the face of the company to both insiders and outsiders. It is no wonder that the company's annual meeting has been dubbed Woodstock for Capitalists.

CEOs' Traditional and New Roles

A traditional view of what makes executives effective points to these eight practices[30]:

1. Asking, "What needs to be done?"
2. Asking, "What is right for the enterprise?"
3. Developing action plans
4. Taking responsibility for decisions
5. Taking responsibility for communicating
6. Focusing on opportunities rather than problems
7. Running productive meetings
8. Thinking "we" rather than "I"

Although these practices are all still important, today the role of CEO is far more complex than even this list suggests. For example, consider that today the idea of "taking responsibility for communicating" involves not only traditional communications to employees and stakeholders, but also presenting a company image to the market. CEOs must communicate in a variety of media, and, often, internationally. More than ever before, CEOs must be skilled at clarifying and presenting their company philosophy and image to journalists, customers, and a variety of other external stakeholders.

Part of this communication process involves the image of the CEO himself or herself. Today the CEO's personal image plays an important role in determining a company's image.[31] Research suggests that the CEO's image or reputation has a significant influence on financial analysts' stock recommendations, investors' stock purchase decisions, and overall company reputation.[32] Being an icon is neither simple nor, necessarily, comfortable. One executive, commenting on what it feels like to be seen as his company's hero, says, "I'm a leader [and] I'm becoming a legend. I see it. It's the most remarkable experience because I don't perceive myself that way. I mean, I've been coming to this office, the same office, for 32 years. I was a schlepper doing the most menial work. It's been a very gradual process."[33]

One aspect of the CEO's image is acting as the moral standard bearer of the organization.[34] The CEO's behavior sends a strong message to employees, affecting what they pay attention to, what they think, and how they behave. In this high-pressure position, CEOs must develop a moral capacity that includes recognizing moral issues, promoting appropriate organizational practices, and being able to stand up in the face of pressures against implementing a moral stand. Effective CEOs are able to see many different sides of any moral issue and to help followers to come to win-win solutions. As always, "actions speak louder than words" certainly holds true.[35] For leaders, in particular, saying one thing and doing another will communicate that what is done, rather than what is said, is what really matters.

As one American executive puts it, "Today . . . people want to see their leaders, hear them talk from their hearts, roll their sleeves up, and spontaneously and genuinely build that trust. Followership is critical, especially in downsizing organizations. People don't want to see you only when there is a downsizing announcement to be made. People want to know what's in it for them and if the person leading them knows and cares about them enough. Today, if you're going to spill your blood for the organization, it will be because of personal loyalty to your team, not to some abstract organization."[36]

How Do Leaders Act as Disciplinarians?

Most of the management techniques we have discussed in this book adopt a positive focus: how to motivate workers using (primarily) positive reinforcement, how to influence organizational commitment, how to enhance productivity through self-directed teams, and so on. Only occasionally have we mentioned the dark side of organizational life. Yet, a common, time-consuming aspect of managing people is dealing with discipline problems. Managers are expected to show authority and leadership in dealing with a variety of discipline-related personnel issues, and they are likely to spend a lot of their time doing this.[37]

Employee deviance is voluntary behavior that violates important organizational norms and threatens the well-being of an organization or its members.[38] Deviant behaviors include harming another's reputation, incivility (rudeness), misrepresenting one's work output or shirking work, and theft. Whereas some deviant behaviors require counseling by managers or counselors, others require disciplinary action or dismissal.

See Table 12.1 for the main types of employee deviance that leaders must manage.

employee deviance
Voluntary behavior that violates important organizational norms and threatens the well-being of an organization or its members.

Recognize Abusive Behaviors and Bullying

Abusive behavior is a frequently encountered form of personal aggression. Both bosses and subordinates can be abusive. Research on abuse suggests that a boss is abusive when he or she:[39]

■ Ridicules subordinates, telling them they are stupid or incompetent.

■ Gives subordinates the silent treatment.

■ Puts people down in front of others.

■ Invades individuals' privacy.

■ Reminds others of their past mistakes and failures.

TABLE 12.1 Types of Employee Deviance

	Definition	Examples
Acts directed at individuals in the organization		
Political deviance	Engaging in social interaction that puts other individuals at a personal or political disadvantage	*One sales rep undermines another with false gossip.* *A manager favors an employee with whom he/she is having a romantic relationship.*
Personal aggression (Abusive behavior and bullying)	Behaving in an aggressive or hostile manner toward other individuals	*In group meetings, a boss frequently singles out one individual for criticism.* *One employee physically attacks another. (Working Americans experience 1.7 million violent victimizations each year.[42])*
Acts directed at an organization		
Production deviance	Behaving in ways that violate formal norms about minimal quality and quantity of work to be accomplished	*A member of the IT support staff surfs the Net for bargains.* *Substance abuse damages an employee's output.*
Property deviance	Acquiring or damaging the tangible property or assets of the organization without authorization	*A consultant exaggerates the number of hours he or she has worked.* *Clerks help themselves to the products they are selling.*

Source: Based on: S. L. Robinson and R. J. Bennett, "A Typology of Deviant Workplace Behaviors: A Multidimensional Scaling Study," *Academy of Management Journal 38* (2), April 1995:555–572.; T. W. Mangione, and R. P. Quinn, R. P. "Job Satisfaction, Counterproductive Behavior, and Drug Use at Work," *Journal of Applied Psychology 60* (1) February 1975:114–116.

- Doesn't give individuals credit for jobs requiring a lot of effort.
- Blames employees to save himself or herself embarrassment.
- Breaks promises he or she makes.
- Expresses anger at subordinates when he or she is mad for another reason.
- Makes negative comments about workers to others.
- Is rude to subordinates.
- Does not allow subordinates to interact with coworkers.
- Lies to subordinates.

Experiencing abuse leads to higher turnover; less favorable attitudes toward one's job, life, and the company; greater work/family conflict; and greater psychological distress. Many countries in the European Union actually have laws against "moral harassment," or bullying.[40] In the United States bullying is not against the law unless it involves sexual, racial, or age discrimination.

Today there is increasing interest in a newly recognized issue: the abuse by subordinates of their organizational superiors. Managers who depend on employees, as many in today's decentralized organizations do, may themselves be the subjects of bullying and verbal abuse. A study in Great Britain found that lower-level supervisors in today's leaner organizations are particularly vulnerable to bullying.[41]

A manager's dependency on staff provides some individuals with the opportunity to misuse their power, and managers may be reluctant to inform higher ups for fear of damaging their own reputations.

Causes of Employee Deviance

There are many causes of deviant workplace behaviors.[43] Personality is one factor. People low in conscientiousness, for instance, are more likely to engage in deviant behaviors.

A second factor is job characteristics. People working in jobs that are low in skill variety, task identity, and autonomy are more likely than others to have high rates of absenteeism.[44]

Work group characteristics also predict deviance. If his or her group exhibits more counterproductive behaviors, so will the individual.[45]

Other factors that are related to organization deviance are organizational culture (for instance, does the company have a climate that promotes honesty?), the organizational control system (for example, are there policies against drug use, or not?), and employees' perception of whether the organization is fair and just (for example, are employee appraisals based on performance or favoritism?).

Managing Workplace Deviance

Little academic research has been done on how to manage workplace deviance. The research described in our chapters on communication and conflict does suggest some useful general approaches. However, advice by consultants and practitioners dominates the practical applications. Their advice on how to manage workplace deviance falls into two areas: interpersonal approaches and organizational approaches.

We have a bit of advice of our own: With either approach, *getting good legal counsel is a prerequisite.* It is crucial to follow proper legally sanctioned procedures at the outset, beginning when you suspect a problem. Even when a company follows all appropriate procedures, the cost of defending itself in court is high.[46]

Interpersonal Approaches to Difficult People

When dealing with difficult people, you need to know how to both counsel and discipline them.

COUNSELING When dealing with employee deviance, the human dimension—yours and theirs—plays a significant role. When an employee is deviant, your first approach is usually to discuss the problem with the individual and then give him or her the time and resources he or she needs in order to change.[47] In general, avoid confronting the individual in front of others so as not to embarrass him or her. However, to protect yourself, both legally and physically, when giving negative feedback you may want to invite another manager, such as an HRM director, into the room. Stay emotionally distant and as professional as possible. During the discussion, elicit more information, and state your concerns. Avoid attacking. Manage your own anger.

Writer Len Leritz describes a number of principles for "taking the bull out of the bully."[48] Here are some key ones: 1) Get the deviant individual's attention by setting a boundary. If he or she crosses the boundary, the person will receive a negative consequence. However, as one expert puts it, "If you don't mean it, don't draw the boundary. And remember, if you don't draw the boundary, nothing will change."[49] 2) Explicitly identify the problem behavior and invite the individual to do something different. 3) Refuse to be punished. When the other person keeps repeating his or her attack or venting anger without telling you how you can help to solve the problem, you are being punished. Tell the person you will not continue the discussion until he or she can tell you how you can help to solve the problem.

At the same time, be realistic about whether difficult people will change, and accept the probability that most likely they will not. The best you may be able to do in the situation is to focus on your own behavior, manage it well, and take pride and comfort in the fact that you are doing all you can.

DISCIPLINING When the employee does not change on his or her own, or when merely annoying behavior becomes a punishable offense, disciplinary action may be necessary. When disciplining an employee, consider these common sense factors:

- How serious was the offense?
- What were the circumstances under which the offense was committed?
- Has the employee committed similar offenses in the past?
- How long has the employee been with the company and what is his or her conduct record over that period?
- What has been company practice in similar cases?

When you believe discipline is necessary, act quickly to influence the employee before the problem has become a habit.[50] Give clear feedback about the specifics of the problem, explain why change is necessary, communicate your expectations, establish consequences for failing to meet those expectations, then follow up with appropriate actions. Apply positive reinforcement for welcome behaviors and punishment for unwelcome behaviors. And, of course, in all instances, know and follow your company's policies.

In general, being personally and socially competent will help you to deal with difficult people.[51] You develop personal competence by paying attention to your own emotional reactions in situations, doing your best to understand exactly why you react the way you do, thinking of a variety of ways to react in emotionally charged situations, and constructively coping with emotional stress. Similarly, you develop social competence by paying attention to the behavior and emotions of others, trying to understand those behaviors and emotions, imagining a variety of responses from which to choose, and observing the effects of your actions.

Remember, the only behavior you truly control is your own. And reinforcement and punishment only increase or decrease the *probability* that a behavior will change.

Organizational Approaches to Difficult People

When dealing with difficult people, having the support of your organization is important. An effective organization will avoid problems by hiring stable individuals in the first place, by establishing a climate of respect, and by having clear policies for employee termination.

AVOIDING PROBLEMS IN THE FIRST PLACE: INTERVIEW FOR STABILITY In hiring and promotion, it is extremely important to distinguish between high-potential managers and those who are merely glib and narcissistic.[52] Unfortunately, this is easier said than done.

narcissism
The characteristic of being self-centered, which, in moderation, is secure self-esteem that allows a person to develop healthy relationships.

In general, **narcissism** is the characteristic of being self-centered. A certain level of narcissism is normal. For instance, having secure self-esteem allows a person to develop healthy relationships. However, **destructive narcissism** is a personality disorder that companies should try to identify in their job candidates. It is characterized by an outward self-confidence that is in reality an attempt to protect what is at base a fragile self-esteem. Destructive narcissism manifests itself in arrogance, grandiosity, the need for admiration, and the devaluation of others.[53]

destructive narcissism
A personality disorder characterized by an outward self-confidence that is actually an attempt to protect what is at base a fragile self-esteem.

Under stress, narcissists frequently protect their self-esteem by stepping on others. Narcissistic managers typically direct their most troublesome behaviors (including bullying, manipulation, failing to reward, and failing to share credit) toward their subordinates, while charming their bosses.

Unfortunately, many of the personality traits that underlie the behavior of difficult people are the very traits that help them to be promoted. These include high levels of expressed self-confidence, charisma, energy, and unrelenting drive for power and prestige. Aside from personality testing, the best way to identify destructive narcissists is to find out how they have treated past subordinates and to ask them questions aimed at identifying empathy.

ESTABLISH A CLIMATE OF RESPECT Elsewhere we have described the motivating potential of establishing fair systems in your organization. These include systems for distributive justice, procedural justice, and interactional justice. We have also discussed using culture to motivate ethical behavior. Applying these principles will establish a climate of respect that may deter deviance.

Treating employees fairly throughout their employment and fostering the belief that the company is concerned about fair treatment can reduce the probability that terminated employees will later sue the company for being wrongfully fired.[54] Leaders can help by giving employees a voice in decision making,[55] and allowing them to give their opinion about organizational outcomes that affect them, even if the organization does not in the end accept their views.[56]

FIRING If terminating an employee is your best option, follow your company's policy guidelines, which should take into account both your ethical and legal responsibilities to your employee. When the bad news is delivered, experts suggest there should be at least two company representatives in the room—the immediate supervisor, who informs the employee of the decision and answers specific job-related questions, and, if possible, a representative of the human resources department, who can answer questions on issues like severance pay and unemployment benefits.[57]

In conclusion, giving negative feedback is an emotionally charged process that is difficult for both employee and manager. Yet effective disciplining has clearly been identified as a characteristic of leadership. (Recall from the earlier chapter on leadership that one characteristic of incompetent managers is unwillingness to use discipline).[58] Practicing professional behavior and anger management, and following company policy, are key components of effective disciplining.

When Should a Leader Stop Leading and Follow Instead?

It may surprise you to hear that being an effective follower is a necessary leadership skill. Yet, consider the reality that hierarchical organizations inevitably have many leaders who are also followers. In fact, leaders must understand and practice how to be good followers if organizations are to be effective.

Some people we think of as leaders are in fact limited in their ability to lead independently. General George Patton, the World War II military hero, was a top troop commander but was judged incapable of holding an independent command. According to General George Marshall, the U.S. chief of staff, "Patton is the best subordinate the American army has ever produced, but he would be the worst commander."[59]

When to Stop Leading

The only person in a company who has no hierarchical superior is the CEO, and even he or she should follow others on some occasions. Consultant and writer Douglas K. Smith points out that leaders must know how to stop leading and be followers when:[60]

1. Individual performance demands it. You must follow another individual, regardless of your or their position in the hierarchy, if that individual, because of experience, skill, and judgment, knows best; or if you want that individual to grow and develop skills and self-confidence; or if only that individual has the capacity to get the job done.

2. Team performance demands it. You must follow the team if the team's purpose and goals demand it; if the team, not you, must develop skills and self-confidence; if the team's approach requires that you do real work just like the other team members.

3. Organizational performance demands it. You must follow others if the organization's purpose and goals demand it; if you need to develop the leadership capacity of others for the organization; or if the vision and values of the company demand it.

Managing Up

Wise followers learn to manage up as well as down. For instance, they learn to let their bosses know, subtly, whether they want less supervision, or more. If less, they might tell their boss, "John, I'd like to get your thoughts on this project, particularly what your own benchmarks are, so I can keep you in the loop but not take up too much of your time." If more, they might say, "Judy, I anticipate there will be several key decision points in this project. Could we go over my plan? I'd like to get your input now and at several points along the way."

Another skill of followers is learning how to push back.[61] Sometimes the boss needs to know that something he or she is doing is ineffective. An effective follower establishes early on whether their boss really wants to know the truth, and, if the boss does, occasionally reminds the boss of his position: "Jack, I know you prefer it straight, right?" Thus, when a problem does arise, the boss knows that the follower equates intellectual honesty with loyalty, not insubordination, and will react accordingly to the negative feedback.

It has been argued that finding a subtle way to help your boss succeed by offering suggestions for improvement or reminding her of her commitments can enhance your probability of being selected as the next leader of the department.[62] By offering suggestions that make your boss look good, you may set yourself up as an equal in your boss's mind, thus escaping the reputation of a lowly underling.

In summary, to manage up you should:[63] Understand your boss's goals and objectives, pressures, strengths, and weaknesses, blind spots, and preferred work style. Assess your own strengths and weaknesses, personal style, and predisposition toward dependence on authority figures. You should develop a relationship with your boss in which you find a fit between your style and your boss's style, establish mutual, not just one-way, expectations, keep your boss informed, and use your boss's time and resources selectively. It goes without saying that you should determine that you and your boss are mutually dependable and honest.

When you are interested in influencing your boss or other higher-ups, what kind of influence are you personally most likely to use? Do you tend to use a rational approach? Do you try to create a coalition? Take the self-test in Table 12.2 to find out.

Now you know which influence strategies you are most likely to depend upon. Establishing this profile of your preferred upward influence strategies helps you to clarify which techniques are easy for you and which are more challenging. Depending on the circumstances, each has some utility. Take a look at your least preferred upward influence strategy. Perhaps it is ingratiation. Why don't you use it much, or at all? Can you imagine a circumstance in which you should use it? Do you have the skills that would allow you to use it if necessary? In general, ask yourself whether you have enough range in the techniques at your disposal.

As a Leader, What Aspects of Your Personal Philosophy Are Likely to Have the Most Influence on Others?

Who a leader is as an individual human being influences not only his or her style but also his or her influence on others. Individual personality, beliefs, and values all contribute to who you are. Since we have discussed these extensively earlier in this book, here we will focus on leaders' personal beliefs and values.

Steve Jobs of Apple describes in memorable fashion his joy at leading a new venture: "The heaviness of being successful was replaced by the lightness of being a beginner again."[64] Jobs is a firm advocate of doing what you love. Having faced down cancer, he says, "Death is very likely the single best invention in life. All external expectations, all pride, all fear of embarrassment or failure—these things just fall away in the face of death, leaving what is truly important."[65]

What personal beliefs and values matter the most? Here we will consider those associated with personal authenticity, spirituality, responsibility, and, specifically, our capitalist system.

Authenticity and Integrity

authentic leaders
Leaders who are characterized in part by the synchronicity of their "inner path" with their leadership style and impact.

Authentic leaders are characterized in part by the synchronicity of their "inner path" and their leadership style and impact.[66] What does this mean exactly?

Former CEO of financial services firm CitiCorp John Reed provides an anecdotal overview of what motivates executives. He believes that to lead people well, you have to reach into yourself for some form of self-assurance that allows you to take on difficult responsibilities. This could come from any of several sources, he points out. However, values-driven motivation is what counts the most and lasts the longest.

According to Reed, self-assurance can come from pure ego, and some leaders rely on "that false sense of themselves that we call an ego in order to be able to persist in playing

TABLE 12.2 The Upward Influence Scale

Never = 1   Seldom = 2   Occasionally = 3   Frequently = 4   Almost always = 5

You want to request something from your boss. How often are you likely to:

1._____ Act very humbly to him or her while making the request.

2._____ Remind him or her of past favors that you did for him/her.

3._____ Use logic to convince him or her.

4._____ Have a showdown in which you confront him or her face-to-face.

5._____ Obtain the informal support of higher-ups.

6._____ Obtain the support of co-workers to back up your request.

7._____ Make him or her feel good about you before making your request.

8._____ Offer an exchange (for example, if you do this for me, I will do something for you).

9._____ Explain the reasons for your request.

10._____ Express your anger verbally.

11._____ Make a formal appeal to higher levels to back up your request.

12._____ Obtain the support of your subordinates to back up your request.

13._____ Act in a friendly manner prior to asking for what you want.

14._____ Offer to make a personal sacrifice if he or she will do what you want (for example, work late, work harder, do his/her share of the work).

15._____ Present him or her with information in support of your point of view.

16._____ Use a forceful manner, such as demanding, setting deadlines, or expressing strong emotion.

17._____ Rely on the chain of command—on people in the organization higher up who have power over him or her.

18._____ Mobilize other people in the organization to help you in influencing him or her.

Score your results as follows:

Questions	Score: How many total points did you score for these three questions?	Interpretation: What general strategy of upward influence do these questions measure?	Rank the upward influence strategies from 1 to 6, with 1 being the highest score.
1, 7, 13	_____	Ingratiation	_____
2, 8, 14	_____	Exchange of Benefits	_____
3, 9, 15	_____	Rationality	_____
4, 10, 16	_____	Assertiveness	_____
5, 11, 17	_____	Upward Appeal	_____
6, 12, 18	_____	Coalition	_____

Source: C. A. Schriesheim and T. R. Hinkin, "Influence Tactics Used by Subordinates: A Theoretical and Empirical Analysis and Refinement of the Kipnis, Schmidt, and Wilkinson Sub-Scales," *Journal of Applied Psychology* 75 (3), June 1990:246–257. This questionnaire has been adapted for individuals who may not be employed currently. Copyright © 2003 by the American Psychological Association. Reproduced with permission.

their role and meeting their responsibilities."[67] Other leaders draw on an analytic sense that they believe gives them deep knowledge of a situation. "You go to a business school and you learn how to make rational decisions and you work in business for a number of years and you get to know the details of the business and you draw on what you consider to be the deep knowledge of the situation. That gives you the self-assurance to persist in playing the leadership role. . . . But . . . if the world changes around you, and you find you have to deal with discontinuities, your leadership skills can be severely tested, because the source of your self-assurance is no longer there. . . ."[68] Still others are motivated by a goal, and draw their sense of themselves as leaders from their commitment to that goal. Yet, Reed notes, "Having clear goals clearly makes you feel good about what you're trying to communicate. But if there isn't anything beneath it that touches something more fundamental, my experience as a leader is that, without those values you can find yourself short and then you have little to draw on."[69]

The most effective leaders are motivated by the sense that they are doing something good and right and that they have a duty to do it. Reed says, "Obviously, if you can draw on deep moral strength . . . it gives you tremendous self-assurance. Many leadership situations do not quite end up as intended, and we must persevere and be patient with our ideas. If you can draw on a deep moral sense, it clearly helps."[70]

Spirituality

spiritual synchronicity
The energy and the influence derived from living in synch with a higher purpose, often based on a worldview of an ultimate transcendent (nonmaterial) reality.

Some thinkers make a similar connection between leadership and spirituality. The path of spirituality is an inner path that also affects leader motivation and effectiveness. They use the term **spiritual synchronicity** to refer to "the energy and the influence derived from living in synch with a higher purpose, often based on a worldview of an ultimate transcendent (nonmaterial) reality."[71]

Research suggests that businesspeople who acknowledge the spiritual component of their work have these characteristics in common:[72]

- They have similar definitions of spirituality, based on the notion of an inner path devoted to a higher purpose.
- They prefer not to compartmentalize their lives. For example, they do not like to separate their work and private lives.
- They differentiate strongly between spirituality and religion.
- They are often afraid to use the word "spirituality" in the workplace.

Influence and Responsibility

Because of leaders' high level of influence, it is especially important that they understand who they are and how they affect others. Writer Parker Palmer describes leadership as a crucial force in people's lives:

> A leader is a person who has an unusual degree of power to project on other people his or her shadow, or his or her light. A leader is a person who has an unusual degree of power to create the conditions under which other people must live and move and have their being—conditions that can either be as illuminating as heaven or as shadowy as hell. A leader is a person who must take special responsibility for what's going on inside him- or herself, inside his or her consciousness, lest the act of leadership create more harm than good.[73]

There are several implications of this view. One is that leadership training programs should include not only the development of skills to manipulate the external world but also the skills necessary to go inward. Parker points out that people who lead tend to be extraverts and may ignore what is going on inside themselves. Often leaders gain power by operating competently and effectively in the external world, but at the cost of internal awareness. Similarly, students are seldom asked to relate their life story to what they are studying; the implication is that their life story does not matter. It follows that education should be more connected to a student's own values and understanding.

Of course, the final implication is that we project our values and spirit onto our interactions with others and our organizations. In an address to the U. S. Congress, Vaclav Havel, dissident and president of the new Czechoslovakia after the fall of the Soviet Union, said, "Consciousness precedes being. . . . The salvation of this human world lies nowhere else than in the human heart, in the human power to reflect, in human meekness and in human responsibility."[74]

Similarly, author James Clawson notes that the first step to effective leadership is "clarifying your center." "Your center, or core, and its content are crucial to your ability to lead. When your center is clear and focused, you are more likely to have a powerful influence on others."[75] Clawson relates that in a Japanese leadership school established by the founder of Matsushita Electric Company, the entire first year (of five) is devoted to knowing one's life mission. During that year there are no faculty and no courses. The final exam has but one question: What is your life's purpose?

Examining Capitalism as a Core Value

Most business leaders subscribe in some way to a core value they call capitalism. Yet, perspectives on the nature and role of capitalist systems differ, and how individuals view capitalist organizations and their role in society influences how they design and run their companies. Although a full discussion of capitalist organizations is beyond the scope of this book, a mention of some basic issues is instructive because it illustrates why confronting one's own assumptions about capitalism is a crucial aspect of clarifying one's personal center.

On the one hand, some business leaders suggest that companies should single-mindedly pursue the making of money without concern for the public interest. As put by the influential business magazine *The Economist:*

> Managers cannot be criticized on ethical grounds for aiming to increase long-term owner-value: that is their job. Assuming that they have also acted within the law, the next question is whether they have violated the standards of ordinary decency and distributive justice within the organization. If they have—if they have lied, or bribed, or coerced, for instance—then they have behaved unethically. But if they have acted in accordance with those two standards of business conduct, they are ethically in the right, even though they have acted against the public interest. . . .
>
> The proper guardians of the public interest are governments, which are accountable to all citizens. . .
>
> The proper business of business is business. No apology required.[76]

On the other hand, some leaders believe capitalist organizations should do more than make money and follow the law.[77] As a case in point, Dennis Bakke, co-founder of the energy company AES, set out to create "a group of people from different cultural backgrounds, with unique talents, skills, and aspirations, stretched and bound together to serve the world." To Bakke, "Principles are the bottom line."[78] His philosophy is based on his view that "The majority of Western investors and corporate executives continue to believe that some people are ordained to lead and others to follow. The followers are replaceable parts in the economic machinery. When practiced this way, capitalism resembles a command economy. It lacks a moral dimension. Individual freedom and human dignity, which are the cornerstones of democracy, are eclipsed by the single-minded pursuit of economic goals."[79] To this end, AES is uniquely designed to maximize employee participation.

In the same vein, Professor Sandra Waddock writes that focusing on the bottom line to the exclusion of all other factors—that is, maximizing shareholder value without regard for the effects on other stakeholders—leads to corruption.[80] As she puts it, "Until business schools teach future accountants and leaders how deep the connections are between business, society, nature, and the world, corporations will continue to be run by hollow leaders who have no sense of ethics or responsibility. Accounting for performance is likely to remain too narrowly focused to be helpful in today's demanding environment."[81]

What do *you* think?

How Do Leaders Act as Talent Scouts and Mentors?

Effective leaders do not hog the limelight. They find and develop talent, they mentor others, and they plan for their own replacement.

Finding and Developing Talent

Developing others is one of an executive's most important roles. According to a survey of more than 500 CEOs, finding and nurturing talented managers and executives is among their top ten challenges.[82] (Succession planning, discussed below, is also in their top ten.) Amazon CEO Jeff Bezos reports that when he is recruiting executives, he spends more than half of his interview time discussing candidates' own track record in recruiting and developing people.[83]

To develop talent for their companies, effective CEOs find good people and make sure they get the right experiences. Effective managers generally have three characteristics—basic intelligence, a variety of experience, and the experience of continuously learning to do something new or different.[84] The kinds of experiences that develop leaders are startup and turnaround assignments, managing projects critical to the business, moving to a different function or line of business, and jumps in scale of their overall responsibility. These experiences demand continuous learning.

At Dell senior managers are measured and compensated on how well they develop people. In addition to holding managers accountable for development, the company identifies high potential employees early in their careers. When Michael Dell was Chairman, and Kevin Rollins was CEO, they travelled every three months to meet with the top 10 percent of Dell managers, and the company ran a 10-day leadership training program in which both Dell and Rollins taught for several days. As Michael Dell notes, "Throughout the first 18 years of our history, we had very specific and measurable financial objectives. The people stuff was there, but we didn't emphasize it the way we did the financial goals. The surveys told us that we had to get more serious about developing managers. This was also what the company needed to grow."[85]

Mentoring

mentor
A senior, more experienced manager who provides support, direction and feedback to a protégé.

protégé
A junior, less experienced manager who receives support, direction and feedback from a mentor.

Mentorship is a relationship between a senior experienced manager, known as a **mentor**, and a less experienced junior manager, called a **protégé**, in which the mentor provides support, direction, and feedback about career plans and personal development.[86] Mentorship can be accomplished through formal programs organized by the company or through informal relationships established based on mutual self-interest. Sometimes a mentor is a protégé's direct supervisor, and sometimes not.

Mentors provide two main kinds of support.[87] The first, career support, includes such activities as coaching, protecting, obtaining challenging assignments, and increasing visibility. The second, psychosocial support, includes serving as a role model, friend, and counselor.[88] Research suggests that mentoring reduces turnover[89] and increases organizational commitment.[90]

Today some managers are turning to not merely one but a network of mentors in order to learn and advance their careers.[91] They also look not only to senior management, but to their peers and even their subordinates for ideas and support. They look to individuals both inside and outside their organizations as well.

Leaders who mentor benefit their companies in several ways.[92] First, they improve employee motivation, job performance, and retention rates. By contributing to the development of a common value base, they also strengthen and assure the continuity of organizational culture. For example, during times of organizational change, such as during times of leadership succession, these mutual values developed between mentors and protégés stabilize the company and the process.

Succession Planning

How well do leaders choose their successors? Not very well, it seems: 40 percent of new CEOs fail within 18 months.[93]

Today a variety of stakeholders, from customers to stockholders, are concerned not only with the efficacy of the CEO selection process but also with its legitimacy. When the Enron Corporation's board of directors hired Jeffrey Skilling as CEO, his ability to motivate his subordinates to take risks was a popular leadership attribute, but he lacked the ability or will to impose discipline and accountability on himself or his company.[94] The Enron debacle and other lesser scandals have raised the issues of what leadership attributes really matter, and, just as importantly, how companies should go about finding the people who have them.

One key question is "What should be the role of the executive himself or herself in finding and choosing his or her own replacement?"

Many stakeholders and observers are doubtful that the CEO should be involved in succession planning. Certainly, in one study of international recruiters, only 11 percent thought the incumbent CEO should be *in charge of* succession planning.[95] One concern is that powerful retiring CEOs strongly influence successor selection, and they prefer successors who are similar to themselves.[96] Another concern is that a chief executive is likely to pick someone inferior to himself.[97] Driven, quick-tempered Andrew Grove of Intel Corporation, for example, selected a protégé and successor who lacked his charisma.[98] Yet another problem is that, under powerful CEOs, heirs apparent typically have to wait many years before taking over the job.[99]

Many observers believe that the choice of successor is better left to those who will have to live with the decision, such as the board of directors.[100] Yet, typically the CEO chooses an heir apparent well in advance and grooms that individual before his or her final promotion.[101] Boards of directors generally limit themselves to monitoring the succession process and counterbalancing the CEO.[102] This pattern suggests that succession planning is more strongly influenced by power than by merit, although research has not yet confirmed this hypothesis.

In Conclusion

In this chapter we have examined some of the specific roles that leaders play in their companies. As you move up in a company, improving the bottom line is only one measure of your success as a leader. It is when you develop a reputation for being an excellent project manager, for dealing well with difficult people, for developing talent for the organization, and for filling a variety of other crucial roles, that you are really on your way to proving your executive potential.

Apply What You Have Learned. . .

World Class Leader: John Tu, Kingston Technology Company

Part I.

Discuss

What makes a leader authentic? Read back over the chapter section on authenticity and list the characteristics of authentic leaders.

Part II.

Watch the film *Kingston Technology* (Prentice Hall video).
   1. What is it about Tu that suggests authenticity?

2. Discuss John Tu's leadership in light of Parker Palmer's idea (quoted in the chapter) that "A leader is a person who has an unusual degree of power to project on other people his or her shadow, or his or her light. A leader is a person who has an unusual degree of power to create the conditions under which other people must live and move and have their being—conditions that can either be as illuminating as heaven or as shadowy as hell."

Advice from the Pros

How to Interview Executives for Integrity

Can a manager really interview a top job candidate for integrity? The answer is yes.

In an article for *Across the Board,* a magazine directed at top-level management, consultant William C. Byham describes the process.[103] He points out that, as the manager-interviewer, it is best to save questions about ethics until late in an interview, after you have developed rapport with the candidate. He counsels that if a candidate answers one of your questions with a recommendation that you think is actually unethical, be empathetic rather than judgmental. Reflect his or her thinking back to the candidate ("So, you felt you had no reason to rethink the sales call"). Use the opportunity to keep the candidate talking, while listening more deeply to what he or she is saying.

Byham suggests interviewers pose at most two or three ethics questions to candidates. Here are some examples of such questions:

   1. We are often confronted with the dilemma of having to choose between what is right and what is best for the company. Give at least two examples of situations in which you faced this dilemma and how you handled them.

   2. Have you ever observed someone stretching the rules at work? What did you do about it?
   3. Have you ever felt guilty about receiving credit for work that was mostly completed by others? If so, how did you handle it?

Individually. . .

For each question, write down what you think would be a good answer. Do not share these with your teammates.

In teams of three persons. . .

   1. For each question, discuss what types of answers are good ones and, based on your discussion, list three criteria for good answers.
   2. For each question, discuss what types of answers are questionable ones and list three criteria for deciding which types are questionable.

Evaluate your answers

Did you answer with integrity or not? Your professor may ask you to write a short paper evaluating your answers.

Gain Experience

Three Discipline Dilemmas

In this exercise, students roleplay three increasingly challenging levels for giving negative feedback to an employee.
Divide the class into groups of three. In each group, assign the following roles:

Manager
Employee
Observer

After each roleplay, switch roles so that each person has a chance to give negative feedback.

1. Giving Negative Feedback: The Sandwich

Eric(a) the Employee: You are a salesperson who has not done very well in your territory. In fact, this year you are at the bottom of the heap in terms of dollar amount of sales. However, you have developed good relationships with your clients over the years and are confident the sales slump is due to their business constraints rather than your own ability and effort. Because you saw your clients' businesses suffering, you did take some extra time off this year. You figured, why beat a dead horse? But you are hopeful business will pick up next year.

Marty the Manager: Eric(a) has underperformed the group this year, and is, in fact, at the bottom of the heap in terms of dollar amount of sales. You must tell him/her that because of this, he/she will not earn the annual end-of-the-year bonus, which usually amounts to about 10 percent of salary. You want to break this gradually, so you first praise, then give the negative feedback about the bonus, and then end with on a note of more praise.

2. A Disciplinary Action

Eric(a) the Employee: The story transpired as above. However, when your boss told you you will not get a bonus, you claimed to other coworkers that he/she is sexist. When you talk with Marty now, you claim you will contact your lawyer and file an official claim of discrimination.

Marty the Manager: As above. After you let Eric(a) know about the loss of bonus, you have heard that Eric(a) is now accusing you to other employees as a sexist. You are determined to let Eric(a) know that this gossiping behavior is unacceptable and will result in disciplinary action if not stopped.

3. Firing for Cause

Eric(a) the Employee: As above. In this interview your goal is to keep Marty talking so you can get even more information to substantiate your lawsuit.

Marty the Manager: As above. Eric(a) has not stopped gossiping. You explain that you have already issued a warning, and that since it has been ignored, you have no alternative but to fire Eric(a).

Discuss

1. Focus on your emotional reactions in these disciplinary situations. Even though it is not a real situation, do you feel angry, hurt, or frustrated? Or do you feel calm and self-assured?
2. To what extent were you able to pay attention to the behavior and emotions of the other party, rather than being caught up in your own issues?
3. Why do you react the way you do in emotionally charged situations?
4. Brainstorm some ways to cope in emotionally charged situations.

Can You Solve this Manager's Problem?

Levi Strauss & Company

Robert Haas is the great-great-grandnephew of Bavarian immigrant Levi Strauss and was the last person from the Strauss family to head up Levi Strauss & Co., the San Francisco organization that invented blue jeans.[104]

Looking back, the question is, "Was Haas a good choice to lead the company?" Unlike his father, an outgoing man who also led the company, Haas was detail-oriented and a very private person. He graduated from the University of California at Berkeley and the Harvard Graduate School of Business. He served in the Peace Corps in the Ivory Coast for two years, and was an associate with the management consulting firm McKinsey & Company for three years. He served in positions in marketing, planning, and operations before assuming the job of CEO in 1984.

When Haas took over, the company was in crisis, with sales dropping, excessive production capacity, and a failing diversification strategy. He felt "stark terror," he says, at the time (he was 43 years old), and had "no bold plan of action."[105] In 1985 Haas took the company private, managing what was at the time the largest buyout ever of a publicly held firm.

The company's sales peaked at $7.1 billion in 1996 and then, buffeted by competitors internationally, fell to $4 billion in 2004. The company was not as responsive as it should have been to fashion trends, and Haas was slow to ship jobs overseas even though his competitors were doing just that. When Levi Strauss did establish factories abroad, it adopted a strong factory-monitoring program and a manufacturing code of conduct.

In 1999, Haas stepped down as head of the company. Phil Marineau, the head of Pepsi's North American operations, became CEO. Marineau brought a strong marketing background to the job.

Haas continued to be an important part of the company. His normal duties included working with the board of directors, the community affairs department, and the company's charitable foundation, and representing the company with shareholders, customers and other external groups. Haas has been described as a paragon of the community. Along with other family members he donates large amounts of both money and time to a variety of local and national charities.

1. Look back over the roles and skills of leaders described in this chapter, and describe which ones Robert Haas has filled.
2. For which roles does he seem particularly well suited? ill suited?

3. Based on this case, do you think Haas was a charismatic, considerate, or structured leader (see Chapter 11)? Was this style appropriate for the company? Was Haas a good choice to lead the company?

Chapter Summary and Key Terms

What is the leader's role in special teams?
Leaders should know how to lead project teams, and adapt their style for e-leadership situations.

project management team   324

What do leaders need to know about negotiation?
Negotiation is a complex activity that requires particular interpersonal skill. Leaders must be able to diagnose a negotiation situation and select the most appropriate behavioral and analytic strategies.

negotiation   325

What is unique about the leadership role of executives and CEOs?
To move into executive (top-level) positions, mid-level leaders must develop new skills. For example, they must drop a task-oriented leadership style in favor of relationship-oriented style. CEOs have a variety of roles. For example, they manage meaning for their company. They present the company philosophy in a variety of media. They themselves become the symbol of the company and its moral standard bearer.

How do leaders act as disciplinarians?
Managers spend significant amounts of time on discipline-related personnel issues, including managing employee deviance through counseling and disciplining. Organizations develop systematic approaches to difficult people that include interviewing for stability, establishing a climate of respect, and using appropriate procedures for firing.

employee deviance   329

narcissism   332
destructive narcissism   332

When should a leader stop leading and follow instead?
Leaders must know when to stop leading. You should stop leading when another individual knows best or needs development, when your team's needs and development demand it, or when your leading will not enhance organizational performance and development.

As a leader, what aspects of your personal philosophy are likely to have the most influence on others?
Authentic leaders experience a synchronicity between who they are and their leadership style and impact. Spiritual synchronicity is the special connection between the leader's inner path with respect to a higher purpose and their leadership style. Because of leaders' high level of influence, it is especially important that they understand themselves and how they affect others.

authentic leaders   334
spiritual synchronicity   336

How do leaders act as talent scouts and mentors?
CEOs have to find and develop talent, mentor less experienced managers, and help their company choose their successor. Powerful retiring CEOs strongly influence successor selection, and they prefer successors who are similar to themselves.

mentor   338
protégé   338

Explorations

1. Leadership roles or skills you want to enhance
Choose a leadership role or skill described in this chapter that you personally would like to develop further in yourself, and research it online. Don't forget to include the academic data-bases owned by your university. Based on what you learn, create a concrete plan for how you can acquire the necessary skills.

2. Leadership and authenticity
Web search for *authenticity* and *leadership*. Further describe authentic leadership based on what you learn. Who cares about authentic leadership enough to put material on the Web? Who exemplifies it? How important is it, really, in running an effective organization?

References

[1] L. H. Summers, "Letter from President Summers on Women and Science," January 19, 2005, http://www.president.harvard.edu/speeches/2005/womensci.html. Accessed September 25, 2005.

[2] J. Turner and R. Muller, "On the Nature of the Project as a Temporary Organization," *International Journal of Project Management 21* (1), 2003:1–8; M. Ives, "Identifying the Contextual Elements of Project Management Within Organizations and Their Impact on Project Success," *Project Management Journal 36,* March 2005:37–50.

[3] H. Woodward, "Integrating SAP and Primavera at AOL," *Project Management World Today: Case Studies and Project Briefs, January 2006,* http://www.pmforum.org/library/cases/2006/01.htm. Accessed September 16, 2006.

[4] G. Laszlo, "Project Management: A Quality Management Approach," *The TQM Magazine 11* (3), 1999:157–160; J. Pinto and P. Rouhiainen, *Building Customer-Based Project Organizations* (New York: John Wiley & Sons, 2001).

[5] B. Hebert, "Tracking Progress," *CMA Management 75* (10), February 2002:24–26.

[6] R. Loo, "Training in Project Management: A Powerful Tool for Improving Individual and Team Performance," *Team Performance Management: An International Journal 2* (3), 1996:6–14.

[7] J. Cannon, "Why IT Applications Succeed or Fail: The Interaction of Technical and Organizational Factors," *Industrial and Commercial Training 26* (1), 1994:10–15.

[8] J. Pinto and P. Rouhiainen, *Building Customer-Based Project Organizations* (New York: John Wiley & Sons, 2001).

[9] L. Crawford and T. Cooke-Davies, "Enhancing Corporate Performance through Sustainable Project Management Communities," *Proceedings of the 30th Annual Project Management Institute Seminars & Symposium,* (Sylva, NC: Project Management Institute, October 10–16, 1999).

[10] M. Cheng and A. R. J. Dainty, "What Makes a Good Project Manager?" *Human Resource Management Journal 15* (1), 2005:25–37.

[11] H. J. Thamhain, "Team Leadership Effectiveness in Technology-Based Project Environments," *Project Management Journal 35* (4), December 2004:35–46, 36.

[12] H. J. Thamhain, "Team Leadership Effectiveness in Technology-Based Project Environments," *Project Management Journal 35* (4), December 2004:35–46, 36.

[13] B. J. Avolio and S. S. Kahai, "Adding the 'E' to E-Leadership: How It May Impact Your Leadership," *Organizational Dynamics 13* (4), 2003:325–338.

[14] B. J. Avolio, *Leadership Development in Balance* (Mahwah, NJ: Lawrence Erlbaum Associates, Publishers, 2005).

[15] R. J. Lewicki, J. A. Litterer, D. M. Saunders, and J. W. Minton, *Negotiation: Readings, Exercises, and Cases,* 2nd ed. (Burr Ridge, IL: Irwin, 1993).

[16] R. J. Lewicki, J. A. Litterer, D. M. Saunders, and J. W. Minton, *Negotiation: Readings, Exercises, and Cases,* 2nd ed. (Burr Ridge, IL: Irwin, 1993).

[17] J. Main, "How to Be a Better Negotiator," in R. J. Lewicki, J. A. Litterer, D. M. Saunders, and J. W. Minton, *Negotiation: Readings, Exercises, and Cases,* 2nd ed. (Burr Ridge, IL: Irwin, 1993):20–24.

[18] R. Fisher and W. H. Davis, "Six Basic Interpersonal Skills for a Negotiator's Repertoire," in R. J. Lewicki, J. A. Litterer, D. M. Saunders, and J. W. Minton, *Negotiation: Readings, Exercises, and Cases,* 2nd ed. (Burr Ridge, IL: Irwin, 1993):407–413.

[19] H. S. Jonas III, R. E. Fry, and S. Srivastva, "The Person of the CEO: Understanding the Executive Experience," *Academy of Management Executive 3* (3), August 1989:205–215.

[20] W. M. McCall and M. M. Lombardo, *Off the Track: Why and How Successful Executives Get Derailed* (Greensboro, NC: Center for Creative Leadership, 1983); M. M. Lombardo and C. McCauley, *The Dynamics of Management Derailment* (Greensboro, NC: Center for Creative Leadership, 1988).

[21] K. R. Brousseau, M. J. Driver, G. Hourihan, and R. Larsson, "The Seasoned Executive's Decision Making Style," *Harvard Business Review 84* (2), February 2006:110–121.

[22] E. Van Velsor and J. B. Leslie, "Why Executives Derail: Perspectives across Time and Cultures," *Academy of Management Executive 9* (4), November 1995:62–72.

[23] G. Ekvall and J. Arvonen, "Leadership Profiles, Situation and Effectiveness," *Creativity and Innovation Management 3,* 1994:139–161.

[24] R. B. Kaiser and R. E. Kaplan, *Leadership Versatility Index: User's Guide* (Greensboro, NC: Kaplan DeVries Inc., 2002); R. E. Kaplan and R. B. Kaiser, "Rethinking a Classic Distinction in Leadership: Implications for the Assessment and Development of Executives," *Consulting Psychology Journal: Research and Practice 55* (1), 2003:15–25; R. E. Kaplan and R. B. Kaiser, "Developing Versatile Leadership," *MIT Sloan Management Review 44* (4), Summer 2003:19–26.

[25] M. Augier and D. J. Teece, "Reflections on (Schumpeterian) Leadership: A Report on a Seminar on Leadership and Management Education," *California Management Review 47* (2), Winter 2005:114–136, 130.

[26] H. S. Jonas III, R. E. Fry, and S. Srivastva, "The Person of the CEO: Understanding the Executive Experience," *Academy of Management Executive 3* (3), August 1989:205–215, 213.

[27] H. S. Jonas III, R. E. Fry, and S. Srivastva, "The Person of the CEO: Understanding the Executive Experience," *Academy of Management Executive 3* (3), August 1989:205–215.

[28] Attributed to David Truman in M. Augier and D. J. Teece, "Reflections on (Schumpeterian) Leadership: A Report on a Seminar on Leadership and Management Education," *California Management Review 47* (2), Winter 2005:114–136, 125.

[29] W. Buffett, "2005 Chairman's Letter: To the Shareholders of Berkshire Hathaway Inc.," February 28, 2006, http://www.berkshirehathaway.com/letters/letters.html. Accessed October 4, 2006.

[30] P. F. Drucker, "What Makes an Effective Executive," *Harvard Business Review 82* (6), June 2004:58–63.

[31] D. Park and B. K. Berger, "The Presentation of CEO's in the Press, 1990–2000: Increasing Salience, Positive Valence, and a Focus on Competency and Personal Dimensions of Image," *Journal of Public Relations Research 16* (1), January 2004:93–123.

[32] L. Gaines-Ross, "CEO Reputation: A Key Factor in Shareholder Value," *Corporate Reputation Review 3*, 2000:366–370.

[33] H. S. Jonas III, R. E. Fry, and S. Srivastva, "The Person of the CEO: Understanding the Executive Experience," *Academy of Management Executive 3* (3), August 1989:205–215, 208.

[34] D. R. May, A. Y. L. Chan, T. D. Hodges, and B. J. Avolio, "Developing the Moral Component of Authentic Leadership," *Organizational Dynamics 32* (3), 2003:247–260.

[35] A. Bandura, *Social Learning Theory* (Englewood Cliffs, NJ: Prentice Hall, 1977).

[36] E. Van Velsor and J. B. Leslie, "Why Executives Derail: Perspectives across Time and Cultures," *Academy of Management Executive 9* (4), November 1995:62–72, 66.

[37] N. Nicholson, "How to Motivate Your Problem People," *Harvard Business Review 81* (1), January 2003:56–65.

[38] S. L. Robinson and R. J. Bennett, "A Typology of Deviant Workplace Behaviors: A Multidimensional Scaling Study," *Academy of Management Journal 38* (2), April 1995:555–572.

[39] B. J. Tepper, "Consequences of Abusive Supervision," *Academy of Management Journal 43* (2), April 2000:178–190.

[40] J. S. Lublin, "Managing Harassment Law in U.S. is Strict, Foreigners Find," *The Wall Street Journal* May 15, 2006:B1.

[41] H. Hoel, C. L. Cooper, and B. Faragher, "The Experience of Bullying in Great Britain: The Impact of Organizational Status," *European Journal of Work & Organizational Psychology 10* (4), December 2001:443–465.

[42] L. W. Andrews, "When It's Time for Anger Management," *HR Magazine 50* (6), June 2005:131–136, 135.

[43] P. R. Sackett and C. J. DeVore, "Counterproductive Behaviors at Work," in N. Anderson, D. S. Ones, H. K. Sinangil, and C. Viswesvaran, eds., *Handbook of Industrial, Work, and Organizational Psychology 1,* (Thousand Oaks, CA: Sage Publications, 2001):145–151.

[44] J. R. Rentsch and R. P. Steel, "Testing the Durability of Job Characteristics as Predictors of Absenteeism over a Six-Year Period," *Personnel Psychology 51,* 1998:165–189.

[45] S. L. Robinson and A. M. O'Leary-Kelly, "Monkey See, Monkey Do: The Influence of Work Groups on the Antisocial Behavior of Employees," *Academy of Management Journal 41* (6), 1998:658–672.

[46] Employment attorney K. Karr, in L. W. Andrews, "When It's Time for Anger Management," *HR Magazine 50* (6), June 2005:131–136, 135.

[47] G. A. Bielous, "Five Ways to Cope with Difficult People," *Supervision 57* (6), June 1996:14–16.

[48] L. Leritz, "Taking the Bull Out of the Bully," in R. J. Lewicki, J. A. Litterer, D. M. Saunders, and J. W. Minton, eds., *Negotiation: Readings, Exercises, and Cases,* 2nd ed. (Burr Ridge, IL: Irwin, 1993):227–236.

[49] L. Leritz, "Taking the Bull Out of the Bully," in R. J. Lewicki, J. A. Litterer, D. M. Saunders, and J. W. Minton, eds., *Negotiation: Readings, Exercises, and Cases,* 2nd ed. (Burr Ridge, IL: Irwin, 1993):227–236, 231.

[50] W. Cottringer, "The ABC's of Employee Discipline," *Supervision 64* (4), April 2003:5–7.

[51] R. H. Lubit, *Coping with Toxic Managers, Subordinates, and Other Difficult People* (Upper Saddle River, NJ: Financial Times/Prentice Hall, 2004).

[52] R. H. Lubit, *Coping with Toxic Managers, Subordinates, and Other Difficult People* (Upper Saddle River, NJ: Financial Times/Prentice Hall, 2004).

[53] R. H. Lubit, *Coping with Toxic Managers, Subordinates, and Other Difficult People* (Upper Saddle River, NJ: Financial Times/Prentice Hall, 2004); J. J. McDonald Jr., "The Narcissistic Plaintiff," *Employee Relations Law Journal (Aspen) 30* (4), Spring 2005:86–98.

[54] J. Greenberg, "Looking Fair versus Being Fair: Managing Impressions of Organizational Justice," in B. M. Staw and L. L. Cummings, eds., *Research in Organizational Behavior 12* (Greenwich, CT: JAI Press, 1990):111–157.

[55] R. Folger and J. Greenberg, "Procedural Justice: An Interpretive Analysis of Personnel Systems," in K. R. Rowland and G. R. Ferris, eds., *Research in Personnel and Human Resources Management 3* (Greenwich, CT: JAI Press, 1985):141–183; E. A. Lind and T. R. Tyler, *The Social Psychology of Procedural Justice* (New York: Plenum, 1988).

[56] E. A. Lind, R. J. MacCoun, R. E. Ebener, W. L. R. Felstiner, D. R. Hensler, J. Resnik, and T. R. Tyler, "In the Eye of the Beholder: Tort Litigants' Evaluations of Their Experiences in the Civil Justice System," *Law and Society Review 24,* 1990:953–996.

[57] G. Bielous, "How to Fire!" *Supervision 57* (11), November 1996:8–10.

[58] V. J. Bentz, "A View from the Top: A Thirty Year Perspective of Research Devoted to Discovery, Description, and Prediction of Executive Behavior," paper presented at the 93rd Annual Convention of the American Psychological Association, Los Angeles, CA, August 1985; M. M. Lombardo, M. N. Ruderman, and C. D. McCauley, "Explanations of Success and Derailment in Upper-Level Management Positions," *Journal of Business and Psychology 2,* 1988:199–216; L. W. Hellervik, J. F. Hazucha, and R. J. Schneider, "Behavior Change: Models, Methods and a Review of the Evidence," in M. D. Dunnette and L. M. Hough, eds., *Handbook of Industrial and Organizational Psychology 3,* 2nd ed. (Palo Alto, CA: Consulting Psychologists Press, 1992); M. W. McCall and M. M. Lombardo, "Off the Track: Why and How Successful Executives Get Derailed," *Technical Report No. 21* (Greensboro, NC: Center for Creative Leadership, 1993).

[59] P. F. Drucker, "Managing Oneself," *Harvard Business Review 83* (1), January 2005: 100–108, 104.

[60] D. K. Smith, "The Following Part of Leading," in F. Hesselbein, M. Goldsmith, and R. Beckhard, eds., *The Leader of the Future: New Visions, Strategies, and Practices for the Next Era* (San Francisco, CA: Jossey-Bass Publishers, 1996):199–207.

[61] M. C. Feiner, "The Law of the Emperor's Wardrobe," *Ivey Business Journal 69* (3), January/February 2005:1–5.

[62] L. Bogomolny, "Taming the Giant," *Canadian Business 76* (23), December 7, 2003:153–155.

[63] J. J. Gabarro and J. P. Kotter, "Managing Your Boss," *Harvard Business Review 83* (1), January 2005:92–98.

[64] "The Resurrection of Steve Jobs," *The Economist* September 15, 2005, http://www.economist.com/research/articles. Accessed October 15, 2005.

[65] "The Resurrection of Steve Jobs," *The Economist* September 15, 2005, http://www.economist.com/research/articles. Accessed October 15, 2005.

[66] C. D. Pielstick, *Authentic Leading: Where the Blue Sky Hits the Road* (Longmont, CO: Rocky Mountain Press, 2003).

[67] J. Reed in M. Augier and D. J. Teece, "Reflections on (Schumpeterian) Leadership: A Report on a Seminar on Leadership

and Management Education," *California Management Review 47* (2), Winter 2005:114–136, 123.

[68] J. Reed in M. Augier and D. J. Teece, "Reflections on (Schumpeterian) Leadership: A Report on a Seminar on Leadership and Management Education," *California Management Review 47* (2), Winter 2005:114–136, 123/124.

[69] J. Reed in M. Augier and D. J. Teece, "Reflections on (Schumpeterian) Leadership: A Report on a Seminar on Leadership and Management Education," *California Management Review 47* (2), Winter 2005:114–136, 124.

[70] J. Reed in M. Augier and D. J. Teece, "Reflections on (Schumpeterian) Leadership: A Report on a Seminar on Leadership and Management Education," *California Management Review 47* (2), Winter 2005:114–136, 123.

[71] C. D. Pielstick, "Teaching Spiritual Synchronicity in a Business Leadership Class," *Journal of Management Education 29* (1), February 2005:153–168.

[72] I. I. Mitroff and E. A. Denton, *A Spiritual Audit of Corporate America: A Hard Look at Spirituality, Religion, and Values in the Workplace* (San Francisco, CA: Jossey-Bass, 1999).

[73] P. J. Palmer, "Leading from Within: Reflections on Spirituality and Leadership," private manuscript, October 1990. I received this manuscript as a gift from Peter J. Frost.

[74] P. J. Palmer, "Leading from Within: Reflections on Spirituality and Leadership," private manuscript, October 1990:2.

[75] J. G. Clawson, *Level Three Leadership: Getting Below the Surface* (Upper Saddle River, NJ: Prentice Hall, 2003):95.

[76] "The Ethics of Business: Good Corporate Citizens, and Wise Governments, Should Be Wary of CSR," *The Economist 374,* January 22, 2005:20–22, 22.

[77] For a full discussion, see W. Greider, *The Soul of Capitalism: Opening Paths to a Moral Economy* (New York: Simon & Schuster, 2003).

[78] D. W. Bakke, *Joy at Work: A Revolutionary Approach to Fun on the Job* (Seattle, WA: PVG, 2005):12–13.

[79] D. W. Bakke, *Joy at Work: A Revolutionary Approach to Fun on the Job* (Seattle, WA: PVG, 2005):239–240.

[80] T. A. Kochan, "Addressing the Crisis in Confidence in Corporations: Root Causes, Victims, and Strategies for Reform," *Academy of Management Executive 16* (3), August 2002:139–141.

[81] S. Waddock, "Hollow Men and Women at the Helm . . . Hollow Accounting Ethics?" *Issues in Accounting Education 20* (2), May 2005:145–150, 145.

[82] M. Lombardo, "Developing Talent: The Magic Bullets," *Strategic HR Review 4* (2), January/February 2005:3.

[83] R. Peters, *Re-Imagine! Business Excellence in a Disruptive Age* (London: Dorling Kindersley Limited, 2003).

[84] M. Lombardo, "Developing Talent: The Magic Bullets," *Strategic HR Review 4* (2), January/February 2005:3.

[85] T. A. Stewart and L. O'Brien, "Execution Without Excuses," *Harvard Business Review,* March 2005:103–111.

[86] J. E. A. Russell and D. M. Adams, "The Changing Nature of Mentoring in Organizations: An Introduction to the Special Issue on Mentoring in Organizations," *Journal of Vocational Behavior 51,* 1997:1–14.

[87] K. E. Kram, "Phases of the Mentor Relationship," *Academy of Management Journal 26* (4), December 1983:608–625.

[88] G. F. Dreher and R. A. Ash, "A Comparative Study of Mentoring among Men and Women in Managerial, Professional, and Technical Positions," *Journal of Applied Psychology 75* (5), October 1990:539–546.

[89] M. Lankau and T. A. Scandura, "An Investigation of Personal Learning in Mentoring Relationships: Content, Antecedents, and Consequences," *Academy of Management Journal 45* (4), 2002:779–790.

[90] S. C. Payne and A. H. Huffman, "A Longitudinal Examination of the Influence of Mentoring on Organizational Commitment and Turnover," *Academy of Management Journal 48* (1), February 2005:158–168.

[91] S. C. de Janasz, S. E. Sullivan, and V. Whiting, "Mentor Networks and Career Success: Lessons for Turbulent Times," *Academy of Management Executive 17* (4), November 2003:78–91.

[92] J. A. Wilson and N. S. Elman, "Organizational Benefits of Mentoring," *Academy of Management Executive 4* (4), November 1990:88–94.

[93] "Bad Heir Days," *The Economist 375* (8425), May 7, 2005:59.

[94] R. Khurana, *Searching for a Corporate Savior: The Irrational Quest for Charismatic CEOs* (Princeton, New Jersey: Princeton University Press, 2002.)

[95] "Bad Heir Days," *The Economist 375* (8425), May 7, 2005:59.

[96] E. J. Zajac and J. D. Westphal, "Who Shall Succeed? How CEO/Board Preferences and Power Affect the Choice of New CEOs," *Academy of Management Journal 39* (1), February 1996:64–90.

[97] According to P. Haspeslagh, in "Split and Stay," *The Economist 375* (8426), May 14, 2005:68. See also "Bad Heir Days," *The Economist 375* (8425), May 7, 2005:59.

[98] "After the Icon Exits," *BusinessWeek Online* July 3, 2006, http:www.businessweek.com/print/magazine/content/06_-27/b3991044.hrm?chang=g1. Accessed October 5, 2006.

[99] A. A. Cannella Jr. and W. Shen, "So Close and Yet So Far: Promotion versus Exit for CEO Heirs Apparent," *Academy of Management Journal 44* (2), April 2001:252–270.

[100] "Bad Heir Days," *The Economist 375* (8425), May 7, 2005:59.

[101] R. M. Vancil, *Passing the Baton* (Boston, MA: Harvard University Press, 1987).

[102] A. A. Cannella Jr. and W. Shen, "So Close and Yet So Far: Promotion versus Exit for CEO Heirs Apparent," *Academy of Management Journal 44* (2), April 2001:252–270.

[103] W. C. Byham, "Can You Interview for Integrity?" *Across the Board* March/April 2004:35–38.

[104] Based on information in P. Sarker, "Haas to Keep Hand On Levi's," *San Francisco Chronicle,* July 24, 2005:E1, E4.

[105] P. Sarker, "Haas to Keep Hand On Levi's," *San Francisco Chronicle,* July 24, 2005:E1, E4.

13

Power and Influence

Preview

What is power?

How can you identify the sources of power in your company?
Power sources versus power tactics
Formal versus informal power
Interpersonal source of power: the soft and the harsh
Other sources of power

How can you acquire power in your organization?
Prepare for the use of power
Apply power tactics
Engage in political behavior
Use networks and mentors
Understand empowerment

As a leader, what should you know about power?
How do leaders differ from power-holders?
Does power corrupt?

How can others acquire power over you?
What factors lead to obedience and resistance?
How are employees subject to routinization and dehumanization?
How do some managers intimidate their employees?
How powerful is deception?
What is the allure of toxic leaders?

How does a person's view of power depend on culture?
Effects of national culture
Effects of organizational culture

What do Donald Trump, Gwyneth Paltrow, and Dr. Phil have in common?

Organizational politics is about who you know rather than what you know. Whether playing politics is a good idea or a bad idea depends on whom you ask.

Many companies strive to be meritocracies, in which the brightest and hardest working people advance based on their merits. Although these companies may not fully succeed, their belief that fair treatment is what motivates most employees keeps them working hard to reduce influences such as nepotism and favoritism. For example, when a position opens up, they make sure to inform all possible candidates and make the selection process impartial.

Other companies are quite open about playing favorites. Nowhere is this more true than in family-owned businesses. The real Trump apprentices are his three children Donald Jr., Ivanka, and Eric, all of whom plan to enter the Trump companies. Getting an MBA is a Trump family tradition, and, The Donald reasons, why start all over again when they can build on a base that already exists? Trump points out that nepotism, whether among friends or families, is the way the world works. "The fact is," he says, "I love my children and I hope they do a real good job."[1]

So what do Donald Trump, Gwyneth Paltrow, and Dr. Phil have in common? Trump's children will enter his business. Paltrow is the daughter of the Hollywood actor Blythe Danner and her husband director Bruce Paltrow. And Dr. Phil's son Jay McGraw is following in his father's footsteps as a talk show host. Are these offspring innately talented, or do they simply know how to use the power of family connections? Or both? How will their presence influence others who work in their companies?

The influence of nepotism is just one example of how power works in organizations. In this chapter you will learn about organizational power and influence—including how to acquire them in today's organizations.

What Is Power?

power
The ability to mobilize resources to accomplish some end.

Power is the ability to mobilize resources to accomplish some end.[2] In organizations, this generally means that it is the ability to get someone to do something. Sometimes power has a negative connotation, implying coercion. For example, "He used his power to get her the job," implies that the candidate's qualifications alone would not have been sufficient and that someone had to be influenced to hire her. Early definitions of power were, in fact, often negative: "A has power over B to the extent that he can get B to do something that B would not otherwise do."[3] However, today's view of power is generally more balanced.

influence
The ability to move or impel someone to some action, typically has a positive connotation, in that it impels someone to go along with something willingly.

The related term **influence** also involves the ability to get someone to do something, and is often used interchangeably with power. However, influence typically has a positive connotation, suggesting that the individuals who have been influenced have gone along somewhat willingly. For example, "He influenced the decision." The term **authority** suggests legitimate control or command over others. For example, "As her superior, he has the authority to tell her what to do."

authority
Legitimate control or command over others.

Of course, in organizational life there are many common terms that suggest some aspect of power, including the expressions "power base," "the powers that be," "power play," "power structure" "personal power," and "political power." Even the term *leadership* suggests power—or is it influence?—over others.

In earlier, simpler societies, the exercise of power was usually direct and face-to-face, whereas today power often operates indirectly.[4] The policy set by a CEO is implemented down through the many levels of the organization. Power extends throughout a corporation in part because of hierarchical relationships, making everyone answerable to someone and, ultimately, to the top person.

How Can You Identify the Sources of Power in Your Company?

There are many sources of power in an organization. They include formal and informal sources, interpersonal sources, indirect sources such as manipulation, and control of resources.

Power Sources versus Power Tactics

power sources
The entire repertoire of behaviors that an individual could potentially call upon to influence others.

Power sources are the entire repertoire of behaviors that an individual could potentially call upon to influence others, whereas **tactics** are the behaviors actually used in a particular situation.[5] Thus, a manager might tell a chronically late employee to change his or her behavior, but it is most likely the fact that the manager is a source of potential punishment, rather than the reminder itself, that has the larger influence on changing the employee's behavior. We will cover interpersonal sources of power next, and power tactics below.

power tactics
The behaviors an individual actually uses in a particular situation to influence others.

Formal versus Informal Power

formal power
Power based on the principle of hierarchy.

Power is a social process that is either formal or informal.[6] **Formal power** originates in the principle of **hierarchy**—the belief that power should be held disproportionately, with those higher in the organization having more and those lower having less. In contrast, **informal power** is reciprocal—individuals help each other out because of anticipated mutual gain, and conflict is minimal. See Table 13.1 for examples of the types of relationships that exemplify formal and informal power.

hierarchy
The disproportionate holding of power, with those higher in the organization having more power and those lower having less.

Interpersonal Sources of Power: The Soft and the Harsh

informal power
A proportionate holding of power, in which individuals help each other out because of anticipated mutual gain.

What are the interpersonal sources of power available to individuals in organizations? There are two main categories: personal ("soft") sources and formal ("harsh") sources.[7] See Table 13.2 for the sources of power in each category.

Using soft sources of power rather than harsh sources is more likely to lead to satisfaction and commitment on the part of subordinates,[8] as well as to a greater willingness to comply.[9] Most new young managers rely on expert power and referent power—establishing a reputation based on their expertise, and developing an interpersonal network.[10]

TABLE 13.1 **Formal and Informal Power Relationships in Organizations**

	Formal Power Relationships	Informal Power Relationships
Individual level	Boss–subordinate relationship Mentoring programs	Friendships Mentoring Romantic relationships
Organizational level	Hierarchical structures Cross-functional workgroups and project teams	Cliques Networks

TABLE 13.2 **Overview: Sources of Power in Organizations**

	Person A influences Person B because Person B. . .	Examples from Organizational Life
Personal ("soft") sources of power		
Referent power	Identifies with, likes, and admires Person A	A subordinate sees the boss as a role model.
Expert power	Believes Person A has relevant experience and knowledge	An employee agrees to implement a policy created by the company's legal advisors.
Information power	Is convinced by Person A's clear logic, argument, or information	A work team is sold on a company redesign because of the way the boss presents it to them.
Formal ("harsh") sources of power		
Coercive power	Fears being punished if he or she does not comply with Person A's wishes	Employees receive tangible punishments such as a pay cut, or intangible punishments such as personal disapproval.
Reward power	Anticipates being rewarded if he or she complies with Person A's wishes	Employees receive tangible rewards such as money, or intangible rewards such as personal approval.
Legitimate power	Accepts that Person A's formal position in the organization gives him or her the right to make certain decisions.	A boss tells a subordinate how to do his or her job.

Sources: J. R. P. French, "A Formal Theory of Power," *Psychological Review 63*, 1956:181–194; J. R. P. French and B. H. Raven, "The Bases of Social Power," in D. Cartwright, ed., *Studies in Social Power* (Ann Arbor, MI: Institute for Social Research, 1959):150–167; B. H. Raven, "The Bases of Power: Origins and Recent Developments," *Journal of Social Issues 49* (4), 1993:227–251; B. H. Raven, J. Schwarzwald, and M. Koslowsky, "Conceptualizing and Measuring a Power/Interaction Model of Interpersonal Influence," *Journal of Applied Social Psychology 28* (4), February 15, 1998:307–332.

Other Sources of Power

The sources of power described in Table 13.2 are all interpersonal and direct, describing how one person influences another. However, not all power is direct. Indirect sources of power include manipulation, providing information indirectly, and influencing third parties.[11] Control of resources is yet another type of power.

MANIPULATION Manipulation is changing some aspect of the targeted individuals or their environment to achieve a desired goal. For example, if your goal is to prevent someone from dominating a meeting, you might assign him or her beforehand a consuming task such as coordinating the slides with the speaker. Or if you do not want your employees to meet and develop interpersonal networks (perhaps you think they will be time-wasters), do not provide a lounge in which they might do so.

PROVIDING INFORMATION INDIRECTLY Telling someone to do something and explaining why they should do it is quite a different process than only hinting and suggesting to them what they might do. People in lower power positions are likely to be more successful using the latter tactic. For example, rather than tell a doctor what medication is appropriate for a patient's illness, a nurse might suggest that a particular medication seemed helpful to a patient down the hall who had a similar illness.

INFLUENCING THIRD PARTIES One way to influence others is to bring in a third party who has some sort of power, such as expertise or referent power (contacts). A person's work group might be used as a third party to apply pressure, too. Of course, sometimes it may be necessary to deal with an interfering third party by undermining the party's legitimacy, expertise, or status as a role model.

CONTROL OF RESOURCES One way to bring others under your power is to take control of the resources that they want or need, thus making them dependent on you. Resources people often want include money, prestige, legitimacy, rewards and sanctions, expertise, and the ability to deal with uncertainty.[12] Resources vary in their importance, scarcity, and nonsubstitutability.[13] For instance, to an employee just out of college and paying off big loans, money is important and scarce, and hardly anything can take its place, whereas to an employee whose children are grown and whose savings are substantial, money is less important and its scarcity does not matter, and more vacation time would be an adequate substitute.

How Can You Acquire Power in Your Organization?

Acquiring power requires setting a goal, acquiring sources of power, assessing which influence strategy is likely to work best, preparing the scene, and taking action.[14] We have already discussed sources of power. Next let's take a look at how to prepare for the use of power and how managers choose among a variety of approaches for obtaining power—power tactics, political behavior, networking, and empowerment.

Prepare for the Use of Power

When you are preparing to apply power, consider each of these factors: setting the stage, enhancing and emphasizing your own power bases, minimizing the strength of the targeted individual, and minimizing the strength of others who might influence the process.[15]

SETTING THE STAGE The first factor is literally setting the scene. Have you ever walked into a professor's office and seen a wall full of diplomas? Or a politician's office and seen a wall full of pictures of him or her with celebrities? Have you noticed that doctors often wear a white laboratory coat? These people are setting the scene by showing you signs of their expert, referent, and legitimate power. (By the way, how do you decorate your own space? Is power a factor?)

ENHANCING AND EMPHASIZING POWER BASES There are various ways people can enhance their own power base in the eyes of others. They may make a point of referring to their role as a person's boss, teacher, or doctor, thus emphasizing their legitimate power over the person. They may self-promote, emphasizing their superior knowledge or connections. They may make a request the other person is not likely to accept, thus inducing guilt in preparation for another request. They may even intimidate, presenting the person with a fearful image and hinting at what harm might come from disobeying them.

MINIMIZING THE OTHER PERSON'S STRENGTH This is another factor to consider when you want to apply power. Subtle put-downs that decrease the other person's self-esteem and confidence may increase your own expert, informational, or legitimate power in the person's eyes.

MINIMIZING THE INFLUENCE OF OUTSIDE PARTIES The final type of preparation is damaging the image of potentially influential outsiders, thus reducing their expert, legitimate, or informational power. For example, you suspect your boss wants to hire a consultant whom you dislike, so you dig up and share some stories about how his or her interventions have failed in other companies.

Obviously, the use of these last two types of preparation must be weighed carefully against ethical and practical considerations. Not only might you have ethical concerns about using them, you also might damage your reputation by using them, and you may also create a backlash from the object of your power play.

Apply Power Tactics

Having established power bases and set the stage, it is now time to choose your tactics, the actual behaviors you will apply. Although there are numerous tactics you can use to gain power in organizations, research suggests a set of fundamental choices.[16] Imagine, for instance, that you want your boss to approve a project you have designed. Rank-order the following tactics in terms of how likely it would be that you would use them to convince your boss to approve your project. (Let 1 equal the most likely tactic. There are 10 tactics.) Place the ranking in the space before the tactic.

1. _____ You explain to your manager how the costs of the project would be offset by improved efficiency.

2. _____ To convince your boss that your project is a good idea, you appeal to your boss's values about innovation and staying competitive.

3. _____ At an early stage of the project development, you ask your boss for ideas.

4. _____ You comment on how successful your boss's latest project has been, then request help with your own.

5. _____ You offer to work longer hours in your usual assignments if you are allowed to do this project.

6. _____ You call a meeting of like-minded peers to convince your boss of the merits of the project.

7. _____ You point out that others at your level in other departments have been given similar opportunities to initiate projects.

8. _____ You make a point of asking your boss about your proposal once every day.

9. _____ You obtain the support of higherups for your project.

10. _____ You ask your manager to initiate the change as a personal favor.

These behaviors exemplify the following tactics, in the same order. From your rank ordering, you can get some idea of which power tactics you prefer.

1. *Rational persuasion*—Using logical arguments and factual evidence to persuade.

2. *Inspirational appeals*—Arousing enthusiasm by appealing to a person's values, ideals, or aspirations, or by increasing his or her self-confidence.

3. *Consultation*—Getting a person involved with the plan or a change in order to enlist his or her support and assistance.

4. *Ingratiation*—Using praise, flattery, or friendly or helpful behavior to establish a positive mood before you ask for something.

5. *Exchange*—Offering an exchange of favors now or in the future, including sharing in the benefits of the proposed project.

6. *Coalitions*—Seeking the aid of others to persuade someone, or using the support of others as a reason for a person to go along.

7. *Legitimation*—Claiming the authority or right to make a request, or showing how the request is consistent with organizational policies or traditions.

8. *Pressure*—Making demands, threats, or frequently checking or reminding someone to do what you want.

9. *Upward appeals*—Getting the support of higher-ups to allow you to do what you want.

10. *Personal appeals*—Appealing to feelings of loyalty and friendship when asking for something.

Now consider which tactics research suggests are the best. When should you use a particular tactic? On the one hand, when targeting peers and subordinates, there are many techniques that can be effective. These include rational persuasion, consultation, collaboration, and inspirational appeals. Using coalitions, legitimation, and pressure are *not* likely to be effective.

On the other hand, not all of these tactics are likely to be effective when you, the subordinate, are trying to influence your boss. When you are trying to influence your boss or other higher-ups, the tactic *most* likely to be successful is rational persuasion.[17]

Engage in Political Behavior

Sometimes people act outside of their organizational roles to get power. We call this **political behavior** or, in the vernacular, "playing politics." Political behavior is defined as activities that are not required as part of a person's organizational role but that influence, or attempt to influence, the distribution of advantages and disadvantages within the organization.[18]

Political behavior has many important impacts on organizational life. To begin with, managers, according to one study, believe that playing politics does lead to a higher level of power, and that more power leads to more opportunities to engage in politics.[19] Second, some, though not all, political behavior does advance organizational goals. Third, in a less positive vein, the perception that people are playing politics can lead to a variety of undesirable outcomes, including job stress, aggressive behavior, reduced organizational commitment, and turnover.[20]

What constitutes political behavior? A critical view suggests it exists when:[21]

- Favoritism, including nepotism, rather than merit determines who gets ahead.
- Yes-men get promoted, and good ideas are not put forward if doing so means disagreeing with supervisors.
- An employee can get along by being a good guy, regardless of the quality of his or her work.
- Employees are not encouraged to speak out frankly when they are critical of well-established ideas.
- Cliques and in-groups hinder effectiveness.

On the other hand, as we will see below, not all political behavior is counterproductive to individuals or organizations.

PATTERNS OF POLITICAL BEHAVIOR Political behavior has distinct patterns.[22] For one thing, it is both internal and external. Internal politics includes the exchange of favors, forming alliances, trading agreements, reprisals, and even symbolic protest gestures.

political behavior
Activities that are not required as part of a person's organizational role but which influence the distribution of advantages and disadvantages within the organization; also known as "playing politics."

External politics involves attempts to engage outsiders. Examples are leaking information to the media, engaging in whistle blowing, or filing a lawsuit.

Political behavior also has a vertical–lateral dimension. Vertical political behaviors include complaining to a supervisor, bypassing the chain of command, and apple-polishing. Lateral political behaviors include exchanging favors, offering help, and organizing coalitions.

Finally, political behavior has a legitimate–illegitimate dimension. Some political behavior is common and acceptable, whereas some violates organizational norms. This dimension invites the question: Is political behavior good or bad for organizations? Sometimes political behavior is good for the organization and sometimes it is not.[23] See Table 13.3, in which the three shaded boxes include political behaviors and the unshaded box includes nonpolitical behaviors, and which suggests which behaviors are functional and dysfunctional for an organization.

Should you play politics? A major consideration is whether you consider playing politics to be ethical. Professor Debra Comer has provided this set of guidelines for determining whether a particular political behavior is personally appropriate for an individual:[24]

- First, is the act of engaging in this political behavior in line with your personal beliefs, values, and style? Do you consider it be ethical?

- Second, what outcomes is this behavior likely to produce? For instance, can you execute it well? Is the behavior appropriate given your organization's culture? How likely is it to be rewarded in your organization's culture? Will key players respond favorably to the behavior? What is your relationship with these key players, and how will this relationship affect their response?

- Third, is engaging in this behavior in line with your personal goals?

- Finally, are the likely outcomes of this behavior in line with organizational goals?

If you can answer "yes" to all of these questions, then playing politics—this time, at least—is for you.

TABLE 13.3 Is Political Behavior Good or Bad for Organizations?

		Are the goals sanctioned by the organization?	
		Yes: The behavior is functional for the organization.	No: The behavior is dysfunctional for the organization.
Are the means sanctioned by the organization?	Yes	It is not political behavior, and it is functional for the organization. Example: A performance appraisal is conducted according to company guidelines.	It is not political behavior, and it is dysfunctional for the organization. Example: Workers threaten to form a union in order to obtain a large raise.
	No	It is political behavior, and it is functional for the organization. Example: A nonsanctioned team works off-site and outside of work hours to initiate an innovation that is subsequently adopted by the company.	It is political behavior and it is dysfunctional for the organization. Example: A network of disgruntled employees secretly sabotages a brilliant new manager.

Source: Based on B. T. Mayes and R. W. Allen, "Toward a Definition of Organizational Politics," *Academy of Management Review* 2 (4), 1977:672–678, 675.

Use Networks and Mentors

There is no question that networking with other individuals is one way to acquire power in organizations. From the individual's perspective, networking plays an important role in organizational success. One goal of networking is to establish effective relationships with key people who have the potential to help you in your career.[25] To this end, most managers develop personal networks both inside and outside their organizations. From a company's perspective, networking plays an important role in disseminating information and ideas throughout the organization.

coalitions

Networks which primarily exchange information and influence, and are characterized by clear norms, easy visibility to outsiders, and moderate representation across organizational levels.

cliques

Networks which primarily exchange information and emotional support, and are characterized by moderately clear norms, moderate visibility to outsiders, and a small representation across organizational levels.

Coalitions and **cliques** are two types of networks.[26] Coalitions exchange primarily information and influence, whereas cliques exchange information and emotional support. Coalitions are characterized by clear norms, easy visibility to outsiders, and moderate representation across organizational levels. Cliques are characterized by moderately clear norms, moderate visibility to outsiders, and a small representation across organizational levels.

CAREER ADVANTAGES OF NETWORKING An interesting study by researcher Fred Luthans took an in-depth look at 44 managers from different levels and types of organizations primarily in the service sector, including retail stores, hospitals, corporate headquarters, government agencies, insurance companies and a few manufacturing companies.[27] The managers were observed by trained researchers who recorded in detail their behaviors and activities. The first thing Luthans discovered was that actual managers engage in four main sets of activities:

1. Communication

   Exchanging information
   Paperwork

2. Traditional management

   Planning
   Decision making
   Controlling

3. Networking

   Interacting with outsiders
   Socializing/Politicking
   (Networking behaviors include non–work-related "chit chat," informal joking around, discussing rumors, hearsay and the grapevine, complaining, griping, putting others down, politicking and gamesmanship, dealing with customers, suppliers and vendors, attending external meetings, and doing/attending community service events.)

4. Human resource management

   Motivating/reinforcing
   Disciplining/punishing
   Managing conflict
   Staffing
   Training/Developing

In terms of how managers allocated their time, Luthans then compared "successful" managers—defined as those who are promoted relatively quickly—with "effective" managers—defined as those who run high-performing units and have satisfied, committed subordinates. Of the four standard managerial activities, *only* networking had a statistically significant relationship with being successful. The most successful managers (those in the top third on being promoted quickly) did much more networking and had slightly more routine communication than the least successful managers (those in the bottom third on being promoted quickly). Furthermore, they did not give much time to traditional management and human resource management activities!

A typical prescription for success from one of the "successful" managers was:

> I find that the way to get ahead around here is to be friendly with the right people, both inside and outside the firm. They get tired of always talking shop, so I find a common interest—with some it's sports, with others it's our kids—and interact with them on that level. The other formal stuff around the office is important but I really work at this informal side and have found it pays off when promotion time rolls around.[28]

In contrast, the study found that for the "effective" managers, the largest contribution to their effectiveness was routine communication and human resource management. Traditional management and networking made by far the least relative contribution to their effectiveness. A typical "effective" manager said:

> Both how much and how well things get done around here, as well as keeping my people loyal and happy, has to do with keeping them informed and involved. If I make a change in procedure or the guys upstairs give us a new process or piece of equipment to work with, I get my people's input and give them the full story before I lay it on them. Then I make sure they have the proper training and give them feedback on how they are doing. When they screw up, I let them know it, but when they do a good job, I let them know about that too.

Is it possible to be both a successful and an effective manager? You be the judge: Less than 10 percent of the managers were within both the top third of successful managers *and* the top third of effective managers. These individuals were the only ones who were able to adopt a balanced approach and still succeed.

NETWORKING ADVANTAGES (AND PROBLEMS) FOR COMPANIES When individuals use their networks to exchange knowledge, the networks contribute to the effectiveness and efficiency of their companies.[29] Therefore, companies in information-intensive industries find that helping individuals grow their knowledge networks helps generate and disseminate knowledge throughout their organization by increasing the number of communication channels and by widening existing channels. Managers can enhance network building by encouraging project teams to be connected with the rest of the organization (and beyond as needed), creating cross-functional teams, organizing social gatherings with different related organizational units, hiring individuals with established networks or a perceived potential of building them, measuring network development/activity as part of the individuals' annual review process, and encouraging individuals to provide assistance to others within the organization.

Just as there are networks of individuals that enhance productivity, so other networks hinder others from doing their work.[30] A group of coworkers who routinely criticize the company, leave work early and encourage others to do the same is an example of a **hindrance network**.

A practice related to networking is **mentoring**, the relationship between a senior, more experienced individual (the mentor) and a junior, less experienced individual (the protégé), in which the mentor helps the protégé navigate the world of work.[31] Mentors give their protégés primarily two kinds of support.[32] The first is career-related support, which includes giving them opportunities to attain visibility, sponsoring them for opportunities, coaching them, and protecting them. Mentors who offer sound career-related support develop protégés who are somewhat likely to have higher salaries and more promotions than others who are not mentored.[33] They are also somewhat likely to be more satisfied in their careers and their jobs.

Protégés report that, when it comes to career development, the most important things mentors can do for them are:[34]

- Offering networking opportunities outside the organization
- Offering opportunities for internal networking opportunities inside the organization including not only up and down the hierarchy but also laterally and cross-functionally
- Finding them intellectually challenging assignments that help them broaden their skills (as opposed to helping them deepen their knowledge in their particular specialty)
- Offering personalized feedback and advice on one's personal career strategy

hindrance network
A group of coworkers which hinders others from doing their work.

mentoring
The relationship between a senior, more experienced individual (the mentor) and a junior, less experienced individual (the protégé), in which the mentor helps the protégé navigate the world of work.

The second type of support that mentors offer is psychosocial support, which includes role modeling, acceptance, counseling, and friendship. In comparison with individuals who have no mentors, protégés that receive this sort of support are also somewhat more likely to receive higher salaries and more promotions, and to be more satisfied in their careers and jobs.

Although the popular press often assumes that having a mentor is a great career builder, the research evidence is not so strong. For one thing, people with mentors are, on average, only somewhat more likely than those without them to experience the benefits just mentioned. Also, these benefits have to be weighed against the costs of having a mentor. For example, building the relationship can be time consuming. It may also have political consequences: Your boss might become jealous of your mentor, for instance. At the same time, the right mentor can make your career. One such situation is presented in the story about how Barry Diller helped Michael Eisner in the case study "The Walt Disney Company" at the end of this chapter.

One factor to consider is that mentorship relationships can be negative as well as positive. For example, you and your mentor might not be well matched in terms of values, work styles, and personality.[35] This is a problem that is more likely to occur when the organization itself arranges the relationship through a formal program, rather than you and your mentor developing your relationship informally. Or your mentor may not have the expertise that you need. Your mentor might be manipulative, too, taking credit for your accomplishments or acting tyrannically. Of course, a mentor-protégé relationship can also mix the positive and the negative.[36] For example, a mentor might introduce his or her protégé to important contacts, but also sexually harass him or her.

Understand Empowerment

empowerment
Giving workers power by deliberately moving power downward in the organizational hierarchy.

Some companies deliberately give their employees power. **Empowerment** is the term used when a company moves power downward in its formal organizational hierarchy. According to researcher Edward Lawler, empowerment provides employees with power, information, knowledge, and rewards,[37] and is accomplished through a variety of employee involvement programs. These programs include quality circle programs, profit-sharing plans, and self-managed teams.

Is employee empowerment reality or rhetoric? Empowerment programs have been used widely in a variety of industries, and have been credited with a variety of positive company and employee impacts.[38] For example, retail giant Best Buy Company, Inc. asked officers of its 130 top-performing stores to mentor 130 executives above them on how to serve customers as well as motivate themselves and their teams.[39] As part of the program, each executive spent three days working in his or her assigned store, and the store managers spent a week visiting the corporate center to sit in on meetings and phone calls and provide ideas for improving executive support. The company credits this program with changing how these managers communicate with each other, adding a coaching dimension to the executive team's roles and making store managers more knowledgeable about how to ask for support.

At the same time, although there is much support for the idea of empowerment, some research suggests that after employees have been exposed to empowerment programs, they are *less* likely to be committed to their company and more likely to be committed to their union.[40] Although contextual issues such as layoffs certainly are a factor in such findings, it is also true that some individuals find that, over time, greater involvement in empowerment programs does not actually give them a greater voice. As a result, they become increasingly skeptical about their companies and more committed to their unions.

Related research in the aerospace industry in the United Kingdom suggests that programs designed to increase empowerment and participation can actually lead to a deficit in workplace decision making and deterioration in the quality of working life.[41] The authors of the research conclude, "Trust and mutuality mean that employees are expected to perform work for an employer to the best of their ability but in return employers should provide both meaningful work and job security. . ., [but] we have found considerable evidence of a one-way street; indeed, [we have found] evidence of inevitable management resistance to the principles of worker participation and security of employment."[42]

By way of explanation, consultant Vincent Caiman points out there is a range of democratic possibilities in today's corporations.[43] Although some companies are command-and-control all the way, others try to "liberate employee talent within an economically viable business model."[44] Most organizations are not highly democratic in the sense that they have a democratic governance system in place, yet many include democratic elements. A few are "democratically designed communities" combining ownership, employment, and viable business processes.

Other observers believe that it is pretty much inevitable that democratic processes in organizations will only be implemented if they contribute to competitive advantage and are accepted by top management. As asserted by Professor Jeffrey Kerr, "Organizational democracy . . . is not an easy system to live with once established. In place of straightforward commands and controls, every interaction is a potential negotiation.. . . Furthermore . . . no one with power naturally gives it up, and no rational person trades in an efficient decision process for one that is almost guaranteed to be less so."[45]

As a Leader, What Should You Know About Power?

Recall that leadership is the ability of an individual to motivate and enable others to contribute toward the effectiveness of his or her organization.[46] If leadership is the *process* of guiding others' actions toward the achievement of organizational goals,[47] power is the *capacity* to guide others' actions toward whatever goals are meaningful to the power-holder.[48] In other words, power is one means of accomplishing the work of leadership.

How Do Leaders Differ from Power-Holders?

Leaders and power-holders are not always one and the same. While leaders aim to enhance the effectiveness of their organization, power-holders seek to influence others for their own ends, independent of whether organizational effectiveness is enhanced. Good leadership is typically attributed to the individual who appears to have had the greatest positive impact on the behavior of many organization members, whereas a person's ability to wield power effectively is judged in terms of the power-holder's personal success and accomplishment.[49] Thus, all effective leaders have power, but not all power-holders are leaders.

Does Power Corrupt?

You have probably heard Lord Acton's famous dictum that, "Power corrupts, and absolute power corrupts absolutely." Do you believe it?

Having power does indeed influence a person's psychology, altering his or her attitudes and behaviors in predictable ways. Early research showed that managers who have power, in contrast with those who do not have much power, are more likely to 1) use more influence tactics, 2) value their subordinate's performance less, and 3) seek more psychological distance from their subordinates.[50] Recently researchers have found that having power causes individuals to have positive feelings, and to focus on rewards instead of punishments. It also causes them to be decisive and disinhibited.[51] Furthermore, as their power increases, individuals become even less deliberate and more action-oriented. Obviously, these changes can be either good or bad for their organizations, depending on whether decisiveness or deliberation is the approach needed at the moment.

Powerful leaders can cause significant organizational problems. One problem is that having power allows leaders to pursue their individual goals at the expense of organizational goals. Various experiments have shown that power-holders are likely to act selfishly and with reduced social inhibitions. For example, one laboratory study found that in contrast to those without power, power-holders will consume food when it is a scarce resource—taking the last cookie from the plate even though others do not get seconds—and will chew with their mouths open and make a general mess.[52] Men and women in positions of high power also flirt more aggressively than non-power-holders.[53] Men in positions of power are more likely than their peers to sexually harass their subordinates.[54] In addition, there are numerous publicized examples that demonstrate how and how often organizational leaders stiff their followers. Of course, when actions benefit the power-holder but not the people who depend on them, an organization has the makings of corruption.

An additional concern is that power-holders have a tendency to objectify other persons.[55] They tend to see others in terms of their physical attributes and material possessions, and to view them as a means to an end. They ignore the others' internal experiences—such human qualities as feelings, beliefs, and preferences. Power-holders would, for example, be more likely to use stereotypes to judge a job applicant, while non-power-holders would be more likely to consider information unique to the individual.[56] Power-holders also are more likely than the non-powerful to inaccurately represent members of minority groups as extremists,[57] to give less-than-deserved credit to their subordinates,[58] and, in group tasks, to fail to acknowledge the contributions of group members.[59]

If you are a leader who has power, is it inevitable that you will abuse your power? The authors of a recent review of leadership and power conclude that leaders should be taught to be aware that:[60]

- Having power is likely to incite them to act even when inaction is the preferable course.
- Power is likely to reduce their feelings of responsibility and empathy for others.
- Power is likely to accentuate the probability that they will use their authority even when other modes, such as encouraging participation, are preferable.

Power has to be managed, and self-awareness is one way to do so. Of course, organizational context also matters, and effective organizations use meritocracy, boards of directors, and organizational democracy as checks on individual power.

How Can Others Acquire Power Over You?

It is all too easy for managers to use organizational processes to induce compliance and obedience in subordinates. Of special concern is that, when power is abused through institutionalized processes, no one individual is accountable. Therefore, the abuse is likely to continue, because those in power are shielded from blame.[61]

In the next sections we will examine three types of power that may lead to abuse: authority, routinization, and dehumanization. We will also consider how some bosses dehumanize their employees through intimidation and lying, and why people stay with such toxic bosses.

What Factors Lead to Obedience and Resistance?

In 1974, psychologist Stanley Milgram asserted that "The social psychology of this century reveals a major lesson: Often, it is not so much the kind of person a man is as the kind of situation in which he finds himself that determines how he will act."[62] Milgram wondered how a civilized country like Germany could support a government as evil as Hitler's Third Reich. His world-famous experiments shed light on why people from any culture, including Americans, may be obedient to authority.[63]

Working out of his experimental laboratory at Yale University, Milgram set up a situation in which his trained confederate took the role of "learner" and the subject of the experiment took the role of teacher. After their initial meeting, the "learner" left the room and was not visible to the teacher. In fact, as soon as he was alone, the "learner" took out a tape recorder and used only prerecorded, standardized responses whenever he communicated (by intercom) with the teacher. The teacher was not aware of the subterfuge.

The teacher tested the "learner" on how well he had memorized word pairs. Whenever the "learner" made a mistake, the teacher was required to give him an electric shock—or at least what he *thought* was an electric shock. The teacher pulled a switch on an electric panel indicating voltage ranges from 15 to 450 volts. He was told to move one level higher on the shock generator each time the "learner" gave the wrong answer. The panel was clearly marked with such designations as "slight shock," "strong shock," "very strong shock," and "danger: severe shock."

At lower levels, the "learner" took the shock quietly, but later he groaned and protested. Whenever the teacher complained to the experimenter about this abuse, he was told, "Please continue," or "The experiment requires that you continue," or "You have no other choice, you *must* go on." The teachers had been told that the experiment was a study of memory, but actually it was of a study of their own obedience. The question was, when the "learner" failed to learn, and the teacher was told by an authority figure to continue shocking him, just how far up the shock scale would the teacher go?

Psychiatrists asked to predict how far up the voltage scale the teachers would go predicted that most people would not go very far at all. Yet Milgram found that 65 percent of

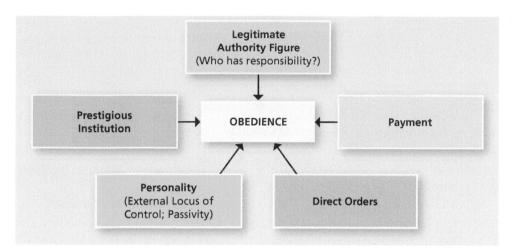

FIGURE 13.1

Why Individuals Obey Authority

the teachers administered the highest level of shocks (450 volts), and none quit before administering 300 volts. This happened despite the fact that the "learner" pleaded to be allowed out of the experiment.

A variety of situational factors explain why the teacher/subjects were obedient even though they believed they were harming the learner. The experiment was performed at a prestigious institution. Subjects were paid to participate. When a subject hesitated to shock the "learner," a legitimate authority figure in a white coat gave him or her direct orders to continue. Analysis of the experiment suggests that the obedient subjects actually saw the experimenter and the "learner" as more responsible for the learner's suffering than they themselves were. To some extent this was related to their personality: Individuals characterized by a high external locus of control and passivity were more likely to interpret their behavior this way.

See Figure 13.1 for a summary of the factors that Milgram determined lead to obedience.

How do the Milgram experiments relate to modern times? Well, imagine yourself at age 40, with a mortgage and two kids to put through college, working for, let's say, Enron in its heyday, when many people saw it as the company of the future. You know that your company is under investigation, and your boss tells you to spend the day shredding documents. Do you ask questions and refuse? Or do you say nothing and obey?

We have just discussed the factors that are likely to lead to your obedience. Now let's examine those that are likely to lead to your resistance.

To begin with, just understanding how authority works will arm you to some extent. Second, if you are not alone in your resistance, if others go along or at least support you in your own actions, you are much more likely to resist. It will help if you are already an assertive person with a high internal locus of control. Also, being materially independent — mortgage-free, with savings for college and money to live on—helps. Finally, having clear ethical beliefs of your own is a definite deterrent: We each need to take the time to think about what these are. (This is one reason why taking a course in business ethics is such a good idea.) These principles are summarized in Figure 13.2.

How Are Employees Subject to Routinization and Dehumanization?

Along with the process of authority just discussed, organizational routinization and dehumanization can also disempower and control workers.[64] **Routinization** is the transformation of an immoral job into a "routine, mechanical, highly programmed operation."[65] Routinization reduces moral resistance to an immoral job because it encourages mechanical, mindless action and inhibits moral questioning. Workers focus on the details of the job rather than on its meaning. For example, a journalist might be directed by her boss to "*always* tell both sides of the story." By this simple act of routinization, the reporter loses the power to interpret in complex ways what he or she is really seeing and believing.[66] Routinization is often accompanied by the use of **euphemisms** that further sanitize a person's work, disguising its immoral and unpleasant actions. To the Nazis, the Jews were

routinization
The transformation of an immoral job into a "routine, mechanical, highly programmed operation" by encouraging mechanical, mindless action and inhibiting moral questioning.

euphemisms
Words with falsely pleasant overtones which disguise their true immoral and/or unpleasant meanings.

FIGURE 13.2

Why Individuals Resist Authority

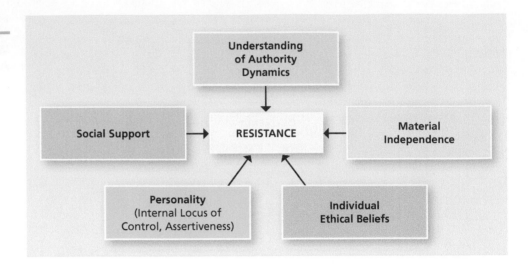

never "people"—they were "items" or "pieces." The Holocaust was "the final solution to the Jewish problem," not mass murder.[67]

amoralization

The absence of moral standards which results from routinization.

Routinization results in **amoralization**, which is the removal of moral standards. To illustrate, consider **corporate greening**, the phenomenon of companies taking responsibility for the environmental effects of their operations. While overall this trend is a positive one, researchers have discovered that there is a tendency for corporate greening to be accompanied by a process of amoralization.[68] This is because, as corporations take on environmentally sensitive changes, their leaders often argue that they do so only because the changes affect the bottom line. In this way, champions of greening policies in companies tend to downplay the moral meaning and significance of the greening efforts, essentially reinventing greening as organizational routine. The result is a fundamental denial of the legitimacy of moral reasoning in the company.

corporate greening

The phenomenon of companies taking responsibility for the environmental effects of their operations.

dehumanization

The process of depriving individuals of their human qualities and attributes, of their individuality.

Dehumanization is the process of depriving individuals of their human qualities and attributes; of their individuality.[69] For example, the process of entering a hospital is often dehumanizing, so much so that patient advocates suggest patients display personal items and pictures to remind their doctors, and themselves, that they have a unique identity that matters. Not allowing individuals to express their individuality at work—for example, by forbidding them to personalize their own work space—is one form of dehumanization. Like routinization, dehumanization reduces the likelihood that an individual will ask moral questions.

How Do Some Managers Intimidate Their Employees?

According to social psychologist Roderick M. Kramer, some leaders gain power through intimidation. They use several different tactics. One is to "get up close and personal,"[70] using direct confrontation and invading the personal space of another individual. For example, Harvey Weinstein, head of Miramax, once attempted to intimidate petite Stacey Snider, chair of Universal Pictures, in public by towering over her, jabbing a finger in her face and screaming, "You're going to go down for this!"[71]

Another intimidation tactic is getting angry. Anger deters potential challengers. Because most people don't like confrontation, they will concede ground or even give up altogether to avoid an unpleasant encounter with an angry intimidator.

A third tactic is to keep people guessing about what you are thinking, including how you are judging them. By not being open and transparent you can more easily change your mind without losing credibility. Also, subordinates of silent, sullen bosses are forced to try to figure out whether their behavior is pleasing their boss or not, and may worry a great deal about how to please him or her. Carly Fiorina of Hewlett-Packard and Michael Eisner of Disney have both been known to give employees the silent treatment.

Examples of intimidating bosses who have inspired loyalty in their followers are Martha Stewart and Steven Jobs. An executive who worked with Stewart has reported, "She had the most amazingly well-organized and disciplined mind I've ever known.... She could be incredibly impatient and brusque if you were slow on the uptake—but if you could keep up with her, and perform to her standard, it was tremendously satisfying."[72] One who worked for Jobs has said, "[He] was the most difficult human being I've ever worked for—but he was also the most technologically brilliant. No one knew technology better than he did, and no one had a clearer sense of where it was going."[73] Another Jobs employee has said, "You just dreaded letting him down. He believed in you so strongly that the thought of disappointing him just killed you."[74]

Some executives believe that in order to use their legitimate power more effectively they should also learn to be intimidating. As one puts it, "I would love to have Carly [Fiorina]'s ability to stare down her opponents."[75] Clearly, more research needs to be done on how effective intimidation may be as a management technique.

How Powerful Is Deception?

Machiavellianism is the extent to which individuals exhibit a cool detachment from others and may be, as a result, more manipulative and impersonal. A Machiavellian individual would be likely to agree with the statements in Table 13.4, and to disagree with statements such as "Most men are brave," or "All in all, it is better to be humble and honest than to be important and dishonest," or "Most people who get ahead in the world lead clean, moral lives."

Over the years, psychological tests for Machiavellianism have failed to meet professional standards for reliability. Yet interest in the concept remains. There is a certain fascination—perhaps an instinct for self-protection—in trying to understand an individual who believes that "the best way to handle people is to tell them what they want to hear."[76] A recent study suggests, for instance, that people higher in Machiavellianism are more likely to make deliberate choices about what power tactics to use, and as a consequence, often use softer tactics such as rational persuasion and consultation rather than harder tactics such as pressure and coalitions.[77] However, more clarification of the concept of Machiavellianism itself has been recommended before we apply it broadly.

What Is the Allure of Toxic Leaders?

Toxic leaders engage in destructive behaviors that inflict serious and enduring harm on their followers and organizations. They do destructive things *including* leaving their followers worse off than when they found them, feeding them illusions that enhance the leader's power while impairing the followers' capacity to act (for example, convincing them that they are the only ones who can save the organization), playing to their basest fears, and stifling constructive criticism.[78] Leaders may become more toxic, as we have seen, by the mere fact of having power. They may also get that way because of their personal narcissism, paranoia, grandiosity, or malevolence.

> **Machiavellianism**
> The extent to which individuals exhibit a cool detachment from others and may be more manipulative and impersonal as a result.

TABLE 13.4 Machiavellian Beliefs

1. Never tell anyone the real reason you did something unless it is useful to do so.
2. The best way to handle people is to tell them what they want to hear.
3. It is safest to assume that all people have a vicious streak and it will come out when they are given a chance.
4. Generally speaking, men won't work hard unless they're forced to do so.
5. Anyone who completely trusts anyone else is asking for trouble.
6. The biggest difference between most criminals and other people is that the criminals are stupid enough to get caught.
7. It is wise to flatter important people.
8. It is hard to get ahead without cutting corners here and there.
9. People suffering from incurable diseases should have the choice of being put painlessly to death.
10. Most men forget more easily the death of their father than the loss of their property.

Source: R. Christie and Others, "Machiavellianism," in J. P. Robinson and P. R. Shaver, *Measures of Social Psychological Attitudes* (Ann Arbor, MI: Survey Research Center, Institute for Social Research, 1973):590–594.

Why do individuals follow Machiavellian, toxic leaders? Of course, the Milgram experiments suggest we might follow them because we accept their authority. Yet why would we accept authority from someone who inflicts harm on *us*?

Professor Jean Lipman-Blumen points out that some potent psychological factors, in ourselves, may explain why people accept toxic leaders.[79] These include our need for reassuring authority figures to fill our parents' shoes, our need for security and certainty and the willingness to sacrifice freedom to achieve them, our need to feel chosen or special, our fear of ostracism and isolation, and our fear of personal powerlessness to challenge a bad leader. Because of these factors, we often fail to challenge toxic leaders; instead, we escape them, or we adapt to the toxic organizations they create.

Perhaps individuals in today's business organizations are becoming more savvy about toxic bosses. A 2002 Aspen Institute poll of MBA students' attitudes toward ethics found an increase in students' willingness to speak up about their ethical objections in their companies, and an interest in trying to get others to join them in addressing their concerns.[80] Certainly these young managers are on the right track. Not only do individuals have to deal with their own anxieties and needs, they have to understand what makes people speak out. The decision to protest toxic leadership depends on many factors. For example, you are more likely to speak out if a harmful act affects someone close to you (for example, someone who works in your department). You are also more likely to speak out if you have a significant amount of information about the problem rather than just the bare outlines, if you identify with the victim because you share a similar history or culture, if you are particularly willing to take risks or have a strong sense of responsibility, if many relatively powerful people know about the toxic behavior, and if someone else also protests.

According to Lipman-Blumen, companies can avoid toxic leaders by selecting leaders who are not neurotically driven to achieve power. They also can create respectable departure options, so difficult leaders do not lose face when they step down to make room for new people with fresh approaches. Companies can design open and democratic policies and practices and protect whistle-blowers from reprisals. Finally, they can design accountability forums into the decision-making process, so that every major decision is scrutinized by independent groups.

How Does a Person's View of Power Depend on Culture?

Reactions to how power is wielded in a company depend in part on how people's cultural differences affect their perceptions of politics, conflict, and networking. We will consider, first, what the research says about differences based on national and ethnic culture, and then about those based on organizational culture.

Effects of National Culture

Some studies have found universal trends in how power is wielded in different cultures. For example, a study in six cultures found that the power tactics universally believed to be effective are rational persuasion, collaboration, and consultation.[81] Pressure, gift-giving, and socializing are considered to be the least effective tactics.

Other studies have found some interesting cultural differences. For example, a comparison of British and Israeli employees facing organizational politics found that the British employees were more likely to be affected by the politics. Faced with political behavior, they developed higher intentions of leaving their organizations and lower levels of loyalty and job satisfaction.[82] In another comparative cross-cultural study, direct, task-oriented power tactics were rated more highly by Western managers than by Chinese managers.[83]

Even in cultures that appear on the surface to be quite similar, differences in the use of power tactics can cause interpersonal problems. For example, pressure is a more acceptable tactic in Hong Kong than in China or Taiwan.[84] Pressure is unexpected and unwelcome by ethnic Chinese and Taiwanese doing business in Hong Kong.

Certainly there is enough evidence to caution managers about how to wield power when they enter another culture. More research is needed on this important subject.

Effects of Organizational Culture

As a new member of an organization, it is important to understand that organizational cultures differ significantly in how people use power and how their employees react to the existing power structures. Consider this description of how power is implemented in one sort of company, referred to as a "jungle":

> Many people will do whatever is necessary—lie, back-bite, rumormonger, sabotage, and so forth—to get what they want....
>
> Participants in this jungle activity often rationalize their actions.. . . These rationalizations lead to jockeying for position, finding an ally base, or any of the other myriad actions that many call appropriate strategy, but really are little more than political maneuvering. Organizations are not guiltless. Some, in fact, may actually support organizational politics, as managers and executives believe the best person for a position is the one who can 'fight their way to the top.'[85]

And here is an interesting description of power relationships in a highly successful Silicon Valley company that supplies high-performance computer products:

> Link.Com [a pseudonym] had a masculine culture, characterized by self-promotion, overt struggles for competition, and interpersonal norms that condoned yelling and other forms of controlled aggression. As the masculinity literature predicts for technical occupations, these competitive struggles were intense at Link.Com. It is possible . . . that these competitions were particularly fierce when one or more of [the] high-ranking women were present.[86]

At Link.Com it was also the case that women who had considerable formal power nevertheless had little informal power. Evidently, the male networks excluded them and rewarded unqualified male group members for their loyalty. Meetings required "forceful, brutally honest, even semiviolent argumentation,"[87] and opportunities for challenging work went to those who promoted themselves most actively. One woman (who subsequently started her own company), was told by an external consultant hired by the company that her open, participative, and collaborative personality would make it hard for her to survive in the company.

In sum, power relationships are crucial influences in any organizational culture, and it is useful for you to understand how power is wielded differently in different companies.

In Conclusion

In this chapter we have explored the dynamics of power and influence, including how you can get power and how power-holders can influence you.

Apply What You Have Learned...

World Class Company: The Walt Disney Company

You may have heard of Michael Eisner and the power struggles that surrounded him during his years as chief executive of the Walt Disney Company. Eisner is known for his feuds not only with Walt Disney's nephew Roy Disney, but also with Apple founder and Pixar boss Steve Jobs, and with Hollywood power-broker Michael Ovitz. In 2004, in an extraordinary move, 45 percent of Disney's shareholders withheld their vote for Eisner's reelection to the board, and soon afterward he agreed to step down as chairman and, later, as chief executive. He had led the company for 20 years. His replacement as Chairman of the Board was his friend and long-time board member and former U.S. Senator George J. Mitchell, who also holds the post of Chairman of a prestigious law firm.[88]

Eisner was criticized for his tightly controlling style, micromanaging both people and strategy. His strategic planning department was nicknamed "department of business prevention," because it so often vetoed ideas it did not create itself.[89] In a letter announcing his resignation (under pressure from Eisner) from the Disney Company, Roy Disney noted that although Eisner had had more than 10 years of early success running the company, he had turned it into a "rapacious, soul-less" organization "always looking for 'the quick buck' rather than the long-term value, which is leading to a loss of public trust."[90] Disney criticized Eisner for strategic failures such as timidity in investing in the theme park business and allowing ABC programming to decline. He asserted Eisner had failed to build constructive relationships with such creative partners as Pixar and Miramax.

Eisner started out in the entertainment industry in a summer job as a page at NBC studios in New York.[91] After graduating from college, he got a job as a clerk at NBC, moved to the programming department at CBS six weeks later, and in 1966 became assistant to the national programming director at ABC, a post he held for two years. By 1976, he had logged a decade of increasing successes in programming, including fostering popular programs such as *All My Children* and *Happy Days*. In 1976 his mentor Barry Diller, chairman of the board of Paramount Pictures, hired him as president and chief operating officer of Paramount Pictures. Eisner was 34. At Paramount Eisner kept costs down and moved the company from last place to first place among the six major studios. In 1984 he left Paramount to become chairman and chief executive officer of The Walt Disney Company. He turned what was mainly an animation studio and theme park operation into a major entertainment company.

In a 2006 interview, Eisner said, "My best bosses were the Disney shareholders, because they were so enthusiastic about the company. This was always true, whether it was a new movie, a park opening, or return on investment. Individually, my best boss was Barry Diller, because he was smart. When you walk in with a good idea and your boss gets it, that's what you want. He or she will either say, 'Yes, go with it' or tell you something that adds value. If she isn't smart, you're in trouble."[92]

Contrast Eisner's style with that of George W. Bodenheimer, president of ESPN Networks and ABC Sports, today a key part of the Disney empire. In this role, Bodenheimer has overseen some 50 different businesses, including on-demand video, wireless, ESPN Zone restaurants, and the daily program *SportsCenter*. Bodenheimer is modest, preferring to remain behind the scenes and to delegate power. For example, when he hired an executive to revamp the company's broadband service, he simply wrote her notes every week or so with suggestions, and gave plenty of encouragement. "He would send hand-written notes.... He would offer up [notes such as] 'Make it the ultimate on-demand product for the sports fan and one that is as flexible as possible,'" the executive says.[93] Bodenheimer has little presence in the media.

Bodenheimer has not changed the high energy, cocky ESPN corporate culture established by his predecessor; he knows that its youthful bent is important to his customers. He personally stays in touch with customers, by doing things like mingling among the crowds, unnoticed, at sports events. Next up for Bodenheimer are battles with competing national sports channels, and extending the ESPN brand to hardware so fans can take it with them anywhere.

Discuss

1. How did Eisner use power in his career? (Consider his preparation, power sources, and power tactics, and whether his political behavior was effective.)
2. Contrast Eisner with Bodenheimer in terms of how they have wielded power.
3. Why do you think the Board replaced Eisner with Senator Mitchell?
4. Do a Web search to find out who is in charge of Disney now. Discuss.

Advice from the Pros

Sharing Power at the Top

Can two people run a company without getting into a power struggle?[94] Although many believe that they cannot, Jerry Greenberg and Stuart Moore, who are the co-CEOs of the consulting firm Sapient, disagree.

Greenberg and Moore offer this advice to companies considering having two people at the top:

- Appoint a referee. From the very beginning of their co-leadership, Greenberg and Moore chose three colleagues who would act as tie-breakers if they could not come to an agreement.
- Don't confuse your employees by having them report to two bosses. Individuals report either to Greenberg or Moore.
- Take distinct roles. Greenberg does the outside contact work, including marketing and investor rela-

tions, whereas Moore handles the day-to-day running of the company.

- Admit that you cannot do everything. The partnership won't work if one person really wants to be running the whole show, or thinks he or she ought to be because of his or her superior talent.

Discuss

1. How is company power increased by the Greenberg–Moore alliance? How is it decreased?
2. How is Greenberg's and Moore's individual power increased or decreased?
3. Would you personally want to be in a CEO-sharing position? Why or why not?
4. Make a summary list of the pros and cons of having two people sharing the CEO position.

Gain Experience

Grow Your Network

1. Think about whom you know, at this time, who might help you in any way in the business world. Include relatives and friends. Draw this network by putting yourself at the center of a page, and then arranging the contacts around you. Follow these guidelines:

A. The ones you put closest to you should be those you can contact by phone pretty much any time.

B. Those farther away should be those whom you would contact by phone only during business hours.

C. If you need to go through a third party to get to a contact (for example, if you need to ask one party to mention you to another party before you would call that person), draw an arrow from the closer contact to the more remote contact.

2. With a partner, describe your network. For example: How many people are in your network? How influential are they? How helpful would they be, really? Exactly how might they help you?

3. Now imagine and draw your ideal business network. Begin by thinking about exactly how people in a network could help you reach your career goals, and then figure out what types of people can fill the positions. You do not need to have specific people in mind. For instance, you might include "Someone with contacts in x industry" and "Someone who knows me well enough to give a thorough recommendation to an employer."

4. Explain your ideal business network to your partner.

5. Discuss with the class: What does a really good business network look like? How do you create one? How do you maintain it over time?

Can You Solve This Manager's Problem?

Should You Play Politics?

Carla is the manager of the women's cosmetics department of a store in a major retail chain. In her first months on the job, Carla observed other managers at her level being particularly nice to and doing many favors for their mutual senior manager, Marguerite. They would often lunch with her, bring her coffee, and schmooze with her after hours. A busy mother of a 1-year-old, Carla herself worked hard but did not worry about

extending herself to please her boss. She was proud of her performance in her job and in terms of sales she was one of the top producers in the entire chain.

Carla had made one friend among her peers—Darlene in sportswear, with whom she had a quick lunch every few days. One day, Darlene said she had been asked to stay on after her shift to watch Marguerite's two children while Marguerite went to a meeting. Carla was surprised. She said, "I sure wish I could get that kind of help with my kid. Don't you have any commitments after work?" "Yes, I did," said Darlene, "But I thought it was really important to help her out. When I do stuff like that I get to know her and her work even better, so maybe one day I can step into her shoes. You should be doing the same thing, by the way."

"What?" asked Carla.

"Play politics," laughed Darlene.

"Oh, right." Carla wasn't so sure. She wondered what would she have done if Marguerite had asked her. What would have been the consequences for refusing?

Discuss

1. Is taking care of Marguerite's children in line with Carla's personal goals?
2. Is taking care of Marguerite's children in line with the company's goals? How could Carla find out whether such requests are appropriate in her organization's culture?
3. If Carla were to refuse this or similar requests, what is likely to happen in her relationship with Marguerite? with other coworkers?
4. Is looking after Marguerite's children after hours a kind of political behavior that is in line with your personal beliefs, values, and style? Do you consider Marguerite's request to be ethical?
5. Which is your position? Defend it.
   a. Effective employees have little time for politics. OR
   b. You always have to play politics to get ahead.
   a. Effective organizations discourage politics. OR
   b. Effective organizations encourage politics.

Chapter Summary and Key Terms

What is power?

Power is the ability to mobilize resources to accomplish some end. The terms *power* and *influence* are used synonymously. *Authority* suggests control or command over others that is legitimized by a group or organization.

power 348
influence 348
authority 348

How can you identify the sources of power in your company?

In organizations, power can be either formal or informal. There are six bases of interpersonal power: Three soft/interpersonal bases are referent, expert, and information power, and three hard/formal bases are coercive, reward, and legitimate power. Other sources of power include manipulation, providing information indirectly, influencing third parties, and control of resources.

power sources 348
power tactics 348
formal power 348
hierarchy 348
informal power 348

How can you acquire power in your organization?

You acquire power in your organization by setting a goal, acquiring sources of power, preparing for the use of power, and then acting. You can apply any of a number of power tactics, including rational persuasion, building coalitions, engaging in political behavior, and networking.

political behavior 352
coalitions 354
cliques 354
hindrance network 355
mentoring 355
empowerment 356

As a leader, what should you know about power?

The idea that power corrupts is true. Managers with power tend to distance themselves from subordinates, for example, and they are somewhat likely to act selfishly and with reduced social inhibitions.

How can others acquire power over you?

Organizations are powerful entities that may use authority, routinization, and dehumanization to induce compliance in their workers. Factors that lead to obedience to authority include working for a prestigious company, being paid well, and being given a direct order by a legitimate authority figure. You resist authority by developing your individual ethical beliefs in advance, by being financially independent, by mustering social support for your views, and by understanding the dynamics of authority.

Toxic leaders engage in destructive behaviors that harm their employees and the organization. To some extent, people follow toxic leaders because of their own needs, including the needs for security and the need to feel chosen.

routinization 359
euphemisms 359
amoralization 360
corporate greening 360
dehumanization 360
Machiavellianism 361

How does a person's view of power depend on culture?

Cultural differences may influence your perceptions of organizational politics, conflict, networking, and related phenomena. For example, applying direct pressure is more acceptable in Hong Kong than in Taiwan.

Explorations

1. Nepotism
Web search "nepotism" to find out more about how, where, and why it is used.

2. Obedience and resistance today
Many people believe individuals today are less conforming than they were at the time of the Milgram experiments. In your university databases and online, look for research confirming or disconfirming this view. Discuss this idea with someone from an earlier generation.

3. Cross-cultural differences
Two classic treatises on power are Sun Tzu's *The Art of War* and Niccolo Machiavelli's *On the Art of War.* Pick up one or both of these books and describe how their views influence today's approaches to organizational power. Consider how they exemplify cross-cultural differences in how power is perceived and implemented.

4. Corporate Boards
Go to the Web site for any corporation and read the bios of the board of directors. What does this information tell you about power in that company?

References

[1] B. Walters, Interview with Donald Trump, (ABC, Prentice Hall Video, 2005).

[2] D. C. McClelland, *Power: The Inner Experience* (New York: Irvington, 1975); N. Roberts, "Organizational Power Styles: Collective and Competitive Power under Varying Organizational Conditions," *Journal of Applied Behavioral Science 22,* 1986:443–458; D. Krackhardt, "Assessing the Political Landscape: Structure, Cognition, and Power in Organizations," *Administrative Science Quarterly 35* (2), June 1990:342–368.

[3] R. Dahl, "The Concept of Power," *Behavioral Science 2,* 1957:201–18, 202–203.

[4] D. Willer, "Power-at-a-Distance," *Social Forces 81* (4), June 2003.1295–1334.

[5] B. H. Raven, J. Schwarzwald, and M. Koslowsky, "Conceptualizing and Measuring a Power/Interaction Model of Interpersonal Influence," *Journal of Applied Social Psychology 28* (4), February 15, 1998:307–332.

[6] D. Krackhardt, "Assessing the Political Landscape: Structure, Cognition, and Power in Organizations," *Administrative Science Quarterly 35* (2), June 1990:342–368; J. M. Peiró and J. L. Meliá, "Formal and Informal Interpersonal Power in Organizations: Testing a Bifactorial Model of Power in Role-Sets," *Applied Psychology: An International Review 52* (1), January 2003:14–35; K. Lamertz and K. Aquino, "Social Power, Social Status and Perceptual Similarity of Workplace Victimization: A Social Network Analysis of Stratification," *Human Relations 57* (7), July 2004:795–822.

[7] B. H. Raven, J. Schwarzwald, and M. Koslowsky, "Conceptualizing and Measuring a Power/Interaction Model of Interpersonal Influence," *Journal of Applied Social Psychology 28* (4), February 15, 1998:307–332; M. Koslowsky, J. Schwarzwald, and S. Ashuri, "On the Relationship between Subordinates' Compliance to Power Sources and Organisational Attitudes," *Applied Psychology: An International Review 50* (3), Summer 2001:455–476.

[8] M. Koslowsky, J. Schwarzwald, and S. Ashuri, "On the Relationship between Subordinates' Compliance to Power Sources and Organisational Attitudes," *Applied Psychology: An International Review 50* (3), Summer 2001:455–476.

[9] J. Schwarzwald, M. Koslowsky, and V. Agassi, "Captain's Leadership Type and Police Officers' Compliance to Power Bases," *European Journal of Work & Organizational Psychology 10* (3), September 2001:273–290.

[10] J. P. Kotter, *Power and Influence* (New York: Free Press, 1985).

[11] B. H. Raven, "The Bases of Power: Origins and Recent Developments," *Journal of Social Issues 49* (4), 1993:227–251.

[12] J. Pfeffer, *Power in Organizations* (Cambridge, MA: Ballinger Publishing Company, 1981).

[13] H. Mintzberg, *Power In and Around Organizations* (Upper Saddle River, NJ: Prentice Hall, 1983).

[14] B. H. Raven, "The Bases of Power: Origins and Recent Developments," *Journal of Social Issues 49* (4), 1993:227–251.

[15] B. H. Raven, "The Bases of Power: Origins and Recent Developments," *Journal of Social Issues 49* (4), 1993:227–251.

[16] D. Kipnis, S. M. Schmidt, and I. Wilkinson, "Intraorganizational Influence Tactics: Explorations in Getting One's Way," *Journal of Applied Psychology 65* (4), August 1980:440–452; C. A. Schriesheim and T. R. Hinkin, "Influence Tactics Used by Subordinates: A Theoretical and Empirical Analysis and Refinement of the Kipnis, Schmidt and Wilkinson Subscales," *Journal of Applied Psychology 75* (3), 1990:246–257; G. Yukl and C. M. Falbe, "Influence Tactics in Upward, Downward, and Lateral Influence Attempts," *Journal of Applied Psychology 75,* 1990:132–140; G. Yukl, C. M. Falbe, and J. Y. Youn, "Patterns of Influence Behaviour for Managers," *Group and Organization Management 18,* 1993:5–28; W. A. Hochwarter, A. W. Pearson, G. R. Ferris, P. L. Perrewe, and D. A. Ralston, "A Reexamination of Schriesheim and Hinkin's (1990) Measure of Upward Influence," *Educational and Psychological Measurement 60* (5), October 2000:755–771; G. Yukl, P. P. Fu, and R. McDonald, "Cross-Cultural Differences in Perceived Effectiveness of Influence Tactics for Initiating or Resisting Change," *Applied Psychology: An International Review 52* (1), January 2003:68–82.

[17] G. Yukl, C. M. Falbe, and J. Y. Youn, "Patterns of Influence Behavior for Managers," *Journal of Organizational Behavior 20,* 1993:5–28.

[18] D. Farrell and J. C. Petersen, "Patterns of Political Behavior in Organizations," *Academy of Management Review 7* (3), 1982:403–412.

[19] D. L. Madison, R. W. Allen, L. W. Porter, P. A. Renwick, and B. T. Mayes, "Organizational Politics: An Exploration of Managers' Perceptions," *Human Relations 33,* 1980:79–100.

[20] R. S. Cropanzano, J. C. Howes, A. A. Grandey, and P. Toth, "The Relationship of Organizational Politics and Support to

Work Behaviors, Attitudes, and Stress," *Journal of Organizational Behavior 18*, 1997:159–180; K. M. Kacmar, D. P. Bozeman, D. S. Carlson, and W. P. Anthony, "A Partial Test of the Perceptions of Organizational Politics Model," *Human Relations 52*, 1999:383–416; L. A. Witt, A. L. Patti, and W. L. Farmer, "Organizational Politics and Work Identity as Predictors of Organizational Commitment," *Journal of Applied Social Psychology 32* (3), March 2002:486–499; E. Vigoda, "Stress-Related Aftermaths to Workplace Politics: The Relationship among Politics, Job Distress, and Aggressive Behavior in Organizations," *Journal of Organizational Behavior 23* (5), August 2002:571–591; K. J. Harris, M. James, and R. Boonthanom, "Perceptions of Organizational Politics and Cooperation as Moderators of the Relationship between Job Strains and Intent to Turnover," *Journal of Managerial Issues 17* (1), Spring 2005:26–42.

21 G. R. Ferris and K. M. Kacmar, "Perceptions of Organizational Politics," *Journal of Management 18* (1), 1992:93–116.

22 D. Farrell and J. C. Petersen, "Patterns of Political Behavior in Organizations," *Academy of Management Review 7* (3), 1982:403–412.

23 B. T. Mayes and R. W. Allen, "Toward a Definition of Organizational Politics," *Academy of Management Review 2 (4)*, 1977:672–678.

24 D. R. Comer, "Preparing Students to Determine Personally Appropriate Political Behavior," *Journal of Management Education 16* (3), 1992:327–340.

25 M. L. Forrett and T. W. Dougherty, "Correlates of Networking Behavior for Managerial and Professional Employees," *Group & Organization Management 26* (3), 2001:283–311.

26 N. M. Tichy, "Networks in Organizations," in P. C. Nystrom and W. H. Starbuck, eds., *Handbook of Organizational Design: Remodeling Organizations and Their Environments 2* (London: Oxford University Press, 1981):225–249.

27 F. Luthans, "Successful vs. Effective Real Managers," *Academy of Management Executive 2* (2), 1988:127–132.

28 F. Luthans, "Successful vs. Effective Real Managers," *Academy of Management Executive 2* (2), 1988:127–132,130.

29 M. Hoegl, P. K. Parboteeah, and C. L. Munson, "Team-Level Antecedents of Individuals' Knowledge Networks," *Decision Sciences 34* (4), Fall 2003:741–770.

30 R. T. Sparrowe, R. C. Linden, S. J. Wayne, and M. L. Kraimer, "Social Networks and the Performance of Individuals and Groups," *Academy of Management Journal 44*, 2001:316–325.

31 K. E. Kram, *Mentoring at Work* (Glenview, IL: Scott, Foresman and Co., 1985).

32 K. E. Kram, *Mentoring at Work* (Glenview, IL: Scott, Foresman and Co., 1985); R. A. Noe, "An Investigation of the Determinants of Successful Assigned Mentoring Relationships," *Personnel Psychology 41* , 1988:457–479.

33 T. D. Allen, L. T. Eby, M. L. Poteet, E. Lentz, and L. Lima, "Career Benefits Associated with Mentoring for Protégés: A Meta-Analysis," *Journal of Applied Psychology 89* (1), 2004:127–136.

34 L. T. Eby and S. E. McManus, "Protégés Most Positive Mentoring Experience," In R. Day and T. D. Allen (Co-Chairs), *Underlying Processes Responsible for Beneficial Mentorships: Iimplications of Emerging Research,* (Toronto, Canada: Annual meeting of the Society for Industrial and Organizational Psychology, 2002).

35 L. T. Eby, S. McManus, S. A. Simon, and J. E. A. Russell, "An Examination of Negative Mentoring Experiences from the Protégé's Perspective," *Journal of Vocational Behavior 57*, 200:1–21.

36 L. Eby, M. Butts, and A. Lockwood, "Protégés Negative Mentoring Experiences: Construct Development and Nomological Validation," *Personnel Psychology 57*, 2004:411–447.

37 E. E. Lawler III, G. E. Ledford Jr., and S. A. Mohrman, *Employee Involvement in America: A Study of Contemporary Practice* (Houston, TX: American Productivity & Quality Center, 1989).

38 E. E. Lawler, III, S. Mohrman, and G. E. Ledford, Jr. *Employee Involvement and Total Quality Management: Practices and Results in Fortune 1000 companies.* (San Francisco: Jossey-Bass, 1992).

39 L. K. Johnson, "Company Debriefing: How Best Buy's Executives Learn from the Front Lines," *Harvard Management Update* 10 (10) October 2005, 3–4. Article reprint U0510B.

40 R. C. Hoell, "How Employee Involvement Affects Union Commitment," *Journal of Labor Research 25* (2), Spring 2004:267–277.

41 A. Danford, M. Richardson, P. Stewart, S. Tailby, and M. Upchurch, "High Performance Work Systems and Workplace Partnership: A Case Study of Aerospace Workers," *New Technology, Work & Employment 19* (1), March 2004:14–29.

42 A. Danford, M. Richardson, P. Stewart, S. Tailby, and M. Upchurch, "High Performance Work Systems and Workplace Partnership: A Case Study of Aerospace Workers," *New Technology, Work & Employment 19* (1), March 2004:14–29, 26–27.

43 V. F. Caimano, "Executive Commentary," *Academy of Management Executive 18* (3), 2004:96–97.

44 V. F. Caimano, "Executive Commentary," *Academy of Management Executive 18* (3), 2004:96–97, 96.

45 J. L. Kerr, "The Limits of Organizational Democracy," *Academy of Management Executive 18* (3), 2004:81–95, 93.

46 R. J. House and M. Javidan, "Overview of GLOBE," in R. J. House, P. J. Hanges, M. Javidan, P. W. Dorfman and V. Gupta, eds., *Culture, Leadership and Organizations: The GLOBE Study of 62 Societies* (Thousand Oaks, CA: Sage Publications, 2004):9–28:15.

47 E. P. Hollander, "Leadership and Power," in G. Lindzey and E. Aronson, eds., *The Handbook of Social Psychology 2*, 2nd ed. (New York: Random House, 1985):485–538.

48 P. M. Blau, *Exchange and Power in Social Life* (New York: Wiley, 1964); D. Keltner, D. H. Gruenfeld, and C. Anderson, "Power, Approach, and Inhibition," *Psychological Review 110*, 2003:265–284; D. H. Gruenfeld, D. J. Keltner, and C. Anderson, "The Effects of Power on Those Who Possess It: How Social Structure Can Affect Social Cognition," in G. Bodenhausen and A. Lambert, eds., *Foundations of Social Cognition: A Festschrift in Honor of Robert S. Wyer, Jr.* (Mahwah, NJ: Lawrence Erlbaum Associates, 2003):237–256.

49 J. C. Magee, D. H. Gruenfeld, D. J. Keltner, and A. D. Galinsky, "Leadership and the Psychology of Power," in D. M. Messick and R. M. Kramer, eds., *The Psychology of Leadership: New Perspectives and Research* (Mahwah, NJ: Lawrence Erlbaum Associates, Publishers, 2005):275–293, 277.

50 D. Kipnis, *The Power-holders* (Chicago, IL: University of Chicago Press, 1976).

51 D. Keltner, D. H. Gruenfeld, and C. Anderson, "Power, Approach, and Inhibition," *Psychological Review 110*, 2003:265–284.

52 G. Ward and D. Keltner, *Power and the Consumption of Resources*, unpublished manuscript, 1998.

53 G. C. Gonzaga, D. Keltner, E. A. Londahl, and M. D. Smith, "Love and the Commitment Problem in Romantic Relations and Friendship," *Journal of Personality & Social Psychology 81*, 2001:247–262.

54 J. A. Bargh, P. Raymond, J. B. Pryor and F. Strack, "Attractiveness of the Underling: An Automatic Power Sex Association and Its Consequences for Sexual Harassment and Aggression," *Journal of Personality & Social Psychology 68*, 1995:768–781.

55 J. C. Magee, D. H. Gruenfeld, D. J. Keltner, and A. D. Galinsky, "Leadership and the Psychology of Power," in D. M. Messick and R. M. Kramer, eds., *The Psychology of Leadership: New Perspectives and Research* (Mahwah, NJ: Lawrence Erlbaum Associates, Publishers, 2005):275–293.

56 J. R. Overbeck and B. Park, "When Power Does Not Corrupt: Superior Individuation Processes among Powerful Perceivers," *Journal of Personality & Social Psychology 81*, 2001:549–565.

57 D. H. Ebenback and D. Keltner, "Power, Emotion and Judgmental Accuracy in Social Conflict: Motivating the Cognitive Miser," *Basic & Applied Social Psychology 20*, 1998:7–21.

58 D. Kipnis, "Does Power Corrupt?" *Journal of Personality & Social Psychology 24*, 1972:33–41.

59 E. T. Fan and D. H. Gruenfeld, "When Needs Outweigh Desires: The Effects of Resource Interdependence and Reward Interdependence on Group Problem Solving," *Basic & Applied Social Psychology 20*, 1998:45–56.

60 J. C. Magee, D. H. Gruenfeld, D. J. Keltner, and A. D. Galinsky, "Leadership and the Psychology of Power," in D. M. Messick and R. M. Kramer, eds., *The Psychology of Leadership: New Perspectives and Research* (Mahwah, NJ: Lawrence Erlbaum Associates, Publishers, 2005):275–293.

61 D. H. Messick and R. K. Ohme, "Some Ethical Aspects of the Social Psychology of Social Influence," in R. M. Kramer and M. A. Neale, eds., *Power and Influence in Organizations* (Thousand Oaks, CA: Sage Publications, 1998):181–202.

62 S. Milgram, *Obedience to Authority* (New York: Harper and Row, 1974):205.

63 S. Milgram, "Behavioral Study of Obedience," *Journal of Abnormal and Social Psychology 67*, 1963:371–378.

64 H. C. Kelman and V. L. Hamilton, *Crimes of Obedience* (New Haven, CT: Yale University Press,1989); D. H. Messick and R. K. Ohme, "Some Ethical Aspects of the Social Psychology of Social Influence," in R. M. Kramer and M. A. Neale, eds., *Power and Influence in Organizations* (Thousand Oaks, CA: Sage Publications, 1998):181–202.

65 H. C. Kelman and V. L. Hamilton, *Crimes of Obedience* (New Haven, CT: Yale University Press, 1989):18.

66 P. J. Bowers, C. Meyers, and A. Babbili, *Journal of Mass Media Ethics 19* (3/4), 2004:223–246.

67 J. Tsang, "Moral Rationalization and the Integration of Situational Factors and Psychological Processes in Immoral Behavior," *Review of General Psychology 6* (1), 2002:25–50.

68 A. Crane, "Corporate Greening as Amoralization," *Organization Studies 21* (4), 2000:673–696.

69 N. Haslam, "Dehumanization: An Integrative Review," *Personality & Social Psychology Review 10* (3), 2006:252–264.

70 R. M. Kramer, "The Great Intimidators," *Harvard Business Review 84* (2), February 2006:88–96, 92.

71 K. Auletta, "Beauty and the Beast," *The New Yorker*, December 16, 2002, Annals of Communications, http://www.kenauletta.com/beautyandthebeast.html. Accessed October 9, 2006.

72 M. Kramer, "The Great Intimidators," *Harvard Business Review 84* (2), February 2006:88–96, 95.

73 M. Kramer, "The Great Intimidators," *Harvard Business Review 84* (2), February 2006:88–96, 95.

74 M. Kramer, "The Great Intimidators," *Harvard Business Review 84* (2), February 2006:88–96, 95.

75 M. Kramer, "The Great Intimidators," *Harvard Business Review 84* (2), February 2006:88–96, 96.

76 J. A. Moss and J. E. Barbuto Jr., "Machiavellianism's Association with Sources of Motivation and Downward Influence Strategies," *Psychological Reports 94*, 2004:933–943.

77 B. Barry and D. Shapiro, "Influence Tactics in Combinations: The Interaction Effects of Soft versus Hard Tactics and Relational Exchange," *Journal of Applied Social Psychology 22*, 1992:1429–1441; J. A. Moss and J. E. Barbuto Jr., "Machiavellianism's Association with Sources of Motivation and Downward Influence Strategies," *Psychological Reports 94*, 2004:933–943.

78 J. Lipman-Blumen, *The Allure of Toxic Leaders: Why We Follow Destructive Bosses and Corrupt Politicians—and How We Can Survive Them* (Oxford: Oxford University Press, 2005).

79 J. Lipman-Blumen, *The Allure of Toxic Leaders: Why We Follow Destructive Bosses and Corrupt Politicians—and How We Can Survive Them* (Oxford: Oxford University Press, 2005).

80 J. Lipman-Blumen, *The Allure of Toxic Leaders: Why We Follow Destructive Bosses and Corrupt Politicians—and How We Can Survive Them* (Oxford: Oxford University Press, 2005).

81 P. P. Fu, G. Yukl, J. C. Kennedy, E. S. Srinivas, A. Cheosakul, T. K. Peng, and J. Tata, "Cross-Cultural Comparison of Influence Behavior: A Preliminary Report," *Academy of Management Proceedings*, 2001:D1–D6.

82 E. Vigoda, "Reactions to Organizational Politics: A Cross-Cultural Examination in Israel and Britain," *Human Relations 54* (11), November 2001:1483–1518.

83 G. Yukl, P. P. Fu, and R. McDonald, "Cross-Cultural Differences in Perceived Effectiveness of Influence Tactics for Initiating or Resisting Change," *Applied Psychology: An International Review 52* (1), January 2003:68–82.

84 P. P. Fu, T. K. Peng, J. C. Kennedy, and G. Yukl, "Examining the Preferences of Influence Tactics in Chinese Societies: A Comparison of Chinese Managers in Hong Kong, Taiwan and Mainland China," *Organizational Dynamics 33* (1), February 2004:32–46.

85 B. W. Sciacca, "Don't Turn Your Back on Organizational Politics," *Pennsylvania CPA Journal 75* (3), Fall 2004:1–2, 1.

86 J. Martin and D. Meyerson, "Women and Power: Conformity, Resistance, and Disorganized Coaction," in R. M. Kramer and M. A. Neale, eds., *Power and Influence in Organizations* (Thousand Oaks, CA: Sage Publications, 1998):339.

87 J. Martin and D. Meyerson, "Women and Power: Conformity, Resistance, and Disorganized Coaction," in R. M. Kramer and M. A. Neale, eds., *Power and Influence in Organizations* (Thousand Oaks, CA: Sage Publications, 1998):339.

88 "Biography: Michael Eisner," Academy of Achievement, http:///www.achievement.org/autodoc/printmember/eis0bio-1. Accessed September 16, 2006.

89 "A New King for the Magic Kingdom," *The Economist* February 17, 2005, http://www.economist.com/research/articles. Accessed October 15, 2005.

90 Text of Roy Disney's resignation letter, November 30, 2003, usatoday.com. Accessed September 16, 2006.

91 "Biography: Michael Eisner," Academy of Achievement, http:///www.achievement.org/autodoc/printmember/eis0bio-1. Accessed September 16, 2006.

92 T. Van Riper, "First Job: Michael Eisner," Forbes.com, May 23, 2006, http://www.forbes.com. Accessed September 16, 2006.

93 T. Lowry, with M. Hyman, R. Grover, and R. Crockett, "In the Zone," *BusinessWeek Online* October 17, 2005, http://www.businessweek.com/print/magazine/content/05. Accessed October 15, 2005.

94 A. Fisher, "Share Power—Without Losing Any," *Fortune 152* (8) October 17, 2005:232.

14 Conflicts Good and Bad

Preview

What is conflict and why is it a major factor in organizational life?
Types of conflict
Patterns of conflict
Is conflict constructive or destructive?

In general, how do managers deal with conflict?
Recognize the myths about conflict
If the conflict is destructive, reduce it
If the conflict is constructive, stimulate it

How should you approach interpersonal conflicts?
Recognize the sources of interpersonal conflict
Understand individual styles for handling interpersonal conflict
What to expect when a conflict occurs between peers
Should you help your subordinates work through a conflict?
What happens when conflict occurs between a boss and a subordinate?
How should you deal with your anger?

What should you do when your team members have a conflict?
How does task conflict affect team performance?
How does relationship conflict affect team performance?
When is conflict useful to teams?
How should you manage the conflicts within your team?

How should you intervene when teams are in conflict with each other?
Why is intergroup conflict destructive?
Why is intergroup conflict constructive?
How should you, as a manager, deal with intergroup conflict?

What happens when employees have a conflict with their organization?
What are the most important employee dispute-resolution techniques?
What is the role of labor unions?
How do companies work with dissent and whistle-blowing?

What are some cross-cultural differences in approaches to conflict, and why do they matter?
Cross-cultural models of conflict
Why do cultural differences matter?

Bertelsmann: Paul and Sylvie Go Head to Head

In the Bertelsmann company, Sylvie is a line manager in a department that has just hired Roger. Her department managed the hiring process jointly with the company's Human Resources Department. The process included advertising the job, interviewing top candidates, choosing the best candidate, and setting the salary. But a terrible mistake has been made. After sifting through 60 résumés, "We got the wrong candidate," Sylvie tells Paul, the Vice President of HR.

Sylvie asserts that the ads for the job were not put in the right places, that HR only gave the department two days to make the final decision, and that the salary offered was not enough. Paul tells Sylvie that the advertising budget was fixed and that, after all, the ad did generate 60 résumés and three decent final candidates. He asserts that HR only interviews for a limited set of characteristics, such as interpersonal skills, and that the final choice is left to the department. Further, if Sylvie needs more time to make a decision, he suggests she should go to the "powers that be" and negotiate a longer recruitment process. As to salary, the candidate was not fully qualified, so did not merit a top rate.

Roger apologizes: "I am sorry if your people felt backed into a corner and felt like they had to pick from the three." Sylvie holds her ground, continuing to try to blame the unfortunate hire on HR. "You admit to hiring Roger even though you knew he did not meet the criteria!" she says accusingly, jabbing her pen at Paul. Paul in turn raises his hand as if to deflect a blow, and also raises his voice. He says, "The onus is on your department," and then tells Sylvie, "I am going to tell you something for your own benefit. . . .you don't listen."

Whose responsibility is it to deal with this conflict? How would you feel if you were in Paul or Sylvie's shoes? What would you do? How can this conflict be turned into a plus for the company?

What Is Conflict and Why Is It a Major Factor in Organizational Life?

conflict
The awareness on the part of two or more parties that they have incompatible goals, and that one party has, or will, negatively influence the other's pursuit of those goals.

Conflict is the awareness on the part of two or more parties that they have incompatible goals, and that one party has, or will, negatively influence the other's pursuit of those goals.[1] When two people are working together on a daily basis, being involved in conflict may affect not only their relationship but their professional reputations and productivity.[2] Conflicts develop over time, and they also consume time. Studies suggest that managers devote nearly 20 percent of their time to managing conflict.[3] Conflict in organizations may be on the rise, too. According to one executive, "Increased market competition and a more rapid business pace are contributing to conflict in the workplace. Company mergers and restructuring have also created a more volatile environment that can increase employee competitiveness and job insecurity."[4]

In organizational life, conflict occurs between individuals, among members of a group, between groups, and between employees and their company. Although conflict is inherent in the process of **negotiation**, it is not the same thing. Negotiation is the act of two parties coming together to decide about the allocation of scarce resources,[5] in other words, to make a deal.

negotiation
The act of two parties coming together to decide about the allocation of scarce resources, in other words, to make a deal.

Conflict can be either manifest or latent. **Manifest conflict** is observed, whereas **latent conflict** remains hidden. In organizations, latent conflict is common because cultural norms often dictate that overt conflict is unacceptable.

manifest conflict
Conflict that is observed.

latent conflict
Conflict that is hidden.

Types of Conflict

All organizational systems experience conflict.[6] When a leader wants to spark innovation, he may invite participation—and conflict. When a boss rewards some subordinates more than others, she may improve motivation—and conflict.

relationship conflict
An awareness of interpersonal incompatibilities that leads to tension and friction.

There are three main types of conflict. The first is **relationship conflict**, an awareness of interpersonal incompatibilities that leads to tension and friction.[7] This type of conflict causes dislike, annoyance, frustration, and irritation, and tends to harm performance.[8]

task conflict
An awareness of differences of opinions and viewpoints while doing a task.

The second type is **task conflict**, an awareness of differences of opinions and viewpoints while doing a task.[9] Many researchers argue that task conflict is beneficial because it heightens understanding of issues and results in higher quality decisions.[10]

process conflict
An awareness of differences of opinion about how a task should be accomplished.

Finally, **process conflict** is an awareness of differences of opinion about how a task should be accomplished, including who will do what and how resources will be allocated.[11] For instance, a disagreement about who is responsible for a particular task is a process conflict. Some research suggests that process conflict, like relationship conflict, should be minimized in order to improve performance.[12]

Patterns of Conflict

Usually a relationship in conflict moves through a series of episodes during which latent conflict becomes manifest and can escalate. Figure 14.1 shows a typical pattern of conflict escalation over time.

FIGURE 14.1

Conflict Escalation

Source: Adapted from R. E. Walton, *Managing Conflict: Interpersonal Dialogue and Third-Party Roles*, 2nd ed. (Reading, MA: Addison Wesley Publishing Company, 1987):67.

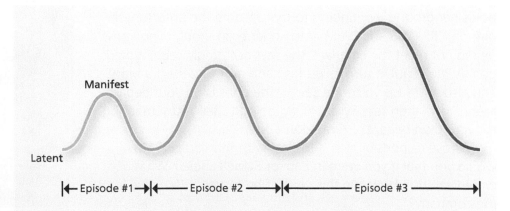

Manifest

Latent

Episode #1   Episode #2   Episode #3

TABLE 14.1 **Stages of Conflict**

Stage 1: Causes of the Conflict	Stage 2: Perceived Conflict	Stage 3: Felt Conflict	Stage 4: Manifest Conflict	Stage 5: Outcomes
• Competition for scarce resources • Desire for autonomy • Incompatible goals • Different opinions • Different values	Thoughts	Emotions	The conflict can be observed in people's behaviors. Individuals have different styles for handling conflict: • Competition • Accommodation • Collaboration • Compromise • Avoidance	Performance is enhanced or reduced when: • The conflict is repressed • The conflict is increased • The parties learn cooperation • The reasons for the conflict disappear

itself, or the parties may develop a resolution before the conflict breaks out into behavioral hostility. Table 14.1 depicts the typical stages of a conflict.

Is Conflict Constructive or Destructive?

Whether a conflict is good or bad depends on who is making the judgment and the measures he or she is using, along with other more subjective criteria.[14] For instance, the conflict process we describe in this chapter is really a Western one rather than a universal one. Other cultures have different ideas about whether conflict is a positive or negative force in their organizations, and some define almost all conflict as destructive.[15] You will learn more about such cultural factors later in the chapter. For now, let's examine some typical reasons why some conflict is constructive and some conflict is destructive.

CONSTRUCTIVE CONFLICT In organizations, conflict can be a constructive force for change.[16] This is because:

1. *Conflict stimulates the search for new facts, methods, or solutions.* When two managers are at odds about what to do, having a high-energy conversation about their alternatives may generate solutions that neither manager alone had imagined. Also, the tension between the two managers may stimulate new methods for its own reduction. For example, when two managers confront each other but manage to resolve their conflict, the resolution process itself may create new, positive relationships between them. One worthwhile outcome of a conflict can be that the conflicting parties learn how to cooperate. Another is that individuals who know how to effectively manage conflict also know how to solve joint problems, establish productive relationships, and feel more in control of their own lives.

2. *Conflict between groups increases the cohesiveness and performance within each group.* During a conflict with an outside group, members of a group tend to become especially loyal and hardworking within their own team. They also tend to choose leaders that are hard-driving and focused, rather than those skilled in building relationships.[17] In these ways, both cohesiveness within the group and group performance are enhanced.

3. *Creating a conflict may reduce perceived power differences and therefore improve problem solving.* In some situations, managers avoid being overly directive with their employees because they do not want to establish a reputation for authoritarianism. Managers who think like this may deliberately invite conflict and dialogue between themselves and their employees in order to prove to their employees that they themselves actually do have some power. Using this approach, the managers expect that their empowered employees will become better problem solvers.

4. *Creating a conflict reduces the probability of a more serious conflict.* Sometimes creating a conflict deliberately is better than waiting for a conflict to erupt on its own, especially if the created conflict is ritualized and relatively indestructive. For instance, in private life, competitive games channel aggressive behavior into socially acceptable formats. In organizational life, institutionalized methods such as routinized labor negotiations release tension and also create relationships between conflicting parties.

DESTRUCTIVE CONFLICT Of course, conflict can also be destructive. Destructive conflict results in problems such as:

1. Conscious efforts by one party to block the goal achievement of another party.
2. Groups that are so intent on competing with each other that they lose their focus on organizational goals.
3. Emotions and attitudes that interfere with problem solving and implementation.

In General, How Do Managers Deal with Conflict?

Organizational conflict should not necessarily be reduced or eliminated, but it must be managed.[18] Effective managers are always on the lookout for conflicts. They identify where a conflict comes from, how people are reacting to it, and how it is affecting, or is likely to affect, key organizational functions. They draw up a plan for dealing with it.

Recognize the Myths About Conflict

Conflict is so common in human relationships that cultures actually develop myths about how to deal with it.[19] When facing a conflict, it is useful to recognize some of the myths that are common in the U.S. culture—myths that, if unrecognized, might cloud your thinking.

Myth 1: There is always an answer or solution to a conflict. Americans tend to assume they can name and analyze, and thus predict and control, their experiences, including conflicts. Yet, the reality is that many conflicts simply do not go away.

Myth 2: Managing conflict is primarily about doing things differently. In pragmatic Western cultures, people equate taking action with progress. But when it comes to managing conflict, it is especially important that action should come after, and follow from, understanding. Learning how to avoid old patterns of creating and encouraging conflict is essential to avoiding similar conflicts in the future.

Myth 3: Peace is the absence of conflict. In fact, the absence of conflict may not be, in the organizational context, cooperation, or, in a larger world context, peace. Conflict may just be lurking, latent, waiting to be triggered by the next resource reduction or personality clash.

Myth 4: More communication always creates more clarity. In our culture, clarity is a cherished value, and we often assume that more talk creates more clarity. Yet, often it is miscommunication that creates a misunderstanding in the first place. Parties in a conflict must work to truly listen to and understand each others' positions before additional talk can become useful.

If the Conflict Is Destructive, Reduce It

Managers should intervene if individuals are not handling a conflict well, or if their group or organization has either too much or too little conflict. Managers can choose either behavioral or structural interventions.[20]

BEHAVIORAL INTERVENTIONS Managers who use behavioral interventions help individuals learn personal strategies for managing conflict and help groups and companies develop more effective conflict management cultures. For example, they might arrange for their employees to get training in a variety of strategies for managing conflict, including interpersonal relations, team building, or problem solving.

They might also work to change their organization's culture by influencing the prevailing beliefs, attitudes, and norms about conflict and its expression. It is fairly common, for example, to find company cultures in which latent conflict is never expressed and, as a result, manifest conflict is inappropriately managed. Through training in interpersonal skills, employees at all levels can learn how to surface latent conflicts effectively, thus improving information sharing and mutual understanding organization-wide.

STRUCTURAL INTERVENTIONS Rather than deal with two warring parties, managers often choose instead to redesign how they interact. These structural interventions might include:

1. *Reducing task interdependence.* Eliminate one party's dependence on another to reduce conflict. For instance, if two workers are in conflict over a project they have to complete jointly, remove one of them from the project.

2. *Increasing resources.* If the root cause of conflict is scarce resources, increase the resources. For example, if two employees are fighting over a piece of equipment, buy a second piece.

3. *Reducing differentiation.* When members of a group are in conflict, create a demographically homogenous group, or put the group through team building activities that encourage the group members to experience their commonalities. Where two or more groups conflict because of their differences, it may be a good idea to rotate group members among the different groups to reduce their in-group–out-group mentality.

4. *Clarifying and applying rules and procedures.* Write rules and procedures to communicate how relationships should work. When such rules are unclear or absent, a relationship has a higher probability of falling into conflict. Allow individuals who must work with each other to participate in decisions about redesigning the rules to make sure they understand and accept them.

5. *Changing reward structures.* Just because individuals understand the existing rules and procedures does not mean they will apply them. Managers should reward behaviors that follow the rules and punish those that do not.

6. *Emphasizing superordinate goals.* A *superordinate goal* is any objective that two parties have in common that is more important to them than the conflict in which they are engaged.[21] If marketing and manufacturing are feuding, for example, pointing out that the feud is causing company sales to go down the tubes should encourage the groups to get over their conflict.

7. *Seeking third-party intervention.* Bring in an outsider to help the parties resolve the conflict. In the case of two individuals in conflict, the outsider could be their boss. In the case of two groups, it could be a boss from higher up or from a neutral group.

See Table 14.2 for a summary of these interventions.

If the Conflict Is Constructive, Stimulate It

Sometimes managers deliberately stimulate conflict because they hope to create an ideal level of tension that, they hope, will improve motivation and productivity.[22] To create conflict they may:[23]

- Bring in employees with new views and styles.
- Alter key organizational structures to foster more interdependence.
- Designate devil's advocates to critique majority opinions.
- Issue threatening or ambiguous messages.

TABLE 14.2 Overview: Structural Interventions to Reduce Conflict

Approach	Example
Reduce task interdependence Increase resources	Give feuding workers totally separate jobs to do. Instead of forcing two busy employees to use one printer, buy two printers.
Reduce differentiation	If the French and British members of a work team can't get along, create two work teams.
Clarify and apply rules and procedures	Tell feuding groups when, where, and how often they should meet. Set their agendas.
Change the reward structure	Reward two feuding groups for their joint product, not for their individual work or separate contributions.
Apply superordinate goals	Prove to both union and management teams that the company will go bankrupt unless they cooperate with each other.
Bring in a third party	When the union and management cannot agree, bring in a National Labor Relations Board mediator.

Interventions such as these will shake things up and motivate people to defend their territory and ideas, and will energize the organization.

Next we will examine more specifically how managers manage conflict between individuals, within groups, between groups, and between individuals and their organization.

How Should You Approach Interpersonal Conflicts?

Recognize the Sources of Interpersonal Conflict

Conflicts between individuals develop because of 1) misunderstandings, resentments, and differences, 2) the belief that goals are competitive, and 3) destructive criticism. Generally, as we have already noted, such relationship conflicts are destructive.

MISUNDERSTANDINGS Communication between individuals is filled with possibilities for misunderstandings that can cause conflict. One reason misunderstanding occurs is because individuals tend to magnify differences between themselves and others. They do this through their own **naïve realism**—the belief that their own views are objective and fact-based, whereas those of others are not. Because of this bias, the parties in a dispute are likely to overestimate the dissimilarity of their views, thus creating a **false polarization** between them.[24]

A second type of misunderstanding occurs because of **incompatibility error**, the belief that the other party's interests are, inevitably, completely opposed to one's own. When two people are emotionally involved in a conflict, this erroneous belief tends to be magnified, thus reducing the prospects for finding common solutions.[25]

A third type of misunderstanding occurs because of our tendency to practice **transparency overestimation**, the belief that what we are saying is perfectly obvious to the other party. In reality, the more interdependent we feel with other people—the more we depend on them and they depend on us— the more likely we are to believe that they understand us even though they do not.[26] This tendency obscures conflict even with relatively friendly others, such as members of a cohesive workgroup, and reduces people's ability to surface tensions and work productively together.

To avoid such misunderstandings, group members should continually check out with each other whether their meanings are really coming across, by asking others to repeat a message in their own words for example. People who really like each other should be especially careful to check out whether their messages are accurately received.

naïve realism
The belief that one's own views are objective and fact-based, whereas those of others are not.

false polarization
An overestimation of the dissimilarity between the views of two parties in a dispute.

incompatibility error
The belief that the other party's interests are, inevitably, completely opposed to one's own.

transparency overestimation
The belief that what one is saying is perfectly obvious to the other party.

RESENTMENTS AND DIFFERENCES Resentments and individual differences also create conflicts. Resentments arise when people perceive they are being treated unfairly, for example. Also, as the popular Dilbert cartoons illustrate, employees resent stupid bosses and the imposition of what they see as dumb management ideas. Individual differences in status, power, race, ethnicity, religion, politics, and class may also create conflicts.

In recent years, sociologists have paid particular attention to income as a source of difference that causes resentment and conflict. Today the United States has the greatest income inequality of all high-income nations.[27] Between 1980 and 2001 the lowest-income 20 percent of U.S. families saw a 7.5 percent increase in earnings, whereas the highest 20 percent saw their incomes jump 59 percent.[28] Also, between 1970 and 2001, the average U.S. family saw a 10 percent increase in income (after taking inflation into account), whereas the average compensation for the 100 highest-paid CEOs grew from $1.3 million (which was about 40 times the earnings of an average worker) to $37.5 million (a 2,500 percent increase and 1,000 times as much as the earnings of the average worker). Although it is hard to imagine an employee in direct conflict with their CEO over the issue of income disparity, it is less difficult to imagine that the disparity contributes to an overall climate of unproductive conflict in some companies.

THE BELIEF THAT GOALS ARE COMPETITIVE A person who enters into a relationship believing it will be competitive rather than cooperative is likely to expect conflict. This belief creates a cycle of competition, as presented in Figure 14.2. Also in Figure 14.2, you can see a quite different cycle—one of cooperation.

Note that when a person is competing rather than cooperating, suspicion replaces trust. Also, developing mutual goals is replaced by outdoing or avoiding the other person. Finally, the possibility of moving forward together is replaced by the thrill of victory. (Winning is, however, tempered by the certainty of even more competition.)

Because of the downside of the competitive cycle, managers must carefully weigh the advantages and disadvantages of deliberately creating competition among their employees. On the one hand, creating competition within groups like salespeople may be a plus. Often it can be done fairly because sales can be measured quantitatively, and opportunities to make a sale can be equalized. On the other hand, creating competition among coworkers working to create a joint product is likely to be a minus.

Some companies favor a steep hierarchy with many organizational levels because this structure increases individuals' opportunities to be rewarded by moving up, and because the inevitable competition to gain a higher rank is seen as productive. In other companies, managers favor flat hierarchies with few levels because they have discovered that flat organizations downplay competition and enhance cooperation, improving overall productivity as a result. Of course, for those who are determined to move up in a flat organization, the competition and conflict may be especially fierce because there are relatively few positions.

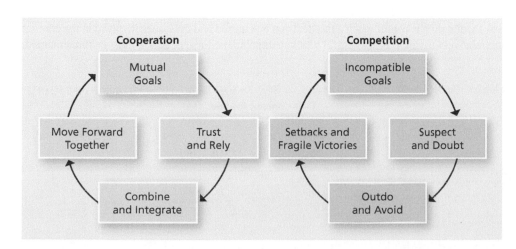

Cooperation

Mutual Goals → Trust and Rely → Combine and Integrate → Move Forward Together → Mutual Goals

Competition

Incompatible Goals → Suspect and Doubt → Outdo and Avoid → Setbacks and Fragile Victories → Incompatible Goals

FIGURE 14.2

The Cycles of Cooperation and Competition

Source: D. Tjosvold, "Cooperation Theory, Consecutive Controversy, and Effectiveness: Learning from Crisis," *Team Effectiveness and Decision Making in Organizations,* (San Francisco, CA: Jossey-Bass, 1995): 79–112, 87. Copyright © 1995, Jossey-Bass. Reprinted with permission of John Wiley & Sons, Inc.

DESTRUCTIVE CRITICISM A final source of interpersonal conflict is destructive criticism. Criticism is often characterized as either constructive or destructive, meant either to help individuals to improve themselves or to tear them down and demean them. Constructive criticism focuses on behavioral and performance problems. For example, you might say to your employee, "This is the third time you have turned in a late report." Destructive criticism globalizes the problem or blames the whole person. A manager (not you, of course) might say, "You never get reports in on time," or "You are such a lazy bum." When individuals receive destructive criticism they are likely to become angry and tense. They are also likely to feel less effective, and as a result they are likely to lower their goals.[29]

It is important to keep in mind that both types of criticism are likely to trigger emotions in the person being criticized. However, whether these emotions escalate into a conflict depends on the ongoing characteristics of the relationship between the parties. For example, a manager who continually lacks tact in approaching employees is likely to generate conflict, whereas one who is generally tactful but only fails on one occasion may not.

In boss–subordinate relationships, criticism is sanctioned by organizational norms, but it is still emotionally charged. Some researchers argue that because of the emotions they incite, performance reviews should be abolished. This is because, no matter how well intended the criticism, the reviews amount to an "annual torture session" that actually accomplishes little in the way of motivation and reward.[30]

Understand Individual Styles for Handling Interpersonal Conflict

You are already familiar with the theory of personal orientation to others—the idea that people differ on how oriented they are to others versus how oriented they are to themselves. People who are more oriented toward themselves are more competitive, whereas those who are more oriented toward others are more cooperative.[31]

Which end of the spectrum best characterizes you? Are you more likely to always want to do better than everyone else and to be the best at everything, or more likely to sacrifice for your team and pitch in to help your team win? One way of thinking about how individuals handle interpersonal conflict is to understand their personal styles in terms of this fundamental difference. This approach yields five styles for managing interpersonal conflict.[32] See Figure 14.3.

Integrators show high concern for both self and others. Because of this orientation, they are willing to be open, to exchange information, and to examine differences to reach a solution that is acceptable to both parties. Integrators are particularly good at getting different groups to work together.

Obligers show high concern for others but not themselves. They attempt to minimize differences and emphasize commonalities to satisfy the other party. Obliging works well when one party believes he or she is wrong, or when one party is particularly invested in the outcome. It is a style that can also used when one party obliges now in order to gain a favor later.

Dominators, also known as competitors, show high concern for themselves but low concern for others. They focus on accomplishing their own objectives and ignore the goals of others. Dominating is useful when a fast decision is required and the issues involved in the conflict are relatively trivial. It is also useful when an unpopular course of action must be implemented.

integrators
People who show high concern for both self and others and are good at getting different groups to work together.

obligers
People who show high concern for others but not themselves, and therefore attempt to minimize differences and emphasize commonalities to satisfy the other party.

dominators
People who show high concern for themselves but low concern for others, and therefore focus on accomplishing their own objectives and ignore the goals of others.

FIGURE 14.3

Styles of Handling Interpersonal Conflict

Source: M. A. Rahim, "A Measure of Styles of Handling Interpersonal Conflict" *Academy of Management Journal* 26 (2): 368–376, 369. Reproduced with permission of The Academy of Management (NY).

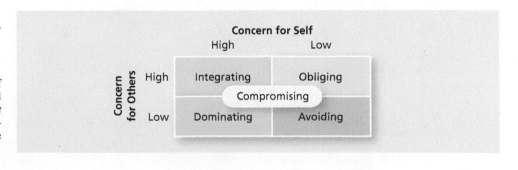

Avoiders have low concern for both themselves and others. They tend to withdraw from conflict situations. Withdrawing is a good approach when issues are trivial or when the potential harm from engaging with the other party is likely to outweigh any potential benefit.

Compromisers are moderately concerned with self and others. Two compromisers in conflict would be likely to engage in mutual sacrifices to accomplish a mutually satisfying decision. Compromising is useful when the parties are equally powerful or when the goals of the parties are mutually exclusive.

What to Expect When a Conflict Occurs Between Peers

Conflict can occur between peers—that is, between individuals who are on the same organizational level—or between bosses and their subordinates. We will take a look at each in turn.

When one peer annoys another, the resulting conflict is quite likely to follow a particular pattern of escalation.[33] This pattern is probably caused by some norms that we have developed in our society: On the one hand, we like to be able to protect an individual's self-interest, but, at the same time, we want to minimize antagonism to a second person. So our conflicts do not abruptly erupt at a high level of violence; instead, they develop gradually. See Figure 14.4 for the typical pattern of conflict escalation.

To illustrate: Jack *requests* a source code from Jane, using a neutral statement that involves no pressure—for example, "I need the source code."

When Jane fails to produce the source code, Jack escalates his request to a *demand*, which is an emotionally neutral request that involves some pressure or indication of impatience: "I need the source code now," or "Come on, Jane, could you please just take a little time to find me the source code?"

When the source code is still withheld, Jack *complains* by objecting to some aspect of Jane's undesirable behavior. "You are holding up my project by not giving me the source code."

If still thwarted, Jack gets *angry*: "I am really getting annoyed with you."

If that doesn't work, he *threatens*, indicating a readiness to punish Jane if she does not comply with his request: "If you don't produce the source code, I am going to have to go over your head to get it."

Next he *harasses*, which is imposing a punishment on Jane or telling her that punishment will continue if she does not comply: Jack actually goes over Jane's head to her boss, or threatens to have a lengthy conversation with her boss about her behavior.

Finally, thwarted, Jack turns *abusive*, making statements that involve name-calling or swearing, or that are extremely forceful: "Jane, you're an idiot." Fortunately, not all conflicts escalate all the way to abuse.

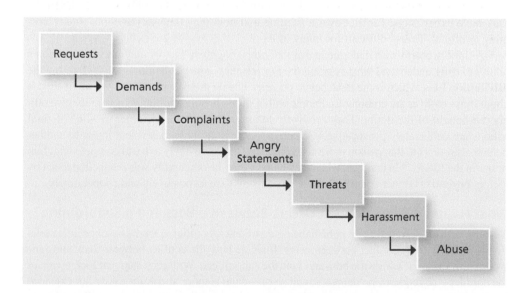

FIGURE 14.4   **The Typical Pattern of Conflict Escalation**

problem-solving
Developing a solution that is acceptable to both parties.

appeals to a third party
Bringing in someone such as a boss or a neutral person to help manage the scarcity of resources or to hear the complaints on both sides.

dialogue
The process in which two conflicting parties directly engage each other and focus on the conflict between them, including aspects of their relationship itself.

hostile attribution bias
The tendency to perceive hostile motives in others even when signals about those motives are ambiguous.

In addition to the steps in this pattern, there are two other common ways to deal with a one-to-one conflict. The first is **problem solving**, which is when two individuals make an effort to find a mutually satisfying agreement. For example, they might agree to trade favors or resources. Jack might say to Jane, "If you can find the time to locate the source code, I'll fix your computer bug."

The second common approach is **appeals to a third party**, which involves bringing in someone such as a boss or a neutral person to help manage the scarcity of resources or to hear the complaints on both sides: Jack asks the IT director to sit down with him and Jane to sort out the reasons for the problem. Research suggests that in real life there is no particular, orderly relationship between these two approaches and the typical steps in the pattern of conflict escalation. However, on average, the feuding parties are most likely to use problem solving and appeals to a third party right after their requests, demands, and complaints have been made and rejected.

It makes common sense that experiencing negative emotions encourages the physical escalation of a conflict. However, the particular emotions associated with having to defend one's honor in the face of demeaning, scornful behaviors are *especially* likely to increase physical escalation.

Should You Help Your Subordinates Work Through a Conflict?

Dialogue is the process in which two conflicting parties "directly engage each other and focus on the conflict between them, including aspects of their relationship itself."[34] Together the parties explore the issues over which they disagree, including the underlying needs or forces involved and their feelings about the situation. The purpose of dialogue is to manage a conflict by resolving or controlling it, thus reducing its costs and improving the quality of the working relationship. In companies, dialogues involving conflict are often held under the watchful eye of a manager or other third party.

Should managers use this process to attempt to resolve a conflict? For instance, would it be a good idea for you to sit down with two conflicting employees and try to help them work things out? There are several factors arguing *against* using it.

One is the fact is that dialogue is only useful when coworkers are personally capable of effective and efficient communication and believe their interaction is more likely to be useful than stressful.[35] The parties must both be motivated to resolve the conflict. Also, they should have equal power to act in the situation. If they do not, the party with more power may think, "Why do I have to explain myself?" and the party with less power may think, "Why bother?" So although dialogue is a potentially powerful tool, as a practical matter, using it to manage interpersonal relationships is fairly rare. This is the case in both organizational and personal life.

A second concern is that sometimes people, whether consciously or unconsciously, avoid dialogue.[36] Facing a conflict may require them to face themselves, including how they have experienced conflict over a lifetime and how they themselves contribute to creating conflicts. This is difficult for many of us.

A third problem with dialogue is that individual cognitive factors may impede a person's ability to truly understand what is going on. For instance, some individuals are high in **hostile attribution bias**, which is the tendency to perceive hostile motives in others even when signals about those motives are ambiguous. People with a strong hostile attribution bias rarely give others the benefit of the doubt. They are likely to assume that even the other person's neutral actions are deliberately provocative.[37] When individuals attribute malevolent intent to another person, they react to that person more negatively and are more likely to try to compete with him or her in the future.[38] In contrast, when they believe that the other party was compelled to act by factors beyond his or her control, they are more likely to react positively and cooperatively.

What Happens When Conflict Occurs Between a Boss and a Subordinate?

Because bosses can reward and punish their subordinates, conflict in the boss-subordinate relationship differs from conflict between peers. Imagine how the conflict between Jack and Jane would play out if Jack were the boss and Jane the subordinate. With each step that Jack escalates the conflict—he requests, he demands, and so on—Jane is more at risk for losing her extended lunch hour, her raise, or even her job. There is little likelihood that the conflict will escalate as predicted for peers, in fact, and there is a high probability that it will either be terminated with a direct order by the boss or be driven underground by Jane's immediate compliance.

Interpersonally, such a situation can become quite complicated. For example, perhaps Jane does not know how to fulfill Jack's request, but is too unassertive to explain this to him. (Lack of assertiveness is not an ideal characteristic in a subordinate, but it is not an unlikely one either.) Or perhaps she has actually tried to explain that she is not able to fulfill his request, but Jack has not understood her, or he disagrees with her. Also, consider the situation in reverse. What if Jane is the boss and Jack is the subordinate? Jack requests the source code, but does not get it. He has made his request and been ignored. He may feel frustrated and try to work around his problem, or he may shrug and give up. Either way, he is unlikely to escalate the conflict, and it does not get resolved.

There are two major concerns when conflict occurs between a boss and a subordinate. The first concern is that conflicts that should be understood and resolved are likely to turn into latent and unresolved conflicts that affect productivity. If Jane does not actually know how to produce the requested source code, and is too unassertive to say so, and if Jack fails to understand her situation, he is likely to punish her for her "failure" and create ill will in their relationship. Furthermore, in the future, Jane is likely to become defensive whenever Jack challenges her to attempt something new. She may not try her best, and ultimately their unresolved conflict will lead to her reduced productivity. How could all these negative consequences be prevented? One antidote is better communication about the conflict when it occurs: Jack could initiate a dialogue with Jane about why she cannot meet his request. Another approach is for Jack and Jane, either alone or together, to reflect upon, and ultimately change, the patterns of conflict in their relationship.

The second major concern is that bosses may abuse their power. **Bullying** is unwanted behavior that causes offense to the injured party and is not justified by the working or professional relationship.[39] It includes verbal intimidation, the undermining of the victims' professional work, the bully taking credit for other people's work, and even physical violence. Jack would be a bully if, just one hour after his first request, Jane still has not produced the source code and Jack sends her a demeaning e-mail.

bullying
Unwanted behavior that causes offense to the injured party and is not justified by the working or professional relationship.

You know you are being bullied when your boss:[40]

- violates your privacy. The boss loads you up with work that has to be done just before a vacation, or asks you to do personal errands.
- fails to honor normal social codes. The boss yells and swears, acts as if he or she is never wrong, and never apologizes.
- belittles you. The boss makes sarcastic or demeaning comments, which may be ill disguised as humor.
- takes things personally. The boss gives you the silent treatment and otherwise communicates resentment.

Experts recommend that when you recognize that you are in a bullying relationship—and you should suspect you are in one when you feel nervous around your boss and drained at the end of the day—you make notes about the important interactions you have with your boss and then analyze them for what was said, how it was said, and how you felt about what was said.[41] Ask yourself whether coworkers have similar problems, and if not, why not. Develop careful strategies for your meetings with your boss. Clarify every assignment with reflective statements such as, "As I understand it, you want me to. . . ." Consider discussing the issue with your human resources department, and even with your boss, but carefully weigh the possible consequences of doing so.

How Can You Deal with Your Anger?

Although conflict can cause any number of emotions, one common and uncomfortable one is anger. On the one hand, anger has positive value.[42] Generally we get angry with people who are important to us—people we value, or people on whom we depend. Expressing our anger gets the other person's attention and motivates him or her to focus on the conflict. Feeling angry also energizes us to act. Our anger motivates us to address the conflict. Anger also educates us, because it forces us to examine what makes us angry and learn more about our own commitments and values.

On the other hand, anger is also destructive. It feels physically unpleasant, and when we are angry we may feel out of control. At the same time, when we feel angry we may feel and be out of sync with the culture of our organization, which is likely to cause us

TABLE 14.3 How Do You Handle Anger?

Respond to the following questions. Be as honest as you can.

	Never = 1	Sometimes = 2	Always = 3
1. When I am angry, it's easy for me to recognize the feeling.	_____	_____	_____
2. When I feel angry, I blame myself.	_____	_____	_____
3. I know how to express my anger appropriately.	_____	_____	_____
4. I let other people press my buttons, causing me to express my anger inappropriately.	_____	_____	_____
5. I am aware of situations in which it is appropriate to express my anger.	_____	_____	_____
6. When I feel angry, I blame others.	_____	_____	_____
7. I know why expressing my anger is appropriate.	_____	_____	_____
8. When someone disagrees with me, he or she is attacking my competence.	_____	_____	_____
9. I realize that the person I express my anger to will be stressed by it.	_____	_____	_____
10. I express anger through sarcasm.	_____	_____	_____
11. When I express my anger, I describe my feelings and their causes.	_____	_____	_____
12. I express anger by being unhelpful.	_____	_____	_____
13. When I express my anger, I am specific about what behaviors angered me.	_____	_____	_____
14. I insult others to express my strong feelings.	_____	_____	_____
15. I avoid smiling when I express my anger.	_____	_____	_____
16. When someone is angry with me, I am likely to get angry back.	_____	_____	_____

In this quiz, the odd numbered questions represent effective tactics for anger management, whereas the even numbered questions represent ineffective anger management. Add up the odd-numbered items to get your effectiveness score, and the even-numbered items to get your ineffectiveness score. Are you more effective or ineffective?

Effectiveness score _____   Ineffectiveness score _____

Source: Adapted from D. Tjosvold, *Learning to Manage Conflict: Getting People to Work Together Productively* (New York: Lexington Books, 1993).

some anxiety. Suppressing anger may lead to self-blame. It may also lead to displacement, which is redirecting one's anger by attacking innocent parties.

Take the quiz in Table 14.3 to get a sense for how you currently handle anger.

How can you manage anger to make the most of this motivating emotion? You can use this list of 16 items in Table 14.3 as a checklist of skills to work on. In summary, effective anger management includes the following behaviors:

- Recognize that you are angry.
- Decide where, how, and why to express your anger.
- Recognize that the target of your anger will be stressed by it.
- Learn to express anger effectively: Describe your feelings and their causes. Be specific about what behaviors have angered you.
- Do not judge the other person. Be consistent in your presentation: Avoid smiling while expressing anger.
- Go out of your way to form strong relationships that will allow direct discussions of anger.

What Should You Do When Your Team Members Have a Conflict?

When the members of your team are sparring with each other, you should carefully consider whether they are in conflict over their mutual task or over their personal relationships.

How Does Task Conflict Affect Team Performance?

As we noted earlier, some level of task conflict within teams probably increases team performance.[43] Conflict is useful in teams in which members feel psychologically safe, there are norms of openness, and the conflict is explicitly induced by means of a devil's advocate.[44] In general, these sorts of teams have high levels of trust and respect. They manage to have open discussions about their conflicts, even during the middle of their work together when their levels of conflict are at their highest.

Yet, the relationship between task conflict and performance is complicated. We know that when conflict grows in intensity, it eventually gets to a level that does reduce performance.[45]

We also know that task conflict is more useful in teams performing complex tasks like project work and less useful, even counterproductive, in teams performing routine tasks like production.[46] This may be because task conflict stimulates group members doing nonroutine work to look deeply and creatively into their task, whereas it interferes with standard procedures when groups are performing routine work.

In addition, teams that bring information diversity to the table are likely to conflict and, because of this conflict, improve their performance. For example, a study of MBA workgroups found that groups that have a large range of different types of information, defined in this instance as having different educational backgrounds, are likely to experience task conflict, and that their task conflict improves performance.[47]

How Does Relationship Conflict Affect Team Performance?

Relationship conflict occurs when people in the team confront each other about things not related to their work, such as their clothing choices. It is likely to occur when team members feel insecure and do not trust each other, or when some people in the team are simply inconsiderate, or when the team is an unhappy blend of shy and dominant people.[48] Relationship conflict within a group results in friction, frustration and personality clashes.

With but a few exceptions, the many studies on relationship conflict have found that it strongly and negatively affects team performance and team member satisfaction.[49] Specifically, it reduces decision quality and understanding, and, also, organizational commitment.[50] In the study of MBA workgroups mentioned in the previous section, groups characterized as having a large social category diversity (including such characteristics as gender, age, and nationality) were likely to experience relational conflict, which reduced their performance.

When Is Conflict Useful to Teams?

In summary, over time, effective teams show distinct patterns of conflict. Good managers learn to recognize and develop effective patterns of conflict.[51] These patterns include:

1. generally low levels of relationship conflict, with a rise in relationship conflict near project deadlines. If they occur at all, the group's relationship conflicts are likely to include minor disagreements over such things as interpersonal style and personal values.

2. moderate levels of task conflict at the midpoint in the group's interactions. The group's task conflicts include disagreements over such things as procedures, policies, interpretations of facts, and the distribution of resources.

3. low but increasing levels of process conflict as a project continues. The group's process conflicts will include disagreements over how members should proceed in accomplishing their task, including who should do what and how responsibility is allocated.

How Should You Manage the Conflicts Within Your Team?

When relationship conflict emerges, managers can be pretty certain that it will impede group performance. They should take steps to resolve or eliminate it. However, when a task conflict emerges, they should thoroughly examine it to see whether it inhibits or enhances group performance, and only then take appropriate steps. (See the earlier sections in this chapter on behavioral and structural interventions, and dialogue.) In addition, team leaders can promote constructive conflict in these ways:[52]

- Apply the golden rule of controversy: Discuss issues with others as you would like them to discuss issues with you.
- Bring in a variety of relevant sources, from print media to experts and independent thinkers, who are likely to disagree with the group.
- Assign subgroups or individuals to play the role of dissenter.
- Respect others by criticizing their ideas rather than their motives, personality, intelligence, or integrity.
- Create solutions by combining ideas from more than one person.
- Establish norms of openness by which all group members are encouraged to express opinions, doubts, and half-formed ideas.
- Protect group members' right to dissent and free speech.

How Should You Intervene When Teams Are in Conflict with Each Other?

Intergroup conflict in organizations may be between formal groups (such as the functional divisions of a company) or between informal coalitions that come together around a common set of issues, beliefs or values. In organizations, as in the rest of society, most people find themselves part of a group that commands their respect and loyalty—an in-group. Unfortunately, where there is an in-group, there is often an out-group—a group towards which the in-group feels competition or opposition.

Why do teams conflict with each other? One reason is that intergroup conflict is a natural outcome of competition for scarce resources. This theory of **realistic group conflict** certainly makes common sense. There is even a commonly used term that describes the phenomenon: turf battles.

However, classic research by Sherif and his colleagues studying boys at summer camps suggests that group conflict also has psychological origins: Interestingly, mere knowledge of another group's presence can be sufficient to trigger intergroup discrimination.[53] The recognition of this phenomenon has led to the theory of **social identity**, the idea that individuals define themselves to a large extent in terms of their social group memberships, and that it is through these memberships that they develop a positive sense of self, or social identity.[54] Unfortunately, individuals achieve their positive social identity in large part by evaluating themselves favorably in comparison with others, and to do this the others must be defined as inferior.

Why Is Intergroup Conflict Destructive?

It follows that intergroup conflict is a destructive force because, as in-group members develop loyalty to one another, they stereotype and malign out-groups. In fact, the very cohesion that is so desired in a real team increases the suspicion and stereotypes of out-groups.[55] In companies where groups need to work with each other, such in-group–out-group conflicts can easily harm the overall effectiveness of the organization. For example, in a company in which a cohesive IT group keeps its distance from other functions, getting the other functions to accept its recommendation for a new integrative software package might be a challenge.

Another problem with intergroup conflict is that it can negatively affect some individuals in the winning group. Although competition rewards the winning group, it may punish some of that group's individual members. Contributing to a group requires personal cost in time, money, physical effort, and in some cases (such as armies or fire departments) even risk of injury or death.[56] Over time, as they perceive their personal sacrifice will outweigh their potential personal gains, sensible group members may decline to participate in their group.[57]

---

realistic group conflict
The theory that intergroup conflict is a natural outcome of competition for scarce resources.

social identity theory
The idea that individuals define themselves to a large extent in terms of their social group memberships, and that it is through these memberships that they develop a positive sense of self, or social identity.

Why Is Intergroup Conflict Constructive?

Of course, intergroup conflict can also be a positive force. For one thing, it encourages more communication between teams and within teams, which leads the teams to increase their understanding of complex problems.[58] For another thing, it sometimes motivates individual group members and in this way improves group performance.

Third, intergroup conflict may positively affect loafers. We know that one of the problems with rewarding all members of a team equally is that some individual group members will loaf, causing the group to fail to realize its highest possible level of performance and the rewards associated with it.[59] A series of experiments has shown that fostering intergroup competition may increase intragroup cooperation and effectiveness, and, as a byproduct, reduce the problem of loafing.[60]

How Should You, as a Manager, Deal with Intergroup Conflict?

When it comes to managing intergroup conflict, team leaders have to make some choices.[61] They might choose to use:

- Problem solving: developing a solution that is acceptable to both parties
- Contention: imposing one group's will on the other
- Yielding: satisfying one group's needs at the expense of the other group
- Avoidance: minimizing the importance of the issues and evading participation in the conflict

From an organizational perspective, there is no one right way, because the best approach depends on what organizational outcomes are sought. However, it is true that often an organization prefers harmony to conflict, perhaps because managers understand what researchers have confirmed: That strong emotional arousal such as that induced by intergroup conflict leads to reduced ability to formulate rational plans of action.[62] This view suggests that the best approach is problem-solving, whereas the worst approach is contention.

What should a manager do when he or she is certain that an intergroup conflict is becoming counterproductive? A manager might try to improve intergroup relations by creating a superordinate social category ("Don't forget we are all working for the same company") or by strengthening an existing one ("I want you to know that the company is watching this conflict closely").[63] Also, intergroup relationships can be improved by weakening the perception of group members that they are separate and different from the other group. In other words, treat both groups equally and discourage any discussion of differences. Finally, a manager may improve the situation by creating positive and cooperative contact between the hostile groups,[64] although he or she has to be careful not to exacerbate the conflict—by allowing one group to discover that the other group has received more resources, for example.[65]

What Happens When Employees Have a Conflict with Their Organization?

At times individual employees or groups of employees have conflicts with their organizations. How do managers deal with such situations?

What Are the Most Important Employee Dispute-Resolution Techniques?

Managers have developed a variety of systems for handling situations in which an employee has a conflict with the company. These employee dispute resolution systems include a variety of conflict resolution methods suited to a wide range of individuals and a broad range of complaints. Today disputes are often supervised by an ombudsperson or administrator who is outside the usual management hierarchy but who has a direct link to upper management.[66] Which form of dispute resolution the administrator uses depends on such environmental factors as government regulation, litigation trends, unionization, and market competition. It also depends on such organizational factors as a company's culture, management commitment, and the nature of the precipitating event.

Historically, U.S. organizations have undergone major changes in how they handle disputes.[67] At one point in time, management's authority to control every aspect of the

mediation
The act of two parties engaging a neutral third party to help them negotiate an agreement.

arbitration
The act of two parties submitting their grievance to a third party who makes a decision for them, which can be either binding or non-binding.

mediation–arbitration
The act of two parties agreeing to use a mediator but also to move on to arbitration should they fail to reach an agreement.

workplace went unchallenged. Subsequently, unions and other legal protections evolved to give more power to employees. Today we are in a new era in which companies use a variety of dispute resolution techniques to avoid escalated disputes. Among the more popular techniques are **mediation**, when two parties engage a neutral third party to help them negotiate an agreement, and **arbitration**, when two parties submit their grievance to a third party who makes the decision for them. Arbitration can be either binding or nonbinding.

A 1997 survey of the corporate legal counsels of the *Fortune* 1,000 companies discovered that 87 percent had used mediation and 80 percent had used arbitration internally at least once in the three years before the survey.[68] About 20 percent had used **mediation–arbitration** (in which the two parties agree to use a mediator but also agree to move on to arbitration should they fail to reach an agreement), minitrials, fact finding, or employee in-house grievance procedures, and about 10 percent had used ombudspersons and peer reviews.

Typically, public and private organizations use different approaches to employee dispute resolution. Managers in the more heavily unionized public sector are more inclined to use mediation and ombudsperson programs, whereas the private sector places more emphasis on non-union arbitration. Some companies even develop private justice systems in order to avoid unions or to address issues concerning individual rights in the workplace.

What Is the Role of Labor Unions?

Labor unions are organizations of employees formed to protect and advance their members' interests, including enhancing wages and benefits, improving working conditions, and increasing job security. The right to form labor unions was established by the National Labor Relations Act of 1935, popularly known as the Wagner Act. The Act established the National Labor Relations Board (NLRB) to supervise union elections and investigate any charges of unfair labor relations practices by management. Subsequent legislation amended and further developed union rights. Not all workers are covered by the National Labor Relations Act. For example, independent contractors and supervisors are excluded.

certified union
A union established through an NLRB-supervised secret ballot election among qualifying employees, which is empowered to engage in collective bargaining.

decertified union
A union abolished through an NLRB-supervised secret ballot election among qualifying employees.

collective bargaining
The negotiation process between a certified union and management over the establishment of human resources practices over the period of a contract.

A union is established, or **certified**, through an NLRB-supervised secret ballot election among qualifying employees. It can be abolished, or **decertified**, in a similar process. Once a union is certified, it is empowered to engage in **collective bargaining** with management to establish human resources practices over the period of a contract. In the first phase of this process, a union negotiating team determines the needs of its members and sets targets for factors such as wages and benefits. Then the union and management negotiators meet to hammer out a contract, which must subsequently be ratified by a vote of the union members. If ratification fails, both parties return to the negotiating table. If it succeeds, the contract establishes certain workplace practices and benefits for its duration.

When business is bad, union workers are better able than nonunion workers to resist employer efforts to make salary and benefit reductions.[69] Although union workers typically enjoy better wages than nonunion workers, between 1971 and 1999, as union representation and power fell, their wage premium also fell.[70]

How Do Companies Work with Dissent and Whistle-Blowing?

Dissent is the expression of conflict between employees and their organization. In organizational life, the dissent of minorities has both negative and positive consequences. On the one hand, it consumes time and disrupts stability and therefore, in the short term, reduces efficiency.[71] On the other hand, dissent can also promote change, innovation and long-term effectiveness.[72]

In general, organizations tend to avoid dissent. One piece of evidence for this view is that historically managers have preferred homogeneous workforces—people who will agree with them.[73] People are attracted to similar others and they tend to select similar others for jobs.[74] We also know that in groups there is higher turnover among deviant group members than among conforming group members. One reason for these choices is that often people are personally uncomfortable with dissent and dissenters.

Given the advantages and disadvantages of dissent for organizational effectiveness, what should managers do about dissenting individuals and minorities? Some choose to reduce and, if possible, eliminate dissent. They do this in three ways.[75] First, they foster an organizational culture that disrespects individual conscience and fails to foster interpersonal trust. Second, they establish reward systems that supervise employees closely and give them relatively little autonomy. Third, they become overtly hostile to dissent, especially during times of trouble and scarcity.

However, other managers choose to sanction and encourage dissent. A company may have an **open door policy**, that allows any employee to bring any issue directly to top management and expect a hearing. In decision-making groups, managers may encourage the use of a devil's advocate or the expression of minority views. Other types of minority dissent, such as whistle-blowing, may be sanctioned or not dependent on the organizational culture.

Whistle-blowing is the disclosure by former or current organization members of illegal, immoral, or illegitimate practices under the control of their employers, to persons or organizations that may be able to correct the wrongdoing.[76] Most research on whistle-blowing has been done in the United States, with little published on this topic outside North America and Great Britain.[77]

What turns an individual into a whistle blower? Interestingly, many whistle-blowers are high performers who are relatively well paid and who believe their job requires them to report wrongdoing.[78] In fact, individuals are less likely to report incidents when they believe their own job performance is below average, or when they are employed by a highly bureaucratic organization.

Whistle-blowers are more likely to report incidents of wrongdoing when:[79]

- They feel compelled morally or by the mandate of their job to do so.
- They feel the public or their co-workers have been harmed by the wrongdoing.
- The wrongdoing involves theft by relatively low-level workers.
- There are few other observers.
- The organization is highly regulated.

Another interesting point is that research has consistently shown that the fear of retaliation does not usually deter whistle-blowers.[80]

From the organization's perspective, it is desirable to encourage *internal* whistle-blowing while avoiding the need for *external* whistle-blowing.[81] Research suggests that the most effective way for companies to manage whistle-blowing internally is to demonstrate to employees that, if a complaint is valid, something will be done to correct the problem. Retaliation against whistle-blowers only encourages them to use external channels and go public with the allegation of wrongdoing.[82] Generally, whistle-blowers do bring their grievances to their company before taking them to an outside party. This suggests that responding effectively to internal complaints is key to preventing the conflict from escalating to parties outside.

To avoid escalation to outside parties, companies publish policies and codes of ethics, and they try be clear about how and to whom employees should report a potential wrongdoing. A key factor is establishing trust and rapport between employees and the individuals to whom they report a wrongdoing. One way of doing this is to assure the employee's confidentiality. IBM has a program under which it receives up to 18,000 letters a year from workers making confidential complaints. Bank of America in San Francisco encourages employees to complain via its "Open Line" program: The program's coordinator contacts the employee at home, rather than at work, to gather information, and then takes the complaint back to the company for a response.[83]

What Are Some Cross-Cultural Differences in Approaches to Conflict, and Why Do They Matter?

Cross-Cultural Models of Conflict

The model of conflict that is the best fit for the U.S. culture is the **confrontation model**, which emphasizes individuality and allows for the aggressive pursuit of individual goals.[84] U.S. managers, being individualistic and aggressive, prefer to confront problems directly and bring conflicts out into the open. They emphasize confrontation,

open door policy
A company's policy of allowing any employee to bring any issue directly to top management and to expect a hearing.

whistle-blowing
The disclosure by former or current organization members of illegal, immoral, or illegitimate practices under the control of their employers, to persons or organizations that may be able to correct the wrongdoing.

confrontation model
A model of conflict which emphasizes individuality and allows for the aggressive pursuit of individual goals.

which includes making rational arguments, presenting factual evidence, and suggesting solutions.[85] Cultures that follow the confrontational model think of organizational conflict as natural and desirable. They see competition between employees as fair and right, and they believe that too little conflict leads to stagnation.[86] Organizations using this model stress norms of due process and the fair treatment of a variety of viewpoints.

harmony model

A model of conflict which emphasizes intragroup harmony, consensus, and absence of conflict.

A second model, the **harmony model**, is a best fit for cultures that emphasize intragroup harmony, consensus, and absence of conflict. For example, in both Japanese and Chinese organizations, fulfilling one's role and downplaying conflicts are norms. Because individuals see differences as part of long-term relationships and networks, conflicts may never be manifested. People in these and similar cultures might describe a troubling relationship not as a conflict in which "we are at odds with each other," but rather as a situation in which "we are all entangled" or "we are caught in a net."[87]

To illustrate, because the Chinese come from a culture that values harmony and personal relationships, they often avoid direct and open conflict, preferring to settle the problem in private or use authority to suppress it. [88] Their style for managing conflict emphasizes negotiation and compromise, and they strongly prefer to avoid overt disagreements.[89] One reason Chinese managers prefer indirect forms of influence is to avoid losing face and damaging guanxi (a kind of harmony in a relationship). To them, open and direct ways of dealing with conflict are embarrassing. When they have conflicts with another party, American managers are reluctant to invest time and effort to enlist the help of other people, but Chinese managers routinely use indirect forms of influence that involve the assistance of a third party.[90] Americans have trouble understanding the roundabout ways that Chinese use to manage even simple conflicts.[91]

regulative model

A model of conflict in which organizations themselves are structured to contain competition and conflict through an emphasis on regulation and bureaucratic rules.

A third model, the **regulative model**, describes cultures that are highly individualistic and, at the same time, highly motivated to avoid uncertainty. In these cultures, organizations themselves are structured to contain competition and conflict by emphasizing regulation and bureaucratic rules. In France, for example, conflicts that might be created by high status differences are minimized because personal contact between organizational levels is minimized and differences are negotiated by means of rules and distant third parties. Similar cultures include Eastern European and Iberic countries, and Germany.

Why Do Cultural Differences Matter?

Understanding different cultural approaches to conflict is important because misunderstandings between cultures can reduce their ability to effectively negotiate together. For example, research in the U.S. and Japanese cultures suggests that one-on-one negotiations involving parties from these quite different cultures are less likely to make joint gains than are one-on-one relationships involving parties within the same culture.[92] As described by cross-cultural experts, "Team members from collective cultures are more likely to look for mutual gain. . ., to focus on building and maintaining the relationship, and to come to the table in a 'humble,' not assertive, posture. *This should not be confused with weakness*" (italics added).[93]

Also, managers moving between cultures must take attitudes toward conflict into account. To illustrate, although Americans find that task conflict is beneficial in groups, this belief does not hold true in every culture. Researchers compared the decision making effectiveness and amount of task conflict in U.S. and Chinese groups.[94] High task conflict did generate more effective decisions among the U.S. groups, although this was the case only when group members were friendly with each other. However, among the Chinese groups, those with high task conflict had relatively low performance, whether group members were friends or not. The researchers interpreted these results as suggesting that the Chinese might be more sensitive to the potential for discord in their groups, and would display less performance improvement as a result. Overall, the results suggest that the task conflict advantage so widely assumed in the U.S. culture may be culture specific, and that, in other cultures, different factors, such as the nature of group cohesiveness, may be more likely to make teams effective. A manager that fails to recognize such differences will have trouble managing a team in another culture.

Finally, managers must be aware that conflict styles in other cultures may be changing. For example, there is some evidence that Hong Kong businesses are increasingly adopting confrontive styles.[95] In today's fast-changing global organizations, managers working cross-culturally should be aware of the potential for cultural differences, but cautious about stereotyping the style of any particular culture.

In Conclusion

Conflict is a normal part of organizational life. You will find yourself engaged in it, and you will probably have to deal with others' conflicts as well. This chapter has outlined some of the basic ideas and approaches that you will need.

Apply What You Have Learned. . .

World Class Companies: Southwest Airlines and Continental Airlines

In recent times economically stressed airlines have tried to cut employee wages, leading to intense labor–management conflict. Although lowering wages can theoretically lead to higher productivity and operating margins, a study of the aviation industry by a research team at MIT suggests that if wage reductions are accompanied by increased conflict and a deterioration of workplace culture, they are likely to cause deterioration in many aspects of firm performance.[96] For example, union–management conflict is related to reduced service quality (defined as the safety and reliability of the travel experience), reduced aircraft productivity, and reduced operating margins.

Southwest Airlines has been the highest-performing firm in the airline industry, and at least part of its success can be attributed to the quality of relations it has with its employees, many of whom are unionized. The cooperative culture at Southwest contributes to faster aircraft turnarounds, higher labor productivity, and higher levels of service quality.

Southwest offers profit-sharing and flexible work rules. Supervisors are highly involved with front-line employees, who are recruited for their teamwork skills. There is a high level of trust and cooperation between employees and their managers. Southwest often earns a place at or near the top of *Fortune*'s "Best Companies to Work For" list.

Another airline known for having a high-quality workplace culture and low levels of conflict is Continental. In the 1980s, Continental followed a union suppression strategy and eventually broke the pilots' and mechanics' unions. However, the strategy did not produce sustained positive performance, as service quality declined and, in 1991, the company was forced into bankruptcy. After emerging from bankruptcy in 1993, unions were created once more and the new management created greater trust between labor and management. Today Continental is known as having a high-quality workplace culture and low levels of conflict.

In the airline industry, employee gains in labor relations do not necessarily lead to company losses; in fact, in the presence of unions, company performance seems to improve on certain dimensions. For example, today both Southwest and Continental negotiate their labor contracts more quickly than other airlines and have a lower probability of work disruptions such as strikes or slowdowns. Although the unions do bring higher wage costs, union members also deliver higher aircraft productivity.

In summary, the research team that studied conflict in the aviation industry asserts, "Efforts to build an effective labor relations system by focusing on the quality of the relationships among employees, supervisors, and managers, and on reaching collective bargaining agreements in a timely and peaceful fashion without resort to extensive use of the NMB [National Mediation Board] procedures, appear to offer considerable potential for improving firm financial performance and the industry's overall service quality."[97]

Discuss

1. What kind of conflict is union–management conflict?
2. When it comes to conflict, what are the advantages to the *employee* of belonging to a union? the disadvantages?
3. When it comes to conflict, what are the advantages to the *company* of having a union? the disadvantages?
4. Do you think that unionization is a positive or a negative force in society?

Source: J. H. Gittell, A. Von Nordenflycht, and T. A. Kochan, "Mutual Gains or Zero Sum? Labor Relations and Firm Performance in the Airline Industry," *Industrial & Labor Relations Review 57* (2), January 2004:163–180.

Advice from the Pros

How to Resolve Your Team's Internal Conflicts

The members of one executive team describe each other as "smart," "team players," and the "best in the business." The members of a different team describe each other as "manipulative," "secretive," and "burned out." Guess which team knows how to manage conflict and, also, makes better decisions?

How do teams fall into unproductive conflict? A comment meant to be on task inadvertently insults someone, who vows to get even. Or, faced with difficult choices, group members feel frustrated and angry and take it out on each other. Or issues become identified with particular personalities.

Productive conflict, on the other hand, emerges from specific types of group process. One executive in a successful team describes such an approach: "We scream a lot, then laugh, and then resolve the issue."[98] Here are some processes successful executive teams use to avoid unproductive conflict in the first place:

1. **Get great facts.** As long as it is objective and current, more information is better. Without good data, executives waste time debating pointless opinions.
2. **Discuss many alternatives.** Deliberately develop many alternatives—perhaps four or five, rather than one or two. Having many choices available prevents choices from becoming black or white, and allows individuals to think more broadly because they have more ideas to work with. Also, when an individual's favorite idea is losing ground, he or she can shift positions without losing face.
3. **Create common goals.** Without common goals, executives are likely to close their minds to others' opinions. Also, as Steve Jobs of Apple, NeXT, and Pixar points out, "It's okay to spend a lot of time arguing about which route to take to San Francisco when everyone wants to end up there, but a lot of time gets wasted in such arguments if one person wants to go to San Francisco and another secretly wants to go to San Diego."[99]
4. **Use humor.** Even if it's contrived, humor can go a long way toward defusing conflict. One company does things like scatter pink plastic flamingos around in its classy headquarters. Another celebrates Halloween and April Fools' Day.
5. **Balance the power structure.** Autocratic leaders create high interpersonal friction. Weak leaders leave a power vacuum. The CEO should be powerful, but so should the other members of the team, especially in their own areas of expertise.
6. **Seek "consensus with qualification."** Sometimes the price of consensus is a decimated team. Instead of pushing too hard and offending and tiring people, if the group cannot reach consensus in a reasonable amount of time, let the more relevant senior manager make the decision using advice from the group.

Discuss

1. Cite several instances of task conflict in this article.
2. Would the approaches to managing intragroup conflict suggested here work for other groups besides executive teams?
3. Which instances of interpersonal conflict are noted? Have you experienced any of these common pitfalls?

Source: Based on K. M. Eisenhardt, J. L. Kahwajy, and L. J. Bourgeois III, "How Management Teams Can Have a Good Fight," *Harvard Business Review,* July–August 1997:77–85.

 ## Gain Experience

I. Guide Your Employees with Dialogue: A Roleplay

Break into groups of four: two employees, a manager, and an observer.

When dialoguing, two individuals directly engage each other and focus on the conflict between them, including aspects of their relationship itself. In this exercise a manager will help two employees who have a disagreement to discuss their issues. Dale and Brenda (or Bob) are both summer interns at a *Fortune* 100 company in which both hope to find very good jobs when they graduate next year with their MBAs. The situation is that Dale has been asking Brenda to help him with his work, which he finds boring. Although Brenda has cooperated many times to help her colleague, she now thinks the situation has gotten out of hand. In this roleplay, imagine yourself in Dale's or Brenda's shoes and react as you personally might react.

Employee No. 1: Dale

The work we have to do this summer is really dull. "Just grind it out" kinds of data analysis. Brenda does this stuff really quickly, so sometimes I ask her to help me. We do have a certain deadline to meet, and we have to work together to finish our mutual reports. But I'm more of an idea kind of guy, really. Although I am not part of the marketing team, on the side this summer, I am working on a marketing plan for our great new product. I really want to impress this company. The way to do that is not to do grunt work. It's to be innovative. I want Brenda to cut me some slack.

Employee No. 2: Brenda (Bob)

I work really hard and I want to have a successful career in the marketing group of this or a similar company. After I have proven myself as a strong market analyst, I hope to join a team that designs marketing campaigns. We have been assigned a lot of detailed work this summer, and I want to make sure we do it effectively and efficiently. I know that the quality of our product may determine whether I get a job offer. In the meantime, Dale asks for my help far too often. He can't seem to get his own work done and meet the deadlines, and he's always asking me to help him out at the last minute. He is jeopardizing our project, and I am sick and tired of doing his work! I want him to do his own work and stop jeopardizing my job prospects.

The Manager

Bring your employees together to discuss this problem. As their manager, your task is to help your employees to do the following things. Encourage them to address them in this order:

1. Clarify the issues over which they disagree.
2. Explore the underlying needs and forces involved.

3. Clarify their feelings about the situation overall.

4. Help them decide what to do.

Discussion

1. For each group, the observers should report on how well the manager was able to do his or her four tasks. Please share techniques the manager used that were especially effective.

2. Research suggests that dialoguing only works when the coworkers:
   - Are personally capable of effective and efficient communication.
   - Believe their interaction is more likely to be useful than stressful.
   - Are both motivated to resolve the conflict.
   - Have equal power to act in the situation.

What happened in this exercise that either supports or refutes this view of the efficacy of dialoguing?

II. The Virtualiens

This is an online group project to be completed outside of class. Use conventional e-mail or, even more conveniently, online chats as provided by services such as Blackboard.

Project Goals

In groups of five, one student, serving as the team leader, is assigned the job of assembling a profile of the team and circulating it to the team for their approval. Because this team only meets virtually, the purpose of the profile is to introduce the team to each other and begin to develop some spirit of group cohesion. What makes the project challenging is that, whereas the leader represents his or her own culture, the other team members represent a culture or cultures that are unknown to the leader and to each other. The professor will teach the team members about their cultures by giving them written profiles that tell them how to act but which they do not share with their leader.

Role description for the team leader/boss

You have been selected to lead a new cross-cultural, cross-functional virtual team. As leader, your first task is to assemble a profile of the team. You must get information from all of your team members, organize it, and circulate it to the team for their approval. All team members must sign off on whether or not they think the profile is both accurate and useful in helping the team develop cohesion. The profile of team members should include the following for each team member:

a. A one paragraph description of his or her professional background

b. His or her current title

c. A one paragraph description of his or her current responsibilities

d. Any other information you think would help the team to develop cohesion

Be creative in soliciting information here!

Your team members may not refuse to answer your e-mails. However, they may not always give you the information you want. Often this occurs because, as a member of a different culture, you have not understood how to approach team members effectively. If an individual refuses to give you information, your job is to find a way to convince them to comply with your requests.

Time limit: To be determined by your professor. Somewhere in the range of 3 to 7 days is recommended. Effort limit: Leaders should try at least four times to elicit information from each individual.

Role description for four or more Virtualiens

Your professor will give you your role description.

Written assignment

Based on what you experienced and learned in this exercise, write a one-page guide for employees who are communicating both cross-culturally and virtually.

Can You Solve This Manager's Problem?

"Hi, I'm from Corporate. . ."

Six months ago Carla Albertson, Chief Financial Officer (CFO) of Cortech, accepted a new member, Ricardo Alvarez, into her department. Alvarez formerly worked in finance at Pytheon, the company that had acquired Cortech just one year ago. When a position had opened up in her group, Albertson was asked by the HR department of Pytheon to interview Alvarez. She had been one of half a dozen persons asked to do so, with all of their input going back to corporate management. Corporate managers made the final decision about who to hire for the position, and Alvarez was their top choice.

Albertson had rated Alvarez among her top three candidates for the job and was reasonably pleased to have him as an employee. Unfortunately, the others in her department were not as comfortable with him. Behind his back they speculated about things such as what his salary was and why he had been hired. Was he there to spy on them in some way? to give corporate managers ideas about who should be laid off, for instance? Was he there to change their policies and procedures? Their suspicions led them to ostracize Alvarez. Although they were polite to him, they seldom invited him to lunch or to outside parties.

Alvarez' job was technical and did not give him regular opportunities to interact with the rest of the group on business matters. So he had few chances to allay the fears and suspicions of his coworkers. Gradually he just withdrew into his office and did his job. He began to hang out with several other people who had also come down from corporate, having lunch with them regularly in the company cafeteria. This behavior only confirmed his coworkers' suspicions that he was from corporate and up to no good.

Discuss

1. Analyze this problem using conflict theory.
2. Suggest what Albertson should do about the situation.

Chapter Summary and Key Terms

What is conflict and why is it a major factor in organizational life?

Conflict is an awareness of incompatible goals and the belief that one party will negatively influence the other party's pursuit of their goals. The three main spheres of conflict are relationships, tasks, and processes.

conflict   372
negotiation   372
manifest conflict   372
latent conflict   372
relationship conflict   372
task conflict   372
process conflict   372

In general, how do managers deal with conflict?

The main sources of interpersonal conflict in organizational life are misunderstandings, resentments and differences, the belief that goals are competitive, and destructive criticism. Dialoguing can be used to manage a conflict, but only when the conflicting parties are effective communicators and believe they can achieve their mutual goals.

How should you approach interpersonal conflicts?

naïve realism   376
false polarization   376
incompatibility error   376
transparency overestimation   376
integrators   378
obligers   378
dominators   378
avoiders   379
compromisers   379
problem-solving   380
appeals to a third party   380
dialogue   380
hostile attribution bias   380
bullying   381

What should you do when your team members have a conflict?

In general, some level of task conflict within a group probably increases its performance. Too much conflict, however, reduces performance. Managers should take immediate steps to reduce relationship conflict, but they should evaluate a task conflict to see whether or not it might be useful to the group decision making.

How should you intervene when teams are in conflict with each other?

Groups conflict because of competition over scarce resources, and because individuals identify themselves with their group and want to see themselves favorably in comparison with others. Intergroup conflict can may enhance intergroup problem solving, and intragroup motivation and performance, but it can also create suspicion and stereotypes of the out-group and punish individual members who sacrifice for their group.

realistic group conflict   384
social identity theory   384

What happens when employees have a conflict with their organization?

Companies use a variety of dispute resolution techniques to avoid escalated disputes. These include mediation, arbitration, and mediation–arbitration. In addition, labor unions protect and advance their members' interests in companies. Whistle-blowers disclose immoral or illegitimate practices under the control of their employers to persons or organizations that may be able to correct the wrongdoing.

mediation   386
arbitration   386
mediation–arbitration   386
certified union   386
decertified union   386
collective bargaining   386
open door policy   387
whistle-blowing   387

What are some cross-cultural differences in approaches to conflict, and why do they matter?

Some cultures favor a confrontational model, whereas others prefer a harmony model or a regulative model

confrontation model   387
harmony model   388
regulative model   388

Explorations

1. More on unions. . .
Check out the AFL-CIO Web site and find three issues that you think would be interesting to discuss in class. Learn enough about these issues to be able to briefly present them if asked.

2. Conflict research
Choose a type of conflict that particularly interests you (interpersonal, intergroup, intragroup, individuals within their organization) and, using an academic database, summarize three research-based articles that address that type. Also find two examples of the type of conflict you have chosen, using the Web or other sources.

3. International Association for Conflict Management
Log on to the International Association for Conflict Management Web site for resources on conflict. This site covers business, academic, and government resources: Find several resources in each category. How do they compare? What resources can businesses obtain from the other areas?

4. Consultants in conflict management
Web search for "conflict management" and check the sponsored links for types of products available for conflict management. What types of conflict do they address? What kinds of products are offered?

References

[1] K. Boulding, *Conflict and Defense* (New York: Harper & Row, 1963); K. W. Thomas, "Conflict and Negotiation Processes in Organizations," in M.D. Dunnette and L.M. Hough, eds., *Handbook of Industrial and Organizational Psychology 3*, 2nd ed. (Palo Alto, CA: Consulting Psychologists Press, 1992):651–717.

[2] E. A. Mannix, C. Tinsley, and M. H. Bazerman, "Negotiating Over Time: Impediments to Integrative Solutions," *Organizational Behavior and Human Decision Processes 62*, 1995:241–251.

[3] K. W. Thomas and W. H. Schmidt, "A Survey of Managerial Interests with Respect to Conflict," *Academy of Management Journal 10*, 1976:315–318; E. McShulskis, "Managing Employee Conflicts," *HR Magazine 41* (9), September 1996:16.

[4] M. Messier quoted in E. McShulskis, "Managing Employee Conflicts," *HR Magazine 41* (9), September 1996:16.

[5] M. Bazerman, E. Mannix, and L. Thompson, "Groups as Mixed-Motive Negotiations," in E. J. Lawler and B. Markovsky, eds., *Advances in Group Processes: A Research Annal 5* (Greenwich, CT: JAI Press, 1988):195–216.

[6] P. M. Kellett and D. G. Dalton, *Managing Conflict in a Negotiated World: A Narrative Approach to Achieving Dialogue and Change* (Thousand Oaks, CA: Sage Publications, 2001).

[7] K. Jehn, "A Multimethod Examination of the Benefits and Detriments of Intragroup Conflict," *Administrative Science Quarterly 40*, 1995:256–282; K. Jehn and E. A. Mannix, "The Dynamic Nature of Conflict: A Longitudinal Study of Intragroup Conflict and Group Performance," *Academy of Management Journal 44* (2), April 2001:238–251.

[8] E. Mannix, "Editor's Comments: Conflict and Conflict Resolution—A Return to Theorizing," *Academy of Management Review 28* (4), October 2003:543–546.

[9] A. Amason and H. Sapienza, "The Effects of Top Management Team Size and Interaction Norms on Cognitive and Affective Conflict," *Journal of Management 23*, 1997:496–516.

[10] L. Coser, *The Functions of Social Conflict* (New York: Free Press, 1956); S. B. Bacharach and E. J. Lawler, *Bargaining: Power, Tactics, and Outcomes* (San Francisco: Jossey Bass, 1981); J. Z. Rubin, D. G. Pruitt, and S. H. Kim, *Social Conflict: Escalation, Stalemate, and Settlement*, 2nd ed. (New York: McGraw-Hill, 1994); C. De Dreu and E. Van de Vliert, eds., *Using Conflict in Organizations* (Thousand Oaks, CA: Sage, 1997).

[11] K. Jehn, "A Qualitative Analysis of Conflict Types and Dimensions in Organizational Groups," *Administrative Science Quarterly 42*, 1997:530–557; K. Jehn, G. Northcraft, and M. Neale, "Why Differences Make a Difference: A Field Study of Diversity, Conflict, and Performance in Workgroups," *Administrative Science Quarterly 44*, 1999:741–763.

[12] K. A. Jehn and E. A. Mannix, "The Dynamic Nature of Conflict: A Longitudinal Study of Intragroup Conflict and Group Performance," *Academy of Management Journal 44* (2), April 2001: 238–251.

[13] L. R. Pondy, "Organizational Conflict: Concepts and Models," *Administrative Science Quarterly 12* (2), September 1967:296–320; K. W. Thomas, "Conflict and Negotiation Processes in Organizations," in M. Dunnette, ed., *Handbook of Industrial and Organizational Psychology 3*, 2nd ed. (Palo Alto, CA: Consulting Psychologists Press, 1992):651–717.

[14] A. C. Filley, *Interpersonal Conflict Resolution* (Glenview, Illinois: Scott, Foresman and Company, 1975).

[15] M. K. Kozan, "Culture and Conflict Management: A Theoretical Framework," *International Journal of Conflict Management 8* (4), October 1997:338–360.

[16] D. Tjosvold, *Learning to Manage Conflict: Getting People to Work Together Productively* (New York: Lexington Books, 1993).

[17] R. R. Blake and J. S. Mouton, "Loyalty of Representatives to In-group Positions during Intergroup Competition," *Sociometry 24*, 1961:177–183.

[18] M. A. Rahim, "A Strategy for Managing Conflict in Complex Organizations," *Human Relations 38* (1), 1985:81–89; P. M. Kellett and D. G. Dalton, *Managing Conflict in a Negotiated World: A Narrative Approach to Achieving Dialogue and Change* (Thousand Oaks, CA: Sage Publications, 2001).

[19] P. M. Kellett and D. G. Dalton, *Managing Conflict in a Negotiated World: A Narrative Approach to Achieving Dialogue and Change* (Thousand Oaks, CA: Sage Publications, 2001).

[20] M. A. Rahim, "Toward a Theory of Managing Organizational Conflict," *International Journal of Conflict Management 13* (3), 2002:206–235.

[21] M. Sherif, "Superordinate Goals in the Reduction of Intergroup Conflict," *American Journal of Sociology 68*, 1958:349–358.

[22] E. Van de Vliert, "Enhancing Performance by Conflict–Stimulating Intervention," in C. De Dreu and E. Van de Vliert, eds., *Using Conflict in Organizations* (Thousand Oaks, CA: Sage, 1997):208–222.

[23] S. P. Robbins, *Managing Organization Conflict: A Nontraditional Approach* (Englewood Cliffs, NJ: Prentice Hall, 1974).

[24] D. K. Sherman, L. D. Nelson, and L. D. Ross, "Naïve Realism and Affirmative Action: Adversaries Are More Similar Than They Think," *Basic & Applied Social Psychology 25* (4), December 2003:275–289.

[25] L. Thompson, "'They Saw a Negotiation': Partisanship and Involvement," *Journal of Personality & Social Psychology 68* (5), May 1995:839–853.

[26] J. D. Vorauer and J. J. Cameron, "So Close, and Yet So Far: Does Collectivism Foster Transparency Overestimation?" *Journal of Personality & Social Psychology 83* (6), December 2002:1344–1352.

[27] J. C. Macionis, *Sociology*, 10th ed. (Upper Saddle River, NJ: Pearson/Prentice Hall, 2005).

[28] U.S. Census Bureau, 2002.

[29] R. A. Baron, "Negative Effects of Destructive Criticism: Impact on Conflict, Self-Efficacy, and Task Performance," *Journal of Applied Psychology 73* (2), May 1988:199–207.

[30] T. Coens and M. Jenkins, *Abolishing Performance Appraisals* (San Francisco, CA: Berrett-Koehler Publishers, Inc., 2002).

[31] D. M. Messick and C. G. McClintock, "Motivational Basis of Choice in Experimental Games," *Journal of Experimental Social Psychology 4*, 1968:1–25; D. M. Kuhlman and A. F. J. Marshello, "Individual Differences in Game Motivation as Moderators of Preprogrammed Strategy Effects in Prisoner's Dilemma," *Journal of Personality and Social Psychology 32*, 1975:922–931; G. P. Knight, A. G. Dubro, and C. Chao, "Information Processing and the Development of Cooperative, Competitive and Individualistic Social Values," *Developmental Psychology 21*, 1985:37–45.

[32] R. R. Blake and J. S. Mouton, *The Managerial Grid* (Houston, TX: Gulf Publishing Company, 1964); K. W. Thomas, "Conflict and Conflict Management," in M. D. Dunnette, ed., *Handbook of Industrial and Organizational Psychology* (Chicago: Rand-McNally, 1976):889–935; M. A. Rahim, "A Measure of Styles of Handling Interpersonal Conflict," *Academy of Management Journal 26* (2), 1983:368–376; E. Van de Vliert and B. Kabanoff, "Toward Theory-Based Measures of Conflict Management," *Academy of Management Journal 33* (1), March 1990:199–209.

[33] J. M. Mikolic, J. C. Parker, and D. G. Pruitt, "Escalation in Response to Persistent Annoyance: Groups Versus Individuals and Gender Effects," *Journal of Personality and Social Psychology 72*, 1997:151–163; D. G. Pruitt, J. C. Parker, and J. M. Mikolic, "Escalation as a Reaction to Persistent Annoyance," *International Journal of Conflict Management 8* (3), July 1997:252–270.

[34] R. E. Walton, *Managing Conflict: Interpersonal Dialogue and Third-Party Roles*, 2nd ed. (Reading, Massachusetts: Addison-Wesley Publishing Company, 1987):5.

[35] R. E. Walton, *Managing Conflict: Interpersonal Dialogue and Third-Party Roles*, 2nd ed. (Reading, Massachusetts: Addison-Wesley Publishing Company, 1987).

[36] P. M. Kellett and D. G. Dalton, *Managing Conflict in a Negotiated World: A Narrative Approach to Achieving Dialogue and Change* (Thousand Oaks, CA: Sage Publications, 2001).

[37] K. A. Dodge, R. R. Murphy and K. Buchsbaum, "The Assessment of Intention–Cue Detection Skills in Children: Implications for Development Psychopathology," *Child Development 55*, 1984:163–173.

[38] R. A. Baron, "Positive Effects of Conflict: Insights from Social Cognition," in C. de Dreu and E. Van de Vliert, eds., *Using Conflict in Organizations* (Thousand Oaks, CA: Sage, 1997):177–191.

[39] R. Simpson and C. Cohen, "Dangerous Work: The Gendered Nature of Bullying in the Context of Higher Education," *Gender, Work and Organization 11* (2), March 2004:163–186.

[40] Adapted from B. Leichtling, "Bullies in the Workplace," *Office Pro 65* (5), June/July 2005: 10–12.

[41] "Coping with Conflict with Your Boss," *Supervisory Management 38* (8), August 1993:11–12.

[42] D. Tjosvold, *Learning to Manage Conflict: Getting People to Work Together Productively* (New York: Lexington Books, 1993).

[43] K. Jehn, "Enhancing Effectiveness: An Investigation of Advantages and Disadvantages of Value-Based Intragroup Conflict," *International Journal of Conflict Management 5*, 1994:223–238; K. Jehn, "A Multi-Method Examination of the Benefits and Detriments of Intragroup Conflict," *Administrative Science Quarterly 40*, 1995:256–282; C. K. W. de Dreu and E. Van de Vliert, *Using Conflict in Organizations* (London: Sage, 1997).

[44] For a full discussion see C. K. W. de Dreu and L. R. Weingart, "Task versus Relationship Conflict, Team Performance, and Team Member Satisfaction: A Meta-Analysis," *Journal of Applied Psychology 88* (4), August 2003:741–749.

[45] For a review see C. K. W. de Dreu and L. R. Weingart, "Task versus Relationship Conflict, Team Performance, and Team Member Satisfaction: A Meta-Analysis," *Journal of Applied Psychology 88* (4), August 2003:741–749.

[46] While K. Jehn, in "A Multimethod Examination of the Benefits and Detriments of Intragroup Conflict," *Administrative Science Quarterly 40*, 1995:256–282, found that task conflict had a stronger positive effect on nonroutine tasks, subsequent research shows the opposite. See for example A. C. Amason, "Distinguishing the Effects of Functional and Dysfunctional Conflict on Strategic Decision Making: Resolving a Paradox for Top Management Groups," *Academy of Management Journal 39*, 1996:123–148; M. Turner and A. Pratkanis, "Mitigating Groupthink by Stimulating Constructive Conflict," in C. K. W. de Dreu and E. Van de Vliert, eds., *Using Conflict in Organizations* (London: Sage, 1997):39–52; C. K. W. de Dreu and L. R. Weingart, "A Contingency Theory of Task Conflict and Performance in Groups and Organizational Teams," in M. A. West, D. Tjosvold, & K. Smith, eds., *International Handbook of Organizational Teamwork and Cooperative Working* (Chichester, UK: Wiley, 2003):151–166.

[47] K. Jehn, C. Chadwick, and S. Thatcher, "To Agree or Not to Agree: Diversity, Conflict, and Group Outcomes,"

International Journal of Conflict Management 8, 1997:287–306.

[48] K. A. Jehn, "Affective and Cognitive Conflict in Work Groups: Increasing Performance through Value-Based Intragroup Conflict," in C. K. W. de Dreu and E. Van de Vliert, *Using Conflict in Organizations* (Thousand Oaks, CA: Sage Publications, 1997):87–100.

[49] C. K. W. de Dreu and L. R. Weingart, "Task versus Relationship Conflict, Team Performance, and Team Member Satisfaction: A Meta-Analysis," *Journal of Applied Psychology 88* (4), August 2003:741–749.

[50] A. Amason, "Distinguishing the Effects of Functional and Dysfunctional Conflict on Strategic Decision Making: Resolving a Paradox for Top Management Teams," *Academy of Management Journal 39* (1), 1996:123–148.

[51] K. A. Jehn and E. A. Mannix, "The Dynamic Nature of Conflict: A Longitudinal Study of Intragroup Conflict and Group Performance," *Academy of Management Journal 44* (2), April 2001:238–257.

[52] Adapted from D. Tjosvold, "Cooperation Theory, Constructive Controversy, and Effectiveness: Learning from Crisis," in R. A. Guzzo, E. Salas, and Associates, eds., *Team Effectiveness and Decision Making in Organizations* (San Francisco, CA: Jossey-Bass, 1995):79–112.

[53] M. Sherif, *Group Conflict and Cooperation* (London: Routledge, 1966).

[54] M. Billig, *Social Psychology and Intergroup Relations* (London: Academic Press, 1976); M. Hewstone and K. Greenland, "Intergroup Conflict," *International Journal of Psychology 35* (2), 2000:136–144.

[55] H. Tajfel, "Social Psychology of Intergroup Relations," *Annual Review of Psychology* (Palo Alto, CA: Annual Reviews, 1982):1–39.

[56] G. Bornstein, "Intergroup Conflict: Individual, Group, and Collective Interests," *Personality & Social Psychology Review 7* (2), 2003:129–145.

[57] R. V. Gould, "Collective Violence and Group Solidarity: Evidence from Feuding Society," *American Sociological Review 64*, 1999:356–380.

[58] L. L. Putnam and M. S. Poole, "Conflict and Negotiation," in F. M. Jablin, L. L. Putnam, K. H. Roberts, and L. W. Porter, eds., *Handbook of Organizational Communication* (Beverly Hills, CA: Sage, 1987):549–599.

[59] J. F. Dashiell, "Experimental Studies of the Influence of Social Situations on the Behavior of Individual Human Adults," in C. Murchison, ed., *A Handbook of Social Psychology* (Dorchester, MA: Clark University Press, 1935):1097–1158; N. L. Kerr, "Motivational Losses in Groups: A Social Dilemma Analysis," *Journal of Personality and Social Psychology 45*, 1983:819–828; T. Yamagishi, "Exit from the Group as an Individualistic Solution to the Free Rider Problem in the United States and Japan," *Journal of Personality and Social Psychology 35,* 1988:1–11.

[60] G. Bornstein and I. Erev, "The Enhancing Effect of Intergroup Competition on Group Performance," in C. De Dreu and E. Van de Vliert, eds., *Using Conflict in Organizations* (Thousand Oaks, CA: Sage, 1997):116–128.

[61] A. Bizman and Y. Yinon, "Intergroup Conflict Management Strategies as Related to Perceptions of Dual Identity and Separate Groups," *Journal of Social Psychology 144* (2), April 2004:115–126.

[62] D. Zillmann, "Cognition-Excitation Interdependencies in the Escalation of Anger and Angry Aggression," in M. Potegal and J. F. Knutson, eds., *The Dynamics of Aggression* (Hillsdale, NJ: Erlbaum, 1994).

[63] A. Bizman and Y. Yinon, "Intergroup Conflict Management Strategies as Related to Perceptions of Dual Identity and Separate Groups," *Journal of Social Psychology 144* (2), April 2004:115–126.

[64] T. F. Pettigrew, "Intergroup Contact Theory," *Annual Review of Psychology 49*, 1998:65–85.

[65] M. Hewstone and K. Greenland, "Intergroup Conflict," *International Journal of Psychology 35* (2), April 2000:136–144.

[66] D. B. Lipsky, R. L. Seeber and R. D. Fincher, *Emerging Systems for Managing Workplace Conflict: Lessons from American Corporations for Managers and Dispute Resolution Profssionals* (San Francisco, CA: Jossey-Bass, 2003).

[67] D. B. Lipsky, R. L. Seeber and R. D. Fincher, *Emerging Systems for Managing Workplace Conflict: Lessons from American Corporations for Managers and Dispute Resolution Professionals* (San Francisco, CA: Jossey-Bass, 2003).

[68] D. B. Lipsky, R. L. Seeber and R. D. Fincher, *Emerging Systems for Managing Workplace Conflict: Lessons from American Corporations for Managers and Dispute Resolution Professionals* (San Francisco, CA: Jossey-Bass, 2003).

[69] D. G. Blanchflower and A. Bryson, "What Effect Do Unions Have on Wages Now and Would 'What Do Unions Do' Be Surprised?" *National Bureau of Economic Research working paper no. w9973*, September 2003.

[70] B. Bratsberg and J. F. Ragan Jr., "Changes in the Union Wage Premium by Industry," *Industrial and Labor Relations Review 56* (1), October 2002:65–83.

[71] D. M. Schweiger, W. R. Sandberg and J. W. Ragan, "Group Approaches for Improving Stategic Decision Making: A Comparative Analysis of Dialectical Inquiry, Devil's Advocacy, and Consensus," *Academy of Management Journal 29* (1), 1986:51–71.

[72] C. K. W. De Dreu and N. K. De Vries, "Minority Dissent in Organizations," in C. De Dreu and E. Van de Vliert, eds.,

Using Conflict in Organizations (Thousand Oaks, CA: Sage, 1997):72–86.

[73] L. Cohen and B. M. Staw, "Fun's Over, Fact-Finders Are Here: A Case Study of Institutional Dissent," paper presented at the Academy of Management meetings, Vancouver, BC, August 11–14, 1995.

[74] B. Schneider, "An Interactionist Perspective on Organizational Effectiveness," in L. L. Cummings and B. Staw, eds., *Research in Organizational Behavior* (Greenwich, CT: JAI Press, 1983):1–31.

[75] J. W. Graham, "Principled Organizational Dissent," in B. M. Staw and L. L. Cummings, eds., *Research on Organizational Behavior 8* (Greenwich, CT: JAI Press 1986):1–52.

[76] J. P. Near and M. P. Miceli, "Organizational Dissidence: The Case of Whistle-Blowing," *Journal of Business Ethics 4* (1), 1985:1–16.

[77] J. P. Near and M. P. Miceli, "Whistle-Blowing: Myth and Reality," *Journal of Management 22* (3), 1996:507–526.

[78] M. P. Miceli and J. P. Near, "Individual and Situational Correlates of Whistleblowing," *Personnel Psychology 41*, 1988:267-282; M. P. Miceli, J. P. Near, and C. Schwenk, "Who Blows the Whistle and Why?" *Industrial and Labor Relations Review 45* (1), October 1991:113–130.

[79] M. P. Miceli and J. P. Near, "Who Blows the Whistle and Why?" *Industrial and Labor Relations Review 45* (1), October 1991:113–130.

[80] M. P. Miceli and J. P. Near, "Whistleblowing: Reaping the Benefits," *Academy of Management Executive 8* (3), August 1994:65–72.

[81] M. P. Miceli and J. P. Near, "Whistleblowing: Reaping the Benefits," *Academy of Management Executive 8* (3), August 1994:65–72.

[82] M. T. Rehg, M. P. Miceli, J. P. Near, and J. R. Van Scotter, "Predicting Retaliation against Whistle-Blowers: Outcomes of Power Relationships within Organizations," *Academy of Management Proceedings*, 2004:E1–E6.

[83] J. L. Sheler, "When Employees Squeal on Fellow Workers," *U.S. News & World Report*, November 16, 1981:81–82. The companies are IBM and Bank of America in San Francisco.

[84] S. P. Robbins, *Managing Organization Conflict: A Nontraditional Approach* (Englewood Cliffs, NJ: Prentice-Hall, 1974); G. Hofstede, *Culture's Consequences: International Differences in Work-Related Attitudes* (Beverly Hills, CA: Sage, 1984).

[85] S. Ting-Toomey and J. G. Oetzel, *Managing Intercultural Conflict Effectively* (London: Sage Publications, 2001).

[86] S. P. Robbins, *Managing Organization Conflict: A Nontraditional Approach* (Englewood Cliffs, NJ: Prentice-Hall, 1974); G. Hofstede, *Culture's Consequences: International Differences in Work-Related Attitudes* (Beverly Hills, CA: Sage, 1984).

[87] J. P. Lederach, "Of Nets, Nails, and Problems: The Folk Language of Conflict Resolution in a Central American Setting," in K. Avruch, J. A. Scimessa, and P. W. Black, eds., *Conflict Resolution: Cross Cultural Perspectives* (New York: Greenwood Press, 1991):165–186.

[88] S. Ting-Toomey, "Toward a Theory of Conflict and Culture," in W. B. Gudykunst, L. P. Stewart, and S. Ting-Toomey, eds., *Communication, Culture and Organizational Processes* (Beverly Hills, CA: Sage, 1985):71–86.

[89] S. Ting-Toomey, "Toward a Theory of Conflict and Culture," in W. B. Gudykunst, L. P. Stewart, and S. Ting-Toomey, eds., *Communication, Culture and Organizational Processes* (Beverly Hills, CA: Sage, 1985):71–86.

[90] G. Yukl, C. M. Falbe, and J. Y. Youn, "Patterns of Influence Behavior for Managers," *Group and Organization Management 18*, 1993:5–28.

[91] K. M. Weaver, "Attitudes toward Cooperative Strategies: A Cross-Cultural Analysis of Entrepreneurs," *Journal of International Business Studies 31*, Fourth Quarter, 2000:591–609.

[92] W. L. Adair, J. M. Brett, and T. Okumura, "Negotiation Behavior When Cultures Collide: The United States and Japan," *Journal of Applied Psychology 86* (3), June 2001:371–385; K. Pan Fan and K. Zhang Zigang, "Cross-Cultural Challenges When Doing Business in China," *Singapore Management Review 26* (1) 1st half, 2004:81–90.

[93] J. L. Graham, and Y. Sano, *Smart Bargaining: Doing Business with the Japanese* (New York: Harper & Row, 1989); S. C. Schneider and J. Barsoux, *Managing Across Cultures* (London: Prentice Hall/Financial Times, 2003): 237.

[94] R. Nibler and K. L. Harris, "The Effects of Culture and Cohesiveness on Intragroup Conflict and Effectiveness," *Journal of Social Psychology 143* (5), October 2003:613–631.

[95] C. C. Cheung and K. B. Chuah, "Intergroup Conflict Management Framework for Hong Kong's Manufacturing Industry," *Engineering Management Journal 12* (3), September 2000:26–33.

[96] J. H. Gittell, A. Von Nordenflycht, and T. A. Kochan, "Mutual Gains or Zero Sum? Labor Relations and Firm Performance in the Airline Industry," *Industrial & Labor Relations Review 57* (2), January 2004:163–180.

[97] J. H. Gittell, A. Von Nordenflycht, and T. A. Kochan, "Mutual Gains or Zero Sum? Labor Relations and Firm Performance in the Airline Industry," *Industrial & Labor Relations Review 57* (2), January 2004:163–180, 177

[98] K. M. Eisenhardt, J. L. Kahwajy, and L. J. Bourgeois III, "How Management Teams Can Have a Good Fight," *Harvard Business Review*, July–August 1997:77–85, 78.

[99] K. M. Eisenhardt, J. L. Kahwajy, and L. J. Bourgeois III, "How Management Teams Can Have a Good Fight," *Harvard Business Review*, July–August 1997:77–85, 80.

15

Designing Effective Organizations

Preview

Total Entertainment Restaurant, Inc.

Located in Wichita, Kansas, Total Entertainment Restaurant is the company behind the Fox and Hound Smokehouse and Tavern restaurant chain. At the time of this writing it is a $100 million company, with 54 restaurants in 19 states. The restaurants are a unique concept, combining an upscale ambiance with sports entertainment.

The company is relatively young and small, and its organizational design is relatively simple. There are four people on the senior management team, and they perform a variety of functions, such as site selection, that in a larger corporation might be performed by specialists. Below this team is a middle management group: eleven district managers, along with managers for information technology, human resources, legal affairs, and construction. Below them are the restaurant managers and employees.

The company prides itself on its district managers, who are carefully chosen and given significant autonomy. Whereas the top management team concerns itself with corporate strategy and related tasks, these managers visit each of the restaurants almost daily, where they exhibit and promote the company's entrepreneurial spirit. They are given financial and operational freedom to run specials of their choosing. Because the full company management team meets often, their great ideas are readily rolled out to the other districts and restaurants.

The chain hopes to grow 20 percent per year to 300 stores, and it realizes that new design features, such as specialist departments, will have to be added. But for now, Total Entertainment Restaurant, Inc., exemplifies the relatively flat, or horizontal, organizational structure that is popular in so many companies today.

Who Designs Organizations and, in General, What Do These Designers Do?

Organizational design is the way in which an organization divides its labor into distinct tasks and then achieves coordination of these tasks.[1] Put simply, it is designing systems that organize employees. After a task has been divided into subtasks to be done by specialists, managers must figure out how to reintegrate the subtasks to meet the organization's goals.[2] For example, the task could be the introduction of a new product. Subtasks would be designing, manufacturing, and marketing the product. Only when these subtasks are well organized will the product launch be a success.

Building on this straightforward definition, organizational design quickly becomes fairly complex. An organization is like a forest, a living, growing, and adapting organism subject to its own biological limitations and its environment. It is comprised of living organisms (people) who work in a hierarchy to sell goods and services in order to survive. To adapt to their environments, organizations must evolve, and managers must try to improve their organization's design to better meet the organization's goals. How managers implement an organizational design becomes "a process of specifying optimal combinations of organizational characteristics to achieve organizational outcomes."[3] The key word here is "optimal": Which organizational design is the best fit to the organization's constraints and challenges?

Organizations are designed by entrepreneurs, top management groups, and company design teams. Companies may bring in change experts trained in organizational psychology and organizational development. The fundamental questions these people pose for the company are: What is the nature of our competitive environment? What work do we as a company perform and how can we best organize that work? Who should perform that work? In summary, what is the optimal combination of organizational characteristics to achieve organizational goals?

What Are the Major Factors Influencing Organizational Design?

Researchers have identified several environmental factors that drive an organization to adopt a particular design. Three of these factors are based on the company's historical origins, whereas three originate in the business the company is in.

The Three Historical Factors That Drive Organizational Design

The three historical factors that drive an organizational design are the personality and style of the founder, the design trends during the period in which the company was founded, and the historic size of the company.

WHO WAS THE FOUNDER? The first driver of organizational design is the personality and style of the individual who started the company. Computer giant Microsoft is brilliant, innovative, and competitive because Bill Gates is all of these, and the ice cream company Ben & Jerry's Homemade Holdings, Inc., has been a participative, flat organization because of Ben Cohen's and Jerry Greenfield's personal philosophies.

The founder's influence on company design and culture may last for decades. For example, McDonalds' founder Ray Kroc was "famously obsessive," and fond of saying "If you've time to lean, you've time to clean."[4] Since he founded the company in 1955, the restaurant chain has thrived on a worldwide reputation for its immutable standards and consistent service. Employees are trained in every detail of the franchise, and there are plenty. Potato peelers are cleaned all over the world on the same day of the year, drink cups are always filled to a point just below the arches logo, and mustard is served in exactly five drops.[5]

Lincoln Electric Company is a manufacturing bureaucracy famous for its philosophy that employees should earn and be promoted in direct proportion to their individual contribution to the company's effectiveness. (See "World Class Companies" in Chapter 8.) In 1907, James A. Lincoln, brother of the founder of Lincoln Electric, designed the company based on his belief that "Competition is the foundation of man's development. . . . Competition will mean the disappearance of the lazy and incompetent. . . . Competition promotes progress. Competition determines who will be the leader. . . . It is completely necessary for anyone, be he worker, user, distributor or boss, if he is to grow."[6] More than 100 years later the legacy of the founders of this enduringly successful company is still strong, and the company's results-based employee incentive program, a keystone of its organizational design, is widely studied by other organizations.

WHAT CHARACTERIZED ORGANIZATIONAL DESIGN DURING THE HISTORIC PERIOD IN WHICH THE COMPANY WAS FOUNDED? An organization founded during the Industrial Revolution of the nineteenth century is likely to have a highly structured, bureaucratic design.[7] In contrast, an organization founded during the technology boom of the late 1990s would be likely to have a flexible design that includes an energetic culture.

You might think that the global electricity company AES Corporation, a utility with an obvious need to be absolutely precise and efficient, would be designed as a bureaucracy. Yet when founders Roger Sant and Dennis Bakke established AES Corporation in 1981, they set out to build a modern company that they themselves would want to work in. Says Bakke, "We just wanted to create a company that embodied the four principles that we felt mattered in any kind of community, be it a business, church, village, or whatever: fairness, integrity, social responsibility, and fun.... If you're interested in gaining power or moving up in a traditional hierarchy, you're not going to choose to work at AES."[8] For nearly three decades, the company has operated successfully using a relatively unbureaucratic organizational design based on the founders' modern belief in empowering rather than controlling their employees.

WHAT HAS BEEN THE HISTORIC SIZE OF THE COMPANY? The third historic factor that influences organizational design is the number of employees in the company. Even though the size of a company may change, the issues that develop once the size of the company is established are themselves fairly fixed. In a small company there is more opportunity for face-to-face and flexible communication, while in a large company there is more need for standardization as the means for control and communication. Often, these established patterns continue to influence a company even as it grows or shrinks.[9]

So an organization that starts out small is likely to be designed around flexible jobs and a laid-back culture, and it will experience pressure to continue that culture even as it grows. On the other hand, a company that starts out large (or grows very quickly) is likely to have much more structure and definition, and to continue to have these. It is also unlikely to shrink. Larger organizations are more specialized, have more rules, more documentation, and a greater decentralization of decision making further down in their hierarchies.[10]

In sum, an organization's history, culture, values, and entrenched ways of doing things are referred to as its **administrative heritage**.[11] Of course, companies also change as they grow, a phenomenon that will be covered in greater detail in Chapter 16.

The Three Business Factors (Constraints) That Drive Organizational Design

The three business factors that drive a company's design are the environment in which it does business, the work that it performs, and the people it employs.[12] Because these three factors are relatively difficult for management to influence, they are often referred to as **constraints**.[13] For example, although it is theoretically possible for a company to influence its government regulators, the process would be long and time-consuming. Further, it is hard to imagine a company changing the nature of the work that it does (although some do) or the nature of its employees (although some have successfully retrained employees, and others change the nature of their workforce through judicious hiring and firing). Next let's take a detailed look at each of a company's constraints.

WHAT CHARACTERIZES THE COMPANY'S ENVIRONMENT? A company's **environment** consists of those elements outside of the organization that have some influence on it. A company's environment includes competitors, government, the economy, suppliers, stockholders, and customers. Note that in the context of organizational design, environment is

administrative heritage
An organization's history, culture, values, and entrenched ways of doing things.

constraints
The three business factors that drive a company's design and are relatively difficult for management to influence: the environment in which it does business, the work that it performs, and the people it employs.

environment
The elements external to an organization which have some influence on it, including competitors, government, the economy, suppliers, stockholders, and customers.

simple environment
An environment which includes a small number of any given element, such as few competitors.

stable environment
An environment which does not change quickly.

complex environment
An environment that has many elements (such as many competitors).

dynamic environment
An environment that changes quickly, such as one in which competitors frequently produce new products.

diversity
Having different types of environmental influences, such as having many different types of clients or products, or operating in a variety of regions.

hostility
The nature of competition, regulation and other related environmental influences, which ranges from "munificent" (friendly) to "hostile."

uncertainty
The degree to which an environment is predictable.

technology
The technical term for an organization's work; the actions that an individual performs upon an object, with or without the aid of tools or mechanical devices, in order to make some change in that object.

programmed work
Work that is planned, scheduled, inflexible and standardized.

nonprogrammed work
Work that is extemporaneous, spontaneous, flexible and creative.

not an internal company factor. Environment is external. It would not be correct to say, for example, "The environment around here is too political for me." It would be correct to say, "The culture around here is too political for me. " Also correct is, "The environment of this company includes a great many regulators but few competitors."

A company is designed to survive and thrive in a particular competitive environment.[14] In reaction to external factors, it develops a particular business strategy. For example, if a company has few competitors it is said to be doing business in a relatively **simple environment**, and if its products do not change quickly, it is said to be doing business in a relatively **stable** competitive **environment**.[15] Generally, companies doing business in a simple and stable environment are highly structured. Why? Because their basis for competition is almost always quality and/or price rather than innovation. To be successful against their competitors, these companies must meet or beat them in quality and/or price, and this means they must streamline their operations to maximize efficiency. Further, companies in this type of competitive environment already know a great deal about how their competitors do business and about their customers' needs, and they need little new information about them. Thus, they do not have to invest heavily in people and systems that are devoted to researching new markets and technologies. They have relatively little need to innovate.

Of course, these days the number of businesses operating in slow paced, unchanging environments is shrinking. Small town banks are a classic example of companies that traditionally operated in such environments, but which now have a large and varied array of competitors who produce a wide range of competing products.

Today many companies operate in **complex** and **dynamic environments**—that is, environments that have many elements and that change frequently. For example, companies often compete against many competitors who are frequently producing new processes and products. To compete effectively, they must know what new products their competitors will introduce, which new products their customers will demand, and what new competitors will be entering the market. And they must be able to put this knowledge to use quickly. Under these circumstances, companies must invest heavily in knowledge and information, and are designed to maximize learning, innovation, and flexibility. They also adjust their production processes frequently in order to utilize their knowledge.

Companies that create computer software operate in such environments. Their managers worry every day about the hot new products their competitors are developing. Sometimes an entire company can be destroyed by the introduction of an unanticipated competitive product. A company must be designed to deal with these uncertainties.

In addition to complexity and change, environments vary in terms of how diverse, hostile, and uncertain they are.[16] **Diversity** refers to having different types of environmental influences, such as having many different types of clients or products, or operating in a variety of regions. **Hostility** refers to the nature of the competition, regulation, and related influences, and ranges from "munificent" to "hostile." For instance, flower growers who share data on pesticides industry-wide refer to their "friendly competitors" in what is a relatively munificent industry, whereas a construction firm that has to bid on all its contracts may find the competition mean-spirited and subversive—that is, hostile. **Uncertainty** refers to the degree in which an environment is predictable. A company facing fickle customers, perhaps preteen music consumers, would decentralize decision making and empower employees so they could constantly be looking for trends. See Table 15.1 for a summary of the characteristics of organizational environments.

WHAT TYPE OF WORK DOES THE COMPANY DO? A second major business influence on an organization's design is the nature of the work that the employees perform. The technical term researchers often use for an organization's work is **technology**, defined as "the actions that an individual performs upon an object, with or without the aid of tools or mechanical devices, in order to make some change in that object."[17]

Work can be characterized as **programmed** or **nonprogrammed**.[18] Work that is so standardized that it can be described with a formula is quite different from work that is creative. In companies where the work can be coordinated easily by giving people clear directions—for example, where work is programmed—employees are generally told what to

TABLE 15.1 **Overview: Characteristics of Organizational Environments**

Characteristic	Environment	
Complexity	Simple (few competitors, regulations, customers)	Complex (many competitors, regulations, customers)
Change	Stable (static, changes slowly)	Dynamic (changes quickly)
Diversity	Low diversity (few clients and products)	High diversity (many clients and products)
Hostility	Munificent (easy)	Hostile (difficult)
Uncertainty	Certain (predictable)	Uncertain (unpredictable)

do, and various rules and procedures are part of the daily routine. Making batches of chemicals is an example. In contrast, in companies in which the work requires individual input and initiative—for example, where work is nonprogrammed—organizational designs that promote flexibility and systems that promote creativity prevail. The work of a lawyer in a law firm is an example. Related characterizations include whether few or many exceptions are encountered in the work process, and whether or not the work is highly routine (readily analyzable) or not (unanalyzable).[19]

When engaged in manufacturing, some companies perform custom work, producing individualized **units**, such as personalized yachts or kitchens or unique types of furniture in small batches.[20] Others produce hundreds of thousands of identical or nearly identical items, such as toys or cars. They often use assembly lines in the technique that is called **mass production**. A third type of work is that which continues around the clock and has to be constantly monitored. **Continuous production** is found in oil refineries, nuclear power generators, internet providers, and water refineries that must keep their operations going around the clock. Researchers have discovered that these three different kinds of work—unit, mass, and continuous—are performed in companies that are designed in three different ways.[21] The custom work is done by flexible, decentralized organizations; the assembly line work is done by centralized, bureaucratic organizations; and the continuous work is done by organizations that maximize both centralized, hierarchical control and decentralized, professional control of the work they do.

unit
Unique, individualized items, such as custom-made yachts or kitchens or small batches of a unique type of furniture.

mass production
The production of large quantities of identical items, which often uses assembly lines.

continuous production
Work that keeps going around the clock.

WHO ARE THE EMPLOYEES? Finally, organizations are designed because of the nature of both their current and their potential employees. To some extent, formal organizations require people who thrive on formality, whereas flexible organizations require people who thrive on change.[22] People differ in their goals, abilities, training, styles, motivation, demographics, life and career states, psychology, and personality, any of which may influence an organizational design.

For instance, an enterprising organization facing a fast-paced, highly competitive environment demanding creativity needs many people who are self-starters and comfortable with change. A bureaucratic organization in a stable and placid environment needs many people who are steady and conforming.

Organizational Constraints Summarized

Different companies face different business constraints. In one company, environmental factors may be known and require minimal reaction on a day-to-day basis. In another company they may have a great deal of impact, changing frequently, and requiring constant attention. The work that the company performs may be programmatic—that is, readily analyzable using logical programs and methods—or it may be nonprogrammatic, heavily reliant on individual and group inspiration and creativity. Finally, the people employed by the organization may be primarily formal people or informal people; they may be linear thinkers, or they may be creative thinkers; they may be introverts who prefer solving problems alone or extroverts who prefer solving problems in groups. All of these constraints require that managers make deliberate choices about how their organizations gather information and make decisions—in short, about how their organizations will be designed.

TABLE 15.2 Overview: Why Organizational Designs Differ

The Six Historic and Business Factors That Motivate Different Organizational Designs	More Structured Organizational Designs. . .	More Flexible Organizational Designs. . .
The company's (external) environment, including its competitors, regulators, customers, and suppliers is. . .	• Not particularly complex • Not particularly diverse • Relatively static • Relatively certain	• Highly complex • Highly diverse • Dynamic and changing • Uncertain
The type of work the company does. . .	• Is highly analyzable • Requires solving problems that are routine—that is, pretty much the same from day to day	• Requires lots of creative problem-solving and innovation • Requires that employees often face new problems to solve, even on a daily basis
The people who are attracted to work in the company. . .	• Like to solve logical problems to achieve efficiencies, often working alone	• Like to solve creative problems to achieve innovation, often working in interactive teams
The size of the company is. . .	• Medium to large	• Small to medium
The historic period in which the company was founded. . .	• Earlier rather than later	• Later rather than earlier (later equals roughly post-1975)
The founder was. . .	• Interested in starting a large, bureaucratic firm focusing on efficiencies	• Focused on bringing new products to market and then creating a company to do this

The executives of the world's most respected companies have not been successful because they espoused a particular theoretical approach. They have been successful because of the way they reacted to the individual circumstances of their companies and industries.[23] One way managers react is by designing their organizations uniquely to meet their unique business challenges.

The factors that drive different company designs are summarized in Table 15.2.

What Do Managers Actually Design?

What is it that organizational designers actually do? What is it, specifically, that they design?

In contrast to the design constraints just discussed, certain aspects of a company are under management's control and can be changed. We call these aspects **design variables**. They include how decisions are made, how the work is coordinated, and so on. How these factors are designed contributes significantly to the development of unique organizational capabilities that provide competitive advantage.[24]

You need to understand design variables both theoretically and practically. First, let's take a look at their theoretical basis.

The Theory of Organizational Design

Three fundamental elements in organizational design are **specialization**, formalization, and centralization.[25]

SPECIALIZATION Specialization is differentiating the tasks individuals do in order to produce better work.[26] In the context of organizational design, there are two types of specialization. **Task specialization** is the way tasks are divided and dispersed in an organization.[27]

design variables
The aspects of a company which are under management's control and can be changed, including such factors as how decisions are made and how the work is coordinated.

specialization
Differentiating the tasks individuals do in order to produce better work.

task specialization
The way tasks are divided and dispersed in an organization.

Organizations may choose to divide their work into increasingly simplified subtasks, which can be performed by unskilled labor, or they may choose to maintain task complexity, utilizing skilled labor or teams. **Personal specialization** is the variety of professional skills available in the organization.[28] It is based on individuals' education, training, and experience. As organizational tasks become increasingly more complex, a greater variety of professional skills, along with more different types of professionals, may be needed to complete them.

Because managers rely on the concept of specialization to design the work of their companies, they must deal with issues of **integration**, coordinating the separate tasks and individual knowledge to create the organization's final product.

FORMALIZATION Formalization is the means by which an organization determines who, when and how tasks are performed.[29] It refers to the amount of rules, regulations, and policies that tell people what to do, the extent to which these are followed and enforced, and also the unwritten norms and traditions that shape people's behavior.[30] Formalization is one way to integrate tasks and persons. When formalization is high, individuals' roles and goals are clearly defined. When formalization is low, people have more discretion about how to do their jobs and are more likely to perform a variety of jobs.

Formalization and **standardization** are often used synonymously. Standardizing behaviors reduces performance variability and promotes coordination. However, too much standardization reduces employee flexibility and creativity.

Older and larger organizations often have more formalization than younger, smaller organizations. Older organizations simply have more time to develop and accumulate policies that have worked, whereas larger organizations turn to increased formalization to integrate more people and more hierarchical levels.[31]

CENTRALIZATION Centralization is the degree to which organizational members participate in decision making.[32] If a decision is centralized, it is made by top managers, whereas if it is decentralized, it is made further down in the hierarchy. Perfect centralization would be having the top manager in the company make all decisions. Perfect decentralization would be having all employees make all decisions.

Typically, organizations that have only a few managers are relatively centralized. When a company has many managers—if, for example, its work requires the input of many specialists or specialized divisions—decision making is more likely to be decentralized.

ON THE CONGRUENCE OF SPECIALIZATION, FORMALIZATION, AND CENTRALIZATION
The **congruence hypothesis** suggests that specialization, formalization, and centralization all affect each other, and that if a manager changes one factor, the other factors must also be changed.[33] Another way of saying this is that the factors are **synergistic**. For instance, in a company that has high task specialization as exemplified in mass production, centralization and formalization are both likely to be high. If a manager were to decentralize decision making, employees would expect that formalization and task specialization would also be reduced.

In contrast, in a company with low task specialization as exemplified in an advertising agency's creative department, centralization and formalization are both likely to be low. Increasing formalization would be counter-cultural, leading employees to wonder whether decision-making authority would be centralized and lateral relationships among the employees would deteriorate.

Although there are no pat answers to finding the right organizational design, the hope of developing organizational synergy is a key factor in choosing one.[34]

The Practice of Organizational Design

At last, we come to what managers actually do when they design organizations. The practice of organizational design is based on systems theory.[35] (See Chapter 1.) Organizations face constraints (inputs), and, because of them, are designed in particular ways (processes, also called throughputs) to achieve organizational effectiveness (outputs). See Figure 15.1 for a model, adapted from theorist Patrick Connor, that illustrates these elements of organizational design.[36]

---

personal specialization
The variety of professional skills available in an organization, which is based on individuals' education, training, and experience.

integration
Coordinating separate tasks and individual knowledge in order to create the organization's final product.

formalization
The means by which an organization determines who, when and how tasks are performed, including the amount of rules, regulations, and policies that tell people what to do; also called "standardization."

standardization
The means by which an organization determines who, when and how tasks are performed, including the amount of rules, regulations, and policies that tell people what to do; also called "formalization."

centralization
The degree to which organizational members participate in decision making.

congruence hypothesis
The hypothesis that specialization, formalization, and centralization are synergistic (all affect each other), and that if a manager changes one of these factors, the other factors must also be changed.

synergistic factors
Factors such as specialization, formalization and centralization, which all affect each other.

FIGURE 15.1

A Systems Model of Organizational Processes

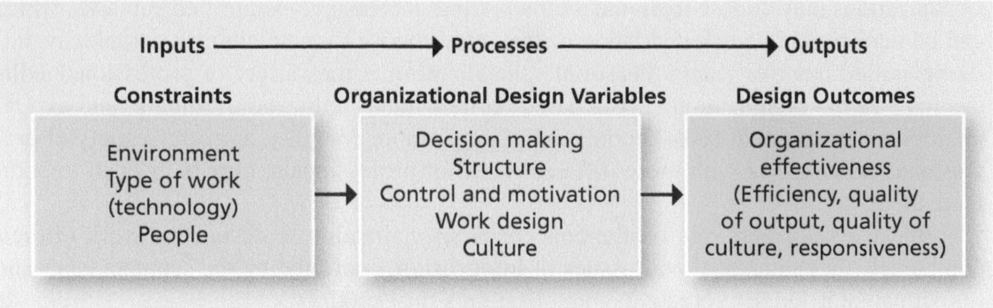

Inputs ——————→ Processes ——————→ Outputs

Constraints	Organizational Design Variables	Design Outcomes
Environment Type of work (technology) People	Decision making Structure Control and motivation Work design Culture	Organizational effectiveness (Efficiency, quality of output, quality of culture, responsiveness)

organizational effectiveness
The extent to which an organization meets its goals.

Inputs to the model are the organizational constraints of environment, type of work, and people, that we discussed previously.

The output to the model is **organizational effectiveness**, the extent to which an organization meets its goals.[37] Although there are numerous outcomes that organizations might pursue, most fall into one of the following four categories.[38]

- Efficiency: This includes minimizing costs, maximizing profits, labor productivity, waste control, proportion of capacity used, accuracy of communication, elimination of dysfunctional procedures, improved work flow, and appropriate information systems.

- Quality of output: This refers to whether goods or services, the quality of an organization's output—in terms of durability, dependability and attractiveness—distinguishes it.

- Quality of the work culture: The employees' satisfaction with the organization as a whole, the job being performed, their supervisors, and interpersonal relationships with colleagues comprise the quality of the work culture.

- Responsiveness: This refers to the organization's adaptability in the face of both environmental conditions and internal developments such as new structures and operating systems.

The throughputs in the model are the five design variables, those characteristics that managers manipulate to achieve organizational outcomes. These are:

1. *Decision making.* Managers decide such processes as whether decisions will be centralized in the top management team or decentralized to a middle level or bottom rung level of the company, and they decide whether decisions will be made individually or in groups.

A fundamental question is whether decision making should be centralized or decentralized. Some advantages of centralized decision making are that decisions can be easily standardized, top management always knows what is going on, and fewer managerial employees are required. Advantages of decentralized decision making are that it motivates lower level managers to be involved, trains them in decision making, solves lower level problems where they arise, and leaves top management free to focus on strategy.

2. *Structure.* Organizational structure is the design through which an organization is administered, including lines of authority and communication between different departments, along with the information that flows through these lines of communication and authority.[39] Usually we think of organizational structure as the organizational chart that indicates the different layers and departments of a company, although it should be recognized that the chart is only one indication of the actual interactions that take place in a company. We will cover the important topic of structure more fully in the next chapter.

steep hierarchy
A structure with many levels, in which there is usually a narrow span of control.

flat hierarchy
A structure with few levels, in which there is usually a large span of control.

A fundamental structural question is whether a company should use a **steep hierarchy** or a **flat hierarchy**.[40] A company with many levels has a steep hierarchy, whereas a company with few levels has a flat hierarchy. See Figure 15.2.

direct reporting
Individuals reporting directly to their managers.

Generally, when a company has a steep hierarchy, individuals report directly to their managers (**direct reporting**) and the boss–subordinate relationship is the key building block of the organization. In contrast, in a company with a flat hierarchy, individuals may report to a boss, but they also work frequently in teams, engaging in a great deal of cross-departmental communication. In companies with steep hierarchies, the number of individuals reporting to one boss is usually smaller than it is in companies with flat hierarchies. The number of individuals reporting to one boss is referred to as the boss's **span of control**. See Chapter 16 for more on this concept.

span of control
The number of subordinates a manager supervises; the number of individuals reporting to one boss.

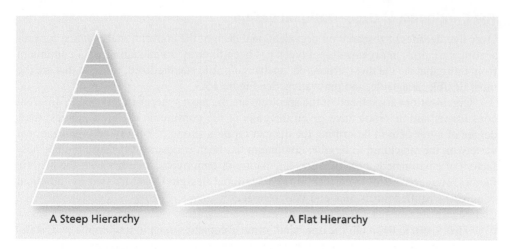

FIGURE 15.2

A Steep Hierarchy Compared with a Flat Hierarchy

A Steep Hierarchy   A Flat Hierarchy

3. *Control and motivation.* Management also decides what motivation systems it will use with its workers, choosing what mix of rewards and punishment, and directive and participatory management, it will employ.

What is the company's fundamental approach to motivation? Does it emphasize extrinsic control, applying strong rules and norms and even the occasional punishment, or does it focus on fostering intrinsic motivation through norms of flexibility and employee autonomy? Generally, companies that are competing on cost and quality fall into the former camp, whereas those that require more innovation fall into the latter camp.

4. *Work design.* Management decides how jobs will be designed within the company. For example, it decides whether the jobs will be complex or simple, done individually or in groups, and whether people will be allowed to participate in the design of their own jobs.

Some companies emphasize that one person does one and only one job, and that the boss has the sole authority to design jobs. Others allow for, and actively encourage, work-sharing between individuals and within groups. They emphasize teamwork and empower teams to distribute work among their members.

5. *Organizational culture.* Organizational culture refers to the values people share and the norms held by the groups in an organization over time.[41] There are a great many variables connected to the concept of culture. (See Chapter 17.) For example, one set of researchers focuses on members' experience of their companies, including their perceptions of the extent of "red tape," feelings of autonomy, feelings related to being assured of appropriate rewards, perceptions of risk and challenge, feelings of warmth and support, and tolerance of different ideas.[42] Other researchers focus on meanings shared by a group of people that are passed on to others.[43] Both approaches are valid and useful.

Management chooses what symbols represent the organization, what special events characterize it, and what emotional climate will be encouraged on a daily basis. Perhaps the most important characteristics they influence are whether a culture will be varied and flexible or homogeneous and fixed.

IN SUM. . . These five variables are the organizational characteristics that managers control. Managers have real choices about how decisions are made, how workers are motivated, and so on. In the next sections we will see that these characteristics are not independent of one another, and that, in fact, over time, a pattern of synergies among them has been widely recognized by organizational researchers and practitioners.

How Can You Predict Whether an Organizational Design Will Be Effective?

As we have seen, organizational designs are synergistic when their different elements interact together in a coherent pattern. A synergistic organization is likely to be an effective organization.

The Continuum of Organizational Design

Over five decades of research on organizational design, the conventional practice for presenting variations in organizational types has been to array organizations on a continuum from those that are the most structured, unchanging, and standardized, to those that are the most flexible, adaptable, and innovative. See Figure 15.3.

Organizations at each end of the spectrum are the most synergistic. Although different consultants and theorists have given the ends of the continuum different names, their degree of agreement in describing the distinct types is strong.[44] Portraying organizational variety on the structured to flexible continuum has been widespread because the business factors of environment, type of work, and nature of employees, together with the historic factors, suggest logical synergies in organizational design. Consider two hypothetical companies: Stuffed Shirts, Inc. and Widgetry, Inc.[45]

STUFFED SHIRTS, INC. On the one hand, some companies exist in uncomplicated, static environments doing highly systematized work because they must compete with other companies on the basis of efficiencies and economies of scale. An example is a clothing manufacturing company—we'll call it Stuffed Shirts, Inc.—that competes with several similar companies for the business of one major customer, a large retailer. Stuffed Shirts strives to make its manufacturing process as logical and efficient as possible and attracts employees and managers who enjoy solving practical, structured problems.

Its design follows this logic:

> A static, sometimes legalistic environment in which cost and quality are the main factors on which companies compete *leads to* planned, prescribed, and programmed work, *which attracts* linear-thinking, often conservative employees *who enjoy* doing one particular job, *who are comfortable* with a respectful but conservative reward structure, *who understand* why the company uses centralized decision-making and has many levels in its hierarchy, and *who are willing* to apply procedures by the book in the context of a day-to-day office routine that is traditional and conservative.

bureaucracy
An organization which is characterized by highly systematized, planned, prescribed and programmed work, linear thinking, conservatism, centralized decision-making, a steep hierarchy, and doing things "by the book."

Organizations with these characteristics are called **bureaucracies**. They are also referred to as mechanistic, System 1, and Theory X organizations.

WIDGETRY, INC. In contrast, companies in complex, changing environments compete on the basis of their ability to be flexible in the face of constant challenges. An example is a manufacturing company we will call Widgetry, Inc., whose customers are constantly demanding new products. Widgetry specializes in the design and production of flexible manufacturing systems. It attracts workers who are interested in solving the dual problems of deciding how to respond to customer demand for new products and then reengineering to meet those demands, problems that are not essentially programmable and that require a great deal of team interaction. It also attracts workers who enjoy making decisions, such as product judgments, in an atmosphere of uncertainty, in addition to the constantly creative work of retooling their manufacturing systems to accommodate new products.

The design of flexible and innovative organizations such as this one follows this logic:

> A fast-changing environment in which creating innovative products is the main factor on which companies compete leads to a spontaneous, team-based decision-making style, which attracts energetic, creative employees who enjoy doing a variety of tasks and taking on new challenges, who expect to be highly and/or creatively rewarded, who understand and enjoy teamwork and networking, and who are willing to go with the flow as the day-to-day work in the company changes, being alternately laid-back and hard-driving, fun and pressured.

FIGURE 15.3

The Continuum of Organizational Designs

Structured ································· Flexible	
(unchanging, standardized, bureaucratic)	(adaptable, innovative, enterprising)
Example: Stuffed Shirts, Inc.	Example: Widgetry, Inc.

Organizations with these characteristics are called **enterprises**.† Other terms for this type are organic, System 4, Theory Y, adhocracy, learning, high performance, and new organizations.

Notice that although Stuffed Shirts and Widgetry are both manufacturers, their business environments, work, and people differ considerably, and so will their organizational designs. Nevertheless, each design is logical, realistic, and synergistic.

How Synergy Is Reduced

It follows that if one or more design factors defy the logic of the rest of the organization, the synergy of the organization's design is reduced. This would happen if, for example, a highly creative, energetic employee ends up in a highly programmed, scheduled job. Likewise, synergy is reduced if a company emphasizes the design characteristics suitable to a flexible organization while trying to compete on cost and quality, or if a company maintains centralized decision-making while promoting a laid-back, participative culture. In organizational design the possibilities for mismatches are many, suggesting just one of the many reasons why managing a business is so fascinating.

See Table 15.3 for a summary of the contingency approach to organizational design, described next.

Should You Adopt the Contingent Design or the Fashionable Design?

Today U.S. business has moved away from manufacturing and toward services, and away from technology-driven businesses toward knowledge-driven businesses. Competition has, in general, become more fast-paced and global. These and related changes have increased the need for what many theorists and consultants describe as the ideal design for modern times—the organic/learning/high performance/new organization—that is, the enterprise.

Of course the **contingency theory** of organizational design, the idea that organizations should be designed to meet their unique constraints, states that not all organizations should be enterprises.[46] Rather, it suggests, organizations should be uniquely designed to face their unique challenges. When we differentiate organizations in terms of their constraints and suggest that designs should match these constraints, we are using a contingency approach. See Table 15.3 for a summary of the contingency approach to organizational design.

Over the last 40 years, many researchers have pointed out how fashion influences organizational design, and that it even induces managements to adopt inappropriate designs.[47] Currently, Western fashion favors flat organizational structures, for example. In contrast, as pointed out by Australian researchers, "Japanese, Korean, and Singaporean corporations look far more like traditional bureaucracies, with levels of middle managers intact and often increasing as these companies become global. . . . Hardly a flat structure, but one that resources and delivers new projects and new opportunities—that is, growth."[48]

What Are Some Unconventional Approaches to Organizational Design?

A couple of unconventional approaches to organizational design are the theories based on equifinality and metaphor.

The Theory of Equifinality

Some researchers challenge contingency theory, asserting that there are actually multiple, equally effective designs that support a given business strategy.[49] The theory of equifinality

enterprise
An organization which is characterized by innovative and creative work, non-linear thinking, spontaneous and team-based decision-making, "going with the flow," and employees being highly and/or creatively rewarded.

contingency theory
The theory that organizations should be uniquely designed to meet their unique constraints or challenges; using a contingency approach means differentiating organizations in terms of their constraints and designing them based on those constraints.

---

†Business theorists have worked hard to put a label on this type of organization. I use the word "enterprise" because it captures the essence of the concept and is more convenient to use than other terms. An "enterprise" is defined in the dictionary as a company organized for commercial purposes, but it is also "a project undertaken, especially one that is of some importance or that requires boldness or energy." Thus, an enterprise organizational design is one that involves not only organicity, learning, and high performance, but also energy and innovation, which nicely reflects existing theory.

TABLE 15.3 Overview: The Contingency Approach to Organizational Design: Contrasting Bureaucratic (Mechanistic) and Enterprise (Organic) Organizations

		The Bureaucracy	The Enterprise
I. Constraints	Environment (external)	Stable, simple, predictable	Dynamic, complex, unpredictable
	Core work of the company ("technology")	Routine with few exceptions	Nonroutine with many exceptions; innovation
	People	Employees enjoy structured tasks, and prefer directive styles of leadership	Employees are self-starters ("internals") and interpersonally skilled
II. Design Variables	Decision making	Centralized	Decentralized
	Structure	Steep hierarchy with direct reporting	Flat hierarchy with cross-functional communication
	Motivation and control	Rules and strong norms; extrinsic control, some punishment	A norm of flexibility, a belief in laissez-faire management, and intrinsic control
	Work design	One person does one job and the boss is the job designer	Autonomous and participative groups; work is shared
	Organizational culture	Homogeneous, inflexible, and unchanging	Varied, flexible, and changing
III. Outcomes	Effectiveness	Both bureaucratic and enterprise organizations are effective if there is a fit between the design constraints and the design variables.	

Source: Early researchers who used a mechanistic–organic continuum were T. Burns and G. M. Stalker, *The Management of Innovation* (London: Tavistock, 1961).

suggests that even given the same constraints, there is more than one way to design organizations to achieve effectiveness.[50] In the complex real world, managers may seek tradeoffs in designs because the use of one design may not be possible, or because of their personal preferences for a certain design based on their personal histories and experiences.[51] More research needs to be done in this area.

The Subjective Side of Organizational Design: Metaphor and the Collective Paradigm

collective paradigm
The invisible agreement in consciousness held by an organization's members.

Some researchers assert that although influences like the external environment and a company's technology are certainly important in determining an organization's design, what actually causes the creation, maintenance, and change of organizations is "the invisible agreement in consciousness" of the organization's members. This invisible agreement is known as the members' collective paradigm.[52]

For example, people often describe their organizations using metaphors. When many people use the same metaphor, it becomes part of their collective paradigm. Here are some common metaphors for organizations, some of which you may have used yourself:[53]

Organizations are machines. . . emphasizing efficiency.

Organizations are organisms. . . with needs and with relationships to their environment.

Organizations are brains. . . they process information and learn.

Organizations are cultures. . . their members share values, beliefs, and patterns of meaning.

Organizations are political systems. . . in which people wield power and influence.

Organizations are psychic prisons. . . in which people are trapped by their own unconscious thoughts, ideas, and beliefs into alienating modes of interaction.

Organizations are flux and transformation. . . creating and changing themselves.

Organizations are instruments of domination. . . exploiting individuals and society.

When a person uses a metaphor to think about an organization, his or her actions may be driven by that metaphor. For example, a person who likens organizations to machines sees members of the organization as parts of the machine and may treat them as though they are rigid and unchanging. One who sees an organization as flux and transformation, on the other hand, may see its members as changing and learning, and is likely to treat them as though they have potential. It is thought that, when many members of an organization share a metaphor, the metaphor can significantly influence their organization's design.

What Characterizes the Fundamental Organizational Types?

It follows from all of the above that there are three fundamental organizational types. These are:

- The bureaucracy
- The enterprise
- The hybrid, which is a combination of bureaucracy and enterprise

You should have a fundamental understanding of how each type achieves synergy.

The Bureaucracy

A bureaucracy is a highly systematized organization aimed at efficiency. Its goals and results are predictable and reliable. Daily work is planned, programmed, prescribed, scheduled, and directed "by the book." When facing pressures from its environment, the organization focuses first on itself and its processes (its main source of competitive advantage), responding fairly slowly to stakeholders such as customers, suppliers, and stockholders.

What does the design of a bureaucracy look like in the real world?

The Case of PharmCo.

Consider a 2,000-person division of a large pharmaceutical manufacturing company and an entity that for our purposes can be considered an organization in its own right. The business of this division, a real organization we will identify by the pseudonym PharmCo, is to produce and market a particular group of pharmaceuticals.

PharmCo's business environment is relatively static. Although the company has several powerful competitors, the number and type of competitors change little because the industry has high barriers to entry: It is extremely expensive to start such a company. The company has to pay strict attention to its regulatory environment, in which the major player is the Food and Drug Administration, and because PharmCo is also an international company, it must follow similar directives from regulators in the many countries in which it does business. However, these regulations change slowly, and with plenty of warning.

The company manufactures and markets a variety of drugs, and its work process for manufacturing is straightforward and logical, with few exceptional problems cropping up. Production at PharmCo follows strict rules defined by the industry's regulators. Even the company's approach to marketing is fairly straightforward, with an emphasis on building a corporate image of dependability and reliability rather than on creating excitement for its new products.

The key decisions at PharmCo are centralized in top management. More important decisions are made at levels well above the level where most of the information to make the decision is held. This assures coordination and alignment with company goals. Communication from the top down is consistent and clear. Approval processes are lengthy and always proceed from the bottom of the company to the top.

The company is divided into three product groups, and is organized in a steep hierarchy with seven levels. The company does not foster thinking "outside the box" or making decisions in groups (except to coordinate the work of individuals). In fact, even in the marketing area most creative decisions are outsourced to an advertising agency.

Each individual employee has a particular job description and is not interested in doing something different, such as helping others. Their work is assigned by their managers. The culture is conservative and traditional, with strong norms and rules, among which is the norm of business casual or more formal dress. PharmCo's employees are highly educated, many with MBAs and Ph.D.'s. They are for the most part conservative and traditional, individual contributors who find personal gratification in doing structured tasks well. They experience a high degree of satisfaction with the company and their work. They are quite loyal, and the employee turnover rate is low.

The company's motivation and control system is founded on the principle of treating employees with respect. Because it is a professional bureaucracy (you will read more on this later in the chapter), this means paying employees salaries that meet or exceed the market rate, offering strong benefits, establishing a merit-based pay system, and maintaining a comfortable working environment. The amount of money the company generates determines the employees' annual bonus.

Historically, bureaucracies have often been found in mature markets in which demand for their product is well established or perhaps even falling. As noted above, efficiency and, often, quality are the main strategies on which they compete. However, it would be a mistake to assume that the bureaucracies of the beginning of the twenty-first century are identical to the bureaucracies that existed at the beginning of the twentieth century. During the last century, the nature of regulation, employees, and tasks have all changed. In general, today's bureaucracies are less punitive, more responsive to their various stakeholders, and more populated with educated employees. Today, taking advantage of new technology, bureaucracies also introduce new products more frequently to a variety of markets.

What sorts of companies are designed as bureaucracies today? Among those industries most likely to favor the bureaucratic type are banks, financial services companies, auditing firms, utilities, construction companies, large retail companies, automated services, and manufacturing companies.

Given this large variety of industries, and the related variety in jobs to be accomplished, it is not surprising that there are also different types of bureaucracy. Next we will consider the differences between the classic, or "machine," bureaucracy, and the professional bureaucracy.[54]

THE CLASSIC (MACHINE) BUREAUCRACY Like all bureaucracies, the classic bureaucracy is characterized by many hierarchical levels and direct reporting. Decision making is centralized.[55] However, it is in the classic form that employees come closest to the "faceless bureaucrats" so often ridiculed by those who enjoy making fun of bureaucracies. There is some validity to this criticism, because, in truth, in classic bureaucracies individuals are not encouraged to speak up as individuals. Discussion of personal opinions and values is time-consuming and inefficient. Rather, employees are expected to participate primarily as people who fill a certain role in the organizational plan.

In a large manufacturing company, for example, employees have little say in how the business is run. If the company is using an assembly line, they may even have little say about how their jobs are organized and performed. Machine bureaucracies deliberately break work down into its smallest parts so that workers who do not fulfill their roles for one reason or another can easily be replaced, thus maintaining the efficiency of the organization. Under this circumstance, it is very easy for employees to feel like mere cogs in a wheel. Autonomy and job satisfaction are likely to be low.

Today many services have been bureaucratized. Unfortunately, the intelligent workers required by these services are easily dissatisfied in their humdrum jobs. Consider telephone call centers, which in the U. S. employ millions of people.[56] Call centers are located wherever labor is cheap and plentiful. Unlike manufacturing plants, they are easy to move because a company only has to transfer its computers. Unlike traditional assembly line workers, telephone call workers are usually high school graduates with one or more years of additional training. Operators who speak with customers about things such as credit card balances and airline rates must be able to handle complaints effectively, and they must develop a sophisticated knowledge of their product or service. Typically, such workers handle about 100 calls per 8-hour day, with 10-minute breaks every hour and 30 minutes for lunch.[57]

Countering the demotivating characteristics of the classic bureaucracy requires commitment and creativity on the part of managers. These days phone center managers attempt to keep employees satisfied by offering flexible work hours, making the workers' cubicles more homey, and giving perks like tuition reimbursement. Even so, they have trouble reducing their employee turnover rate below 25 percent per year.[58] Probably the classic bureaucracy will always face pressure from workers who want more job satisfaction and who are not particularly committed to the company.

THE PROFESSIONAL BUREAUCRACY In modern times we can state emphatically that, historic reputation to the contrary, not all bureaucracies are boring and dehumanizing places to work. Professional bureaucracies can provide excellent work cultures and career opportunities. In contrast to the classic bureaucracy, which is designed to maximize efficiency through simplified work, a professional bureaucracy does complex (though not especially creative) work that demands a highly educated worker, also with the goal of efficiency. Decision making is more decentralized than in classic bureaucracies.[59]

PharmCo, discussed earlier in this chapter, is a professional bureaucracy. The work of the highly educated professionals at PharmCo is more complex than either the work of an assembly line worker or the work of a telephone call employee, although all three jobs are routine. It is more intellectually challenging to test a new drug using prescribed scientific methodology than it is to assemble a simple product or answer a phone using the correct script. Workers at PharmCo can use many more of their skills, and their jobs have more variety. Because of their expertise, their opinions have more weight in the company.

Many of the workers in professional bureaucracies are knowledge technologists— computer technicians, software designers, analysts in clinical labs, or manufacturing technologists. They often do manual work based on the substantial knowledge that they acquired through formal education. These workers have good job mobility through their specialty. Their company is committed to helping them to continue to update their knowledge.

Clearly, professional workers and knowledge technologists are not as readily replaceable as assembly line workers, which gives them more power to demand status, high wages, and good working conditions. An important way in which the professional bureaucracy differs from the classic bureaucracy is that workers have a real voice in their organization, at least at their own level.

Historically, some classic bureaucracies have attempted to improve productivity by giving workers a voice. By increasing employee participation and encouraging teams, some companies have succeeding in increasing their employees' satisfaction and motivation. In so doing they have moved as close as they could to the design of a professional bureaucracy, which itself has become one of the more successful organizational types in the business world today.

HOW BUREAUCRATIC DESIGNS CAN FAIL When the classic bureaucracy is taken to its extreme, it becomes an exploitive, authoritarian bureaucracy. Work is broken down into its smallest parts without any regard whatsoever to how demotivating the resulting jobs might be. Managers emphasize punishment and minimize reward. Workers are paid as little as possible. While the workers are cajoled to be a part of the team, they are exploited financially with low wages, and physically and emotionally with stressful conditions. This kind of company succeeds only when it has an endless supply of captive, or neurotic, workers.

Professional bureaucracies employ many professionals and quasi-professionals who have some control over their jobs and who contribute to organizational planning. Their very flexibility causes problems, including overdecentralized decision making and managers' inability to make the system coherent.[60]

The Enterprise

Enterprise organizations adapt quickly in business environments that are dynamic, complex, and uncertain. Enterprises attract people who are themselves enterprising—who thrive on solving frequent and varied problems, often in interactive teams, and who tolerate risk and uncertainty well. Goals and results are custom-designed and creative/innovative. Daily work is not preprogrammed; rather it is extemporaneous, improvised, spontaneous, and directed by discussion and teamwork. When facing pressures from its environment, the organization thinks creatively and holistically (its main source of competitive advantage), considering impacts on all stakeholders before taking action to change its processes.

Here is an example.

The case of EBiz

EBiz (another real company with a fictitious name) is a moderate-sized marketing company whose mission is to integrate its clients' marketing strategies with the Web and other developing technologies. Its synergistic enterprise organizational design makes extraordinary use of teamwork, communication and learning in order to react, create, and produce. EBiz is known as a great place to work (hard) and is a rising marketing firm.

The industry in which the company operates experiences rapid shifts in consumer preferences. Because client demands and technology change constantly, so must the products that the company produces. The company offers a broad range of services both domestically and internationally. Clearly, its business environment is highly complex and changing. Also, its competitors are often hostile, ruthlessly competing for suppliers and customers and even playing dirty tricks.

The work the company does is highly creative, with little room for the routine or the programmatic. Decision making is moderately decentralized, with daily operational decisions made at many levels and client decisions made only at the level of top management. The company's structure is based on client teams (some as large as 60 people) organized in steep hierarchies. When making recommendations, these groups are highly participative.

The company promotes flexibility in how people structure their jobs and make decisions. Few rules exist, and punishment is not apparent. Whereas each person is assigned a particular job, within teams the lines of job responsibility are often blurred. There is also a strong focus on learning, with many free employee workshops and sharing sessions across client teams. At EBiz a manager's job is to guide and facilitate discussions rather than to make decisions personally. Physically its offices are designed on an open concept that facilitates this interaction, with team "breakout" rooms available for their frequent meetings. The culture is flexible and loose. Dress is business casual, or even more informal.

EBiz attracts creative people who are flexible self-starters. They enjoy creative problem solving under conditions of uncertainty and stress. It seeks individuals who have excellent communication skills and a strong personal drive to succeed. EBiz is known as young, hip, fast-paced and innovative.

Overall, EBiz is a flexible business organization in which management delegates some, but not most, decision-making authority. While a still more flexible design can be imagined (it would be one in which the hierarchies are flatter, or nonexistent, and client decisions are moved further down in the company), the company's widespread teamwork and commitment to learning suggest a typical modern enterprise.

HOW ENTERPRISE DESIGNS CAN FAIL Enterprise designs fail when the required teamwork fails to function effectively. If teams fail systematically across an organization, if they merely eat up time while inadequately reacting, creating and producing to meet the competition, the result is chaos. Management may pull back on the reins and become more bureaucratic, causing confusion and frustration.

People caught up in this mess are likely to try to appear energized and excited on the outside, while feeling angry and betrayed on the inside. Often the energy that should be put into putting out the best product is directed instead towards intergroup bickering and territorial struggles aimed at group survival. Despite the fact that it might have a public image as modern and flexible, the chaotic enterprise is a poor place to work. Mobile people will leave.

The Hybrid Organization

No doubt you have already figured out that many organizations actually do more than one type of work and therefore should include different designs.[61] Although a company's core work is to mass produce widgets, suggesting that it should be organized as a bureaucracy, it may also design widgets, suggesting it—or at least a part of it—should be organized as an enterprise. If a company's core work is to produce computer software, which would logically suggest an enterprise design, it still has to manage its financing and accounting, which require bureaucracy.

A hybrid is an organization comprised of distinct elements, some of which are bureaucratic and some of which are enterprising, with one overarching culture. A hybrid organization is designed to meet the different constraints on its subunits.[62] It includes both bureaucratic and enterprising units, under one dominant culture. On the continuum of organizational designs the hybrid does not fall in the middle. Rather than being a compromise between a bureaucracy and an enterprise, it is an organization that recognizes that its subparts perform different work in different business environments, and therefore should be designed differently. Hybrids are highly adaptive organizations whose designs match the different types of work performed. Typically their designs have important strategic value for their companies.

Having the finance and accounting functions of a company run more bureaucratically than the rest of the organization is typical of a hybrid. Another typical example is when the research and development group is run flexibly even though it exists in the context of a bureaucratized manufacturing company. In general, when the main company design is bureaucratic, the secondary, enterprise designs are likely to be found in the sales divisions, marketing groups, business and new product development groups, or new business start-ups and turnarounds.

Here are two examples of hybrids that are differentiated by unit.

Red House Brewery (fictitious name, real place) is a 60-person operation that produces a dozen ales and beers. The business environment of the company, with its strong competitors and broad market, suggests a flexible design, but manufacturing a food item requires precision. How should the company be designed?

In this hybrid, two different types of work have spawned a design that is an even balance of programmed and flexible approaches. The beer production side of the company is programmed and routinized, whereas the marketing and sales side is flexible and team-oriented. Decision making in the company is centralized in top management. At the same time all employees have easy access to the CEO, and the overall hierarchical structure of the company is flat.

Southern Financial Services (SFS) (fictitious name, real place) is a small financial services company that manages portfolios for about 100 investors. Much of its work is routine and programmed, and, of course, it is regulated by strict accounting rules. At the same time, the company's elite clients require personal attention.

SFS centralizes key decisions. However, unlike its competitors, all of which are larger firms, SFS has a flat hierarchy, encourages participative groups, and has an informal culture. These enterprise characteristics originate in its small size and its core work of client contact. The company has created a strategic niche for itself by combining flexible, highly service-oriented client contact work with routine financial services work. Its core work is really the client contact, and the overall design of the company reflects that. At the same time, the technical programmed work is accomplished efficiently. We would expect that SFS will become more bureaucratized if the company were to grow, but that growth may never occur because it would be antithetical to the company's mission of serving a small group of elite clients.

Managing a hybrid can be challenging. When two cultures—the flexible, personalized culture and the buttoned-down programmed culture—exist side by side on a daily basis over a period of years, they may misunderstand each other, they are likely to stereotype each other, and resentments about different groups having different privileges may fester. Workers in SFS, for instance, report some confusion and distractions in their jobs because of the need to interface with the opposite culture on a daily basis. On the other hand, at Red House Brewery, an emphasis on employee communication, including frequent social events and training, has tied a diverse and educated workforce into a loyal team.

HOW HYBRIDS FAIL Hybrid designs fail when management tries to pretend that the differences between its bureaucrats and its enterprisers do not exist, ignoring intergroup stereotyping and other symptoms of dysfunction and repeating ineffectually that the company has common goals and should act as a team. As individuals become overly identified with their own group, personalities and group identity can develop into major obstacles to effective problem solving. Disorganization, miscommunication, and impaired decision making become the hallmarks of the company overall.

Hybrid designs can also fail if management tries to impose one culture on the other, ignoring employees' perceptions of the real need to meet environmental constraints.

When management is caught between the two cultures that it has created, it is forced to devote time to negotiating between the two groups. Only when management squarely faces the design differences between sub-groups can a hybrid organization achieve optimal functioning. Management has to name these differences, explain the reasoning underlying them, and work consistently to convince employees to accept and value them. It must inform some employees why others get privileges such as flexible hours, and it must convince others to value the bureaucratic elements that produce a good product reliably every day. Management must continue to clarify these differences for as long as they exist. At the same time, it must create a corporate culture that keeps the company's common goals firmly in focus.

In Conclusion

Understanding the fundamentals of organizational design helps you to avoid falling victim to some common prejudices about organizations. Chief among these are that all bureaucracies are inherently bad, whereas all enterprises are inherently good. Also, by understanding organizational types, you are more likely to discover the type of organization that best fits your personality, skills, and goals.

Although the design of organizations is usually logical, we have seen in this chapter that it is not simple. Having learned about designs in all their complexity, we are now ready to study organizational structures to see how they adapt and evolve over time.

Apply What You Have Learned. . .

World Class Company: IDEO Product Development

Part I.

IDEO Product Development is the world's largest product design firm and arguably the most successful.[63] In 2005 it won seven Best Product Design awards (the most) from the Industrial Designers Society of America. Its products are as varied as a new Sam Adams tap handle for Boston Beer Company, Pringles Prints (potato chips with trivia facts printed on them) for Proctor & Gamble, the original mouse for Microsoft, and a way to expedite kidney transport for Organ Recovery Systems.

Founder David Kelley is known widely as a creative guy. For example, in a recent article, he describes how he uses mind maps for creative work.[64] He notes that when he wants to do something analytical, he makes a list and then simply works to complete it. But when he wants to strategize and be creative, he draws a mind map because it allows him to generate new ideas. To draw a mind map, put your problem in the center of the page and then think up all the different ideas you can that relate to it, putting them around the edge of the problem. Each one of these ideas then becomes a road on the map, and you follow that road by free association to see what additional ideas crop up. Using this kind of technique is something in which Kelley's company excels.

To foster creativity, IDEO is structured into small units. Kelley vowed that his company would never be larger than 40 people, so, as necessary, groups of 40 or fewer are spun off into their own facilities. Design work is done by project teams, diversified in terms of their skills. For example, you are likely to find psychologists, design engineers, and biologists on the same team. When they are working on a new project, it is common for teams to spend 50 to 60 hours on the job. They engage in a process called the "Deep Dive," a playful exploration of a huge variety of ideas over a period of days, weeks or even months, before developing a product prototype.

At IDEO, disagreeing with the boss is a very good idea. People are encouraged to ask forgiveness instead of permission, which suggests that failure is accepted and punishment is almost nonexistent. Project leaders often emerge, rather than being appointed.

In general, the company has a playful culture. Employees decorate their own offices. Craziness is okay: A wing from a DC-3 can be an item of decor. There is no dress code and titles are discouraged. High performers are rewarded with more opportunity to lead challenging projects and, often, with equity deals, such as shares in the client's venture capital base.

Discuss

Why is IDEO an enterprise (organic) organization? Consider the five design variables:

    a. How the company makes decisions
    b. How the company is structured
    c. How employees are controlled and motivated
    d. How work is designed
    e. What the organizational culture is like

Part II.

Is having a flat, small enterprise organization such as IDEO the only way to innovate? Large companies try to innovate as well, oftentimes by employing R & D (research and development) specialists. Some organizational designers believe it is important to house their R & D specialists in the same offices with people who are currently working with customers, whereas others like to separate them into centers of their own. And some companies do both.

For example, Bell Labs is the innovation arm of Lucent Technology. More than 90 percent of Bell's scientists and engineers work directly with service providers. However, some of them aim at maintaining the company's broader technical capability and become part of Bell Lab's small but highly productive, long-term research program. This program is separately housed. It examines phenomena such as the future of wireless and optical networking, the Internet, multimedia communications, physics, and mathematics. It is considered to be the "seed corn" that ensures that Lucent will always have a leading position in technological knowledge.[65]

Discuss

Compare the design of innovation at Bell Labs with IDEO. How might being part of a large bureaucracy reduce innovation? How might being part of a large bureaucracy enhance innovation?

Advice from the Pros

How Do Executives Achieve an Optimal Organizational Design?

Organizational designs often develop haphazardly, evolving over time and being shaped more by politics than policies. To help management teams regain control of their companies' designs, British authors Michael Goold and Andrew Campbell have synthesized information from the design experiences of dozens of companies in a variety of industries. Among their practical suggestions to managers who are contemplating a design overhaul are:

1. Get the fit right.
   a. Make sure the company's design directs enough management attention to the company's main sources of competitive advantage.

      For example, do you know your market segments, and does the design focus enough attention on them?
   b. Make sure the design reflects the strengths, weaknesses, and motivations of your people.

      Look at your top management team and other highly talented, key individuals. Will the design include and motivate them?
   c. Make sure the design is feasible. For example, can it be done, given government regulations, stakeholder preferences, the company's information systems, and the company's culture?

      For example, you will have trouble moving from a country-based design to a product-based design if your company's information systems are unable to report performance by product.
2. Plan for the potential impacts of a redesign.
   a. Make sure specialist cultures that need protecting, such as e-business groups or new-product development teams, will indeed be protected.

      To accomplish this, put a high-ranking executive in charge of that unit.
   b. Where unit to unit communication links are likely to be damaged, be sure to strengthen them.

And if this is not possible, set up separate units. For example, in a restructuring, IBM had to create a Global Services Division to be sure customer service was integrated across the company.
   c. If levels in the hierarchy will be redundant, plan to cut them.

      Pay particular attention to levels above the operating units. One rule of thumb is that if the unit cannot add at least 10 percent to the performance of the units it manages, cut it.
   d. Make sure the proposed design is flexible to allow for future strategic changes.

      Assume for the moment that your people and design are smart and flexible. What roadblocks do you anticipate? Assemble a group of well-informed managers from different parts of the company and have them create a list of about 10 opportunities, including remote possibilities, for the company in the future.

      Does your design allow for the incorporation of these?

Discuss

1. Several of these suggestions include opportunities for key players. What are they?
2. Which of these suggestions will create resistance to the redesign? Which are aimed at dealing with employee resistance to the redesign? Name them and describe what type of resistance they imply.
3. Have you ever been part of an organizational redesign? Does the prospect of being involved in one interest you?

Gain Experience

Stuffed Shirts and Widgetry: A Roleplay

Do organizational designs really affect how businesses are run day-to-day? In this exercise you will have the opportunity to create, or observe, two fundamental types of organizations in action.

Two teams of five people will be selected from volunteers. One team will roleplay as Stuffed Shirts, Inc., and one will roleplay as Widgetry, Inc., a bureaucracy and an enterprise, respectively. Each team will operate in its assigned style: The bureaucrats will act "bureaucratically," and the enterprisers will act "flexibly." Review the chapter descriptions of these types of organizations.

Your challenge is to use your creativity to portray these styles to the best of your ability. In front of the class, the teams will meet to select a candidate to head their company's new manufacturing plant in Japan. (See the list of candidates below.) After the roleplay the consultants will discuss how well each team portrayed its ideal type.

Process

1. Students volunteer for the roles, as below.
2. In their respective groups, Stuffed Shirts, Widgetry, and the consultants meet outside the classroom to figure out how to portray their type, or, in the case of the consultants, to list the criteria for evaluating each type. Meanwhile, back in the classroom, the remaining students break into groups of five to brainstorm and write down five ways they expect Stuffed Shirts and Widgetry will be different. (10 minutes)
3. The roleplays: Stuffed Shirts and Widgetry run their meetings to decide which candidate will get the job. (5 to 7 minutes each)
4. Consultants meet to decide which team did the best job of portraying its assigned type, and report their choice and their reasons for it to the class.
5. Class discussion
   a. How well did the teams exemplify their type? What more could they have done?
   b. How did the companies treat Middle Manager #2, the deviant?
   c. Have you ever worked in an organization that exemplifies one of these types? Which design did you prefer? Why?
   d. Do organizational designs really affect how businesses are run day-to-day? Yes!

The Roles

President of Stuffed Shirts: You have called this meeting to select a new manager of your plant in Tokyo (part of a joint venture with the Japanese). Run the meeting according to the norms of a bureaucratic/mechanistic organization.

President of Widgetry: You have called this meeting to select a new manager for your plant in Tokyo (part of a joint venture with the Japanese). Run the meeting according to the norms of an organic organization.

CFO of Stuffed Shirts: Your concern is with the bottom line: How much will this selection procedure cost in time, resources, and money?

CFO of Widgetry: Your concern is with the bottom line: How much will this selection procedure cost in time, resources and money?

HRM Director of Stuffed Shirts: Your business experience to date has been in accounting firm and manufacturing firms. You really emphasize the bureaucratic approach, lobbying for it in any way you can.

HRM Director of Widgetry: Your business experience to date has been in a software development company and a large advertising agency. You really emphasize the enterprise/organic approach, lobbying for it in any way you can.

Middle Manager #1, Stuffed Shirts: As an up-and-coming young manager, you fully support top management's view of this matter. You help in any way you can with a bureaucratic method for selecting the new plant manager.

Middle Manager #1, Widgetry: An up and coming young manager, you fully support top management's view of this matter. You help in any way you can with an organic method for selecting the new plant manager.

Middle Manager #2, Stuffed Shirts: Although you work for Stuffed Shirts, you would prefer a more enterprise/organic organization. You see your job as advocate for a different approach to the selection process.

Middle Manager #2, Widgetry: Although you work for Widgetry, you would prefer a more bureaucratic selection procedure. You see your job as advocate for a different approach to the selection process.

The Candidates

JAMES LOGAN has had a varied career within your company, holding positions of increasing responsibility for five years in financial planning, and then moving over to manufacturing as head of your plant in Buffalo, New York, for two years. James is 35 years old. His international experience consists of several weeks in France after he graduated from college and half a dozen trips to Europe and the Far East to coordinate financial planning activities of several subsidiaries.

CAROL BROWN is the 40-year-old vice-president of purchasing for your company. She started working for the company 12 years ago as a line supervisor in manufacturing, and has worked her way up through the hierarchy. Brown has been studying Japanese for a year at night because she has actively sought an assignment in that region. She recently visited Japan for a week on a vacation.

RENALDO OBREGON has worked in the corporate office for three years as special assistant to the Comptroller. Before coming to "corporate" he headed up the manufacturing plant in Corazon, Mexico, for three years (his father is corporate vice-president for Latin America). Thirty-twoyear-old Obregon speaks Spanish fluently. He has traveled extensively in the United States and Latin America.

Chapter Summary and Key Terms

Who designs organizations and, in general, what do these designers do?

Organizational designers, typically top managers or consultants, look for optimal combinations of organizational characteristics to achieve organizational outcomes.

organizational design   400

What are the major factors influencing organizational design?

Three primary factors in the company's history affect its design. These factors are the personality and values of founder, the era in which the company was founded, and the historic size of the company.

Company designs are also affected by such constraints as the company's (external) environment, the nature of its employees, and the type of work that it does.

What do managers actually design?

From a theoretical point of view, designers consider formalization, centralization, and specialization when designing their organizations. Typically, when one of these changes, the others should also change.

In practice, organizational designers focus on five factors, called design variables, that managers can influence in their organizations. The design variables are decision making, structure, control and motivation, work design, and organizational culture.

How can you predict whether an organizational design will be effective?

In a synergistic organizational design different elements of the company interact together in a coherent pattern. Examples of synergistic designs are bureaucracies and enterprises. According to contingency theory, as long as its organizational design fits its organizational constraints, either a bureaucracy or an enterprise can be effective.

What are some unconventional approaches to organizational design?

Some researchers challenge contingency theory, arguing that there are many designs that can be effective. Their theory is called the theory of equifinality.

Theorists who believe in what is called the collective paradigm point out that although the effects of organizational constraints on design are important, it is only through changes in the collective consciousness of organizational members that organization design changes can really be made.

What characterizes the fundamental organizational types?

A bureaucracy is a highly systematized organization aimed at efficiency. Classic bureaucracies differ from professional bureaucracies. An enterprise is a highly flexible organization that adapts quickly in dynamic business environments. A hybrid is an organization comprised of distinct elements, some of which are bureaucratic and some of which are enterprising.

Explorations

1. Restructuring: The case of Cisco Systems

Look for information on how the computer-networking firm Cisco Systems restructured itself in 2001. What was its structure like before and after the change? What was the company's philosophy during the restructuring?

2. Organizational design services

Web search for "organizational design" and report on what kinds of services are available to companies in this area. What new concepts are available that go beyond this chapter?

3. Designing small and large companies for innovation

For more information on IDEO and its creative processes, go to www.ideo.com.
To learn more about Bell Labs go to www.bell-labs.com.

4. Many people believe that American car companies such as Ford and GM have fallen behind international companies in the creation of innovative products.

Web search to see if you can discover any organizational design explanations for this failure to innovate.

References

[1] H. Mintzberg, *The Structuring of Organizations* (Englewood Cliffs, NJ: Prentice Hall, 1979).

[2] J. R. Galbraith, "Organizational Design: An Information Processing View," in P. E. Connor, *Organizations: Theory and Design* (Chicago: Science Research Associates, Inc., 1980):43–49.

[3] P. E. Connor, *Organizations: Theory and Design* (Chicago: Science Research Associates, Inc., 1980):58.

[4] "Face Value: Where's the Beef," *The Economist*, November 3, 2001.

[5] A. G. Bedeian and R. F. Zammuto, *Organizations: Theory and Design* (Chicago: Dryden Press, 1991); K. Deveny, "Bag Those Fries, Squirt That Ketchup, Fry That Fish," *BusinessWeek,* October 13, 1986:86; G. Morgan, *Creative Organization Theory: A Resourcebook* (Newbury Park, CA: Sage, 1989).

[6] J. F. Lincoln, *Incentive Management* (Cleveland: Lincoln Electric Company, 1951):33.

[7] A. L. Stinchcombe, "Bureaucratic and Craft Administration of Production: A Comparative Study," *Administrative Science Quarterly*, 1959–1960:168–187; H. Mintzberg, *The Structuring of Organizations* (Englewood Cliffs, NJ: Prentice-Hall, 1979).

[8] S. Wetlaufer, "Organizing for Empowerment: An Interview with AES's Roger Sant and Dennis Bakke," *Harvard Business Review,* January–February 1999:110–123.

[9] H. Mintzberg, *The Structuring of Organizations* (Englewood Cliffs, NJ: Prentice Hall, 1979).

[10] J. Child, "Predicting and Understanding Organization Structure," *Administrative Science Quarterly 18,* 1973:168–185.

[11] C. A. Bartlett and S. Ghoshal, *Managing Across Borders: The Transnational Solution* (Cambridge: Harvard Business School Press, 2001).

[12] R. Duncan, "What Is the Right Organizational Design?" *Organizational Dynamics*, Winter 1979:59–80.

[13] P. E. Connor, *Organizations: Theory and Design* (Chicago: Science Research Associates, Inc., 1980).

[14] T. Burns and G. M. Stalker, *The Management of Innovation* (London: Tavistock, 1961); S. M. Davis and P. R. Lawrence, *Matrix* (Reading, MA: Addison-Wesley, 1977); J. R. Galbraith, E. E. Lawler III, *Organizing for the Future: The New Logic for Managing Complex Organizations* (San Francisco: Jossey-Bass, 1993).

[15] T. Burns and G. M. Stalker, *The Management of Innovation* (London: Tavistock, 1961); H. Mintzberg, *The Structuring of Organizations* (Englewood Cliffs, NJ: Prentice Hall, 1979).

[16] P. R. Lawrence and J. W. Lorsch, "New Management Job: The Integrator," *Harvard Business Review*, November–December 1967:142–151; S. M. Shortell, "The Role of the Environment in a Configurational Theory of Organizations," *Human Relations 30*, 1977:275–302; H. Mintzberg, *The Structuring of Organizations* (Englewood Cliffs, NJ: Prentice Hall, 1979).

[17] C. Perrow, "A Framework for the Comparative Analysis of Organizations," *American Sociological Review 32* (April, 1976):194–208.

[18] H. A. Simon, *The New Science of Management Decision* (Englewood Cliffs, NJ: Prentice Hall, Inc., 1960).

[19] C. Perrow, "A Framework for the Comparative Analysis of Organizations," *American Sociological Review 32*, April 1976:194–208.

[20] J. Woodward, *Industrial Organization: Theory and Practice* (London: Oxford University Press, 1965).

[21] J. Woodward, *Management and Technology* (London: Her Majesty's Stationery Office, 1958); J. Woodward, *Industrial Organization: Theory and Practice* (London: Oxford University Press, 1965).

[22] J. W. Lorsch, "Contingency Theory and Organizational design: A Personal Odyssey," in R. H. Kilman, L. R. Pondy, and D. P. Slevin, eds., *The Management of Organizational Design* (New York: Elsevier, North Holland Publishing Company, 1976):141–165; I. B. Myers, M. H. McCaulley, N. L. Quenk, and A. L. Hammer, *MBTI Manual: A Guide to the Development and Use of the Myers-Briggs Type Indicator*, 3rd ed. (Palo Alto, CA: Consulting Psychologists Press, Inc., 1998).

[23] M. Skapinker, "Ruthless Individuality Is the Key: Executives Prefer Honest Nonconformity to Conventional Management Qualities," *Financial Times,* January 20, 2003:II.

[24] J. R. Galbraith, *Competing with Flexible Lateral Organizations*, 2nd ed. (Reading, MA: Addison-Wesley Publishing Company, 1994).

[25] H. Mintzberg, *The Structuring of Organizations* (Englewood Cliffs, NJ: Prentice Hall, 1979).

[26] H. Fayol, *General and Industrial Management* (London: Sir Isaac Pitman & Sons, Ltd., 1949).

[27] D. S. Pugh, D. J. Hickson, C. R. Hinings, K. M. MacDonald, C. Turner, and T. Lupton, "A Conceptual Scheme for Organizational Analysis," *Administrative Science Quarterly 8*, December 1963:289–315.

[28] J. Hage, "An Axiomatic Theory of Organizations," *Administrative Science Quarterly 10*, December 1965:289–320.

[29] H. A. Simon, *The New Science of Management Decision* (New York: Harper & Row, 1960); P. E. Connor, *Organizations: Theory and Design* (Chicago: Science Research Associates, Inc., 1980).

[30] H. Mintzberg, *The Structuring of Organizations* (Englewood Cliffs, NJ: Prentice Hall, 1979).

[31] P. M. Blau, "Decentralization in Bureaucracies," in M. M. Zald, ed., *Power in Organizations* (Nashville, TN: Vanderbilt University Press, 1970); J. Child, "Strategies of Control and Organizational Behavior," *Administrative Science Quarterly 18* (1973):1–17.

[32] J. Child, "Organization Structure and Strategies of Control: A Replication of the Aston Study," in D. S. Pugh and C. R. Hinings, *Organizational Structure: Extensions and Replications* (Farnborough, England: Saxon House, 1976):27–44.

[33] H. Mintzberg, *The Structuring of Organizations* (Englewood Cliffs, NJ: Prentice Hall, 1979).

[34] M. Goold and A. Campbell, *Designing Effective Organizations: How to Create Structured Networks* (San Francisco: Jossey-Bass, 2002).

[35] P. R. Lawrence and J. W. Lorsch, *Organization and Environment: Managing Differentiation and Integration* (Boston, MA: Harvard University, Graduate School of Business Administration, Division of Research, 1967); P. E. Connor, *Organizations: Theory and Design* (Chicago: Science Research Associates, Inc., 1980).

[36] Adapted from P. E. Connor, *Organizations: Theory and Design* (Chicago: Science Research Associates, Inc., 1980). Given the extensive research on changing organizational culture

published since Connor's model, I have included culture as a variable rather than an outcome. For simplicity, I have also combined goals and effectiveness.

[37] D. K. Banner and T. E. Gagné, *Designing Effective Organizations: Traditional & Transformational Views* (Thousand Oaks, CA: Sage Publications, 1995).

[38] P. E. Conner, D. M. Egan, and B. Karmel, "Organizational Relationships: Context, Action, and Effectiveness," *Proceedings of the Mountain–Plains Management Association, 15th Annual Meeting,* 1973; P. E. Connor, *Organizations: Theory and Design* (Chicago: Science Research Associates, Inc., 1980).

[39] A. Chandler, *Strategy and Structure: Chapters in the History of the American Industrial Enterprise* (Cambridge, MA: MIT Press, 1962).

[40] W. F. Joyce, V. E. McGee, and J. W. Slocum, Jr., "Designing Lateral Organizations: An Analysis of the Benefits, Costs and Enablers of Nonhierarchical Organizational Forms," *Decision Sciences 28* (1), Winter 1997:1–25.

[41] J. P. Kotter and J. L. Heskett, *Corporate Culture and Performance* (New York: The Free Press, 1992).

[42] J. P. Campbell, M. D. Dunnette, E. E. Lawler III, and K. E. Weick Jr., "Environmental Variation and Managerial Effectiveness," in J. P. Campbell, M. D. Dunnette, E. E. Lawler III, and K. E. Weick Jr., *Managerial Behavior, Performance and Effectiveness* (New York: McGraw-Hill, 1970).

[43] M. R. Louis, "Organizations as Culture-Bearing Milieu," in L. R. Pondy et al, eds., *Organizational Symbolism* (Greenwich, CT: JAI Press, 1980).

[44] See D. McGregor, *The Human Side of Enterprise* (New York: McGraw-Hill Book Company, Inc., 1960):33–34; R. Likert, *The Human Organization* (New York: McGraw Hill Book Company, 1967); P. Senge, *The Fifth Discipline: The Art and Science of the Learning Organization* (New York: Currency Doubleday, 1990); D. Ancona, T. A. Kochan, M. Scully, J. Van Maanen, and D. E. Westney, eds., *Organizational Behavior & Processes* (Cincinnati: South-Western College Publishing, 1996):Module 1:3; J. Boyett and J. Boyett, *The Guru Guide: The Best Ideas of the Top Management Thinkers* (New York: John Wiley & Sons, 1998).

[45] The cases in this chapter have been adapted from R. André, *The Type Factor* (unpublished manuscript), and are used by permission of the author.

[46] T. Burns and G. M. Stalker, *The Management of Innovation* (London: Tavistock, 1961); P. R. Lawrence and J. W. Lorsch, *Organization and Environment: Managing Differentiation and Integration* (Homewood, IL: Richard D. Irwin, Inc., 1969); J. W. Lorsch, "Contingency Theory and Organizational design: A Personal Odyssey," in R. H. Kilman, L. R. Pondy, and D. P. Slevin, eds., *The Management of Organizational design* (New York: Elsevier, North Holland Publishing Company, 1976):141–165.

[47] H. Mintzberg *The Structuring of Organizations* (Englewood Cliffs, NJ: Prentice Hall, 1979), and L. Donaldson and F. G. Hilmer, "Management Redeemed: The Case Against Fads That Harm Management," *Organizational Dynamics 26* (4) Spring 1998:7–20.

[48] L. Donaldson and F. G. Hilmer, "Management Redeemed: The Case Against Fads That Harm Management," *Organizational Dynamics 26 (4)*, Spring 1998:7–20.

[49] A. H. Van de Ven and R. Drazin, "The Concept of Fit in Contingency Theory," in B. M. Staw & L. L. Cummings, eds., *Research in Organizational Behavior 7* (Greenwich, CT: JAI Press, 1985):333–365.

[50] L. von Bertalanffy, *General System Theory* (New York: Braziller, 1968); L. Hrebiniak and W. Joyce, "Organizational Adaptation: Strategic Choice and Environmental Determinism," *Administrative Science Quarterly 30,* 1985:336–349; D. A. Nadler and M. L. Tushman, *Strategic Organizational design* (Glenwood, IL: Scott, Foresman, 1988); D. C. Galunic and K. M. Eisenhardt, "Renewing the Strategy–Structure–Performance Paradigm," in L. L. Cummings and B. M. Staw, eds., *Research in Organizational Behavior 16* (Greenwich, CT: JAI Press, 1994):215–255.

[51] C. Gresov and R. Drazin, "Equifinality: Functional Equivalence in Organizational design," *Academy of Management Review 22 (2)*, April 1997:403–428.

[52] D. K. Banner and T. E. Gagné, *Designing Effective Organizations: Traditional and Transformational Views* (Thousand Oaks, CA: Sage Publications, 1995):xv.

[53] G. Morgan, *Images of Organization* (Newbury Park, CA: Sage, 1996).

[54] T. A. Leitko, "Why Traditional OD Strategies Fail in Professional Bureaucracies," *Organizational Dynamics 15* (3), Winter 1987:52–65.

[55] H. Mintzberg, *The Structuring of Organizations* (Englewood Cliffs, NJ: Prentice-Hall, 1979).

[56] L. Uchitelle, "For Answerers of '800' calls, Extra Income but No Security," *The New York Times,* March 27, 2002:A1, C5.

[57] L. Uchitelle, "For Answerers of '800' Calls, Extra Income but No Security," *The New York Times,* March 27, 2002:A1, C5.

[58] L. Uchitelle, "For Answerers of '800' Calls, Extra Income but No Security," *The New York Times,* March 27, 2002:A1, C5.

[59] H. Mintzberg, *The Structuring of Organizations* (Englewood Cliffs, NJ: Prentice-Hall, 1979).

[60] T. A. Leitko, "Why Traditional OD Strategies Fail in Professional Bureaucracies," *Organizational Dynamics 15* (3), Winter 1987:52–65.

[61] P. R. Lawrence and J. W. Lorsch, "Differentiation and Integration in Complex Organizations," *Administrative Science Quarterly 12*, June 1967:1–47.

[62] H. Mintzberg, "Structure in 5's: A Synthesis of the Research on Organizational Design," *Management Science 26* (3), March 1980:322–341.

[63] Based on information in S. Thomke and A. Nimgade, "IDEO Product Development," Harvard Business School Case 9-600-143, October 2000; A. Holland, "Apple and IDEO Prove They Are Full of Innovative Ideas," *Design Week 19*(28), July 8, 2004:7; B. Nussbaum, "The Best Product Design of 2005," *Business Week 3941* July 4, 2005:60–63; T. Brown, "Strategy by Design," *Fast Company 95* June 2005:52–54.

[64] "A Mind Map from IDEO's David Kelley," *BusinessWeek* online, September 25, 2006, http://www.businessweek.com/magazine/content/06_39/b4002408.htm?chan=search. Accessed September 27, 2006.

[65] "About Bell Labs," http://www.bell-labs.com/about/#difference. Accessed September 27, 2006.

16 Organizational Structure as a Design Tool

Preview

After managers divide up the organization's work, how do they coordinate their employees to get it done?
Differentiation
Span of control
Integration

How can you expect an organizational structure to evolve?
Why do organizational structures evolve?
How do organizational structures evolve?

What are some recent trends in organizational structure?
Structured networks
The front–back structure
The boundaryless organization

How do managers use organizational structure to advance their company's strategy?
Different business strategies suggest different organizational structures
Structure affects how strategic decisions are made

How do international organizational structures typically evolve?
Direct reporting
The international division
The global structure

What are international strategic alliances?

SAS Institute Inc.

SAS Institute is a North Carolina company that makes business analytics software. Even though it has more than eleven thousand employees worldwide (in 2009), the company is run using a flat hierarchical structure. Management believes that this policy reduces administrivia and creates product involvement. Also, the president's view is if you treat people as if they make a difference, they will. Founder Jim Goodnight designed his company to be as much fun and as meaningful to employees as to top management.

What exactly does having a flat structure mean in the company? For one thing, the president has a large number of direct reports (at one point, the number was 20.) Also, people may move in and out of management because becoming a manager is not necessarily an opportunity to get higher status. Rather, managing is seen as an opportunity to serve. And, almost everyone in the company has a private office. Finally, the company has what is called "a culture of sanity," as exemplified by facilities at its world headquarters in Cary, North Carolina: on-site and near-site childcare, recreation and fitness facilities, free soft drinks and coffee, excellent health care, a 35-hour standard work week, unlimited sick time, and free M&M's on Wednesdays.

With such a widespread reputation as a great place to work, SAS sometimes attracts applicants whose main interest is in the benefits. A rigorous hiring process, which often involves interviews with future co-workers, weeds out those candidates.

In the last chapter we observed that what organizations do, fundamentally, is divide up labor into its most logical units (which is the process called differentiation) and then create ways to integrate those units to meet the organization's goals (which is the process called integration). In this chapter we look more closely at the ways in which organizations manage these important processes.

After Managers Divide Up the Organization's Work, How Do They Coordinate Their Employees to Get It Done?

Differentiation

horizontal differentiation
The degree to which labor is divided.

horizontal firms
Companies that emphasize decision making through teams rather than through the organizational hierarchy.

vertical differentiation
The distribution of authority from lower to higher level managers.

vertical firms
Companies in which decision making depends on a hierarchical process such as centralization and employee–manager communication, rather than on teams.

Horizontal differentiation is the degree to which labor is divided. A company with a large horizontal differentiation ordinarily has a flat structure. **Horizontal firms** are companies that emphasize decision making through teams rather than through the organizational hierarchy. See Figure 16.1.

Horizontal differentiation encourages the input of a large variety of specialists, but it also creates the challenge of managing the conflict among them. When differences among the organization's units are not well managed, counterproductive in-group–out-group dynamics may develop.

Vertical differentiation is the distribution of authority from lower to higher level managers. A company with a large horizontal differentiation has a steep structure. **Vertical firms** are companies in which decision making depends on a hierarchical process such as centralization and employee–manager communication, rather than on teams. See Figure 16.2.

In these types of companies conflicts between levels in the hierarchy are likely to develop when subordinates feel they cannot achieve their personal goals through their jobs—when, for instance, their upward mobility is limited.

Span of Control

Span of control is the number of subordinates a manager supervises. In Figure 16.1, a horizontal firm, the spans of control for units A, B, and C are 7, 4, and 10, respectively. The concept of span of control is an old one. As Napoleon asserted, "No man can command more than five distinct bodies in the same theatre of war."[1]

The number of individuals a manager can supervise effectively depends on several factors. One is the nature of the employees' tasks. When employees' tasks are routine, a manager can manage more people. In Figure 16.1, Unit C has the broadest span of control and, probably, the most routine work in the company. It might represent the clerical division of a small insurance firm, for instance.

A second factor is the nature of a company's available strategies for integration. If, for example, a company utilizes technology that allows employees to post project results to a common Web site, its managers can spend less time coordinating and can take on more subordinates.

Span of control also varies according to the business the company is in and the company's size. In the health care sector, the median number of employees per manager is 16,

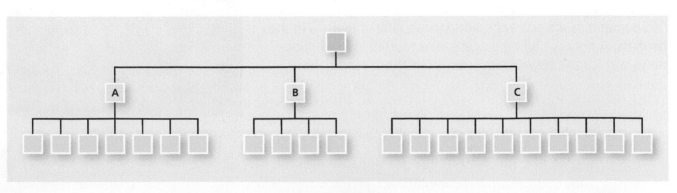

FIGURE 16.1 A Horizontal Firm

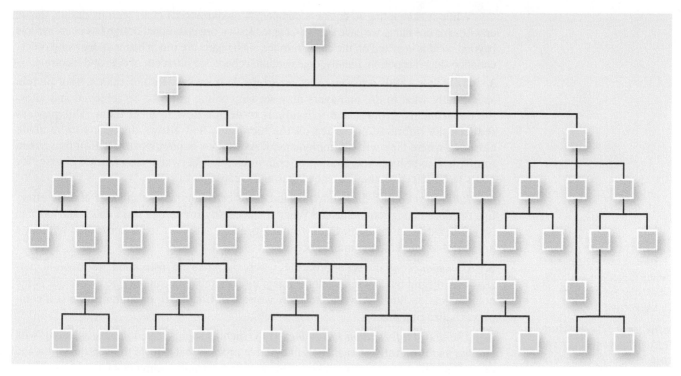

FIGURE 16.2 A Vertical Firm

whereas in information services, the median number is 4.[2] Some companies in retail have more than 100 employees per manager. In companies with 500 or fewer employees the median span of control is 4, whereas in companies with 2,000 to 5,000 employees the median is 9. In general, the span of control in U.S. companies is about 7.

In recent years the average span of control in U.S. firms has trended upward because of widespread changes in organizational structures, including the increased use of process and customer-oriented teams, and the use of decentralized processes to swiftly meet competitive challenges. Increasing an organization's average span of control has the additional advantage of reducing the need for expensive managers. When many employees report to one manager, sometimes natural groups form among them to perform such functions as the coordination and support that were once performed by managers.[3]

Integration

The greater an organization's differentiation, the greater is the challenge of integration. Naturally, the greater the challenge, the more time and expense are needed to meet it. Nevertheless, research suggests that when competing in uncertain environments, the most successful organizations are the ones that are the most highly differentiated *at the same time* that they are the most integrated.[4]

Companies have many options for achieving integration, the most common of which are described next.

1. *Hierarchy,* as you know from our earlier discussion, is a system in which some individuals are ranked higher than others.[5] The more highly ranked individuals are empowered to make most of the decisions that coordinate and integrate. Hierarchical integration is usually effective in smaller, less complex companies. However, as companies grow larger and more complex, the hierarchy can become overwhelmed with information and decisions, so companies adopt other methods for integration.

2. *Departmentalization* is the process of dividing up the company's work into integrating subunits. Each subunit coordinates a specified aspect of the company's work. An **organizational chart,** also known as an "organigram," depicts these subunits.[6]

departmentalization
The process of dividing up the company's work into integrating subunits, each of which coordinates a specified aspect of the company's work.

organizational chart
A chart depicting a company's departmentalized subunits; also called an "organigram."

While it is tempting to equate a company's organizational chart with its design, this is unwise. For one thing, we have seen in Chapter 15 that organizational design has many aspects beyond what is depicted on the chart. Further, such charts are much better at depicting differentiation than integration. Finally, organizational charts are often out of date and incorrect.

3. *Goals* also help organizations integrate their tasks.[7] Rather than telling people specifically what to do, managers may set targets and goals to be achieved and allow the departments, groups, and individuals to decide how to meet them. This process reduces the information burden on the hierarchy, and allows decisions to be made closer to where they will be implemented. As long as behaviors stay within prescribed limits, it also reduces the amount of communication between subunits. Of course, for goals to be effective, they must be clear and meaningful.

4. *Rules, procedures, and policies* standardize behaviors across subunits and are effective in coordinating routine tasks.[8] When the necessity for certain tasks and behaviors can be predicted in advance, they allow interdependent activities to be performed without a great deal of interunit communication.

5. *Communication* is a set of processes whose purposes are instruction, information, persuasion, integration, and innovation.[9] Integration of subunits can only be as smooth as the communication flows between them. As we saw in Chapter 7, communication is a complex, challenging process.

6. *The use of **information technology** (IT)*, such as sophisticated databases, along with storage and retrieval systems, is an integrative process that affects the centralization and decentralization of decision making. Because of IT, some companies have been able to decentralize decision making to the level of business units, whereas others have been able to centralize decision making.[10] Lower-cost telecommunications have also facilitated data center consolidation, making it possible for one central location to service far-flung subsidiaries.

Using information technology effectively is especially important in knowledge industries. In companies such as consulting firms, the widespread need to share information has created the job of **knowledge integrator**. These individuals are responsible for keeping the company's knowledge data-base orderly and current, cajoling consultants to actually use it, and adding new research.[11]

7. *Some companies create a formal **integrator role*** by appointing individuals or groups to act as liaisons between subunits.[12] This role may supplement or replace that of the managers above the subunits in the organizational hierarchy. For example, an integrator might be responsible for coordinating the production, sales, and research and development departments as they develop and market a new product, or a business group might be created to oversee worldwide research and development,[13] as illustrated in Figure 16.3.

---

information technology
The development of computer systems to organize, store and communicate information electronically, a process that affects the centralization and decentralization of decision making.

knowledge integrator
An individual who is responsible for keeping the company's knowledge database orderly and current, cajoling consultants to actually use it, and adding new research.

integrator role
A formal role, assigned to individuals or groups, of acting as liaisons between subunits.

FIGURE 16.3

An Integrating Department (the Business Development Group) for R&D

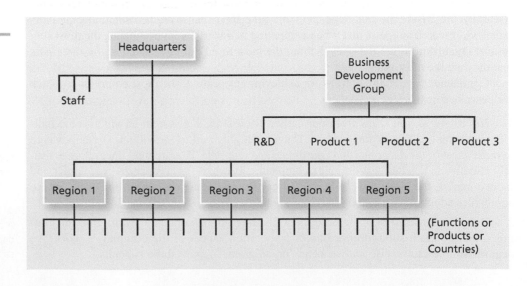

The failure to integrate effectively undermines the whole idea of "organization." At the individual level, the failure to integrate causes confusion and frustration, and at the organizational level it reduces a company's ability to compete effectively. It is also one of the main reasons why well intended efforts to change company cultures fail. For example, when companies establish separate departments to promote workplace ethics, workforce diversity, or environmental responsibility, they may fail to integrate the goals of these departments throughout the company, perpetuating the idea that these issues are outside of the realm of basic business concerns.[14]

How Can You Expect an Organizational Structure to Evolve?

As we have just seen, an organizational chart shows the departmentalization of a company. The presentation of departments on a chart is a company's **structure**. As companies change, they rewrite their organizational charts to indicate new emphases and changed reporting relationships.

structure
The departmentalization of a company; the presentation of departments on a chart.

Why Do Organizational Structures Evolve?

One reason a company revises its structure is because it is growing. Imagine you have grown your own small business over a period of years. You have been so successful that you decide that, rather than relying on one person for financial and accounting expertise, the company now needs its own accounting department. Similarly, a strictly domestic company may decide to go international, so it adds an international division.

Another reason a company changes its structure is to align it with a new company strategy. A company's **strategy** is the determination of its long-term goals and objectives, along with the adoption of actions and the allocation of resources to carry out these goals.[15] When a company adopts a new strategy, it examines its organizational design to see whether it fits that strategy. It may then change its structure, and other aspects of its organizational design, to align with that strategy. Research suggests that fitting a company's design to its strategy is a good idea. For instance, if a company adopts a low-cost product strategy (selling its product at the lowest cost that will defeat the competition), it will want to closely control manufacturing and materials management processes, and the best design for doing this is the bureaucracy.[16] A bureaucracy generally has a relatively tall structure and functional units.

strategy
The determination of a company's long-term goals and objectives, and the adoption of actions and the allocation of resources to carry out those goals.

A third reason a company may change its structure is because it is facing a business crisis. Researcher Larry Greiner suggests that as companies evolve, they pass through a predictable set of challenges that they must successfully resolve before moving on.[17] In the early, innovative stage of starting a company, the typical entrepreneur creates and develops new products and services and downplays the need to be efficient. Ignoring efficiency concerns precipitates a *crisis of leadership* in which he or she realizes that running a company is a very different process from starting one. In response, the company hires a management team that grows the company by centralizing authority and formalizing decision making. Eventually this move toward more bureaucracy leads to a *crisis of autonomy*, in which employees working in innovative functions like R & D and marketing become dissatisfied with their inability to creatively generate new products. So the company delegates authority, empowering lower-level managers and, perhaps, even creating profit centers throughout the company. This change precipitates, in turn, a *crisis of control*, in which top managers and lower-level managers compete for company resources. In the next stage a *crisis of red tape* occurs when bureaucracy fails to improve organizational collaboration and efficiency. In the final stage, the company develops growth through collaboration by using the product team or matrix structures, which we will examine in the following section.

How Do Organizational Structures Evolve?

As organizations grow and evolve, they take on a variety of structures.[18] In the next sections we will examine the most important ones, presented in the order in which they typically occur as a company grows.

simple structure
The organizational form in which a small number of support staff report to one person.

THE SIMPLE STRUCTURE The **simple structure** evolves in a simple, dynamic environment in which an entrepreneur finds a strategic niche that can be filled by one person with a few supporting staff.[19] Simple structures tend to be small enterprises, and they stay small so their owner-managers can maintain tight control. The classic simple structure is the entrepreneurial firm. These companies search for niches, often risky environments in which they can be aggressive and innovative, and which larger bureaucracies tend to avoid.

Because the barriers of entry (such as the costs to enter the business) are low in their markets, and because they themselves are small, these firms are vulnerable to threats from their competitors. Their markets are characterized as hostile. In these types of companies, strategy tends to be intuitive rather than analytical, residing in the ideas and vision of the owner-manager. The environment is simple enough that an entrepreneur working alone can understand it, and the owner makes most of the decisions. Generally, the company emphasizes operations rather than strategy, there is little planning, and time horizons are short.[20] If we were to draw a simple structure, it would consist of the owner-manager and the employees.

functions
Specialties within an organization.

functional structure
The organizational form in which employees are expected to specialize in their particular function and to report to a manager who heads up and also specializes in that function.

THE FUNCTIONAL STRUCTURE As entrepreneurial firms grow, owner-managers find themselves unable to deal with all of the resulting complexities, so they begin to hire specialists. For example, they might hire a marketing specialist, a production specialist, or an accounting specialist to help them out. These specialties are **functions** that need to be performed in the organization, and the resulting organizational form is called the **functional structure.**

In a functional structure, employees are expected to specialize in their particular function, and they report to a manager who heads up and also specializes in that function. Typical functions within the organization are manufacturing, accounting, finance, sales, marketing, supply-chain management, and research and development. See Figure 16.4.

Functional structures are best for small- to medium-size companies that are producing one or only a few products using a routine technology. Functional structures operate best in environments that have little uncertainty and are relatively stable, or unchanging. Functional structures do very well in accomplishing their specialized goals and in developing in-depth skills in their personnel. Furthermore, there are economies of scale within the functions.

A major weakness of the functional structure is its slow response time to environmental changes. Whenever employees have a problem, they have to go through top management in order to determine how to react. This takes time, and decisions may pile up on top of the company. A related issue is that customer contact points with the company are unclear. If you have a problem with your widget, whom do you call—the manufacturing group, the marketing group, or the CEO? Other weaknesses of the functional structure are that the individual functions have only a limited view of the overall goals of the organization, there is a minimal amount of innovation, and there may be poor coordination among the functional units.

From the standpoint of your career, one of the advantages of working in a functional organization is that you can acquire in-depth expertise in a functional area. If you work in the human resources group, for instance, you will be exposed to the variety of responsibil-

FIGURE 16.4

A Functional Structure

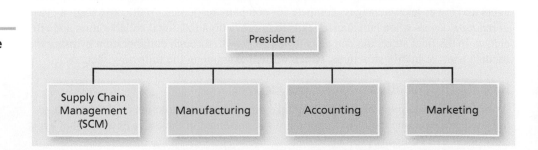

ities in that group, and if you manage that group, you will have gained experience in all areas of personnel management. Your broad-based expertise should enhance your marketability in your specialty.

THE DIVISIONAL STRUCTURE As the organization continues to grow, it increases its number of products, develops a broader geographical range, and reaches a wider customer base. At some point, the functional structure cannot accommodate these complexities. If, for example, manufacturing is producing half a dozen different products, marketing is marketing all of them, and purchasing is buying the materials for them, integrating these functions across all of the products becomes complicated. Often the result is that one or more products fails to get the attention that it deserves. At the same time, the customers for those products may be neglected.

To solve these sorts of problems, organizations are reorganized into the **divisional structure** (also called a "unit structure"). In this organizational structure, a layer is added below top management, delegating at least some responsibility for profit-making and customer responsiveness to vice presidents in charge of products or regions. Sometimes the divisional subunits become **strategic business units**, which have profit goals and a great deal of autonomy. The most common divisional structure is the product structure. Other divisional structures are the regional and the market structures. See Figure 16.5, in which the divisions could be any of these.

The divisional structure is used primarily by large corporations operating in fast-changing environments characterized by moderate to high uncertainty. The work these companies perform is likely to be nonroutine. The divisional structure is particularly adaptable in unstable environments because it is relatively easy to add or drop a product line: Without affecting the other divisions, a product (or regional) division can be closed or sold. The divisional structure also promotes client satisfaction because the contact points with the company are clear. Another advantage of this structure is that giving managers profit responsibility increases the probability that there will be adequate coordination across the functions within a division. Finally, creating these new organizational subunits allows for smaller, more manageable units within the organization.

The two weaknesses of this structure include, first, that the company loses economies of scale across functions. That is, because there is a separate marketing group for each product, clearly there will be inefficiencies. Second, the company loses the kind of broad-based expertise that an individual who manages a function across the whole company would have.

One of the career advantages of working in a divisionalized structure is that, by ascending to the vice presidential level, individuals whose career goal is to be a CEO can get experience coordinating a variety of functions. A career disadvantage is that if an individual remains a specialist, he or she may never move beyond their division.

THE MATRIX STRUCTURE The matrix structure is an organizational form that is widely known but not widely adopted. A **matrix structure** is a multiple command system, including a related structure and the necessary support mechanisms, culture and behaviors.[21] See Figure 16.6.

The defining characteristic of a matrix is that one manager reports to two (and sometimes more) bosses. Can you find this type of manager in Figure 16.6? In a product and

---

divisional structure
An organizational form created to address complexities that a functional structure cannot, in which a layer is added below top management; also called a "unit structure."

strategic business units
Divisions which have profit goals and a great deal of autonomy.

matrix structure
An organizational form which has a multiple command system, in which one manager reports to two or more bosses.

FIGURE 16.5

A Divisional Structure

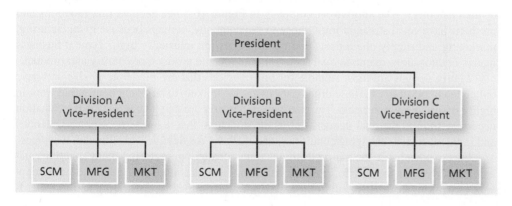

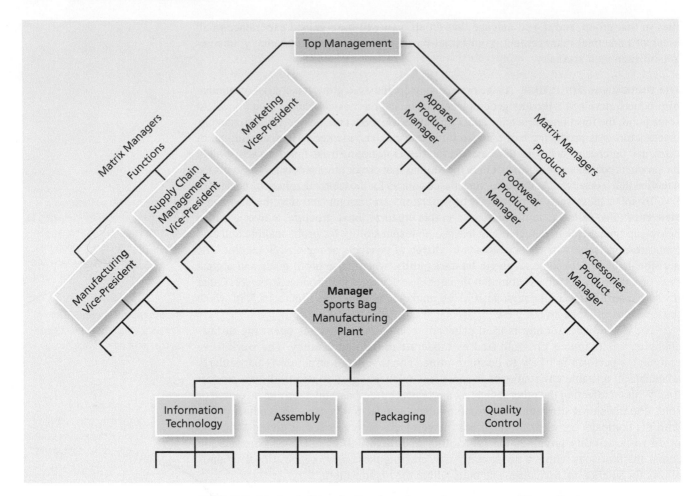

FIGURE 16.6 **A Matrix Design for a Sportswear Manufacturer**

market matrix, a person who markets widgets would report to the product vice-president in charge of widgets and also to the marketing vice-president. In Figure 16.6, the manager of the sports bag manufacturing plant reports to both the manufacturing vice-president and the accessory product manager. This dual reporting relationship allows for intensive information exchange and integrated decision making.

In Figure 16.6, you will note that below the middle management level, the employees who actually manufacture the product are managed using a more bureaucratic design. They work in a programmed style, report to one boss, do one routine job, and, most important, their part of the organization has a functional structure.

One of the reasons companies move to a matrix is environmental pressure for a dual strategic focus. The form originated in the aerospace industry, in which firms must focus intensive attention on both complex technical issues and on the unique project requirements of the customer.[22] The sportswear company in Figure 16.6 has decided that functions and products have equal strategic importance to the company, perhaps because manufacturing, marketing and supply chain costs and complexities are unusually high. Typical business matrix organizations maintain dual focus on function and product, or country and product.

Matrix designs are most suitable for organizations that are moderate in size and have only a few product lines. These organizations are most likely to be doing nonroutine work in highly uncertain environments. The strengths of a matrix are that it achieves the coordination necessary to meet the dual demands of its environment, that it supports complex decisions and rapid reaction to changing conditions, and it allows for flexible use of human resources.

On the other hand, the matrix design is time-consuming, requiring many meetings and an extensive focus on how to integrate its parts.[23] In addition, some people do not adapt well to working in a matrix environment; they find it confusing, frustrating and unrewarding. Matrix organizations are subject to power struggles between product and functional managers, and their decision making can easily be paralyzed because all strategies seem to have equal importance in the minds of decision makers.[24]

Often, the matrix structure is only a temporary design option for a company. Once the dual pressures on the company are resolved into a single strategic direction, management is happy to return to a divisionalized structure.

Would you like to work in a matrix? Individuals who succeed in these types of organizations must have a high tolerance for ambiguity, in part because they actually do report to two bosses who both direct them and evaluate them. Employees working in a matrix need excellent interpersonal and communication skills, including skills in conflict resolution. Working in a matrix is an excellent opportunity to gain broad-based experience, including both functional skills and teamwork skills.

What Are Some Recent Trends in Organizational Structure?

In this section, we will take a look at several organizational design innovations that are related to structure but which deviate from the typical patterns and evolution that we have just described.

Structured Networks

If you were to take a divisionalized organization that is based on strategic business units—that is, one in which each unit is a profit center—and spin off all of those units into separate but still interacting companies, you would have what is variously called a "networked organization," a "network form of organization,"[25] and a **structured network**."[26] Less often, such sets of organizations are known as "economic webs"[27] or "virtual organizations."[28]

structured network
A network form in which each organization is independent but interacting with other companies.

ADVANTAGES Because each of the units in the network is an organization in its own right, with its own legal status, it is easy for a network to be flexible and adaptable. "To the outside observer, [the network] will appear almost edgeless, with permeable and continuously changing interfaces between company, suppliers, and customers. From inside the firm the view will be no less amorphous, with traditional offices, departments, and operating divisions constantly reforming according to need."[29]

The idea of organizational networks is now an important metaphor driving business development. Rather than owning all of the activities that it wishes to control, an organization sub-contracts for many or all of these activities. However, being in the network still implies ongoing relationships and interdependencies.[30]

Another important advantage of a network is that each company can focus on its core competency, the thing it does the best. Another advantage is that the network can be large or small depending on environmental demands. It can be small when specialized work needs to be done by experts, but it can be large when it needs to purchase in volume for better terms and discounts.[31]

An example of a company that operates as a network is Nike, the large sports-shoe manufacturer. The core of the Nike network is the product design and research function, which is located in Oregon. Most of the other functions have been outsourced to companies around the world. For example, Nike might send the blueprints for the various parts of a shoe to various factories located throughout Southeast Asia. Each of these factories produces the component in which it specializes, then ships it to a manufacturing facility with which Nike partners in China. The Chinese factory in turn ships the shoes to the distributors around the world with whom Nike has a contractual relationship.

DISADVANTAGES Networks do have certain disadvantages. One is the potential loss of control over parts of the business. The companies in the network are there voluntarily, and if enticed away by other competitors, can create significant disruptions.

In addition, networks risk losing proprietary knowledge to any one of their members that chooses to steal it. For example, Apple Computer taught software vendor

Microsoft about its Macintosh operating system so that the company could write applications that would run on the Mac. However, Microsoft also incorporated what it had learned about the Mac into its own Windows operating system, costing Apple much of its competitive advantage. Another example is that after Schwinn contracted its bicycle manufacturing to a Taiwanese firm, the subcontractor subsequently used its manufacturing knowledge to sidestep Schwinn and sell directly to such mass merchandisers as Wal-Mart.[32]

A third disadvantage is that although it seems simple to outsource an activity, the fact is that often complicated adjustments and coordination must be arranged. As a general rule, the more complex the company's production and marketing, the more problems there are that are associated with having a network structure. In sum, the structure works best for simpler, more straightforward situations.[33]

The large network is a key organizational design for the future. *The Economist* writes, "In the next society, the biggest challenge for the large company—especially for the multinational—may be its social legitimacy: its values, its mission, its vision. Increasingly, in the next society's corporation, top management will, in fact, be the company. Everything else can be outsourced."[34]

The Front–Back Structure

The front–back or "front-end-back-end" model divides an organization into two components: 1) those that are oriented to the customer and/or the geographical region in which the company is doing business, called the front end, and 2) a back end that is organized by product and technology.[35] Typical functions in the front end include sales, marketing, and service, whereas typical functions in the back end include purchasing, manufacturing, and new product development.

There are two ways to depict this structure. One uses a traditional organizational chart and divides it into two; the other draws the front end and back end, literally in those places. See Figure 16.7, in which manufacturing, engineering and R & D make up the back end.

ADVANTAGES As you can see from Figure 16.7, the front end of the company provides value added by emphasizing service, customer education, and application software. Front–back organizations make companies more competitive by allowing them to focus on more than one dimension at a time, with the front end focusing on customers or channels of distribution, and the back end units focusing on products or technologies. This ability to focus on more than one dimension allows a company to cope with the complex business world.[36] Large computer companies are often designed with front ends and back ends. For example, at the front end, companies such as IBM and Digital provide systems integration, application software, and consulting services. Meanwhile,

FIGURE 16.7 Front-End–Back-End Structure

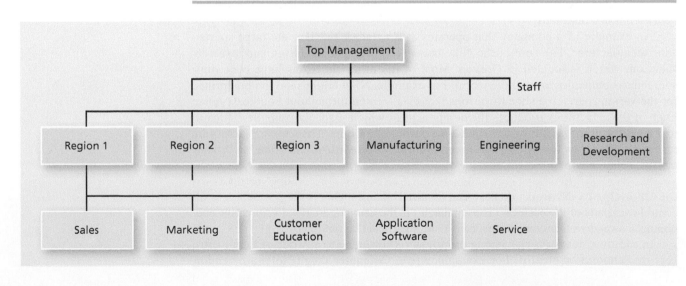

the companies' back ends create new products.[37] There are many possible variants on front–back structures.

In addition, the front end of a company is often designed to manage cross-product strategies and coordination. These include **cross-selling**, which is presenting a single face to the customer. Such processes have been created to meet the demands of large buyers like Wal-Mart. Large and powerful customers prefer to buy complete systems rather than stand-alone products, and they want to have systems custom-designed for them rather than having to face a bidding process and developing new relationships with many suppliers. Further, they prefer that the seller rather than they themselves coordinate the variety of products that they need.

cross-selling
Presenting a single face to the customer; one of the cross-product marketing strategies which are addressed through the design of the front end of a company.

DISADVANTAGES One concern with the front–back structure is that there is often a lack of clarity about how the front end is supposed to work with the back end. Also, it is similar to the matrix structure, with all its strengths and weaknesses including the high need for collaboration along with the high possibility for conflict.

The Boundaryless Organization

General Electric's former chairman Jack Welch popularized the term "**boundaryless organization**" as he worked to break down both the interior and exterior barriers to communication and cooperation in his company.[38] Welch argued that a company should do all it could possibly do to break down hierarchical barriers to communication as well as functional barriers to communication, and that it should, as well, break down the boundaries of the organization so that it could be closer to customers. These goals could be accomplished through the extensive use of technology to empower everyone involved. In the boundaryless organization, decision making is decentralized, and cross-functional teams have a great deal of power.

boundaryless organization
An organizational form that breaks down hierarchical and functional barriers to communication through extensive use of technology, decentralized decision making, and cross-functional teams.

However, since Welch, the term "boundaryless" has taken on other meanings as well. For example, one researcher suggests that the boundaryless organization is one in which people rarely or never see each other face to face, but rather are linked by computers, video teleconferencing, computer-aided design systems, and so on.[39] A similar idea is that some individuals are not formal parts of an organization at all, but rather form an alliance with an organization through their contractual obligations, and when the particular project they are working on is finished, they move on.[40]

How Do Managers Use Organizational Structure to Advance Their Company's Strategy?

As you have seen, companies sometimes change their organizational designs because they believe that doing so will make them more competitive. Clearly strategy and structure are interrelated. How, exactly?

Different Business Strategies Suggest Different Organizational Structures

Company A is pursuing a "differentiation strategy" whereby it hopes to improve its market share by developing different, innovative products that outshine the competition. Company B, in contrast, is pursuing a "low-cost strategy," whereby it hopes to beat its competitors on price. Should both companies use the same organizational structure? The answer is "no."[41]

The company following the differentiation strategy must be capable of acting quickly to meet customer needs and exploit its advantage. Its functions, including marketing, research and development, and manufacturing, must work together effectively and efficiently. Its design should be organic/enterprising, and its structure should be organized around products, with many cross-functional teams.

The company following the low-cost strategy, in contrast, needs to closely supervise the costs of materials and manufacturing. It does not invest heavily in research and development, but rather imitates existing products while specializing in producing them cheaply. It should use the simplest possible structure, probably a functional one.[42]

Structure Affects How Strategic Decisions Are Made

The process of making strategic decisions is likely to be influenced by the nature of an organization's structure in the following ways.[43]

First, as the structure becomes more centralized or vertically differentiated—that is, when it is more likely that decisions are made at the top—there is a stronger probability that the strategic decision-making process will be initiated by only those few dominant individuals who run the company, and that it will be the result of their proactive seeking for business opportunities. Their strategy is likely to be opportunistic rather than defensive, and to be deliberately rational and innovative. A main limitation on the decision making will be the cognitive limitations of the top managers themselves.

Second, as the structure becomes more formalized (for instance, when it has more procedures and policies), the strategic decision making process is likely to become reactive rather than proactive. Strategic actions will be the result of standardized organizational processes and any changes in organizational direction will be incremental rather than major. Emphasis on detail can become a constraint on the comprehensiveness of the decision making process.

Third, as the level of complexity of the structure grows (that is, when it becomes more horizontally differentiated), so does the probability that members will either not recognize the strategic impacts of a policy or will ignore these impacts in favor of the interests of the immediate unit in which they work. Strategic actions will come about only after an internal process of political bargaining, and these actions are likely to be incremental rather than major. In this instance, the major constraint on the decision making process is the organizational members' limited, self-serving view of organizational strategy.

How Do International Organizational Structures Typically Evolve?

Taking a company international adds new dimensions to its organizational design. Check out Figure 16.8 to see how international companies evolve and read on to see why this happens.

Direct Reporting

In the earliest stages of internationalization, a company often explores a relatively simple foreign involvement in order to achieve production efficiencies or tap a new market. Often, in order to test its ability in the international arena, it chooses to enter into just one country. To accommodate this change into its structure, it merely adds a new unit onto its organizational chart that represents the country. Usually, home country presidents want an intimate view of operations in their new ventures, so they require the new venture managers to report directly to them. Hence the name "direct reporting" for this type of organizational structure.

Whether or not a company decides to go international at all depends in part on the country in which it originates. Companies operating in large markets such as the United States, Japan, and Germany are often preoccupied with those markets and are less likely to go international, whereas companies from smaller countries go international quickly because they have no other choices for expansion.[44]

The International Division

Next, after succeeding in one country, a company may want to pursue operations in additional countries. As the company enters more countries, the complexity of the international operation increases. The company president soon needs help integrating all the information flowing from all of the countries, so the company creates a new division, termed the "international division," with its own vice-president.

Irrespective of how the home country is organized, an international division is organized by country. For example, even though the home country has a functional or product structure, the international division has a country structure.

There are several reasons why having an international division is effective at this point in time for the company.[45] First, it enables a focus on international operations separate from

FIGURE 16.8

The Evolution of International Organizational Structures

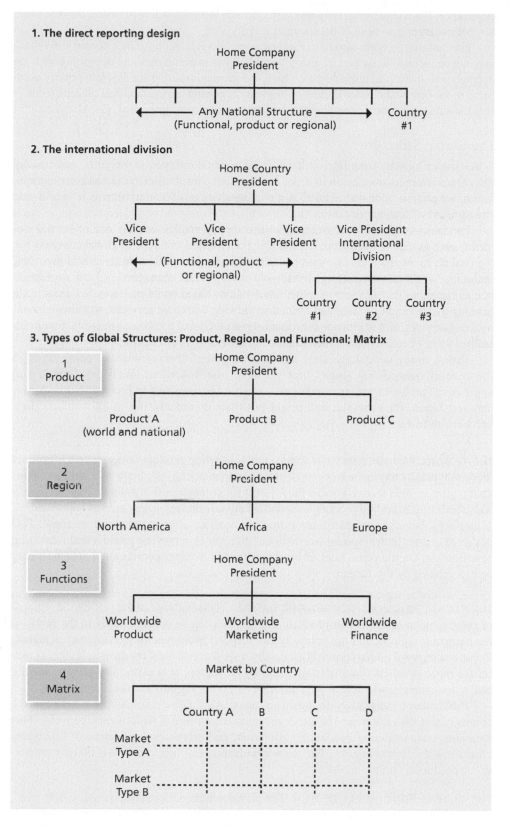

the domestic operations. Second, it allows the international division to develop critical mass and thus compete effectively for scarce resources, both within and outside the company. This ability to compete is enhanced by the vice president who reports directly to the home company president. Finally, having an international division economizes on what is still a scarce resource in most companies—that is, finding general managers with international experience. If a company has only one manager with international experience, the best place for that manager is as head of the international division.

International divisions also have disadvantages, however. A company's domestic divisions may not be inclined to support it, giving low priority to export orders and competing with the international division as profit centers. Often, the international division has low priority compared to the better established domestic divisions. In general, an international division tends to be a transitional structure, preceding the development of a more integrated, global structure.[46]

The Global Structure

When the influence of the international division has developed sufficiently, and usually this means when its sales begin to make an important contribution to the company, companies move on to a "global structure." A global structure is also referred to as a "worldwide structure" or a "transnational structure."

Fundamentally, the structure of a global company emphasizes any one of several elements, such as regions, functions, or products. For example, one type of global company has regional divisions and regional vice-presidents. Another has worldwide functional divisions, including worldwide marketing, worldwide supply chain management, and worldwide human resources management. Another has divisions based on its products. For example, a banking group might be designed around worldwide corporate services, worldwide small business services, and worldwide individual services. Global companies may function in literally dozens of countries, and their operations and designs can become quite complex.

Today, many companies start right out as global designs without going through the several transitional stages that we have just described. Well capitalized and aggressive, such companies immediately open sales divisions in Europe, North America, and Japan, for example, and might put their manufacturing in Taiwan and their software in India.[47]

THE GLOBAL PRODUCT DESIGN Under the worldwide product structure, each product division typically has its own export department, manufacturing plants, and sales and marketing groups. This format is especially useful for companies that are growing, because it adds flexibility in adding product lines and taking advantage of new market opportunities. A company can add a product line or drop one without a major structural overhaul. This design also does better than an international division in achieving product and marketing coordination. On the other hand, if local expertise is lacking, coordination problems may be exacerbated by this design.

THE GLOBAL REGIONAL/GEOGRAPHIC DESIGN The advantage of the worldwide regional or geographic structure is that products and services can be adapted easily to the needs of the particular regions, and the company can respond more readily to consumer demands. Because a regional global format is especially responsive to local conditions, it is most useful for those products that differ significantly by region. It is especially popular among banks, for example, which deal with different monetary systems and legal constraints.

Problems of integration do, however, arise. Although communication between the company and the region may be good, communication across regions may be weak. This structure tends to inhibit product coordination, and promotes duplication of functional efforts in the different regions. The major disadvantage of this structure is that the emphasis on product is compromised.

THE GLOBAL FUNCTIONAL DESIGN The global functional structure is not widely used, because it primarily suits companies with a very limited product line. Companies whose product is a natural resource, such as copper, are most likely to adopt it. Also, because the form is not easily altered, it is best suited to companies that are operating in stable environments.

One problem with the functional global format is that local, functional operations tend to preempt the company's strategic concerns. Also, like functional organizations in general, the format does not tend to develop general managers who can then move up and bring international expertise to the company as a whole.

THE MATRIX DESIGN A global structure can also be a matrix. Among the possibilities, the market-by-country matrix is the most common. For example, a large bank may operate in several different countries, employing both country managers and managers responsible for, respectively, individual banking needs and corporate banking needs in those countries. As we have already discussed, matrix organizations suffer from complexity and ambiguity, while allowing companies to have a dual focus. Even international companies tend to use them primarily as a transitional form.

What Are International Strategic Alliances?

Networked organizations can, of course, be international.[48] Generally, organizations network to achieve a particular competitive advantage.

For example, one kind of international alliance develops based on "licensing agreements," by which international firms can quickly and inexpensively develop manufacturing capability in other countries. Another sort, the "joint venture," occurs when existing companies that are already networked together develop new organizations. Finally, "consortia" are groups of firms that take on new products and technologies together. Airbus Industrie, for instance, is a consortium of European businesses that produces commercial aircraft.

In Conclusion

Business strategy theorist Henry Mintzberg points out that in a sense, the structures presented here do not exist at all. They are just words and pictures on pieces of paper, not reality itself.[49] Reality is far more complex.

How strong is the link between organizational structure and actual organizational functioning? The experience of many companies that have changed their organizational structures suggests that it is at least worth paying attention to, and that, having changed their organizational structures, they become more efficient. However, there are a large number of factors that influence a company's effectiveness, including its strategy, technology, marketing, leadership, culture, work design, and management control system. In the struggle to stay competitive, organizational structure is only one factor of many that managers must weigh.

Apply What You Have Learned. . .

World Class Company: Dell, Inc.

Dell, Inc. designs, manufactures, and sells computer systems and services worldwide. It markets its products directly to its customers, which include large corporations, governments, small and medium businesses, and consumers. Only about 15 percent of its business is direct sales to individuals.[50] In its 15 biggest markets the company increased its market share routinely over the period from 1996 to 2004.

Michael Dell is a predictable type of guy who runs a predictable type of business. As one commentator put it, among technology executives, he is an anomaly. Larry Ellison of Oracle has a huge yacht and a fighter jet; Jeff Bezos of Amazon is funding a space-rocket start-up; Bill Gates has his enormous high-tech house; and Michael Dell has "four kids, a wife, and three dogs."[51] His company, the world's largest maker of personal computers, takes a lean approach to manufacturing, cutting costs wherever possible, and utilizing a state of the art supply-chain management system. Its approach of marketing direct to customers is also lean. Also, the company does not do defensive research and development.[52]

Today the company is facing criticism that it is not as nimble as it once was, that it is too large to react quickly to changing market conditions. Also, because its competitiveness depends on milking economies of scale, it is vulnerable to Asian competitors that can cut costs even more. However, its worldwide market share, which is about 19 percent, does mean there is room for growth.[53] Michael Dell argues that Dell is itself an Asian vendor. It has factories in both Malaysia and China, for example. He himself sometimes takes customer calls in his call centers to be sure he is on top of market demands. On one such visit to a call center he was deluged with calls, which convinced him that he had cut a particular price too low.

The company attributes its success not to its business model alone, but to terrific execution. "We drummed into our people's heads, through presentation after presentation, what's good performance and what's bad performance. They saw data on inventory every day. They got rewarded when inventory came down and punished when inventory went up . . . the reward and punishment didn't come from us, it came from our people seeing for themselves how much better their businesses worked when they didn't have inventory."[54] Also, "To succeed as a GM [general manager] here you have to be smart and you have to be tough. You have to be a team player, and you have to understand the P&L. You're in trouble if you don't understand the P&L. Sometimes our managers think that what we've asked them to do is irrational. But the fact of the matter is our general managers have succeeded time and time again. When we hold somewhat irrational expectations and convince them they can do it, they come up with fantastic breakthroughs. We challenge our people to substitute ingenuity for investment."[55]

Dell has about 55,000 employees.[56] They are organized in a matrix of sales regions and product groups.[57] These are in turn broken down into sub-products and sales sub-segments. In addition, it utilizes a variety of business councils. For instance, there is a worldwide small-business council made up of all their small-business general managers and product managers. In late 2006, Dell set out to hire 500 new engineers to add to its more than 4,000 engineers and developers.[58] These engineers will work on all its product lines. We are not just a "screwdriver shop," the company asserts; encouraging innovation and ensuring quality are important aspects of the business.

Dell's main competitors are Hewlett-Packard, IBM, and Sun Microsystems Inc. In 1992, at the age of 27, Michael Dell became the youngest CEO in the *Fortune* 500.

Discuss

1. Describe the organizational design of Dell.
2. Describe the strengths and weaknesses of the design with respect to the business the company is in.
3. What is the organization's structure? Often, for competitive reasons, companies do not publish their organizational charts. However, you can develop your own chart by going to the company's Web site (www.dell.com) and finding the page that shows their executive leadership team, which numbers about 20 people. Note the team members' titles and develop a chart based on them.

Advice from the Pros

Is a Flatter Organization a Better Organization? Do the Math

In their award-winning book *Management Redeemed: Debunking the Fads That Undermine Corporate Perfor-* *mance,* Lex Donaldson and Frederick G. Hilmer make the case *against* flattening organizations. They do some interesting math: Assume a corporation has 15,000 employees (production workers and sales personnel), with a total of

2,500 managers in five levels, and the average span of control of these managers is 7. Now let's cut one entire level, or 1,000 expensive managers, for a 40 percent saving in managerial salaries and benefits. Sounds great, doesn't it?

Here's the problem: Now the average span of control is 11, and as Donaldson and Hilmer put it, "this is not a trivial increase in the burden faced by each manager and may well have an adverse impact on supervision quality, communication, and decision speed."[59] Furthermore, the total workforce has only been reduced about 5.7 percent, and estimated payroll savings are only around 9 percent. If total payroll costs make up about a quarter of the company's total costs, then cutting 1,000 managers has only saved about 2 percent in total costs.

"The likely results: a delirious financial press, happy shareholders (for this year at any rate), reduced corporate effectiveness, and long-term satisfaction among overseas competitors!"[60]

Discuss

1. List 10 ways in which organizational processes and effectiveness might be improved by getting rid of a layer of people.
2. Now list 10 ways in which organizational processes and effectiveness might be damaged by eliminating a layer of people.
3. Which type of company is better to work for, a flatter one or a steeper one?

Gain Experience

Analyze the Design of an Organization You Know Well

In teams of five or more, describe the organizational design of your university.

1. Obtain an organization chart of your university. What are the main parts of the university?
2. What historic factors still play a part in the design of your university today?

3. What characterizes the university's environment?
4. Is the university a bureaucracy, enterprise, or hybrid?
5. Use Table 15.3 on page 410 to describe the bureaucratic and enterprising elements of your university.
6. In what ways does the organization chart reflect your university's strategy?
7. Can you improve the chart to better reflect the university's strategy?

Can You Solve This Manager's Problem?

Asea Brown Boveri (ABB)

In 1988 the Swedish company ASEA merged with the Swiss company Brown Boveri to form ABB (Asea Brown Boveri), the world's leading supplier in the $50 billion electric power industry.[61] ABB's businesses include power plants, power transmission, power distribution, and industrial equipment. At the time of the merger, the organization controlled as much as a third of the European market and more than 20 percent of the world market. The new ABB had 180,000 employees, all but 30,000 of them in Europe.

It sold its products in 140 countries. After merging, the company immediately initiated an emphasis on profit centers, which are the local operating companies, and adopted a matrix structure.

Discuss

1. What do you think would be a good matrix structure for ABB? Draw it.
2. How would you select the matrix managers? What would be their qualifications?

Chapter Summary and Key Terms

After managers divide up the organization's work, how do they coordinate their employees to get it done?

Theoretically speaking, organizational design is dividing up the work of a company into jobs (the process called differentiation) and then finding ways to coordinate the people in these different jobs (the process called integration). The greater a company's differentiation, the greater the challenge of integration. Integration can be achieved through such means as hierarchy, departmentalization, goals, integrating departments, and integrator roles.

How can you expect an organizational structure to evolve?

Company structures change because companies grow, change their strategies, or face crises. As a company grows, a typical structural evolution is from a simple structure to a functional structure to a divisional structure.

What are some recent trends in organizational structure?

Today companies are likely to spin off strategic business units into separate but still interacting companies. The resulting form is called a network. Another modern form is the front-back structure, in which one part of the company, the front, is oriented to the customer, and another, the back, is oriented toward manufacturing and new product development. A concept popularized in recent years is the boundaryless organization, in which boundaries between levels and units and also between the company and its customers are reduced.

How do managers use organizational structure to advance their company's strategy?

Companies change their designs because they believe that doing so will give them a competitive advantage. For example, a company following a differentiation strategy, in which it plans to develop a variety of innovative products, should be an enterprise, whereas a company following a low-cost strategy should be a bureaucracy.

How do international organizational structures typically evolve?

A company that is going international typically starts out using a direct reporting structure, then later moves to an international division. Finally, it may adopt a global structure. Global structures are based on product, region, or function, although they may also be matrixes.

What are international strategic alliances?

In today's competitive global environment, companies are likely to pursue relationships with companies in other countries through licensing agreements, joint ventures, and consortia.

Explorations

1. Organizational charts

Find an interesting organizational chart on the Internet. (It may or may not be a chart of a corporation.) Bring it into class and be prepared to describe what it means and why it is of particular interest.

2. Structure and innovation

Web search for organizational structure and innovation and report on what you learn about how some structures foster innovation better than others.

3. Matrix structures today

Web search for matrix structures to find out which companies are using them today, and why many companies find them to be a problem.

References

[1] D. D. Van Fleet and A. G. Bedeian, "A History of the Span of Management," *Academy of Management Review 2* (3), 1977:356–372.

[2] B. Davison, "Management Span of Control: How Wide Is Too Wide?" *Journal of Business Strategy 24* (4), 2003:22–29.

[3] J. S. McClenahen, "Flexible Structures to Absorb the Shocks," *Industry Week 18,* April 1988: 41–42.

[4] M. B. McCaskey, "An Introduction to Organizational Design," *California Management Review 17* (2), 1974:13–20.

[5] H. Fayol, *General and Industrial Management* (London: Sir Isaac Pitman & Sons Ltd, 1949).

[6] H. Mintzberg, *The Structuring of Organizations* (Englewood Cliffs, NJ: Prentice Hall, 1979).

[7] J. R. Galbraith, "Organizational design: An Information Processing View," in P. E. Connor, *Organizations: Theory and Design* (Chicago: Science Research Associates, Inc., 1980):43–49.

[8] J. R. Galbraith, "Organizational design: An Information Processing View," in P. E. Connor, *Organizations: Theory and Design* (Chicago: Science Research Associates, Inc., 1980):43–49.

[9] C. W. Downs, P. G. Clampitt, and A. L. Pfeiffer, "Communication and Organizational Outcomes," in G. M. Goldhaber and G. A. Barnett, eds., *Handbook of Organizational Communication* (Norwood, NJ: Ablex Publishing Corporation, 1988):171–212.

[10] L. Fried, *Managing Information Technology in Turbulent Times* (New York: John Wiley & Sons, Inc., 1995); G. G. Dess, and A. M. A. Rasheed, "The New Corporate Architecture," *Academy of Management Executive 9,* 1995:7–18.

[11] T. A. Stewart, *Intellectual Capital: The New Wealth of Organizations* (New York: Doubleday/Currency, 1997).

[12] P. R. Lawrence and J. W. Lorsch, "New Management Job: The Integrator," *Harvard Business Review,* November–December 1967:142–151.

[13] J. R. Galbraith, *Competing with Flexible Lateral Organizations,* 2nd ed., (Reading, MA: Addison-Wesley Publishing Company, 1994).

[14] M. H. Bazerman and A. H. Hoffman, "Sources of Environmentally Destructive Behavior: Individual, Organizational, and Institutional Perspectives," *Research in Organizational Behavior 21,* 1999:39–79.

[15] A. D. Chandler Jr., *Strategy and Structure: Chapters in the History of the American Industrial Enterprise* (Cambridge, MA: MIT Press, 1962).

[16] G. R. Jones, *Organizational Theory: Text and Cases,* 3rd ed. (Upper Saddle River, NJ: Prentice Hall, 2001).

[17] L. Greiner, "Evolution and Revolution as Organizations Grow," *Harvard Business Review,* July–August 1972:37–46.

[18] R. Duncan, "What Is the Right Organization Structure: Decision Tree Analysis Provides the Answer," *Organizational Dynamics,* Winter 1979.

[19] H. Mintzberg, "Structure in 5's: A Synthesis of the Research on Organization Design," *Management Science 26* (3), March 1980:322–341.

[20] A. C. Filley and R. J. House, *Managerial Process and Organizational Behaviour* (New York: Scott Foresman, 1969).

[21] S. M. Davis and P. R. Lawrence, *Matrix* (Reading, MA: Addison-Wesley, 1977).

[22] S. M. Davis and P. R. Lawrence, *Matrix* (Reading, MA: Addison-Wesley, 1977).

[23] S. M. Davis and P. R. Lawrence, *Matrix* (Reading, MA: Addison-Wesley, 1977); H. F. Kolodny, "Managing in a Matrix," *Business Horizons 24 (2),* March/April 1981:17–24.

[24] J. Brown and N. Agnew, "The Balance of Power in a Matrix Structure," *Business Horizons 25* (6), 1982:51–54.

[25] R. E. Miles and C. C. Snow, "The New Network Firm: A Spherical Structure Built on a Human Investment Philosophy," *Organizational Dynamics 23* (4), Spring 1995:5–18.

[26] M. Goold and A. Campbell, *Designing Effective Organizations: How to Create Structured Networks* (San Francisco, CA: Jossey-Bass Publishers, 2002).

[27] T. A. Stewart, *Intellectual Capital: The New Wealth of Organizations* (New York: Doubleday/Currency, 1997).

[28] W. H. Davidow and M. S. Malone, *The Virtual Corporation* (New York: Harper Collins Publishers, 1992).

[29] W. H. Davidow and M. S. Malone, *The Virtual Corporation* (New York: Harper Collins Publishers, 1992):6

[30] R. E. Miles and C. C. Snow, "Network Organizations: New Concepts for New Forms," *California Management Review 28,* 1986: 62–73.

[31] J. R. Galbraith, "Designing the Networked Organization: Leveraging Size and Competencies," in S. A. Mohrman, J. R. Galbraith, Edward E. Lawler III, and Associates, *Tomorrow's Organization: Crafting Winning Capabilities in a Dynamic World* (San Francisco, CA: Jossey-Bass Publishers, 1998):51–75.

[32] J. R. Galbraith, "Designing the Networked Organization: Leveraging Size and Competencies," in S. A. Mohrman, J. R. Galbraith, Edward E. Lawler III, and Associates, *Tomorrow's Organization: Crafting Winning Capabilities in a Dynamic World* (San Francisco, CA: Jossey-Bass Publishers, 1998):51–75.

[33] C. C. Snow, R. E. Miles, and H. J. Coleman Jr., "Managing 21st Century Network Organizations," *Organizational Dynamics,* Winter 1992:5–20.

[34] "Will the corporation survive?" *The Economist,* November 3, 2001:14–18.

[35] J. R. Galbraith, "The Value-Adding Corporation: Matching Structure with Strategy," in J. R. Galbraith, E. E. Lawler III, and Associates, *Organizing for the Future: The New Logic for Managing Complex Organizations* (San Francisco, CA: Jossey-Bass Publishers, 1993):15–42.

[36] M. Goold and A. Campbell, *Designing Effective Organizations: How to Create Structured Networks* (San Francisco, CA: Jossey-Bass Publishers, 2002).

[37] J. R. Galbraith, "The Value-Adding Corporation: Matching Structure with Strategy," in J. R. Galbraith, E. E. Lawler III, and Associates, *Organizing for the Future: The New Logic for Managing Complex Organizations* (San Francisco, CA: Jossey-Bass Publishers, 1993):15–42.

[38] J. Welch, *Jack: Straight from the Gut* (New York: Warner Books, 2003).

[39] J. Fulk and B. Desanctis, "Electronic Communication and Changing Organizational Forms," *Organizational Science 6,* 1995:337–349.

[40] G. R. Jones, *Organizational Theory: Text and Cases,* 3rd ed. (Upper Saddle River, NJ: Prentice Hall, 2001).

[41] G. R. Jones, *Organizational Theory: Text and Cases,* 3rd ed., (Upper Saddle River, NJ: Prentice Hall, 2001)

[42] D. Miller, "Strategy Making and Structure: Analysis and Implications for Performance," *Academy of Management Journal 30,* 1987:7–32.

[43] J. W. Fredrickson, "The Strategic Decision Process and Organizational Structure," *Academy of Management Review 11,* 1986:280–297.

[44] S. A. Mohrman, J. R. Galbraith, E. E. Lawler III and Associates, *Tomorrow's Organization: Crafting Winning Capabilities in a Dynamic World* (San Francisco, CA: Jossey-Bass Publishers, 1998).

[45] S. A. Mohrman, J. R. Galbraith, E. E. Lawler III and Associates, *Tomorrow's Organization: Crafting Winning Capabilities in a Dynamic World* (San Francisco, CA: Jossey-Bass Publishers, 1998).

[46] S. Ronen, *Comparative and Multinational Management* (New York: John Wiley & Sons, 1986).

[47] S. A. Mohrman, J. R. Galbraith, E. E. Lawler III and Associates, *Tomorrow's Organization: Crafting Winning Capabilities in a Dynamic World* (San Francisco, CA: Jossey-Bass Publishers, 1998).

[48] See, for example, the discussion of ABB in M. F. R. Kets de Vries, "Charisma in Action: The Transformational Abilities of Virgin's Richard Branson and ABB's Percy Barnevik," *Organizational Dynamics 26* (3), Winter 1998:7–21.

[49] H. Mintzberg, *The Structuring of Organizations* (Englewood Cliffs, NJ: Prentice Hall, 1979).468–469.

[50] "Technology's Mr. Predictable," *The Economist,* September 22, 2005, http://www.economist.com/research/articles. Accessed October 15, 2005.

[51] "Technology's Mr. Predictable," *The Economist,* September 22, 2005, http://www.economist.com/research/articles. Accessed October 15, 2005.

[52] T. A. Stewart and L. O'Brien, "Execution without Excuses," *Harvard Business Review 83* (3) March 2005:102–111,105.

[53] "Technology's Mr. Predictable," *The Economist,* September 22, 2005, http://www.economist.com/research/articles. Accessed October 15, 2005.

[54] T. A. Stewart and L. O'Brien, "Execution without Excuses," *Harvard Business Review 83* (3) March 2005:102–111,105.

[55] T. A. Stewart and L. O'Brien, "Execution without Excuses," *Harvard Business Review 83* (3) March 2005:102–111,106.

[56] "Dell Inc.," Yahoo! Finance, www.yahoo.com. Accessed October 16, 2005.

[57] T. A. Stewart and L. O'Brien, "Execution without Excuses," *Harvard Business Review 83* (3) March 2005:102–111.

[58] F. Norrod, "Looking for a Few Good Engineers," http://www.direct2dell.com/one2one/archive/category /1010.aspx. Accessed September 26, 2006.

[59] L. Donaldson and F. G. Hilmer, "Management Redeemed: The Case Against Fads That Harm Management," *Organizational Dynamics 26* (4), Spring 1998:7–20, 10.

[60] L. Donaldson and F. G. Hilmer, "Management Redeemed: The Case Against Fads That Harm Management," *Organizational Dynamics 26* (4), Spring 1998:7–20, 11.

[61] http://www.abb.com/global/. Accessed July 19, 2005; D. E. Westney, "ABB—Through the Strategic Design Lens," in D. Ancona, T. Kochan, M. Scully, J. Van Maanen, and D. E. Westney, *Organizational Behavior & Processes* (Cincinnati, OH: South-Western College Publishing, 1999): Module 2, 27–39.

17 Organizational Culture

Preview

Why is organizational culture so important to companies?
Where do organizational cultures originate?
What is the difference between culture and climate?
How does national culture affect organizational culture?
What companies have built a reputation around their corporate cultures?

How do you discover an organization's culture?
What do you need to know?
How do new employees learn an organization's culture?

How do managers use organizational culture to improve organizational effectiveness?
How does culture . . .
. . . motivate performance?
. . . create commitment?
. . . integrate organizational units?
. . . motivate ethical behavior?
. . . enhance corporate branding? (And how does branding enhance culture?)
. . . enhance service?

What happens when organizations with different cultures merge?
How can managers foster acculturation?
What is the effect of merging business systems on merging organizational cultures?

How can an existing organizational culture be changed?

How can you find an organizational culture in which you will thrive?
What kind of culture do you prefer?
Will you face the glass ceiling?

Patagonia, Starbucks, and Army Boot Camp

Founder Yvon Chouinard uses his company Patagonia as a tool for social change. Dedicated to green causes, it serves as a model for other organizations that want to be environmentally responsible.

Starbucks connects with its customers through its partners (its employees). It listens carefully to partners' suggestions, provides them with extensive training, and offers good benefits. The company believes that if it takes care of its partners, they will in turn take good care of its customers. The result is a highly successful worldwide business.

The Army is all about discipline. Boot camp is designed to break people down so they will submit to the organization's rules and control. If people are to adapt to the Army's highly structured world, a rigorous orientation is believed to be absolutely necessary.

The question is, what do Patagonia, Starbucks, and Army boot camp have in common? The answer: Their unique organizational cultures. Each has a published organizational philosophy and a distinctive style. Each has become famous for its unique methods. Though very different, each culture is a strong one, and each of these three organizations is more effective because of that strength.

culture

An organization's system of shared values and norms, along with related behaviors, which defines for organizational members what is important in the company and what attitudes, beliefs, and behaviors are appropriate.

An organization's **culture** is its system of shared values and norms, along with related behaviors.[1] Culture defines for organizational members what is important in the company and what attitudes, beliefs, and behaviors are appropriate.

Why Is Organizational Culture So Important to Companies?

Culture sounds like a pretty soft concept, yet many companies today are investing significant amounts of money to improve theirs. One reason organizational cultures are important is that they affect bottom lines, as you will see in a moment. In addition, unlike formal control systems using rules and policies, culture shapes employee behavior in subtle ways without reducing individual autonomy.[2]

dominant culture

The system of values and norms held by most of a company's member; also called a company's "core values."

The **dominant culture** in a company is the system of values and norms held by most members. Often this system is referred to as a company's **core values**. In some circumstances, it is important to differentiate between **espoused values** and **enacted values**—those that people say they value versus those that actually guide their actions.

core values

Values and norms held by most organizational members.

Subcultures are formal and informal groups and networks that may subscribe to some of these values and norms, but also have their own. **Counter-cultures** are those subcultures whose values and norms oppose those of the dominant culture of the company. Subcultures and counter-cultures in an organization create both productive and counterproductive conflict, allowing for the expression of alternative values and innovative ideas that can be either a distraction from, or an important source of diversity for, organizational problem-solving.[3]

espoused values

Values which people profess to hold.

enacted values

Values which actually guide people's actions.

Where Do Organizational Cultures Originate?

Perhaps you remember from our chapter on design that the three historical factors that drive a company's design, including its culture, are the personality and style of the founder, the historic period in which the company was founded, and the historic size of the company. The norms and values of any organization originate in those of its founder personally and in the fashions for organizational design during the period in which the company was founded.

subcultures

Formal and informal groups and networks that may subscribe to some of the dominant values and norms, but also have their own.

They also originate in the norms and values that typify organizations of different sizes. For instance, norms for behavior are relatively flexible in small organizations and relatively standardized in large organizations. In addition, an organization's culture is determined by the business the company is in and the national and regional cultures in which the company is embedded. Often, all of these factors are reflected in a company's published philosophy.

counter-cultures

Subcultures whose values and norms oppose those of the dominant culture.

What Is the Difference Between Culture and Climate?

In recognition of how important individual perception and interpretation are in describing culture, researchers sometimes use the word **climate** to refer to organizational members' *perceptions* of an organization's policies, practices, and procedures, including its structure, reward systems, warmth and support, and other aspects.[4]

climate

Organizational members' perceptions of an organization's policies, practices, and procedures.

According to the **social information processing model**, organizational climate is influenced by organizational culture. For example, how individuals feel about their jobs is influenced by what people around them say.[5] If a boss or coworker comments on the amount of challenge or autonomy there is in a job, an employee is likely to adopt that attitude toward his or her work.[6]

social information processing model

A model of organizational culture which suggests that organizational climate is influenced by organizational culture (for example, that an individual's feelings about his or her job are influenced by what the people around him or her say).

Conceptually, researchers are still figuring out precisely how organizational climate differs from organizational culture.[7] Although the definition of climate does depend on perception, perception itself includes the idea that meaning is attached to the perceived event or thing, and this notion of shared meaning is central to the conceptualization of culture. Perhaps the two concepts cannot really be differentiated.

How Does National Culture Affect Organizational Culture?

Although organizational culture and national culture are not one and the same, they are related. For example, the Japanese emphasis on conformity is displayed in Japanese organizational cultures through norms of demonstrating the appropriate attitude, spirit, and way of thinking.[8] Similarly, anthropologists report that American society emphasizes individualism, which, in American work cultures, can be found in norms that emphasize individual rewards and value charismatic leaders.

Another example is that national cultures whose members prefer to avoid uncertainties tend to have companies with closed-system, bureaucratic cultures rather than open-system, enterprise organizational cultures.[9] Dutch organizations, for instance, are more likely to have bureaucratic cultures than are Danish organizations.

What Companies Have Built a Reputation Around Their Corporate Cultures?

In this text we have already mentioned several companies that have famous organizational cultures, including Lincoln Electric and Southwest Airlines. Other companies with famous cultures are IBM, Hewlett-Packard, Goldman Sachs, and Starbucks. Companies with infamous cultures that are now out of business were Enron and Arthur Anderson.

Consider the case of Wal-Mart, one of the most famous organizational cultures of all time.

Wal-Mart created its organizational culture around the image of its founder, Sam Walton, a small town merchant who became an American tycoon. Sam Walton opened his first Walton's 5 & 10 in 1950 in Bentonville, Arkansas, and when he died in 1992 he was running a phenomenally successful empire of retail stores nationwide. At the time, he was the world's second richest man, behind Bill Gates. Today his company has successfully entered such international markets as Mexico, Canada, Argentina, Brazil, South Korea, China, and Puerto Rico.

"Genuine, polite, civic-minded, and wholesome," are characteristics of both Walton and Wal-Mart.10 Walton was one of the earlier employers to call his employees "associates," give them stock, and share store data with them. He was "enthusiastic, positive, folksy, and nurturing," a charismatic leader who did the hula dance down Wall Street when Wal-Mart's net profits exceeded 8 percent.11

Wal-Mart's employees don't "work for" someone, they "help out." The Wal-Mart message to them is that the people who work hard and take part in the company's profit-sharing program become rich and happy.

As we discuss various aspects of organizational culture, we will continue to use Wal-Mart to illustrate our points.

How Do You Discover an Organization's Culture?

It's your first day on the job and you have just walked through the door of your new company. How do you figure out what its culture is?

What Do You Need to Know?

Think of a company's culture as existing on four levels, from the most concrete and obvious to the most abstract and unconscious.[12] Understanding each level demands some observation and thought on your part.

LEVEL 1: BEHAVIORS AND ARTIFACTS At the first, most superficial level, take note of the organization's behaviors and artifacts, the visible but not always decipherable indicators of the company culture. Level 1 includes all behaviors, and also such subtle aspects as the language and metaphors people use, corporate rituals and ceremonies, and stories and legends.[13] Also consider how the company designs its physical space—from its architecture to the art it hangs on the walls.

Some visible aspects of an organization's culture have symbolic value. One reason researchers and practitioners alike are so interested in corporate culture is that they recognize the importance of these symbols in helping people make sense of their organizational life.[14] When assessing an organization's culture, always consider the potential symbolic value of its behaviors and artifacts.

Using your observations, determine whether a company's culture is:[15]

Process-oriented or results-oriented.

Does it emphasize bureaucratic routines to the detriment of organizational outcomes?

Job-oriented or employee-oriented.

Does it focus more on job performance than it does on members' well-being?

Professionally or parochially oriented.

Do members identify primarily with their professions or with the organization?

An open system or a closed system.

Is the company open to internal and external communication, and does it easily admit outsiders and newcomers, or not?

Tightly controlled or loosely controlled.

Is the company formal and punctual or informal and casual?

Pragmatic or normative.

Is the company flexible or rigid in dealing with its environment, particularly its customers?

> You can learn a lot about Wal-Mart's culture by taking a walk through its stores. Shoppers can shop on Sundays. Buying guns is easy and inexpensive.
>
> Also, the culture is adaptive. A 1998 report pointed out that officials were removing certain magazines and marking some compact disks "Sanitized for your protection."[16] In late 2006, the company was stocking the morning-after pill and had signed up with the national Gay and Lesbian Chamber of Commerce.[17]
>
> The annual meeting also demonstrates the company's culture.[18] Held in Bud Walton and Barnhill Arenas, the home of the basketball dynasty the Arkansas Razorbacks, the meeting features celebrities like Nolan Ryan, Marie Osmond, Barbara Bush, and Joe Montana. Athletes often lead the crowd in the Wal-Mart cheer—"Give me a W, an A.. .." Little criticism is tolerated at the annual meeting. Most questions from the floor come from supporters asking questions such as, "When will Wal-Mart came to my area?" Challenging questions are quickly dismissed.

LEVEL 2: SHARED PERSPECTIVES The second level of organizational culture is the level of shared perspectives, the underlying rules and norms that guide solutions to the typical problems encountered by organizational members. Perspectives are relatively concrete ideas, and organizational members are usually aware of them. For example, employees can typically describe how their organization approaches problems, and they can define what constitutes acceptable behavior in their company.

> Wal-Mart has three basic rules. The first is that the customer is boss. The second is "Get it done by sundown." And the third is "Greet any customer who is within 10 feet."[19] A company slogan is "Exceed customer expectations."[20] In 1997, because it was going global, the company changed its "Buy American" program with a "Made Right Here" program, which promotes Canadian products in Canada and Brazilian products in Brazil.

LEVEL 3: AWARENESS The level of awareness consists of the ideals, standards, and goals held in consensus in the organization. These are the ideas held in common by which people judge other people and their behaviors.

Some of these values are expressed in a company's mission statement or statement of philosophy, whereas others are not. Some values are clear and can be agreed upon, while others are complex, ambiguous, conflicting, and in flux. For example, there may be inconsistencies between what people say they value and what they actually do, or ambiguities about what statements and symbols actually mean.[21]

> Wal-Mart culture emphasizes religion, patriotism, a classless collective identity, science, rationality, ecology, progressiveness, and low costs. The company's values are embodied in the life and myth of Sam Walton, who "went to great lengths to emphasize his old pick-up, his cheap haircuts, and his hunting dogs," and who bought his clothes at Wal-Mart.[22]

LEVEL 4: UNCONSCIOUS ASSUMPTIONS The deepest level of organizational culture is the unconscious assumptions that people hold about the nature of human beings, human relationships, reality, time, space, and the relationship of individuals and organizations to their environments. You discover both values and basic assumptions by listening thoughtfully to what people say and watching carefully what people do.

> Sam Walton was a highly competitive person whose company reflects that ethic. Although he maintained that the competition was always in fun, the evidence suggests a more serious component, with managers and department heads being held closely accountable. The company is the epitome of successful capitalism. An investor who bought 100 shares in 1970 for $1,650 would have $3 million only 30 years later.
>
> The company is also a capitalistic "cultural force that both remakes and destroys our idealized past world and our emotional links to it. Wal-Mart is a participant in the destruction of the small town culture that it mythologizes, while it also is recreating new patterns and identities."[23]
>
> The commentator Paul Harvey has said that in Wal-Mart there is "something better than communism, socialism, and capitalism. We have created Enlightened Consumerism. The customer is king again."[24]

See Table 17.1 for an overview of the levels of organizational culture.

How Do New Employees Learn an Organization's Culture?

The main way for an employee to learn an organization's culture is to become immersed in it. By processes of socialization, employees learn a culture and adapt to it.

ORGANIZATIONAL SOCIALIZATION New employees learn and adapt to their organization's culture through organizational socialization, the process by which new members' values, norms, and behaviors align with those of the organization and permit them to participate as members of the organization.[25] New members are often uncertain about how to do their job, how their performance will be evaluated, what is expected in terms of social behavior, and what personal relationships will be useful to them.[26] In short, they have a lot to learn.

Organizations often help newcomers to adapt by deliberately structuring the early stages of their entry into the organization. This helps them to deal with their uncertainty and anxiety, and instructs them in desired or necessary attitudes, behaviors, and knowledge.[27] For example, IBM's new hire orientation continues throughout the employee's first year.[28] During that time, employees who want to learn more about the company can utilize a one-and-a-half-day

TABLE 17.1 Overview: The Levels of Organizational Culture

Level	Description	Examples
Behaviors and artifacts	Visible indicators	How the offices are decorated, who represents the company in the media, how people dress
Shared perspectives	Shared rules and norms that employees use to guide problem solving	Axioms such as "the customer always comes first"
Awareness	Ideals, standards, and goals held by most people in the organization; the company's philosophy, whether written down or not	Religion matters (or does not matter) in this company
Unconscious assumptions	Unconscious beliefs people hold about the nature of human beings, human relationships, reality, time, space, and the relationship of individuals and organizations to their environments	Competition is a necessary way of life

learning lab, up to 60 hours of e-learning, and opportunities for creating a personal action and development plan. They also have access to an employee Web site.

However, not all socialization processes are, or should be, identical. New organizational members differ in their need for organizational socialization.[29] Some bring with them values that are already similar to those of the organization, while others do not. In addition, the intensity of the socialization process depends on the nature of the company's prevailing value system: Some organizations have unique core values that differ significantly from general societal values and thus, they require more intense processes of socialization. Although the process of organizational socialization is particularly relevant to new members, it also applies to existing members, who may need to be reminded of particular norms and values or who may benefit from having them reinforced.

Specifically, what can you expect when you are a new entrant to an organization? The process of organizational socialization has three stages.

Stage 1: Anticipatory Socialization. Socialization begins even before you start work.[30] Anticipatory socialization occurs when you read the company's literature and interact with interviewers, current employees, and other applicants. Already you are forming impressions.

The selection interview is part of this first step because it is a two-way communication in which a candidate and an interviewer exchange information about their norms and values, including the fit of the candidate to the organizational culture. In the typical job interview, the interviewer spends more time talking than the candidate does, often because the interviewer is answering the candidate's questions about the company or telling him or her about the company.[31]

realistic job preview
Information that an interviewer gives an applicant about the realities—both good and bad—of working for the company.

Generally, job applicants have unrealistically positive impressions about the organization, [32] and many companies augment this positive impression by selling themselves as great places to work. Some companies, however, take a different approach. Although their literature may be laudatory, in person their interviewers make a point of informing applicants about the realties—the good *and* at least some of the bad aspects—of working for the company. This **realistic job preview** is likely to inoculate applicants against the trials and tribulations they will soon face on the job, and create trust between them and the company, because, after all, they told the truth.[33] Research results support the idea that realistic job previews can significantly lower new employees' job expectations.[34] Of course, companies also hope that they will reduce the costs of hiring by reducing disappointment, disillusionment, and turnover once a newcomer is on the job. The fact is that realistic job previews do increase retention about 9 percent above and beyond traditional methods of hiring.

organizational assimilation
The process by which an individual is actually integrated into the culture of the organization.

Stage 2: Encounter. Encounter is the "breaking-in" period during which the newcomer confronts the realities of his or her new organization.[35] Encounter begins **organizational assimilation**, the process by which an individual is actually integrated into the culture of the organization. It includes both the deliberate and unintentional efforts by the organization to socialize the newcomer, along with the newcomer's own attempts to modify their new organizational roles and environments to better accommodate their own needs, ideas, and values.[36] For example, the law firm you join suggests to you that when dealing with clients the dress code is formal. You indulge your need for self-expression by buying several stylish suits.

reality shock
An intense experience of unpleasant surprise at the realities in your new company.

Generally, encounter is a pattern of day-to-day events in which you experience some surprises as your expectations clash with the realities and you try to make sense of the new information. Occasionally, you will experience **reality shock**, an intense experience of unpleasant surprise at the realities in your new company. For example, as a young engineer you may have been sold on how innovative the company is, only to learn that it is actually highly bureaucratic.

Stage 3: Metamorphosis. Finally, you enter the metamorphosis stage of assimilation, in which you attempt to become an accepted member of the culture by learning new attitudes and behaviors or modifying existing ones to conform.[37] During this phase, learning from existing organizational members is crucial, and individuals who are not welcomed will struggle to integrate. For example, you take up golf in order to join an important informal network. Meanwhile, a coworker who does not play is passed over for important assignments.

SUCCESSFUL SOCIALIZATION After all is said and done, what makes for a successful socialization process?[38] From the organization's perspective, this depends on its established goals. Some companies want a high level of conformity to their culture, while others want less conformity and, indeed, some even want nonconformity. At a minimum, organizations want employees who accept aspects of their roles that are pivotal to the organization's mission so they can at least do their jobs at an acceptable level, and they expect a certain style and decorum.[39] If these goals are achieved, the socialization is successful. From the individuals' viewpoint, the socialization is successful if they are meeting career goals without compromising essential aspects of their identity.

THE POTENTIAL IMPACT OF TECHNOLOGY AND RELATED TRENDS ON THE SOCIALIZATION PROCESS Recent developments in communication technology, and part-time and temporary workm suggest that in some cases the organizational socialization process may not quite work as it has traditionally. When new organizational members will be part of a virtual team, for example, their socialization depends less on learning traditional cultural signs and symbols, and less on face–to-face interaction, than on what they learn through electronically enhanced communication. Interestingly, for some newcomers, socializing individuals remotely may be even more effective than traditional means. This is likely to be true for individuals who are especially nervous about interpersonal communications, or for those who prefer an anonymous or noninteractive way to acquire information about their organizations.[40]

How Do Managers Use Organizational Culture to Improve Organizational Effectiveness?

In this section we will take a look at several ways that organizational culture contributes to organizational effectiveness.

How Does Culture Motivate Performance?

Culture motivates individuals, and it affects organizational performance overall. One way to understand these effects is to compare strong and weak cultures. A second approach is to identify several different types of cultures and compare their effectiveness in a variety of environments. We will take a look at both approaches.

COMPARE THE PERFORMANCE OF STRONG AND WEAK CULTURES Companies with strong organizational cultures are often recognized by both insiders and outsiders as having a certain style. In a strong organizational culture, the shared values and norms are clear, consistent, and comprehensive.[41] Values are intensely held and widely shared.[42]

To determine whether a culture is strong, you might ask the following questions:[43]

1. Have managers in competing firms commonly spoken of this company's style or way of doing things?

2. Has this firm both made its values known through a creed or credo and made a serious attempt to encourage managers to follow them?

3. Has the firm been managed according to long-standing policies and practices other than those of just the incumbent CEO?

Consider the culture of Microsoft.

> Microsoft's legendarily strong organizational culture is competitive and intense, a reflection of founder Bill Gates' own personal style. One of its features has been a norm of criticism throughout the company—people challenge everything from what the company is doing in the marketplace to how it is run internally. Another feature is its harsh performance appraisal system: The company uses a bell curve to rate employees in each group, so that for every high scorer there is also a low scorer. And this in a company that hires only the best! Yet, 85 percent of the company's employees feel strongly that they are proud to work for Microsoft,[44] and more than 90 percent of the applicants who are offered jobs accept.[45]

Strong organizational cultures enhance individual performance by energizing employees with engaging ideals,[46] providing identity and meaning,[47] and shaping and coordinating employees' behavior.[48] Strong cultures can also enhance corporate performance. There is a positive relationship between strength of corporate culture and companies' long-term economic performance, but the relationship is modest, and some firms with weak cultures also have strong performance.[49] When they are operating in relatively stable environments, firms with strong cultures exhibit superior and more reliable performance than firms with weak cultures.[50] However, when the company's environment becomes more volatile, this advantage is often lost.

Sometimes strong cultures are maladaptive. As one researcher puts it, "In firms with strong corporate cultures, managers tend to march energetically in the same direction in a well-coordinated fashion. That alignment, motivation, organization, and control can help performance, but only if the resulting actions fit an intelligent business strategy for the specific environment in which a firm operates. . . . Strong cultures with practices that do not fit a company's context can actually lead intelligent people to behave in ways that are destructive—that systematically undermine an organization's ability to survive and prosper."[51]

> Financially, Microsoft is arguably the most successful technology company of all time. But in recent years its stock has struggled, and a big question for the company today is whether its increased size, along with its strong culture, will be its downfall. In recent years employees have complained about oppressive bureaucracy. The company's compensation system has created a culture of haves and have-nots, with newer employees in the have-nots category because stock deals are less lucrative than in the past. Also, efforts to trim costs, such as asking employees to make a $40 co-payment on prescription drugs, have been met with disbelief.

Researchers Jeffrey Pfeffer and John Veiga estimate that only about 12 percent of today's companies have a sufficiently motivating culture to give them a competitive advantage.[52] Worse, some companies actively weaken or even destroy their organizational cultures because they ignore their human resources in favor of the short-term bottom line. Based on their research and consulting experience, Pfeffer and Veiga suggest that companies should build their cultures in a variety of ways, including offering job security, using teams to minimize bureaucracy, reducing status differences, sharing information, and making compensation contingent on organizational performance.

> Will Microsoft's strong culture continue to enhance its competitive advantage? Will the company maintain its entrepreneurial capabilities, or evolve into something less innovative? In 1995, Bill Gates, having ignored the Internet, led the company in an inspiring comeback to deal with it. But Gates is now focusing on product development, and his friend Steve Ballmer is the chief executive officer. Stay tuned.

COMPARE THE PERFORMANCE OF DIFFERENT TYPES OF ORGANIZATIONAL CULTURES
A second approach to organizational culture and performance examines different types of cultures and compares how they perform in different circumstances.[53] This approach looks for a **cultural fit**.

For example, if you think of organizational culture as a way of controlling and governing an organization, you can imagine three distinct types of cultures. One type, the **bureaucracy**, governs through developing in organizational members shared understandings about legitimate authority and fair treatment of employees. Another type, the **market culture**, controls by sharing among organizational members complex understandings about competition and prices. The third type, the **clan**, controls by developing in its members a deep social understanding, specific to their organization, about its general objectives, methods and values. Although in reality organizations use all three types of control, their emphases differ.

Because it emphasizes participation and openness, the clan is the most time-consuming culture to develop and maintain.[54] Building a clan is worth the effort, however, because it is likely to be more efficient than other cultures when the organization faces conditions of ambiguity and complexity. On the other hand, the clan is less efficient than bureaucratic or market cultures when the organization faces conditions characterized by low to moderate complexity and uncertainty. For example, small high tech companies determined to launch a new product often operate like clans, with intense interpersonal interactions and shared

cultural fit
The extent to which an organizational culture suits the organization's circumstances, and predicts how well an organization will perform under those circumstances.

bureaucracy
A type of organizational culture which controls mainly by developing in its members shared understandings about legitimate authority and fair treatment of employees.

market culture
A type of organizational culture which controls mainly by sharing among its members complex understandings about competition and prices.

clan
A type of organizational culture which controls mainly by developing in its members a deep social understanding, specific to their organization, about its general objectives, methods and values.

hard work. Later, however, as their market flattens out, they are likely to lose business to cultures that are designed to focus on efficiency and customers.

A clan is not the same thing as a strong culture, although a strong culture might be a clan. It is unlikely that very large organizations will adopt clan cultures because subcultures within the organization, notably functional and professional groups, will more easily develop shared social understandings than will the organization as a whole. Individuals will more readily identify with these more intimate groups than with their company.

How Does Culture Create Commitment?

Organizational commitment, as you will recall, is being involved with, identifying with, and having an emotional attachment to one's organization.[55] Having employees who are committed to the company predicts many desirable organizational outcomes, including higher job satisfaction, reduced intention to quit, lower absenteeism, and lower turnover.[56] Strong cultures enhance commitment because there is a comfortable match between an individual's characteristics and the organizational culture, and because having a sense of shared values make people feel good about working for their company.[57]

A study by consulting firm Watson Wyatt based on a sample of 7,500 U.S. workers in all industries found that the top seven factors leading to employee commitment are, in order of importance:[58]

1. Trust in senior leadership

2. The chance to use one's skills and abilities

3. Pay satisfaction

4. Job security

5. The quality of the company's products and services

6. Absence of work-related stress

7. Honesty and integrity of the company's business conduct

The same study found that only about half of all workers are committed to their employers. It also discovered that there is a strong relationship between worker commitment and higher returns for shareholders. Companies with low employee commitment had a three-year total return to shareholders of 76 percent, whereas those with high employee commitment had a return of 112 percent.

Of the seven commitment factors, trust is the most important. This crucial component of strong organizational cultures also predicts the bottom line. In the Watson Wyatt study, companies in which employees had a high level of trust and confidence in their senior management had a 108 percent return to shareholders as opposed to a 66 percent return for those with low trust and confidence. Of course, it is impossible to tell from these data which came first, the success, or the trust. Most likely, effective companies strive for both.

How Does Culture Integrate Organizational Units?

One function that culture performs in an organization is to create commonalities across units that direct people collectively toward organizational goals. An organizational unit is any formal or informal group in the organization, including teams, divisions, and subcultures.

ORGANIZATIONAL CULTURE AS COMMUNITY For example, many people view organizational culture as a force that creates community and thus improves organizational effectiveness.[59] It is thought that creating a sense of community reduces competition and increases cooperation among organizational units. For example, participating in company outings may reduce tensions between two factions of a company's sales force.

To create community, companies can work to enhance sociability, which is sincere friendliness among members, and they can try to increase solidarity, which is the ability of members to pursue shared objectives quickly and effectively regardless of personal ties. Specifically, they can improve sociability by recruiting compatible people who are likely to share interests, ideas, and emotions; by increasing social interaction among employees inside and outside the office; by reducing formality; by limiting hierarchical differences; and by modeling friendship themselves. They can increase solidarity by developing employee awareness of competitors, creating a sense of urgency, stimulating the will to win, and encouraging commitment to shared corporate goals.

Unfortunately, the depiction of an organization's culture as a community may be simplistic. Culture is a highly complex phenomenon and predicting which of its factors is most likely to improve organizational effectiveness is difficult and perhaps impossible.[60] Perhaps organizations are not really like societies, after all, and are characterized by processes that are quite different from those of communities. In support of this point of view, consider that the culture of an organization is much more amenable to change than is the culture of a society.[61] Nevertheless, although counting on community building to integrate subunits may be ineffectual, it is still quite a popular idea.

superordinate culture
A strong organizational culture with which all nationalities can identify.

CORPORATE CULTURE AS GLOBAL INTEGRATOR In a similar way, multinational companies operating in a variety of national cultures often look to corporate culture to help them coordinate and integrate their personnel. They deliberately create a **superordinate culture**, which is a strong organizational culture with which all nationalities can identify.

Multinationals use a variety of techniques to develop strong corporate cultures, including integrating human resources practices worldwide; pursing career management strategies such as international transfers of employees; instituting cross-national projects and training programs; holding worldwide meetings; sending corporate senior managers on frequent visits; and, finally, creating managerial career paths and reward systems that strengthen manager's commitment to corporate visions and objectives.[62]

Although companies hope to improve control of their subsidiaries by superimposing a superordinate corporate culture, the reality is that fundamental assumptions about people and the world vary widely around the globe. People's assumptions differ not only from country to country but between a country culture and the corporate culture of the multinational.[63] It goes without saying that adopting a superordinate culture that is closely identified with one country undermines efforts to create a culture that all nationalities can relate to.

So developing an effective superordinate corporate culture is quite challenging. For one thing, it may be useless to present new forms of management to people culturally unable to accept them. Another problem is that multinational companies have a hard time submerging the particular identities of different cultures.[64] In some instances, asserting a strong corporate culture may incite locals to aggressively assert their own autonomy by promoting their own national culture.

A French researcher who has examined management practices in 10 Western countries believes that national culture strongly determines views of what proper management should be. He suggests, "It may very well be that the management process in these . . . countries is as much culture bound as their cooking, and that international management has to avoid the trap of international cuisine. National cultures may still offer some genuine recipes."[65]

How Does Culture Motivate Ethical Behavior?

Culture motivates ethical behavior in many ways. Let's consider three important ones: How culture helps people express their personal values at work, how it encourages moral expression, and how it encourages the appreciation of human diversity.

RECONCILING PROFESSIONAL AND PERSONAL VALUE SYSTEMS Today some company cultures are attempting to respond to individuals' needs to fulfill personal values at work. It makes common sense that being able to fulfill personal values on the job improves job satisfaction, and the evidence supports this view.[66] Today many employees hope to be able to express and develop their complete selves at work,[67] bringing their personal as well as professional values to bear on the decisions they make.

There are several reasons why reconciling professional and personal values is of particular interest right now.[68] One reason is that people are spending significantly more time at work than previous generations did. Another is that baby boomers are trying to maintain their idealistic roots. Also, with individuals being less loyal to companies, they are more loyal to their own personal values.

Individuals are members of multiple social groups, including professions, religions, social activist groups, and political organizations, and they want to reconcile the values they express in these groups with those they express at work. For example, many Americans think that environmental protection and economic development are compatible processes.[69] Yet, individuals' personal values about the merits of environmental protection often clash with normative professional beliefs about the necessity for increasing economic growth and maintaining the autonomy of firms. Companies that hope to attract and keep top employees respond by developing organizational cultures that can absorb employee values that are widely held in the population from which they draw their employees. By the early 1990s, for example, many American companies had adopted environmental policies and standards, including 11 percent that had added environmental responsibility to their existing company ethics statements.[70] Today such company environmental policies are widespread.

DESIGNING ORGANIZATIONAL CULTURES TO ENCOURAGE MORAL EXPRESSION In a company, managers as individuals may share similar views regarding morally appropriate standards, yet their views are held "privately and tacitly, and not collectively and publicly."[71] Because they are not expressed, an individual's moral views never influence corporate values, and, as a consequence, they are not expressed in the corporate culture.

Moral stress occurs when an individual recognizes the moral issues in a decision or action but is uncertain how to act on them in his or her company culture.[72] A key source of moral stress for individual managers is the absence in their company culture of institutionalized procedures for raising, discussing, and resolving moral issues. Researchers James Waters and Frederick Bird assert that it is only through public discussion of the particular moral issues facing people in their own organization that individuals can develop clarity of, and commitment to, moral views.

> **moral stress**
> The tension an individual experiences when he or she recognizes the moral issues in a decision or action but is uncertain how to act on them in his or her company culture.

Unfortunately, in most organizations, corporate codes of ethics suggest the importance of morality, but they suggest how to make ethical decisions.[73] Yet moral expression is achieved only when the organizational culture includes specific structures for moral decision making.

According to Waters and Bird, moral company cultures must include the following structures for moral decision making:

1. An expression of top management's philosophy and values in the form of direct communications from the leadership, including policies and speeches, to the effect that meeting legal and moral constraints is more important than conventional economic goals. These messages should focus on specific examples rather than on exhortations to "do good and avoid evil."[74]

2. Discussion among those immediately involved in moral issues. These discussions can take place in training programs, group meetings, and planned sessions across the organization.

3. Encouraging managers to openly discuss moral issues with their subordinates, to the point that discussing moral issues becomes a comfortable and familiar part of a manager's job.

DESIGNING CULTURES TO VALUE DIVERSITY Having a corporate culture that is demographically diverse may challenge a company's traditional standards for moral behavior.[75] For example, one of a company's traditional values may be that treating employees fairly means treating them uniformly. Every employee is treated exactly like every other employee. Yet, when a culture is not homogeneous, this moral belief may work against particular subcultures. For example, what works for parents may not work for non-parents; what works for one race may not work for another.

Companies today strive to create moral cultures that meet the needs of a variety of employees. See Figure 17.1 for an overview of the dimensions of diversity that a company culture might have to take into account.

In recent decades companies have invested heavily in programs to help them work with their diverse U.S. and multinational workforces. A key approach has been to educate all employees about the impact and value of diversity in a company. In addition, managers

FIGURE 17.1

Dimensions of Diversity

Source: L. Gardenswartz and
A. Rowe, *Diverse Teams at Work*
(New York: McGraw-Hill, 1994).
Copyright © 2003 by the Society for
Human Resource Management.
Reproduced with permission of the
Society for Human Resource
Management.

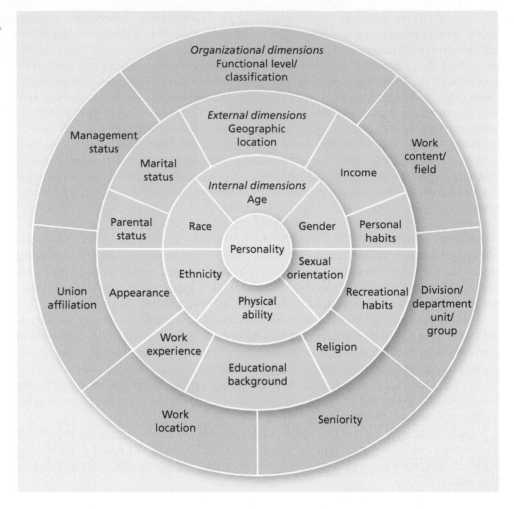

are trained to be fair by appreciating diversity rather than imposing homogeneity, using such approaches as:[76]

■ Using equal performance standards for all workers

■ Providing feedback often and equally to all members of the workforce

■ Recognizing and confronting the issue of discomfort—their own and others'—in dealing with a diverse workforce

■ Appreciating and using the different perspectives and styles of diverse workers

■ Confronting racist, sexist, or other stereotypic or discriminatory behavior

Along these lines, managers are learning to tailor organizational practices to organizational subcultures. For instance, when it comes to benefits, young people and individuals without children generally do not need life insurance, yet their companies often require them to pay for it. Recognizing the need to examine the traditional values of the company is the first step toward a new idea of fairness. In this example, instituting **cafeteria benefits** plans, in which individuals can choose how to spend their benefit dollars, resolves an issue of cultural diversity.

How Does Culture Enhance Corporate Branding? (And How Does Branding Enhance Culture?)

If you have taken a marketing course, you are no doubt familiar with the concept of **corporate branding**, the process by which a distinct identity is created for a company.[77] Today companies often develop and display their cultures as part of their corporate branding strategy. Especially when a company has a heavy service component, the attitude and culture of

cafeteria benefits
Benefit plans in which individuals can choose how to spend their benefit dollars.

corporate branding
The process by which a distinct identity is created for a company, often through the company developing and displaying its culture.

its workforce influences how customers view it and its products. Employees who are engaged, interested in customers, empowered, responsive, and competent create greater respect, liking, and loyalty among customers.[78]

It turns out that corporate branding affects company culture, as well. The emerging phenomenon of **employer branding** means creating the same experience for employees that a company promises to its customers.[79] This includes, in part, focusing on engaging employees mentally and physically in their jobs, involving them mentally and emotionally with the business and the brand, and giving them the skills and capabilities to act effectively. Southwest Airlines practices employer branding by valuing both employees and customers, sometimes even putting employees first. Because the employees know they are valued and taken care of, they in turn take care of their customers.

Cause branding, whereby a company is associated with supporting particular social causes, also affects organizational culture. Helping the larger community beyond the corporation involves employees socially and spiritually, and adds a dimension to a corporate culture that goes beyond the bottom line.[80] In particular, pursuing a cause by involving employees as volunteers develops loyalty and commitment.[81] In companies with volunteer programs, 62 percent of employees recommend their companies as good places to work, whereas at companies without such programs only 39 percent make this recommendation.

In organizations that have both strong brands and a strong organizational culture, a problem that sometimes develops is that established internal values differ from those associated with the brand. Companies end up with two competing value sets, thus confusing and demotivating their employees.

How Does Culture Enhance Service?

When companies fail at customer service, it is often because they lack a service climate and culture.[82] It is not enough to train employees how to deliver superior service, for instance. Exhortations to be pleasant and answer the phone within three rings only go so far. Employees need to feel empowered by the whole corporate culture to deliver quality service. One reason culture enhances service is that the emotions displayed by employees are related to how customers feel and how they evaluate the quality of the service they receive.[83] Simply, happy employees create happy customers.

Employees are **boundary spanners**, individuals who represent the company to actors in its environment, in this case, to its customers. For individuals in the boundary spanning role, believing they are supported by their organization is important for job satisfaction and organizational commitment.[84] They want and need the whole organization behind them, including managerial practices, the physical facility, human resources practices, operations management, and marketing management. It is important for managers to consult with them, too, since they possess valuable information and insights about what customers experience. As one writer concludes, "In the absence of this patterning of activities with service as a frame of reference, a service climate cannot exist."[85] (Of course, as you recall, climate and culture are intimately related.)

What Happens When Organizations with Different Cultures Merge?

When organizations merge, they typically address their differences and decide whether, and how, to merge their cultures and business systems.

How Can Managers Foster Acculturation?

Acculturation is "the process by which two or more cultures come into contact and resolve the conflict that arises as a result of this contact,"[86] and **acculturative stress** is the "individual states and behaviors that are mildly pathological and disruptive" that accompany an unsuccessful acculturation.[87] When two companies merge, or when they work closely

---

employer branding
The marketing concept in which a company creates the same positive experience for its employees that it promises to its customers.

cause branding
The phenomenon in which a company is associated with supporting particular social causes, which can add a social and spiritual dimension to the company's organizational culture.

boundary spanners
Individuals who represent a company to actors in its environment (such as customers).

acculturative stress
The upsetting individual states and behaviors that accompany an unsuccessful acculturation.

together to develop and manage a joint venture, they address issues of acculturation. They examine their separate values and assumptions about how their businesses are run so that the merger is not disrupted by cultural conflicts. Before they merge, they may perform a **bicultural audit** to determine differences that need to be managed and commonalities that can be built upon.[88] Such audits include a thorough examination of the culture of each company, followed by an analysis of potential conflicts and commonalities, and the development of a strategy for dealing with the issues that arise.

bicultural audit
A thorough examination of the cultures of merging companies, followed by an analysis of potential conflicts that are likely to occur and commonalities, and the development of a strategy for dealing with the issues that arise.

Having done such an audit, some companies decline to merge, but most determine to forge ahead and simply deal with their cultural differences. The late-1980s merger of Burroughs and Sperry, two mainframe computer companies, is an example of a successful cultural merger that has lasted to this day.[89] Burroughs, which had a strength in sales, acquired Sperry, which had a strength in engineering. The companies had distinctively different product lines and cultures, but were committed to forging a new corporate culture. With the assistance of internal task forces and external consults, the companies merged successfully into the company that is today known as Unisys. Few top executives left, customers were retained, and orders increased.

Companies choose among four modes for merging their cultures.[90] Which mode they choose depends on such factors as which company is more powerful, the strength of the respective organizational cultures, the companies' motivation to preserve their own cultures, and how similar their cultures are. The four modes are assimilation, integration, separation, and deculturation.

ASSIMILATION When the members of the acquired firm willingly adopt the identity and culture of the acquiring firm, their firm "assimilates" to the acquirer's culture. In the acquisition process, the acquired firm is fully absorbed and ceases to exist as a cultural entity.

Acquiring companies that have a strong culture, and have no strong subcultures, are comfortable assimilating another company's culture. Acquired companies that have weak or ineffective cultures may be quite willing to be acquired and to adopt the acquirer's culture.

INTEGRATION When the acquired firm wants to be autonomous and generally maintain its own culture but is willing, nevertheless, to be acquired and share some cultural aspects, the two cultures are said to "integrate." Each culture changes to some extent, but, on the whole, neither group attempts to dominate the other and the cultural change is balanced on either side.

Cultural integration is a strategy that works best for acquirers that routinely tolerate and encourage organizational subcultures. Already accustomed to managing this diversity, taking on one more different unit is for them relatively easy. The same might be said of the acquired firm, which must be flexible enough to make some changes while culturally strong enough to maintain its identity.

SEPARATION Sometimes the acquired firm wants total independence and refuses to become culturally assimilated at any level with the acquirer. Sometimes, too, the acquirer wants only financial ties with the acquired. In these cases, each company maintains its separate cultural identity and there is little exchange between the two organizations.

Often companies that maintain separate identities are in separate industries, and are acquired by a holding group that has a financial interest in them but no interest in managing them.

DECULTURATION When the acquired firm values neither its own culture nor that of its acquirer, the acculturation process is likely to be a rocky one. The acquired company disintegrates as a cultural entity, with accompanying feelings of stress among its members. Under pressure from the acquirer to adopt its culture, organizational members of the acquired company may become confused and alienated and experience a loss of identity.

This is obviously a destructive mode of acculturation, the sort practiced by corporate raiders bent on a takeover, often of a company in a different industry. The acquired company members despise and resist the acquirer, and, indeed, their fears are realistic because their company is likely to be dismantled.

What Is the Effect of Merging Business Systems on Merging Organizational Cultures?

Business systems are the company's particular methods and technologies for doing business. The extent to which the business systems of the two merging companies can be integrated affects the potential success of the cultural aspects of the merge.[91] Think of merging business systems as occurring on three levels. At the level of minimal integration, only a few corporate and staff functions are merged and consolidated, whereas all strategic and day-to day-operating decisions remain autonomous. Only a few requirements are negotiated by which the acquired company must report to the parent company.

At a moderate level of integration, certain key functions, such as sales and marketing or manufacturing, are merged and consolidated and managed from the top, while other day-to-day operations remain autonomous.

At a full level of integration, all areas and processes of both companies are integrated into one system. It is believed that cultural integration can only be accomplished when a moderate or full level of business systems integration is also part of the plan.

How Can an Existing Organizational Culture Be Changed?

Once established, organizational cultures tend to be self-perpetuating.[92] New members are chosen because they fit the established culture, and when their original fit is not strong, they are socialized to work in the style of that culture. Managers model the culture and tell stories and legends about how it developed. People who embody the culture are rewarded and celebrated, while those who deviate from it are punished and ignored.

At the same time, cultures are always evolving. Competitive influences spark behavioral and attitudinal changes. Crises force the reevaluation of values and perspectives.[93] Culture evolves, too, when key members leave and new members enter, or when a company diversifies into a new business or enters a new region.[94]

Sometimes companies decide to deliberately change their cultures. What is it that they actually do when they attempt cultural change? Here are some examples:

- They create new policies, procedures, and rules that reinforce new ways of operating, and eliminate those that reinforce old methods.
- They establish new rituals and tell new stories about the new organization.
- They provide training that teaches and reinforces new ways of leading and following.
- They hire people who fit into the new culture.

In Table 17.2 you can examine the dimensions of organizational culture that are typical targets of organizational change:[95]

Researchers diverge widely in their opinions about how to initiate a cultural change. Some believe that change can be achieved through transformational leadership, in which a charismatic leader inspires employees.[96] Others criticize this approach as being too dependent on leadership alone, and argue that it is irrelevant for non-Western countries.[97] Another belief is that it is both leaders and followers, not either party alone, who change a culture.[98] By this view, leaders redefine meanings and present associated artifacts, but followers interpret the meanings in terms of their work and roles.

One view is that management should strive to change effectiveness rather than culture, because culture is so complicated that only some aspects of it are likely to be directly related to effectiveness anyway.[99] It follows that because cultural change is an expensive, long-term proposition with an uncertain outcome, it should only be attempted after other innovations have been tried and failed.

TABLE 17.2 **When Changing an Organizational Culture, What Behaviors Should You Target?**

1. Organizational values and norms—what is the corporate philosophy and "the way things are done around here"?

2. The managerial culture—including which leadership styles dominate, what mental frameworks are used, and how people behave and solve problems

3. Organizational heroes—the role models who personify organizational values and norms

4. Organizational myths and stories—the indirect narrative expressions of what people believe and value

5. Organizational rites, rituals, and taboos—which can be observed in special awards and ceremonies, annual parties, daily meetings, and in commonly held definitions of acceptable and unacceptable behaviors

6. Cultural symbols and other aspects of objective culture, including the physical work environment, the corporate logo, the style of dress, and similar aspects

Source: Adapted from: A. F. Buono and J. L. Bowditch, *The Human Side of Mergers and Acquisitions* (San Francisco, CA: Jossey-Bass, 1989).

After experiencing important losses in market share, General Motors Corporation underwent years of attempting to develop a more flexible and innovative culture. Finally, it opted to create an entirely new organization, Saturn, with a totally different culture from the rest of GM, including different structures, technologies, manager–employee relations, and customer–company relations.[100] Today Saturn has the feel of a unique culture that employees and customers both recognize. GM's experience confirms how difficult it is to effect organization-wide cultural change. The case of Saturn illustrates that sometimes it is simply easier to start afresh.

How Can You Find an Organizational Culture in Which You Will Thrive?

cultural preferences
Fundamental values that differentiate between cultures and are relatively enduring and conscious.

Individuals have **cultural preferences**, fundamental values that differentiate between cultures and are relatively enduring and conscious.[101] Your cultural preferences are relatively stable over time, and they are likely to endure even after you have changed your job or your company.[102]

What Kind of Culture Do You Prefer?

For example, individuals differ on whether they prefer cultures that have a concern for people or cultures that have a concern for goal accomplishment.[103] Having a supervisor with high concern for people (and thus, by inference, a culture that has this concern) predicts whether or not a newcomer is committed to the company and plans to stay. When their supervisor has high concern for people, newcomers who also have high concern for people are committed and plan to stay. However, newcomers with low concern for people are uncommitted and say they might leave, irrespective of the attitude of their supervisors.

One study worked with 32 personality traits and 24 dimensions of corporate culture to see if personality traits predict a preference for particular types of culture.[104] It found that each personality trait predicts a preference for those cultural dimensions that are clearly related to it in the first place. In other words, if you are an achiever you will prefer corporate cultures that value high performance, and if you value rule-following you will prefer cultures that value caution, and if you are unconventional you will prefer cultures that are flexible. The implication is that finding a cultural fit is a straightforward matter if you know your own personality and get an accurate, complete overview of a company's culture.

Will You Face a Glass Ceiling?

To identify a culture in which you will fit, you also need to understand organizational sub-cultures. Consider, for example, the important subculture known as top management. The **glass ceiling** is the invisible barrier between middle and top management positions that is said to exist for women and other minorities. Maybe the reason women and minorities hit the glass ceiling is cultural.[105] Maybe, rather than facing outright discrimination, women and minorities face a CEO culture in which they simply do not fit.

For example, if top management represents a culture in and of itself, a culture that might be described as masculine, do women turn away from that culture because of a personal cultural preference? A study in the Netherlands defined masculine culture as a rational goal culture focusing on achievement, rewards, and competition, and defined feminine culture as a human relations culture reflecting concern for people through emphasis on cohesion, participation, and cooperation. It found that in contrast with non-managers, both male and female managers with positions in middle and higher organizational levels have a stronger preference for masculine culture. However, women, regardless of their level, have a weaker preference than men do for masculine culture, especially its competition and work pressure. Also, female middle managers' ambition to ascend to a higher management position is weaker than that of men. Even ambitious women think conflicts between their work and home life will be an important barrier in accepting a top management job.

The implication is that, as long as the culture of top management stresses the need to sacrifice one's personal life, it will fail to attract even ambitious women in large numbers. High salaries and status are less important to most women than having a balanced work/family life.

A major study of executives in 10 global companies endorses this perspective.[106] It suggests that companies that are seriously interested in developing women as top managers should make several cultural interventions, including auditing the top leadership group not only for its gender and racial diversity, but also for personal styles, family status, career paths, and nationalities. It suggests that the top management team should broaden its range of accepted leadership styles. Of course, these suggestions are relevant to integrating other groups from the diverse workforce as well.

glass ceiling
The invisible barrier between middle and top management positions that is said to exist for women and other minorities.

In Conclusion

These days company culture is a hot topic because organizations have learned that managing the company culture well improves the bottom line. A great way for you to understand the concept of corporate culture better, and to know which type of culture is best suited to your goals and values, is to spend some time in companies with distinctly different cultures. Then figure out what types of cultures you prefer and look for companies that have them. Understanding culture can help you to become a more productive and happier employee, as well as a more effective manager.

Apply What You Have Learned...

A Once World Class Company: Arthur Andersen

For more than 80 years, Arthur Andersen[107] held a stellar reputation as an accounting firm of the highest integrity. Yet in 2002 the firm was found guilty of obstruction of justice in the investigation of Enron Corporation. Subsequently, a whole list of Andersen clients announced their accounts had to be redone because of irregularities. For example, among these clients was telecommunications giant WorldCom, which had to restate $9 billion in revenues, and whose chief financial officer was subsequently arrested for fraud. Clearly, Andersen's organizational culture itself had undergone a transformation from ethical to unethical. But how did this occur?

In the early 1990s, Arthur Anderson was a highly respected company with 85,000 employees worldwide. People were proud to be a part of the Andersen team, and their Anderson experience helped them build their careers. At that time, Andersen had formal ethical standards and ethics training, although no ethics office. It even had a consulting group whose actual business was training other companies in ethics. A key company motto originated by founder Arthur Andersen and cherished over the years was "Think straight—talk straight." Company lore included the story of a young Arthur Andersen pushing back on a railway executive who wanted him to cook the books. Andersen replied, "There's not enough money in the city of Chicago to induce me to change that report."

However, over the years the company's profits came increasingly from consulting rather than from auditing. According to Barbara Toffler, author of *Final Accounting: Ambition, Greed, and the Fall of Arthur Andersen* and an Anderson employee beginning in 1995, the company's emphasis on ethics morphed into an emphasis on profits. A mismatch of standards and approaches between the accounting side and the consulting side of the company developed, but was never addressed. This failure to clearly define corporate values left such determinations to individuals and groups, who were encouraged to focus on the bottom line and retain customers by keeping them happy.

In addition, the firm's culture favored working with hot New Economy companies, high-risk clients who were doing massive acquisitions and who were taking advantage of government deregulation to transform themselves. In this fast-paced environment, new and complicated ethical considerations were easily overlooked.

Furthermore, according to researchers Linda Klebe Treviño and Michael E. Brown, at Arthur Anderson, "tradition became translated into unquestioning obedience to the partner, no matter what one was asked to do. For example, managers and partners were expected to pad their prices. Reasonable estimates for consulting work were simply doubled or more as consultants were told to back into the numbers."[108] New consultants were advised not to bother with corporate training because it interfered with lucrative client contacts.

In the end, it was the loss of its ethical culture that led to the downfall of Arthur Anderson. According to Toffler, employees had adopted the attitude that people in the company are all good and ethical people, so ethics training and ethics manuals and ethics offices were all irrelevant. If we put ourselves in their shoes at the time, we can imagine that this was a legitimate view. But it could also have been a convenient rationalization.

Discuss

1. How could having a formal ethics office have helped Arthur Andersen?
2. How could having moral people as leaders have helped Arthur Andersen? What would be the contribution of such people? What would be their limitations?
3. What should the company have done to preserve its ethical culture?

Advice from the Pros

Fun Cultures

Pierre Bellon is founder of the global diversified service business Sodexho Alliance,[109] which includes among its services campus, school, and corporate dining and catering. Bellon describes his business philosophy:

> My observation has been that what are most sustainable over time are the world's religions. If you consider Christians or Muslims or Buddhists, you will see that what is most permanent, most sustainable, is religion. My dream is that the company is sustainable like that.

> I don't want us to create some new religious order—I don't want us to become priests. My vision is to create a corporate religion of value. It is not a sad religion. It is a religion where you can drink, you can play, you can be a comedian, you can dance, you can love. It is a religion of joy. You must be able to work and dance at the same time.[110]

Fun corporate cultures encourage and support enjoyable and pleasurable activities. They attract new employees and increase employee commitment. They may improve customer satisfaction. Employees in fun work cultures are said to complain less about boredom and to be less stressed.[111] What do companies do to promote fun? This kind of stuff:

- Recognizing personal milestones such as birthdays
- Organizing social events
- Holding public celebrations of professional achievements
- Offering opportunities for volunteerism in the community
- Offering stress release activities like exercise facilities and massages
- Providing humor in newsletters and e-mails
- Organizing game like bingo or darts, and company-sponsored athletic teams
- Encouraging friendly competition among employees
- Providing opportunities for personal development such as book clubs and fun classes
- Sponsoring entertainment like bands and skits

Is there a downside to fun? Too much of a good thing can be inappropriate, especially when it detracts from organizational goals like productivity. And humor sometimes has a way of going overboard, hurting some individuals. Yet, a national study of human resources managers reported that most employees don't think there's enough fun at work, and only 3 percent said there was too much fun in their organizations.[112] It seems that most companies have a long way to go before having too much fun becomes a problem.

FYI, researchers who study fun have taken to describing their work as funology. Now, that's funny.

Discuss

What companies have you worked in that have fun cultures? How did the fun affect you?

Defend Your Position

1. In pairs, defend one of these positions:
   Fun has little or no place at work. Some people will inevitably take it too far, and it is likely to interfere with productivity.
   OR
   Fun organizational cultures are good for the organization, the work team, and the individual employee and should be strongly encouraged by management.
2. The two most enthusiastic supporters for each side will duke it out in front of the class.

Gain Experience

Assess an Educational Culture

Step One

In groups of four, use the table 17.3 on page 464 to assess the *educational culture* of your program or university. Educational culture includes how students are taught, how they learn, and how they are motivated.

Fill in as many spaces as you can.

Step Two

One or two groups will be asked to describe the university culture. Other groups will join in with additional information.

Step Three

As a class, explore:

- How the university's culture could be improved to enhance student learning.
- Which other universities might provide role models for a cultural transformation.
- Whether a cultural transformation would be practical at your university.

Table 17.3 **Assess the Educational Culture of Your University**

	How students learn and are motivated in general	How students are taught and motivated in their classes	The faculty and how it interacts with students each other	The extent to which students collaborate with learning culture	What is absolutely unique about the university's
In its publications, what image does the university project about. . .					
What does the Admissions Office say about. . .					
What do the university's students say about. . .					
What do students from other universities say about. . .					
What do faculty members say about. . .					
What do outside sources, like Web sites, say about. . .					
What have you personally learned about. . .					

Can You Solve This Manager's Problem?

Daimler-Benz and Chrysler

When Daimler-Benz Chairman Juergen E. Schrempp initiated the $40 billion acquisition of Chrysler Corporation, the deal was touted as a "merger of equals."[113,114] On November 17, 1998, he and Chrysler's chief executive Robert J. Eaton together rang the opening bell on the New York Stock Exchange to celebrate the first day of trading in DaimlerChrysler's stock. The merger brought together the German luxury car maker, which had had trouble introducing mass market vehicles, and Chrysler, with its vast experience in selling cars in volume, in what many saw as a highly synergistic alliance. The new company became the third-largest manufacturer of motor vehicles in the world.

Part I.

Discuss

When organizations with different cultures emerge, they choose one of four paths as described in this chapter: assimilation, integration, separation, or deculturation. Which path do you think Daimler-Benz and Chrysler should choose? Defend your answer.

Part II.

1. Your professor will tell you which path the companies actually chose. Discuss why this may have happened.
2. What should the company do next?

Chapter Summary and Key Terms

Why is organizational culture so important to companies?

An organization's culture may affect a company's profitability, and it acts as a subtle control mechanism on employee

behavior. In addition, subcultures and counter-cultures create both productive and counterproductive conflict in an organization. Cultures originate in the historical foundations of the company, the business the company is in, and the company's national and regional origins. Companies such as Wal-Mart, Starbucks, and Patagonia have built their reputations, in part, around their organizational cultures.

culture   446
dominant culture   446
core values   446
espoused values   446
enacted values   446
subcultures   446
counter-cultures   446
climate   446
social information processing model   446

How do you discover an organization's culture?

A company's culture exists on four levels: behaviors and artifacts; shared perspectives on rules and norms; general awareness of ideals, standards, and goals; and unconscious assumptions. Employees learn a company's culture through the process of organizational socialization.

realistic job preview   450
organizational assimilation   450
reality shock   450

How do managers use organizational culture to improve organizational effectiveness?

Strong organizational cultures have a certain style. For example, the norms and values of the company are clear and comprehensive, and values are intensely held and widely shared. Strong organizational cultures may enhance individual and company performance; they can also lead a company energetically in the wrong direction. Among other benefits, they may enhance corporate branding through the processes of employer branding and cause branding.

cultural fit   452
bureaucracy   452

market culture   452
clan   452
superordinate culture   454
moral stress   455
cafeteria benefits   456
corporate branding   456
employer branding   457
cause branding   457
boundary spanners   457

What happens when organizations with different cultures merge?

Companies that merge go through one of these processes for acculturation: assimilation, integration, separation, or deculturation. Performing a bicultural audit before the merger can help avoid acculturative stress and merger failure.

acculturative stress   457
bicultural audit   458

How can an existing organizational culture be changed?

Once established, cultures are hard to change. Companies that do try to change their cultures emphasize new policies, new rituals, and new ways of leading. Typically they hire people who fit into the new culture.

How can you find an organizational culture in which you will thrive?

Individuals have cultural preferences. Individuals who are achievers prefer corporate cultures that value high performance, for example. Sometimes you do not fit into your company's corporate culture or subculture, a fact that may create serious career consequences.

cultural preferences   460
glass ceiling   461

Explorations

1. Organizational culture now
Web search for "organizational culture" to find more information and examples that answer the question that opens this chapter, namely: What's so important about organizational culture?

2. Find a strong culture
Select an organization that you believe has a strong culture and find 10 facts to support your belief.

3. Corporate mergers
Research some corporate mergers online. Find one merger that has worked because of cultural reasons, and one that has not, and describe what happened.

References

[1] R. E. Walton, "Establishing and Maintaining High Commitment Work Systems," in J. R. Kimberly, R. H. Miles, and Associates, eds., *The Organizational Life Cycle: Issues in the Creation, Transformation, and Decline of Organizations* (San Francisco, CA: Jossey-Bass, 1980):208–290; C. A. O'Reilly and J. A. Chatman, "Culture as Social Control: Corporations, Culture and Commitment," in B. M. Staw and L. L. Cummings, eds., *Research in Organizational Behavior 18* (Greenwich, CT: JAI Press, 1996):157–200.

[2] M. L. Tushman and C. A. O'Reilly, *Winning Through Innovation: A Practical Guide to Leading Organizational Change and Renewal* (Boston, MA: Harvard Business School Press, 1997).

[3] A. Boisnier and J. Chatman, "The Role of Subcultures in Agile Organizations," in R. Petersen and E. Mannix, eds., *Leading*

and Managing People in Dynamic Organizations (Mahwah, NH: Lawrence Erlbaum Asssociates, 2003):87–112; A. Sinclair, "Approaches to Organizational Culture and Ethics," *Journal of Business Ethics 12*, 1993:63–73.

[4] G. H. Litwin and R. A. Stringer, *Motivation and Organizational Climate* (Cambridge, MA: Harvard Business School, Division of Research, 1968).

[5] J. Thomas and R. W. Griffin, "The Social Information Processing Model of Task Design: A Review of the Literature," *Academy of Management Journal,* October 1983:672–682.

[6] G. W. Meyer, "Social Information Processing and Social Networks: A Test of Social Influence Mechanisms," *Human Relations*, September 1994:1013–1045; K. J. Klein, A. B. Conn, D. B. Smith, and J. S. Sorra, "Is Everyone in Agreement? An Exploration of Within-Group Agreement in Employee Perceptions of the Work Environment," *Journal of Applied Psychology,* February 2001:3–16.

[7] A. E. Reichers and B. Schneider, "Culture: An Evolution of Contructs," in B. Schneider, ed., *Organizational Climate and Culture* (San Francisco, CA: Jossey-Bass Publishers, 1990):5–39.

[8] M. Y. Brannen and J. Kleinberg, "Images of Japanese Management and the Development of Organizational Culture Theory," in N. M. Ashkanasy, C. P. M. Wilderom and M. F. Peterson, eds., *Handbook of Organizational Culture and Climate* (Thousand Oaks, CA: Sage Publications, Inc., 2000):387–400.

[9] G. Hofstede, B. Neuijin, D. D. Ohayv, and G. Sanders, "Measuring Organizational Cultures: A Qualitative and Quantitative Study Across Twenty Cases," *Administrative Science Quarterly 35*, 1990:286–316.

[10] M. J. Schneider, "The Wal-Mart Annual Meeting: From Small-Town America to a Global Corporate Culture," *Human Organization 57* (3), 1998:292–299, 293. Many of the details about Wal-Mart's culture are taken from this article.

[11] M. J. Schneider, "The Wal-Mart Annual Meeting: From Small-Town America to a Global Corporate Culture," *Human Organization 57* (3), 1998:292–299, 293.

[12] E. H. Schein, "Does Japanese Management Style Have a Message for American Managers?" *Sloan Management Review 23* (1), Fall 1981:55–68; W. G. Dyer, "Patterns and Assumptions: The Keys to Understanding Organizational Culture," *Office of Naval Research Technical Report TR-ONR-7*, 1982; D. R. Denison, *Corporate Culture and Organizational Effectiveness* (New York: John Wiley & Sons, 1990).

[13] L. A. Krefting and P. J. Frost, "Untangling Webs, Surfing Waves, and Wildcatting: A Multiple-Metaphor Perspective on Managing Organizational Culture," in P. J. Frost, L. F. Moore, M. R. Louis, C. C. Lundberg and J. Martin, eds., *Organizational Culture* (Newbury Park, CA: Sage Publications, 1985):155–168; D. R. Denison, *Corporate Culture and Organizational Effectiveness* (New York: John Wiley & Sons, 1990).

[14] L. R. Pondy, P. J. Frost, G. Morgan, and T. C. Dandridge, eds., *Organizational Symbolism* (Greenwich, CT: JAI Press, 1983).

[15] G. Hofstede, B. Neuijen, D. D. Ohayv, and G. Sanders, "Measuring Organizational Cultures: A Qualitative and Quantitative Study Across Twenty Cases," *Administrative Science Quarterly 35*, 1990:286–316.

[16] M. J. Schneider, "The Wal-Mart Annual Meeting: From Small-Town America to a Global Corporate Culture," *Human Organization 57* (3), 1998:292–299, 298.

[17] "Wal-Mart: From Both Sides Now," *The Economist,* November 25, 2006:30.

[18] M. J. Schneider, "The Wal-Mart Annual Meeting: From Small-Town America to a Global Corporate Culture," *Human Organization 57* (3), 1998:292–299, 298.

[19] M. J. Schneider, "The Wal-Mart Annual Meeting: From Small-Town America to a Global Corporate Culture," *Human Organization 57* (3), 1998:292–299, 294.

[20] M. J. Schneider, "The Wal-Mart Annual Meeting: From Small-Town America to a Global Corporate Culture," *Human Organization 57* (3), 1998:292–299, 297.

[21] Joanne Martin, *Organizational Culture: Mapping the Terrain* (Thousand Oaks, CA: Sage Publications, 2002).

[22] M. J. Schneider, "The Wal-Mart Annual Meeting: From Small-Town America to a Global Corporate Culture," *Human Organization 57* (3), 1998:292–299, 297.

[23] M. J. Schneider, "The Wal-Mart Annual Meeting: From Small-Town America to a Global Corporate Culture," *Human Organization 57* (3), 1998:292–299, 299.

[24] M. J. Schneider, "The Wal-Mart Annual Meeting: From Small-Town America to a Global Corporate Culture," *Human Organization 57* (3), 1998:292–299, 297.

[25] J. Van Maanen, "Breaking In: Socialization to Work," in R. Dubin, ed., *Handbook of Work, Organization and Society* (Chicago, IL: Rand McNally College Publishing Company, 1976): 67-130; A. Etzioni, *A Comparative Analysis of Complex Organizations* (New York: Free Press, 1961).

[26] V. D. Miller and F. M. Jablin, "Information Seeking during Organizational Entry: Influences, Tactics, and a Model of the Process," *Academy of Management Review 16*, 1991:92–120.

[27] J. Van Maanen and E. H. Schein, "Toward a Theory of Organizational Socialization," in B. M. Staw, ed., *Research in Organizational Behavior 1* (Greenwich, CT: JAI Press, 1979):209–264; G. R. Jones, "Socialization Tactics, Self-Efficacy, and Newcomers' Adjustments to Organizations," *Academy of Management Journal 29*, 1986:262–279; T. N. Bauer, E. W. Morrison, and R. R. Callister, "Organizational Socialization: A Review and Directions for Future Research," *Research in Personnel and Human Resource Management 16*, 1998:149–214:; D. G. Allen, "Do Organizational Socialization Tactics Influence Newcomer Embeddedness and Turnover?" *Academy of Management Proceedings*, 2004:B1–B6.

[28] "Training Top 100: Top Five Profile & Ranking," *Training,* March 2004:42, www.trainingmag.com. Accessed October 15, 2005.

[29] Y. Wiener, "Forms of Value Systems: Focus on Organizational Effectiveness and Cultural Change and Maintenance," *Academy of Management Review 13* (4), October 1988:534–545.

[30] F. M. Jablin, "Organizational Entry, Assimilation and Exit," in F. M. Jablin, L. L. Putnam, K. H. Roberts and L. W. Porter., eds., *Handbook of Organizational Communication* (Beverly Hills, CA: Sage, 1987):679–740.

[31] C. D. Tengler and F. M. Jablin, "Effects of Question Type, Orientation, and Sequencing in the Employment Screening Interview," *Communication Monographs 50*, 1983:245–263.

[32] F. M. Jablin, "Assimilating New Members into Organizations," in R. N. Bostrom, ed., *Communication Yearbook 8* (Newbury Park, CA: Sage, 1984):594–626.

[33] J. P. Wanous, *Organizational Entry: Recruitment, Selection and Socialization of Newcomers* (Reading, MA: Addison-Wesley, 1980).

[34] R. A. Dean and J. P. Wanous, "Effects of Realistic Job Previews on Hiring Bank Tellers," *Journal of Applied Psychology 69*, 1984:61–68.

35 F. M. Jablin, "Organizational Entry, Assimilation and Exit," in F. M. Jablin, L. L. Putnam, K. H. Roberts and L. W. Porter., eds., *Handbook of Organizational Communication* (Beverly Hills, CA: Sage, 1987):679–740.

36 J. Van Maanen, "Breaking In: Socialization to Work," in R. Dubin, ed., *Handbook of Work, Organization, and Society* (Chicago, IL: Rand McNally, 1976):67–120.

37 F. M. Jablin, "Assimilating New Members into Organizations," in R. N. Bostrom, ed., *Communication Yearbook 8* (Newbury Park, CA: Sage, 1984):594–626.

38 J. Van Maanen, "Breaking In: Socialization to Work," in R. Dubin, ed., *Handbook of Work, Organization, and Society* (Chicago, IL: Rand McNally, 1976):67–120.

39 E. H. Schein, "The Individual, the Organization, and the Career: A Conceptual Scheme," (Cambridge, MA: Massachusetts Institute of Technology, unpublished paper, 1968.)

40 A. J. Flanagin and J. H. Waldeck, "Technology Use and Organizational Newcomer Socialization," *Journal of Business Communication 41* (2), April 2004:137–165.

41 J. A. Chatman and S. E. Cha, "Leading by Leveraging Culture," *California Management Review 45* (4), Summer 2003:20–34.

42 Y. Wiener, "Forms of Value Systems: A Focus on Organizational Effectiveness and Cultural Change and Maintenance," *Academy of Managmenet Review,* October 1988:534–545.

43 J. P. Kotter and J. L. Heskett, *Corporate Culture and Performance* (New York: Free Press, 1992):159.

44 "Steve Ballmer Shrugs Off the Critics," *BusinessWeek* Issue 3952, September 26, 2005:102–103, 102.

45 J. Greene, S. Hamm, D. Brady, and M. Der Hovanesian, "Troubling Exits at Microsoft," *BusinessWeek* Issue 3952, September 26, 2005:98–108.

46 C. O'Reilly and J. Chatman, "Cultures as Social Control: Corporations, Cults, and Commitment," in L. Cummings and B. Staw, eds., *Research in Organizational Behavior 18* (Greenwich, CT: JAI Press, 1996).157–200, 166.

47 R. E. Baumeister, "The Self," in D. T. Gilbert, S. T. Fiske, and G. Lindzey, eds., *The Handbook of Social Psychology*, 4th ed. (New York: McGraw-Hill, 1998):680–740.

48 J. R. Kotter and J. L. Heskett, *Corporate Culture and Performance* (New York: Free Press, 1992).

49 J. P. Kotter and J. L. Heskett, *Corporate Culture and Performance* (New York: Free Press, 1992):159.

50 J. B. Sørensen, "The Strength of Corporate Culture and the Reliability of Firm Performance," *Administrative Science Quarterly 47* (1), March 2002:70–91.

51 J. P. Kotter and J. L. Heskett, *Corporate Culture and Performance* (New York: Free Press, 1992):141–142.

52 J. Pfeffer and J. F. Veiga, "Putting People First for Organizational Success," *Academy of Management Executive 13,* May 1999:37–48.

53 A. L. Wilkins and W. G. Ouchi, "Efficient Cultures: Exploring the Relationship between Culture and Organizational Performance," *Administrative Science Quarterly 28,* 1983:468–481.

54 A. L. Wilkins and W. G. Ouchi, "Efficient Cultures: Exploring the Relationship between Culture and Organizational Performance," *Administrative Science Quarterly 28,* 1983:468–481.

55 R. T. Mowday, L. W. Porter, and R. M. Steers, *Employee Organizational Linkages: The Psychology of Commitment, Absenteeism, and Turnover* (New York: Academic Press, 1982).

56 D. A. Yousef, "Validating the Dimensionality of Porter et al.'s Measurement of Organizational Commitment in a Non-Western Culture Setting," *International Journal of Human Resource Management 14* (6), September 2003:1067–1079.

57 E. J. Wallach, "Individuals and Organizations: The Cultural Match," *Training and Development Journal 37* (2) February 1983: 29–36.

58 B. N. Pfau, "WorkUSA 2000–Employee Commitment and the Bottom Line," Watson Wyatt, www.watsonwyatt.com. Accessed January 22, 2005.

59 R. Goffee and G. Jones, "What Holds the Modern Company Together?" *Harvard Business Review 74* (6), November/December 1996:133–148.

60 E. H. Schein, "What Holds the Modern Company Together?" *Harvard Business Review 75* (6), November/December 1997:174–175.

61 A. L. Wilkins and W. G. Ouchi, "Efficient Cultures: Exploring the Relationship between Culture and Organizational Performance," *Administrative Science Quarterly 28,* 1983:468–481.

62 M. K. Welge, "The Effective Design of Headquarter-Subsidiary Relationships in German MNCs," in L. Otterbeck, ed., *The Management of Headquarters-Subsidiary Relationships in Multinational Corporations* (1981); S. C. Schneider, "National vs. Corporate Culture: Implications for Human Resource Management," *Human Resource Management 27* (2) 1988:231–246;G. Aldershot, C. A. Bartlett, S. Ghoshal, and G. Sumantra, G, "Matrix Management: Not a Structure, a Frame of Mind," *Harvard Business Review 68* (4), 1990:138–45; P. Evans, "Management Development as Glue Technology," *Human Resource Planning 15* (1), 1992:85–106.

63 S. C. Schneider, "National vs. Corporate Culture: Implications for Human Resource Management," *Human Resource Management 27* (2) 1988:231–246.

64 A. Laurent, "Management Style a Matter of Nationality, Study Suggests," *Management Review 72* (4), April 1983:31.

65 A. Laurent, "The Cultural Diversity of Western Conceptions of Management," *International Studies of Management & Organization 13* (1/2), Spring/Summer 1983:75–96, 95.

66 W. A. Hochwarter, P. L. Perrewe, G. R. Ferris, and R. A. Brymer, "Job Satisfaction and Performance: The Moderating Effects of Value Attainment and Affective Disposition," *Journal of Vocational Behavior,* April 1999:296–313.

67 I. Mitroff and E. Denton, "A Study of Spirituality in the Workplace," *Sloan Management Review 40,* Summer 1999:83–92.

68 Andrew J. Hoffman, "Reconciling Professional and Personal Value Systems: The Spiritually Motivated Manager as Organizational Entrepreneur," in R. A. Giacalone and C. L. Jurkiewicz, eds., *Handbook of Workplace Spirituality and Organizational Performance* (Armonk, NY: M.E. Sharpe, 2003):193–208.

69 Seventy percent of Americans think that environmental protection and economic development are compatible, according to *The Environmental Two Step: Looking Forward, Moving Backward* (New York: Times, Mirror, 1995).

70 R. Berenbeim, *Corporate Ethics Practices* (New York: Conference Board, 1992).

71 J. A. Waters and F. Bird, "The Moral Dimension of Organizational Culture," *Journal of Business Ethics 6,* 1987:15–22, 15.

72 J. A. Waters and F. Bird, "The Moral Dimension of Organizational Culture," *Journal of Business Ethics 6,* 1987:15–22, 15.

73 J. A. Waters and F. Bird, "The Moral Dimension of Organizational Culture," *Journal of Business Ethics 6,* 1987:15–22, 18.

74 J. A. Waters and F. Bird, "The Moral Dimension of Organizational Culture," *Journal of Business Ethics 6,* 1987:15–22, 21.

75 R. André, "Diversity Stress as Morality Stress," *Journal of Business Ethics 14*, 1995:489–496.

76 R. Blank and S. Slipp, *Voices of Diversity* (New York: Amacom, 1994).

77 C. L. Bovée and J. V. Thill, *Business in Action* (Upper Saddle River, NJ: Prentice Hall, 2001).

78 D. A. Aaker, "Leveraging the Corporate Brand," *California Management Review 46* (3), Spring 2004:6–18.

79 F. Rogers, "Engaging Employees to Live the Brand," *Strategic HR Review 2* (6), September/October 2003:34–37.

80 F. Wagner-Marsh and J. Conley, "The Fourth Wave: The Spiritually Based Firm," *Journal of Organizational Change Management 12* (4), 1999:292–302.

81 C. L. Cone, M. A. Feldman, and A. T. DaSilva, "Causes and Effects," *Harvard Business Review 81* (7), July 2003:95–101.

82 B. Schneider, D. E. Bowen, M. G. Ehrhard, and K. M. Holcombe, "The Climate for Service: Evolution of a Construct," in N. M. Ashkanasy, C. P. M. Wilderom and M. F. Peterson, eds., *Handbook of Organizational Culture and Climate* (Thousand Oaks, CA: Sage Publications, Inc., 2000):21–36.

83 S. D. Pugh, "Service with a Smile: Emotional Contagion in the Service Encounter," *Academy of Management Journal 44* (5), October 2001:1018–1027.

84 C. L. Stamper and M. C. Johlke, "The Impact of Perceived Organizational Support on the Relationship between Boundary Spanner Role Stress and Work Outcomes," *Journal of Management 29* (4), August 2003:569–588.

85 B. Schneider, D. E. Bowen, M. G. Ehrhard, and K. M. Holcombe, "The Climate for Service: Evolution of a Construct," in N. M. Ashkanasy, C. P. M. Wilderom and M. F. Peterson, eds., *Handbook of Organizational Culture and Climate* (Thousand Oaks, CA: Sage Publications, Inc., 2000):21–36, 35.

86 A. Nahavandi and A. R. Malekzadeh, *Organizational Culture in the Management of Mergers* (Westport, CT: Quorum Books, 1993):3.

87 J. W. Berry, "Social and Cultural Change," in H. C. Triandis and R. W. Brislin, eds., *Handbook of Cross-Cultural Psychology 5* (Boston, MA: Allyn & Bacon, 1980):211–279, 261.

88 K. J. Fedor and W. B. Werther Jr., "The Fourth Dimension: Creating Culturally Responsive International Alliances," *Organizational Dynamics 25* (Autumn 1996):39–53; E. H. Schein, *The Corporate Culture Survival Guide* (San Francisco, CA: Jossey-Bass, 1999).

89 A. R. Malekzadeh and A. Nahavandi, "Making Mergers Work by Managing Cultures," *Journal of Business Strategy 11* (3), May/June 1990:55–57.

90 A. Nahavandi and A. R. Malekzadeh, "Acculturation in Mergers and Acquisitions," *Academy of Management Review 13* (1), January 1988:79–90; A. R. Malekzadeh and A. Nahavandi, "Making Mergers Work by Managing Cultures," *Journal of Business Strategy 11* (3), May/June 1990:55–57.

91 T. J. Galpin and M. Herndon, *The Complete Guide to Mergers and Acquisitions: Process Tools to Support M&A Integration at Every Level* (San Francisco, CA: Jossey-Bass Publishers, 2000).

92 J. P. Kotter and J. L. Heskett, *Corporate Culture and Performance* (New York: Free Press, 1992).

93 G. Donaldson and J. Lorsch, *Decision Making at the Top* (New York: Basic Books, 1983).

94 V. Sathy, *Culture and Related Corporate Realities* (Homewood, IL: Richard D. Irwin, 1985); E. H. Schein, *Organizational Culture and Leadership* (San Francisco, CA: Jossey-Bass, 1985).

95 A. F. Buono and J. L. Bowditch, *The Human Side of Mergers and Acquisitions* (San Francisco, CA: Jossey-Bass, 1989).

96 B. M. Bass and B. J. Aviolo, *Improving Organizational Effectiveness Through Transformational Leadership* (Thousand Oaks, CA: Sage Publications, 1994), J. A. Conger and R. N. Kanungo, "Toward a Behavioral Theory of Charismatic Leadership in Organizational Settings," *Academy of Management Review* 12 (4):837–847.

97 P. B. Smith and M. F. Peterson, "Cross-Cultural Leadership," *Blackwell Handbook of Cross-Cultural Management* (Oxford: Blackwell Publishing, 2002):217–235; J. M. Meindl, "On Leadership: An Alternative to the Conventional Wisdom," in B. M. Staw and L. L. Cummings, eds., *Research in Organizational Behavior 12,* (Greenwich, CT: JAI Press, Inc., 1990):159–203.

[98] M. J. Hatch, "The Dynamics of Organizational Culture," *Academy of Management Review 18*, 1993:657–693.

[99] E. H. Schein, "Sense and Nonsense About Culture and Climate," in N. M. Ashkanasy, C. P. M. Wilderom, and M. F. Peterson, eds., *Handbook of Organizational Culture and Climate* (Thousand Oaks, CA: Sage Publications, Inc., 2000):xxiii–xxxiii.

[100] B. Schneider and A. P. Brief, "Creating a Climate and Culture for Sustainable Organizational Change," *Organizational Dynamics 24* (4), Spring 1996:7–19.

[101] J. R. Edwards, "An Examination of Competing Versions of the Person-Environment Fit Approach to Stress," *Academy of Management Journal 39*, 1996:292–339.

[102] A. E. M. van Vianen and M. G. Prins, "Changes in Newcomers' Person–Climate Fit following the First Stage of Socialization," *International Journal of Selection and Assessment 5*, 1997: No page numbers available.

[103] A. E. M. van Vianen, "Person–Organization Fit: The Match between Newcomers' and Recruiters' Preferences for Organizational Cultures," *Personnel Psychology 53* (1), Spring 2000:113–149.

[104] P. Warr and A. Pearce, "Preferences for Careers and Organisational Cultures as a Function of Logically Related Personality Traits," *Applied Psychology: An International Review 53* (3), 2004:423–435.

[105] A. E. M. van Vianen and A. H. Fischer, "Illuminating the Glass Ceiling: The Role of Organizational Culture Preferences," *Journal of Occupational & Organizational Psychology 75* (3), September 2002:315–337.

[106] E. Galinsky, K. Salmond, J. T. Bond, M. B. Kropf, M. Moore, and B. Harrington, *Leaders in a Global Economy: A Study of Executive Women and Men* (Families and Work Institute, Catalyst, and Boston College Center for Work & Family, www.familiesandwork.org, www.catalystwomen.org, and www.bc.edu/cwf, 2003).

[107] Based on information in B. L. Toffler with J. Reingold, *Final Accounting: Ambition, Greed, and the Fall of Arthur Andersen* (New York: Broadway Books, 2003) and L. K. Treviño and M. E. Brown, "Managing to Be Ethical: Debunking Five Business Ethics Myths," *Academy of Management Executive 19* (2), 2004:69–81.

[108] L. K. Treviño and M. E. Brown, "Managing to Be Ethical: Debunking Five Business Ethics Myths," *Academy of Management Executive 19* (2), 2004:69–81.

[109] Based on information in R. C. Ford, "Pierre Bellon, Founder and President-Director General of Sodexho Alliance, on Working Hard and Having Fun," *Academy of Management Executive 17* (1), February 2003:38–45, and R. C. Ford, "Having Fun at Work," *Engineering Management,* April/May 2004:32–33.

[110] R. C. Ford, "Pierre Bellon, Founder and President-Director General of Sodexho Alliance, on Working Hard and Having Fun," *Academy of Management Executive 17* (1), February 2003:38–45, 45.

[111] R. C. Ford, "Having Fun at Work," *Engineering Management* April/May 2004:32–33.

[112] R. C. Ford, F. S. McLaughlin and J. W. Newstrom, "Questions and Answers about Fun at Work," *Human Resource Planning 26* (4), 2003:18–33.

[113] Based on information in D. Ostle, "The Culture Clash at DaimlerChrysler was Worse Than Expected," *Automotive News Europe 4* (24), November 22, 1999:3–4; J. Muller, "Lessons from a Casualty of the Culture Wars," *BusinessWeek 3657* November 29, 1999:198; R. Wilson, "The Culture Clash Pays Off," *Automotive Industries 185* (1), January 2005:31.

[114] R. Wilson, "The Culture Clash Pays Off," *Automotive Industries 185* (1), January 2005:31.

18 Changing Organizations

Preview

What is large-scale organizational change and why do companies attempt it?
Planned and unplanned change
Forces for stability versus forces for change

In large-scale organizational change, what, exactly, changes?
Company strategy and systems
Power and decision making
Culture

How do managers structure a planned change?
Traditional change: Implementing a corporate strategy
Organizational development
Appreciative inquiry
Positive organizational behavior

How does the change process work?: Models
A three-stage model of change
Punctuated equilibrium change
Continuous change

During planned change, how do individuals and organizations learn?
Where do people learn best?
What do people learn?
How do organizations learn?

What are some key ethical dilemmas during organizational change?

What are some common problems during organizational change?

Which assumptions about change are important?
Should the change focus on the process or the problem?
Is change logical, or emotional?
Does change start at the top or the bottom of the company?
How is change disseminated?

How do individuals react to change and how do managers deal with their reactions?
Individual predispositions toward change
When change is threatening
What managers can do to foster change

Are Western approaches to change exportable?

Student Advantage, Inc.

At Student Advantage, competition, technology, and a changing marketplace have all been forces for change. Add to these the CEO's desire to grow the company, and you have a classic scenario for organizational evolution. What changes as a company grows? Everything from strategy to culture to decision making.

In terms of strategy, the leaders of Student Advantage first established a successful business, then decided to acquire their competitors, and ultimately took their company public. They have considered going international.

In the process the number of employees more than doubled, to about 500 nationwide. With this rapid growth, the company culture became more formal, although it maintained its high energy. Effective communication became crucial. Integrating individuals who had formerly worked for acquired companies was a challenge that was met in part by assigning new employees to a buddy in the home office. When acquiring companies, the process of due diligence involved figuring out whether the culture of that company should be integrated with that of the parent, or left alone because it met the needs of a unique market niche. Successful integration also involved a sense of timing, allowing the acquired company to gradually adjust to new ways of doing things.

Decision making changed, too. The CEO has to delegate more and was not seen as often by each individual employee. Employees who once knew everything about the company and its product could no longer keep track of all these details, and were forced to specialize. With more specialization, more important decisions were made in teams.

Student Advantage is an example of a company that has changed as it has grown. Other companies have already grown, yet still need to change. In this chapter we will examine the basic principles of organization-wide change.

What Is Large-Scale Organizational Change and Why Do Companies Attempt It?

large-scale organizational change
Change that is organization-wide.

Change is a core phenomenon of organizational life. When you get right down to it, most of OB is about change—from motivating yourself and your employees to improving team processes. This chapter covers, in particular, **large-scale organizational change**, change that is organization-wide. Examples include restructuring a company, including all of its systems; changing a company's processes for decision making; and changing an organization's culture.[1] Changes such as these are often needed when a company alters its business strategy, adopts a new technology, or seeks more innovation. They are the kinds of changes that thriving companies such as GE have successfully undertaken, and that struggling companies such as General Motors would like to achieve.

Many observers argue that companies that do not change do not survive. As evidence for this point of view, consider the fate of the 500 benchmark companies selected in 1957 to comprise Standard and Poor's stock market index.[2] Guess how many of these companies remained on the list in 1998? Also, how many do you think outperformed the index during that time period?† It has been predicted that over the next 25 years, two-thirds of our most prominent corporations will either die or be acquired.[3] Unless they change.

Planned and Unplanned Change

Organizational change can be either planned or unplanned.[4] This chapter examines primarily planned change—that is, change that is systematic and relatively controlled. A major reason managers institute change is to control change rather than being victimized by it.

Keep in mind that organizations are changing all the time in response to the various demands that are placed on them. Unplanned change is sometimes effective. But unplanned change also has a tendency to cause the members of an organization to draw wrong conclusions from events—essentially, to mislearn. When the unplanned actions people invent to solve problems on the fly come to be seen as the "correct" way to solve problems, an organization is likely to become inflexible and ineffective.[5] For example, a powerful department in a company might adopt a new software program and pressure other departments into adopting it, too—even though it does not optimally meet their needs. A better approach to would be to ensure that, when software is purchased, the needs of the entire company are evaluated and met.

Forces for Stability versus Forces for Change

In organizational life, forces for change coexist with forces for stability. From the point of view of a company, both stability and change have their virtues. Companies pursue organizational stability when they value:[6]

- Institutionalism. Sometimes managers prefer stability simply because it is easier. (And sometimes they cannot think of any alternative.)

- Reduction of transaction costs. Organizational restructurings that emphasize employee reductions can be expensive, and may strain relationships with such stakeholders as employees, communities, and governments.[7] When employment is stable, on the other hand, the costs of firing, hiring, socializing, and training workers are reduced.

- Sustained competitive advantage. If, over time, companies can design workforce relationships that are not easily copied, these relationships can themselves be a source of competitive advantage. For example, sustained international networks are difficult and time-consuming to put in place, but are helpful to a company trying to adapt to global competition. A company would want to preserve them rather than change them.

Companies pursue organizational change when they value:[8]

- Adaptability. As their environments become increasingly unpredictable, organizations must become more adaptable.[9] Why are environments unpredictable? Primarily because of global competition, rapid advances in technology, and mobile capital.

† Seventy-four companies (about 15 percent) remained on the list. Only 12 companies outperformed the index.

Additional factors are world politics, economic conditions, social trends, changing workforce composition, and government regulation.

■ Cost containment. To keep costs down, companies shrink by firing workers and outsourcing work. The remaining employees may be organized in new ways.

■ Meeting the demands of impatient capital markets. With investors demanding quick returns on their money, companies do whatever it takes to meet short-term financial targets and avoid making long-term investments. All aspects of the organization, including human systems, must adapt.

■ Consolidation of control. When an organization decentralizes, managers can set targets and require employees to figure out how to meet them. In this way, managers consolidate their power, and employees must become more flexible and adaptable.[10]

■ Competitive advantage through organizational design. Being able to change quickly is itself a source of competitive advantage for a company. Organizing a company's work and processes so they can be quickly altered may create considerable cost savings over competitors.

In Large-Scale Organizational Change, What, Exactly, Changes?

In most cases, large-scale organizational change is driven by new management thinking in one or more of three general areas: 1) company strategy and systems, 2) organizational decision making and power, and 3) organizational culture.[11] We will take a look at each of these in turn.

Company Strategy and Systems

When management changes a company's strategy, it often redesigns its systems, including its organizational structure and processes, to better implement that strategy. The people charged with implementing these changes must adapt, learning new ways of working and even new attitudes.

A modern example of change in processes organization-wide is **reengineering**, which is the redesign of business processes to achieve improvements in "critical, contemporary measures of performance, such as cost, quality, service and speed."[12] Reengineered companies change structures, jobs, and people; in fact, any key process that gets the company's product or service into the hands of the customer.

Duke Energy (formerly Duke Power Company) is a *Fortune* 500 energy company that chose to reengineer. As part of a new cost cutting strategy, the company's top executives first identified and mapped their basic processes. They wanted to figure out how they could minimize the number of steps in any given process and at the same time widen managers' span of control (recall that "span of control" is the number of workers reporting to a manager). One thing the company management did was to determine how long a job should take. Then they took steps to streamline various processes. For example, they stopped sending workers out into the field with less than a day's work to do. They also standardized their trucks, and although linemen who had set up their vehicles to suit their own personal tastes were disturbed by the change, standardizing the trucks allowed the company to cut its fleet size. Duke Energy even centralized vacations and time off. Employees no longer negotiated these things with their supervisors. Instead, a central office created a process for requesting vacation time, calling in sick, and getting time off for doctors visits. Using this centralized process, the company could know in advance what the size of its workforce would be on any given day. Finally, the company eliminated its middle layer of managers, about 130 to 140 positions out of 4,500 jobs, and replaced them with cross-functional teams.

Reengineering is just one example of system-wide change. Other types you may encounter in businesses today are concurrent engineering[13] and business model reinvention.[14]

Power and Decision Making

Sometimes management decides that it should change how organizational power and decision making are distributed. For instance, management may decide that customer contact points must be established much lower in the organization, and that employees should be empowered to make on-the-spot decisions about how best to serve their customers.

reengineering
The redesign of business processes to improve various measures of performance, such as cost, quality, service and speed, and which may involve changes in structures, jobs, people, or any key processes.

To make changes that move decision making down in the hierarchy, management first evaluates who makes decisions and controls resources. Then it empowers individuals at lower levels in the organization by giving them some of the resources and decision making authority that was formerly reserved for managers. For instance, it might give them more data about how well customers are being served and more time in their work schedule to think about how this knowledge could actually be used to improve customer service. This type of change may disadvantage some groups, such as middle managers, and may require on-going negotiation as power shifts from one group to another.

Two important examples of employee empowerment are total quality management (TQM) and industrial democracy. Other organizational change programs that have done similar things in the past have been called quality of working life programs (QWL), quality circles, and labor–management cooperation.

total quality management
A management strategy aimed at developing high awareness of quality in all organizational processes; a system for organization-wide change which originally helped companies to improve measurable factors such as their products' conformance to specifications.

TOTAL QUALITY MANAGEMENT Once a widely practiced system for organization-wide change, **total quality management** (TQM) originated in part as a response to the belief that U.S. companies must compete on quality in the global marketplace. Originally, TQM helped companies to improve measurable factors such as their products' conformance to specifications, reliability, and serviceability, as well as intangible factors such as product aesthetics and perceived quality.[15] Today the influence of TQM is diffused throughout the business world, and the term "TQM" itself has declined in use. Yet the approach continues to be used in businesses as diverse as water utilities services and semiconductor packaging.[16]

Focusing on quality requires adopting specific output criteria and being able to effectively measure a company's performance against those criteria. Because today's production processes are quite complex, it is often not feasible for managers at the upper levels of an organization to understand the details of what is going on at the level of production. Therefore, the workers at the lower levels must themselves know how to use statistics to measure and control defects, scrap, and deadlines.

benchmarking
The process by which a company compares its own processes and products with the best processes and products available in the industry and then sets goals for improvement.

Benchmarking is the process by which a company compares its own processes and products with the best processes and products available in the industry and then sets goals for improvement. In companies that use benchmarking extensively, most employees learn to use sophisticated statistical techniques effectively because they personally contribute to internal audits, reliability analyses, and benchmarking against competitors.[17] Every year the prestigious Malcolm Baldridge Award recognizes American companies that have achieved the highest standards for quality. A recent winner is The Bama Companies, Inc., a developer and manufacturer of frozen food products for restaurant chains that has 1,100 employees and production facilities in Tulsa, Oklahoma, and Beijing, China.[18] In recent years, Bama's sales have increased 72 percent, in an industry that has remained relatively flat.

Another award-winner is Zytec Corporation, which designs and manufactures electronic power supplies for original equipment manufacturers.[19] Zytec has converted its process measurements to be extremely precise (measured in parts per million) on all product lines. The company benchmarks every important manufacturing process, and also 18 different processes for gathering data and information about its customers. Also, quality training for all its employees, from clerical workers to engineers and executives, is extensive, including courses in statistical process control and just-in-time manufacturing. The employees receive an average of 72 hours of such training.

Unfortunately, TQM programs have often failed to create sustained change.[20] Usually the problems lie with the management teams that are charged with the TQM implementation. Often these teams fail to develop enough commitment to TQM, and to behave and make decisions that are consistent with it. Another problem has been that they fail to develop the leadership skills, cross-functional communication, and team cultures necessary for implementing TQM.

INDUSTRIAL DEMOCRACY Sometimes organizational change is spurred by external, societal pressures to empower workers. For example, some labor unions and governments have lobbied to have workers participate in managing their companies, a practice known as **industrial democracy**. Industrial democracy is found worldwide in a variety of formats, from worker self-management to extensive trade union representation in company governance.

In Germany, for example, employees have the legal right to have representatives on their company's influential supervisory board. This board appoints and fires top managers, determines their compensation, and advises on company policy. Also, in all German companies with more than five employees, groups called "works councils" have extensive consultation, information, and even veto rights on certain financial and personnel issues in their companies. A study in the United States, Germany, the United Kingdom, and Australia suggests that in recent decades the ability of unions to strengthen industrial democracy has been curtailed in all of these countries except Germany.[21] However, today even Germany is under pressure to change, as some view industrial democracy as costly and inflexible.

Culture

An organization's culture is comprised of its shared values and norms, which define for organizational members what is important to the company and what attitudes and beliefs are appropriate.[22] (See Chapter 17.) When a company changes its organizational culture, it first analyzes its values and norms, and then sets out to alter them. As you can imagine, it is essential to involve employees in this type of change.

Some of the important types of cultural change in modern organizations are enhancing organizational learning, valuing workforce diversity, and implementing Six Sigma precepts.

LEARNING CULTURES **Organizational learning** is the manner in which organizations preserve knowledge, behaviors, mental maps, norms, and values over time, despite the fact that some of their individual members leave.[23] Together these are referred to as a company's **intellectual capital**. Learning, and thus enhancing intellectual capital, is often a source of competitive advantage, whether the learner is an individual, a group, or an organization.[24] Research suggests that effective organizational learning leads to increased product innovation[25] and the ongoing strategic renewal of companies.[26]

In a learning culture each employee develops the motivation, understanding, capability, and opportunity to interpret what is happening in the business. Employees are supported by organizational systems that encourage the sharing, integration, and institutionalization of their knowledge.[27] A company that values learning makes time for it, has approachable leaders who act as teachers and stewards of change, and encourages shared commitment to learning and thinking systemically.[28] Top learning organizations also devote many hours to educating their employees. Annual average training hours per employee stand at 40 for pharmaceutical giant Pfizer Inc., 54 for the semiconductor equipment manufacturer KLA-Tencor, 54 for technology giant IBM, and 70 for consulting firm Booz Allen Hamilton.[29] Notably, Pfizer's training budget as a percentage of its payroll is 14 percent.

Learning cultures are **knowledge-centered cultures**, which means that they encourage knowledge creation and dissemination.[30] Hewlett-Packard has many of the characteristics of a learning and knowledge-centered culture. For example, it was one of the first companies to create a version of an internal electronic yellow pages in which company experts and their expertise are listed.[31] However, such organizations do much more than simply accumulate information. They develop effective **knowledge management systems** that not only manage data and information, but also the processes of learning, understanding, and applying information. Under this way of working, a company's formal databases are used as tools for strategy rather than being mere storage facilities, and individual knowledge must be captured for use by the organization.[32]

CULTURES THAT VALUE DIVERSITY In recent decades the composition of the U.S. workforce has changed significantly, incorporating larger percentages of women and racial minorities.[33] As a result, many companies have gone through a deliberate process of cultural change, moving away from cultures that reflect primarily the values and norms of white males to cultures that reflect the diverse values and norms of their varied

---

industrial democracy
A practice in which workers participate in company management.

organizational learning
The manner in which organizations preserve knowledge, behaviors, mental maps, norms, and values (their "intellectual capital") over time.

intellectual capital
An organization's knowledge, behaviors, mental maps, norms, and values.

knowledge-centered cultures
Cultures which encourage the creation and dissemination of knowledge, and which develop effective knowledge management systems.

knowledge management systems
Systems for managing data and information and also learning, understanding and applying information.

employees.[34] In this context, diversity refers to any number of demographic and cultural identities, such as race, gender, age, and nationality.

Many companies have made the cultural change to valuing diversity because they want to attract and keep the best people in the available employment pool. In addition, heterogeneous organizational cultures have other advantages. Diversity brings a useful variety of views and approaches to problem solving.[35] For example, diversity has been shown to improve group performance on creative tasks (in those situations in which individuals' self-concepts are supported by their group).[36] Another advantage is that members who differ from each other are likely to tap into different interpersonal networks, thus increasing the amount of information available for organizational decision making.[37] Even investors see the value of cultural diversity in modern companies: They tend to bid up the stock price of firms that receive national recognition for their high quality affirmative action programs.[38]

On the other hand, cultural diversity also brings challenges. A key one is that heterogeneous work groups tend to experience more conflict and turnover than homogeneous work groups.[39] As one research report puts it, "Simply having more diversity in a group is no guarantee that the group will make better decisions or function effectively. In our view . . . diversity is a mixed blessing and requires careful and sustained attention to be a positive force in enhancing performance."[40]

The negative factors associated with increased diversity can be minimized by creating an organizational culture that emphasizes collectivism rather than individualism.[41] Companies with collectivist cultures emphasize people's membership in their organization and develop the sense that everyone has a shared fate. Creating a culture that all employees can identify with might include such obvious changes as holding a "holiday party" rather than a "Christmas party," or turning the annual golf outing into an annual picnic. It generally includes a variety of more systemic changes, as well, such as establishing a mentoring program for minorities, partnering with educational institutions and nontraditional groups to attract minorities, inclusion of management of diversity as an issue on performance evaluations, and diversity training programs.[42]

Six Sigma
A multifaceted approach to organizational change that attempts to alter a company's entire culture; a "Six Sigma Organization" is designed to measure and improve all organizational processes, with the objective of creating a culture of continuous renewal.

SIX SIGMA CULTURES **Six Sigma** is a multifaceted approach to organizational change that attempts to alter a company's entire culture. A Six Sigma Organization is designed to measure and improve all organizational processes, with the objective of creating a culture of continuous renewal.[43] Originally conceived at Motorola to achieve near-perfect quality by comparing customer needs with how well the company was meeting them, Six Sigma became famous as the system adopted by GE: "Six Sigma has forever changed GE. Everyone [here] . . . is a true believer in Six Sigma, the way this Company now works."[44]

When practicing the Six Sigma culture, managers follow the critical processes of their functions but also communicate with other functions to share useful data and ideas. They also stay in regular touch with their customers and competitors, and they have key facts on hand at all times. The Six Sigma organization is created to be adaptable, positioned for "continuous renewal."[45]

The result is what some would call an ideal blend of bureaucratic and organic (in this book termed "enterprising") organizational design factors. The bureaucratic aspect of Six Sigma includes reliance on detailed measures of business performance and emphasizing process improvement. The organic/enterprising aspects include focusing on the customers and their ever-changing needs, and expanding opportunities for employees to interact with customers, suppliers, and supply chain partners.

How Do Managers Structure a Planned Change?

There are many ways to implement organizational change. In this section we will examine some of the most widely used techniques, including the traditional approach of implementing an organizational strategy, the people-centered approach called "organizational

TABLE 18.1 Overview: Types of Systemic Change

What is the focus of the change?	What actually changes?	What is the process of change?	What is the role of leadership in making the change?	Examples
Company strategy	Organizational structures and processes	Analysis and redesign	Creating a strategy, then making sure it is implemented effectively	• Establishing profit centers • Other restructuring • Reengineering
Organizational power and decision making	Who makes decisions and controls resources	Mobilization and empowerment	Understanding and coordinating groups that have vested interests	• Employee participation including TQM • Employee stock ownership plans (ESOPs)
Organizational culture	Patterns of interaction and mutual meanings	Development of shared meanings and images; socialization	Providing a vision that fosters commitment and shared values	• Organizational learning • Organizational development

Source: Adapted from theory presented in D. Ancona, T. Kochan, M. Scully, J. Van Maanen, and D. E. Westney, *Managing for the Future: Organizational Behavior & Processes,* 2nd edition (Cincinnati: South-Western College Publishing, 1999).

development," and newer approaches called "appreciative inquiry" and "positive organizational behavior." We will also take a look at learning and training, which is a core tool used by all approaches. Finally, we will examine some of the common errors that companies make when attempting an organization-wide change.

Traditional Change: Implementing a Corporate Strategy

When organizations engage in strategic planning, they define their goals, assess their internal strengths and weaknesses, examine their opportunities and threats, and then develop, communicate, implement, and, finally, evaluate the results of their plan. Sometimes this process is routine, an annual or biannual exercise that results in a published strategic plan that is then implemented (or, perhaps, ignored); other times, strategic planning occurs in response to an organizational threat or opportunity.

You can learn how to do the analysis underpinning a company strategy in any course on business strategy. However, it is one thing to perform an analysis, and it is another thing to turn an entire organization in the direction it needs to go. To effectively implement a change in a company's strategy, managers must have certain applied, organizational behavior skills.[46] These include:

- Being able to mobilize the executive team and the rest of the organization
- Responding to those organizational members who raise objections and resist
- Creating a sense of urgency to motivate others to want to change
- Articulating the strategy clearly and convincingly
- Building coalitions to support the strategy
- Locating the right people for key jobs while removing others
- Preventing managers from letting day-to-day concerns distract them from the change

Inviting people to participate in developing a strategy may have a direct effect on implementation, because people who are involved with and informed about a change are more likely to accept and implement it.[47] For example, involving middle managers in the analysis that leads to adopting a particular strategy is likely to positively impact the implementation process.[48] Establishing fair processes is also important. Managers should engage people in decisions that affect them, explain the final decisions, and establish clear expectations for employees' actions and deliverables. "Fair process is a key organizational practice for effectively conceiving and executing any strategy, but is particularly efficacious when companies wish to break from the status quo. . . ."[49]

Organizational Development

organizational development (OD)

Generally, the use of social science knowledge to improve organizational effectiveness; specifically, any organizational improvement effort which is planned, organization-wide, managed from the top, and makes use of behavioral science knowledge.

In a general sense, **organizational development (OD)** is the use of social science knowledge to improve organizational effectiveness. The term can be used more specifically, too, to describe any organizational change effort that is planned, organization-wide, and managed from the top, with the goals of improving organizational effectiveness and health through interventions in organization processes using behavioral science knowledge.[50] Many OD practitioners emphasize a set of core values that include respect and inclusion for all organizational members, the encouragement of collaboration, and the importance of self-awareness.[51]

OD focuses on the human systems of an organization. It is a total process for behavioral systems change that includes the five steps of diagnosis, feedback, planning, intervention, and follow-up evaluation.

change agent

Any individual who is responsible for implementing an organizational change.

The term **change agent** refers to any individual who is responsible for implementing an organizational change, and it is used frequently in connection with those who do OD. A change agent can be a manager, an external or internal consultant, or even an employee who is charged with implementing change.

Let's next take a look at the five steps in a typical OD process to understand one way that planned change can be designed.

ORGANIZATIONAL DIAGNOSIS How do companies determine what they need to do to improve their behavioral systems? One method is to count on top management to know and understand the company and everybody in it. Naturally, the larger and more complex the company, the more difficult it is for executives to know what is going on. Also, top managers are not immune to bias; sometimes their particular functional, organizational, and industry experiences influence their beliefs and perceptions.[52] For example, a top manager whose professional specialty is marketing is likely to see the organization through that lens, and perhaps to miss opportunities in production or supply chain management.

In general, for a complex company, a better way to learn an organization's strengths and weaknesses is to perform a systematic organizational diagnosis. Often companies hire OD consultants to assist them in this effort. The advantages of using these trained outsiders are that they have learned to recognize and overcome their inherent biases, and they take a broad view of the possibilities for change.

There are many ways to do an organizational diagnosis. Common methods include interviewing, observation, and surveys. Each has its strengths and weaknesses. See Table 18.2 for a summary of these. However, all diagnostic methods create the expectation that something will be done with the data that has been gathered. To avoid creating ill will with employees who have taken the time to offer their opinions, managers should carefully consider this factor before launching any data-gathering process.

survey guided development

A method for organizational change that relies heavily on surveys of employees' perceptions about which aspects of organizational functioning are affecting performance, satisfaction, and motivation.

A particular OD method for organizational change that relies heavily on surveys is **survey guided development**. This method surveys employees' perceptions of which aspects of organizational functioning are affecting performance, satisfaction, and motivation.[53] Often the survey results are compared with some standard, such as previously collected data from similar organizations. In this way, areas of weakness are identified before a plan for change is developed.

FEEDBACK In the next step in the OD process, the data from the organizational diagnosis are fed back to the participants. Often the data are presented to groups, which discuss the findings and elaborate upon them. For example, a questionnaire might reveal that many employees think their workload is extremely high. In the feedback session, participants have the opportunity to discuss how they developed those perceptions and what can be done to improve the situation.

PLANNING Information from the diagnosis and the subsequent feedback sessions is collected and analyzed, and a plan for change is proposed. Sometimes at this stage managers invite participation from employees on a variety of organizational levels. For example, the groups that make recommendations might include representatives of line workers, supervisors, middle managers, and top management.

TABLE 18.2 Methods for Organizational Diagnosis

	Strengths	Weaknesses
Interviews	The interviewer can probe for more information The interviewee can volunteer ideas A skilled interviewer builds trust through the interview	Time-consuming Expensive May elicit information the company does not want to know or deal with (personal problems, for example)
Observation	The information obtained is complex and credible	The presence of an observer may affect the behavior being observed
Surveys	Inexpensive to administer to large numbers of people Quick to administer Anonymity allows for the expression of strong opinions Data can be statistically analyzed Quantified results are received favorably by many audiences Results are useful for structuring feedback sessions	The survey may not ask all the right questions There is no ability to probe for more information Some cultures dislike and distrust surveys

All individuals involved in planning must learn what options for change are available to them. For example, they must know how much time and money the organization is willing to invest in change, and they must learn what sorts of training and support are available to implement a change. This often requires a significant time investment in learning about available training and development programs.

INTERVENTION The entire organization is informed about the need for change and about how change will proceed. Patterns of organizational behavior are modified through goal setting, training, learning, practice, and feedback.

FOLLOW-UP EVALUATION Was the intervention a success? A second diagnosis of the organization is performed in order to assess whether the planned change has actually occurred, and, assuming it has, to determine whether it has had the predicted influence on organizational effectiveness. For example, a company might introduce total quality management techniques in order to improve sales. The follow-up evaluation measures how well the TQM techniques were really learned and applied, and also whether they actually affected sales. It is at this point that organizational learning is confirmed. Oftentimes, change agents also return to the organization over a period of years to assess whether the change has been continued.

An OD process is called **action research** when the follow-up leads to generalized knowledge that is published for use by the changed organization and other similar organizations. Of course, companies often prefer not to share their improvements with their competitors. A representative example of action research disseminated beyond the changed organization would be a community mental health center that learns to better integrate its professional and volunteer staffs, and then shares its new approaches with other centers.

You may have noticed that OD is patterned after the scientific method: Select a subject (the organization), study the subject (collect behavioral data), perform an intervention (try to change behaviors), and collect more data (see if behaviors have changed.) This is an effective approach because it is systematic and data-based, thus minimizing bias. The most effective change agents approach the change process with an open mind. Rather than hiring a consultant who advocates a particular type of solution, or following the latest management fad, they scientifically investigate the organization and its issues, and only afterward select an appropriate intervention.

action research
Any OD process in which the outcome leads to generalized knowledge that is published for use by the changed organization and other similar organizations.

appreciative inquiry

An approach to organizational change that identifies an organization's positive characteristics in order to build on them.

positive psychology

The idea that too much of psychology focuses on problem behaviors and difficult people instead of helping people build upon their passions and strengths.

Appreciative Inquiry

In recent years some companies have adopted an approach to organizational change called **appreciative inquiry**, which identifies the positive characteristics of an organization and builds on them.[54] This approach contrasts to the more conventional approaches that discover organizational problems in order to fix them. The appreciative inquiry approach is related to **positive psychology**, the idea that too much of psychology focuses on problem behaviors and difficult people instead of helping individuals build upon their passions and strengths.

The appreciative inquiry approach is based on the assumptions, among others, that how people understand their organization and construct a personal view of it is at the center of every attempt at change, and that change comes from first changing our images of the future.[55] The steps in appreciative inquiry are: 1) discovering and valuing the best of what has already existed in the organization, 2) dreaming and envisioning what might be, 3) dialoguing about what can be, and 4) co-constructing—democratically discussing and creating—what will be.

While the British Broadcasting Corporation (BBC) has historically been known for its creative culture, a culture in which challenging ideas and decisions is the norm, around the turn of the century the culture seemed to be in a slump.[56] It had begun to be seen as less creative, with higher levels of individual competition and lower levels of teamwork. The company's executive committee decided to do a version of an appreciative inquiry intervention to regain a positive focus. In 2002, 10,000 individuals, about 40 percent of the total BBC operation, attended about 200 voluntary meetings at their offices around the world. As part of the intervention, individuals paired up and talked about their positive experiences at the BBC, including successful moments and times of special pride. They were asked to focus on three key questions:[57]

1. What has been the most creative/valued experience in your time at the BBC?
2. What were the conditions that made that experience possible?
3. If those experiences were to become the norm, how would the BBC have to change?

The most powerful stories were then shared with larger groups. According to Sam Berrisford, a participant and an internal communications partner for BBC Radio and Music, the process, "reconnected people with their emotions and gave them a positive sense of what could be. This positive energy created a powerful momentum, people felt that their opinions mattered and that they could make a difference. The organizational mindset was significantly changed.[58]"

Positive Organizational Behavior

A related approach to change is positive organizational behavior, the study and application of positively oriented human resource strengths and psychological capacities that can be measured, developed, and effectively managed to improve performance.[59] You may recall that the trait of self-efficacy describes whether individuals believe that they can actually accomplish a task. Having a positive self-perception leads to the expectation of personal efficacy, and to positive outcomes like making positive choices, such as welcoming a new task; increasing one's effort, such as trying harder on a difficult task; and persevering in the face of problems and even failures.[60]

Researcher Fred Luthans argues that self-efficacy can actually be strengthened by giving people challenging experiences, in which they can master a task, and providing vicarious positive experiences, in which people observe models similar to themselves achieving their goals. Strengthening self-efficacy strengthens organizations, he suggests.

How Does the Change Process Work?: Models

Now that we have examined the fundamental processes of large-scale organizational change, let's take a look at some of the theoretical approaches that underlie the change process itself.

A Three-Stage Model of Change

Social psychologist Kurt Lewin proposed a three-stage model of change that has been widely adopted by managers.[61] Lewin suggested that when undergoing change, organizations normally pass through the following stages: 1) unfreezing, a period in which individuals become aware of the forces for change and begin to see that their own behaviors will have to adapt; 2) changing, or movement, when people develop a plan for, and begin to implement, new behaviors and systems; and 3) refreezing, when the new behaviors are reinforced to become organizational norms. The new organizational norms are expected to continue indefinitely, until a new set of forces suggests the need for more change.

Why is this model useful when applied?[62] The first step in the model, unfreezing, reminds managers that they need to do whatever they can to increase the odds that a change will be successful. They need to pay attention to what significant unfreezing events occurred, and whether these really motivated the people who will have to implement the change. Was it a crisis that motivated the change? Was it managers' analysis of a pending problem? Did affected employees know about these events or this information? During the second step, changing, the model reminds all interested parties that they should be engaged in planning the change effort and outcomes. Finally, as the change is implemented during refreezing, the model directs both management and employees to be involved in the process in a mutually supporting way.

Since Lewin, other researchers have suggested similar models, such as the awakening–mobilizing–reinforcing model[63] and the energizing-envisioning-enabling model.[64] Although there are some differences, these models all pretty much come down to the same thing: awareness of the need for change, mobilizing the organizational members to accept and learn new behaviors, and applying the new behaviors consistently over time in the organization.

Lewin also created **force-field theory**, which has also been quite influential in how managers think about change.[65] The theory is that in organizational life there are always two sets of opposing forces—forces for change and forces against change. When these forces are in balance, the organization will not change. However, if managers can either increase the forces for change, or reduce the forces against change, the organization will change. Too often managers become excited about the possibilities inherent in an organizational change and fail to assess the potential problems. Force-field analysis is a useful model because it encourages managers to recognize both the forces for and the forces against change.

Punctuated Equilibrium Change

The **punctuated equilibrium model** of change suggests that in some organizations, long periods of equilibrium, when change is minimal and incremental, are interrupted by brief periods of radical organizational change.[66] By this way of thinking, organizations coast along indefinitely until forced to change by some mobilizing event.

Continuous Change

In contrast, many organizations experience continuous change,[67] which is significant change that is ongoing. As researchers Shona Brown and Kathleen Eisenhardt put it, "For firms such as Intel, Wal-Mart, 3M, Hewlett-Packard, and Gillette, the ability to change rapidly and continuously, especially by developing new products, is not only a core competence, it is also at the heart of their cultures. For these firms, *change* is not the rare, episodic phenomenon described by the punctuated equilibrium model, but, rather, it is endemic to the way these organizations compete. Moreover, in high-velocity industries with short product cycles and rapidly shifting competitive landscapes, the ability to engage in rapid and relentless continuous change is a crucial capability for survival."[68]

Companies undergoing continuous change neither rigidly plan for change nor chaotically react to it.[69] Their managers may use **semistructures**, an organizational design in which some organizational features are determined and structured, whereas others are undetermined and flexible. For example, a company might determine its project priorities, but not the process by which its products are designed. In this way the company maintains both stability and innovation.

Another way companies manage continuous change is by helping managers create **links in time**. In this process managers continuously and literally envision present and future projects and the transitions between them. Managers who use the links in time approach tend to place more emphasis on time than on events. They see themselves as opportunistic and aggressive. In this way they actually make change a part of their philosophy for doing business.

force-field theory
The theory that change involves forces for organizational change and forces against it—and that managers must either increase the forces for change or reduce the forces against change in order for change to occur.

punctuated equilibrium model
A model of change which suggests that in some organizations, long periods of equilibrium are interrupted by brief periods of radical organizational change caused by some mobilizing event.

semistructures
An organizational design in which some organizational features are determined and structured while others are undetermined and flexible, which help a company manage continuous change.

links in time
Managers' continuous and literal envisioning of present and future projects and the transitions between them, to help a company manage continuous change.

During Planned Change, How Do Individuals and Organizations Learn?

Whatever the method or the theory behind a large-scale organizational change, individuals involved in the change must learn new behaviors. Large-scale organizational change always challenges people to learn new processes, such as altered leadership styles, improved interpersonal skills and enhanced problem solving. Organizations also "learn" in the sense that they retain knowledge.

Where Do People Learn Best?

People can learn in a variety of settings. To develop interpersonal skills, some companies hire consultants to teach their people either on site or off site. Larger companies are likely to use their own corporate universities for this purpose. Sometimes, participants diagnose their own processes and essentially train themselves on the job, as in the hospital case you are about to read. Training that emphasizes only cognitive learning, such as the statistical analysis training that is important to Six Sigma cultures, is often offered online.

Today most companies emphasize the importance and efficacy of learning in real-world settings. Learning on the job helps to assure that what is learned is applicable to the company, and also that what is learned is immediately applied and continually practiced.

What Do People Learn?

Essentially, people learn whatever they need to learn to move the organization in the proposed direction. Maybe everyone in the organization has to learn a new computer program in order to facilitate coordination. Maybe the whole company needs to learn the system-wide process improvements associated with Six Sigma change. The range of possibilities, from straightforward cognitive knowledge to complicated behavioral patterns, is huge.

How Do Organizations Learn?

Consider the case of Huddings Hospital, a university hospital in Sweden that embarked on a quality improvement project. This case exemplifies how learning actually takes place in organizations.[70] The goal of the Huddings project was to improve clinical processes, such as treating heart failure or hip fractures, throughout the hospital. The head facilitator/change agent was a senior cardiologist who had championed successful improvement in his own department.

The first thing the facilitators did at Huddings was to give the hospital staff an overview and framework for the proposed change. The project was to last five years, and eventually it would include 93 separate improvement projects. The facilitators emphasized that the project would utilize experiential learning rather than lecturing. They felt that lecturing on methods for quality improvement would create more resistance to the change than willingness to get going on actual improvements.

Groups throughout the hospital, from doctors and their staffs to administrators, determined what their own improvement projects would be. During the five-year period, these groups developed extensive experience, which they documented and shared with other teams so that all teams could benefit from lessons learned elsewhere. Their documentation included process flow charts, notes on brainstorming sessions, notes on management team decisions on the improvement projects, and progress notes kept by the facilitators. The facilitators routinely solicited feedback from the individuals participating in the program, and encouraged them to reflect on their experience. They made time and space for all participants who requested support for their projects.

What specifically did participants learn? About 60 percent of their learning involved participants developing a new understanding of their own work and how to continually improve it, and about 40 percent involved the particulars of how to solve complex clinical problems.

In some instances, organizations hire outside consultants to assist them in diagnosis, change and follow-up. The case of Huddings Hospital, however, illustrates one way in which an organization can diagnose its own problems and institute system-wide change. Of course, the case also demonstrates how an organization learns. In this setting, the knowledge accumulated by many individuals was systematically collected, retained, and disseminated to organizational members. If any member left the organization, most of what that member had learned about process improvements was retained, either in documents or, because it had been shared, in the collective memory of that person's colleagues. Holding such data in **organizational memory** is a key goal in organizational change. Building an organizational memory involves understanding how organizations learn, how knowledge is retained and transferred within an organization, and how errors are detected.[71]

Of course, the process used at Huddings is not the only way to build organizational memory. To foster learning without decreasing efficiency, some organizations implement **parallel learning structures**, which are groups that operate in parallel with the formal organization. Rather than attempting to change their existing bureaucratic structures and processes, companies create the supplemental structures to enhance organizational learning, innovation and other issues related to organizational adaptation.[72] For example, a company might create a cross-functional team to foster learning and innovation and ask a set of employees to work both on that team and in their traditional roles. The key difference between parallel learning structures and taskforces is that the former are designed specifically to foster learning and innovation, whereas the latter reflect existing company values and norms. The culture of the parallel learning team is designed to foster creativity and openness. For example, when making decisions, using a formal chain of command in which managers decide and employees implement, is minimized.

IBM and Pfizer Inc. are examples of learning organizations. IBM is noted for its investment in employee and organizational learning.[73] Its annual training budget is about $700 million. In addition, in 2004 it initiated a two-year company-wide learning initiative costing $85 million. Some 32,000 IBM executives and managers participated in this program, which focused on changing the role of the manager. The program included a Web-based learning event, an e-coach to help individuals tailor their learning plan, and a large scale, collaborative e-space for sharing best practices and decisions.

Pfizer Inc. has a program called "Retaining Knowledge" that helps the company keep valuable knowledge. Specifically, it helps senior leaders and other key employees who are changing roles to transfer their knowledge and their networks to their successor. Part of the process is meeting with a trained advisor, who facilitates knowledge transfer meetings between the experts and their successors.

An overview of the design of learning organizations is presented in Table 18.3, which contrasts learning organizations with organizations that inhibit learning.

What Are Some Key Ethical Dilemmas During Organizational Change?

As you can imagine, changing an organization raises a variety of ethical dilemmas.

One dilemma concerns the nature of the information individuals are required to give to their organization for purposes of the change. For instance, cultural changes typically require the collection of information about individual values and norms. Individuals may feel that being required to reveal such personal information is a violation of their privacy and independence, and being forced to reveal them may undermine the mutual trust between employee and employer.[74]

Another dilemma concerns the nature of the changes that are espoused. In the case of organizational learning, for example, the question arises whether learning can really occur without challenging the assumptions, ideas, and power of management.[75] As suggested by theorists Tony Huzzard and Katarina Östergren, "The quest for shared meanings and consensus as prerequisites for learning is likely to be problematic. If organizational learning is to have any meaning beyond that of being merely another device for organizational control, *there has to be an explicit recognition of organizational diversity.*"[76] Diversity, in this case, means diversity of viewpoints. The implication is that, for organizations to be effective learners, top-down influence must be minimized and democratic governance that respects diverse views must be an explicit value. There is a fine line between persuasion and coercion.

A related issue is who is to have a voice in creating the targeted organizational values. In the past, unions have challenged such changes as quality of work life (QWL) programs

organizational memory
The storage of many individuals' accumulated knowledge in an organization's documents and/or collective memory.

parallel learning structures
Groups created with the purpose of enhancing organizational learning, innovation and other issues related to organizational adaptation, that operate in parallel with the formal organization.

TABLE 18.3 Organizational Designs That Advance, or Inhibit, Organizational Learning

	The organizational design that inhibits learning. . .	The organizational design that advances learning. . .
Motivational Philosophy	Pays lip service to "soft" issues, such as people relationships, and considers that which can be quantified as the "real" work. People are merely a resource like capital and raw materials.	Assures that no one stakeholder, whether customers, employees, suppliers, the community, or stockholders, dominates management thinking.
Motivational System	• Believes in individual competition. • Is lean and mean, preoccupied with short-term coping and adapting.	• Believes in teamwork. • Makes time for learning.
Decision Making	Has charismatic leaders making the major decisions.	Has leaders who act as teachers and stewards of change.
Culture	Has controlling leaders who are decisive and dominant.	Has approachable leaders who acknowledge their own vulnerability and uncertainty.
Structure	Has functions that are highly separated.	Encourages a shared commitment to learning and thinking systemically.
Job Design	Creates jobs that are compartmentalized.	Takes a holistic approach to problem solving.

Source: Based on information in P. Senge, *The Fifth Discipline: The Art and Science of the Learning Organization* (New York: Currency Doubleday, 1990); E. H. Schein, "Organizational and Managerial Culture as a Facilitator or Inhibitor of Organizational Learning." Working paper for the MIT Organizational Learning Network, May 19, 1994; Joseph Boyett and Jimmie Boyett, *The Guru Guide: The Best Ideas of the Top Management Thinkers* (New York: John Wiley & Sons, 1998).

because they believe the programs usurp their role as the voice of workers. Indeed, recent research suggests that the more strongly union members are committed to their company, the less committed they are to their union.[77] On the other side, research also suggests that the more exposure employees have to employee involvement programs, including QWL, the more committed they are to their unions.[78] It seems that some experienced employees decide that so-called employee involvement programs do not really give them more voice in their organizations.

What Are Some Common Problems During Organizational Change?

According to change expert John Kotter, organizations attempting a system-wide change commit several typical errors. These are[79]:

1. Permitting complacency
2. Failing to create a sufficiently powerful guiding coalition
3. Underestimating the power of vision
4. Undercommunicating the vision
5. Allowing obstacles to get in the way of the new vision
6. Failing to create short-term wins
7. Declaring victory too soon
8. Neglecting to anchor changes firmly in corporate culture

Of these errors, undercommunicating the vision is of particular note. Kotter points out that given that the average total amount of communication to an employee in three months is about 2,300,000 words and numbers, and given that the typical communication of a change vision over that time is 13,400 words or numbers (about the length of one 30-minute speech or one 2,000-word memo), the typical "vision communication" accounts for only .58 percent of the employee's total received communication!

In addition to these factors noted by Kotter, another typical problem in organizational change is weak **transfer of training**. What employees learn in a classroom is often "forgotten," and also not reinforced, when they return to their regular jobs and routines. It was for this reason that the Huddings hospital encouraged employees to develop learning goals and problem solutions while actually on the job. Behaviors and processes learned and developed on the job are more likely to be retained over time.

transfer of training
The transfer of knowledge gained in a classroom setting to other settings.

A final impediment to change is employee silence.[80] Because true empowerment is not the norm in most organizations, companies' dominant tendency may actually be to create a climate of silence in which upward communication is stifled. Under these circumstances, employees believe that speaking up is useless and even dangerous—beliefs that are clearly at odds with any change that requires empowerment, involvement, and different viewpoints.

Which Assumptions About Change Are Important?

Perhaps because it is so complicated and human, the topic of changing organizations sometimes seems to generate as many questions as it does answers. What follows are some of the key assumptions that change consultants and concerned managers are likely to debate when considering large-scale organizational change.

Should the Change Focus on the Process or the Problem?

Managers that want to solve practical business problems face a major question: Are their organization's current processes—including structure, decision making, and culture—up to the task? Can they take on virtually any problem and be confident their people can solve it? Or do they need to change their organization's processes first, and only then (or perhaps simultaneously) tackle the business problems?

Focusing first on organizational process has some pitfalls. For one thing, if they choose to focus first on changing their organization, managers then face the daunting question of what organizational processes, exactly, they should change. This is difficult in part because there are so many factors and so many consulting products from which to choose. Another pitfall is that some people are simply uncomfortable dealing in any way with process issues. Not all businesspeople have had the opportunity to discuss and practice new organizational processes (motivation, group decision making, leadership, conflict management, and so on) in a course like organizational behavior, and some of those who have still resist discussing process in a real life business setting. Furthermore, as change agents repeatedly point out, change is not merely a matter of telling people how to change their processes and then assuming they will be able to implement the instructions. As one executive says, "I had witnessed some very disturbing experiences the past several years with programs such as zero defects, quality circles, and so on. So often these programs were seen as gimmickry by the working people and as magic by the managers. In most cases they were implemented through management edicts and directives. I am not interested in just another short-lived program."[81]

Interestingly, as consultant Mike Beer has observed, sometimes it is the companies that do *not* use high-profile corporate programs for process that are most proficient at large-scale change.[82] And consultants Rosabeth Moss Kanter, Barry A. Stein, and Todd D. Jick suggest that, "Both the popular press and the academic literature tend to consider organizational change as a step-by-step process leading to success. . . . This unrealistic portrayal of the change process [gives] an illusion of control that in fact does not exist. Managers are sometimes misled by consultants or authors who make change seem like a bounded, defined, discrete process with guidelines for success. They feel deceived; instead of a controllable process, they discover chaos."[83]

Reluctant to take on the uncertainty and expense of changing organizational processes, it is no wonder that many managers choose to focus on solving business problems by applying their habitual organizational practices, and hoping for the best.

Is Change Logical or Emotional?

Does change occur primarily because people make logical choices, or because they have emotional reactions? Although both processes are undoubtedly important, today emotional issues are considered more important than ever before. Emotions are aroused particularly at the stages when people develop a sense of urgency about the need for change, and when they buy into—that is, commit to—the change.

Again, consultant John Kotter asserts, "The central issue is never strategy, structure, culture, or systems. All those elements, and others, are important. But the core of the matter is always about changing the behavior of people, and behavior change happens in highly successful situations mostly by speaking to people's feelings. This is true even in organizations that are very focused on analysis and quantitative measurement, even among people who think of themselves as smart in an MBA sense. In highly successful change efforts, people find ways to help others see the problems or solutions in ways that influence emotions, not just thought. Feelings then alter behavior sufficiently to overcome all the many barriers to sensible large-scale change."[84]

Does Change Start at the Top or the Bottom of the Company?

In a traditional, centralized bureaucracy you might expect change to be top down. However, change sometimes appears to occur from the bottom up, initiated by lower level employees. And sometimes it moves from the periphery of the organization to the core, as when a new plant or troubled business unit initiates it.[85] With the popularity of flat, decentralized organizations, modes other than top-down seem more likely than ever before.

In large organizations, programs that are conceived at the top are often out of touch with the realities in different plants, branches and divisions. Such programs may be appropriate for general corporate problems, but they are unlikely to address the highest-priority problems in organizational subunits.[86] Of course, when employees in lower levels of the company do not participate in the diagnosis and planning, they are likely to dismiss the proposed solution as irrelevant to their units.

How Is Change Disseminated?

diffusion of change
The process of disseminating a successful change from one unit to other units in the organization.

A related problem is how to disseminate a successful change from one unit to other units in the organization. This process is known as **diffusion of change**. Managers and other change agents often need help in mapping and supporting the connections needed to turn local improvements into applications elsewhere in the company.[87]

Generally speaking, whether pilot projects disseminate to other units is a function of such factors as how interdependent the units are and whether they use similar measures for performance. Organizational change efforts that do not recognize such factors are more likely to fail. For example, teaching and rewarding a participative leadership style in one division of a company will only be useful in another division if that division is also willing to actually reward participative teams.

How Do Individuals React to Change and How Do Managers Deal with Their Reactions?

Try this: Cross your arms across your chest. Notice which arm is on top. Now cross your arms with the other arm on top. Feel weird? As this demonstration shows, even minor change can be disturbing. Change challenges us to think and act outside of the box. In organizational life, change can feel not merely uncomfortable, but downright threatening. Of course, having negative feelings and concerns about a change is a perfectly normal part of the process.[88] Responding appropriately to change ensures your survival, and your organization's survival as well.

People react to a change in complex ways that can be understood in terms of three factors: beliefs, emotions, and behaviors.[89] First, people develop beliefs about a change. They believe it will succeed or fail, for example. Second, they react emotionally to the change. They may find it exciting or worrisome. Third, they plan or resolve to take some action based on the change. They may volunteer to work the change agent, for example, or they may secretly decide to passively resist. To illustrate how these aspects all come into play, consider the example of an employee who learns that his budget for offering incentives to his distributors will soon be cancelled. The announcement shocks him, especially because he has already planned around having the money. However, despite his initial, emotional reaction, he believes the change is a good one because the savings will be used to improve the product. He decides to support and implement the change.

Individual Predispositions Toward Change

Individuals differ in their readiness for change.[90] Some people resist change because they strongly prefer routine, they react emotionally to change, or they have a short-term focus. Others resist because, regardless of the circumstances, they seldom change their mind. Still others enjoy change.

When change is in the air in your organization, it is helpful to be clear about your own attitude toward change. Take the self-test in Table 18.4 to discover yours.

When Change Is Threatening

Sometimes change poses actual threats to individuals in terms of losing things they value. When a company is purchased, redundant workers are usually laid off. When a company is downsized, some people lose their jobs. When companies are redesigned, some people may gain power and some may lose it. Under such circumstances, resisting the change is a realistic approach for some employees.

Unfortunately, given the likelihood of such events in modern business, many employees are likely to become nervous whenever large-scale organizational change is proposed. Individuals may resist change not only because it is likely to adversely affect them, but simply because they imagine it will.

What Managers Can Do to Foster Change

When managers want to make a change, they should first assess whether their employees are ready for change. See Figure 18.1 for a summary based on two crucial factors describing an individual's readiness for change. The two factors are whether the employee is uncomfortable with the current situation and whether he or she perceives the change as threatening.

Then managers must convince their employees to accept and implement a change.[91] At the same time, they must work hard to prevent resistance to change. To accomplish these goals, they must make special efforts to:

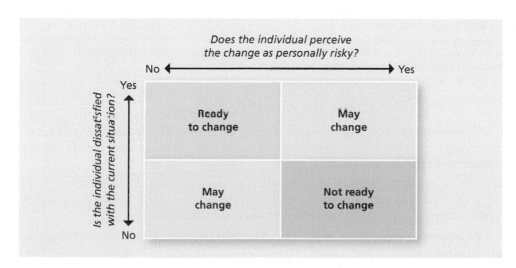

FIGURE 18.1

Is Your Employee Ready to Change?

Source: Adapted from Y. Zeira and J. Avedisian, "Organizational Planned Change: Assessing the Chances for Success," *Organizational Dynamics 17* (4), Spring 1989: 31–45

TABLE 18.4 **Is Change Your Idea of a Good Time?**

Listed below are several statements regarding a person's general beliefs and attitudes about change. Please indicate the degree to which you agree or disagree with each statement by selecting the appropriate number on the scale next to it. Describe yourself as you generally are now, not as you wish to be in the future.

Scale

1 = strongly disagree   2 = disagree   3 = inclined to disagree   4 = inclined to agree   5 = agree   6 = strongly agree

1. _____I generally consider change to be a negative thing.

2. _____I'll take a routine day over a day full of unexpected events any time.

3. _____I like to do the same old things rather than try new and different ones.

4. _____If I were to be informed that there's going to be a significant change regarding the way things are done at work, I would probably feel stressed.

5. _____When I am informed of a change of plans, I tense up a bit.

6. _____When things don't go according to plans, it stresses me out.

7. _____Changing plans seems like a real hassle to me.

8. _____Often, I feel a bit uncomfortable even about changes that may potentially improve my life.

9. _____When someone pressures me to change something, I tend to resist it even if I think the change may ultimately benefit me.

10. _____I often change my mind.

11. _____Once I've come to a conclusion, I'm not likely to change my mind.

12. _____My views are very consistent over time.

Scoring: To obtain your overall average score, add up your points and divide by 12. Research to date on hundreds of subjects has produced a mean score of 2.8, with the range of average scores falling between 2 and 3.5. Scores lower than 2 suggest that you particularly like change. Scores higher than 3.5 suggest you are likely to resist change.

In addition, you can further interpret your score by looking at some question subsets. Questions 1 to 3 measure the extent to which you like routine (the average score is 3.3, with high scores suggesting you do like routine). Questions 4 to 6 measure the extent to which you react emotionally to change (the average score is 3.0, and high scores suggest you do react emotionally). Questions 7 to 9 measure the extent to which you have a short-term focus (the average score is 3.3, and high scores suggest you do have a short-term focus). Questions 10 to 12 measure the extent to which you demonstrate cognitive inflexibility (the average score is 3.1, with high scores suggesting you are inflexible in your thinking).

Source: Adapted from S. Oreg, "Resistance to Change: Developing an Individual Differences Measure," *Journal of Applied Psychology* 88 (4), 2003:680–693. Copyright © 2003 by the American Psychological Association. Reproduced with permission.

1. *Communicate* to their employees the need for the change. This requires an often time-consuming effort and a good working relationship between the initiators of change and the resistors to the change.

2. *Involve* any likely resistors in some aspect of the design and implementation, especially when the managers do not have all the information they need to design and implement the change, or when they need the help of the potential resistors.

3. *Be supportive,* offering training in new skills, and providing emotional support.

4. *Negotiate* by offering incentives to active or potential resistors.

Sometimes, especially when speed is essential, managers may adopt two additional approaches. However, these approaches are not generally recommended, because they are likely to cause such long-term problems as mistrust and sabotage. These approaches are:

5. *Manipulate and co-opt.* Use information selectively in order to scare people into thinking there is a crisis coming and co-opt people by giving them a role but no real influence in the change process.

6. *Coerce* people to accept the change by explicitly or implicitly threatening them.

Are Western Approaches to Change Exportable?

A 1992 study found that less than half of companies with international operations implement OD efforts outside of the United States and Canada.[92] One reason for this is the difficulty of finding OD consultants with the necessary understanding of different cultures. Because the process of change is culture-dependent, change agents must be thoroughly familiar with the culture, both organizational and national, in which they are operating. They must ask themselves which of the culture's values are most deeply held and therefore unlikely to change.[93] They must also make a judgment about how their own values fit with those of the organizational culture.

The approaches to organizational change that are described in this chapter have been developed primarily in the United States, with some applications in other Western countries. International consultants and companies interested in instituting change in other cultures should take into account national values, characteristics, and culture as they approach the change process.[94]

For example, consider the issue of values. As we have seen, OD practitioners often apply a set of values that includes treating individuals as human beings, trusting people, and emphasizing cooperation.[95] Such values are similar to those of companies in Denmark, Norway, and Sweden, but quite different from those of Belgium, Japan, Mexico, Taiwan, and Brazil. OD practitioners in the latter set of cultures should expect resistance if they attempt to impose their own values on the change process by, for example, insisting on employee participation.

Also consider cultural assumptions about the process of change itself. Compared to Chinese managers, Western managers (U.S. and Swiss) prefer to use direct, task-oriented tactics when implementing a change.[96] Chinese managers are more likely than Westerners to value tactics involving personal appeals, the avoidance of confrontation, and an informal approach. For another thing, U.S. organizations value people who take personal risks to help their organizations overcome resistance to innovative ideas. Yet, such innovation champions are much less valued in cultures that rank high on the need for uncertainty avoidance. In these cultures, managers prefer change agents who work through existing rules, norms and procedures to create change.[97]

Another case in point is the differences in attitudes toward OD interventions as practiced in U.S. and Hong Kong firms.[98] A 1996 study suggested that Hong Kong firms have their own understanding of "strategic change." Hong Kong firms are less likely than U.S. firms to emphasize organization-wide interventions aimed at changing organization systems and culture, and are more likely to allow the organization as traditionally designed to implement new company strategies. They are also more likely to implement team-building that is task-oriented rather than team-building that is relationship-oriented.

Finally, consider how the change process works in companies in transitional economies. Estonia is a country that is in transition from communism to a free market. In this society, employees are used to being taken care of, and are less likely to understand the need for change. They may not even be ready for training and learning,[99] let alone ready for full scale organizational change.

In Conclusion

Charles Darwin is quoted as saying, "It is not the strongest of the species that survive, nor the most intelligent, but the one most responsive to change."[100] Although Darwin was not talking about organizations, his comment certainly applies to them. Today's executives know they must understand change and, when possible, manage it.

Apply What You Have Learned. . .

World Class Company: BP

BP is one of the largest oil companies in the world. With more than 100,000 employees,[101] it seeks collaborative, problem-oriented change to enhance innovation throughout its organization.[102] For example, when BP's North American Mid Continent business unit changed its primary business strategy from cost containment to aggressive growth, management developed several new company-wide programs to achieve its goal. These programs included Quick Hits, Action Learning Events, and the Helios awards.

Quick Hits

A foundation of the Quick Hits program was the belief that those closest to actual day-to-day operations would be most likely to come up with innovative ideas for improvements. The corporate purpose behind Quick Hits was to make immediate improvements and thus demonstrate to people in the field that top managers were serious about change that would lead to growth. The Mid Continent organization had a high workload and a performance-driven culture, factors that suggested that its employees would respect real, measurable change.

The Quick Hits program involved employees in coming up with ideas for innovation and implementing their own recommendations. Innovations had to be relatively inexpensive, costing up to about $15,000. The employees were given the power to drop their idea at any time, depending on what they observed about its effect on business results.

When a corporate team interviewed field personnel for their Quick Hits ideas, in two-weeks time more than 300 ideas were submitted. Using a peer voting process, 50 of these were approved for implementation. An example of an improvement was removing some physical restrictions on wellheads to increase production. The Quick Hits initiative challenged, successfully, the assumption that this was impossible, and the change resulted in an annual benefit to the company of about $750,000.

Action Learning Events

In another change program, called Action Learning Events, cross-functional teams of 10 to 15 employees tackled complex business problems that demanded careful analysis by a diverse group. Company leaders assisted in identifying the problem. They also helped by finding ways to free up group members from their day-to-day tasks in order to work on the team.

The teams used a variety of group problem-solving strategies, including brainstorming, to develop a solution to the problem. They then wrote up the problem as a business case, and discussed and further refined their solution. Finally, they made a formal proposal to their managers. If the proposal was approved, they then implemented the solution. An example of a successful project was the development of an electronic tool to identify bottlenecks in the company's production cycle.

Helios Awards

An ongoing project of BP is its Helios Awards program.[103] The program recognizes successful innovations anywhere in the company, and is open to all employees as well as third parties working for the company. By encouraging employees to formally share their innovations, it provides the company with data on innovation throughout the organization and facilitates the sharing of best practices across the company.

The 2005 winner of the Helios Award was an American team working in the Gulf of Mexico. The team developed a new way to estimate pressure in deepwater drilling situations, thus preventing blow-outs and oil spills.

Discuss

1. What has changed at BP?
2. What assumptions about change does BP make?
3. What does this company do to motivate individuals during the change, and prevent any resistance to the change?

Advice from the Pros

Anne M. Mulcahy, President, Xerox Corporation

Anne Mulcahy assumed the presidency of Xerox Corporation on May 11, 2000.[104] The previous president had just been fired after a tenure of one year, during which the company lost $9 billion in market value. Interviewed in *Fast Company,* Mulcahy says, "You can move a company too fast—but you can create a bigger problem by moving it too slowly. Finding the right 'clock speed' for change is all about judgment, about knowing what you can accomplish and who you need to accomplish it. . . . I look at Xerox and think that we've changed more in the past 12 months than in all the 25 years I've been here."

What establishes the success of large-scale organizational change, according to Mulcahy? These are some of the factors that matter:

- Having a team in place that is large enough to get the job done
- Having a team that understands the company culture
- Being able to act aggressively and quickly in a crisis so that the change does not lose momentum when people realize the company and their jobs are at risk
- Being able to deliver tough decisions, such as layoffs, by establishing credibility and making sure people understand the rationale
- Not backing off from tough issues, but also knowing when to stop and take time out to make sure you are not doing stupid things
- When it comes to critical parts of the company, being "damned careful" to be sure you have the best

possible solution (Even announce you will do something without telling people exactly what.)
- Being highly visible (In one three-week period, Mulcahy and Xerox Chairman Paul Allaire met with nearly 60,000 of the 88,000 Xerox employees live, by phone bridges, or in town meetings.)

Mulcahy asserts it is not practical to maintain a level of turnaround, crisis intensity forever. Her goal is to maintain a company culture with a higher level of intensity than before.

Discuss

1. Anne Mulcahy's advice addresses which of the problems that are common in organizational change?
2. Think about Mulcahy's remarks in terms of Lewin's stages of change. What does Mulcahy do to unfreeze, change, and refreeze behaviors? How does she reinforce continuous change?
3. According to this article, what assumptions about change does Mulcahy appear to make?

 Gain Experience

I. Basic Chemical Company: Organizational Diagnosis

The Basic Chemical Company has asked you, a management consultant, to help them improve company decision making. You have just met the company's new president and heard about his needs. The president was chosen by Basic's parent corporation just after they bought out what had been a family-owned business. (Even though the former owners have departed from the scene, there are still half a dozen uncles, cousins, and in-laws scattered throughout the approximately 200-person organization.) Since the new management took over, the company has lost less money each year. Last year it was thought that it might break out of the red, but it missed by a small margin.

Basic's product line is a series of primary chemicals that the company supplies to manufacturers of commercial products such as cosmetics, soaps, and foods. Each order results in a batch run made to the customer's specifications. In a period of 2 weeks, the company may process as many as 75 different orders, ranging in size from several million to hundreds of millions of gallons. Company policy is to process orders according to the date of their receipt, and also to give priority to high-volume customers.

The president takes you on a tour of the plant. You follow an order from its receipt by sales, to the lab, through processing, quality control, and supply chain management. Walking through the plant, you notice that some employees are African-American and others speak in a strange-sounding language that you think might be Portuguese. The president confirms that the company has a high proportion (about 60

percent) of minority (non-white) employees. He says that the company has had no trouble with the various ethnic groups. (Later you learn that one of the company's most trusted black employees was fired recently for stealing scrap materials.)

The president tells you that what he really wants to do is establish better teamwork among the people in his organization. He'd like you to discover some of the factors that prevent full cooperation among key individuals and groups in the system. You find the president to be moderately informed about current management techniques and the science of organizational change.

Next you attend a meeting of the company's executives. The group includes the assistant to the president, general manager, head of sales, head of manufacturing, director of the laboratory, head of quality control (QC), and head of supply chain management. Also present at the meeting are the office manager and a personnel manager/accountant. The president introduces you, gives his reasons for inviting you, and presents a résumé of your professional credentials. You give your pitch about the merits of objective organizational diagnosis and data collection and end by inviting questions from the group.

The head of manufacturing points out that departments within the company vary greatly in size. His own group has 125 people. You ask about the other departments and learn the number of employees in each:

Sales: 15
Laboratory: 5
Quality Control (QC): 25
Supply chain management: 15
Office: 6

Next you ask the group for its impressions of the personnel problems in the company. A lively debate among Sales, Manufacturing, and QC breaks out on the subject of the importance of people versus production in running an organization. QC emphasizes the importance of group cohesion and high morale for getting the job done. Manufacturing seems to disagree with QC, indicating that he believes that the main thing is to get good people into the company to begin with. You notice that whenever Manufacturing speaks, Sales leans forward in his chair with his fist clenched. Sales emphasizes again and again the importance of communication between departments.

While this action is going on, the other managers remain silent. You try to read their expressions but find this difficult. Your only guess is that they don't feel part of the discussion. The conversation ends when the head of the Lab tells a joke about a psychiatrist who cheated on his wife. No one laughs very loud; they all look embarrassed.

Design a Diagnosis

1. Working in small groups, design a diagnosis for this company.

2. Write your main points up on the board and be prepared to present them to the class for discussion.

II. Clarifying Your Assumptions about Change: Defend Your Position

Here are several of the key assumptions that managers should address before they institute a change. On each issue, based on your own organizational experience and what you have read in the text about these issues, decide your position, and then defend it. Your professor will tell you whether to do this in pairs, groups, or a fishbowl in front of the class.

1. In any large-scale organizational change, management should focus on the change process itself.
versus
In any large-scale organizational change, management should focus on the business problem that the company is trying to solve.
2. Change is primarily logical.
versus
Change is primarily emotional.
3. Effective change starts at the top of the company.
versus
Effective change starts at the bottom of the company.

Can You Solve This Manager's Problem?

JW, Inc.

You are the new CEO of JW, Inc., an American company that competes worldwide in a variety of consumer and defense-related products. It has 404,000 employees, with as many as 12 levels between the factory floor and the top management team. Its 25,000 managers average 7 direct reports. More than 130 executives hold the title of vice president or above.

You can expect to have quite a lot of control in the company. Thick planning books containing detailed forecasts for the next five years are an important tool. These plans are given grades, including points for their cover design. Traditionally, the CEO submits questions about them at meetings with the company's business leaders, questions that are designed to test the executives' mettle.

Almost every request for a significant capital expenditure will eventually make it to your desk for a signature, after many others below you have already signed it. JW emphasizes cost cutting.

The company's reward system emphasizes loyalty. Managers think of their positions as rewards for long service, and are quite comfortable in their jobs. Informal meetings are opportunities to put in face time and earn points. Conflict, even when productive, is driven underground.

Discuss

1. What's the problem here?
2. What would be your solution to this problem?
3. Describe how you would implement your solution.

Chapter Summary and Key Terms

What is large-scale organizational change and why do companies attempt it?

Large-scale organizational change is organization-wide. Companies attempt planned, large-scale organizational change because they seek adaptability, cost containment, or competitive advantage, among other things.

large-scale organizational change   472

In large-scale organizational change, what, exactly, changes?

Typically, companies change 1) their strategy and their systems for implementing their strategy, 2) power and decision making, or 3) organizational culture.

reengineering   473
total quality management   474

How do managers structure a planned change?

The traditional way that companies change is by choosing a new corporate strategy and changing organizational systems accordingly. Other ways of structuring an organizational change include organizational development, appreciative inquiry, and positive organizational behavior.

How does the change process work?: Models

Models of change include Lewin's model, the punctuated equilibrium model, and the continuous change model.

During planned change, how do individuals and organizations learn?

Individuals learn either in training settings or on the job. Organizations are also said to learn, by developing such processes as organizational memory and parallel learning structures.

What are some key ethical dilemmas during organizational change?

Change raises such ethical concerns as the nature of the information individuals are asked to give to their organization (should they have to reveal their individual values?) and the nature of the changes to be adopted.

What are some common problems during organizational change?

Typical problems in organizational change are failures of communication, weak transfer of training from the training class to the organization, and employee silence.

Which assumptions about change are important?

Assumptions to examine include whether a change should focus on the process or the problem, whether it is logical or emotional, whether it should start at the top or the bottom of the company, and how change is disseminated.

How do individuals react to change and how do managers deal with their reactions?

Some individuals enjoy change and some don't. Managers can deal with individual reactions by, among other things, communicating clearly the need for the change and involving potential resistors in the change.

Are Western approaches to change exportable?

Only to some extent. Although some change is logically based, many aspects of change are culture-dependent.

Explorations

1. The Organization Development Network

This organization's Web site lists U.S. and international programs and conferences designed for individuals who specialize in change management. Does this career appeal to you?

2. The business of diversity training

Web search for "diversity training" to check out the multi-million-dollar diversity training industry. What sorts of training are currently popular?

3. Minorities in business

To get up-to-date information on: a) women in management, see the Web site for the Catalyst organization;

b) blacks, Hispanics, Asian-Americans, Native Americans, and other racial minorities in business, Web search for each race and "business" and you will find a variety of professional organizations; c) older workers in business, Web search for "older workers in business."

4. Appreciative inquiry

Web search for "appreciative inquiry" and find out what advances are taking place using this approach to organization change.

5. Learning organizations

Web search for "learning organizations" and find 10 different processes that characterize such organizations.

References

[1] J. P. Kotter and D. S. Cohen, *The Heart of Change: Real-Life Stories of How People Change Their Organizations* (Boston, MA: Harvard Business School Press, 2002).

[2] R. Foster and S. Kaplan, *Creative Destruction: Why Companies That Are Built to Last Underperform the Market—and How to Successfully Transform Them* (New York: Doubleday, 2001).

[3] R. Foster and S. Kaplan, *Creative Destruction: Why Companies That Are Built to Last Underperform the Market—and How to Successfully Transform Them* (New York: Doubleday, 2001).

[4] P. C. Nutt, "Helping Top Management Avoid Failure during Planned Change," *Human Resource Management 31* (4), 1992:319–354.

[5] M. D. Cohen, J. G. March, and J. P. Olsen, "Garbage-Can Model of Organizational Choice," *Administrative Science Quarterly 17,* 1972:178–184.

[6] C. R. Leana, "Stability and Change as Simultaneous Experiences in Organizational Life," *Administrative Science Quarterly 25* (4), 2000:753–759.

[7] P. P. M. A. R. Heugens and H. Schenk, "Rethinking Corporate Restructuring," *Journal of Public Affairs 4* (1), January 2004:87–101.

[8] C. R. Leana, "Stability and Change as Simultaneous Experiences in Organizational Life," *Administrative Science Quarterly 25* (4), 2000:753–759.

[9] T. Burns and G. M. Stalker, *The Management of Innovation* (London: Tavistock, 1961).

[10] R. Sennett, *The Corrosion of Character: The Personal Consequences of Work and the New Capitalism* (New York: Norton, 1998).

[11] D. Ancona, T. Kochan, M. Scully, J. Van Maanen, and D. E. Westney, *Managing for the Future: Organizational Behavior & Processes,* 2nd ed. (Cincinnati, OH: South-Western College Publishing, 1999).

[12] M. Hammer and J. Champy, *Reengineering the Corporation: A Manifesto for Business Revolution* (New York: HarperBusiness, 2001). The cases of IBM and Duke Power are also summarized from this book.

[13] N. Bhuiyan, V. Thomson, and D. Gerwin, "Implementing Concurrent Engineering," *Research Technology Management 49* (1), January/February 2006:38–43.

[14] S. C. Voelpel, M. Leibold, and E. B. Tekie, "The Wheel of Business Model Reinvention: How to Reshape Your Business Model to Leapfrog Competitors," *Journal of Change Management 4* (3), September 2004:259–276.

[15] J. E. Ross, *Total Quality Management* (Delray Beach, FL: St. Lucie Press, 1993):102.

[16] "TQM Models and Their Effectiveness in New Zealand Water Utilities Services," *TQM Magazine 18* (5), September 2206:440–454; K.B. Ooi, A. Veeri, L.K. Yin, and L.S. Vellapan, "Relationships of TQM Practices and Employees' Propensity to Remain: An Empirical Case Study," *TQM Magazine 18* (5), September 2006:528–541.

[17] J. E. Ross, *Total Quality Management* (Delray Beach, FL: St. Lucie Press, 1993):102.

[18] "Malcolm Baldrige National Quality Award: 2004 Award Winner," http://www.nist.gov/public_affairs/BamaPDFfinal.pdf. Accessed October 16, 2005.

[19] The Malcolm Baldrige National Quality Award was instituted in 1987. See http://www.quality.nist.gov/Zytec_91.htm.

[20] M. Beer, "Why Total Quality Management Programs Do Not Persist: The Role of Management Quality and Implications for Leading a TQM Transformation," *Decision Sciences 34* (4), Fall 2003:623–642.

[21] M. Poole, R. Lansbury, and N. Wailes, "A Comparative Analysis of Developments in Industrial Democracy," *Industrial Relations 40* (3), July 2001:490–525.

[22] R. E. Walton, "Establishing and Maintaining High Commitment Work Systems," in J. R. Kimberly, R. H. Miles and Associates, eds., *The Organizational Life Cycle: Issues in the Creation, Transformation, and Decline of Organizations* (San Francisco, CA: Jossey-Bass, 1980):208–290; C. A. O'Reilly and J. A. Chatman, "Culture as Social Control: Corporations, Culture and Commitment," in B. M. Staw and L. L. Cummings, eds., *Research in Organizational Behavior 18* (Greenwich, CT: JAI Press, 1996):157–200.

[23] R. L. Daft and K. E. Weick, "Toward a Model of Organizations as Interpretation Systems," *Academy of Management Review 9,* 1984:284–295; M. M. Crossan, H. W. Lane, R. E. White, and L. Djurfeldt, "Organizational Learning: Dimensions for a Theory," *International Journal of Organizational Analysis 3* (4), October 1995:337–360. See also C. Argyris and D. Schön, *Theory in Practice* (San Francisco, CA: Jossey-Bass, 1974); C. Argyris, "Reflection and Beyond in Research on Organizational Learning," *Management Learning 35* (4), 2004: 507–509.

[24] M. M. Crossan, H. W. Lane, R. E. White, and L. Djurfeldt, "Organizational Learning: Dimensions for a Theory," *International Journal of Organizational Analysis 3* (4), October 1995:337–360.

[25] I. Nonaka and H. Takeuchi, *The Knowledge Creating Company* (Oxford: Oxford University Press, 1995).

[26] M. M. Crossan, H. W. Lane, and R. E. White, "An Organizational Learning Framework: From Intuition to Institution," *Academy of Management Review 24* (3), July 1999:522–537.

[27] M. M. Crossan, H. W. Lane, and R. E. White, "An Organizational Learning Framework: From Intuition to Institution," *Academy of Management Review 24* (3), July 1999:522–537.

[28] P. Senge, *The Fifth Discipline: The Art and Science of the Learning Organization* (New York: Currency Doubleday, 1990); E. H. Schein, "Organizational and Managerial Culture as a Facilitator or Inhibitor of Organizational Learning," Massachusetts Institute of Technology, working paper for the MIT Organizational Learning Network, May 19, 1994.

[29] "Training Top 100: Top Five Profile & Ranking," *Training,* March 2004:42, http://www.trainingmag.com. Accessed October 15, 2005.

[30] B. D. Janz and P. Prasarnphanich, "Understanding the Antecedents of Effective Knowledge Management: The Importance of a Knowledge-Centered Culture," *Decision Sciences 34* (2), Spring 2003:351–384.

[31] "Brain Teasing," *The Economist,* October 13, 2005, http://www.economist.com/research/articles. Accessed October 15, 2005.

[32] C. Soo, T. Devinney, D. Midgley, and A. Deering, "Knowledge Management: Philosophy, Processes, and Pitfalls," *California Management Review 44* (4), Summer 2002:129–150.

[33] W. B. Johnston and A. E. Packer, *Workforce 2000: Work and Workers for the 21st Century* (Indianapolis, IN: Hudson Institute, 1987).

[34] S. Rynes and B. Rosen, "A Field Survey of Factors Affecting the Adoption and Perceived Success of Diversity Training," *Personnel Psychology 48* (2), Summer 1995:247–270.

[35] W. E. Watson, K. Kumar and L. K. Michaelsen, "Cultural Diversity's Impact on Interaction Process and Performance: Comparing Homogeneous and Diverse Task Groups," *Academy of Management Journal 36*, 1993:590–602; R. J. Ely and D. A. Thomas, "Cultural Diversity at Work: The Effects of Diversity Perspectives on Work Group Processes and Outcomes," *Administrative Science Quarterly 46*, 2001:229–273.

[36] J. T. Poizer, L. P. Milton, and W. B. Swann Jr., "Capitalizing on Diversity: Interpersonal Congruence in Small Work Groups," *Administrative Science Quarterly 47* (2), June 2002:296–324.

[37] A. Donnelion, "Crossfunctional Teams in Product Development: Accommodating the Structure to the Process," *Journal of Product Innovation Management 10*, 1993:377–392.

[38] P. Wright, S. P. Ferris, J. S. Hiller, and M. Kroll, "Competitiveness through Management of Diversity: Effects on Stock Price Valuation," *Academy of Management Journal 38* (1), February 1995:272–287.

[39] T. R. Zenger and B. S. Lawrence, "Organizational Demography: The Differential Effects of Age and Tenure Distributions on Technical Communication," *Academy of Management Journal 32*, 1989:353–376; C. A. O'Reilly, D. F. Caldwell, and W. P. Barnett, "Work Group Demography, Social Integration, and Turnover," *Administrative Science Quarterly 34*, 1989:21–37.

[40] K. Y. Williams and C. A. O'Reilly, III, "Demography and Diversity in Organizations: A Review of 40 Years of Research," in B. M. Staw and L. L. Cummings, eds., *Research in Organizational Behavior 20*, 1998: 77–140.

[41] J. A. Chatman, J. T. Polzer, S. G. Barsade, and M. A. Neale, "Being Different Yet Feeling Similar: The Influence of Demographic Composition and Organizational Culture on Work Processes and Outcomes," *Administrative Science Quarterly 43* (4), December 1998:749–780.

[42] A. M. Morrison, *The New Leaders: Guidelines on Leadership Diversity in America* (San Francisco, CA: Jossey-Bass, 1992).

[43] P. S. Pande, R. P. Neuman, and R. R. Cavanagh, *The Six Sigma Way* (New York: McGraw-Hill, 2000).

[44] P. S. Pande, R. P. Neuman, and R. R. Cavanagh, *The Six Sigma Way* (New York: McGraw-Hill, 2000):4.

[45] P. S. Pande, R. P. Neuman, and R. R. Cavanagh, *The Six Sigma Way* (New York: McGraw-Hill, 2000):77.

[46] L. E. Greiner, A. Bhambri, and T. G. Cummings, "Searching for a Strategy to Teach Strategy," *Academy of Management Learning & Education 2* (4), December 2003:402–420.

[47] F. Heller and G. Yukl, "Participation, Managerial Decision Making, and Situational Variables," *Organizational Behavior and Human Performance 4*, 1969:227–241; J. L. Cotton, D. A. Vollrath, K. C. Frogatt, M. L. Lengnick-Hall, and K. R. Jennings, "Employee Participation: Diverse Forms and Different Outcomes," *Academy of Management Review 13*, 1988:8–22; W. C. Kim and R. Mauborgne, "Procedural Justice, Strategic Decision Making and the Knowledge Economy," *Strategic Management Journal 19*, 1998:323–328; R. Lines, "Influence of Participation in Strategic Change: Resistance, Organizational Commitment and Change Goal Achievement," *Journal of Change Management 4* (3), September 2004:193–215.

[48] S. W. Floyd and B. Wooldridge, "Middle Management's Strategic Influence and Organizational Performance," *Journal of Management Studies 34* (3), May 1997:465–488.

[49] W. C. Kim and R. Mauborgne, "Strategy, Value Innovation, and the Knowledge Economy," *Sloan Management Review 40* (3), Spring 1999:41–54, 52.

[50] R. Beckhard, *Organization Development: Strategies and Models* (Reading, MA: Addison-Wesley, 1969).

[51] OD Network, "Principles of Practice," www.odnetwork.org/principlesofpractice.html. Accessed March 2, 2005.

[52] C. Bowman and K. Daniels, "The Influence of Functional Experience on Perceptions of Strategic Priorities," *British Journal of Management 6* (3), September 1995:157–167.

[53] D. L. Hausser, P. A. Pecorella and A. L. Wissler, *Survey-Guided Development II: A Manual for Consultants Consultants* (La Jolla, California: University Associates Publishers and Consultants, 1977); S. E. Seashore, "Surveys in Organizations," in J. W. Lorsch, ed., *Handbook of Organizational Behavior* (Englewood Cliffs, NJ: Prentice Hall, Inc., 1987):140–154.

[54] D. L. Cooperrider and S. Srivastva, "Appreciative Inquiry in Organizational Life," in W. W. Pasmore and R. W. Woodman, eds., *Research in Organization Change and Development 1* (Greenwich, CT: JAI Press, 1987):129–169.

[55] F. Barrett and R. Fry, "Appreciative Inquiry in Action: The Unfolding of a Provocative Invitation," in R. Fry, F. Barrett, J. Seiling, and D. Whitney, eds., *Appreciative Inquiry and Organizational Transformation* (Westport, CT: Quorum Books, 2002):1–26.

[56] S. Berrisford, *Strategic Communication Management 9* (3), April 2005:22–25.

[57] S. Berrisford, *Strategic Communication Management 9* (3), April 2005:22–25,23.

[58] S. Berrisford, *Strategic Communication Management 9* (3), April 2005:22–25,24.

[59] F. Luthans, "Positive Organizational Behavior: Developing and Managing Psychological Strengths," *Academy of Management Executive 16* (1), February 2002:57–75.

[60] F. Luthans, "Positive Organizational Behavior: Developing and Managing Psychological Strengths," *Academy of Management Executive 16* (1), February 2002:57–75.

[61] K. Lewin, "Frontiers in Group Dynamics," *Human Relations 1*, 1947:5–41.

[62] R. E. Levasseur, "People Skills: Change Management Tools—Lewin's Change Model," *Interfaces 35* (4), July/August 2001:71–73.

[63] N. Tichy and M. Devanna, *The Transformational Leader* (New York: John Wiley, 1986).

[64] D. Nadler and M. Tushman, "Organizational Framebending: Principles for Managing Reorientation," *Academy of Management Executive 3*, 1989:194–202.

[65] K. Lewin, "Frontiers in Group Dynamics," *Human Relations 1*, 1947:5–41; K. Lewin, *Field Theory in Social Science* (New York: Harper and Row, 1951).

[66] E. Romanelli and M. L. Tushman, "Organizational Transformation as Punctuated Equilibrium: An Empirical Test," *Academy of Management Journal 5*, 1994:1141–1166.

[67] S. L. Brown and K. M. Eisenhardt, "The Art of Continuous Change: Linking Complexity Theory and Time-Paced Evolution in Relentlessly Shifting Organizations," *Administrative Science Quarterly 42* (1), March 1997:1–34; K. E. Weick and R. E.

Quinn, "Organizational Change and Development," *Annual Review of Psychology 50,* 1999:361–386.

[68] S. L. Brown and K. M. Eisenhardt, "The Art of Continuous Change: Linking Complexity Theory and Time-Paced Evolution in Relentlessly Shifting Organizations," *Administrative Science Quarterly 42* (1), March 1997:1–34, 1.

[69] S. L. Brown and K. M. Eisenhardt, "The Art of Continuous Change: Linking Complexity Theory and Time-Paced Evolution in Relentlessly Shifting Organizations," *Administrative Science Quarterly 42* (1), March 1997:1–34.

[70] J. Thor, K. Wittlöv, B. Herrlin, M. Brommels, O. Svensson, J. Skår, and J. Øvretveit, "Learning Helpers: How They Facilitated Improvement and Improved Facilitation—Lessons from a Hospital-Wide Quality Improvement Initiative," *Quality Management in Health Care 13* (1), January–March 2004:60–74.

[71] R. Vince, K. Sutcliffe, and F. Olivera, "Organizational Learning: New Directions," *British Journal of Management 13* (3) (Supplement 2), September 2002:S1.

[72] G. R. Bushe, "Use of a Parallel Learning Structure to Implement System Transforming Innovations: The Case of Statistical Process Control," *Journal of Managerial Psychology 4* (4), 1989:25–31.

[73] "Training Top 100: Top Five Profile & Ranking," *Training,* March 2004:42, www.trainingmag.com. Accessed October 15, 2005.

[74] J. M. Stanton and E. M. Weiss, "Organisational Databases of Personnel Information: Contrasting the Concerns of Human Resource Managers and Employees," *Behaviour & Information Technology 22* (5), September 2003:291–304.

[75] M. Easterby-Smith, M. Crossan, and D. Nicolini, "Organizational Learning: Debates Past, Present, and Future," *Journal of Management Studies 37* (6), 2000:783-796.

[76] T. Huzzard and K. Östergren, "When Norms Collide: Learning under Organizational Hypocrisy," *British Journal of Management 13* (3) (Supplement 2), September 2002:s47–s59, s49.

[77] R. C. Hoell, "How Employee Involvement Affects Union Commitment," *Journal of Labor Research 25* (2), Spring 2004:267–277.

[78] M. W. Fields and J. W. Thacker, "Influence of Quality of Work Life on Company and Union Commitment," *Academy of Management Journal 35* (2), June 1992:439–450; R. C. Hoell, "How Employee Involvement Affects Union Commitment," *Journal of Labor Research 25* (2), Spring 2004:267–277.

[79] J. P. Kotter, *Leading Change* (Boston, MA: Harvard Business School Press, 1966).

[80] E. W. Morrison and F. J. Milliken, "Organizational Silence: A Barrier to Change and Development in a Pluralistic World," *Academy of Management Review 25* (4), October 2000:706–725.

[81] M. Beer, "The Critical Path for Change: Keys to Success and Failure in Six Companies," in R. H. Kilmann, T. J. Covin and Associates, *Corporate Transformation: Revitalizing Organizations for a Competitive World* (San Francisco, CA: Jossey-Bass Publishers, 1989):17–45, 25.

[82] M. Beer, "The Critical Path for Change: Keys to Success and Failure in Six Companies," in R. H. Kilmann, T. J. Covin and Associates, *Corporate Transformation: Revitalizing Organizations for a Competitive World* (San Francisco, CA: Jossey-Bass Publishers, 1989):17–45.

[83] R. M. Kanter, B. A. Stein and T. D. Jick, "The Challenges of Execution: Roles and Tasks in the Change Process," in D. Ancona, T. Kochan, M. Scully, J. Van Maanen, and D. E. Westney, *Managing for the Future: Organizational Behavior & Processes,* 2nd ed. (Cincinnati, OH: South-Western College Publishing, 1999):M–8, 11–30, 13.

[84] J. P. Kotter and D. S. Cohen, *The Heart of Change: Real-Life Stories of How People Change Their Organi-*

zations (Boston, MA: Harvard Business School Press, 2002):x.

85 M. Beer, "The Critical Path for Change: Keys to Success and Failure in Six Companies," in R. H. Kilmann, T. J. Covin and Associates, *Corporate Transformation: Revitalizing Organizations for a Competitive World* (San Francisco, CA: Jossey-Bass Publishers, 1989):17–45.

86 M. Beer, "The Critical Path for Change: Keys to Success and Failure in Six Companies," in R. H. Kilmann, T. J. Covin and Associates, *Corporate Transformation: Revitalizing Organizations for a Competitive World* (San Francisco, CA: Jossey-Bass Publishers, 1989):17–45.

87 P. S. Goodman and D. M. Rousseau, "Organizational Change That Produces Results: The Linkage Approach," *Academy of Management Executive 18* (3), August 2004:7–19.

88 M. Jarrett, "Tuning into the Emotional Drama of Change: Extending the Consultant's Bandwidth," *Journal of Change Management 4* (3), September 2004:247–258.

89 S. K. Piderit, "Rethinking Resistance and Recognizing Ambivalence: A Multidimensional View of Attitudes Toward an Organizational Change," *Academy of Management Review 25* (4), *2000: 783–794.*

90 S. Oreg, "Resistance to Change: Developing an Individual Differences Measure," *Journal of Applied Psychology 88* (4), August 2003:680–693.

91 J. P. Kotter and L. A. Schlesinger, "Choosing Strategies for Change," *Harvard Business Review 57* (2), March/April 1979:106–114.

92 G. C. McMahan and R. W. Woodman, "The Current Practice of Organization Development within the Firm," *Group and Organization Management 17* (2), 1992:117–134.

93 A. M. Jaeger, "Organization Development and National Culture: Where's the Fit?" *Academy of Management Review 11* (1), January 1986:178–190.

94 P. Sorensen Jr., T. Head, N. Mathys, J. Preston and D. Cooperrider, *Global and International Organizational Development* (Champaign, IL: Stipes, 1995).

95 R. Tannenbaum and S. A. Davis, "Values, Man and Organizations," *Industrial Management Review 10* (2), 1969:67–83.

96 G. Yukl, P. P. Fu, and R. McDonald, "Cross-Cultural Differences in Perceived Effectiveness of Influence Tactics for Initiating or Resisting Change," *Applied Psychology: An International Review 52* (1), January 2003:68–82.

97 S. Shane, S. Venkataraman, and I. MacMillan, "Cultural Differences in Innovation Championing Strategies," *Journal of Management 21* (5), 1995:931–952.

98 C.-M. Lau, G. C. McMahan, and R. W. Woodman, "An International Comparison of Organization Development Practices: The USA and Hong Kong," *Journal of Organizational Change Management 9* (2), 1996:4–19.

99 R. Alas and S. Sharifi, "Organizational Learning and Resistance to Change in Estonian Companies," *Human Resource Development International 5* (3), September 2002:313–331.

100 J. McLean, "Responding to Change Ensures Survival," *British Journal of Administrative Management 44,* December 2004/January 2005:16.

101 BP.com, accessed May 23, 2006.

102 This case draws largely on the following article: R. Ziegler, "Anyone Here Have Any Bright Ideas?" *Outlook Journal,* January 2002, http://www.accenture.com. Accessed May 18, 2006.

103 http://www.bp.com/genericarticle.do?categoryId=9002633&contentId=2000564. Accessed May 23, 2006.

104 Based on information in K. H. Hammonds, "The Not-So-Quick Fix," *Fast Company,* July 2001, in http://www.fastcompany.com/lead/lead_feature/mulcahy.html. Accessed November 11, 2001; and A. Mulcahy, "CRN Interview: Anne Mulcahy, Xerox," CRN Interview, March 28, 2005, Issue 1139:22.

19

OB Is for Life

Preview

Beyond this book, how can you continue to learn about OB?

What more do you need to know about the scientific approach to human behavior?
How do social scientists apply the scientific method?

How do social scientists test hypotheses?
Analizing Hypotheses
What some key ethical issues in social science research?

How do you read a scientific journal article?
How are articles structured?
How do articles integrate practical applications?
What are some basic types of statistical analyses?
What are the different roles of academic and practitioner journals?

What are some current controversies that may affect the study and practice of OB in the future?
Who should organizations serve?
What should OB professors study and teach?
What you see is what you learned to look for. But is it the truth?

What resources can you use to learn even more about human behavior in organizations?
Further education
Further reading
Use the human resource management (HRM) department in your company
Current techniques and fads

Conclusion to this chapter. . . and this book

Honest Tea

Should OB researchers pay more attention to organizational processes and outcomes that serve the good of society? Are alternative organization design the wave of the future? What do you think?

Consider Honest Tea, the company that makes the first fully organic bottled tea. With more than twenty bottle varieties and outlets in 10,000 food and convenience stores, the company has had an annual compound growth rate of 65% for the past ten years. It measures its outcomes not only in growth, but in factors like its donations to community partners, its purchases from those partners, and its support of organic growers in terms of the pounds of organic ingredients it purchases.

To illustrate, Honest Tea partners with farmers in Haarlem, South Africa, to produce several of its red tea varieties. The company makes fair trade purchases from that community that helps address community development and capacity building. In the U.S., it partners in a similar way with the Crow Nation to produce First Nation Peppermint tea.

Co-Founder, President and TeaEO Seth Goldman (see accompanying photo) is not interested in running a business that just does business as usual. He is interested in how many bottles the company can sell to expand this model of business, to make the impact of the model more dramatic and powerful. The company's mission is a powerful internal motivator: Associates in the company know they are doing more than selling a bottle of tea, they are creating relationships and helping disadvantaged communities across the globe.

Would you want to work for a company like Honest Tea? Figuring out how to integrate your personal values with your organizational life is just one of the questions that this textbook cannot answer. In this chapter we offer some guidelines on how and where to learn more.

Beyond This Book, How Can You Continue to Learn About OB?

Having added the contents of this book to your store of practical knowledge, you are now much better equipped to deal with life in organizations. From here on out your tasks are to:

■ Hone your interpersonal and organizational understanding and skills.

■ Gain experience. Look for feedback on your strengths and weaknesses. Identify your unique challenges and work on them. Determine how to factor your personal values into your organizational life.

■ Launch your career successfully, building the necessary expertise, reputation, and networks to create a power base to advance yourself, or perhaps run your own company.

Along the way, you may want to refer back to what you have studied here. This book offers two key takeaways:

1. *Your personal profile.* By working through the various tests and exercises you have created an extensive profile of your personality, preferences, and tendencies. Knowing that you have a tendency to be a bit autocratic in your leadership style may help you to see why people try to avoid you. Or reminding yourself that one of your strengths is to be an extravert, but that managing with this strength may intimidate some individuals, should help you to manage a technically excellent but shy employee.

2. *Guidelines for approaching common problems you will face in organizations.* Having studied the problem-solving approaches described here, you can now easily use the chapters as guides for thinking through common organizational problems. For example, do you have a major decision to make? The approaches posed in the chapter on decision making walk you through the key issues you should consider. From teams to leadership, you have here succinct summaries of some of the best and most current approaches, tested by a cast of thousands of researchers and their subjects. You can take advantage of these carefully crafted ideas throughout your career.

Alas, absorbing this book is not enough. It is not much of an exaggeration to say that in organizational life you will be either a student of human behavior or a victim of it. One reason is that every one of us has a lot to learn about human behavior, and we continue learning throughout our lives. Another reason is that because business is so fast-paced, complex, and changing, managers face new, previously unimagined people problems all the time, and to be effective they must stay up-to-date. Looking forward, what else would you like to learn about life in organizations? Where will you learn what you need to know?

The purpose of this last chapter is to outline for you the fundamentals of a strategy for lifelong learning in OB. We will examine:

1. What you need to know to follow future scientific research on human behavior in organizations.

2. Some current debates and controversies in the field that may influence your thinking. For example, should the field focus more on outcome variables such as social impact, as illustrated in the case of Honest Tea?

3. Resources that can help you to learn more, including human resources experts, training and further education, and some classic reads.

4. Whether to take seriously popular techniques and fads.

What More Do You Need to Know about the Scientific Approach to Human Behavior?

Most of what you have read here is based on the social psychology of organizations—the study of organizations and organizational phenomena using research techniques developed by the disciplines of psychology and sociology, and, to a lesser extent, political science and anthropology. While textbook writers could base their books on the opinions of senior executives and other organizational members, they choose, instead, to present a synthesis of research. Why do we textbook writers generally favor this research-based approach?

One reason is that individuals who work for particular organizations, whatever their level, naturally tend to have a narrow view of the world. The CEO of Widgetry has typically spent most of his or her working life understanding how to manufacture and market widgets, and when a broader picture is needed—say, for instance, a new organizational design seems warranted—he or she knows it is a good idea to call in a generalist. The generalists are the professors and consultants whose business is to know about a wide variety of possibilities, as well as to have researched these possibilities to determine which are most likely to be effective in a given situation. It is certainly true that you can learn a great deal from the CEO of Widgetry, and his or her advice is especially likely to be useful if you are in a similar type of company, facing similar problems, in a similar industry. However, if you want a broader picture that allows you to weigh alternatives, you are probably better off learning from someone who has synthesized information from 20 CEOs, or who has studied 30 companies in as many industries, and who has identified and weighed a variety of approaches to problems.

Another reason we favor basing a textbook on social science research is that researchers pursue answers to questions in a systematic way. Of course, over the years, countless individuals have debated what "systematic" should mean in social science research. While this debate will continue as long as there are social scientists, at the same time researchers today have clear standards for determining whether something is "true" and whether they can reasonably assert that x causes y.

Studies of human beings and their organizations do not predict future behavior as accurately as analyzing a chemical reaction predicts the effects of mixing ammonia and chlorine. Individual human beings and their interactions are complicated indeed, so much so that research results can only suggest some probability, and often not a very high one, that given x, y will occur. Thus you must read social science results a bit differently than hard science results: As a manager, you should probably think of them as hypotheses to be further tested in the real world situation you are facing.

How Do Social Scientists Apply the Scientific Method?

At the beginning of an investigation, a social scientist develops a theory. The theory is usually based on what has been learned in previous research, or on ideas derived from the study of a particular case. The purpose of theory is to explain reality, and generally theories are rather abstract. An example of a theory is, "Behavior in organizations can be influenced by reward and punishment." Such a statement is a generalization that, if proven by subsequent research, can be a useful guide for managers.

Next the scientist creates hypotheses, which are ideas about what relationships might be true given the theoretical framework in which the scientist is operating. An example of a hypothesis is, "Absenteeism can be reduced by docking the pay of individuals who fail to come to work." Note that this statement is concrete: Both pay and absenteeism can be observed and measured. The theory that behavior is influenced by reward and punishment is **operationalized** by testing the hypothesis.

Hypotheses have two fundamental components. On the one hand, **independent variables** (sometimes called "predictor variables") are the factors that influence some outcome. On the other hand, the outcomes are called **dependent variables** (also, "criterion variables"). In the example we have been using, cutting pay is the independent variable whereas the rate of absenteeism is the dependent variable. *If* we cut pay, we *may* reduce absenteeism.

In studies of business organizations, independent variables might be anything from the nature of the boss–subordinate relationship to perceived group cohesiveness, or even organizational culture. Typical dependent variables are performance, absenteeism, and turnover. Of course, each of these is itself a complex concept and must be handled carefully. For instance, culture is a multifaceted concept, and absenteeism is not always a negative for a company.[1]

A further complexity is that sometimes a concept is an independent variable, whereas at other times it is a dependent variable. For example, we might test the hypothesis that commitment to one's company affects one's productivity, or, in contrast, we might test the hypothesis that one's productivity, perhaps because it improves a person's mood at work, affects commitment to one's company.

operationalize
To make a theory practical by using it to form specific hypotheses that can be tested.

independent variable
A variable that influences some outcome; also called a "predictor variable."

dependent variable
An outcome; also called a "criterion variable."

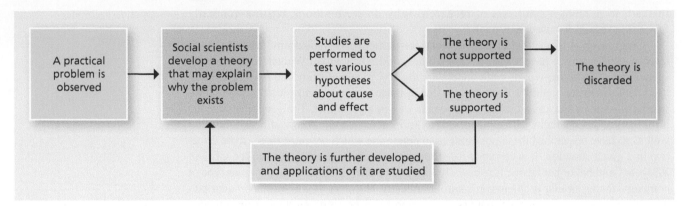

FIGURE 19.1 **How Social Scientists Develop and Test Theories**

Figure 19.1 depicts the process by which social scientists develop, test, and, ultimately, refine theories.

How Do Social Scientists Test Hypotheses?

Here are several common ways in which researchers operationalize and test hypotheses[2]:

Field studies.

Researchers interact with their subjects in their real-life organizations. They observe them, and may even participate or live with them. The researchers make "field notes," which may be based on the researcher's real time observations and impressions or on a pre-determined list of behaviors and activities to observe.

Questionnaire studies.

Researchers ask participants to fill out a survey, relying on language and its interpretation to investigate participants' thoughts and behaviors.

Laboratory experiments.

Research is done in settings that allow the researcher to rigorously control the conditions under which observations are made. In organizational research, such settings might be anywhere, even an office. They are not limited to the stereotypical laboratory with two-way mirrors and experimenters in white coats.

Examining secondary-source materials.

Researchers examine organizational records, such as transcripts of meetings, policy manuals, newsletters, and personnel files. They review available data on absences, turnover, and performance.

Sometimes researchers use more than one method. For example, it would be common to examine a company's existing data on employee turnover while doing a field study of employee dissatisfaction. See Table 19.1 for an examination of the pros and cons of using these different methods.

Analyzing Hypotheses

Generally, researchers test hypothesis using one of two methods.

qualitative methods
Hypothesis-testing methods which are based on the observations and interpretations of one or more individuals.

   Qualitative methods are based on the observations and interpretations of one or more individuals. For example, a trained observer might sit in on a meeting of a board of directors and comment on the interpersonal processes she or he observes there. Qualitative research is usually designed to provide information-rich cases for studying a specific experience in depth, rather than to produce generalizations.[3]

TABLE 19.1 Overview: Strengths and Weaknesses of Four Common Research Methodologies

Strengths	Weaknesses
Field studies	
Are good for exploring tentative ideas and generating hypotheses	Draw conclusions based on the researcher's subjective interpretation of the behaviors observed
Promote in-depth information and understanding	
Allow for immediate follow-up on new insights that emerge as the study develops	Allow the observation itself to influence the behavior of those observed
	Are based on observations that are hard to quantify
	Are time-consuming and expensive
Questionnaire studies	
Allow researchers to choose their subjects	Are sometimes based on samples whose representativeness of the population of interest is questionable
Generate large amounts of data for the purpose of making comparisons	
Are fast and inexpensive	Do not allow the subjects and the researchers to communicate
Allow statistical data analysis	Are difficult to validate beyond the subjects' opinions
Are especially suited to collecting data on employee values, attitudes and beliefs, as well as organizational characteristics	Are subject to individuals' fallibility, including holding a perceptual slant, failure to tell the truth, and inability to remember
Laboratory experiments	
Allow for control of situational variables	Generate results that are hard to generalize to real-life situations
Establish conditions that might be difficult to establish in the field	May seem artificial to subjects
Are good for sharpening concepts and improving measurements	
Secondary-source materials	
Are inexpensive	May not be easily accessible
Are typically plentiful	Are often unsuitable for a project's specific purpose
Are helpful in providing background material	Raise issues of privacy of subjects
May be untrustworthy	

Source: Based on ideas in A. G. Bedeian and R. F. Zammuto, *Organizations, Theory and Design* (Chicago, IL: The Dryden Press, 1991):634.

In recent years, there has been a significant effort to make qualitative methods as credible and rigorous as possible.[4] For example, one standard requires researchers to present "an explicit description of the data collection process, including a clear articulation of how participants and/or sites were selected, the kinds of questions asked, and the documentation of observations."[5]

Quantitative methods use statistical analysis to summarize and analyze measurable data points to yield results. We will have more to say about this method shortly.

quantitative methods Hypothesis-testing methods which use statistical analysis to summarize and analyze measurable data points to yield results.

AN EXAMPLE An OB professor observes that 30 percent of the students in his class have failed the first exam. Because this is an unusually high number, he decides to investigate the problem. The professor decides to test the hypothesis that the failing students are students who do not study enough.

In his role as a social scientist, he creates several different types of studies to test his hypothesis. One study is a field study in which, over the course of a week, trained observers shadow some of the students who flunked and some of those who passed to assess how much they study. Another study is a questionnaire study of the entire class in which the students who flunked and the students who passed are compared in terms of their report of the number of hours studied for the test, their attitude towards studying, their interest in the course material, and their beliefs about the importance of a college degree. A third study is a laboratory experiment to test personal initiative. In it the performance of a sample of students who passed is compared with that of a sample of students who flunked. Their task is one that requires personal initiative— choosing to exercise, or not, while watching TV. The professor's final study is based on secondary sources: He compares the overall grade point averages of the students who passed with those of the students who failed.

The professor analyzes the data from all these studies to see whether or not they confirm the hypotheses. Based on these findings, he decides whether the flunked students are lazy or not, or perhaps somewhere in between. His research has real-world consequences, too. Based on it the professor will decide whether to make the next exam easier, harder, or just the same.

Designing experiments for the social sciences is a highly complex process. Learning how to do it is a core topic in some master's degree programs and all Ph.D. programs in organizational behavior. To be able to take advantage of the latest social science research, many professionals who use organizational behavior information, including human resources experts, consultants, and managers, strive to achieve at least some familiarity with experimental design.

What Are Some Key Ethical Issues in Social Science Research?

In the process of research, numerous ethical issues arise. A key one is that researchers performing studies on human subjects must take precautions that protect their subjects from physical and psychological harm. Psychologists can no longer do experiments like those Stanley Milgram did on obedience, for example, because it is now believed that the subjects who were induced to harm others, or so they believed, cannot be sufficiently debriefed to prevent them from eventually feeling guilty. (Milgram did debrief his subjects, by the way, and found no ill effects. Nevertheless, the experiment was controversial at the time.)[6]

The topic of protection of human subjects is so important that when U.S. government funds research using human subjects, it oversees their protection. For instance, the U.S. Department of Health & Human Services includes the Office for Human Research Protections. Most colleges, universities, and independent research centers also have their own policies.

Other ethical issues in research include the possibility of manipulating data to get desired results, suppressing data that might not be desirable to a funding authority, the fact that many published studies are never replicated, and the possibility of manipulating the peer review process.

How Do You Read a Scientific Journal Article?

Being able to read research reports in academic journals is a useful skill. Suppose your boss assigns you to draft a recommendation on how your company can improve the productivity of its manufacturing teams. To do a good job, you must include the findings of the latest research on this topic. Using the appropriate online databases in your library, it is a relatively simple matter to identify key words and pull up the relevant articles. But then what?

Reading an academic article can be a daunting task, sometimes even for professionals. This is because academic articles tend to be narrowly focused, filled with jargon, and, often, based on complex statistical analyses. Of course, there are good reasons for these characteristics. The research is focused because it is testing particular hypotheses that test broader theories. Jargon is the shorthand of the field, as it is in any professional field, and allows researchers to communicate succinctly. As we will discuss later in this chapter, particular types of statistical analyses have been shown to be the most useful in revealing the relationships between independent and dependent variables.

Despite these challenges, it is important that you find ways to absorb academic research, at least at some level. What follows are some suggestions on how to read a journal article without having a Ph.D.

How Are Articles Structured?

The typical data-based article has several parts, and, as it turns out, these provide a handy framework for skimming.

The first part is the **abstract**, which tells you the purpose of the study and its major findings, and sometimes suggests what the implications of the findings are for future research and for managerial (also referred to as "applied") use. The abstract consists of a paragraph immediately after the title of the article and before the body of the article.

abstract
The first part of an article, which states the purpose of the study and its major findings.

The first part of the body of the article is the **introduction**. Often it is untitled. Among other things, it tells you why the study makes a contribution to the field. This section is followed by a discussion of the **theoretical background** of the research, placing the hypotheses to be tested in the larger context of the research and theory that have been published previously.

Next is a **methodology** section covering which research method (field study, questionnaire study, and so on) was used for collecting data and, often, why it was chosen above other methods. This section also covers what sample of individuals was used to test the hypothesis.

Next you will come to the **results** section, which presents the conclusions drawn from statistical analysis of the data collected. This is followed by a **discussion** section that includes implications of the study for the advancement of theory (often termed "theoretical implications"), limitations on interpretations of the study given the chosen methodology, practical implications, and implications for future research. If you are lucky—and many journals today do specifically include this—the last section has a subheading called something like "Practical Implications."

How Do Articles Integrate Practical Applications?

People read journal articles at different levels to achieve their unique goals. Some, more practice-oriented individuals such as yourself, just want to get the gist of it. Others, researcher-oriented people such as your professor, may want to dissect each detail. Consider approaching a journal article at one of the following levels, based on how deeply you want to delve into it:

Level 1: Your goal is to learn the implications of this research for practitioners (for example, for a paper you are writing for a course).

Read the abstract and introduction, and, in the discussion section, search for the practical implications. If these seem to be of interest, go back to the section on the theoretical origins of the research and the full discussion section to learn more about the context for the findings.

This is the level at which any educated layperson, including undergraduate students and managers who have not specialized in OB, can approach an article. If you might need to defend why this research is valid, read on. . . .

Level 2: Your goal is to understand exactly how useful this research is as a guide to practical applications.

The purpose of reading at this level is to determine whether you agree that the message to practitioners is warranted given the methods used. Suppose you were to base a recommendation to the top management of your company on a piece, or related pieces, of research. You would not want to make the mistake of accepting the researcher's conclusions without understanding them in detail. For example, you would want to be ready to fend off disagreements based on the nature of the sample of individuals studied. Your manager might say, "I don't believe this stuff. All the research was done on college students, not managers!" You need to anticipate such criticisms.

Naturally, this requires much more sophistication than a Level 1 reading. You must read the article closely enough to understand the logic of the theory and the hypotheses. You may have to read related articles in order to do this. You should have an understanding of some basic ideas about sampling populations and applying statistical methodology.

This is the level at which a student who has mastered a course in basic statistics should be able to approach the article.

Level 3: Your goal is to understand the research methodology and findings in every detail in order to build on them for future research.

This is the level at which Ph.D. students and research professionals approach the article. If they are specialists in the area researched, they will read not only the article,

introduction
The first part of the body of an article, which is often untitled, and which states why the study makes a contribution to the field.

theoretical background
The part of an article which discusses the hypotheses to be tested in the larger context of the research and theory that have been published previously.

methodology
The part of an article which covers which research method was used and why that method was chosen.

results
The part of an article which presents the conclusions drawn from statistical analysis of the data.

discussion
The final part of an article, which covers the study's implications for the advancement of theory, limitations on interpretations of the study given the chosen methodology, practical implications, and implications for future research.

but many of the references as well. They will have training in research methodology and statistical analysis that allows them to see the holes in the research as well as its contribution.

What Are Some Basic Types of Statistical Analyses?

When you want to move to a Level 2 or Level 3 reading of academic articles, you should be familiar with some fundamental types of statistical analysis. Taking a course or two in statistics would be a good idea.

Multiple regression is used when a researcher wants to explain the relationship between multiple independent variables and a dependent variable. It allows you to answer the question, what is the best predictor of (whatever your dependent variable is)? For example, if you want to know what predicts worker satisfaction, it helps you to compare the relative contributions of whatever independent variables you specify, such as workload, peer support, and salary.

One of the pitfalls of multiple regression analysis is that, although the strength of the ability of the independent variables to predict the dependent variable may be high enough to excite a researcher, it may not be high enough to be useful to a practitioner. For example, although the statistical relationship between job satisfaction and individual productivity is considered by researchers to be strong, the correlation of the two may not be high enough to allow managers to say with reasonable certainty that other variables are not just as important.[7]

Correlation shows the relationship between two variables. For example, what is the relationship between job satisfaction and productivity? If satisfaction goes up, will productivity go up, too (a "positive" correlation), or will productivity go down (a "negative" correlation)?

A common pitfall in the interpretation of correlation analyses is the belief that when two variables are correlated, one can be said to cause the other. Nothing could be further from the truth. The correlation technique merely tells you that the two variables are related and does not say which one causes the other. Referring back to the theory that prompted the investigation in the first place may convince you for all practical purposes which was the cause and which is the effect, but you should always be wary when you draw this conclusion. For example, for years researchers explored the relationship between satisfaction and productivity, and results were interpreted as the former causing the latter. Now many researchers argue that performance causes satisfaction, and are investigating how the relationship may be circular.[8]

Factor analysis finds relationships between and among variables and then organizes similar variables into factors. Thus, if in a questionnaire you ask 100 questions about what motivates people in their jobs, you might find that there are five sets of questions, or five factors, that have strong correlations with each other and correspondingly weak correlations with the other factors. This is the type of analysis that was done to discover the five factors that motivate people in their jobs. (See Chapter 5.)

Meta-analysis is a way to synthesize the results of many previous studies. In recent years it has been widely used because it allows researchers to objectively integrate and interpret years of research on a topic.[9]

What Are the Different Roles of Academic and Practitioner Journals?

So far in this section we have been talking about articles in **academic journals**, also called scholarly journals, those journals in which research and the research process are the primary focus. The vast majority of academic journals are **blind peer reviewed**, which means that anonymous reviewers in the field critique the article without knowing who submitted it, and then recommend whether or not to accept it. These peer reviewers may also suggest that the authors make changes, such as improving their statistical methodology or collecting more data. Sometimes the editor has the final say as to whether the article is published or not, and sometimes the editor relies solely on the reviewers' opinions.

In this review process, most technical problems with a manuscript, and certainly all elementary ones, are cleared up. Of course, in academic journals, not all articles that are submitted are accepted for publication. In top journals, it is common that fewer than one in 20 articles submitted actually make it into print.

---

multiple regression
A type of statistical analysis used to explain the relationship between multiple independent variables and a dependent variable, by determining what the best predictor is of the dependent variable.

correlation
A type of statistical analysis which determines whether two variables are related, but not whether one causes the other.

factor analysis
A type of statistical analysis that finds relationships between and among variables and then organizes similar variables into factors.

meta-analysis
A type of analysis which synthesizes the results of many previous studies, enabling researchers to objectively integrate and interpret years of research on a topic.

academic journals
Journals in which research and the research process are the primary focus; also called "scholarly journals."

blind peer review
The critique of an article by anonymous reviewers in the field who do not know who submitted it.

Examples of academic journals that present research studies are *Administrative Science Quarterly* and the *Journal of Applied Psychology*. The *Academy of Management Review* is an academic journal that focuses on theory alone.

Articles in **practitioner journals** have their own publishing standards and goals. They are more likely than academic journals to focus on practice than on theory, and are likely to be stylistically different from articles in academic journals.[10] Overall, they focus less on the process of research and more on the findings. For example, although the academic article will make an effort to scrutinize potential biases in the research findings, the practitioner article will not, on the assumption that generalizations are acceptable. Practitioner articles include more prescriptions about how to solve practical problems. They are often written with an eye to translating complicated research for lay audiences. Some practitioner journals are blind peer reviewed, and some are not.

Examples of journals that are practitioner oriented are *California Management Review* and the *Harvard Business Review*.

> **practitioner journals**
> Journals with independent publishing standards and goals, which tend to focus more on practice (rather than theory) and the findings (rather than the process) of research.

What Are Some Current Controversies That May Affect the Study and Practice of OB in the Future?

The OB research of the future will no doubt be influenced by some of the current debates about the fundamental assumptions of the field. Discussion about the purpose of OB research will affect what variables are studied, for example. Here are a few of the more important issues that theorists have been debating.

Who Should Organizations Serve?

The Academy of Management (AoM) is the major professional organization for academics in business, including, of course, OB specialists. At its founding, AoM established a dual purpose: to meet society's social and economic needs and, at the same time, to serve the public interest.[11] Today one of the organization's strategic themes echoes this dual commitment: "Our collective and individual scholarship should remain relevant, responsible, and make a valuable contribution to society and its institutions."[12]

Professors James Walsh, Klaus Weber, and Joshua Margolis argue that today the AoM needs to do more to honor the field's historic social values.[13] The authors studied 1,738 data-based articles in several key journals to determine whether researchers were most interested in organizational productivity or human welfare. "Human welfare" was defined to include outcomes such as health, satisfaction, justice, social responsibility, or environmental stewardship. Walsh and his associates discovered that since the 1970s, the number of research studies in which some form of human welfare is the dependent variable has fallen. Specifically, in 1978, 32 percent of the academic articles were interested in the causes of human welfare, whereas in 1999 only 19 percent were.

Who should organizations serve? Walsh and his colleagues point out that more than a hundred years ago Henry Ford himself tried to withhold some of the dividends of his company to serve a public purpose. He was sued by a stockholder, and he lost. A 1919 court decision unambiguously stated that, "A business organization is organized and carried on primarily for the profit of the stockholders."[14] It is to this decision that many people point when they argue that business organizations have no role in improving society.[15]

Walsh and his colleagues disagree. They state that, unfortunately, "Organization and management scholars either line up squarely behind the economic objectives of the firm . . . reframe their interests to reflect an economic logic . . . graft their work to this economic logic . . . or simply ignore the effects of the firm on society."[16] They urge researchers to pay more attention to outcome variables that reflect the public good and to do more research on the relationships between organizations and such societal institutions as government, civil society, and transnational organizations.

In the same vein, **critical theorists** would like to see OB take a more challenging approach toward business organizations, including critiquing their design (business organizations are not,

> **critical theorists**
> Theorists who would like to see OB take a more challenging approach toward business organizations, including critiquing their design and their role in society.

for example, democratic) and their role in society (business organizations are often powerful yet not always ethical).[17]

What Should OB Professors Study and Teach?

Another of the ongoing debates in the field is whether teachers and researchers should focus on what has been learned through social science or what has been learned through managerial experience. The latter sort of information is found in sources such as in-depth case studies (including books), descriptions of "best practices," and stories from managers. How should professors study organizational life so that they can then impart their knowledge to their students? Should they focus primarily on gaining personal experience in organizations, or should they craft research that is as objective as possible? Then, too, what should they teach? Should they focus on case studies and examples as told by practitioners, or on theory and research findings?

Historically, according to commentators Warren Bennis and James O'Toole, business schools suffered from an excess of "good ole boys dispensing war stories, cracker-barrel wisdom, and the occasional practical pointer. We remember when MIT's Sloan School of Management was known as MIT School of Industrial Management and its production class was taught by the manager of a nearby General Motors assembly plant."[18] However, they argue, now the emphasis on scientifically based knowledge has gone too far. They note, "Though scientific research techniques may require considerable skill in statistics or experimental design, they call for little insight into complex social and human factors and minimal time in the field discovering the actual problems facing managers. . . . When applied to business—essentially a human activity in which judgments are made with messy, incomplete, and incoherent data—statistical and methodological wizardly can blind rather than illuminate. . . . Broad, multifaceted questions do not easily lend themselves to scientific experiment or validation."[19]

Others make the opposite case—that organizational behavior should follow a natural science model. Orlando Behling notes that the advantages of using social science are that research procedures are public, definitions are precise, data collection is objective, findings are replicable (meaning that the methodology is described in enough detail that any future researcher could redo the study), and the approach is systematic and cumulative (meaning that one study builds on others). The purposes of this kind of research, he says, are explanation, understanding, and prediction.[20]

Still others argue that there is more than one way of knowing. James March and Robert Sutton suggest that some ways of knowing are impossible to confirm through standard social science methods, hence the need for reports from individuals.[21]

Perhaps we should just live with the tension between practitioner and scientific findings, valuing both ways of getting at the truth. One interesting idea is that more research should be performed in teams of academics and practitioners, who jointly decide what methods are best for the particular problem and context.[22]

What You See Is What You Have Learned to Look For. But Is It the Truth?

Some researchers argue that people interpret their worlds through different conceptual lenses, and that these lenses are colored by the way others around them experience the same phenomena. In recent times, the chief trends in the way individuals interpret the world have been **modernism** and **postmodernism**.

When people see their social world through the lens of modernism they tend to focus on how that world is becoming increasingly defined by economic and organizational logic and forces.[23] They believe that progress is made through "the rigorous application of rationality to different arenas of life—regardless of whether it is mathematics, organization of people, or decision making that shapes the future of the community."[24] In organizational life, modernists concern themselves with management and management theory and how to improve these, and how improving them improves society. Modernism is the dominant view in today's organizations.

In contrast, to see the social world through the lens of postmodernism is to be skeptical that any one conceptual lens is the correct one. Postmodern thought assumes that "realities

modernism
A way of seeing the world which focuses on how the world is becoming increasingly defined by economic and organizational logic and forces, and which believes that progress is made through the rigorous application of rationality to different arenas of life.

postmodernism
A way of seeing the world which is skeptical of the idea that any one conceptual lens is the correct one; it believes that all social science is subjective.

are value laden and contain contradictions."[25] Postmodernists assert that all social science is subjective, and that objectivity itself is an illusion. One implication of this way of thinking is that it is important to pay attention to the variety of different human perspectives, to the different "voices," that exist in any given situation or in any given organization. One should pay attention, therefore, not only to science and management, which are said to give even more power to those who already have it, but also to people who are not necessarily included in or empowered by science and management. These include less powerful groups such as ethnic minorities, women, and third world people.[26]

One way the postmodern view has been utilized in the field of OB is in teaching. Today professors are increasingly interested in teaching with stories. Eliciting people's personal stories and views, often called **narratives** or discourses, is believed to create a more valid view of organizational life than simply accepting one version of reality. It is argued, for example, that stories usually have two sides. To fully understand an organization, a person needs to ask: What is the other side of the story in your organization? in any organization? It is important to try to tell "the side of the story" of people who have been underrepresented, marginalized, or silent.[27] Professors might give their students a set of organizational details and ask them to write out not just one, but a set, of alternative interpretations of those details. In short, they are asking their students to walk in other people's shoes.

One application of postmodern thinking in OB has been the use of feminist approaches in organizational studies. For example, some feminists criticize bureaucracies because they require so much conformity and control.[28] As researchers Marta Calás and Linda Smircich describe such applications, "'Feminist' theories are *not* only about 'women's' issues: by using feminist theories as conceptual lenses, we believe a more inclusive organization studies can be created, one that brings in the concerns of others, not just women, who are directly affected by organizational processes and discourses."[29]

> **narratives**
> People's personal stories and views, which can create a more valid view of organizational life than simply accepting one version of reality also called "discourses."

What Resources Can You Use to Learn Even More About Human Behavior in Organizations?

Now that you have thought about how both social science and current controversies are shaping the field, consider your own future: After you finish this course, where can you learn more about OB? Once you get out into the real world, problems will come up for which this book does not offer specific approaches. Then what? The information that might be considered to fall within the field of OB is widely dispersed. You will run into it everywhere, from the popular press in its many mediums to academic journals in a variety of far-flung disciplines. Here are some ideas that will help you to guide your explorations.

Further Education

Of course, further education is always a possibility. You may want to consider courses in communications, negotiation, labor relations, leadership, organizational change, psychology, group dynamics, and sociology. In an MBA program, you can expect to take at least one more basic OB course, along with courses in strategic management that will build on your knowledge of organizational design.

You might consider getting a specialty degree, including an M.A. or Ph.D. in human resource management, organizational psychology, or labor relations, among many other related disciplines.

Further Reading

You will also want to explore on your own. Thousands of business books are published each year, many of them written by consultants, business executives, and professors.[30] If a manager gets even one good idea from a book, reading it is probably worth the effort.

Some people make the case for reading great books—defined in this case as books from the field of OB that "focus our thinking but do not dominate it," and that "continue to be relevant to today's issues."[31] Consider, for example, some of the classics we will describe next.

CLASSIC WORKS IN OB AND MANAGEMENT How does the field of OB advance over time? Some believe that the field develops by investigating new, unexplored areas. When an organizational innovation—take matrix organization design, for instance—comes along that might provide a competitive edge, companies adopt it and researchers study it. Others believe that the field progresses through a process of action and reaction. By this way of thinking, it is inevitable that after the theory of bureaucracy was popularized and developed, it was criticized and fell out of favor.[32] Probably both views are right to some extent.

It is interesting to realize that at the end of the nineteenth century, all large American companies were highly centralized bureaucracies, and most writers assumed the bureaucratic organization design was the best one. Belief in bureaucracy was so dominant at that time that Henry Ford, founder of the Ford Motor Car Company and inventor of the assembly line, could comment that, as an employer, he always got stuck with a whole person, along with that person's troublesome body and annoying ideas, when what he *really* wanted was just a pair of hands.[33] In this context, researchers' main interest was on improving worker efficiency. Eventually, decades later, the effectiveness of bureaucratic organizational design itself was questioned, and researchers began to focus on variables like employee participation that might improve upon bureaucracies.

Over time, the following early writers have been particularly influential in influencing the field, and their work suggests some ideas worth considering even today:

Frederick W. Taylor (1856–1915). Early in the twentieth century at Bethlehem Steel, Frederick W. Taylor performed a large number of data-based time and motion studies to figure out how individual workers could be made more productive. His most famous study demonstrated that, in contrast to an average worker, a man using the right shovel could load almost four times the amount of pig-iron per day. As you can imagine, such a finding was of great interest to managers. Taylor's work was lauded as an effective application of scientific principles to management, and his approach came to be known as **scientific management**.

scientific management
An approach to management which determines how to improve labor productivity by precise procedures developed after careful scientific study of an individual at work.

Historically, scientific management has been equated with treating workers as parts of machines, cogs in a wheel whose labor is to be studied and exploited. However, there is another side to this story. According to a recent reanalysis of Taylor's results:

> The secret to this success was partially the shovel but primarily the utilization of time. The phenomenal results were obvious, but Taylor never emphasized to Bethlehem Steel that [his subject] was resting 57 to 58 percent of the work day. . . .

> The emphasis of Taylor's study was placed on timed work habits that measured performance. Resting was considered idle time and not productive. Employers gave employees breaks only because the unions fought for those rights, especially at the turn of the century when Taylor was at Bethlehem Steel.[34]

It seems that Taylor had been dismissed from Midvale Steel Company in 1890 for his radical ideas, the next company he worked for went out of business, and, perhaps as a result of these traumatic events, he interpreted his study to tell management what it wanted to hear. Had he described the full study and pointed out the human element of rest, he might have been known as an early advocate of the human relations approach to management (which we will describe next). As it was, he became famous as a theorist who enhanced the effectiveness of bureaucracies.

Taylor published *The Principles of Scientific Management* in 1911.

Mary Parker Follett (1868–1933). In the era when Frederick Taylor's principles of scientific management were widely influential, Follett emphasized teamwork, responsibility, and empowerment.[35] A social worker and writer, her first business-oriented book was *Creative Experience* (1924). Follett was the first woman to publish a book specifically about management, entitled *Dynamic Administration* (1941).[36]

Follett emphasized the importance of power in organizations, and argued that power in organizations should be democratized. As summarized by Stewart R. Clegg and his associates, Follet believed that, "We should welcome [human] difference because it feeds and enriches society, whereas differences that are ignored feed *on* society and eventually corrupt it."[37] Interestingly, Parker also recognized the relationship between leadership and teaching. She wrote, "The relation of the rest of the group to the leader is not a passive one, and I think teachers see this more clearly than most people and therefore in their teaching are doing more than teaching; they are helping to develop one of the fundamental conceptions of human relations."[38]

Elton Mayo (1880–1949). Elton Mayo was, along with Dean Donham and L. J. Henderson, one of the early proponents of the human relations approach to management.[39] These theorists argued that managers should not treat workers merely as economic rationalizers determined to make the most money with the least effort, but rather should recognize that workers have strong social needs that they try to fulfill through informal groups at work.[40]

Between 1924 and 1933 a series of influential studies on how worker motivation affects productivity were carried out at the Hawthorne Works of the Western Electric Company. The results of these studies were, in their day, surprising, and were later referred to as the "Hawthorne Effect."[41] However, what the Hawthorne Effect is, exactly, has been described in several different ways.[42] One of the most popular interpretations is that merely paying attention to workers and giving them special treatment increases productivity.[43] This finding has generally failed to be replicated by other researchers.[44] Other interpretations say productivity depended on group cohesiveness, a participatory supervisory style, employee learning through feedback, or the small group wage incentive. Recent analysis of the Hawthorne studies suggests that the most important factors leading to productivity were probably group cohesiveness and the incentive system.[45]

Chester I. Barnard (1886–1961). Chester I. Barnard was an executive who was also a major theoretician in the human relations approach to management. One of his peers described him as "the one and only executive in captivity who not only could run a successful organization but could also talk intelligently about what he was up to in the process."[46] In 1937 Barnard gave a series of lectures, subsequently published as *The Functions of the Executive,* in which he emphasized cooperative approaches to managing people and downplayed money as a motivator.[47]

Barnard is generally credited with early work on the concept of corporate culture, and theories of organizational learning can also be traced back to him.[48] His contributions to leadership theory are also notable. For instance, he pointed out that a key management role is to harness the power of informal groups and that having authority is only useful if people accept it.[49]

Max Weber (1864–1920). Max Weber was a German sociologist and political economist whose important work on bureaucracy was written early in the twentieth century but not translated into English until the 1940s. According to scholars:

> Weber . . . was the first to focus on the totality of the organizational forms that were becoming significant when he wrote—the model for which was bureaucracy. Bureaucratic organization, seen at the turn of the nineteenth century as the hallmark of modern organization, depended above all else on the application of what Weber termed "rational" means for the achievement of specific ends. . . . However, the stress on rationality symptomatic of Taylor and the engineers was analyzed critically by Weber. His interest was in the link between rationality, rules, and their social impact.[50]

One of Weber's most influential books is *The Protestant Ethic and the Spirit of Capitalism.*

POST WORLD WAR II DEVELOPMENTS AND MODERN TIMES Immediately following World War II, U.S. business practices were admired across the globe. Since the 1980s, however, business methods have become increasingly internationalized. In the 1980s, in fact, U.S. companies were scrutinizing Japanese companies to learn what they could from them. Going full circle, the quality circle movement that Americans imported at that time from Japan was based on earlier work exported to Japan by American W. Edwards Deming.

Today in the United States the field of OB has a host of dedicated researchers. These include professors in business and related academic departments, organizational consultants, and in-house company researchers. The major themes they are investigating include:

- Integrating bureaucratic and enterprise (organic) elements in organizations
- Continuing focus on organizations as open, learning systems that must adapt to their environments
- International differences in motivation and organizational design

Along with these themes, companies continue to be interested in classic issues such as improving efficiency (which can be traced back to scientific management), enhancing creativity and commitment (which can be traced back to the human relations school), and improving organizational design (which can be traced back to contingency theories of bureaucracy).

Use the Human Resource Management (HRM) Department in Your Company

human resource management
The programmed and strategic management of an organization's people.

In the organizations in which you will work, there will probably be a **human resource management (HRM)** department or manager. This unit or person can be a key resource for your ongoing learning. As mentioned in Chapter 1, HRM is the managerial function that is concerned with employees as a company resource.[51] The larger the organization, the larger and more complex the department. In small companies, HRM functions may be delegated to just one person; in larger companies, there will be a variety of specialists. Whatever the situation, the HRM specialists are trained individuals who can help you understand not more only about OB in your company, but about OB in general.

Some of the main functions of HRM departments and how they might be of use to you are the following:

Staffing includes analyzing the work of the company to determine what jobs should be created, developing profiles of the ideal candidates to fill those jobs, recruiting, selection, and socialization to the firm. As you move through this process yourself, you can get answers to a great many questions that will help you understand the culture and design of your company. You will see how OB concepts such as impression management and socialization are put into action.

Compensation and benefits includes developing and administering pay and benefit systems for the company. Professionals in this area must know how pay and benefit systems are structured. To attract the best people, they must also know how their systems compare with those of their competitors. They may also be trained in the psychology of motivation.

Training and development is the function that manages the ongoing learning of a company's employees. This department influences a range of decisions, from whether a company should institute a tuition-reimbursement benefit to what should be taught at the corporate training center. Obviously it is a good idea to know about and take advantage of that learning opportunities they may offer to you. Some of these will be technical, but many will be interpersonal and managerial.

Industrial relations is the function that is concerned with union–management relations. It involves maintaining relationships among employees, their unions if any, management, and government agencies. Professionals in this area are versed in such areas as negotiation, conflict, and legal aspects of the employee-management relationship.

Strategic human resource planning helps a company predict how many employees will be needed in the future and plans career systems to develop employees. It also suggests how the company's overall strategy should be shaped by its human resource needs. Today, this function includes a significant international component. HRM professionals know a great deal about how to develop international managers and executives, and how to move individuals from one culture to another. Especially if your international experience is limited, you may learn a lot from them.

Current Techniques and Fads

It seems that every decade or so, new behavioral techniques emerge to meet current organizational needs.[52] For instance, in the latter half of the twentieth century, all of the following influential approaches were developed: management by objectives (MBO) (1950s), sensitivity training (1960s), quality circles (1970s), total quality management (TQM) (1980s), and self-managed teams (1990s). Over time each of these has influenced how organizations view and manage change. For instance, although MBO is seldom seen in its pure form today, it has influenced current thinking on goal setting. The influence of sensitivity training, which is a process for enhancing interpersonal development, is seen in today's communication training and team building. Quality circles and total quality management are still widely used, although often under different names and tailored to different situations, and self-managed teams are a natural outgrowth of all of these.

Often referred to as "fads," popular techniques are actually important for managers and organizations. According to researchers Jane Whitney Gibson and Dana V. Tesone, understanding fads and applying them in the workplace can be a reputation builder for managers, suggesting that they are staying current in both theory and practice.[53] Also, organizations that are closely associated with popular management fads are more admired by the public and are considered to be particularly innovative.[54] A 1995 study of the 100 largest industrial companies in the United States found that companies that adopt fads are seen as having better managers. Irrespective of their company's performance, their CEOs receive increased compensation.

Are fads really useful to companies? To date no research has definitively answered this question. However, to decide whether a fad you are considering might actually be useful in your company, and whether you should champion it, consider the following questions[55]:

1. Has the fad been around long enough to have a proven track record?
2. Does the goal of the fad complement the needs of the organization?
3. Does implementation of the fad mesh with the organizational culture?
4. Will adopting the fad help the organization remain competitive?
5. Does the organization have the resources needed to implement the fad?
6. Do the expected benefits of the fad outweigh the direct and indirect costs of implementing it?
7. Can the fad be implemented in small sections of the organization to test the new concepts with minimum risk?
8. Has the organization's track record with implementing previous fads been positive?
9. Can the organization afford to wait for the long-term benefits from adopting this fad?
10. Can organizational inertia and resistance to change be managed to successfully implement the fad?
11. Do you have a choice?

Conclusion to This Chapter . . . and This Book

Students sometimes wonder why they should take a course in OB, because, after all, isn't understanding human behavior just common sense? After reading this book I hope you understand why this view is less than accurate.

Could you start and run a successful business without ever having read a single paragraph about human behavior? Of course you could. But would you be armed as well as someone who has thought more deeply about motivating workers, leading teams, and designing effective organizations? Probably not.[56] Could you learn as you went along? Maybe so—especially in a small, simple business—but at what cost? Certainly you would be at a competitive disadvantage compared to those who do know how to manage themselves and others well.

So, take advantage of the education provided to you in your OB course, and then, keep on learning about human behavior. Soon you will leave your university and move on to your life in organizations. I hope this book will help you on your journey. May you find your passion and fulfill your dreams. And may you serve your community and improve our world, one organization at a time.

Apply What You Have Learned. . .

Advice from the Pros

Keep on Learning

A recent list of 20 great ideas for doing business today contains the following ones on learning more about organizations:

On understanding the complexities of human behavior in organizations. . .

"Many managers eager to pursue ambitious growth strategies suspect that their organizations lack the right stuff to deliver. These leaders want desperately to crack the code of high-performance DNA. But performance anatomies are highly individual and delicately balanced. New research initiatives are making the *je ne sais quoi* of success more decodable, teachable, and learnable."

—Julie Kirby

On selecting topics for further exploration. . .

"Organizations tiptoe around politically or socially risqué subjects—especially perennial cringe-inducers like sex, death, and God. But if a subject makes you uncomfortable, chances are it's exactly what you should be discussing."

—Leigh Buchanan

On learning from business books. . .

"Publishers churn out around 3,500 business titles a year, and—wonder of wonders—not all of them offer good advice. Managers who can't afford to waste time on dreck need help navigating the ideas marketplace. Some rules of thumb: Be skeptical of anything touted as "new," keep an eye out for half-truths, and if someone calls himself a guru, run the other way."

—Jeffrey Pfeffer

Discuss

1. Discuss each of these ideas with your class.
2. Take 10 minutes to write down some personal goals for what you would like to learn and how you will keep on learning after graduation.

Source: Adapted from Roderick M. Kramer, Julia Kirby, Joseph L. Bower, Jeffrey E. Rayport, Eric Bonabeau, Roger L. Martin, Kirthi Kalyanam, Monte Zweben, Robert C. Merton, Thomas A. Stewart, Mohanbir Sawhney, Denise Caruso, Thomas H. Davenport, Leigh Buchanan, Henry W. Chesbrough, Kenneth Lieberthal, Jochen Wirtz, Loizos Heracleous, Mary Catherine Bateson, and Jeffrey Rosen, "The HBR List," *Harvard Business Review* 83 (2), February 2005:25–29, 26 (Julia Kirby), 29 (Leigh Buchanan), 28 (Jeffrey Pfeffer). Reprinted by permission of *Harvard Business Review*, 'Keep On Learning', from "The HBR List", Feb 2005. Copyright © 2005 by the Harvard Business School Publishing Corporation; all rights reserved.

Gain Experience

Current Controversies in OB: Defend Your Position

Your professor will tell you how to divide up the class for this debate. You will debate one or both of these topics:

1. Who should organizations serve?
2. What should OB professors study and teach?

To prepare for the debate, reread "What are some current controversies that may affect the study and practice of OB in the future?" in this chapter.

Design the Professor's Research

In this chapter you read about how a professor investigated the phenomenon of a large number of students flunking an exam. In this exercise you will critique the professor's research.

Discuss in small groups:

Part I: *An OB professor observes that 30 percent of the students in his class have failed the first exam. Since this is an unusually high number, he decides to investigate the problem. The professor decides to test the hypothesis that the failing students are students who do not study enough.*

   a. Why do you think the professor chooses this particular hypothesis?
   b. Think of some other hypotheses he might have chosen.
   c. Why might students and professors looking at the same problem choose different hypotheses to test? What do these differences suggest about the research process?

Part II: *In his role as a social scientist, the professor creates several different types of studies to test his hypothesis. One study is a field study in which, over the course of a week, trained observers shadow some of the students who flunked and some of those who passed to assess how much they study. Another study is a questionnaire study of the entire class in which the students who flunked and the students who passed are compared in terms of their report of the number of hours studied for the test, their attitude towards studying, their interest in the course material, and their beliefs about the importance of a college degree. A third study is a laboratory experiment to test personal initiative. In it the performance of a sample of students who passed is compared with that of a sample of students who flunked. Their task is one that requires personal initiative—choosing to exer-cise, or not, while watching TV. The professor's final study is based on secondary sources: He compares the overall grade point averages of the students who passed with those of the students who failed.*

   a. Choose one of the hypotheses you created in Part I and tell how to operationalize it for each type of study.

Part III: *The professor analyzes the data from all these studies to see whether or not they confirm the hypotheses. Based on these findings, he decides whether the flunked students are lazy or not, or perhaps somewhere in between. His research has real-world consequences, too. Based on it the professor will decide whether to make the next exam easier, harder, or just the same.*

   a. Should the professor base the difficulty of the next exam on the research findings? Why or why not?

Chapter Summary and Key Terms

Beyond this book, how can you continue to learn about OB?

Build on your personal interests and the problem-solving approach used in this book by deepening your knowledge of OB history, the latest research, and current controversies. Understand current research more completely by understanding its context in history. The field is often summarized by surveying the work of major writers, such as Taylor, Follett, Mayo, Barnard, and Weber. In the companies for which you work or will work, use organizational resources to help you.

What more do you need to know about the scientific approach to human behavior?

Learn as much as you can about the scientific method in social science, including how researchers test hypotheses and what types of statistical analysis are common. Understand ethical issues such as the treatment of human subjects.

operationalize 501
independent variable 501
dependent variable 501

How do social scientists test hypotheses?

qualitative methods 502
quantitative methods 503

How do you read a scientific journal article?

Understand the parts of a journal article, which include the abstract, introduction, theoretical background, methodology, results and discussion. Learn to read scientific studies for their practical implications. Grasp at least the basics of statistical analysis, including multiple regression, correlation, factor analysis, and meta-analysis. Understand the difference between a scholarly journal and a practitioner journal.

abstract 504
introduction 505
theoretical background 505
methodology 505
results 505
discussion 505
multiple regression 506
correlation 506
factor analysis 506
meta-analysis 506
academic journals 506
blind peer reviewed 506
practitioner journals 507

What are some current controversies that may affect the study and practice of OB in the future?

Important current issues are based on the questions "Who should organizations serve?" "What should OB professors study and teach?" and "What different perspectives should be included in organizational research?"

critical theorists 507
modernism 508
postmodernism 508
narratives 509

What resources can you use to learn even more about human behavior in organizations?

There are many sources for information on OB. Look to your human resource management group for expertise, read the history and current science, and observe on your own. Staying up on the current fads can build your reputation as an effective manager.

scientific management 510
human resource management 512

Explorations

1. Compare databases and the internet for exploring a topic

Sign on to Business Source Premier or a similar database of articles in academic business and related journals through your university library. Be sure the database gives you full articles, not just abstracts. Choose a topic and compare academic versus practitioner articles and approaches to it. Note that in some databases you can tailor your search to select only peer-reviewed journals.

Now go to www.ceoexpress.com and check out the sections on business magazines and business knowledge. How does the information you find there compare with what you find in your organizational journals data base?

2. Become familiar with professional organizations

Many OB academics and other professionals belong to the *Academy of Management.* Learn a lot about the field at the Academy's Web site: www.aomonline.org.

The professional association for academics interested in labor issues is the *Labor and Employment Relations Association* (LERA), formerly the Industrial Relations Research Association. See www.lera.uiuc.edu.

The Society for Industrial and Organizational Psychology (SIOP) is a division of the American Psychological Association whose mission is to enhance well-being and performance in work settings by promoting the science and practice of industrial-organizational psychology. See www.siop.org.

References

[1] B. M. Staw and G. R. Oldham, "Reconsidering Our Dependent Variables: A Critique and Empirical Study," *Academy of Management Journal 21* (4), December 1978:539–559.

[2] A. G. Bedeian and R. F. Zammuto, *Organizations, Theory and Design* (Chicago, IL: The Dryden Press, 1991).

[3] M. Q. Patton, *Qualitative Evaluation and Research Methods* (Newbury Park, CA: Sage Publications, 1990).

[4] R. P. Gephart Jr. in S. Rynes and R. P. Gephart Jr., "From the Editors," *Academy of Management Journal 47* (4), August 2004:454–462.

[5] D. Choudhuri, A. Glauser, and J. Peregoy, "Guidelines for Writing a Qualitative Manuscript for the Journal of Counseling & Development," *Journal of Counseling & Development 82* (4), Fall 2004:443–446, 444.

[6] S. Milgram, *Obedience to Authority* (New York: Harper and Row, 1974).

[7] M. M. Petty, G. W. McGee, and J. W. Cavender, "A Meta-Analysis of the Relationships between Individual Job Satisfaction and Individual Performance," *Academy of Management Review 9* (4), October 1984:712–721.

[8] M. M. Petty, G. W. McGee, and J. W. Cavender, "A Meta-Analysis of the Relationships between Individual Job Satisfaction and Individual Performance," *Academy of Management Review 9* (4), October 1984:712–721.

[9] J. E. Hunter and F. L. Schmidt, *Methods of Meta-Analysis: Correcting Error and Bias in Research Findings* (Newbury Park, CA: Sage Publications, 1990); P. Bobko and E. F. Stone-Romero, "Meta-Analysis May Be Another Useful Tool, but It Is Not a Panacea," in G. R. Ferris, ed., *Research in Personnel and Human Resource Management 16* (Stamford, CT: JAI Press, 1998):359–397.

[10] M. Kelemen and P. Bansal, "The Conventions of Management Research and Their Relevance to Management Practice," *British Journal of Management 13* (2), June 2002:97–108.

[11] J. P. Walsh, K. Weber, and J. D. Margolis, "Social Issues and Management: Our Lost Cause Found," *Journal of Management 29* (6), 2003:859–881, quoting the Editor's preface to the *Journal of the Academy of Management 1* (1), 1958:5–6.

[12] "Statement of Strategic Direction," 2003–2005 Academy of Management, http://www.aomonline.org/aom.asp?ID=&page_ID=49. Accessed July 17, 2005.

[13] J. P. Walsh, K. Weber, and J. D. Margolis, "Social Issues and Management: Our Lost Cause Found," *Journal of Management 29* (6), 2003:859–881, quoting the editor's preface to the *Journal of the Academy of Management 1* (1), 1958:5–6.

[14] *Dodge Brothers v. Ford Motor Company* (Michigan, 1919):170 N. W. 668.

[15] M. Friedman, "The Social Responsibility of Business Is to Increase Its Profits," *New York Times Magazine,* September 13, 1970:32–33, 122, 124, 126.

[16] J. P. Walsh, K. Weber, and J. D. Margolis, "Social Issues and Management: Our Lost Cause Found," *Journal of Management 29* (6), 2003:859–881, 867.

[17] "Business Schools: But Can You Teach It?" *The Economist,* May 20, 2004:61–63.

[18] W. G. Bennis and J. O'Toole, "How Business Schools Lost Their Way," *Harvard Business Review 83* (5), May 2005:96–104, 98. See also R. A. Gordon and J. E. Howell, *Higher Education for Business* (New York: Columbia University Press, 1959) and F. C. Pierson, *The Education of American Businessmen* (New York: McGraw-Hill, 1959).

[19] W. G. Bennis and J. O'Toole, "How Business Schools Lost Their Way," *Harvard Business Review 83* (5), May 2005:96–104, 99.

[20] B. Berelson and G. A. Steiner, *Human Behavior* (New York: Harcourt, Brace & World, 1964); O. Behling, "The Case for the Natural Science Model for Research in Organizational Behavior and Organization Theory," *Academy of Management Review 5* (4), 1980:483–490.

[21] J. G. March and R. I. Sutton, "Organizational Performance as a Dependent Variable," *Organizational Science 8* (6), November/December 1997:698–706.

[22] M. Kelemen and P. Bansal, "The Conventions of Management Research and Their Relevance to Management Practice," *British Journal of Management 13* (2), June 2002:97–108.

[23] M. Sarup, *An Introductory Guide to Post-Structuralism and Postmodernism* (Atlanta, GA: University of Georgia Press, 1993).

[24] S. Clegg, M. Kornberger, and T. Pitsis, *Managing and Organizations: An Introduction to Theory and Practice* (Thousand Oaks, CA: Sage Publications, 2005):60.

[25] S. Rynes and R. P. Gephart Jr., "From the Editors," *Academy of Management Journal 47* (4), August 2004:454–462.

[26] M. E. Spiro, "Postmodernist Anthropology, Subjectivity, and Science: A Modernist Critique," *Comparative Studies in Society and History V,* 1996:759–780.

[27] D. M. Boje and R. F. Dennehy, *Managing in the Postmodern World: America's Revolution against Exploitation,* 1st ed. (Dubuque, IA: Kendall-Hunt, 1993). Free online version at http://cbae.nmsu.edu/~dboje/pages/mpw.html.

[28] K. E. Ferguson, *The Feminist Case Against Bureaucracy* (Philadelphia, PA: Temple University Press, 1984).

[29] M. Calás and L. Smircich, "From 'The Woman's' Point of View: Feminist Approaches to Organization Studies," in S. R. Clegg, C. Hardy, and W. R. Nord, *Handbook of Organization Studies* (Thousand Oaks, CA: Sage Publications, 1996):218–257.

[30] J. Micklethwait and A. Wooldridge, *The Witch Doctors: Making Sense of the Management Gurus* (New York: Times Business, 1996); J. Pfeffer and C. T. Fong, "The End of Business Schools? Less Success Than Meets the Eye," *Academy of Management Learning & Education 1* (1), 2002:78–95.

[31] W. J. Duncan, "A Case for Great Books in Management Education," *Academy of Management Learning & Education 3* (4), December 2004:421–428, 422.

[32] For a discussion of these trends, see S. Clegg, M. Kornberger, and T. Pitsis, *Managing and Organizations: An Introduction to Theory and Practice* (Thousand Oaks, CA: Sage Publications, 2005).

[33] S. Clegg, M. Kornberger, and T. Pitsis, *Managing and Organizations: An Introduction to Theory and Practice* (Thousand Oaks, CA: Sage Publications, 2005):55.

[34] J. J. Clark, "Frederick Winslow Taylor," *PA Times 23* (12), December 2000:8. For additional interpretations, see S. Kakar, *Frederick Taylor: A Study in Personality and Innovation* (Cambridge, MA: MIT Press, 1970).

[35] M. P. Follett, "Mary Parker Follett: A Prophet Gaining Honour," *Business Strategy Review 14* (1), Spring 2003:75–76.

[36] S. Clegg, M. Kornberger, and T. Pitsis, *Managing and Organizations: An Introduction to Theory and Practice* (Thousand Oaks, CA: Sage Publications, 2005).

[37] S. Clegg, M. Kornberger, and T. Pitsis, *Managing and Organizations: An Introduction to Theory and Practice* (Thousand Oaks, CA: Sage Publications, 2005):30.

[38] M. P. Follett, "The Teacher–Student Relation," in E. M. Fox and L. Urwick, eds., *Dynamic Administration: The Collected Papers of Mary Parker Follett* (New York: Hippocrene Books, Inc., 1982), 303.

[39] E. Walter-Busch, "Chester Barnard and the Human Relations Approach at Harvard Business School," *Academy of Management Proceedings,* 1985:139–143.

[40] "Human Relations Movement," *Blackwell Encyclopedic Dictionary of Organizational Behavior,* 1995:215–216.

[41] J. G. Adair, "The Hawthorne Effect: A Reconsideration of the Methodological Artifact," *Journal of Applied Psychology 69,* 1984:334–345.

[42] G. W. Yunker, "An Explanation of Positive and Negative Hawthorne Effects: Evidence from the Relay Assembly Test Room and Bank Wiring Observation Room Studies," *Academy of Management Proceedings,* 1993:179–183.

[43] S. R. G. Jones, "Was There a Hawthorne Effect?" *American Journal of Sociology 98* (3), November 1992:451–468.

[44] S. M. Johnson and O. D. Bolstad, "Methodological Issues in Naturalistic Observation: Some Problems and Solutions for Field Research," in L. A. Hamerlynck, L. C. Handy, and E. J. Mash, eds., *Behavior Change: Methodology, Concepts, and Practice* (Champaign, IL: Research Press, 1973):7–68; J. G. Adair, "The Hawthorne Effect: A Reconsideration of the Methodological Artifact," *Journal of Applied Psychology 69,* 1984:334–345.

[45] G. W. Yunker, "An Explanation of Positive and Negative Hawthorne Effects: Evidence from the Relay Assembly Test Room and Bank Wiring Observation Room Studies," *Academy of Management Proceedings,* 1993:179–183. See also S. R. G. Jones, "Worker Interdependence and Output: The Hawthorne Studies Reevaluated," *American Sociological Review 55* (2), April 1990:176–190.

[46] F. Roethlisberger, *The Elusive Phenomena* (Cambridge, MA: Harvard University Press 1977):67.

[47] E. Walter-Busch, "Chester Barnard and the Human Relations Approach at Harvard Business School," *Academy of Management Proceedings,* 1985:139–143.

[48] M. Rowlinson, "Organization Theory: From Chester Barnard to the Present and Beyond (Book)," *Journal of Management Studies 34* (1), January 1997:153–156; W. G. Scott, *Chester I. Barnard and the Guardians of the Managerial State* (Lawrence, KS: University Press of Kansas, 1992).

[49] S. Clegg, M. Kornberger, and T. Pitsis, *Managing and Organizations: An Introduction to Theory and Practice* (Thousand Oaks, CA: Sage Publications, 2005).

[50] S. Clegg, M. Kornberger, and T. Pitsis, *Managing and Organizations: An Introduction to Theory and Practice* (Thousand Oaks, CA: Sage Publications, 2005):43.

[51] See G. R. Ferris, S. D. Rosen and D. T. Barnum, *Handbook of Human Resource Management* (Cambridge, MA: Blackwell Business, 1995).

[52] J. W. Gibson and D. V. Tesone, "Management Fads: Emergence, Evolution, and Implications for Managers," *Academy of Management Executive 15* (4), November 2001:122–133.

[53] J. W. Gibson and D. V. Tesone, "Management Fads: Emergence, Evolution, and Implications for Managers," *Academy of Management Executive 15* (4), November 2001:122–133.

[54] B. M. Staw and L. D. Epstein, "What Bandwagons Bring: Effects of Popular Management Techniques on Corporate Performance, Reputation, and CEO Pay," *Administrative Science Quarterly 45* (3), 2000:523–556.

[55] J. W. Gibson and D. V. Tesone, "Management Fads: Emergence, Evolution, and Implications for Managers," *Academy of Management Executive 15* (4), November 2001:122–133.

[56] For a discussion of how MBA students, CEOs and other educated individuals compare in their ability to use contingency theories of design and strategy, see R. L. Priem and J. Rosenstein, "Is Organization Theory Obvious to Practitioners? A Test of One Established Theory," *Organization Science: A Journal of the Institute of Management Sciences 11* (5), September/October 2000:509–524.

Appendix 1: World Countries and U.S. Trading Partners

World countries, with the United States' top five trading partners in mauve.
The map also includes, in green, the country's top five trading states.

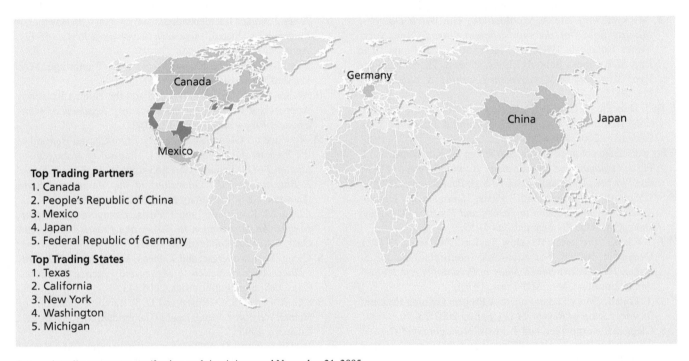

Top Trading Partners
1. Canada
2. People's Republic of China
3. Mexico
4. Japan
5. Federal Republic of Germany

Top Trading States
1. Texas
2. California
3. New York
4. Washington
5. Michigan

Source: http://www.census.gov/foreign-trade/top/. Accessed November 21, 2005.

Appendix 2: Answers for: "Who Is the American?"

Count yourself as a self-aware American if you got 5 or 6 correct.

1. Y
2. Y
3. X
4. Y
5. X
6. X

Appendix 3: Where Are The Groups in Organizations?

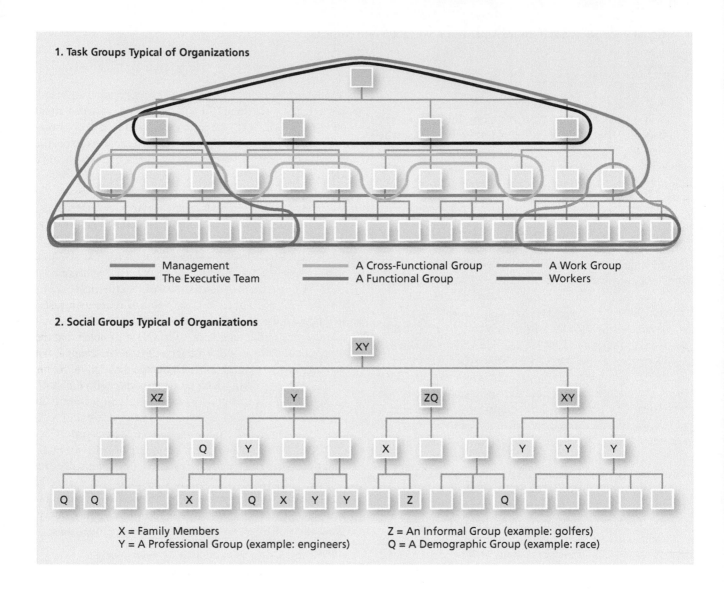

1. Task Groups Typical of Organizations

Management	A Cross-Functional Group	A Work Group
The Executive Team	A Functional Group	Workers

2. Social Groups Typical of Organizations

X = Family Members
Y = A Professional Group (example: engineers)
Z = An Informal Group (example: golfers)
Q = A Demographic Group (example: race)

Case 1 Western Distribution Center, Inc.

Part 1. The Problem

"This is a can-do company, a company that people are proud to work for," Mike Henley told himself. "Then why is it that we can't solve our safety problem? I love this company, too. I am fully committed to it and to my people! But right now I certainly could use some inspiration. . . ."

Mike Henley was the middle-level manager responsible for daily operations in the regional distribution center of a major mail-order catalog company. The subsidiary was located in a small and cohesive community in which such traditional values as close-knit families and patriotism were highly regarded. Mike had been working for the company for 12 years, and many of his employees had been with the company for even longer. The company was run like a large and friendly family in which the norm was to work with diligence and enthusiasm. Employees were seldom fired.

Depending on the time of year, Mike supervised between 60 and 100 hourly and salaried associates (non-union). Their duties were to receive, store, and ship merchandise advertised in the quarterly catalog. More specifically, the associates packed orders, hand-carried merchandise, ran a forklift operation, counted stock, stacked and opened cartons, and handled related paperwork. The company was known locally as a good, even inspiring place to work, and turnover was low.

In recent months Mike had become deeply concerned about an upward trend in the frequency of accidents in the facility. Injuries had been up over the same period last year, and fall and the December holidays—traditionally the busiest months of the year—were still to come. At the same time, cost reductions had become a special concern in the highly competitive mail-order business, and upper management had been urging middle-level supervisors to closely examine expenditures. Over recent years the average cost per injury at Western, including first aid, medical care, and time lost from work, had been high.

Mike was determined to reverse the trend for accidents. He decided to challenge himself, and his associates: Even though his busiest season was yet to come, involving more associates and more orders, he wanted to end the year with some improvement and, in the subsequent year, he wanted a major change.

Mike consulted his corporate organizational development (OD) people in the Chicago office, who suggested that he might want to use behavior modification and feedback techniques to influence associates to work more safely. The OD staff suggested that even though the company already had a highly positive culture, setting specific goals and carefully managing rewards could still have strong payoffs. Mike was a willing listener; he felt as though he had tried everything else without success.

However, the OD staff tried to temper his eagerness to get started right away. In fact, they cautioned him on several issues. For instance, to use these techniques effectively he would have to know exactly what the problem was. Also, he would have to make a commitment to involving and training the associates. Furthermore, if he wanted the program to be a success for more than just a few months, he would have to understand how behavior is maintained for the long term. The OD staff noted that the corporate culture would probably support the change, but that he must be careful not to challenge that culture by his efforts. After several detailed discussions with the staff, Mike decided to commit himself to taking a course on behavior modification techniques and to designing a "b mod" program to reduce the warehouse accident rate.

As he learned more about the theory of behavior modification, Mike decided to research systematically the causes of the accident rate. He wanted to "know exactly what the problem is." Initially, he nominated a representative team of workers and managers to study facility safety. Their job was to get answers to the following questions:

■ Have conditions in the facility been unsafe?

■ Have the workers lacked training in safety procedures?

■ Is there some factor of human fallibility that contributes to the accident rate?

To answer these questions, the task force first tested workers on their knowledge of safety procedures: Each associate was interviewed by his or her immediate manager about safety procedures pertinent to their job. Next, through additional interviews and examination of records, a detailed review of the causes of previous accidents was assembled.

The results of this investigation indicated that workers' actual knowledge of safety procedures was extremely high. Accidents occurred most frequently when people "forgot" about safety—for example, when they were distracted from their task or were in a hurry. The task force's conclusion was that 97 percent of all accidents had been caused by mistaken acts, not by inadequate training or unsafe conditions.

Mike accepted the task force's analysis that it was people's behavior on the job that should be targeted for change. He believed that improving people's attention to issues of safety would translate into improved safety behaviors. He decided that his next step should be to design a program to motivate people to behave safely.

Questions for Discussion—Part 1

1. Why has the OD staff cautioned Mike about the proper way to approach behavior modification? Discuss the issues the staff has raised in light of what you know about application of behavior modification principles in the workplace.

2. What additional problems should Mike anticipate, if any?

3. How would you design the program? Consider each step, from diagnosis of the problem through implementation and follow-up.

4. Why should Mike use behavior modification instead of other approaches (for example, a change in leadership style or team building or employee training) to this issue?

Part II. The Program

Students: Please do not read this part until asked to do so.

First Mike concerned himself with getting his team to buy into the idea of using behavior modification. He invited an internal OD consultant to the plant to explain such programs and the evidence of their effectiveness. The consultant emphasized the positive aspects of behavior modification and worked for nearly two hours with the associates discussing thoroughly their concerns about the negative images and associations ("punishment," "manipulation," "shock treatment") they had with the term "behavior modification." The consultant's main theme was "empowerment": Knowing behavior modification empowers people to work more efficiently and effectively.

Subsequently, Mike and his team decided to run a four-month pilot project for the remainder of the year. Based on what was learned in the pilot, the final implementation would take place in the next year, with continual monitoring in subsequent years. To emphasize that the goal of the project was safety and to focus people's attention on the fact that the project would be ongoing, Mike named his intervention the MAIM project: *measure, analyze, implement, maintain.*

His study of behavior modification had convinced Mike that he would need to identify observable and quantifiable behaviors in order to effectively implement the program. His examination of current safety standards in the warehouse indicated a standard operating procedure that was too vague to be really useful. Managers generally believed that their goal was "to work as quickly, accurately, and safely as possible." When pressed, a few remembered that the company policy handbook suggested that the safety standard was "to have fewer injuries than last year." Mike decided to set two new, specific goals. First, for the current year the target would be to not exceed the previous year's total number of chargeable injuries (which was 17). Second, for the subsequent year the goal would be to reduce the figure to zero, though an intermediate goal of 50 percent reduction would be acceptable.

Baseline information on current safety behavior was collected. This included the total number of accidents and the amount of lost time for accidents for the current and past year. The method of measurement Mike used for determining an annual injury rate is shown in Table 1.

The MAIM team drew up a matrix of recent accidents which showed type of accident, location of the injury on the body, cause of the accident, time of occurrence, age and length of service of the injured, and job classification of the injured. Finally, the baseline data included the cost of the accidents to the department.

Mike met with Tom Alexander, the operations manger of the warehouse, to explain in detail how the program would work. Tom, who had a degree in operations management, had been with the company for three years.

Together Mike and Tom reviewed current baseline performance, and Mike had no trouble convincing Tom to buy into the program based on the various payoffs that would result from improved performance. They discussed and agreed upon the behavioral emphasis of the program, the new safety performance goals, and various feedback methods. Together they determined that the best way to secure authorization from top management was to emphasize the projected performance improvements and the minimal funds outlay required to get the program off the ground. Subsequently, they did obtain this authorization.

Finding the best way to provide feedback to associates was a key part of Mike and Tom's discussion. For some time the two men discussed the merits of positive reinforcement of safe behaviors versus punishment of unsafe behaviors. Should the program use one or the other method, or perhaps both? They considered the corporate culture, the seriousness of the problem, and the long-term effects on their associates, and in the end decided to first attempt the project using positive feedback alone. They would provide a comprehensive list of positive-feedback components to their managers, and suggest to the managers that they each select from this list the kinds of reinforcement they would be most comfortable using. Table 2 shows the list of potential rewards Mike and Tom used.

Despite the fact that "pay in its various forms" was on the list, such a strict budget was established that large monetary rewards were out of the question. Also, Mike and

TABLE 1 Method of Measurement

This is a standard industry method for computing the injury rate at any particular week of the fiscal or calendar year for a company, or part of a company. For example, if a department with 75 employees has 1 injury in its first week, that extrapolates into a rate of 1 injury on average per week for the year. If after 13 weeks there have been 3 injuries, that extrapolates into 12 injuries for the year. Obviously, choosing an appropriate reference year is crucial in determining this statistic.

Number of injuries × annual hours = hours of exposure	Total department injury frequency rate per hours worked
Example: After 1 week: 1 injury × 156,000 annual hours (department) = 3,000 hours of exposure (1 week)	52 injuries on average per year
Example: After 13 weeks: 3 injuries × 156,000 annual hours (department) = 39,000 hours of exposure (13 weeks)	12 injuries on average per year
Example: After 39 weeks: 5 injuries × 156,000 annual hours (department) = 117,000 hours of exposure (39 weeks)	6.7 injuries on average per year

Tom planned to initiate a top-down, tiered approach, in which all managers would be responsible for providing feedback to those individuals on the organizational level immediately below them. In addition, they felt that all managers should emphasize the positive results of the program by posting performance on a daily basis where every associate could see it and by sending the results to their associates at home.

A schedule of reinforcement was also discussed. It was decided that during the first two weeks managers should reward associated with praise whenever a safe working procedure was being followed. This meant that during the first two weeks workers would frequently receive positive feedback. In weekly meetings during this period, managers would require supervisors to cite specific examples of how they had used positive reinforcement during that week. The managers in turn would reward the supervisors with praise. Gradually, as perfor-

mance improved, less emphasis would be placed on direct personal praise, but performance feedback would continue.

Mike then scheduled several meetings involving Tom, the supervisors, and the team leaders in the warehouse. In the first meeting, the details of the program were reviewed. In the second meeting, basic principles of positive reinforcement were conducted. At the same time the principles of timing feedback were reviewed and application exercises were run.

The next step was to communicate all of this information to associates in a condensed form. The operations manager and supervisors met with the associates to explain the details of the program implementation and to tell them what the new goals would be. Questions and objects were handled at this time.

Once the implementation of the pilot program began, a safety performance information graph was posted in the warehouse on the wall across from the time clock. The graph was updated daily.

After the first month Mike distributed the following letter:

TABLE 2 Potential Rewards

- Pay in its various forms: salary, bonuses, stock options, benefits, perquisites
- Promotion: both upward mobility and transfers laterally into desirable positions
- Management praise
- Career opportunities: longer-term chances for growth and development
- Appreciation from customers and/or clients of the organization
- Personal sense of well-being: feeling good about oneself for accomplishing things
- Opportunity to learn: chances to expand one's skills and knowledge base
- Security: sense of job and financial security
- Responsibility: providing individuals with a sense of organizational responsibility
- Respect from coworkers
- Friendship of coworkers

To: All Catalog Associates

As you know, we are all making an all-out effort to reduce the number of accidents in our department. Our goal, of course, is to not have any more during the rest of the calendar year.

The key to not having accidents is in working safely—lifting correctly, being very careful when using a knife, and always being on the alert for potential hazards. Having an accident is not a pleasant experience. If you've never had one, ask someone who has.

We are glad to report that our department had no reportable accidents this past week. This shows that we're thinking and practicing safety. You are to be commended for your contribution toward decreasing our accident frequency rate. The line on the graph looks great going down, doesn't it?

Keep up the good work!

The letter was signed by Mike and Tom and all of the other supervisors.

The information was also sent to the division director, the company safety manager, and to associates at their homes. Associates received the information at home after the first week of implementation, the third week, the sixth week, the tenth week, and once a month thereafter.

Questions for Discussion—Part II

1. What are the strengths and weaknesses of the MAIM program?
2. Estimate how much you believe the company should have invested in this program. How much do you think it did invest?
3. What else might Mike have done to maximize the program's chances of success?
4. Predict the results of the pilot project and the outcome of the project in the subsequent year.

Part III. The Results

Students: Please do not read this part until asked to do so. The result of the pilot project was that the trend toward an increase in injury frequency was reversed. In the first year of full implementation there was an improvement of 94 percent in the accident frequency rate, despite a 64 percent increase in orders processed and an 80 percent increase in merchandise handled. After five months of the following year, only one injury was charged. This happened in spite of the fact that there had been a 76 percent increase in orders processed, an 89 percent increase in the amount of merchandise handled, and an approximate 30 percent increase in the number of people in the department over the same period in the previous year.

Total investment in the project was approximately $3,000, about $300 of which was materials and the rest was salary.

An additional result of the program was that it served as a model for the application of behavior modification principles in other areas of the company. The same approach was used to modify safety procedures in manufacturing, receiving, and building and grounds, and significant positive results were achieved. The legal assistance department adapted the principles to reduce a five-month correspondence backlog within six weeks.

Mike Henley had more than met his challenge, and his program eventually won a regional industry award for excellence in organizational change.

Questions for Discussion—Part III

1. The MAIM program achieved improved safety over a period of several years. What were the reasons for this success? What would be required to ensure continued success for the program?
2. What sort of corporate culture supports this kind of program?
3. Do you believe this success is typical of safety programs? From a behavioral standpoint, why do some safety programs succeed while others fail?
4. What do we learn from corporate success stories such as this one, as opposed to stories of corporate problems and failures? Under what circumstances are companies likely to keep their successes to themselves? Under what circumstances are they likely to publicize them?

Source: This case was written by Rae André under a grant from the Minerva Education Institute with funding from NIOSH, and is in the public domain.

Case 2 International Rose Growers, Inc.: Managing a Small Business Start-up in the Caribbean

Introduction

David Langley was the 58-year-old president of International Rose Growers, Inc., a New York–based firm with annual sales close to $8 million. Like his father and grandfather before him, Langley grew flowers for distribution to wholesale markets along the eastern coast of the United States. Domestically, he ran about 12 acres of greenhouses, putting the company among the top ten greenhouse operations in the United States in 1995.

To compete with flower growers from Latin America, Langley started a subsidiary in Santa Nueva (not the real name), an island republic in the Caribbean. The following text is a transcript of discussions with him two years after he successfully started the new operation.

Managing the International Startup

We first became interested in going abroad when we heard about it from one of our competitors. We had decided it might be a good idea to hedge our bets and move to a climate where there is no fuel requirement. So we went down to Santa Nueva to see the competitor's operation and we thought he was doing a good job. Sixty percent of the flowers used in the United States today are imported. Those flowers are grown with labor at $2 a day, versus what we have to pay at minimum wage, around $3.35 per hour. We thought there was money in it.

But establishing yourself in a foreign country is not easy. There are pitfalls. The laws of these governments look like they welcome business coming in. It's all on the books: the laws are there to help you. The government itself wants you there in a lot of these countries. What they spend nationally on oil alone exceeds the money they get from exports, which constantly puts them in the doghouse internationally. They can't buy anything outside, so they're constantly in a state of devaluation relative to everybody else. In addition to that, they have an enormous birthrate which constantly keeps their poverty in place.

There's a lot of money to be made if you know how. You go down there and start spending your money and then you find out that the laws have to be administered by people, and the people are where the hang-ups come because they don't obey the law. They circumvent it to their own benefit. In other words, they make it difficult for you for various reasons.

For example, we have to import a lot of things into the country because they don't have them. Well, they can let that stuff sit down at that dock until some guy clears it. They let our crates of greenhouses sit there for two to three *months*. It threw us way back, cost us thousands of dollars. We had importers down there who knew their business. All the paperwork was right, but all the government guy says is "I don't think this is right," and it gets kicked back and forth.

One problem is that a lot of the government income is taxes on imports, so that they're very strict, particularly if it's an American company that's shipping. This holdup means that everybody's benefiting except the poor guy who has to cut the flowers, because they've made work for the phone operator and everybody else. You're constantly checking, checking, checking. It's a make-work scheme, in any sense of the word, whether it's in Detroit or the Caribbean, and they're masters at it. A lot of these foreign countries, they don't operate, they make work.

For example, down where we are, the bureaucracy has increased 50 percent in four years—50 percent more government employees. Going through the airports, there's a guy who puts the tag on your thing and there's a guy who takes it off, five feet away. You can tell them your problem, but they don't understand the problem of business having to get that money moving that's sitting there. They don't realize that they have to collect their taxes and build their country from business. Even having a conversation on the phone is hard. The conversations are long, the conversations are flowered. They don't get to the point, and this, of course, is frustrating if you're not used to it. And especially if you're paying for a long distance phone call. It takes them a half hour to say good morning!

Back about six months ago, we needed this particular type of spreader for an insecticide and I wanted to make sure it was there. We wanted it the following morning and I wanted it delivered that day. And my secretary is on the phone talking to this guy 25 miles away. He kept saying, "Mañana" (tomorrow), and I kept saying, "Ayer" (yesterday). The secretary kept saying, "Mañana," and I kept saying, "Ayer." Finally, with negotiations back and forth, I got it.

So you have to tighten things. They don't respect you if they know they're getting away with it, because everybody is watching everybody else. We made that mistake. We were too easy. Of course, these people are very hungry. Their unemployment rate is tremendous. The established rate is 40 percent, but they don't count everybody. If they counted everybody, it's around 80 percent. You learn as you go, and you learn from talking to people. They don't respect softness and, yet, they don't respect anybody who's going around shouting and yelling either. You've got to have them understand who's boss.

We had a guy who was coming in late all the time, so we gave him a written notice. After you hire him for three months, the government says you own him: it costs you money to let him go. If he's there three months, you might have to give him another three months pay. After a year, you might have to give him another six months pay. The guy was late. We gave him the notice. He still was late, so we had to let him go. It didn't cost us anything. If he breaks the company rules and they're allowable rules according to the law, then you can get rid of him without any pay. But we had to get tougher and tougher and tougher. It's so easy to be easy because the labor's cheap. But you have to realize that any time you're not making money, it's coming out of capital, so labor's not cheap then.

We weren't knowledgeable about the culture. We assumed that they're like us—sort of like us—if you have the language. That's the mistake you make. You can hire a Nuevan to run the place if you've got the language yourself, but you have to know the language so well that you get the innuendoes and that's something none of us have. Very few Americans have that. You could hire a Cuban, Mexican, or a Puerto Rican, but even they do not think like we do. They're more apt to identify with the person instead of identifying with the problem. They identify with their emotions and they think, "Well, poor guy."

We hadn't taken one dime out of there yet, and we were asked for a raise. They'll say, "Look at these poor people here. Don't you think they ought to be given hope?" Well, we hired them and they had 60 percent unemployment in the town, and yet I didn't give them hope? They're big on expectations and poor on execution down there.

You have to have an American boss, period. When we went into the village there the only means of transportation was the truck that we had bought. Now, almost everybody rides up in a new Honda motorcycle. The standard of living has gone up because of us. All those guys underneath can be Nuevans, but you got to have an American boss because you have to teach the Nuevan middle managers how you want it. If you go down there and take their way of doing it, you've lost everything you've ever had.

There was a lot of petty thievery when we built the place. A bar down the end of the street was built in the last year since we built. The owner didn't have a thing before. He's the guy that plowed our property and worked the field before we put our greenhouses up. Right after we built, he was able to build himself a bar and a dance hall from similar materials that were used to construct our greenhouses. I call it Langley's bar. It's right at the end of our road. I often stop in for a cerveza.

All the foreigners do better than we Americans do. Number one, they can bribe the governments. We put strings on our businessmen that are absolutely abominable and then holler that we can't export anything. Another thing is the gringo approach. The Japanese are a new face in there and they operate a little differently than we do. They always say, "Yes." We say, "No," but they say "Yes" and don't mean it, so it doesn't hurt as much. It's a different approach and they've sold one hell of a lot of cars. In fact, I have never driven an American car down there. If you want to go buy an American truck, just forget it. We have a little two-cylinder Japanese truck that's running up and down those hills for 50 kilometers per gallon.

Personnel in the Local Operations

Our manager there came originally from Puerto Rico. I hired him when he was 15 or 16 years old. He has worked for me for 17 years. We usually have about 75 percent Puerto Ricans working for us up North. I am like a father to him. He had a child and named it after me. I sent him down and he's been as happy as a lark, but that's Jorge. That's not everybody. You can't generalize on Jorge. He's doing a good job and he loves it there. However, Jorge's also losing his English. And he is getting maybe too friendly with the locals. He's fitting in too well, you might say.

Also, the girls will come and work for you, but if they get pregnant, you have to give them at least a month off with pay. Sure enough, they'll come when they're already pregnant. First thing you know, you have five young ladies pregnant, nobody to do the work and you're paying for it. When we hired our first secretary, we thought she could speak English, took me nine months to get rid of her. I fired her. She couldn't speak a word of English. "Yes" or "No." She had the books all fouled up. Pregnant, too. She lied to us about it.

We have 3 managers and 20 employees. That's what we call the office help: managers. We have an office manager, a pack and ship manager, and an overall manager. These people can all speak Spanish. Then we have about 12 men and 8 women. The women do the bunching. The men do the cutting, are night watchmen and all kinds of things.

You look in that packing shed down there and it's probably identical to this one up here, only there are no conveyer belts. God forbid I ever put a conveyer down there because it'll only work about three hours. And that's when I'm working. The more we check up on them, the more controls we put on them in equipment, the more apt they are to say, "This doesn't work now." It's so simple to break a computer. You spit at it or push the wrong damn buttons and it's done. We sent down one of the finest little power mowers you can buy. We started it up before it went down. It worked perfectly. It was eight or nine months later and three mechanical overhauls before we got that thing working.

Last year I arrived and found 10 or 15 men cutting the fields with machetes. I'm still not sure that isn't the cheapest. If you hire them for $2 a day, they're telling you something. They really are telling you something. You can hire their people, on certain jobs anyway, cheaper than you can use the damned equipment. You won't see a lot of bookkeeping machines in Santa Nueva. They use people and they'll get it right. They'll have a calculator, but that's about the extent of it. You might in a very big American company, but not generally.

We have parameters for the manager: checklists for his rounds, a checklist for his maintenance, a checklist for his night man. You must be specific. You don't just walk out and say "clean." You've got to say, "Clean this table, clean that table, clean this." Write it down and give it to him. If you don't do that some of it will be forgotten, some of it just won't be done. And then you can't come in and holler, because the guy will say he didn't hear you. They're really sharp this way. You have to be specific. You have to draw it step by step or they just won't do it. If they have a package of cigarettes, the empty packs will go onto the floor, until you tell them, "The next time you do that ... out. We are not going to have that. This is not the way we're going to be." You go to the company next door to ours where he never enforced these things and it's a dump. Not that he doesn't make money, but it's a dump, a literal dump. It's terrible.

We have the manager take videotape pictures around the plant every week so we see what the plants look like, see what the surroundings look like, see what the house-keeping looks like. We also have him send all the bills, the bank balances, and the payroll up each week.

We have a problem with visitors, too. We have to keep them out. They'll just drop in and say, "Can I see the place?" and they'll take up the manager's time and they'll take up the office time. When they get to talking, they'll talk about their grandfather, their father, their brothers, their sisters, and it's on your time. So we had to discourage that. We had to fence the place to keep the horses out, the cows out, and the people out. Just so you can keep control of the flowers. I don't know if we stopped it. If you have a fence, you have to say, "Don't crawl over the fence."

A lot of growers don't do things the way we do them, even up North. I like it written down. I hate verbal orders, unless it's just a day order. If it's a long-term deal it should be written down and put in the policy. "This is what we do in this way at this particular time." We're known to have the best place in Santa Nueva and there are a lot of flower growers. In the town, we're known as operating a very tight ship.

The President's Personal Involvement

I've spent a lot of hard times down there. When I go down there, I'm alone most of the time. There are many, many nights you're all alone. There's no one in the hotel. That's why I like to take somebody with me to play gin or to go out to eat. You're just there in the mountains and you're all alone. It's not a bad hotel as hotels go. Jorge has a list he puts in my room for me. I have a toaster, coffee, water, coke, beer, vodka, insecticides, and other stuff. Of course, they haven't changed the linen in the three years we've been going there. They say you don't go in the kitchen or you'll never eat there again. I spray the room for cockroaches and watch them wiggling. In the middle of the night you hear them. I spray all over the room every time I go out.

The hotels are owned by the government and they're rented from the government. It's amazing. These beautiful hotels rent for two or three hundred dollars a month. And you should see the way they keep it. Terrible. You can't swim in the swimming pool. It's green. It's a beautiful swimming pool and I know how to tell them to keep it, but they won't. If I were going to be down there a lot, I'd take my own chlorine and fix it. It would only cost $100 to use the pool the whole time I was there. Probably, they'd give me free drinks out of it, they'd make it up. They just don't know how to do things. They fool around.

When I was robbed at the hotel, I went to the police station and gave them a list just because I wanted it for the insurance company. Nothing happened. Nobody found anything. I didn't eat in that hotel for the next two months, the next two times I was there. I wouldn't go in their dining room, because I knew those guys knew who did it. I was there alone. Somebody had to be watching and the town is too small not to know the thief and I knew the police knew. I found out the hotel was responsible, but you can't get blood out of a stone, so I said, "All right, I want a 10 percent discount rate until this is paid off on my hotel room," which they went along with. After that, they put a guard on me. Every night I have a guard, a private guard. They give him a peso. He's sitting right outside my door. I've never felt physically afraid, just alone, that's all.

I went down to town one night trying to negotiate for this land. Downtown at night looks like a country road. The house lights are on, but there are no street lights. I went down there negotiating with this family right in their house. (The guy who said that he owned the land just buzzed me bigtime. I had it all negotiated and later found out we couldn't get a clear title.) Anyway, I'm sitting there in this house with this family. Nobody can speak English, and I can't speak Spanish, but we're negotiating. It was this guy and his son, who could speak English a little, and the whole family—his wife and relatives. They all come in to look at me. Everybody was just staring. All of a sudden, I started to wiggle my ears, and I'll tell you, they had a hilarious time. My wife was up in the hotel. She was worried I'd disappeared in the middle of the night down in a strange country. I didn't get home till one or two o'clock in the morning.

It's just a new ball game and you should detail it right from the beginning. We should have had notebooks, which was my fault. We should have had everything detailed— the duties, the laws of the country, the work rules. If I were to do it now, I would have all this stuff researched and if we ever expand again, we'll know what the hell we're doing. And there'll be no problem. I spent quite a bit of time down there last June when we were planting, but I should have spent two months down there. I did spend practically that much time down there off and on, but I should have been right there and taken over the job of doing it. It's not the Nuevan's fault at all. I might lose it if I don't get down there more.

Our government insures us if we're taken over down there because of riot or insurrection or government acquisition. Otherwise, you couldn't get any loans. You'll see people with jobs there and you wouldn't believe it. Take the waiters in the hotels. You'll go down there today and five years from now and they're practically working for nothing. There's nobody in the hotels from one day to the next. Yet, they'll be there. They have no place to go. There's no place to go except the United States and there are 500,000 Nuevans working in the United States. You literally can't get a plane reservation back to the States during the first two weeks of January.

But it's gorgeous. It's a paradise. You couldn't believe it until you see it. Everything grows. You can have a terrific amount of flowers; I love to go there. I'm getting homesick for it. I would say they've treated us very well. After all, it's their country. It's not up to them to change ... we've trying to take a profit out of it.

Discuss

1. From the standpoint of cross-cultural OB, what does a business need to know about the country in which it plans to operate? List these needs and then prioritize them according to which personnel and OB issues are absolutely crucial to making a major financial investment.

2. How can a small business find out what it needs to know about the culture of the country in which it plans to operate?

3. Describe Langley's leadership style. Is it appropriate to the situation?

4. Describe the personal characteristics of the company president who would be most likely to succeed in this venture.

5. What are the current OB problems in the business, and what should Langley do about them?

Source: © Copyright Rae André 1995. Used with permission.

Part I

A German multinational went out of the business of producing mobile phones and related products, and sold its two U.S. divisions—the Baker Company and the Eiger[†] Company—to separate small groups of investors. As a result, Baker and Eiger became competitors for a variety of telephone development projects involving creating prototypes and then producing phones in quantities specified by the customer. Quantities varied significantly, but typically fell somewhere between 50,000 and 500,000 units.

Baker and Eiger each had close to 300 employees. Both had been startup divisions for their German parent, a typical, formal German company in which major production and manufacturing decisions were made at corporate headquarters in Stuttgart. Both Baker and Eiger realized that, upon becoming independent from their parent company, their management approaches would have to be reexamined.

Baker Company made no changes in its U.S. management team. The team was accustomed to producing high-quality products to meet parent company specifications, and the new owners of the company reasoned that one advantage of keeping it intact would be to send a message to customers that the company was not losing control over either its design processes or its production setup. The owners felt fortunate in having Karl Meyers as president. Meyers had spent 10 years in the Stuttgart offices in various managerial capacities, and he had been involved as an engineer on several new product designs. With an American wife and two children in high school, he was happy to stay on for an indefinite period to run Baker. He was totally familiar with the systems and processes that Baker employees were used to, and he would provide stable leadership.

The owners of Eiger Corporation had similar goals. They wanted both stability and continuity, but also the capacity for innovation. However, when the company was spun off from the parent, their most likely internal candidate for president had returned to Germany. After much searching and discussion, the company hired as their president Sam Jackson, the former head of new product development for a medium-sized consumer products company. Jackson was an American with 15 years of increasing levels of responsibility in three companies. He came well rec-

ommended as someone who could develop employees to their fullest and motivate them to enhance profitability.

The Baker Philosophy

Karl Meyers believed that his company's success at producing a high volume of top quality products depended on its streamlined and efficient management processes. Upon stepping into his job as president, he immediately sent a memo to all employees and customers reassuring them that he would run Baker with the same attention to detail and the same efficiency as before. Also, to provide the necessary coordination, he and his management team personally supervised all major decisions. Under Meyers' leadership, the detailed organizational charts, job descriptions, and procedures manuals that were utilized by the German parent were updated to reflect the company's new status as an independent entity. Individuals knew exactly what to do in their jobs. Through regularly scheduled meetings, their work was efficiently coordinated. Although some engineers personally preferred more latitude in their jobs, most accepted that, when it came to making a profit for the company, efficiency mattered more than their personal preferences.

The Eiger Philosophy

Believing that organization charts should not dictate how decisions are made, Sam Jackson organized his engineers into teams and gave the teams responsibility for different products. Typically teams had some of their products in the manufacturing stage and some in the development stage. The manufacturing wing of the company was also organized into teams, which were made responsible for monitoring product quality. Jackson invested a significant chunk of money in training teams to take on more responsibility for decision making. Because of this new philosophy, some managers worried that their jobs might be on the line. Jackson chose not to replace two managers who retired, and also one who left because he disliked the new management philosophy.

Jackson felt that the company was small enough to have a family-like atmosphere. He eliminated preferred parking and the executive dining room. In manufacturing, he made clear that everyone was expected to pitch in. For example, faster workers should help slower workers to

[†] pronounced "eye-grr"

complete the day's quota. Jackson also established weekly 90-minute seminars so engineers could learn about each others' areas of expertise. Occasionally he brought in outside experts to teach new technologies. Most engineers appreciated the new opportunities for growth and sharing, though a few grumbled that the seminars were a waste of time.

The Challenge

Baker and Eiger often competed for the same customers, typically large consumer products firms wanting to outsource the design and development of some of their products. It happened that Certex Corporation was looking for a company to design a cell phone and produce 500 prototypes for test marketing. Being successful in this project could lead to a two-year contract to produce a large quantity of phones. There was a catch, however: Certex was under pressure to get the product into the market for the December holidays. The whole process, from creating the prototype design through manufacturing the 500 prototype phones, had to be accomplished in less than one month.

Discuss

1. How do the organizational constraints for Baker and Eiger differ? Consider environmental factors, the nature of their people, and the nature of their work.

2. Which company will do the best job producing the prototypes?

Part II

Baker and Eiger agreed to enter into a competition to produce the prototype. Certex, interested in obtaining the best possible phone design, agreed to compensate each company for its costs. Certex's decision about who would get the final contract to produce the phones would be made after the winning prototype was selected. However, the company made clear that producing the best prototype was only one of many criteria it would consider in awarding the final contract, which would be for a minimum of 200,000 phones.

Both Baker and Eiger received Certex's specifications for the phone on September 1, with the goal of delivering the 500 phones by September 29.

Baker's Approach

September 1, Friday. As soon as he received the specifications from Certex, Meyers sent e-mails to his various departments with directions on how to proceed. The best engineering design team in the firm was assigned to the project. The industrial engineering group was directed to begin work on designing the methods of production. Purchasing was authorized to buy the necessary materials. Manufacturing was told to schedule in manufacturing time later in the month. To the other industrial engineering

groups, executives and key managers, Meyers spelled out the project's time constraints and its value to the company. He urged them to give the project their full cooperation.

Meyers kept in touch with Certex management through phone conversations at least twice a week. He also copied them on most internal memos.

September 5, Tuesday. After returning from the long September 4 weekend, each of the groups concentrated on its assigned problems. A couple of issues became clear rather quickly. One was that certain materials would not be available in a reasonable amount of time. Another was that if manufacturing was to schedule in enough time for production, other major projects would have to be set aside. The industrial engineers met and decided to do nothing for a few days until the design engineers were closer to a final design. Meyers called a meeting of the principals for September 8 to assess progress.

September 8, Friday. At the meeting, Meyers learned that the industrial engineers had not yet begun working on the project. He could not believe his ears. He angrily ordered the design engineers to work through the weekend to produce the design, and he told the industrial engineers to be on call to come into the office as soon as the design had taken shape. He ordered purchasing to get the needed materials "or else." Preoccupied by these immediate issues, he did not deal with the issue of scheduling manufacturing time.

September 10, Sunday. During the weekend, Meyers was in the office constantly, working with his design engineers. Late Sunday evening they finally settled on a design. Because it was too late to call in the industrial engineers, Meyers scheduled a meeting with them for 8 a.m. on Monday.

September 11, Monday. At the meeting, Meyers and the head of the design engineering team presented the design to the industrial engineers. Meyers directed them to begin organizing the manufacturing process. After the meeting, Meyers communicated the status of the project to others in the company in a lengthy memo. In the memo, he also reminded everyone that there were only 18 days to deadline.

September 13, Wednesday. The industrial engineers learned from purchasing that a particular part was not yet available. They decided to begin assembly of the phones anyhow, and to incorporate the part later.

September 18, Monday. In a phone call with Certex, Meyers learned that a part in the already partially assembled phones was defective. (Eiger had discovered the problem and relayed it to Certex management, who informed Meyers.) Meyers called an emergency meeting of industrial engineers and manufacturing managers to iron out how to coordinate replacement of the defective part with inclusion of the missing part and still complete the phones on time. The decision was made to stop partial assembly and wait until all parts were available before completing assembly.

During the week, the purchasing managers were constantly on the phone. Although it had taken them several days, they had finally identified an out-of-country source for the missing part. Meyers wanted frequent updates on where the part was in the shipping process. The purchasing managers also discovered a new supplier for the defective part, and kept Meyers informed about where that part was in the shipping process as well.

September 25, Monday, and the rest of the week. . . . By Monday morning all components were available, and by Monday afternoon manufacturing had cleared time to begin making the phones. Managers pushed their assemblers to finish by Friday. By Tuesday afternoon, the first batch of 100 phones was sent to the quality control department, where three were found to be defective. By Thursday morning, the process for fixing the defect was put in place. However, by Friday only 350 phones had been built. The assemblers complained that preassembling some phones had actually slowed them down. Not wanting to incur overtime expenses, Meyers did not authorize weekend work. On Monday and Tuesday, the remaining 150 phones were completed. Meyers waived the quality control inspection and shipped to Certex only two business days late.

Eiger's Approach

On June 28 Jackson notified the leaders of his key teams to schedule a meeting for Friday, September 1, to discuss the specifications they would receive from Certex. Like the president of Baker, he put his top engineering design team on the project and kept others in the loop via e-mail.

September 1, Friday. The leaders of the design, industrial engineering, purchasing and manufacturing teams convened early in the morning to discuss the specifications, followed by separate meetings for all teams and their members. Many individuals expressed concern that the long holiday weekend should be utilized to jump-start the project. Jackson asked for volunteers to come in over the weekend to work on moving the project forward and several people volunteered.

In the afternoon, teams proceeded with their various assignments. By mid-afternoon purchasing had learned that a key part would not be readily available and emailed this information to all the groups and the rest of the company. Purchasing called a meeting of all the teams for Tuesday, September 5, at 8 a.m. to resolve this problem.

September 2–4, the weekend. Four people—one manufacturing manager, two production design engineers, and one industrial engineer—spent Saturday afternoon and Sunday producing a mock-up of the product. In the process they discovered several ready-made components that did not appear to work as advertised. They decided to bring this problem to the Tuesday morning meeting.

September 5, Tuesday. At 8 a.m. the team leaders met as planned. Several problems still needed to be addressed.

Like Baker, Eiger had been missing a key part. However, the problem of the key part had been resolved over the weekend when a design engineer not working on the project remembered an obscure Korean supplier who made it.

The weekend team, which dubbed themselves the "Weekend Warriors," reported on the component problems they had uncovered and agreed to continue to work on these as an informal group, in addition to their other duties in their formal workgroups.

Eiger also had to decide when to assemble. The manufacturing managers agreed to keep production capacity fully available the last week (September 26–30) for assembly of the 500 phones. Meanwhile, they would clean up other projects. They would also discuss with their assembly teams the likely quality issues they would encounter and would reinforce team processes for checking quality before the phones left the team. Two production design engineers agreed to double as quality control checkers by sampling 5 phones in each 100 that were produced. Teams with five perfect phones were promised an afternoon off.

September 12, Tuesday. The Weekend Warriors had debugged the component problems and resolved all except one. It had become clear to them that one ready-made component was clearly defective. To save time, it would have to be reengineered by Eiger. Jackson created a project team of highly capable engineers to work with the Weekend Warriors on the problem.

September 25, Monday. All components were finally available. Manufacturing worked hard all week, and by noon on Friday, 500 phones had been assembled, checked for quality by their teams, and sampled for quality by the volunteer production design engineers. On Friday afternoon, the 500 units were shipped to Certex on schedule.

Discuss

1. Which company was more effective at producing the prototype?

2. Compare the organizational designs of Baker and Eiger. How do they differ in terms of decision making, structure, control and motivation, job design, and culture?

3. Which organization should win the contract to produce the phones?

Source: © Copyright Rae André 2000. Used with permission. Acknowledgment. Some aspects of the structure of this case were suggested by "The Paradoxical Twins: Acme and Omega Electronics," by John F. Veiga.

The Assignment

Evaluate yourself with respect to your career goals. To do this:

1. Research your chosen career to find out what personality and other personal characteristics predict success in that career.

For example, an overview of personality factors can be found in: P. D. Tieger and B. Barron-Tieger, *Do What You Are: Discover the Perfect Career for You Through the Secrets of Personality Type,* 2nd ed. (Boston, MA: Little, Brown and Company, 1995).

In addition, search academic databases for studies of the MBTI factors and the Big Five personality factors that predict performance in your chosen career.

2. Describe yourself based on the self-assessments in this textbook, including the online Big Five (see IPIP-NEO) survey described in the Explorations section of Chapter 2.

3. Compare your characteristics with those of the ideal characteristics for a person in your chosen career (as discovered in Step 1 above).

4. Write a paper based on the specifications given by your instructor.

Prerequisite

Students must have access to a company that someone in their group knows fairly well, or can readily learn about. Typically, either the student or someone he or she knows has worked there, or the student has access through personal connections. The kind of information required for the presentation is not typically available on the Internet or even in books.

Presentation Assignment

Analyze the organizational design of a company someone in your group knows well. Present your analysis to the class assuming you are presenting to the board of directors of the company. After your presentation, students in the class will also ask you questions about your analysis.

Consult the evaluation form below for details of how your presentation will be evaluated by the professor.

Instructions for the content of your presentation:

1. Using the model of organizational design from Chapter 15, present your company's current design. Present the design part by part, from constraints through design variables. (See Chapter 15, Table 3.)

Use course concepts as much as you can. That is, throughout your presentation, use the material from our lecture notes and readings to deepen your analysis. Be sure to include lots of company-specific examples that indicate your company's actual design.

Also, include an organizational chart under the "structure" section (a hand drawing is okay), telling what type of structure the company has.

2. Analyze the company's design fit: currently, how well do the company's design variables fit the company's design constraints? What strengths and weaknesses does this fit, or lack thereof, suggest?

3. Given what you can predict about likely changes in the organization's constraints, describe how the design of this organization should be altered, or not, in the short term (1 to 2 years).

4. Given what you can predict about likely changes in the organization's constraints, describe how the design of this organization should be altered, or not, in the long term (3 to 10 years).

You should strive to make your presentation:

- Well-organized
- Interesting to the class
- You must hand your slides to the professor at the beginning of your presentation.
- Your presentation must be 15 to 16 minutes long, not including questions.

All students must present. A question-and-answer period will follow each presentation. Your group members should be prepared to ask pertinent questions, as though they were members of the board.

Company Design Presentations Evaluation Form

Group number: _____ Company: _____ Start time: _____ End time: _____

Criteria: The group uses these concepts correctly and thoroughly, or answers the questions well, and uses specific examples to support their analysis.

Scale: 0 = omitted, 1 = to a very little extent, 3 = to some extent, 4 = to a great extent, 5 = to a very great extent

Concepts and Questions	Points	Comments
Design Constraints		
Environment (external)		
People		
Core work of the company ("technology")		
Design Variables		
Decision making		
Structure (include an organizational chart, and name the type of structure)		
Control and motivation		
Work design		
Organizational culture		
Fit		
Does the company's current design fit its constraints? What strengths and weaknesses do you detect in the fit?		
Will the company's design continue to fit its constraints in the short term (1 to 2 years)?		
Will the company's design continue to fit its constraints in the long term (3 to 10 years)?		
Presentation Overall		
The presentation content is well organized. (Topics are presented in order, etc.)		
The team is well organized. (The slides are given to the professor in advance. Members are on time and prepared. A unified team culture is apparent.)		
The group made the presentation interesting to the class (for example, by using graphics, site visit report, handouts, or other engaging supplementary material).		
Total Points		
Letter Grade		

**The Connections Project and Paper:
An Integrative Project on Leading Teams**

The Assignment

In the Connections Project you will be making connections between 1) the textbook theory and 2) your own and your classmates' behaviors as you observe them in a number of in-class team projects. During the course of the semester, you will have the opportunity to lead, and also to be a member of, various one-class-session project teams, and you will write a term paper about your experiences.

The Paper

Your paper will include these sections:

Part I: A commentary/diary on each of the Connections project days, including your role *and* the role of others. Each daily analysis should *draw on the theory* that we have covered to that point in the course, including the readings for the day of the project. The course concepts you use will evolve as you learn, of course, and will also depend on what happens in your group. Do not describe the assigned problem and its solution (the "content" for the day); instead, describe the *process* your group used to deal with the problem. Each daily entry must be at least 300 words, with no maximum. Of course, it is a really good idea to write up each Connections project shortly after attending the Connections class and reading the relevant theory.

An A-range paper will make extensive use of multiple course concepts (including but not limited to personality factors, group roles and processes, decision making, leadership types, motivational principles, stress, and one-to-one interaction) and will illustrate these by examples from your group's process; it will demonstrate how your style and observational capability of self and others have evolved during the term; a B-range paper does what the A-range paper does but somewhat less effectively; a C-range paper

discusses group process to some extent but fails to give convincing examples of it, and probably relies too much on description of the project; a D-range paper is one that describes the project you did on a given day and hardly discusses the group process.

Part II: An analysis of your style, including your personality and leadership style, based on :

a. Your IPIP-NEO/Big Five results (do not use the Myers-Briggs test, although you may use the Myers-Briggs letters). Consider using the subscales as well as the major categories. Add anything else you think relevant, such as information from other tests you have taken in our textbook, or feedback from having asked others to take tests with you in mind.

b. Feedback you have gathered from group members during the term (350 word minimum, no maximum).

Part III: Imagine you are facing an interview with a company that emphasizes team work. Describe to the interviewer how the group experience you have gained in this project will help you to be effective in the company (250 word minimum, no maximum).

Appendix: Feedback forms from all participants for the day you lead.

Append:

a. A list of all participants for that day and whether or not they gave you the written feedback. If they did not, please provide an explanation of your attempts to entice them to do so. Be sure to make a reasonable attempt, and document it. You will lose points if you don't attempt to get the feedback, and they will lose points if they do not provide it.

b. All of their forms.

The Connections Project: Feedback Form for Group Leaders

Leader's name: _____   Evaluator's name: _____

Connections Problem # and topic _____   Date of class _____

Answer each question with a number, and write additional comments on the back:

5 = to a very great extent   4 = to a great extent   3 = to some extent   2 = to a little extent   1 = to a very little extent   NA = not applicable to this assignment

Questions	Points
To what extent did I address these questions for you:	
a. "Why am I here?"	_____
b. "What are we going to do?"	_____
c. "What's in it for me?"	_____
To what extent did I create a culture that encourages participating by:	
• Being sure people come to the meeting prepared.	_____
• Posing open-ended questions to the group.	_____
• Calling on people directly.	_____
• Summarizing and re-stating ideas that come from the group.	_____
• Maintaining eye contact.	_____
• Waiting for answers and not jumping into awkward pauses.	_____
• Describing to the group what I have observed about their process.	_____.
To what extent did I:	
• Reinforce on-task comments: Answer them, make eye contact with the speaker, and build on them.	_____
• Re-state the objectives of the meeting.	
• When an individual went on a tangent, summarized the discussion to that point, and then asked someone to comment on the summary.	_____
• When someone went off-task, asked them a yes/no question, and then asked someone else an open-ended question.	_____
• Used an easel or similar device to collect information, so people could stay on track with the ideas that are being expressed. If appropriate to the nature of the problem being solved, used an agenda, and stuck to it.	_____
To what extent did I:	
• End by being sure people have clear assignments?	_____
• Take time to reinforce those members who stayed on task?	_____
• Acknowledge the group's accomplishments?	_____
Leaders: Add here a few questions that reflect your own leadership concerns and goals for improvement:	
_____	_____
_____	_____
_____	_____
_____	_____
_____	_____
_____	_____
_____	_____
Total Points (of _____ possible)	_____

Required: On the back of these sheets (or typed below) please provide:

Some positive feedback, about my style and ability in leading.

Some constructive criticism about my style and ability to lead.

Chapter Glossaries

A note to students

To help you study key terms, this glossary is organized by chapter. We also designed it so that you can easily cover a definition while trying to remember it.

Chapter 1: Why Mastering Organizational Behavior Is Essential to Your Career

boundaryless career
A (linear) career characterized by increased movement between organizations.

boundaryless organization
Organization in which the internal barriers to communication and information are removed among the organization's functions (such as engineering, marketing, and manufacturing) and between domestic and foreign operations.

career anchor
An occupational self-concept based on one's self-perceived talents, abilities, values, needs, and motives.

career plateau
Stage at which one is seen as a solid company citizen, but not in line for advancement.

closed systems
Systems that do not easily absorb inputs from their environments.

contingent jobs
Jobs that are temporary and not expected to last.

core competencies
The operations in which a company excels.

downsize, rightsize
To grow smaller by cutting employees..

employability skills
Social and behavioral skills necessary for fitting into the workplace.

employee empowerment
Allowing employees to make decisions that traditionally were made by managers alone.

employment
Working for someone.

globalization
The increased internationalization of business based on the movement of trade, resources, and personnel across borders and regions.

human resources management (HRM)
The particular organizational function responsible for selecting employees, establishing compensation systems, managing benefits, implementing training programs, and coordinating labor relations.

impermeable boundaries
Boundaries that restrict information flow.

independent contributor
Someone who works without subordinates to do an important organizational job.

job
A specified task or set of tasks an individual does as part of an occupation.

knowledge work
Work that requires high levels of analysis and is performed by well-educated individuals; often requires specialists.

linear career
A career in which one stays within the same profession, but changes jobs and companies fairly frequently, moving up the ladder.

macro level OB
OB theory covering how human systems are organized, structured, and controlled.

manager
Someone who works through people to accomplish the work of an organization.

micro level OB
OB theory covering individual, interpersonal, and group behaviors.

networked organization
An organization comprised of loosely joined companies that may have quite different designs, each adapted to a separate environment, but that are organized through one core holding company.

offshore
To outsource jobs to other countries.

open systems
Systems that easily absorb inputs from their environments.

organization
A coordinated set of individuals working together on a relatively continuous basis toward common goals.

organizational behavior (OB)
The study of how people behave in organizations.

organizational learning
The process by which knowledge acquired by individuals is embedded in organizational memory.

organizational theory (OT)
Term reserved for macro level concepts.

outsource
To send jobs to other companies or other countries.

permeable boundaries
Boundaries that permit the free flow of information both into and out of the organization.

primary labor market
The market that includes professional, managerial, and other white-collar jobs.

protected classes
Factors such as age, gender, and race, on the basis of which it is illegal to discriminate.

re-engineering
The redesign of business processes to improve performance on such outcomes as cost, quality, service, and speed.

role

The behavior expected of someone who holds a particular status.

secondary labor market

The market of jobs with few benefits and little security.

spiral career

A career in which one follows a variety of interests based on one's skills centered around one core interest.

steady state career

A career in which one remains in one job long-term, changing employers infrequently.

system

A set of elements that combine to form a complex whole.

systems theory

The theory that organizations are entities that transform inputs into outputs and operate within constraints imposed on them by their environments.

total quality management (TQM)

Organization-wide processes that emphasize excellence in outcomes such as product reliability and durability.

transitory career

A career in which one moves among many different unrelated positions.

transparency

Visibility into organizational decision making to assess its truthfulness.

wage differential

The increment of the median salary of union members compared to non union workers,

work

An activity an individual engages in to earn money.

Chapter 2: Your Personality and Style

affect

The manner in which one expresses one's emotions.

analytic ability

Reasoning and problem-solving skills.

antisocial personality disorder

A disorder characterized by the lack of anxiety, remorse, or guilt; psychopathy, sociopathy.

attitude

The combination of one's beliefs about something (one's cognitions) with one's feelings (affect) and actions (behavior) toward it.

attitude surveys

Written questionnaires that tap job satisfaction, organizational commitment, and company-specific attitudes.

belief

The conviction that a particular matter is true or false.

bounded emotionality

An approach in which certain constrained emotional expressions are encouraged at work in order to encourage community building and personal well-being.

cognitions

Ways of knowing.

cognitive dissonance

Anxiety that results from simultaneously holding contradictory attitudes, or from behaving in ways that contradict one's beliefs.

continuum

A continuous series.

creative ability/creativity

The ability to produce innovative, high-quality ideas and products.

display rules

Guidelines about how employees doing emotional labor must interact with others, usually customers.

displayed emotions

The emotions which one expresses to others.

emotion

A momentary, elementary feeling of pleasure or displeasure, and of activation or deactivation.

emotion cultures

The characteristic emotional styles of different societies.

emotional competence

Emotional intelligence or "EQ"; a multi-faceted personal characteristic that includes self-awareness, psychological self-management, social awareness and empathy, and relationship management.

emotional display

The manner and extent of emotional expression.

emotional dissonance

The inconsistency experienced between one's felt emotion(s) and one's emotional expression.

emotional incompetence

Lack of emotional intelligence.

emotional labor

The effort, planning, and control needed to express certain specific emotions while performing a job.

environment

Non-genetic factors.

ethical business values

Principles/standards governing the handling of ethical situations in the workplace.

external locus of control

The tendency to believe that powerful others, fate, or chance primarily determine events.

felt emotions

Emotions which are experienced; may or may not be appropriate to express to others.

heredity

Genetic factors.

intelligence quotient (IQ)

The most widely used measure of analytic ability.

internal locus of control

The tendency to believe that events result primarily from one's own behavior and actions.

IQ test

Any test used to measure analytic intelligence on an objective, standardized scale.

job involvement

The belief that there is a relationship between an individual's performance in a job and his or her own self-worth.

job satisfaction

A person's positive or negative evaluation of his or her job.

locus of control

The extent to which individuals believe that they can control events that affect them.

mood

An ongoing cycle of feelings that are *not* intense enough to interrupt one's ongoing thought processes.

narcissistic personality disorder

A disorder characterized by arrogance, self-importance, a feeling of entitlement to special treatment by others, and a marked lack of empathy for others.

normal distribution

A distribution of scores with a bell-shaped curve or "normal curve," the results of which tell us about the majority of a population and also about the unusual members of that population.

organizational commitment

A person's emotional attachment to and identification with his or her organization.

peer group influences

The influences of people of approximately the same age, social status, and interests.

personality

The unique pattern of enduring thoughts, feelings, and actions that characterize an individual, the expression of the sum total of who you are biologically, psychologically, and behaviorally.

personality profile

A test that describes an individual's whole personality, rather than just the separate traits that make up that personality.

personality traits

Characteristics that individuals display over time and across situations.

practical intelligence

Common sense, also called "situational judgment".

psychological disorder

A psychological condition which causes significant pain, stress, and maladaptive functioning, due to biological factors, learned habits, or mental processes, rather than situational influences.

reliable test

A test that will give similar results if it is repeated.

self-perception theory

A theory which suggests that under some circumstances people do not experience cognitive dissonance when their attitudes and behaviors differ, but rather observe their own behavior and deduce what their attitude must be from what they see.

stereotype threat

A phenomenon in which individuals have impaired performance on a test after being reminded about the negative stereotypes of their groups' cognitive abilities.

subjective well-being

Happiness.

tacit knowledge

The action-oriented knowledge one acquires that allows one to achieve goals one personally values.

test anxiety

The impairment of one's ability to perform on a test due to high emotional arousal.

transparent

Easy to manipulate to attain desired results.

triarchic theory of intelligence

A model of cognitive abilities which includes analytic, creative, and practical components.

turnover

When an individual leaves a company.

valid test

A test that measures what it says it measures.

value

A broad principle underlying one's beliefs; an abstract standard of goodness that is often defined by the culture one lives in.

work centrality

The general importance of work in an individual's life compared with other activities, such as leisure, spending time with friends, or family events.

work-life balance

A proportioning of time and commitment between work life and personal life.

Chapter 3: Decision Making

administrative model

A model of decision-making which emphasizes that decision makers 1) process only limited, manageable amounts of information rather than identifying all alternatives, 2) use shortcuts and rules of thumb when processing information, and 3) choose solutions that seem adequate but are actually less than optimal .

availability heuristic

Making judgments based on the information that is mentally "available" at any given moment rather than conducting a thorough, realistic appraisal.

behavioral economics

The study of a variety of psychological and situational influences on decision making.

bounded rationality

Herbert Simon's idea that rationality is constrained, or "bounded," by numerous individual and environmental factors, including the limitations of the human mind, the complexity and uncertainty of problems, and time pressures.

confirmation bias

The tendency to seek out and favor evidence that supports one's beliefs.

convergent thinking

The ability to apply logic and knowledge to narrow down the number of possible solutions to a problem.

divergent thinking

The ability to think along many paths to generate many solutions to a problem.

escalation of commitment

The tendency to continue on a course of action once money has been spent or effort has been invested, despite signals that a project is failing.

ethical dilemma

Any situation or decision that requires moral judgment.

expert systems

Computer programs that mirror some aspects of human decision-making processes.

forced-choice test

A test which requires one to make subtle choices about one's preferences.

formal reasoning

Deductive reasoning, which uses rules of logic to make a decision.

gambler's fallacy

The tendency to believe that random events will correct themselves.

heuristic

A mental decision-making shortcut.

image theory

A theory which says that how a decision-maker manages and coordinates images is the essence of the intuitive decision-making process.

implementation

Putting a solution into effect using a definite plan or procedure.

implicit egotism

The tendency to prefer things which are connected with one's positive associations about oneself.

informal reasoning

Inductive reasoning, which is guided to some extent by the rules of formal reasoning, but has no deterministic methods (that is, its methods are debatable).

interactional justice

Treating people respectfully when formal organizational procedures are carried out.

intuition

An unconscious or relatively automatic decision-making process that integrates experience, goals, and values without using direct reasoning.

loss aversion

The tendency to choose not losing as the preferred outcome, when faced with an equal probability of gaining or losing.

naturalistic decision making

Decision making that occurs in real-world settings, often under time pressure.

nonprogrammed decisions

Decisions that are made by using judgment, rather than by following explicit rules.

optimizing

Maximizing one's decision-making effectiveness.

over-confidence

Over-reliance on one's ability to make accurate predictions.

procedural justice

Using formal decision-making procedures that are fair; "procedural fairness".

programmed decisions

Decisions that are made by following explicit (often written) rules.

rational-economic model

A model of behavior rooted in Adam Smith's work which assumes that a person making a decision has complete and perfect information and is able to process this information accurately and without bias.

representativeness heuristic

Looking for familiar patterns without assessing why certain patterns exist or whether they are likely to continue.

risk propensity

The tendency to take risks.

satisficing

Choosing solutions that seem adequate but are actually less than optimal.

satisficing heuristic

Selecting the first alternative one thinks of that meets one's minimum requirements, instead of taking the time to weigh and choose the best alternative among a large array of options.

unconscious bias

The illusion that one is an objective observer and actor; reliance on preconceived opinions about someone or something.

Chapter 4: Fundamentals of Motivation

A-B-C's of behavior modification

Study of the interaction of the antecedents to a behavior, a behavior, and the consequences of that behavior.

behaviorally anchored rating scheme (BARS)

An approach which rewards target behaviors and is generally perceived to be fair.

behaviorally based evaluation

An approach in which observable behaviors are rated on their frequency or other quantifiable measure, and these ratings are summarized in a "behaviorally anchored rating scheme" (BARS).

collectivism

An emphasis on social harmony and stability that is often found in Asia and the Southern Hemisphere.

contingent

Given on the condition that a particular behavior is performed.

distributive justice

The perceived fairness of outcomes in terms of how rewards and resources are allocated in an organization.

employee stock ownership plans (ESOPs)

Particular plans that allow employees to buy stock.

equity theory

A theory which predicts that one will weigh the ratio of one's effort (and other job inputs such as one's experience and ability) to one's rewards against that of others.

expectancy

The belief that one's effort will lead to an acceptable level of performance.

expectancy theory

A theory of motivation which proposes that one's effort is determined primarily by one's beliefs in three key areas: expectancy, instrumentality, and valence.

explicit motives

The reasons people give for their actions; conscious motives.

extinction

Stopping all rewards.

extrinsic aspirations

Explicit motives that are materialistic and social, such as wishing to enhance one's wealth, image, and popularity.

extrinsic motivators

External influences that cause a person to act, including both rewards and punishments.

fading out

Reducing reinforcers systematically over a period of time.

halo effect

The influence of a manager's overall impression of the employee on every item of the evaluation.

humanistic capitalism

The idea that companies should foster humane behavior and the appreciation and preservation of human achievements.

independents

People who think of themselves as autonomous individuals, whose rights and feelings outweigh those of the groups to which they belong.

individualism

An emphasis on the importance of individual freedoms and rights that is often found in developed Western countries such as the United States.

instrumentality

The belief that the performance level one achieves will result in specific positive and/or negative outcomes.

interdependents

People who think of themselves as linked with others through their status and social roles.

intrinsic aspirations

Explicit motives that are psychological and interpersonal, such as wishing to enhance one's self-acceptance, personal affiliations, and community contribution.

intrinsic motivators

Inner influences that cause a person to act, such as personality, emotion, needs, motives, goals, and expectations.

judgment-based evaluation

Rating employees based on traits that management deems to be important.

learning goals

Goals concerned with developing competence in an activity.

Management by Objectives (MBO)

A system in which supervisors and their subordinates jointly decide the individual employee's goals for the year, and in which pay is contingent on meeting these goals.

merit-based pay systems

Pay systems in which pay is based on performance.

motivation

An individual's direction, intensity, and persistence of effort in attaining a goal.

need for achievement

The desire to succeed by setting and reaching goals.

need for affiliation

The desire to establish and deepen social relationships.

need for power

The desire for dominance and social control.

needs

Unconscious patterns, some developed early in life and some perhaps instinctive, that lead to emotional and behavioral preferences.

negative reinforcement

Removing something a person dislikes, to increase the probability that he or she will behave in a particular way.

OB Mod

Organization behavior modification: An approach that focuses on changing behavior using reward and punishment.

pay for performance

Making pay contingent on general performance.

pay for targeted behaviors

making pay contingent on the achievement of specific targets.

performance goals

Goals concerned with demonstrating competence one has already acquired.

positive reinforcement

Giving a person something he or she wants, to increase the probability that he or she will behave in a particular way.

punishment

Any event that decreases the probability of a behavior.

punishment by application

Doing something to a person that he or she dislikes.

punishment by removal

Taking away from a person something that he or she wants.

quality circles

Teams of employees who meet to discuss quality improvements.

reinforcement

Any event that increases the probability of a behavior.

results-based evaluation

Rating employees based on their performance over time.

reward

A desired consequence which is typically given for general performance, rather than being contingent on specific behaviors.

self-actualization

Achieving one's full personal potential.

self-efficacy

A person's generalized belief in his or her ability to execute a course of action in any given situation.

self-managed teams

Autonomous groups that take on some of the tasks typically done by supervisors, with the theory that empowering workers will motivate them to work harder and be more committed to their organization.

seniority-based pay systems

Pay systems in which pay is based on years with the company.

shaping

Reinforcing small improvements made along the way.

sociobiology

A controversial field that studies how natural selection, previously used only to explain the evolution of physical characteristics, shapes behavior in animals and humans.

Theory X managers

Managers who tell their people what to do, judge their performance, and reward and punish them.

Theory Y managers

Managers who emphasize relationships, encourage self-control, and encourage active and responsible participation of individuals in decisions affecting their careers.

universal reinforcer

Money, because it can be exchanged for so many things (food, shelter, safety. . .).

valence

The belief that the attained outcome will be personally valued.

variable-pay programs

Programs that blend a (sometimes relatively modest) set salary with pay contingent on some output measure.

Chapter 5: Motivating Individuals in Their Jobs

360 degree performance appraisal

An appraisal of an employee by his or her bosses, coworkers, and subordinates.

autonomy

The degree to which the job provides freedom and discretion in scheduling the work and in determining the procedures to be used.

cellular spaces

Traditional, individual work spaces.

compressed workweek

A form of flextime in which employees are allowed to work a certain number of hours during a certain number of days or weeks.

continuance commitment

Employees' objective (non-emotional) decision that it is in their best interest to remain with the organization.

core job characteristics

Five characteristics that describe what makes a job motivating. The five characteristics (skill variety, task identity, task significance, autonomy, and feedback) foster the development of the three psychological states which are critical to a person's intrinsic motivation to do a job: 1) the extent to which a person experiences the job to be meaningful, 2) the extent to which a person experiences responsibility for doing the job fully and well, and 3) the extent to which a person sees the results of her or his labor.

employability

The idea that workers' abilities and competencies are the basis for their job security.

employee customer profit chain model

A model which suggests that employees' satisfaction with their jobs and company leads to less turnover, more motivated staff, and consistent service.

EVLN model

A model of job dissatisfaction comprised of two active behaviors: exit (quitting an organization altogether), and voice (staying in one's company and actively trying to improve conditions there); and two passive behaviors: loyalty (accepting the status quo without trying to change it) and neglect (staying in the company and exhibiting passive withdrawal behaviors).

exit

Dissatisfied employees quit an organization in response to job satisfaction.

feedback

The extent to which performing the job results in the worker receiving clear information about the effectiveness of his or her performance.

flextime

Allowing employees to choose their own hours.

gliding schedule

A form of flextime in which employees are allowed to choose their own hours around a common core of time during which they are required to be in the office.

growth need strength

The degree to which an individual values complex, challenging work; one of the measures included in the job diagnostic survey.

job

A specified task or set of tasks an individual does as part of an occupation.

job analysis

The first step in the process of fitting a person to a job: determining what work needs to be done and what skills and abilities are necessary to perform the work.

job description

The second step in the process of fitting a person to a job: the details of what the work will be.

job diagnostic survey

A survey created by J. R. Hackman and G. R. Oldham which assesses any job based on the five core job characteristics and some related factors.

job enlargement

Broadening an individual's work; "horizontal loading".

job enrichment

Redesigning jobs so that workers have more autonomy, responsibility, and feedback; also called "vertical loading" because it moves decision making lower in the hierarchy .

job rotation

Giving workers more variety by rotating them from one kind of job to another kind of job.

job satisfaction

A collection of attitudes about the various parts of a job, which can be measured simply by asking "overall, how satisfied are you with your job?".

job sharing

Allowing two or more persons to share the responsibilities and the benefits of one job position, each working part time.

job specifications

The third step in the process of fitting a person to a job: the details of what skills, education, and experience are required to perform the work.

loyalty

Dissatisfied employees accept the status quo without raising any objections or making suggestions for improvements.

meritocracy

A system in which people are rewarded according to established standards of performance (such as how many clients they see, how much money they bring in, or how many calls they answer in a set amount of time) and sometimes also factors such as effort and circumstances.

motivating potential score (MPS)

An employee's score on the job diagnostic survey, which shows with some precision which characteristics of his or her job are motivating to him or her.

neglect

Dissatisfied employees stay in the company and exhibit passive withdrawal behaviors such as minimizing their effort

normative commitment

Feeling of obligation to remain with one's company.

open plan office

An office design in which traditional, individual (cellular) spaces are replaced by individual work units organized into one large room.

organizational citizenship

Behaviors on behalf of the organization that go well beyond normal job expectations and may even serve a larger societal purpose.

organizational commitment

Employees' involvement with, identification with, and emotional attachment to their organization.

performance appraisal

The formal evaluation of an employee's performance.

person-job fit

The extent to which an individual's abilities and traits match the requirements of a particular job.

procedural process

How the selection process is performed; which procedures are used to select candidates.

psychological contract

The individual's belief about the exchange between himself or herself and his or her employer.

scientific management

Principles introduced by Frederick Winslow Taylor early in the twentieth century, including the principle that breaking work down into its smallest parts maximizes efficiency because each part is relatively simple to learn

and do, and that when a job is easily learned, workers can easily be replaced.

skill variety

The extent to which the job involves a variety of different activities that require different skills and abilities.

social process

The process of enhancing the social and emotional aspects of candidate selection, including how much participation and control of the process the candidate has, how the candidate receives feedback during the process, and how candidate privacy is respected.

task identity

The extent to which the job involves the completion of a whole identifiable piece of work.

task performance

The behaviors, both mental and physical, that individuals exhibit in pursuit of organizational goals.

task significance

The degree to which the job is perceived by the worker as being important and having a significant impact on others.

telecommuting

Any work arrangement that allows employees to do some of their work at home.

virtual relationship

Telecommuting that is primarily conducted through technology.

voice

Dissatisfied employees choose to stay in their company and actively try to improve conditions.

Chapter 6: Health and Stress at Work

AHA! Syndrome

Tendency to experience anger, hostility, and aggressiveness, which some research suggests are major predictors of cardiovascular disorders.

biogenic triggers

Foods that create a stress response all by themselves irrespective of other conditions, including coffee, tea, caffeinated soda, and amphetamines.

burnout

A mismatch between a person and his or her job, or between a person and his or her workplace, that is frequently associated with stress.

challenge

The belief that change is normal and interesting rather than a threat to your security.

Circadian rhythms

Patterns in our bodies (including body temperatures, heart rate, and hormone production) that are kept in cycle by environmental cues, especially light.

cognitive restructuring

Substituting more solution-oriented ideas for emotionally charged ideas about a stressor.

commitment

The tendency to involve yourself in, rather than being alienated from, whatever you encounter or are doing.

control

The tendency to feel and act as if you are influential rather than helpless in life.

eustress

A state of stress which is experienced as positive.

fight or flight

A set of survival responses passed down to modern human beings from their ancestors, in which humankind either flees or fights back in response to stressors; our bodily response equips us for these strategies.

hardiness

The possession of three attitudes (commitment, control, and challenge) which buffer you from the negative effects of stress.

insufficient authority

Situation in which someone needs to complete a job but doesn't have enough authority to make important decisions.

job burnout

A mismatch between a peson and job, or between a person and workplace, that is associated with stress.

job stress

The harmful physical and emotional responses that occur when the requirements of the job do not match a worker's capabilities, resources, or needs.

noise

Unwanted sound.

overload

Situation in which the amount of work in a person's job is beyond his or her ability to do alone.

repetitive stress injuries

Injuries caused by repetitive motions while working, including wrist pain from typing or back injuries from awkward lifting.

role

The behavior expected of someone who holds a particular job.

role ambiguity

The confusion that occurs when people do not know clearly what has to be done in their jobs.

role conflict

The existence of two or more sets of role expectations for an individual's work which are incompatible with each other (i.e., the individual cannot comply with both).

stress

A state of tension experienced when one's usual modes of coping are insufficient.

stress response

The body's reaction to a stressor.

stressor

Any event that causes someone to feel stress.

tend and befriend

Responding to stressors by seeking the nurturing and support of familiar people, rather than using a fight-or-flight response.

the relaxation response

The elicitation of a relaxed state, in which one's metabolism, heart rate, blood pressure, breathing rate, and muscle tension all decrease.

Type A—Type B personality

A constellation of personality traits related to stress.

workaholism

Excessively high ranking on the traits of work involvement and a drive to work.

Chapter 7: Communication and Interpersonal Relationships

active listening

A strategy of paying attention in order to assess the emotional and informational content of a message and establish rapport with the speaker.

agonism

A warlike, oppositional style of interaction used to accomplish a range of interactional goals that have nothing literally to do with fighting.

assessment centers

Training and development facilities staffed by professional interviewers and assessors, and designed with amenities such as rooms with one-way mirrors.

attitudes

Tendencies to think, feel, or act either positively or negatively toward stimuli in our environment.

attribute framing effect

People's tendency to think positively about a characteristic when it is described in positive terms.

attribution

The process of explaining the causes of people's behavior, including your own; this process is prone to errors.

augmented cognition systems

Media that know when to interrupt you, and when not to.

calculus-based trust

Trust based on the belief that another person may be deterred from acting against our interests.

central route

A persuasion strategy which focuses on the argument that one is trying to make.

closed questions

Questions which can be answered with a yes or no; tend to pause or even end a dialogue.

cognitive dissonance theory

A theory about why attitudes change which suggests that individuals want their attitudes and beliefs to be consistent with each other and also with their behavior.

communication

The exchange of thoughts, opinions, or information by speaking, writing, or other means.

conduit metaphor

The idea that language transfers thoughts and feelings from person to person rather like a pipe transfers water from place to place.

credible communicator

A communicator with sufficient competency (knowledge in one's field) and trustworthiness (the extent to which one is believed to be telling the truth).

distrust

The expectation that another will not act in one's best interests and may deliberately seek to cause harm.

double-bind

The idea that a woman who acts the passively feminine role that society has traditionally dictated for women may be perceived as weak, while a woman who acts assertively may be perceived as bossy.

first impression bias

The phenomenon in which raters are more highly influenced by a candidate's first impression once it is established than by that candidate's later performance.

framing

Describing a message in a way that is most likely to lead to the outcome you want, which is an effective strategy because of people's somewhat predictable patterns of decision making.

fundamental attribution error

Mistakenly believing that an action was caused by the actor rather than the situation.

identification-based trust

Trust based on the belief that another person identifies (empathizes) with our interests and values, and is likely to look out for them.

illusory correlation

The process by which we categorize an entire group based on the behavior of a handful of people in that group.

impression management

The attempt to manage the impression one makes on others, partly to protect one's self-concept.

information filtering

Focusing only on useful knowledge rather than miscellaneous information.

jargon

Language which is comprehensible only to certain groups.

likable communicator

A communicator with personal traits (often including personal attractiveness and demographic similarity) that endear him/her to the receiver.

medium

Communication channel, such as face to face conversation, telephone, or email.

open door policy

A policy that encourages employees to go "around" their bosses, when necessary, to take their message to someone higher up in the organization.

open questions

Questions which encourage elaborate responses; tend to move a dialogue along.

peripheral route

A persuasion strategy which focuses on the communicator, using personal cues such as confidence and attractiveness.

personal space

The area around a person that he or she claims in order to maintain privacy.

possible selves

Concrete ideas about what our psychological identity is or may become.

prejudice

A preconceived opinion, either favorable or unfavorable, of others.

rapport talk

Conversation that is aimed at relationship building.

realistic job preview

A recruitment procedure in which organizations give both favorable and unfavorable work information to candidates.

report talk

Conversation in which information is exchanged.

risky choice framing effect

People's tendency to become risk averse when possible gains to be made are emphasized, but to become more interested in taking the risk when possible ills to be escaped are emphasized.

personal orientation to others

The extent to which an individual is interested in other people.

selective attention

Focusing only on some stimuli while disregarding others.

self-monitoring

An individual's tendency to actively construct his or her public image to achieve social goals.

self-perception theory

A theory about why attitudes change which suggests that when people are not sure of their attitudes, they simply infer them from their behavior (this also makes attitudes consistent with behavior).

self-presentation strategy

A type of impression management which seeks to make the actor more appealing through both verbal and nonverbal cues such as smiling, eye contact and touching.

self-serving bias

The tendency to attribute one's successes to one's personal attributes while attributing one's failures to external causes.

social exchange

The ongoing give-and-take between the employee and the organization.

stereotypes

Social categories.

trust

One party's optimistic expectation of the behavior of the other, when the other must decide how to act.

unintentionality

The communication of unintended meanings.

Chapter 8: Cross-Cultural Relationships

culture
A set of shared beliefs and values about what is desirable in a community, and the set of behaviors and practices that support these values.

cultural assimilator
A cross-cultural training method in which an individual is presented with a scenario that takes place in the country to which he or she will travel and is asked to describe how he or she would react in such a situation.

cultural intelligence
The ability to "think about thinking" and to develop and expand one's behavioral repertoire, often on the spot.

cultural interpreter
A person who can explain the psychological and social basis of local behaviors and attitudes.

culture shock
A sense of disorientation in interpreting the myriad unfamiliar environmental, business, and social cues one encounters in a new culture; "acculturative stress".

high context cultures
Cultures in which people rely extensively on situational cues such as physical context, body language, and status when interacting with others.

low context cultures
Cultures in which people rely extensively on explicit codes, especially the spoken and written word, when interacting with others.

monochronicity
The preference for scheduling tasks separately and for focusing on just one task at a time.

national culture
The thoughts, emotions, and behaviors rooted in common values and societal conventions of a particular society.

polychronicity
The preference for having multiple activities occurring at the same time.

reentry shock
Culture shock that happens in reverse upon returning to one's own culture.

tolerance for ambiguity
The extent to which someone enjoys complexity and novelty, and tolerates problems in which there is no clear answer; a trait which helps one relate to others cross-culturally.

Chapter 9: Groups and Their Influence

cohesion
The sum of all the forces acting on members to remain in a group, including the degree to which members of a group are personally attracted to each other.

co-located work team
A team that always works together in the same place.

conformity
The tendency for people to change their behavior to match group norms.

content
The task that the group is involved in; *what* the group is deciding.

deindividuation
The loss of your objective self-awareness, reducing your desire to adhere to personal and societal values.

formal group
A group which is officially designated by an organization to accomplish its tasks.

group
Two or more people who spend time with each other, experience emotional ties, share a common frame of reference, and are behaviorally interdependent.

high-performance team
A rare type of real team whose members are deeply committed to each other's personal growth and success, and which significantly outperforms other teams.

informal group
A social group which has no official designation by the organization, in which individuals have some common interests and personal ties.

in-group
A group that commands members' esteem and loyalty.

interrole conflict
The situation that arises when someone finds that he or she is trying to fill two roles that conflict, such as mentoring a junior employee and also evaluating that employee's performance.

Köhler effect
A gain in motivation in which a less capable member of a group actually increases his or her effort, when he or she perceives that his or her contribution is crucial to the group, or when the member's evaluation within the group is crucial to him or her personally, or when their group is involved in intergroup competition.

motivation gain
Situation in which group members exert greater task effort than comparable individuals working alone.

networked team
A virtual team which consists of people who collaborate to achieve a common goal across time, distance, or organizational boundaries.

norms
Informal rules which regulate and standardize group members' behaviors.

out-group
A group toward which the group members feel some opposition or competition.

parallel team
A virtual team which carries out special assignments that the regular organization does not want to do, and also works across time, distance, or organizational boundaries.

potential team
A team which is trying to improve its performance but has not yet achieved some of the goals of a real team.

process

The pattern of interpersonal relationships in the group; *how* the group decides.

process consultant

Someone who helps a group interact more effectively.

punctuated equilibrium model

A model for the behavior of short-term groups which suggests that time-pressured groups progress through long periods of inertia, punctuated by concentrated, creative periods of significant change.

real team

A group whose members are committed to a common purpose and working collectively toward their goals, while holding themselves mutually accountable for achieving them.

risky shift

The tendency to make risky decisions; accepting a plausible early solution rather than working to find an optimal solution.

roles

Shared expectations about how a particular person in a group ought to behave, including what tasks a person should perform, and what socioemotional support a person should provide.

role strain

The strain someone experiences when he or she lacks the knowledge, ability, or motivation to perform a role well.

self-directed team

A group that is responsible for a whole product or service and makes its own decisions about task assignments and work methods.

social compensation

A gain in motivation which occurs when individuals increase their own efforts to compensate for the anticipated poor performance of other members of their group.

social identity

A part of your self concept that depends on your beliefs about the groups to which you belong.

team

A group whose members act collectively to produce joint work products.

virtual team

A group of employees situated in distant locations whose members have unique skills and must collaborate using technology to accomplish their assigned tasks.

working group

A group whose members do not have to interact very much to complete a task.

Chapter 10: Improving Team Effectiveness

alignment

The process of promoting individual buy-in to team goals while at the same time stimulating individual learning.

cautious shift

The phenomenon in which a group behaves more conservatively than individuals would behave.

expert loss

The minimization of the inherent value of experts in a group because of the tendency of groups to base discussions on information that is already collectively known by the group members, while failing to integrate new knowledge from individual expertise; also called the "shared versus unshared information paradigm".

group task roles

Roles of team members which involve facilitating and coordinating group problem-solving and directly improving the content of the decision.

group-building and maintenance roles

Roles of team members which involve building group-centered attitudes and a group orientation, and maintaining and perpetuating such group-centered behavior.

groupthink

The mode of thinking people adopt when the desire to agree becomes so dominant in a cohesive group that it overrides realistic appraisal of alternative courses of action.

groupware

Collaboration software tools which are intended to improve interpersonal interaction by simplifying group processes and reducing social barriers to effective communication, and by allowing team members in different locations worldwide to communicate.

hybrid culture

A culture which a manager encourages a multinational team to develop in which rules, expectations, and roles are understood and shared by all members.

polarization

The tendency of groups to make more extreme decisions than individuals, in either a more adventurous direction (risky shift) or more conservative direction (cautious shift).

production blocking

The fact that only one person can speak at a time, which limits the ability of the group to make ideas.

social facilitation

The enhancement of or detraction from a person's performance which results from that person being in the presence of others.

social loafing

A reduction in motivation and effort when individuals work in groups compared to when they work individually.

sociogram

A visual representation of who talks to whom.

Chapter 11: The Challenge of Leadership

charismatic leader

A leader who is able to exert an unusual amount of influence on his or her followers, often through a combination of his or her personal characteristics, goals and also some extraordinary circumstances.

consideration

The degree to which a leader shows concern and respect for followers, looks out for their welfare, and expresses appreciation and support for them.

contingency theory

A leadership theory that takes into account both the leader and the situation in which the leader is performing, because the leader's effectiveness is contingent upon that situation.

derailing traits

The loss of your objective self-awareness, reducing your desire to adhere to personal and societal values.

emergent leader

A leader who exerts significant influence over others despite having no formal authority.

formal leader

A leader who has formal or legal authority to direct others in his or her organization.

implicit leadership theory

The study of leadership prototypes, which individuals hold implicitly.

independent contributor

Someone who is concerned with improving the quality of products and services, and whose main responsibility is to produce as much as possible; a "professional contributor" (as distinct from a **leader** or a **manager**).

leadership

The ability of individuals to influence, motivate, and enable others to contribute to the effectiveness and success of their organizations.

leadership antiprototype

The two negative prototypical traits of an ideal leader: tyranny (being dominant, selfish, and manipulative) and masculinity (being male and masculine).

leadership prototype

The four positive prototypical traits of an ideal leader: sensitivity/compassion, intelligence, dedication, and dynamism/energy.

manager

An individual who is concerned with developing competitive advantage for a company by creating predictable results.

peer-to-peer leadership development

A model for leadership development which involves peers sitting down and sharing with each other their leadership problems and solutions, and which is able to create knowledge based on first-hand experience in fast-paced environments in which traditional leadership ideas may quickly become outdated.

prototypes of leadership

The models of ideal leadership that are held by the individuals in a company.

structure

The degree to which a leader defines and organizes his or her role and the roles of followers, is oriented toward goal attainment, and establishes clearly defined patterns and channels of communication; also called "initiating structure".

transactional leader

A leader who manages his or her followers, contingently reinforcing them based on whether they meet organizational goals, and who is unlikely to encourage initiative.

transformational leader

A leader who motivates his or her followers to move beyond their personal self-interest for the good of the group or organization, and who is likely to encourage initiative.

Chapter 12: Leadership Roles and Skills

authentic leaders

Leaders who are characterized in part by the synchronicity of their "inner path" with their leadership style and impact.

destructive narcissism

A personality disorder characterized by an outward self-confidence that is actually an attempt to protect what is at base a fragile self-esteem.

employee deviance

Voluntary behavior that violates important organizational norms and threatens the well-being of an organization or its members, such as harming another's reputation, misrepresenting one's work output or shirking work, and theft.

mentor

A senior, more experienced manager who provides support, direction and feedback to a protégé.

narcissism

The characteristic of being self-centered, which, in moderation, is secure self-esteem that allows a person to develop healthy relationships.

negotiation

A situation in which two or more parties must make a decision about their interdependent goals and objectives.

project management team

A group that comes together for a finite period of time to perform a variety of tasks to meet an organizational objective.

protégé

A junior, less experienced manager who receives support, direction, and feedback from a mentor.

spiritual synchronicity

The energy and the influence derived from living in synch with a higher purpose, often based on a worldview of an ultimate transcendent (nonmaterial) reality.

Chapter 13: Power and Influence

amoralization

The absence of moral standards which results from routinization.

authority

Legitimate control or command over others.

cliques

Networks which primarily exchange information and emotional support, and are characterized by moderately clear norms, moderate visibility to outsiders, and a small representation across organizational levels.

coalitions

Networks which primarily exchange information and influence, and are characterized by clear norms, easy visibility to outsiders, and moderate representation across organizational levels.

corporate greening
The phenomenon of companies taking responsibility for the environmental effects of their operations.

dehumanization
The process of depriving individuals of their human qualities and attributes, of their individuality.

empowerment
Giving workers power by deliberately moving power downward in the organizational hierarchy.

euphemisms
Words with falsely pleasant overtones which disguise their true (underlying) immoral and/or unpleasant meanings; the use of such words often accompanies routinization.

formal power
Power based on the principle of hierarchy.

hierarchy
The disproportionate holding of power, with those higher in the organization having more power and those lower having less.

hindrance network
A group of coworkers which hinders others from doing their work, through behavior such as routinely criticizing the company, leaving work early and encouraging others to do the same.

influence
The ability to move or impel someone to some action; affect; typically has a positive connotation, in that it impels someone to go along with something willingly.

informal power
A proportionate holding of power, in which individuals help each other out because of anticipated mutual gain and there is minimal conflict.

Machiavellianism
The extent to which individuals exhibit a cool detachment from others and may be more manipulative and impersonal as a result.

mentoring
The relationship between a senior, more experienced individual (the mentor) and a junior, less experienced individual (the protégé), in which the mentor helps the protégé navigate the world of work, often by giving career-related and psychosocial support.

political behavior
Activities that are not required as part of a person's organizational role but which influence, or attempt to influence, the distribution of advantages and disadvantages within the organization; also known as "playing politics".

power
The ability to mobilize resources to accomplish some end (in organizations, this often means the ability to get someone to do something); can have a negative connotation in that it forces someone to do something he or she wouldn't do otherwise.

power sources
The entire repertoire of behaviors that an individual could potentially call upon to influence others.

power tactics
The behaviors an individual actually uses in a particular situation to influence others.

routinization
The transformation of an immoral job into a routine, mechanical, highly programmed operation by encouraging mechanical, mindless action and inhibiting moral questioning.

Chapter 14: Conflicts Good and Bad

appeals to a third party
Bringing in someone such as a boss or a neutral person to help manage the scarcity of resources or to hear the complaints on both sides.

arbitration
The act of two parties submitting their grievance to a third party who makes a decision for them, which can be either binding or non-binding.

avoidance
Minimizing the importance of the issues and evading participation in the conflict.

avoiders
People who have low concern for both themselves and others, and therefore tend to withdraw from conflict situations.

bullying
Unwanted behavior that causes offense to the injured party and is not justified by the working or professional relationship.

certified union
A union established through an NLRB-supervised secret ballot election among qualifying employees, which is empowered to engage in collective bargaining.

collective bargaining
The negotiation process between a certified union and management over the establishment of human resources practices over the period of a contract.

compromisers
People who are moderately concerned with self and others, and therefore are likely to engage in mutual sacrifices with another person to accomplish a mutually satisfying decision.

conflict
The awareness on the part of two or more parties that they have incompatible goals, and that one party has, or will, negatively influence the other's pursuit of those goals.

confrontation model
A model of conflict which emphasizes individuality and allows for the aggressive pursuit of individual goals, which is the best fit for the U.S. culture.

contention
Imposing one group's will on the other.

decertified union
A union abolished through an NLRB-supervised secret ballot election among qualifying employees.

dialogue
The process in which two conflicting parties "directly engage each other and focus on the conflict between them, including aspects of their relationship itself".

dominators

People who show high concern for themselves but low concern for others, and therefore focus on accomplishing their own objectives and ignore the goals of others.

false polarization

An overestimation of the dissimilarity between the views of two parties in a dispute.

harmony model

A model of conflict which emphasizes intragroup harmony, consensus, and absence of conflict, which is the best fit for cultures which value harmony and personal relationships, such as the cultures of Japan and China.

hostile attribution bias

The tendency to perceive hostile motives in others even when signals about those motives are ambiguous.

incompatibility error

The belief that the other party's interests are, inevitably, completely opposed to one's own.

integrators

People who show high concern for both self and others, and therefore are willing to be open, to exchange information, and to examine differences to reach a mutually acceptable solution.

latent conflict

Conflict that is hidden.

manifest conflict

Conflict that is observed.

mediation

The act of two parties engaging a neutral third party to help them negotiate an agreement.

mediation-arbitration

The act of two parties agreeing to use a mediator but also to move on to arbitration should they fail to reach an agreement.

naïve realism

The belief that one's own views are objective and fact-based, whereas those of others are not.

negotiation

The act of two parties coming together to decide about the allocation of scarce resources; in other words, to make a deal.

obligers

People who show high concern for others but not themselves, and therefore attempt to minimize differences and emphasize commonalities to satisfy the other party.

open door policy

A company's policy of allowing any employee to bring any issue directly to top management and to expect a hearing.

problem-solving

Developing a solution that is acceptable to both parties.

process conflict

An awareness of differences of opinion about how a task should be accomplished, including who will do what and how resources will be allocated.

realistic group conflict

The theory that intergroup conflict is a natural outcome of competition for scarce resources.

regulative model

A model of conflict in which organizations themselves are structured to contain competition and conflict through an emphasis on regulation and bureaucratic rules, which is a best fit for cultures that simultaneously emphasize individuality and the avoidance of uncertainty, such as the cultures of France, Eastern Europe, Iberia, and Germany.

relationship conflict

An awareness of interpersonal incompatibilities that leads to tension and friction and tends to harm performance.

social identity theory

The idea that individuals define themselves to a large extent in terms of their social group memberships, and that it is through these memberships that they develop a positive sense of self, or social identity.

task conflict

An awareness of differences of opinions and viewpoints while doing a task, which can be beneficial because it heightens understanding of issues and results in higher quality decisions.

transparency overestimation

The belief that what one is saying is perfectly obvious to the other party.

whistle-blowing

The disclosure by former or current organization members of illegal, immoral, or illegitimate practices under the control of their employers, to persons or organizations that may be able to correct the wrongdoing.

yielding

Satisfying one group's needs at the expense of the other group.

Chapter 15: Designing Effective Organizations

administrative heritage

An organization's history, culture, values, and entrenched ways of doing things.

bureaucracy

An organization which is characterized by highly systematized, planned, prescribed and programmed work, linear thinking, conservatism, centralized decision-making, a steep hierarchy, and doing things "by the book;" also called a "mechanistic," "System 1," or "Theory X" organization.

centralization

The degree to which organizational members participate in decision making; a centralized decision is made by top managers, whereas a decentralized decision is made further down in the hierarchy.

collective paradigm

The invisible agreement in consciousness held by an organization's members.

complex environment

An environment that has many elements (such as many competitors).

congruence hypothesis

The hypothesis that specialization, formalization, and centralization are synergistic (all affect each other), and that if a manager changes one of these factors, the other factors must also be changed.

constraints

The three business factors that drive a company's design and are relatively difficult for management to influence: the environment in which it does business, the work that it performs, and the people it employs.

contingency theory

The theory that organizations should be uniquely designed to meet their unique constraints or challenges; using a contingency approach means differentiating organizations in terms of their constraints and designing them based on those constraints.

continuous production

Work that keeps going around the clock; continuous production work is performed by organizations that are centralized in terms of their hierarchical control structures and decentralized in terms of professional control over their work.

design variables

The aspects of a company which are under management's control and can be changed, including such factors as how decisions are made and how the work is coordinated; these design choices contribute significantly to the development of unique organizational capabilities that provide competitive advantage.

direct reporting

Individuals reporting directly to their managers, which is a common feature among companies with a steep hierarchy.

diversity

Having different types of environmental influences, such as having many different types of clients or products, or operating in a variety of regions.

dynamic environment

An environment that changes quickly, such as one in which competitors frequently produce new products.

enterprise

An organization which is characterized by innovative and creative work, non-linear thinking, spontaneous and team-based decision-making, "going with the flow," and employees being highly and/or creatively rewarded; also called an "organic," System 4," "Theory Y," "adhocracy," "learning," "high performance" or "new" organization.

environment

The elements external to an organization which have some influence on it, including competitors, government, the economy, suppliers, stockholders, and customers.

flat hierarchy

A structure with few levels, in which there is usually a large span of control.

formalization

The means by which an organization determines who, when, and how tasks are performed; the amount of rules, regulations, and policies that tell people what to do, the extent to which these are followed and enforced, and the

unwritten norms and traditions that shape people's behavior; also called "standardization".

hostility

The nature of competition, regulation and other related environmental influences, which ranges from "munificent" (friendly) to "hostile" (mean-spirited and subversive).

integration

Coordinating separate tasks and individual knowledge in order to create the organization's final product.

mass production

The production of large quantities of identical items, which often uses assembly lines; mass production work is performed by centralized, bureaucratic organizations.

nonprogrammed work

Work that is extemporaneous, spontaneous, flexible, creative, and directed by discussion and teamwork.

organizational design

The way in which an organization divides its labor into distinct tasks and then coordinates these tasks.

organizational effectiveness

The extent to which an organization meets its goals.

personal specialization

The variety of professional skills available in an organization, which is based on individuals' education, training, and experience; as tasks become more complex, more personal specialization may be needed.

programmed work

Work that is planned (prescribed), scheduled, inflexible, and standardized, in which people are given clear directions.

simple environment

An environment which includes a small number of any given element, such as few competitors.

synergistic factors

Factors such as specialization, formalization and centralization, which all affect each other.

span of control

The number of subordinates a manager supervises; the number of individuals reporting to one boss.

specialization

Differentiating the tasks individuals do in order to produce better work.

stable environment

An environment which does not change quickly.

standardization

The means by which an organization determines who, when, and how tasks are performed; the amount of rules, regulations, and policies that tell people what to do, the extent to which these are followed and enforced, and the unwritten norms and traditions that shape people's behavior; also called "formalization".

steep hierarchy

A structure with many levels, in which there is usually a narrow span of control.

task specialization

The way tasks are divided and dispersed in an organization.

technology

The technical term for an organization's work; the actions that an individual performs upon an object, with or without the aid of tools or mechanical devices, in order to make some change in that object.

uncertainty

The degree to which an environment is predictable; companies doing business in a highly uncertain environment tend to decentralize decision making and empower employees so they can constantly be looking out for trends.

units

Unique, individualized items, such as custom-made yachts or kitchens or small batches of a unique type of furniture; unit work is performed by flexible, decentralized organizations.

Chapter 16: Organizational Structure as a Design Tool

boundaryless organization

An organizational form that breaks down hierarchical and functional barriers to communication through extensive use of technology, decentralized decision making, and cross-functional teams.

core competency

The operation at which a company excels.

cross-selling

Presenting a single face to the customer; one of the cross-product marketing strategies which are addressed through the design of the front end of a company.

departmentalization

The process of dividing up the company's work into integrating subunits, each of which coordinates a specified aspect of the company's work.

divisional structure

An organizational form created to address complexities that a functional structure cannot, in which a layer is added below top management, delegating at least some responsibility for profit-making and customer responsiveness to vice presidents in charge of products or regions; also called a "unit structure".

front–back structure

An organizational form in two parts, a front-end that is oriented to the customer and a back-end that is oriented to such functions as purchasing and new product development.

functional structure

The organizational form in which employees are expected to specialize in their particular function and to report to a manager who heads up and also specializes in that function.

functions

Specialties within an organization.

horizontal differentiation

The degree to which labor is divided; a company with a large horizontal differentiation usually has a flat structure.

horizontal firms

Companies that emphasize decision making through teams rather than through the organizational hierarchy.

information technology (IT)

The development of computer systems to organize, store and communicate information electronically, a process that affects the centralization and decentralization of decision making.

integrator role

A formal role, assigned to individuals or groups, of acting as liaisons between subunits, which may supplement or replace that of the managers above the subunits in the organizational hierarchy.

knowledge integrator

An individual who is responsible for keeping the company's knowledge database orderly and current, cajoling consultants to actually use it, and adding new research.

matrix structure

An organizational form which has a multiple command system, including a related structure and the necessary support mechanisms, culture and behaviors, in which one manager reports to two or more bosses.

organizational chart

A chart depicting a company's departmentalized subunits; also called an "organigram".

simple structure

The organizational form in which a small number of support staff report to one person.

strategic business units

Divisions which have profit goals and a great deal of autonomy.

strategy

The determination of a company's long-term goals and objectives, and the adoption of actions and the allocation of resources to carry out those goals.

structure

The departmentalization of a company; the presentation of departments on a chart.

structured network

A network form in which each organization is independent but interacting with other companies.

vertical differentiation

The distribution of authority from lower to higher level managers; a company with a large vertical differentiation usually has a steep structure.

vertical firms

Companies in which decision making depends on a hierarchical process such as centralization and employee-manager communication, rather than on teams.

Chapter 17: Organizational Culture

acculturative stress

The upsetting individual states and behaviors that accompany an unsuccessful acculturation.

bicultural audit

A thorough examination of the cultures of merging companies, followed by an analysis of potential conflicts that are likely to occur and commonalities that can be built upon, and the development of a strategy for dealing with the issues that arise.

boundary spanners

Individuals who represent a company to actors in its environment (such as customers).

bureaucracy

A type of organizational culture which controls mainly by developing in its members shared understandings about legitimate authority and fair treatment of employees.

cafeteria benefits

Benefit plans in which individuals can choose how to spend their benefit dollars.

cause branding

The phenomenon in which a company is associated with supporting particular social causes, which can add a social and spiritual dimension to the company's organizational culture.

clan

A type of organizational culture which controls mainly by developing in its members a deep social understanding, specific to their organization, about its general objectives, methods and values.

climate

Organizational members' perceptions of an organization's policies, practices, and procedures, including its structure, reward systems, warmth, and support

core values

The values held by most of a company's members.

corporate branding

The process by which a distinct identity is created for a company, often through the company developing and displaying its culture.

counter-cultures

Subcultures whose values and norms oppose those of the company's dominant culture.

culture

An organization's system of shared values and norms, along with related behaviors, which defines for organizational members what is important in the company and what attitudes, beliefs, and behaviors are appropriate.

cultural fit

The extent to which an organizational culture suits the organization's circumstances, and predicts how well an organization will perform under those circumstances.

dominant culture

The system of values and norms held by most of a company's members; also called a company's "core values".

employer branding

The emerging marketing concept in which a company creates the same positive experience for its employees that it promises to its customers.

enacted values

Values which actually guide people's actions.

espoused values

Values which people profess to hold.

glass ceiling

The invisible barrier between middle and top management positions that is said to exist for women and other minorities.

market culture

A type of organizational culture which controls mainly by sharing among its members complex understandings about competition and prices.

moral stress

The tension an individual experiences when he or she recognizes the moral issues in a decision or action but is uncertain how to act on them in his or her company culture.

organizational assimilation

The process by which an individual is actually integrated into the culture of the organization, which includes both the deliberate and unintentional efforts by the organization to socialize the individual(newcomer), and the individual's(newcomer's) own attempts to modify their new organizational roles and environments to better accommodate their own needs, ideas, and values.

realistic job preview

Information that an interviewer gives an applicant about the realities—both good and bad—of working for the company, which can help to inoculate applicants against problems they will face on the job, and create trust between the applicant and the company.

reality shock

An intense experience of unpleasant surprise at the realities in your new company.

social information processing model

A model of organizational culture which suggests that organizational climate is influenced by organizational culture (for example, that an individual's feelings about his or her job are influenced by what the people around him or her say).

subcultures

Formal and informal groups and networks that may subscribe to some of the company's dominant or "core" values and norms, but also have their own.

superordinate culture

A strong organizational culture with which all nationalities can identify.

Chapter 18: Changing Organizations

action research

Any OD process in which the outcome leads to generalized knowledge that is published for use by the changed organization and other similar organizations.

appreciative inquiry

An approach to organizational change that identifies an organization's positive characteristics in order to build on them, in contrast to more conventional approaches that identify an organization's negative characteristics in order to fix them.

benchmarking

The process by which a company compares its own processes and products with the best processes and products available in the industry and then sets goals for improvement.

change agent
Any individual who is responsible for implementing an organizational change; this term is often used in connection with those involved in OD.

diffusion of change
The process of disseminating a successful change from one unit to other units in the organization.

force-field theory
A theory created by social psychologist Kurt Lewin which says that in organizational life there are always two sets of opposing forces—forces for organizational change and forces against it—and that managers must either increase the forces for change or reduce the forces against change in order for change to occur (if those two forces are in balance, change will not occur).

industrial democracy
A practice in which workers participate in company management.

intellectual capital
An organization's knowledge, behaviors, mental maps, norms, and values, which it preserves over time.

knowledge management systems
Systems for managing data and information and also learning, understanding, and applying information, in which a company's formal databases are not just knowledge storage facilities but are also strategic tools for using knowledge.

knowledge-centered cultures
Cultures which encourage the creation and dissemination of knowledge, and which develop effective knowledge management systems.

large-scale organizational change
Change that is organization-wide.

links in time
Managers' continuous and literal envisioning of present and future projects and the transitions between them, to help a company manage continuous change.

organizational development (OD)
Generally speaking, the use of social science knowledge to improve organizational effectiveness; specifically speaking, any organizational improvement effort which is planned, organization-wide, managed from the top, and makes use of behavioral science knowledge .

organizational learning
The manner in which organizations preserve knowledge, behaviors, mental maps, norms, and values (their "intellectual capital") over time, despite the fact that some of their individual members leave.

organizational memory
The storage of many individuals' accumulated knowledge in an organization's documents and/or collective memory; the building of organizational memory is a key goal in organizational change and involves understanding how organizations learn, how knowledge is retained and transferred within an organization, and how errors are detected.

parallel learning structures
Groups created with the purpose of enhancing organizational learning, innovation, and other issues related to organizational adaptation that operate in parallel with the formal organization, which allows the organization to foster learning without decreasing efficiency.

positive psychology
The idea (which underlies the appreciative inquiry approach) that too much of psychology focuses on problem behaviors and difficult people instead of helping people build upon their passions and strengths.

punctuated equilibrium model
A model of change which suggests that in some organizations, long periods of equilibrium, in which change is minimal and incremental, are interrupted by brief periods of radical organizational change caused by some mobilizing event.

reengineering
The redesign of business processes to improve various measures of performance, such as cost, quality, service, and speed, and which may involve changes in structures, jobs, people, or key processes.

semi-structures
An organizational design in which some organizational features are determined and structured while others are undetermined and flexible, which can help a company manage continuous change.

Six Sigma
A multifaceted approach to organizational change that attempts to alter a company's entire culture; a "Six Sigma Organization" is designed to measure and improve all organizational processes, with the objective of creating a culture of continuous renewal.

survey guided development
A method for organizational change that relies heavily on surveys of employees' perceptions about which aspects of organizational functioning are affecting performance, satisfaction, and motivation.

total quality management (TQM)
A management strategy aimed at developing high awareness of quality in all organizational processes ; a system for organization-wide change which originally helped companies to improve measurable factors such as their products' conformance to specifications, reliability, and serviceability, as well as intangible factors such as product aesthetics and perceived quality.

transfer of training
The transfer of knowledge gained in a classroom setting to other settings; weak transfer of training is a typical problem in organizational change because what employees learn in a classroom is often not remembered or reinforced when they return to their regular jobs and routines.

Chapter 19: OB Is for Life

abstract
The first part of a data-based article, consisting of a paragraph immediately after the title and before the body of the article,

which states the purpose of the study and its major findings, and sometimes suggests what the implications of the findings are for future research and for managerial (or "applied") use.

academic journals

Journals in which research and the research process are the primary focus; also called "scholarly journals".

blind peer review

The critique of an article by anonymous reviewers in the article's field of study who do not know who submitted it, which is often the deciding factor in whether the article is published; sometimes the reviewer(s) will suggest that the authors make changes, such as improving their methodology or collecting more data.

correlation

A type of statistical analysis which determines whether two variables are related, but not whether one causes the other.

critical theorists

Theorists who would like to see OB take a more challenging approach toward business organizations, including critiquing their design (such as the fact that they are not democratic) and their role in society (such as the fact that they are often powerful yet not always ethical).

dependent variable

An outcome; also called a "criterion variable".

discussion

The final part of a data-based article, which covers the study's implications for the advancement of theory (or "theoretical implications"), limitations on interpretations of the study given the chosen methodology, practical implications, and implications for future research; it may have a subheading with a title like "Practical Implications".

factor analysis

A type of statistical analysis that finds relationships between and among variables and then organizes similar variables into factors.

human resource management (HRM)

The programmed and strategic management of an organization's people; many companies have an HRM department or manager, who can be a key resource for an employee's ongoing learning about OB in the company and also OB in general.

independent variable

A variable that influences some outcome; also called a "predictor variable".

introduction

The first part of the body of a data-based article, which is often untitled, and which states why the study makes a contribution to the field, among other things.

meta-analysis

A type of statistical analysis widely used in recent years which synthesizes the results of many previous studies, enabling researchers to objectively integrate and interpret years of research on a topic.

methodology

The part of a data-based article which follows the theoretical background and which covers which research method (field study or questionnaire study, for example) was used for collecting data and often why that method was chosen, as well as the sample of individuals that was used to test the hypothesis.

modernism

A way of seeing the world which focuses on how the world is becoming increasingly defined by economic and organizational logic and forces, and which believes that progress is made through the rigorous application of rationality to different arenas of life; in organizational life, modernists are concerned mainly with how to improve management and management theory, and thus improve society.

multiple regression

A type of statistical analysis used to explain the relationship between multiple independent variables and a dependent variable, by determining what the best predictor is of the dependent variable.

narratives

People's personal stories and views, which can create a more valid view of organizational life than simply accepting one version of reality; also called "discourses".

operationalize

To make a theory practical by using it to form specific hypotheses that can be tested.

postmodernism

A way of seeing the world which rejects many principles of modernism and is skeptical of the idea that any one conceptual lens is the correct one; it believes that all social science is subjective.

practitioner journals

Journals with independent publishing standards and goals, which tend to focus more on practice (rather than theory) and the findings (rather than the process) of research, and which are often stylistically different from articles in academic journals.

qualitative methods

Hypothesis-testing methods which are based on the observations and interpretations of one or more individuals, and which are generally used to study a specific experience in depth rather than to produce generalizations.

quantitative methods

Hypothesis-testing methods which use statistical analysis to summarize and analyze measurable data points to yield results.

results

The part of a data-based article which follows the methodology section and which presents the conclusions drawn from statistical analysis of the collected data.

scientific management

An approach to management which determines how to improve labor productivity by precise procedures developed after careful scientific study of an individual at work.

theoretical background

The part of a data-based article which follows the introduction and which discusses the hypotheses to be tested in the larger context of the research and theory that have been published previously.

Photo Credits

Subject Index

Note: Pages in **bold** locate definitions

A

ABB, 250
A-B-C's of behavior modification, **107**
ABC Sports, 364
Ability characteristics, 293
Absenteeism, 130, 331
Abstract, **504**
Abusive behaviors, 329–330
Academic articles, reading, 504–507
  integration of practical applications in, 505–506
  statistical analyses in, 506
  structure of articles, 504–505
Academic journals, **506**
  articles in, 504–507
Academy of Management (AoM), 507
Acceptance, mentors and, 356
Accountability forums, 362
Acculturation, 457–459
Acculturative stress, 225–226, **457**
Achievable goals, setting, 104
Achievement, need for, 102
Achievement motivation, competitiveness and, 43
Achievement-oriented leader behavior, 304
Across the Board, 340
Action Learning Events, 490
Action research, **479**
Active coping, 162
Active listening, 192–194, **192**
Acton, Lord, 357
Adaptability, 472–473
  assessing one's cross-cultural, 224
  person-job fit and, 136–137
Adaptations in organizational design, 14–15
Adhocracy. *See* Enterprise
Adjourning stage of group development, 246, 247
Administrative heritage, **401**
Administrative model, **64**
Administrator, dispute resolution by, 385
Advanced Software Systems, Inc., 95
Adventurous vs. traditional, 37–38, 39
Aerospace industry, 356, 432
AES Corporation, 337, 401
Affect, **44**
Affiliation, need for, 102
Affinity groups, 239
Age, U.S. workforce by, 10, 11
Agenda, cultural differences in, 277
Aggression, 330
Agonism, **185**
Agor, W. H., 74
Agreeableness
  leadership and, 296
  tough-mindedness vs., 38, 39
The AHA! Syndrome, **160**
Airbus Industrie, 439
Airline industry, labor relations in, 390
Alexander, Marie, 291–292
Alibaba (e-commerce firm), 301
Alignment, **266**
Allen, R. W., 353
Altruism, 64
Amae, Japanese concept of, 221
Ambiguity
  role, 154
  tolerance for, 224
American characteristics, 210. *See also* United
    States
  American way of business, 211
  in cultural perspective, 212
  style of communication, 216
American Management Association, 13
America Online, 324
Amoralization, **360**
Amy's Ice Creams, 31
Analytic ability, 46–47, **46**
Analytical style of decision making, 69, 70
Ancona, D., 477
Andersen, Arthur, 462
Anger

dealing with, 381–382
  intimidation by, 360
  susceptibility to illness and, 158
Antecedents-behaviors-consequences (A-B-C's)
    analysis, 107
Anticipatory socialization, 450
Antisocial personality disorder, **43**
Anxiety
  low pain tolerance and high, 158
  test, 45
Appeals
  inspirational, 351
  as power tactic, 352
Appeals to a third party, **380**
Apple Computer, 334, 364, 433–434
Appreciative inquiry, **480**
"The Apprentice on Steroids," 315
Arbitration, **386**
Aristotle, 293
Army, U.S., 445
Arthur Andersen, 447, 462
Articles, academic, 504–507
Artifacts, discovering organizational culture
    through, 447–448, 449
Asch, Solomon, 77–78, 242–243
Asea Brown Boveri (ABB), 441
Asians in U.S. workforce, 12
Aspen Institute, 362
Aspirations, 103
Assertiveness
  cultural differences in, 217
  negotiation and, 326
  in subordinate, 381
Assessment centers, **196**
Assimilation
  acculturation through, 458
  cultural assimilator, 227
  organizational, 450
Assumptions, unconscious, 449
Attention, selective, 179–180
Attitude(s), **48**, **188**
  changing, 50–51, 190
    persuasive communication and, 188–190
    reasons for, 189–190
  cultural differences in, 214–216, 217, 218
    toward time, 211, 212
  hardiness and, 161
  personal style and, 50
  work-related, 36, 48–49, 127–129
Attitude surveys, 50
Attractiveness, first impressions and, 194
Attribute framing effect, **189**
Attribution, **181**
  hostile attribution bias, 380
Audience
  matching message to, 188
  persuasive communication and, 189–190
Audit, bicultural, 458
Augmented cognition systems, **180**
Australia, meaning of equality in, 219
Authentic leaders, **334**
Authority, **348**
  distribution of, 426
  insufficient, 154
  power of, 358–359, 360
Autocratic approaches to decision making, 78
Autonomous leadership, 313
Autonomous work groups. *See* Self-directed team
Autonomy, 18, **131**
  crisis of, 429
  job diagnostic survey of, 133
"Autonomy" stage of culture shock, 226
Availability heuristic, **75**, 76
Avedisian, J., 487
Avoidance, intergroup conflict management
    through, 385
Avoiders, **379**
Awakening–mobilizing–reinforcing model, 481

B

Baker, Wayne E., 215

Baker Company, case study of, 529–531
Bakke, Dennis, 337, 401
Ballmer, Steve, 452
The Bama Companies, Inc., 474
Banesto, 139
Bank of America, 387
Barnard, Chester I., 511
Barnevik, Percy, 250
Barrett, L. F., 101
Barriers of entry, 430
BARS (behaviorally anchored rating scheme), 111
Bartunek, J. M., 101
Baseline for target behavior, establishing, 107
Bateson, Mary Catherine, 514
Baye's theorem, 279
Bedeian, A. G., 503
Beer, Mike, 485
Behavior(s)
  Big Five personality factors predictive of, 40
  changing attitudes and, 50–51, 190
  coping with stress through, 164–165
  discovering organizational culture through,
    447–448, 449
  organizational. *See* Organizational behavior (OB)
  rational-economic model of, 64
  scientific approach to human, 500–502
  structured interviews anchoring questions to, 196
  target, OB Mod approach to, 107–109
Behavioral economics, **64**
Behavioral interventions, conflict management
    through, 375
Behaviorally anchored rating scheme (BARS), **111**
Behaviorally based evaluation, **111**
Behavioral style approach to leadership, 293
Behavioral style of decision making, 69, 70
Behavior modification theory, 106–113
  business applications of, 109–110
  case study of applied, 521–524
  five-step OD mod approach, 107–109
  limitations of, 113
  misuse of rewards and, 112–113
  performance appraisal design based on, 110–111
  reward systems design based on, 111–112
Behling, Orlando, 508
Belgium, 489
Belief, **48**. *See also* Culture; Value(s)
  in expectancy theory, 105
  intrinsic motivation and, 105–106
Bell Labs, 417
Bellon, Pierre, 462
Benchmarking, **474**
Benefit systems
  cafeteria benefits, 456
  developing and administering, 512
Benjamin, E. J., 160
Ben & Jerry's Homemade Holdings, Inc., 400
Bennis, Warren, 508
Benson, Craig, 274
Benson, Herbert, 164
Bentley College Center for Business Ethics, 80
Berger, Mel, 253
Berggren, Christian, 143
Berkshire Hathaway, 328
Bernanke, Ben, 7
Berrisford, Sam, 480
Best Buy Company, Inc., 356
Bethlehem Steel, 510
Bezos, Jeff, 337–338, 440
Bias
  confirmation, 75, 76
  first impression, 194
  hostile attribution, 380
  in managers, 478
  monitoring, 79–80
  naïve realism, 376
  overconfidence, 76
  self-serving, 181
  structured interviews to reduce, 196
  unconscious, 75–76
Bicultural audit, **458**
Bies, R. J., 186